Health Education

Health Education
Elementary and Middle School Applications

SIXTH EDITION

Susan K. Telljohann
University of Toledo

Cynthia W. Symons
Kent State University

Beth Pateman
University of Hawaii

 **Higher Education**

Boston   Burr Ridge, IL   Dubuque, IA   New York   San Francisco   St. Louis
Bangkok   Bogotá   Caracas   Kuala Lumpur   Lisbon   London   Madrid   Mexico City
Milan   Montreal   New Delhi   Santiago   Seoul   Singapore   Sydney   Taipei   Toronto

The McGraw-Hill Companies

Mc Graw Hill **Higher Education**

Published by McGraw-Hill, an imprint of The McGraw-Hill Companies, Inc., 1221 Avenue of the Americas, New York, NY 10020. Copyright © 2009, 2007, 2004, 2001, 1995, 1992. All rights reserved. No part of this publication may be reproduced or distributed in any form or by any means, or stored in a database or retrieval system, without the prior written consent of The McGraw-Hill Companies, Inc., including, but not limited to, in any network or other electronic storage or transmission, or broadcast for distance learning.

This book is printed on acid-free paper.

Printed in China

2 3 4 5 6 7 8 9 0 CTP/CTP 0 9

ISBN: 978-0-07-338080-3
MHID: 0-07-338080-6

Editor in Chief: *Michael Ryan*
Editorial Director: *William R. Glass*
Executive Editor: *Christopher Johnson*
Marketing Manager: *William Minick*
Director of Development: *Kathleen Engelberg*
Senior Developmental Editor: *Kirstan Price*
Production Editor: *Holly Paulsen*
Manuscript Editor: *Cheryl Smith*
Design Manager: *Ashley Bedell*
Text Designer: *Maureen McCutcheon*
Cover Designer: *Ashley Bedell*
Illustrator: *Lotus Art, ICC Macmillan Inc.*
Photo Research Coordinator: *Sonia Brown*
Production Supervisor: *Tandra Jorgensen*
Composition: *10/12 ITC Legacy Serif Book by ICC Macmillan Inc.*
Printing: *CTPS*

Cover: © Ariel Skelley/gettyimages.com

Credits: The credits section for this book begins on page 435 and is considered an extension of the copyright page.

Library of Congress Cataloging-in-Publication Data has been applied for.

The Internet addresses listed in the text were accurate at the time of publication. The inclusion of a Web site does not indicate an endorsement by the authors or McGraw-Hill, and McGraw-Hill does not guarantee the accuracy of the information presented at these sites.

www.mhhe.com

BRIEF CONTENTS

CONTENTS

PREFACE

VISION AND GOALS

The ideas, concepts, and challenges presented in this text have developed out of many different experiences: teaching elementary and middle-level children; teaching a basic elementary/middle school health course to hundreds of preservice elementary, early childhood, and special education majors; working with numerous student teachers; and serving on a variety of local, state, and national curriculum and standards committees. Two of the authors of this book have taken sabbatical leaves from their university teaching positions and taught for a term in a local elementary and middle school. The third author receives ongoing feedback on health education strategies from preservice elementary education majors who teach health education lessons as part of their field experience in elementary K–6 classrooms. This has provided opportunities to use the strategies included in this sixth edition.

We have written this textbook with several groups in mind: (1) the elementary and middle-level education major who has little background or experience in health education but will be required to teach health education to her or his students in the future, (2) the health education major who will be the health specialist or coordinator in an elementary or middle school, (3) the school nurse who works in the elementary/middle school setting, and (4) those community health educators and nurses who increasingly must interact with elementary and/or middle school personnel. Our goal is to help ensure that elementary and middle school teachers and health specialists obtain the information, skills, and support they need to provide quality health instruction to students.

CONTENT AND ORGANIZATION

The sixth edition is divided into three sections. Section I, "Foundations of Health Education," includes Chapters 1 through 4. This section introduces the coordinated school health program, the relationship between health and learning, the national health initiatives, the development of the elementary/middle school health education curriculum, the concept of developmentally appropriate practice, lesson and unit planning, and assessment. The basics of effective health education and effective instruction approaches are provided, including a critical analysis of standards-based approaches to health education and strategies for creating a positive learning environment, managing time constraints, and handling controversial topics and issues.

Sections II and III reflect the Centers for Disease Control and Prevention's new Health Education Curriculum Analysis Tool. Section II, "Helping Students Develop Skills for Positive Health Habits," includes Chapters 5 through 9 and focuses on the positive health habits students can adopt and maintain to help them live a healthy life. The chapters in Section II cover mental and emotional health, healthy eating, physical activity, safety and unintentional injury prevention, and personal health and wellness. Section III, "Helping Students Translate Their Skills to Manage Health Risks," focuses on the health risks students need to avoid or reduce to promote health. These chapters (10 through 14) cover intentional injury prevention and violence; tobacco use; the use of alcohol and other drugs; sexual health; and managing loss, death, and grief.

Sections II and III present the content and the personal and social skills that comprise the National Health Education Standards. Each chapter in these sections begins by discussing the prevalence and cost of *not* practicing the positive health behavior, the relationship between healthy behaviors and academic performance, and relevant risk and protective factors. Readers then are provided with information about what schools are currently doing and what they should be doing in relation to the health behavior. Chapters in these sections also provide background information for the teacher, developmentally appropriate strategies for learning and assessment, sample student questions with suggested answers (Chapters 11–14), and additional recommended resources, including evaluated commercial curricula, children's literature, and websites.

Four Appendices (three in the text and one available at the Online Learning Center) provide students with resources they can keep and use in the future:

- Appendix A, "2007 National Health Education Standards for Grades Pre-K–8," includes the latest version of the NHES standards and performance indicators.

- Appendix B, "RMC Rubrics for the National Health Education Standards," provides a standards-based framework teachers can use to evaluate student work. The rubrics were developed by the Rocky Mountain Center for Health Promotion and Education of Lakewood, Colorado.
- Appendix C, "Development Characteristics and Needs of Students in Elementary and Middle Grades," summarizes common growth and development characteristics and the corresponding needs of students in kindergarten through grade 9 that can serve as a foundation for age appropriate practice.
- Appendix D, "Activity Listings by Content Area, Grade Level, and NHES Standard," contains an overall index of all the teaching activities in the text and at the Online Learning Center. This appendix is available at the book's Online Learning Center (see below) as a downloadable Excel file that can then be sorted electronically by any category.

FEATURES OF THE SIXTH EDITION

The sixth edition has been substantially revised and updated. Key changes include the following:

Updated coverage of Health Education Curriculum Analysis Tool (HECAT). Coverage of HECAT has been completely revised throughout the text to reflect the latest version available from the Centers for Disease Control and Prevention. This coverage includes new versions of the listings of developmentally appropriate concepts and skills in each of the health content chapters.

Coverage of national standards and key data sources. The sixth edition includes the 2006 National Health Education Standards. They are introduced in Chapter 3 and used as the organizing principle for all the teaching activities presented in the content chapters (5–14). The new edition also provides relevant current data from Healthy People 2010, the Youth Risk Behavior Survey (YRBS), and the School Health Policies and Programs Study (SHPPS).

Emphasis on theory to practice. The content chapters include teaching activities that support the constructs of the theory of planned behavior, and they provide lists of desired behavior outcomes to help teachers focus on the most important goals for their students. The text presents many real-world experiences from elementary and middle school classrooms.

Expanded teaching activities. The "Strategies for Learning and Assessment" sections have been expanded to include many new activities (additional activities are provided at the text's Online Learning Center). These activities, found in Chapters 3 and 5–14, are organized by National Health Education Standards and developmental levels and include assessment items. The hundreds of activities provided focus not only on knowledge acquisition but also on skill development. Look for the special "Strategies for Learning and Assessment" icon to locate these activities throughout the text. New online Appendix D indexes all the activities from the text and the Online Learning Center according to content area, standard, and other criteria.

Updated and expanded coverage of key topics. Updated topics in the sixth edition include lesson plan design, assessment, teaching to standards, diversity and student interaction, and No Child Left Behind. Updated and expanded topics in the health content chapters include mental disorders affecting children and adolescents, self-esteem, overweight and obesity, immunizations, physical activity pyramid, injury prevention, bullying and cyberbullying, children of alcoholics, abuse of prescription drugs, and common sexually transmitted diseases.

Updated and refined pedagogy and resources for future teachers. Health Education offers strong pedagogical features and learning aids such as chapter objectives and Teacher's Toolbox and Consider This boxes, which present information to support successful health education. The colorful design highlights the children's art and enhances the illustrations and other pedagogical features of the text. Listings of suggested children's literature, evaluated curricula and instructional materials, websites, and additional resources have all been updated for the sixth edition. A complete list of all the children's books recommended in the text is available at the Online Learning Center, along with live links to all the websites listed in the text.

SUPPLEMENTS

The sixth edition of *Health Education: Elementary and Middle School Applications* is accompanied by an expanded package of supplementary materials designed to enhance teaching and learning. Contact your local McGraw-Hill sales representative to obtain a password to access the instructor materials that are available online.

Online Learning Center
www.mhhe.com/telljohann6e

The Online Learning Center for the sixth edition of *Health Education* provides key teaching and learning resources in an easy-to-use format. It includes the following teaching tools:

- *Instructor's Manual to Accompany Health Education: Elementary and Middle School Applications.* Updated and expanded for the sixth edition by Denise Seabert of Ball State University, the manual includes objectives, lecture outlines, classroom activities, and student Internet exercises.

- *PowerPoint slides.* A complete set of PowerPoint slides is available for download from the book's Online Learning Center. Keyed to the major points in each chapter, these slide sets can be modified or expanded to better fit classroom lecture formats. Also included in the PowerPoint slides are many of the illustrations from the text, including the children's art.
- *Test bank.* The test bank, prepared for the sixth edition by Denise Seabert of Ball State University, includes true-false, multiple choice, short-answer, and essay questions. The test bank is also available with EZ Test computerized testing software. EZ Test provides a powerful, easy-to-use test maker to create printed quizzes and exams. For secure online testing, exams created in EZ Test can be exported to WebCT, Blackboard, PageOut, and EZ Test Online. EZ Test comes with a Quick Start Guide; once the program is installed, users have access to a User's Manual and Flash tutorials. Additional help is available at www.mhhe.com/eztest.

For students, the Online Learning Center provides free resources to help them succeed in the course and in their teaching experiences. Learning objectives and self-quizzes allow students to review key concepts and prepare for exams. Suggested teaching and portfolio activities help students expand their personal collection of teaching resources and experiences. Additional Online Learning Center tools include extensive sets of Web links, lists of recommended children's books, and Appendix D, a searchable electronic index to all the teaching activities presented in the text.

Course Management Systems

Instructors can combine Online Learning Center resources with popular course-management systems. Contact your local sales representative for more information.

Primis Online (www.mhhe.com/primis)

Primis Online is a database-driven publishing system that allows instructors to create customized textbooks, lab manuals, or readers for their courses directly from the Primis website. The custom text can be delivered in print or electronic (eBook) form. A Primis eBook is a digital version of the customized text sold directly to students as a file downloadable to their computer or accessible online by password. *Health Education* can be customized using Primis Online.

ACKNOWLEDGMENTS

The authors would like to thank Dr. I. Renee Axiotis for her contributions to this text. Her work in compiling lists of the most current, developmentally appropriate, and relevant children's literature for this edition is greatly appreciated. We are also grateful for the guidance of Nicole Kerr and Krista Hopkins Cole in the areas of nutrition and safety education, respectively.

We express deep appreciation to Donna Rodenhurst and Jimmy Edwards, health education teachers at King Intermediate School in Kaneohe, Hawaii, and to their seventh-grade students who provided the artwork on health education standards and risk areas. And we thank Mary Doyen and Debra Sandau Christopher of the Rocky Mountain Center for Health Promotion and Education for the use of their cutting edge work in assessment of the National Health Education Standards.

We also want to thank the following reviewers for their helpful comments:

Lisa Alastuey, *University of Houston*

Judith Ausherman, *Cleveland State University*

Sally Champlin, *California State University, Long Beach*

Matt Flint, *Utah State University*

Deborah A. Fortune, *North Carolina Central University*

Douglas Q. Frisk, *Bethel University*

Gina A. Goebel, *Texas State University—San Marcos*

Claudia Maria Guedes, *San Francisco State University*

Alexandra Loukas, *University of Texas at Austin*

Mary M. O'Leary, *Wayne State University*

Adele S. Ruszak, *Millersville University*

Maureen C. Smith, *San Jose State University*

We hope that you enjoy the changes and additions made in this sixth edition. We welcome any comments or suggestions for future editions. We wish all the best and success in teaching health education to children and preadolescents.

Susan K. Telljohann
Cynthia W. Symons
Beth Pateman

Foundations of Health Education

Section I begins with a review of important definitions and concepts that frame current understandings of health and health promotion, then presents a rationale for the importance of school health programming to reduce health risks and promote school success. Undergirded by the *Healthy People 2010* agenda and findings from the most recent School Health Policies and Programs Study, this section reviews the eight critical components of the Coordinated School Health Program. Teachers in elementary and middle schools will be enriched by the translation of the broad science about education and brain-based learning into ways to improve health instruction. Information about the value of using health education theory to inform practice is introduced. A critical analysis of standards-based approaches to health education is provided. Finally, this section highlights strategies for creating a positive learning environment, managing time constraints, and dealing with controversial issues.

1

(Grischa, age 12; Jessica, age 12)

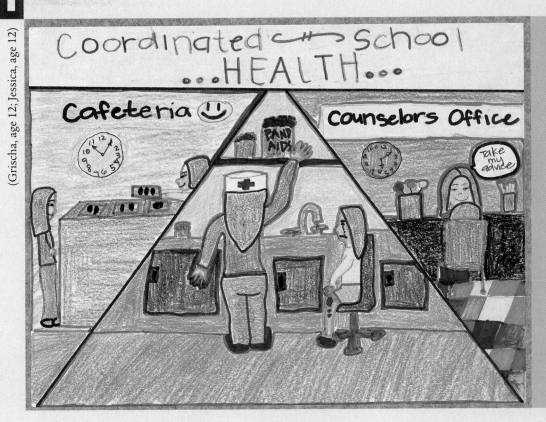

The Coordinated School Health Program

A Foundation for Health Promotion in the Academic Environment

DESIRED LEARNER OUTCOMES

After reading this chapter, you will be able to . . .

- **Define each of the domains of personal health.**

- **Identify behavioral risk factors that influence illness and death.**

- **Describe the link between student health and academic achievement.**

- **Discuss the influence of school health programs on improving school success.**

- **Summarize the role of each element of the Coordinated School Health Program in improving the health of all stakeholders in the school community.**

- **Discuss the combined impact of the elements of the Coordinated School Health Program on improving the health of all stakeholders in the school community.**

HEALTH: DEFINITIONS

When we review our understanding of the concept of health, most of us think in terms of our physical well-being. Our thoughts most often focus on preventing or managing illnesses, participating in fitness activities, or modifying our dietary behaviors. It is important, however, for teachers in elementary and middle schools to understand that health is a very broad concept that extends far beyond a foundation defined by physical parameters.

In 1947, the World Health Organization provided a definition confirming that health is "a state of complete physical, mental, and social well-being and not merely the absence of disease or infirmity."[1] This definition clarifies that our health status is influenced by a number of interrelated elements.

Today, health is best understood as our capacity to function in effective and productive ways, influenced by complex personal, behavioral, and environmental variables that can change quickly. Bedworth and Bedworth defined health as "the quality of people's physical, psychological, and sociological functioning that enables them to deal adequately with the self and others in a variety of personal and social situations."[2] Carter and Wilson further clarified that "health is a dynamic status that results from an interaction between hereditary potential, environmental circumstance, and lifestyle selection."[3] This confirms that, though we can exert a great deal of personal control over elements of our health, our control over other influential factors is limited. In summary, the most enriching definitions of health clarify the independent strength as well as the interaction among six influential elements: the physical, mental/intellectual, emotional, social, spiritual, and vocational domains.

Physical Health

The physical domain of health is the most conspicuous and is influenced by the combined effects of our hereditary potential, infectious agents to which we have been exposed, medical care to which we have access, and the consequences of our personal behaviors. Our physical health is the result of a complex and changing set of personal, family, and environmental variables.

Our initial and often lasting impression of the well-being of a friend or classmate is based on observations of superficial physical characteristics, including height, weight, energy level, and the extent to which the person appears to be rested. Also, we make judgments about the health of others based on observable behaviors. If we see our friends participating in regular exercise or always wearing a seatbelt, we might conclude that they are healthy. Conversely, we make very different judgments about the health of friends who appear overweight or who use tobacco products. Though a person's health prospects could improve if behavioral risks were addressed, such individuals may be very healthy in other domains.

Mental/Intellectual Health

The capacity to interpret, analyze, and act on information establishes the foundation of the mental or intellectual domain of health. Additional indicators of mental or intellectual health include the ability to recognize the sources of influence over our beliefs and to evaluate the impact of those influences on our decision making and behaviors. We can examine another's degree of mental health by observing the person's processes of reasoning, capacity for short- and long-term memory, and expressions of curiosity, humor, logic, and creativity.[4]

Our mental or intellectual health status can influence our general health in many ways. Personal health is enriched when we are able to analyze the quality of available health information. The ability to interpret and apply accurate information to our circumstances is critical for personal and family health promotion. Individuals who are unwilling to evaluate or change risky behavior patterns after they gain new insights are more likely to be confronted with long-term health challenges. For example, many of us have family members whose health has been compromised by their failure or inability to participate in early-detection screenings, yet some remain resistant to seeking preventive medical care.

Emotional Health

The emotional domain of health is characterized by our feelings and the ways we express them. Emotionally healthy people communicate self-control and self-acceptance and express a full range of feelings in socially acceptable ways. Experiencing positive emotions and managing negative ones in productive ways contribute balance for our emotional health. Emotionally robust individuals have equipped themselves with a range of coping skills that enable them to express negative feelings—including sadness, anger, or disappointment—in ways that are not self-destructive or threatening to others. In this way, emotional health contributes to and is reflected in our perceived quality of life.

Many people who feel isolated, inadequate, or overwhelmed not only express their feelings in excessive or abusive ways but also might suppress or bottle up strong emotions. Keeping negative feelings inside has been shown to contribute to stress-related illnesses, including susceptibility to infections and heart disease. Fortunately, emotional health assistance and support networks are available to help us live emotionally healthy lives.

Social Health

The social domain of health is reflected in the manifestation of our social skills. As humans, we all live and interact in a variety of social environments, including our homes, schools, neighborhoods, and workplaces. Social health is characterized by the ability to navigate these environments effectively while maintaining comfortable relationships in which we experience connection, mutuality, and intimacy. Socially healthy people communicate respect for and acceptance of the uniqueness of others,[5] and recognize ways that they enrich and are enriched by their relationships.

Unfortunately, many people are unable to function comfortably or effectively in the company of others. Such individuals may not know how to integrate a range of important social skills into daily living, being so focused on themselves that they compromise effective interaction by failing to recognize the needs and issues of others. Ineffective social skills and behaviors place a limit on their ability to initiate and maintain healthy relationships. Such limitations compromise their health and the quality of life of others with whom they live and work.

Spiritual Health

The spiritual domain of health is best understood in the context of a combination of three important elements:

- Comfort with ourselves and with the relationships we have with others
- The strength of our personal value system
- The pursuit of meaning and purpose in our lives[6]

Spiritually healthy people have developed the capacity to integrate such positive moral and ethical standards as integrity, honesty, and trust into their relationships. These individuals demonstrate strong concern for others regardless of gender, race, nationality, age, sexual orientation, or economic status. Some people believe that spiritual well-being is enriched by their participation in formal religious activities, but the definition of spiritual health is not confined by sacred terms or practices.

People with compromised spiritual health might not be guided by broadly accepted moral or ethical principles nor believe that a higher process or being contributes meaning to life. Among such individuals, short-term economic objectives, self-interest, or personal gain at the expense of others might become a priority. During times of compromised spiritual health, a person might feel isolated and have difficulty finding meaning in activities, making decisions about significant issues, or maintaining productive relationships with others.

Vocational Health

The vocational domain of health relates to our ability to collaborate with others on family, community, or professional projects. Vocationally healthy people are committed to contributing their share to projects and activities. This commitment is demonstrated by the high degree of integrity with which individuals approach tasks. The vocational domain of health also is manifested in the degree to which a person's work makes a positive impact on others or on the community. The behaviors of people with compromised vocational health threaten personal work-related goals and have a negative impact on the productivity of professional associates and the collaborative community of the school or workplace.

Thinking About Health in Hawai'i
The Lōkahi Wheel

Lōkahi
(Harmony, Balance, Unity)

Physical/Body	Spiritual/Soul
Friends/Family	Work/School
Thinking/Mind	Feelings/Emotions

FIGURE 1–1 | **The Lōkahi Wheel**

SOURCE: Native Hawaiian Safe and Drug-Free Schools Program, *E Ola Pono (Live the Proper Way): A Curriculum Developed in Support of Self-Identity and Cultural Pride as Positive Influences in the Prevention of Violence and Substance Abuse* (Honolulu, HI: Kamehameha Schools Extension Education Division, Health, Wellness, and Family Education Department, 1999).

Lōkahi: A Model of "Balance, Unity, and Harmony"

When evaluating the quality of our health, it is important to remember that balance among the domains is as important as maintaining an optimal level of functioning within each. An individual who is very healthy in the physical domain might be ineffective or inappropriate when expressing emotions. Also, it is quite possible for physically healthy people to behave in ways that confirm a poorly developed moral or ethical code. Conversely, a student in a middle school who uses a wheelchair because of a disabling condition might produce very high-quality academic work and have confident and effective relationships with classmates.

All cultures value balance within their own set of beliefs and behaviors. In Hawaiian culture the term *lōkahi*, meaning "balance, unity, and harmony," is used to express this ideal. This concept is depicted in Figure 1–1.[7] The illustration offers a foundation for learning about each critical element and for understanding the delicate balance that is necessary in the relationships among them that influence individual, family, and community health.

By examining the Lōkahi Wheel, readers can review the importance of maintaining balance within each domain of health:

- Physical/body (physical health),
- Thinking/mind (mental/intellectual health),
- Feelings/emotions (emotional health),
- Friends/family (social health),
- Spiritual/soul (spiritual health), and
- Work/school (vocational health).

In addition, examination of the Lōkahi Wheel reinforces the negative impact an imbalance in the health of one person can exert on the "balance, unity, and harmony" in the health of their family and community. A student who is addicted to tobacco, alcohol, or other drugs will be challenged by personal, legal, and health consequences. At the same time, such addictive behaviors can threaten the health of family and friends. Also, addictive behaviors of one student will disrupt the functional "balance" at school, in the workplace, and in the community. In this way, unhealthy risk behaviors can have far-reaching negative consequences.

Lōkahi serves as a foundation for the Hawaiian term *e ola pono*. Though this term has a number of related interpretations, it is generally translated as "living in the proper way" or "living in excellence." When we live our lives in a way that is orderly, successful, and true to what is in our best interest, the elements of our health are in balance and contribute to the enriched well-being of our family, school, and community.[8]

When planning developmentally appropriate and meaningful health education learning activities for elementary and middle school students, teachers must pay attention to each domain of health, plus reinforce the interrelated nature of these dimensions. To begin this process, it would be helpful for teachers to participate in a personal evaluation of their own health, as suggested in Consider This 1.1.

DETERMINANTS OF HEALTH

In 1979, the U.S. government embarked on a sweeping initiative to improve the health status of all Americans. This multidecade agenda was launched with the publication of *Healthy People: The Surgeon General's Report on Health Promotion and Disease Prevention*. This document contained confirmation that the leading causes of illness and death among Americans had undergone dramatic change between the beginning and the end of the twentieth century. In the early 1900s, the greatest number of Americans died as a result of infectious or communicable diseases, including influenza and pneumonia, tuberculosis, and diarrhea and related disorders. Fortunately, due to measures such as improved sanitation and waste disposal and medical discoveries, Americans living just 100 years later were enjoying significantly longer, healthier lives.[9]

Data have confirmed that, since 1900, the average life span of Americans has lengthened by greater than thirty years. Many factors improved the health of Americans during the twentieth century, but the Centers for Disease Control and Prevention (CDC) compiled a list of ten specific achievements that had a "great" impact on improving citizens' health between 1900 and 1999. Each achievement is reviewed in Table 1-1.[10] The extent to which each achievement contributed to preventing or reducing death, illness, and disability among U.S. citizens served as the criterion for inclusion on this list.[11]

Although there have been dramatic increases in the length and the quality of life of Americans since 1900, *Healthy People* reminded us of the need to address factors that continue to cause premature death. This report confirmed that approximately 50 percent of premature morbidity (illness) and mortality (death) among Americans was linked to variables largely beyond personal control. These variables include heredity (20 percent); exposure to environmental hazards, toxins, and pollutants (20 percent); and inadequate access to quality medical care (10 percent).[12] Also, *Healthy People* revealed that the remainder of premature illness and death (approximately 50 percent) could be traced to our participation in risky health behaviors.[13] Table 1-2[14, 15] contrasts past and current causes of death among Americans. Examination of this table reminds us of the devastating impact of communicable diseases on the health of our ancestors.

Importantly, chronic diseases (those that last a year or longer and require medical attention or limit daily activity) are the leading cause of death and disability in the United States.[15] Almost one in ten Americans are limited in their daily living by a chronic condition, and such

TABLE 1–1

Ten Great Public Health Achievements in the United States, 1900–1999

1. *Vaccination:* resulted in eradication of smallpox, elimination of polio in the Americas, and control of measles, rubella, tetanus, and other infections in the United States and around the world
2. *Improvements in motor-vehicle safety:* include engineering advancements in highways and vehicles, increased use of safety restraints and motorcycle helmets, and decreased drinking and driving
3. *Safer workplaces:* better control of environmental hazards and reduced injuries in mining, manufacturing, construction, and transportation jobs, contributing to a 40 percent decrease in fatal occupational injuries since 1980
4. *Control of infectious disease:* resulted from clean water, improved sanitation, and antibiotic therapies
5. *Decline in deaths due to heart disease and stroke:* a 51 percent decline in cardiovascular death since 1972—related to decreased smoking, management of elevated blood pressure, and increased access to early detection and better treatment
6. *Safer and healthier foods:* decreased microbe contamination, increased nutritional content, and food-fortification programs that have nearly eliminated diseases of nutritional deficiency
7. *Healthier moms and babies:* better hygiene and nutrition, available antibiotics, greater access to early prenatal care, and technological advances in maternal and neonatal medicine—since 1900, decreases in infant (90 percent) and maternal (99 percent) death rates
8. *Family planning:* improved and better access to contraception, resulting in changing economics and roles for women, smaller families, and longer intervals between births; some methods related to reduced transmission of human immunodeficiency virus (HIV) and other sexually transmitted diseases
9. *Fluoridation of drinking water:* tooth decay prevented regardless of socioeconomic status; reduced tooth loss in adults
10. *Recognition of the health risks of tobacco use:* reduced exposure to environmental tobacco smoke; declining smoking prevalence and associated deaths

As we begin the twenty-first century, we should celebrate each of these achievements and their contribution to helping us live longer and healthier lives. The public health accomplishments identified in this list are not ranked in order of importance.

SOURCE: Centers for Disease Control and Prevention, "Ten Great Public Health Achievements—United States, 1900–1999," *MMWR 48*, no. 12 (1999): 241–43.

TABLE 1–2

Leading Causes of Death Among Americans in 1900 and 2004
(ranked in order of prevalence)

1900	2004
Pneumonia	Heart disease
Tuberculosis	Cancer
Diarrhea/enteritis	Stroke
Heart disease	Unintentional injuries
Liver disease	Chronic lung disease
Injuries	Diabetes
Cancer	Influenza and pneumonia
Senility	Suicide
Diphtheria	Chronic liver disease and cirrhosis

SOURCES: U.S. Department of Health and Human Services, *Healthy People 2010: Conference Edition, in Two Volumes* (Washington, DC: U.S. Government Printing Office, 2000), 22; *Health, United States, 2007* (Hyattsville, MD: National Center for Health Statistics, 2007), 178.

NOTE: In 1900, the leading causes of death for most Americans were communicable or infectious conditions. Today, however, most Americans die as a result of chronic conditions.

TABLE 1–3

Underlying Risk Behaviors—Actual Causes of Death in the United States in 2000

Risk Behavior	Approximate Number of Deaths	Approximate Percent of Annual Deaths
Tobacco	435,000	18.1
Obesity	112,000	4.7
Alcohol	85,000	3.5
Infections	75,000	3.1
Toxic agents	55,000	2.3
Motor vehicles	43,000	1.8
Firearms	29,000	1.2
Sexual behavior	20,000	0.8
Drug use	17,000	0.7

SOURCES: A. H. Mokdad et al., "Actual Causes of Death in the United States, 2000," *Journal of the American Medical Association* 291, no. 10 (March 10, 2004): 1238–45; K. M. Flegal et al., "Excess Deaths Associated with Underweight, Overweight, and Obesity," *Journal of the American Medical Association* 293, no. 15 (April 20, 2005): 1861–67.

NOTE: We can exert influence over the common lifestyle risk behaviors linked to many of the causes of premature death. These health risks represent the actual leading causes, rather than the clinical diagnoses provided at the time of death for the majority of Americans.

diseases account for 70 percent of all U.S. deaths.[17] Our system for delivering medical care was designed to treat acute illnesses, yet over 75 percent of today's health-related spending is devoted to caring for people suffering from the consequences of chronic conditions.

A change in focus is critical. In addition to the need to retool medical-care delivery, Americans would be wise to embrace a new orientation focused on preventing chronic conditions among all age groups.[18]

First, we must recognize that the majority of chronic conditions have been linked to participation in relatively few health-risk behaviors. These include activities over which each of us can exercise significant personal control. Teachers are encouraged to examine Table 1–3 for clarification of this important point. Data in this table identify the risk behaviors that undergird the actual causes of most

American deaths.[19, 20] In this context, a physician might indicate a clinical diagnosis of heart disease on a death certificate. The actual cause of the heart disease, however, often can be traced to the cumulative effects of participation in any number of underlying risk behaviors.

The great majority of adults who participate in risk behaviors initiated those health habits during their youth. Public health professionals at the CDC identified six priority health behaviors to guide educational programmers and intervention specialists. Due to the demonstrated link between these behaviors and the leading causes of illness and death among Americans, curriculum developers and teachers should target educational strategies at reducing the risks associated with the following:

- Tobacco use
- Poor eating habits
- Alcohol and other drug risks
- Behaviors that result in intentional or unintentional injuries
- Physical inactivity
- Sexual behaviors that result in HIV infection, other sexually transmitted diseases, or unintended pregnancy[21]

In addition to addressing personal health risks, school-based professionals must remember that human behavior in general, and health behavior specifically, is influenced by a complex set of variables. Though we must empower students to manage personal risks, it is equally important to recognize that such behaviors do not happen in a vacuum. Public health researchers have identified six important sources of influence over the health of individuals and communities. Similar to the causes of premature death identified in the 1979 *Healthy People,* these variables determine the health of today's Americans:

- *Biology:* genetic factors with which an individual is born, family history that may suggest a risk for disease, and health problems acquired during life.
- *Behaviors:* individual responses or reactions to internal stimuli and external conditions influenced by personal choices and physical and social environmental factors; they might or might not be under immediate or individual control.
- *Social environment:* social institutions, housing circumstances, cultural customs, and interactions with family, friends, and others in the community; individual behaviors both influence and are influenced by the social environment.
- *Physical environment:* health-promoting elements (clean, safe places) or health-threatening elements (toxic substances, irritants, infectious agents, and physical hazards) in the home, school, or community.
- *Public policies and interventions:* community campaigns and legislation (tobacco-free workplaces, indoor air-quality mandates, child restraint and immunization laws) that might be implemented by citizen groups, community agencies, schools, businesses, or government agencies in response to public activity.
- *Access to quality health care:* medical settings, schools, and community service providers.[22]

In the context of the discussion about chronic diseases, it becomes clear that the combination of individual behaviors and environmental factors is responsible for approximately 70 percent of all premature deaths in the United States. Only when we better understand and can address critical sources of influence and their combined effects can we hope to achieve the highest quality of health for all. This will require the coordinated efforts of individuals, families, schools, civic groups, faith-based organizations, and governmental agencies.[23]

HEALTHY AMERICANS, HEALTHY YOUTH

Since the publication of *Healthy People* in 1979, local, state, and federal agencies have been committed to a long-term broad and collaborative initiative. For three decades the U.S. Department of Health and Human Services (HHS) has established and monitored national health objectives targeting a broad range of current health issues. These specific and measurable objectives provide a framework to help individuals and communities take actions to improve their health.

Published in 2000, *Healthy People 2010* contains 467 health objectives based on the best science available. Like those in previous *Healthy People* ten-year plans, these objectives specify health outcomes targeted for achievement by the end of the first decade of the twenty-first century. This systematic plan was organized to address two overarching goals:

- To help individuals of all ages increase their life expectancy and improve their quality of life;
- To eliminate health disparities among different segments of the population, including those that occur as a result of sex, race or ethnicity, education, income, disability, place of residence, or sexual orientation.[24]

Of these objectives, 107 place a specific focus on improving some aspect of the health of children, adolescents, and young adults. Because the number of objectives relevant to this age group was so large, a task force of experts was convened to identify those objectives that address the most serious health and safety challenges facing the population. As a result, 21 critical health objectives were highlighted for attention, action, and cooperation among key stakeholders including families, schools, communities, agencies, and policymakers. This list included objectives that specified a role for K–12 schools.[25]

Midway through the decade, HHS conducted a midcourse review to assess the status of progress toward accomplishing the objectives in *Healthy People 2010*. Federal agencies and other experts assessed data trends and reviewed the newest and best research. As a result, a number

TABLE 1–4

Healthy People 2010 Objectives That Specify Action for Schools

Objective 6-9	Increase the proportion of youth with disabilities who spend at least 80 percent of their time in regular education programs
Objective 7-2	Increase the proportion of middle, junior high, and senior high schools that provide school health education to prevent health problems in the following areas: unintentional injury; violence; suicide; tobacco use and addiction; alcohol and other drug use; unintended pregnancy, HIV/AIDS, and STD infection; unhealthy dietary patterns; inadequate physical activity; and environmental health
Objective 7-4	Increase the proportion of the nation's elementary, middle, junior high, and senior high schools that have a nurse-to-student ratio of at least 1:750
Objective 8-20	Increase the proportion of the nation's primary and secondary schools that have official school policies ensuring the safety of students and staff from environmental hazards, such as chemicals in special classrooms, poor indoor air quality, asbestos, and exposure to pesticides
Objective 9-11	Increase the proportion of young adults who have received formal instruction before turning age 18 years on reproductive health issues, including all of the following topics: birth control methods, safer sex to prevent HIV, prevention of sexually transmitted diseases, and abstinence
Objective 14-23	Maintain vaccination coverage levels for children in licensed daycare facilities and children in kindergarten through the first grade
Objective 15-31	Increase the proportion of public and private schools that require use of appropriate head, face, eye, and mouth protection for students participating in school-sponsored physical activities
Objective 15-38	Reduce physical fighting among adolescents
Objective 15-39	Reduce weapon carrying by adolescents on school property
Objective 19-15	Increase the proportion of children and adolescents aged 6 to 19 years whose intake of meals and snacks at schools contributes to good overall dietary quality
Objective 21-13	Increase the proportion of school-based health centers with an oral health component
Objective 22-8	Increase the proportion of the nation's public and private schools that require daily physical education for all students
Objective 22-9	Increase the proportion of adolescents who participate in daily school physical education
Objective 22-10	Increase the proportion of adolescents who spend at least 50 percent of school physical education class time being physically active
Objective 22-12	Increase the proportion of the nation's public and private schools that provide access to their physical activity spaces and facilities for all persons outside of normal school hours (before and after the school day, on weekends, and during summer and other vacations)
Objective 24-5	Reduce the number of school or work days missed by persons with asthma due to asthma
Objective 27-2	Reduce tobacco use by adolescents
Objective 27-11	Increase smoke-free and tobacco-free environments in schools, including all school facilities, property, vehicles, and events

SOURCE: U.S. Department of Health and Human Services, *Healthy People 2010: Understanding and Improving Health*, 2nd ed. (Washington, D.C.: U.S. Government Printing Office, 2000).

NOTE: Education professionals are encouraged to evaluate the extent to which their schools have established policies and practices that bring them into compliance with these national health objectives.

of the original objectives were revised to ensure that all goals targeted for accomplishment by the end of the decade were current, relevant, and based on the most accurate data. Those revised objectives included a number focused on improving the health of children, adolescents, and young adults.[26] In particular, Table 1–4 lists objectives contained in the *Healthy People 2010 Midcourse Review* that have particular relevance for schools in promoting the health of students in elementary and/or middle schools.[27]

Prior to 2000, the average life span among Americans continued to increase steadily for over 200 years. In 2005, however, U.S. researchers concluded, "the steady rise in life expectancy during the past two centuries may soon come to an end."[28] It is now projected that between 2000 and 2050, life expectancy in the United States will level off or get shorter. Further, medical discoveries like those noted in Table 1–1 that reduced death rates during the 1900s will make a positive impact on the nation's health, but an "onrushing disaster will overshadow such advances."[29] Though tobacco use will continue to exert a negative influence on death rates,

research has confirmed that the "childhood obesity epidemic is an impending catastrophe. Nothing like this has happened before. Data have confirmed that the risks associated with this epidemic of childhood obesity will overwhelm any changes that medical science will make to affect longevity."[30]

Over the course of the *Healthy People* agenda, a systematic approach to promoting and protecting the nation's health was established. Individuals, organizations, and communities were given a formal structure around which activities could be organized and the success of these activities measured. At the state and federal level, the *Healthy People* agenda provided a system for collaboration, efficiency, and effectiveness in addressing complex public health issues. An organized and systematic structure to eliminate duplication of services and reduce costs associated with public health activities was established.

It is now more important than ever that all resources be mobilized to confront current public health challenges. If continuing increases in longevity are to be in our future, the complex problem of childhood obesity must be managed.

Quality health education can help empower children in all domains of health.

HEALTH IN THE ACADEMIC ENVIRONMENT

Today, youth are confronted with health, educational, and social challenges on a scale not experienced by previous generations of young Americans. Violence, alcohol and other drug use, obesity, unintended pregnancy and STDs, and disrupted family situations can compromise both short- and long-term health prospects.[31]

Educational institutions are in a unique and powerful position to improve health outcomes for youth. In the United States, over 55 million students are enrolled in approximately 125,000 public and private elementary and secondary schools. Each school day, over 95 percent of all 5- to 17-year-olds experience approximately six hours of instruction.[32] Schools represent the only public institution that can reach nearly all young people.[33]

Beyond offering efficient access to a critical mass, schools provide a setting in which friendship networks develop, socialization occurs, and norms that influence behavior are developed and reinforced.[34] Such social norms prevail in the environment before the health behaviors of most youth become habitual. Educators are academically prepared to organize developmentally appropriate learning experiences to empower children to lead safer, healthier lives.

However, advocates committed to promoting child and adolescent health in schools have struggled to co-exist with a sweeping national priority to reform public education. Since the early 1980s, many research reports, position statements, and legislative initiatives have been directed at improving the quality of education for all students. This reform agenda has taken many forms, including experimentation with strategies to improve teacher preparation, evaluation of student performance, and the U.S. Supreme Court decision supporting vouchers to promote school choice options for parents. Most school improvement plans have targeted specific quantitative measures of student performance in the basic, or core, academic subjects: language arts, mathematics, social studies, and the physical sciences.

Support for academic activities designed to address the complex health issues confronting students has been very limited in calls for education reform. *A Nation at Risk*, a report by the National Commission on Excellence in Education, included health education on a list of academic subjects categorized as part of the "educational smorgasbord." This prestigious and powerful 1983 report, sponsored by the U.S. Department of Education, asserted that American education curricula had become "diluted . . . and diffused" and recommended that educational programs in this "smorgasbord" category be either eliminated or significantly reduced in emphasis.[35] The legacy of such findings is found in the federal No Child Left Behind legislation, discussed in Chapter 2.

In an effort to respond to concerns about the competing demands placed on limited instructional time in the school day, the Mid-continent Regional Educational Laboratory (McRel) conducted an analysis revealing public perceptions concerning the importance of health knowledge and skills for today's students. Research has confirmed that between the time most students start their formal schooling in kindergarten and the time they graduate, schools have about 9,042 hours of instructional time with which to work. McRel's analysis revealed that over 15,000 hours of instruction would be necessary to adequately address all the content and skills specified in the national and state standards across all content areas for which standards have been developed. Given current time parameters, students would need to stay in school through grades 21 or 22 just to meet all national and state mandates. Clearly, within the current education system that solution is impossible.

Responding to the problem of too much content and too little time, McRel conducted an analysis of the American public's perception of the relative importance of the standards in published national and state documents. Specifically, this study was designed to gauge adult perceptions of what should and should not be included in the K–12 educational experience of American students. The knowledge and skills specified in the National Health Education Standards received the highest overall rating among respondents. In this study, an average of 73.9 percent of adults responded that it was "definitely" necessary for students to master skills in this subject before high school graduation. No one would suggest that public perception should be the sole criterion for judging the relative value of academic content areas to the lives of students, but these findings do lend strong support for addressing student health issues during school.[36]

In addition, a growing body of science has emerged to support the assertion that student health behaviors and the way schools address them are "inextricably intertwined."[37] The American Cancer Society and representatives of over forty national organizations concluded that "healthy children are in a better position to acquire knowledge" and cautioned that no curriculum is "brilliant enough to compensate for a hungry stomach or a distracted mind."[38] To reinforce this position, Harriet Tyson asserted,

> While there are no signs of any political retreat from the steely focus on academic outcomes, there is an awakening to the notion that education reform may require creative interventions that lower the barriers to learning and reduce risky behavior. First among those barriers are poor physical and mental health conditions that compromise students from showing up for school, paying attention in class, restraining their anger, quieting their self-destructive impulses, and refraining from dropping-out.[39]

In 2004, the Council of Chief State School Officers (CCSSO), the professionals responsible for education programming and policy in each state, issued *Policy Statement on School Health*. Recognizing that "healthy kids make better learners and that better students make healthy communities," this policy statement urged education leaders "to recognize the enormous impact that health has on the academic achievement of our nation's youth." Consistent with Tyson, this policy statement urged the education community to "look beyond standards setting and systems of accountability and join with public and private sector mental health, health, and social services providers to address the widespread conditions that interfere with student learning and students' prospects for healthy adulthood."[40]

Beyond making this statement of advocacy, the CCSSO specified a number of recommendations for state and local education leaders. States were encouraged to demonstrate their commitment to linking health and academic success by engaging in activities such as the following:

- Disseminating data that confirm the impact of health-promoting activities on academic achievement
- Designating senior-level staff to oversee school health-related activities
- Supporting policies that promote student health, including restricting vending machine sales, prohibiting tobacco use on school property, and ensuring health insurance coverage for all students and staff
- Ensuring curricular compliance with the National Health Education Standards
- Allocating adequate funding for school health promotion[41]

A variety of advocacy and professional organizations recognized that a focus on school-based health promotion initiatives must occur in context of, rather than in competition with, strategies to improve education outcomes. To that end, the Association for Supervision and Curriculum Development (ASCD) convened the Commission on the Whole Child in 2006. This esteemed group was charged with the responsibility of re-defining the definition of the "successful learner."[42] Their specific task was to reframe the understanding of a "successful learner" from a student whose achievement is measured only by scores on academic tests, to one who is knowledgeable, emotionally and physically healthy, engaged in civic activities and events, involved in the arts, prepared for work and for economic self-sufficiency, and ready for the world after completing formal schooling.[43]

The Position Statement on the Whole Child, developed by this group, affirms that academics remain essential, but are only one element of student learning and development. Rigorous testing can be only one part of a complete system of educational accountability. In an expansion of conventional thinking about education reform, the "new compact" established by ASCD calls on teachers, schools, and communities to collaborate to ensure that

- "Each student enters school healthy and learns about and practices a healthy lifestyle,
- Each student learns in an intellectually challenging environment that is physically and emotionally safe for students and adults,
- Each student is actively engaged in learning and is connected to the school and broader community,
- Each student has access to personalized learning and to qualified, caring adults, and
- Each graduate is prepared for success in college or further study and for employment in a global environment."[44]

Achieving these ambitious outcomes for learners requires a foundation of supportive and involved families, community volunteers, and advocates for health promotion networks and school health councils, and the support of governmental, civic, and business organizations. Schools must develop challenging and engaging curricula, provide professional development and planning time for high-quality teachers and administrators, cultivate a safe, healthy, orderly, and trusting learning environment, promote strong relationships between adults and students, and support health promotion networks and school health councils. Teachers must use evidence-based instruction and assessment practices, engage learners in rich content, make connections with students and families, manage their classrooms effectively, and model healthy behaviors.[45]

Given the complex health and learning challenges facing today's students it is critical for educators, families, and other advocates to remember that children don't grow and learn in isolation. They grow physically, emotionally, ethically, expressively, and intellectually in networks of families, schools, neighborhoods, and communities. Educating the whole child won't happen with emphasis only on measures of academic achievement.[46]

Health promotion activities are gaining credibility as an effective and efficient way to promote student success. Mounting evidence has confirmed the destructive impact of student health risks on attendance, class grades, performance on standardized tests, and graduation rates.[47] The kinds of programs and policies adopted by school communities have been demonstrated to improve both health and achievement outcomes for students. Although schools can't be expected to assume sole responsibility for addressing the health and social problems confronting youth, they provide an institutional and organizational focal point for student health education and promotion.[48]

THE COORDINATED SCHOOL HEALTH PROGRAM

A Foundation for Understanding

Those concerned about student health risks and their impact on academic outcomes are encouraged to advocate for effective school health programming in conjunction with activities to promote achievement. It is clear that even the most talented students are confronted with risks for alcohol or other drug-related behaviors, pregnancy, or the negative outcomes of violence. Unfortunately, crisis intervention approaches to health issues are all too common in school communities. Rather than developing sound and sustained programming, it is common for educators to mobilize to confront complex student health risks only when there is a problem or a newsworthy event. Such strategies meet the needs of only limited numbers of students and have been demonstrated to produce short-lived outcomes.

The 1979 *Healthy People* initiative provided a starting point for organizing effective school health programs by defining the key concepts of medical care, disease prevention, and health promotion. It is crucial for student health advocates to understand these concepts as a foundation for framing boundaries of professional practice, identifying realistic program expectations, and targeting key stakeholders with shared responsibility for the health of learners.

In *Healthy People*, "medical care" is defined with a primary focus on "the sick" and involves activities designed "to keep these individuals alive, make them well, or minimize their disability."[49] Each day, children enrolled in America's schools receive medical care consistent with this definition. They have diagnosed conditions and clinicians have prescribed a treatment regimen. School-based education professionals are not equipped to provide diagnostic and therapeutic intervention. Exceptions exist only in circumstances in which first aid or emergency care must be provided. Even in such cases, only trained individuals in the education community should render emergency care. The appropriate role for school-based professionals in managing students requiring medical care includes referral, support, and compliance with the prescriptions and proscriptions made by attending clinicians. Educators should help parents and trained others carry out care plans developed by clinicians.

By contrast, disease prevention "begins with a threat to health—a disease or environmental hazard—and seeks to protect as many people as possible from the harmful consequences of that threat."[50] Disease prevention is best understood as the process of "reducing risks and alleviating disease to promote, preserve, and restore health and minimize suffering and distress."[51] Often, teachers emphasize hand washing and proper disposal of soiled tissues as part of daily classroom practice. Education professionals collaborate with school nurses, administrators, parents, and medical care providers to manage outbreaks of infectious conditions, including chicken pox, head lice, and the flu. School policymakers work with public health officials in screening and enforcing compliance with immunization policies. Whether working independently in the classroom setting or collaborating with others on issues of a broader scope, teachers assume a much more active role in disease prevention than in medical care strategies within the school setting.

Though there are circumstances in which medical care and disease prevention strategies are warranted, school-based professionals must be most comfortable with activities that focus on student health promotion. *Healthy People* defined all strategies that begin with "people who are basically healthy" as the target for health promotion activities. Health promotion "seeks the development of community and individual measures which can help [people] develop healthy lifestyles that can maintain and enhance the state of well-being."[52] The definition of health promotion was updated in the Report of the 2000 Joint Committee on Health Education and Promotion Terminology. This document clarified that health promotion is best understood as any "planned combination of educational, political, environmental, regulatory, or organizational mechanisms that support actions and conditions of living conducive to the health of individuals, groups, and communities."[53]

In this context, the primary task for education professionals who work with the majority of students who are "basically healthy" is to plan, coordinate, and implement health promotion programming for individuals in the school community. As concluded in *Healthy People*,

> Beginning in early childhood and throughout life, each of us makes decisions affecting our health. They are made, for the most part, without regard to, or contact with, the health care delivery system. Yet their cumulative impact has a greater effect on the length and quality of life than all the efforts of medical care combined.[54]

A commitment to health promotion at the school site provides a foundation for proactive collaboration by many stakeholders invested in the health of learners and school success. The contrast between conventional approaches to school health and implementation of the health promotion philosophy previously discussed is highlighted in Consider This 1.2, "A Fence or an Ambulance." This poem, written in the 1800s, clarifies the value of making a commitment to a health promotion philosophy based on a commitment to prevention.

A Program Model for Best Practice

Built on the foundation of a health promotion philosophy, the best approach to managing complex student health challenges rests in organizing all available resources,

A Fence or an Ambulance   Joseph Malins

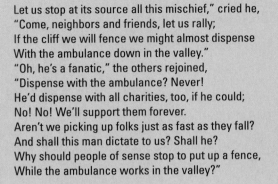

'Twas a dangerous cliff, as they freely confessed,
Though to walk near its crest was so pleasant;
But over its terrible edge there had slipped
A duke and full many a peasant.
So the people said something would have to be done,
But their projects did not at all tally;
Some said, "Put a fence around the edge of the cliff,"
Some, "An ambulance down in the valley."

But the cry for the ambulance carried the day,
For it spread through the neighboring city;
A fence may be useful or not, it is true,
But each heart became brimful of pity
For those who slipped over that dangerous cliff;
And the dwellers in highway and alley
Gave pounds or gave pence, not to put up a fence,
But an ambulance down in the valley.

"For the cliff is all right, if you're careful," they said,
"And, if folks even slip and are dropping,
It isn't the slipping that hurts them so much,
As the shock down below when they're stopping."
So day after day, as these mishaps occurred,
Quick forth would these rescuers sally
To pick up the victims who fell off the cliff,
With their ambulance down in the valley.

Then an old sage remarked: "It's a marvel to me
That people give far more attention
To repairing results than to stopping the cause,
When they'd much better aim at prevention.

Let us stop at its source all this mischief," cried he,
"Come, neighbors and friends, let us rally;
If the cliff we will fence we might almost dispense
With the ambulance down in the valley."
"Oh, he's a fanatic," the others rejoined,
"Dispense with the ambulance? Never!
He'd dispense with all charities, too, if he could;
No! No! We'll support them forever.
Aren't we picking up folks just as fast as they fall?
And shall this man dictate to us? Shall he?
Why should people of sense stop to put up a fence,
While the ambulance works in the valley?"

But a sensible few, who are practical too,
Will not bear with such nonsense much longer;
They believe that prevention is better than cure,
And their party will soon be the stronger.
Encourage them then, with your purse, voice, and pen,
And while other philanthropists dally,
They will scorn all pretense and put up a stout fence
On the cliff that hangs over the valley.

Better guide well the young than reclaim them when old,
For the voice of true wisdom is calling,
"To rescue the fallen is good, but 'tis best
To prevent other people from falling."
Better close up the source of temptation and crime
Than deliver from dungeon or galley;
Better put a strong fence round the top of the cliff
Than an ambulance down in the valley.

---

expertise, and activities into a model representing best practice. Most schools invest considerable time and expertise in managing a range of health problems, but it is common for such activities to take place as isolated or competing entities. Schools organize categorical activities, including Red Ribbon Week campaigns to reduce drug risks, transportation safety activities at the start of the school year, physical education instruction, and free or reduced-cost lunches for children living in poverty, with little thought for focus or coordination. Most school health programs operate under a "more of anything" rather than a "better is better" philosophy.

By contrast, in the report of the 2000 Joint Committee on Health Education and Promotion Terminology, a coordinated school health program model is defined as "an organized set of policies, procedures, and activities designed to protect, promote, and improve the health and well-being of students and staff, thus improving a student's ability to learn. It includes, but is not limited to comprehensive school health education; school health services; a healthy school environment; school counseling; psychological and social services; physical education; school nutrition services; family and community involvement in school health; and school-site health promotion for staff."[55]

The CDC and many other national organizations endorse the model of the Coordinated School Health Program (CSHP). The CSHP provides a formal model around which the talents and efforts of many disciplines within the school are coordinated with those of families and community groups to promote student health and school success. With an emphasis on coordination, all activities are organized to deliver consistent, health-promoting messages that are reinforced across multiple communication channels in the school and throughout the community. The resources and professionals identified in such a program already exist and function in some fashion in most school communities. As such, rather than demanding the investment of additional tax dollars, developing a CSHP requires an investment of intentional coordination and collaboration.

Dr. Lloyd Kolbe, one of the architects of CSHP, revisited his original work and concluded that the goals of the modern school health program are consistent with the agenda of educational reform. Consistent with the advocacy

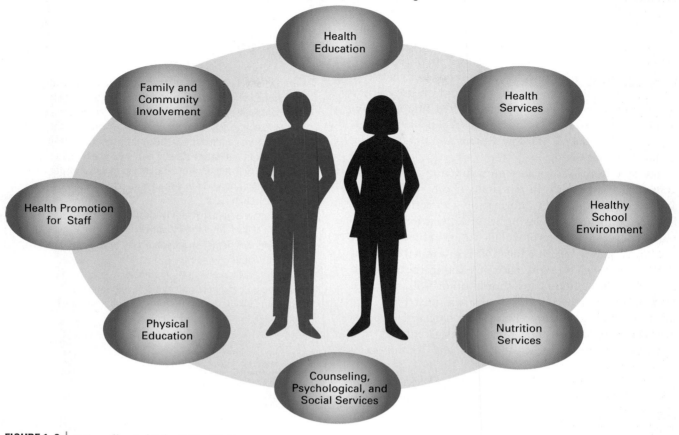

FIGURE 1–2 | **A Coordinated School Health Program**

Source: Centers for Disease Control and Prevention. (www.cdc.gov/HealthyYouth/cshp)

position taken by ASCD for education for the "whole child," Dr. Kolbe asserted that modern school health programs develop when the efforts of education, health, and social service professionals are integrated purposefully to tackle four overlapping and interdependent types of goals for students:

- Goals focused on improving health knowledge, attitudes, and skills
- Goals focused on improving health behaviors and outcomes
- Goals focused on improving educational outcomes
- Goals focused on improving social outcomes among learners[56]

Rather than emerging from a competitive position, such programs put both student health and academic achievement at the heart of the matter and provide an efficient and effective way to improve, protect, and promote the well-being of students, families, and professionals in the education system.

Student health advocates should review Figure 1–2, a depiction of the CSHP model, which is designed to

- Maximize the impact of all available expertise and resources directed toward risk reduction and health promotion

- Conserve taxpayer dollars by reducing duplication of services for health issues
- Maximize use of public facilities in the school and community to promote health
- Enhance communication and collaboration across health promotion professionals in the school and community
- Address student health risks in the context of, rather than in competition with, the academic mission of the school

Health Education: The Keys to Quality Health Instruction

The most familiar element of the CSHP is its educational, or instructional, foundation: comprehensive school health education. This element of an effective school-based health promotion program is defined as "the part of the CSHP that includes the development, delivery, and evaluation of planned, sequential, and developmentally appropriate instruction, learning experiences, and other activities designed to protect, promote, and enhance the health literacy, attitudes, skills and well-being of students, pre-kindergarten through grade 12. The content is derived from the National Health Education Standards, and guidelines that are available in some states."[57] As such, a program of quality health instruction is focused on enabling and empowering students to gather accurate health information, evaluate attitudes that influence personal and community health, and practice the skills needed to integrate health-enhancing behaviors into daily living. To accomplish this, the health education program of study must be addressed with the same commitment and integrity as any other academic discipline. Review selected findings from SHPPS 2006 concerning comprehensive school health education in the Chapter 1 "More Resources" section of the Online Learning Center.

Student health advocates must update conventional approaches to health instruction. Those instructional approaches grounded in information acquisition are not likely to influence complex health-risk behaviors. Consistent with best-practice protocol identified in the education literature, quality health education is grounded in activities that bridge all three domains of learning: the (1) cognitive, (2) affective, and (3) psychomotor, or skill, domains. In addition, health education curricula must reflect the most current and accurate knowledge base and incorporate developmentally appropriate, ability centered, and culturally relevant learning materials and technological resources.

Consistent with such an approach to best practice, a collaborative committee representing national health and advocacy organizations published *National Health Education Standards: Achieving Excellence* (2nd ed.) in 2007. This publication outlined national standards developed to set ambitious goals for improving health education for all students. The developers also specified a rationale for each standard and performance indicators to be achieved by students in grades 2, 5, 8, and 12. Elementary and middle school teachers should examine Appendix A, containing the health education performance indicators for students in grades Pre-K–2, 3–5, and 6–8. Teacher's Toolbox 1.1 shows the broad range of health content areas of the National Health Education Standards. The standards provide a framework for developing a rigorous health education instructional scope and sequence and meaningful evaluation protocol for students in all grade levels.[58] The School Health Policies and Programs Study (SHPPS) conducted in 2006, confirmed that 74.5 percent of states mandating standards-based health education have used the National Health Education Standards as a starting point for curriculum update or revision.[59] Chapter 3 contains an expanded discussion of the National Health Education Standards and their applicability for improving health education practice.

In addition to standards-based approaches, state legislatures and boards of education often require that certain time allocations be mandated for health instruction, and there is great variability among state mandates. It is common for more formal instructional time to be devoted to health education in the upper-elementary and middle-level grades than in the primary grades. SHPPS 2006 confirmed that the percentage of schools mandating health

---

Teacher's Toolbox 1.1

National Health Education Standards

1. Students will comprehend concepts related to health promotion and disease prevention to enhance health.
2. Students will analyze the influence of family, peers, culture, media, technology, and other factors on health behaviors.
3. Students will demonstrate the ability to access valid information and products and services to enhance health.
4. Students will demonstrate the ability to use interpersonal communication skills to enhance health and avoid or reduce health risks.
5. Students will demonstrate the ability to use decision-making skills to enhance health.
6. Students will demonstrate the ability to use goal-setting skills to enhance health.
7. Students will demonstrate the ability to practice health-enhancing behaviors and avoid or reduce risks.
8. Students will demonstrate the ability to advocate for personal, family, and community health.

NOTE: "This list of health education standards represents the work of the Joint Committee on National Health Education Standards. Copies of *National Health Education Standards: Achieving Excellence* can be obtained through the American School Health Association, the Association for the Advancement of Health Education, or the American Cancer Society."

SOURCE: Reprinted with permission, from the American Cancer Society, *National Health Education Standards: Achieving Excellence*, 2nd ed. (Atlanta, GA: American Cancer Society, 2007). www.cancer.org/bookstore

---

instruction increases by the greatest percentage between kindergarten and grade 5. Only 8.5 percent of schools mandate health instruction for students in grade 12, a time when most young people confront a broad range of health risks.[60]

Across both the standards- and time-based models of health education, research has revealed that more hours of formal health instruction are necessary to produce changes in the affective domain than in either the cognitive or the psychomotor domain of learning. Further, forty to fifty hours of formal health education is necessary to produce stable improvements across all three domains: knowledge, attitudes, and skills.[61]

In addition to instructional time, there is great variability in the health topics addressed in the curricula of local school districts. Choosing or developing the best possible health education curriculum is an important step in making sure that the program of instruction is effective at promoting healthy behaviors among all students. Unfortunately, in many districts, the process of curriculum selection or development lacks structure and focus. A diffuse approach can result in inadequate and ineffective health instruction.

In response, the CDC has developed the Health Education Curriculum Analysis Tool (HECAT), which contains guidance, tools, and resources for completing a clear, complete, and consistent analysis of health education curricula. Districts that use HECAT will find help in selecting

Teacher's Toolbox 1.2

Sound Health Education: Instructional Topics for Which HECAT Criteria Have Been Developed

- Mental and emotional health
- Healthy eating
- Physical activity
- Safety/unintentional injury prevention
- Personal health and wellness
- Violence prevention
- Tobacco-free lifestyle
- Alcohol- and drug-free lifestyle
- Sexual health

SOURCE: Centers for Disease Control and Prevention, *Health Education Curriculum Analysis Tool* (Atlanta, GA: Centers for Disease Control and Prevention, 2007).

TABLE 1–5

Keys to Quality Health Instruction: A Checklist of Important Questions That Confirm a Commitment to Comprehensive School Health Education

Has your school community developed a planned, sequential, developmentally appropriate pre-K through grade 12 health curriculum focused on the six CDC problem priorities and the HECAT instructional health topics?

Does the district curriculum extend beyond knowledge acquisition and structure sufficient learning activities for students to practice skills necessary for the adoption of health-promoting behaviors?

Has the health education curriculum been developed with attention to the national or state school health standards?

Are credentialed certified health educators employed to coordinate and deliver the program of health instruction?

Is sufficient time built into the academic year at each grade level for meaningful health education?

Have provisions been made to evaluate, update, and improve the health education curriculum at regular intervals?

Do parents and designees from community health agencies participate as active partners in health instruction?

Is an ongoing program of health-related staff development provided for administration, faculty, and staff?

---

or developing evidence-based, appropriate, and effective health education courses of study. Schools that implement HECAT will implement curricula that will improve health education instruction and promote healthy behaviors among students.[62]

This book is organized around HECAT curricular themes. In addition to an expanded discussion of HECAT in Chapter 2, curricular topics are organized into two sections:

- Section II: Helping Students Develop Skills for Positive Health Habits
- Section III: Helping Students Translate Their Skills to Manage Health Risks

Teacher's Toolbox 1.2 highlights priority health issues that should be addressed in a developmentally appropriate way with all students in elementary and middle grades.[63]

Unlike secondary schools, in which content specialists are employed, elementary and middle school classroom teachers often are expected to deliver the health education program. In such cases, it is common for the school nurse or community resource personnel to provide instructional support or supplemental expertise. Many elementary and middle school teachers report that they have inadequate academic preparation to teach complex or often controversial health education topics, and lack confidence or enthusiasm for health instruction due to limitations from their teacher preparation program. Unfortunately, state departments of education often specify only minimal requirements for teacher certification or licensure for those who will teach health education concepts to younger learners.

As a solution, responsibilities and competencies have been developed for the professional preparation of elementary and middle school classroom teachers who assume the primary responsibility for teaching health education to young students. These responsibilities and competencies, developed by representatives of professional health education associations, are identified in the Chapter 1 "More Resources" section of the Online Learning Center.[64, 65]

Readers can use the competencies as a foundation for conducting a self-check of strengths and weaknesses in their own expertise. Classroom teachers who feel ill prepared or uncomfortable managing health education topics or a range of instructional activities are encouraged to participate in staff development or continuing education opportunities for in-service professionals. Such programs are designed to help teachers update content expertise and develop skills to improve classroom instruction.

In summary, SHPPS 2006 reminds us that over 85 percent of elementary and middle schools have been mandated by their state departments of education to teach some health education to enrolled students.[66] Administrators, curriculum developers, and teachers can review Table 1–5 for a checklist of important questions regarding the elements of a comprehensive school health education program, the keys to quality health instruction. Readers will also find more information about comprehensive school health education in Chapter 2.

Health Services

The practice of providing health services in the school setting began in the early twentieth century as a way to improve academic outcomes for students. Public health nurses began working in schools to reduce student absenteeism related to outbreaks of communicable diseases.[67] Today, although communicable diseases are still an issue for many students, there are many other complex health-related barriers to academic achievement. Asthma, child abuse and neglect, domestic and school violence, adolescent pregnancy and parenting, alcohol and other drug use, mental health concerns, and a lack of health insurance coverage are among the issues addressed by today's school health service providers.[68]

School health services include a range of policies and programs designed to assess the health status of children, as well as measures to protect the health of all children. Although various school personnel contribute to the school health service program, the school nurse assumes primary responsibility for leadership in this component of the CSHP. With the support of parents, teachers, administrators, support staff, community agency professionals, and a range of medical care providers, the school nurse leads the collaborative effort to

- Direct patient care, including screening, diagnostic, treatment, and health counseling services
- Maintain referral and linkages with other community health service providers
- Collaborate in health promotion and injury and disease prevention education[69]

The school nurse assumes a pivotal role in assuring the continuity of care for students with health-related barriers to school success. The school nurse coordinates, plans, provides, and evaluates the range of school health services for all re-enrolled students. School nurses, physicians, and others on the school health services team support student health and learning by acting as liaison among the school, home, and medical communities. For example, many school nurses take an active role in the collaborative development and management of individual health plans (IHPs) and individualized education programs (IEPs) to enrich learning for students with special needs. To fulfill their complex assignment, school nurses share the following responsibilities for all patients with their counterparts in other medical care settings:

1. "Providing age-appropriate, and culturally, and ethnically sensitive care,
2. Maintaining safe environments,
3. Educating patients [students] about healthy practices and treatment modalities,
4. Assuring continuity of care,
5. Coordinating care across settings and among care givers,
6. Managing information, and
7. Communicating effectively."[70]

The effective and timely delivery of such services is affected by the number of nurses available at the school site to respond to students' needs. The number of trained nurses needed to manage the student caseload effectively and efficiently within a district is influenced by a number of factors, including

- Education/professional preparation of the school nurse
- Functions mandated by the board of education for the school nurse
- The number and location of buildings within the district to be served
- Social attributes, economic characteristics, cultural status, and access to medical care within the community
- Special health problems of students
- Licensed or unlicensed personnel to provide assistance
- Presence or absence of a school-based clinic[71]

The National Association of School Nurses (NASN) has issued an important position statement in which it is asserted that, to meet the health and safety needs of all students, the maximum ratio of nurse to student should be

- One school health nurse to no more than 750 students in the general school population,
- One school health nurse to no more than 225 students who may require daily professional nursing services or interventions,
- One school health nurse to no more than 125 students in the severely chronically ill or developmentally disabled population (those with complex healthcare needs), and
- A potential one-to-one ratio for individual students who need daily and continuous professional nursing services.[72]

This NASN position statement quantified recommendations for best practice. These recommendations have been reinforced in *Healthy People 2010,* and by important federal actions. In 1999, the U.S. Supreme Court ruled that schools must provide all nursing services required by students to attend school, including one-on-one nursing care.[73] Unfortunately, SHPPS 2006 confirmed that, although slightly over 50 percent of schools have a part-time or full-time nurse to provide health services, only 45.1 percent of schools are in compliance with the 1:750 recommended nurse-to-student ratio.[74] (Readers can review selected findings from SHPPS 2006 concerning school health services in the Online Learning Center (OLC).)

Although debate continues about the kinds and extent of direct health services that should be provided at the school site, school nurses must manage care plans for students with special health care needs. In addition, nurses must institute policy and protocol approved by the board of education for administering medication to students. As the number of students with special needs attending schools grows, new, expensive, and often labor-intensive demands are placed on school districts and their health service providers. School administrators have legal responsibility for the safety of all students enrolled in the district, including providing and supervising the program of health services. Unfortunately, many school districts have assigned these tasks to untrained classroom teachers and secretaries. Such practices are dangerous for the student, the school employee, and the school district.

The National Association of State School Nurse Consultants has asserted that health services should be provided directly by licensed professional school nurses or delegated to qualified paraprofessionals or trained unlicensed assistants under the supervision of the trained school nurse.[75] Consistent with this assertion, Teacher's Toolbox 1.3 includes minimum policy recommendations (provided by NASN) to guide safe and effective administration of medications in schools.[76] Boards of education and district administrators are encouraged to review local policies to affirm that they ensure the safety and legal protection of all concerned.

Although school nurses assume primary leadership for the provision of health services, many other educators and advocates are engaged in responding to student health issues that can compromise achievement. Classroom teachers are in an important position to participate in initial observation and referral of any conditions evident in students with whom they have contact. Reports of such observations should be made to the school nurse or other designees specified in school district policy. In response, the coordinated team of health service providers can plan appropriate interventions to address the problem.

School nurses also collaborate with a range of allied health professionals in providing a formalized program of student health status assessments. In most school districts, a child must have a health examination before enrolling in school. Some school districts require additional periodic health examinations for students. These requirements vary from state to state. Most states also require vision and hearing screening at some point in the child's schooling. Often, vision and hearing difficulties are not identified until the child enters school. Scoliosis screening is a simple, but very effective, procedure to identify spinal curvatures in schoolchildren in upper-elementary grades. During the elementary school years, the child's weight and height also are recorded. These measurements provide a record of basic childhood growth and development. A review of a chart containing student growth data can provide quick confirmation that a child's physical development is on pace with chronological age.

School health service professionals also coordinate disease prevention measures and participate in activities to protect the health of students, faculty, and staff. To this end, policies must be developed in collaboration with public health officials to exclude from school activities those children who are infected with contagious conditions. All district policies governing communicable disease risk reduction should be available for school staff and caregivers to promote collaboration in risk reduction. Classroom teachers must be informed about when and under what circumstances a child excluded from school due to a communicable disease can be permitted to return.

Every state has a legislative mandate requiring that children be immunized against certain communicable diseases before they can enroll in school. Although these state requirements differ slightly, immunization requirements for polio, diphtheria, pertussis, tetanus, measles (rubeola), German measles (rubella), and hepatitis are common. Accurate record keeping and communication with immunization providers are very time-consuming, but important, roles of the school nurse.

Finally, it is imperative that school districts develop written policies for managing sick and injured students. In addition to a protocol for managing emergencies, staff development programs must ensure full compliance with universal precautions for handling body fluid spills in the educational environment. Such training should be extended to all school staff, including playground monitors, bus drivers, and other classified staff.

Clearly, the program of school health services fills a critical role in promoting student health and advancing the

Confirming a Commitment to a Quality Program of Health Services: A Checklist of Important Elements

Has your board of education adopted plans and policies concerning

- Prevention and control of communicable diseases?
- Provision of emergency care and first aid?
- Health status appraisal of all students?
- Response to students with special needs?
- Screening, referral, management, and record keeping for students within these areas:

Vision	Hearing
Height/weight	Scoliosis
Blood pressure	Dental health

- Physical exams for all students prior to participation in co-curricular activities?

Have policies and protocol been institutionalized for record keeping and compliance with state immunization mandates?

Have staff development activities been implemented to promote sanitation and compliance with universal precaution recommendations?

Are instructional, transportation, and physical activity areas stocked with universal precaution supplies?

Are plans implemented for the safe distribution of student medications?

Have interagency networks been established to assure confidential, quality, and collaborative services for students?

Do health service professionals participate in the academic program of health instruction?

Are sufficient numbers of licensed health service staff members employed?

Do employed professionals participate in a program of continuing professional education?

academic mission of schools. Table 1–6 provides a checklist for effective review of important elements in a quality program of school health services.

Healthy School Environment

Like other elements of the CSHP depicted in Figure 1–2, the school environment in which a student spends a large part of each day makes an impact on both health status and achievement. The most conspicuous element of a healthy school environment is related to the physical condition of the buildings, vehicles, playgrounds, sport facilities, and other school district properties. Policies adopted by the local board of education govern safety and management of noise, temperature, lighting, and air and water quality in physical learning environments.

The quality of the physical learning environment of any school district is maintained through the consistent implementation of such health-promoting policies. Thus, the school principal assumes primary responsibility for maintaining a healthy and safe environment through the enforcement of district policies at the building level.

Though school leaders adopt policies to ensure health and safety within all facilities in the district, it is the responsibility of all school personnel to ensure that children do not become injured in their classrooms or during activities for which they are the designated supervisors. Although this does not mean that the classroom teacher must make necessary repairs to school equipment, it is important to report any potential health hazards to designated district personnel. To ensure that potential hazards are addressed quickly, teachers should make such reports in writing.

A primary source of concern for school environmental advocates is the management of specific physical health hazards. Physical hazards include the temperature of the rooms in which the students spend the school day. Rooms that are too warm or too cold can detract from the learning experience and can cause health problems. The physical surroundings of the classroom, including lighting, glare, and room color, affect students' attitude as well as their ability to function to their full capacity. Distracting, repetitive noise can also affect students, both psychologically and physically. Finally, the U.S. Environmental Protection Agency and other researchers have confirmed that poor indoor air quality can cause illnesses that lead to increased absences, create health symptoms that decrease school performance, and reduce student ability to perform mental tasks requiring concentration, memory, or calculation.[77]

School districts also are responsible for the safety of students being transported on school buses and in other school vehicles. Because the potential for injury is always present, all school vehicles must be in safe operating condition. In addition, bus drivers should be provided with continuing education opportunities concerning the operation of the bus, the management of the behaviors of their young passengers, and compliance with universal precautions in the event of an emergency in which someone could be exposed to blood or other body fluids.

The role of the classroom teacher with regard to transportation issues includes the provision of instruction and supervision. Children need to learn appropriate ways to get on and off buses and safe and appropriate behavior when they are being transported. Also, students should receive information about safe places to wait for the bus along the roadways and how to proceed from the bus after disembarking.

Students need to learn safe routes for other modes of transportation to and from school. Each year, teachers of elementary students would be wise to review policies established to protect students who don't travel by bus, addressing neighborhood traffic patterns, designated pedestrian areas, and safe bicycle routes on and around school grounds. In addition, students should be familiar with the names of transportation safety supervisors with whom they will come in contact.

In cooperation with community police departments, many school districts participate in school safety patrol programs. These programs, intended to meet the needs of students who attend schools within walking distance

TABLE 1–7

Confirming a Commitment to Promoting and Maintaining a Healthy School Environment: A Checklist of Important Questions

Does your school district maintain compliance with state standards for cleanliness, lighting, heating, ventilation, and management of environmental hazards in public buildings?

Does your district participate in periodic health and safety inspections and staff development for certified and classified staff?

Are board-adopted policies consistently enforced to ensure a safe and tobacco-, alcohol-, and other drug–free school campus?

Are board-adopted policies consistently enforced to ensure that fund-raising and celebration activities do not contradict the commitment to health promotion?

Is a districtwide/community school health advisory council in operation?

Does the administration demonstrate support for the CSHP?

Is there a designated coordinator/director of the CSHP?

What formal provisions are made to maintain a supportive and caring emotional climate to which students feel connected?

Are health promotion activities extended beyond the district and into the community?

of their homes, are designed to teach pedestrian safety to students in elementary grades. Older students volunteer or are selected and receive training in how to help younger students cross intersections and roadways. The importance of proper selection and rigorous training of members of the student safety patrol cannot be overstated. In addition, many districts employ adults to monitor student safety at the busiest, or most hazardous, intersections in the district.

Another critical, but often overlooked, aspect of a healthy environment is the social and psychological climate of the school. Schools need to be places where all students and staff feel cared for, included in events, and personally valued.[78] School personnel must collaborate to establish an inviting, safe, and nurturing learning environment that extends throughout the school campus. Research has confirmed that students who feel like engaged citizens of their schools report greater enjoyment of their academic experience than do their counterparts attending less healthy schools. These engaged students also demonstrate patterns of higher academic achievement.[79]

Research involving fifth graders has found that the environment, or social context, of a school is related to a range of student attitudes and behaviors. In this study, social context was defined as a school environment that students perceived to be caring. Student participation in co-curricular activities, development of shared norms, and involvement in decision making concerning school matters all were shown to be important components of healthier social context. This study confirmed that those students who attended schools with a stronger sense of community tended to engage in less drug taking and delinquent behavior.[80]

Educators are reminded that the important elements of a healthy school environment are not limited to the maintenance of physical facilities and the establishment of a welcoming emotional climate. School districts must consistently enforce policies managing student behaviors in priority risk areas. These include bullying; weapon carrying; tobacco, alcohol, and other drug possession; and instances of acting-out. Such policies must be enforced consistently for all students and personnel within the school community. Enforcement of tobacco-free campus policies during all school activities and elimination of fund-raising activities that threaten the nutritional health of students are examples of such policies under review in many school districts.

Creating and maintaining a safe and healthy school environment is consistent with two objectives specified in *Healthy People 2010*. Review Table 1–4, for highlights of specific goals concerning managing environmental hazards at the school site and promoting tobacco-free school campuses. Unfortunately, SHPPS 2006 revealed that only 65.5 percent of elementary and 58.7 percent of middle schools had policies that (1) prohibited smoking and smokeless tobacco use among all students, visitors in buildings and on school grounds, buses or other school vehicles, and at off-campus school-sponsored events, and (2) prohibited cigar or pipe smoking by all students, faculty, staff, and visitors.[81] Clearly, we have a long way to go in meeting this national health objective in school communities.

All school personnel and child health advocates share a responsibility for maintaining the highest standards of a healthy, safe, and nurturing learning environment. Examine Table 1–7 for a review of important elements that confirm a commitment to a healthy school environment.

Nutrition Services

As indicated on Figure 1–2 schools are in a unique position to promote healthy dietary behaviors and help ensure appropriate nutrient intake among America's youth. Nutrition services should provide a variety of nutritious and appealing meals that meet the health and nutrition needs of all students. In addition, the school nutrition services program should offer students a learning laboratory for classroom nutrition and health education. This role has intensified since a national epidemic of childhood obesity has been documented. This program should serve as a resource for links with nutritionally related community service agencies.[82]

Adequate nutrition is critical to the physical and emotional well-being of children, as well as their academic success. School breakfast and lunch programs comprise a key source of nutrition for many students.

The dietary behaviors of elementary and middle school students have a significant impact on their physical development. Educators should take particular note of the growing body of literature confirming the strong relationship between nutritional behaviors and student achievement. Researchers have noted that hungry children manifest behaviors such as apathy and shorter attention spans. These students often have lowered energy levels and a compromised ability to concentrate, factors that threaten attention to detail and the general quality of academic work. Hungry children are at increased risk for infections and tend to be absent from school more often than children who are well fed. There is little question that students who are absent frequently tend to fall behind in their studies.[83]

In response to the inadequate nutritional intake of many students, the national school lunch and breakfast programs were initiated. School lunch programs were begun in 1946 with the enactment of the National School Lunch Act. This legislation provided local districts with surplus agricultural commodities and federal funds to defray the costs of providing nutritious meals delivered through the mechanism of a school-based lunch program. Management of this program is the responsibility of the U.S. Department of Agriculture.

Educators must remember that the school lunch and breakfast programs in most districts operate under strict budgetary constraints. However, research has demonstrated that these school-based meals serve as a significant source of nutrition for many children. Nearly two-thirds of all students in the United States receive about one-third of their daily nutrient density from participation in a school food service program. The meals served in the school lunch program constitute the majority of the daily food volume consumed by many students.[84] Recent research has confirmed that more than half eat either breakfast or lunch, and one in six students consume both of these meals at school.[85]

Beyond the amount and enriching nutritional density of foods in school-based programs, research has confirmed that student participants have better school attendance, greater class participation, and more greatly improved achievement than do hungry students.[86] Although schools are not mandated to participate in the national school lunch program, most do, as there is little question of the value of such programs for many students.

Recognizing the potential of a sound school nutrition program to promote both health and school success, the U.S. Congress voted in 2004 to apportion federal funding for the Child Nutrition Reauthorization Act. This important piece of legislation provided for expanded access to fruits and vegetables for school children and required every school district that receives federal funds for school meals to have a school wellness policy in place no later than the first day of the 2006–2007 academic year. Though the law does not dictate that schools take specific actions, such as the removal of vending machines or the elimination of unhealthy fundraising practices, it does require schools to collaborate with concerned stakeholders to

- Set goals for nutrition education, physical activity, and other school-based activities designed to promote student wellness, and
- Include nutrition guidelines for all foods available on the school campus during the school day.[87]

Unfortunately, SHPPS 2006 confirmed that less than 40 percent of states adopted policies stating that all school districts will employ an overseer or coordinator for nutrition services in the district.[88] Many school districts fail to incorporate this element of the CSHP into the nutrition education program. If a kitchen is located in the building, it provides the only access to such a learning laboratory for teachers and their students.

Wise teachers have learned to collaborate with food service personnel to enrich the nutrition education curriculum. The food service personnel in some school districts provide nutrition education activities that are developmentally appropriate and meaningful for all students. Some schools have organized student/food service advisory councils, which collaborate on special meal planning and nutrition education activities. Special event luncheons, nutrition newsletters, cafeteria bulletin boards or posters, food-tasting parties, and nutritional labeling of breakfast or lunch line food choices are activities with the potential to enrich the nutrition education curriculum.[89]

Beyond its use as a location for breakfast and lunch, the cafeteria in many middle schools is used only for large-group study halls. Wisely, some districts have developed ways to use this area for more academically enriching activities. Special mini-lectures on a range of topics can be targeted to particular students during their lunch meal. In addition, student organizations, teachers, and administrators can construct table tents to highlight important content matters or upcoming events on the school calendar.[90] In this way, nutrition education is enhanced without sacrificing valuable classroom instruction time, and the use of valuable instruction space is expanded.

Unfortunately, it has become more and more common for food industry marketers to invest in getting their products and messages to children. Experts in marketing to children realize that targeting adult policymakers in schools is sound short- and long-term practice. In return for needed funds and materials, marketers gain access to captive audiences of children who have money to spend, who can influence the purchasing patterns of their families, and who are the consumers of the future. Marketing strategies that focus on children in schools are very successful, as brand-name foods are marketed in school cafeterias and hallways, products and coupons are distributed on holidays and as rewards for achievement, and students and their parents sell products to raise funds for their schools.[91]

Many elementary and middle schools provide access to less-than-healthy foods. SHPPS 2006 findings revealed that such foods are available in vending machines, at snack bars, or at school stores. As a result, students don't have to go far to buy the following foods:

- Soft drinks, sports drinks, or fruit drinks that are not 100 percent fruit juice,
- Salty snacks (high in fat),
- Cookies or other baked goods (high in fat).

Over 20 percent of schools offering vending machines have not established policies restricting their use during the lunch period. As a result, the more nutritionally sound school lunch program must compete with machines containing almost exclusively high-fat, high-salt, and highly sweetened food options. In addition, some elementary and middle schools allow students to purchase such foods and beverages before school starts in the morning and throughout the school day.[92]

In light of growing concerns about childhood obesity and related negative health outcomes, administrators, parents, and child health advocates need to explore alternative funding options that do not compromise the health of enrolled students. To this end, Table 1–8 provides a checklist of key questions to guide school health advocates toward a strong commitment to quality school nutrition

TABLE 1–8
Confirming a Commitment to Quality School Nutrition Services: A Checklist of Important Questions
Does your school district provide a breakfast and lunch program supported by the U.S. Department of Agriculture?
Are the meals provided by your school nutrition program in compliance with the Dietary Guidelines for Americans?
Does the federally mandated school wellness policy include nutrition guidelines for all foods available on the school campus?
Are kitchen and cafeteria facilities used as nutrition education learning laboratories?
Are qualified personnel employed in the food service program?
Are only nutritionally sound products sold in all fund-raising activities and vending machines throughout the school district?
Is nutrition information shared with faculty, staff, parents, and students?
Are students and other stakeholders invited to collaborate with food service staff in menu planning and nutrition education activities?
Has an advisory council been organized to support and inform the school nutrition program?
Do food service personnel act as resource persons for nutrition education curriculum matters?

services. (Readers can find much more information about promoting healthy eating in Chapter 6 of this text.)

Counseling, Psychological, and Social Services

In a 1999 report on mental health, the Surgeon General estimated that approximately one in five U.S. children had a diagnosable mental or addictive disorder. Unfortunately, about 70 percent of youth in need of treatment do not receive necessary mental health services. Of those who do get care, about 70 percent receive services from schools, about 40 percent use mental health specialists, and 11 percent are treated in other medical care settings. Although these percentages overlap because some youth are cared for in multiple settings, the Surgeon General's report confirmed that schools are the primary providers of mental health services for children. The report concluded that offering such treatment at the school site improves treatment access for the broad range of students in need.[93] In this context, it is clear why counselors, psychologists, and other social service providers are critical contributors to a CSHP as indicated in Figure 1–2.

Resources to provide such services often are limited, but educators and student advocates cannot overlook the impact of mental health concerns on academic success. Psychologist Dr. Howard Adelman has identified five important barriers to learning:

- Inadequate basic resources—food, clothing, housing, and a sense of security at home, at school, and in the neighborhood

- Psychosocial problems—difficult relationships at home and at school; emotional upset; language problems; sexual, emotional, or physical abuse; substance abuse; delinquent or gang-related behavior; and psychopathology
- Stressful situations—inability to meet the demands made at school or at home, inadequate support systems, and hostile conditions at school or in the neighborhood
- Crises and emergencies—death of a classmate or relative, a shooting at school, or natural disasters such as earthquakes, floods, or tornadoes
- Life transitions—onset of puberty, entering a new school, and changes in life circumstances (moving, immigration, loss of a parent through divorce or death)[94]

Although there are a number of models and approaches around which school-based mental health services are organized, three kinds of professionals most frequently offer such care: school counselors, psychologists, and social workers. Originally, school counselors provided vocational guidance for students. Today, they help students solve relationship problems, make decisions to improve learning outcomes, and address developmental challenges. School psychologists evaluate the psychological functioning and needs of students and coordinate referral networks and collaborative activities with other community service providers. In this way, school psychologists play a critical role in responding to learners with special needs. Many school psychologists also provide individual and group counseling for students, and they conduct informational sessions concerning student needs for parents, faculty, and staff. Finally, school social workers serve as the formal link among the school, the home, and the community, offering case management, group counseling, home visits, advocacy for students, parent education, and coordination of programs for youth.[95]

In addition to providing intervention services for students and their families, counselors and social workers participate in the instructional program in elementary and middle schools. These resource professionals organize learning activities in areas such as nonviolent conflict resolution, problem solving, communication, and decision-making skill development. In some districts, counselors, psychologists, and social workers collaborate in curriculum and staff development activities.

SHPPS 2006 has documented that slightly over three-fourths of schools have a part- or full-time counselor on staff. In addition, less than two-thirds of schools have access to a school psychologist, but less than half have a social worker who provides mental health or social services for students.[96]

In order to evaluate the program of mental health services in local schools, readers should consult Table 1–9, a checklist of important questions that confirm a commitment to a quality program of school counseling, psychological, and

social services. (Readers can find additional information about promoting mental and emotional health in students in Chapter 5.)

Physical Education

In 1996, the Surgeon General published the landmark report on physical activity and health. This document confirmed the following significant benefits of regular participation in physical activity: a reduced risk of premature death and a decreased likelihood of developing heart disease, diabetes, and colon cancer. Further, this report documented that the health benefits of physical activity are not limited to adults. Regular activity among children and youth helps build healthy bones, muscles, and joints; helps control weight; supports development of lean muscle mass; addresses risks for high blood pressure; and reduces feelings of depression and anxiety.[97]

In addition to the health benefits, emerging literature has established a link between participation in physical activity and enhanced academic outcomes for students. In particular, research concluded that a consistent, organized program of school-based physical activity is related to increased concentration and improved scores on tests of math, reading, and writing skills.[98] Further, people who exercise on a regular basis are more likely to participate in other healthy behaviors, including less cigarette use, improved dietary behaviors, and more effective stress management practices.[99] In light of these findings, the American

---

TABLE 1–9

Confirming a Commitment to a Quality Program of School Counseling, Psychological, and Social Services: A Checklist of Important Questions

Are an appropriate number of licensed, credentialed professionals employed to meet the counseling, psychological, and social service needs of all students in the district (1:200–250 provider-to-student ratio)?

Do students have access to a developmentally appropriate, planned, and sequential guidance and counseling program?

Have the school district and community collaborated in the development of an interagency network of counseling, psychological, and social service providers?

Have interdisciplinary patterns of collaboration been established to identify students at risk in the school community?

Do students have access to the following school/community-linked services to support academic outcomes?

Individual counseling	Tutoring
Crisis counseling	Developmental programs
Group counseling	

Do counseling, psychological, and social service professionals provide consultation and staff development to update and inform curricular matters?

Has a student assistance program been established?

Association of School Administrators has concluded that "children need to be attentive to maximize the benefits of participation in learning tasks. Attention takes energy, and students who are physically fit, well-nourished, and stress-free have more energy."[100]

Schools are an ideal location for students to be active and can play an important role in motivating young people to stay active. The CDC has identified elements of a comprehensive approach to school-based physical activity in programs that include

- Daily physical education
- Health education that provides students with knowledge and self-management skills to maintain an active lifestyle
- Extracurricular physical activities, including intramural programming, physical activity clubs, and interscholastic sports[101]

In this context, sound programs of physical education are the backbone of school-based fitness activities. Such programs are developed to include a range of learning activities targeting cardiovascular health, muscular endurance, flexibility, strength, agility, balance, coordination, and good posture. Emphasis is placed on physical fitness and the development of skills that lead to lifelong habits of physical activity. As children learn basic exercise movement skills, they are more likely to develop lifelong activity patterns. As in other content areas, national physical education standards have been developed to provide guidelines for program development.

Physical education experiences that are most effective in addressing these fitness components involve participation in vigorous, aerobic activity. Research has confirmed that the five activities most commonly incorporated into physical education in the primary grades are movement experiences and body mechanics, soccer, jumping or skipping rope, gymnastics, and basketball.[102] Instructional activities for students in the upper-elementary grades primarily focus on more team-related activities. Softball, basketball, soccer, volleyball, football, and track and field are given greater emphasis in each higher grade.[103] School physical education programs should be developed that emphasize individual fitness and skill development, not just team sport participation.

The amount of time allotted for the physical education class varies from as little as fifteen to twenty minutes at some schools to as much as forty-five minutes to one hour at others. The average length of elementary school physical education classes is 33.4 minutes.[104]

The amount of vigorous aerobic activity in which each student is a participant is also worthy of discussion. While observing an elementary physical education class, it is common for concerned adults to witness large blocks of time when many students are standing or sitting while few are active or the teacher is instructing. Relays and team games tend to result in limited participation for the majority of students. In the average physical education

Daily physical activity for children—during physical education class and recess—enhances academic performance and sets the stage for lifelong healthy activity habits.

class, the typical student may participate in only two to three minutes of individual exercise.[105] Clearly, this is not an acceptable level of participation if there is to be any positive impact on the physical fitness or achievement of students.

An important addition to the program of formal physical education is the provision of recess for most elementary school children. Unfortunately, many schools reduce recess time in favor of preparation for proficiency testing or count recess time periods toward compliance with state requirements for participation in physical education. This practice is unacceptable, as it implies that physical education learning experiences are less important than experiences in other academic subjects. Unfortunately, SHPPS 2006 confirmed that only 57 percent of school districts required local schools to provide regularly scheduled recess periods for students in grades K–5.[106] Table 1–10 reviews the key elements in a quality program of physical education. Further findings are available for reader review in the Online Learning Center, and in Chapter 7.

Confirming a Commitment to a Quality Physical Education Program: A Checklist of Important Questions

Does the federally mandated wellness policy set goals for physical activity?

Has a planned, sequential physical education curriculum been implemented in grades pre-K through 12?

Has the curriculum been developed with attention to the national physical education standards?

Are credentialed teachers employed in the physical education program?

Do all students participate in a program of organized daily physical activity?

Is the physical education curriculum organized with a focus on lifetime activities rather than acquisition of team-sport skills?

Do students participate in an ongoing program of health-related fitness assessments?

Does the physical education faculty collaborate with health service personnel to record results of fitness assessments on students' permanent health records?

Are noncompetitive co-curricular fitness activities organized for student participation?

Is participation in co-curricular fitness activities promoted for elementary and middle school students?

Confirming a Commitment to a Quality School-Site Health Promotion Program for Faculty and Staff: A Checklist of Important Questions

Have health promotion programs for faculty and staff been organized to focus on the following health-promoting practices?

Weight management	Physical fitness
Tobacco use cessation	Blood pressure screening
Stress management	Cholesterol screening
Cancer screening	Back injury prevention

Do health promotion programs include employee assistance activities, screening, referral, and education?

Is the expertise of school district and community professionals incorporated into the school-site health promotion program?

Have policies and incentives been developed to promote faculty/staff participation in health promotion activities?

Do the faculty and staff participate in an ongoing program of health risk appraisals?

Have record keeping and referral protocols been developed to maintain confidentiality of all faculty and staff health information?

Do administrators participate in health promotion activities with other district employees?

Has a relationship been developed among the district, insurance providers, and coordinators of the district health promotion program to help contain health care costs?

Does the designated coordinator of this program receive release time for organizational, management, and record-keeping tasks?

Has an oversight committee involving diverse stakeholders been organized?

Health Promotion for Faculty and Staff

Since the 1970s, corporate America has demonstrated an increased interest in health promotion initiatives for employees. Providing long-term hospitalization for an aging American public has led many businesses and industries to seek ways to reduce costs for hospital, medical, and other types of insurance. Many in the health promotion and medical care professions are committed to the notion that, with appropriate health promotion and disease prevention initiatives, these costs can be reduced. Corporations with work-site health promotion programs formalize opportunities for employees and their families to assume more responsibility for their health and well-being. In turn, the employees tend to be more productive, are absent less frequently, and demonstrate improved attitudes and morale.

Boards of education and administrators are faced with the same issues as their colleagues in corporate management positions. Schools represent one of the largest employers in the United States. There are over 6.5 million faculty and staff employed in the nation's public schools.[107] A significant portion of a school district budget is earmarked for health insurance and related benefits for faculty and staff.

School districts are ideal locations for work-site health promotion programs. School buildings are constructed with a wide range of facilities, and school districts employ resource professionals skilled in planning and implement-

ing quality health promotion programs. Screenings, health education, employee assistance programs, health care, immunizations, and implementation of organizational policies that support safe and healthy lifestyles are among the formalized activities integrated into the employee contracts in some school districts.

School-based health promotion programs for faculty and staff have been shown to reduce health care costs, decrease absenteeism, and improve quality of life.[108] In addition, an investment in such activities is associated with improved physical health, reduced health risks, and improved psychosocial well-being. Faculty and staff participants in such programs have been identified as positive role models for students.[109]

Healthy teachers, administrators, and support staff not only are less costly to taxpayers but also have fewer absences that require temporary employment of substitute teachers. Better continuity of instruction for students is maintained and costs are contained. Elementary and middle school teachers interested in exploring the advantages of such programs in their local district should review Table 1–11. This checklist reviews key elements in a quality school-site health promotion program for faculty and staff.

TABLE 1–12

Confirming a Commitment to Quality Family and Community Collaboration with the Schools: A Checklist of Important Questions

Does an active school/community coalition or committee meet on a regular basis to address student health problems and curriculum matters, as well as to plan health promotion activities?

Is there conspicuous administrative/board of education involvement or support for integrated school and community health promotion activities?

Have policies and protocol been established to encourage active parental involvement in school health activities?

Has a pattern of collaborative programming been established between the school district and public and community health agencies and advocates?

Have protocol and communication networks been established to expedite interagency referral and record keeping concerning student health issues?

Have policies and communication networks been established to manage controversial health issues that confront the school community?

Family and Community Involvement

The school is an agency of the community that cannot function effectively in isolation. Today, many associate a range of student problems with shortcomings in the school program, yet there are many entities in every community with whom children and their families interface. Children who attend local schools also are influenced by practices in the neighborhoods, churches, and stores and by medical care providers with whom they have contact. No school district is solely responsible when a community is confronted with children who have developed problems with tobacco, alcohol or other drugs, or violence. Rather, every student who is at risk is a part of some kind of family arrangement, resides in a neighborhood, shops in local stores, and might participate in chosen religious celebrations. All student advocates must remember that the complexity of today's health and social problems require that no one agency or group be blamed or held responsible for intervening in such matters in the absence of other stakeholders. Student risk behaviors are influenced by a complex set of variables. Thus, effective prevention and intervention are based on collaborative approaches.

As an important step in confronting such challenging issues, the school health literature has confirmed the need for local districts to establish a school health advisory council. Such organizations focus the efforts of school, medical, safety, and advocacy services on health promotion in the school community. Specifically, such coalitions or committees work to increase the quantity and quality of school-based health promotion efforts. Such groups also help reduce duplication of services and enhance the visibility and potential impact of all participant agencies. With pooled resources, advocacy initiatives and projects that are too large for any one agency become realistic health promotion options.[110]

In addition to addressing more global concerns, elementary and middle school classroom teachers would be wise to cultivate relationships with student health advocacy organizations and agencies in their communities. Many of these organizations offer support for classroom instruction by providing resource materials developed to focus on a broad range of health content matters.

SHPPS 2006 confirmed that most activities related to family and community involvement in school health programs are based in the local community rather than at the state level.[111] Table 1–12 contains a checklist of key questions to confirm a quality program of family and community collaboration with the schools. Parent engagement is discussed in greater detail in Chapter 4 and throughout this text. Other findings from SHPPS 2006 can be found in the Online Learning Center.

Pulling It All Together

The health status and academic achievement of students who attend elementary and middle schools are threatened by many complex variables. Some students are absent due to allergies or communicable infections, others have difficulty maintaining their attention to schoolwork because of dietary risks. The key to confronting such complex issues is to capitalize on the many resources and talents of professionals who are committed to promoting the health of children and youth.

The CSHP represents best practice in health promotion. The successful integration of this eight-component model into the active life of the school community depends on several key elements. As a foundation, all school and community personnel with expertise in any aspect of student health are invited to be active participants in this proactive health promotion agenda. The likelihood of successful application of the model is related to the extent of cooperation, collaboration, and communication among the stakeholders. Participants representing the eight component programs of the model must organize their efforts in a coordinated manner. Table 1–13 provides a summary of ways in which professionals, policies, and activities in a coordinated school health program can enhance academic outcomes among students.

Many schools offer a range of programs to address students who are at risk. Additionally, many districts offer

TABLE 1–13

The Coordinated School Health Program: A Foundation for School Success

- *Comprehensive school health education*
  Reading and math scores of third- and fourth-graders who received comprehensive health education were significantly higher than among those students who did not receive comprehensive school health education.[112]
- *School health services*
  Fewer student absences due to medical reasons occur in schools that have full-time nurses on staff.[113]
- *Healthy school environment*
  Students who develop a connection or positive affiliation with their school are more likely to remain academically engaged and less likely to be involved in misconduct than their counterparts who don't have such a bond.[114]
- *School nutrition services*
  School breakfast programs have been demonstrated to increase achievement, improve attention span, reduce visits to the school nurse, and decrease behavioral problems.[115]
- *School counseling, psychological, and social services*
  School-based social services programs that target students who are at risk for dropping out of school have been linked to improvements in self-esteem and increased grade-point average.[116]
- *Physical education*
  Participation in physical education programming does not threaten academic instruction. While less time was available for other academic subjects, students who participate in physical education do not experience a harmful effect on standardized test scores.[117]
- *School-site health promotion for faculty and staff*
  Teachers who participate in health promotion programs focusing on nutrition, exercise, and stress management have reported increases in their ability to manage job stress.[118]
- *Family and community collaboration with the schools*
  Students whose parents are involved in their education have greater achievement gains in reading and math, better attendance, and more consistently completed homework than students whose parents are not.[119]

diverse activities to prevent participation in any number of health-risk behaviors. These activities must be offered in a coordinated and intentional manner to increase the probability of their longevity and success. For example, nutrition education is a common content area in health instructional programs. The school food service program should provide nutritionally sound meals, and students with eating disorders may be referred for intervention counseling. Unfortunately, professionals involved in these nutritional health promotion activities rarely are involved in collaborative planning.

The approach to nutritional health promotion in a school district with a Coordinated School Health Program is very different. Such a district, with an established school health council, might collaborate in planning proactive and well-organized activities, including the following:

- *Health education:* Provide a developmentally appropriate nutrition education curricular scope and sequence.
- *Health services:* Provide consultation and resources for planning a nutritional health week in which cross-curricular instruction focuses on healthy foods.
- *Healthy environment:* Review, by administrators and the board of education, all fund-raising policies and practices to make sure that none sabotage the district commitment to nutritional health promotion.
- *School food services:* Establish training tables for athletes, students involved in co-curricular activities,

and interested others, including building faculty and staff.
- *Counseling:* Provide support groups and appropriate referral activities for students with eating disorders or other risky dietary behaviors.
- *Physical education:* Develop exercise prescriptions that feature healthy weight management practices for all students.
- *Faculty and staff:* Organize a "Healthy Nutrition for Life" support group open to all faculty and staff.
- *Family engagement:* Have students plan a healthy meal with their families.
- *Healthy community:* Organize "a taste of [name of your community]" event. Invite local restaurants and food outlets to the school campus to prepare samples of their healthy entrees for school district residents. Proceeds can support a range of health promotion activities.

Finally, many school health advocates have identified the need for a person or leadership group to coordinate and champion all activities of the school health program. The primary responsibility of this person or group is to translate the CSHP into specific programming activities to meet local needs. In particular, the program coordinator(s) focus(es) professional time and energies on heading the school health advisory committee, maintaining the program budget, and organizing advocacy and liaison activities with district, community, and state agencies. The coordinator provides direct health promotion activities and services and organizes evaluation activities to ensure quality control of the many aspects of the CSHP.[120]

In 2004, the Association for Supervision and Curriculum Development (ASCD), one of the nation's largest and most respected education organizations, issued *Position Statement on Health and Learning*. This important statement was based on the assertion that "successful learners are not only knowledgeable and productive but also emotionally and physically healthy, motivated, civically engaged, and prepared for work and economic self-sufficiency, and ready for the world beyond their own borders." Because both emotional and physical health are critical to accomplishing such short- and long-term goals for the educational process, ASCD concluded that health should be "fully embedded into the educational environment for all students." Consistent with the text in this chapter, this national organization concluded that both the health and the learning needs of children are best addressed when

- Health is recognized as a multifaceted concept best enriched by supporting the intellectual, physical, civic, and mental attributes of learners
- Health and learning are supported by coordinated and comprehensive teacher, school, family, community, and policy resources
- Communities, families, schools, teachers, and policymakers assume reciprocal responsibility for enriching health and learning among students[121]

Within such a structure, the talents of many can be focused efficiently and effectively on promoting student health while maintaining a focus on the primary mission of schools: to maintain the highest standards of academic achievement.

INTERNET AND OTHER RESOURCES

Visit the Online Learning Center (www.mhhe.com/telljohann6e) for links to these sites, quizzes and other study aids, and many additional resources.

WEBSITES

Action for Healthy Kids
www.actionforhealthykids.org

Alliance for a Healthier Generation
www.healthiergeneration.org

American School Health Association
www.ashaweb.org

Center for Health and Health Care in Schools
www.healthinschools.org

Centers for Disease Control and Prevention—Division of Adolescent and School Health
www.cdc.gov/Healthy Youth

Centers for Disease Control and Prevention—Health and Academic Achievement web page
www.cdc.gov/healthyyouth/health_and_academics/publications.htm

National Alliance for Nutrition and Activity (NANA)
www.nanacoalition.org

National Association of School Nurses
www.nasn.org

National School Boards Association—School Health Programs
www.nsba.org/schoolhealth

Office of the Surgeon General
www.surgeongeneral.gov

Robert Wood Johnson Foundation
www.rwjf.org

School Health Profiles: surveillance characteristics of health programs among secondary schools (profiles 2006)
www.cdc.gov/healthyyouth/profiles/index.htm

Society of State Directors of Health, Physical Education, and Recreation
www.thesociety.org

U.S. Department of Agriculture's Team Nutrition Website
www.fns.usda.gov/tn

OTHER RESOURCES

Batada, A., and M. G. Wootan. "Nickelodeon Markets Nutrition-poor Foods to Children." *American Journal of Preventive Medicine* 33, no. 1 (2007): 1–3.

Cornwell, L., S. R. Hawley, and T. St Romain. "Implementation of a Coordinated School Health Program in a Rural, Low-income Community." *Journal of School Health* 77, no. 9 (2007): 601–606.

Federal Interagency Forum on Child and Family Statistics. *America's Children: Key National Indicators of Well-Being*, 2007 (Washington, DC: Federal Interagency Forum on Child and Family Statistics, 2007).

Food and Nutrition Service, U.S. Department of Agriculture, Centers for Disease Control and Prevention, U.S. Department of Health and Human Services, and U.S. Department of Education. *Making It Happen! School Nutrition Success Stories* (Alexandria, VA: USDA, 2005).

Institutes of Medicine. *Schools and Health: Our Nation's Investment* (Washington, DC: National Academy Press, 1997).

Joyner, A. "The Healthy Approach." *American School Board Journal* (June 2007): 42–44.

Murray, N., B. Low, C. Hollis, A. Cross, and S. Davis. "Coordinated School Health Programs and Academic Achievement: A Systematic Review of the Literature," *Journal of School Health* 77, no. 9 (2007): 589–600.

Rothstein, R., T. Wilder, and R. Jacobson. "Balance in the Balance." *Educational Leadership* (May 2007): 8–14.

The Education Alliance. *Positive Youth Development: Policy Implications and Best Practices* (Charleston, WV: The Education Alliance, 2007).

U.S. Department of Health and Human Services. *Stories from the Field: Lessons Learned About Building Coordinated School Health Programs* (Atlanta, GA: CDC, 2003).

Wilson, T. K., and J. Bogden. *Fit, Healthy, and Ready to Learn: A School Health Policy Guide, Part III* (Alexandria, VA: National Association of State Boards of Education, 2005).

1. World Health Organization, "Constitution of the World Health Organization," *Chronicle of the World Health Organization* (1947): 1.
2. D. Bedworth and A. Bedworth, *The Profession and Practice of Health Education* (Dubuque, IA: Wm. C. Brown, 1992).
3. G. F. Carter and S. B. Wilson, *My Health Status* (Minneapolis, MN: Burgess Publishing, 1982), 5.
4. J. Thomas Butler, *Principles of Health Education and Health Promotion* (Belmont, CA: Wadsworth/Thomson Learning, 2001), 6.
5. Ibid., 5.
6. B. L. Seaward, "Spiritual Wellbeing: A Health Education Model," *Journal of Health Education* 22, no. 3 (1991): 166–69.
7. Native Hawaiian Safe and Drug-Free Schools Program, *E Ola Pono (Live the Proper Way): A Curriculum Developed in Support of Self-Identity and Cultural Pride as Positive Influences in the Prevention of Violence and Substance Abuse* (Honolulu, HI: Kamehameha Schools Extension Education Division, Health, Wellness, and Family Education Department, 1999).
8. Ibid.
9. U.S. Department of Health, Education, and Welfare, Public Health Service, *Healthy People: The Surgeon General's Report on Health Promotion and Disease Prevention* (Washington, DC: U.S. Government Printing Office, 1979).
10. Centers for Disease Control and Prevention, "Ten Great Public Health Achievements—United States, 1900–1999," *MMWR* 48, no. 12 (1999): 241–43.
11. Ibid.
12. U.S. Department of Health, Education, and Welfare, Public Health Service, *Healthy People.*
13. Ibid.
14. U.S. Department of Health and Human Services, *Healthy People 2010: Conference Edition, in Two Volumes* (Washington, DC: U.S. Government Printing Office, 2000), 22.
15. U.S. Department of Health and Human Services, *Health, United States, 2007* (Hyattsville, MD: National Center for Health Statistics, 2007), 178.
16. G. Anderson and J. Horvath, "The Growing Burden of Chronic Disease in America," *Public Health Reports* 119 (May/June 2004): 263–70.
17. National Center for Chronic Disease Prevention and Health Promotion, *Chronic Disease Prevention* (www.cdc.gov/NCCdphp/index.htm, 2007).
18. Ibid.
19. A. H. Mokdad et al., "Actual Causes of Death in the United States, 2000," *Journal of the American Medical Association* 291, no. 10 (10 March 2004): 1238–45.
20. K. M. Flegal et al., "Excess Deaths Associated with Underweight, Overweight, and Obesity," *Journal of the American Medical Association* 293, no. 15 (20 April 2005): 1861–67.
21. L. Kolbe, "An Epidemiological Surveillance System to Monitor the Prevalence of Youth Behaviors That Most Affect Health," *Health Education* 21, no. 3 (1990): 24–30.
22. U.S. Department of Health and Human Services, *Healthy People 2010,* 19–20.
23. Ibid., 18–20.
24. U.S. Department of Health and Human Services, *Healthy People 2010,* 8–11.
25. U.S. Department of Health and Human Services, *Improving the Health of Adolescents and Young Adults: A Guide for States and Communities* (Atlanta, GA: Centers for Disease Control and Prevention, 2004), 3–16.
26. U.S. Department of Health and Human Services, *Healthy People 2010 Midcourse Review* (Washington, DC: U.S. Government Printing Office, 2006).
27. Ibid.
28. S. J. Olshansky et al., "A Potential Decline in Life Expectancy in the United States in the 21st Century," *The New England Journal of Medicine* 352, no. 11 (March 17, 2005): 1138–45.
29. Ibid.
30. D. J. DeNoon, "Will Obesity Shorten the American Life Span?" *MedicineNet.com* (www.medicinenet.com/script/main/art.asp?articlekey=56059, 2007).
31. U.S. Department of Health and Human Services, *Healthy People 2010. Understanding and Improving Health, and Objectives for Improving Health,* 2d ed. (Washington, DC: U.S. Government Printing Office, 2000).
32. National Center for Education Statistics, *Fast Facts. Elementary and Secondary Education* (http://nces.ed.gov/fastfacts/display.asp?id=372, 2008).
33. L. Kolbe et al., "Enabling the Nation's Schools to Help Prevent Heart Disease, Stroke, Cancer, COPD, Diabetes, and Other Serious Health Problems," *Public Health Reports* 119, no. 3 (May 2004): 286–302.
34. U.S. Department of Health and Human Services, *Healthy People 2010: Conference Edition, in Two Volumes,* 7–4.
35. National Commission on Excellence in Education, *A Nation at Risk: The Imperative for Educational Reform* (Washington, DC: U.S. Department of Education, 1983).
36. R. J. Marzano, J. S. Kendall, and L. F. Cicchinelli, *What Americans Believe Students Should Know: A Survey of U.S. Adults: Executive Summary* (Aurora, CO: Mid-Content Regional Educational Laboratory, 1998), 1–6.
37. A. Novello et al., "Healthy Children Ready to Learn: An Essential Collaboration Between Health and Education," *Public Health Reports* 107, no. 1 (1992): 3–15.
38. American Cancer Society, *National Action Plan for Comprehensive School Health Education* (Atlanta, GA: American Cancer Society, 1992), 4–7.
39. H. Tyson, "A Load Off the Teacher's Backs," K2.
40. Council of Chief State School Officers, *Policy Statement on School Health* (Washington, DC: CCSSO, 17 July 2004), 1.
41. Ibid., 7–8.
42. Association for Supervision and Curriculum Development, *The Learning Compact Redefined: A Call to Action, A Report of the Commission on the Whole Child* (Alexandria, VA: ASCD, 2007), 43.
43. Ibid.
44. Ibid., 20.
45. Ibid., 3.
46. Ibid., 11.
47. C. Wolford Symons et al., "Bridging Student Health Risks and Academic Achievement Through Comprehensive School Health Programs," *Journal of School Health* 67, no. 6 (1997): 220–27.
48. L. Kann et al., "The School Health Policies and Programs Study (SHPPS): Rationale for a Nationwide Status Report on School Health Programs," *Journal of School Health* 65, no. 8 (1995): 291–94.
49. U.S. Department of Health, Education, and Welfare, Public Health Service, *Healthy People,* 119.
50. Ibid.
51. "Report of the 2000 Joint Committee on Health Education and Promotion Terminology," *American Journal of Health Education* 32, no. 2 (2001): 90–103.
52. U.S. Department of Health, Education, and Welfare, Public Health Service, *Healthy People,* 119.
53. "Report of the 2000 Joint Committee on Health Education and Promotion Terminology," 90–103.
54. U.S. Department of Health, Education, and Welfare, Public Health Service, *Healthy People,* 119.
55. "Report of the 2000 Joint Committee on Health Education and Promotion Terminology," 90–103.
56. L. J. Kolbe, "Education Reform and the Goals of Modern School Health Programs," *Education Standard* (autumn 2002): 4–11.
57. "Report of the 2000 Joint Committee on Health Education and Promotion Terminology."
58. Joint Committee on National Health Education Standards, *National Health Education Standards: Achieving Excellence,* 2d ed. (Atlanta, GA: American Cancer Society, 2007).
59. L. Kann, S. Telljohann, and S. Wooley, "Health Education: Results from the School Health Policies and Programs Study 2006," *Journal of School Health* 77, no. 8 (2007): 413.
60. Ibid., 420.
61. D. B. Connell et al., "Summary of Findings of the School Health Education Evaluation: Health Promotion Effectiveness, Implementation, and Costs," *Journal of School Health* 55, no. 8 (1985): 316–22.
62. Centers for Disease Control and Prevention, *Health Education Curriculum Analysis Tool* (Atlanta, GA: Centers for Disease Control and Prevention, 2007).
63. Ibid.
64. American Association for Health Education, *Health Instruction Responsibilities and Competencies for Elementary (K–6) Classroom Teachers* (Reston, VA: AAHE, 1992).
65. American Association for Health Education, *Responsibilities and Competencies for Teachers of Young Adolescents in Coordinated School Health Programs for Middle Level Classroom Teachers* (Reston, VA: AAHE, 1999).
66. Kann, "Health Education: Results from the School Health Policies and Programs Study 2006," 413–415.
67. C. M. Smith and F. A. Mauer, eds., *Community Health Nursing: Theory and Practice,* 2d ed. (Philadelphia: Saunders, 2000).
68. National Association of School Nurses (NASN), *The Role of the School Nurse* [brochure] (Scarborough, ME: NASN, 1999).
69. P. Duncan and J. Igoe, "School Health Services," in *Health Is Academic: A Guide to Coordinated School Health Programs,* eds. E. Marx, S. Wooley, and M. Northrop (New York: Teachers College Press, 1998).
70. American Nurses Association (ANA), *Standards of Clinical Nursing Practice,* 2d ed. (Washington, DC: ANA, 1998).
71. National Association of School Nurses, *Position Statement. Caseload Assignments* (www.nasn.org/Default.aspx?tabid=209, 2008).
72. Ibid.
73. *Cedar Rapids Community School District v. F. Garret,* 526 US 66, 1999.
74. N. Brener et al.,"Health Services: Results from the School Health Policies and Programs Study 2006," *Journal of School Health 77,* no. 8 (2007): 477.
75. National Association of State School Nurse Consultants (NASSNC), *Delegation of School Health Services Position Statement* (Kent, OH: NASSNC, 2000).
76. National Association of School Nurses, *Position Statement: Medication Administration in the School Setting* (www.nasn.org/Default.aspx?tabid=230, 2008).
77. U.S. Environmental Protection Agency, *Indoor Air Quality and Student Performance* (Washington, DC: U.S. Environmental Protection Agency Indoor Environments Division, 2003).
78. J. F. Bogden, *Fit, Healthy, and Ready to Learn: A School Health Policy Guide* (Alexandria, VA: National Association of State Boards of Education, 2000).

79. V. Battistich et al., "Schools as Communities, Poverty Levels of Student Populations, and Students' Attitudes, Motives, and Performance: A Multilevel Analysis," *American Education Research Journal* 32 (1995): 627–58.

80. V. Battistich and A. Hom, "The Relationship Between Students' Sense of Their School as a Community and Their Involvement in Problem Behaviors," *American Journal of Public Health* 87, no. 12 (December 1997): 1997–2001.

81. S. E. Jones, C. Fisher, B. Greene, M. Hertz, and J. Pritzl, "Healthy and Safe School Environment, Part 1: Results from the School Health Policies and Programs Study 2006," *Journal of School Health* 77, no. 8 (2007): 537.

82. J. Bogden, *Fit, Healthy, and Ready to Learn.*

83. K. B. Troccoli, "Eat to Learn, Learn to Eat: The Link Between Nutrition and Learning in Children," *National Health/Education Consortium: Occasional Paper* 7 (April 1993): 1–33.

84. K. Bushweller, "Health on the Menu," *American School Board Journal* (July 1993): 94.

85. U.S. Department of Agriculture, *School Breakfast Program Participation and Meals Served,* 2007 (www.fns.usda.gov/pd/sbsummar.htm, 2007).

86. American School Food Service Association, "Impact of Hunger and Malnutrition on Student Achievement," *School Food Service Research Review* 13, no. 1 (1989): 17–21.

87. Child Nutrition Reauthorization Act (PL 108-265), 30 June 2004.

88. T. O'Toole, S. Anderson, C. Miller, and J. Guthrie, "Nutrition Services and Foods and Beverages Available at School: Results from the School Health Policies and Programs Study 2006," *Journal of School Health* 77, no. 8 (2007): 504.

89. D. Allensworth and C. Wolford, *Achieving the 1990 Health Objectives for the Nation: Agenda for the Schools* (Bloomington, IN: American School Health Association, 1988).

90. Ibid., 26.

91. J. Levine, "Food Industry Marketing in Elementary Schools: Implications for School Health Professionals," *Journal of School Health* 69, no. 7 (1999): 290–91.

92. O'Toole, "Nutrition Services and Foods and Beverages Available at School," 518–19.

93. U.S. Department of Health and Human Services, *Mental Health: A Report of the Surgeon General* (Washington, DC: U.S. Department of Health and Human Services, 1999).

94. H. Adelman, "School Counseling, Psychological, and Social Services," in *Health Is Academic: A Guide to Coordinated School Health Programs,* eds. E. Marx, S. Wooley, and M. Northrop (New York: Teachers College Press, 1998).

95. N. Brener et al., "Mental Health and Social Services: Results from the School Health Policies and Programs Study 2000," *Journal of School Health* 71, no. 7 (2001): 305–12.

96. N. Brener, M. Weist, H. Adelman, L. Taylor, and M. Vernon-Smiley, "Mental Health and Social Services: Results from the School Health Policies and Programs Study 2006," *Journal of School Health* 77, no. 8 (2007): 494.

97. U.S. Department of Health and Human Services, *Physical Activity and Health: A Report of the Surgeon General* (Atlanta, GA: Centers for Disease Control and Prevention, 1996).

98. L. Kolbe et al., "Appropriate Functions of Health Education in Schools: Improving Health and Cognitive Performance," in *Child Health Behavior: A Behavioral Pediatrics Perspective,* eds. N. Krairweger, J. Arasteli, and J. Cataldo (New York: John Wiley, 1986).

99. C. Bouchard et al., *Exercise, Fitness, and Health: A Consensus of Current Knowledge* (Champaign, IL: Human Kinetics Books, 1990).

100. American Association of School Administrators, *Critical Issues Report: Promoting Health Education in Schools—Problems and Solutions* (Arlington, VA: American Association of School Administrators, 1985).

101. Centers for Disease Control and Prevention, "Guidelines for School and Community Programs to Promote Lifelong Physical Activity Among Young People," *MMWR* 46, no. RR-6 (1997): 1–36.

102. J. G. Ross et al., "What Is Going On in the Elementary Physical Education Program?" *Journal of Physical Education, Recreation and Dance* (November/December 1987): 81.

103. Ibid.

104. J. G. Ross et al., *What Is Going On in the Elementary Physical Education Program? Summary of Findings from National Children and Youth Fitness Study II* (Washington, DC: U.S. Department of Health and Human Services, 1987), 78–84.

105. G. S. Parcel et al., "School Promotion of Healthful Diet and Exercise Behavior: An Integration of Organizational Change and Social Learning Theory Interventions," *Journal of School Health* 57, no. 4 (1987): 150–56.

106. S. M. Lee, C. Burgeson, J. Fulton, and C. Spain, "Physical Education and Physical Activity: Results from the School Health Policies and Programs Study 2006," *Journal of School Health* 77, no. 8 (2007): 446.

107. D. Eaton, E. Marx, and S. E. Bowie, "Faculty and Staff Health Promotion: Results from the School Health Policies and Programs Study 2006," *Journal of School Health* 77, no. 8 (2007): 557.

108. Association for Supervision and Curriculum Development, "Investing in Teacher Health Pays Off," *Educational Leadership* (January 2006): 4–5.

109. J. Allegrante and J. L. Michela, "Impact of a School-Based Workplace Health Promotion Program on Inner-City Teachers," *Journal of School Health* 60, no. 1 (1990): 25–28.

110. D. Allensworth and C. Wolford, *Achieving the 1990 Health Objectives for the Nation: Agenda for the Schools,* 26.

111. S. Michael, P. Dittus, and J. Epstein, "Family and Community Involvement in Schools: Results from the School Health Policies and Programs Study 2006," *Journal of School Health* 77, no. 8 (2007): 567–579.

112. J. Schoener, F. Guerrero, and B. Whitney, *The Effects of the Growing Healthy Program upon Children's Academic Performance and Attendance in New York City* (New York: Office of Research, Evaluation, and Assessment to the New York City Board of Education, 1988).

113. G. Allen, "The Impact of Elementary School Nurses on Student Attendance," *Journal of School Nursing* 19, no. 4 (August 2003): 225–31.

114. B. Simons-Morton et al., "Student Bonding and Adolescent Problem Behavior," *Health Education Research* 14, no. 1 (1999): 99–107.

115. J. Murphy et al., "The Relationship of School Breakfast to Psychosocial and Academic Functioning," *Archives of Pediatric Adolescent Medicine* 152 (1998): 899–907.

116. L. Eggert et al., "Preventing Adolescent Drug Abuse and High School Dropout Through an Intensive School-Based Social Network Development Program," *American Journal of Health Promotion* 8, no. 3 (1994): 202–15.

117. J. Sallis et al., "Effects of Health-Related Physical Education on Academic Achievement: Project SPARK," *Research Quarterly for Exercise and Sport* 70, no. 2 (1999): 127–34.

118. S. Blair et al., "Health Promotion for Educators: Impact on Health Behaviors, Satisfaction, and General Well-being," *American Journal of Public Health* 74, no. 2 (1984): 147–49.

119. A. V. Shaver and R. T. Walls, "Effect of Title 1 Parent Involvement on Student Reading and Mathematics Achievement," *Journal of Research and Development in Education* 61, no. 3 (1998): 379–406.

120. K. Resnicow and D. Allensworth, "Conducting a Comprehensive School Health Program," *Journal of School Health* 66, no. 2 (February 1996): 59–63.

121. Association for Supervision and Curriculum Development, *What We Believe: ASCD 2004 Adopted Positions* (Alexandria, VA: ASCD, 2004).

(Shayna, age 12)

Comprehensive School Health Education

Applying the Science of Education to Improving Health Instruction

DESIRED LEARNER OUTCOMES

After reading this chapter, you will be able to . . .

- **Identify key policymakers and ways in which they influence education practice in the United States.**

- **Summarize ways in which findings from the growing body of brain science can be applied to improve teaching and learning.**

- **Describe the application of developmentally appropriate practice to improving health instruction for students in elementary and middle schools.**

- **Summarize characteristics of effective health education curricula.**

- **Describe effective strategies for engaging children in curriculum planning.**

- **Use the Internet and other resources for assistance in improving health education policy and practice.**

INTRODUCTION

One important way to begin to address the problem of developing effective health education curricula and instructional practices is to review important findings about learning from education literature. Educators who understand how students learn are better equipped to translate information into meaningful health education learning experiences. A review of literature about schools and educational effectiveness can be revealing for parents, teachers, and administrators involved in making decisions about their local health education course of study.

INFLUENTIAL POLICYMAKERS IN THE EDUCATION COMMUNITY

The education enterprise in the United States is grounded in a commitment to decentralization. Rather than being controlled by the federal government, the education of our youth is the responsibility of each state. State-specific mandates and recommendations are interpreted and put into practice within each local school district. As such, the system for educating American children is designed so that the determination of curricular topics and their boundaries, teacher licensure requirements, and the planning, development, implementation, and evaluation of instruction reflect the unique interests and education standards adopted by each state.

As the voice for education reform has become more powerful, experimental models for educating students have emerged and are being tested. Today's parents can choose from several schooling options for their children. As models for educating youth have become more varied, it has become more difficult for teachers and other stakeholders to understand who controls the structure, policy, and practices governing schools.

Although exercised by relatively few parents, the education option of charter, or community, schools is being selected by some caregivers. Recent data from the National Center for Education Statistics confirm that less than 1 million students attend approximately 3,300 such schools in the United States.[1] Charter or community schools operate with public monies and must conform to state standards for health and safety. Charter schools must also operate in full compliance with federal civil rights laws. These schools, however, are granted considerable autonomy in developing policies, curricula, and programs.[2]

As another option, a growing number of students are being educated in their homes by parents or caregivers. Since 1999, when national prevalence data about home schooling began to be collected, the estimated percentage of the school-age population being home schooled has risen to over 1 million or just over 2 percent of American students.[3] In most states, adult family members in charge of educational activities must submit education plans and maintain records with their state department of education. Parents and caregivers who are opting to home school their children can find an increasing volume of educational resource materials, including Internet resources specifically developed to meet their needs.[4]

First tested in the cities of Milwaukee and Cleveland, tuition voucher programs were proposed initially by politicians and education reform advocates. Tuition vouchers were intended to give economically disadvantaged families access to the widest range of schooling alternatives promising a better education for their children. Vouchers were challenged by many groups of professional educators who saw such programs as a drain on already limited allocations of public monies for public education. A Supreme Court decision in 2002 confirmed that states have the legal right to distribute public tax dollars *to parents* for use as tuition vouchers for their children to attend private schools.[5]

Private schools represent a more established and historically significant educational alternative in the United States. More broadly available and widely accessed by parents and their children than alternative models, private schools operate with a minimum of government influence or control. In the 2007–2008 school year, just over 6 million attended private schools in the United States.[6] There is great variability among the states concerning government oversight of matters such as curriculum, performance evaluation, and professional preparation requirements for teachers and administrators. Many private schools were established by religious organizations to meet the educational needs of the children of early settlers, others were organized around secular unifying missions or goals. To this day, the largest private schooling enterprise in the United States operates under the auspices of the Catholic Church. In most cases, boards of directors or trustees comprised of prominent members of the community, volunteers, religious leaders, and/or alumni of the school are responsible for setting policies for individual schools or groups of schools. The majority of funding for private schools is generated from the tuition and fees charged to attendees.[7]

By contrast, the governance structure of public schools is very complex. Attended by the majority of U.S. students (nearly 50 million in the 2007–2008 academic year), public schools must operate in full compliance with several layers of federal, state, and local laws.[8] In addition, public schools and their employees must respond to the expectations and concerns of parents and other taxpayers in the local community. As a result, many stakeholders have a voice in public school policy and practice.

Federal Influence

Throughout U.S. history, the federal government has exerted only narrow and limited influence over education policy. Until recent years, Congress specified that the U.S. Department of Education would maintain a very broad role in public education by participating in activities such as the following:

- Enforcing civil rights laws, prohibiting discrimination, and ensuring equity
- Exercising leadership by sponsoring research and evaluating policy strategies and pilot programs
- Providing funds for activities to enrich economically disadvantaged students and children with special needs
- Promoting educational effectiveness through support of state-developed tests of proficiency in core content areas[9]

No Child Left Behind (NCLB)

With the signing of the reauthorization of the Elementary and Secondary Education Act on January 8, 2002, the role of the federal government in influencing public education in the United States was expanded and strengthened. This act, termed "No Child Left Behind (NCLB)," established a multiyear national agenda to improve academic achievement among all students. As a result of this legislation, the federal government assumed leadership for specific activities in state education agencies and local school districts with regard to

- Improving student performance on test scores in selected content areas;
- Eliminating achievement gaps among different racial, ethnic, income, and disability groups of learners;
- Upgrading the qualifications of teachers and paraprofessionals working in schools.

The original purpose of No Child Left Behind was a worthy one. This act was intended "to ensure that all children have a fair, equal, and significant opportunity to attain a high-quality education and reach, at a minimum, proficiency on challenging state academic achievement standards and state academic assessments."[10] This federal law affecting public education policy and practice in all schools was built with a focus on four key elements:

- Accountability for results
- Emphasis on policies and instructional practices demonstrated by research to be effective
- Expansion of options for parents
- Extension of local control and flexibility in the management of schools.[11]

This sweeping federal initiative was intended to unite all stakeholders in the education enterprise in the following ways:

Parents were to have access to information about the academic performance of their children and the schools they were attending, with options and resources available to them if their children were attending failing schools.

Teachers were to have the training they needed to teach effectively, use curricula demonstrated to be effective,

and, as a result of testing, know which students were in need of extra attention.

Principals were to have the information to address school weaknesses and to implement evidence-based methods and strategies.

Superintendents were to have evidence to distinguish between strongly performing and more poorly performing schools and personnel.

School boards were to have data to compare the performance of local district schools to others in their state and have evidence on which to base decision making about financial and policy priorities.

State school leaders were to know how the performance of schools in their state compared to that in other states and have data to help pinpoint needed guidance and resources.

Governors were to be able to base education decision making on a yearly report card of school performance in their state.

Community leaders and volunteers were to have information at their disposal to help target advocacy activities for children and schools most in need of help.[12]

Data on the impact of this federal legislation has shown mixed results. Education officials in many states and school districts report that scores on tests of math and reading have gone up, and achievement gaps are narrowing or at least remaining constant. In general, schools are paying more attention to aligning curricula with standards and many are using assessment data to inform decision making about school improvement. Nearly 90 percent of teachers in core subjects have met the NCLB definition of "highly qualified," and the federal and state governments are more engaged in local education matters. However, NCLB is a mandate that is grossly underfunded. Federal funding to support NCLB implementation has stagnated. Nearly 80 percent of school districts report that they have had to use local tax dollars to cover associated costs.

In addition to managing the financial burdens of NCLB compliance, school districts have had to change instructional time allocation to accommodate mandated testing and increased demands for reading and math instruction.[13] Although 91 percent of school districts have made no changes to the length of the elementary school day since NCLB was enacted, over 35 percent of districts have reduced instructional time in social studies, 28 percent have reduced time devoted to science instruction, 16 percent have reduced time devoted to art and music education, and 9 percent have reduced the time that students participate in physical education. In addition, 20 percent of elementary schools have decreased time devoted to recess and 5 percent have shortened the length of the lunch period. Similar shifts in instructional time have been documented in middle schools, most of which are spending significantly more instructional time on reading and math than on science, social studies, foreign languages, physical education, art, and music.[14]

Given these constraints, many local districts have very limited time, financial, and human resources to invest in such activities as science fairs, foreign language competitions, instruction in the arts, life-skills development, and activities that support student health.[15] Unfortunately, data throughout this text confirm that there have been negative and increasingly more evident consequences of such decisions. Education researchers are beginning to conclude that when schools cut back on activities that address the health and comprehensive developmental needs of learners to concentrate on testing and instruction in a few specific priority content areas, it is proving to be "short-sighted and counterproductive."[16]

Children with special needs are increasingly integrated into general education classrooms, where instructional adaptations can help meet their needs.

Deliberations over the federal reauthorization of NCLB have focused on such critical issues as increasing funding to support its implementation, placing expanded instructional priorities on more equal footing, and striking a better balance between supporting student learning and the emphasis on accountability. Though standards-based reform, rigorous assessment, and increased accountability have been positive legacies of NCLB, many stakeholders are convinced that education reform must be broad enough to ensure that all children learn and develop to their fullest potential. This includes increasing the capacity of schools, communities, and parents to help students adopt healthy lifestyles, a neglected element in the original NCLB legislation.[17]

Federal Monitoring and Supervision of School Health Activities

A number of federal agencies have been charged with the responsibility of monitoring and providing support for school-based health education and promotion activities. The U.S. Department of Education manages the Safe and Drug-Free School and Communities funding program, and the U.S. Department of Agriculture oversees school food service activities, including the National School Breakfast and National School Lunch Programs.

While it has no direct policy authority over state and local education agencies, the U.S. Department of Health and Human Services (USDHHS) manages grant activities that support school health efforts. In particular, the Centers for Disease Control and Prevention, a subdivision of the USDHHS, manages a funding program to support HIV/AIDS education and supports the implementation of the Coordinated School Health Program (described in Chapter 1) across the states. In addition, the Public Health Service of

the USDHHS and the Office of the Surgeon General have produced a number of reports focusing national attention and resources on the health issues confronting children and youth, discussed in later chapters. One is the 2002 Report of the Surgeon General's Conference on Health Disparities and Mental Retardation titled *Closing the Gap: A National Blueprint for Improving the Health of Persons with Mental Retardation.* While this document makes a number of recommendations for managing age-associated medical needs of individuals with mental retardation, it also asserts that "health promotion programs should accommodate people with MR . . . including a particular focus on . . . smoking cessation, weight control, fitness, safe sex, drugs and alcohol."[18]

Teaching Students with Exceptional Needs: A Brief Introduction

The important actions contained in NCLB to improve academic outcomes for all students also were foundational to the reauthorization in December 2004 of the Individuals with Disabilities Education Act (IDEA) of 1997. The new Individuals with Disabilities Education Improvement Act (IDEIA) incorporated NCLB mandates into educational programs specifically targeted at students with disabilities. IDEIA (also known as IDEA 2004) stipulates that a free appropriate public education in the least restrictive environment must be made available for students diagnosed with disabilities who require special education services. IDEIA identifies specific disability categories that qualify students for special education and/or related services, including specific learning disability, serious emotional disturbance, mental retardation, autism, other health impairments, and orthopedic impairments. Students with disabilities also can access educational services under Section 504 of the federal Rehabilitation Act.[19]

About 10 percent of American school-age children have been diagnosed with a specific disability, and an increasing number of children with disabilities are being integrated into general education classrooms.[20] In most cases, it is the classroom teacher who assumes instructional responsibility for students with disabilities. As such, teachers, regardless of their training, must adapt and accommodate instruction to manage the educational needs of learners with disabilities. Teachers or other support staff with particular expertise in special education or related services might be identified to assist classroom teachers with necessary classroom and/or instructional modifications. Classroom teachers have become an integral part of a multidisciplinary team of professionals engaged in decision making about what represents best practice for each student with a disability. These decisions are reflected in the specific Individualized Education Program (IEP) or 504 plan developed to meet the needs of each child.

An often overlooked aspect is the critical need for educators and parents to meet both the academic and the health needs of students with disabilities. To support both school success and healthy behavioral outcomes for all students, teachers must be skilled at and comfortable with implementing a wide range of instructional strategies, including learning centers, computer-assisted instruction, cooperative learning, peer-based learning activities, and skill development in self-management. All students—including those with disabilities—who interact with highly skilled teachers are offered the best chance for success in both of these critical areas. This text will discuss many of these strategies in detail.

All students benefit from diversified instruction complemented by instructional adaptations or accommodations when necessary. Most accommodations are simple and easily implemented (e.g., more time for completing tasks, adapted assignments, the use of special equipment, and so on). Other accommodations can be extensive. Having a large repertoire of strategies that support academic and health outcomes is the key to success.[21]

As a starting point, teachers working with diverse groups of learners are encouraged to seek the expertise of colleagues in the local school community. Many national and state professional, governmental, and advocacy groups have established clearinghouses and information centers to help teachers meet the needs of the widest range of learners.

State Influence

The U.S. Constitution asserts that education is a responsibility of each state. At the state level, the governor is responsible for developing the state budget and proposing initiatives of importance. However, the state legislature has final authority over state policies, state budgets, and the distribution of state funds. Across the United States, states contribute about 48 percent of the funds necessary to cover public education costs.[22] Many governors and legislators have found that it is politically wise at least to verbalize a commitment to improving education outcomes and the management of funding issues as a way to generate support and popularity among constituents. Unfortunately, competing political pressures, budgetary realities, and turnover among officials in state government can challenge continuity and implementation of such intentions.

Although the scope of influence varies from state to state, it is the state board of education (SBE) that is responsible for policymaking and enforcement and for governance of the public schools. In some states, members of the SBE are elected. In others, they are appointed by the governor. In most states, a chief state school officer chairs the SBE. This professional, usually trained as an educator, holds the title of state superintendent, commissioner, secretary, or director of education. Typically, the SBE is responsible for maintaining a broad long-term vision for education. Further, this body must provide bipartisan leadership over matters such as education goals and standards, graduation requirements, teacher licensure requirements, and assessment programs to ensure school performance.

In this way, the SBE sets many policies that influence school health programming within each state. This body has the power to require that all students receive nutrition education or daily physical education. Many SBEs have wrestled with questions concerning the amount and type of sexuality education to be delivered within their state. (Teachers in elementary and middle schools would be wise to examine specific policy mandates concerning a requirement for an "abstinence-only" or an "abstinence emphasis" approach to sexuality education within their state.)

Under the guidance of the chief state school officer and the SBE, the state education agency (SEA) or state department of education enforces regulations governing federal and state programs, distributes funds to local school districts, and offers technical assistance and training for employees. Consistent with the statutes in NCLB, the state department of education, sometimes referred to as department of public instruction, must develop curricular guidelines, performance standards in specific content areas, and tests of student performance. This body is also responsible for evaluating school improvement plans. As such, SEA employees collaborate with community agencies and school leaders to support continuous improvement in local school districts. Finally, many specialists in the areas of HIV/AIDS risk reduction, nutritional health promotion, substance abuse prevention, and school health services are funded by federal grants. These programs, intended to promote student health, are managed by SEA staff.[23]

Local Influence

At the local level, school districts must comply with all federal and state education laws. However, the local school board is responsible for establishing policies and practices that define the day-to-day operations in the schools within each school district. This model of governance grew from a commitment to the belief that local citizens should control the policies and practices of the public schools in their communities. Currently, there are more than 15,000 local school boards operating in the United States. Their responsibilities include hiring personnel, approving the district curricula, selecting texts, managing the budget, and contracting for services.[24] Local tax dollars account for approximately 43 percent of local public education costs.[25]

With very few exceptions, local school boards are composed of elected members. The number of school board members varies from state to state, but there are three general eligibility requirements for candidates:

1. *Age.* In most states, those seeking a seat on the board must be at least 18 years of age.
2. *Residence.* Candidates must live within the geographic boundaries of the school district they will represent.
3. *Financial affiliation.* To avoid the potential for conflict of interest, persons running for a seat on the school board must not be employed by the school district.

In this context, a wide range of professional expertise and interest is reflected in the deliberations and decisions made by a local school board.

Every school board member has strong beliefs about what constitutes the best education for local children. Disagreements about how this ideal is translated into practice are common among members of local boards of education. In addition to personal passions about education issues, elected members must represent what they believe to be the values and interests of their constituents. Activist residents and special interest groups can exert a powerful influence over school district policies and practices.

In all communities, there are many health and social service agencies and juvenile justice providers who serve local students and their families. Poor communication between independently functioning school personnel and agency representatives can lead to duplication of services to students. In some unfortunate cases, the needs of students may be overlooked. This is particularly true for students with disabilities, those with complex medical problems, or cases in which the school board can't resolve a policy matter regarding a controversial health issue.

To help bridge gaps that emerge between the education ideals of members of the board and the education needs of students, school districts employ a superintendent, or chief executive officer, of schools, responsible for implementing policies and practices adopted by the school board. Typically, the superintendent is supported by a number of professional assistants. Depending on the size and budget of the school district, a number of trained specialists serve as staff in the central office of the district. Collectively, these professionals oversee curriculum, budget, personnel, operations, and policy implementation.

Unions and other employee associations influence the budget and operations within school districts. Many school communities have organized unions for teachers (the National Education Association [NEA] and American Federation of Teachers [AFT]) and administrators. Local chapters of unions for noncertified or classified staff can be very active. These groups participate in activities such as contract negotiations, employee health and advocacy initiatives, and resolution of conflicts or grievances.

Within each school building, a variety of employees manage daily operations. The principal supervises the instructional program, maintains a safe and nurturing learning environment, evaluates teachers and other staff, and represents the school to parent and community groups. Assistant principals and "school improvement" or "site-based management" teams assist many principals. These teams are composed of teachers, coaches, custodial and school support staff, and parents or other community representatives. A growing body of literature confirms the importance of engaging parents and concerned others in the management, policies, and program implementation of the school.[26]

Teachers in elementary and middle schools confronted with curricular decisions and threats to student success would be wise to identify committed stakeholders within their school community from whom they can seek counsel and support. Only in this way can they feel fully equipped to serve as advocates for the instructional and health needs of their students.

Understanding the organization and sources of influence over public schools is important for educators and other student advocates. Though the structure of the public education system appears to be cumbersome and inconsistencies between local policies and practices may be evident, it is designed to maximize input from taxpayers and other concerned stakeholders. With this sound philosophical underpinning, children can be educated in ways that reflect the best education practice mediated by parental concerns and community needs, values, and standards.

LESSONS FROM THE EDUCATION LITERATURE

The sources of influence over school policy and practice may be varied, but the call for education reform has been nearly universal. Beyond the call for overall school improvement, student populations have become more diverse, and schools are being asked to deliver more services to meet learner needs. As a result, school staff are struggling to improve academic success while meeting social, emotional, occupational, and health needs among increasingly diverse groups of learners.

A range of educational innovations, including school councils, parent involvement task forces, continuous improvement teams, and authentic assessment protocols, have been proposed as ways to improve the quality of instruction to maximize academic success for all students. Many approaches, including those that place students in roles of active or cooperative learners, have been promoted in both the education literature and the popular press. As discussed in Chapter 3, a great deal of energy has been devoted to developing and refining standards on which to base curriculum development and student evaluation.

Unfortunately, many proposals to reform education have a political, financial, procedural, or operational motivation. These strategies might not be based on sound education theory or evaluated to confirm that they are scientifically sound. The highest standards, the most rigorous proficiency testing protocol, and the most creative curricula can undermine meaningful learning unless they are planned and implemented with specific attention to how students process information and learn.[27]

Connecting Brain Research with Learning

As a foundation for improving teaching and learning, educators have begun to explore ways to translate research from the neurological and cognitive sciences into effective classroom practices. Such brain-based research has begun to show promise for improving teaching and learning, particularly among students with diverse learning needs.[28]

Brain-based research has given educators a way to translate neuroimaging data into classroom activities that stimulate parts of the brain demonstrated to be active during information processing, memory, and recall. Research suggests that the most successful strategies are those that teach for meaning and understanding, and that learning is most likely to occur in classrooms in which students feel low levels of threat but reasonable degrees of challenge. In addition, such brain research has begun to confirm that students who are active, engaged, and motivated devote more brain activity to learning than do their counterparts. Findings from this growing body of literature cluster into the following categories.[29]

Findings About Acquiring and Integrating Knowledge

Brain-based research has confirmed that learning must occur within the context of what the learner already knows, has experienced, or understands.[30] In addition, new information must be processed so that it can be retrieved for use in different situations or contexts. The more a student repeats a learning activity, the more developing nerve connections in the brain are stimulated. Further, different parts of the brain store different parts of a memory. For example, singing a song is the result of complex brain activity. One part of the brain stores the tune, while another area stores the song's lyrics. As a result, the brain must reconstruct the parts of that memory before the person can re-create the whole song.[31]

To promote learning, teachers are encouraged to

- Present new information within the context of prior knowledge or previous experience.
- Structure opportunities for students to repeat learning activities as a way to cement information or skills in their memories.
- Use mnemonics to promote associations in memory tasks.

- Incorporate visually stimulating learning materials and hands-on manipulatives to activate the right hemisphere of the brain and incorporate text-based presentations to activate the left hemisphere.
- Integrate art, music, and movement into learning experiences to promote learning by activating different parts of the brain.[32]

Teacher's Toolbox 2.1 contains brain-friendly techniques for improving memory.[33]

Findings About Positive Attitudes Toward Learning

Teachers have long suspected that attitudes affect learning, and brain research has confirmed this link between the cognitive and affective domains. Interestingly, the concept of "emotional intelligence" has been characterized as the best predictor of life success.[34] Though understandings of emotional intelligence have been debated, brain science has confirmed that nerve pathways connect the emotional and cognitive processing centers in the brain. It has been demonstrated that hormones alter brain chemistry in students under stress. When we are stressed, chemicals are released into the brain that can impair memory and learning.[35] Research confirms that teachers should consider the following emotionally supportive classroom practices as a foundation for promoting learning:

- Establish a challenging but supportive classroom environment that reduces the stress associated with academic difficulties and peer conflicts. Pair students with a homework buddy, arrange for peer-based tutoring or practice sessions focusing on study skills, and conduct one-on-one meetings with students to reinforce trust.
- Structure learning experiences that enable students to practice social skills and peer acceptance. Hold class meetings and use literature- and history-based learning materials that celebrate diversity. Model appreciation for contributions of students with different learning styles and needs.
- Create and reinforce a climate of civility in the classroom. Model saying "please" and "thank you" for specific student behaviors.
- Use humor, movement, or the expressive arts to promote an engaging learning environment and ease instructional transitions. Such activities arouse emotional centers in the brain, a foundation for peak academic performance.[36]

Findings About Extending and Refining Knowledge

Thinking skills have to be practiced for students to be able to extend and refine knowledge. Classroom activities should require students to go beyond the basic tasks of recognizing or memorizing. Learning strategies must be constructed in such a way that students explore information more deeply and analytically. Specifically, students must practice manipulating information by comparing, contrasting, deducing, analyzing errors, and analyzing perspective. Further, brain research supports activities in which students are engaged in classifying concepts and using complex retrieval and integration systems in the brain.[37] To this end, teachers are encouraged to consider the following classroom strategies:

- Design learning activities that require students to build on prior knowledge or experience.
- Structure opportunities for students to compare their work with model responses.
- Create rubrics that require students to develop models or visual representations of error patterns in their work.
- Structure learning experiences in which students identify patterns of events and compare or contrast characteristics or attributes among ideas.[38]

Findings About Meaningful Use of Knowledge

We learn best when we believe that information is needed to accomplish a goal. Evidence suggests that experiential learning activities that require students to make decisions, conduct experiments, and investigate ways to solve real-world problems activate those areas within the brain responsible for higher-order thinking. In this context, productive learning experiences extend beyond hands-on activities. When physical activities are paired with problem-solving tasks, memory and learning are enhanced.[39] Examples of such strategies include the following:

- Assignments in which students are actively engaged in investigating, analyzing, and solving problems from the world around them
- Learning activities that require students to demonstrate learning in multiple ways, including inventions, experiments, displays, and musical or oral presentations[40]

Findings About the Learning Habits of the Mind

Learning is promoted for students who are able to establish and practice important habits, including goal setting, monitoring their own thinking, setting standards for self-evaluation, and regulating behaviors, including their own work habits. Research has confirmed the value of exploring, understanding, and applying concepts in the context of individual ways of thinking and interpreting. In this context, Gardner has asserted that intelligence is difficult to reduce to a single number, or IQ score. Intelligence and learning have more to do with the capacity of a student to solve problems and develop products in a natural setting. In this spirit, teachers are encouraged to review the extensive bodies of research focused on learning styles and multiple intelligence theory as a context for translating brain research into teaching strategies. Teacher's Toolbox 2.2 contains a checklist for identifying and responding to the range of intelligences represented in a group of learners.[41]

Pertinent classroom strategies include the following:

- Use thinking logs and reflective journals with students of varying abilities.
- Embed group discussions into cooperative learning structures.
- Model classroom habits that foster reflection about learning. Holding class discussions that reinforce reflection and recording important concepts and facts learned in a lesson are very productive strategies.[42]

Although researchers agree that exploration of brain function is in the early stages, the field of neurology and cognitive science has experienced an explosion in recent years. As this field develops, it will continue to shed light on thinking and learning patterns among the broadest range of learners. In addition, as more inroads are made in translating this body of research into meaningful classroom practice, decision making about reforming education in classrooms and schools will become easier for teachers, curriculum developers, and school administrators. A summary of brain research and related applications can be found in Teacher's Toolbox 2.3.[43, 44]

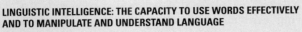

A Checklist for Identifying and Responding to Multiple Intelligences

LINGUISTIC INTELLIGENCE: THE CAPACITY TO USE WORDS EFFECTIVELY AND TO MANIPULATE AND UNDERSTAND LANGUAGE

Does the student:
- Write better than average for age?
- Have an advanced vocabulary for age?
- Enjoy reading books?
- Enjoy word games?
- Tell tall tales, stories, or jokes?
- Re-create tongue twisters and rhymes?
- Verbalize memories of names, dates, and other facts?

Planning question for teacher:
- How can I incorporate the written or spoken word into daily classroom practice?

Helpful teaching materials:
- Books, tape recorders, stamp sets, books on tape, walkie-talkies, comic books, word games

LOGICAL-MATHEMATICAL INTELLIGENCE: THE ABILITY TO USE NUMBERS EFFECTIVELY, UNDERSTAND ABSTRACTIONS, OR DEMONSTRATE AWARENESS OF LOGICAL PATTERNS AND RELATIONSHIPS

Does the student:
- Enjoy logic puzzles or brainteasers?
- Enjoy math and science classes?
- Organize things into categories or hierarchies?
- Play chess or other strategy games?
- Compute math quickly in head?
- Ask questions about how things work?
- Enjoy experiments?

Planning question for teacher:
- How can I incorporate numbers, calculations, classification, or logic activities into daily classroom practice?

Helpful teaching materials:
- Calculators, math manipulatives, number games, and equipment for experiments

SPATIAL INTELLIGENCE: THE CAPACITY TO PERCEIVE, REPRESENT, OR TRANSFORM VISUAL OR SPATIAL CONSTRUCTS OR TO ORIENT SELF IN SPACE

Does the student:
- Report clear visual images?
- Read maps, charts, and diagrams more easily than text?
- Enjoy puzzles or mazes?
- Respond more positively to illustrations than to text?
- Enjoy art activities?
- Draw figures that are advanced for age?
- Doodle on learning materials?

Planning question for teacher:
- How can I use visual aids, color, art, or metaphor in daily classroom practice?

Helpful teaching materials:
- Graphs, maps, videos, cameras, optical illusions, art materials, and LEGO or block sets

BODY-KINESTHETIC INTELLIGENCE: THE ABILITY TO USE THE WHOLE BODY TO EXPRESS IDEAS AND FEELINGS OR TO PRODUCE OR TRANSFORM OBJECTS

Does the student:
- Excel in one or more sports?
- Mimic the gestures or mannerisms of others?
- Take things apart and put them back together?
- Move, tap, or fidget when seated for a period of time?
- Integrate fine-motor coordination or skill into a craft?
- Report physical sensations while thinking or working?
- Dramatically express ideas or feeling?

Planning question for teacher:
- How can I involve the whole body or integrate hands-on experiences and dramatic depictions into daily classroom practice?

Helpful teaching materials:
- Building tools, clay, sports equipment, manipulatives, theater props

MUSICAL INTELLIGENCE: THE ABILITY TO RECOGNIZE, DISCRIMINATE, TRANSFORM, AND EXPRESS MUSICAL FORMS

Does the student:
- Have a good singing voice?
- Remember melodies of songs?
- Play a musical instrument?
- React to environmental noises or anomalies in music (off-key)?
- Unconsciously hum to self?
- Enjoy and work well while music is played in the classroom?
- Tap rhythmically while working?

Planning question for teacher:
- How can I integrate music, environmental sounds, rhythmic patterns, or melodic frameworks into daily classroom practice?

Helpful teaching materials:
- Musical instruments, tape recorders, CD players, improvised musical instruments

INTERPERSONAL INTELLIGENCE: THE ABILITY TO PERCEIVE AND MAKE DISTINCTIONS IN THE MOODS, FEELINGS, INTENTIONS, AND MOTIVATIONS OF OTHERS

Does the student:
- Enjoy socializing with peers?
- Give advice to friends with problems?
- Demonstrate leadership skills?
- Have a strong sense of empathy for others?
- Have several close friends?
- Have others seek out his or her company?
- Appear to be street-smart?

Planning question for teacher:
- How can I engage students in peer sharing, cooperative learning, or large-group activities?

Helpful teaching materials:
- Board games, party supplies, props and costumes for role-playing

INTRAPERSONAL INTELLIGENCE: THE ACCURATE AWARENESS OF PERSONAL STRENGTHS AND WEAKNESSES, A STRONG KNOWLEDGE OF SELF, AND THE ABILITY TO ADAPT ACTIONS BASED ON THAT KNOWLEDGE

Does the student:
- Display a sense of independence and strong will?
- "March to the beat of a different drummer" in learning and living style?
- Play and work well alone?
- Have a strong sense of self-direction?
- Prefer working alone to collaboration?
- Accurately express feelings?
- Have strong and positive self-esteem?

Planning question for teacher:
- How can I evoke feelings and memories or give students more choices in daily classroom practice?

Helpful teaching materials:
- Journals, personal progress charts, materials to reinforce self-checking, equipment for projects

NATURALISTIC INTELLIGENCE: SENSITIVITY TO FEATURES IN THE NATURAL WORLD OR THE ABILITY TO DISCRIMINATE AMONG OBJECTS IN THE ENVIRONMENT

Does the student:
- Bring insects, flowers, or other natural things to share with classmates?
- Recognize patterns in nature?
- Understand the characteristics of different species?
- Demonstrate interest and ability in classification of objects?
- Recognize and name natural things?
- Collect environmental artifacts?
- Care for classroom pets and plants?

Planning question for teacher:
- How can I incorporate living things, natural phenomena, or ecological exploration into daily classroom practice?

Helpful teaching materials:
- Plants, animals, binoculars, tools to explore and document the environment, gardening equipment

Source: T. Armstrong, *Multiple Intelligences in the Classroom,* 2d ed. (Alexandria, VA: Association for Supervision and Curriculum Development, 2000).

Summarizing and Applying Brain Research to Health Promotion

Each number below highlights a research finding from the growing body of brain science. Each finding is interpreted for better understanding (A), general implications for improving classroom practice are discussed (B), and an example for improving student health promotion is provided (C).

1. *The brain is a complex parallel processor.*
   A. Thoughts, emotions, and imagination all operate simultaneously, allowing elements of the system to interact and to exchange input from the environment.
   B. Because no single teaching method or learning strategy can address all the variations of brain operation, teachers need to create learning environments that engage as many aspects of the brains of students as possible.
   C. To promote nutritional health, teachers would be wise to include pertinent music, visual depictions, menu planning, and food preparation and tasting into units of instruction.
2. *Learning involves the whole body and its processes.*
   A. Learning is natural for the brain, but it is a process that can be supported or influenced negatively by student health status.
   B. Classroom practice is enriched when teachers help minimize stress, threats, and boredom. Such states affect brain function differently than do peace, challenge, and contentment. In addition, teachers must recognize that health is not just an instructional class or body of information. Despite the fact that they might be the same chronological age, it is unrealistic to expect children of unequal health status to reach the same level of achievement. Healthy kids may differ by as much as five years in acquisition of basic skills.
   C. Regardless of the health unit of instruction, teachers should create health class practices that encourage children to drink enough water to keep their brains properly hydrated.
3. *The search for meaning is innate.*
   A. Making sense of our experiences is linked to survival and is a basic brain function. Our brains register the familiar while searching out and responding to novel stimulation.
   B. While teachers would be wise to establish classroom policies and routines that communicate stability and behavioral boundaries, they must balance the familiar with learning opportunities that satisfy curiosity, discovery, and challenge.
   C. The kinds of alcohol risk reduction activities developed to engage and challenge learners identified as gifted and talented should provide guidance for developing learning opportunities about this topic for all students.
4. *The brain searches for meaning by patterning.*
   A. The brain is designed to identify and generate patterns, to organize and categorize information into meaningful groupings.
   B. For learning activities to be effective, they must be based on or associated with things that make sense to students. Teachers should avoid basing lessons on elements of isolated or disconnected pieces of information.
   C. Tobacco lessons based on repetition of facts are far less successful than thematic units of instruction that require students to use math skills to calculate costs of tobacco use or to explore the history of tobacco as a cash crop in various states in the United States.

5. *Emotions are critical to patterning.*
   A. Emotions, expectations, and thoughts can shape one another and can't be separated in the brain.
   B. Teachers must remember that the degree to which students feel supported by them and their colleagues will affect student learning.
   C. When teachers model consistent communication patterns across the school day that convey respect and value for learners, students are more likely to practice similar communication skills with classmates and others when confronted with health issues.
6. *The brain processes parts and wholes simultaneously.*
   A. Research has demonstrated that there are significant differences between the left and right lobes of the brain. However, both hemispheres work to organize information by reducing it to parts and by working with wholes or series of whole sets of inputs.
   B. Learning is cumulative and developmental.
   C. As a way to address decision-making skill development, many teachers create units of instruction focused on practicing such skills outside the context of genuine experiences. It is far more effective to teach and practice decision-making skills in the context of daily dietary experiences or field trips to the grocery store.
7. *We understand and retain best when facts and skills are embedded in spatial memory.*
   A. Learning experiences are enriched by both internal processes and social interaction.
   B. To maximize learning experiences, teachers should connect them to real-life experiences as often as possible. Examples include field trips, stories, metaphors, drama, and meaningful homework experiences that connect learners with their families, neighborhood, and community.
   C. The impact and value of bullying risk reduction activities are enriched when students are immersed in complex and interactive learning experiences. Rather than only lecturing about the negative consequences of bullying, teachers should construct activities in which students read developmentally appropriate and pertinent stories, participate in dramatic play activities and simulations, and practice personal management and advocacy skills with others.
8. *Complex learning is enhanced by challenge but is inhibited by threat.*
   A. The brain is able to maximize connections when risk taking is encouraged within a safe context. Similarly, the brain processes stimulation less efficiently and effectively when the individual perceives threat.
   B. Creating a safe learning environment for relaxed alertness, thinking, and risk taking is critical for understanding and learning.
   C. While sexual health instruction should be regarded with as much academic rigor as other subject matter, the threat of failure or of a low grade might inhibit critical thinking and learning about developmentally appropriate sexual health issues.

Sources: R. N. Caine and G. Caine, *Unleashing the Power of Perceptual Change: The Potential of Brain-Based Teaching* (Alexandria, VA: Association for Supervision and Curriculum Development, 1997); B. Samek and N. Samek, 'It's a Brain Thing: Keeping Students Focused and Learning,' a presentation at the 78th Annual Meeting of the American School Health Association, 16 October 2004

TABLE 2–1

Six Characteristics of Deep Understanding

We confirm that we truly understand something when we are able to

1.	*Explain it.*	By providing thorough, justifiable accounts of facts, data, or issues
2.	*Interpret it.*	By telling meaningful stories, providing meaningful personal interpretations of ideas or events, or making issues accessible through images or analogies
3.	*Apply it.*	By using and adapting what we know in another context or circumstance
4.	*Reflect perspective.*	By demonstrating that we can see the big picture or other points of view through a critical lens
5.	*Empathize.*	By affirming the value of things that others find odd or implausible
6.	*Be self-aware.*	By recognizing personal attributes that shape or limit our capacity for understanding

SOURCE: G. Wiggins and J. McTighe, *Understanding by Design* (Alexandria, VA: Association for Supervision and Curriculum Development, 1998).

Authentic Instruction and Achievement

Once district curricula are updated and teachers have participated in staff development activities to enrich their expertise with brain-based approaches to learning, the next step to improve classroom practice is to maximize authenticity across all learning activities. Newmann and Wehlage describe *authentic learning* as that which has meaning and significance. This is contrasted with many conventional approaches to instruction and testing that are trivial or useless.[45] As a quick test, teachers can evaluate the extent to which current classroom practice is likely to result in authentic outcomes by asking several questions as they plan and organize learning activities. Teachers are encouraged to reflect on the extent to which, as a result of student participation,

- Students will practice the construction of meaning as a foundation for producing knowledge.
- Students will be engaged in disciplined inquiry as a basis for constructing meaning.
- Students will produce work directed toward discussion, outcomes, and/or performances that have value or meaning beyond the confines of the classroom or school.[46]

Specifically, it is the responsibility of teachers to make sure that their approach to instruction is consistent with the following five criteria, or standards, of authentic instruction:

1. *To what degree are students encouraged to use higher-order thinking skills?* Lower-order thinking occurs when students are asked to receive or recite facts. At this level, learners are called on to apply rules though repetitive experiences. In contrast, higher-order thinking requires students to manipulate, synthesize, explain, or draw conclusions about ideas. The goal of all instructional activities should be for students to transform the original meaning of an idea in some way. While higher-order thinking implies a challenge for students, it ensures that they will be engaged in solving problems and making meaning that has applicability or relevance. For example, student learning and violence risk reduction are enhanced when learners engage in translating district violence policies into meaningful classroom practice rather than simply reading or memorizing local codes of conduct.

2. *What is the depth of knowledge included in the lesson?* Depth of knowledge is the substantive character of ideas included in a lesson and the level of understanding students demonstrate as they work with these ideas. Knowledge is characterized as thin or superficial if it does not deal with significant issues or ideas within a topic or content area. Superficiality is inevitable if students grasp only a trivial understanding of important concepts, or if they cover large amounts of fragmented information. Knowledge is characterized as deep when it focuses on developmentally appropriate ideas that are central to a topic or discipline. Students are engaged in work that is deep when they participate in making distinctions, developing arguments, and constructing explanations. Though fewer topics might be addressed within a specified time period, this approach is far more sound. By attending to the depth of instruction, teachers are formalizing the connections between topics.[47] Table 2–1 clarifies six characteristics associated with deep understanding.[48] Chapter 3 provides a discussion about how to apply this standard to promoting student health.

3. *To what extent do instructional activities and class content have meaning beyond the classroom?* Many learning activities have no impact on others. Some certify only that students have been compliant with the rules and norms of their school. In such cases, instructional activities support successfully navigating systems established to support efficiency rather than learning in the school environment. Lessons gain authenticity when instruction is connected to the larger community in which students live. As a framework for understanding or applying knowledge, students must address real-world problems or incorporate experiences or events from outside the school into classroom learning experiences.[49] For example, student learning and nutritional health can be enriched when learning opportunities extend beyond content mastery of the importance of selected vitamins and minerals. Functional knowledge and decision-making skill development are supported by visiting local food producers, conducting product analyses at local grocery stores, or carrying out vitamin and mineral scavenger hunts in home kitchens.

4. *How much class time is involved in substantive conversation about the subject?* It is all too common for teachers to engage students in unsophisticated classroom conversation.

Social support for achievement promotes positive learning experiences.

Professionals are reminded that authentic instructional approaches are useful for all content areas and teaching methods. This approach is demonstrated when any instructional activity—new or old, in or out of school—engages students in using complex thinking skills to confront issues and solve problems that have meaning or value beyond simple measures of school performance. Classroom practices then are consistent with the emerging body of science related to brain-based learning.

Developmentally Appropriate Practice

Regardless of the age of students or the focus of a lesson (increasing functional knowledge, helping students examine their health beliefs or attitudes, practicing essential skills to live healthier lives), developmentally appropriate practice criteria should serve as the foundation for translating content recommendations contained in the district curriculum document into sound classroom practice. Researchers have found that "the use of developmentally appropriate practices is one of the best current strategies to ensure that individual children will have opportunities for engaging in meaningful and interesting learning on a daily basis."[51]

The National Association for the Education of Young Children reminds all teachers that planning developmentally appropriate learning activities for any content area has two important dimensions. These involve instructional practices that respond to

- The age-appropriate attributes of learners
- Individually appropriate characteristics of students

Age-Appropriate Activities

Teachers in elementary and middle grades are advised to focus their lesson-planning energies on organizing age-appropriate learning activities for students. Age-appropriate practices are based on research in human development that confirms the universal and predictable sequences of growth and change that occur in the physical, emotional, social, and intellectual, or cognitive, dimensions of all children.[52] Appendix C of this text contains a summary of common growth and development characteristics and the corresponding needs of students in kindergarten through grade 9 that can serve as a foundation for age-appropriate practice.[53]

Wise teachers will use this general information about the typical or predictable developmental sequences of students as a foundation for cultivating a functional learning environment and for planning instructional activities that correspond to the developmental attributes, needs, and abilities of students of a given age.[54] With the foundation of a developmental framework, teachers who have had only limited personal contact with a particular group of

Typically, interaction between students and teachers is one-directional with a planned body of information delivered. This part of the lesson is followed by a recitation period, in which students respond to predetermined questions in pursuit of predetermined answers. This process is the oral equivalent of true-false or short-answer test items. In contrast, high-level, substantive conversation is framed by three characteristics:

- Conversation is focused on higher-order ideas about the topic, including making distinctions, applying ideas, and raising questions rather than simply reporting facts, definitions, or procedures.
- Ideas are shared in an unscripted forum—students are encouraged to explain their thinking, ask questions, and respond to the comments of classmates.
- Conversation builds improved collective understanding of lesson themes or topics.

For example, instruction about injury risk reduction is enriched when teachers make time to cultivate discussions about ways to manage potentially dangerous play spaces at school, at home, and in local neighborhoods.

5. *Is there a high level of social support for the achievements of peers?* Low levels of social support for achievement are evident in classrooms in which the behaviors or comments of teachers and classmates discourage effort, experimentation, creativity, and engagement among all students. High-level social support is evident in classrooms in which teachers and classmates reinforce norms of high expectations for all students. In such classrooms, everyone communicates mutual respect and celebrates risk taking and hard work in confronting challenging tasks.[50] To support cognitive and skill development about physical activity, opportunities should be provided for students to experience activities that feature group problem solving, celebrate the contribution of diverse skills, and eliminate rewards for individual success.

students, such as at the start of the school year, can maximize their planning time. Further, age-appropriate cues are helpful for teachers as they introduce new, potentially emotionally charged, or controversial health education topics.

Individually Appropriate Activities

As teachers have more contact with particular groups of students they can recognize that students have different patterns and/or timing in their personal growth and development that can influence their ability to integrate education concepts into daily behavior.[55] Teachers are encouraged to build individually appropriate learning activities into lessons. The ability to add activities with specific applicability to classroom practice evolves as specific student characteristics become evident.

It is important to remember that there may be a discrepancy between age and ability. While all students need structured opportunities to practice health-promoting skills, students with cognitive disabilities might need instruction adaptation in order to learn age-relevant skills. By paying attention to individual learner attributes, teachers are better equipped to develop lessons that are both age appropriate and ability centered.

Conclusion

In relation to planning from either an age- or an individually appropriate practice perspective, teachers should begin their decision making and planning with a review of the following student characteristics:

- *Physical* abilities and limitations
- *Mental,* or *cognitive,* attributes, including variables such as time on task, attention span, and interests
- *Social* interaction patterns with family, friends, teachers, and influential others
- *Emotional* characteristics and reaction patterns
- *Language* skills and attributes as a foundation for understanding and communication[56]

Such information about students can serve as a foundation for best practice when teachers integrate the following considerations into their curriculum development and lesson planning:

- *What is known about child development and learning, including*
  1. Age-related human characteristics to support decisions about meaningful instruction
  2. General age-related clues about activities, materials, interactions, or experiences that will be safe, healthy, interesting, achievable, and challenging to learners
- *What is known about the strengths, interests, and needs of individual learners in a group, as a foundation for*
  1. Identifying individual variations in students
  2. Adapting classroom policy, practice, and learning activities to respond to needs, interests, and abilities of diverse students

- *What is known about the social, cultural, and family contexts in which children live, as a way to*
  1. Make sure that learning experiences are meaningful and relevant
  2. Ensure that respect for the uniqueness among learners and their families is communicated

The content and skills to be learned and how best to construct or organize the learning environment should be based on

- The body of literature confirming attributes of best practice about the topic (evidence-based practice guidelines)
- Family and community standards
- Policy mandates of the state and the local board of education
- Developmental characteristics and abilities of students
- The relationship between previous learning experiences and the new content and/or skills to be mastered.[57]

Such a foundation is most likely to increase the functional knowledge and essential skills among students, but teachers should remember that many variables not grounded in developmentally appropriate practice criteria can influence the district curriculum development process. This is particularly true of health instruction. Factors such as teacher expertise and comfort levels, priorities included in a selected textbook series, community traditions, social or cultural values, and parental desires can play a significant role in the development and adoption of the course of study. For example, in many communities, health teachers face pressure to take an approach to tobacco, alcohol, and other drug prevention that is based on the notion that children are "never too young" to receive unconditional messages about abstinence and peer refusal concerning the use of such products ("Just Say No" campaigns).

As a balance for less sound approaches, the National Association for the Education of Young Children reminds health educators that developmental needs and characteristics of learners must serve as the guide for best practice. For this reason, tobacco, alcohol, and other drug prevention instruction for primary-grade children should focus on developmentally appropriate concepts such as

- Recognizing the differences of medicine and items that are unsafe for play from safe play objects
- Complying with rules about safe and adult-supervised use of medication
- Identifying community health helpers who provide directions and prescriptions for medication
- Identifying safety risks associated with smoking and using other tobacco products (e.g., recognizing that matches and lighters should be used only by grown-ups)
- Practicing fire prevention and safe escape strategies

In this way, the needs and abilities of the learners, rather than other pressures, become the basis for planning and implementing lessons. Learner attributes, needs, and

Consider This **2.1**

Developmental Missions Confronting Students in Elementary and Middle Grades

1. *Sustain self-esteem.* Experience a range of experiences and interactions with others, bounce back after difficulties, and establish a loving, trusting relationship with significant adults.
2. *Be liked and accepted by peers.* Establish a range of behaviors, dress, and language patterns to be an insider with peers.
3. *Fit in while remaining unique.* Compromise on preferences without sacrificing individuality—often in conflict with establishing peer acceptance.
4. *Identify acceptable role models.* Experiment with identities and behaviors recognized in others—an evolving process helpful for self-discovery and goal setting.
5. *Question family beliefs/values.* Evaluate previously accepted "truths" and begin development of personal philosophy—consistent with increased exposure to a range of environments and people.
6. *Earn respect with family.* Gain affirmation from parents or caregivers—pride about and from the family is essential to self-worth.

7. *Seek independence/test limits.* Rehearse adolescent roles, test abilities to manage increasing independence—often leading to struggles with parents over boundaries of authority.
8. *Gather information/master skills.* Seek knowledge and practice a range of requisite life skills—limited defenses against failure can lead to embarrassment.
9. *Accept physical appearance.* Compare and contrast physical attributes with those of others—concern over differences contributes to worry and extreme modesty.
10. *Manage fears.* Establish coping skills to manage common worries—the future, loss, or humiliation.
11. *Control drives and desires.* Compromise about wants, accept reasonable alternatives, and manage passions.
12. *Define a realistic sense of self.* Express strengths and weaknesses in skills and abilities—a foundation for meeting adolescent challenges.

Source: P. Keener, *Caring for Children: Useful Information and Hard-to-Find Facts about Child Health and Development* (Indianapolis, IN: James Whitcomb Riley Memorial Association, 2001), 106–8.

---

concerns must take center stage in lesson planning and curriculum development. To this end, the Riley Hospital for Children in Indianapolis has summarized important developmental missions, or tasks, that children will confront during the elementary and middle grades. Consider This 2.1 can assist in creating developmentally appropriate curricula and lesson plans.[58]

When organizing learning strategies that are both age and individually appropriate, health educators of students in elementary and middle grades should remember the following:

• The most effective activities tend to be those that help students connect the content issues and health-promoting behaviors addressed in health class to other aspects of their lives.
• The most effective lesson planning is based on a combination of developmental and/or observed characteristics of students, the body of literature in the content area, and teachers' best professional judgments.
• Learning, particularly about health-promoting behaviors, is rarely successful if teachers approach it as a spectator sport for students. Students of all ages learn best in an active learning environment that encourages exploration and interaction with materials, other children, teachers, and other adults.
• Learning activities and materials should be concrete, real, and relevant to the lives of the students, rather than focused on some possible negative future outcome.

• Flexibility, resourcefulness, and humor often are helpful teacher characteristics. Children's interests and abilities often violate developmental expectations (think about young children and their fascination with the language and lore of dinosaurs), and even well-planned lessons sometimes flop. Teachers must be prepared to adapt, adjust, and think on their feet.
• Planning to celebrate human diversity is critical. Given the range of health beliefs and practices, activities should be carefully structured to omit sexist and culturally biased language, examples, and stereotypes (firefighters vs. firemen, mail carriers vs. mailmen, police officers vs. policemen, flight attendants vs. stewardesses, exclusive male references to physicians, exclusive female references to nurses).[59]

Research-Based Strategies for Improving Achievement

Until recently, many people were convinced that achievement and learning were influenced, in large part, by non-school factors, including the student's home environment, socioeconomic status, and/or natural aptitude or ability. Before the 1970s, teaching and instructional methodologies were regarded largely as an issue of teacher passion or art, rather than being based on a foundation of scientific research. In 1966, the landmark Coleman Report asserted that the actions taken by schools contributed little to student achievement.[60]

In the 1970s, however, researchers began to narrow the focus of their work. Rather than attempting to explain the influence of the activities of an entire school district or of individual schools on achievement, scholars began to analyze the influence of teachers and their instructional practices on student success. Findings from this growing body of research confirmed that classroom teachers have the potential to significantly affect student achievement. Effective teachers are successful with students of all ability levels, whereas students of ineffective teachers generally make less than adequate academic progress.[61]

In 1998, a comprehensive study identified those instructional strategies most likely to enhance student achievement among all students, in all grade levels, and across all subjects. Though the study did not reveal the influence of particular teaching strategies within identified content areas, the findings revealed nine categories of instructional strategies that have a strong and positive influence on student achievement.[62] Teachers planning health lessons for students in elementary and middle grades are encouraged to examine the descriptions and recommendations contained in Teacher's Toolbox 2.4.[63]

Though other elements of classroom practice, including classroom management techniques, have been shown to influence student success, this research has established a firm foundation on which curriculum development and lesson planning should be based.[64]

In summary, drawing from the literature in learning theory, behavioral psychology, and education, teachers, administrators, and parents are reminded that students learn best when

1. Information or skills seem relevant to them.
2. Students are actively involved in the learning process.
3. Learning experiences are organized.
4. Learning experiences enable students to derive their own conclusions.
5. Students become emotionally involved with or committed to the topic.
6. Students can interact with others.
7. Information can be put to immediate use or skills can be practiced rather than simply discussed.
8. Students recognize the reason for or value of the information or tasks to be mastered.
9. Positive teacher–learner relationships are cultivated.
10. A variety of teaching methods and learning strategies are used.[65]

THE STATE OF THE ART IN HEALTH EDUCATION

Health education is integral to the primary mission of schools. It provides students with functional knowledge and essential skills to be successful learners and healthy and productive adults.[66] By increasing the number of schools that provide effective education about health

problems of youth, a critical objective for improving the health of our nation is addressed.[67]

Grounded in the body of sound education research, the health education curriculum in local school districts must be organized into a scope and sequence that support the development and demonstration of increasingly sophisticated functional knowledge, attitudes, and essential skills. A Comprehensive Health Education Program is designed to promote healthy living and discourage health-risk behaviors among all students (see Chapter 1). Sound health education curricula include structured learning opportunities in which students are engaged as active learners. Through sound instructional approaches, learners increase functional health knowledge and are challenged to compare and contrast their beliefs and perceptions about health issues. Finally, students practice essential skills to maintain healthy daily lifestyles. Such a foundation is reflected in the National Health Education Standards (see Chapters 1 and 3).

Like other content areas, health instruction must comply with state learning standards or guidelines. In addition, the health education curriculum should be responsive to student health risks confirmed by local data. As a starting point for program evaluation, local school board members, administrators, teachers, and parents should examine elements that have been shown to contribute to student learning. To meet the needs of the widest range of learners, health education should:

- Base classroom practice on a foundation of theories and methods that have credible evidence of effectiveness.
- Emphasize learning and practicing skills for healthy daily living.
- Build on knowledge and skills from year to year.
- Include only the most accurate and current information.
- Include active and learner-centered instructional approaches.
- Feature developmentally appropriate and community and culturally relevant learning materials and activities.
- Structure learning activities for students in all grades that enable them to evaluate their personal behaviors, to set goals for continuous improvement, and to practice managing peer and social influences that reinforce health risks.
- Reinforce the positive and enjoyable elements of a healthy lifestyle.
- Use learning materials that are gender-neutral and do not reinforce stereotypes when addressing student health concerns.
- Include adaptations to meet the needs of students with differing abilities, those with limited English proficiency, and those in alternative education settings.
- Align assessment of student knowledge and skills with instructional activities.

Instructional Strategies That Influence Student Achievement

IDENTIFYING SIMILARITIES AND DIFFERENCES

Presenting students with explicit direction for identifying similarities and differences between and among objects or ideas enhances understanding and the ability to use knowledge. The following classroom strategies are suggested to support learning:

1. Comparison tasks
2. Classification tasks
3. Metaphors
4. Analogies

SUMMARIZING AND NOTE TAKING

The creation of a summary requires students to delete, substitute, and retain selected information. This requires students to analyze the organization, structure, and sequence of the information beyond the superficial level. The following classroom strategies are suggested to support learning:

1. Rule-based strategies for summarizing
2. Summary frames (organizing summary by responding to a series of teacher-developed questions)
3. Teacher-prepared notes or outlines
4. Webbing notes (visual "web" depictions of key concepts)
5. Narrative/visual note combinations

REINFORCING EFFORT AND PROVIDING RECOGNITION

Although these strategies do not engage the cognitive skills of learners, they help students examine attitudes and beliefs they hold about themselves and others. In particular, reinforcement and recognition highlight the importance of investing effort in tasks and affirm accomplishments with meaningful rewards. The following classroom strategies are suggested to support learning:

1. Using literature, art, or other references to reinforce the value of investing effort when confronting tasks
2. Charts or rubrics depicting effort and achievement
3. Personalizing recognitions (e.g., "personal bests")
4. "Pause, prompt, then praise"
5. Verbal and concrete symbols of recognition (nothing that compromises student health—candy, pizza parties, etc.)

HOMEWORK AND PRACTICE

These familiar strategies enable students to deepen their understanding and to master requisite skills. The purpose of homework should be made clear to students and the volume of work should be variable as students get older. In addition, sufficient class time should be allocated for focused practice sessions. The following classroom strategies are suggested to support learning:

1. Establish, communicate, and reinforce homework policies.
2. Design assignments with clearly identified purposes and outcomes.
3. Vary feedback.
4. Chart accuracy, efficiency, and speed in using skills.
5. Segment complex skills.
6. Clarify the importance of skills or processes to be mastered.

NONLINGUISTIC REPRESENTATIONS (IMAGES OF IDEAS)

There are many ways for students to create images of ideas to reinforce their understanding. In all cases, these representations should clarify, refine, or elaborate on student knowledge. The following classroom strategies are suggested to support learning:

1. Graphic organizers
2. Physical models
3. Mental pictures
4. Movement representations or depictions

COOPERATIVE LEARNING

Please refer to Chapter 4 for an extensive discussion, recommendations, and examples of cooperative learning applications.

SETTING OBJECTIVES AND PROVIDING FEEDBACK

The skills associated with setting clear goals enable students to establish direction for their learning and help them realize both short- and long-term desires. Instructional goals help students narrow and refine the focus of their work and personalize tasks assigned by teachers. To be most meaningful, teacher feedback should be corrective, constructive, complimentary, and timely and should reinforce a specific task or goal specified by the teacher or the student. The following classroom strategies are suggested to support learning:

1. Contracts
2. Criterion-referenced feedback
3. Student-led feedback (peer-based or self-directed)
4. Progress monitoring

GENERATING AND TESTING HYPOTHESES

These processes require students to engage in higher-order thought. To accomplish such learning tasks, students must make predictions or draw conclusions about an event or an idea. Students should be encouraged to practice making clear explanations about their hunches and the outcomes they expect. The following classroom strategies are suggested to support learning:

1. Problem-solving tasks
2. Historical investigations
3. Inventions
4. Decision-making exercises
5. Templates and rubrics for reporting work

CUES, QUESTIONS, AND ADVANCE ORGANIZERS

This category of activities is intended to help students retrieve and activate what they already know about a topic. The activation of prior knowledge is critical to all types of learning, as it enables students to focus on important concepts and to reflect on issues from a higher-order perspective. The following classroom strategies are suggested to support learning:

1. Questions that elicit inferences
2. Questions that require analysis
3. Narratives as advance organizers
4. Skimming information prior to reading for depth
5. Graphic advance organizers

Source: R. Marzano, D. Pickering, and J. Pollock, *Classroom Instruction That Works* (Alexandria, VA: Association for Supervision and Curriculum Development, 2001).

- Be taught by instructors who are professionally prepared and who are given sufficient administrative support.
- Be allocated sufficient instructional time to enable students to achieve curricular objectives.
- Be taught in classes that are the same average size as that for other subject areas.
- Engage parents and families as active partners.
- Receive robust program evaluation at regular intervals.[68]

It is important to remember that, regardless of local district practices, all health education classrooms include heterogeneous groups of students. In addition to intellectual ability, students in all health education classrooms vary with regard to interest, background, and health experiences. As such, the school district health education course of study must be developed to meet the highest standards, be regularly and rigorously evaluated, be consistent with community standards, and respond to the needs of the widest range of learners.

Supporting Sound Teaching

Research has confirmed that the majority of us began to experiment with all kinds of health-risk behaviors when we were young. Most of us had our first personal exposure to such risks long before we were required to participate in formal and sound health instruction. To address this obvious case of developmentally inappropriate practice, health education advocates have invested considerable energy in trying to make planned and intentional health education a more prominent and consistent part of the course of study in elementary schools.[69]

In school districts in which sound practices have been adopted, evidence has emerged that supports the effectiveness of a comprehensive approach to health education. As years of sound health instruction increase, so do student knowledge, reflections of healthy attitudes, and practice of health-enhancing behaviors. The following behavior changes were noted between students with one year of health education and those with three years of similar study:

- Forty-three percent of students with one year of health education reported that they drank alcohol "sometimes or more often," whereas 33 percent of students with three years of education reported the same behavior.
- Thirteen percent of students with less education reported having taken drugs, but only 6 percent reported similar behavior following more education.
- Seventy-two percent of students with less health education reported participation in exercise outside of school, whereas 80 percent of students with more health education reported participating in exercise.[70]

In addition to its potential to promote health-enhancing student behavior, health education can contribute to cost containment, according to research by the Centers for Disease Control and Prevention. Estimates suggest that, for every dollar spent on quality school health education, society saves more than $13 in direct costs (medical treatment, addiction counseling, alcohol-related motor-vehicle injuries, and drug-related crime) and indirect costs, such as lost productivity associated with premature death and social welfare expenses related to teen pregnancy.[71]

Barriers to establishing such educational practice for students who are just beginning to form health habits include time limitations, policy constraints, teacher priorities, the pressure to focus on subjects included in high-stakes tests, and a general lack of reinforcement by state and local education policymakers. Though a 2002 study confirmed that many teachers have an interest in addressing health issues with their students, it identified another important barrier; very few teachers working in elementary and middle schools expressed a feeling that they were adequately prepared to manage meaningful and timely health instruction. As a result of an emphasis on other matters in teacher education programs, teachers reported that they were ill-equipped to plan developmentally appropriate health instruction for young learners. Consequently, health education is relegated to a very low status in most elementary schools.[72]

Regardless of professional preparation, all health educators must participate in an ongoing program of staff development activities. Many school districts regard staff development as a responsibility to be managed within the district, others collaborate with state or regional colleagues to plan meaningful and timely enrichment activities for in-service professionals. In addition, it is common for teachers to attend conferences of state or national education organizations for professional enrichment.

Staff development programming should focus on several specific issues as a way to refine teacher expertise. It is important for all teachers to increase their comfort in using interactive teaching methods across a range of health topics. Furthermore, staff development activities must update teachers to refresh their knowledge of the most current health information and build the skills necessary to find the most credible resources. Teachers are encouraged to enrich their comfort and expertise by taking advantage of staff development opportunities that provide support for and comfort with

- Using standards-based, theory-driven, and research-based approaches to health instruction
- Identifying and collaborating with appropriate community and agency health promotion resources
- Cultivating meaningful parent engagement in health education
- Evaluating and integrating sound web-based resources and other current materials into classroom practice
- Practicing advocacy skills for student health promotion[73]

Consistent with these expectations for staff development programs, teacher education students will find help with unit and lesson planning throughout this text.

Translating Health Education Theory into Practice

Although most elementary and middle school teachers believe that health education is important, it is difficult to dedicate sufficient instructional time to adequately address all health education essential content and skills within the school day. As a result, teachers must use limited instructional time wisely. Because not all health education strategies are equally successful, teachers in the elementary and middle grades should remember the following when planning lessons targeting student health behaviors:

- What students know and think influences the health behaviors in which they participate (specific health behaviors are influenced by the functional knowledge base that students have about the health issues confronting them).
- Though knowledge is necessary, it is not enough to produce most changes in student health behavior.
- Health behavior does not occur in a vacuum, but is influenced by perceptions, motivations, skills, and the social environment in which it takes place.[74]

Research has confirmed that the most promising health education practice extends beyond the goal of content mastery to address the health determinants, social factors, attitudes, values, norms, and skills that influence specific health behaviors. Effective health educators acknowledge that health behaviors are complex and base their lessons on theoretical approaches.[75]

Theories present a systematic way to understand health behaviors by identifying and addressing the important factors that influence them. Most theories used to explain health behavior have come from other disciplines including psychology, sociology, anthropology, consumer behavior, and marketing. Theories equip teachers with tools to move beyond intuition or content, resources, and methodologies used with previous groups of students. Theories can help teachers understand why their students pursue common risky health behaviors and how to organize lessons that are most likely to be successful. Finally, theories can help teachers identify key times and factors to enrich student assessment or evaluation of lesson effectiveness.[76]

Health educators use many theories to guide their professional practice. When focused on the heath behaviors of individuals, professionals often base programming and research on such theories as the health belief or stages of change models or the theory of planned behavior. Social cognitive theory can be useful when trying to understand the influence of family or friends on the health behaviors of a student, and the diffusion of innovations, communication theory, or community organization models can help guide health promotion programming among larger and more diverse groups of people.[77]

It is not important for classroom teachers in elementary and middle schools to understand the underpinnings of all health behavior theories. However, one way to enrich instruction with a theoretical foundation is to apply the theory of planned behavior. This theory is based on the belief that the most important factor that influences health behavior is behavioral intention. The theory of planned behavior asserts that behavioral intention is influenced by three major variables:

- *Attitudes toward the behavior*. This variable reflects the degree to which the student has made a favorable or an unfavorable evaluation of the behavior. This includes the individual's belief about what will happen if he or she participates in the behavior and the extent to which he or she cares about the outcome of engaging in the behavior.
- *Subjective norms*. The perceived social pressure to participate in or to refuse to participate in a behavior constitutes the foundation of this variable. Norms reflect how much an individual's families and friends will approve of a behavior and how much motivation there is to comply with the wishes of family and friends.
- *Perceived behavioral control*. This variable includes the individual's belief about the ease or difficulty of performing a behavior, based on the individual's beliefs about his or her level of control over the behavior and perceived ability to do the behavior.[78]

Figure 2–1 illustrates the theory of planned behavior in practice. Following are some examples of how a teacher might apply each element of this theory in actual classroom practice:

1. Students express intentions to act in healthy ways.
   A. Teachers can encourage students to sign and post pledges (to wear safety belts, to drink plenty of water, to eat five fruits and vegetables a day).
   B. Teachers can ask students to stand or raise their hands if they intend to practice a healthy behavior.
2. Attitudes toward the behavior.
   A. Students can investigate the short-term effects of smoking and determine how those effects might influence their quality of life.
   B. Teachers can ask students to explain possible outcomes if they had a wreck on their bike while not wearing a bike helmet. Would they anticipate a different outcome if wearing a bike helmet?
3. Subjective norms.
   A. Teachers can help students clarify actual norms (e.g., students often overestimate the number of students who practice an unhealthy behavior, such as smoking. It is important that students understand that the majority of their peers do not smoke. Teachers can use local and state data to help students understand actual smoking rates).

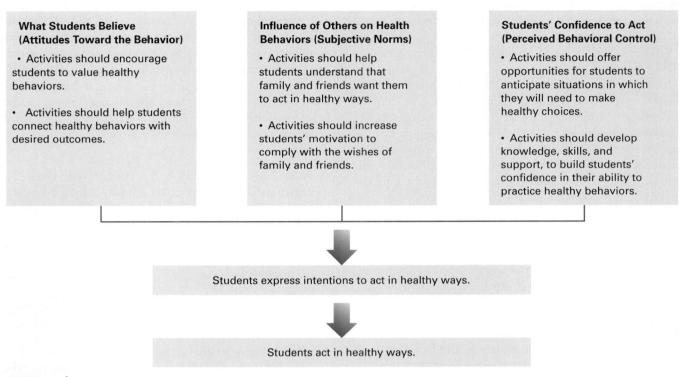

Theory of Planned Behavior

| **What Students Believe (Attitudes Toward the Behavior)** | **Influence of Others on Health Behaviors (Subjective Norms)** | **Students' Confidence to Act (Perceived Behavioral Control)** |

What Students Believe (Attitudes Toward the Behavior)

• Activities should encourage students to value healthy behaviors.

• Activities should help students connect healthy behaviors with desired outcomes.

Influence of Others on Health Behaviors (Subjective Norms)

• Activities should help students understand that family and friends want them to act in healthy ways.

• Activities should increase students' motivation to comply with the wishes of family and friends.

Students' Confidence to Act (Perceived Behavioral Control)

• Activities should offer opportunities for students to anticipate situations in which they will need to make healthy choices.

• Activities should develop knowledge, skills, and support, to build students' confidence in their ability to practice healthy behaviors.

Students express intentions to act in healthy ways.

Students act in healthy ways.

FIGURE 2–1 | Theory of Planned Behavior in Practice

SOURCE: W. Kane, S. Telljohann, and F. Quiroz, *HealthSmart Program Foundation: Standards, Theory, Results* (Santa Cruz, CA: ETR Associates, 2001).

B. Teachers can encourage students to write about or verbalize healthy behaviors in which they participate (e.g., ask students to identify their favorite fruit or vegetable. This will confirm the norm that most students eat fruits and vegetables.)

4. Perceived behavioral control.

A. Encourage students to practice peer-resistance skills before they are pressured to engage in risky or unhealthy behaviors.

B. Teach students how and where to access valid and reliable health information.

C. Encourage students to participate in a health behavior change project.

With the foundation of a health behavior theory, teachers can focus their planning more directly on influencing health behavior. Sections II and III of this text offer a variety of teaching activities that feature parts of the theory of planned behavior in applied instructional practice.

Characteristics of Effective Health Education Curricula: Foundations for Decision Making and Best Practice

Health instruction in schools is shaped most commonly by the district-approved health education curriculum. Informed by national and state content standards, a sound health education curriculum provides a foundation for instruction that is most likely to promote healthy behaviors among local students.

As in other academic content areas, the term *curriculum* applied to health education can have several meanings:

• A written course of study that describes what students will know and be able to do (behavioral expectations and learning objectives) by the end of a single grade or multiple grades and for a particular health content area (health education, tobacco prevention education)

• Content that will be taught to achieve these objectives

• A detailed plan including a set of directions, strategies, and materials to support student learning and teacher delivery of health education content

Throughout this text, curriculum will apply to those health education teaching activities and learning experiences that provide students with opportunities to acquire functional knowledge, practice essential skills, and evaluate attitudes that are necessary to make health-promoting decisions, achieve health literacy, and adopt health-enhancing behaviors.[79]

Some school districts assemble teams of local professionals to develop curriculum materials with a specific focus on meeting learner needs in that district, others buy curriculum packages produced by for-profit companies, community agencies (American Cancer Society/American

Lung Association tobacco risk–reduction curricula), government agencies, or other national groups with an interest in particular issues (DARE curricula offered by local police departments). Regardless of how it is developed, a common set of elements make up a sound health education curriculum:

- A set of expected learning outcomes or learning objectives that contribute to health-promoting decisions, achieving health literacy, and adopting health-enhancing behaviors, including promoting the health of others
- A planned progression of lessons or learning experiences that lead to achieving these objectives
- Continuity between lessons or learning experiences that clearly reinforce adoption and maintenance of specific health-enhancing behaviors
- Accompanying content or materials that correspond with the sequence of learning experiences and help teachers and students meet the learning objectives
- Assessment strategies to determine if students achieved the desired outcomes

Though some educators and advocates consider a textbook, a collection of activities, or a website to be a curriculum, such materials typically do not contain all these identified elements. They can, however, serve as potentially valuable resources of support materials.[80]

Selecting an effective prevention program from the range of those that have been developed by corporate entities, community health or government agencies, or other advocacy groups can be challenging. Prevention programs should address the specific needs of a particular group and be able to produce similarly positive outcomes across different settings and populations. Various federal agencies have identified youth-targeted programs that they consider to be worthy of recommendation based on rigorous review. The list of websites at the end of this chapter includes these resources.

But even curricula and other school/community partnership programs that have been shown to be effective do not always meet the needs of local schools. A number of barriers to implementing such programs in school-based instructional environments have been identified:

- Relatively few health curricula show evidence of effectiveness.
- Few identified curricula target multiple health-risk behaviors.
- Many health education curricula, including those that have been locally developed, have not been rigorously evaluated.
- For a number of reasons, schools cannot implement the curriculum (with fidelity) as it was implemented in evaluation studies.[81]

The Health Education Curriculum Analysis Tool (HECAT) developed by the Centers for Disease Control and Prevention (CDC) contains guidance, tools, and valuable resources to conduct an analysis of health education curricula (see Chapter 1). HECAT results can help local districts select or develop an appropriate and effective curriculum, strengthen their delivery of health instruction, and improve their ability to influence healthy behavioral outcomes among local students. Based on scientifically demonstrated evidence of effective curricula and the National Health Education Standards (see Chapters 1 and 3), HECAT contains the following:

- An overview of school health education
- Background about reviewing and selecting health education curricula
- Guidance for undertaking a curriculum review
- Tools to analyze a variety of health education curricula

HECAT facilitates assessment of comprehensive curricula that address multiple topics and grade levels, a single-topic or single-grade focus, and the health education component of a more comprehensive intervention (part of a Coordinated School Health Plan). HECAT was specifically developed to enable local school districts to assess comprehensive health education curricula and curricula developed to focus on promoting the following:

- An alcohol- and other drug-free lifestyle
- Healthy eating
- Physical activity
- Tobacco-free lifestyle
- Violence prevention
- Other emerging health issues[82]

HECAT is based on the growing body of research that confirms the value of teaching functional health information (essential concepts), shaping personal values that support healthy behaviors, shaping social norms that reinforce a healthy lifestyle, and developing essential health skills to adopt, practice, and maintain healthy behaviors. Readers can review Table 2-2 for a summary of evidence-based characteristics of effective health education curricula.[83]

As long ago as 1990, former President Jimmy Carter asserted, "The bottom line of what needs to be done in improving American health is through the public elementary and secondary schools in our country. In the past, health has been a kind of appendage, a kind of novelty, forced upon quite often unwilling superintendents, teachers and administrators in the school system, and part of it is our own fault."[84] As parents, teachers, government agencies, and concerned health and education advocates demand accountability for all school-based activities, health educators must respond. Only when the local curriculum is research-based, theory-driven, developmentally appropriate, and meaningful can we hope to reduce health risks among students in elementary and middle schools. Using HECAT and integrating the lessons reviewed in this chapter into classroom practice will equip teachers to support health behavior risk reduction among the students in their care.

TABLE 2–2

Characteristics of an Effective Health Education Curriculum

Focuses on specific behavioral outcomes
Supported by strategies and learning activities with an exclusive focus, the curriculum has a clear set of behavioral outcomes.

Is research-based and theory-driven
Strategies and learning experiences are built on theory as discussed in this chapter and go beyond the cognitive domain of learning.

Addresses individual values and group norms that support health-enhancing behaviors
Learning activities help students assess the level of risk taking among their peers, correct their misconceptions, and reinforce healthy values and beliefs.

Focuses on increasing the personal perception of risk and harmfulness of engaging in specific health-risk behaviors as well as reinforcing protective factors
The curriculum enables students to assess their actual vulnerability to risk behaviors and situations and supports the affirmation of health-promoting behaviors.

Addresses social pressures and influences
The curriculum provides opportunities for students to address personal and social pressures to participate in risky behavior.

Builds personal and social competence and self-efficacy by addressing skills
Learning activities build essential skills to manage social pressures and avoid or reduce risk-taking behaviors.

Provides functional health knowledge that is basic and accurate, and directly contributes to health-promoting decisions and behaviors
The curriculum provides accurate, reliable, and credible information to enable students to assess risks, correct inaccuracies, build personal and social competence. A curriculum that disseminates information for the sole purpose of increasing knowledge is inadequate and incomplete.

Uses strategies designed to personalize information and engage students
Learning activities are student centered, interactive, and experiential and enable students to personalize information while being engaged.

Provides age-appropriate and developmentally appropriate information, learning strategies, teaching methods, and materials
Learning activities and materials are relevant and applicable to the daily lives of learners.

Incorporates learning strategies, teaching methods, and materials that are culturally inclusive
Curricular materials are free of culturally biased information and include activities and examples inclusive of diverse cultures and lifestyles.

Provides adequate time for instruction and learning
The curriculum maintains adequate time for students to build on prior knowledge and to practice skills to maintain healthy behaviors.

Provides opportunities to reinforce skills and positive health behaviors
Learning activities build on previously learned concepts and skills and provide opportunities for reinforcement across health content areas and grade levels.

Provides opportunities to make positive connections with influential others (parents or other caregivers, teachers, youth leaders, clergy, etc.)
Learning activities link students with influential others who can affirm and reinforce healthy norms, beliefs, and behaviors.

Includes teacher information and plans for professional development and training that enhances effectiveness of instruction and student learning
With staff development support, teachers believe in what they are teaching, are knowledgeable about the content, and are skilled and comfortable when implementing instructional strategies.

SOURCE: Centers for Disease Control and Prevention, *Health Education Curriculum Analysis Tool (HECAT)* (Atlanta, GA: CDC, 2007). www.cdc.gov/HealthyYouth/Hecat/index.htm

INVOLVING CHILDREN IN CURRICULUM PLANNING

As an alternative to teacher-developed curriculum models, educators have been exploring the value of involving children in the planning process. Unfortunately, it is not a practice that is widely implemented in elementary and middle school classrooms. Although most administrators and teachers would not want to develop all health curricula this way, there are compelling reasons to supplement conventional instruction with instruction based on children's interests. When students are invited into the process of determining the focus of their learning activities, they become active in practicing communication skills. With teacher support, children are better able to connect health issues to other content areas, including language arts and social studies. A collaborative approach to planning also can bring richness to classroom instruction, because it is grounded in the identified interests of a particular group of students. In this way, it capitalizes on the elements of individually appropriate practice.

Curriculum scholars recommend a four-step procedure for teachers interested in engaging students in a collaborative approach to planning. It is recommended that these steps be implemented after the teacher has identified potential instructional topics or themes. Themes can emerge from student comments or questions.[85] The recommended sequence of steps involves students in seeking answers to four specific questions:

Step 1: *What do you wonder?* During this stage of planning, students are given the opportunity to express ideas,

A collaborative approach to planning helps keep students energized and involved in learning.

Step 3: *What materials do we need?* In this step in the process, students are encouraged to make a connection between the methods that they identify to solve problems or answer questions and the materials they will need to achieve their goals. As students identify necessary materials, teachers are urged to clarify responses and reinforce the connection between problem-solving methods and materials.

Step 4: *What will you bring (do)? What would you like me to bring (do)?* As concepts, methods and materials to be explored are clarified, specific contributions to the process are collected from volunteers. Consistent with the tenets of authentic instruction, students reinforce the connection between classroom topics and events or experiences from their own lives. This step also provides fertile opportunities for parent engagement, as "expert" consultation or support can be solicited from supportive adults.

questions, or concerns about an identified topic. As questions about the topic emerge, teachers can gain insight into development, language skills, misconceptions, and thinking processes among students.

Step 2: *What can we do to find out?* This step in the collaborative process is based on the fundamental idea that learning is a social, or collaborative, process. As a result, activities in this phase of planning reinforce the importance not only of students' questions but also of their involvement in finding answers or solutions. In this context, the teacher and students brainstorm ways in which they can work together to "find out." As an outgrowth of this process, students practice brainstorming and problem-solving skills, and their creativity is reinforced when they help design learning activities.

When children are involved in planning curricula for their classrooms, both teachers and students are rewarded. As curriculum and learning activities emerge from mutual interests, teachers are freed from the constraints of artificial time lines, children are energized by concepts and issues that are of interest to them, parent engagement can be formalized, and the benefits of integrated or cross-curricular instruction can be realized for everyone (see Chapter 4). Although unconventional, a collaborative model is a perfect vehicle for implementing a developmentally appropriate practice approach to health instruction.[86]

INTERNET AND OTHER RESOURCES

Visit the Online Learning Center (www.mhhe.com/telljohann6e) for links to these sites, quizzes and other study aids, and many additional resources.

WEBSITES

Blueprints for Violence Prevention
(Sponsored by the Office of Juvenile Justice and Delinquency Prevention, U.S. Department of Justice)
www.colorado.edu.cspv/blueprints

Compendium of HIV Prevention Interventions with Evidence of Effectiveness
(Sponsored by the Centers for Disease Control and Prevention, U.S. Department of Health and Human Services)
www.cdc.gov/hiv/resources/reports/hiv_compendium/index.htm

Exemplary and Promising Safe, Disciplined, and Drug-Free Schools Programs
(Sponsored by the Office of Safe and Drug-Free Schools, U.S. Department of Education)
www.ed.gov/admins/lead/safety/exemplary01/index.html

National Registry of Evidence-based Programs and Practices
(Sponsored by the Substance Abuse and Mental Health Services Administration, U.S. Department of Health and Human Services)
www.modelprograms.samhsa.gov

Preventing Drug Use Among Children and Adolescents: A Research-based Guide
(Sponsored by the National Institute on Drug Abuse, National Institutes of Health, U.S. Department of Health and Human Services)
www.nida.nih.gov/Prevention/Prevopen.html

Research-tested Intervention Programs
(Sponsored by the National Cancer Institute, U.S. Department of Health and Human Services)
http://cancercontrol.cancer.gov/rtips/index.asp

OTHER RESOURCES

American School Boards Journal. *Education Vital Signs 2008, U.S. Schools: Facts and Figures* (Alexandria, VA: National School Boards Association, February 2008).

Bogden, J. *How Schools Work and How to Work with Schools: A Primer for Professionals Who Serve Children and Youth* (Alexandria, VA: National Association of State Boards of Education, 2003).

Bracey, G. W. "The First Time 'Everything Changed:' The 17th Bracey Report on the Condition of Public Education." *Phi Delta Kappan* (October 2007): 119–36.

Costa, A. "The Thought-filled Curriculum." *Educational Leadership* (February 2008): 20–24.

Garner, B. *Getting to Got It* (Alexandria, VA: Association for Supervision and Curriculum Development, 2007).

Kauffman, J. M. "Waving to Ray Charles: Missing the Meaning of Disabilities." *Phi Delta Kappan* (March 2005): 520–21, 524.

Lapkoff, S., and R. Li. "Five Trends for Schools." *Educational Leadership* (March 2007): 8–15.

Littky, D., and S. Grabelle. *The Big Picture: Education Is Everyone's Business* (Alexandria, VA: Association for Supervision and Curriculum Development, 2004).

Marzano, R. *The Art and Science of Teaching* (Alexandria, VA: Association of Supervision and Curriculum Development, 2007).

Packer, J. "The NEA Supports Substantial Overhaul, Not Repeal of NCLB." *Phi Delta Kappan* (December 2007): 265–69.

Sack-Min, J. "The Issues of IDEA." *American School Board Journal* (March 2007): 20–25.

Stover, D. "Will ED in '08 Succeed?" *American School Board Journal* (January 2008): 21–23.

ENDNOTES

1. National Center for Education Statistics, *Fast Facts: Elementary and Secondary Education* (http://nces.ed.gov/fastfacts/display.asp?id=372, 2008)
2. J. F. Bogden, *Fit, Healthy, and Ready to Learn: A School Health Policy Guide* (Alexandria, VA: National Association of State Boards of Education, 2000).
3. National Center for Education Statistics, *Fast Facts*.
4. J. F. Bogden, *Fit, Healthy, and Ready to Learn.*
5. Ibid.
6. National Center for Education Statistics, *Fast Facts*.
7. J. F. Bogden, *Fit, Healthy, and Ready to Learn.*
8. National Center for Education Statistics, *Fast Facts*.
9. J. F. Bogden, *Fit, Healthy, and Ready to Learn.*
10. U.S. Congress, *No Child Left Behind Act of 2001: Conference Report to Accompany H.R. 1, Report 107–334* (Washington, DC: Government Printing Office, 2001).
11. U.S. Department of Education, *No Child Left Behind: A Parent's Guide* (Washington, DC: U.S. Department of Education, Office of the Secretary, Office of Public Affairs, 2003).
12. Ibid., 5.
13. J. Jennings and D. S. Rentner, "Ten Big Effects of the No Child Left Behind Act on Public Schools," *Phi Delta Kappan* 88, no. 2 (October 2006): 110–13.
14. Center on Education Policy, *Choices, Changes, and Challenges: Curriculum and Instruction in the NCLB Era* (Washington, DC: CEP, 2007).
15. E. W. Crane, S. Rabinowitz, and J. Zimmerman, *Locally Tailored Accountability: Building on Your State System in the Era of Accountability* (San Francisco, CA: WestEd, 2004).
16. T. L. Hanson, G. Austin, and J. Lee-Bayha, *How Are Student Health Risks and Resilience Related to the Academic Progress of Schools: Ensuring That No Child Is Left Behind* (San Francisco, CA: WestEd, 2004).
17. AAHPERD, "Prospects for No Child Left Behind," *Update Plus* (January/February 2007): 5.
18. U.S. Public Health Service, *Closing the Gap: A National Blueprint for Improving the Health of Persons with Mental Retardation, Report of the Surgeon General's Conference on Health Disparities and Mental Retardation* (Washington, DC: U.S. Department of Health and Human Services, 2002).
19. U.S. Department of Education, *Individuals with Disabilities Education Improvement Act of 2004 (H.R. 1350)*, December 2004.
20. J. L. Meece, *Child and Adolescent Development for Educators* (New York: McGraw-Hill Higher Education, 2002), 315–74.
21. D. J. Bernert, "Educators Who Integrate Students with Disabilities into Sexuality Education Programs," in *Partners in Prevention: Whole School Approaches to Prevent Pregnancy and Sexually Transmitted Infections* (Kent, OH: American School Health Association, 2006).
22. Hoover Institution, *Facts on Policy: School Funding Shift* (www.hoover.org/research/factsonpolicy/facts/4249156.html, 2008)
23. J. F. Bogden, *Fit, Healthy, and Ready to Learn.*
24. Ibid.
25. Hoover Institution, *Facts on Policy: School Funding Shift.*
26. J. F. Bogden, *Fit, Healthy, and Ready to Learn.*
27. F. M. Newmann and G. G. Wehlage, "Five Standards of Authentic Instruction," *Educational Leadership* (April 1993): 8–12.
28. M. M. Hardiman, "Connecting Brain Research with Dimensions of Learning," *Educational Leadership* 59, no. 3 (November 2001): 52–55.
29. J. Willis, "Which Brain Research Can Educators Trust?," *Phi Delta Kappan* (May 2007): 697–99.
30. B. Perry, "How the Brain Learns Best," *Instructor* 11, no. 4 (2000): 34–35.
31. R. Leamnson, "Learning as Biological Brain Change," *Change* 32, no. 6 (2000): 34–40.
32. M. M. Hardiman, "Connecting Brain Research with Dimensions of Learning."
33. J. King-Friedrichs, "Brain-Friendly Techniques for Improving Memory," *Educational Leadership* 59, no. 3 (November 2001): 76–79.
34. D. Goleman, *Emotional Intelligence* (New York: Bantam Books, 1995).
35. E. Jensen, "How Julie's Brain learns." *Educational Leadership* 56, no. 3 (1998): 41–45.
36. M. M. Hardiman, "Connecting Brain Research with Dimensions of Learning."
37. L. Lowery, "How New Science Curriculums Reflect Brain Research," *Educational Leadership* 56, no. 3 (1998): 26–30.
38. M. M. Hardiman, "Connecting Brain Research with Dimensions of Learning."
39. R. Leamnson, "Learning as Biological Brain Change."
40. M. M. Hardiman, "Connecting Brain Research with Dimensions of Learning."
41. T. Armstrong, *Multiple Intelligences in the Classroom*, 2d ed. (Alexandria, VA: Association for Supervision and Curriculum Development, 2000).
42. M. M. Hardiman, "Connecting Brain Research with Dimensions of Learning."
43. R. N. Caine and G. Caine, *Unleashing the Power of Perceptual Change: The Potential of Brain-Based Teaching* (Alexandria, VA: Association for Supervision and Curriculum Development, 1997).
44. B. Samek and N. Samek, "It's a Brain Thing: Keeping Students Focused and Learning," a presentation at the 78th Annual Meeting of the American School Health Association (16 October 2004).
45. F. M. Newmann and G. G. Wehlage, "Five Standards of Authentic Instruction."
46. D. Archbald and F. M. Newmann, *Beyond Standardized Testing: Assessing Authentic Academic Achievement in the Secondary School* (Reston, VA: National Association of Secondary School Principals, 1988).
47. F. M. Newmann and G. G. Wehlage, "Five Standards of Authentic Instruction."
48. G. Wiggins and J. McTighe, *Understanding by Design* (Alexandria, VA: Association for Supervision and Curriculum Development, 1998), 44–62.
49. F. M. Newmann and G. G. Wehlage, "Five Standards of Authentic Instruction."
50. Ibid.
51. S. L. Ramey and C. T. Ramey, "The Transition to School," *Phi Delta Kappan* 76, no. 3 (November 1994): 197.
52. S. Bredekamp, ed., *Developmentally Appropriate Practice in Early Childhood Programs Serving Children from Birth Through Age 8* (Washington, DC: National Association for the Education of Young Children, 1987), 1–2.
53. J. W. Lochner, "Growth and Developmental Characteristics," in *A Pocketguide to Health and Health Problems in School Physical Activity*, ed. B. Petrof (Kent, OH: ASHA, 1981), 4–9.
54. S. Bredekamp, *Developmentally Appropriate Practice*, 2.
55. Ibid.
56. Ibid., 1–3, 5.
57. S. Bredekamp and C. Copple, eds., *Developmentally Appropriate Practice in Early Childhood Programs* (Washington, DC: National Association for the Education of Young Children, 1997), 8–15.
58. P. Keener, *Caring for Children: Useful Information and Hard-to-Find Facts About Child Health and Development* (Indianapolis, IN: James Whitcomb Riley Memorial Association, 2001), 106–8.
59. S. Bredekamp, *Developmentally Appropriate Practice*, 2–5.
60. J. S. Coleman et al., *Equality of Educational Opportunity* (Washington, DC: U.S. Government Printing Office, 1966).
61. S. P. Wright, S. Horn, and W. Sanders, "Teacher and Classroom Context Effects on Student Achievement: Implications for Teacher Evaluation," *Journal of Personnel Evaluation in Education* 11 (1997): 57–67.
62. R. J. Marzano, *A Theory-Based Meta-Analysis of Research on Instruction* (Aurora, CO: Mid-Continent Research for Education and Learning, 1998).
63. R. Marzano, D. Pickering, and J. Pollock, *Classroom Instruction That Works: Research-Based Strategies for Increasing Student Achievement* (Alexandria, VA:

Association for Supervision and Curriculum Development, 2001).

64. Ibid., 9–10.

65. R. M. Pigg, "20 Concepts of Learning," *Journal of School Health* 63, no. 9 (November 1993): 375.

66. Centers for Disease Control and Prevention, *Health Education Curriculum Analysis Tool* (Atlanta, GA: CDC, 2007).

67. U.S. Department of Health and Human Services, *Healthy People 2010. Two Volumes. 2d ed.* (Washington, DC: U.S. Government Printing Office, 2000).

68. J. F. Bogden, *Fit, Healthy, and Ready to Learn,* C-33, C-34.

69. D. Wiley, "Elementary School Teachers' Perspectives on Health Instruction: A Commentary," *American Journal of Health Education* 33, no. 2 (March/April 2002): 83–85.

70. L. Harris, *An Evaluation of Comprehensive Health Education in American Public Schools* (New York: Metropolitan Life Foundation, 1988).

71. Centers for Disease Control and Prevention, *Is School Health Education Cost Effective? An Exploratory Analysis of Selected Exemplary Components,* unpublished manuscript, 1997.

72. R. Thakery et al., "Elementary School Teachers' Perspectives on Health Instruction: Implications for Health Education," *American Journal of Health Education* 33, no. 2 (March/April 2002): 77–82.

73. D. Duffy, "The Right Stuff: Two Perspectives on What It Takes to Be an Effective Health Teacher," *RMC Health Educator* 2, no. 3 (spring 2002): 1–4.

74. U.S. Department of Health and Human Services, *Theory at a Glance: A Guide for Health Promotion Practice* (Washington, DC: National Cancer Institute, 2005).

75. Centers for Disease Control and Prevention, *Health Education Curriculum Analysis Tool.*

76. U.S. Department of Health and Human Services, *Theory at a Glance: A Guide for Health Promotion Practice.*

77. Ibid.

78. I. Aizen, *Theory of Planned Behavior Diagram* (www.people.umass.eduaizen/tpb.diag.html), 2002.

79. Centers for Disease Control and Prevention, *Health Education Curriculum Analysis Tool.*

80. Ibid.

81. Ibid.

82. Ibid.

83. Ibid.

84. J. Carter, "The Challenge of Education for Health in America's Schools," *Journal of School Health* 60, no. 4 (April 1990): 129.

85. K. C. Williams, "What Do You Wonder? Involving Children in Curriculum Planning," *Young Children* (September 1997): 78–81.

86. Ibid.

Standards-Based Planning, Teaching, and Assessment in Health Education

DESIRED LEARNER OUTCOMES

After reading this chapter, you will be able to . . .

- Describe the focus of school health education reflected in the National Health Education Standards.

- Summarize the concepts and skills included in the National Health Education Standards.

- Describe the process of integrating standards, content areas, healthy behavior outcomes, and theoretical constructs for yearly, unit, and lesson planning.

- Summarize strategies for including students with diverse backgrounds, interests, and abilities in health education lessons.

- Explain the role of rubrics in health education assessment.

- Describe interactive, standards-based learning and assessment strategies.

- Use the Internet and other resources for assistance in standards-based planning, assessment, and teaching.

INTRODUCTION

When adults are asked what they remember about school health education in their own K–12 experience, they frequently reply, if they remember health education at all, that they mainly learned facts and information about health topics. Indeed, until recently the primary focus of health instruction was knowledge acquisition. In contrast, today's school health education helps young people learn and practice the skills they need to deal with the important health issues and decisions that they encounter as they grow from childhood and adolescence into young adulthood.

The publication of *National Health Education Standards* in 1995 marked this important change in focus for school health education.[1] The National Health Education Standards, revised and updated in 2005 (see Teacher's Toolbox 1.2), reflect important personal and social skills that elementary and middle school students can apply in the context of important content areas. For example, students learn to demonstrate a variety of effective communication skills and to compare and contrast the best use of those skills in situations such as refusing tobacco or suggesting alternatives to risky, potentially injurious behaviors.

This change from an information-based to a skills-based focus is grounded in promising curriculum evaluation research of programs that include a strong skills component. Federal health agencies have identified school and community programs that have been rigorously evaluated for their effectiveness in reducing youth risk behaviors.[2] Parents, teachers, administrators, and community members support school health efforts designed to increase healthy behaviors rather than merely to increase health knowledge. For example, schools want to prevent and reduce tobacco use on and off campus rather than simply ensure that students can name the carcinogens in tobacco smoke.

A skills-based approach helps students acquire tools for making sense of the enormous amount of new health information generated each year. Rather than memorizing countless health facts, students learn to access valid health information and the quality of various information sources for themselves. When students take an active role in acquiring information, they build their content knowledge as astute investigators rather than as passive receivers.

The National Health Education Standards and related performance indicators (see Appendix A) focus on important health-promoting concepts and skills for students in grades kindergarten through 8. Many state and local education agencies used the National Health Education Standards as a basis for creating their own standards and curriculum documents. The personal and social skills reflected in the standards that students should develop include the following:

1. *Core concepts*—learning "functional knowledge" or the most important information and ideas essential to health promotion and disease prevention

2. *Analysis of internal and external influences*—examining internal influences (feelings, likes, dislikes, curiosity, values, beliefs, fears, moods) and external influences (family, peers, culture, technology, and media, such as advertising, music, television, and movies) on health decisions and behaviors

3. *Access to information, products, and services*—learning to locate and use the best sources of health information, products, and services to fulfill health needs

4. *Interpersonal communication*—practicing and comparing verbal and nonverbal strategies for clear communication and peer resistance in various content areas

5. *Decision making*—learning and applying age-appropriate processes for making health-promoting decisions

6. *Goal setting*—learning and applying age-appropriate processes for working toward achievable health-related goals

7. *Self-management*—learning to practice skills for healthy behaviors, such as positive self-talk, stress management, anger and conflict management, injury and disease prevention, and personal health care

8. *Advocacy*—learning to act in effective ways to promote personal, family, and community health

This manner of naming the National Health Education Standards (e.g., Standard 7: self-management) originated with the work of the Council of Chief State School Officers (CCSSO), the State Collaborative on Assessment and Student Standards (SCASS), and the Health Education Assessment Project (HEAP).[3] HEAP provided groundbreaking leadership in assessing the National Health Education Standards. The Rocky Mountain Center for Health Promotion and Education (RMC) provided further leadership through the development of analytic rubrics and checklists for assessing the standards.[4] The criteria used to assess standards in this text are adapted from the RMC rubrics (see Appendix B).

Elementary and middle school students need many opportunities to practice health-related skills in the context of the content areas described in Chapters 5 through 14. Thus, each content chapter includes learning and assessment strategies organized by the National Health Education Standards and grade levels. To reinforce the standards, health educators Donna Rodenhurst and Jimmy Edwards had their seventh-grade health education classes make classroom posters to illustrate what the standards mean in "kid terms." The work of Rodenhurst's and Edwards's students appears throughout this text.

MEETING THE NATIONAL HEALTH EDUCATION STANDARDS

The idea of meeting the health education standards is twofold in this chapter. Students in grades K–12 meet standards when they demonstrate the ability to apply essential concepts and skills to help keep themselves and others healthy and safe. The overall goal of health education is for students to adopt and maintain healthy behaviors. Thus, health education should contribute directly to a student's ability to engage in health-enhancing behaviors and to avoid or reduce behaviors that can lead to poor health.

Before educators can help their students meet standards, however, they must get to know the standards for themselves. The description of each of the National Health Education Standards provides a user-friendly introduction. This section on standards is followed by information on planning, assessment, and teaching with the standards. The chapter ends with examples of learning and assessment strategies that teachers can apply across content areas.

NHES 1 | *Students will comprehend concepts related to health promotion and disease prevention to enhance health.* (Alyssa, age 12; Rochelle, age 12)

Standard 1: Core Concepts

Students Will Comprehend Concepts Related to Health Promotion and Disease Prevention to Enhance Health

Acquiring core concepts refers to learning functional knowledge, or the information and ideas most essential to health promotion and disease prevention. Many educators think of core concepts as the content knowledge of health education. Rather than being passive receivers of information, young people should be active seekers of information. Thus, National Health Education Standard (NHES) 1, core concepts, is closely linked to NHES 3, access to information, products, and services.

Given the overwhelming amount of health information generated each year and the limited time available for teaching about health, how can teachers make decisions about the information that is essential for students to acquire? They can consider the following guidelines:

• *Focus first on the important content areas identified in this text.* Health education in the elementary and middle school curricula must share time with many other content areas. Ensure that the most important public health priorities for children are the focus of the school health education curriculum.

• *Build on what children already know and what they want to know.* The Know-Wonder-Learn (KWL) chart, described in the section "Strategies for Learning and Assessment" is a wonderful tool for assessing students' current knowledge and questions before proceeding with health instruction. How many children in the elementary and middle grades are introduced to the food pyramid each year as if they have never seen it before? Teachers model respect for students when they take the time to start where students are and provide opportunities for them to build their own content knowledge.

• *Articulate health instruction within and across grade levels.* Teachers spend a great deal of time articulating math and language arts instruction. Ideally, teachers should have time for articulation in the other important curriculum areas as well (science, social studies, health education, the arts, and physical education). What should the health education focus be at each grade level? What topics belong in the health curriculum, as compared to the science or physical education curriculum? How can teaching in other content areas support student learning about health?

• *Integrate health instruction into other content areas in deliberate ways.* Children in the elementary and middle grades read a variety of books related to personal and social health skills. Teachers can go the extra mile for health education by having their students discuss the goals, decisions, communication skills, and self-management strategies of the characters in the stories. (Each content chapter includes ideas for children's literature for health education.) Similarly, mathematics instruction can engage students in a "health problem of the day," which requires the estimation and calculation of answers to problems such as determining the percentage of calories from fat in various snack foods, the stopping time for cars traveling at various speeds, or the time required to walk or run three times around a large play area.

• *Identify functional knowledge, or that which is truly essential for health promotion and disease prevention.* Identifying the ways in which HIV and other sexually transmitted diseases are and are not transmitted is functional knowledge essential for disease prevention. However, explaining the ways in which retroviruses work is not essential for self-protection and might more appropriately be part of the science or biology curriculum. Similarly, learning to name the bones of the body is not nearly as important in terms of health promotion as learning the effects of healthy nutrition and regular physical activity on the bones. When setting priorities for health information, teachers should consider what students must know to stay healthy and safe.

The Health Education Curriculum Analysis Tool (HECAT) from the Division of Adolescent and School Health, Centers for Disease Control and Prevention (CDC), identifies healthy behaviors in nine important topic areas for today's pre-K–12 school health education (Teacher's Toolbox 3.1).[5] These topics mirror the content chapters (Chapters 5–14) in this text.

The theory of planned behavior (see Chapter 2), can help teachers focus lesson time on those ideas most likely to influence healthy behavior. Lessons related to core concepts can help students develop positive attitudes toward health by connecting healthy behaviors with positive results. Learning core concepts can also help students care about the consequences of their behaviors.

Health education lessons should engage students in scratching beneath the surface to discover how the concepts and skills they learn connect with their lives. A student might reason, "Breakfast is important because it helps people stay alert. I want to stay alert because I want to do well in school." On the other hand, a student might reason, "I know smoking is unhealthy for me, but it's more important right now that I have friends, and all of my friends smoke." Health education can help students first make connections with their lives and then dig deeper to explore alternatives. For example, in the latter example, the student could explore a new array of choices related to wanting to maintain the important relationship with friends. The student might decide to spend time with these friends primarily when they are involved in nonsmoking activities, such as sports or movies; try low-key refusals to smoking ("No thanks, not right now"); or give reasons for not wanting to smoke ("Nah—my Mom will smell it on my clothes and I'll be so busted").

Standard 2: Analyze Influences

Students Will Analyze the Influence of Family, Peers, Culture, Media, Technology, and Other Factors on Health Behaviors

Elementary and middle school students often find this standard to be a favorite. Working on this standard helps students consider answers to the perplexing health behavior question "Why do we do what we do—especially when what we do doesn't always seem to be the smartest thing?"

NHES 2 | *Students will analyze the influence of family, peers, culture, media, technology, and other factors on health behaviors.* (Kylie, age 12; Kimberly, age 12)

In practicing the skill of analyzing influences, students look first at factors inside themselves (internal influences), such as feelings, likes, dislikes, curiosity, moods, needs, values, fears, and desires. How do these factors influence what we decide to do in terms of our health? Students then examine outside factors (external influences) in all their variety—friends, family, culture, technology, advertising, and media of all kinds. Are these influences real? In terms of advertising and media, who's working behind the scenes, and what do they want to convince us to do? Children and adults find these topics fascinating.

Media, parents and family, peers, community, cultural and peer norms, and personal values and beliefs are important influences on health behavior that students should examine. The theory of planned behavior supports lessons that help students examine social pressures to participate or refuse to participate in health behaviors. Complex personal, family, religious, and sociocultural factors influence health-related decisions. Health education lessons can be structured to help students understand that family and friends want them to act in healthy ways and that most of their peers practice healthy behaviors. Teachers can use data from the national and local Youth Risk Behavior Surveillance System[6] and Global Tobacco Surveillance System[7] for an important reality check on other students' health behaviors and health behavior norms among young people.

Though students may perceive that they and others are influenced by families, friends, feelings, and culture, they may be less willing to believe that they are influenced by advertisers. ("Who, me? Not!") An interesting start to lessons on media influences is to have students identify and count the product logos on their clothes, shoes, book bags,

HECAT Health Topics and Healthy Behaviors

A pre-K–12 school health education curriculum should enable students to:

1. Promote mental and emotional health
   - Express feelings in a healthy way.
   - Engage in activities that are mentally and emotionally healthy.
   - Prevent and manage conflict and stress in healthy ways.
   - Use self-control and impulse-control strategies to promote health.
   - Seek help for troublesome feelings.
   - Be empathetic toward others.
   - Carry out personal responsibilities.
   - Establish and maintain healthy relationships.
2. Promote healthy eating
   - Eat a variety of whole-grain products, fruits and vegetables, and fat-free or low-fat milk or equivalent milk products every day.
   - Eat the appropriate number of servings from each food group every day.
   - Choose foods that provide ample amounts of vitamins and minerals.
   - Eat the appropriate amounts of foods that are high in fiber.
   - Drink plenty of water.
   - Limit foods and beverages high in added or processed sugars.
   - Limit the intake of fat, avoiding foods with saturated and trans fats.
   - Eat breakfast every day.
   - Eat healthy snacks.
   - Eat healthy foods when dining out.
   - Prepare food in healthful ways.
   - Balance caloric intake with caloric expenditure.
   - Follow a plan for healthy weight management.
3. Promote physical activity
   - Engage in moderate to vigorous physical activity for at least sixty minutes every day.
   - Regularly engage in physical activities that enhance cardio-respiratory endurance, flexibility, muscle endurance, and muscle strength.
   - Perform warm-up and cool-down activities before and after exercise.
   - Drink plenty of water before, during, and after physical activity.
   - Avoid injury during physical activity.
4. Promote safety
   - Wear seatbelts in motor vehicles.
   - Sit in booster seats in the rear of the vehicle when age appropriate.
   - Sit in the back seat of the vehicle when age appropriate.
   - Avoid using alcohol and other drugs when driving a motor vehicle.
   - Avoid riding in a car with a driver who is under the influence of alcohol or other drugs.
   - Use appropriate safety equipment.
   - Refuse to engage in or encourage others to engage in risky behaviors.
   - Practice safety rules and procedures to avoid injury.
   - Plan ahead to avoid dangerous situations and injuries.
   - Seek help for poisoning, sudden illness, and injuries.
   - Provide immediate help to others with a sudden illness or injury.
5. Promote personal health and wellness
   - Brush and floss teeth daily.
   - Practice appropriate hygiene habits.
   - Get an appropriate amount of sleep and rest.
   - Prevent vision or hearing loss.
   - Prevent damage from the sun.
   - Practice behaviors that prevent infectious diseases.

- Practice behaviors that prevent chronic diseases.
- Prevent serious heath problems that result from common chronic diseases and conditions among youth, such as allergies, asthmas, diabetes, and epilepsy.
- Practice behaviors that prevent food-borne illnesses.
- Seek out help for common chronic disease and conditions.
- See health care professionals for appropriate screenings and examinations.
- Practice behaviors that support and improve the health of others.
- Prevent health problems that result from fads or trends.
6. Prevent violence
   - Engage in positive, helpful behaviors.
   - Manage interpersonal conflict in nonviolent ways.
   - Manage emotional distress in nonviolent ways.
   - Avoid bullying, being a bystander to bullying, or being a victim of bullying.
   - Avoid engaging in violence, including coercion, exploitation, physical fighting, and rape.
   - Avoid situations where violence is likely to occur.
   - Avoid associating with others who are involved in or encourage violence or criminal activity.
   - Get help to prevent or stop violence including harassment, abuse, bullying, hazing, fighting, and hate crimes.
   - Get help to address inappropriate touching.
   - Get help to stop being subjected to violence or physical abuse.
   - Get help for self or others who are in danger of hurting themselves.
   - Argue persuasively against the use of violence.
7. Promote a tobacco-free lifestyle
   - Avoid using (or experimenting with) any form of tobacco.
   - Avoid second-hand smoke.
   - Support others to be tobacco free, including supporting a tobacco-free environment.
   - Seek help for stopping the use of tobacco for self and others.
   - Quit using tobacco if already using.
8. Promote an alcohol and other drug-free lifestyle
   - Use over-the-counter and prescription drugs properly and safely.
   - Avoid experimentation with alcohol and other drugs.
   - Avoid the use of alcohol.
   - Avoid the use of illegal drugs.
   - Avoid driving while under the influence of alcohol and other drugs.
   - Avoid riding in a car with a driver who is under the influence of alcohol and other drugs.
   - Seek help for stopping the use of alcohol and other drugs (for self and others).
9. Promote sexual health
   - Establish and maintain healthy relationships.
   - Practice and maintain sexual abstinence.
   - Seek support to be sexually abstinent.
   - Avoid pressuring others to engage in sexual behaviors.
   - Return to sexual abstinence if sexually active.
   - Support others to avoid sexual risk behaviors.
   - Seek health care professionals to promote sexual health.

Additional risk-reduction outcomes not addressed in a risk-avoidance curriculum are

- Limit the number of sexual partners if sexually active.
- Use condoms consistently and correctly if sexually active.
- Use birth control consistently and correctly if sexually active.
- Discuss contraception, disease prevention, and HIV and STD risk and status with sexual partners if sexually active or experienced.

SOURCE: Centers for Disease Control and Prevention, *Health Education Curriculum Analysis Tool (HECAT)*. (Atlanta, GA: CDC, 2007) www.cdc.gov/HealthyYouth/Hecat/index.htm.

Teacher's Toolbox 3.2

Advertising Techniques

1. *Bandwagon.* Everyone is doing it or using the product.
2. *Testimonials.* Famous people or celebrities use and talk about the product.
3. *Snob appeal.* Well-dressed, wealthy-looking people use and talk about the product.
4. *Fun and friendship.* Friends have fun using the product.
5. *Just plain folks.* Ordinary people (the people next door) use and talk about the product.
6. *Humor.* Humor is used to sell the product.
7. *Emotion.* Attempts to stir the emotions are used to sell the product.
8. *Statistics.* Statistics and the results of studies are used to sell the product.
9. *Romance.* A romantic situation between two people is used to sell the product.
10. *Sex appeal.* Sexy models or spokespersons use and talk about the product.
11. *Cultural or group pride.* Pride in identity with a culture or another group is used to sell the product.
12. *Fear appeal.* Fears about negative consequences (unsafe tires) or social consequences (bad breath) are used to sell the product.
13. *Exaggeration.* It's "the best ever!" It's "one of a kind!"
14. *Problem solvers.* This product will take care of everything.
15. *Repetition.* The same message or phrase is used over and over.

and lunchboxes. In her book *Born to Buy: The Commercialized Child and the New Consumer Culture,* Juliet Schor stated,

> The United States is the most consumer-oriented society in the world. . . . ads have proliferated far beyond the television screen to virtually every social institution and type of public space, from museums and zoos, to college campuses and elementary school classrooms, restaurant bathrooms and menus, at the airport, even in the sky. The architects of this culture—the companies that make, market and advertise consumer products—have now set their sights on children. . . . Kids and teens are now the epicenter of American consumer culture. They command the attention, creativity, and dollars of advertisers. . . . Yet few adults recognize the magnitude of this shift and its consequences for the futures of our children and of our culture.[8]

Schor identified important ways adults can act to nurture the development processes of childhood through decommercializing the home, school, and community environments. Teachers also can engage students in spotting and analyzing the media messages that bombard them every day. Teacher's Toolbox 3.2 provides a list of techniques that students can use to examine the strategies marketers use to target their messages. Students also can use these techniques to create their own student-designed media messages.

Media literacy researcher Donna Grace calls for educators to think beyond the notion that students are passive victims of advertising. Dr. Grace works with students to help them purposefully produce their own media, rather than just consuming messages in the environment. She states that in the process students are provided with the opportunity to think and talk about the images they have created and to construct their own critiques. The production process allows students to play with, mediate, and, in some cases, rework media messages rather than absorbing them uncritically.[9]

The theory of planned behavior is linked strongly to the skill of analyzing internal and external influences on health behaviors. As students examine social approval and pressures to participate or refuse to participate in a behavior, they are exploring the variable of subjective norms. The learning and assessment strategies in this text provide many hands-on opportunities to engage students in the process of taking direct action in understanding and responding to diverse influences.

Standard 3: Access Information, Products, and Services

Students Will Demonstrate the Ability to Access Valid Information and Products and Services to Enhance Health

NHES 1 and 3 are closely connected. Learning to access valid health information is as important as learning the information itself in promoting positive health behaviors among youth. NHES 3 also requires that students learn to identify, access, and evaluate the health-enhancing products and services they need.

Students make many health-related decisions in their lives, and they often do so while being bombarded with incomplete and inaccurate information. Students need to be able to identify credible sources of information and then use that information to make healthy choices. Increasingly, students may find health sources through technology, such as the Internet or health-related software packages. Other situations require students to seek advice from community health helpers.

Children are far more capable of conducting their own health investigations than many educators realize. Fourth-grade teacher Nadine Marchessault engaged her students in co-creating an integrated health and language arts curriculum, based on their questions and interests. The students worked in small groups to plan and complete research on building strength, divorce and resolving conflict, exercising safety and first aid, food pyramid and food groups, learning strategies and cheating, snacks and nutrition labels, and tobacco—a very close match for the priority health topics addressed in this text. The students identified trustworthy information sources, interviewed knowledgeable adults, surveyed peers, compiled their research, and made oral presentations, which included developing visuals and handouts for the audience, extending formal invitations to other classes, and videotaping their presentations. Because the students selected their own topics, they worked tirelessly to complete their reports. As one student wrote in reflection, "It was scary, but we did good!" Perhaps most

NHES 3 | *Students will demonstrate the ability to access valid information and products and services to enhance health.* (Keegan, age 12)

Mrs. Marchessault's students work on Lōkahi Wheels as part of their health research projects.

used to temporarily paralyze muscles. Tiny amounts of injected Botox relax the facial muscles used in frowning and raise the eyebrows, temporarily removing wrinkles.[10] The students found striking before-and-after pictures on the Web and excitedly recommended the Botox regimen to their peers, saying "Got wrinkles? Get Botox!" Questioning by their instructor revealed that the students had consulted only commercial (.com) websites for their report and had not ventured into education (.edu), professional organization (.org), or government (.gov) websites to more critically evaluate the information that was available. The students obviously did not meet NHES 3, and they were asked to conduct further investigations on the topic and report back to the class.

Teaching students to evaluate information, products, and services with a critical eye is consistent with the theory of planned behavior. As students explore information about and the claims made for various products and services in depth, they shape their attitudes toward health behaviors. For example, if the students in the preceding example had investigated Botox more thoroughly, they would have learned that repeated Botox treatments can result in permanent thinning of the muscles, weakness in neighboring muscles, droopy eyebrows or eyelids, and headaches. Botox injections also can interfere with the abilities to eat, speak, and blink.[11] Practicing skills—such as accessing valid information—can increase perceived behavioral control and self-efficacy as students gain confidence in their ability to practice healthy behaviors.

Standard 4: Interpersonal Communication

Students Will Demonstrate the Ability to Use Interpersonal Communication Skills to Enhance Health and Avoid or Reduce Health Risks

Students need to learn and practice communication skills in the context of their relationships with family, friends, and others. To become effective communicators, students need a wide variety of realistic learning opportunities to try out their skill at resisting pressure, communicating empathy and support, managing conflicts, and asking for assistance. Practicing communication skills provides a natural link to language arts and performing arts as students engage in script writing, editing, rehearsing, and performing in various scenarios.

The theory of planned behavior supports communication lessons that provide the opportunity for students to express their intention to behave in a certain way, describe

interesting, the students said at the beginning of the project that they were interested in learning new things but no so interested in school. At the end of the project, their interest increased in both categories. Working toward this standard provides opportunities for students to become questioning consumers of health information, products, and services. Questions such as "Who says?" and "What are their qualifications?" are part of NHES 3. Another important NHES 3 question is "Who benefits?"

With the advent of the World Wide Web, older individuals need these skills, too. To model their understanding of NHES 3, a group of elementary teacher education students reported to their classmates on the topic of Botox (botulinum toxin)

NHES 4 | *Students will demonstrate the ability to use interpersonal communication skills to enhance health and avoid or reduce health risks.* (Kelli, age 13; Nicole, age 12)

their attitudes, ascertain the position of others, and affirm their perceived ability to practice the behavior. For example, in dealing with a misunderstanding among friends, a student might state the intention to get the friends together to talk things out, explain why talking things out is a good idea, refer to others who use this practice successfully, and express confidence that the group of friends has the ability to come to a positive solution to the problem. The importance of teaching communication and peer resistance/refusal skills is explained further in the rest of this section.

Communication Skills

Although speech develops in most children in a predictable developmental sequence, effective communication includes many skills that do not come naturally—they must be learned. Just as doctors practice medical skills and athletes practice sport skills, students need structured opportunities to practice effective communication skills. Southern Illinois University professor Joyce Fetro stated,

> A young person's ability to communicate can have a direct effect on his or her sense of self-worth, ultimately affecting the quality of relationships with others. Communication patterns can make or break relationships. Good communication skills can help a person learn more about the self and others. Poor communication can cause misunderstandings leading to feelings of anger, mistrust or frustration in relationships with teachers, friends, family and others.[12]

Good communication skills are important in the classroom, in relationships, and in the workplace. The two main types of verbal communication skills are speaking and listening. Speaking skills include the ability to clearly convey a specific message. Many plans have been ruined because a person did not clearly convey information to a listener. Another speaking skill that can be important to children is the use of I statements.[13] Children can practice expressing their feelings by saying "I feel . . . when you. . . ." I messages may be more well received than the accusatory "you" statement (e.g., "You always want to have it your way, and you make me sick!"). The way a person says something also is important. Two people can say the same thing but use a different tone of voice or nonverbal cue, resulting in very different interpretations.[14]

Listening is the second skill in oral communication. People feel good when they talk to a person who listens. On the other hand, they may feel discouraged when they try to have a conversation with a person who interrupts, never looks at them, or continues to watch television while they are speaking. Teacher's Toolbox 3.3 identifies important strategies for listeners.

People tend to communicate in three ways: aggressively, passively, or assertively. Fetro explained,

> Passive people will do something they don't want to do or make up an excuse rather than tell others how they really feel. Aggressive people will overreact to situations, blame or criticize others, and may even physically attack other people, with no consideration of the other's rights. Assertive people can say what they think and stand up for what they believe without hurting others.[15]

Educators should provide opportunities for students to practice the steps in assertive communication, which include stating a position, offering a reason, and acknowledging others' feelings.

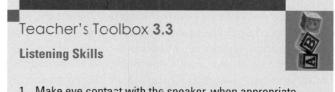

Teacher's Toolbox 3.3

Listening Skills

1. Make eye contact with the speaker, when appropriate.
2. Give nonverbal cues, such as nodding and facing the speaker.
3. Paraphrase what the speaker says.
4. Ask appropriate questions.
5. Give feedback that is genuine and sincere.
6. Respond in an empathetic manner.

Teacher's Toolbox 3.4

Peer Pressure Resistance Techniques

Give an excuse or a reason. This technique is familiar to most students, who use it in other types of situations, such as when they forget their homework or when they don't clean their room. Following are examples of reasons or excuses (here, for not smoking):

- I promised my dad I would go straight home after school.
- I'm allergic to smoke.
- I'm going to the movies with my older brother and his friends.

Avoid the situation or walk away. Have students think of ways to leave a situation to avoid being confronted with peer pressure to engage in an unhealthy behavior. For example, students may think that there will be alcohol at a party and choose not to go. If they find alcohol at a party when they get there, they may choose to leave. Following are examples of avoiding the situation or walking away:

- I can't right now—I'm busy with a project.
- I can't go to the party because I'm grounded.
- I have to go—I'm supposed to be home in five minutes.

Change the subject. Students refuse an offer and then change the subject. For example, if a friend offers you a cigarette, say, "No, thanks. What did you do last night after the ballgame?" Following are other examples of changing the subject:

- What did you watch on TV last night?
- Let's go play some basketball.
- Let's go to my house and get something to eat.

Repeat the refusal. Students repeat the same response, with no additional response. Following are examples of repeated refusals:

- I don't want to.
- Not right now.
- No, thanks.

Strength in numbers, or recruit an ally. When students find friends who have the same values, they can find strength in numbers. Pressure situations become less difficult when friends support their decisions. Following are examples of strength in numbers:

- What would you do in this situation?
- What do you think I should do?
- Do you go along with what they want me to do?

Suggest alternatives. Students suggest healthy alternatives. Following are examples of alternatives:

- Let's go watch a video.
- Let's go play soccer.
- Let's call Sherry and see what she's doing

Peer Resistance/Refusal Skills

Adolescents report that some of the most common reasons they initiate risky behaviors (experimenting with drugs, engaging in sexual activity) are they believe that their friends do, they want to fit in with others, and they want to belong to a group. Being accepted into a group is important at every age, but it is especially important during early adolescence. In contrast, lower-elementary children generally are egocentric and family-focused, which may result in a lack of attention toward other children. Upper-elementary children begin to extend beyond their family and to practice the important task of establishing their own identities. Although establishing an identity is developmentally appropriate and necessary, children may begin to participate in negative behaviors because of peer influence or because they want to be accepted by a group. For example, some children are influenced by friends to cheat on homework, lie to parents, or join in cruel teasing of another student.

Research about social influence resistance skills training identifies important skills to counteract the peer pressure by friends and pressure from media messages that students experience.[16] This research suggests that teachers should develop instructional activities to expose elementary and middle school students to the kinds of social pressures to use drugs and engage in other negative health behaviors they may encounter in the future. These activities should be conducted in the safe and controlled environment of the classroom, under the supervision of a skilled and nurturing teacher before students actually confront these social pressures in real life. In this context, teachers can show students video/movie/television clips about social pressures that young people experience, or students can role-play the types of social pressure situations they think they will encounter in the future. Teachers should follow the video clips or role-plays with well-planned discussions and demonstrations on how to get out of pressure situations and still maintain positive peer relationships. Because younger students (grades 3–5) admire older students, an excellent strategy is to have older students (grades 6–8) role-play pressure situations and demonstrate successful peer resistance skills.

Children need time to practice peer resistance skills in the classroom beginning about third grade. Around this time, children show increased independence from adults and begin to rely more heavily on their peers. Teacher's Toolbox 3.4 provides peer pressure resistance techniques students can practice in the classroom.

Standard 5: Decision Making

Students Will Demonstrate the Ability to Use Decision-Making Skills to Enhance Health

NHES 5, decision making, is closely related to NHES 6, goal setting. The short- and long-term, realistic goals that students set for themselves can provide important reasons to make good decisions for their health and future.

NHES 5 | *Students will demonstrate the ability to use decision-making skills to enhance health.*
(Brandy, age 12)

Thinking through the steps involved in making decisions does not come naturally to most elementary and middle school students. In fact, parents and teachers often are bewildered by the impulsivity of the young people in their care. R. E. Dahl indicated that, although adolescence generally is the healthiest and most resilient phase of the human life span, overall morbidity and mortality rates increase from childhood to adolescence, with the primary causes of death and disability in this age group related to problems with control of behavior and emotions.[17] These problems appear to be related to changes that occur in the brain before, during, and independently of adolescence.

Behaving as an adult requires the development of self-control over behavior and emotions. Adults modify their behaviors to avoid negative future consequences, initiate and persist in certain courses of action, manage complex social situations even when strong emotions are involved, and self-regulate their feelings and behaviors to attain long-term goals. All these behaviors involve the prefrontal cortex of the brain, which is among the last regions of the brain to achieve full functional maturation. Dahl likened the challenge facing adolescents to "starting the engines without a skilled driver." Today's adolescents experience earlier puberty, resulting in several years of living in a sexually mature body with sexually activated brain circuits—but with relatively immature neurobehavioral systems involved in self-control and emotional regulation.[18]

Western societies want adolescents to demonstrate increasing self-control over their emotions and behavior, consider long-term consequences, abide by complex social rules, and use strategies and planning to move toward goals. Furthermore, adolescents are expected to accomplish these tasks during a time when they often experience strong and conflicting emotions. To complicate matters, Dahl observed that many young adolescents are faced with an enormous amount of freedom in trying to navigate complex decision making. Adolescents often show extremely poor decision making in real-life situations.[19]

In its report *Teenage Brain: A Work in Progress,* the National Institute of Mental Health (NIMH) reported that MRI studies are shedding new light on how teens process emotions differently from adults.[20] Researchers scanned brain activity as subjects identified the emotions on pictures of faces displayed on a computer screen. Young teens, who characteristically perform poorly on the task, activated the amygdala, a brain center that mediates fear and other gut reactions, more than the frontal lobe. As teens grow older, their brain activity during this task tends to shift to the frontal lobe, leading to more reasoned perceptions and improved performance. NIMH concluded that while studies show remarkable changes occurring in the brain during the teen years, they also demonstrate what every parent can confirm: The teenage brain is a very complicated and dynamic arena that is not easily understood and definitely is in progress.

Given the complexity of brain development and its relationship to emotional and behavioral control, the theory of planned behavior should be considered in its entirety. As demonstrated in other NHES discussions in this chapter, a simple one-shot approach (e.g., teaching a series of steps for decision making and then moving on to a new topic) is not sufficient for helping students develop their thought processes and skills. Identifying behavioral intentions, attitudes, subjective norms, and perceived behavioral control are all involved in thorough planning and teaching. Students need well-structured opportunities to identify the important issues for themselves and others inherent in the decisions they make. Health education can be planned to help them do this more thoughtfully.

Decision making is an important social skill that can empower students. Students, and even adults, often make decisions without really thinking about them. From a young age, children should be given opportunities and encouraged to make some decisions of their own, with the help of caring adults.

Children learn two important lessons when they are allowed to make some of their own choices. First, they learn that every choice is connected to a consequence. They learn that some choices produce results that are unpleasant or even dangerous. When children are allowed to experience minor unpleasant results, with adult support, they begin to understand decision making and its consequences in ways that serve them well as independent thinkers. Second, children learn that they will be held accountable for their choices. If parents, caregivers, and teachers hold children accountable for their decisions, children increasingly learn responsibility for their actions.

Young children don't need to learn a formal decision-making model. Instead, children in the early elementary

SAMPLE DECISION-MAKING PROCESS (FIVE STEPS FOR YOUNGER STUDENTS)

1. *Problem.* Define the problem to be solved.
2. *Alternatives.* List alternative solutions for the problem.
3. *Pros and cons.* List the positive and negative consequences of each alternative.
4. *Choose.* Make a choice and try it.
5. *Evaluate.* How did it go? What would you do next time?

SAMPLE DECISION-MAKING MODEL (EIGHT STEPS)

Define the problem. Figure out and define the specific decision to be made.

Identify a support group. Make a list of people who may be able to help in making the decision. Include at least one adult on this list.

List alternatives. Brainstorm a list of all possible alternatives. Try to think of all the different ways this situation could be handled. The more ideas to choose from, the better the chance of finding the one that works best. Questions for brainstorming include

- What has worked in the past in a similar situation?
- What would an adult I respect do to solve this problem?
- What are some things I haven't tried that might work?

Identify pros and cons. List the pros and cons (positive and negative consequences) of each alternative. Consider both short- and long-term outcomes. Ask questions about each alternative:

- What are my responsibilities to my family?
- What are my feelings and fears about each alternative?
- How does each alternative fit into my value system?

Eliminate alternatives. Cross out the alternatives that no longer seem acceptable.

Rank the remaining alternatives. List the remaining solutions in the order you want to try them. (Eliminate this step if only one solution remains.)

Try the chosen alternative.

Evaluate the choice. If the alternative didn't work well, try another from the list.

---

grades should be encouraged to make choices and then experience the resulting positive or negative outcomes of their choices. Children need opportunities to talk about their choices and the outcomes with caring adults. Upper-elementary and middle-level students are capable of using a formal decision-making model as a means of organizing their thoughts into a process for making the increasingly complex decisions that confront them. A variety of decision-making models can be found in health education curricula and other texts. Teacher's Toolbox 3.5 shows two decision-making models that work well with upper-elementary and middle-level students.

An aspect of teaching decision making that teachers must consider is the ideas and beliefs that students take away from their classroom when discussions end. Upper-elementary and middle-level students may use a decision-making model to rationalize exactly what they want to do, even if that behavior isn't healthy. Caryn Matsuoka[21] found that middle school students were adept at using the reasoning and inquiry skills they had learned in elementary school (i.e., Habits of the Mind,[22] Good Thinker's Toolkit[23]). Although most students were using their reasoning skills in positive ways to navigate their new middle school environments, at least one student indicated that he was using his reasoning skills to justify an action—stealing—that most of his peers and most adults would consider harmful. Educators can use the theory of planned behavior to help students dig deeper into their thinking by linking their intentions and attitudes (in this case, potentially hurtful ones) to additional information to act in more health-enhancing ways. This information might involve subjective norms ("What do other classmates think? Do they think

this is right or wrong? What do parents, teachers, and other family members think? Why? How would I feel if I made a decision like this that went against their values and my values?") or perceived behavioral control ("There are at least three other ways I can solve this problem"). Teachers can ask other students to weigh in on perplexing issues by asking "What do others think about this? Is this a good decision for everyone involved? Why or why not? What could happen? What could happen then? How could we look at this problem from another angle?" Students can help each other when they are allowed the opportunity to reason together in honest conversation within a safe environment.

Standard 6: Goal Setting

Students Will Demonstrate the Ability to Use Goal-Setting Skills to Enhance Health

NHES 6 calls for students to practice skills in goal setting. A goal is an aim related to something a person would like to do, have, or be. An achievable goal is within a person's power to accomplish in the short or long term. Without goals, children and adolescents, and even adults, may lose their sense of direction and make poor choices.

Health education lessons can help students assess their current health status and make plans to improve their health, taking into account variables such as their level of commitment, diverse alternatives, positive and negative consequences, barriers to progress, important steps toward their goals, and supports for their actions. Students also need to create ways to track their progress and evaluate their accomplishments—a tall order for most young people.

Joyce Fetro's series of books on teaching personal and social skills are an excellent source of information and

NHES 6 | *Students will demonstrate the ability to use goal-setting skills to enhance health.*
(Brittany, age 12; Chevante, age 12)

strategies for teaching goal setting.[24] Fetro states that without clear goals, students' personal efforts and hard work may not lead to the results they want. Conversely, learning to set achievable short- and long-term goals can help young people prioritize what's most important to them and work meaningfully toward getting where they want to go. Teacher's Toolbox 3.6 provides a series of goal-setting steps for students.

Identifying supports for and barriers to achieving goals is an important part of the goal-setting process. Students can name family members and friends who want to see them succeed and can enlist their help in accomplishing their goals. Students need supporters who can provide a caring but honest appraisal. Similarly, students should think hard about attitudes, beliefs, experiences, or people who might intentionally or unintentionally block their progress. Teachers and peers can help students plan strategies in advance to deal with barriers when they arise.

Learning to set a clear, achievable goal is a skill that young people need to master. Fetro recommends that students take time to perform a reality check on who and where they are and to develop a mental picture of where they want to go.[25] In terms of actually setting goals, students need practice in identifying aims that truly are important to them. For example, a young person who sets a goal of becoming a teacher mainly because his or her parents are teachers may find that teaching isn't the right career choice. Goals should be observable, measurable, and defined in manageable steps. How will a person know if steps toward the goal are having the desired effect? What would real progress look like?

Determining whether a goal is under a person's control is an essential step in the goal-setting process.[26] Health education lessons can lead students to realize that the only behavior they can manage is their own. A student might enlist family support in collecting and taking bottles and cans from home to a new recycling center in the neighborhood each Saturday. The student also can ask other families in the neighborhood to join the effort, but the decision to participate rests with each family. Thus, the goal that is within the student's control is to manage the recycling effort at home.

Making plans to track progress and evaluate how things are going is another important aspect of goal setting. Students might create personalized charts or graphs to provide a visual reminder of their goals. Students also might make plans to celebrate progress along the way, whether by themselves or with others. The content chapters provide additional learning and assessment strategies for helping students learn and practice successful goal setting.

Teacher's Toolbox 3.6

Goal-Setting Steps

Set a long-term goal. What do you want to accomplish?

- Think about something specific you want to improve or do better at.
- Be sure your goal is achievable and measurable.

Assess your situation. Where are you now, and where do you want to be in the future?

- How are you doing now?
- How do you want to change?

Make a plan. What steps do you need to take to achieve your goal?

- What resources will you need?
- Who will support your efforts?
- What short-term goals should you set to meet your long-term goal?
- What obstacles will you need to overcome?
- How long will it take to meet your goal? Develop a timeline.

Evaluate your progress. How did you do?

- If you reached your overall goal, celebrate your success and thank those who helped.
- If you have difficulty reaching your goal, rethink the goal-setting steps. Celebrate your successes along the way and make plans to try again.

Standard 7: Self-Management

Students Will Demonstrate the Ability to Practice Health-Enhancing Behaviors and Avoid or Reduce Risks

Having students actually practice healthy behaviors is an important goal of school health education. Providing opportunities for students to learn and practice a range of personal and social skills to promote health is the focus in the classroom. Ultimately, young people and adults choose their own course of action in health-related matters. Teachers can ensure that children are prepared with a ready tool kit of health skills and knowledge to assist them in making the decisions and taking the actions that are best for them. Teachers don't assess students on the health behaviors they actually practice. Rather, teachers assess them on their ability to demonstrate personal and social skills to facilitate and promote healthy behavior.

NHES 7 | *Students will demonstrate the ability to practice health-enhancing behaviors and avoid or reduce risks.* (Tisha, age 12; Janna, age 12; Kuulei, age 12)

The content chapters contain teaching strategies for helping children learn to be good self-managers. In many instances, self-management skills naturally overlap with other personal and social skills, such as communication and decision making. Teachers and students can think of self-management as the "doing" skill—the steps students actually take to keep themselves and others healthy and safe in real-life situations.

In the classroom, students can work together to create strategies to use in potentially challenging situations. For example, middle school students might plan to carry a cell phone or money for a phone call and cab with them whenever they are riding with others to social events, such as parties or ball games. If the person they are supposed to ride home with begins drinking, the students then have a way to call for a ride with a sober driver, whether a parent, older sibling, friend, or taxi driver. Performing healthy practices such as hand washing and flossing and learning life-saving practices such as the Heimlich maneuver are other examples of self-management.

Behavioral rehearsals are an important part of learning self-management. Practicing ways to deal with strong emotions (e.g., counting to ten) and stress (e.g., going for a walk) is helpful to students of all ages, even those in kindergarten. For example, when young children demonstrate alternatives such as walking away, saying "Stop it!" or asking a teacher for help when troubled by classmates who persist in mean-spirited teasing, they are practicing self-management skills. Relieving stress during exam periods by taking deep breaths to clear the mind, standing for stretch breaks between testing sessions, or using positive self-talk also helps students build their tool kit of personal self-management strategies.

The intention to practice healthy behavior is an important component of the theory of planned behavior. However, intention by itself is not enough—it must work together with the other components of the model (attitudes, subjective norms, and perceived behavioral control). A study using data from the 1995 National Longitudinal Study of Adolescent Health reported on the effectiveness of virginity pledges in reducing sexually transmitted disease (STD) infection rates among young adults ages 18–24.[27] A nationally representative sample of students enrolled in grades 7–12 were asked on three different occasions during the initial study whether they had ever taken a virginity pledge. During a follow-up study, a sample of respondents provided urine samples to be tested for four sexually transmitted diseases. Data analysis revealed that though pledgers were consistently less likely to be exposed to risk factors across a wide range of indicators, their STD infection rates were no different from those of nonpledgers. The researchers suggested that pledgers, 88 percent of whom reported sexual intercourse before marriage, were less likely than others to use condoms at first intercourse and to be tested for and diagnosed with STDs. They concluded that virginity pledges alone might not be the optimal approach to preventing STD acquisition among young adults.

A related commentary cautioned that these results represent data from a survey rather than an experiment and are not representative of all adolescents.[28] The study design could not take into account the complex personal, family, religious, and sociocultural factors that might influence the decision to make a virginity pledge. However, the commentary concluded that the most important lesson from the data is the confirmation that absolutist approaches to prevention incompletely serve those at risk. Abstinence-only prevention efforts such as those represented by virginity pledges ignore adolescents who initially heed the prevention message but become sexually active later. From a public health perspective, educators must get past the notion that simple, perfectly effective, and completely harm-free interventions exist for the negative consequences of sexuality.

How can educators move beyond simplistic classroom activities such as telling students they should make public pledges of a certain kind? The theory of planned behavior advocates using the whole model to create learning opportunities for students. To start, students need accurate and complete information (e.g., individuals can contract STDs from oral and anal sex as well as from vaginal intercourse) to help them develop healthy attitudes and make informed decisions. Students also need to examine norms related to the behavior of their peers (e.g., most middle and high school students do not have intercourse during their secondary school years) and explore the beliefs of their families and friends about sexuality. Finally, students need assistance in building their perceived behavioral control and self-efficacy with respect to decisions and actions related to sexuality. For example, carefully planned health education lessons can provide opportunities for students to anticipate challenging situations (e.g., potential risks involved in going to someone's house when parents are not at home) and to practice peer resistance and other self-management skills before they face actual risk-taking situations. In summary, telling students the attitude that they "should" have (the familiar "Just say no") without further education results in many students just not buying it.

Standard 8: Advocacy

Students Will Demonstrate the Ability to Advocate for Personal, Family, and Community Health

NHES 8 calls for students to learn the skills they need to advocate for personal, family, and community health. Becoming an advocate for health means learning to promote and encourage positive health choices and to take a stand to make a difference on a health-related issue.

Students must learn to declare their positions clearly when they try to educate and influence others about important issues. As advocates, students also assume the role of supporting others to promote healthy social norms. Any advocacy effort should have a healthy norms component.

NHES 8 | *Students will demonstrate the ability to advocate for personal, family, and community health.* (Sterling, age 12; Taylor, age 12; Samantha, age 12)

Advocacy campaigns can be especially effective when older students work with younger children. Students often believe that "everyone is doing it" in terms of health-risk behaviors. Well-planned advocacy efforts can help young people recognize that same-age and older peers are making healthy choices.

The theory of planned behavior supports health education lessons that help students understand that their family and friends want them to act in healthy ways. Students also gain perceived behavioral control when they see that their classmates and older students support and engage in healthy behaviors. Health education lessons about advocacy should be relevant to students' interests and development. If students aren't interested in an issue, advocacy efforts might be a shallow exercise. For example, social pressures to use tobacco usually begin in early adolescence. Thus, upper-elementary and middle-level students will be more attuned to tobacco prevention campaigns than will lower-elementary students.

Educators can invite students to tackle health advocacy issues for their whole school by framing their efforts around the Coordinated School Health Program (CSHP) model (see Chapter 1). How can students envision each component of the CSHP contributing to a health-related advocacy effort? Upper-elementary and middle-level students might plan and carry out an advocacy effort to promote daily physical activity in the following ways:

- *Health education·* Help design and present hands-on lessons for younger students that teach them about the health benefits of cardio-respiratory (aerobic) endurance, muscular strength and endurance, flexibility, and body composition.

- *Health services:* Consult with school health services personnel for guidelines on how individuals with asthma, allergies, or other chronic conditions can participate safely in physical activity.
- *Healthy environment:* Work with administrators to ensure plenty of access to water fountains and bottled water. Ask school administrators for permission to design a walking trail on the school grounds.
- *School food service:* Work with school food service personnel to design table tents and posters for the cafeteria and school that promote healthy eating for optimal participation in physical activity.
- *Counseling:* Ask school counselors to help students understand the social and emotional benefits of physical activity.
- *Physical education*: Help design and teach lessons for younger students that focus on ways to increase activity (three students per long jump rope, alternating often as turners and jumpers, rather than one long line waiting for one jump rope) during physical education and recess periods.
- *Faculty and staff:* Interview teachers and staff about the kinds of physical activity that interest them, and design opportunities that are student-led.
- *Healthy community:* Involve parents and community members in a campaign to increase physical activity by recording their activity on student-designed posters and charts. Ask community businesses to donate funds for Frisbees, jump ropes, and soccer balls for use during recess periods.

PLANNING EFFECTIVE SCHOOL HEALTH EDUCATION

Building on Evaluation Research

"Healthy kids make better learners" is a reminder often given by educators to stress the importance of effective health education in K–8 classrooms. As discussed in Chapter 1, research data indicate that school health education can contribute to students' increased well-being and school achievement.

The overall goal of health education is for students to adopt and maintain healthy behaviors. To this end, health education should contribute directly to students' ability to engage in health-enhancing behaviors and to avoid behaviors that can lead to poor health. Unfortunately, common approaches to health education (having students listen to long lectures, memorize information for a test, or complete worksheets day after day) show little or no evidence of being effective.

Chapter 2 described the characteristics of health education lessons that are consistent with evaluation research. These characteristics are the foundation of the recommendations and strategies for teaching health education in this text. The theory of planned behavior serves as a starting point for planning. The introductory and content

chapters focus on teaching the most important concepts using a skills-based approach to achieve healthy behavior outcomes. This chapter and the content chapters assist educators with planning health education that is effective, engages students, and fits naturally into the K–8 curriculum.

Working with the Big Picture in Mind

Earlier in this chapter, readers were introduced to the eight National Health Education Standards. A math education professor asked during a curriculum presentation, "What makes these standards unique to health education? Mathematics teachers also want students to communicate with each other, make good decisions, and learn core concepts as they engage in mathematics." The answer to this question lies in the content areas in which students learn the health education standards.

How can the standards and the content areas be integrated into a cohesive, manageable, and memorable approach to curriculum planning? The Hawaii Department of Education provides one example: an eight-by-eight focus for the health curriculum (Teacher's Toolbox 3.7). A grid of the standards and content areas can be created to pinpoint the emphasis at the elementary, middle, and high school levels. Teachers and students find the eight-by-eight idea easy to remember.

Teaching to Standards

What does it mean to teach to standards? For many educators, this is a new way of thinking. When teachers begin to plan around standards, they sometimes find that some of their long-used classroom ideas don't match up with important learning. For example, middle school health educator Lynn Shoji stated that she realized she was spending too much time on content (facts) and not enough time on the personal and social skill development outlined in the health education standards. Still, the content was important. Shoji solved this dilemma by increasingly teaching her students to conduct their own research (NHES 3) and to share their findings with the rest of the class. Her students learned communication (NHES 4) and advocacy (NHES 8) skills in making their presentations. Having the courage to examine familiar teaching habits can lead to the discovery of engaging and meaningful new ways to help students succeed.

Another challenge is rethinking or reworking activities that have become classroom favorites because students find them so enjoyable. If the activity under scrutiny can be linked to standards, content areas, healthy behaviors, and theoretical constructs, it deserves a closer look. A teaching activity called "Balloon-Up," found in Chapter 5, is engaging and interactive—and also links directly to standards-based teaching. Balloon-Up allows students to experience a simple decision-making model first-hand in the classroom, which meets part of NHES 5. The model then can be applied in the context of any content area to help students consider healthy behaviors, their intentions toward

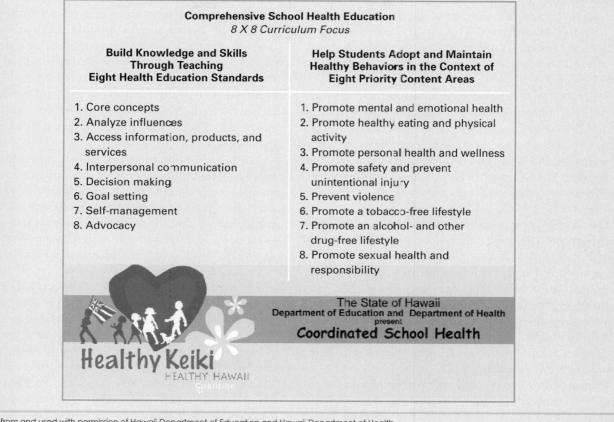

Comprehensive School Health Education
8 X 8 Curriculum Focus

Build Knowledge and Skills Through Teaching Eight Health Education Standards	**Help Students Adopt and Maintain Healthy Behaviors in the Context of Eight Priority Content Areas**
1. Core concepts	1. Promote mental and emotional health
2. Analyze influences	2. Promote healthy eating and physical activity
3. Access information, products, and services	3. Promote personal health and wellness
4. Interpersonal communication	4. Promote safety and prevent unintentional injury
5. Decision making	5. Prevent violence
6. Goal setting	6. Promote a tobacco-free lifestyle
7. Self-management	7. Promote an alcohol- and other drug-free lifestyle
8. Advocacy	8. Promote sexual health and responsibility

Healthy Keiki
HEALTHY HAWAII
Coalition

The State of Hawaii
Department of Education and Department of Health
present
Coordinated School Health

Adapted from and used with permission of Hawaii Department of Education and Hawaii Department of Health.

a behavior, what they believe their family and friends think about a behavior, and how successful they believe they would be at carrying out the behavior. Students can demonstrate learning through story or script writing about a decision they need to make, and demonstrate each step of the decision-making model in their writing. Used simply as an activity to fill class time, Balloon-Up has little relevance other than as a class break. However, if Balloon-Up is used to engage students in deeper discussion about the decision making they wrestle with in and out of school, alternatives, and the consequences of their decisions, it becomes the means to carry out a teaching strategy with purpose in the curriculum.

This chapter and the content chapters (Chapters 5–14) are filled with standards-based learning strategies. Thoughtful planning means more than choosing an activity for the day. Strategies should be selected carefully to help students learn what they need to know and how to apply it.

Readers can conduct an Internet search to compare and contrast the health education standards for their own and other state education agencies. How do the state standards align with national standards? How do states differ in terms of the topic areas covered? Suggestions for getting started include:

Health Framework for California Public Schools (*www.cde.ca.gov/ci/cr/cf/documents/healthfw.pdf*)

Maine Health Education Standards (*www.maine.gov/education/lres/hpe.htm*)

Michigan Content Standards and Benchmarks for Health Education (*www.emc.cmich.edu/cshp/hesb.htm*)

Texas Essential Knowledge and Skills for Health Education (*www.tea.state.tx.us/rules/tac/chapter115/index.html*)

Wisconsin Model Academic Standards for Health Education (*http://dpi.state.wi.us/standards/pdf/health.pdf*)

Readers also should locate the health education curriculum for their district education agency and school.

Yearly Planning

An excellent planning resource is Grant Wiggins and Jay McTighe's book *Understanding by Design.*[29] Wiggins and McTighe's "backward design" process encourages educators to begin with the end in mind by first identifying the results they want their students to achieve.

The authors of this text begin by identifying the healthy behavior outcomes that health education can help students learn and practice across important content areas. When educators are clear on desired results ("Where do we want to go?"), they can move on to identifying acceptable evidence of achievement ("How can students show what they have learned?") and to planning learning opportunities ("How should we teach so that students learn best?").[30]

Educators can use the information in this text to make a yearly plan for health education. Teacher's Toolbox 3.8, an example of a yearly health education plan, is based on the healthy behavior outcomes that serve as a basis for teaching concepts and skills across the content areas explored in this text. The healthy behavior outcomes build on one another and grow in complexity from one grade cluster to the next.

The sample yearly plan focuses each month on a particular content area. Lessons might or might not be taught daily, but they should at a minimum be taught weekly. Educators don't expect children to learn to read with an occasional hit-or-miss language arts lesson. Similarly, devoting sufficient instructional time to health education increases the potential for helping students develop healthy behaviors. In middle schools, where semesters or quarters might be the norm, appropriate scheduling adjustments can be made.

Working from this broad yearly plan, educators at the local level can develop a more detailed weekly scope (concepts and skills) and sequence (order) appropriate for the students in their school community. For example, the healthy behavior outcome "practicing safety rules and procedures" in grades K–2 typically includes learning concepts and practicing skills related to fire, school bus, pedestrian, and playground safety. However, the decisions need to be local. Children who live in coastal or island communities, for example, also need to learn ocean and sun safety, whereas children who live in very cold climates need to learn how to protect themselves during winter conditions such as low temperatures, snow, and ice.

The Health Education Curriculum Analysis Tool (www.cdc.gov/HealthyYouth/HECAT/pdf/HECAT_Append_4.pdf) provides information on developing scope and sequence in health education. The HECAT notes that scope and sequence should address the concepts and skills students need *before* problems emerge, help coordinate instruction within standards and across grade levels, and show reinforcement of skills and concepts without excessive repetition.

Unit Planning

From a yearly plan, educators move to decisions about units or "chunks" of study related to a particular topic or theme. Units are more than a collection of daily lesson plans or health activities for the day. They address important questions and ideas that invite students' curiosity and engagement. Common threads of inquiry connect one lesson to the next and to children's lives. In health education, units can be created to answer important questions about a content area (What does it mean for elementary students to express feelings in healthy ways?) or a skill (How can middle school students apply the skill of interpersonal communication across all the content areas?). The authors encourage unit developers to focus on intriguing questions that students want to answer (How would health be affected if people ate from only one part of the food guide pyramid all the time?) rather than single-word topics or themes that likely are too broad to be covered in one unit (a unit on the topic "nutrition").

Teacher education programs and education agencies use a variety of unit formats. Educators can ask for information on local methods and sample units. Wiggins and McTighe state that "the first requirement of effective, user-friendly curriculums is that the designer must make the goals clear to students."[31] Effective unit design means involving students early in what they will learn and do and in how they will be assessed.

In their book *Integrating Differentiated Instruction + Understanding by Design,* Carol Ann Tomlinson and Jay McTighe expand on the backward design process.[32] Teacher's Toolbox 3.9 provides a backward design template that can be used to design health education units or lessons. Readers may be especially interested in the health education unit "You Are What You Eat": A Unit Planned with Backward Design, included in the Tomlinson and McTighe text.

In addition to the HECAT, teachers can locate excellent web-based resources for health education unit and lesson planning. The following websites provide a good starting place:

> Education Materials Center, Central Michigan University (Michigan Model for Health) (*www.emc.cmich.edu*)
>
> Health Teacher: Teaching Concepts and Skills (*www.healthteacher.com*)
>
> PE Central (*www.pecentral.org*)
>
> WebQuest.org (*www.webquest.org*)

Units offer great possibilities for curriculum integration with other subject areas. A unit on helping students express their feelings in healthy ways could explore the skills of interpersonal communication, decision making, and self-management within the content area of promoting mental and emotional health. Teaching through children's literature provides a natural link with language arts. Suggestions for children's literature are included in each content chapter; a combined list of recommended books can be found on the Online Learning Center.

The CDC's School Health Education Resources (SHER) provides user-friendly access to the myriad school health

Teacher's Toolbox 3.8

Sample Yearly Plan Based on Healthy Behaviors, Grades K–8

Month	Content Area (chapter)	Grades K–2* Build for 3–8 ⇒	Grades 3–5* ⇐ Build ⇒	Grades 6–8* ⇒ Build from K–5
July–August	Promoting mental and emotional health (5)**	• Express feelings in healthy ways • Use self-impulse control • Be kind and empathetic • Carry out personal responsibilities	• Engage in mentally and emotionally healthy activities • Manage conflict and stress in healthy ways • Establish and maintain healthy relationships	• Seek help for troublesome feelings • Manage pubertal changes in healthy ways • Support others in healthy ways
September	Promoting healthy eating (6)	• Eat healthy snacks • Eat a variety of foods • Eat breakfast every day • Drink plenty of water • Limit sugary foods and drinks • Limit foods high in fat	• Make healthy food choices • Eat in moderation • Prepare foods in healthy ways • Eat foods high in fiber • Limit salt intake	• Eat appropriate number of food group servings • Balance caloric intake with expenditure • Eat healthy at restaurants • Prevent eating disorders • Follow healthy body-weight practices
October	Promoting physical activity (7)	• Get recommended amount of moderate and vigorous physical activity • Drink plenty of water	• Regularly engage in cardio-respiratory, flexibility, and strengthening activities • Do warm-ups and cool-downs	• Avoid injury during physical activity
November	Promoting safety and preventing unintentional injury (8)	• Wear safety belts • Use booster seats • Sit in the backseat • Practice safety rules and procedures • Seek emergency help	• Use appropriate safety equipment • Refuse to dare others or take dares • Plan ahead to prevent injury	• Avoid riding with drivers under AOD influence • Provide immediate help for a sudden illness or injury
December	Promoting personal health and wellness (9)	• Brush and floss teeth • Practice good hygiene • Get plenty of sleep • Prevent communicable disease (wash hands) • Prevent sun damage	• Prevent vision and hearing loss • Prevent chronic disease problems (asthma) • Prevent food-borne illness • Support health of others	• Prevent chronic diseases by eating healthy • Seek help for chronic disease and conditions • Seek medical help for screenings/exams • Prevent problems from trends or fads
January	Preventing violence (10)	• Avoid bullying • Get help when needed • Engage in positive, helpful behaviors • Get help for inappropriate touching	• Manage interpersonal conflict nonviolently • Get help for others in danger of self-harm • Argue against the use of violence	• Avoid engaging in violence, situations with high potential for violence, and people who engage in or encourage violence
February	Promoting a tobacco-free lifestyle (11)	• Avoid using or trying any form of tobacco • Avoid second-hand smoke	• Avoid being influenced to use or try tobacco • Seek support for being tobacco-free	• Support others to be tobacco-free • Avoid pressuring others • Quit using tobacco
March	Promoting an AOD-free lifestyle (12)	• Use medicines correctly, as directed by parents, caretakers, and doctors	• Avoid experimentation with AOD • Avoid use of AOD	• Avoid riding with drivers under influence of AOD • Avoid pressuring others • Quit using AOD • Seek help for stopping
April	Promoting sexual health (13)	• Practice being a good family member and friend • Take good care of both body and mind	• Build and maintain respectful relationships • Set and respect boundaries • Learn about what puberty will entail	• Manage puberty in healthy ways • Practice and support abstinence • Avoid pressuring others • Return to abstinence
May–June	Revisiting mental and emotional health (5)	• Help students prepare for a healthy summer break!	• Help students prepare for a healthy summer break!	• Help students prepare for a healthy summer break!

*Adapted from the Health Education Curriculum Analysis Tool (HECAT), Centers for Disease Control and Prevention.

**Include material on managing loss, death, and grief here or later in the year (Chapter 14).

Teaching about health through children's literature helps engage students and allows for curriculum integration with language arts.

education offerings available from the U.S. Department of Health and Human Services. Included with the SHER materials are the related National Health Education Standards and CDC's Characteristics of Effective Health Education Curricula. CDC's Health Education Curriculum Analysis Tool (HECAT) can help schools conduct a clear, complete, and consistent analysis of health education curricula based on the National Health Education Standards and CDC's Characteristics of Effective Health Education Curricula. The HECAT results can help schools select or develop appropriate and effective health education curricula and improve the delivery of health education. Educators can find SHER online at http://apps.nccd .cdc.gov/sher/.

Lesson Planning

The task of lesson planning can seem overwhelming to teacher education students, student teachers, and beginning teachers, especially when their mentor teachers and more experienced colleagues appear to work from brief notes jotted in their planning books. Effective lesson planning is a skill that new teachers can sharpen with experience and with feedback from other educators.

Building on Wiggins and McTighe's idea of backward design, this text offers a format consisting of four major parts:

Step 1: Desired results (Where do we want to go?)
Step 2: Assessment evidence (How can students show what they learn?)
Step 3: Active learning plan (How should we teach so that students learn best?)
Step 4: Reflection (What did my students and I learn?)

Teacher's Toolbox 3.9 illustrates this four-part lesson plan, customized for the health education standards and content areas discussed in this text. A step-by-step look at this lesson design process follows.

1. Desired Results

The backward design process begins with *desired results.* What do we want students to understand and be able to do as a result of our plan? What "end" do we have in mind? Thinking through the following ideas can help teachers create a meaningful plan. This example focuses on interpersonal communication skills (NHES 4).

Standards: Health education standard(s) and performance indicator(s) or benchmark(s) Teachers begin by selecting standards and performance indicators or benchmarks to focus the lesson. A standard provides a broad target for the lesson (e.g., students demonstrate the ability to use interpersonal communication skills to enhance health). Performance indicators or benchmarks give more detail about how the standard looks in practice and the purpose of the lesson (students demonstrate healthy ways to express needs, wants, and feelings). A unit or lesson based on this standard and performance indicator should help students learn to communicate openly and honestly in ways that are beneficial to everyone concerned. Focusing on one standard and performance indicator is perfectly acceptable, especially for those who are new to unit and lesson planning. However, units and lessons can focus on several standards at once, including standards from other content areas (an integrated lesson that addresses standards in both health education and performing arts). See health standards and performance indicators in Appendix A.

Context: Health content area(s) The health content areas provide the context or backdrop for teaching communication skills that promote good health. For younger children, the content area of Promoting Mental and Emotional Health provides an excellent context for learning to communicate needs, wants, and feelings in ways that are helpful rather than hurtful. Elementary teachers can help children think through and practice the difference between tattling (trying to get someone in trouble) and helping (getting adult help when someone is in danger, upset, or might get hurt), both of which involve interpersonal communication. Upper-elementary students can learn to communicate needs, wants, and feelings in ways that promote calm rather than confrontation in tense situations. Middle-level students can compare and contrast communication skills in pressure situations across content areas. For example, though a student might say in response to pressure to smoke, "Nah, not now, let's go play basketball." The same response wouldn't work at all in a pressure situation to have sex! What could students say instead? Chapters 5–14 provide communication skill strategies across health content areas.

Behavior: Healthy behavior(s) Identifying the healthy behavior focus for the unit or lesson provides the underlying reason for teaching. What healthy behaviors do educators want students to have the knowledge and skills to practice throughout their lives? In the content area of Safety or Promoting an Alcohol and Other Drug-Free

Backward Design Planning Template for Health Education

Title: _____

Developed by: _____ Grade level: _____ Date: _____

Step 1: Desired Results (Where do we want to go?)

• **Standards:** Health education standard(s) and performance indicator(s) or benchmark(s)
• **Context:** Health content area(s)
• **Behavior:** Healthy behavior(s)
• **Theory to Practice:** Theory of Planned Behavior Construct(s)
• **Differentiation:** Enrichment, IEP objectives, or other plans for diverse learners

Step 2: Assessment Evidence (How can students show what they learn?)

• **Performance Task:** What will students *do* to demonstrate learning?
• **Criteria:** How good is good enough? (Show checklists, rubrics, or other criteria.)
• **Other Evidence:** Self-reflections, quizzes, tests, observations, journals, homework

Step 3: Active Learning Plan (How should we teach so that students learn best?)

• **Steps for Students:** Learning strategies (detailed sequence of lesson)	• **Reminders for Teachers:** What do I need to remember to say and do?

• **Materials:** What I need to have ready
• **Time:** Approximate time I need for lesson(s)
• **Resources:** Where I got my ideas

Step 4: Reflection (What did my students and I learn?)

• What happened during my lessons (what did the students and I say and do)? How effective was my lesson design and teaching?
• What evidence can I show that my students learned about health (e.g., student work or other response)? How effective was my assessment plan for getting information about what they learned?
• How did I do in meeting my desired results for these health lessons? What are my next steps to improve student learning for health?

Source: Adapted from Tomlinson and McTighe, 2006.

Lifestyle, units or lessons might focus on the healthy behavior of "Avoid riding in a car with a driver who is under the influence of alcohol or other drugs." The communication skills a young person needs to promote this healthy behavior can be tremendously complex. Young people may have no choice about riding with an adult who is inebriated and might well risk an abusive response if they protest. Respectfully asking to ride with someone else ("I'd like to ride with Auntie Lynn") or to stay behind ("Could I stay over at Sam's house tonight?") might be viable alternatives students could consider in the safe environment of the classroom. The healthy behaviors teachers are trying to effect over time are an important component of health units and lessons. See a summary of healthy behaviors in Teacher's Toolbox 3.1.

Theory to Practice: Theory of Planned Behavior Construct(s) Educators often speak of linking theory to practice. The Theory of Planned Behavior (see Chapter 2) provides a guide to key factors that are most likely to influence students' health behavior. With limited time for health education in the K–8 curriculum, the constructs help in planning units and lessons that truly can make a difference. The constructs are:

1. Intentions to act
2. Attitudes toward a behavior
3. Subjective norms (perceived social pressures related to a behavior)
4. Perceived behavioral control (perceived ease or difficulty of performing a behavior)

Educators can fine-tune units and lessons by thinking through which of these constructs they are trying to influence. A lesson on interpersonal communication within the context of Promoting a Tobacco-Free Lifestyle, designed to help students avoid being influenced to use tobacco, could be drawn from the constructs *intention to act* ("I will use my words and actions to say no to tobacco, even if older kids pressure me after school") and perceived behavioral control ("I've practiced in lots of situations with my friends in the classroom, and I believe I can use repeated refusals without making a big deal out of it or losing my friends"). The teaching strategies in this textbook are aligned with one or more constructs, which can help educators think carefully about assessment. For example, older students could interview family members and friends about their views on dating (subjective norms). To demonstrate their learning, students could design a questionnaire, conduct interviews, compile data, display results, and draw conclusions about the healthy ways in which their friends and families want them to act.

Differentiation: Enrichment, IEP objectives, or other plans for diverse learners

Differentiation means planning to help all learners. Educators must consider the needs and characteristics of all the children in their classroom to make learning meaningful, rather than one size fits all. For example, the learning strategy *Punahele Bear: How Do We Talk to Each Other?* in Chapter 5 provides several considerations for differentiation. One is that some students may want to watch and listen rather than actually provide examples of words or actions that they hear or see at school. In particular, young children may not want to say "mean words" they've heard, even as part of a learning activity. Another consideration for differentiation might involve planning for children in the class who are unable to speak, hear, or walk. What modifications can a teacher make to allow them to participate in the activity? Teachers also can provide differentiation by permitting students to choose one of several performance tasks to work on alone or with a partner. For example, students might choose from creating a four-panel cartoon about using kind words, demonstrating a tableau "stop action" performance to demonstrate different responses to an unkind remark, or keeping a tally of the ratio of kind to hurtful words and actions they hear and observe at school over a period of three days.

2. Assessment Evidence

Assessment should have the same characteristics as instruction—it should be meaningful and significant for students and their families. Educators call this kind of assessment "authentic," which is another way of saying something is valued in the world outside the school.[33] Assessment should be planned concurrently with instruction, rather than as an afterthought (when a grade is needed). Educators can think beyond pencil-and-paper testing for assessment. Teacher's Toolbox 3.10 provides an extensive list of strategies that allow students to demonstrate their knowledge and skills.

Performance Task: What will students do to demonstrate learning?

A performance task describes what students will do to show learning and meeting standards. As indicated in Teacher's Toolbox 3.10, tasks might include creating a brochure, designing a questionnaire, conducting an interview, composing a song, illustrating a cartoon, drawing a Venn diagram, acting in a play, or participating in a service learning project. Educators should think of the word *do* in relation to designing performance tasks. What will students do to demonstrate their learning that others can read, see, hear, and feel? The key is to ensure that performance tasks fit well with the standards and performance indicators students will use to demonstrate. Students enjoy getting involved in designing and demonstrating their knowledge and skills in engaging performance tasks.

Criteria: How good is good enough? (Show checklists, rubrics, or other criteria.)

Students also enjoy collaborating to determine the qualities of a good performance. The question teachers and students want to answer in terms of criteria is, "How good is good enough?" To illustrate, there are many ways to create a brochure, which students might use for the advanced kind of communication required for advocacy (NHES 8). Criteria for creating a good brochure as a performance task might require students to provide information from at least three valid sources, ensure that all their information is correct, make two or more connections between behaviors and health, and show evidence of targeting their message to a particular audience (classmates). Educators should note that criteria relating to technical matters such as layout, grammar, spelling, and use of computer graphics are not health related. If such procedural criteria are part of the overall assessment, they should be identified clearly and scored separately from the health criteria.

Other Evidence: Self-reflections, quizzes, tests, observations, journals, homework

In addition to a performance task that is the culminating or *summative* assessment of a student's work, teachers often collect other evidence about a student's progress. Teachers might use quizzes, observations of how students work together, journals, homework, or self-reflections as additional evidence of learning. These in-progress checks on learning are called *formative* assessments. Teachers can learn more about formative assessment in the excellent resource, *Checking for Understanding: Formative Assessment Techniques for Your Classroom,* by Douglas Fisher and Nancy Frey.[34] Fisher and Frey explore formative assessment through oral language, questions, writing, projects and performances, tests, and common assessments and consensus scoring.

3. Active Learning Plan

New and even experienced teachers sometimes find it tempting to plan by choosing activities. Educators often see engaging hands-on teaching ideas at workshops and

Assessment Strategies for Health Education Concepts and Skills

Students can complete many kinds of individual and group projects to demonstrate their understanding of the concepts and skills in the National Health Education Standards.

Written	Oral	Visual	Kinesthetic
Advertisement	Audiotape	Advertisement	Community outreach
Biography	Debate	Banner	Dance
Book report	Discussion	Campaign flyer	Dramatization
Book review	Dramatization	Cartoon	Field trip
Brochure	Haiku	Chart	Letter writing
Campaign speech	Interview	Collage	Oral interviews
Crossword puzzle	Newscast	Collection	Pantomime
Editorial	Oral presentation	Computer graphic	Play
Electronic portfolio	Oral report	Construction	Role play
Essay	Poetry reading	Data display	Scavenger hunt
Experiment record	Rap	Design	Service learning
Game	Role play	Diagram	Simulations
Journal	Skit	Diorama/shoebox	Skit
Lab report	Song	Display	
Letter	Speech	Drawing	
Log	Teaching a lesson	Graph	
Magazine article		Map	
Memo		Mobile	
Newspaper article		Model	
Paper portfolio		Painting	
Poem		Photograph	
Position paper		Poster	
Proposal		Scrapbook	
Questionnaire		Sculpture	
Research report		Slide show	
Script		Storyboard	
Story		Venn diagram	
Test		Videotape	
Yearbook			

Adapted with permission from the Rocky Mountain Center for Health Promotion and Education (RMC), Lakewood, CO (www.rmc.org).

understandably are eager to try them with their students. In keeping with the recommendations of Wiggins and McTighe, however, the authors of this text recommend that educators start with desired results and assessment evidence and then identify the active teaching strategies that will best help students learn and demonstrate learning.

There are many ways to structure learning plans. Teacher candidates should seek out the format used in their teacher education program. New teachers can talk with experienced teachers and the curriculum directors in their school or district to learn whether there is a preferred planning style.

A learning plan should begin with an introduction that grabs students' interest. Some educators refer to this "hook" as the anticipatory set. For example, to start a lesson on interpersonal communication skills, a teacher

might arrange for someone to call on the classroom phone or a cell phone, at the beginning of the lesson. The teacher could use words, tone, and facial expressions to heighten the students' interest in the call. In other words, teachers can do much more than simply state, "Today, boys and girls, we are going to learn about communication."

Interesting introductions are followed by a logical sequence of learning activities that flow one to another. In the learning plan featured in Teacher's Toolbox 3.9, the authors suggest thinking first in terms of what *students* will do, with notes alongside that provide important reminders for teachers. This procedure gets the focus where it should be—on the students and what they are doing to learn. In learning plans of this type, teachers might write, "Students will participate in the "Lilo and Stitch" learning strategy about pressure situations (see Chapter 5) and then brainstorm about different ways that they saw classmates use their words, voices, facial expressions, and body movements to communicate effectively. This approach moves from the teacher's role as, "I will explain, I will model, I will demonstrate," to one of questioner and guide, as students explore a real-time situation in which they just participated. In any learning plan, teachers must play the role of keeping the classroom environment safe and positive.

Good learning plans end with a closing that helps students think back on what they've learned. A new teacher recalled a surprising result to illustrate the importance of helping children pull together the pieces of the lesson. Her second-graders had participated in a parachute lesson for physical education, during which the children spontaneously chanted, "Shake, shake, shake!" They were flapping the parachute to send lightweight plastic balls high in the air and catch them, send them through the hole in the center of the chute, or bounce certain balls off the chute while keeping others aloft by adjusting their shakes all together. The teacher, confident that the children had understood the importance of teamwork, asked one little boy what they had done and learned that day. To her chagrin and amusement, the student shrugged, scratched his head, and responded, "I don't know—shake your booty, I guess." What is clear to the lesson designer is not always clear to students. Thus, a closing time to reflect together is important.

A plan should include sufficient detail for another teacher to follow it. Notes on materials to have ready, the approximate time needed, and resources used for the lesson are helpful. The Strategies for Learning and Assessment in each content chapter can be used to build standards-based learning plans.

4. Reflection

Educators today talk a great deal about reflection. Charlotte Danielson and Thomas McGreal claim that few activities are more powerful for professional learning than reflection on classroom practice.[35] Teachers may learn more from thinking, writing, and talking about their classroom experiences than from the experiences themselves. Educators find that taking the time to pause and systematically consider their work improves their teaching. To assist in a structured approach to reflection, the authors of this text pose three questions for consideration at the conclusion of health education lessons:

1. What happened during my lessons (what did the students and I say and do)? How effective was my lesson design and teaching?
2. What evidence can I show that my students learned about health (student work or other response)? How effective was my assessment plan for getting information about what they learned?
3. How did I do in meeting my desired results for these health lessons? What are my next steps to improve student learning for health?

Retelling the story of the lesson and what occurred helps teachers examine it for themselves and explain it to readers or listeners. Often the events are highly entertaining in the retelling, even if they didn't seem so at the time. A student teacher taught a well-planned lesson on dengue fever to her first-grade students, as requested by her mentor teacher. Dengue fever, spread by mosquitoes, was a concern in the community at the time. The student teacher finished reading a picture book about mosquitoes and was well into the lively discussion portion of her lesson when one of the children, who had been especially quiet that period, vomited on the carpet. The student teacher immediately had a number of challenges on her hands—contacting the custodian and the health aide, comforting the sick child, and keeping the other children from touching his clothes or the carpet in their desire to help. One of the children suddenly made a connection to the lesson and cried, "Russell threw up. He must have dengue fever! Oh, nooooo!" Needless to say, a great deal of excitement ensued. In retelling the story, the student teacher understandably described it as "the worst hour of my life!" In this case, the student teacher was prepared for her lesson and handled the emergency well. In answer to what her students learned, she certainly could say that they knew the symptoms of dengue fever and made a connection right before her eyes. They also learned, after calming down, that Russell simply didn't feel well and might have eaten something that upset his stomach, that not all vomiting indicates dengue fever. The student teacher learned that even the most brilliant educators can't anticipate every eventuality and that a cool, calm approach is valuable in a classroom filled with anxious first graders.

Including Learners with Diverse Backgrounds, Interests, and Abilities

Students differ in many ways—sex, gender role, culture, religion, race, ethnicity, age, national origin, ancestry, ability, learning needs, talents, interests, language, sexual orientation, socioeconomic status, home community, aspirations, desires, temperament, and physical characteristics, to name a few. Making the classroom a place where all students feel safe and welcome is one of the most important and challenging aspects of promoting child and adolescent health. Chapters 4 and 5 provide a variety of ideas for building classroom community for everyone. An excellent resource for learning to bring students together is Jeanne Gibb's book *Tribes: A New Way of Learning and Being Together.*[36] *Tribes* describes an ongoing process—more than a series of activities—that K–8 teachers can use to engage all students in the life of the classroom.

In addition to helping all students feel safe and welcome, educators must do their utmost to help all students learn. Educators can make careful observations about how different students learn best and incorporate a variety of engaging approaches to learning into their lessons. Sometimes the modifications that are needed are clear. Students with a visual impairment might need large-print pages to assist

Classrooms are diverse places. Making all students feel welcome and included sets the stage for successful learning.

them in reading for a research assignment. Other students might benefit from having a reading assignment recorded on tape by a classmate so they can listen as they read the printed pages.

Special education professor Rhonda Black provides the following suggestions, which she calls "just good teaching," for making instruction more effective for students with cognitive disabilities:

1. *Use visual aids.* Use realistic photos and simple diagrams. Complicated abstract charts can be confusing.
2. *Repeat key information.* Ask students for feedback to check their understanding. Reinforce important concepts and provide small amounts of information spaced out over time.
3. *Provide opportunities to practice interpersonal skills.* Behavioral rehearsals are an excellent technique to help young people prepare for situations they are likely to encounter.
4. *Use many approaches.* Use a variety of teaching methods—verbal discussions, movement, signs, colors, the senses.
5. *Use humor when appropriate.* Life is sometimes comical. Having a sense of humor (and teaching students to find their own sense of humor) is a valuable teaching asset.
6. *Encourage questions.* Set aside time for questions. Say to students, "I don't know the answer. How can we find out together?"
7. *Keep it simple.* Present ideas and their practical applications in logical ways.
8. *Be concrete.* Abstract reasoning is often difficult for students with cognitive disabilities. Don't use abstract metaphors and analogies (learning about the birds and the bees) or phrases that can be misunderstood (*cat got your tongue, in over my head*).

9. *Find out the words and terms that students know, and use those to make new connections.* A word like *cardio-respiratory* might be totally unknown to students, but they might be familiar with the idea of "aerobics."
10. *Check how the communication is going.* Teachers might be saying one thing and their students hearing something completely different. If a teacher says "vagina" and the students hear "China," confusion is inevitable.[37]

As educators get to know their students, they learn about the different cultures, beliefs, and circumstances that are part of students' home communities. Remaining open to listening, learning, and responding with genuineness and empathy is of paramount importance in drawing students together as a learning family.

Linking Health Education with Other Curriculum Areas

Planning for the elementary and middle grades provides many opportunities to link health education with other curriculum areas. Units of study related to a particular theme, such as a middle-level unit on "Staying Healthy in a Rapidly Changing World," could easily incorporate investigations related to social studies and geography, mathematics, science, physical activity, and health, while resulting student presentations could build on performing arts, language arts, and technology. These types of units take careful planning and collaboration among teachers in various subject areas.

Linking health education to other curriculum areas also can be done at a simpler level. Many children's books tell stories that deal with managing strong feelings, making a natural connection between health education and language arts. Teacher's Toolbox 3.11 provides examples of standards-based curriculum links between health education and other subject areas in the K–8 curriculum.

ASSESSING STUDENT WORK

As adults remember their own school experiences, they often equate paper-and-pencil testing with the term *assessment*. In speaking of today's focus on performance assessment, Wiggins and McTighe state,

> Beginning with a quest for alternatives to prevailing modes of assessment, the performance movement has put performance itself at stage center. It no longer makes sense, if it ever did, to call test scores "performance." Performance is doing something that is valued in the world outside schools. . . . for our evaluations to be valid, we must assess performance.[38]

Sample Standards-Based Learning Opportunities That Link Health Education to Other Subjects in the K–8 Curriculum

Learning Opportunity	Subject Area	Health Education
Write and perform an original song or theater production that tells the story of resolving a difficult decision.	Fine arts • Music	• Analyze influences • Decision making
Sponsor a showing of class drawings, paintings, and sculptures to promote various aspects of health.	• Theater • Visual arts	• Self-management • Interpersonal communication • Advocacy
Read child and adolescent literature to initiate discussions about mental, emotional, social, and physical health concepts and how they influence health behaviors.	Language arts • Reading	• Core concepts • Analyze influences
Write about personal decision-making and goal-setting processes in the practice of health-enhancing behaviors.	• Writing	• Decision making • Goal setting • Self-management
Measure and record personal changes in physical growth over time.	Mathematics • Measurement	• Core concepts
Access and analyze public health statistics to establish the incidence and prevalence of various types of injuries and estimate the probability of injury related to specific risk behaviors.	• Data analysis and probability	• Access information
Describe ways students can promote a physically active lifestyle for themselves and their families.	Physical education • Exhibiting a physically active lifestyle	• Self-management • Advocacy
Design a plan for a physical activity facility that includes access for and conveys welcome and respect for all participants.	• Demonstrating understanding and respect for differences among people in physical activity settings	• Access information • Interpersonal communication • Advocacy
Investigate the influence of various substances on the function of the body systems and use this information to advocate for a tobacco-, alcohol-, and other drug–free lifestyle.	Science • Life science	• Core concepts • Advocacy
Determine how research in earth and space science can contribute to improved health, quality of life, and longevity.	• Earth and space science	• Core concepts • Access information
Contrast the approaches that various cultures take in public health messages about preventing HIV infection.	Social studies • Culture	• Core concepts • Advocacy
Determine the extent to which public health practices in one part of the world can affect health status in other parts of the world.	• Global connections	• Access information • Analyze influences
Access health-related information through the Internet and design a web page to communicate recommendations for personal health.	Technology • Access and exchange information in a variety of ways	• Access information • Self-management • Advocacy
Design a questionnaire on the STD knowledge of classmates, teachers, and parents. Organize and present data with a computer presentation application (PowerPoint).	• Compile, organize, analyze, and synthesize information	• Access information • Analyze influences

Although well-designed tests have a place in the world of assessment, the authors of this text encourage educators to consider a much broader array of assessment strategies that allow students to demonstrate what they know, understand, and can do. Teacher's Toolbox 3.12 provides a framework of assessment approaches and methods, indicating those that are performance-based. See Teacher's Toolbox 3.10 for a more detailed list of written, oral, visual, and kinesthetic strategies that educators can consider for assessing student work in health education.

Framework of Assessment Approaches and Methods

Selected Response Items		**Performance-Based Assessment**		
	Constructed Responses	Products	Performances	Process-Focused Responses
Multiple-choice	Fill-in-the-blank (words,	Essay	Oral presentation	Oral questioning
True-false	phrases)	Research paper	Dance or movement	Observation (kid
Matching	Short answer	Log/journal	Science lab	watching)
	(sentences,	Lab report	demonstration	Interview
	paragraphs)	Story/play	Athletic skills	Conference
	Label a diagram	Poem	performance	Process description
	Show your work	Portfolio	Dramatic reading	Think aloud
	Representations (web,	Art exhibit	Enactment	Learning log
	concept map, flow-	Science project	Debate	
	chart, graph, table,	Model	Musical recital	
	matrix, illustration)	Video or audiotape	Keyboarding	
		Spreadsheet		

Used with permission from the Rocky Mountain Center for Health Promotion and Education (RMC), Lakewood, CO (www.rmc.org).

	Health-Enhancing Position	**Support for Position**	**Audience Awareness**	**Conviction**
4 Exceeds standards	• Extremely clear, health-enhancing position	• Thoroughly supports position using relevant and accurate facts, data, and evidence	• Strong awareness of the target audience (e.g., the audience's perspective, interests, prior knowledge)	• Displays strong and passionate conviction for position
3 Meets standards	• Generally clear, health-enhancing position	• Adequately supports position using facts, data, evidence; support may be incomplete and/or contain minor inaccuracies	• Adequate awareness of audience	• Displays conviction for position
2 Does not meet standards	• Unclear or conflicting positions	• Inadequately supports position due to limited information and/or some inaccuracy, irrelevant facts, data, or evidence	• Some evidence of awareness of audience	• Displays minimal conviction for position
1 Does not meet standards	• No position stated OR position is not health-enhancing	• No accurate or relevant support for position provided	• No evidence of awareness of audience	• Conviction for position not evident

FIGURE 3–1 | Analytic Rubric for National Health Education Standard 8, Advocacy Students will demonstrate the ability to advocate for personal, family, and community health.

Adapted from and used with permission from the Rocky Mountain Center for Health Promotion and Education (RMC), Lakewood, CO (www.rmc.org).

Engaging Students in Assessment

One of the most important aspects of authentic assessment—that is, assessing what matters beyond the school grounds—is inviting students to participate in decisions about what is of value and how it can be fairly assessed. Although the health education standards provide specific criteria for meeting standards, students can add their own ideas to build ownership and investment into their work.

To illustrate, meeting the health education standard of advocacy (NHES 8) involves stating a health-enhancing position, providing support for the position, demonstrating audience awareness, and showing strong conviction (Figure 3-1). To get students' input, teachers can pose these questions: "What do you think would make a great advocacy presentation? What do you want to see, hear, and do during your classmates' presentations?" The students might decide that they want presenters to choose topics that kids care about, involve them in active participation rather than having them just sit and listen, and explain topics with colorful posters in everyday language. When students plan with these ideas in mind, they find themselves better able to meet the NHES 8 criterion of demonstrating audience awareness and can target their presentation with greater precision.

The authors of this text encourage educators to involve their students in assessment by making sure students understand and have a say in what is required of them from the very beginning of a new unit of study. Most educators remember situations as students when they felt they needed to "guess" what the instructor wanted in terms of a research paper or test material. Involving students early in the assessment process leads to higher-quality work and minimizes misunderstandings.

Developing and Using Rubrics

Rubric is a term that educators hear often in relation to assessment. A rubric is simply a framework for evaluating student work. Appendix B includes scoring rubrics developed by the Rocky Mountain Center for Health Promotion and Education (RMC) for each National Health Education Standard. RMC developed its analytic rubrics in collaboration with respected education author Jay McTighe.[39]

Teachers and students can practice the idea of using a rubric by scoring a familiar activity. For instance, what might individuals consider when judging their last movie experience? If someone simply says that the experience was "great," "okay," or "a bummer," listeners don't know why. To paint a more comprehensive picture of their experience, moviegoers could design a rubric to allow a more informative assessment. Patrons could evaluate the quality of the story (*truly engaging, somewhat interesting, boring*), the acting (*totally believable, somewhat convincing, not into it*), the picture (*sharp and clear, mostly in focus, blurry or jumpy*), and the sound (*just right for my ears, sometimes a bit too loud or soft, annoyingly loud or soft*). In addition, the temperature of the theater (*very comfortable, mostly comfortable, too hot or too cold*) and the price of refreshments (*very reasonable, mostly affordable, a rip-off*) could be considered in students' overall assessment of movie enjoyment.

The RMC rubrics show four possible scores for student work. As teachers and students look at the advocacy rubric (see Figure 3–1), they will note scores of 3 and 4 meet and exceed standards, respectively, and that scores of 1 and 2 do not meet standards. This initial distinction is important in addressing the assessment question "How good is good enough?" The RMC rubrics clearly describe those performances that are acceptable (meet standards) and those that go beyond basic requirements (exceed standards) or do not measure up to requirements (does not meet stan-

dards). When teachers and students develop rubrics, they should designate clear distinctions related to the categories and descriptors they use. The first and most important distinction is that between work that meets standards and work that does not. Figure 3–2 provides an example of a rubric stated in kid terms, with descriptors in language selected by students.

Rubistar (www.rubistar.4teachers.org) is a web-based tool to help teachers create quality rubrics for project-based teaching activities. Registration is free. Registered users can access their rubrics at any time, and save and edit them online. Rubistar contains templates for oral projects, multimedia, math, writing, products, reading, art, work skills, science, and music. Teachers can enter health-related keywords (health, nutrition, mental health, bully prevention) to search Rubistar by rubric titles, author's name, or author's email address. Teachers can explore a tremendous variety of health-related rubrics that already are posted online.

The content chapters provide a wide variety of learning strategies for standards-based health education. Each learning strategy is followed by simple suggestions for assessment. When learning strategies and assessment are planned together, teachers increase opportunities for both instructional improvement and student achievement.

Designing Performance Tasks

RMC conceptualizes assessment as a shift in thinking, from "teach and test" to the alignment and congruence of standards (concepts and skills), assessment, and instruction. Educators at RMC assert that classroom assessment should (1) promote learning, (2) incorporate multiple sources of information, and (3) provide fair, valid, and reliable information.[40] Similarly, the National Council of Teachers of Mathematics (NCTM) states, "Assessment should not merely be done *to* students; rather, it should also be done *for* students, to guide and enhance their learning."[41]

How can teachers design standards-based performance tasks that are linked to instruction? RMC provides a performance assessment template that includes three steps:

1. Select National Health Education Standards (or local standards) and content areas.
2. Construct a "prompt" or item for student response.
3. Determine criteria for success in terms of concepts (NHES 1) and skills (NHES 2–8).

Teacher's Toolbox 3.13 provides an example of a teacher-created performance task for upper-elementary and middle-level students based on NHES 4 and 8, interpersonal communication and advocacy, and the content area promoting a tobacco-free lifestyle. Educators should note that the performance task emphasizes skills demonstration as well as conceptual knowledge.

Portfolio assessment is a type of performance task that is widely used in elementary and middle school classrooms. When students design portfolios, they select their best and

Score	Standard: Advocacy	Self-Assessment
4	• I stated my position very clearly—I know where I stand. • I backed up what I said with accurate information. • I really targeted my audience—I understand them well. • I was very strong in my statements—I showed conviction. **Bull's Eye! Hits the Standards Target**	
3	• I stated my position clearly, but I still have a few questions about it. • I backed up what I said with information—I'm sure of most of it. • I targeted my audience fairly well—I understood them for the most part. • I was fairly strong in my statements—I showed some conviction. **Meets Standards**	
2	• I wasn't exactly sure about my position or where I stand. • I couldn't really back up my position—I needed more information. • I sort of knew my audience—I may have missed what they really are like. • I made statements, but I really didn't feel that strongly about what I said. **Does Not Yet Meet Standards**	
1	• I didn't know what to say or think. • I didn't research my topic. • I didn't know my audience—I didn't think about them before now. • Either way is okay with me—I don't have a real opinion. **Does Not Meet Standards**	

FIGURE 3–2 | **Student Rubric for National Health Education Standard 8, Advocacy**
Adapted with permission from the Hawaii Department of Education.

most representative work to illustrate how they meet standards. For example, a portfolio related to the health education standards might require middle school students to select two samples of their work for each standard studied during their semester-long health education course. A further requirement might specify that at least four different content areas should be addressed in the student work samples. Students might present their portfolios during designated class times or during special parent nights at their schools.

Portfolios can be completed with file folders, notebooks, display boards, or other physical organizers. Students increasingly are learning to compile electronic portfolios, scanning their work directly into computer files for assessment and presentation. Electronic portfolios (e-portfolios) are easily transported on disks or other small drives and can be e-mailed to teachers for assessment and feedback.

Providing Feedback to Promote Learning and Skill Development

Using teacher- and student-created rubrics provides far more information for students on their progress than do simple letter grades (B+) or general written phrases such as "Well done!" When a student receives feedback that indicates she has done a thorough job of stating an extremely clear health-enhancing position and displaying strong and passionate conviction for the position but has not yet demonstrated a strong awareness of the target audience, she knows exactly where to fine-tune her upcoming advocacy presentation. Teachers can give meaningful feedback by communicating to students on the rubrics—circling the level of performance within a particular category, writing comments and suggestions at the bottom of the rubric, and attaching it to student work. Many educators find this way of providing feedback to be thorough and time-saving.

In addition to providing feedback through rubrics, teachers should think about the way they interact with students as they observe them at work. Though praising children with generic phrases such as "Good job!" and "Great!" often is sincere and well intended, students might benefit more from a more genuine and informative conversation about their work. For example, a teacher who is circulating around the classroom as children draw pictures to illustrate their self-management strategies for dealing with strong feelings might say, "Tell me more about your picture and what you are thinking—I see you are using lots of bright colors." This comment invites students to express their thought processes and intentions.

Another consideration in measuring students' progress is looking at the quality of their work over time. An undergraduate chemistry major earned a score of only 9 percent out of a possible 100 percent on her first advanced calculus test. With hard work and group study sessions, her grades were in the range of 90 to 95 percent by the end of the semester. In traditional grading—averaging—this student likely would fail the course, but an examination of the student's scores throughout the semester could lead to a different assessment.

Communicating About the New Smoke-Free City Ordinance in Our Hometown
Upper Elementary and Middle School

Step 1: Identify standards and content areas
Standards: Interpersonal Communication (NHES 4) and Advocacy (NHES 8)
Content Area: Promoting a Tobacco-Free Lifestyle

Step 2: Construct the prompt
Instructions to Students:

Setting and role: You are a restaurant owner in Our Hometown. The city has a new ordinance that bans smoking in all restaurants. Your customers may or may not know about the new rule, and they may or may not agree with it. Your may employees are concerned about explaining the new rule to customers.

Challenge: Your challenge is to model, for your employees, communication with customers who ask about, complain about, or break the rules. You need to model positive communication that provides a clear and respectful message to customers in a way that helps you maintain positive relationships with them (so they will stay and eat in your restaurant!). You also need to help customers understand why the new rule is healthy for employees and other customers. Remember that some customers merely will be asking about the rule, but others may be unhappy or angry about it.

Products and performance: Write a script for a scenario in your restaurant that happens on the Friday night that the rules go into effect. During the scenario, you will have to deal with three different customers who (1) ask about the rules, (2) complain about the rules, and (3) light up. You must inform your customers about the new rule, modeling positive communication for your employees, and convince your customers that the new no-smoking rule is a good change and that they should stay and eat in your restaurant.

Scoring: Your work will be scored on two standards: Interpersonal Communication and Advocacy.

Step 3: Determine criteria for success and share with students

Interpersonal Communication	Advocacy
• Demonstrate appropriate verbal and nonverbal communication strategies. • Demonstrate appropriate communication skills. • Demonstrate appropriate communication behaviors.	• State a clear position. • Support the position with information. • Target the message to your customers. • Show strong conviction for your position.

Adapted with permission from the Hawaii Department of Education (content) and the Rocky Mountain Center for Health Promotion and Education (format).

Many educators say that they love teaching and dislike assigning grades. Assessing student performance and providing feedback is important for learning, however. Applying the assessment strategies in this text and other resources and participating in professional development can place assessment in a new and inviting light for educators, students, and families alike.

The learning and assessment strategies presented here provide building blocks for standards-based lessons and units that can be tailored to local needs. Assessment criteria are used with permission from the Rocky Mountain Center for Health Promotion and Education (RMC). See Appendix B for Scoring Rubrics.

STRATEGIES FOR LEARNING AND ASSESSMENT

This section provides an example of a standards-based learning and assessment strategy for each NHES standard. The examples in this chapter can be applied to any content area. Chapters 5–14 include content-specific learning and assessment strategies organized by standard and grade cluster (K–2, 3–5, and 6–8). Each set of strategies begins with a restatement of the standard and a reminder of the assessment criteria, drawn from the RMC rubrics in Appendix B. Strategies are written as directions for teachers and include applicable theory of planned behavior (TPB) constructs—intention to act in healthy ways, attitudes toward behavior, subjective norms, perceived behavioral control—in parentheses.

NHES 1 | Core Concepts

Students will comprehend concepts related to health promotion and disease prevention to enhance health.

ASSESSMENT CRITERIA

- Connections—Describe relationships between behavior and health; draw logical conclusions about connections between behavior and health.
- Comprehensiveness—Thoroughly cover health topic, showing breadth and depth; give accurate information.

Know-Wonder-Learn (KWL) Chart A KWL chart can be used with any curriculum topic. Using newsprint or a chalkboard, draw three columns labeled *Know*, *Wonder*, and *Learn*. For the given topic (e.g., bullying), have students list all the facts that they know or think they know. Record all information offered by students in the *Know* column—verification comes later. Some teachers write students' names next to the information they volunteer as a record of the class discussion. When the *Know* column is completed, go on to the *Wonder* column. What do the students wonder and want to know about this topic? Record all questions, along with students' names.

To integrate this activity with NHES 3 (access information, products, and services) decide with the students how class members will verify their facts (*Know* column) and answer their questions (*Wonder* column). Who will be responsible for finding out about each fact or question? Learning the skill of accessing information can mean making trips to the library, inviting guest speakers to address the class, interviewing parents or community members, e-mailing an expert, reading resource books in the classroom, and using the Internet to investigate websites.

When the work is done, have students complete the *Learn* column to answer the question "What did we learn?" Help students focus on the core concepts they need to know to stay safe and healthy.

ASSESSMENT | Completing the KWL chart is an assessment task in itself as well as a record of what the class investigated and learned. Students also can write and draw in journals about what they learned. Criteria for assessing the KWL chart or journals include ensuring that all final information is accurate and that students can provide the breadth and depth of information appropriate for their grade level. In addition, students should be able to describe one or more relationships and make one or more connections between behaviors and health. (Construct: Attitudes toward behavior.)

NHES 2 | Analyze Influences

Students will analyze the influence of family, peers, culture, media, technology, and other factors on health behaviors.

ASSESSMENT CRITERIA

- Identify both external and internal influences on health.
- Explain how external and internal influences interact to impact health choices and behaviors.
- Explain both positive and negative influences, as appropriate.

External Influences: Family Health Practices Ask students to think about and list all the things their families do to stay healthy. The teacher or students can display the list on newsprint or a chalkboard. The class list might include eating healthy meals and snacks, drinking skim milk, exercising regularly, playing games or other activities together, practicing personal health care, and getting to bed early. Have children make a list of their family health practices to take home and share with their families. Ask students to discuss how their family's choices (choice of cereal or toothpaste) affect their preferences. Have students ask themselves, "How does my family influence my choices and my health?"

ASSESSMENT | As an assessment task, have students create posters depicting their family health practices. Have them take their poster home to share with their families. As assessment criteria, have students describe a minimum of three healthy family habits and explain how the family habits influence their own health actions. (Construct: Subjective norms.)

NHES 3 | Access Information, Products, and Services

Students will demonstrate the ability to access valid information and products and services to enhance health.

ASSESSMENT CRITERIA

- Access health information—Locate specific sources of health information, products, or services relevant to enhancing health in a given situation.
- Evaluate information sources—Explain the degree to which identified sources are vaild, reliable, and appropriate as a result of evaluating each source.

Phone Book Scavenger Hunt Have students work in small groups to complete a scavenger hunt using the telephone directory. Ask colleagues and friends to save their old directories for your classroom. Make a scavenger hunt worksheet with questions that require students to find the agency or person who can help in a specific situation. For example, what agency would you call if you wanted to help a friend who has begun using alcohol? Whom would you call if you suspected a classmate is developing an eating disorder? Whom would you call if you think a neighborhood swimming pool is inadequately fenced? Whom would you call if you think your water supply is contaminated? Whom would you call if your dad has lower-back pain? Students likely will think of other resources they want to find. After students complete the scavenger hunt, have the groups compare their answers with those of other groups and debrief them on the appropriateness of their answers.

ASSESSMENT | Completing the scavenger hunt worksheet is the assessment task. Assessment criteria include having students identify one or more appropriate resources for all of the questions after the class discussion. Students might also identify counterexamples, or inappropriate resources, for various questions. For example, a massage parlor might not be the best solution for Dad's lower-back pain! (Construct: Perceived behavioral control.)

NHES 4 | Interpersonal Communication

Students will demonstrate the ability to use interpersonal communication skills to enhance health and avoid or reduce health risks.

ASSESSMENT CRITERIA

- Use appropriate verbal/nonverbal communication strategies in an effective manner to enhance health or avoid/reduce health risks.
- Use appropriate skills (negotiation skills, refusal skills) and behaviors (eye contact, body language, attentive listening).

Tableau: Pressure Points   Have students work in small groups to discuss the times others have pressured them to participate in an uncomfortable or unwanted behavior. The situations do not have to be health-related—students need peer resistance skills in a wide variety of situations. Ask students to share how they felt and how they responded. Ask students if they knew what to say or what to do. Ask what they wanted to say and do and whether they were able to do it. After gathering students' ideas, share the list of peer pressure resistance techniques from this chapter (see Teacher's Toolbox 3.4).

ASSESSMENT | For an assessment task, have students work in small groups to plan and perform a short scenario that demonstrates a realistic pressure situation. At the point where students need to use peer resistance skills, have the actors freeze in place to form a still picture or *tableau* (a new vocabulary word for most students). Ask class members to advise the actors on what to say or do to resist pressure in healthy ways. Have class members recommend a health-enhancing way to end the story, and have the actors act it out. For assessment criteria, agree with students that they will demonstrate at least two verbal and one nonverbal peer pressure resistance strategies to deal with the tableau situation in healthy ways. (Constructs: Perceived behavioral control, subjective norms.)

NHES 5 | Decision Making

Students will demonstrate the ability to use decision-making skills to enhance health.

ASSESSMENT CRITERIA

Reach a health-enhancing decision using a process consisting of the following steps:

- Identify a health-risk situation.
- Examine alternatives.
- Evaluate positive and negative consequences.
- Decide on a health-enhancing course of action.

The Courageous Thing to Do: Decision Making Through Literature Circles and Decision Trees   Students read many books that involve challenges and decision making. Reading and discussing picture and chapter books provide important opportunities to talk about acting with courage or doing the courageous thing in the face of opposing influences. Have students read (or read aloud to younger students) only up to a certain point at which a decision must be made. Identify the stopping point in advance. Next, students can work in small groups or literature circles to talk about the book and apply the steps in the decision-making model (see Teacher's Toolbox 3.5) by making a decision tree. Students can draw a tree trunk labeled with the decision the book characters need to make, large branches growing out from the trunk to show alternatives, and smaller branches stemming from the large branches to show positive and negative consequences of each alternative. Be sure students identify at least three alternatives. Students tend to see choices as either-or, but additional choices often come to mind when they think harder. Ask students to show their decision trees to the class and to identify the choices they think are the best ones and those that require the most

courage or bravery. Ask students why the healthy choices often take courage to carry out, and ask how they can gather courage for what they need to do. What kind of help do they need? From whom? What do they think their family and friends would want them to do? Can their family and friends help them do it or be ready to do it? After the discussion, read or have students read the remainder of the story and compare their decisions with those of the book characters.

ASSESSMENT | The assessment tasks are the decision trees that students develop and their accompanying explanations for courageous decision making. For assessment criteria, check to see that students have stated the decision to be made, at least three alternatives, positive and negative consequences of each alternative, the action they think is most courageous and healthy, and the reason they believe it is best. Have students compare their decisions to those of the book characters. (Construct: Perceived behavioral control.)

NHES 6 | Goal Setting

Students will demonstrate the ability to use goal-setting skills to enhance health.

ASSESSMENT CRITERIA

- Goal statement—Give goal statement that identifies health benefits; goal is achievable and will result in enhanced health.
- Goal setting plan—Show plan that is complete, logical and sequential, and includes a process to assess progress.

The Little Engine That Could: **A Closer Look at Goal Setting**   Watty Piper's book *The Little Engine That Could* provides students with an opportunity to examine the steps involved in goal setting through a familiar story. Teachers can ask students to listen for evidence of the important goal-setting steps as the story is read: (1) a clear, achievable goal; (2) a plan that includes logical, sequential steps; (3) ways to build support and deal with obstacles; and (4) a process to assess progress. The goal is clear—the little train needs to deliver cars of wonderful things to boys and girls on the other side of the mountain. What was the little train's plan? What obstacles did she encounter, and how did she deal with them? Whose support did she need? What can students learn about providing support for themselves and others? How did the Little Blue Engine know she was making progress and reaching her goal? What is the most important lesson about reaching a goal in this story? Teachers can ask students to talk together to identify a goal they would like to reach as a class and to make a plan that includes the basic goal-setting steps. Examples include a "no-name-calling" week, a "saying please and thank you" week, or a "healthy snacks only" week.

ASSESSMENT | The assessment task is the class goal the students set. For assessment criteria, students should identify an achievable class goal, the steps to achieve it, plans to build support and deal with obstacles, and a process to assess class progress. (Construct: Perceived behavioral control.)

NHES 7 | Self-Management

Students will demonstrate the ability to practice health-enhancing behaviors and avoid or reduce risks.

ASSESSMENT CRITERIA

- Application (transfer)—Initiate health-enhancing behaviors; apply concepts and skills appropriate and effectively.
- Self-monitoring and reflection—Monitor actions and make adjustments; accept feedback and make adjustments; able to self-assess, reflect on, and take responsibility for actions.

Stress Busters Adults must remember that students experience stress just as keenly as older people do. Begin this activity by having children describe situations that stress them out. Help them realize that people experience good stress (eustress), which keeps them on their toes and helps them perform better, as well as bad stress (distress), which can make people ill if it goes on for too long. Invite students to think about how people can control their responses to stress, even if they can't control the stressor, and how they might respond to stress in healthy and unhealthy ways. Following this discussion, have students make a list of their favorite stress-buster strategies. Students can create a class book by having each student contribute an illustrated page. Students might want to share their book with other classes.

ASSESSMENT | The class book or list is the assessment task. Have students develop their own criteria for "great pages" in the stress-buster book, making sure, at a minimum, that all stress busters are health-promoting. Use the criteria that the students develop to assess and help them assess their work. (Constructs: Perceived behavioral control, subjective norms.)

NHES 8 | Advocacy

Students will demonstrate the ability to advocate for personal, family, and community health.

ASSESSMENT CRITERIA

- Health-enhancing position—Give clear, health-enhancing position.
- Support for position—Support position with facts, concepts, examples, and evidence.

- Audience awareness—Show awareness of target audience; choose words, tone, and examples to suit audience.
- Conviction—Display conviction for position.

What Do Kids Really Do? Establishing Social Norms by Using Data from the Youth Risk Behavior Survey and the Global Youth Tobacco Survey Most states and many large cities conduct the Youth Risk Behavior Survey (YRBS), funded by the Centers for Disease Control and Prevention (CDC). Countries around the world conduct the Global Youth Tobacco Survey (GYTS), also funded by the CDC. Students can type YRBS or GYTS into the search line at www.cdc.gov to locate data. Have students work in small groups to explore results for various states and cities (YRBS) and counties (GYTS). Students can prepare their data for a health advocacy presentation to classmates. Alternatively, teachers can print tables from the Internet in advance for students' use. An important way to use these data is to ask students to concentrate on the number and percentage of students who practice healthy behaviors. For example, what percentage of U.S. high school students did not smoke during the past thirty days? Students can work on one topic (tobacco use) or a variety of topics (alcohol and other drug use, injury and violence, nutrition) to search for data on what "kids really do." This activity links with NHES 3 (accessing information, products, and services). Using and interpreting the YRBS and GYTS data tables make an excellent link with mathematics.

ASSESSMENT | The advocacy presentations that students make as a result of their research into YRBS and GYTS data are the assessment tasks. For assessment criteria, remind students to focus on advocacy by stating a clear, health-enhancing position; supporting the position with data; targeting the message to classmates; and showing strong conviction. (Construct: Subjective norms.)

INTERNET AND OTHER RESOURCES

Visit the Online Leaning Center (www.mhhe.com/telljohann6e) for links to these sites, quizzes and other study aids, and many additional resources.

WEBSITES

American Association for Health Education
www.aahperd.org/aahe

American School Health Association (ASHA)
www.ashaweb.org

Association for Supervision and Curriculum Development (ASCD)
www.ascd.org

BAM! (Body and Mind)—Site for Students with Teacher's Corner
www.bam.gov

Education Materials Center, Central Michigan University (Michigan Model for Health)
www.emc.cmich.edu

Federal Agencies' Lists of Programs Considered Exemplary, Promising, or Effective
www.cdc.gov/HealthyYouth/HECAT/pdf/HECAT_Append_2.pdf

Global Tobacco Surveillance System (GTSS)
www.cdc.gov/tobacco/global/index.htm

Health Teacher: Teaching Concepts and Skills
www.healthteacher.com

Healthy Youth, Division of Adolescent and School Health, CDC
www.cdc.gov/healthyyouth

Kid's Health
www.kidshealth.org

PE Central
www.pecentral.org

Rocky Mountain Center for Health Promotion and Education (RMC)
www.rmc.org

Rubistar
http://rubistar.4teachers.org/index.php

School Health Education Resources
http://apps.nccd.cdc.gov/sher

State Collaborative on Assessment and Student Standards, CCSSO
www.ccsso.org/projects/SCASS

Surgeon General's Website for Kids
www.healthfinder.gov/kids

WebQuest.org
www.webquest.org

Youth Risk Behavior Surveillance System (YRBSS), CDC
www.cdc.gov/HealthyYouth/yrbs/index.htm

OTHER RESOURCES

Fetro, J. V. *Personal and Social Skills: Levels I, II, III.* Santa Cruz, CA: ETR Associates, 2000.

D. Fisher and N. Frey, *Checking for Understanding: Formative Assessment Techniques for Your Classroom.* Alexandria, VA: Association for Supervision and Curriculum Development, 2007.

Gibbs, J. *Tribes: A New Way of Learning and Being Together.* Windsor, CA: Center Source Systems, 2001.

Joint Commission on National Health Education Standards. *National Health Education Standards.* Atlanta, GA: American Cancer Society, 1995.

C. A. Tomlinson and J. McTighe. *Integrating Differentiated Instruction + Understanding by Design.* Alexandria, VA: Association for Supervision and Curriculum Development, 2006.

Wiggins, G., and J. McTighe. *Understanding by Design.* Alexandria, VA: Association for Supervision and Curriculum Development, 1998.

ENDNOTES

1. Joint Commission on National Health Education Standards, *National Health Education Standards* (Atlanta, GA: American Cancer Society, 1995).

2. Centers for Disease Control and Prevention, *Federal Agencies' Lists of Programs Considered Exemplary, Promising, or Effective* (www.cdc.gov/HealthyYouth/HECAT/pdf/HECAT_Append_2.pdf).

3. Council of Chief State School Officers, *Assessing Health Literacy: Assessment Framework* (Soquel, CA: ToucanEd, 1998).

4. J. McTighe, "Assessing Student Learning in the Classroom: Part II," *RMC Health Educator* 1, no. 3 (2001): 1–7.

5. Centers for Disease Control and Prevention, *Health Education Curriculum Analysis Tool—HECAT* (www.cdc.gov/HealthyYouth/HECAT/index.htm).

6. Centers for Disease Control and Prevention, *YRBSS: Youth Risk Behavior Surveillance System* (www.cdc.gov/HealthyYouth/yrbs/index.htm).

7. Centers for Disease Control and Prevention, *Global Tobacco Surveillance System—GTSS* (www.cdc.gov/tobacco/global/surveys.htm).

8. J. B. Schor, *Born to Buy: The Commercialized Child and the New Consumer Culture* (New York: Scribner, 2004).

9. D. Grace, "Gender, Power and Pleasure: Integrating Student Video Production into the Elementary Literacy Curriculum," *Curriculum Perspectives* 23, no. 1 (2002): 21–27.

10. British Broadcasting Corporation, *Extreme Cosmetics* (www.bbc.co.uk/science/hottopics/extremecosmetics/index.shtml).

11. Ibid.

12. J. Fetro, *Personal and Social Skills* (Santa Cruz, CA: ETR Associates, 2000), 50.

13. Ibid., 58.

14. Ibid., 59.

15. Ibid., 57.

16. Centers for Disease Control and Prevention, *Federal Agencies' Lists of Programs Considered Exemplary, Promising, or Effective.*

17. R. E. Dahl, *Adolescent Brain Development: A Framework for Understanding Unique Vulnerabilities and Opportunities* (www.wccf.org/pdf/dahl.pdf).

18. Ibid.

19. Ibid.

20. National Institute of Mental Health, *Teenage Brain: A Work in Progress* (www.nimh.gov/publicat/teenbrain.cfm).

21. C. N. Matsuoka, conversation with author, Honolulu, HI, March 2007.

22. A. L. Costa and B. Kallick, *Discovering and Exploring Habits of the Mind* (Alexandria, VA: Association for Supervision and Curriculum Development, 2000).

23. M. Lipman, *Philosophy Goes to School* (Philadelphia: Temple University Press, 1988).

24. J. Fetro, *Personal and Social Skills.*

25. Ibid.

26. Ibid.

27. H. Bruckner and P. Bearman, "After the Promise: The STD Consequences of Adolescent Virginity Pledges," *Journal of Adolescent Health* 36, no. 4 (2005): 271–78.

28. J. D. Fortenberry, "The Limits of Abstinence-Only in Preventing Sexually Transmitted Infections, *Journal of Adolescent Health* 36, no. 4 (2005): 269–70.

29. G. Wiggins and J. McTighe, *Understanding by Design* (Alexandria, VA: Association for Supervision and Curriculum Development, 1998).

30. Ibid.

31. Ibid., 117.

32. C. A. Tomlinson and J. McTighe, *Integrating Differentiated Instruction + Understanding by Design* (Alexandria, VA: Association for Supervision and Curriculum Development, 2006).

33. G. Wiggins and J. McTighe, *Understanding by Design*, vi.

34. D. Fisher and N. Frey, *Checking for Understanding: Formative Assessment Techniques for Your Classroom* (Alexandria, VA: Association for Supervision and Curriculum Development, 2007).

35. C. Danielson and T. McGreal, *Teacher Evaluation to Enhance Professional Practice* (Alexandria, VA: Association for Supervision and Curriculum Development, 2000).

36. J. Gibbs, *Tribes: A New Way of Learning and Being Together* (Windsor, CA: Center Source Systems, 2001).

37. B. Pateman, R. S. Black, K. Serna, L. Shoji, and A. S. Murai, "Promoting Sexual Health and Responsibility: Healthy Sexuality Education for Hawaii's Youth," *Educational Perspectives* 34, no. 2 (2001): 25–30.

38. G. Wiggins and J. McTighe, *Understanding by Design*, vi.

39. J. McTighe, "Assessing Student Learning in the Classroom: Part II."

40. Ibid.

41. National Council of Teachers of Mathematics (NCTM), *Principles and Standards for School Mathematics* (Reston, VA: NCTM, 2000).

4

(Kiana, age 13)

A safe and Positive CLASSROOM

Building and Managing the Safe and Positive Learning Environment

DESIRED LEARNER OUTCOMES

After reading this chapter, you will be able to . . .

- Describe activities that contribute to a safe, engaging, and enriching classroom environment.

- Summarize a range of learning activities that enrich instruction with a direct focus on child and adolescent health issues.

- Discuss the strengths and weaknesses of interdisciplinary instructional approaches.

- Evaluate electronic resources to enhance health education practice.

- Summarize the roles of school personnel in managing potentially controversial health issues with students and their caregivers.

- Develop an action plan for engaging parents in promoting achievement and reducing health risks.

INTRODUCTION

Although the structure and time frame of the school day have remained relatively stable, the knowledge base across all content areas has grown exponentially. As a result, teachers are challenged to fit an ever-expanding body of knowledge and skill development opportunities into the school day.[1] Elementary school teachers in self-contained classrooms must manage the allocation of time resources to accommodate effective instruction in the diverse content areas of reading, mathematics, science, social studies, computer literacy, and health education and to accommodate the transition to other learning environments for music, art, and physical education.

In middle schools, it is the norm for school districts to hire content specialists to provide health instruction for students. Health teachers in middle schools are confronted with the time constraints associated with a fixed "bell" schedule signaling students to move quickly and efficiently from one class to another. Thus, middle school health teachers have well-defined time periods in which to deliver meaningful and developmentally appropriate learning experiences for students.

All teachers, including those most highly motivated to advance a health promotion agenda, are challenged by the time constraints of the school day. Mandated testing, special enrichment programs, and other events on the master schedule of the school can interrupt the continuity of instruction. Competing community priorities and the lack of teacher comfort with health issues also threaten dedicated time for quality health instruction. Learning can be disrupted for students in elementary grades by predetermined recess and lunch periods, and teachers must manage the time devoted to instruction in art, music, and physical education. Even when the health education course of study and classroom practice are developmentally appropriate, evidence based, and consistent with state and national standards (see Chapters 2 and 3), demands on instruction time exert a negative impact. It is an all too common and unfortunate practice for important learning activities or even whole units of health education to be sacrificed.

This chapter suggests practical ways to manage the challenges confronting teachers who organize health instruction. Tools to help teachers weave effective health education activities into the fabric of the school day include learning activities that can be incorporated into a range of health education content areas and cooperative learning applications for health education lesson planning.

Beyond direct approaches to health issues, this chapter examines correlated and integrated health education strategies that extend health education across the curriculum. Suggestions for managing potentially controversial health topics are offered, and the importance of parental engagement in health promotion activities is reviewed. Specific ways to engage parents in student health promotion are suggested.

Most of the recommendations included in this chapter are strategies with which teachers in the elementary and middle grades are familiar. Importantly, however, the tools in this chapter are applied specifically to Comprehensive School Health Education. These practical recommendations are offered to help teachers who feel that, though important, health promotion activities are just one more thing to add to an already overcrowded school day.

INSTRUCTIONAL APPROACHES TO ENHANCE EFFECTIVE HEALTH EDUCATION

Although a great deal of time in professional education programs is devoted to helping teachers learn to organize effective and meaningful ways for students to engage with learning materials (texts, curriculum materials, online resources, etc.) or with themselves and other education professionals, how students interact with each other is largely ignored. Yet how teachers structure student–student interaction exerts significant influence over how students learn, how they feel about each other, their sense of connectedness with the adults at their school, and even student self-esteem.[2]

In this context, as a starting point for effective instruction in any content area, teachers must plan how they can create a positive learning environment by cultivating safety, engagement, and inclusivity in their classroom. This is particularly important as today's classrooms reflect an increasingly diverse population. To maximize academic productivity, all students must feel safe, be skilled at communicating both self-respect and respect for others, understand classroom rules and procedures, and celebrate the academic successes they and their classmates experience. To promote such an environment, teachers must structure policies and practices in ways that enhance student engagement and a sense of connectedness to classroom learning experiences and with their school.

Building a Positive Learning Environment

Establishing and maintaining a safe and positive learning environment is a very important responsibility for all teachers. When students feel comfortable, challenged, safe, and cared for in the learning environment, they are much more likely to be academically successful.[3,4] Such a climate in the classroom also helps students feel a sense of connection to their school. Research has confirmed that feelings of connectedness provide a protective factor in helping prevent violence, suicidal thoughts, and tobacco, alcohol, and other drug use among students;[5] the importance of a sense of connection and ways it can be cultivated will be discussed in greater detail later in this chapter.

When we think of our favorite teachers, many of our memories focus on those who were warm, caring, fair, challenging, easy to talk with, enthusiastic, interesting, approachable, and interested. These are the attributes that contribute to students' feelings of connectedness with their teachers and their school. A number of classroom activities make an important contribution, but the most important element in cultivating connectedness is the teacher's consistent and

Strategies such as spreading attention around the class and communicating interest in each student and his or her work help build a sense of connectedness and a positive learning environment.

tive learning environment into regular classroom practice. Such activities support academic achievement and promote or reinforce emotional health among students. Students who are emotionally healthy

- Feel comfortable with themselves
- Are able to interact effectively with classmates and grown-ups with whom they have contact
- Are able to think and act independently
- Appropriately manage disappointment, stress, problems, and accomplishments
- Effectively express concern for others

Learning activities that enrich emotional health and academic achievement can be used with a range of age groups and health education content areas. Teachers can vary the use of such strategies to best meet the needs and interests of their students. Readers are encouraged to explore the implications of the classroom environment for promoting mental and emotional health (see Chapter 5). Following is a discussion of a number of learning activities to help communicate that the classroom environment is safe and engaging. Each activity is described for general classroom application, but teachers are encouraged to apply them to enhance health instruction.

positive attitude toward and engagement with students. Teachers who communicate an inviting and open attitude through their words and deeds communicate to children that they belong and are important to the success of the community of learners. Though teachers, like everyone else, have good and bad days, they are professionally obligated to behave consistently with students, to help students feel less confused and able to act on consistent expectations for behavior and achievement.

As a self-test to make sure the focus is on students rather than on teaching content (or simply supporting the mastery of subject matter), readers can review the work of William Purkey. In his book *Self-Concept and School Achievement*, Dr. Purkey identified seven questions for educators to assess their personal characteristics as educators. Teachers who can answer yes to these questions are on the right track to developing their students' sense of connectedness.

1. Do I learn the name of each student as soon as possible and use it often?
2. Do I share my feelings with my students?
3. Do I practice courtesy with my students?
4. Do I arrange some time when I can talk quietly, alone with each student?
5. Do I spread my attention around and include each student, keeping special watch for the student who might need special attention?
6. Do I notice and favorably comment on the things that are important to students?
7. Do I show students who return after being absent that I am happy to have them back in class and that they were missed?[6]

In addition to making sure they strive to communicate respect, enthusiasm, and an invitation to learn, teachers can integrate learning activities that promote a safe and posi-

Clustering

Clustering allows students and teachers to interact in several different groups to talk with many people during a short period of time. The class will need enough space to walk around the room freely. Consider pushing desks and chairs toward the walls to allow space in the center of the room. Explain that you will call out categories to form small groups. When students cluster in groups, they introduce themselves to each other and try to learn every person's name. For younger students, teachers should select categories with limited choices (favorite season, number of siblings, eye color), designate an area of the room for each choice, and facilitate students' movement to appropriate areas. Teachers might want to post pictures in assigned areas of the room to reduce confusion. For older students, have children write responses to categories on an index card, select students to share their choices, and then group students with like-minded peers. Repeat this process until all students are grouped. In addition to sharing their names, older students can share a rationale for each choice. Teachers can participate in clustering as an icebreaker to help learn students' names and to help students feel comfortable. When students return to the larger group, ask them, "What happened?" "How did you feel?" "What did you learn?"

Whip Around

Whip Around helps students learn names quickly. Have the class sit or stand in a circle, so that everyone can see everyone else. Ask students to say their names and tell something about themselves, as specified. You can start the activity, followed by one of the students sitting to either side and continuing around the circle. Topics can include students' favorite subject in school, one thing they did during the summer, what they had for breakfast, what they'll do after school, and what they want to be when they grow up. A favorite topic of elementary students during Whip Around is their "claim to fame." In claim to fame, students tell their name, followed by something they are famous for or hope to be famous for in the future. The students become creative during this activity. Whip Around takes only a short time to complete and functions as an icebreaker activity, giving students and teachers the opportunity to learn names and other information about classmates.

Boundary Breaking

Boundary breaking develops connectedness and communication skills. Ask students to stand or sit with a partner. If there is an odd number of students in the class, teachers can participate. Ask one student to be the talker and the other the listener. Ask a question, and talkers have thirty seconds to answer the question while the listener listens quietly. If the talker runs out of things to say, the listener can ask questions. Call time after thirty seconds; talkers and listeners switch roles and repeat the activity, asking a new question. Have students choose a new partner after each pair of questions. Conduct Boundary Breaking throughout the year to help students get to know each other on a more personal level and to practice speaking and listening skills. Sample questions include

What was the title of the last book you read, and what was it about?

What is your favorite hobby and why?

What is your favorite subject and why?

How do you select your friends, and what is the most important characteristic in a friend?

If you could be any animal (other than a human), what animal would you choose and why?

What is something about yourself that you are really proud of and why?

Who is your hero and why?

If you could meet any person in the world today, who would you meet and why?

What was the most fun thing you have ever done in your life?

How could the world be a better place?

What do you like to do on Saturday?

What makes you happy and why?

A good resource for questions is *The Kids' Book of Questions,* by Gregory Stock.[7] This book contains 260 questions that are developmentally appropriate for elementary and middle school youth. Students can also make up questions to use.

Four Corners

Put up large sheets of paper in the four corners of the classroom at the end of the school day or while students are out of the room. Each sheet of paper should have one word written on it that represents a category. Examples of categories that can be used include kinds of circus animals (lion, elephant, monkey, seal), colors, pizza toppings, sports or activities, and geometric shapes. To begin the activity, ask students to think about which of the four corners they prefer. On signal, have students go to the corner of their choice. Students will introduce themselves by name and tell why they chose that corner. Teachers can use this activity as a trigger for instruction and as a grouping strategy.

Snow Cones

Use brightly colored paper to represent the flavors of snow cones (crushed ice doused with flavored syrup in a paper cone). Have students sit in a circle. Place one sheet of colored paper in the center of the circle. Pass around paper of various colors, allowing students to choose the color they like. They'll need a pencil or marker and a hard surface to write on (a book or notebook). When everyone has a sheet of paper, have students fold their sheet in fourths. In the upper-left-hand corner (vertical or horizontal—students choose), ask students to write their name. Then ask a question and have them write the answer in that block. You can ask questions of all kinds or questions about an instructional topic. When students have finished, have them crumple their papers up in a ball and toss them at the paper in the center of the circle. When all the colored balls of paper are in the center, ask students to get up and retrieve a piece of paper that is a different color than their own, without bumping anyone else (students might need to practice this part first). Students should go back to their place in the circle and read in turn what is written on the paper they selected. Next, ask students to write their names in the upper-right-hand corner of the paper. Ask another question. Students write their answer, toss the papers in again, retrieve, read, and write names and the answer to a new question. Repeat until all four squares are filled. When applied as a strategy to enrich instruction, "snowcones" can provide an opportunity to review or assess student knowledge or attitudes. (This activity is adapted from Jeanne Gibbs's *Tribes.*[8])

Time to Move!

Activities that include a gross-motor element make for a more pleasant learning environment for everyone. This activity lets students and teachers learn more about each other and move about. Have students start by sitting in a circle in chairs or at desks (that don't slide easily). Start by standing in the center of the room and having students get up on signal, walk across the circle, and sit at another chair.

When students show they can move without bumping, start the activity. Say "It's time to move if . . ." and continue with a description of some of the students in the classroom—for example, "It's time to move if you are wearing blue" or "It's time to move if you like chocolate milk." When students get the idea, remove one chair as they are moving around the room. This means one student won't have a seat. That student goes to the center of the circle and continues the activity. To end the activity, simply slip the chair that was originally removed back into place so that everyone gets a seat. (This activity is adapted from Jeanne Gibbs's *Tribes*.[9])

Greetings Before School Begins

Before school begins for the year, teachers send a postcard to each student. Indicate your excitement about working with the students throughout the next school year. Students and their parents or caregivers will be pleasantly surprised to receive this early and affirming communication.

Positive Letters and Phone Calls

Sometimes, parents and caregivers say that they hear from teachers only when their child has done something wrong or has a problem. An excellent way to connect with parents or caregivers is to call or write when things are going well for their child. You may tell parents and caregivers that their child is improving his or her behavior or performance in a certain subject or that you enjoy the creativity their child brings to the class. By using e-mail or computer-generated reinforcement or affirmation messages, teachers can encourage parent engagement in school activities. Teachers must make sure that such "good news" communications are shared frequently with caregivers of all students. Parents and caregivers especially enjoy newsletters when students help create them. Many strategies will be discussed later in this chapter to help establish communication and trust between teachers and parents or caregivers.

The Appreciation Activity

This activity is enjoyable for students and can be accomplished in a relatively short amount of time. First, ask students what it means to appreciate someone or something. Then ask students for examples of statements that show appreciation ("I appreciate you because you help me with my homework"; "I appreciate you because you smile a lot"; "I appreciate you because you always say 'Good morning'"). Next, have students help each other tape a piece of paper to their backs, with the following words at the top: "I appreciate you because you. . .". On signal, have students move around the room with a pen or pencil to write an appreciation statement on the backs of as many classmates as possible, without signing their names. After time is called, have students take their papers off their backs and read them. Students' faces light up when they read all the ways their classmates appreciate them. (Before doing this activity, be certain that students understand the difference between appreciations and put-downs and that there is a sense of trust in the class.)

Popcorn Appreciation

At the end of the school day, have students gather in a circle for Popcorn Appreciation. You or any student can start by saying "Today, I appreciated [student's name] for [reason]"—for example, "Today, I appreciated Neil for helping me on the computer"; "Today, I appreciated Lola and Cathy for helping me put away the art supplies"; or "Today, I appreciated Eric for sharing his snack with me." Allow students to volunteer their appreciations for the day, rather than going around the circle. Teachers should share their appreciation of children who may be overlooked or who are not affirmed by classmates to help reinforce a classroom norm of acceptance and respect for all in the classroom community. Popcorn Appreciation is a way to allow children to leave school with the positive aspects of the day ringing in their ears. The idea of appreciation encourages noticing the efforts of others in a wide variety of contexts rather than praising only those who did especially well at academic tasks. Expressing appreciations goes beyond the "good job" feedback that carries no real information. Hearing and saying specific appreciations helps students and teachers improve both reflection and communication skills.[10]

Interviews

Conducting interviews can help students improve their oral and written communication skills. In addition, interviewing family members or neighbors can personalize academic content. Interviewing a family member might help students learn more about their heritage. Interviewing a classmate might help students make new friends. Regardless of the questions, students will get to know the person they interview better and might feel more connected to that person. Following are examples of general questions that can be used for a classmate interview:

What is your favorite activity to do at home?

What is your favorite activity to do outdoors?

What is your favorite TV show?

What is your favorite thing to eat?

What is your favorite subject in school?

How would you describe yourself?

Students can share the results of their interviews with classmates by reporting something new that they learned.

Class Picture Inspection (for Teachers)

You can use a class picture or roster on a daily basis to ensure that you connect with every student. At the end of each day, look at the class picture and try to remember at least one positive comment you made to each student. For those students who did not receive a positive comment for the day, begin the next day by making a positive comment to them. It is easy to forget the quiet students who never cause trouble, but this activity quickly brings them to mind. Positive comments do not always have to relate to schoolwork or be expressed as praise. Positive comments and appreciations can relate to any aspect of students' personalities and interests and can be expressed as questions and conversations. Students feel valuable when their teachers show genuine interest in their lives ("How did your soccer team do yesterday?" "Have you been working on some of your drawings this week?" "Wow—how's it going being the new big sister in the family?").

Featured Student of the Week

Every week of the school year, select a different student as the Student of the Week. Teachers must make sure that every child is chosen. Notify parents and caretakers in advance, so that students can bring in items from home or make items for the Student of the Week bulletin board. Students might want to display pictures or information about their favorite food or sport, things they are good at, and things they enjoy doing. Sometimes, students bring family pictures or baby pictures to class. To support the development of this display, teachers can list potential things to include, from which a maximum of five can be chosen. While encouraging creativity, such a process ensures that depictions provide equal representations for all students. The bulletin board allows other students in the class to learn more about the featured student's interests and capabilities, and can provide an opportunity to discuss and honor unique family or cultural customs.

Student Collage

Have students make a collage that represents things they like to do and things they do best. Students can draw, write, or cut pictures out of magazines to make their collages. Younger students might want to make their collage on an outline of their bodies (students can trace each other on butcher paper). Display the completed collages in the classroom and have students explain them so they can all learn more about one another. This project correlates with the content area of fine arts.

Graffiti Wall

Cover a large bulletin board or wall in the classroom with butcher paper. Allow students to write or draw on the graffiti wall whenever they complete their work or during any free time. Teachers might want to have specific themes for graffiti walls, including seasonal health issues or ways to be a friend, appreciations for classmates, favorite activities, or favorite foods. Make an agreement with students that they will write or draw only positive representations or comments on the graffiti wall. If negative comments or pictures are placed on the wall, use a class meeting to allow students to decide how to manage this or other problems with the graffiti wall.

Journal Writing

Have students keep a journal throughout the school year. Journaling reinforces students' writing skills. Ask students to respond to instructional activities or class events, write creative stories or poetry, or just write about their feelings for the day. Be sure to collect student journals frequently and respond to the entries each child has written. Although responding takes time, teachers build relationships with students by writing back to them. Write questions for students to think about for their next journal entry to promote conversation.

Role-Playing

Role-playing is particularly effective with middle school students. Acting allows students to be creative while practicing a range of skills, including resistance, communication, friendship, affirmation, and decision making. Use scripted and half-scripted role-plays to help students get started. Then turn the role-play design over to students with open-ended scenarios.

Success of the Day

At the end of each school day, ask students to write down a success they experienced that day. Students can keep these successes in a journal or a separate notebook, so that they can look back at them whenever they need to lift their spirits. Students can share their success with the class at the end of each school day or can write them on a teacher-developed form to share with family members. Use this activity to end the school day on a positive note that helps students remember their accomplishments.

Class Contracts

It is important for teachers to promote the idea that classrooms are communities of learners that are shared by students and teachers together—not just to teachers. Allowing students to have input in establishing the rules of the class, through a class contract or a positive behavior contract, helps reinforce this concept. Although there are several ways to develop a class contract, a suggested format follows. First, introduce the concept of a *contract* (an agreement in which everyone gives something and gets something back in return). Discuss circumstances or jobs for which people make and sign contracts. Next, ask students to discuss the meaning of the word *privilege*. Ask them to think of privileges they have liked having in school or at home. Explain that they will be able to have some of those privileges by creating a class contract. List these privileges on the board or on newsprint under the heading "Students Get." Suggestions might include several five-minute activity breaks during the school day, additional time during which the teacher reads a book aloud, or extra library time each week.

Review the list and decide or negotiate which items can be given to the students. For instance, a student might suggest that there should be no tests. Although most teachers have to give tests, they might offer to not give any tests on Friday.

Next, remind students that very few things in life are free, and, if they want to get these privileges they must give something in return. Ask students what they would be willing to give and write these suggestions on the board or on newsprint under the heading "Students Give." Suggestions from elementary students might include good effort, cooperation, attention, positive attitude, participation, and respect. Ask the students if they can live up to the items on the "Students Give" list. If students cannot live up to a certain item under "Students Give," then it must be removed. Remind students that this is a class contract for everyone.

Next, share your list under "Teacher Gives." Preprint the list to save class time. Some sample items from a "Teacher Gives" list are time, energy, knowledge, humor, kindness, fairness, and extra help. Students appreciate this part of the contract, because they feel the teacher is also willing to give things to make the class succeed. Then share a preprinted list of "Nonnegotiables." These are the rules that must be followed—no negotiation is possible. Some "Nonnegotiables" are "Follow all school rules," "No tobacco use by anyone," "Never say I can't," and "No put-downs allowed." Next, discuss the consequences of breaking a rule in the contract, in case either side (students or you) does not live up to the contract. Most of the time, the students come up with stiffer consequences than the teacher does.

Some consequences suggested by elementary students are staying after school, apologizing to the class, and doing extra homework. Be sure that consequences are appropriate. For example, doing extra homework as a consequence doesn't help students enjoy learning, because homework is being used as a punishment. A more appropriate consequence is to have students write an explanation of what went wrong and why and then create a plan to behave more responsibly if the situation arises again.

In the last part of the contract, build in a plan for celebration. For example, when the class follows the contract they created for a week, have a celebration time that includes all class members, with healthy snacks, music, and time to participate in favorite activities. Help students think of these times as celebrations of their work together, rather than as rewards. Rewards sometimes are used to exclude certain children and engender a sense of competition instead of collaboration.

After students agree on the contract, make a copy for everyone in the class with your signature and send it home to parents or caregivers. Have parents or caregivers and students sign the contract and return it to you. Post a large copy of the contract in the room for the entire school year. If there is a student in the class who does not agree with the contract, have an individual conversation with the student to discuss the benefits for all concerned. As a foundation for establishing classroom norms of safe, healthy, and productive behavior, it is important that all students engage in the contract despite potential disagreement with some element of it.

Students usually create class contracts with the rules most teachers would initiate without student input, but students are more willing to follow the rules if they develop them. (Teachers who try making a class contract for the first time should remember that students probably will need a period of time to adjust to their contract.) If the contract is broken, use these incidents as an opportunity for learning—don't give up. Some teachers might feel that it is easier to throw out the contract and come up with their own rules and consequences. Though this might seem efficient, as the school year progresses teachers typically find that it becomes increasingly difficult to use this method as a foundation for effective classroom management.

Once students get accustomed to the idea that they can influence class rules and consequences, they begin to hold other students accountable to the contract. Students can hold their teachers accountable as well. Health educator Lynn Shoji shares that she knows she needs to

watch her comments when her middle school students say, "Mrs. Shoji, that was a put-down."[11]

Contracts also provide an effective method for working with individual students on skill development. Teachers can develop specific contracts with students to work on goal setting, planning, time management, and so on. Such contracts can be used daily, weekly, or as needed. See Teacher's Toolbox 4.1, "Sample Contracts for a Third-Grade Class."

Teacher's Toolbox 4.1

Sample Contracts for a Third-Grade Class

Class Contract

Students Get
- Field trips
- No Friday test
- Good grades
- Fun
- Friends
- Extra help
- To learn

Students Give
- Try hard
- Study
- No talking when others are talking
- Pay attention
- Be prepared

Teacher Gives
- Fairness
- Understanding
- Extra help
- Humor
- Enthusiasm
- Praise
- Kindness
- Good explanations

Nonnegotiables
- Follow school rules
- No put-downs

Consequences
- Apology to class
- Stay after school
- Go to principal

I agree to this contract for the school year.

Student's signature: _____

Parent's/caregiver's signature: _____

Teacher's signature: _____

Individual Student Contract

My goal is to _____
_____(state goal)

I can do this if I _____
_____(plan of action)

If I do this, I will _____
_____(reward)

If I don't do this, I will _____
_____(consequence)

Student's signature: _____

Parent's/caregiver's signature: _____

Teacher's signature: _____

Class Jobs

Brainstorm a list of class jobs with students and allow them to apply as individuals or small groups for jobs that appeal to them. Class jobs may include line leader, lunch money collector, chalkboard cleaner, trash can monitor, pencil sharpener monitor, bulletin board designer, calendar monitor, attendance taker, plant caretaker, and animal caretaker. Students who perform class jobs feel responsible when helping the class function effectively. Be sure that all jobs are equal-opportunity—girls and boys should be able to hold any class job. Elementary teacher Diane Parker initiates the idea of "helper families" in her classroom.[12] Students work in groups to perform jobs for a given period of time. The jobs rotate among the "helper families" in the classroom.

Participation in Classroom Decisions

Although many decisions are made for elementary and middle school students, it is important to equip students with essential skills to make their own decisions when possible and appropriate. For example, students might get to decide such things as where they will sit for a particular activity, which book they will read, which of two assignments they will complete first, or the format for a particular assignment (poster, skit, dance, or rap). As discussed in Chapter 3, decision making is complex and includes defining problems, generating and evaluating choices, and selecting and acting on best options. In addition to cultivating opportunities for students to practice decision-making skills, it is helpful to discuss the positive and negative consequences that can result—for example, "What will happen if I choose to sit by my best friend during science? Will we both do our best work, or will we distract each other? What's the best decision for me and why?"

Class Meetings

Regular class meetings with students sitting in a circle to openly discuss current class issues, are an important way to increase students' sense of control and self-management. Rules for class meeting might include

- Only one person speaks at a time.
- Stick to the topic.
- Be honest.
- Be thoughtful of the feelings of others.
- Speak only for yourself.

Have students set class meeting rules, and review the rules before each class meeting. During the class meeting, teachers can act as facilitators by sitting outside the circle, answer questions or clarify comments when necessary, and summarize meeting content. In this scenario, students run the meeting themselves. Students might want to choose different student discussion leaders for each meeting. Alternatively, teachers can sit in the circle, participating as a class member who has an equal voice (but not the discussion leader, unless the children need assistance).

All kinds of topics are appropriate for class meetings. Students might want to discuss a specific class project or issue. If the class has conducted a health fair for parents, a class meeting could be used for students to express both the positive and negative outcomes or to make suggestions for improving the activity in the future. Another topic that could be used for a class meeting is the most and least favorite activities of the week—and how to make the least favorite activities work more productively. Some teachers have class meetings for students to work out the way things will be done—for example, "We are going on a field trip with our grade level. We have 103 students and four buses. Two buses hold 25 and two buses hold 45 students. How many students should go on each bus? How will we decide who goes on which bus?"

A good time to have a weekly class meeting is on Friday afternoons so that students have the opportunity to evaluate the week. Active participation in class meetings can take time, especially if students have never had this kind of voice before. Over time, and with practice, students will begin to give useful feedback about the week's activities and other issues. Reinforce the notion that students will not be punished for discussing negative aspects of the class. Rather, encourage students to suggest ways to improve activities.

Teachers who use the class meeting must feel confident enough to view negative comments as feedback that can be used to improve their teaching. You will be surprised at how many creative ideas students suggest during a class meeting. The class meeting helps teachers understand their students better and helps students feel comfortable, confident, and valued. It is best for teachers to resist the natural temptation to take over and run the meetings, unless the children really need assistance. Students need experience in working through issues for themselves, and they can learn to do so.

Question Box

Create a class question box to promote a positive learning environment. Students can write anonymous questions about topics discussed in class, but the questions need to pertain to class issues and students' activities and interests, rather than personal questions about the teacher or other students. A question box allows students who may hesitate to speak in class to get answers to their questions. It is common for teachers to use this activity for sexuality questions, but the question box is a great classroom tradition to maintain for the entire year. You should be clear with students that you are required to tell and get help if students reveal that they or another person is in any type of danger. It is also vital for teachers who create question boxes to establish a consistent time each week to respond to student questions.

Guest Speakers

Expose students to careers, skills, and other specific information by inviting a variety of respected individuals from the community to share their interests or areas of expertise. Hearing from community members or parents helps students to get to know people with unique skills or careers. Be sure you know any classroom guest and the topic of their remarks before adults from the community have any interaction with students.

Correlating "He-roes" and "She-roes" with Language Arts (Cross-Curricular Activity)

Correlate health education with social studies by having students investigate the lives of men ("he-roes") and women ("she-roes") who have made a difference for good in the world throughout history. To create a link with language arts, ask students to identify local he-roes and she-roes (parents, older brothers or sisters, community helpers) as the main characters of short stories they write to share with the class.

Peer Tutoring/Cross-Age Teaching

Have upper-elementary and middle-level students tutor or help teach lower-elementary students. It is common for older students to take their roles as models for younger students very seriously, and students of both age groups have the opportunity to learn from each other. Some schools initiate "reading buddy" programs in which older students read with younger students and discuss the books together. Finally, if your school has resource or special education classrooms, consider developing a collaborative peer tutoring program.

Goal Setting

Younger elementary students should learn what the word *goal* means and be encouraged to work on short-term, daily goals. Examples of daily goals are giving three appreciations to classmates, completing a math lesson, and cleaning their desks. Upper-elementary and middle-level students can be encouraged to set weekly, monthly, or even longer-term goals. An important goal project for older students is a personal health promotion project. Have students decide on a positive health behavior they want to incorporate into their lives and develop a plan for reaching their goal, including the steps they will take, plans to overcome potential barriers, and a method for assessing their progress.

Community Service/Service Learning Projects

Ask students to brainstorm various community service projects in which they could participate. Community service projects reinforce a value system that includes helping and contributing to better the total community. Ideas include cleaning up parks or playgrounds, bringing in food for needy families, visiting and performing for residents of a nursing home, and raising money for a community project. Help students make arrangements to carry out their community service projects by allowing them to take developmentally appropriate responsibility for planning, permissions, and implementation.

Instruction Organized with a Specific Focus on Health Issues

Once teachers have invested in establishing and reinforcing a safe and nurturing learning environment, a common starting point for a discussion about instruction is to view all information as divided or clustered into segments or disciplines. Many education researchers assert that each content area in the school curriculum represents a discrete form of knowledge. As such, academic disciplines or content areas have their foundation in unique sets of issues and questions. Developmental psychologist Jean Piaget defined a discipline as a specific body of teachable knowledge, with its own background of education, training, methods, and areas of focus.[13] In this context, the organization of instructional delivery into discrete academic disciplines in American middle and high schools is based on the goal of enhancing efficiency.[14]

Many local district curricula have been developed around strictly focused subjects or content areas. Schools adopting such a time management and instructional approach organize instructional delivery into discrete and predetermined blocks of time and employ content specialists to deliver instruction.

Direct instruction delivered in this way represents the most common curricular and scheduling model in U.S. education. It is associated with the following advantages for students, teachers, administrators, and parents:

- Parents, teachers, and students are familiar and comfortable with it.
- The approach is consistent with courses of study, standards, and testing protocol developed in most states.
- Textbooks and supplementary learning materials are readily available.
- Students are empowered with specialized information and skills.
- Secondary teachers academically prepared as content specialists are equipped with limited range but a great depth of expertise within a given discipline.
- All content areas, including those perceived to be of less importance, are afforded a portion of formal instructional time.

Supporters of such an approach to health education base their endorsement on the belief that health education is grounded in a discrete body of knowledge. As such, health education has its own philosophical underpinnings and content integrity, and it is worthy of specific and dedicated instructional time.[15]

Instructional Activities with Many Uses

It is not uncommon for teachers to associate a particular learning activity with a specific grade level, health issue, or unit of instruction. Teachers must remember, however, that there are countless instructional activities and learning strategies that can be adapted to address a wide range of health issues and diverse target audiences. Teachers interested in activities with applicability for a range of students and health topics are encouraged to examine the activities in Teacher's Toolbox 4.2. Each of these can be applied to all of the National Health Education Standards.

Teacher's Toolbox 4.2 provides a starting point for teachers to experiment with cross-topical application of learning activities. Recommendations for their use in the context of specific health issues can be found in later chapters of this text organized around specific health issues. Finally, these activities can be applied across the curriculum to reinforce instruction in a range of academic subjects, including reading, social studies, math, and science.

Selected Activities with Applicability to a Range of Health Topics and Grade Levels

Anonymous Cards Strategy

The Anonymous Cards activity enables students to compare and contrast their knowledge, beliefs, and self-reported practices with classmates. This activity can be used to explore health issues across all three learning domains (cognitive, affective, psychomotor) while protecting students' anonymity. Nonwriters can use drawings, colors, or shapes to respond.

1. Each student receives an identical 3 × 5 inch card or piece of paper. All students must have similar writing implements.
2. Students are instructed to provide no personal identification on the card or paper.
3. Students respond to a series of teacher-developed questions on their card.
4. Questions are reviewed and cards are collected when all students have completed their responses.
5. The teacher shuffles the cards and redistributes them. Students receive a card that is not their own. Students who receive their own card in this process are encouraged to proceed with the activity as though the responses were provided by a classmate. It is important to assure the presumption of anonymity as cards are redistributed.
6. The teacher cues the discussion with the following: "Who has a card on which someone said . . . ?" or "What did your classmate who wrote on the card that you received have to say about . . . ?"

Human Scavenger Hunts/People Scrambles

This activity works well for any group of students with reading and writing skills. Developmentally appropriate accommodations must be made. The Human Scavenger Hunt is an effective trigger activity, or it can be used to summarize a unit of instruction.

1. Prior to class, teachers construct a handout asking students to conduct a self-assessment of their knowledge, attitudes, or self-reported practices about the health issue on which the unit is focused. Space is provided for student reflections on the handout.
2. One self-assessment sheet is distributed to each student.
3. Developmentally appropriate time limits are set for students to address all questions or items on the sheet.
4. When all students have completed this portion of the activity, they are encouraged to seek classmates with additional knowledge, different beliefs, or alternative health practices. Classmates from whom this information is gathered are asked to place their signature on the sheet confirming that they shared their alternative response.
5. Teachers are encouraged to place strict time limits on this final phase of the activity. In addition, the activity may be structured to limit the number of signatures that students may gather from any one classmate.

Carousel Activity

Structuring developmentally appropriate time blocks for all phases of this activity is imperative. The advantage of this activity is that each student responds to each item independently in relative anonymity to classmates outside their small group before small groups process the responses. This activity can be used to introduce, reinforce, or summarize units of health instruction.

1. Prior to the class, the teacher prepares a series of trigger questions, phrases, or words about the health topic. Each is placed at the top of a large sheet of newsprint paper.
2. Students are organized into appropriately sized groups. Each student has something with which to write. Each group receives a sheet of newsprint for consideration. For older students, the groups can assemble around sheets that have been taped to the wall. For younger students, working on the floor might be appropriate.

FIGURE 4–1 | **The Fishbone Diagram**

3. In carefully monitored time periods, all students are encouraged to provide written feedback to the question or issue on their large sheet of paper. As students respond concurrently, it must be reinforced that no student may write on top of the work provided by any other student.
4. When the time period has elapsed, all students are asked to stop writing. The groups of students are instructed to rotate to another issue or question to which they will respond. When they reach the next sheet, they are to provide as complete a response as possible in the available time. Teachers are urged to remind students to ignore the work of previous responders. This process continues until all students have responded to all items.
5. When groups return to the sheet on which they provided their original responses, they are to read all responses, tally and react to the comments, and prepare to share a summary of the remarks with the class as a whole.

Fishbone Diagrams

This activity can be part of an art or social studies correlation. Adapted from the body of literature on total quality management, it is also referred to as Ishikawa Charts, a tool for brainstorming. This brainstorming format has the advantage over its counterparts of enabling students to compare and contrast information, beliefs, or self-reported skills.

1. Prior to the lesson, the teacher prepares a blank fishbone diagram for each student or for each small group (Figure 4–1). In addition, the teacher identifies a theme with contrasting points of view.
2. Each student places the theme on which he or she is working in the "head" of the fishbone diagram. Then opposing viewpoints, conflicting information, or alternative practices are brainstormed. Contrasting responses are written on opposing "bones" of the diagram.
3. When completed, responses are shared with partners, small groups, or the whole class.

Cooperative Learning: An Instructional Alternative

As teachers engage in the process of selecting effective learning strategies to respond to student needs, they must remember that the diversity of the student body in their classrooms is increasing each school year. Teachers will recognize this change in cultural, ethnic, racial, religious, economic, social, and language terms. Such diversity can manifest itself with positive or negative outcomes for students, teachers, and the learning process. If structured and managed with intention, diversity among students can result in increased achievement and productivity, creativity in problem solving, growth in cognitive and moral reasoning, and increased ability to recognize and accept the point of view of others. Unfortunately, diversity among students also has been associated with such negative outcomes as lowered achievement, closed-minded rejection of new information, and increasingly negative relationships characterized by hostility, bullying, rejection, and racism; a prescription for student difficulties and classroom management problems for teachers and school leaders.[16]

Teachers play a critical role in structuring the learning environment and the kinds and quality of interactions that occur between students. Research has confirmed that there are three basic ways in which students interact during classroom learning experiences:

- the *competitive* model in which students vie for recognition as the "best" (spelling bees or races to see who gets a correct answer first during a review game),
- *individualistic* approaches in which students work toward meeting set criteria, with their success depending only on their own performance without influence by other students (achievement tests of proficiency), and
- *cooperative* learning, in which interaction occurs in the context of learning in small groups within which students must collaborate to achieve shared goals while maintaining individual accountability.

The value systems that provide the foundation for each approach to learning exist as a "hidden curriculum" under the surface of the formal and intentional activities that permeate school life for students. Because everyone faces situations in which these engagement patterns are in operation, all students must learn to function effectively in each.[17]

Not all of the identified student interaction patterns have been demonstrated to be equally effective in helping learners to master concepts and skills. Cooperative learning, used in only about 7 percent of U.S. classrooms, has been demonstrated to have a powerful impact on learner outcomes in the areas of achievement, interpersonal relationships, psychological health and social competence, and converting diversity into strength.[18] Hundreds of studies have confirmed the following important and positive results:

- Working together to achieve a common goal results in higher achievement and greater productivity than working alone. Cooperative learning produces higher-level reasoning, more frequent generation of new ideas, and a greater ability to transfer what is learned across situations.
- When students work together to achieve a common goal, they care more about each other and are more committed to the success and well-being of classmates than when they work independently or compete to see who is the best.
- When students learn to value collaboration through accomplishing a shared success, they experience greater psychological health and higher self-esteem than when they compete with peers or work independently.
- When cooperative rather than competitive or individualistic approaches are used across the school day, diversity among students becomes a source of creative enrichment and increased productivity.[19]

Commonly used in upper-elementary and middle-school classrooms, cooperative learning is both a teaching philosophy and a collection of instructional strategies (structures). This approach has been incorporated into lessons in diverse content areas including language arts, math, social studies, and science.[20] Regardless of the context in which it is applied, cooperative learning makes each individual group member stronger by learning in collaboration with others.[21]

Cooperative learning involves much more than randomly arranging clusters of students into discussion groups.[22] Cooperative learning groups are intentionally organized to include students with a range of abilities. Consider This 4.1 reviews the differences between traditional approaches to group work and the cooperative learning group approach.[23] In addition, Gardner's work on multiple intelligences, discussed in Chapter 2, provides an interesting and effective way to organize students into cooperative learning groups.[24]

Cooperative learning requires students to be responsible not only for their own achievement but also for that of their groupmates. This practice reinforces collaboration and encourages a more reciprocal status among group members.[25] Specifically, cooperative learning implies that students depend on one another for rewards by contributing to the achievement of the whole group through participation in peer-based learning.[26] Cooperative learning groups and activities are organized with consistency around the following common elements:

- *Positive interdependence* (sink or swim together): This is ensured through assigning mutual goals, providing joint rewards, and dividing tasks, materials, resources, and information among group members.
- *Face-to-face interaction* (assist and encourage others to achieve): Students seated in close physical proximity are supported in mutual discussion of all aspects of the assignment. Such practices reinforce positive interdependence.
- *Individual accountability* (individuals are responsible for doing their part): Although there is a focus on group outcomes, it is important that individual student achievement not be compromised. To this end, teachers can support

individual learning by assigning individuals to bring completed work to the group, picking random students to answer questions, and assigning a challenging job or role to each student.

• *Interpersonal and small-group skills* (skills are required to be an effective group member): Rather than assuming that students possess social and collaborative skills, teachers must teach them as a foundation of cooperative learning. Reinforcement of these skills is enhanced by establishing the following expectations for groups: Everyone contributes and helps, everyone listens carefully to others, group members praise good work, and quiet voices are used unless otherwise specified.

• *Group processing* (discuss how well the group is functioning and make suggestions for improvement): Formal acknowledgment is provided for assessing group achievement and working relationships. This can be accomplished by having students identify at least three group members or specific things that enhanced collaborative success. Such positive outcomes are supported when role assignments (recorder, timekeeper, etc.) are rotated within cooperative learning groups.[27-28]

Researchers have identified a number of cooperative learning strategies or structures for use with diverse age groups and content areas. These structures make an effective contribution to instruction by supporting academic growth in the cognitive, affective, and psychomotor learning domains. Commonly used cooperative learning strategies, or structures, include Round-Robin, Corners, Numbered Heads Together, Pairs Check, Think-Pair-Share, Team Word Webbing, and Roundtable. A brief overview of each strategy is found in Table 4–1.[29]

Though there is a robust body of literature about uses and effectiveness of cooperative learning across various ages of learners and content areas, little information confirms its effectiveness in enriching health education practice. The National Commission on the Role of the School and the Community in Improving Adolescent Health has asserted that a new kind of health education should be developed, an approach focused on enriching student skills in making decisions, dealing with group pressure, avoiding fights, and working cooperatively.[30] Consistent with this call, early research has confirmed that cooperative learning has been associated with improving some health outcomes including content mastery of HIV/AIDS information and enhanced self-esteem, conflict resolution skills, and social and resiliency skills.[31, 32]

In an effort to expand health education applications of cooperative learning, readers will find an example of a "jigsaw" structure focused on promoting healthy eating in Teacher's Toolbox 4.3.[33] In this example, middle-grade students organized into cooperative learning groups increase their understanding of the Dietary Guidelines for Americans developed by the U.S. Departments of Agriculture and Health and Human Services. Group members are responsible for developing expertise in one segment of a similar body of information that is distributed to each group. Students then teach this information to group members.

Although cooperative learning requires teachers to do a different kind of preparation, impressive student outcomes can be achieved in context of rather than in place of instructional goals. Valuable instructional time is conserved without compromising academic goals.

Teachers are encouraged to explore the extensive body of literature on cooperative learning. It is unlikely that this model will completely replace the more traditional, or competitive, classroom approach to learning, but cooperative learning approaches help diverse groups of students benefit from both formats when used as an instructional supplement from one-third to one-half of the time.[34]

TABLE 4–1

An Overview of Selected Cooperative Learning Strategies

Structure	Brief Description
Round-Robin	Students take turns sharing information, attitudes, or skills with their teammates.
Corners	Group designees move to a predetermined corner of the room. Students in corner groups then discuss and prepare to paraphrase ideas for their reassembled cooperative learning groups.
Numbered Heads Together	Questions or challenges are posed to groups by the teacher. Group members who have been previously assigned numbers consult on the answer or response, reflecting the best collective wisdom of the group. When the teacher calls a number at random, the student with that assigned number shares the group response.
Pairs Check	Groups of students work in pairs to alternate in the roles of problem solver and coach. After two problems, each pair compares answers with its counterpart in the group.
Think-Pair-Share	Working independently, then with a partner, students identify a solution or response for a teacher-posed challenge. Pairs then share responses with classmates.
Team Word Webbing	Group members respond simultaneously on a large sheet of paper to identify main concepts, supporting elements, and bridges between concepts.
Roundtable	Learners take turns providing responses as a pencil and paper are passed around the group.

SOURCE: Bethann Cinelli, Cynthia W. Symons, Lori Bechtel, and Mary Rose-Colley, "Applying Cooperative Learning in Health Education Practice," *Journal of School Health 64,* no. 3 (March 1994): 99–102.

Reprinted with permission. American School Health Association, Kent, Ohio.

Teacher's Toolbox 4.3

Applying Cooperative Learning to Promoting Healthy Eating: Using a "Jigsaw"

- Teachers provide identical and complete packets of nutrition information and resources to each cooperative learning group (predetermined heterogeneous "base groups").

- Within groups, each student is assigned one subsection of material with which to work. Group members should negotiate the distribution of packets.

- Students seek out peers with identical assignments (and packets of information) from other base groups. This temporary group of "experts" reads, discusses, and formulates a plan for presenting the information to their peers in a way they think will be most effective.

- The experts return to their base groups and present the content to peers in the manner determined to be most effective.

- Once all base group members have had the opportunity to present their portion of content to their peers, critical information disseminated using the "jigsaw" is summarized and reviewed by the teacher. Teachers might randomly call on students in a rapid-fire question period, have base groups develop a visual depiction of a model school lunch for a middle school student, or evaluate content mastery of functional knowledge through a written assessment. It is important that this critical processing step not be overlooked.

SOURCE: B. Cinelli, C. W. Symons, L. Bechtel, and M. Rose-Colley, "Applying Cooperative Learning in Health Education Practice," *Journal of School Health 64,* no. 3 (March 1994): 102.

Individualized Instruction: An Important Alternative

Although the majority of health education curricula are developed around a discipline-specific focus with the inclusion of some commitment to cooperative learning, individualized instructional approaches can enrich instructional practice. This less common instructional format has enjoyed wide use in learning resource centers as a better way to meet the needs of students with learning or developmental disabilities. In addition, individualized learning approaches are used to provide remediation or as a supplement to more conventional educational approaches.[35]

Specific applications of individualized instruction that have particular potential to enrich health education practice include the use of learning centers and health fairs. Learning centers and health fairs that focus on timely health issues add an important individualized dimension to elementary and middle school classrooms.

Learning Centers A learning center consists of an organized sequence of student-centered activities, each of which increases functional knowledge, develops essential skills, and/or helps students examine their attitudes or beliefs about a health topic. While working at a learning center, students are active, independent, and can process information in the context of their personal experiences or understandings. Learners are encouraged to work at their own pace, selecting from any number of interesting and multisensory activities organized to supplement more formal or larger-group instruction.

Learning centers usually are arranged in a compact location in the classroom. To develop a learning center, teachers collect sets of materials, instructions, and/or complete activities in a designated, often separate, classroom space. The physical

Exploring Safe Play Spaces in My School, Neighborhood, and Community

Learning objectives/organizing concepts:

- Learners will identify safe and unsafe play spaces on their school campus.
- Learners will map routes from their home to the closest playground.
- Learners will create a visual depiction of all the physical activities in which they could participate within walking or biking distance of their home.
- Learners will explore their community (Chamber of Commerce) website to evaluate the commitment to safe and noncompetitive physical activity for local children.
- Learners will serve as advocates for safe play spaces in their local community.

Materials needed for students working at the center:

- Laminated task lists with suggested procedures (creative expression should be encouraged)
- Rubrics clarifying task elements and evaluation criteria
- School campus maps
- Drawing materials (markers, paper, rulers, etc.)
- Poster board, scissors, magazines, glue sticks, and so on
- Computer access to local Internet resources and/or text and visual material provided by city, Chamber of Commerce, local police department, and so on
- Materials to write letters, samples of letters to the editor from the local newspaper, materials to make buttons or bumper stickers, contact information for local officials

Resource samples or models to display in learning centers:

- Previous letters to the editor written by students
- Samples of political or campaign buttons
- Maps developed by students
- Posters/collages assembled by students
- Sample bumper stickers

Strategies for introducing and/or sequencing activities:

- Teachers are encouraged to number task lists or organize materials in numbered packets if a developmental progression is important to successfully completing learning center tasks.
- While teachers are encouraged to be clear with directions, they are cautioned against being overly directive, because such an approach can compromise the positive independence fostered by learning centers.

Evaluation tools:

- Checksheets for self-evaluation (formative and summative)
- Rubrics
- Bullet points to guide peer evaluation of work products
- Presentations or opportunities to share work with classmates
- Suggestions for ways to share work with parents, school administrators, and community leaders

---

space of a learning center often is large enough for several students to work simultaneously but independently on self-selected tasks. This reinforces the notion of "parallel play," particularly appropriate for students in pre-primary and primary grades. Commonly, student work is displayed at the learning center as a way to stimulate thinking and reinforce creativity among others. Projects also can be shared with broader school audiences in hall, library, or lobby displays.

Learning centers designed to promote student health provide extended time for in-depth exploration of health concepts. As discussed earlier in this chapter, health education is not given the highest priority by many classroom teachers who must allocate and manage limited instruction time. Learning centers provide a way to both support and extend basic health instruction without taking time away from whole-group instruction. With learning centers, engaged students can move beyond mastery of basic content to explore beliefs and norms and practice health-promoting skills. Well-designed learning centers can

- Organize resource materials for students
- Encourage students to work independently
- Respond to individual learning pace

- Incorporate both independent and collaborative activities
- Supplement or reinforce basic instruction
- Provide opportunities for applying higher-order thinking skills and working in multiple learning domains
- Combine a well-organized structure with freedom for independent thinking and creative expression
- Provide opportunities for peer-based learning

Though it is common for teachers to organize classroom interest areas that feature a range of materials and resources, learning centers must be instructionally sound. Planning should be focused on the following common elements:

- Developmentally appropriate learning objectives or organizing concepts
- Directions for students working at the center
- Samples or models of previously completed work
- Media or computer applications
- Strategies for introducing and sequencing activities
- Evaluation protocol based on the identified objectives

Learning center suggestions for promoting physical activity among students in the upper-elementary grades can be found in Teacher's Toolbox 4.4.

Health Fairs An interesting and effective alternative to the conventional use of learning centers within the classroom is to organize multiple student-developed centers into a health fair. Students and teachers may be familiar with the format of health fairs from having participated in similar events at a hospital, shopping mall, or community center. A health fair or health carnival can be an exciting, useful trigger or reinforcement activity when it is incorporated into the district's approved health education graded course of study.

When describing a county or state fair, words such as *fun, excitement, noise, rides, food, booths, games, prizes, music, color,* and *exhibits* often come to mind. The same words have been used to describe health fairs or carnivals. Health fairs provide opportunities to teach health concepts in a hands-on, fun, creative, and exciting way. Student stations or learning centers developed for school health fairs focus direct health instruction about topics as diverse as substance abuse prevention, disability awareness, the senses, and fire safety. Although health screening (including vision and hearing testing, reaction-time testing, and blood typing) often is conducted at community health fairs for adults, such activities are not developmentally appropriate ways to enrich student understanding.

Although health fairs provide valuable supplemental health education learning experiences, they should not be perceived as the foundation for direct health instruction in any school. The purpose of a health fair is to stimulate interest in health issues and to expose participants to a variety of developmentally appropriate health issues in a compressed period of time. In addition, students can gain in-depth understanding about a health topic when they create a learning center for a health fair. The health fair also can serve as an effective organizational umbrella for collaborative activities among community groups, parents, teachers, and students. As such, health fairs can provide unique and memorable learning experiences.

Health fairs can be incorporated into an elementary and middle school health curriculum in a variety of ways. First, they can be organized for elementary students by college students enrolled in health education classes, by junior or senior high school health classes, or by community health agencies. Such collaboration between elementary and middle school students and their secondary or university counterparts or local agency professionals can be mutually enriching.

Second, health fairs can be integrated into the academic program of studies in elementary and middle schools by having students in the upper grades develop learning centers and organize a health fair for their primary-grade counterparts. Teachers who supervise student planning for such cross-age approaches to learning should pay attention to developmentally appropriate practice concerns for younger students invited to the health fair.

Third, middle-grade students can organize a health fair for parents and the local community. When organizing a fair for parents, appropriate topics for adults—including

Teacher's Toolbox 4.5

Sample Health Fair Outline

Following is a model of an outline that students can be asked to submit to the teacher clarifying plans and procedures for their health fair learning center:

 I. General health topic of the learning center
 II. Specific theme or concept on which the center is focused
 III. Learning center number
 IV. Organization or sequence of activities
    A. How will your topic be introduced?
    B. What functional information will be shared?
    C. What multisensory activities have been planned?
    D. What summary/closure activities have been planned?
 V. Diagram or drawing of the layout of the booth
 VI. List of equipment and materials needed
 VII. List of things to be distributed

diabetes prevention, tobacco use, cardiovascular disease prevention, and osteoporosis prevention—should be the focus. Such an activity allows students to learn more about the health concerns of grown-ups while promoting health in their community.

Fourth, a group of students can organize a health fair for other students in their own school. For example, seventh graders can develop a health fair for sixth and eighth graders in their middle school.

Regardless of the format and target audience served by a health fair, such critical student skills as organizing, planning, implementing, and evaluating are enriched. To maximize the academic benefit of creating a learning center to contribute to a larger health fair, a sample organizational outline has been provided in Teacher's Toolbox 4.5. Although they are special events that supplement rather than replace effective and developmentally appropriate comprehensive health education (discussed in Chapter 2), health fairs are an effective way to correlate or integrate health education concepts with a range of other content areas (approaches discussed later in this chapter).

Limitations of Direct Instructional Approaches

Although familiar and comfortable for many education stakeholders, discipline-specific instruction presents challenges for teachers and students. Regardless of content area, the major problem associated with direct instructional approaches rests with the fragmentation of instructional time. In practical application, as students in secondary schools move from one subject to another, they also change rooms. In this model, teachers are forced to structure learning activities within time boundaries rather than in response to the developmental needs or pace of learning among students.

Because concepts and information are fragmented in direct instructional approaches, an unrealistic and often inaccurate view of problems and issues is offered to students. This model implies that students need to be equipped to manage situations and questions one at a time or only within content categories. A review of the research on brain-based instruction from Chapter 2 reminds us that learning is most likely to occur when students make connections between new concepts and pre-existing knowledge. Direct instruction does not formalize learning experiences that will capitalize on students' abilities to draw relationships between or across issues. To be equipped to manage the tasks that confront them in their daily lives, students must participate in learning experiences in which they practice making connections within and between concepts.[36]

In addition, discipline-specific instruction can reinforce the value of competition. This common competitive teaching/learning philosophy is implemented in today's classrooms more than 90 percent of the time.[37] The underpinning of this model implies that all students are expected to do their own work. As discussed earlier in this chapter, classmates are discouraged from seeking assistance from their peers, and providing support or assistance for classmates usually is regarded as cheating. As a result of intentional or unintentional teacher behaviors, students are reinforced for working against one another to accomplish personal goals. In this way, the potential benefits of collaborative problem solving and decision making about academic challenges are not realized for many learners. Even under the best of circumstances, a hierarchy of student performance emerges that influences academic performance, classroom climate, and student interaction in negative ways.[38] Such negative consequences can be reduced with cross-curricular approaches.

Interdisciplinary Instructional Approaches

In 1977, educator Lionel Elvin provided an analogy to help educators see the value of alternatives to direct instructional approaches. He suggested that, when we are walking outside, we are not confronted with fifty minutes of exclusive contact with flowers, followed by fifty minutes of exclusive contact with animals.[39] As discussed in Chapter 2, brain research has confirmed that, in the process of learning, the brain searches for patterns and interconnections as a way to make meaning from new concepts. If students learn by making connections, then educators must explore ways to teach through formalizing connections among concepts.[40]

Interdisciplinary approaches to instruction are defined as a view of knowledge (and, thus, a curriculum) that formally applies information, beliefs, and skills from more than one discipline to a problem, topic, theme, or experience.[41] Natural links among content areas serve as the foundation for implementing interdisciplinary instruction in classroom practice. For example, ideas for cross-curricular instruction might be stimulated among readers who review Teacher's Toolbox 3.11, which contains links between the National Health Education Standards and standards developed in other content areas. Experimental applications of interdisciplinary approaches have become more common for the following reasons:

- The growth of knowledge in fields that often fall between, rather than neatly within, the confines of traditional content areas
- Fragmentation of the school day and associated time management problems
- Concerns about the relevancy of many issues included in the school curriculum
- The preparation of students to manage complex tasks that will confront them in the professional adult world[42]

Correlated Health Instruction

Although educators have identified a variety of interdisciplinary approaches to instruction, correlation is very common in health education practice. In correlated instructional approaches, complementary, discipline-specific units of study or related disciplines are brought together to answer common questions, solve problems, or address complex issues. The advantages of correlated instruction are evident for health education:

- Connections between previously unrelated content areas are formally reinforced.
- Realistic and complex health issues can be addressed.
- Complementary resource materials have begun to emerge.
- Time management problems can be eased with a correlated instruction approach.

Teachers who are interested in correlating health education with another content area are urged to examine the treatment of health concepts in textbooks in other subjects. This exploration can provide teachers with a starting point for reducing repetition and expanding the use of correlated learning activities. Teachers are most likely to find such material in science textbooks. Though a useful starting place, teachers and administrators must not consider the text developed for science instruction or any other content area to be the primary source of information about health issues for students.

As with conventional approaches to instruction, problems can be associated with correlated instructional practice. Any change in organizational structure that deviates from the familiar might be met with resistance from parents, teachers, administrators, or students. In addition, scheduling problems, lack of teacher training and comfort, and lack of clarity about appropriate assessment protocol are common.

Teachers in self-contained classrooms who attempt correlated instruction can place unintentional emphasis on one content area over another. For example, if a teacher has greater expertise in language arts than in health education, it is unlikely that the health issue explored in a trade book, play, or poem will receive equal attention or emphasis. This imbalance can be exaggerated in response to topical emphasis on state tests of proficiency.

Health-specific content areas serve as the organizational structure for the chapters in this text, but to reinforce the importance of interdisciplinary or cross-curricular

TABLE 4–2

Children's Literature with Themes or Characters with Disabilities or Special Needs

Ages 5–8

Aseltine, Lorraine, and Nancy Taut. *I'm Deaf and It's Okay.* Albert Whitman, 1991.

Brown, Tricia. *Someone Special, Just Like You.* Holt, Henry Books, 1995.

Cairo, Shelly, Jasmine Cairo, and Tara Cairo. *Our Brother Has Down's Syndrome.* Firefly Books, 1993.

Edwards, Becky. *My Brother Sammy.* Millbrook Press, 1999.

Fassler, Joan. *Howie Helps Himself.* Albert Whitman, 1991.

Graff, Lisa. *The Thing About Georgie.* Laura Geringer, 2007.

Moss, Deborah. *Lee, the Rabbit with Epilepsy.* Woodbine House, 1990.

Shriver, Maria. *What's Wrong with Timmy?* Little, Brown, 2001.

Ages 8–12

Gantos, Jack. *Joey Pigza Swallowed the Key.* HarperCollins, 2000.

Greenberg, Jan, and Sandra Jordan. *Chuck Close, Up Close.* DK, 2000.

Konigsberg, E. L. *The View from Saturday.* Simon & Schuster, 1998. (Newbery Award)

Meyer, Donald J., ed. *View from Our Shoes: Growing Up with a Brother or Sister with Special Needs.* Woodbine House, 1997.

Peacock, Carol A., and Abby Levine, ed. *Sugar Was My Best Food: Diabetes and Me.* Albert Whitman, 1998.

Polacco, Patricia. *Thank You, Mr. Falker.* Putnam, 1998.

Teacher's Toolbox 4.6

Promoting a Tobacco-Free Lifestyle Across the Curriculum

With tobacco risk reduction as a central theme, instructional activities in other content areas might be organized in the following way:

- *Integrated language arts.* Students dictate or write a newspaper story about examples and types of tobacco use that they have seen around their school. Younger students' stories could focus on the risk of playing with matches or lighters that a child might find in the home, school, or neighborhood.
- *Mathematics.* After gathering information about the costs of a pack of cigarettes in the local community, students calculate the costs of smoking for a week, a month, and a year. Following this activity, they create a list of healthy alternative purchases.
- *Geography.* Students map and graphically code locations of tobacco production, transportation, and sales in their region or state.
- *Science.* Students trace the path of cigarette smoke for primary smokers and for second-hand and side-stream tobacco exposure as smoke enters the body, passes through the lungs and bloodstream, and is exhaled.
- *Health education.* Students collect information about the location and types of tobacco advertising in their community. Following this collection of data, they analyze the types of messages and the intended target audiences of each message.
- *Art.* Students develop a "Tobacco-Free Me and We" campaign for the local school community.
- *Social studies.* Students examine the history and economic impact of tobacco production in the United States as a foundation for current local, state, and national policies and practices.

---

approaches to learning, each content chapter features a list of recommended children's and adolescent books. In addition, many learning activities include links to topic-specific, developmentally appropriate literature. Many of the books have been selected because they have been recognized with the Newbery Award for their literary merit. Other books have been suggested because they contain multicultural characters, themes, or illustrations. Still others appear on the lists because they have received the Caldecott Award for noteworthy illustrations. Finally, other books have been used successfully in classroom applications.

These lists are not intended to serve as a complete catalog of all appropriate books that address health-related issues. Rather, they are included to reinforce the value of sound correlated instructional approaches. These and other trade books can provide a starting place for integrating health education concepts into classrooms and districts that have made a commitment to a whole-language approach to reading instruction. As a place to begin, teachers are urged to examine Table 4–2, which contains a list of children's trade books with themes about characters with disabilities or special needs. Consistent with the National Health Education Standards, the characters and stories in these books can provide a framework for better understanding of diversity and a context for practicing a range of health-promoting skills.

As is the case with all children's and adolescent literature, teachers must ensure that selected books are developmentally appropriate and have received thorough review. Readers who are concerned about the potential for controversy about this curricular approach or student health issue are urged to read the section "Controversy Management in Health Education" found later in this chapter.

Integrated-Health Instruction: Thematic Units

In integrated approaches to instruction, the insights from multiple discrete content areas contribute to thematic units of instruction. Units organized around a theme can last a few days or can emerge over longer periods of time. Thematic or integrated instruction is common in early childhood learning environments. Integrated instruction shares similar, yet exaggerated, advantages and disadvantages with correlated instructional approaches. The most compelling reason to incorporate integrated instruction into classroom practice is that it is consistent with life outside the classroom. Consequently, it is stimulating and motivating for students and teachers.

Readers interested in thematic units of instruction are encouraged to review the example contained in Teacher's Toolbox 4.6. Caution is urged, as time, resource, and assessment challenges are common when attempting integrated instruction. Funding constraints, preparation time, and staff development are practical issues that compromise long-range integrated planning. In addition, parents and taxpayers from the community often need to be educated about the value of integrated educational approaches if such approaches are to have widespread application and acceptance.[43]

As with cooperative learning, the developmental needs of students should drive decision making about which curricular approaches are best. Though teachers are not likely to abandon direct instruction, they might find that interdisciplinary education approaches can enrich instruction about the complex health issues facing elementary and middle school students.

Use of computers can challenge students and enrich learning, but teachers must conduct careful evaluation of all materials on the Internet before allowing students access. Many schools limit student access to Internet content.

USING ELECTRONIC RESOURCES IN HEALTH EDUCATION

Anyone who has visited an elementary or middle school in recent years has noticed a changing learning landscape. Though many of the conventional approaches to teaching and learning remain, there is ever-increasing evidence of the use of instructional technologies. In classrooms and/or in school-based learning labs, computers almost universally are used as tools to enrich learning and assessment (see the discussion about electronic portfolios and rubrics in Chapter 3). In many cases, computers provide access to challenging and enriching learning experiences for students of wide-ranging abilities. In addition, volumes of information are accessible to students, who have increasingly sophisticated computer expertise. In fact, the computer literacy of students often surpasses that of their teachers, parents, and other significant adults. A review of the use of computer-based technologies to enrich classroom instruction follows.

• *The Internet.* The Internet is a global network of computers linking commercial online communication services (America Online, CompuServe) with many and varied university, government, and corporate networks. Composed of many parts (the World Wide Web, documents, e-mail, newsgroups, mailing lists, chat rooms, etc.), the Internet provides users with access to in-depth information about health promotion topics, the latest research on health issues, and individuals from around the world who share an interest in specific health concerns.

To reach the Internet, students and teachers need a computer, a modem, access to the network through a provider, and browser software that provides navigation potential. Students, teachers, schools, and families often gain access to the Internet through local or state governmental or academic sources (public libraries or local public universities). Many people gain access through a commercial Internet service provider. Such services vary

considerably, from bare-bones services for which additional browser software must be purchased (Netscape Navigator or Microsoft Internet Explorer) to more expensive but more comprehensive providers that include all necessary software and features, including e-mail, access to newsgroups, and web browsers (America Online, CompuServe, NetZero, Microsoft Network.).[44]

• *The World Wide Web.* The World Wide Web is composed of a collection of files called web pages or websites created by individuals, companies, organizations, or government agencies. The Web, a user-friendly part of the Internet, offers easy access, navigation, and media such as audio, video, and animation.

Each website is identified by an address or uniform resource locator (URL), such as www.healthfinder.gov. To access a site, a user can either type the URL into the appropriate screen of the browser or click on a hyperlink that provides a shortcut to another web page or a different part of the current page. Hyperlinks appear as images, in a different color, or underlined in the text. Clicking on links allows the user to jump to related sites anywhere on the Internet.

Search engines or directories are used to find information about a particular health issue. Users must understand that search engines each scrutinize unique databases of web pages, so different results will emerge from the use of different search engines. Search engines include

AllTheWeb (www.alltheweb.com)

AltaVista (www.altavista.com)

Ask (www.ask.com)

Excite (www.excite.com)

Google (www.google.com)

Lycos (www.lycos.com)

Northern Light (www.northernlight.com)

Yahoo! (www.yahoo.com)

Teacher's Toolbox 4.7

Evaluation of Web-Based Resources: Criteria for Teachers

Here is a list of questions to guide evaluation of electronic content and resources for use with students.

Authority with regard to the topic (Who is responsible for the site?):

- Who is the author of the site (individual, institution, or organization)?
- What are the credentials, expertise, and experience of those responsible for the site?
- Is contact information available for those responsible for the site (name, e-mail address, other information)?
- Does the URL type suggest that the site has a reputable affiliation (.edu, or educational; .org, or nonprofit organization; .com, or commercial enterprise; .net, or Internet Service Provider; .gov, or governmental body; .mil, or military)?

Objectivity (Is the purpose or any particular viewpoint of the site made clear to users?):

- Is there a statement of purpose or scope of the site?
- Is an intended audience identified?
- Is the information that is presented primary or secondary in origin?
- Is information on the site presented as fact or opinion?
- Are the criteria for including content on the site clarified for users?
- Is any sponsorship or underwriting made clear?

Accuracy (Is the information on the site evidence-based?):

- Does the site contain evidence that the facts and other information are well documented and researched?
- Are facts and information posted on this site consistent with those in print or on other online sources?
- Do links that are provided connect to other quality resources?

Currency (Is posted information up-to-date?):

- Does the site contain current information?
- Are pages on the site date-stamped with the latest update?

Usability (Is the site well designed and stable?):

- Does the organization of the site seem logical and make the site easy to navigate?
- Is the content of the site readable by the intended audience?
- Is information free of spelling, grammar, and punctuation errors?
- Do users have ready access to the institutional or organizational home of the site?
- Is the site readily accessible?
- Do pages on the site load quickly?

SOURCE: Kent State University, Libraries and Media Services, 19 July 2004, *Criteria for Evaluating Web Resources* (www.library.kent.edu/webeval; retrieved 2 February 2008). Used with permission.

In addition to these individual search engines, meta-search engines are available. Examples include the following, which simultaneously submit a topic to multiple search engines:

Dogpile (www.dogpile.com)

Ixquick (www.ixquick.com)

Vivisimo (www.vivisimo.com)

When searching, it is best to make the search topics or issues as specific as possible. The use of broad keywords such as "nutrition" will reveal thousands or even millions of matches. Most search engines have help sections that contain suggestions about how best to enter keywords. If one search engine fails to give helpful results, try another. The list of websites at the end of this chapter includes search engines, directories, and websites to help users find information about student health issues.[45]

Note that anyone can post anything on the Internet without its being subjected to any evaluation or review for accuracy or quality. Teachers must conduct a scrupulous evaluation of all Internet resources and materials to be shared with students. Teacher's Toolbox 4.7 reviews important criteria for teachers and older students to use

to support informed decision making about web-based resources.[46] In addition, such issues as cyberbullying will be addressed in pertinent content chapters in this text.

- *Usenet newsgroups.* Similar to electronic bulletin boards, newsgroups consist of a collection of messages, articles, and postings about a topic that has been archived. Commercial online services maintain newsgroups for subscribing members only, but many are available on the Internet for anyone to use. Users seeking a newsgroup about a particular health issue can use a search engine or a site devoted to searches of newsgroups, such as Deja.com (http://groups.google.com).

Browsers of a newsgroup will find that related topics are collected in a "thread" containing the message that started a discussion and all responses to that original posting. Older articles are deleted from newsgroups to make room for newer messages, so readers are encouraged to print or save information of particular interest.

In addition to browsing, reading, and saving newsgroup postings of interest, users can become active participants. Individuals can respond to one or all newsgroup participants, or they can post a new message to start a new thread of the discussion. Before becoming an active member of a newsgroup, users are encouraged to observe postings for a brief time or review the "frequently asked questions" (FAQs) section to make sure that postings are appropriate.[47]

- *Listserv mailing lists.* Listservs are similar to newsgroups, but rather than being posted on a public site, messages are delivered by e-mail to mailing list subscribers. Subscribers to a mailing list can post messages and receive messages posted by other subscribers. It is common for teachers to create listservs for students and/or their parents or caregivers. To locate listservs focused on a particular topic, users can do a keyword search or enter a health topic of interest into a search engine, followed by the word *listserv*. An extensive mailing list directory can be found at Topica (http://lists.topica.com).[48]

- *Real-time online communication: chat rooms.* Another online tool with educational potential is the real-time chat room. After careful screening, teachers and students can sign on and communicate with a group of people from around the world about a health topic of interest. To maximize safety, teachers are urged to use extreme caution before engaging students in even academically focused chat rooms. Though much of the conversation is public, it is possible for smaller groups or pairs of chat room subscribers to have private conversations.[49]

- *WebQuests.* Teachers and students interested in learning about health issues through an inquiry and online format are encouraged to explore the world of WebQuests. These electronic resources are made up of a series of classroom-based learning experiences in which most or all of the information students explore and evaluate comes from the World Wide Web. Through participation in short-term (one to three class meetings) or longer-term (one week to one month) WebQuest learning experiences, students can participate in independent, group, or role-playing activities that have a single-issue or cross-curricular focus.

WebQuests contain six essential components (Introduction, Task, Process, Resources, Evaluation, and Conclusion) and commonly are tied to national or state content standards. Unlike many other web-based learning applications, WebQuests require students to move beyond lower-order cognitive skills. In addition, student ownership of learning is increased as teachers assume the role of guide or facilitator. Students and teachers also can develop their own WebQuests reflecting particular health issues of interest.

To ensure maximal utility, evaluation of WebQuests is critical. Teachers should review the following list of questions as a starting point in their decision making about the use or development of WebQuests as a learning strategy:

1. Is the Introduction understandable?
2. Are the goals clear and attainable?
3. Does this WebQuest require only appropriate use of the Internet?
4. Are students required to use higher-order thinking skills?
5. Is group collaboration required?
6. Are activities suggested that can be done without using the Internet?
7. Is the identified Evaluation appropriate?

Interested readers are encouraged to review the list of WebQuest resources at the end of this chapter.[50]

The effects of using instructional technologies to target health-risk reduction are unclear. Little research has been done to define the nature of this relationship, particularly among students in elementary and middle schools. However, it has been documented that many computer-based learning applications for young learners tend to focus on lower-order cognitive processes.

As computer access increases and more instruction is delivered using identified technologies, more developmentally appropriate learning resources will emerge. Although computers will never replace the relationship between students and teachers, they do offer a vehicle for exploring an increasingly exciting and sophisticated range of resources to enrich learning and classroom practice.

CONTROVERSY MANAGEMENT IN HEALTH EDUCATION

Controversy involves a conflict of values and beliefs. Such conflict is an inevitable part of life in a pluralistic society. School-based professionals and programs are particularly vulnerable to controversy because their primary source of funding is public tax dollars. In addition, the U.S. education enterprise is based on mandatory participation for all children and youth. Controversy about school policies and practices takes two common forms:

1. Conflict about what content and issues are addressed
2. Disagreement about the proper parameters for implementation of the curriculum[51]

In the context of both sources of conflict, the subject matter and curricular approaches that provide a foundation for sound health education practice can provide fertile ground for dispute. In some school districts, the notion of including a Comprehensive School Health Education program in the approved district curriculum is regarded as an inappropriate use of instructional time. Advocates for a back-to-basics approach to education often view attention to anything other than core content as a waste of valuable academic time. Still others view the process of organizing a Coordinated School Health Program as a way to formalize intrusion into family issues or to attempt to usurp parents' rights.

Some health topics are likely to evoke little or no heated response, but others (sexual health promotion, stress management, death education, and some approaches to tobacco, alcohol, and other drug risk reduction) can serve as a lightning rod for parental and public concern. In addition, HECAT and the National School Health Education Standards imply that the primary focus of instruction should be skill development in potentially controversial areas.

Like education professionals, parents and taxpayers who express concern about curricular or policy matters in their schools are motivated by a commitment to creating the best possible learning environment for students. Consequently, the best way to avoid controversy is to formalize open and effective communication among all stakeholders.[52] The Coordinated School Health Program model provides an effective mechanism for anticipating discrepancies in values and even formalizes a structure for community and parental review of all curricular and policy matters.

There is no guarantee that controversy can be avoided, but, recommendations have been offered for the school community to manage any negative outcry in a way that will reduce its impact on the quality and continuity of health instruction. Though many such recommendations are taken from the body of research in human sexuality, school personnel might find them also helpful when confronted with controversy about reading or math curricula or literature selections in the school library.

Anticipation: Strategies for School Leaders

The most effective strategy for managing controversy in a school district is to anticipate the potential for a negative reaction. The following recommendations have been suggested by Jacquelyn Sowers, a nationally regarded school health and education consultant, and are offered to help in developing proactive, districtwide plans:

1. *Do your homework.* Knowledge of demographic facts about the community and state, as well as data about the health risks of children and youth, is critical. In addition, school administrators must be fluent in information about local health agencies, counseling services, medical facilities, and law enforcement agencies. Finally, it is vital for school personnel to have an accurate understanding of the social norms and standards in their school community.

2. *Engage a broad base of planners.* For best results, all planning groups must reflect the community. Efforts must include input from students, parents, advocates, opponents, and leaders of faith-based organizations in the school district.

3. *State goals clearly.* Standards and testing parameters developed by state departments of education are best regarded as a starting point for activities within local districts. Although potentially time-consuming, the investment in reaching consensus on goals will minimize controversy in the long run.

4. *Cultivate support networks.* Administrators would be wise to seek support from those community providers who see the result of myth and misinformation among youth. Public health professionals, medical care providers, youth counselors, the faith community, and senior citizen representatives often are aware of such negative consequences.

5. *Identify articulate spokespersons.* Regardless of profession, there are individuals within every community who can serve as respected and articulate advocates and respond to concerns about school-based health promotion programming.

6. *Create awareness within the community.* Often, controversy can be reduced if the community is aware of the needs of its students. Wise administrators cultivate the media, hold open forums, and provide presentations to civic and religious organizations to provide information about health issues confronting local youth.

7. *Be positive.* Negativism on the part of administrators can become a self-fulfilling prophecy for controversy. All efforts must be made to manage each confrontation as it arises rather than to interpret activities as a conspiracy against health promotion activities.[53, 54]

School districts that have established school health advisory committees are far more likely to manage controversy successfully than are their less proactive counterparts. The importance of well-planned, developmentally appropriate, board-approved health curricula cannot be overstated. School district officials must provide staff development activities for teachers delivering potentially controversial instructional activities. Finally, classroom-based professionals must be assured that they have administrative support at all times.

In the event that controversy surfaces, the following strategies are suggested for school leaders:

- Know your goals and be able to communicate them positively and effectively.
- Listen and find common ground.
- Don't get defensive.
- Keep supporters informed and involved.
- Step up an information campaign.
- Be honest and forthright.
- Respect differences.
- Remain positive.[55]

Recommendations for Teachers

Although most of the activities listed in "Anticipation: Strategies for School Leaders" are beyond the responsibility of classroom teachers, it is the teachers who must translate district policy into instructional practice. As a starting point, many teachers look to district-approved texts and instructional materials. Unfortunately, these materials often provide very little help in teaching potentially controversial topics. A review of currently available elementary and middle school health textbooks revealed a lack of coverage of certain subjects. Most noteworthy is the omission of information about human reproduction, sexuality, and childbirth. No information can be found in the same textbooks on the subject of death and dying. Although drug abuse is a major problem in American society, elementary and middle school health textbooks provide little developmentally appropriate information about current drugs of choice with which children might be familiar.

As discussed earlier in this chapter, teachers must be prepared to create a safe and nurturing learning environment for all students about all subject matter in the district course of study. As a starting point, Chapter 13 provides guidelines for teaching sexuality that can be generalized to address any health education content area. In addition, teachers must be prepared to provide accurate and timely information about classroom content matters. To this end, participation in staff development opportunities is advised. Also, teachers must seek the support of their local administrators and would be wise to consult colleagues in professional associations to which they belong.

Finally, the following recommendations can help teachers respond to the many questions children have about their health. In general, the reaction to student questions can be as important as the response that is provided. In this context, teachers are encouraged to

- Know local district policies and approved curricular parameters.
- Affirm and clarify questions.
- Separate personal emotions from responses.
- Maintain the lines of communication.

The following types of questions and corresponding response strategies are particularly relevant to questions about potentially controversial topics.[56]

Requests for Information

Many times, students will be very curious about a subject or will need something clarified. If the teacher thinks the question is appropriate for the grade level and knows the answer, then it is certainly appropriate to answer the question. If the teacher does not know the answer, he or she should tell the student so and should ask students to identify a strategy for finding the answer. In addition, it is important for the teacher to make sure student questions get correct, developmentally appropriate responses.

If the teacher feels the question is inappropriate for the grade level, the teacher should tell the class that he or she does not feel comfortable answering that question. However, it is important to find out from the student why he or she asked it. The teacher should try to find out more information about what motivated the question before answering it.

Finally, it is critical for teachers to know about any local policies concerning responding to student questions about selected issues (contraception, same-sex relationships). Some school districts have established a list of responses for teachers to read in addressing inquiries about these matters.

"Am I Normal?" Questions

"Am I normal?" questions generally focus on concerns about students' bodies and the physical and emotional changes that are occurring in them. It is important to validate their concerns by informing them that many young people of their age share those concerns. Next, the teacher should provide information about what students can expect as their bodies continue to change, grow, and develop over the next few years. In addition, it is appropriate to suggest that they can talk to parents, counselors, or clergy or consult other community resources if they need additional information.

Permission-Seeking/Personal Belief Questions

Generally, these questions are intended to ask permission to participate in a particular behavior. For example, "Is it normal for kids my age to . . . ?" "Did you participate in . . . activity when you were growing up?" or "Do you think it is okay to . . . ?" are cues for parents and teachers that permission might be being sought. It is important to avoid using the word *normal* or *typical* when answering questions. Morality enters into these questions, and it is not up to teachers to decide what is right or wrong for students. The exception to this is something that is against the law. Also, it is important to establish ground rules at the beginning of the year and to emphasize that personal sexual behavior is not open for discussion. In particular, teachers are urged not to share personal experiences with students when such information can be construed as permission to act in a similar way.

Shock Questions

Sometimes, students ask questions to shock the teacher. Many questions are shocking because of the vocabulary used. To deal with this situation, the teacher should reword the question, using proper terminology. In any case, it is important for the teacher to stay calm and not act embarrassed. Finally, it might be necessary for teachers to remind students when questions are inappropriate and/or require a private conversation.

Conclusion

The keys to managing potential controversy lie in having a Coordinated School Health Program in place and anticipating community response to curricular matters. While maintaining fidelity to school policies and curricular boundaries, teachers can serve as advocates for change when student health needs are not being met. Successful implementation of controversy management lies in knowing parents and key stakeholders in the community. Increasing parental engagement in all aspects of the education process is an important goal for all school districts.

PARENTAL ENGAGEMENT: A FOUNDATION FOR IMPROVED SCHOOL PERFORMANCE AND HEALTH PROMOTION

Confirming the value of partnerships between the home and the school has been the focus of intense public debate and the subject of a growing body of scholarly research. Educators and politicians recommend that energy be devoted to increasing parental engagement in the academic lives of their children. Most major educational reform efforts have identified parental involvement as an important factor in improving the education process. To this end, government and education agencies have made recommendations to help schools organize parent participation programs. In addition, documents have been published describing the characteristics of exemplary parent involvement programs.[57] In this spirit, the National PTA

TABLE 4–3

National Standards for Parental/Family Involvement

Standard I	**Communicating**—communication between home and school is regular, two-way, and meaningful.
Standard II	**Parenting**—parenting skills are promoted and supported.
Standard III	**Student learning**—parents play an integral role in assisting student learning
Standard IV	**Volunteering**—parents are welcome in the school, and their support and assistance are sought.
Standard V	**School decision making and advocacy**—parents are full partners in the decisions that affect children and families.
Standard VI	**Collaborating with community**—community resources are used to strengthen schools, families, and student learning.

SOURCE: National Standards for Parent/Family Involvement, National PTA 2004 (www.pta.org/archive_article_details_1118251710359.html; retrieved 1 February 2008). Used with permission.

has developed standards for parental/family involvement programs. These standards are listed in Table 4–3.[58]

As the call has gone forth for an increased and more formal role for parents in their children's education, a growing body of research has confirmed specific positive effects that engaged families can have on student achievement. Following is a summary of important outcomes that can result from sound programming that engages parents:

- When families support learning in their homes, students experience higher achievement.
- Achievement gains occur regardless of socioeconomic status, ethnic/racial background, or the education level of parents.
- Children of engaged parents have higher grades and test scores, better attendance, and more consistently complete homework. In addition, these students have higher graduation rates and are more likely to enroll in postsecondary education.
- Among children who are socioeconomically disadvantaged, learning improves to levels similar to those of children of middle-income families when their parents become engaged as partners in their learning.
- When parents don't participate in school events and fail to cultivate productive working relationships with school personnel, children are more likely to fall behind in their academic performance.[59]

In addition to their role in influencing improved academic outcomes, parents and other significant adults can exert a powerful influence over the health behaviors of young people. A longitudinal study confirmed that, among the most basic socially contextual influences, "the family and school contexts are among the most critical."[60] Across all health-risk domains, the role of the family in shaping the health of adolescents is significant. Specifically, when students perceive that their parents have high expectations for their success in school, there is decreased likelihood they will participate in health-risk behaviors. This study confirmed the particular importance of feelings of warmth, love, and caring from parents in reinforcing healthy lifestyle choices. Parental availability has been confirmed as an influential factor in "family connectedness," and adolescents who feel such a connection to parents or adult caregivers are

- Three times less likely to smoke cigarettes
- Two times less likely to use marijuana
- Three times less likely to drink alcohol to excess
- Five times less likely to participate in risky sexual behaviors
- Five times more likely to participate in regular exercise[61]

The home environment has been demonstrated to play an important role in shaping specific health risks. Students who have easy access to guns, alcohol, tobacco, and other drugs in their homes are at higher risk for suicide, violence, and substance use.[62]

The amount and type of communication that occurs between caregivers and their children have been demonstrated to influence sexual risks among youth. Research has confirmed that effective communication between parents and teens is likely to deter teens from participating in sexual experimentation at an early age. Such communication between parents and their teens has also been linked to the use of contraception among young people if or when they engage in sexual behaviors. Further, when teens and their mothers discuss contraception, such conversations *do not* cause or give implied permission to teens to engage in risky sexual behavior.[63]

Finally, the health behaviors of parents have been linked to the health risks of youth. Although parents who use tobacco are more likely to have children who smoke, this factor is not causal. Due to many complex sources of influence over teen tobacco use, parents who smoke might or might not influence their children to smoke. The value that parents place on a tobacco-free lifestyle is very influential in respect to tobacco use among children. Regardless of parental tobacco use, children who understand that their parents are negative about tobacco use among youth are less likely than the children of permissive parents to smoke.[64]

In addition to the importance of a strong connection with parents or other caregivers, a connection to their school exerts a protective influence over youth. Students who feel connected to their school, parents, family, and other adults tend to participate in far fewer health-risk behaviors.[65] Consistent with the philosophy and practice of the Coordinated School Health Program model, collaborative approaches to pooling home, school, and community resources in health promotion agendas can result in very positive outcomes.

The key to confirmed academic gains and health-risk reduction rests in the implementation of sound programs that extend beyond increasing the in-school visibility of parents and other caregivers. In a call for effective efforts, and not just gestures, an article in *American School Board Journal* asserted that "the cookie-baking, word-processing,

Parents who are engaged in homework activities with their children communicate that they are committed to success in school.

candy-selling, paper-shuffling, showing-up activities are not likely to have much impact on achievement."[66] In contrast with less effective efforts, research has identified several types of parental engagement in the educational process that have been linked consistently with improved academic performance.[67] These activities primarily are based in the home and reinforce the commitment students must make to their schoolwork. The kinds of behaviors most likely to improve academic outcomes for students include

• *Managing and organizing children's use of time.* Parents of successful students help their children organize their schedules and check to see that their children are following routines.[68] In addition, parents would be wise to stay informed about school activities, performance, and assignments and to provide a place and time for homework to be completed. Finally, academic outcomes are improved for students whose parents know where they are, with whom they are spending time, and when they plan to come home. Engaged parents also supervise and exercise control over nonschool activities, including time devoted to television viewing.

• *Helping with homework.* Participating in homework provides parents with the opportunity to confirm their interest and take a direct role in their children's schooling. Specific suggestions for supporting academic success include making certain that assignments are completed, checking accuracy, and asking questions about the nature of assignments.

• *Discussing school matters with children.* It is important for children and their parents to talk regularly about school activities. The kind of conversation also is important: Parents should be willing to discuss problems as well as successes and reinforce persistence in confronting challenges. In addition, research supports developmentally appropriate collaborative decision making about matters such as participation in activities, projects undertaken, and, for older students, course selection.

• *Reading to and being read to by children.* A large body of research confirms the importance of reading activities for developing reading proficiency in younger learners. In addition, there is a connection between achieving school success and living in a home that is literacy-laden—that is, one that contains newspapers, books, magazines, and a computer or word processor.[69]

Teachers can support parental involvement in student learning by providing engaging and developmentally appropriate assignments that parents and children can complete together at home, but it is important to remember that strong parent–teacher relationships are based on reciprocal elements. The literature is clear that parents have consistent concerns about teacher performance. Specifically, parents are concerned about how well teachers know and care about

• Teaching
• Their children
• Communication with parents

As a means of evaluating the often unintentional messages being sent to parents, teachers are encouraged to ask themselves the following questions:

Concerning My Teaching

1. Do I appear to enjoy teaching and believe in the value of what I do?
2. Do I set high expectations and help children reach them?
3. Do I know my subject matter and practice effective teaching methods?
4. Do I create a safe and inviting learning environment in which students are encouraged to pay attention, participate, and learn?
5. Do I deal with behavior problems consistently and fairly?
6. Do I assign meaningful homework that can be completed in a timely manner?
7. Do I make learning expectations clear to students and parents?
8. Do I provide constructive feedback using positive communication in a timely manner?

Concerning My Students

1. Do I understand the diverse ways in which children learn and create correspondingly diverse learning activities?
2. Do I treat students fairly and with respect?
3. Do I contact parents promptly about academic or behavioral concerns?
4. Do I provide helpful information during conferences?

Concerning Communicating with Parents

1. Do I provide parents with clear information about expectations?
2. Do I use a variety of tools to communicate with parents?

3. Am I accessible and responsive when contacted by parents?
4. Do I cooperate with parents to develop strategies that are helpful for students?
5. Do I communicate with parents in language that they can understand easily?
6. Do I communicate in ways that invite and support parents as partners in the learning process?
7. Do I do my best to accommodate the time and schedules of parents?[70]

To support parental engagement, the Education Commission of the States has made seven recommendations for teachers to improve student achievement by reaching out to parents. While not surprising, this list of suggestions, found in Teacher's Toolbox 4.8, can help teachers build bridges and improve communication networks to influence student health and academic performance.[71] In addition, readers are encouraged to examine the websites focused on improving parental engagement in the education of their children located under "School and Family Partnerships" in the "Internet and Other Resources" section.

Engaging parents in the learning process has been demonstrated to influence academic outcomes and student participation in health-risk behaviors in a positive way. Developing a strategy to engage these important caregivers depends more on the attitude and personal characteristics

of teachers and administrators than on the sophistication of any organizational or recruitment plan. To create mutually rewarding relationships between parents and school personnel requires honesty, humility, and authenticity.

Teacher's Toolbox 4.8

Communication Tips for Parents and Teachers

RECOMMENDATIONS FOR IMPROVED STUDENT SUCCESS FROM THE EDUCATION COMMISSION OF THE STATES

1. Listen to people first; then talk later.
2. Expect to fail if you don't practice communicating well.
3. Make involving interested parties from the community a top priority.
4. Be clear about what it means to set and meet high standards for all students.
5. Show concerned others how new ideas can enhance, rather than replace, old ones.
6. Educate parents about the choices available to them.
7. Help parents and community residents understand how student progress is evaluated and what the results mean.

SOURCE: Education Commission of the States (ECS), *Listen, Discuss, and Act* (Denver: ECS, 1996), 15–17.

INTERNET AND OTHER RESOURCES

Visit the Online Learning Center (www.mhhe.com/telljohann6e) for links to these sites, quizzes and other study aids, and many additional resources.

WEBSITES

WEBSITES WITH A FOCUS ON HEALTH AND HEALTH PROMOTION

American Academy of Pediatrics
www.aap.org

CDC Health Information A to Z
www.cdc.gov/az.do

Healthfinder
www.healthfinder.gov

InteliHealth
www.intelihealth.com

Mayo Clinic
www.mayoclinic.com

NIH Health Information Index
www.health.nih.gov

U.S. Consumer Gateway: Health
www.consumer.gov/health.htm

WebMD
www.webmd.com

WEBSITES WITH A FOCUS ON WEBQUESTS

www.eduscapes.com/tap/topic4.htm
www.webquest.org
www.bestwebquests.com

www.questgarden.com
http://webquest.sdsu.edu/LessonTemplate.html

OTHER RESOURCES

COOPERATIVE LEARNING

Johnson, D., R. Johnson, and M. B. Stanne. *Cooperative Learning Methods: A Meta Analysis* (Minneapolis, MN: University of Minnesota, 2000).

STUDENT CONNECTEDNESS

Association for Supervision and Curriculum Development. *The Learning Compact Redefined: A Call to Action* (Alexandria, VA: ASCD, 2007).

Bean, S., and L. A. Rolleri. *Parent-Child Connectedness: Voices of African-American and Latino Parents and Teens* (Santa Cruz, CA: ETR Associates, 2005).

Lezin, N., L. A. Rolleri, S. Bean, and J. Taylor. *Parent-Child Connectedness: Implications for Research, Interventions, and Positive Impacts on Adolescent Health* (Scotts Valley, CA: ETR Associates, 2004).

Libbey, H. P. "Measuring Student Relationships to School: Attachment, Bonding, Connectedness, and Engagement." *Journal of School Health* 74, no. 7 (September 2004): 274–83.

McNeely, C., and C. Falci. "School Connectedness and the Transition Into and Out of Health-Risk Behavior Among Adolescents: A Comparison of Social Belonging and Teacher Support." *Journal of School Health* 74, no. 7 (September 2004): 284–92.

EDUCATIONAL TECHNOLOGY

Caeuso, C. "Bringing Online Learning to Life." *Educational Leadership* (May 2008): 70–72.

Colgan, C. "What's in a BLOG?" *American School Board Journal* (July 2005): 16–21.

National Association for the Education of Young Children. *Technology and Young Children—Ages 3 Through 8* (Washington, DC: NAEYC, 1996).

Snyder, T. D. "Online Education: Closing Opportunity Gaps." *The RMC Health Educator* 6, No. 2 (Spring 2006): 1–5.

Whalen, S., and L. H. Fiorentino. *Teaming Up on Technology: Lessons for Health Education and Physical Education Teachers* (Reston, VA: AAHE/AAHPERD, 2006).

SCHOOL AND FAMILY PARTNERSHIPS

Christie, K. "Changing the Nature of Parent Involvement." *Phi Delta Kappan* (May 2005): 645–46.

Dillon, N. "The Parent Trap." *American School Board Journal* (February 2008): 30–33.

Educational Testing Service. *The Family: America's Smallest School* (Princeton, NJ: ETS, 2007).

Gerne, K. M., and J. L. Epstein. "The Power of Partnerships: School, Family and Community Collaborations to Improve Children's Health." *RMC Health Educator* 4, no. 2 (winter 2004): 1, 2, 4–7.

Redding, S., J. Langdon, J. Meyer, and P. Sheley. *The Effects of Comprehensive Parent Engagement on Student Learning Outcomes* (Cambridge, MA: Harvard Family Research Project, 2004).

ENDNOTES

1. H. H. Jacobs, "On Interdisciplinary Curriculum: A Conversation with Heidi H. Jacobs," *Educational Leadership* (October 1991): 24.

2. R. T. Johnson and D. W. Johnson, "An Overview of Cooperative Learning," in *Creativity and Collaborative Learning*, eds., J. Thousand, A. Villa, and A. Nevin (Baltimore, MD: Brookes Press, 1994).

3. M. Demaray and C. Malecki, "Critical Levels of Perceived Social Support Associated with School Adjustment," *School Psychology Quarterly* 17, no. 3 (2002): 213–41.

4. K. Wentzel, "Are Effective Teachers Like Good Parents? Teaching Styles and Student Adjustment in Early Adolescence," *Child Development* 73, no. 1 (2002): 287–301.

5. M. Resnick et al., "Protecting Adolescents from Harm: Findings from the National Longitudinal Study on Adolescent Health," *Journal of the American Medical Association* 278, no. 10 (1997): 823–32.

6. William W. Purkey, *Self-Concept and School Achievement* (Englewood Cliffs, NJ: Prentice-Hall, 1970), 49.

7. G. Stock, *The Kids' Book of Questions* (New York, NY: Workman, 1988).

8. J. Gibbs, *Tribes: A New Way of Learning and Being Together* (Sausalito, CA: Center Source Systems, 1995).

9. Ibid.

10. Ibid.

11. L. Shoji, conversation with author, November 2001.

12. D. Parker, conversation with author, February 2001.

13. J. Piaget, *The Epistemology of Interdisciplinary Relationships* (Paris: Organization for Economic Cooperation and Development, 1972).

14. H. H. Jacobs, ed., *Interdisciplinary Curriculum: Design and Implementation* (Alexandria, VA: Association for Supervision and Curriculum Development, 1989), 7.

15. E. E. Ames, L. A. Trucano, Julia C. Wan, and Margo H. Harris, *Designing School Health Curriculum,* 2d ed. (Dubuque, IA: Wm. C. Brown, 1995), 90.

16. D. Johnson and R. T Johnson, *Cooperation and Competition: Theory and Research* (Edina, MN: Interaction Book Company, 1989).

17. R. T. Johnson and D. W. Johnson, "An Overview of Cooperative Learning," in *Creativity and Collaborative Learning.*

18. S. Friedland, "Bridging the Gap," *Executive Educator* 16, no. 10 (October 1994): 27.

19. D. Johnson and R. T Johnson, *Cooperation and Competition: Theory and Research.*

20. B. Cinelli, C. W. Symons, L. Bechtel, and M. Rose-Colley, "Applying Cooperative Learning in Health Education Practice," *Journal of School Health* 64, no. 3 (March 1994): 99–102.

21. R. Johnson and D. Johnson, 1997; *Cooperative Learning and Conflict Resolution* (www.newhorizons.org/strategies/cooperative/johnson.htm; retrieved 1 February 2008).

22. Cinelli et al., "Applying Cooperative Learning," 100.

23. Ibid.

24. Ibid., 101.

25. S. Friedland, "Bridging the Gap."

26. B. Cinelli et al., "Applying Cooperative Learning," 100.

27. R. Johnson and D. Johnson, *Cooperative Learning and Conflict Resolution.*

28. S. Friedland, "Bridging the Gap."

29. B. Cinelli et al., "Applying Cooperative Learning," 103.

30. National Commission on the Role of the School and the Community in Improving Adolescent Health, *Code Blue: Uniting for Healthier Youth.* (Alexandria, VA: National Association of State Boards of Education and AMA, 1990), 37–38.

31. B. Cinelli et al., "Applying Cooperative Learning," 99–100; Gist, "Problem-Based Learning," 12.

32. G. Tanaka, J. Warren, and L. Tritsch, "What's Real in Health Education?" *Journal of Health Education* 24, no. 6 (1993): 57–58.

33. B. Cinelli et al., "Applying Cooperative Learning," 102.

34. S. Friedland, "Bridging the Gap."

35. Ibid.

36. H. H. Jacobs, *Interdisciplinary Curriculum,* 1.

37. S. Friedland, "Bridging the Gap."

38. Ibid.

39. L. Elvin, *The Place of Common Sense in Educational Thought* (London: Unwin Educational Books, 1977).

40. Susan M. Drake, *Planning Integrated Curriculum* (Alexandria, VA: Association for Supervision and Curriculum Development, 1993), 3.

41. H. H. Jacobs, *Interdisciplinary Curriculum,* 8.

42. Ibid., 3–6.

43. Drake, *Planning Integrated Curriculum,* 2.

44. P. M. Insel and W. T. Roth, *Core Concepts in Health* (New York, NY: McGraw-Hill, 2004), A-13–A-15.

45. Ibid.

46. Kent State University, Libraries and Media Services, 19 July 2004; *Criteria for Evaluating Web Resources* (www.library.kent.edu/webeval; retrieved 9 March 2005).

47. P. M. Insel and W. T. Roth, *Core Concepts in Health.*

48. Ibid.

49. Ibid.

50. Mary H. Tipton, WebQuest Workshop, Kent State University, conversation with author, May 2005.

51. Loren B. Bensley and Elizabeth Harmon, "Addressing Controversy in Health Education," *Alliance Update* (May/June 1992): 9–10.

52. Ibid.

53. J. G. Sowers, *Guidelines for Dealing with Resistance to Comprehensive Health Education* (Hampton, NH: Sowers Associates, 1994).

54. J. Sowers, "Building Bridges to Common Ground," in *Partners in Prevention,* eds., M. Rubin and S. Wooley (Kent, OH: American School Health Association, 2006): 19–23.

55. J. G. Sowers, *Guidelines for Dealing with Resistance to Comprehensive Health Education.*

56. K. Middleton, B. Hubbard, W. Kane, and J. Taylor, *Contemporary Health Series: Making Health Education Comprehensive* (Santa Cruz, CA: ETR Associates, 1991), 31–33.

57. B. Rutherford, B. Anderson, and S. Billig, *Parent and Community Involvement in Education* (Washington, DC: U.S. Department of Education, Office of Educational Research and Improvement, 1997).

58. National PTA, 2002; *National Standards for Parent/Family Involvement* (www.pta.org/archive_article_details_1118251710359.html; retrieved 1 February 2008).

59. A. Henderson, T. Mapp, and A. Averett, *A New Wave of Evidence: The Impact of School, Family, and Community Connections on Student Achievement* (Austin, TX: National Center for Family and Community Connections with Schools, 2002).

60. Michael D. Resnick et al., "Protecting Adolescents from Harm," *Journal of the American Medical Association* 278, no. 10 (10 September 1997): 823–32.

61. Ibid., 830.

62. Ibid., 831.

63. C. Dailard, "Recent Findings from the 'Add Health' Survey: Teens and Sexual Activity," *Guttmacher Report on Public Policy* (August 2001): 9–16.

64. U.S. Department of Health and Human Services, *Got a Minute? Give It to Your Kid* (Atlanta: Centers for Disease Control and Prevention, Office on Smoking and Health, 2002).

65. Michael D. Resnick et al., "The Impact of Caring and Connectedness on Adolescent Health and Well-Being," *Journal of Pediatric Child Health* 29 (Suppl. 1): S3–S9.

66. R. Jones, "How Parents Can Support Learning," *American School Board Journal* (September, 2001): 18–22.

67. Jeremy D. Finn, "Parental Engagement That Makes a Difference," *Educational Leadership* 55, no. 8 (May 1998): 20–24.

68. R. M. Clark, *Family Life and School Achievement* (Chicago: University of Chicago Press, 1983).

69. R. M. Wolf, "The Measurement of Environments," in *Invitational Conference on Testing Problems,* ed. A. Anastasi (Princeton, NJ: Educational Testing Service, 1964).

70. Dorothy Rich, "What Parents Want from Teachers," *Educational Leadership* 55, no. 8 (May 1998): 37–39.

71. Education Commission of the States (ECS), *Listen, Discuss, and Act* (Denver: ECS, 1996), 15–17.

Helping Students Develop Skills for Positive Health Habits

This section focuses on the *positive health habits* students can adopt and maintain to help them live a healthy life. It contains the content and the personal and social skills found in the National Health Education Standards. Each chapter in this section begins with an introduction that provides information about the prevalence and cost of *not* practicing the positive health behavior, about the relationship between the healthy behavior and academic performance, and about the risk and protective factors related to the behavior. Readers learn what schools currently are doing and what they should be doing in relation to the health behavior. Each chapter also provides background information for the teacher, developmentally appropriate strategies for learning and assessment, and children's literature and Internet and other resources related to each content area.

5

(Joyce, age 12; Michelle, age 12)

Promoting Mental and Emotional Health

DESIRED LEARNER OUTCOMES

After reading this chapter, you will be able to . . .

- Describe the prevalence and cost of mental and emotional health problems among youth.

- Explain the relationship between mental and emotional health problems and compromised academic performance.

- Identify factors that influence mental and emotional health.

- Summarize current guidelines and practices for schools and teachers related to mental and emotional health.

- Summarize developmentally appropriate mental and emotional concepts and skills for K–8 students in the context of the National Health Education Standards and target healthy behavior outcomes.

- Demonstrate developmentally appropriate learning strategies and assessment techniques that incorporate concepts and skills shown to promote mental and emotional health among youth.

- Identify effective, evaluated commercial mental and emotional health promotion curricula.

- Identify websites and children's literature that can be used in cross-curricular instructional activities promoting mental and emotional health.

INTRODUCTION

In every child there lies a promise
There's great potential in their hearts and minds
They only need a little kindness
Patience and guidance to help them fly
....
In every child lies our future
Teach them the past so they can find their way
Life's greatest lessons come from sharing
Each child through knowledge will shine one day
....
In every child a promise
Let's show them we believe
Each one is very special
Let them live their dream

These words from Robi Kahakalau's beautiful song "Every Child a Promise"[1] set the tone for this chapter on promoting the mental and emotional health of children and adolescents. Although many educators are familiar with the extensive literature on children who are considered at risk for problems of many kinds, new research in the field of positive psychology focuses on qualities such as hope, wisdom, creativity, courage, spirituality, and responsibility rather than on the more limited perspective of problems and deficits.[2] In keeping with this focus, Mervlyn Kitashima, one of the participants in the Kauai Longitudinal Study of Resilience, encourages educators to think of all students as "at promise" rather than at risk.[3]

Longitudinal studies indicate that the majority of children come from an at-risk background become healthy, competent adults.[4] This chapter helps educators build on the qualities and strengths that allow children to build *resilience*, the term used to describe those who "bounce back" despite difficulties and who learn to "love well, work well, play well, and expect well."[5]

Mental and emotional health problems are growing among children and adolescents in the United States.[6] The world is a scary, uncertain, and even violent place for many young people. School needs to be a tremendously safe place—physically, emotionally, mentally, and socially—in their lives. Educators can work to encourage the positive capacities of young people as well as to facilitate access to the services they and their families need when problems arise. All students have strengths that can be put to productive use, and resilience efforts in schools can help students succeed.[7] In the words of Martin Krovetz, educators can help all students learn to use their minds and hearts well.[8]

Prevalence and Cost of Mental Health Problems

Mental health in childhood and adolescence is characterized by the achievement of expected developmental cognitive, social, and emotional milestones and by secure attachments, satisfying social relationships, and effective coping skills. The Surgeon General's Report on Mental Health stated that mentally healthy children and adolescents enjoy a positive quality of life and function well at home, in school, and in their communities. The report cautioned that children are not "little adults." They must be viewed in the context of their social environments, which include families, peer groups, and larger physical and cultural surroundings.[9]

Mental health disorders and illnesses are serious threats to the health of children in the United States. Health scientists have reported sharp declines in major infectious and medical problems among young people during the past century. In contrast, mental health problems appear to be increasing. The National Mental Health Association (NMHA) reported that one in five children and adolescents may have a mental health problem. At least one in ten—as many as 6 million young people—may suffer from a serious emotional disturbance. An estimated two-thirds of young people with mental health problems are not getting the help they need.[10] The National Institute of Mental Health (NIMH) identified the following mental disorders that affect children and adolescents:

Attention deficit hyperactivity disorder (ADHD)

Autism spectrum disorders (pervasive developmental disorders)

Bipolar disorder

Borderline personality disorder

Depression

Eating disorders

Childhood-onset schizophrenia[11]

See Table 5–1 for more information.

Mental health problems produce more impairment than almost any other condition among children and adolescents. In contrast to most disabling physical diseases, mental illnesses begin early in life. Researchers supported by NIMH have found that half of all lifetime cases of mental illness begin by age 14, and three-quarters begin by age 24. Thus, mental illnesses can be considered the chronic diseases of the young. Researchers have reported pervasive and long delays between the onset of a mental disorder and the first treatment contact—the median delay across disorders is nearly a decade.[12]

Although the need for mental health services has increased, public mental health institutions and services for children and adolescents have decreased during the past forty years.[13] Treatment for mental health problems is expensive. The costs to families and society are enormous, with direct treatment costs estimated at $12 billion per year in the United States. This estimate does not include additional costs from lost productivity and school performance, time away from work for parents and families, and other indirect costs associated with child and adolescent mental health problems. Inequities in financing for mental health care mean less availability of insurance, more restrictions on payments and the types of conditions covered, and larger cost sharing by patients and families.

The National Mental Health Association reported that the cost of unmet needs is just a small part of the price U.S.

TABLE 5–1

Mental Disorders Affecting Children and Adolescents

Attention Deficit Hyperactivity Disorder (ADHD)

Attention Deficit Hyperactivity Disorder, ADHD, is one of the most common mental disorders that develop in children. Children with ADHD have impaired functioning in multiple settings, including home, school, and in relationships with peers. If untreated, the disorder can have long-term adverse effects into adolescence and adulthood. Symptoms of ADHD appear over the course of many months, and include

- *Impulsiveness*—A child who acts quickly without thinking first.
- *Hyperactivity*—A child who can't sit still, walks, runs, or climbs around when others are seated, talks when others are talking.
- *Inattention*—A child who daydreams or seems to be in another world, is sidetracked by what is going on around him or her.

Autism Spectrum Disorders (Pervasive Developmental Disorders)

Autism Spectrum Disorders (ASD), also known as Pervasive Developmental Disorders (PDDs), cause severe and pervasive impairment in thinking, feeling, language, and the ability to relate to others. These disorders are usually first diagnosed in early childhood and range from a severe form, called autistic disorder, through pervasive developmental disorder not otherwise specified (PDD-NOS), to a much milder form, Asperger syndrome. They also include two rare disorders, Rett syndrome and childhood disintegrative disorder. Parents are usually the first to notice unusual behaviors in their child. In some cases, the baby seemed "different" from birth, unresponsive to people or focusing intently on one item for long periods of time. The first signs of an autism spectrum disorder can also appear in children who had been developing normally, when an affectionate, babbling toddler suddenly becomes silent, withdrawn, self-abusive, or indifferent to social overtures.

Bipolar Disorder

Bipolar Disorder, also known as manic-depressive illness, is a serious medical condition that causes shifts in a person's mood, energy, and ability to function. Unlike the normal ups and downs that everyone goes through, the symptoms of bipolar disorder are severe. Dramatic mood swings go from overly "high" and/or irritable to sad and hopeless, and back again, often with periods of normal mood between. Severe changes in energy and behavior go along with these changes in mood. The periods of highs and lows are called episodes of mania and depression.

Borderline Personality Disorder

Borderline personality disorder (BPD) is a serious mental illness characterized by pervasive instability in moods, interpersonal relationships, self-image, and behavior. This instability often disrupts family and work life, long-term planning, and the individual's sense of self-identity. Originally thought to be at the "borderline" of psychosis, people with BPD suffer from a disorder of emotion regulation. Patients often need extensive mental health services. Yet, with help, many improve over time and are eventually able to lead productive lives. A person with depression or bipolar disorder typically endures the same mood for weeks, but a person with BPD may experience intense bouts of anger, depression, and anxiety that last only hours, or at most a day. These may be associated with episodes of impulsive aggression, self-injury, and drug or alcohol abuse.

Depression

Only in the past two decades has depression in children been taken very seriously. The depressed child may pretend to be sick, refuse to go to school, cling to a parent, or worry that the parent may die. Older children may sulk, get into trouble at school, be negative, grouchy, and feel misunderstood. Because normal behaviors vary from one childhood stage to another, it can be difficult to tell whether a child is just going through a temporary "phase" or is suffering from depression. Sometimes the parents become worried about how the child's behavior has changed, or a teacher mentions that "your child doesn't seem to be himself." In such a case, if a visit to the child's pediatrician rules out physical symptoms, the doctor will probably suggest that the child be evaluated, preferably by a psychiatrist who specializes in the treatment of children.

Eating Disorders

An eating disorder is marked by severe disturbances in eating behavior, such as extreme reduction of food intake or extreme overeating, or feelings of overwhelming distress or concern about body weight or shape. The types of eating disorders are

- *Anorexia Nervosa*—Anorexia nervosa is characterized by emaciation, a relentless pursuit of thinness and unwillingness to maintain a normal or healthy weight, a distortion of body image and intense fear of gaining weight, a lack of menstruation among girls and women, and extremely disturbed eating behavior. Some people with anorexia lose weight by dieting and exercising excessively; others lose weight by self-induced vomiting, or misusing laxatives, diuretics, or enemas.
- *Bulimia Nervosa*—Bulimia nervosa is characterized by recurrent and frequent episodes of eating unusually large amounts of food (binge eating) with a feeling of lack of control over the eating. This binge eating is followed by a type of behavior that compensates for the binge, such as purging (vomiting, excessive use of laxatives or diuretics), fasting, and/or excessive exercise.
- *Binge-Eating Disorder*—Binge-eating disorder is characterized by recurrent binge-eating episodes during which a person feels a loss of control over his or her eating. Unlike bulimia, binge-eating episodes are not followed by purging, excessive exercise, or fasting. As a result, people with binge-eating disorder often are overweight or obese. They also experience guilt, shame, and/or distress about the binge eating, which can lead to more binge eating.

Schizophrenia

Schizophrenia is a chronic, severe, and disabling brain disorder. People with schizophrenia sometimes hear voices others don't hear, believe that others are broadcasting their thoughts to the world, or become convinced that others are plotting to harm them. These experiences can make them fearful and withdrawn and cause difficulties when they try to have relationships with others. Symptoms usually develop in men in their late teens or early twenties and women in their twenties and thirties, but in rare cases, can appear in childhood. They can include hallucinations, delusions, disordered thinking, movement disorders, flat affect, social withdrawal, and cognitive deficits.

SOURCE: National Institute of Mental Health (www.nimh.nih.gov/health/topics/child-and-adolescent-mental-health/index.shtml).

Youth Risk Behavior Survey Data Related to Mental and Emotional Health, 2007

Risk Behavior	Percent Reporting Behavior		
	Total	Females	Males
Felt so sad or hopeless almost every day for two or more weeks in a row that they stopped doing some usual activities	28.5	35.8	21.2
Seriously considered attempting suicide during the past twelve months	14.5	18.7	10.3
Made a suicide plan during the past twelve months	11.3	13.4	9.2
Actually attempted suicide during the past twelve months	6.9	9.3	4.6
Suicide attempt required medical attention during the past twelve months	2.0	2.4	1.5
Described themselves as slightly or very overweight	29.3	34.5	24.2
Were trying to lose weight	45.2	60.3	30.4
Engaged in unhealthy behaviors associated with weight control during the past thirty days (went without eating for twenty-four or more hours to lose weight or keep from gaining weight)	11.8	16.3	7.3
Took diet pills, powders, or liquids to lose weight or keep from gaining weight during the past thirty days	5.9	7.5	4.2
Vomited or took laxatives to lose weight or keep from gaining weight during the past thirty days	4.3	6.4	2.2

SOURCE: Centers for Disease Control and Prevention. "Youth Risk Behavior Surveillance—United States, 2007," *Morbidity and Mortality Weekly Report*, 57, no. SS-4 (6 June 2008): 1–131.

society pays. The nation's failure to provide mental health services for children and families also causes unnecessary long-term suffering.[14]

The good news is that mental disorders increasingly are treatable. Researchers and clinicians have made considerable progress in defining ADHD and treating children with the condition. More children than ever before receive outpatient mental health care from specialists, and schools provide mental health services for more youth now than at any previous time.[15]

Despite these advances, mental health care in the United States is fragmented, and routine care often is available only to those who can pay for it out of their own pocket. Even when resources are available, families often need considerable skill to locate services in a poorly coordinated system of professionals in clinical settings. Many young people who are less financially able must seek care through schools or child welfare, primary care, and juvenile justice systems. These youth face many financial and organizational barriers to effective care and receive ongoing care infrequently. Although crisis services may be available for short-term management, long-term comprehensive care is rarely an option for children and families who cannot afford it. Changes in research, practice, and policy are necessary to make mental health interventions more effective for children and adolescents.[16]

The Centers for Disease Control and Prevention (CDC) conducts the Youth Risk Behavior Survey (YRBS) in odd-numbered years to monitor priority health-risk behaviors among youth, including behaviors related to mental and emotional health. Table 5–2 provides data on risk behaviors reported by high school students across the United States related to depression, suicide, and unhealthy weight loss

Mental health is positively associated with academic achievement. Attachment to peers, emotional resiliency, and a belief in a positive future all promote mental and emotional health in young people.

TABLE 5-3

***Healthy People 2010* Objectives Related to the Mental Health of Children and Adolescents**

Objective 18-1	Reduce the suicide rate.
Objective 18-2	Reduce the rate of suicide attempts by adolescents.
Objective 18-5	Reduce the relapse rates for persons with eating disorders including anorexia nervosa and bulimia nervosa.
Objective 18-7	Increase the proportion of children with mental health problems who receive treatment.
Objective 18-8	Increase the proportion of juvenile justice facilities that screen new admissions for mental health problems.
Objective 7-2	Increase the proportion of middle, junior high, and senior high schools that provide comprehensive school health education to prevent health problems in the following areas: unintentional injury; violence; suicide; tobacco use and addiction; alcohol or other drug use; unintended pregnancy, HIV/AIDS, and STD infection; unhealthy dietary patterns; inadequate physical activity; and environmental health.

SOURCE: U.S. Department of Health and Human Services. *Healthy People 2010: Understanding and Improving Health,* 2nd ed. (Washington, DC: U.S. Government Printing Office, 2000).

practices. Female students reported higher rates than male students of feeling sad or hopeless, considering suicide, making suicide plans, attempting suicide, and needing medical attention as the result of suicide attempts. Female students also were more likely to report participating in unhealthy weight loss behaviors. Although approximately 35 percent of female students considered themselves overweight, more than 60 percent reported that they were trying to lose weight.[17]

In *Healthy People 2010,* the U.S. Department of Health and Human Services identified major public health objectives for mental health among children and adolescents (Table 5-3).[18] This chapter addresses the ways families, schools, and communities can work together to promote mental and emotional health and to facilitate access to appropriate mental health services in a timely manner.

Mental and Emotional Health and Academic Performance

Mental health problems among young people often are recurrent illnesses that ebb and flow over time, with many children and adolescents experiencing problems that persist into adulthood. Adolescents miss more school as a result of emotional and behavioral symptoms than for any other condition. Young people with mental health problems are more likely to drop out of school and fail than any other group of children with disabilities.[19]

Health, Mental Health and Safety Guidelines for Schools, developed by more than three hundred health, education, and safety professionals from more than thirty different national organizations and by parents and other supporters, states,

Health, mental health, and safety . . . are inextricably linked to student achievement. . . . Substance abuse, anxiety about home life, anxiety about relations with peers, exposure to violence, and any unaddressed symptoms are examples of health and safety issues associated with less than optimal achievement in school.[20]

For U.S. children ages 1 to 19, the group of conditions that lowers quality of life and reduces life chances the most consists of emotional and behavioral problems and associated impairments. No other set of conditions comes close to the magnitude of deleterious effects on this age group. Children with these disorders have a greatly increased risk of dropping out of school and not being fully functional members of society in adulthood.[21]

The National Association of School Psychologists (NASP) identified the following mental health challenges as being among the problems children face that can affect their learning and behavior at school:

- *stress* and anxiety
- *worries* about being bullied
- *problems* with family or friends
- *disabilities*
- *depression*
- *thoughts* of suicide or of hurting others
- *concerns* about sexuality
- *academic* difficulties
- *alcohol* and substance abuse
- *fear* of violence, terrorism, and war.[22]

New research conducted by the Collaborative for Social and Emotional Learning (CASEL) revealed that academics improve when schools take time out of the curriculum to teach students to manage their emotions and to practice empathy, caring, and cooperation. The four-year study of 207 school-based programs designed to foster children's social and emotional skills revealed that children who participated in such programs were better behaved, more positive, less anxious, and measured higher on grades and test scores than children who were not involved in such programs. CASEL president Roger P. Weissberg stated, "When kids are disaffected or they're not motivated and engaged, improving academic test scores is a real challenge, and that can't be done unless you address students' social, emotional, and cognitive needs."[23] In keeping with these findings, the Illinois State Board of Education identified three goals for social and emotional learning for students in grades K–12 (see Table 5-4).

The ways schools and classrooms operate can have a tremendous effect not only on the mental health and well-being of young people but also on their opportunity to achieve academically and to develop mentally, emotionally, socially, and physically. A compilation of research linking health status, health behavior, and academic achievement, titled *Making the Connection,* stated, "[Children] . . . who face violence, hunger, substance abuse, unintended pregnancy, and despair cannot possibly focus on academic excellence.

Illinois Learning Standards for Social and Emotional Learning (SEL)

Social and emotional learning (SEL) is the process through which children develop awareness and management of their emotions, set and achieve important personal and academic goals, use social awareness and interpersonal skills to establish and maintain positive relationships, and demonstrate decision making and responsible behaviors to achieve school and life success. A strong research base indicates that these SEL competencies improve students' social/emotional development, readiness to learn, classroom behavior, and academic performance.

Goal 1: Develop self-awareness and self-management skills to achieve school and life success.

Goal 2: Use social awareness and interpersonal skills to establish and maintain positive relationships.

Goal 3: Demonstrate decision-making skills and responsible behavior in personal, school, and community contexts.

Source: Illinois State Board of Education, Illinois Learning Standards, Social and Emotional Learning (SEL) (www.isbe.net/ils/social_emotional/standards.htm).

There is no curriculum brilliant enough to compensate for a hungry stomach or a distracted mind."[24] The report included many important school health practices that positively influence mental and emotional health and academic achievement, including these:

- Students whose parents are involved in their education show significantly greater achievement gains in reading and math, as well as better attendance and more consistently completed homework, than students with uninvolved parents.
- Early childhood and school-age intervention programs that provide parental support and health services are associated with improved school performance and academic achievement.

School failure is a strong predictor of high-risk behaviors.

- A comprehensive intervention combining teacher training, parent education, and social competency training in children had long-term positive impacts, including enhanced commitment and attachment to school, less school misbehavior, and better academic achievement.
- Students who develop a positive affiliation or social bonding with school are more likely to remain academically engaged and less likely to be involved with misconduct at school.
- Students who had taken part in a two-year social decision-making and problem-solving program in elementary school showed more pro-social behavior and less antisocial and self-destructive behavior when followed up in high school four to six years later.
- Physical activity is positively associated with academic performance.
- School breakfast programs positively influence academic performance, absenteeism, and tardiness among low-income elementary school students.

The report quoted the National Governors Association as saying,

> Policymakers need to focus on eliminating the barriers that affect these lower-performing students' readiness to learn. Among these barriers are physical and mental health conditions that impact students' school attendance and their ability to pay attention in class, control their anger, and restrain self-destructive impulses.[25]

Making the Connection reflects the intent of this chapter—to help educators support the mental and emotional health of students in all aspects of their school experience and facilitate timely access to the services students and their families need.

Factors That Influence Mental and Emotional Health

Mental disorders and mental health problems appear in families of all social classes and all backgrounds. No one is immune. Yet some children are at greater risk by virtue of a broad array of factors.[26] There is good evidence that both biological factors and adverse psychosocial experiences during childhood influence, but don't necessarily cause, the mental disorders of childhood. Adverse experiences can occur at home, at school, or in the community. A stressor or risk factor may have no, little, or a profound impact, depending on individual differences among children, the age at which the child is exposed to the stressor, and whether it occurs alone or in association with other risk factors.[27]

Risk Factors

Risk factors are characteristics, variables, or hazards that, if present for a given individual, make it more likely that that individual, rather than someone selected at random from the general population, will develop a disorder. Risk factors are not static but rather change in relation to a developmental phase or a new stressor in a person's life. Risk factors for developing a mental disorder or experiencing problems in social-emotional development include

- prenatal damage from exposure to alcohol, illegal drugs, and tobacco
- low birth weight
- difficult temperament or an inherited predisposition to a mental disorder
- external risk factors such as poverty, deprivation, abuse, and neglect
- unsatisfactory relationships
- parental mental health disorder
- exposure to traumatic events[28]

The roots of most mental disorders lie in some combination of genetic and environmental factors, the latter biological or psychosocial. Biological factors appear to exert a pronounced influence on disorders such as pervasive developmental disorder, autism, early-onset schizophrenia, social phobia, and Tourette's disorder. Psychosocial risk factors—dysfunctional aspects of family life such as severe parental discord, parent psychopathology or criminality, overcrowding, or large family size—can predispose children to conduct disorders and antisocial personality disorders. Children who do not have a loving relationship with at least one parent or caregiver are particularly at risk. Economic hardship and exposure to acts of violence also are possible causes of stress-related mental health problems.[29]

The mental health of parents, especially mothers, is a major factor in the mental health of children. The impact of maternal depression, including postpartum depression, across all of childhood and adolescence has become more widely recognized.[30] For infants and young children, both major and low levels of depression in the mother have been shown to affect emotional and cognitive development. Children of a depressed parent are at increased risk of developing a psychiatric disorder due to both genetic and environmental factors and are four times more likely than other children to develop an affective disorder. Daughters of depressed mothers are particularly vulnerable.[31]

Child maltreatment is a widespread problem—it is estimated that more than 3 million children are maltreated every year in the United States.[32] Child maltreatment is behavior that causes physical or emotional harm. It can result from acts of commission or omission. Categories of child maltreatment include physical abuse, sexual abuse, neglect, and emotional abuse.[33] Physical abuse is associated with insecure attachment and psychiatric disorders. Psychological abuse, believed to occur more frequently than physical abuse, is associated with depression, conduct disorder, and delinquency, and it can impair social and cognitive functioning.[34] The American Academy of Pediatrics stated,

> Psychological maltreatment makes a child feel worthless, unloved, endangered, or as if his or her only value is in meeting someone else's needs. Some examples include:

belittling, degrading, or ridiculing a child; terrorizing a child by committing life-threatening acts or making him or her feel unsafe; exploiting or corrupting a child; failing to express affection, caring, and love; and neglecting mental health, medical or education needs. When such behaviors are severe and/or repetitious, children may experience problems that include: emotional troubles ranging from low self-esteem to suicidal thoughts; antisocial behaviors; low academic achievement; and impaired physical health.[35]

Child maltreatment is discussed more extensively in Chapter 10 on preventing violence.

The relationship between stressful life events, such as parental death or divorce, and risk of child mental disorders is well established. The influence of maladaptive peers also can be damaging to children and greatly increases the likelihood of adverse outcomes such as delinquency. Sibling rivalry can contribute to family stresses and, in the presence of other risk factors, may be the origin of aggressive behavior that extends beyond the family.[36]

Protective Factors

Quackenbush, Kane, and Telljohann reviewed research to compile a series of protective factors that increase the chances a young person will succeed in school, friendships, family, and reaching important goals in life.[37] Prevention focuses not only on the risks associated with a particular illness or problem but also on these protective factors. Protective factors improve response to some environmental hazard, resulting in an adaptive outcome. They can reside within the individual, the family, or the community. The construct of resilience, which focuses on the ability of an individual to withstand chronic stress or recover from traumatic life events, is related to the concept of protective factors.[38] Examples of environmental, social, and individual protective factors follow.

Environmental Protective Factors

Community recognition of young people's value

Opportunities for positive adult–youth interactions

Schools with high academic standards and low drop-out rates

Reception of research-proven health curricula

Social Protective Factors

Family support and connectedness

Parental monitoring, clear rules of behavior consistently enforced

Attachment to prosocial peers

Attachment and connectedness to school

Individual Protective Factors

Value for school and academic achievement

Sense of purpose and belief in a positive future

Critical thinking and problem-solving skills

Emotional resilience and ability to manage feelings[39]

TABLE 5–5

School Health Policies and Programs Study (SHPPS) 2006 Data Related to Mental and Emotional Health Topics

Percentage of All Schools in Which Teachers Taught Emotional and Mental Health Topics as Part of Required Instruction, by School Level	% of All Elementary Schools	% of All Middle Schools
Appropriate ways to express and deal with emotions and feelings	67.0	74.1
Being sensitive to the feelings of others	67.7	75.1
Causes, signs, and effects of depression	30.1	63.5
Causes, signs, and effects of stress	47.3	73.1
Establishing and maintaining healthy relationships	63.9	73.3
Feelings and emotions associated with loss and grief	53.7	62.2
Healthy ways to express affection, love, friendship, and concern	65.8	70.1
How emotions change during adolescence	NA	70.1
How mental illness is diagnosed and treated	12.1	39.1
How students can influence or support others to promote emotional and mental health	54.2	67.6
How to find valid information or services related to emotional or mental health	23.6	58.4
Influence of families on emotional and mental health	44.0	65.6
Influence of the media on emotional and mental health	26.9	53.2
Interrelationships of physical, mental, emotional, social, and spiritual health	42.9	68.1
Positive and negative ways of dealing with stress	56.9	74.9
Social or cultural influences on emotional and mental health	33.8	61.4
Strategies for controlling impulsive behaviors	59.5	58.3
When to seek help for mental health problems	29.6	59.5

NA, not asked at this level.

* In at least one elementary school class or in at least one required health education course in middle schools.

SOURCE: Centers for Disease Control and Prevention, *School Health Policies and Programs Study 2006 (SHPPS)* (Atlanta, GA: CDC, 2007). www.cdc.gov/HealthYouth/shpps

Clearly, many of the risk factors for mental and emotional health problems are beyond the control and influence of schools. However, educators shouldn't be discouraged—research on resiliency and on mental and emotional health provides a wealth of strategies for helping to protect young people and to promote their mental and emotional health. This chapter explores those strategies with the aim of helping educators put them into practice.

GUIDELINES FOR SCHOOLS

State of the Practice

The CDC's Division of Adolescent and School Health (DASH) conducts the School Health Policies and Programs Study (SHPPS) every six years to monitor efforts to improve school health policies and programs.[40] Table 5–5 provides data on the mental and emotional health concepts and skills that elementary and middle school teachers reported teaching in at least one required class or course. The data are encouraging in that many teachers reported teaching concepts and skills to promote mental and emotional health. However, the data also indicate a need for increased, consistent school-based efforts in this critically important area.

State of the Art

Promoting mental and emotional health is most effective when schools and communities work in partnership. Students, teachers, parents, school staff, and community members all play important roles. To help schools deal with issues that vary from violence to substance abuse to obesity, more than three hundred health, mental health, safety, school health, and education professionals developed *Health, Mental Health and Safety Guidelines for Schools*.[41] The purpose of the guidelines (available at www.schoolhealth.org) is to provide help for those who influence the health, mental health, and safety of students and school staff while they are in school, on school grounds, on their way to or from school, or involved in school-sponsored activities.

The guidelines also provide definitions, information, and resources for a wide variety of mental and emotional health topics and issues, including abuse, ADHD, bullying, eating disorders, diversity, grief, parenting, relationships, sexual identity, social skills, substance abuse, suicide, and violence. This material provides recommendations, but not standards. Each community, with the help of its own health, safety, mental health, and educational experts and community members, should decide which guidelines are basic, which do not apply, and which to work toward. The guidelines can help community and school leaders determine the breadth of school health, mental health, and safety issues and set priorities for future action.[42]

The Centers for Disease Control and Prevention released the Health Education Curriculum Analysis Tool (HECAT), an exciting new resource to help educators achieve state-of-the-art practice in health education. The MEH module contains the tools to analyze and score curricula that are intended to promote mental and emotional health. The module uses the National Health Education Standards as the framework for determining the extent to which the curriculum is likely to enable students to master the essential knowledge and skills that promote mental and emotional health. Educators will find curriculum fundamentals, such as teacher materials, instructional design, and instructional strategies and materials analyses. This chapter includes the HECAT's healthy behavior outcomes and developmentally appropriate concepts and skills for promoting mental and emotional health. The HECAT is available at the Healthy Youth website of the Division of Adolescent and School Health (DASH) at CDC (www.cdc.gov/Healthy Youth/HECAT/index.htm).

GUIDELINES FOR CLASSROOM APPLICATIONS

Important Background for K–8 Teachers

This section includes important topics for teachers to consider in establishing a mentally and emotionally healthy classroom environment. These considerations include

- Creating a safe and caring classroom community
- Examining self-esteem: what it is and what it's not
- Fostering resilience: helping students use their minds and hearts well
- Recognizing and helping students who have problems
- Taking care means teachers, too

Creating a Safe and Caring Classroom Community

Many teachers involve their students in setting rules or agreements for the classroom. Clear expectations and norms or agreed-on behaviors are an important foundation of a classroom that is physically, mentally, emotionally, and socially safe. Approaches to setting rules or expectations are as varied as the teachers and students who inhabit classrooms. Three of many possible approaches to establishing classroom expectations and norms are addressed here: Tribes, invitational education, and the "take cares."

Tribes Jeanne Gibbs advocates classroom community building in *Tribes: A New Way of Learning and Being Together:*

> Tribes is not a curriculum, not a program or list of activities. It is a "process"—a way to establish a positive culture for learning and human development throughout a school community. The process . . . is based on a synthesis of studies on children's development, cooperative learning, cognition, systems theory, multiple intelligences, human resilience and the skills needed for the 21st century.[43]

The outcome of the tribes process is to develop a positive environment that promotes human growth and learning through three stages of group development: inclusion, influence, and community. The four community agreements of tribes classrooms are

- Attentive listening
- Appreciation/no put-downs

- The right to pass
- Mutual respect[44]

Students work together to determine what each agreement looks, sounds, and feels like in action. In the tribes process, professional development for schools involves all school members in the philosophy and process of building community.

Invitational Education In their book *Inviting School Success,* Purkey and Novak describe the evolving theory of practice that they call invitational education.[45] They discuss examples of inviting messages that students report having received from their teachers and other school staff during their years of schooling. Based on students' perceptions, these messages fall into three categories: *able, valuable, and responsible.* The teachers students remembered as positive influences in their lives demonstrated the capacity to help students feel able, valuable, and responsible through their words and actions. In contrast, teachers who made students feel disinvited spoke and acted in ways that made the students feel *worthless, unable, and irresponsible.*

Purkey and Novak developed an extensive list of inviting and disinviting signals that apply to verbal comments (good morning vs. keep out), personal behaviors (asking for an opinion vs. yawning in someone's face), physical environments (fresh paint vs. dead plants), and printed signs (Open, come in vs. Do not disturb). Their most recent edition has a chapter titled "Inviting in the Rain," to help teachers behave in inviting ways even in the face of challenging situations. Purkey and Novak advocate handling difficult situations in the most decent, respectful, and caring ways possible through expressing concern, conferring, consulting, and, when needed, confronting and combating the stressful situation.

The Take Cares: A Story from Waikele Elementary The take cares approach to building classroom and school community comes from Waikele Elementary School and other schools in Hawaii. The three take care agreements adopted throughout the school are

- Take care of yourself.
- Take care of others.
- Take care of this place.

As in the tribes process, students and teachers work together to identify what each take care looks, sounds, and feels like in action. Posting a chart of the students' words provides a ready source of discussion when problems arise in the classroom or on the school grounds, as they inevitably do. The take cares are meant to teach children and adolescents to consider the effects of their actions on themselves, their classmates and others, and their environment. As one teacher said, "I can't think of anything the take cares don't cover."

How do the take cares work in practice—especially when a dangerous behavior problem calls for stern measures?

An example from Waikele Elementary School deals with a serious infraction in which a student brought razor blades to school and a group of boys was found playing with them at recess. In addition to disciplinary action—notification of parents and detention—the students had to complete a reflection exercise in which they wrote up what they had done; why their action was not "taking care of self, others, or this place"; and what they thought a better reaction would be in the future. The students also had to ask their teacher and classmates permission to return to class. This last step was the most difficult for the students and left an enduring impression, evidenced by their use of this incident in completing writing assignments the following school year. Read more about this incident, the way the students asked to come back to class, and the take cares philosophy by visiting the Online Learning Center.

Serious infractions always warrant stern consequences. The important difference between the approach at Waikele Elementary and approaches used in other places, in the words of teacher Diane Parker, is that "the responsibility for thinking has to be placed on the child in order for growth to occur. You're looking toward fundamental change in the child's sense of ethics and social consciousness, not toward simply 'managing' behavior. You want your kids to learn to do the right thing, not because they're afraid of being punished, but because it's the right thing to do—and you want them to do it whether anyone's watching them or not!"

Pulling the Learning Community Together Classroom management and community-building strategies "determine the weather" in the classroom. Teachers who plan carefully—ideally with the full support of the school's administration, faculty, and staff—have an important opportunity to create a classroom environment in which students can flourish both academically and in terms of their health. In the words of Barbara Landau, author of *The Art of Classroom Management: Building Equitable Learning Communities,*

> Inclusive and welcoming management and curricular practices are a necessity. They are the most powerful means by which to ensure that all students have an equal opportunity to be successful regardless of the languages they speak, the beliefs they hold, the disabilities that challenge them, their gender, or the color of their skin.[46]

One of the most important reminders for new teachers as well as for those who want to create more inclusive and caring classroom communities is *don't give up*. New ways of thinking and acting take time to teach and time to learn. Students in elementary and middle school truly are a work in progress. The wonderful news is that with caring and persistent teaching, revisited as needed, they can learn to act in respectful ways that are inviting to others and to themselves.

Examining Self-Esteem: What It Is and What It's Not

An education cartoon illustrating a common problem with understanding the role of self-esteem in school settings showed a young teacher talking with her principal. The caption read, "I didn't have time to teach them anything. I was too busy building their self-esteem." These words pinpoint what many educators, parents, and community members have come to believe about attempts to build self-esteem—it's an empty process consisting of puffing up children's ideas about themselves with no basis in reality that takes time away from the real work of schools, which is academics. This section looks into the research on self-esteem and suggests ways to put important concepts into practice in the classroom.

An excellent review of research and implementation of mental and emotional health practices in the classroom by Quackenbush, Kane, and Telljohann acknowledges questions about self-esteem:

> Self-esteem presents a puzzle to teachers who want to promote emotional and mental health. It makes sense that feeling good about oneself would be an essential element of positive mental health. But a number of reports have cast doubt on the value of self-esteem teaching, and some have even suggested that efforts to boost self-esteem are wasteful.[47]

Given this confusion, just what is self-esteem? Robert Reasoner, writing for the National Association for Self-Esteem (www.self-esteem-nase.org), stated that, "Efforts to convey the significance and critical nature of self-esteem have been hampered by misconceptions and confusion over what is meant by the term self-esteem." The term is difficult to define because of its multiple dimensions, which include cognitive, affective, and behavioral elements. Reasoner cautioned, however, that the significance of self-esteem should not be lost in the confusion over what it means. The National Association for Self-Esteem defines self-esteem as "The experience of being capable of meeting life's challenges and being worthy of happiness. . . . This concept of self-esteem is founded on the premise that it is strongly connected to a sense of competence and worthiness and the relationship between the two as one lives life. . . . The value of this definition is that it is useful in making the distinction between authentic or healthy self-esteem and pseudo or unhealthy self-esteem. A sense of personal worth without competence is just as limiting as competence without worthiness."[48]

Quackenbush, Kane, and Telljohann stated that self-esteem is not, in and of itself, predictive of better health practices, greater social responsibility, or less participation in antisocial behaviors.[49] Various studies indicate that self-esteem is a complex and seemingly bewildering concept. Some people who test high on measures of self-esteem act in aggressive and antisocial ways. Others, who have high self-esteem based primarily on external markers such as physical appearance or the approval of others, show high stress levels, conflicts in relationships, and increased use of alcohol and other drugs. However, young people who measure high on self-esteem are more likely to be protected against emotional distress, whereas those who measure low on self-esteem have more suicidal thoughts.[50]

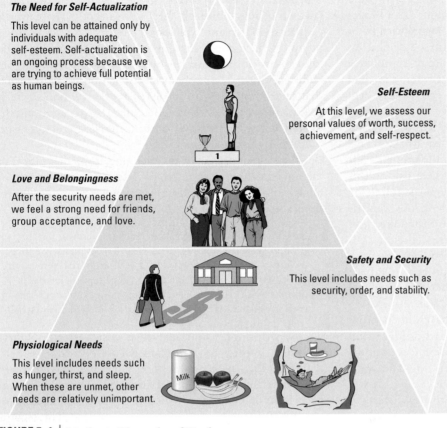

The Need for Self-Actualization

This level can be attained only by individuals with adequate self-esteem. Self-actualization is an ongoing process because we are trying to achieve full potential as human beings.

Self-Esteem

At this level, we assess our personal values of worth, success, achievement, and self-respect.

Love and Belongingness

After the security needs are met, we feel a strong need for friends, group acceptance, and love.

Safety and Security

This level includes needs such as security, order, and stability.

Physiological Needs

This level includes needs such as hunger, thirst, and sleep. When these are unmet, other needs are relatively unimportant.

Milk

FIGURE 5–1 | **Maslow's Hierarchy of Needs**

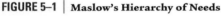

TABLE 5–6
The Four Conditions of Self-Esteem

- *Sense of connectiveness.* Children must to be able to gain satisfaction from the people, places, or things to which they feel connected. Children with a high sense of connectiveness feel that they are part of something, that they are important, and that they belong.
- *Sense of uniqueness.* Children must acknowledge and respect the qualities and characteristics about themselves that are special and different, and they must receive confirmation from other people that those qualities and characteristics are important and good. Children with a high sense of uniqueness feel there is something special about themselves and know that other people think they are special.
- *Sense of power.* Children need to have the competence to do what they must do, the resources required to effectively express their competence, and the opportunity to use their competence to influence important circumstances of their lives. Children with a high sense of power believe that they can do what they set out to do and feel confident that they can handle challenges.
- *Sense of models.* Children must be able to refer to human, philosophical, and operational models to help them make sense of the world. Children with a high sense of models know people they want to emulate and feel confident that they can tell right from wrong and good from bad.

SOURCE: R. Bean, *The Four Conditions of Self-Esteem* (Santa Cruz, CA: ETR Associates, 1992).

Maslow's familiar hierarchy of needs (Figure 5–1) lists the needs of human beings in order of urgency. People must meet basic needs (food, water, shelter, sleep, and safety) before attempting to meet needs for love and belonging (friends, group acceptance, and love) and self-esteem (personal value of worth, success, achievement, and self-respect). Individuals with adequate self-esteem can work toward self-actualization, an ongoing process of achieving full potential as human beings.

Reynold Bean, author of *The Four Conditions of Self-Esteem,* provides a list of key behaviors that indicate high self-esteem. For example, children who have high self-esteem:

- Are proud of their accomplishments ("I really like this picture I painted.")
- Act independently ("I wrote this story about the dinosaurs all by myself.")
- Assume responsibility easily ("I'll water the plants for you.")
- Tolerate frustration ("This model is hard to put together, but I know I can do it.")
- Approach new challenges with enthusiasm ("We get to start learning long division today.")
- Feel capable of influencing others ("I think we should let Sara play, too.")[51]

Teachers are likely to buy into this kind of evidence of self-esteem, through which children indicate that they indeed see themselves as able, valuable, and responsible. Conceptualizing self-esteem in this manner is a far cry from instilling falsely inflated self-worth. See Table 5–6 for information on the four conditions of self-esteem.

Another important component of self-esteem is self-efficacy, defined by Quackenbush, Kane, and Telljohann as young people's sense of competence or ability: Do they feel capable of reaching their goals or completing the tasks they set for themselves?[52] For many educators, self-efficacy is the crux of the matter. Educators want to help students believe that they can set tasks for themselves and succeed in those tasks, even when the work is challenging or difficult.

Martin Seligman spoke directly to concerns about self-esteem:

Armies of American teachers, along with American parents, are straining to bolster children's self-esteem. That sounds innocuous enough, but the way they do it often erodes children's sense of worth. By emphasizing how a child feels, at the expense of what the child does—mastery, persistence, overcoming frustration and boredom, and meeting challenge—parents and teachers are making this generation of children more vulnerable to depression.[53]

Seligman goes on to say that children soon learn to ignore the puffery and constant flattery—often with no real basis—that they hear in some classrooms. Thus, teachers need to think carefully about how they talk with children. Many teachers have been trained to praise children constantly and to direct a comment to one child ("I like the way Neil is sitting up so straight and tall") to get other children to behave. Although praising Neil for sitting up straight certainly is better than yelling at the other students, and might get Joe and Sandy to sit up some of the time, it might also cost Neil socially in terms of friends, playmates, and name-calling. Quackenbush, Kane, and Telljohann summarized research showing that when troubled young people learn to feel unwarranted high self-esteem (when they are praised in the absence of anything exemplary about their performance), they are more likely to behave violently or aggressively when they receive criticism in the future. Thus, research indicates that self-esteem without foundation is not useful for young people and might even be detrimental.[54]

What can teachers do, then, to build children's sense of competence and self-efficacy as a genuine source of self-esteem? Seligman encourages teachers to think in terms of helping children "do well" rather than merely "feel good" about themselves. Seligman stated,

> Feelings of self-esteem in particular, and happiness in general, develop as side effects—of mastering challenges, working successfully, overcoming frustration and boredom.... The feeling of self-esteem is a byproduct of doing well. Once a child's self-esteem is in place, it kindles further success.... There is no question that feeling high self-esteem is a delightful state to be in, but trying to achieve the feeling side of self-esteem directly, before achieving good commerce with the world, confuses profoundly the means and the end.[55]

Teachers can help children learn and love to read, answer mathematical questions that are real to them, explore how the world around them works from a scientific perspective, understand people and places around the world, express their ideas and emotions through the fine and performing arts, and experience the joy of physical movement. In talking with children about their work, teachers can stop to ask real questions and listen to children's answers rather than sweeping around the room saying "Good job!" to everyone they pass. To illustrate, a teacher education student shared that she hadn't really taken to heart the seminar discussions on engaging children in genuine conversations about their work. Instead, she said in passing to a little girl who was hard at work on a painting, "Good job—I like your boat!" The little girl looked up at her, looked down at the picture, and burst into tears. "It's not a boat!" she wailed. The teacher education student said ruefully that she wished she had simply said "Tell me about your picture" and waited to hear what the little girl would say.

Teachers should provide the support and resources children need to learn about themselves and their world and give the constant message that they'll help them learn even when learning is a challenge. Mathematics education professor Neil Pateman tells preservice teachers, "Your job is not to make mathematics fun—your job is to make it understandable. When mathematics is understandable, then it really can become fun." In the same vein, health education professor Mohammad Torabi tells his statistics students, "Squeeze your brain!" Perhaps the Little Engine That Could said it best of all: *I think I can, I think I can.*[56]

Fostering Resilience: Helping Students Use Their Minds and Hearts Well

In his university counselor education courses, Mike Salzman asks his students, "What kind of young people are you trying to grow?" After the counselors respond with their ideas, he then asks "Why?" The first why is followed by another, and then by the question of what they will do as counselors to help those things happen. These questions are an excellent starting place for a discussion of resilience.

Martin Krovetz, author of *Fostering Resiliency: Expecting All Students to Use Their Minds and Hearts Well*, explained resiliency theory as the belief in the ability of every person to overcome adversity if important protective factors are present in that person's life. He expressed the belief that when the school community works to foster resiliency, alongside the efforts of family and community, a large number of students can overcome great adversity and achieve bright futures. Krovetz stated,

> Fostering resiliency starts by challenging our underlying beliefs about student potential and how students learn. This strikes at the heart of not only who we are as educators but who we are as people. It involves far more than altering the discipline policy, adding social service support to the school, adopting a new curriculum program, buying computers, or having teachers go through a new staff development program.... For a school to attempt to foster resiliency for all its students honestly, school practices must be examined. What we teach, how we teach, and how we assess are all central to fostering resiliency. How we organize the school and how we group students are central. Likewise, expecting and supporting all students to be literate and to demonstrate the habits of mind to think critically are directly related to fostering resiliency.[57]

Bonnie Bernard defined resiliency as the ability to bounce back successfully despite exposure to severe risks.[58] A resilient community focuses on the protective factors that foster resiliency for its members. These factors include caring, high expectations and purposeful support, and ongoing opportunities for meaningful participation.[59]

Judith Deiro, in her book *Teachers DO Make A Difference*, acknowledged that teachers face more intense challenges with students today than they did thirty years ago.[60] Teachers need effective ways to deal with the complicated human situations they encounter in today's classrooms. Deiro affirmed that teachers do not want to be social workers—

A caring teacher can make all the difference in helping children build resilience.

they are teachers and want to act in a teacher's role. She described effective, role-appropriate ways for teachers to make a difference for their students, to help students who live in high-risk situations—without becoming social workers or adding more work to their busy schedules. Deiro stated that *the most powerful and effective way teachers can help students overcome the negative influences in their environment is by developing close and caring connections with them.* Research indicates that today's youth have too few pro-social adults (individuals who obey the laws of society, respect social norms, and care about the well-being of others) in their lives. The healthy development of children in today's society depends on having more caring adults meaningfully involved in children's lives.[61]

Research on bonding also shows powerful ways teachers can make a positive change in students' lives. The Kauai Longitudinal Study on Resilience, which studied children born into adverse home conditions in Hawaii in 1955, documented factors that helped these children grow up to be successful, well-adjusted adults.[62] More often than not, the key factor was a caring, responsive teacher. The resilient adults these children grew up to be often mentioned a favorite teacher as the person who really made the difference for them. Other studies have found similar results.

How do teachers put these ideas into practice in the classroom? If the number one prerequisite for student learning is establishing caring, respectful, inviting relationships with young people, how do teachers structure their thinking, actions, and classrooms to go about doing this? Deiro studied the behaviors of teachers to learn how they established healthy, nurturing connections with students. She summarized the strategies the teachers used, often in combination:[63]

• *Creating one-to-one time with students.* Teachers did this by making themselves accessible to students before classes,

between classes, and after school; opening their classrooms early and keeping them open after school; stationing themselves in the doorway between classes; encouraging and being open to personal conversations; getting involved in extracurricular activities; maximizing individual and small-group contact during lessons; interspersing personal talk during lectures; providing personally written comments on student papers; and using nonverbal communication, such as eye contact and standing close to students.

• *Using appropriate self-disclosure.* Deiro defined appropriate self-disclosure for student–teacher relationships as the act of sharing or disclosing the teacher's own feelings, attitudes, and experiences with students in ways that are helpful to the students and enhance their learning process. Appropriate disclosure can build a bridge between students and teachers on a common human level.

• *Having high expectations of students while conveying a belief in their capabilities.* A school culture of high expectations is a critical factor in increasing academic achievement. Students need adults in their lives who believe they can achieve. Students enjoy being around teachers who see them as bright and capable with bright futures in front of them. The key seems to be conveying a belief in student capabilities while holding high expectations. Teachers can help most by expressing their belief in students by problem-solving with them to help them achieve, even when they are struggling, rather than by expressing discouragement or disappointment about what students haven't been able to do.

• *Networking with parents, family members, and friends of students.* In schools situated in functional communities, parents know the parents of their children's friends, and teachers know the family, friends, and neighbors of their students. These "intergenerational closures" provide a common circle of friends and acquaintances and create additional sources of information about students. Teachers can strengthen their connection with students by living in the communities where they work.

• *Building a sense of community among students within the classroom.* The word *community* refers to a relational association within which human interactions and social ties draw people together. A genuine sense of community comes after group members commit themselves to taking significant risks and sharing meaningful experiences. Group members are accepting and tolerant of one another, with a sense of belonging and relatedness extending to everyone in the group. *Inclusive* is another important word used to describe relational classroom communities. The tribes process, described earlier in this chapter, is built on building safe, inclusive, productive, and caring classroom communities.

• *Using rituals and traditions within the classroom.* Rituals and traditions bond individuals with their families, communities, institutions, or even countries. Rituals are activities that are performed the same way each time they are introduced, such as beginning each health lesson with a related news item brought in by a student. Traditions are customs, practices, or special events that are routinely acknowledged and honored, such as Martin Luther King Jr. Day. Rituals and traditions help build a sense of community.

This introduction to the important area of fostering resilience in children can provide a springboard for further study among interested teachers. In addition to the resources cited in this section, teachers might explore the books listed in "Internet and Other Resources" at the end of the chapter.

Recognizing and Helping Students Who Have Problems

Teachers who provide safe, caring, and resilience-building classrooms contribute enormously to the mental and emotional well-being of their students. However, in almost every school situation, individual students will need additional support due to mental, emotional, learning, or health difficulties. Some occurrences, such as a trauma at school or in the larger community, affect everyone in the school population and the community.

Quackenbush, Kane, and Telljohann included an excellent chapter for teachers, titled "Helping Troubled Students," in their text *Teach and Reach: Emotional and Mental Health*.[64] The authors advise that the two types of events most likely to call for teacher intervention are individual students with emotional problems (a student who is being bullied) and events that affect students as a group (a serious injury to a student in the school or community). Chapters 10 and 14 in this text, on preventing violence and on managing loss, death, and grief, provide guidance for teachers in responding to school and community events that affect students.

Common emotional and mental problems that affect individual students at school include ADHD, learning disabilities, eating disorders, depression, and anxiety disorders.[65] Education on assisting children with specific disabilities is beyond the scope of this text. The authors strongly recommend that all teachers pursue professional development opportunities for learning to work with children who have special physical, mental, emotional, social, and other health needs and disabilities. In addition, teachers should avail themselves of all possible assistance from qualified special education teachers and resource staff at the school, district, and state levels. The necessity of providing a safe and welcoming environment applies to all students, including those with special learning needs and disabilities.

The National Mental Health Association (NMHA) provides helpful information for teachers, parents, and community members seeking to understand and recognize signs and symptoms of mental and emotional health conditions among children and adolescents. Teachers must remember that they are neither counselors nor mental health professionals—they should not attempt to make diagnoses, interview children, or express opinions about diagnoses to parents and caregivers.

The teacher's responsibility is to make appropriate referrals to help children and their families access the mental health services they need. Mental Health America (www.mentalhealthamerica.net), formerly known as the National Mental Health Association, provides an excellent Children's Mental Health Resource List. These resources provide a great starting place for learning to help and get help for children who are experiencing difficulty. In particular, the role of stress and family stress in children's lives cannot be overstated. The Strategies for Learning and Assessment section in this chapter also provides ideas for helping children learn about and deal with stress (NHES 7: Self-Management) in healthy ways. Examples from Children's Mental Health Resource List include:

- ADHD and kids
- Anxiety disorders and kids
- Autism in children
- Bullying: what to do about it
- Coping with separation and divorce
- Depression in children
- Helping children cope with loss resulting from war or terrorism
- Learning disabilities
- Recognizing mental health problems in children
- Talking to kids about fear and violence
- Talking to kids about school safety

Teachers need to know where to go to find more information on specific problems that arise in their classrooms. Teachers should identify those specialists in their schools, districts, and states who can provide the assistance they need. In addition, teachers can access valid and reliable resources on the Internet, including those listed at the end of this chapter in "Internet and Other Resources." See Table 5-7 for NMHA's tips for promoting children's mental health.

Taking Care Means Teachers, Too

Teachers want to help their students grow to become resilient people who demonstrate mental and emotional health, persist when work or life circumstances are challenging, and are justly proud of their hard-earned accomplishments. However, Deiro[66] acknowledged that consistently caring without achieving consistent returns creates an imbalance in the caring cycle—the mutual giving and receiving of caring—and is the root of emotional burnout among teachers. Teachers who are too exhausted mentally, emotionally, or physically to come to school and perform at their best are unlikely to be able to help anyone, including students. Teachers can practice the health education standard of self-management, by taking care of themselves as well as their students. Ideas for a teacher's "take care of yourself" list include eating nutritiously, getting plenty of sleep, and learning to manage stress in healthy ways. (Visit the Online Learning Center for more advice from Diero's research.)

A final recommendation is for teachers to choose to spend time with other educators who value students and

TABLE 5–7

Children's Mental Health Matters: General Tips for Promoting Mental Health from the National Mental Health Association

The best way to promote children's mental health is to build up their strengths, help to protect them from risks, and give them tools to succeed in life.

- *Help children relate to others and build their confidence.* Give children a chance to talk about experiences and feelings; offer encouragement and praise; acknowledge positive and negative behavior; and provide consistent and fair expectations with clear consequences for misbehavior.
- *Be a role model.* Talk about your own feelings, apologize when you are wrong, don't express anger with violence, and use active problem-solving skills.
- *Encourage exercise and sports.* Researchers have linked a variety of psychological benefits to exercise, including decreased depression and anxiety, and improved mood states, self-confidence, sense of life quality, and general psychological well-being. Participation in exercise and sports has also been shown to reduce delinquent behavior and boost academic performance.
- *Suggest involvement in after-school activities.* A questionnaire on body image and self-esteem found that girls who were active in a greater number of after-school activities had higher body image, self-esteem, and feelings of competence than girls who participated in fewer.
- *Encourage strong family relationships.* Researchers at Baylor College of Medicine in Houston found that adolescents who were from closely knit families and maintained an intimate connection with their parents based on trust and open communication were less likely to use alcohol.
- *High expectations can go a long way.* Studies indicate that high parental or family expectations for a child's performance may serve as a protective factor against child substance abuse.

Tips for Teachers and School Officials
- Think about mental health as an important component of a child being "ready to learn"; if a child is experiencing mental health problems, he or she will likely have trouble focusing in school.
- Incorporate mental health into the classroom and ensure that all students are treated with respect.
- Know the signs of mental illness and be aware of available resources.
- If you have concerns, contact a child's parent or caretaker and seek consultation from school mental health professionals.
- Use the mental health professional(s) at your school as resources for preventive interventions with students, including social skills training; education for teachers and students on mental health; crisis counseling for teachers and students following a traumatic event; and classroom management skills training for teachers.

Children's Mental Health Matters is an initiative of the National Mental Health Association's Campaign for America's Mental Health. This nationwide public education campaign is supported by a coalition of national organizations and state and local mental health associations and their partners. Through this program, NMHA, its affiliates and partners offer educational materials for children and their families on a variety of topics including anxiety disorders, attention deficit/hyperactivity disorder, bipolar disorder, and childhood depression, and mental wellness.

Source: National Mental Health Association (www1.nmha.org/children/children_mh_matters/promoting.cfm).

teaching as much as they do. Staying away from complainers, the teacher's lounge (if it's a negative place), and other people and places that disparage children, families, school administration, and the teaching profession is a great self-management strategy!

Recommendations for Concepts and Practice

Healthy Behavior Outcomes

The goal of health education is to help students adopt or maintain health-enhancing behaviors. School districts and teachers should identify the health-enhancing behaviors they would like their students to adopt or maintain. The following list from the HECAT identifies some possible healthy behavior outcomes related to promoting mental and emotional health. Though not all of the suggestions are developmentally appropriate for students in grades K–8, this list can help teachers understand how the learning activities they plan for their students support both short- and long-term desirable behavior outcomes.

Ways to Promote Healthy Behavior Outcomes for Mental and Emotional Health

Express feelings in a healthy way.

Engage in activities that are mentally and emotionally healthy.

Prevent and/or manage internal conflict and stress in healthy ways.

Use self-control and impulse-control strategies to promote health.

Seek help for troublesome feelings.

Be empathetic toward others.

Carry out personal responsibilities.

Establish and maintain healthy relationships.

Developmentally Appropriate Concepts and Skills

Teaching to promote mental and emotional health should be developmentally appropriate and based on the physical, cognitive, social, emotional, and language characteristics of specific students. Teacher's Toolbox 5.1 lists some developmentally appropriate concepts and skills to help teachers create lessons that encourage students to practice the desired healthy behavior outcomes. Teachers may notice that some of these concepts and skills are reinforced in other content areas (e.g., the concept "explain the importance of talking with parents about feelings" also applies to preventing violence and promoting sexual health).

Developmentally Appropriate Concepts and Skills for Promoting Mental and Emotional Health

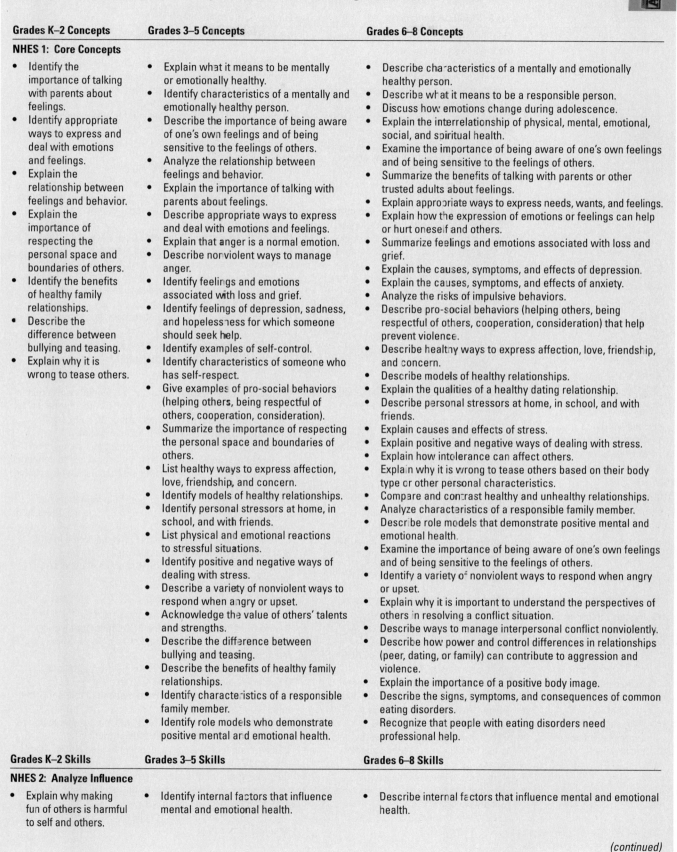

Grades K–2 Concepts	Grades 3–5 Concepts	Grades 6–8 Concepts
NHES 1: Core Concepts		
• Identify the importance of talking with parents about feelings.	• Explain what it means to be mentally or emotionally healthy.	• Describe characteristics of a mentally and emotionally healthy person.
• Identify appropriate ways to express and deal with emotions and feelings.	• Identify characteristics of a mentally and emotionally healthy person.	• Describe what it means to be a responsible person.
• Explain the relationship between feelings and behavior.	• Describe the importance of being aware of one's own feelings and of being sensitive to the feelings of others.	• Discuss how emotions change during adolescence.
• Explain the importance of respecting the personal space and boundaries of others.	• Analyze the relationship between feelings and behavior.	• Explain the interrelationship of physical, mental, emotional, social, and spiritual health.
• Identify the benefits of healthy family relationships.	• Explain the importance of talking with parents about feelings.	• Examine the importance of being aware of one's own feelings and of being sensitive to the feelings of others.
• Describe the difference between bullying and teasing.	• Describe appropriate ways to express and deal with emotions and feelings.	• Summarize the benefits of talking with parents or other trusted adults about feelings.
• Explain why it is wrong to tease others.	• Explain that anger is a normal emotion.	• Explain appropriate ways to express needs, wants, and feelings.
	• Describe nonviolent ways to manage anger.	• Explain how the expression of emotions or feelings can help or hurt oneself and others.
	• Identify feelings and emotions associated with loss and grief.	• Summarize feelings and emotions associated with loss and grief.
	• Identify feelings of depression, sadness, and hopelessness for which someone should seek help.	• Explain the causes, symptoms, and effects of depression.
	• Identify examples of self-control.	• Explain the causes, symptoms, and effects of anxiety.
	• Identify characteristics of someone who has self-respect.	• Analyze the risks of impulsive behaviors.
	• Give examples of pro-social behaviors (helping others, being respectful of others, cooperation, consideration).	• Describe pro-social behaviors (helping others, being respectful of others, cooperation, consideration) that help prevent violence.
	• Summarize the importance of respecting the personal space and boundaries of others.	• Describe healthy ways to express affection, love, friendship, and concern.
	• List healthy ways to express affection, love, friendship, and concern.	• Describe models of healthy relationships.
	• Identify models of healthy relationships.	• Explain the qualities of a healthy dating relationship.
	• Identify personal stressors at home, in school, and with friends.	• Describe personal stressors at home, in school, and with friends.
	• List physical and emotional reactions to stressful situations.	• Explain causes and effects of stress.
	• Identify positive and negative ways of dealing with stress.	• Explain positive and negative ways of dealing with stress.
	• Describe a variety of nonviolent ways to respond when angry or upset.	• Explain how intolerance can affect others.
	• Acknowledge the value of others' talents and strengths.	• Explain why it is wrong to tease others based on their body type or other personal characteristics.
	• Describe the difference between bullying and teasing.	• Compare and contrast healthy and unhealthy relationships.
	• Describe the benefits of healthy family relationships.	• Analyze characteristics of a responsible family member.
	• Identify characteristics of a responsible family member.	• Describe role models that demonstrate positive mental and emotional health.
	• Identify role models who demonstrate positive mental and emotional health.	• Examine the importance of being aware of one's own feelings and of being sensitive to the feelings of others.
		• Identify a variety of nonviolent ways to respond when angry or upset.
		• Explain why it is important to understand the perspectives of others in resolving a conflict situation.
		• Describe ways to manage interpersonal conflict nonviolently.
		• Describe how power and control differences in relationships (peer, dating, or family) can contribute to aggression and violence.
		• Explain the importance of a positive body image.
		• Describe the signs, symptoms, and consequences of common eating disorders.
		• Recognize that people with eating disorders need professional help.
Grades K–2 Skills	**Grades 3–5 Skills**	**Grades 6–8 Skills**
NHES 2: Analyze Influence		
• Explain why making fun of others is harmful to self and others.	• Identify internal factors that influence mental and emotional health.	• Describe internal factors that influence mental and emotional health.

(continued)

Grades K–2 Skills *(continued)*	**Grades 3–5 Skills** *(continued)*	**Grades 6–8 Skills** *(continued)*
	• Identify external factors that influence mental and emotional health. • Explain how families can influence mental and emotional health. • Identify how media can influence mental and emotional health. • Identify characteristics of a positive role model. • Describe how culture, media, and others influence what we think about attractiveness and relationships. • Explain that most young people do not use violence to deal with problems. • Describe how culture, media, and others influence what a person thinks about people who have infectious or chronic diseases (HIV, infection, AIDS, cancer).	• Describe external factors that influence mental and emotional health. • Analyze how personal, family, and cultural values can influence mental and emotional health. • Explain how ethnic and cultural diversity both enrich and challenge society. • Discuss how media can influence mental and emotional health. • Describe characteristics of a positive role model. • Identify socioeconomic influences that affect mental and emotional health. • Summarize how culture, media and others influence what we think about attractiveness and relationships. • Describe how personal values and feelings influence choices. • Describe strategies to minimize negative influences on mental and emotional health. • Describe how alcohol use affects a person's ability to effectively deal with emotional and mental health issues. • Explain that most young people do not use violence to deal with problems. • Discuss how values influence decisions about sexual behavior and relationships. • Explain why stereotypes exist about people with mental disabilities and illness. • Explain why stereotypes exist about people with infectious diseases (HIV, tuberculosis).

NHES 3: Accessing Information, Products, and Services

• Identify people who are caring and supportive. • Demonstrate ways to seek help from trusted adults.	• Identify accurate sources of information about mental and emotional health. • Demonstrate the ability to access appropriate people in school who can help with mental and emotional health concerns. • Identify when a person would benefit from asking for help for a mental and emotional health problem. • Demonstrate ways to seek help from trusted adults or friends. • Explain that getting help for mental and emotional health problems is appropriate and sometimes necessary.	• Distinguish accurate information about mental and emotional health products and services from inaccurate information. • Demonstrate the ability to access accurate sources of information about mental and emotional health. • Demonstrate the ability to access school and community resources to help with mental and emotional health concerns. • Explain when a person would benefit from asking for help for an emotional health problem. • Explain when it is necessary to seek help for mental and emotional health problems (depression, mood disorders, and anxiety disorders). • Explain that getting help for mental and emotional health problems is appropriate and sometimes necessary. • Demonstrate the ability to access sources of accurate information about eating disorders.

NHES 4: Interpersonal Communication

• Identify techniques of effective listening. • Demonstrate verbal and nonverbal ways to ask for help from trusted adults. • Demonstrate empathy for others. • Demonstrate how to express emotions in healthy ways.	• Describe techniques of effective listening. • Demonstrate communication skills necessary to express personal needs and wants appropriately. • Demonstrate ways to communicate directly, respectfully, and assertively. • Demonstrate appropriate ways to respond to feedback from others. • Demonstrate verbal and nonverbal ways to ask for help from trusted adults or friends. • Demonstrate empathy for others. • Demonstrate how to express emotions in healthy ways.	• Demonstrate techniques of effective listening. • Demonstrate ways to communicate respect for diversity. • Demonstrate effective communication skills to express feelings appropriately. • Demonstrate how to communicate clear expectations, boundaries, and personal safety strategies. • Demonstrate appropriate ways to respond to feedback from others. • Demonstrate ways to ask for help with mental and emotional health problems from trusted adults or friends. • Demonstrate methods for responding to problems of others with empathy and support. • Describe steps for effective negotiation. • Demonstrate effective strategies for resolving conflicts with another person in nonviolent ways. • Demonstrate communication skills necessary to maintain a healthy relationship.

Grades K–2 Skills *(continued)*	Grades 3–5 Skills *(continued)*	Grades 6–8 Skills *(continued)*
		• Demonstrate how to express emotions in healthy ways. • Demonstrate ways to communicate support for a peer with a suspected eating disorder.

NHES 5: Decision Making

• Describe the importance of thinking about the effects of one's actions on other people.	• Discuss the importance of thinking about the effects of one's actions on other people. • Discuss methods for making decisions to avoid conflicts or violence.	• Discuss how mental and emotional health affect decision making. • Discuss the short- and long-term consequences of the decision to choose a violent or nonviolent solution to a problem. • Explain how decisions regarding alcohol and drug use affect relationships with friends and family.

NHES 6: Goal Setting

• Set a goal to spend more time with people who are respectful, supportive, and positive and less time with people who engage in negative behaviors.	• Set a goal to spend more time with people who are supportive and positive and less time with people who engage in negative behaviors. • Demonstrate the ability to identify signs when becoming upset or angry. • Demonstrate the ability to set goals to prevent and manage stress. • Demonstrate the ability to monitor personal stressors and reactions to stress. • Demonstrate the ability to set a goal for helping at home and show responsibility as a family member. • Make a personal commitment to show respect and consideration for others.	• Set a goal to spend more time with people who engage in positive behaviors and less time with people who engage in negative behaviors. • Describe barriers to mental and emotional health and ways to address those barriers. • Demonstrate the ability to monitor personal feelings. • Demonstrate the ability to set goals to prevent and manage stress. • Demonstrate ways to monitor personal stressors and techniques for managing them. • Demonstrate ability to set goals to be successful in school. • Make a personal commitment to show respect and consideration for others. • Describe steps needed to reach personal goals for the future.

NHES 7: Self-Management

• Demonstrate techniques to manage stress. • Demonstrate the ability to use self-control when angry. • Demonstrate ways to show respect, consideration, and caring for classmates. • Demonstrate pride in personal qualities and accomplishments.	• Demonstrate appropriate ways to accept and carry out personal and family responsibilities. • Demonstrate techniques to manage stress. • Demonstrate how to express feelings appropriately. • Demonstrate the ability to use self-control when angry. • Demonstrate strategies to manage loss and grief. • Demonstrate ability to use nonviolent alternatives to conflict (walking away, negotiation). • Express intentions to resolve conflicts nonviolently. • Express intentions to treat others with caring and respect.	• Demonstrate appropriate ways to accept and carry out personal and social responsibilities. • Demonstrate techniques to manage stress. • Demonstrate strategies for expressing feelings appropriately. • Demonstrate actions that express personal values. • Demonstrate the ability to use self-control. • Demonstrate tolerance for individual differences. • Demonstrate methods for coping with disappointment and loss. • Demonstrate ways to replace negative thoughts with positive ones. • Demonstrate ability to use multiple nonviolent alternatives to conflict (walking away, negotiation). • Describe the perspectives of all sides in a conflict situation. • Express intentions to resolve conflicts nonviolently. • Express intentions to treat others with caring and respect.

NHES 8: Advocacy

• Object to teasing of peers.	• Demonstrate support and respect for people with differences (cultural, disabilities, gender, religious). • Explain how to be supportive to peers. • Object to teasing of peers based on their body types.	• Demonstrate support and respect for people with differences (cultural, disabilities, gender, and sexual orientation). • Identify strategies to advocate for needs and rights of others effectively and respectfully. • Object to teasing of peers based on their body type or other personal characteristics. • Identify ways to advocate for an emotionally healthy social environment at school. • Advocate for a positive and respectful school environment that supports pro-social behavior.

SOURCE: Centers for Disease Control and Prevention, *Health Education Curriculum Analysis Tool (HECAT)* (Atlanta, GA: CDC, 2007). www.cdc.gov/HealthyYouth/Hecat/index.htm

STRATEGIES FOR LEARNING AND ASSESSMENT

Promoting Mental and Emotional Health

This section provides examples of standards-based learning and assessment strategies for promoting mental and emotional health. The strategies begin with a restatement of the standard and a reminder of the assessment criteria, drawn from the RMC rubrics in Appendix B. Strategies are written as directions for teachers and include applicable theory of planned behavior constructs in parentheses (intention to act in healthy ways, attitudes toward behavior, subjective norms, perceived behavioral control). These learning and assessment strategies provide building blocks for standards-based lessons and units that can be tailored to local needs. Assessment criteria are used with permission from the Rocky Mountain Center for Health Promotion and Education (RMC). See Appendix B for Scoring Rubrics.

Many of the learning and assessment strategies in this first content chapter can be applied to other content areas. The strategies focus on actively engaging students in their own learning and having them take responsibility for it. Teachers should remember that almost all health education topics affect students' mental and emotional health. For example, a lesson that teaches no name-calling relates both to preventing violence and to promoting mental and emotional health. Additional strategies for learning and assessment for Chapter 5 can be found at the Online Learning Center. A complete list of all the strategies is available at the Online Learning Center.

NHES 1 | Core Concepts

Students will comprehend concepts related to health promotion and disease prevention to enhance health.

ASSESSMENT CRITERIA

- Connections—Describe relationships between behavior and health; draw logical conclusions about connections between behavior and health.
- Comprehensiveness—Thoroughly cover health topic, showing breadth and depth; give accurate information.

Grades K–2

Children's Literature for Mental and Emotional Health   The "Children's Literature" section at the end of the chapter lists more than 150 books that teachers can use to initiate discussions about mental and emotional health. All the books describe situations or issues that impact the characters in ways that relate to their mental and emotional health. The stories help children see that others have problems and challenges similar to theirs—for example, a new baby in the family. Elementary teachers can expand their discussions of children's books to encompass health concepts and health skills (analyzing influences, accessing information, communication, decision making, goal setting, self-management, and advocacy) in relation to a particular topic of interest to their students. Students might act out their ideas for an ending to the book before the teacher finishes the story, tell a story of their own about a similar situation and what they did about it, help create a class book about a particular

topic (each student contributes a page), make puppets to dramatize a story, or make a shoebox display of how the characters felt inside and acted outside.

ASSESSMENT | Students can demonstrate their understanding of mental and emotional health concepts and skills in a wide variety of ways (see the list of sample assessment tasks in Chapter 3). For assessment criteria, students should provide accurate information about the mental and emotional health issue under discussion and make connections between behaviors and health. (Constructs: Perceived behavioral control, attitudes toward behavior.)

Read Aloud by Older Students   Teachers can work across grade levels to allow opportunities for older students to select and read to younger students books with mental and emotional health themes. For example, older students might select books about having and working toward a goal (links to NHES 6), using books such as those listed under "Goals and Decisions" at the end of the chapter. Teachers should work with older students before the lesson to help them plan questions for the younger students to discuss about the topic of interest and to make sure the older students provide health-enhancing messages.

ASSESSMENT | For an assessment task, younger students should be able to answer the questions the older students ask about meeting challenges in ways that are mentally and emotionally healthy. For assessment criteria, younger students should be able to provide accurate information and make connections between behaviors and health. (Construct: Subjective norms.)

Is There Really a Human Race?   This book by Jamie Lee Curtis and Laura Cornell (see booklist at end of chapter) asks questions children can relate to about the way people live their lives and the importance of making good choices. In contrast to the rushing that children see all around them, this book reminds them to take their time, try their best, lend a helping hand, and speak up for those who can't speak for themselves—to make the world a better place. Teachers can use these messages to help build a positive learning environment and to talk with children about the "take cares" described earlier in this chapter: Take care of yourself, take care of each other, and take care of this place.

ASSESSMENT | For an assessment task, each child can identify special things they can do for the take cares. The class can make a take cares poster for the classroom to remind everyone of the way they want to work together. The actual examples children provide tell about their understanding of the take cares idea. For assessment criteria, children should explain how each of their ideas connects to creating a positive and healthy classroom. (Construct: Attitudes toward behavior.)

Grades 3–5

Emotions from A to Z: Feelings Alphabet   Students can work in small groups to brainstorm a list of as many "feeling words" as they can. To test whether a word is a feeling word, students can try filling in the blank: "I feel . . .". If students find themselves saying "I feel *like* . . . " or "I feel *that* . . . ," they need to keep working to get to the actual feeling word or emotion. For example, students might say, "I feel like throwing up when we have a test." Throwing up isn't the feeling—scared, anxious, or agitated might be the emotion they are after. (A sample feelings alphabet of words is posted at the "Other Resources" section of the Online Learning Center; teachers can give parts of this list to students to help get them started.) Students can put their group lists together to make a class list to post on the wall or bulletin board.

A feelings alphabet list is a great reference tool for lessons on mental and emotional health and discussions throughout the day. To add to the list, teachers can prepare strips of paper with new words (appropriate for the vocabulary level of learners) for students to "draw out of the hat," look up, and report back on to classmates. (Note: Teachers should remember that the purpose of this list is to help students identify strong feelings and act in healthy ways in response to them. Mental and emotional health means recognizing and dealing with feelings of all kinds, including those that aren't pleasant at the time.)

ASSESSMENT | For assessment criteria, students should provide an accurate description of a word drawn out of the hat in kid terms and make connections between behaviors and health related to the word. For example, when people feel quixotic, they might set goals that sound wonderful but are unrealistic. (Construct: Attitudes toward behavior.)

BAM! Welcome to Your Life! The Body and Mind (BAM!) website at www.bam.gov is provided by the Centers for Disease Control and Prevention (CDC). The "Welcome to Your Life!" link helps students explore topics such as getting along with others, dealing with bullies, and tips to keep you cool, calm, and collected. Teachers can have pairs of students choose and explore different parts of the website and report back to class members. If students don't have computer access at school, teachers can print out the information for the class.

ASSESSMENT | For an assessment task, students can identify one source of stress they are facing and select three tips for managing their stress in healthy ways. Students can create a bookmark to remind them of the strategies they want to try and report back to classmates on how their strategies worked for them. For assessment criteria, students should make connections between their behaviors and health. (Constructs: Perceived behavioral control, attitudes toward behavior.)

Grades 6–8

Student-Generated Game Shows, PowerPoints, and Other Creative Ways to Learn Core Concepts Many educators will recall health education lessons that marched straight through a textbook—read the chapter, do the questions at the end, take a test on Wednesday. Middle school students are quite capable of researching mental and emotional health topics of interest and creating game shows, newsletters, dramatic presentations, PowerPoints, and other creative presentations. Class members can agree on topics of interest (see the previous two learning strategies for ideas) and work in small groups to present the content to class members in memorable and engaging ways. The students should literally run the show for this activity.

ASSESSMENT | The creative presentation students make on their mental and emotional health topic of interest is the assessment task for this activity. For assessment criteria, students should provide accurate information and draw conclusions about connections between behaviors and health. (Construct: Perceived behavioral control.)

NHES 2 | Analyze Influences

Students will analyze the influence of family, peers, culture, media, technology, and other factors on health behaviors.

ASSESSMENT CRITERIA
- Identify both external and internal influences on health.
- Explain how external and internal influences interact to impact health choices and behaviors.
- Explain both positive and negative influences, as appropriate.

Healthy Families Help Me Stay Strong The idea of this activity is to help students understand how family habits and practices help them stay mentally and emotionally healthy. Teachers can begin with the question "What kinds of things do you and your family do to stay healthy and strong?" Students might start with physical health practices, such as eating healthy, exercising, not smoking, and getting a good night's sleep. Teachers can help students dig deeper by asking "What do you and your family do to stay healthy and strong when you have a problem?" Students might say that they talk things out or watch a funny television show. Students can draw from their family practices and habits to make a class book about healthy families. Teachers should know their students and families well before undertaking a lesson like this. If teachers know that several students are experiencing difficult times in their families, they might want to restructure this lesson to include healthy practices in general, rather than practices related directly to students' families. In addition, teachers should remind students not to use family members' names when talking about problems. The purpose of the activity is to help children understand how their families influence their health habits and practices, not to pry in any way into what goes on in children's homes.

ASSESSMENT | The pages students create for a class book are the assessment task for this activity. For assessment criteria, students should explain at least one way their families influence them to stay healthy and strong. (Construct: Subjective norms.)

Curious George and Healthy Risk Taking Although the area of risk taking often is linked to unintentional injury, it also can be linked to emotional and social risk taking, such as trying out for a part in a school play, reading aloud in class, or talking with a new student. Teachers can read any of the Curious George books by H. A. Rey to generate a discussion on curiosity and taking a healthy risk. This activity can link to discussions of NHES 5 and 6, decision making and goal setting.

ASSESSMENT | For an assessment task, students can identify one new thing they want to try (singing a solo, asking for help, joining the community soccer team, taking swimming lessons, learning to dive). For assessment criteria, students should be able to explain what makes them want to try something new and what makes them hesitate to try (internal and external influences). Students can report back to the class on their experiences when they are able to carry out their ideas. (Construct: Intention to act in healthy ways.)

Grades 3–5

Don't Buy It—Get Media Smart! Students sometimes are surprised to learn that commercials and advertisements are targeted directly to kids their age. Teachers can find helpful information for talking about advertising with their students on the PBS website "Don't Buy It—Get Media Smart!" (pbskids.org/dontbuyit/ teachersguide.html). Classroom activities should help students build critical thinking skills and media literacy—that is, the ability to access, evaluate, analyze, and produce print and electronic media by dissecting advertisements and other products of pop culture. The "Tips for Teachers" section of the site includes creative strategies for helping students concentrate on different aspects of advertising.

In terms of mental and emotional health, teachers can help students focus on aspects of advertising designed to make them want to buy products to make themselves feel better, feel cool, feel accepted, and feel good enough. Teachers can help students examine the veracity (a new vocabulary word) of such claims.

ASSESSMENT | For an assessment task, students can, with parent or caregiver permission, watch television for a specified amount of time (half hour, one hour) to take notes on commercials and advertising. Students can note what the product is, strategies used to sell it (see the advertising techniques in Chapter 3), how the product is pictured (what's around it, what the lighting is like), and whether the claims probably are truthful or not. Teachers and students might want to make a grid, such as the one featured on the PBS website, to record their data. For assessment criteria, students should explain at least three ways advertisers try to influence them to buy products and the relation to mental and emotional health. How do advertisers promise consumers will feel if they buy the product? Are those claims true? Students also should discuss how advertisements are intended to make a person feel—not good enough, not attractive enough—and should refute those images. (Construct: Perceived behavioral control.)

Challenging Stereotypes Teachers will find that collecting pictures of people of all ages, nationalities, and walks of life—people pictures—can be useful for this and other activities. For example, social studies teacher Shannon Lowrey uses people pictures from *National Geographic* to ask students "What does it mean to be civilized?" Students examine the pictures and discuss whether each depicts people who are civilized or not civilized and why. Lowrey then introduces the idea of stereotypes and biases from one's own culture and has the students look at the pictures again.

Similarly, students can be asked to examine pictures of people with this question in mind: "Who will get HIV/AIDS?" Working in small groups, students should select three pictures and explain to the class why they think those people will become infected with the virus. Students might say that they can "tell" who will get HIV because of the way a person dresses (e.g., a female dressed in revealing clothing), because a person looks gay or is a professional athlete, or simply because a person looks "weird" to them. Teachers can introduce the idea of stereotypes and bias based on appearances and ask students to challenge their own statements and the statements of others. For example: Just because people are tall, are they good basketball or volleyball players? Just because a woman wears a short skirt, does she necessarily engage in risk behaviors? Teachers can help students debrief by making a chart with columns labeled "stereotypes" and "facts about HIV infection," emphasizing that no one can tell who is infected or might become infected based on appearance only. Students also should discuss how people treat others they regard with stereotyping or bias and how stereotyping and bias can lead to hurtful words or actions and even violence.

ASSESSMENT | For an assessment task, students can complete a two-column chart that lists stereotypes and facts about HIV infection. For assessment criteria, students should explain how stereotypes and biases can influence behavior, including hurtful and harmful behavior, toward others. In addition, students should refute each stereotype in their chart with facts and explain how they can be supportive of others who have HIV/AIDS or other chronic illnesses. (Constructs: Perceived behavioral control, attitudes toward behavior.)

Grades 6–8

Healthy Laughter—the Best Medicine Laughter helps boost mood and immunity, reduce stress and blood pressure, and connect people to each other. How can teachers use laughter in the classroom? Shannon Lowrey shared that she allowed her high school students to spend the first minute of homeroom each day telling jokes to get everyone off to a good start. Middle school teacher Georgia Goeas tells her students, "Your job is to entertain me—and you better be

good. I have television, CDs, and DVD!" Research indicates that students learn better when they feel safe, capable, and supported in their classrooms. Teachers can allow students classroom time to research laughter on the Web and recommend ways to bring humor into the classroom in a healthy way—with the kind of humor that makes everyone feel warm and invited versus hurtful laughter or words that makes some students feel put down.

ASSESSMENT | For an assessment task, students can make a list of ten ways to bring humor and laughter into the classroom in healthy ways. For assessment criteria, students should explain how the strategies can help everyone feel included and part of the class and why hurtful humor or laughter is not allowed. (Construct: Perceived behavioral control.)

My Family, My Culture, My Pride in Who I Am An important aspect of analyzing influences is examining the roles family and cultural tradition play in people's lives. For this activity, students can identify traditions that are important in their lives, such as huge celebrations to mark a young person's sixteenth or twenty-first birthday. Religious traditions are important in many families and cultures, and include celebrations at specific times of the year. With parent or caregiver permission, students can share pictures, videotapes, or other keepsakes that mark their celebrations. Students should describe their traditions and answer two questions:

- How do my family and cultural traditions influence my pride in who I am?
- How do my family and cultural traditions influence my health?

In many instances, family and culture create a sense of belonging, which influences mental and emotional health in important ways. This activity can be a powerful one for dispelling misperceptions about people from different cultures and for inviting appreciation of diversity. Students might want to invite family members to visit the classroom to share more about their family and cultural traditions. As a follow-up activity, students can develop special traditions to celebrate their culture as a community of learners.

ASSESSMENT | The family and cultural traditions students share are the assessment task for this activity. For assessment criteria, students should describe how their family and cultural traditions influence their pride and sense of belonging and their mental and emotional health. (Construct: Subjective norms.)

Media Messages About Attractiveness—Says Who? Students can dig into popular music, movies, television shows, and print advertising to look for messages about what boys and girls are like and what they should be like. Students can display their findings as "media images and messages" versus their own "truth ads" to show what males and females are like in the real world. For example, media images often indicate that men should be muscular, tough, strong, unemotional, and violent, whereas women often are portrayed as very thin, sometimes physically fit, large-breasted, empty-headed, and passive. Students might be interested in what one female celebrity said about preparing for a photo shoot. Asked whether she dieted to get ready, she replied, "Of course not. That's what air-brushing is for!" Students can share their findings with other middle school students.

ASSESSMENT | Students can create PowerPoint, poster, or shoebox (internal and external influences) presentations to display their findings. For assessment criteria, students should contrast the media images and messages they found with their truth ads about what males and females are like and should be like to foster mental and emotional health. (Construct: Perceived behavioral control.)

Dying to Be Thin: **Eating Disorders in America** Teachers might watch and, if appropriate, screen the television production of *Dying to Be Thin* with middle school students. Teachers can find information on the show from PBS (www.pbs.org/wgbh/nova/thin/). The film looks at the media's focus on very thin models and celebrities, the conflict between real and fashionable body images, and the complications of and treatments for eating disorders. This production shines a spotlight on the internal and external factors that affect the incidence and prevalence of eating disorders in the United States.

ASSESSMENT | For an assessment task, students can write a reaction paper to the film, following substantial class discussion. For assessment criteria, students should explain how unhealthy weight loss techniques can initiate disordered eating behavior and should affirm the importance of using health self-management techniques for achieving healthy body weight, healthy body image, and fitness. (Constructs: Perceived behavioral control, attitudes toward behavior.)

NHES 3 | Access Information, Products, and Services

Students will demonstrate the ability to access valid information and products and services to enhance health.

ASSESSMENT CRITERIA

- Access health information—Locate specific sources of health information, products, or services relevant to enhancing health in a given situation.
- Evaluate information sources—Explain the degree to which identified sources are valid, reliable, and appropriate as a result of evaluating each source.

Grades K–2

Interview an Adult As suggested in Chapter 4, students can interview a parent, a caregiver, another adult family member or friend, or a neighbor about mental and emotional health questions of interest. For example, students can interview three adults about questions such as these:

- What do you do to feel better when you are sad?
- What do you do to feel better when you are angry?
- What do you do to feel better when someone hurts your feelings?
- What do you say or do if someone is rude or mean to you?

Students can share their findings with the class. Teachers should remind students not to use anyone's real name when relating a personal story.

ASSESSMENT | The students' reports on their interviews are the assessment task for this activity. For assessment criteria, students can select three smart ways they found to deal with mental and emotional health issues and tell why their interviews were valid sources of information. (Constructs: Subjective norms, perceived behavioral control.)

Visits with School and Community Health Helpers Teachers can help students write class letters of invitation, which they all sign, to invite health helpers from the school (counselor, nurse, health aide) and community (9-1-1 operator, doctor, nurse, psychologist, public health educator) to visit their classroom. On some occasions, teachers might be able to arrange field trips for students to visit health helpers at their place of work. Students should prepare a list of questions in advance of the visits and decide who will ask them.

ASSESSMENT | For an assessment task, students should review the answers to their list of questions for the health helper. For assessment criteria, students explain why their interviews were valid sources of information and tell when and how they would contact these health helpers. (Construct: Perceived behavioral control.)

Getting Help in Emergencies Even young students should know how to call 9-1-1 in case of an emergency. Teachers should help students understand the kinds of questions they will be asked, the importance of staying on the line until the operator tells them they can hang up, and the seriousness of a 9-1-1 call. Students should know that 9-1-1 calls are logged and can be traced to the caller's number—calls should never be made as a prank. One of the best ways to help students understand how to make 9-1-1 calls is to use a disconnected phone to role-play, with the teacher or another adult acting as the operator. Because a cell phone might be the only phone available, students also should learn to use cell phones. Teachers and students can find more information on making 9-1-1 calls at KidsHealth (www.kidshealth.org); click on "Kids Site," "Watch Out," and "How to Use 9-1-1."

ASSESSMENT | For an assessment task, teachers can give students a scenario. For example, "Your friend falls while the two of you are riding your skateboards, and she says her leg hurts too much to stand up. You have your mom's cell phone with you, but your mom isn't home when you call." For assessment criteria, students should be able to answer the "operator's" questions and stay on the line until the operator tells them to hang up. Students also should be able to explain when and when not to call 9-1-1. (Construct: Perceived behavioral control.)

Grades 3–5

Ask the Experts: Broadcast News Students can work in pairs to select and investigate a mental and emotional health topic for a class report. Students become the class experts on their topic and should be able to provide accurate information and answer questions about it. The websites given in NHES 1 and NHES 3 are good places to start. Teachers and school librarians can help students locate additional information sources. Students can decide as a class on criteria for great presentations. Students could present their findings in a headline news format, complete with interviews and graphics.

ASSESSMENT | The news presentations students make are the assessment task for this activity. Teachers can allow students to select from a variety of formats, including PowerPoint or other computer-generated report formats. For assessment criteria, students should provide accurate information and draw conclusions about connections between behavior and health (NHES 1) and should provide their information sources and explain why they are valid (NHES 3). (Construct: Perceived behavioral control.)

Safe Surfing on the Web Health Finder for Kids (www.healthfinder .gov/kids) and other websites for students provide important information on staying safe on the Web. For example, the Health Finder for Kids link "Safe Surfing" states,

> Before you start using Healthfinder® Kids or any other Web site, talk with your parents about "safe surfing" on the Web. Here are some basic tips to get started:
> - Talk with your parents first about sites you're visiting.
> - Look at a site's "Privacy" link to see how it will use the information you give it.
> - Keep your password, last name, phone number, and address to yourself.
> - Stay away from chatting with people on the Web if you don't know them. They may not be who they are pretending to be.

- Tell your parents, caregivers, or a teacher if a site makes you feel uncomfortable in any way.

Students can check out these and other safe surfing tips on the Web to create a list of class safety rules for using the Internet. See the websites listed in "Internet and Other Resources" at the end of the chapter. Students might be interested to learn which government agencies have put this safety information on the Web for them (the Federal Bureau of Investigation). Internet safety for students is a serious business!

ASSESSMENT | The safe surfing rules students create for the class are the assessment task for this activity. For assessment criteria, students should explain where they obtained their information, why their information sources are valid, and how they plan to stay safe while surfing the Web. (Construct: Perceived behavioral control.)

Interviewing Counselors and Administrators About Safe Schools
A safe school should be safe mentally, emotionally, socially, and physically. Teachers can assist their students in writing a letter of invitation to their school principal, vice-principal, or counselors to learn more about policies and programs in place in their school to make sure everyone stays safe. For example, what are the rules about name-calling, bullying, or harassment? What happens if someone brings a weapon to school? What happens if there is a fight at school? How should students report a problem? What happens when students make a report? What if someone threatens to "get" someone if they make a report? What should students do if they feel stressed out over an important test? Students should make a list of questions for their guest visitors. As an extension, students might also enjoy the books listed under "Safe and Healthy Classrooms and Schools" in the list of children's literature at the end of the chapter.

ASSESSMENT | For an assessment task, students should provide correct answers for all their questions after the interviews and tell where to go for help in a safety situation of any kind. For assessment criteria, students should provide accurate information (NHES 1), explain why their interviews were valid sources of information (NHES 3), and tell what they can do to keep their school mentally and emotionally healthy. (Construct: Perceived behavioral control.)

Grades 6–8

Cover Stories: Health in the News   Teachers and students can start a class collection of magazine covers that deal with mental and emotional health issues such as depression, eating disorders, ADHD, and the science of happiness. Students can display the covers on a "Mental and Emotional Health in the News" bulletin board and use the accompanying stories as starting points for class reports and presentations on various mental and emotional health topics.

ASSESSMENT | The reports and presentations students make are the assessment task for this activity. For assessment criteria, students should provide accurate information and draw conclusions about connections between behaviors and health (NHES 1) and should provide their information sources and explain why they are valid (NHES 3). (Construct: Perceived behavioral control.)

Phone Book Scavenger Hunt   Teachers and students can collect old phone books for this class activity. Teachers can prepare a scavenger hunt page of questions or have students brainstorm a list of questions they have about finding services for mental and emotional health issues. For example, questions might address what local community agencies students can call if they, a friend, or a family member experiences problems with

- Sadness or feeling down for two weeks or more
- An alcohol or drug problem
- Cutting or other self-abusive behavior
- Refusal to eat, or binge eating and throwing up afterward
- Ongoing problems at school with classwork or behavior
- Problems with a prescription medication
- A situation in which someone feels afraid of being hurt or abused
- A situation in which abuse is taking place

Students also can investigate websites that provide accurate and valid information on mental and emotional health issues.

ASSESSMENT | The list of mental and emotional health resources students compile as a result of their scavenger hunt is the assessment task for this activity. For assessment criteria, students should cite their sources for information, products, and services and explain why they are valid and reliable. (Construct: Perceived behavioral control.)

Healthy Kids and Families Directory   Students can take the information they compiled in the previous activity a step further to make a Healthy Kids and Families Directory. For each listing, the directory should include the name of the agency, a short description of services, contact information (phone, fax, e-mail), and hours of operation, if applicable. Students can work with their school technology specialist to design an attractive cover for the directory and have it duplicated for students in their grade level or school. Students should create an attention-getting title for their directory that will appeal to middle school students.

ASSESSMENT | The directory students create is the assessment task for this activity. For assessment criteria, students should provide accurate information (NHES 1), tell why their resources are valid (NHES 3), and explain when and how to use the directory to promote good mental and emotional health. (Construct: Perceived behavioral control.)

NHES 4 | Interpersonal Communication

Students will demonstrate the ability to use interpersonal communication skills to enhance health and avoid or reduce health risks.

ASSESSMENT CRITERIA
- Use appropriate verbal/nonverbal communication strategies in an effective manner to enhance health or avoid/reduce health risks.
- Use appropriate skills (negotiation skills, refusal skills) and behaviors (eye contact, body language, attentive listening).

Grades K–2

Lilly's Purple Plastic Purse: **Children's Literature for Communication Skills**   Teachers and students will enjoy Kevin Henke's tale of Lilly and her purple plastic purse. Students will sympathize with Lilly when she makes an impulsive mistake, is nasty to a favorite teacher, and then has to find a way to make things right. This book and others listed under "Communication" at the end of the chapter can help children consider the dilemmas of communication. Sometimes people say things in the heat of the moment that they don't mean. How can they make it better? Sometimes people don't communicate clearly. How can they make their ideas make sense to others? Sometimes people don't tell the truth because they worry about what will happen if they do. What should they do? Teachers and students can use these books to spark discussions about being a good communicator—giving clear messages, being a good listener, and being mindful of body language and facial expression.

Punahele Bear: How Do We Talk to Each Other?   This activity about the importance of using kind words, from family counselor Dr. Allana Coffee, can be tremendously successful with both younger and older children.[67] To begin the activity, children should sit in a circle. The teacher shows the children a stuffed animal, such as a teddy bear, and asks them to describe it (cuddly, friendly). Coffee calls her teddy bear "Punahele" (pronounced Poon-ah-hel-ay), which means "cherished" or "favorite" in Hawaiian. The teacher can place Punahele Bear in the middle of the circle. Next, the teacher tells the children a story about how excited Punahele Bear is to go to school and how much he is looking forward to it. However, sometimes things happen at school or people at school say things that make kids feel bad or ashamed. The teacher can ask students if they can think of things (without using real names) that kids or adults say or do that might make Punahele Bear feel bad or not want to come to school and should then ask students to volunteer things people say or do that might make others feel bad. As children volunteer ideas ("You can't play with us," "Your clothes are ugly," "You talk funny"), the teacher should have them place an old piece of cloth, a rag, or a paper towel over Punahele Bear. Children should go one at a time, be given plenty of time to think, and be allowed to volunteer their ideas. When the bear is covered up, the teacher should ask the children how they think he or she feels now (scared, in the dark, sad). Children can be asked to share instances when things have happened to them at school that might make them feel this way (remember, no names). As children share, everyone should listen carefully to understand how unkind words and actions can make classmates feel.

After the discussion, the teacher should ask students how they can help Punahele Bear feel better by using kind words to take off the rags, one at a time. Allow students to volunteer their kind words ("Come sit with us," "Thank you," "Let's go and play") and remove a rag, returning it to the teacher. This part of the activity often takes longer than naming the put-downs. Coffee shared that one kindergarten class told her not to take off all the rags. When she asked why, the children said, "Because even if you say sorry, it still hurts." Some teachers end this activity by leaving Punahele Bear in the classroom (on a bookshelf) to watch over class members and remind them to use kind words and actions. One lesson on kindness won't take care of all problems, of course, just as one reading lesson won't teach children to read. However, Punahele Bear provides a concrete reminder that teachers can refer to as situations arise during the school day.

Many teacher education students and teachers have reported success with this activity. One student teacher said that a kindergarten girl said as a put-down statement, "You're too fuzzy!" To remove her rag, she simply said, "You're not too fuzzy." Her words showed that she understood the intent of the activity. A middle school student teacher who tried this activity with his older students reported that they liked it very much (the students later wanted to take turns holding the bear) and that he heard one boy say to another on the way to the bus, "Hey, don't put those rags on me, man!" Teachers can expect children to giggle or laugh when the activity starts; however, most students stop laughing as the activity goes on because the words so obviously are hurtful. Teachers also should note that some children will listen but not want to participate. Young children, in particular, may not want to say "mean words," even as an activity.

ASSESSMENT | For an assessment task, students should be able to explain, write about, or draw using kind words and actions with classmates and others. For assessment criteria, students should tell how kind words can help them be better communicators. (Construct: Perceived behavioral control.)

Tattling or Helping? Communicating So Adults Will Listen   Anyone who has worked with young children is familiar with the phenomenon of tattling. Weary teachers may routinely tell students "Settle it yourselves," but students sometimes genuinely need adult intervention. Teachers can help children think about their communication by making a two-column chart labeled "tattling" and "helping." Children should first define the terms in kids' words—tattling is telling to get someone in trouble, and helping is telling because someone is in danger, is upset, or might get hurt. Students can give examples of each, and teachers can help them link to the take cares discussed earlier in this chapter: Will telling help take care of yourself, others, and this place? One lesson won't solve the dilemma of tattling, because children are still learning about their world and about communication. However, the discussion gives teachers and students a reference point for future conversations that develop around real incidents. Allana Coffee recommends teaching children to ask adults for help in this way:

- Say "I need your help."
- In one sentence, tell what the person has done.
- In one sentence, explain what you have done to solve the problem yourself.
- Repeat "I need your help."[68]

For example, a student might say, "Mrs. Serna, I need your help. Lola and Lynn climbed up in the big tree on the playground when Kelvin was chasing them, and they don't know how to get down. I told them to hold on tight while I came to get you, and we need your help!"

ASSESSMENT | For an assessment task, students can work in pairs to dramatize a situation in which they tattle or ask for help from their teacher. Other students can guess which kind of communication, tattling or helping, they are demonstrating. For assessment criteria, students should be able to explain the difference between the two kinds of communication (telling to get someone in trouble versus telling because someone is in danger, is upset, or might get hurt) and give at least one communication tip on helping rather than tattling. (Construct: Perceived behavioral control.)

Grades 3–5

Same Words, Different Messages   Joyce Fetro created this activity to help students try out different tones of voice, facial expressions, and body language.[69] Students can work in small groups to give different interpretations to the same sentences, either of their choosing or distributed by their teacher. Students should decide on (or draw from a hat) a different feeling or emotion to convey when they say the sentence. Following are some examples of sentences for students to interpret:

The coach says to stay and talk with her after practice.

We're getting our science test back today.

My teacher gave me a note for my parents.

I'm going to the mall with my sister after school.

My English teacher gave me a book to read over the holidays.

Jamie left a message for me to call back.

My Mom said we'll talk with my Dad about the party when he gets home today.

Students might express these statements with joy, disgust, exhaustion, worry, excitement, or some other emotion. Groups can have each person express a different feeling for their sentence with their tone of voice, facial expressions, and body language.

ASSESSMENT | The students' demonstrations are the assessment task for this activity. For assessment criteria, groups should be able to explain how differences in tone, facial expression, and body language changed the intended message of their sentence. (Construct: Perceived behavioral control.)

Pressure Lines: Making a Healthy Comeback Joyce Fetro recommended that students practice their peer refusal skills (see Chapter 3) by responding to a list of pressure lines.[70] Students can draw teacher-prepared slips of paper with pressure lines printed on them, or students can write pressure lines on index cards to exchange with other students. Examples of pressure lines include the following:

Hurry! Shana is holding the back door open so we don't have to pay for the movie.

Don't be a baby—we're all going to jump our bikes over the ditch.

Everyone is doing it. Drinking beer is the bomb, and no one will know.

Can't you handle it? We're all into smoking, and we never get caught.

Nobody eats just one. Have some more chips.

We're cutting school at lunch—we're heading to the lake for a swim.

Students can work in small groups, with one student reading the pressure line and the others offering different peer resistance responses (repeat the refusal, use humor, suggest an alternative).

ASSESSMENT | For an assessment task, students should demonstrate their responses to the pressure lines for other class members. For assessment criteria, students should be able to identify and demonstrate at least three peer resistance strategies and tell how and when they would use them. (Construct: Perceived behavioral control.)

Grades 6–8

Triple Your Resistance: The Power of Repeating Refusals Students might be interested to know that they often will need to repeat a refusal at least three times before people take them seriously and decide to stop pressuring them. Thus, students shouldn't be discouraged if they have to repeat a refusal. Students can work in small groups to practice their peer resistance skills, discussed in Chapter 3. Students can create scenarios to share with other groups and practice repeating a refusal three times or using three different kinds of refusals. Students can discuss how this strategy compares with saying something one time. Remind students to communicate a clear no message through their words, tone of voice, facial expressions, and body language.

ASSESSMENT | The repetition skills students demonstrate for their classmates are the assessment task for this activity. For assessment criteria, students should demonstrate three refusals, either by repeating the same refusal or by using different types of refusals, in a health-enhancing way. (Construct: Perceived behavioral control.)

Respecting Limits and Boundaries: No Pressuring Others Middle school students in health education classes often work on resisting

pressure. However, sometimes middle-level students are the ones doing the pressuring. This activity involves looking at oneself and asking hard questions about communication and behavior toward others. Students should remember not to call anyone by name when giving examples. Students can start this discussion with the question "Why do people pressure and even bully other people to do things they don't want to do?" Students can first discuss this question in small groups and then share their answers with the class. From their list of possible reasons, students can go on to discuss responsible and respectful behaviors toward others, such as the following:

- Considering another person's point of view
- Respecting another person's physical and emotional comfort zone
- Using self-talk to think through words and actions, considering how they will affect another person
- Backing off when someone says, or acts in ways that say, no

Students might remember from their work in self-management that having a support group is a good strategy for resisting pressure. Students in a given classroom can commit to coming to each other's aid in pressure situations by simply being close by physically, helping a friend get out of a situation, or even saying "Don't pressure my friend."

ASSESSMENT | For an assessment task, students can designate words for the letters in the words *respect, limits,* or *support* or create a rap, slogan, poem, or song to communicate support for others and for the idea that pressuring others is wrong. For assessment criteria, students should communicate health-enhancing messages about respecting boundaries, not pressuring others, and coming to the support of friends. (Construct: Attitudes toward behavior.)

NHES 5 | Decision Making

Students will demonstrate the ability to use decision-making skills to enhance health.

ASSESSMENT CRITERIA
Reach a health-enhancing decision using a process consisting of the following steps:

- Identify a health-risk situation.
- Examine alternatives.
- Evaluate positive and negative consequences.
- Decide on a health-enhancing course of action.

Grades K–2

Children's Literature for Decision Making Many children's books focus on making a decision; see the list of appropriate books at the end of the chapter. Teachers and students can read these books and then talk about how people make good decisions (see Chapter 3). Young students don't need elaborate models. They do need to understand that they and other people make decisions every day that affect their health and well-being and to talk about how to make good decisions.

ASSESSMENT | For an assessment task, students can make pages for a class book about a good decision they made. For assessment criteria, students should identify health-enhancing decisions and write one or more sentences about how their decisions can help them stay strong and healthy. (Construct: Perceived behavioral control.)

"The Rules" and Other Decisions in the Classroom Teachers can help young students learn about decision making by engaging them in class meetings and community circles on topics of interest to the whole class. For example, many teachers involve their students in making rules for the classroom, as being allowed a say in the class rules gives students a greater investment in following them. Children's books that teachers can use to introduce the subject of making class rules and decisions about school are listed under "Safe and Healthy Classrooms and Schools" in the children's literature section at the end of the chapter. Teachers will find that engaging students in making rules and decisions for the classroom can positively affect the climate of the classroom. At a minimum, teachers should keep in mind that all rules and decisions should help students live up to the take cares: take care of yourself, take care of others, and take care of this place.

ASSESSMENT | For an assessment task, students can share their reflections on how they feel about being involved in making class rules and decisions. For assessment criteria, students should be able to explain why their ideas for rules and decisions support the mental and emotional health of everyone involved. (Construct: Attitudes toward behavior.)

Grades 3–5

Deciding About Ground Rules for Class Discussions   Many teachers find it useful to set ground rules with students before engaging in conversations and discussions about health issues. Examples of ground rules include

- Listen with your eyes, ears, and heart when others are talking.[71]
- Use encouraging words—no put-downs.
- Try to put yourself in someone else's situation.
- No gossiping about others or about class discussions outside the classroom.
- Don't ask personal questions about classmates or teachers.

Students can decide on the ground rules they want to follow for class discussions to keep everyone safe and willing to participate. For starters, teachers can go back to the take cares (take care of yourself, take care of others, take care of this place) and ask students to specify what these should look, sound, and feel like during class discussions.

ASSESSMENT | The ground rules students set are the assessment task for this activity. For assessment criteria, all rules should be health-enhancing and should have the take cares as a basis. (Construct: Intention to act in healthy ways.)

"What's Up?" Basket: Getting Help from Others About Issues and Decisions   An important aspect of mental and emotional health is being able to ask others for help in decision making. This activity helps students put this idea into practice in a nonthreatening way. Students can write a question or an issue that they need help with on a piece of paper and put it in the teacher's "What's up?" basket or box. From time to time, the teacher can draw a piece of paper from the basket and read the question or issue aloud to the class. Teachers should screen the papers first, be careful not to read aloud anything that might upset a particular child or be so personal that a child would be identified, and follow up with individual children when a serious problem is revealed. When the teacher reads a question or an issue, students can volunteer their ideas and advice about how to handle the situation. For example, students might wonder what to do when a bully grabs their book bag and takes whatever he or she wants. Students might offer advice, such as hanging out with two or three good friends when the bully might be around or telling a parent or teacher about it. Sharing problems and questions in this way helps students realize that they are not alone and that others want to

help them. Teachers also can get a good idea of the kinds of experiences students are having from the questions they write.

ASSESSMENT | For an assessment task, students can write a short story about a student who needs help and asks for it from friends, family members, or other caring adults. For assessment criteria, students should explain why the characters in their stories decided to ask for help and why that was a good decision. (Construct: Perceived behavioral control.)

Decision Trees: A Graphic Organizer for Decision Making   Upper-elementary students tend to see their decisions as black and white—only two choices available. A graphic organizer such as a decision tree can help them see that often there are more than two options. In fact, many options may be available when they expand their thinking. Teachers can demonstrate making a decision tree by drawing a tree trunk and writing a problem or question about a decision across the trunk. The teacher then can draw three to five branches coming from the tree and ask students to name alternative methods for handling the problem or decision. Teachers can write the students' ideas at the end of each branch, making sure the students suggest at least three alternatives. For example, students might want to attend a party on the weekend, but they've heard alcohol will be present and they don't want to drink. What can they do? Two obvious alternatives students will think of first are stay home or go to the party and drink. Other alternatives include go to the party with a couple of friends who also don't want to drink; go somewhere else, such as the movies, with other friends; and go to the party with a friend and be sure to take a cell phone to call for a ride home if things get out of hand.

Students then should identify the positive and negative consequences of each alternative. For example, going to a movie instead means that students miss the party (negative) but have a good time with their friends seeing the movie (positive). The decision tree can open students' eyes to the idea that more than two choices are available in most situations. To illustrate, a class was working on the problem of deciding whether to go to someone's house (the home of someone they really liked) when the parents weren't home, realizing there might be pressures to have sex. While students were naming alternatives (e.g., go, don't go), one student suddenly said, "Yeah, go—but take your sister with you!" The class laughed at the option that so clearly would remove the pressure to have sex.

ASSESSMENT | For an assessment task, students can work individually, in pairs, or in small groups to create a decision tree to share with the class. For assessment criteria, students should identify the problem or decision and at least three alternatives, name the positive and negative consequences of each alternative, select an action, and predict the outcome. (Constructs: Perceived behavioral control, attitudes toward behavior.)

Grades 6–8

Balloon Up for Decision Making   Middle school health educator Lynn Shoji created this activity to help students learn the steps in a simple decision-making model (see Chapter 3).[72] Following is a step-by-step approach for teachers to use to implement the activity.

1. Before class, blow up and tie five or six large helium-quality balloons. Put them where students can see them.
2. Begin the health lesson by holding one balloon and telling students you have a problem for them to solve. The problem is to work together as a class to keep the balloon in the air for thirty seconds.

3. *Problem:* Write "problem" on the board and tell students the first step in making a decision is to state the problem. Ask the students, "What is the problem today?" To keep the balloon in the air for thirty seconds.

4. *Alternatives:* Write "alternatives" on the board. Tell students that the next step in making a decision is thinking of all the possible alternatives or choices they can make. Tell students that they can ask questions about alternatives, and you will let them know what is and is not allowed. (Rules: Students must stay in their seats with their bottoms in the chairs at all times, can hit the balloon with one hand at a time, can hit only once until another student hits and then can hit the balloon again, cannot move the chairs once the activity starts, can talk and call out to each other, and can move the chairs anywhere they want before the activity starts.)

5. *Consequences:* Write "consequences" on the board. Tell students that each alternative has a consequence, some positive and some negative. Students can ask questions about what consequences follow each alternative. (Examples: We have to stop and start over if the balloon touches the floor, the balloon comes to rest and stops moving, someone catches it or holds it, someone gets out of the chair or moves the chair, someone hits the balloon two times in a row. The class gets to be a "one-balloon class" if the balloon stays up for thirty seconds. Next the class can try to be a two-balloon class, a three-balloon class, and so on.)

6. *Action:* It's time to choose an action. Students should get into the position they want with their chairs before the activity starts (don't give advice; let students work out their own plan). When students are ready, say "Go," bat the balloon into the air, and time it for thirty seconds. Stop the action if any rules are broken, and start again. When the class keeps the balloon in the air for thirty seconds, stop the action and congratulate them for being a one-balloon class.

7. *Evaluate:* Whether or not the students kept the balloon up, ask them if what they did worked. Go back through the list of steps and ask if there's anything they want to change (new alternatives). Try the activity again, either with one balloon or, if they were successful, with two balloons.

8. Try the activity several more times, either repeating or going on to a greater number of balloons. Important: Each time, stop and go back over the steps (problem, alternatives, consequences, action, evaluation). Ask the students each time if they want to change anything to help them work together better.

9. Stop with four or five balloons the first day. Tell students what "number" their class is, and tell them they can try the activity again the next week. Go back over the steps a final time, asking students to apply them to a real-life problem.

ASSESSMENT | For an assessment task, have students write a one-page story about a real-life situation in which they are being pressured to do something they know their parents don't want them to do (cut class, go swimming unsupervised, let someone copy their homework, go with friends instead of coming straight home after school, smoke, drink, stay out past curfew). Students can choose their own pressure situation. For assessment criteria, students must state the problem in their story and then discuss each step in the decision-making process, ending with an action and an evaluation of how they think things will turn out. (Construct: Perceived behavioral control.)

Lilo and Stitch: Angels on My Shoulder Many middle-level students will have seen the movie *Lilo and Stitch* when they were younger. The characters provide students with a reference point: Lilo will try to get them to make the best decision, and Stitch will try his best to get them to engage in a risky behavior that could hurt them or others. Whether students use the Lilo and Stitch roles or the idea of "good angel/bad angel," this activity is one that middle-level students enjoy and learn from. Teachers should note that it can get very noisy! Be sure to do this activity in a location where other classes won't be disturbed.

Teachers can start this activity by having students work in groups of three. Each group has three roles for members:

- Decision maker
- Lilo ("good angel," or healthy influence)
- Stitch ("bad angel," or unhealthy influence)

If needed, some groups can have four students, with two decision makers, depending on the number of students in the class.

Teachers next should demonstrate the activity with two volunteers, who will play Lilo and Stitch. The teacher plays the decision maker in the demonstration and provides a scenario, such as the following:

> You worked hard on your math homework last night and finished all of it. You are feeling very good about your effort. When you get to school, however, a friend asks to copy your homework—he stayed up late playing computer games and didn't get his work done. What do you decide, and what do you say and do?

The decision maker's role in the first part of the activity is just to listen. Lilo and Stitch, however, will try with all their might to persuade the decision maker to follow their way of thinking. Lilo will try to convince the decision maker not to let the friend copy; Stitch will try to convince the decision maker to go ahead and let the friend copy. Teachers should give Lilo and Stitch a couple of minutes to think about their most persuasive arguments and then, on a signal, give them thirty seconds to argue their case, calling time at the end of the thirty seconds. What makes this activity noisy is that both Lilo and Stitch can talk at the same time.

When time is called, the teacher, as the decision maker, shares what he or she heard and which side was more persuasive. The teacher should then ask the class what they thought about the arguments and which side they thought was most persuasive. At this point, students should simply get the idea of how to do the activity. In the next round, the teacher will take the debriefing further.

When students have the idea, each group should designate roles (Lilo, Stitch, decision maker). Give a scenario; the persuaders have a couple of minutes to think about their arguments. Then signal "Go!" Following are some sample scenarios to get started:

- You've had a good morning at school, and you have a social studies test in the afternoon. During lunch, several students say that they are going to cut school in the afternoon to go skateboarding at the park when it's not crowded. They want you to come, too, and you have your board in your locker. What do you decide? What do you say and do?
- You and a friend are in a music shop at the mall. Your friend has been wanting to get a new DVD, but she doesn't have enough money to pay for it today, so she decides to shoplift it. She asks you to stand as a lookout to watch for the store manager and clerks to make sure she doesn't get caught. She doesn't want you to do the stealing—just to stand at the end of the aisle while she slips the DVD into her purse. What do you decide? What do you say and do?
- There's a new girl at school who wears a headscarf each day. Some of the kids in the class have been making fun of her behind her back. Someone passes you a slam book with really mean comments written about the girl and tells you to write in it, too. What do you decide? What do you say and do?

Learning to set goals and work toward achieving them builds self-esteem and self-efficacy.

- You and your friends want to play basketball in the driveway, but your Dad's car is blocking the way. He took the subway into town today for a conference, and your Mom is at the grocery store in her car. You decide to move the car out of the way, but you wind up scraping it on the fence post, leaving a mark down the side. You can tell your parents what you did—or you can move the car back into place and act as if nothing happened. What do you decide? What do you say and do?

After the first role-play, stop the action and call on the decision maker in each group to tell what they heard from Lilo and Stitch, what was persuasive to them, and why. After hearing from every decision maker, use a "decision tree" to talk about alternatives and consequences. This debriefing is essential. Otherwise, the activity becomes mere entertainment and could even lead students to go away with the idea that dangerous and unhealthy behaviors are okay.

Teachers can have students work through several scenarios, giving each student the chance to play each of the three roles. Teachers and students should thoroughly debrief every scenario. If a student insists that an unsafe or unhealthy behavior is best, the teacher can ask, "What do others think? What could happen if this is what the decision maker does? Who would be affected? How?"

Teachers also can use this activity to discuss two other standards. Students can step back and examine communication style (NHES 4): What kind of communication—words, tone of voice, face, body language—makes a person want to listen to someone? Students also can analyze influences (NHES 2): How do students put pressure on one another? What is most persuasive? How can students deflect or resist that kind of pressure?

ASSESSMENT | For an assessment task, students can create and demonstrate an original Lilo and Stitch scenario for the class. For assessment criteria, students should perform the scenario and then lead the debriefing on decision making (NHES 5), communication style (NHES 4), and analyzing influences (NHES 2). (Construct: Perceived behavioral control.)

NHES 6 | Goal Setting

Students will demonstrate the ability to use goal-setting skills to enhance health.

- Goal statement—Give goal statement that identifies health benefits; goal is achievable and will result in enhanced health.
- Goal setting plan—Show plan that is complete, logical and sequential, and includes a process to assess progress.

Grades K–2

Children's Literature for Goal Setting Many children's books tell stories of characters who have an important goal they work hard to reach. Teachers can use these books to talk with children about the importance of having achievable goals, making plans that include concrete steps to reach goals, overcoming obstacles, finding and building on sources of support, and monitoring progress. The resilience research says that learning to persist and work hard is important for children to grow to be healthy adults. See the list of books at the end of the chapter for stories about goal setting.

ASSESSMENT | For an assessment task, students can select a book and explain what various characters did to reach their goals. For assessment criteria, students should tell what the characters did in terms of (1) setting an achievable goal, (2) making a plan, (3) building on supports and dealing with obstacles, and (4) monitoring progress. Students also can tell alternative steps the characters could have taken. (Construct: Perceived behavioral control.)

Setting Behavioral and Academic Goals Teachers will recall from earlier discussion in this chapter that building self-esteem, self-efficacy, and resilience hinges on helping students learn to achieve things for themselves. Former first grade teacher Diane Parker shared that she helped her students do this by setting an academic and a behavioral goal for each quarter of the school year. Although educators generally focus on helping young students set short-term goals (for a whole day washing their hands before they eat, using kind words all morning), Parker found that her first-grade students were able, with her help, to set achievable long-term goals and define steps toward reaching them. One of her students set the goal of not hitting others when she was upset or angry and to find other ways to let others know what she needed. When she and her teacher went over her goals at the end of the quarter, including the one about not hitting, she exclaimed with happiness, "I don't do that anymore!" Setting these kinds of goals means working with children one-on-one to find the specific issues that they feel their teachers—and their parents or caregivers—believe are important for their success. Students, with their teachers' help, choose the goals and set the steps for reaching them.

ASSESSMENT | The assessment task for this activity is for students to set, with their teachers' help, one academic and one behavioral goal to work on for a specified time period. For assessment criteria, the students' goals should be achievable and should include at least three concrete steps they will take to reach their goals. Students also should identify markers of success—that is, how they will know they have achieved their goals. (Constructs: Intention to act in healthy ways, perceived behavioral control.)

Grades 3–5

The Blue Ribbon Day: **We're All Good at Something!** Katie Couric's book *The Blue Ribbon Day* deals with the disappointment children and adults experience when a goal they care about doesn't work out for them. In this story, one sister makes the soccer team and the other does not. Teachers can use the book to help children think about ways to turn their disappointment into an opportunity to try new things. Children can discuss the importance of having strong sources of support (a parent) and of looking at challenges from new perspectives (submitting a project for the school science fair). This activity links to NHES 7, self-management.

ASSESSMENT | For an assessment task, children can trace the goal-setting steps throughout the story. What goals did the characters have? What steps did they take to reach their goals? What obstacles did they encounter, and how did they handle them? How did they find and build on supports? How did the characters monitor their progress? For assessment criteria, students should be able to identify at least two ideas for dealing with obstacles and two ideas for finding and building on supports. (Construct: Perceived behavioral control.)

■ **Webbing It: Supports for and Barriers to Reaching Goals** Upper-elementary students are ready to think about people and conditions that help them meet their goals and those that keep them from reaching their goals. For example, a student who attends a school and lives in a community with lots of opportunities for physical activity could count those opportunities as a "support" for reaching the goal of being more physically active. A student who lives in an area with little opportunity for participation in physical activity could count that lack of opportunity as a "barrier" to the goal of being physically active. Neither the support nor the barrier dictate what the student will be able to do. However, the student who has more opportunity might find it easier to be active, and the student with less opportunity might have to work harder to be active. Similarly, friends who say "Go ahead—you can do it, and we'll be there to watch you play" are a support. Friends who say "Why would you want to do that—let's go smoke" are a barrier. For this activity, students first identify several goals that are important to them, in both the short term and, if appropriate, the long term. Students then make a web of supports for and barriers to reaching their goals, using a different color for each. Around each support or barrier, students can write how they can take advantage of or overcome the supports and barriers, respectively.

ASSESSMENT | The web of supports and barriers students create is the assessment task for this activity. For assessment criteria, students should make a written plan for taking advantage of and overcoming each support and barrier. Students also can keep track of their experiences with the supports and barriers for a specified time period (one or two weeks). (Constructs: Intention to act in healthy ways, perceived behavioral control.)

Grades 6–8

Lōkahi for Mental and Emotional Health The Lōkahi Wheel, symbolizing balance, harmony, and unity (see Chapter 1), provides an important visualization of mental and emotional health. If the parts of the wheel are in balance, students are likely to experience mental and emotional health, even in the face of challenges. For this activity, students can draw and decorate (linking to fine arts) their own Lōkahi Wheel, showing each of the six parts of the wheel: friends/family, feelings/emotions, thinking/mind, work/school, spiritual/soul, and physical/body. Teachers can review the parts of the wheel with students (spiritual/soul refers to the ways students renew themselves, which may or may not be related to faith-based practices) and have them answer two questions for each part:

1. How is it going?
2. How do I want it to go?

This very personal activity helps students look at the big picture of how things are going with their health and what issues they might like to work on for better health. Students show the six parts of their wheels as being of equal size or make the parts larger or smaller depending on how the parts apply to their lives. For example, many teacher education students show work/school taking up most of their wheel at this point in their lives. They often choose to work on improving the way they take care of themselves in physical/body (more sleep, regular exercise, better nutrition) and taking the time for more renewal in spiritual/soul.

ASSESSMENT | The Lōkahi Wheels students create are the assessment task for this activity. For assessment criteria, students should explain how things are going and how they want them to go in each part of the wheel and should set one goal and list steps to achieve it. (Construct: Intention to act in healthy ways.)

A Letter from Nic: Building Your Support System in Middle School Building a support system in middle school is an important key to mental and emotional health, resilience, and reaching goals of all kinds. Teachers can use the story in this activity to bring the topic of support systems to life. Teacher's Toolbox 5.2 offers a letter from a sixth-grade student, named Nic, who encountered an unexpected problem with a group of boys at his new middle school. Students can read Nic's story to start a discussion on friendship. What is a real friend? Would a friend behave in a hurtful way around other kids? How long should a person try to fit in, and how far should someone go to fit in? When does it make sense to look for new friends? How can a friend help another friend who is being singled out and picked on? What should Nic do, and why? To dig more deeply, teachers can ask students to think about what they really want in friends—how to be that kind of friend and how to find those kinds of friends as a support system. Students can identify the kinds of friendships they want to develop and the kind of relationships they want to stay away from in middle school. After students have completed their discussion, they will be interested to know what Nic actually decided to do. His mom wrote several months later:

> He never stopped riding his bike to school. He found ways to place himself in the group so that it would be difficult for the lead bully to target him. He had to be very strategic. The teasing and taunting still happened, though not as frequently, but he just didn't want to give up the social connection, painful as it was at times. Nic did finally report the behaviors to his homeroom teacher and she and the counselor did some intervening, but it didn't help the problem much. Eventually, one of the boys got so angry with the way "the pack" was treating Nic that he and Nic started riding their bikes to school together (without the pack). He and Nic have become very good buddies. Since then, a couple of other boys have asked to ride with them because they are being bullied, too. He has also made some good friends with boys who are outside the group and has formed strong relationships with his teachers. I think this has been a critical piece in his resilience.

Nic used his support system—his family, teachers, and new friends—to work this problem out for himself, even when the going was really hard. Developing and maintaining a strong support system is an important aspect of middle school for students to consider.

ASSESSMENT | For an assessment task, students can write letters of response giving their best advice on how to deal with Nic's situation. Students can exchange letters to discuss the similarities and differences in their approaches to dealing with problems that involve classmates. For assessment criteria, students should describe how they will find and keep friends who stand up for them throughout their middle school years and beyond. (Construct: Perceived behavioral control.)

Health Behavior Projects: Trying Out a Theory-to-Practice Approach Sabo, Telljohann, and Kane published a helpful guide for working with students on health behavior change, titled *Improving*

Hi. My name is Nicolas and I am 11 years old and I am in 6th grade in middle school. I ride my bike to school with about 9 other boys. One day they said "Let's go" and got on their bikes. We were all riding until we were about half way home from school. Then I saw that they were not there so I stopped and waited for them. When they came around the corner they were whispering and they all hit their brakes and said "What are you doing, Nic?" I said, "I am waiting for you guys." So they started to pedal as fast as they could and when I caught up to them they turned around, saw me and slammed on their brakes. I just kept on going and went home. The next day at lunch I came in to sit with them and they were sitting there talking. I sat down and I saw one of the boys look up and see me. He turned to the boy who was talking and was saying "Be quiet, he is right there." The next morning I rode my bike and met the boys again at our meeting place. They said "hi" and we were OK until about 10 minutes later when they said "Let's go." They all got on their bikes, pedaled just once and then hit their brakes and stayed there while I started riding and rode all the way to school all by myself.

A few days later it was cold outside and raining. Not very many people were going outside to recess. Two of the boys got up and started walking toward the door. As soon as I got up to go with them they turned around and went and sat down. I turned around and sat back down with them. As soon as I sat down they got up and headed for the door again and when I got up to follow they went and sat down. Finally, I just sat there and waited until they were out the door and then I got up and went out with them. I felt like I was being teased and excluded. Now I just wait long enough to see them go out the door and then I go. Otherwise it makes me look stupid when I go out and come back and go out and come back.

Then the next day the routine was the same with the bikes. They started to pedal, slammed on the brakes and I rode to school all by myself. I felt like they didn't want to be around me and I felt sad and mad and left out.

Later that day, they came out and one of them said, "I have a joke to tell all of you but you can't listen to it Nic because it is too inappropriate for you," so I just sat there until we went inside.

I keep going back because they call me a baby or laugh at me if I don't show up.

They are still teasing me sometimes but not as much because I figured out how to make it so they can't. I get in the back of the group on bikes and I make sure they are leaving before I get on my bike and leave.

They are nice to me and talk to me as long as there isn't more than one boy.

Used with permission.

Health Behaviors, as part of the *HealthSmart* series for middle and high school students.[73] In these lessons, students learn to

- Identify unhealthy behaviors.
- Establish a goal to change an unhealthy behavior.
- Develop a plan and implement strategies for achieving a healthy goal.

The lessons are based on a modified version of the transtheoretical model (TTM), which many educators know as "stages of change." This model views behavior changes as a process over time, rather than as a one-time event. Sabo, Telljohann, and Kane explain the five stages of change as follows:

1. *Precontemplation:* People in this stage are not aware that their unhealthy behavior is a problem, or they may know it is a problem but don't intend to change.
2. *Contemplation:* People in this stage are aware that their unhealthy behavior is a problem and are thinking about changing it. They are more open to feedback and information from others.
3. *Preparation:* People in this stage are committed to changing their unhealthy behavior in the near future. They have been taking small steps to help them get ready to change the behavior.
4. *Action:* People in this stage are taking action to change their unhealthy behavior. They have put a plan in place and are making progress in practicing healthier behaviors.
5. *Maintenance:* People in this stage have followed their plan and have changed the unhealthy behavior. Their practice of healthier behaviors is becoming a habit.

Relapse may occur in the action or maintenance stage. Students can benefit from understanding the triggers or events that can bring on relapse and learn how to prepare for and successfully deal with them. Relapse should be seen not as a failure but as a temporary setback that can be overcome.[74] Middle-level students are ready to deal with unhealthy behaviors and are fascinated by working to change them with a "theory into action" approach. Teachers may find it helpful to explore the stages of change model more extensively through the ETR unit or other resources and provide their students with opportunities to try it for themselves.

ASSESSMENT | For an assessment task, students should select a health behavior they want to change, identify the stage they are in, establish a goal based on their stage of change, and develop and implement a plan. Students should keep records of their progress over time for class discussion and should summarize their experience in a health goal summary paper. For assessment criteria, students should be able to explain each step involved in working toward their goal. (Constructs: Intention to act in healthy ways, perceived behavioral control.)

NHES 7 | Self-Management

Students will demonstrate the ability to practice health-enhancing behaviors and avoid or reduce health risks.

ASSESSMENT CRITERIA

- Application (transfer)—Initiate health-enhancing behaviors; apply concepts and skills appropriate and effectively.
- Self-monitoring and reflection—Monitor actions and make adjustments; accept feedback and make adjustments; able to self-assess, reflect on, and take responsibility for actions.

Grades K–2

Table Drumming: Go, Slow Down, and Stop Feelings   Allana Coffee uses this activity to help children develop a sense of self-control and self-management with regard to how they handle strong feelings.[75] Teachers need three pieces of paper—green, yellow, and red—for this activity. Teachers also could create three stoplight pictures that feature the green, yellow, and red signals. Students can tell what these colors mean on a traffic light (go, slow down, stop). Some teachers have reported that their students say the yellow light means speed up. This can be a teachable moment! Teachers should tell students to drum on their desks in response to the color being held up, drumming fast on green, slowing down on yellow, and stopping on red.

Teachers next can ask students to think of feeling words (referring to the feelings alphabet at the Online Learning Center) that apply to the different signals. What feeling words tell students it's okay to go, to slow down, and to stop altogether? Teachers can write these words on the board, or older students can make lists in small groups. For example, "go" words might include happy, calm, peaceful, excited, and rested; "slow down" words might include frustrated, irritated, tired, scared, and sad; and "stop" words could include furious, exhausted, stressed out, agitated, and terrified. Students might find it simpler to start by listing go and stop words, adding slow down words in between. This activity is a good vocabulary builder and helps students identify progressions of feelings (irritated, mad, furious, enraged). Table drumming provides a memorable way for students to think and talk about feelings.

Self-management is an important skill for mental and emotional health. (Lawren, age 12)

Teachers can use various scenarios to ask students what kinds of feelings might result—whether the person might be feeling "green," "yellow," or "red"—and what they should do about it. Coffee asks students what kind of day they are having, using the color words to help the children talk about situations and feelings in their lives.

ASSESSMENT | For an assessment task, students can describe green, yellow, and red feelings or draw a picture that shows them having a green, yellow, or red day, feeling, or experience. For assessment criteria, students should be able to explain what they do when they have that feeling or experience that helps them feel better and stay healthy. (Construct: Intention to act in healthy ways.)

Chilling and Jazzing: Relaxing and Energizing Through Music, Movement, and Imagination Many teachers and students find that they enjoy working as soft music plays in the background. Teachers can introduce students to various kinds of music in this way, as well as help students feel calm in the classroom. Teachers might also want to have students close their eyes and "take a trip" to one of their favorite places, by themselves or with someone they care about, as a way of feeling calm. When students have been sitting and working for a long time, teachers can play music that's a bit more lively and can have students get up and stretch and move around to wake up their minds and their muscles.

ASSESSMENT | For an assessment task, teachers can allow students to have a turn leading the class in either a relaxation or energizer activity, once they are clear on the idea. For assessment criteria, the students leading the activity should explain why they selected their activity as a relaxation or energizer self-management strategy. (Construct: Perceived behavioral control.)

Children's Literature on Taking Care of Family and Friends Maintaining relationships in families and friendships is an important aspect of mental and emotional health. Many children's books lend themselves to discussions about being good family members and friends and about dealing with problems and challenges in healthy ways. See especially the books listed under "Family and Friends" in

the list of children's literature at the end of the chapter. Teachers can lead students in a discussion of their experiences about being good family members and friends and encourage them to identify ways they can be good family members and friends.

ASSESSMENT | For an assessment task, students can make a class list of self-management strategies for being good family members and friends. For assessment criteria, students should be able to give at least three concrete examples of how they will put their strategies into practice at home or school. (Construct: Intention to act in healthy ways.)

Grades 3–5

Children's Literature on Dealing with Worries Childhood might seem like a carefree time to adults, but many children worry about lots of things. One of the authors remembers deciding to say "Present" during roll call in elementary school because she was sure the other children were laughing at the way she said "Here." Similarly, and more seriously, a kindergarten teacher shared that one of her students cried at school when he heard that they had kindergarten aides—he heard "kindergarten AIDS." To help children learn to take positive steps to tackle their fears and help them know they are not alone, teachers can choose books such as those listed under "Worries" in the list of children's literature at the end of the chapter. Teachers can focus discussions on identifying what the characters were worried about and what they did to feel better. Teachers can help children feel able, valuable, and responsible when it comes to thinking through their own problems and acting to solve them.

ASSESSMENT | For an assessment task, students can share orally, in writing, or through pictures a time when they were worried and had a problem and how they solved it. For assessment criteria, students should explain the self-management steps they took to solve their problem and tell how things turned out for them. (Constructs: Intention to act in healthy ways, perceived behavioral control.)

***A Bad Case of Stripes:* Children's Literature on Being Okay with Being Unique** Many children's books deal with learning to accept and appreciate differences and unique attributes in oneself and others. Discussions on these kinds of issues can move well beyond the idea of tolerance to being actively interested in and open to learning about how human beings vary, in all kinds of ways. *A Bad Case of Stripes,* by David Shannon, is a wonderful example. Camilla Cream finds that she indeed has come down with a case of stripes—and the stripes are just the beginning of the changes Camilla experiences until she determines to be herself, rather than trying to be like others. Other books teachers can use are listed under "Diversity and Uniqueness" at the end of the chapter. Teachers can initiate the discussion by asking students what they noticed about the characters in the story. What was unique (a new vocabulary word for some students) about them? What was good, interesting, and valuable about the ways they were unique? How did other characters treat them with respect to the ways they were unique? How do students want to be treated with respect to their unique characteristics? How do they think it is best to treat others who are different from them?

ASSESSMENT | For an assessment task, students can describe unique characteristics of themselves and others and explain how they see those characteristics as valuable. For assessment criteria, students can explain a self-management strategy they use when they meet someone new for finding out and appreciating that person's unique characteristics. (Construct: Perceived behavioral control.)

High Five: My Personal Support System   Having a support system of family members and friends is an important aspect of mental and emotional health. Students can identify important people they know they can go to for talking things over, listening, and support—people they can count on every time. Students can make a visual display of their support system by tracing the outline of their hand (a "high five") and writing on each finger the name of a person who is part of their support system. Students might also draw a support tree, naming people who support them on the tree branches. An activity called "Roles and Relationships," described by ETR Associates in *Actions: Emotional and Mental Health,* helps students visualize the important people in their lives by drawing a web (starting with the student in the middle) of family, friends, teachers, neighbors, and other adults.[76] Students go on to select five people and explain why those people are important to them. The activity encourages students to think about what they get from and give to each relationship. Regardless of the graphic organizer, naming the people in their personal support system helps students realize that they are not alone when the going gets tough.

ASSESSMENT | For an assessment task, students create a graphic organizer (hand, tree, web) to show their personal support system. For assessment criteria, students should name five individuals, including at least three adults, and explain how these people are there for them in terms of support and why a personal support system is important for mental and emotional health. As an extension, students can write a letter of appreciation to each person in their support system. Students also can identify people for whom they can serve as supporters. (Constructs: Subjective norms, perceived behavioral control.)

Grades 6–8

Healthy Self-Talk: Reframing Doom and Gloom into Optimism
Adults sometimes remark that early adolescents are hard on each other in terms of gossip and judgments. However, students in this age group may be even harder on themselves. At an age when their bodies are growing and changing in many ways, young adolescents often spend a great deal of time finding fault with themselves. Talking with students about practicing healthy self-talk can help them

reframe what they say to themselves and others. For example: "My hips are getting huge!" might be replaced with "I'm beginning to look like a woman instead of a little girl, and that's a normal, healthy change—and it looks good, too!" "Everyone will notice this giant pimple on my chin!" might be replaced with "No one will notice if I don't call attention to it, and it will be gone in a few days. Besides, everyone is worrying about their own pimples." "I'm afraid to talk to that new girl in class" might be replaced with "She probably would like some of us to help her feel like she fits in here. I'll ask Sandy to go with me to ask her how she likes it here so far." "I'll never, ever get this work done—I'm doomed!" might be replaced with "I'll make a schedule and do one thing at a time until it's all done. I'll get my friends to help me stick to my schedule." Students will scoff at self-talk that is unrealistic or silly. However, with practice, they can learn to turn their thinking into positive action when their thoughts about themselves or others are unnecessarily negative.

Teachers can provide students with starting statements such as those above and ask students to work on turning them into healthy—and realistic—self-talk. Students can also make a list of doom-and-gloom statements and use them to create healthy self-talk statements.

ASSESSMENT | For an assessment task, students can work in small groups to combine their doom-and-gloom statements, along with their reframed self-talk statements, into a poster to share with class members. Working in groups helps take the focus off any one student. For assessment criteria, students should be able to tell how they used healthy self-talk as a self-management strategy for staying optimistic throughout the day. Students also can share which situations were easy to manage and which were more challenging. (Construct: Intention to act in healthy ways.)

Adolescent Survival Book   "Puberty—how many of you think you will go through it?" Adolescent sexuality educator Amy Stone Murai uses this humorous question to get kids thinking about the fact that "it's going to happen to me." Middle-level students can work in small groups to take a proactive and positive stance toward puberty by working on different sections of an adolescent survival book. Students can learn about helpful websites (www.kidshealth.org) and other resources from their teachers and librarians. Ideas for sections of the book include

> Emotional changes in puberty
> Physical changes for boys and girls
> Being a good family member
> Responsible relationships with friends and significant others
> Handling pressures
> Talking things over
> Supporting myself and others

Students can find other ideas for puberty topics at the websites listed at the end of the chapter.

Students should generate the list of topics they want to cover, research their topics, verify their sources, and prepare their information and survival recommendations for publication in a class book. Students also can decide on a title for their book (*Staying Cool in the Middle*). Teachers can help students duplicate their booklets for distribution to class members and others.

ASSESSMENT | The assessment task for this activity is the survival book students produce. For assessment criteria, students should provide accurate information and draw conclusions about connections between behaviors and health (NHES 1), cite and verify their information sources (NHES 3), and recommend healthy self-management strategies (NHES 7). (Construct: Perceived behavioral control.)

Finding Your Courage: Standing Strong Even When It's Hard to Do   An important and often difficult self-management task for middle-level students, and older people, is finding the courage to take a stand in the face of popular opinion or opposition. Teachers can use literature as a springboard to talk with students about this issue; see the books listed under "Courage" at the end of the chapter. To engage students in a discussion about courage, Dr. Nan Stein recommends that teachers ask students to consider "courage by degrees"—that is, addressing a list of scenarios by asking which take more or less courage.[77] A sample list might be

- Standing up for a friend whom other students are teasing
- Standing up for a new student you don't know very well whom other students are teasing
- Saying no to a younger student who offers you a cigarette
- Saying no to an older student who offers you a cigarette
- Walking away from a fight when you and one other student are involved
- Walking away from a fight when lots of other kids are watching
- Raising your hand to offer an answer you are very sure of in class
- Raising your hand to offer an opinion that differs from what other students have said
- Refusing to sign a slam book
- Volunteering to head a committee for a school party

Students should discuss why each scenario takes more or less courage and how students can find the courage to act in ways that are best for everyone and don't hurt anyone. Students also can add to the list of scenarios for discussion.

ASSESSMENT | For an assessment task, students can make a list of self-management strategies for finding courage when the going gets tough—for example, hanging out with friends who feel the same way about important issues (not drinking). For assessment criteria, students should explain how they will use three of the strategies in real situations. (Construct: Intention to act in healthy ways.)

NHES 8 | Advocacy

Students will demonstrate the ability to advocate for personal, family, and community health.

ASSESSMENT CRITERIA
- Health-enhancing position—Give clear, health-enhancing position.
- Support for position—Support position with facts, concepts, examples, and evidence.
- Audience awareness—Show awareness of target audience; choose words, tone, and examples to suit audience.
- Conviction—Display conviction for position.

Grades K–2

Sharing Time for Health   In this activity, students can share a way they keep themselves healthy. For example, a student might bring a jump rope to class and explain why and how she spends time jumping each day for better health, or a student might bring in a low-sugar or unsweetened cereal to share with the class and explain why the cereal is a healthy choice. Another student might describe listening to music, singing, or dancing to manage stress. Teachers can assign each child a particular day to share a habit for staying healthy. By sharing, students advocate good health.

ASSESSMENT | The healthy practices students share are the assessment task for this activity. For assessment criteria, students should take a health-enhancing stand and explain their practice by giving reasons why it's healthy. (Construct: Subjective norms.)

You Can't Say "You Can't Play"   The idea for this activity comes from Vivian Paley's book of the same title.[78] Paley told her kindergarten students that the one thing they couldn't say to each other on the playground was "You can't play." Teachers can help students start a similar campaign with their classmates and others on the playground. For one week, the children can make a concerted effort to allow everyone who wants to play with them to be included. Teachers can debrief the children on the activity at the end of the week, and students can decide whether they want to continue their advocacy campaign. This activity links to NHES 5, decision making, and NHES 6, goal setting.

ASSESSMENT | The children's campaign is the assessment task for this activity. For assessment criteria, students should describe two positive things that happened on the playground during the week and take a health-enhancing stand on including others in their play. (Constructs: Subjective norms, attitudes toward behavior.)

Grades 3–5

Letter Writing for Health   Students should learn from an early age that they can make a difference. With their teacher's help, students can compose a letter to their principal or someone in their community about a mental and emotional health issue of interest to them. For example, students might want to ask the principal for permission to play music in the cafeteria during lunchtime to make it a more pleasant experience for students and faculty. In this case, students could offer to publicize the idea, soliciting agreement from students in all grades about acceptable behavior at lunch. Students can sign the letter after it is composed—with their teacher's help—to their satisfaction.

ASSESSMENT | The letter the students help compose is the assessment task for this activity. For assessment criteria, students should state a request, back it up with reasons, target their audience, and speak with conviction. (Constructs: Subjective norms, perceived behavioral control.)

No Name-Calling Week   Students might be interested in participating in an advocacy project called No Name-Calling Week, held in January. Teachers and students can find more information at www.nonamecallingweek.org. The website states, "Words hurt. More than that, they have the power to make students feel unsafe to the point where they are no longer able to perform in school or conduct normal lives." Through the website, teachers and students can learn how to conduct a no name-calling week in their school.

ASSESSMENT | Planning and implementing a no name-calling week, with the help of adults, is the assessment task for this activity. For assessment criteria, students should state a health-enhancing position, back it up with reasons, target their audience, and show strong conviction. Students also should explain how name-calling can affect mental and emotional health. (Constructs: Intention to act in healthy ways, subjective norms, attitudes toward behavior.)

***Thank You, Mr. Falkner:* Thanking a Teacher or Other Caring Adult**   Patricia Falacco's book *Thank You, Mr. Falkner* is the story of a struggling reader for whom a new teacher made all the difference. Students can identify a teacher or another caring adult who has made a difference for them and write and send a letter of thanks.

ASSESSMENT | The letters students write are the assessment task for this activity. For assessment criteria, students should explain to classmates how and why this person made a difference for them and tell at least one way they can advocate and support the health of others. This activity links to having a sense of models, one of the conditions of self-esteem. (Construct: Intention to act in healthy ways.)

Meet Our School Counselors Upper-elementary students can plan a poster and speaking campaign to introduce their school counselors to all the students in the school. Students should help their classmates and schoolmates learn who the counselors are, how they can help, and how students can contact them for health concerns.

ASSESSMENT | The campaign students plan and carry out is the assessment task for this activity. For assessment criteria, students should specify how counselors can help and how students can contact them. (Constructs: Subjective norms, perceived behavioral control.)

Grades 6–8

Eating Disorders Are Illnesses, Not Choices Students can learn more about eating disorders at websites such as those listed in "Internet and Other Resources" at the end of the chapter. Students can conduct research on eating disorders and develop a schoolwide campaign on recognizing and getting help for eating disorders. The campaign should help students know how to talk with friends they are concerned about and how to get help for their own personal concerns.

ASSESSMENT | The campaign students plan is the assessment task for this activity. For assessment criteria, students should develop a strong, health-enhancing position; back it up with facts and reasons; target their audience; and speak with conviction. (Constructs: Subjective norms, perceived behavioral control.)

More Than the Moody Blues: Teaching Classmates and Families About Depression Another issue that middle school students might want to explore is depression. What is it? How can students recognize it? How can students get help for themselves and others? Many of the sites listed in "Internet and Other Resources" at the end of the chapter provide extensive information on depression. Students might want to participate in Childhood Depression Awareness Day through the National Mental Health Association (www.nmha .org) or plan a campaign tailored for their school community.

ASSESSMENT | The campaign students plan is the assessment task for this activity. For assessment criteria, students should develop a strong, health-enhancing position; back it up with facts and reasons; target their audience; and speak with conviction. (Constructs: Subjective norms, perceived behavioral control.)

Mental and Emotional Health Night or Health Fair Middle school students are capable of planning, organizing, and conducting a health night or health fair for other students and their families with a focus on mental and emotional health. Students can work in small groups to create a booth or table to provide information and answer questions about any of the mental and emotional health topics in this chapter. A health night or health fair could serve as a culminating activity for a unit on mental and emotional health.

ASSESSMENT | The health night or health fair students organize and conduct is the assessment task for this activity. For assessment criteria, students should provide accurate information; develop educational materials; develop a strong, health-enhancing position; back it up with facts and reasons; target their audience; and speak with conviction. (Constructs: Subjective norms, perceived behavioral control.)

EVALUATED CURRICULA AND INSTRUCTIONAL MATERIALS

The Health Education Curriculum Analysis Tool (HECAT) provides a list of programs that federal agencies consider exemplary, promising, or effective (www.cdc.gov/Healthy Youth/HECAT/pdf/HECAT_Append_2.pdf). These agencies focus on different health topics and risk behaviors and therefore have somewhat different strategies and criteria for identifying effective programs.

For more information on the wealth of effective programs in the area of social and emotional competence, teachers can access these websites:

- National Registry of Effective Programs (www .modelprograms.samhsa.gov)

- Exemplary and Promising: Safe, Disciplined, and Drug-Free Schools Programs (www.ed.gov/admins/lead/ safety/exemplary01/index.html)
- Preventing Drug Use Among Children and Adolescents: A Research-Based Guide (www.nida.nih .gov/Prevention/Prevopen.html)
- Blueprints for Violence Prevention (www.colorado .edu/cspv/blueprints)
- Compendium of HIV Prevention Interventions with Evidence of Effectiveness (www.cdc.gov/hiv/resources/ reports/hiv_compendium)
- Research-tested Intervention Programs (http://rtips .cancer.gov/rtips/index.do)

INTERNET AND OTHER RESOURCES

Visit the Online Learning Center (www.mhhe.com/telljohann6e) for links to these sites, quizzes and other study aids, and many additional resources.

WEBSITES
American Academy of Child and Adolescent Psychiatry
www.aacap.org

American Association of Suicidology
www.suicidology.org

American Psychiatric Association
www.psych.org

American Psychological Association
www.apa.org

Anorexia Nervosa and Related Eating Disorders, Inc. (ANRED)
www.anred.com

BAM! Body and Mind
www.bam.gov

Centers for Disease Control and Prevention/Healthy Youth (Division of Adolescent and School Health)
www.cdc.gov/HealthyYouth

FDA Kids
www.fda.gov/oc/opacom/kids/default.htm

Federation of Families for Children's Mental Health
www.ffcmh.org

FirstGov for Kids
www.kids.gov

Get Your Angries Out
www.angriesout.com

Girl Power!
www.girlpower.gov

GirlsHealth.gov
www.4girls.gov

Head Start Mental Health Resources
www.headstartinfo.org

Health Finder for Kids
www.healthfinder.gov/kids

Health, Mental Health and Safety Guidelines for Schools
www.schoolhealth.org

Helpguide (expert, noncommercial information on mental health and lifelong wellness)
www.helpguide.org

KidsHealth
www.kidshealth.org

Kidz Privacy
www.ftc.gov/bcp/conline/edcams/kidzprivacy/index.html

Mental Health America
www.mentalhealthamerica.net

National Association of School Psychologists
www.nasponline.org

National Center for Kids Overcoming Crisis
www.kidspeace.org

National Eating Disorders Association
www.nationaleatingdisorders.org

National Education Association Health Information Network
www.neahin.org/programs/mentalhealth

National Institutes of Health, National Institute of Mental Health
www.nimh.nih.gov

National Mental Health Association
www.nmha.org

Online Safety Rules for Kids
www.fema.gov/kids/on_safety.htm

Parents, Families, and Friends of Lesbians and Gays (PFLAG)
www.pflag.org

Rules in Cyberspace
www.cybercrime.gov/rules/rules.htm

Safety Tips for Internet Safety
www.fbi.gov/kids/k5th/safety2.htm

School Mental Health Project/Center for Mental Health in Schools at UCLA: ENEWS
http://smph.psych.ucla.edu

Southern Poverty Law Center: Tolerance.Org
www.tolerance.org

Substance Abuse and Mental Health Services Administration (SAMHSA), National Mental Health Information Center
www.mentalhealth.samhsa.gov

OTHER RESOURCES

Elias, M. J., et al. *Promoting Social and Emotional Learning: Guidelines for Educators.* Association for Supervision and Curriculum Development, 1997.

Gardner, H. *Intelligence Reframed: Multiple Intelligences for the 21st Century.* Basic Books, 2000.

Golemen, D. *Emotional Intelligence: Why It Can Matter More Than IQ.* Bantam Books, 1994.

Kohn, A. *What to Look for in a Classroom and Other Essays.* Jossey-Bass, 2000.

Landau, B. M. *The Art of Classroom Management: Building Equitable Learning Communities.* Pearson, 2004.

Seligman, M. E. P. *The Optimistic Child: A Proven Program to Safeguard Children Against Depression and Build Lifelong Resilience.* HarperPerennial, 1995.

CHILDREN'S LITERATURE

AGES 5–8

COMMUNICATION

Cosby, Bill. *The Meanest Thing to Say.* Cartwheel, 1997.

Cosby, Bill. *My Big Lie.* Cartwheel, 1999.

Henkes, Kevin. *Lilly's Purple Plastic Purse.* Greenwillow Books, 1996.

Joslin, Sesyle, and Maurice Sendak. *What Do You Say, Dear?* HarperTrophy, 1986.

Ljungkvist, Laura. *Toni's Topsy-Turvy Telephone Day.* Harry N. Abrams, 2001.

Scieszka, Jon. *The True Story of the 3 Little Pigs.* Viking, 1989.

Sharmat, Marjorie Weinman. *A Big Fat Enormous Lie.* Puffin Books, 1978.

Verdick, Elizabeth. *Words Are Not for Hurting.* Free Spirit, 2004.

Wheeler, Valerie. *Yes, Please! No, Thank You!* Sterling, 2005.

Willems, Mo. *Knuffle Bunny: A Cautionary Tale.* Hyperion Books for Children, 2004.

Willems, Mo. *Time to Say Please!* Hyperion Books for Children, 2005.

Williams, Suzanne. *Mommy Doesn't Know My Name.* Houghton Mifflin, 1990.

Other books with a focus on communication include *Courage* (Waber) and *The Honest-to-Goodness Truth* (McKissack).

COURAGE

Angelou, Maya. *Life Doesn't Frighten Me.* Stewart, Tabori & Chang, 1993.

Crist, James J. *What to Do When You're Scared and Worried: A Guide for Kids.* Free Spirit, 2004.

Demi. *The Empty Pot.* Henry Holt, 1990.

Heide, Florence P. *Some Things Are Scary.* Candlewick, 2000.

McKissack, Patricia C. *The Honest-to-Goodness Truth*. Atheneum Books for Young Readers, 2000.

Waber, Bernard. *Courage*. Houghton Mifflin/Walter Lorraine Books, 2002.

See also the books listed under "Dealing with Worries."

DIVERSITY AND UNIQUENESS

Appelt, Kathi. *Incredible Me!* HarperCollins, 2003.

Carlson, Nancy. *I Like Me!* Viking, 1988.

Couric, Katie. *The Brand New Kid*. Doubleday, 2000.

Curtis, Jamie Lee, and Laura Cornell. *Is There Really a Human Race?* Joanna Cotler Books, 2006.

Davol, Marguerite W. *Black, White, Just Right!* Albert Whitman, 1993.

Emmett, Jonathan. *Ruby in Her Own Time*. Scholastic, 2003.

Fierstein, Harvey. *The Sissy Duckling*. Simon & Schuster Books for Young Readers, 2002.

Graff, Lisa. *The Thing About Georgie*. Laura Geringer, 2007.

Hamanaka, Sheila. *All the Colors of the Earth*. HarperTrophy, 1999.

Henkes, Kevin. *Chrysanthemum*. Greenwillow Books, 1991.

Hoffman, Mary. *Amazing Grace*. Scott, Foresman, 1991.

Johnson, Angela. *Violet's Music*. Dial Books for Young Readers, 2004.

Katz, Karen. *The Colors of Us*. Henry Holt, 1999.

Kindersley, Barnabas, and Anabel Kindersley. *Children Just Like Me: A Unique Celebration of Children Around the World*. DK, 1995.

Kotzwindle, William, and Glenn Murray. *Walter the Farting Dog*. Frog, 2001.

Kraus, Robert. *Leo the Late Bloomer*. Windmill Books, 1971.

Lithgow, John. *The Remarkable Farkle McBride*. Simon & Schuster Books for Young Readers, 2000.

Lucado, Max. *You Are Special*. Crossway Books, 1997.

Munsch, Robert. *The Paper Bag Princess*. Annick, 2002.

Parr, Todd. *It's Okay to Be Different*. Little, Brown, 2001.

Parr, Todd. *This Is My Hair*. Little, Brown, 1999.

Pfister, Marcus. *Just the Way You Are*. North-South Books, 2002.

Root, Phyllis. *Oliver Finds His Way*. Candlewick, 2002.

Shannon, David. *A Bad Case of Stripes*. Blue Sky, 1998.

Tyler, Michael. *The Skin You Live In*. Chicago Children's Museum, 2005.

Wells, Rosemary. *Yoko*. Hyperion, 1998.

Whitcomb, Mary E. *Odd Velvet*. Chronicle Books, 1998.

Willis, Jeanne, and Tony Ross. *I Want to Be a Cowgirl*. Henry Holt, 2001.

Woodson, Jacqueline. *The Other Side*. GP Putnam's Sons, 2001.

FAMILY AND FRIENDS

Aliki. *We Are Best Friends*. Greenwillow Books, 1982.

American Girl Library. *Care and Keeping of Friends*. Pleasant Company, 1996.

Anholt, Catherine, and Laurence Anholt. *Big Book of Families*. Candlewick, 1998.

Axelrod, Amy. *My Last Chance Brother*. Dutton Children's Books, 2002.

Beaumont, Karen. *Being Friends*. Dial Books for Young Readers, 2002.

Brown, Laura K., and Marc Brown. *How to Be a Friend*. Scholastic, 1998.

Carlson, Nancy. *My Best Friend Moved Away*. Penguin Putnam Books for Young Readers, 2001.

Downey, Roma. *Love Is a Family*. Regan Books, 2001.

Edwards, Becky. *My Brother Sammy*. Millbrook, 1999.

Edwards, Pamela Duncan. *Gigi and Lulu's Gigantic Fight*. Katherine Tegen Books, 2004.

Kroll, Virginia. *Hands*. Boyds Mill, 1997.

Lewis, Rob. *Friends*. Henry Holt, 1999.

Lobel, Arnold. *Frog and Toad Are Friends*. HarperTrophy, 1970.

Parr, Todd. *The Best Friends Book*. Little, Brown, 2000.

Parr, Todd. *The Family Book*. Little, Brown, 2003.

Rodman, Mary Ann. *My Best Friend*. Viking, 2005.

GOALS AND DECISIONS

Bridges, Shirin Yim. *Ruby's Wish*. Chronicle Books, 2002.

Carter, Sharon. *The Little Book of Choices*. Island Heritage, 2004.

Couric, Katie. *The Blue Ribbon Day*. Doubleday, 2004.

Crowe, Ellie. *Duke's Olympic Feet*. Island Heritage, 2002.

Dorfman, Craig. *I Knew You Could: A Book for All the Stops in Your Life*. Platt & Munk, 2003.

Hamm, Mia. *Winners Never Quit!* HarperCollins, 2004.

Henkes, Kevin. *Sheila Rae, The Brave*. Mulberry Books, 1987.

Joslin, Sesyle. *What Do You Do, Dear? Proper Conduct for All Occasions*. HarperTrophy, 1986.

Newby, John. *Heart of the Game*. John Newby, 2002.

Pearson, Emily. *Ordinary Mary's Extraordinary Deed*. Gibbs Smith, 2002.

Piper, Watty. *The Little Engine That Could*. Platt & Munk, 1976, original edition 1930.

Reynolds, Peter H. *Ish*. Candlewick, 2004.

Seuss, Dr. *Oh, The Places You'll Go!* Random House, 1990.

Troiano, Joe. *It's Your Cloud*. Barnes & Noble, 2004.

Other books about setting goals and making decisions include *Courage* (Waber); *I Want to Be a Cowgirl* (Willis/Ross); *Life Doesn't Frighten Me* (Angelou); *Oliver Finds His Way* (Root); and *What Do You Say, Dear?* (Joslin).

IALAC (I AM LOVABLE AND CAPABLE)

Andreae, Giles. *Giraffes Can't Dance*. Orchard Books, 1999.

Curtis, Jamie Lee. *I'm Gonna Like Me: Letting Off a Little Self-Esteem*. Joanna Cotler Books, 2002.

Petty, Kate, and Charlotte Firmin. *Feeling Left Out*. Barron's, 1991.

Philips, Barbara. *Don't Call Me Fatso*. Raintree Steck-Vaughn, 1993.

Prelutsky, Jack. *Me I Am!* Farrar, Straus & Giroux, 2007.

Schwartz, Amy. *Annabelle Swift, Kindergartner*. Orchard Books, 1998.

Seskin, Steve. *Don't Laugh at Me*. Tricycle, 2002.

Seuss, Dr. *The Sneetches and Other Stories*. Random House, 1989.

Shannon, David. *David Gets in Trouble*. Blue Sky, 2002.

Shannon, David. *David Goes to School*. Blue Sky, 1999.

Shannon, David. *No, David!* Blue Sky, 1998.

Viorst, Judith. *Alexander and the Terrible, Horrible, No Good, Very Bad Day*. Atheneum Books for Young Readers, 1972.

Other appropriate books include *Walter the Farting Dog* (Kotzwindle/Murray); *Leo the Late Bloomer* (Kraus); *Lilly's Purple Plastic Purse* (Henkes); *The Meanest Thing to Say* (Cosby); and *The Sissy Duckling* (Fierstein).

MOODS AND STRONG FEELINGS

Bang, Molly. *When Sophie Gets Angry—Really, Really Angry. . . .* Blue Sky, 1999.

Bluthenthal, Diana Cain. *I'm Not Invited?* Atheneum Books for Young Readers, 2003.

Cain, Janan. *The Way I Feel*. Parenting, 2000.

Curtis, Jamie Lee. *Today I Feel Silly and Other Moods That Make My Day*. Joanna Cotler Books, 1998.

Curtis, Jamie Lee, and Laura Cornell. *It's Hard to Be Five: Learning How to Work My Control Panel*. Joanna Cotler Books, 2004.

Cutler, Dave. *When I Wished I Was Alone*. GreyCore, 2003.

Danziger, Paula. *Barfburger Baby, I Was Here First*. GP Putnam's Sons, 2004.

Evans, Lezlie. *Sometimes I Feel Like a Storm Cloud*. Mondo, 1999.

Everit, Betty. *Mean Soup*. Harcourt Children's Books, 1992.

Freymann, Saxton, and Joost Elffers. *How Are You Peeling? Foods with Moods*. Arthur A. Levine Books, 1999.

Henkes, Kevin. *Julius the Baby of the World*. Greenwillow Books, 1990.

Hogan, Paul Z. *Sometimes I Get So Mad*. Raintree Steck-Vaughn, 1991.

Leonard, Marcia. *How I Feel Jealous*. Smart Kids, 2002.

Lichtenheld, Tom. *What Are You So Grumpy About?* Little, Brown, 2003.

Oram, Hiawyn. *Badger's Bad Mood*. Scholastic, 1998.

Parr, Todd. *The Feel Good Book*. Little, Brown, 2002.

Raduncky, V. *What Does Peace Feel Like?* Atheneum Books for Young Readers, 2004.

Saltzman, David. *The Jester Has Lost His Jingle*. Jester, 1995.

Sanzo, Stephen. *Cranky Pants*. Cranky Pants, 2005.

Seuss, Dr., Steve Johnson, and Lou Fancher. *My Many Colored Days*. Knopf, 1998.

Shuman, Carol. *Jenny Is Scared! When Sad Things Happen in the World*. Magination Press, 2003.

Vail, Rachel. *Sometimes I'm Bombaloo*. Scholastic, 2002.

Willis, Jeanne, and Tony Ross. *Misery Moo*. Henry Holt, 2003.

Other appropriate books include *Lilly's Purple Plastic Purse* (Henkes); *Alexander and the Terrible, Horrible, No Good, Very Bad Day* (Viorst); and *This Is My Hair* (Parr).

SAFE AND HEALTHY CLASSROOMS AND SCHOOLS

Catrow, David. *We the Kids*. Dial Books, 2002.

Creech, Sharon. *A Fine, Fine School*. Joanna Cotler Books, 2001.

Finchler, Judy. *Testing Miss Malarkey*. Walker & Company, 2000.

Harper, Jessica. *Lizzy's Do's and Don'ts*. HarperCollins, 2002.

Kelley, Marty. *The Rules*. Zino Press Children's Books, 2000.

Seuss, Dr. *Hooray for Diffendoofer Day!* Alfred A. Knopf, 1998.

Teague, Mark. *Dear Mrs. LaRue: Letters from Obedience School*. Scholastic, 2002.

Another appropriate book is *David Goes to School* (Shannon).

DEALING WITH WORRIES

Best, Cari. *Shrinking Violet*. Farrar, Straus & Giroux, 2001.

Cuyler, Margery. *100th Day Worries*. Simon & Schuster Books for Young Readers, 2000.

Henkes, Kevin. *Wemberly Worried*. Greenwillow Books, 2000.

McKee, David. *Elmer*. Lothrop, Lee & Shepard Books, 1968.

Morrison, Toni, and Slade Morrison. *The Book of Mean People*. Hyperion Books for Children, 2002.

Sherman, Allan, and Lou Busch. *Hello Muddah, Hello Faddah! A Letter from Camp*. Dutton Children's Books, 2004).

Viorst, Judith. *If I Were in Charge of the World and Other Worries: Poems for Children and Their Parents*. Aladdin, 1981.

Other books about worries include *Mommy Doesn't Know My Name* (Williams); *My Big Lie* (Cosby); *It's Okay to Be Different* (Parr); *Leo the Late Bloomer* (Kraus); *The Brand New Kid* (Couric); *Yoko* (Wells); *Ish* (Reynolds); *Feeling Left Out* (Petty/Firmin); *Giraffes Can't Dance* (Andreae); *It's Hard to Be Five* (Curtis/Cornell); *I'm Not Invited?* (Bluthenthal); *Some Things Are Scary* (Heide); *What to Do When You're Scared and Worried* (Crist); and many of the books listed under "Courage."

OTHER BOOKS WITH AN EMOTIONAL HEALTH THEME

Andreasen, Dan. *A Quiet Place*. Simon & Schuster Books for Young Readers, 2002.

Anholt, Catherine. *Sophie and the New Baby*. Albert Whitman, 1995.

Calmenson, Stephanie. *The Principal's New Clothes*. Scholastic, 1989.

Cosby, Bill. *The Best Way to Play*. Scholastic, 1997.

Coyle, Carmela LaVigna. *Do Princesses Wear Hiking Boots?* Rising Moon, 2003.

Davis, Gibbs. *The Other Emily*. Houghton Mifflin, 1984.

Ericsson, Jennifer A. *She Did It*. Melanie Drooupa Books, 2002.

Fox, Mem. *Whoever You Are*. Voyager Books, 2001.

Frasier, D. *On the Day You Were Born*. Harcourt, 1991.

Grindley, Sally. *What Are Friends For?* Kingfisher, 1998.

Haan, Amanda. *I Call My Hand Gentle*. Penguin Putnam Books for Young Readers, 2003.

Harris, Robie H. *Don't Forget to Come Back!* Candlewick, 2004.

Hennessy, B. G. *Because of You*. Candlewick, 2005.

Hest, Amy. *The Purple Coat*. Macmillan, 1986.

Kirk, David. *Miss Spider's Tea Party*. Scholastic, 1994.

Krauss, Ruth. *The Carrot Seed*. HarperFestival, 1993.

Krosoczka, Jarrett J. *Baghead*. Alfred A. Knopf, 2002.

Munsch, Robert. *We Share Everything!* Scholastic, 1999.

Munson, Derek. *Enemy Pie*. Chronicle Books, 2000.

Parr, Todd. *Reading Makes You Feel Good*. Little, Brown, 2005.

Penn, Audrey. *The Kissing Hand*. Child & Family, 1993.

Pfister, Marcus. *The Rainbow Fish*. North-South Books, 1992.

Sanders, Mark D., and Tia Sillers. *I Hope You Dance!* Rutledge Hill, 2003.

Simms, Laura. *Rotten Teeth*. Houghton Mifflin, 1998.

Smith, Jada Pinkett. *Girls Hold Up This World*. Scholastic, 2005.

Spelman, Cornelia. *Your Body Belongs to You*. Albert Whitman, 1997.

Verdick, Elizabeth. *Feet Are Not for Kicking*. Free Spirit, 2004.

Verdick, Elizabeth. *Hands Are Not for Hitting*. Free Spirit, 2002.

Wilson, Karma. *Hilda Must Be Dancing*. Margaret K. McElderry Books, 2004.

AGES 8–12

Anderson, Laurie Halse. *Speak*. Puffin Books, 1999.

Applegate, Katherine. *Home of the Brave*. Feiwel & Friends, 2007. (multicultural)

Atkins, Jeannine. *A Name on the Quilt: A Story of Remembrance*. Atheneum Books for Young Readers, 1999.

Avi. *Nothing but the Truth*. Orchard Books, 1991. (Newbery Honor Book)

Blackstone, Margaret, and Elissa Haden Guest. *Girl Stuff: A Survival Guide to Growing Up*. Harcourt Paperbacks, 2006.

Blos, Joan. *Old Henry*. Scribner's, 1987.

Blume, Judy. *Tales of a Fourth Grade Nothing*. Penguin Putnam Books for Young Readers, 2003.

Boynton, Sandra. *Yay, You! Moving Out, Moving Up, Moving On*. Simon & Schuster Children's Books, 2001.

Brooks, Bruce. *The Moves Make the Man*. Harper & Row, 1984. (Newbery Honor Book)

Child, Lauren. *Clarice Bean Spells Trouble*. Orchard Books, 2004.

Choldenko, Gennifer. *Al Capone Does My Shirts*. Penguin Group, 2004. (Newbery Honor Book)

Copsey, Susan Elizabeth, Barnabas Kindersley, Anabel Kindersley, and Harry Belafonte. *Children Just Like Me*. New York: DK, 1995.

Corey, Shana. *Players in Pigtails*. Scholastic, 2003.

Creech, Sharon. *Ruby Holler*. HarperCollins, 2003. (Carnegie Medal winner)

Criswell, Patti Kelley. *A Smart Girl's Guide to Friendship Troubles*. Pleasant Company, 2003.

Discovery Girls. *Fab Girls Guide to Friendship Hardship*. Discovery Girls, 2007.

Erlich, Amy. *When I Was Your Age*. Candlewick, 1996.

Estes, Eleanor. *The Hundred Dresses*. Harcourt, 1944.

Fletcher, Ralph. *Flying Solo*. Clarion Books, 1996.

Hansen, Joyce. *The Gift Giver*. Clarion Books, 1980.

Holm, Jennifer. *Middle School Is Worse than Meatloaf: A Year Told Through Stuff*. Ginee Seo Books, 2007.

Holmes, Sara Lewis. *Letters from Rapunzel*. HarperCollins, 2007.

Holyoke, Nancy. *The Big Book of Help*. American Girl, 2004.

Kadohata, Cynthia. *Kira-Kira*. Simon & Schuster, 2004. (Newbery Medal winner)

Kindersley, Anabel, and Barnabas Kindersley. *Children Just Like Me: Celebrations!* DK, 1997.

Kroeger, Mary, and Louis Borden. *Paper Boy.* Clarion Books, 1996.

Krull, Kathleen. *Wilma Unlimited: How Wilma Rudolph Became the World's Fastest Woman.* Harcourt, 2000.

Lord, Cynthia. *Rules.* Scholastic Press, 2006. (Newbery Honor Book)

Lupika, Mike. *Travel Team.* Penguin, 2004.

Madison, Linda. *The Feelings Book: The Care and Keeping of Your Emotions.* Pleasant Company, 2002.

Madonna. *The English Roses.* Callaway, 2003

Madonna. *Mr. Peabody's Apples.* Callaway, 2003.

Moss, Peggy. *Say Something.* Tilbury House, 2004.

Munsch, Robert. *Love You Forever.* Firefly Books, 1986.

Munson, Erek, and Tara Calahan King. *Enemy Pie.* Chronicle Books, 2000.

Naylor, Phyllis Reynolds. *Shiloh.* Atheneum, 1991. (Newbery Medal winner)

Peterson, Stacey. *Friends: Making Them & Keeping Them.* American Girl, 2006.

Philbrick, Rodman. *Freak the Mighty.* Scholastic, 1993.

Polacco, Patricia. *Thank You, Mr. Falkner.* Philomel Books, 1998.

Silverstein, Shel. *The Giving Tree.* HarperCollins, 1964.

Smith, Robert Kimmel. *The War with Grandpa.* Bantam Books, 1984.

Tarshis, Lauren. *Emma Jean Lazarus Fell Out of a Tree.* Dial, 2007.

Urban, Linda. *A Crooked Kind of Perfect.* Harcourt Children's Books, 2007.

Westcott, Nadine Bernard. *The Care and Keeping of Friends.* Pleasant Company, 1996.

Wiles, Deborah. *Aurora County All Stars.* Harcourt Children's Books, 2007. (multicultural)

Winthrop, Elizabeth. *Squashed in the Middle.* Henry Holt, 2005.

Woodson, Jacqueline. *The Other Side.* GP Putnam's Sons, 2001.

ENDNOTES

1. R. Kahakalau, "Every Child a Promise," *Keiki O Ka 'Aina*, Kanai'a Records, 1997.
2. M. Quackenbush, W. M. Kane, and S. K. Telljohann, *Teach and Reach: Emotional and Mental Health* (Santa Cruz, CA: ETR Associates, 2004).
3. M. Kitashima, conversation with author, June 2007.
4. M. L. Krovetz, *Fostering Resiliency: Expecting All Students to Use Their Minds and Hearts Well* (Thousand Oaks, CA: Corwin Press, 1999).
5. E. Werner and R. S. Smith, *Overcoming the Odds: High Risk Children from Birth to Adulthood* (Ithaca, NY: Cornell University Press, 1992).
6. K. Kelleher, "Mental Health," in *About Children: An Authoritative Resource on the State of Childhood Today*, eds. A. G. Cosby, R. E. Greenberg, L. H. Southward, and M. Weitzman (Elk Grove Village, IL: American Academy of Pediatrics, 2005), 138–41.
7. M. Quackenbush et al., *Teach and Reach.*
8. M. L. Krovetz, *Fostering Resiliency.*
9. U.S. Department of Health and Human Services, *Mental Health: A Report of the Surgeon General* (Rockville, MD: U.S. Department of Health and Human Services, Substance Abuse and Mental Health Services Administration, Center for Mental Health Services, National Institutes of Health, National Institute of Mental Health, 1999, www.surgeongeneral.gov/library/mentalhealth).
10. National Mental Health Association, *Children and Families.* (www.nmha.org/children/index.cfm; Sept. 2007)
11. National Institute of Health, *Child and Adolescent Mental Health.* (www.nimh.nih.gov/health/topics/child-and-adolescent-mental-health/index.shtml; Sept. 2007).
12. National Institutes of Health, *Mental Illness Exacts Heavy Toll, Beginning in Youth.* (www.nih.gov/news/pr/jun2005/nimh-06.htm; 6 June 2005)
13. K. Kelleher, "Mental Health."
14. National Mental Health Association, *Inadequate Funding for Children's Mental Health Services Costs Money Every Year.* (www.nmha.org; Sept. 2007)
15. M. L. Wolraich, "ADHD: Attention Deficit Hyperactivity Disorder," in *About Children: An Authoritative Resource on the State of Childhood Today*, eds. A. G. Cosby, R. E. Greenberg, L. H. Southward, and M. Weitzman (American Academy of Pediatrics, 2005), 150–53.
16. K. Kelleher, "Mental Health."
17. D. K. Eaton et al., "Youth Risk Behavior Surveillance—United States, 2007." *Morbidity & Mortality Weekly Report* 57, no. SS-4 (2008): 1–131.
18. U.S. Department of Health and Human Services, *Healthy People 2010: Understanding and Improving Health*, 2d ed. (Washington, DC: U.S. Government Printing Office, November 2000).
19. K. Kelleher, "Mental Health."
20. H. Taras, P. Duncan, D. Luckenbill, J. Robinson, L. Wheeler, and S. Wooley, *Health, Mental Health and Safety Guidelines for Schools.* (www.schoolhealth.org; 2004)
21. U.S. Department of Health and Human Services, Report of the Surgeon General's Conference on Children's Mental Health: A National Action Agenda. (www.hhs.gov/surgeongeneral/topics/cmh/childreport.htm; Sept. 2007)
22. National Association of School Psychologists, *School Psychologists: Providing Mental Health Services to Improve the Lives and Learning of Children and Youth.* (www.nasponline.org/advocacy/mhbrochure.html; Sept. 2007)
23. D. Viadero, "Social-Skills Programs Found to Yield Gains in Academic Subjects," *Education Week* 27, no 16 (2007): 1, 15.
24. Society of State Directors of Health, Physical Education and Recreation (SSDHPER) and Association of State and Territorial Health Officials (ASTHO), *Making the Connection: Health and Student Achievement.* (www.thesociety.org; Sept. 2007)
25. Ibid.
26. U.S. Department of Health and Human Services, *Mental Health: A Report of the Surgeon General.*
27. Ibid.
28. Ibid.
29. Ibid.
30. A. L. Olson, "Maternal Depression," in *About Children: An Authoritative Resource on the State of Childhood Today*, eds. A. G. Cosby, R. E. Greenberg, L. H. Southward, and M. Weitzman (American Academy of Pediatrics, 2005), 142–45.
31. Ibid.
32. U.S. Department of Health and Human Services, *Mental Health: A Report of the Surgeon General.*
33. R. W. Block and R. M. Reece, "Maltreatment," in *About Children: An Authoritative Resource on the State of Childhood Today*, eds. A. G. Cosby, R. E. Greenberg, L. H. Southward, and M. Weitzman (American Academy of Pediatrics, 2005), 126–29.
34. U.S. Department of Health and Human Services, *Mental Health.*
35. American Academy of Pediatrics, *Failure to Make Children Feel Valued and Loved Causes Lasting Damage.* (www.aap.org/advocacy/archives/aprvalued.htm; Sept. 2007)
36. U.S. Department of Health and Human Services, *Mental Health.*
37. M. Quackenbush et al., *Teach and Reach.*
38. U.S. Department of Health and Human Services, *Mental Health.*
39. M. Quackenbush et al., *Teach and Reach.*
40. L. Kann, S. K. Telljohann, and S. F. Wooley, "Health Education: Results from the School Health Programs and Policies Study 2006," *Journal of School Health* 77, no. 8 (2007): 408–34.
41. H. Taras et al., *Health, Mental Health and Safety Guidelines for Schools.*
42. Ibid.
43. J. Gibbs, *Tribes: A New Way of Learning and Being Together* (Windsor, CA: Center Source Systems, 2001).
44. Ibid.
45. W. W. Purkey and J. M. Novak, *Inviting School Success: A Self-Concept Approach to Teaching, Learning, and Democratic Practice* (Belmont, CA: Wadsworth, 1996).
46. B. M. Landau, *The Art of Classroom Management: Building Equitable Learning Communities* (Upper Saddle River, NJ: Pearson Education, 2004).
47. M. Quackenbush et al., *Teach and Reach.*
48. R. Reasoner, *The True Meaning of Self Esteem* (www.self-esteem-nase.org/whatisselfesteem.shtml; Sept. 2007)
49. M. Quackenbush et al., *Teach and Reach.*
50. Ibid.
51. R. Bean. *The Four Conditions of Self-Esteem* (Santa Cruz, CA: ETR Associates, 1992).
52. M. Quackenbush et al., *Teach and Reach.*
53. M. E. P. Seligman, *The Optimistic Child* (New York: HarperPerennial, 1995).
54. M. Quackenbush et al., *Teach and Reach.*
55. M. E. P. Seligman, *The Optimistic Child.*
56. W. Piper, *The Little Engine That Could* (New York: Platt & Munk, 1976).
57. M. L. Krovetz, *Fostering Resiliency.*
58. B. Bernard, "Fostering Resiliency in Kids," *Educational Leadership* 51 (3): 44–48.
59. M. L. Krovetz, *Fostering Resiliency.*
60. J. A. Deiro, *Teachers DO Make a Difference* (Thousand Oaks, CA: Corwin Press, 2005).
61. Ibid.
62. E. E. Werner and R. S. Smith, *Overcoming the Odds: High Risk Children from Birth to Adulthood* (Ithaca, NY: Cornell University Press, 1992).
63. J. A. Deiro, *Teachers DO Make a Difference.*
64. M. Quackenbush et al., *Teach and Reach.*
65. Ibid.
66. J. A. Deiro, *Teachers DO Make A Difference.*

67. A. W. Coffee, J. Coffee, and J. N. Elizalde, *Peace Signs: A Manual for Teaching School Children Anger Management and Communication Skills* (Honolulu: CoffeePress, 2000).

68. Ibid.

69. J. Fetro, *Personal and Social Skills* (Santa Cruz, CA: ETR Associates, 2000).

70. Ibid.

71. J. Gibbs, *Tribes*.

72. L. Shoji and B. Pateman, "Balloon Up! Engaging Early Adolescents in a Hands-on Decision-Making Process," *American Journal of Health Education* 34 (6): 49–51.

73. T. M. Sabo, S. K. Telljohann, and W. M. Kane, *Improving Health Behaviors* (Santa Cruz, CA: ETR Associates, 2004).

74. Ibid.

75. A. W. Coffee et al., *Peace Signs*.

76. M. Quackenbush et al., *Teach and Reach*.

77. N. Stein, E. Gaberman, and L. Sjostrom, *Bully Proof: A Teacher's Guide on Teasing and Bullying for Use with Fourth and Fifth Grade Students* (Wellesley, MA: Joint publication of the Wellesley College Center for Research on Women and the NEA Professional Library, 1996).

78. V. Paley, *You Can't Say You Can't Play* (Cambridge, MA: Harvard University Press, 1993).

(Lisa, age 12)

Promoting Healthy Eating

DESIRED LEARNER OUTCOMES

After reading this chapter, you will be able to . . .

- Describe the prevalence and cost of unhealthy eating among youth.

- Explain the relationship between unhealthy eating and compromised academic performance.

- Identify factors that influence healthy eating.

- Summarize current guidelines and practices related to healthy eating promotion for schools and teachers.

- Summarize developmentally appropriate healthy eating concepts and skills for K–8 students in the context of the National Health Education Standards and target healthy behavior outcomes.

- Demonstrate developmentally appropriate learning strategies and assessment techniques that incorporate concepts and skills shown to promote healthy eating among youth.

- Identify effective, evaluated commercial curricula on healthy eating.

- Identify websites and children's literature that can be used in cross-curricular instructional activities that promote healthy eating.

INTRODUCTION

Good nutrition is vital to good health and essential for the healthy growth and development of children and adolescents. The U.S. secretaries of Health and Human Services and Agriculture introduced *Dietary Guidelines for Americans 2005* with these words:

> The more we learn about nutrition and exercise, the more we recognize their importance in everyday life. Children need a healthy diet for normal growth and development, and Americans of all ages may reduce their risk of chronic disease by adopting a nutritious diet and engaging in regular physical activity. However, putting this knowledge into practice is difficult. More than 90 million Americans are affected by chronic diseases and conditions that compromise their quality of life and well-being. Overweight and obesity, which are risk factors for diabetes and other chronic diseases, are more common than ever before. To correct this problem, many Americans must make significant changes in their eating habits and lifestyles.[1]

The guidelines were developed to assist Americans in living longer, healthier, and more active lives. This chapter is devoted to helping schools, students, families, and community members make informed, science-based decisions to ensure that good nutrition is a happy and healthy reality in the lives of American youth.

Prevalence and Cost of Unhealthy Eating

The *Dietary Guidelines for Americans 2005* affirm that the major causes of morbidity and mortality in the United States are related to poor diet and a sedentary lifestyle. Specific diseases linked to poor diet and physical inactivity include cardiovascular disease, Type 2 diabetes, hypertension, osteoporosis, and certain cancers. Poor diet and physical inactivity are the most important factors contributing to the increase in overweight and obesity in the United States.[2]

Few other pediatric health problems have increased as rapidly or pose such grave concerns as the epidemic of overweight among children and adolescents.[3] Between 1980 and 2000, the prevalence of overweight children doubled, and the prevalence of overweight adolescents tripled. Boys and girls seem to have been equally affected, but African Americans and Hispanics of both sexes were at greater risk than Caucasians.[4]

Overweight in childhood often has been regarded as a cosmetic problem, with attendant social and psychological costs. However, childhood overweight also carries substantial physical health costs. Overweight children often have cardiovascular risk factors, such as elevated blood pressure, elevated cholesterol or triglycerides, or high insulin levels. The recent emergence of Type 2 diabetes among children and adolescents represents a consequence of obesity previously thought to occur only in adults. Newly diagnosed Type 2 diabetes in adolescents accounts for up to 45 percent of all new cases in some settings.[5]

At the opposite end of the spectrum, food insecurity—that is, limited or uncertain availability of nutritionally adequate and safe foods or uncertain ability to acquire acceptable foods in socially acceptable ways—is a reality in the lives of many children. In 2002, 11.1 percent (12.1 million) of U.S. households experienced food insecurity sometime during that year.[6] In 3.5 percent (3.8 million) of U.S. households one or more household members were hungry sometime during that year because they could not afford enough food. The prevalence of food insecurity was higher in African American and Hispanic households than in households composed of other racial and ethnic groups. The rate was even higher in households with family income below the federal poverty line, in all regions of the United States and in all types of households. Households with children had a much greater prevalence of food insecurity than households overall.[7]

Healthy eating for children and adolescents is essential for young people to grow strong, succeed in school, and establish healthy lifetime habits. The status of eating habits among young people in the United States falls short of the mark:

- More than 60 percent of children and adolescents eat too much fat and saturated fat and not enough fruits and vegetables.
- Only 39 percent of children eat enough fiber.
- Among adolescent females, 85 percent do not consume enough calcium.
- Children and adolescents consume between 18 and 20 percent of their calories from added sugars.[8]

Young children also are at great risk of iron deficiency because of rapid growth and increased iron requirements. Iron deficiency can occur from a lack of iron in the diet, which, if continued, can result in anemia. Anemia is a manifestation of iron deficiency when it is relatively severe, although not all anemia is due to iron deficiency.[9] The Economic Research Service of the U.S. Department of Agriculture found that poor or inadequate diets are linked to four of the top ten causes of death—heart disease, cancer, stroke, and diabetes—and to other health conditions such as overweight, hypertension, and osteoporosis. These diseases cost more than $200 billion annually in treatment and lost productivity.[10]

The Centers for Disease Control and Prevention conducts the Youth Risk Behavior Survey (YRBS) in odd-numbered years to monitor priority health-risk behaviors among youth, including unhealthy dietary behaviors and overweight. See Table 6-1 for 2007 data.

In *Healthy People 2010*, the U.S. Department of Health and Human Services identified objectives focused on nutritional risk reduction among school-age children and youth. Table 6-2 summarizes the major public health concerns related to healthy eating among youth.

Healthy Eating and Academic Performance

The link between learning, academic achievement, and nutrition is well established. Simply put, children who practice healthy eating habits on a regular basis do better in school. Unfortunately, many unhealthy eating patterns begin early in life and result in learning difficulties and health problems during the school years and into adulthood.

TABLE 6–1

Youth Risk Behavior Survey Data Related to Healthy Eating, 2007

Risk Behavior	Percent Reporting Behavior		
	Total	Females	Males
Ate fruits and vegetables five or more times per day during the past seven days (consumed 100% fruit juice, fruit, green salad, potatoes—excluding French Fries, fried potatoes, or potato chips—carrots, or other vegetables)	21.4	19.9	22.9
Drank three or more glasses per day of milk during the past seven days	14.1	8.8	19.4
Drank a can, bottle, or glass of soda or pop (not diet) at least one time per day during the past seven days	33.8	29.0	38.6
Were overweight (body mass index equal to or greater than 85% but less than 95%)	15.8	15.1	16.4
Were obese (body mass index equal to or greater than 95%)	13.0	9.6	16.3
Described themselves as slightly or very overweight	29.3	34.5	24.2
Were trying to lose weight	45.2	60.3	30.4
Engaged in healthy behaviors associated with weight control to lose weight or keep from gaining weight during the past thirty days (ate less food, fewer calories, or foods low in fat)	40.6	53.2	28.3
Engaged in unhealthy behaviors associated with weight control during the past thirty days (went without eating for twenty-four or more hours to lose weight or keep from gaining weight)	11.8	16.3	7.3
Took diet pills, powders, or liquids to lose weight or keep from gaining weight during the past thirty days	5.9	7.5	4.2
Vomited or took laxatives to lose weight or keep from gaining weight during the past thirty days	4.3	6.4	2.2

SOURCE: Centers for Disease Control and Prevention, "Youth Risk Behavior Surveillance—United States, 2007," *Morbidity and Mortality Weekly Report* 57, no. SS-4 (6 June 2008): 1–131.

TABLE 6–2

Healthy People 2010: National Health Promotion Objectives to Improve the Nutritional Health of American Youth

Objective 19-3	Reduce the proportion of children and adolescents who are overweight or obese.
Objective 19-5	Increase the proportion of persons aged 2 years and older who consume at least two daily servings of fruit.
Objective 19-6	Increase the proportion of persons aged 2 years and older who consume at least three daily servings of vegetables, with at least one-third being dark green or deep yellow vegetables.
Objective 19-7	Increase the proportion of persons aged 2 years and older who consume at least six daily servings of grain products, with at least three being whole grains.
Objective 19-8	Increase the proportion of persons aged 2 years and older who consume less than 10 percent of calories from saturated fat.
Objective 19-9	Increase the proportion of persons aged 2 years and older who consume no more than 30 percent of calories from fat.
Objective 19-10	Increase the proportion of persons aged 2 years and older who consume 2,400 mg or less of sodium daily.
Objective 19-11	Increase the proportion of persons aged 2 years and older who meet dietary recommendations for calcium.
Objective 19-15	Increase the proportion of children and adolescents aged 6 to 19 years whose intake of meals and snacks at schools contributes proportionally to good overall dietary quality.

SOURCE: U.S. Department of Health and Human Services, *Healthy People 2010: Understanding and Improving Health*, 2nd ed. (Washington, DC: U.S. Government Printing Office, 2000).

The Council of Chief State School Officers (CCSSO) called for educators to recognize the enormous impact health status has on the academic achievement of young people.[11] CCSSO stated, "We believe that healthy kids make better students and that better students make healthy communities." CCSSO identified the nutrition-related conditions that threaten students' health and their ability to make academic progress as obesity, diabetes, and hunger. The council also identified behaviors and environments related to nutrition as important factors that can put the health of young people at risk.

Action for Healthy Kids (AFHK), a nonprofit organization formed specifically to address the U.S. epidemic of undernourished, overweight, and sedentary youth by focusing on changes at school, summarized research from the many studies that show a direct link between nutritional intake and academic performance.[12] Evidence indicates that children who eat poorly or engage in too little physical activity do not perform as well as they could academically, whereas improvements in nutrition and physical activity can result in improved academic performance. Poor nutrition, physical inactivity, and the increasing prevalence of weight problems among students, besides taking an economic toll on schools in terms of reduced state funding, can have indirect costs such as physical and emotional problems among students and staff.[13] AFHK's report, *The Learning Connection: The Value of Improving Nutrition and Physical Activity in Our Schools,* provides these examples:

- Well-nourished students tend to be better students than poorly nourished students, who tend to demonstrate weaker academic performance and score lower on standardized achievement tests.
- Increased participation in breakfast programs is associated with increased academic test scores, improved daily attendance, better class participation, and reduced tardiness.
- Association between weight problems and lower academic achievement (e.g., from absenteeism).[14]

AFHK identified two important areas related to academic achievement: nutrition and weight.

Nutrition

Nutrition and academic achievement are linked for a variety of reasons. *The Learning Connection* explained,

- Children who don't eat healthy diets lack the essential vitamins, minerals, fats, and proteins for optimal cognitive functioning.
- Iron deficiency has been linked to shortened attention span, irritability, fatigue, and difficulty concentrating.
- Low protein intake has been associated with lower achievement scores.
- Poor nutrition and hunger interfere with cognitive functions and are associated with lower academic achievement. These conditions can be present in underweight, normal-weight, or overweight children.
- Students who were "food-insufficient" had significantly lower math scores and were more likely to repeat a grade, see a psychologist, and be suspended from school.
- Hungry children and those at risk for being hungry were twice as likely to have impaired functioning. Teachers reported higher levels of hyperactivity, absenteeism, and tardiness among hungry and at-risk children than among their peers who were not hungry.

Even short-term hunger from missed meals and moderate undernutrition can compromise cognitive development and school performance. Chronically undernourished children not only attain lower scores on standardized achievement tests, are more irritable, have difficulty concentrating, and have lower energy levels but also have less ability to resist infection and thus are more likely to become sick and miss school. School attendance is positively correlated with school completion and academic success.[15]

Research from published studies by Howard Taras and William Potts-Datema examined the association between nutrition in school-age children and their performance in school and on tests of cognitive functioning.[16] Four categories were examined: food insufficiency, iron deficiency and supplementation, deficiency and supplementation of micronutrients, and the importance of breakfast. Children with iron deficiencies sufficient to cause anemia were found to be at a disadvantage academically; however, their cognitive performance seemed to improve with iron therapy. No evidence was found that population-wide vitamin and mineral supplementation leads to improved academic performance. Food insufficiency was identified as a serious problem affecting children's ability to learn, but more research is needed in this area. On a positive note, the research indicated that school breakfast programs seem to improve attendance rates and decrease tardiness. Among children who are severely undernourished, school breakfast programs appear to improve academic performance and cognitive functioning.[17]

Weight

The Learning Connection acknowledged that evidence about the direct effect of weight on academic achievement is less than conclusive.[18] Only a few studies have attempted to examine this relationship directly, and many factors must be controlled for in this type of research. Though drawing definitive conclusions is difficult, overweight students do face additional barriers to learning that are likely to lead to poorer academic achievement. AFHK (www.actionforhealthykids.org) provided these findings from research related to weight and academic achievement:

- Severely overweight children and adolescents were four times more likely than healthy children and adolescents to report impaired school functioning.
- Severely overweight inner-city schoolchildren tended to have abnormal scores on the Child Behavior Checklist and were twice as likely to be placed in special education and remedial class settings than were children who were not overweight.
- Overweight kindergarten students had significantly lower math and reading test scores at the beginning of the year than did their nonoverweight peers, and those lower scores continued into first grade.[19]

Correlations between weight problems and academic achievement do not indicate causation—results must be interpreted cautiously. Researchers recommend that overweight be considered a marker for poor performance rather than the underlying cause.

Being overweight may trigger or exacerbate certain kinds of health conditions (asthma, Type 2 diabetes, joint problems), resulting in school absences. Some conditions, such as asthma, are significant sources of absenteeism. In addition to missing school, overweight children might face physical, psychological, and social problems related to their weight that might lead to academic problems. For example, overweight students are more likely to be the targets of bullying. One study reported a strong association between being overweight in kindergarten and anxiety, loneliness, low self-esteem, sadness, anger, arguing, and fighting. In other studies, severely overweight adolescent girls were found to be more likely to report being held back a grade and to consider themselves poor students. Similarly, severely overweight and underweight boys were more likely to dislike school and to consider themselves poor students.[20]

Taras and Potts-Datema also reviewed published research related to obesity, school performance, and rates of student absenteeism.[21] Overweight and obesity were found to be associated with poorer levels of academic achievement. Overweight and obese children are more likely to have low self-esteem and higher rates of anxiety disorders, depression, and other psychopathology. These mental health problems may be the mediating factor that leads a child to score poorly in school, but a cause-and-effect link between obesity and poor academic performance has not been established through research. Data on the association between child overweight or obesity and attendance were too sparse to allow conclusions, indicating the need for research that compares absenteeism rates with levels of obesity. Studies are needed to investigate whether missed school days could be related to factors such as embarrassment over participating in physical activity, health problems such as asthma or obstructive sleep apnea, or bullying or teasing. Based on the correlation between overweight and poor academic achievement, Taras and Potts-Datema stated the need to influence change in school policies and practices related to soft drink and food contracts on campus as well as to physical education and nutrition education, which often are supplanted for instruction considered more important to academic achievement. The knowledge that obesity and overweight may be detrimental to academic performance might tip the balance in administrators' decisions about school nutrition and physical activity.[22]

Factors That Influence Healthy Eating

Nutrition and dietary patterns are known to influence academic achievement and health. This section focuses on three factors that influence students' eating practices: food insecurity, dietary patterns that contribute to overweight and obesity, and healthy school food environments.

Food Insecurity

Patrick Casey, chief of the division of developmental/behavioral pediatrics at Arkansas Children's Hospital, stated that children in food-insecure or food-insufficient households have lower general health status, more negative general health symptoms, and more iron deficiency than other children.[23] Children in food-insufficient households are more likely to report stomachaches, headaches, and colds. In addition, food insufficiency has been associated with mental health problems and academic difficulties, including significantly lower arithmetic scores

and a greater likelihood of having repeated a grade, seen a psychologist, and had difficulty getting along with other children.[24]

Families who live in poverty are at greater risk for food insecurity. Cutting back on food purchases might be necessary to make it financially until the end of the month. Depending on its severity and duration, food insecurity can have significant negative impacts on the nutrition and health status of household members, including children.[25]

Household food insecurity is relatively common among African American and Hispanic children, particularly those who live in female-headed households with income below the federal poverty line. Child health advocates and clinicians fear that this trend will worsen as a result of the downturn in the U.S. economy and as a consequence of welfare reform activities.[26] Loss of food stamps is of particular concern because use of food stamps has been shown to increase the nutrient intake of children in impoverished families. According to Casey,

> While research has not shown that food insecurity is an independent cause of negative child and adult physical and mental health status, one can conclude that food insecurity is independently associated with negative physical and mental health status. Researchers, clinicians, and policy makers should consider food insecurity as one of the important cumulative risk factors for children, particularly those who live in families in poverty.[27]

Dietary Patterns That Contribute to Overweight in Youth

Poor nutrition and low fitness levels are factors in the rising rates of overweight among U.S. children and adolescents. Body mass index, expressed as weight/height^2 (BMI;kg/m^2) is commonly used to classify overweight and obesity among adults, and is also recommended to identify children who are overweight or at risk of becoming overweight. Based on current recommendations of expert committees, children with BMI values at or above the 95th percentile of the sex-specific BMI growth charts are categorized as overweight. Results from the 1999–2002 National Health and Nutrition Examination Survey (NHANES), using measured heights and weights, indicate that an estimated 16 percent of children and adolescents aged 6–19 years are overweight. This represents a 45 percent increase from the overweight estimates of 11 percent obtained from NHANES III (1988–94). See Figure 6–1 for comparisons between 1963 and 2002.[28]

Most American children consume fewer than the recommended daily number of servings from the five major food groups. In addition, young people increasingly consume soda on a daily basis. More than half of children consume soda on any given day, and more than one-third of teenagers consume more than three servings of soda per day.[29]

Action for Healthy Kids reported that more than 80 percent of children and adolescents consume too much total fat, and more than 90 percent consume too much saturated fat.[30] Some of this fat intake results from too frequent snacking. Most students report having at least

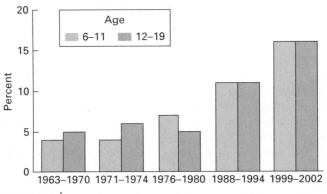

FIGURE 6–1 │ Prevalence of overweight among children and adolescents ages 6–19 years

NOTE: Excludes pregnant women starting with 1971–74. Pregnancy status not available for 1963–65 and 1966–70. Data for 1963–65 are for children 6–11 years of age; data for 1966–70 are for adolescents 12–17 years of age, not 12–19 years.

SOURCE: CDC/NCHS, NHES, and NHANES.

Eating breakfast, whether at home or at school, is associated with better school performance.

three snacks per day, and more than 50 percent report having five or more snacks per day. This unbalanced eating pattern leads to lowered intake of nutrients essential for growth, cognitive functioning, and prevention of chronic conditions. William Dietz, director of the CDC's Division of Nutrition and Physical Activity, stated that sufficient evidence exists to justify increased physical activity, control of television time, and breastfeeding as prevention strategies for childhood obesity.[31] Other promising strategies to prevent or treat overweight include reductions in soft drink consumption, reductions in portion size, and increased fruit and vegetable consumption.

Dietz also recommended that parents or caregivers should be in charge of what children are offered, and children should be allowed to choose what and how much to eat from the foods offered.[32] Parents should persist in their efforts to offer new foods to children. However, some strategies thought to regulate children's intake might actually increase the desirability of certain foods. For example, labeling some foods (cookies or candy) "forbidden," especially when they are in the house but denied to the child, can make those foods more attractive and more likely to be eaten to excess when children have access to them. In the same way, withholding dessert to ensure that children eat a certain amount of other foods (vegetables) may be counterproductive. This strategy may promote overeating by children and suggest to them that the food they are being encouraged to eat is not "good" food—otherwise, why would parents need to bribe them with dessert?

Healthy School Food Environments

The School Nutrition Association (SNA) provides information on the National School Lunch Program (NSLP), the School Breakfast Program (SBP), and other food programs delivered through schools.[33] The NSLP was established officially in 1946 as a measure of national security, to safeguard the health and well-being of the nation's children and to encourage the domestic consumption of nutritious agricultural commodities. The SBP, signed into law in 1966, is a federally assisted meal program that provides nutritionally balanced low-cost or free breakfasts to children in public and nonprofit private schools and residential childcare institutions.

School nutrition programs have the potential to contribute to children's health and academic achievement during their school years and to their future health status as adults. School cafeterias can provide practice for children in choosing healthy foods and establishing healthy habits. Kids' Health (www.kidshealth.org), an initiative established to help kids choose health-enhancing behaviors, reported,

- Children who eat breakfast learn better. Studies indicate that students who eat breakfast at school score higher on standardized tests and have improved math, reading, verbal fluency, and vocabulary scores.
- Children who eat breakfast behave better. Participation in a breakfast program has improved the classroom climate. Studies have shown reduced hyperactivity, depression, and anxiety; improved behavior; and improved emotional functioning.
- The school lunch and breakfast programs can improve children's health status and reduce rates of absenteeism and tardiness; improved nutritional status; and increased intake of food energy, calcium, phosphorous, and vitamin C.[34]

Omitting breakfast can interfere with learning even in well-nourished children. Numerous studies have found that increased participation in the School Breakfast Program is associated with increases in academic test scores, daily attendance, and class participation and with reductions in absences and tardiness. Parents and teachers report that students who participate in breakfast programs are calmer in class and have more energy for studying.[35]

The School Nutrition Association has called for greater access to school meals for children who cannot afford to pay for them. The SNA stated that approximately 1 million children living in the United States are eligible for a reduced-price school lunch but do not participate in the National School Lunch Program. Although the cost for the lunch is only 40 cents each day, many children cannot participate because their parents cannot afford the fee. Lunch participation records show that children who purchase reduced-price lunches early in the month often tend not to purchase them toward the end of the month, only to participate again at the beginning of the next month. For the past three years, SNA has sought funding for a pilot program to study the effectiveness of eliminating the reduced price category. The House Education and Labor Committee sent a letter to the Government Accounting Office (GAO) in February 2008 requesting a study on state and local initiatives to fund programs that provide free meals to students in the reduced price category. SNA hopes the results will be available for the 2009 reauthorization of the 2004 Child Nutrition and WIC Reauthorization Act.[36]

Action for Healthy Kids has raised concerns about food being offered at school outside the school lunch and breakfast programs. Faced with funding shortfalls, schools often sign exclusive contracts with vendors in order to generate additional revenue. Most vendors make high-calorie, low-nutrient foods and beverages available. Some 80 percent of American school districts sell competitive foods—foods and beverages sold in competition with school meal programs—in a la carte lines, school stores, snack bars, and vending machines. These practices contribute to poor eating habits, can aggravate weight and other health problems, and undermine the nutritional contribution of school meal programs.[37] Schools that sell competitive foods might not actually help their overall financial situation. Schools lose federal revenues when school meal participation declines.

Other factors contribute to a school food environment that is less healthy than it could be. In some schools, lunch periods are extremely short because schools have so many meals to serve; therefore, students might not feel they have enough time to eat a full meal. Some students might opt out of school meals because they don't want to be identified publicly as participants in the free or reduced-cost meal program. However, students who do participate in the National School Lunch Program enjoy better nutrition. They consume more vegetables and grains; drink more milk and fewer sugary drinks; and eat fewer cookies, cakes, and salty snacks. School lunch and breakfast programs also may protect some students against overweight.[38] School districts and schools that are working to improve the healthfulness of food and beverage choices while simultaneously maintaining or increasing total revenues from school meal programs are experiencing positive results.[39]

At the school and classroom levels, some educators are trying policies that allow only healthy foods at school, including snacks that children bring from home and foods sold for fund-raising. Fifth-grade teacher Kelly Hong conducted a class project as part of a nutrition unit during which she permitted only healthy snacks at breaks and recess. She and the students worked together to define healthy snacks. She informed parents and caregivers about the project with a letter home and asked for their cooperation. At first, the students complained—no more chips, cookies, or candy at break time. If students brought foods that weren't on the healthy list, Hong collected the foods and returned them to the students at lunch. Over time, the students became interested in the idea of healthy snacks and foods. They especially watched every bite their teacher brought to school to eat! She often brought fruit or vegetable snacks to share with the class, encouraging them to try new foods. Students reflected on their experiences each week during the spring semester. At the end of the school term, students wrote that they had learned about healthy eating, enjoyed the food rule, and were glad they had participated in the class project.

GUIDELINES FOR SCHOOLS

State of the Practice

As described in Chapter 1, the CDC conducts the School Health Policies and Programs Study (SHPPS) every six years to monitor efforts to improve school health policies and programs; SHPPS 2006 is the largest and most complete assessment of school health programs undertaken to date.[40] Table 6-3 provides SHPPS 2006 data about the healthy eating concepts and skills that elementary and middle school teachers reported teaching in at least one required class or course. Comparisons between the 2000 and 2006 SHPPS data demonstrate a decided drop in teaching about nutrition topics at the elementary and middle levels. These changes likely reflect the overall reduction in teaching of subjects other than mathematics and reading at the K–6 level as schools strive to meet Adequate Yearly Progress goals as required by federal law (NCLB).

State of the Art

Promoting healthy eating is most effective when schools, families, and communities work in partnership. Students, teachers, parents, school staff, and community members all play important roles. The CDC published *Guidelines for School Health Programs to Promote Lifelong Healthy Eating* to assist educators in making good nutrition a reality in the school setting.[41] The guidelines are based on solid evidence that school health programs can help children and adolescents attain full educational potential and good health by providing them with the skills, social support, and environmental reinforcement they need to adopt long-term healthy eating behaviors.

In the school environment, classroom lessons alone probably aren't enough to lead to lasting changes in students' eating behaviors. Students also need access to healthy food and the support of the people around them. The influence of school goes beyond the classroom and includes messages from peers and adults regarding foods and eating patterns. Students receive a strong, consistent message when healthy eating is promoted through a Coordinated School Health Program, as described in Chapter 1. The CDC's guidelines,

TABLE 6–3

School Health Policies and Programs Study 2006 Data Related to Healthy Eating

Topics and Skills	Percent of Schools Teaching Topic/Skill in a Required Class	
	Elementary Schools	Middle and Junior High Schools
Topic		
Accepting body size differences	71.2	77.0
Balancing food intake and physical activity	80.9	83.1
Benefits of healthy eating	87.9	84.3
Choosing foods that are low in fat	72.5	81.2
Dietary Guidelines for Americans	NA	67.0
Eating a variety of foods	87.2	82.9
Eating disorders	NA	74.0
Eating more calcium-rich foods	66.4	69.1
Eating more fruits, vegetables, and grain products	86.6	83.1
Food Guide Pyramid	76.9	76.1
Food safety	59.7	61.7
Importance of eating breakfast	84.6	81.1
Importance of water consumption	82.1	81.7
Influence of families on dietary behavior	51.1	68.3
Influence of the media on dietary behavior	60.7	73.7
Making healthy choices while eating at restaurants	51.4	61.6
Preparing healthy meals and snacks	76.4	75.9
Risks of unhealthy weight-control practices	53.7	82.5
Social or cultural influences on dietary behavior	48.5	71.9
Using food labels	68.0	76.9
Using salt and sodium in moderation	NA	70.6
Using sugars in moderation	83.3	79.6
Skill		
How students can influence or support others' healthy dietary behavior	55.5	60.4
How to find valid information or services related to dietary behavior	42.1	63.9
Resisting peer pressure related to unhealthy dietary behavior	43.4	61.0

SOURCE: Centers for Disease Control and Prevention *School Health Policies and Programs Study 2006 (SHPPS)* (Atlanta, GA: CDC, 2007). www.cdc.gov/HealthyYouth/shpps

summarized in Teacher's Toolbox 6.1, include recommendations on seven aspects of a coordinated school health program to promote healthy eating.[42]

Nutrition education helps young people develop lifelong healthy eating patterns. Schools are ideal settings for nutrition education, for several reasons:

- Schools can reach almost all children and adolescents.
- Schools provide opportunities to practice healthy eating. More than 50 percent of young people eat one of their three main meals in school; 10 percent of young people eat two of three main meals in school.
- Schools can teach students how to resist social pressures. Eating is a socially learned behavior that is influenced by social pressures. School programs can directly address peer pressure that discourages healthy eating and direct the power of peer pressure to reinforce healthy eating habits.
- Skilled personnel are available. After appropriate training, teachers and food service personnel can contribute their expertise to nutrition education programs.
- Evaluations suggest that school-based nutrition education can improve the eating behaviors of young persons.[43]

School-based nutrition education is particularly important today because young people frequently decide what to eat with little adult supervision. The increase in one-parent families, families with two working parents, and the availability of convenience foods and fast-food restaurants can affect parents' monitoring of their children's eating habits. In addition, young people's food choices are influenced by television advertisements for low-nutritive foods. Most foods advertised during children's programming are high in fat, sugar, or sodium. Almost no advertisements are for healthy foods, such as fruits and vegetables. School programs should help counter the effect of television on young persons' eating habits.[44]

School policies on nutrition should ensure that students attend school in a healthy food environment. Competitive foods appear at first glance to provide additional revenues for schools. However, studies indicate that such foods can undermine the school meal program, decrease student nutrition, put the school in a position to lose federal funds through decreased school meal participation, and stigmatize children who eat in the school meal programs as children who can't afford the other foods.

Exciting ideas are available from *Making It Happen! School Nutrition Success Stories,* developed by Team Nutrition (U.S. Department of Agriculture) and the Division of Adolescent and School Health (CDC).[45] *Making It Happen!* tells the stories of thirty-two schools and school districts across the United States that have implemented innovative strategies to improve the nutritional quality of food and beverages sold outside the federal school meal programs. One of the most important insights in *Making It Happen!* is that students will buy and consume healthful foods and beverages and schools can make money from selling healthful options.

GUIDELINES FOR CLASSROOM APPLICATIONS

Important Background for K–8 Teachers

Teachers will find a world of nutrition information at their fingertips with new online sources such as *Dietary Guidelines for Americans 2005,* MyPyramid Food Guidance System, and Food Labeling and Nutrition. Accurate, up-to-date nutrition information has never been easier for teachers and their students to find. However, the sheer volume of

Recommendations for School Health Programs: Promoting Healthy Eating

Policy: Adopt a coordinated school nutrition policy that promotes healthy eating through classroom lessons and a supportive school environment. This policy should include a commitment to

- Provide adequate time for nutrition education.
- Provide healthy and appealing foods (fruits, vegetables, and low-fat grain products) when these foods are available.
- Discourage availability of foods that are high in fat, sodium, and added sugars (soda, candy, and fried chips) on school grounds and as part of fund-raising activities.
- Discourage teachers from using food to discipline or reward students.
- Provide adequate time and pleasant and safe space for consumption of meals.
- Formalize links with professionals who can provide counseling for nutrition problems, refer families to nutrition services, and plan health promotion activities for faculty and staff.

Curriculum: Implement a sequential, comprehensive nutrition education curriculum to help students in preschool through grade 12 adopt healthy eating behaviors. This instructional program should

- Help students practice nutrition-related skills (planning healthy meals and comparing food labels).
- Ensure that students practice general health promotion skills (assessing health habits, setting goals, and resisting pressures to make unhealthy eating choices).

Instruction: Integrate cross-curricular nutrition education strategies that are fun, developmentally appropriate, culturally relevant, and learner-centered into classroom practice. These teaching methods should

- Emphasize health-enhancing and appealing aspects of eating, rather than the long-term, harmful effects of unhealthy dietary behaviors.
- Present the benefits of healthy eating in the context of what is important and relevant to involved students.
- Give students many chances to taste healthy foods (low in fat, sodium, and added sugars and high in vitamins, minerals, and fiber).

Program Coordination: Coordinate school food service and nutrition education with other components of the school health program to reinforce messages about healthy eating.

Staff Training: Provide pre-service and in-service nutrition education staff with training focused on strategies that promote healthy behaviors.

Family and Community Involvement: Involve families and the community in reinforcing nutrition education.

Evaluation: Integrate regular evaluation and modification into nutritional health promotion programming.

SOURCE: Centers for Disease Control and Prevention, "Guidelines for School Health Programs to Promote Lifelong Healthy Eating," vol. 45, no. RR-9 (14 June 1996): 11–23.

---

information on nutrition and health can be overwhelming. This section focuses on key resources for teachers.

Dietary Guidelines for Americans 2005

The *Dietary Guidelines for Americans* were published most recently in 2005 by the U.S. Department of Agriculture (USDA) and the U.S. Department of Health and Human Services (DHHS).[46] The guidelines, published every five years, provide the latest science-based advice on promoting health and reducing risk for major chronic diseases through diet and physical activity. Teachers should note this important connection: A nutritious diet and physical activity go hand in hand to promote good health. The guidelines state that physical activity combined with a diet that does not provide excess calories, according to recommendations, should enhance the health of most individuals. The guidelines aim to summarize and synthesize knowledge about nutrients and foods to make recommendations for healthy eating that can be adopted by the public. In short, they provide a framework to promote healthier lifestyles. A summary of key recommendations is provided in Teacher's Toolbox 6.2.

A basic premise of the *Dietary Guidelines* is that people should get their nutrients primarily from consuming foods. Supplements can be useful when they fill a specific gap that is not otherwise being met by an individual's food intake,

but they cannot replace a healthful diet. Individuals who are already consuming the recommended amount of a nutrient in food will not achieve any additional health benefit if they also take the nutrient as a supplement. Another important premise of the guidelines is that foods should be prepared and handled in a way that reduces the risk of food-borne illness.

Many Americans need to consume fewer calories, be more active, and make wiser choices about the foods they eat. The guidelines, intended for Americans older than 2 years, group key recommendations under nine interrelated focus areas meant to be implemented as a whole (see Teacher's Toolbox 6.2). The following discussion summarizes important background for teachers about each focus area.

Adequate Nutrients Within Calorie Needs Many Americans consume more calories than they need without getting the nutrients they require for good health. Most people need to choose meals and snacks that are high in nutrients but low to moderate in energy content—that is, foods that meet nutrient recommendations while keeping calories under control. Benefits include the normal growth and development of children, health promotion among people of all ages, and reduction of risk for a number of chronic diseases that are major public health problems. For children and adolescents, intake levels of calcium, potassium, fiber, magnesium,

Key Recommendations for the General Population—*Dietary Guidelines for Americans 2005*

ADEQUATE NUTRIENTS WITHIN CALORIE NEEDS

- Consume a variety of nutrient-dense foods and beverages within and among the basic food groups while choosing foods that limit the intake of saturated and trans fats, cholesterol, added sugars, salt, and alcohol. (Nutrient-dense foods provide substantial amounts of vitamins and minerals and relatively few calories.)
- Meet recommended intakes within energy needs by adopting a balanced eating pattern, such as the U.S. Department of Agriculture (USDA) Food Guide or the Dietary Approaches to Stop Hypertension (DASH) Eating Plan.

WEIGHT MANAGEMENT

- To maintain body weight in a healthy range, balance calories from foods and beverages with calories expended.
- To prevent gradual weight gain over time, make small decreases in food and beverage calories and increase physical activity.

PHYSICAL ACTIVITY

- Engage in regular physical activity and reduce sedentary activities to promote health, psychological well-being, and a healthy body weight.

  To reduce the risk of chronic disease in adulthood: Engage in at least thirty minutes of moderate-intensity physical activity, above usual activity, at work or at home on most days of the week.

  For most people, greater health benefits can be obtained by engaging in physical activity of more vigorous intensity or longer duration.

  To help manage body weight and prevent gradual, unhealthy body weight gain in adulthood: Engage in approximately sixty minutes of moderate- to vigorous-intensity activity on most days of the week while not exceeding caloric intake requirements.

  To sustain weight loss in adulthood: Participate in at least sixty to ninety minutes of daily moderate-intensity physical activity while not exceeding caloric intake requirements. Some people may need to consult with a health care provider before participating in this level of activity.

- Achieve physical fitness by including cardiovascular conditioning, stretching exercises for flexibility, and resistance exercises or calisthenics for muscle strength and endurance.

FOOD GROUPS TO ENCOURAGE

- Consume a sufficient amount of fruits and vegetables while staying within energy needs. Two cups of fruit and 2 1/2 cups of vegetables per day are recommended for a reference 2,000-calorie intake, with higher or lower amounts depending on the calorie level.
- Choose a variety of fruits and vegetables each day. In particular, select from all five vegetable subgroups (dark green, orange, legumes, starchy vegetables, and other vegetables) several times a week.
- Consume three or more ounce-equivalents of whole-grain products per day, with the rest of the recommended grains coming from enriched products. In general, at least half the grains should come from whole grains.
- Consume 3 cups per day of fat-free or low-fat milk or equivalent milk products.

FATS

- Consume less than 10 percent of calories from saturated fatty acids and less than 300 milligrams per day of cholesterol, and keep trans fatty acid consumption as low as possible.
- Keep total fat intake between 20 and 35 percent of calories, with most fats coming from sources of polyunsaturated and monounsaturated fatty acids, such as fish, nuts, and vegetable oils.
- When selecting and preparing meat, poultry, dry beans, and milk or milk products, make choices that are lean, low-fat, or fat-free.
- Limit intake of fats and oils high in saturated and/or trans fatty acids, by choosing products low in these fats and oils.

CARBOHYDRATES

- Choose fiber-rich fruits, vegetables, and whole grains often.
- Choose and prepare foods and beverages with little added sugars or caloric sweeteners, such as amounts suggested by the USDA Food Guide and the DASH Eating Plan.
- Reduce the incidence of dental caries by practicing good oral hygiene and consuming sugar- and starch-containing foods and beverages less frequently.

SODIUM AND POTASSIUM

- Consume less than 2,300 milligrams (approximately 1 tsp of salt) of sodium per day.
- Choose and prepare foods with little salt. At the same time, consume potassium-rich foods such as fruits and vegetables.

ALCOHOLIC BEVERAGES

- Those who choose to drink alcoholic beverages should do so sensibly and in moderation—defined as the consumption of up to one drink per day for women and up to two drinks per day for men.
- Alcoholic beverages should not be consumed by some individuals, including those who cannot restrict their alcohol intake, women of childbearing age who may become pregnant, pregnant and lactating women, children and adolescents, individuals taking medications that can interact with alcohol, and individuals with specific medical conditions.
- Alcoholic beverages should be avoided by individuals engaging in activities that require attention, skill, or coordination, such as driving or operating machinery.

FOOD SAFETY

- To avoid microbial food-borne illness
  - Clean hands, food contact surfaces, and fruits and vegetables. Meat and poultry should not be washed or rinsed.
  - Separate raw, cooked, and ready-to-eat foods while shopping, preparing, or storing foods.
  - Cook foods to a safe temperature to kill microorganisms.
  - Chill (refrigerate) perishable food promptly and defrost foods properly.
  - Avoid raw (unpasteurized) milk or any products made from unpasteurized milk, raw or partially cooked eggs or foods containing raw eggs, raw or undercooked meat and poultry, unpasteurized juices, and raw sprouts.

NOTE: *Dietary Guidelines for Americans 2005* (www.healthierus.gov/dietaryguidelines) contains additional recommendations for specific populations.

and vitamin E may be of concern. In addition, most Americans consume too many calories and too much saturated and trans fat (vegetable fat that has been treated with hydrogen to make it more solid and give it a longer shelf life), cholesterol, added sugars, and salt. Compared to most American diets, a balanced eating pattern includes *more* dark green vegetables, orange vegetables, legumes, fruits, whole grains, and low-fat and fat-free milk and milk products and *less* total fat, refined grains, added sugar and salt, and calories.[47]

Weight Management During the past two decades, the prevalence of overweight among children and adolescents has increased substantially. For overweight children and adolescents, the goal is to slow the rate of weight gain while achieving normal growth and development. Maintaining a healthy weight throughout childhood may reduce the risk of becoming an overweight or obese adult. Consuming fewer calories while increasing physical activity is the key to controlling body weight.

Preventing weight gain is critical. Both preventing weight gain and losing weight require the same kinds of behaviors, but the extent of the behaviors required to lose weight makes weight loss more challenging. Because many adults gain weight slowly over time, even small decreases in calorie intake can help avoid weight gain, especially if accompanied by increased physical activity. For example, for most adults, a reduction of 50 to 100 calories per day can prevent gradual weight gain, whereas a reduction of 500 calories or more per day is a common initial goal in weight loss programs. Key weight management recommendations for children include

- Reduce the rate of body weight gain while allowing growth and development.
- Consult a health care provider before placing a child on a weight reduction diet.

The healthiest way to reduce calorie intake is to reduce the intake of added sugars, fats, and alcohol, all of which provide calories but few or no essential nutrients. Individuals should give special attention to portion sizes, which have increased significantly over the past two decades. Studies indicate that controlling portion sizes, particularly of calorie-dense foods, helps limit calorie intake, so it's important to understand how portion sizes compare to recommended servings from each food group at a specific caloric level.

Lifestyle changes in diet and physical activity are the best choice for weight loss. When it comes to body weight, it is calories that count—not the proportions of fat, carbohydrates, and protein in the diet. However, diets that provide very low or very high amounts of protein, fat, or carbohydrates are likely to provide low amounts of some nutrients and are not advisable for long-term use. Although these kinds of weight loss diets have been shown to result in weight reduction, maintaining a reduced weight ultimately depends on lifestyle changes.[48]

Physical Activity Regular physical activity and physical fitness make important contributions to health, a sense of well-being, and maintenance of a healthy body weight.

Maintaining good physical fitness enables people to meet the physical demands of work and leisure comfortably. People with higher levels of physical fitness also are at lower risk of developing chronic disease. Conversely, a sedentary lifestyle increases risk for overweight and obesity and many chronic diseases, including coronary artery disease, hypertension, Type 2 diabetes, osteoporosis, and certain types of cancer. Overall, mortality rates from all causes of death are lower in physically active people than in sedentary people. Also, physical activity can help manage mild to moderate depression and anxiety. Key recommendations for children include

- Engage in at least sixty minutes of physical activity on most, preferably all, days of the week.

Individuals should limit sedentary behaviors during their leisure time, such as television and video watching, and replace them with activities requiring more movement. Limiting these sedentary activities appears to be helpful in treating and preventing overweight among children and adolescents.

The excuse often given for a failure to be physically active is lack of time. Setting aside thirty to sixty consecutive minutes each day for planned exercise is one way to obtain physical activity, but it is not the only way. Physical activity can consist of short bouts (ten minutes) of moderate-intensity activity. The accumulated total is what is important, both for health and for burning calories.[49] Promoting physical activity is covered extensively in Chapter 7.

Food Groups To Encourage Increased intake of fruits, vegetables, whole grains, and fat-free or low-fat milk and milk products is likely to have important health benefits for most Americans. Although protein is important in the diet, most Americans already consume enough protein and do not need to increase their intake. Diets rich in foods containing fiber, such as fruits, vegetables, and whole grains, may reduce the risk of coronary artery disease. Diets rich in milk and milk products can reduce the risk of low bone mass throughout the life cycle. The consumption of milk products is especially important for children and adolescents, who are building their peak bone mass and developing lifelong habits. The adequate consumption of all food groups contributes to overall health. Key recommendations for children include

- Consume whole-grain products often; at least half the grains in the diet should be whole grains.
- Children age two to eight should consume 2 cups per day of fat-free or low-fat milk or equivalent milk products.
- Children age nine and older should consume 3 cups per day of fat-free or low-fat milk or equivalent milk products.[50]

Fats Saturated fats, trans fats, omega-3 fats—fats are in the news! Educators and students can learn more at www.nutrition.gov. Fats and oils are part of a healthful diet, but the type of fat makes a difference for healthy hearts. The total amount of fat consumed also is important. High intake of saturated fats, trans fats, and cholesterol increases the risk of unhealthy blood lipid levels, which, in turn, may increase the risk of coronary artery disease.

The Dietary Guidelines recommend that all Americans consume adequate amounts of fruits, vegetables, and whole grains.

Dietary fat is found in foods derived from both plants and animals. To decrease their risk of elevated low-density lipoprotein (LDL) cholesterol in the blood, most Americans need to decrease their intake of saturated fats and trans fats, and many need to decrease their dietary intake of cholesterol. In meeting the total fat recommendation of 20 to 35 percent of calories, most dietary fats should come from sources of polyunsaturated and monounsaturated fatty acids. Sources of omega-6 polyunsaturated fatty acids are liquid vegetable oils, including soybean oil, corn oil, and safflower oil. Plant sources of omega-3 polyunsaturated fatty acids include soybean oil, canola oil, walnuts, and flaxseed. Omega-3 fatty acids are contained in fish and shellfish, particularly those that contain more oil (salmon, trout, herring). Plant sources rich in monounsaturated fatty acids include nuts and vegetable oils (canola, olive, high oleic safflower, and sunflower oils) that are liquid at room temperature.

The recommended total fat intake for adults is between 20 and 35 percent of calories. Few Americans consume less than 20 percent of their calories from fat. Fat intakes that exceed 35 percent of calories are associated with increases in both total saturated fat and calories. Key recommendations for children and adolescents include

- Keep total fat intake between 30 and 35 percent of calories for children age 2 to 3 and between 25 and 35 percent of calories for children and adolescents age 4 to 18, with most fats coming from sources of polyunsaturated and monounsaturated fatty acids, such as fish, nuts, and vegetable oils.[51]

Carbohydrates Carbohydrates should make up 45 to 65 percent of total calories in a healthful diet. Carbohydrates are compounds made of carbon, hydrogen, and oxygen, and take the form of simple sugars (sugary sweets) and complex

carbohydrates (vegetables, grains, breads, beans). Foods in the basic food groups that provide carbohydrates—fruits, vegetables, grains, and milk—are important sources of many nutrients. Choosing plenty of these foods, within the context of a calorie-controlled diet, can promote health and reduce the risk of chronic disease. However, the greater the consumption of foods containing large amounts of added sugars, the more difficult it is to consume enough nutrients without gaining weight. Consumption of added sugars provides calories while providing few, if any, essential nutrients.

The majority of servings from the fruit group should come from whole fruit (fresh, frozen, canned, or dried) rather than from juice to increase fiber intake. However, inclusion of some juice, such as orange juice, can help meet recommended levels of potassium intake.

Legumes—such as dry beans and peas—are especially rich in fiber and should be consumed several times per week. They are considered part of the vegetable group and the meat and beans group because they contain nutrients found in both of these food groups. Consuming at least half the recommended grain servings as whole grains is important for all ages, at each calorie level, to meet the fiber recommendation.

Individuals who consume food or beverages high in added sugars tend to consume not only more calories but also fewer micronutrients (vitamins and minerals). Although more research is needed, studies show a positive association between the consumption of calorically sweetened beverages and weight gain. For this reason, decreased intake of foods high in added sugars, especially beverages with caloric sweeteners, is recommended to reduce calorie intake and help achieve recommended nutrient intakes and weight control. Examine the ingredient list on food labels to find out whether a food contains added sugars.

Carbohydrate intakes of children need special consideration with regard to obtaining sufficient fiber, avoiding excessive calories from added sugars, and preventing dental caries. Several cross-sectional surveys on U.S. children and adolescents have found inadequate dietary fiber intakes that could be improved by increasing the consumption of whole fruits, vegetables, and whole-grain products. Sugars can improve the palatability of foods and beverages that otherwise might not be consumed, which might explain why the consumption of sweetened dairy foods and beverages and presweetened cereals is positively associated with young people's nutrient intake. However, beverages with caloric sweeteners, sugars and sweets, and other sweetened foods that provide few or no nutrients are negatively associated with diet quality and can contribute to consuming too many calories. Most studies of preschool children suggest a positive association between sucrose consumption and dental caries, though other factors (particularly infrequent brushing or not using fluoridated toothpaste) are more predictive of caries incidence. Key recommendations for children include

- Choose fiber-rich fruits, vegetables, and whole grains often.
- Choose and prepare foods and beverages with few added sugars or caloric sweeteners.

- Reduce the incidence of dental caries by practicing good oral hygiene and consuming sugar- and starch-containing foods and beverages less frequently.[52]

Sodium and Potassium On average, the higher an individual's salt intake, the higher that individual's blood pressure. Nearly all Americans consume substantially more salt than they need. Decreasing salt intake is advisable to reduce the risk of elevated blood pressure. Keeping blood pressure in the normal range reduces risk of coronary artery disease, stroke, congestive heart failure, and kidney disease. Lifestyle changes—including reducing salt intake, increasing potassium intake, losing excess body weight, increasing physical activity, and eating an overall healthful diet—can prevent or delay the onset of high blood pressure and lower elevated blood pressure.

When reading a Nutrition Facts panel on a food product, look for the sodium content. (Salt is sodium chloride—food labels list sodium, rather than salt, content.) Look for foods low in sodium (less than 140 mg or 5 percent of the Daily Value). Reading labels, comparing the sodium contents of foods, and purchasing lower-sodium brands can all lower total sodium intake.

Another dietary measure for lowering blood pressure is to increase consumption of potassium. A potassium-rich diet blunts the effects of salt on blood pressure, may reduce the risk of developing kidney stones, and may decrease age-related bone loss. Potassium-rich fruits and egetables include leafy green vegetables, fruit from vines, and root vegetables. Meat, milk, and cereal products also contain potassium but may not have the same effect.[53]

Food Safety Avoiding foods that are contaminated with harmful bacteria, viruses, parasites, toxins, and chemical and physical contaminants is vital for healthful eating. The signs and symptoms of food-borne illness range from gastrointestinal symptoms such as upset stomach, diarrhea, fever, vomiting, abdominal cramps, and dehydration to more severe systemic illness such as paralysis and meningitis. Consumers can take simple measures to reduce their risk of food-borne illness, especially in the home.

When preparing and consuming food, it is essential to wash hands often, particularly before and after preparing food and after handling raw meat, poultry, eggs, or seafood. A good hand-washing protocol includes wetting hands; applying soap; rubbing hands together vigorously for twenty seconds; rinsing hands thoroughly under clean, running warm water; and drying hands completely using a clean disposable or cloth towel.

Washing fresh produce that will not be either peeled or cooked may be the only way to reduce the pathogen load. A good protocol for washing fresh fruits and vegetables includes removing and discarding outer leaves, washing produce just before cooking or eating under running potable water, scrubbing with a clean brush or with hands, and drying the fruits or vegetables using a clean disposable or cloth towel.

Raw meat and poultry should not be washed, because washing may cause cross contamination and is not

FIGURE 6–2 | Food Safety Children can be encouraged to take steps to prevent food-borne illness.
Source: Partnership for Food Safety Education (www.fightbac.org).

necessary if they are cooked. Separating raw foods from cooked and ready-to-eat foods while shopping for, preparing, or storing them is important to prevent contamination from one food to another. Refrigerator surfaces can become contaminated from high-risk foods such as raw meats, poultry, fish, uncooked hot dogs, certain deli meats, and unwashed raw vegetables. If not cleaned, contaminated refrigerator surfaces can, in turn, serve as a vehicle for contaminating other foods.

Uncooked and undercooked meat, poultry, and eggs and egg products are potentially unsafe. These foods should be cooked to a safe internal temperature (use a food thermometer). Leftover refrigerated foods, which may become unsafe within three to four days, should be reheated to the proper internal temperature. If there is any question about whether a food is safe to eat: "If in doubt—throw it out."

Infants and young children, pregnant women, older adults, and those who are immunocompromised should not eat or drink raw (unpasteurized) milk or any products made from unpasteurized milk, raw or partially cooked eggs or foods containing raw eggs, raw or undercooked meat and poultry, raw or undercooked fish or shellfish, unpasteurized juices, or raw sprouts.[54]

Up-to-date information on food safety is available online from the FDA (www.foodsafety.gov) and the Partnership for Food Safety Education (www.fightbac.org) (see Figure 6–2). (Key recommendations about food safety for the

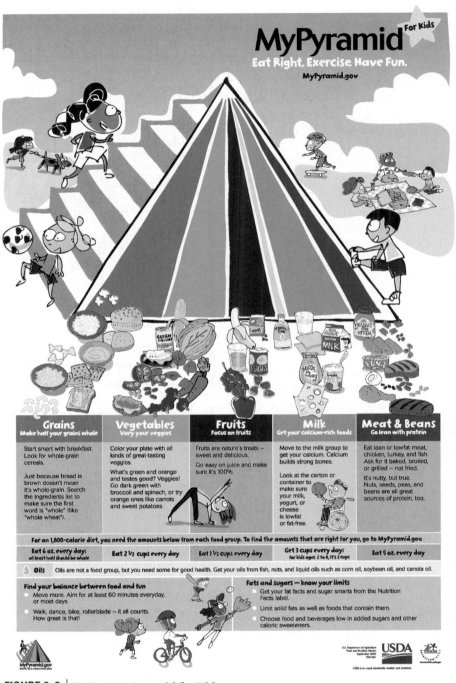

FIGURE 6-3 | **USDA's MyPyramid for Kids**

SOURCE: U.S. Department of Agriculture. Center for Nutrition Policy and Promotion (MyPyramid.gov).

general public are summarized in Teacher's Toolbox 6.2.) CDC also provides a *Food-Safe Schools Action Guide* at www .cdc.gov/healthyyouth/foodsafety/actionguide.htm.

MyPyramid Food Guidance System

MyPyramid Plan (Figure 6-3) was released by the U.S Department of Agriculture in 2005. The colorful, vertically organized MyPyramid replaces the familiar Food Guide Pyramid and offers personal Web-based dietary information based on age, sex, and physical activity level. The website (www.mypyramid .gov) provides easy-to-use tips on how to put the recommendations into practice. The "For Kids" section provides

materials designed specifically for children ages 6-11, such as the MyPyramid Blast Off Game.[55] Educators also will be interested in the *Anatomy of MyPyramid* available on the website.

Key Messages of MyPyramid
The main messages of MyPyramid focus on areas in which many Americans' diets need improvement:

*   *Make half your grains whole.* Eat at least 3 ounces of whole-grain bread, cereal, rice, crackers, or pasta every day. Choose whole grains in place of refined—whole wheat bread instead of white bread, and brown rice instead of white rice—rather than

FIGURE 6–4 | Sample Food Label for Macaroni and Cheese

1. Start here:
Check the serving size and number of servings in the package to determine how many servings of the food you are consuming. Your typical portion size may contain more than one serving.

3. Limit these nutrients:
For health, keep your intake of fat, saturated fat, trans fat, cholesterol, and sodium low. Look for foods low in these nutrients—meaning they provide 5% or less of the Daily Value.

5. Footnote:
This footnote is the same on all food labels and indicates that the Daily Value percentages that appear on the label are based on a 2,000-calorie diet. For reference, the Daily Values for 2,000-calorie and 2,500-calorie diets appear on the label.

2. Check calories:
Many Americans consume too many calories; check the calories you'll get from a serving of the food, adjusted for the number of servings you are consuming. As a general guide, 40 calories is low, 100 calories is moderate, and 400 calories or more is high.

4. Get enough of these nutrients:
Many Americans don't get enough fiber, vitamin A, vitamin C, calcium, and iron in their diets. Look for foods high in these nutrients—meaning they provide 20% or more of the Daily Value.

Nutrition Facts

Serving Size 1 cup (228g)
Servings per Container 2

Amount per Serving

Calories 250   Calories from Fat 110

	% Daily Value*
Total Fat 12g	18%
Saturated Fat 3g	15%
Trans Fat 3g	
Cholesterol 30mg	10%
Sodium 470mg	20%
Total Carbohydrate 31g	10%
Dietary Fiber 0g	0%
Sugars 5g	
Protein 5g	

Vitamin A 4%	•	Vitamin C 2%	
Calcium 20%	•	Iron 4%	

*Percent Daily Values are based on a 2,000 calorie diet. Your daily values may be higher or lower depending on your calorie needs:

		Calories	2,000	2,500
Total Fat	Less than		65g	80
Sat Fat	Less than		20g	25g
Cholesterol	Less than		300mg	300mg
Sodium	Less than		2,400mg	2,400mg
Total Carbohydrate			300g	375g
Dietary Fiber			25g	30g

SOURCE: U.S. Food and Drug Administration, Center for Food Safety and Applied Nutrition. 2004, *How to Understand and Use the Nutrition Facts Label* (www.cfsan.fda.gov/~dms/foodlab.html: retrieved 16 September 2005).

adding servings of grains to your daily diet. Look for *whole* as the first word on the list of ingredients for a grain product.

• *Vary your veggies.* Eat more dark green vegetables, orange vegetables, and legumes (dry beans and peas). Try buying fresh vegetables in season, when they cost less and are likely to be at their peak flavor.

• *Focus on fruits.* Eat a variety of fruit—fresh, frozen, canned, or dried. Keep a bowl of whole fruit on the table or counter or in the refrigerator. Go easy on fruit juices.

• *Get your calcium-rich foods.* Choose low-fat or fat-free milk and milk products. Include milk at meals if you need to increase servings of calcium-rich foods. If you don't or can't consume milk, try lactose-free products or other calcium-rich foods.

• *Go lean on proteins.* Choose low-fat or lean meats and poultry and then bake, broil, or grill your choices. Boneless, skinless chicken breasts and turkey cutlets are lean poultry choices. Consume more fish, beans, peas, nuts, and seeds to add variety.

• *Know your fats.* Your main sources of fats should be fish, nuts, and vegetable oils. Limit solid fats such as butter, stick margarine, shortening, and lard.

• *Be more active.* Choose activities that you enjoy and can do regularly. Fit activity into your daily routine—for example, take a brisk walk to and from the parking lot, bus stop, or subway station—or join an exercise class. Vary your activities to keep up your interest and motivation. What is most important is being active every day.[56]

Many more tips for making healthy food and activity choices can be found at MyPyramid.gov and the other websites listed at the end of this chapter.

Food Labeling and Nutrition

The HealthierUS initative (www.healthierus.gov) recommends linking the Dietary Guidelines for Americans, MyPyramid Food Guidance System, and nutrition labeling to promote healthy eating. For nutrition information, "to know the facts, use the label."[57] Most packaged foods have a Nutrition Facts label that consumers can use to make nutritious food choices quickly and easily (Figure 6–4). Key strategies when reading food labels include the following:

• *Check servings and calories.* Look at the serving size and how many servings you are actually consuming. If you double the number of servings, double the calories and nutrients, including the % Daily Value (DV).

• *Make your calories count.* Look at the calories on the label and compare them with what nutrients you are getting to decide whether the food is worth eating. When one serving of a single food item has over 400 calories per serving, it is high in calories.

• *Don't sugarcoat it.* Because sugars contribute calories with few, if any, nutrients, look for foods and beverages low in added sugars. Read the ingredient list and make sure added sugars are not one of the first few ingredients. Some

Teacher's Toolbox 6.3

School Strategies to Promote Healthy Eating

Lower-Elementary Students	Upper-Elementary Students (build on lower-elementary strategies)	Middle-Level Students (build on upper-elementary strategies)
Strategies to Make the Food Environment More Health-Enhancing		
• Make healthy foods (fruits, vegetables, whole grains) widely available at school, and discourage the availability of foods high in fat, sodium, and added sugars. • Involve parents in nutrition education through homework. • Provide role models (teachers, parents, other adults, older children, celebrities, or fictional characters) for healthy eating. • Provide cues, through posters and marketing-style incentives, that encourage students to make healthy choices about eating and physical activity. • Do not use food for reward or punishment of any behavior.	• Through class discussions and small-group exercises, provide social support for making healthy changes in eating and physical activity. • Have students design posters and marketing-style incentives to encourage others to make healthy choices about eating and physical activity.	• Use peers as role models, and use peer-led nutrition education activities.
Strategies to Enhance Personal Characteristics to Support Healthy Eating		
• Make basic connections between food and health (you need food to feel good and to grow). • Teach the importance of balancing food intake and physical activity. • Identify healthy snacks (fruits, vegetables, low-fat milk). • Increase students' confidence in their ability to make healthy eating choices by gradually building up their food selection and preparation skills and giving them practice.	• Explain the effects diet and physical activity have on future as well as current health concerns (physical appearance, obesity, sense of well-being, capacity for physical activity). • Teach the principles of the Dietary Guidelines for Americans and the MyPyramid Plan. Encourage pride in choosing to eat healthy meals and snacks. • Help students identify foods high and low in fat, saturated fat, cholesterol, sodium, added sugars, and fiber. • Teach the importance of eating adequate amounts of fruits, vegetables, and whole grains. • Help students increase the value they place on health and their sense of control over food selection and preparation. • Have students analyze food preferences and factors that trigger eating behaviors.	• Have students identify reasons to adopt healthy eating and physical activity patterns. • Teach students how to identify foods high and low in fat, saturated fat, cholesterol, sodium, and added sugars. • Teach students how to identify foods that are excellent sources of fiber, complex carbohydrates, calcium, iron, vitamin A, vitamin C, and folate. • Teach the effects of unsafe weight loss methods and the characteristics of a safe weight loss program. • Help students examine what motivates persons to adopt particular eating habits. Have students keep a food diary noting what cues their own eating behavior (mood, hunger, stress, or other persons).

common added sugars (caloric sweeteners) are sucrose, glucose, high fructose corn syrup, corn syrup, maple syrup, and fructose.

• *Know your fats.* Look for foods low in saturated fats, trans fats, and cholesterol to help reduce the risk of heart disease (5% DV or less is low, 20% DV or more is high). Most of the fats you eat should be polyunsaturated and monounsaturated fats. Keep total fat intake between 20 and 35 percent of calories.

• *Reduce sodium (salt), increase potassium.* Research shows that eating less than 2,300 milligrams of sodium (about

1 tsp of salt) per day may reduce the risk of high blood pressure. Most of the sodium people eat comes from processed foods, not from the saltshaker. Also look for foods high in potassium, which counteracts some of sodium's effects on blood pressure.[58]

Teachers can find more information on using food labels at *How to Understand and Use the Nutrition Facts Label* (www.cfsan.fda.gov/~dms/foodlab.html). Students and teachers also will be interested in comparing and contrasting the food labels they can access online for foods of all kinds at Nutrition Data (www.nutritiondata.com).

Lower-Elementary Students (continued)	Upper-Elementary Students (build on lower-elementary strategies) (continued)	Middle-Level Students (build on upper-elementary strategies) (continued)
Strategies to Enhance Behavioral Capability to Support Healthy Eating		
• Provide many healthy foods for students to taste in an enjoyable social context. • Let students prepare simple snacks. • Have students try unfamiliar and culturally diverse foods that are low in fat, sodium, and added sugars.	• Let students prepare healthy snacks or simple meals. • Encourage students to try unfamiliar and culturally diverse foods that are low in fat, sodium, and added sugars and high in fiber. • Have students select healthy foods from a fast-food restaurant menu. • Teach students how to recognize the fat, sodium, and fiber contents of foods by reading nutrition labels. • Help students record and assess their food intake. • Teach students how to use MyPyramid Plan to assess their diet for variety, moderation, and proportionality. • Have students set simple goals for changes in eating and physical activity, and devise strategies for implementing these changes and monitoring progress in reaching their goals. • When appropriate, let students practice (through role-plays) encouraging parents to make healthy choices about eating and physical activity at home. • Have students examine media and social influences on eating and physical activity; teach students how to respond to these pressures.	• Let students plan and prepare healthy meals. • Have students select healthy foods from restaurant and cafeteria menus. • Teach students how to use nutrition labels to make healthy food choices. • Teach students ways to modify recipes and prepare foods to reduce fat and sodium content and to increase fiber content. • Help students identify incentives and reinforcements for their current eating and physical activity behaviors. • Have students identify their own resistance strategies to respond to media and social influences on eating and physical activity. • Have students analyze environmental barriers to healthy eating and physical activity; explore strategies for overcoming these barriers. • Teach students to record their food intake; then have them assess and compare their diets with the standards set forth in the Dietary Guidelines for Americans and MyPyramid Plan. Have them assess their intake of key nutrients (e.g., calcium and iron). • Have students set goals for healthy changes in eating and physical activity, identify barriers and incentives, assess alternative strategies for reaching their goals, and decide which strategies to follow. Show students how to monitor their progress, revise their goals if necessary, and reward themselves for successfully attaining their goals. • Teach students how to evaluate nutrition claims in advertisements and nutrition-related news stories.

SOURCE: Adapted from Centers for Disease Control and Prevention. *Guidelines for School Health Programs to Promote Lifelong Healthy Eating* 45, no. RR-9 (14 June 1998): 11–23.

School Strategies to Promote Healthy Eating

The CDC's *Guidelines for School Health Programs to Promote Lifelong Healthy Eating* provides a list of sample strategies for teaching about healthy eating to lower-elementary, upper-elementary, and middle and high school students. The list includes many of the concepts critical to improving the diet and health of young persons. Interventions that promote healthy changes in eating behaviors need to target three interacting spheres of influence:

• Environment, which influences the likelihood that healthy eating behaviors will be adopted through social norms, influential role models, cues to action, reinforcements, and opportunities for action

• Personal characteristics (knowledge, attitudes, beliefs, values, confidence in one's ability to change eating behaviors, and expectations about the consequences of making changes)

• Behavioral skills and experience, which are related to selecting or preparing specific foods, dietary self-assessment, and decision making

The strategies are summarized in Teacher's Toolbox 6.3.[59]

Learning About Nutrition with Your Students

One of the best pieces of advice the authors of this book can give educators is to learn about nutrition along with their students. Two real classroom stories illustrate this point. In one, a fourth-grade teacher began her health lesson by saying to her students, "Who can give me an example of a carbohydrate? We talked about those last week." A student raised his hand and said, "An apple!" The teacher began to say yes, and then frowned to herself. "No-o-o," she said hesitantly, "carbohydrates are pasta, remember?" As the teacher went on with the lesson, the students (and the author who heard the interchange through the window) wondered what the teacher thought an apple was—a fat or a protein? The truth is that most adults don't know a great deal about nutrition, and information changes rapidly. Practicing the health education standard of accessing information is an important one for students and for teachers. Teachers aren't the "answer machine," and shouldn't hesitate to say, "Hmm . . . how can we find out?"

In the other story, a parent reported that her kindergartener was eating an after-school snack (chips, unfortunately) on the drive home. During the ride, the mother realized that her daughter was talking to herself ("Well, that one is no good. Nope. That one's no good either.") and throwing her chips, one by one, out the car window, which was lowered a bit to catch the breeze. When she asked her daughter what she was doing, the little girl replied, "Well, my teacher said that if a food is bad, it will make a greasy spot on the napkin. So, all the ones I've tried are no good!" She was testing the chips, one after another, and throwing them out if they made a greasy spot on the napkin. However, rather than rejecting the bag outright, she was searching busily for a "good one" that she could eat. The teacher's lesson made an impression on this kindergarten student, but it stopped short of helping the child see the bigger picture. The child's age and development certainly were part of this story, but talking about health lessons with students and checking for understanding, rather than just telling information, can help correct these kinds of misperceptions, including that some foods are "bad."

The Strategies for Learning and Assessment, coming up later in this chapter, provide many opportunities for teachers to investigate topics with their students, including fast foods, portion sizes, fats and cholesterol, carbohydrates, body image and size, and fiber. Teachers should dive in and learn right along with their students because, hey—what's a cruciferous vegetable anyway?

Recommendations for Concepts and Practice

Healthy Behavior Outcomes

The goal of health education is to help students adopt or maintain health-enhancing behaviors. School districts and teachers should identify the health-enhancing behaviors they would like their students to maintain or adopt. The following list identifies possible healthy behavior outcomes related to promoting healthy eating. Although not all of the suggestions are developmentally appropriate for students in grades K–8, this list can help teachers understand how the learning activities they plan for their students support both short- and long-term desired behavior outcomes.

Ways to Promote Healthy Behavior Outcomes for Healthy Eating

Make healthy food choices.

Eat a variety of foods every day.

Eat the appropriate number of servings from each food group each day.

Eat in moderation.

Balance calorie intake with calorie expenditure.

Eat healthy snacks.

Eat healthy foods when eating at restaurants.

Prepare foods in healthy ways.

Eat breakfast every day.

Drink plenty of water.

Eat the appropriate amount of foods that are high in fiber.

Limit foods and drinks that are high in sugar.

Limit salt intake.

Limit foods that are high in fat.

Prevent eating disorders.

Follow a plan for healthy weight management.[60]

Developmentally Appropriate Concepts and Skills

As with other health topics, teaching related to promoting healthy eating should be developmentally appropriate and based on the physical, cognitive, social, emotional, and language characteristics of specific students. Teacher's Toolbox 6.4 contains a list of suggested developmentally appropriate concepts and skills to help teachers create lessons that will encourage students to practice the desired healthy behavior outcomes by the time they graduate from high school. Teachers will notice that some of these concepts and skills are reinforced in other content areas (e.g., the concept "identify the benefits of healthy eating" also applies to personal health and wellness).

Developmentally Appropriate Concepts and Skills for Promoting Healthy Eating

Grades K–2 Concepts	Grades 3–5 Concepts	Grades 6–8 Concepts
NHES 1: Core Concepts		
• Explain the importance of choosing healthy foods and beverages.	• Name the food groups and a variety of nutritious food choices for each food group.	• Summarize a variety of nutritious food choices for each food group.
• Identify a variety of healthy snacks.	• Explain the importance of eating a variety of foods from all the food groups.	• Classify the number and appropriate sizes of servings of food from each food group that a person needs each day.
• Identify the benefits of drinking plenty of water.	• Identify the number of servings of food from each food group that a child needs daily.	• Explain why some food groups have a greater number of recommended portions than other food groups.
• Describe the benefits of eating breakfast every day.	• Summarize the benefits of healthy eating.	
• Describe the type of foods and beverages that should be limited.	• Explain the concept of eating in moderation.	• Analyze the benefits of healthy eating.
	• Describe the benefits of eating plenty of fruits and vegetables.	• Describe the federal dietary guidelines for teens.
• Describe body signals that tell people when they are hungry and when they are full.	• Summarize the benefits of drinking plenty of water.	• Explain the similarities and differences among protein, fats, and carbohydrates regarding nutritional value and food sources.
• Describe how to keep food safe from harmful germs.	• Identify nutritious and nonnutritious beverages.	• Describe the benefits of eating in moderation.
• Identify eating behaviors that contribute to maintaining a healthy weight.	• Identify foods that are high in fat and low in fat.	• Summarize the benefits of eating plenty of fruits and vegetables.
	• Identify foods that are high in added sugars.	• Analyze the benefits of drinking plenty of water.
	• Describe the benefits of limiting the consumption of fat and added sugar.	• Differentiate between nutritious and nonnutritious beverages.
	• Conclude that breakfast should be eaten every day.	• Identify foods that are high in fiber.
	• Summarize body signals that tell people when they are hungry and when they are full.	• Identify food preparation methods that add less fat to food.
	• Describe methods to keep food safe from harmful germs.	• Identify examples of whole grain foods.
	• Explain that both eating habits and level of physical activity can affect a person's weight.	• Describe the benefits of consuming an adequate amount of calcium and a variety of foods high in calcium.
	• Explain how eating disorders impact proper nutrition.	

Grades K–2 Skills	Grades 3–5 Skills	Grades 6–8 Skills
NHES 2: Analyze Influence		
• Explain how family can influence food choices.	• Describe how family and cultural traditions influence food choices.	• Describe how personal values and feelings influence food choices.
• Describe how television advertisements can influence food choices.	• Describe how personal preferences influence food choices.	• Analyze how family and culture influence food choices.
	• Identify the various strategies used by the media to influence food choices.	• Summarize how peers influence food choices.
	• Describe how peers can influence food choices.	• Describe how advertising and marketing influence food choices.
	• Describe the influence of culture and media on body image.	• Explain how the media influence food choices.
		• Describe how technology affects the food supply and food choices.
		• Describe the influence of culture and media on body image.
		• Describe the influence of family and peers on body image.
		• Describe how personal economics influences food choices.
		• Explain how school policy can influence healthy or unhealthy eating.

(continued)

Grades K–2 Skills *(continued)*	Grades 3–5 Skills *(continued)*	Grades 6–8 Skills *(continued)*

NHES 3: Accessing Information, Products and Services

• Identify people who can provide accurate information about healthy eating. • Identify nutrition information on food labels.	• Identify sources of reliable information about healthy eating. • Demonstrate the ability to access accurate information about healthy eating. • Demonstrate the ability to access people who can provide accurate information and advice on healthy eating. • Use the nutrition information on food labels to compare products. • Demonstrate the ability to access sources of accurate information about healthy eating and safe weight management.	• Distinguish accurate nutrition information from inaccurate information. • Summarize reliable sources of information about healthy eating. • Demonstrate the ability to access people who can provide accurate information and reliable advice on healthy eating. • Analyze the nutrition information on food labels to compare products. • Demonstrate the ability to access sources of accurate information about eating disorders. • Analyze the accuracy of claims of nutrition supplements and weight loss pills. • Distinguish accurate from inaccurate information about healthy eating and safe weight management.

NHES 4: Interpersonal Communication

• Demonstrate how to politely refuse less nutritious foods. • Demonstrate how to politely request foods that are more nutritious. • Demonstrate how to refuse foods that cause an allergic reaction.	• Demonstrate how to politely refuse less nutritious foods. • Demonstrate how to politely request foods that are more nutritious. • Demonstrate how to refuse foods that cause an allergic reaction. • Demonstrate interpersonal skills for dealing with peer influence to eat less nutritious foods.	• Demonstrate how to politely refuse less nutritious foods. • Summarize how to politely request foods that are more nutritious. • Demonstrate how to make a special request, related to healthy food preparation. • Discuss plans to maintain healthy eating habits with parents and friends. • Demonstrate negotiation skills for dealing with pressure to eat less nutritious foods.

NHES 5: Decision Making

• Choose healthy foods and beverages instead of less healthy foods and beverages.	• Choose healthy foods and beverages instead of less healthy foods and beverages. • Demonstrate the ability to select healthy from unhealthy foods on a fast-food restaurant menu. • Describe positive outcomes from choosing healthy foods.	• Choose healthy food and beverages instead of less healthy foods and beverages. • Demonstrate the ability to select healthy from unhealthy foods on a fast-food restaurant menu. • Explain positive outcomes from choosing healthy foods. • Describe the consequences of an unhealthy diet. • Choose restaurants that serve more healthy foods rather than ones that serve fewer healthy foods.

NHES 6: Goal Setting

• Set a goal to eat more fruits and vegetables. • Describe ways that parents and other trusted adults can help meet a goal of eating more fruits and vegetables.	• Assess the strengths and weaknesses of personal diet. • Set a goal to improve food choices. • Make a personal commitment to improve food choices. • Demonstrate the ability to keep track of foods and beverages consumed. • Monitor progress toward meeting the goal of improving food choices.	• Assess food intake in relation to established food groups. • Set a goal to improve one's personal food choices that leads to a healthier diet. • Design a plan for implementing a healthier diet. • Make a personal commitment to achieve a healthier diet. • Identify barriers to achieving a healthier diet. • Develop strategies for overcoming barriers to achieving a healthier diet. • Monitor progress toward achieving a healthier diet goal.

Grades K–2 Skills	Grades 3–5 Skills	Grades 6–8 Skills

NHES 7: Self-Management

Grades K–2 Skills	Grades 3–5 Skills	Grades 6–8 Skills
• Choose a variety of healthy snacks. • Express intentions to eat breakfast every day. • Express intentions to drink plenty of water every day. • Express intentions to eat a variety of nutritious foods every day. • Express the intention to eat fruits and vegetables every day.	• Use information on food labels to make healthy eating choices. • Choose healthy foods in appropriate portion sizes. • Plan and prepare a healthy snack. • Choose a variety of nutritious breakfast foods. • Identify ways a person can eat more fruits and vegetables. • Identify ways a person can drink more water and nutritious beverages. • Identify ways a person can eat less fat. • Identify ways a person can eat less sugar. • Develop strategies for making healthier choices at restaurants. • Identify ways a person can keep from overeating. • Plan a meal based on the food groups. • Express the intention to eat a variety of nutritious foods daily. • Describe the importance of assuming personal responsibility for healthy eating. • Demonstrate safe food handling and storage practices.	• Use information on food labels to make healthy eating choices. • Choose healthy foods in appropriate portion sizes. • Plan and prepare a healthy snack. • Develop strategies for making healthier choices at restaurants. • Plan and prepare nutritious breakfasts. • Describe strategies for eating more fruits and vegetables. • Describe strategies for drinking an appropriate amount of water and nutritious beverages. • Describe strategies a person can use to reduce the amount of fat consumed. • Describe strategies a person can use to reduce the amount of sugar consumed. • Describe strategies a person can use to keep from overeating. • Plan a day's meals based on all of the food groups. • Summarize the importance of assuming personal responsibility for healthy eating. • Express the intention to eat a variety of nutritious foods in moderation. • Demonstrate safe food handling, preparation, and storage practices.

NHES 8: Advocacy

Grades K–2 Skills	Grades 3–5 Skills	Grades 6–8 Skills
• Ask parents, guardians, and other caretakers to offer more nutritious food choices at home. • Encourage parents, guardians, and other caretakers to make healthy eating choices. • Provide support to peers for choosing healthy foods.	• Explain to others why healthy eating is important. • Persuade parents or guardians to offer more nutritious food choices at home. • Provide support to peers and family members for choosing healthy foods. • Object to teasing of peers based on their body types.	• Advocate to others about how healthy eating enhances personal health and wellness. • Negotiate with parents or guardians for healthy food choices at home and at restaurants. • Advocate for healthy and appealing food choices at school. • Educate family and peers to choose healthy foods. • Advocate for tolerance for a diversity of body types. • Provide support to peers for choosing healthy foods. • Advocate that others properly prepare and handle food.

SOURCE: Centers for Disease Control and Prevention, *Health Education Curriculum Analysis Tool (HECAT)* (Atlanta, GA: CDC, 2007). www.cdc.gov/HealthyYouth/HECAT/index.htm

STRATEGIES FOR LEARNING AND ASSESSMENT

Promoting Healthy Eating

This section provides examples of standards-based learning and assessment strategies for promoting healthy eating. The strategies begin with a restatement of the standard and a reminder of the assessment criteria, drawn from the RMC rubrics in Appendix B.

Strategies are written as directions for teachers and include applicable theory of planned behavior constructs in parentheses (intention to act in healthy ways, attitudes toward behavior, subjective norms, perceived behavioral control). These learning and assessment strategies provide building blocks for standards-based lessons and units that can be tailored to local needs. Assessment criteria are used with permission from the Rocky Mountain Center for Health Promotion and Education (RMC). See Appendix B for Scoring Rubrics.

Additional strategies for learning and assessment for Chapter 6 can be found at the Online Learning Center. Appendix D, a complete list of all the strategies, is also available at the Online Learning Center.

NHES 1 | Core Concepts

Students will comprehend concepts related to health promotion and disease prevention to enhance health.

ASSESSMENT CRITERIA

- Connections—Describe relationships between behavior and health; draw logical conclusions about connections between behavior and health.
- Comprehensiveness—Thoroughly cover health topic, showing breadth and depth; give accurate information.

Grades K–2

MyPyramid for Kids Teachers can download simplified mini-posters of MyPyramid (www.mypyramid.gov) and ask children what they notice. In addition to the bright colors and different kinds of foods, the students will notice the figure walking up the stairs on the side of the pyramid and other illustrations of active children. Teachers can ask students to brainstorm a list of the foods they can think of that are fruits, vegetables, grains, milk, and meats and beans, as well as healthy ways to exercise. Teachers also can ask questions to help the students realize that foods such as breads and cereals are made from grains. Similarly, meats include fish, chicken, and turkey. If school budgets allow—or if parents or caregivers can help—teachers can share healthy snacks with students to allow them to try different and new kinds of healthy foods. Teachers can have students experiment with different kinds of healthy exercise (walking, jogging, skipping, galloping) during recess and physical education periods.

ASSESSMENT | For an assessment task, students can name nutritious foods for the fruit, vegetable, grain, milk, and meat and bean groups and describe healthy ways to exercise. For assessment criteria, students should be able to give at least two examples of foods in each food group and healthy ways to exercise. (Construct: Attitudes toward behavior.)

SuperKids! The Dole 5-A-Day website (www.dole5aday.com) features SuperKids Heroes, such as Bam-Nana, Broco, Bluebrainy, and Power Pine. The site provides a Kids Cookbook, Nutrition Database, Super Tips, and Games. The link for teachers gives information on healthy classrooms, exercise, and lesson plans. Teachers will find assistance in teaching about the Food Pyramid, portion sizes, healthy snacks, and nutrition adventures. This colorful website is one that children can explore in class and at home, with a section also included for parents.

ASSESSMENT | For an assessment task, students can explore different parts of the site to report on to classmates. For example, one group might help others understand important information on portion sizes, while others talk about MyPyramid. For assessment criteria, students should give accurate information and make connections between nutrition behaviors and health. (Construct: Attitudes toward behavior.)

Go, Slow, and Whoa Foods The National Heart, Lung, and Blood Institute (NHLBI) found that educating kids about good nutrition can help them develop smart eating habits. Providing kids with the knowledge and education they need to make healthier dietary choices is key. Of course, educating children about healthy eating and helping them apply that knowledge can be difficult. To help, the institute classified food into three groups (Teacher's Toolbox 6.5):

- The *Go* group includes heart-healthy foods that should be eaten every day because they are low in saturated fat and cholesterol (low-fat milk, whole-grain cereals).
- The *Slow* group includes foods that should be eaten only a few times a week (waffles, pancakes).
- The *Whoa* group includes foods that should be eaten only once in a while because they are high in saturated fat and cholesterol (French fries, doughnuts).

The trick is to teach children balance in selecting their diet. That means that the Whoa group isn't completely off limits but should be recognized as containing foods that aren't too healthy and should be eaten only every now and then. Parents and teachers can provide a good example by following the Go, Slow, and Whoa approach. The key is to give children choices and to stock plenty of Go group foods that they like. Remember, the Whoa group isn't entirely off-limits—make sure children know that foods from this group are occasional treats.[61]

ASSESSMENT | For an assessment task, students can brainstorm a list of foods and then try categorizing them according to the Go, Slow, and Whoa chart. Teachers can share the NHLBI chart with students for comparison and discussion. For assessment criteria, students should explain how and why foods are categorized as they are in the chart, providing accurate information and drawing conclusions about connections between eating and health. (Construct: Attitudes toward behavior.)

The Peanut-Free Café—What are Food Allergies? This picture book by Gloria Koster and Maryann Cocca-Leffler (see book list at end of chapter) provides a great opportunity to discuss food allergies. A new student who has a peanut allergy comes to Nutley Elementary. Principal Filbert makes a peanut-free lunch table, and anyone who has a peanut-free lunch can eat there. At first, the student sits there alone, but other students join in to make a peanut-free café that features snacks, arts, and crafts. Children learn about the seriousness of food allergies and how they can support each other for good health.

ASSESSMENT | For an assessment task, students can survey their friends, family members, and teachers to learn whether any of them have food allergies. Students can investigate different types of food allergies and report on how they can help friends and family members who have them. For assessment criteria, students give accurate information and make connections between nutrition behaviors and health. (Construct: Attitudes toward behavior.)

Grades 3–5

Sentences About Healthy Eating Teachers can combine learning about nutrition with language arts by having students complete sentence stems about eating. Teachers should select sentence stems that can have a variety of correct answers. When students have completed the sentences, they can work with a partner or a small group to compare their answers. Students should help each other determine whether their sentences are correct and investigate further if they have questions (What's a whole-grain food?). Each group can share something they learned with the class. Examples of sentence stems for core concepts about nutrition are

My two favorite fruits are . . .
An example of a green vegetable I like is . . .

Healthy Eating with Go, Slow, and Whoa Foods

Food Group	GO (almost anytime)	SLOW (sometimes)	WHOA (once in a while)
Vegetables	Almost all fresh, frozen, and canned vegetables without added fat (such as butter) or sauces	All vegetables with added fat or salt Oven-baked fries Avocado	Any vegetable fried in oil, such as French fries or hash browns
Fruits	All fresh and frozen fruits Canned fruits packed in juice	100% fruit juice Fruits canned in light syrup Dried fruits	Fruits canned in heavy syrup
Breads and cereals	Whole-grain breads, pitas, and tortillas Whole-grain pasta Brown rice Hot and cold unsweetened whole-grain cereals	White bread and pasta that's not whole grain Taco shells French toast, waffles, and pancakes Biscuits Granola	Doughnuts, muffins, croissants and sweet rolls Sweetened breakfast cereals Crackers that have hydrogenated oils (trans fats)
Milk and milk products	Skim and 1% milk Fat-free and low-fat yogurt Part-skim, reduced-fat, and fat-free cheese Low-fat and fat-free cottage cheese	2% milk Processed cheese spreads	Whole milk Full-fat cheese Cream cheese Yogurt made from whole milk
Meats and other sources of protein	Beef and pork that has been trimmed of its fat Extra-lean ground beef Chicken and turkey without skin Tuna canned in water Fish and shellfish that's been baked, broiled, steamed, or grilled Beans, split peas and lentils Tofu Egg whites and substitutes	Lean ground beef Broiled hamburgers Ham Canadian bacon Chicken and turkey with the skin Low-fat hot dogs Tuna canned in oil Peanut butter Nuts Whole eggs cooked without added fat	Beef and pork that hasn't been trimmed of its fat Fried hamburgers Ribs Bacon Fried chicken Chicken nuggets Hot dogs Lunch meats Pepperoni Sausage Fried fish and shellfish Whole eggs cooked with fat
Sweets and snacks	Ice milk bars Frozen fruit-juice bars Low-fat frozen yogurt Low-fat ice cream Fig bars Ginger snaps Baked chips Low-fat microwave popcorn Pretzels		Cookies, cakes, and pies Cheesecake Ice creams Chocolate candy Chips Buttered microwave popcorn
Butter, ketchup, and other stuff that goes on food	Ketchup Mustard Fat-free creamy salad dressing Fat-free mayonnaise Fat-free sour cream Olive oil Vegetable oil Oil-based salad dressing Vinegar	Low-fat creamy salad dressing Low-fat mayonnaise Low-fat sour cream	Lard Salt pork Gravy Regular creamy salad dressing Mayonnaise Tartar sauce Sour cream Cheese sauce Cream sauce Cream cheese dips
Drinks	Water Fat-free and 1% milk Diet soda Diet and unsweetened iced teas and lemonade	2% milk 100% fruit juice Sports drinks	Whole milk Regular soda Drinks with added sugar Fruit drinks with less than 100% fruit juice

SOURCE: U.S. National Heart, Lung, and Blood Institute, National Institutes of Health.

A low-fat, healthy snack is . . .

Vegetables that come in other colors besides green are . . .

A low-fat dairy product is . . .

A high-fat dairy product is . . .

Two foods that belong in the meat food group are . . .

For better nutrition, I want to eat more . . .

For better nutrition, I want to eat less . . .

My favorite food that is high in vitamin C is . . .

Some healthy foods with really bright colors are . . .

A whole-grain food is . . .

A favorite healthy food in my family is . . .

A tip for healthy eating is . .

ASSESSMENT | The students' completed sentences and discussions are the assessment task for this activity. For assessment criteria, students should share accurate information and draw conclusions about connections between eating and health. (Construct: Attitudes toward behavior.)

Twenty Questions (or More) About Foods Students can play a game of "twenty questions" to learn more about different kinds of foods. (Note: Any number of questions is allowed.) In preparation teachers can make index cards with the names or pictures of foods on them, one food per card (chicken, fish, apple, grape, cereal, yogurt, rice, tomato—including some combination foods, e.g., pizza, vegetable soup). Teachers should explain that students will have a card taped to their back, but they won't know what is on the card. Classmates will be able to read what is on each person's back. Students circulate around the room, asking yes or no questions (Is it eaten hot? Does it have a round shape? Is it green? Is it a breakfast food?). Students should talk to several different classmates to get information. Classmates can respond only with "Yes," "No," or "I don't know." Students cannot give any other information, no matter what the question, and students cannot tell classmates the names of the foods on their backs. Students who guess their foods correctly may take off their cards and then help other students.

Teachers can call time after five or ten minutes. When time is called, students should return to their seats. Students who haven't guessed their foods should continue to wear their cards on their backs without looking at them. Teachers should ask students who guessed their foods what kinds of questions they asked and what worked well in helping them find out the answer. Teachers also can suggest that students use the major food groups in MyPyramid Plan (fruits, vegetables, grains, milk, meat and beans) to narrow their questions. Students who haven't yet guessed correctly can be given a few more minutes to try more questions. When time is called, all students should look at their cards. To end the activity, students should group their foods according to the MyPyramid Plan. Foods like pizza and vegetable soup provide an opportunity to discuss combination foods that fit into more than one category.

ASSESSMENT | For an assessment task, play another round of the game, with students writing the food names and taping them to other students' backs. Students might enjoy trying a different configuration, such as a circle within a circle (outside circle facing in, inside circle facing out), moving around the circle to talk with different partners on a signal. Encourage students to write foods that are more difficult to guess this time (sweet potato, sushi, tamale, croissant). For assessment criteria, teachers can circulate and listen to students' questions to learn whether they have improved their skill at categorizing foods. For example, rather than asking, "Is it cookies, is it cake, is it candy?" students might ask, "Is it in the fruit group? Is it a bright color? Is it round? Is it orange?" (Construct: Attitudes toward behavior.)

Serving Size Card:
Cut out and fold on the dotted line. Laminate for longtime use.

FIGURE 6–5 | **Portion Size Card**

SOURCE: National Heart, Lung, and Blood Institute (http://hin.nhlbi.nih.gov/portion/servingcard7.pdf).

Grades 6–8

Portion Distortion! The National Heart, Lung, and Blood Institute (NHLBI) features an educational tool called "Portion Distortion" (http://hp2010nhlbihin.net/portion/index.htm) that middle school students should find interesting.[62] The website includes slide shows that students can download to see how portion sizes of foods (bagels, cheeseburgers, French fries, soda) have changed during the past twenty years—and the changes in number of calories that have come with the distortions! Students also can download serving size cards to remind them of what a serving looks like (Figure 6–5). Teachers also can explore NHLBI's "We Can!" link on ways to enhance children's activity and nutrition.

ASSESSMENT | For an assessment task, students can collect various containers (clean, empty, washed) that they purchase foods in that often are thought of as a "serving" (popcorn box or bucket from the movies; other bags, boxes, bottles, cups, cans). Using the information on the serving size cards and the food labels, students can find "portion distortion" in their everyday lives. For assessment criteria, students should be able to show at least one portion distortion and contrast it with an actual serving size. Students should provide accurate information and draw conclusions about connections between behaviors and health. (Construct: Attitudes toward behavior.)

Menu Planning Online   Middle school students can work with the NHLBI online Menu Planner (http://hin.nhlbi.nih.gov/menuplanner/menu.cgi), starting with a number of planned calories for a day and working through a series of food selections for different meals. The website keeps track of calories for the day as the students plan their meals.

ASSESSMENT | For an assessment task, students can work in pairs to plan menus for a day on the website and then share their work with others in the class. For assessment criteria, students should explain what they learned about healthy eating and menu planning, providing accurate information and drawing conclusions about connections between behaviors and health. (Construct: Attitudes toward behavior.)

MyPyramid Blast Off Game   The MyPyramid website features a "For Kids" section that provides information and activities for students ages 6–11. The MyPyramid Blast Off Game is an interactive computer game in which kids can reach Planet Power by fueling their rocket with food and physical activity. The game notifies students when they have selected the correct amounts of fruits, vegetables, grains, meats and beans, milk, and physical activity. As students select various foods for breakfast, lunch, dinner, and snacks, the game gives information on the food group and on the amount of oils, solid fats, and sugar. Students must make healthy selections of foods and activity to be able to blast off.

ASSESSMENT | Blasting off in the game is an assessment task for this activities. For assessment criteria, students can describe their trial-and-error process in selecting foods and activities and how and why they modified their selections. (Construct: Attitudes toward behavior.)

NHES 2 | Analyze Influences

Students will analyze the influence of family, peers, culture, media, technology, and other factors on health behaviors.

ASSESSMENT CRITERIA
- Identify both external and internal influences on health.
- Explain how external and internal influences interact to impact health choices and behaviors.
- Explain both positive and negative influences, as appropriate.

Grades K–2

Pinkalicious—What Influences Our Food Choices?   *Pinkalicious* (see book list at end of chapter), by Victoria Kann and Elizabeth Kann, provides a fanciful way to introduce the idea of influences on food choices. Pinkalicious eats so many pink cupcakes that she wakes up with pink hair and skin. Though the little girl is delighted with her new color, her mother takes her to the doctor, who describes a variety of healthy foods to help her return to normal. Teachers can pair this book with *A Bad Case of Stripes,* by David Shannon, which also involves food choices and appearance.

ASSESSMENT | *Pinkalicious* can lead to investigations of foods of many different colors. For an assessment task, students can categorize foods according to colors and select their favorites for a healthy eating plan. For assessment criteria, students can identify the factors that influence their selections of favorites (color, family or friends' preferences, taste). (Construct: Perceived behavioral control.)

Cultural and Family Celebrations with Food   Foods play an integral role in cultural and family celebrations and traditions of all kinds. Students can write stories and draw pictures about the celebrations and traditions in their families and cultures. Students might want to talk with their families about the significance and preparation of the foods they share. Children can share their artwork and stories with classmates. Children can explain who gathers, who prepares the food, and how they and family members feel during the celebrations and traditions. What do students like best about these times together? Teachers can help students think about how their celebrations and traditions influence their feelings about family, food, and well-being.

ASSESSMENT | The students' artwork and stories are the assessment task for this activity. For assessment criteria, students should explain how the celebrations and traditions make them feel (how they are influenced). (Construct: Subjective norms.)

An Eye-Level Investigation   Children are eager consumers and often have an important influence on what their parents and caregivers buy. Teachers can challenge children to investigate advertising aimed at them. With parental permission (send a letter home), students can investigate the products placed on low shelves on their next trip to the grocery store. Where are the sugary cereals? Where are the candies? Where are the snack foods and sodas? Students might find that certain kinds of products are placed at their height and eye level. Students can discuss whether they found healthy or less healthy products (go, slow, or whoa foods) at their eye level. What conclusions do they draw about marketing to kids? Who does the marketing and why? How do children feel about being targeted this way?

ASSESSMENT | For an assessment task, students can report their findings to class members. For assessment criteria, students should name at least two places in the grocery store where they found products they thought were being targeted to kids. Students also should tell whether the placement makes the products more noticeable or inviting to kids. (Construct: Perceived behavioral control.)

Grades 3–5

Moods and Foods   Teachers can introduce this activity with the book *How Are You Peeling? Foods with Moods,* by Saxton Freymann and Joost Elffers. Students can list ten of their favorite foods on one side of a paper or poster. On the other side, students can write people, places, or feelings they associate with those foods. Students can assess their favorites in terms of the go, slow, and whoa concept. Can students think of healthier replacements for any of their favorites? If so, what people, places, or feelings do they associate with the replacements? Can they still make positive connections? Students can discuss the associations people often make between favorite foods and good feelings. Students can list ways to keep those positive feelings while choosing healthier foods (more "go" foods).

ASSESSMENT | The students' associations between foods and moods, people, and places are the assessment task for this activity. For assessment criteria, students should select one healthy choice or improvement and explain how to keep a positive association with that food. (Construct: Perceived behavioral control.)

Super Size Me!   Students might have seen or heard about the documentary *Super Size Me!* Filmmaker Morgan Spurlock focused on fast food, interviewing people ranging from legislators and the former U.S. surgeon general to gym teachers and school cooks. He also tracked the changes in his body and health as he consumed nothing but food from McDonald's for a month. More information is available on the film's website (www.supersizeme.com/home.aspx); however, teachers and students should note that this is a .com site—it has products, including an educational video, for sale. Whether or not students and teachers visit the website, they might be interested in exploring the idea of eating only fast food for a month and the potential effects on healthy eating. This activity links to personal health and wellness.

ASSESSMENT | For an assessment task, students can work in pairs or in small groups to imagine a week of meals at the fast-food restaurant of their choice. Using menus from the fast-food restaurant, students should select a week of meals. For assessment criteria, students should explain the potential effect on their health and explore the American phenomenon of super sizing in restaurants and its potential influence on health. (Construct: Perceived behavioral control.)

PBS Kids—Don't Buy It! Students can explore being media smart with PBS Kids (http://pbskids.org/dontbuyit). Students can check out "Food Advertising Tricks You Should Know About," where they will learn the tricks a food stylist uses to make the following:

- The Perfect Burger (with brown food coloring, tweezers, and superglue)
- Roasted Chicken (with dishwashing soap, needle and white thread, blowtorch)
- Ice Cream (with shortening, corn syrup, and plastic wrap)

Teachers can find many more teaching ideas from the Education Development Center at www.youthlearn.org.

ASSESSMENT | For an assessment task, students can put themselves in the driver's seat by making a video commercial or print advertisement for an imaginary product. Students can use the advertising techniques described in Chapter 3 or the information from www.pbskids.org or www.youthlearn.org to try to "sell" their product to classmates. For assessment criteria, students should identify the advertisement techniques they are using and their potential influence on middle school consumers of health-related products. (Construct: Perceived behavioral control.)

Grades 6–8

Advertising Bites With parents' or caregivers' permission (send a letter home), students can watch television for a specific period of time (half hour or one hour) to collect information about food and beverage commercials. Teachers should remind students to watch only one channel the entire time they are collecting data. Teachers and students can make a data collection log to record the time of each commercial, what's being sold, and the advertising techniques used to make the product attractive (see Chapter 3). Students can report their findings and compare them with those of other class members. What conclusions can students draw about advertising techniques that target kids their age? Did students find any exaggerations or misrepresentations? Teachers can extend this activity by having students create and perform commercials for nutritious products (or to tell the truth about products that are not nutritious).

ASSESSMENT | The students' analysis of the commercials they watch is the assessment task for this activity. If students make commercials, these also can be used as an assessment task. For assessment criteria, students should identify two or more advertising techniques used in television and in commercials and tell how they can refute false advertising. (Construct: Perceived behavioral control.)

Body Image in the Media The University of Michigan Health System noted that studies report that kids spend the equivalent of a full-time workweek using media each week.[63] Media literacy can help students learn to

- Recognize how media messages influence and manipulate us
- Develop critical thinking about media messages—to uncover hidden messages and values
- Interpret media messages in ways that do not damage students' self-esteem

The American Academy of Pediatrics (AAP) states that media education can help kids with body image problems. AAP recommends that parents and caregivers encourage critical thinking and critical viewing habits as critical thinking and critical viewing habits are integral components. Teachers can work on these ideas with middle school students by having them examine body image portrayals in magazines that are popular with early adolescents. Students can bring magazines to class (with parent or caregiver permission) to cut up for making collages of pictures, words, and phrases to show what the media tell boys and girls they should look like to be attractive or cool. Students can display their collages on a bulletin board with the heading "Health Education Standard 2: Analyzing Media Messages About Attractiveness—Fact vs. Fiction." Students can discuss the media messages they find and how they might influence students' decisions about dieting, fitness, and clothing and other purchases and then write a short essay about their conclusions. Teachers can post the essays around the border of the bulletin board or right over the media messages for added effect. In the words of PBS Kids, students might conclude about media messages, "Don't buy it!"

ASSESSMENT | The students' collages and essays are the assessment task for this activity. For assessment criteria, students should identify at least two ways middle-level students might be influenced by media messages and tell how friends can stick together to refute the messages. (Constructs: Subjective norms, perceived behavioral control.)

NHES 3 | Access Information, Products, and Services

Students will demonstrate the ability to access valid information and products and services to enhance health.

ASSESSMENT CRITERIA

- Access health information—Locate specific sources of health information, products, or services relevant to enhancing health in a given situation.
- Evaluate information sources—Explain the degree to which identified sources are valid, reliable, and appropriate as a result of evaluating each source.

Grades K–2

Children's Literature About Healthy Eating TEAM Nutrition from the U.S. Department of Agriculture provides an extensive list of children's books that teachers can use to introduce discussions about healthy eating (www.fns.usda.gov/tn/Students/Fun/Readers/index.html). An edited list of the TEAM Nutrition booklist is provided at the end of the chapter under "Children's Literature." Students can use the stories to discuss their own experiences and to relate their experiences to what they are learning in the classroom about nutrition.

ASSESSMENT | For an assessment task, students can relate the stories to their own experiences with food and healthy eating. Students can design a page for a class book on healthy eating after hearing and discussing several books. For assessment criteria, students should explain where they got the information for their pages (their families, their experiences, ideas from a book or story). (Construct: Attitudes toward behavior.)

Sorting Foods for Healthy Eating   To reinforce the activity "Go, Slow, and Whoa Foods" in NHES 1, core concepts, teachers can ask students and their families (send a letter home to parents and caregivers) to bring in empty, clean or washed food containers of all kinds. Students then can sort the collection of containers into three large boxes or bags labeled "Go," "Slow," and "Whoa." (Students might enjoy decorating boxes with pictures and words to illustrate the kinds of foods they have discussed.) For example, students could place a skim or 1% milk carton in the "Go" box, a 2% milk carton in the "Slow" box, and a whole-milk container in the "Whoa" box. This activity generates discussion about foods and what's in them, which is where the learning takes place. If students are stuck on how to categorize a food, they can access more information by reading labels with their teacher or investigating the food online or in books.

ASSESSMENT | The students' categorization of foods is the assessment task for this activity. For assessment criteria, students should be able to explain their reasoning, providing accurate information and telling where they got their information about the foods. (Construct: Attitudes toward behavior.)

Kids Only—Fight Bac!   The Partnership for Food Safety Education offers an engaging website for young students called Fight Bac! (www.fightbac.org/kids.cfm) to help them understand the causes and prevention of food-borne illness. Students also can become food detectives to fight bacteria at www.fooddetectives.com. Teachers can download information and activities from the sites for students to work on and discuss in class.

ASSESSMENT | Students can take the Food and Drug Administration's Food Safety for Kids Quiz (www.fda.gov/oc/opacom/kids/html/wash__hands .htm) as an assessment task for this activity. For assessment criteria, students should provide accurate information and explain valid sources of information for food safety. (Construct: Attitudes toward behavior.)

Grades 3–5

What's Up with Vitamins and Minerals? Going Live to the Micronutrients.   One of the book's authors remembers the drudgery of memorizing charts about vitamins and minerals as part of health and home economics classes—boring! How can teachers make this important information come alive for today's students? One solution is to have pairs of students select a vitamin or mineral to investigate and report on as an action news team to the rest of the class. Students can find out

- Where do we find it?
- What does it do for us?
- What happens if we don't get enough—or too much?

Teachers can encourage students to use their creativity (props, costumes, visuals, camcorders) to make their investigative reporting come alive. Students might enjoy the opportunity to video their presentations in advance and show them to the class via television. The schools' technology specialists could be enlisted to teach students how to use recording equipment.

ASSESSMENT | The students' action reports are the assessment task for this activity. For assessment criteria, students should tell where they got their information and why their information sources are reliable and valid. (Construct: Attitudes toward behavior.)

To Get the Facts, Read the Label!   The U.S. Food and Drug Administration provides excellent resources for learning to read and use food labels at www.cfsan.fda.gov/~dms/foodlab.html. Students and teachers can download sample labels and educational information. Kids' Health also provides information at http://kidshealth.org/kid/ stay_healthy/food/labels.html. Students can work in pairs or small groups to explain a particular part of a food label to class members. Students and teachers should try to collect many food containers (empty, washed, clean, and dry) to show how to comparison shop for good nutrition. As an extension activity, students can bring in advertisements they find for particular food products and compare the promises in the ads with the facts of the nutrition label. Students can access and print food labels for almost any kind of food at www .nutritiondata.com.

ASSESSMENT | For an assessment task, students can compare two or more products (different kinds of cereals, milk, or snack foods) and explain their nutrition analysis to the class. For assessment criteria, students should provide accurate information on the best choice and explain why the food label provides valid information. (Construct: Attitudes toward behavior.)

Kids' Health on Nutrition   Students and teachers can access information on nutrition from the Kids' Health website (www.kidshealth .org). By clicking on the kids' site and then on "Fabulous Food," students can learn more about food allergies, food groups, snacking, labels, dieting, and many other nutrition topics. Using the topics discussed on the site, students can select a research project and teach one another. Students can prepare a poster presentation on their topic for a poster session, during which a certain number of class members present their posters as others circulate around the room to view the posters and ask questions. Teachers might want to work with parents or caregivers to provide healthy snacks during the poster sessions.

ASSESSMENT | The posters the students prepare and present are the assessment task for this activity. For assessment criteria, students should provide accurate information, draw conclusions about connections between behaviors and health, and provide valid sources for their information. Students also might like to set their own criteria for "great posters." (Construct: Attitudes toward behavior.)

Grades 6–8

Chew on This—Investigating What's Goes into Your Food.   The following books (see list at end of chapter) provide a great kick-off for middle school students to access information about fast food:

- *Chew On This: Everything You Don't Want to Know About Fast Food* by Eric Schlosser and Charles Wilson.
- *Fast Food Nation* by Eric Schlosser.
- *Fast Food Nation Tie-in: The Dark Side of the All-American Meal (P.S.)* by Eric Schlosser.
- *Processed Food (What's In Your Food? Receipe for Disaster)* by Paula Johanson.
- *Restaurant Confidential: The Shocking Truth About What You're Really Eating When You're Eating Out* by Michael F. Jacobson, Jayne G Hurley, and the Center for Science in the Public Interest.

Middle school students can work in teams to select a fast-food topic that they want to research and report on to classmates. Students may want to write and film their own mini-documentaries, based on viewing recent movies such as *Supersize Me* and *Fast Food Nation 2006*. They can focus especially on the amount of fat, sugar, and salt in the fast foods they choose. Students should collaborate to decide what makes a great presentation and use those criteria to assess themselves and their classmates.

ASSESSMENT | The investigation and report that students generate is the assessment task for this activity. For assessment criteria, students should identify the components of a thorough investigation and top-notch report for their own classroom. (Construct: Attitudes toward behavior.)

Nutrients in a Nutshell Students can access information on the six essential nutrients at Kids' Health by logging onto www.kidshealth.org and visiting "Fabulous Food." Students should work in six groups to investigate and report on the six nutrients. They should identify criteria in advance for "great presentations." During their presentations, students should be able to make links between the grain, vegetable, fruit, meat and bean, and milk groups in MyPyramid Plan and essential nutrients.

ASSESSMENT | The presentations students make are the assessment task for this activity. Teachers and students can use the criteria that students identify for great presentations as the assessment criteria. At a minimum, students should provide accurate information, draw conclusions about connections between behaviors and health, and explain their valid sources of information. (Construct: Attitudes toward behavior.)

See the Label with NutritionData.Com The NutritionData website (www.nutritiondata.com) provides a fantastic opportunity for students to learn about healthy eating by accessing Nutrition Facts labels for foods of all kinds. When students visit the Nutrition Facts and Calorie Counter home page, they can select among a tremendous number of foods for analysis, including brand-name foods, fresh fruits and vegetables, and restaurant foods. The site provides a Nutrition Facts label and other information that students can print to learn about foods of interest. Making food comparisons is a breeze with this Web tool.

ASSESSMENT | For an assessment task, students can access labels on a wide variety of favorite foods. For assessment criteria, students should summarize what they've learned about the nutritional value of their favorite foods and present their information to classmates, including where they found valid information. (Construct: Attitudes toward behavior.)

NHES 4 | Interpersonal Communication

Students will demonstrate the ability to use interpersonal communication skills to enhance health and avoid or reduce health risks.

ASSESSMENT CRITERIA

- Use appropriate verbal/nonverbal communication strategies in an effective manner to enhance health or avoid/reduce health risks.
- Use appropriate skills (negotiation skills, refusal skills) and behaviors (eye contact, body language, attentive listening).

Grades K–2

Green Eggs and Ham **Food Poetry** Children can practice their communication skills (speaking in front of a group) by writing, illustrating, and reading couplets or poems to classmates about their favorite and least favorite foods. Children can write their poems individually or in small groups. If children work in a group, they might want to write their poems as a conversation among group members. Teachers can use the book *Green Eggs and Ham,* by Dr. Seuss, to introduce this activity. Children can read their poems and share their illustrations with classmates. Teachers can then post the poems and illustrations in the classroom.

ASSESSMENT | Having children present their poems and illustrations to classmates is the assessment task for this activity. For assessment criteria, children should use at least one verbal (tone of voice) and some non-verbal (facial expressions, gestures) communication skills to enhance the reading of their poems. (Construct: Attitudes toward behavior.)

Grades 3–5

Fruits and Veggies Tea Party Students can choose a fruit or vegetable to portray. (Students can get ideas at www.dole5aday.com.)

Students can make a mask or hat from construction paper, along with other details (stems, vines, seeds, branches, leaves) to complete their "look." Students should research to find out more about the healthy qualities of their fruits and vegetables. At the "tea party," students should circulate around the room and meet other fruits and vegetables, introducing themselves to each other and telling about why they are so nutritious. This activity allows students to demonstrate their content knowledge (NHES 1, core concepts) while practicing their conversational skills. Teachers can provide a healthy drink (water, skim milk, or 100% juice) for the "tea" party. To end, students can introduce each other to the class.

ASSESSMENT | The introductions students do for each other are the assessment task for this activity. For assessment criteria, students should be able to introduce their new friend in a clear and understandable tone of voice. (Construct: Attitudes toward behavior.)

Grades 6–8

Bet You Can't Eat Just One! Responding to Pressures to Overeat Teachers can begin this activity by asking students to think of times they have been pressured to overeat by friends, family, or peers. Using these ideas, students and teachers can develop a list of pressure lines to overeat, for example:

"Go ahead and eat up! You can eat healthy tomorrow."
"One more won't hurt—you don't have a weight problem."
"Bet you can't eat just one—Cindy made these herself!"
"Stop being so silly. We're all having dessert!"
"Don't spoil the fun. Just have a bite!"
"I've been cooking all day for this dinner. You mean you aren't going to have more?"
"Now, Sherry, you know that children are starving in other parts of the world. Clean your plate like Susan did!"

Next, students can use different kinds of refusal skills (see Chapter 3) to eat only what they want to eat. The important idea is that students decide for themselves what they want to eat, rather than being pressured into poor choices by others.

ASSESSMENT | The pressure lines and refusal skills students demonstrate are the assessment task for this activity. For assessment criteria, students should be able to demonstrate refusals in at least three different ways. (Construct: Perceived behavioral control.)

NHES 5 | Decision Making

Students will demonstrate the ability to use decision-making skills to enhance health.

ASSESSMENT CRITERIA

Reach a health-enhancing decision using a process consisting of the following steps:

- Identify a health-risk situation.
- Examine alternatives.
- Evaluate positive and negative consequences.
- Decide on a health-enhancing course of action.

Grades K–2

Milk Matters The National Institute of Child Health and Human Development initiated a Calcium Education Campaign, *Milk Matters,* to increase calcium consumption among children and teens. The simple message is "Calcium is critical to our health." Teachers can find more information at www.nichd.nih.gov/milk/. The Kids' Page (www.nichd.nih.gov/milk/milk.cfm) offers games and activities to engage children in learning about and increasing their calcium intake with the character "Bo Vine."

ASSESSMENT | For an assessment task, students can brainstorm ways to get more calcium into their diets. Students can decide on one idea to try and set a goal to follow their strategy for one week and report back to the class. For assessment criteria, students should be able to explain what their decision is (which strategy to try) and why they made that decision. Students also can name supports for and barriers to putting their decision into practice as a goal. (Note: If some students don't have access to a variety of foods, teachers can focus this activity on increasing calcium intake during the school meal programs.) (Construct: Intention to act in healthy ways.)

Grades 3–5

Fiber Up Your Cereal Decisions. Elementary and middle school students often eat cereal for breakfast. In addition to being high in sugar, some cereals that students commonly choose are quite low in fiber. Teachers can challenge students to collect nutrition information panels from cereal boxes from home and the web to help make decisions on which cereals deliver the best taste and nutrition at the same time. As part of their research, students can investigate soluble (dissolves readily in water) and insoluble fiber and learn more about the foods in which these two types of fiber are found. Students might also want to conduct a taste test of different kinds of cereals and compare taste and nutrition value, including fiber, for each. Which of the cereals list whole grain as the first ingredient? Is there a lot of sugar? Is there partially hydrogenated or trans fat in the cereal? What cereal is most nutritious and most appealing at the same time?

ASSESSMENT | For an assessment task, students can work through the steps of a simple decision-making process to choose a nutritious, good-tasting cereal.

- What's the problem?
- What are the alternatives?
- What are the consequences, positive and negative?
- What's the action the class recommends?
- What's their evaluation of their choices?

For assessment criteria, students should be able to work through all the steps to make a health-enhancing choice. (Construct: Intention to act in healthy ways.)

Grocery Store Field Trip Teachers can arrange (or help students arrange) a field trip to a local grocery store. The store manager might have someone conduct a tour, during which students take notes about what types of foods are located in what parts of the store. Students can list choices and consequences (positive and negative) about shopping in different parts of the store. What decisions would students make when they next go grocery shopping and why?

ASSESSMENT | The choices and consequences students identify are the assessment task for this activity. For assessment criteria, students should be able to demonstrate steps in a simple decision-making process (state the problem or decision, identify choices, identify positive and negative consequences, act, evaluate). (Construct: Perceived behavioral control.)

Grades 6–8

Getting the Scoop on Fats—Butter, Margarine, or Neither? Information about fats sometimes confuses adults as well as young people. As students prepare to investigate the topic of fat, teachers

should remember that health education is not a chemistry class. Students need to know how different types of fats affect them, where the fats are found, and the amount that is recommended. Fat performs important functions in the body, but all fats are not created equal. Students can break into groups to find out more about and report to classmates on

- Triglycerides
- Monosaturated fats
- Polyunsaturated fats (check out the omega-3 fatty acids in fish)
- Saturated fats
- Trans-fatty acids

One additional group of students can investigate cholesterol and its relation to saturated fat in the diet. Students should also note that "no cholesterol" claims on some food labels are misleading, because plant-based foods don't have cholesterol to begin with!

ASSESSMENT | The investigations and reports students create are the assessment task for this activity. For assessment criteria, students should provide accurate information that classmates need to make healthy choices about the fat in their diet.

"No White At Night" and Other Questionable Advice on Carbohydrates. Carbohydrates are in the news, too, and students wonder what they should eat for good health and healthy body weight. Popular advice abounds (such as no white at night, which means no white bread, pasta, or potatoes in the evening), but how can students and adults make sense of it? As with other nutrition topics, students enjoy investigating and learning from each other more than being lectured to by adults. For this topic, students might investigate

- Simple sugars
- Complex carbohydrates
- "Starchy" carbs
- Sweeteners
- Fruits and fruit juices
- The glycemic index

Teachers and students can find a great resource in *The Complete Idiot's Guide to Total Nutrition* by Joy Bauer.[64] This book, in its fourth edition, contains the basics about nutrition, written in an engaging format that everyone can understand.

ASSESSMENT | As with other similar activities, the investigations and reports the students complete are the assessment task. From a decision-making standpoint, students should provide accurate information that classmates need to make healthy choices. (Construct: Intention to act in healthy ways.)

NHES 6 | Goal Setting

Students will demonstrate the ability to use goal-setting skills to enhance health.

ASSESSMENT CRITERIA
- Goal statement—Give goal statement that identifies health benefits; goal is achievable and will result in enhanced health.
- Goal setting plan—Show plan that is complete, logical and sequential, and includes a process to assess progress.

Grades K–2

Plant a Garden Children can work on the goal of planning, planting, and harvesting a class garden. Children can brainstorm the kinds of

Planting a class garden can help students build decision-making and goal-setting skills as well as teach them more about the foods they eat.

Grades 6–8

Nutrition Behavior Change Project Students should identify one specific nutrition behavior they want to change or improve. For example, some students may routinely skip breakfast, have a soda every day after school, or eat no fruit on most days of the week. As part of their goal setting, students should write a clear, measurable goal for a specific amount of time (two weeks), specific steps to achieve their goal, plans to build support from others and overcome potential barriers, and a plan to assess progress. Students can keep a diary or journal for a specific period of time and report back to the class on their experiences.

ASSESSMENT | The goal-setting plan and journal are the assessment tasks for this activity. For assessment criteria, students should demonstrate their ability to fulfill all the steps in goal setting (goal, steps, support, obstacles, plan to assess progress) over a specific period of time.

foods they would like to grow and investigate (search the Internet, talk with an expert, consult gardening books) the kinds of foods that are feasible to grow for the time of year and soil in the community. The class can make their selections, design and draw out a plan for their garden, and decide on all the jobs class members will need to do to tend the garden (preparing the soil, planting, protecting the plants, watering, weeding, checking weather reports, and harvesting). Small groups of students can take responsibility for different sections of the garden and make a written plan for their work. Teachers can schedule a regular time in the week for garden work and have children keep a class journal about their garden. Children can celebrate the achievement of the class goal by preparing and eating the foods they have grown.

ASSESSMENT | Completing the class journal and garden are the assessment tasks for this activity. For assessment criteria, children should make a clear plan for their garden with achievable steps, identify potential obstacles (not enough rain, small-animal invasion) and strategies to overcome them, and specify a way to assess progress. (Construct: Perceived behavioral control.)

Grades 3–5

Healthy Habits for Families Students can talk in small groups about a healthy nutrition goal they would like to set with their families. Their goals should be clear, achievable, and measurable. Students should think about supports for and barriers to reaching their family goal. Students also should design a simple assessment plan for a given period of time. Students can take their goals home to get family input and to find out whether their families would be willing to try to reach the goal for a given period of time. Students can report back to the class on their progress.

ASSESSMENT | The students' plans and reports are the assessment task for this activity. For assessment criteria, students should be able to demonstrate the steps in goal setting (making a plan with specific steps, identifying supports and obstacles, assessing progress). (Constructs: Intention to act in healthy ways, subjective norms.)

Building on Supports and Overcoming Barriers An important part of achieving a goal is identifying and making plans to deal with supports and barriers. Supports are those people, places, beliefs, conditions, circumstances, and cues that help people achieve a goal. For example, a friend who goes walking with you each day is a support. Barriers are those things that make achieving a goal more difficult—discouraging words from a family member, little personal belief that the goal can be achieved, conditions, and circumstances. For example, going out for a run in the southern United States is difficult in August because of the heat and humidity. Students can identify a healthy eating goal they would like to work toward and at least one support they can build on and one barrier they need to plan to overcome. Students can keep a journal during the course of working toward their goal to track their responses to supports and barriers.

ASSESSMENT | For an assessment task, students can report on their progress in terms of supports for and barriers to their goal periodically throughout the goal period. For assessment criteria, students should be able to tell at least two ways they've dealt with each support or barrier and describe the progress they've made as a result. (Construct: Intention to act in healthy ways.)

NHES 7 | Self-Management

Students will demonstrate the ability to practice health-enhancing behaviors and avoid or reduce health risks.

ASSESSMENT CRITERIA

- Application (transfer)—Initiate health-enhancing behaviors; apply concepts and skills appropriate and effectively.
- Self-monitoring and reflection—Monitor actions and make adjustments; accept feedback and make adjustments; able to self-assess, reflect on, and take responsibility for actions.

Grades K–2

Preparing Healthy Snacks Kids' Health (www.kidshealth.org) offers healthy snacks that kids can make or help make (with an adult assistant). The list includes peanut butter muffins, frozen yogurt pops, veggie bowls, smoothies, and many other kid-friendly snacks.

Students and teachers can make healthy snacks in the classroom, with the help of parent assistants, if needed. Alternatively, students can download recipes to try at home or to bring from home for classmates to try. Be sure to check on student allergies.

ASSESSMENT | For an assessment task, students can describe their favorite choices for healthy snacks and what makes them healthy. For assessment criteria, students should explain the self-management skills they use to eat a healthy snack rather than a junk food snack. (Construct: Perceived behavioral control.)

***Bread and Jam for Frances* and Other Picky Eaters**   Helping students try new healthy foods and snacks is a big part of teaching self-management for healthy eating. Teachers can use popular children's books, like *Bread and Jam for Frances* by Russell Hoban, to talk about trying different foods. In this story, Frances turns up her nose at any food other than bread and jam—so her mother gives her bread and jam at every meal. Frances soon realizes that variety is the spice of life. Other books with similar themes (see the book list at the end of the chapter) include

- *D. W. the Picky Eater,* by Marc Brown
- *Don't Let the Peas Touch!* by Deborah Blumenthal
- *Eat Your Peas,* by Kes Gray
- *Gladys Goes Out to Lunch,* by Derek Anderson
- *I Will Never NOT EVER Eat a Tomato,* by Lauren Child
- *Little Pea,* by Amy Krouse Rosenthal
- *No More Cookies!* by Paeony Lewis
- *Sweet Tooth,* by Margie Palatini
- *Yoko,* by Rosemary Wells.

ASSESSMENT | For an assessment task, students can sample and write about trying one new food during the week (in the cafeteria, during a classroom tasting party, at home). Teachers might want to have a tasting party at school because some children might not have access to a variety of foods at home. For assessment criteria, students should give at least two reasons why trying new foods can help them grow healthy. (Construct: Perceived behavioral control.)

Grades 3–5

Recipe Doctor: Update a Family Favorite   Students and teachers can bring in recipes from home to update for good health. Students can work in small groups of "Recipe Doctors" to examine the ingredients in recipes for possible substitutions to make foods healthier. The Mayo Clinic (www.mayoclinic.com) Tools for Healthier Lives recommends strategies to reduce the amount of fat, sugar, and sodium. The site also contains substitution ideas, such as using extra-lean ground beef, chicken, or turkey in place of regular ground beef. If facilities permit, let students cook some of their improved recipes for a taste-testing party, or have students cook them at home with their families and bring the products to try in class.

ASSESSMENT | The students' improved recipes are the assessment task for this activity. For assessment criteria, students should explain the strategies they used and the reasons why the strategies make the recipes healthier. (Construct: Perceived behavioral control.)

Eating Breakfast—the Right Stuff   Students might have heard that breakfast is the most important meal of the day. Breakfast is the fuel that gets people going after a long night of sleep. Many students are in a hurry in the morning, but eating breakfast is important for everyone. Kids' Health (www.kidshealth.org) suggests a range of ideas for a healthy breakfast at the link "Ready, Set, Breakfast!" It includes traditional foods such as cereal, toast, and eggs as well as choices such as breakfast tacos, sandwiches, and banana dogs. Students can volunteer other ideas for breakfast that they eat at home or are interested in trying. Students can set a goal of eating breakfast every day for a week, whether at school or at home. For example, they might need to make sure they get up early enough to eat breakfast at home or get to school early enough to eat breakfast at school. This activity links to NHES 5 and 6, decision making and goal setting. Teachers might also work with parents to have a special "breakfast at school day," for which teachers, students, and parents or caregivers contribute different types of foods.

ASSESSMENT | For an assessment task, students can discuss various self-management steps they need to take to be sure they eat breakfast, whether at home or at school. For assessment criteria, students should select one self-management strategy to try for the week and report back to the class on their progress. (Note: This activity is based on the assumption that all students have access to breakfast, at home or through the School Breakfast Program. If this is not the case, teachers should talk with school administrators about being certain that all students have access to breakfast.) (Construct: Perceived behavioral control.)

Smart Ways to Quench Your Thirst   *Dietary Guidelines for Americans* recommends that children consume beverages with few added sugars or caloric sweeteners (sugars and syrups added to foods at the table or during processing or preparation, such as high-fructose corn syrup). The National Heart, Lung, and Blood Institute recommends selecting beverages this way:

- *Almost anytime or "go" drinks:* water, fat-free and 1% milk, diet soda, diet and unsweetened iced teas and lemonade
- *Sometimes or "slow" drinks:* 2% milk, 100% fruit juice, sports drinks
- *Once in a while or "whoa" drinks:* whole milk, regular soda, drinks with added sugar, fruit drinks with less than 100% fruit juice

The best choices for children and adolescents are skim and 1% milk, water, and 100% fruit juice. (Note: 100% juice may not be appropriate for children who are diabetic.) Although artificial sweeteners are considered generally safe when consumed as part of a balanced diet, researchers disagree on their appropriateness for children. Students can set goals of drinking more healthy drinks—and less soda of any kind—to link self-management to NHES 5 and 6, decision making and goal setting. Teachers and parents will be interested to know that major soft drink companies (Coca-Cola and PepsiCo) recommend that schools not sell carbonated drinks in elementary schools during the school day. Further guidelines include making juices, water, and other products available where soft drinks are sold, at the same price.

ASSESSMENT | For an assessment task, students can keep track of everything they drink for five days (a school week). Students can combine their data to make a graph of class beverage consumption. Students can set individual or class goals to increase consumption of healthy drinks (water, skim or 1% milk, 100% juice) during the next week. For assessment criteria, students should report on the progress they made in increasing their consumption of healthy drinks and identify supports for and barriers to reaching their goals. Students also should identify at least two self-management strategies they used to increase healthy beverage consumption. (Construct: Perceived behavioral control.)

Grades 6–8

Eating Out, Eating Healthy   Middle school students increasingly eat meals away from home, whether with their friends or with their families. What self-management skills can students develop to make

Water, fat-free or 1% milk, and sometimes 100% fruit juice are the best beverage choices for children and adolescents.

healthier selections when they eat out? Students can access nutrition data for a wide variety of restaurants at these websites:

- Nutrition Data (www.nutritiondata.com)
- The Fast Food Nutrition Fact Explorer (www.fatcalories.com)

At the Nutrition Data website, students also can create Food Facts labels for all kinds of foods, including fruits and vegetables. For this activity, students can collect menus from restaurants in their community and "order" several different meals. Using the websites, students can then analyze the nutritional value of the meals and recommend modifications for healthier choices, which they can also analyze.

ASSESSMENT | For an assessment task, students can work in small groups to "visit" a restaurant and order a meal (different orders for everyone). Students should analyze the nutritional value of their meals and then make recommendations, which they also analyze, for healthier choices, if needed. For assessment criteria, students should describe what they learned and explain the self-management strategies they used to make healthy selections. (Construct: Perceived behavioral control.)

Kids' Health on Teen Dieting Adolescents often worry about their body size and weight. The Kids' Health website (www.kidshealth.org) has some helpful information for students who believe they need to lose weight. Topics include evaluating one's weight and different types of diets and dietary supplements. Students can work in pairs or small groups to learn more about a topic related to healthy body weight.

ASSESSMENT | For an assessment task, students can create a game show (*Jeopardy, Wheel of Fortune*) or another television show format (news, talk show) to teach classmates about their topic. For assessment criteria, students should provide accurate information about three or more self-management tips for safe and healthy ways to maintain healthy body weight. (Construct: Perceived behavioral control.)

Powerful Bones, Powerful Girls The National Bone Health Campaign has a website through the Centers for Disease Control and Prevention called "Powerful Girls Have Powerful Bones" (www.cdc.gov/powerfulbones/index_content.html). At this site, girls (and boys) can learn about how to build strong bones through a healthy diet and weight-bearing physical activities. The site features games, quizzes, and a dictionary of key concepts. (Additional information is available at other girls' health websites; see the list at the end of this chapter.)

ASSESSMENT | For an assessment task, students can make a list of tips for bone health. For assessment criteria, students should explain how to practice at least three self-management strategies for healthy and strong bones. (Construct: Perceived behavioral control.)

NHES 8 | Advocacy

Students will demonstrate the ability to advocate for personal, family, and community health.

ASSESSMENT CRITERIA

- Health-enhancing position—Give clear, health-enhancing position.
- Support for position—Support position with facts, concepts, examples, and evidence.
- Audience awareness—Show awareness of target audience; choose words, tone, and examples to suit audience.
- Conviction—Display conviction for position.

Grades K–2

Building MyPyramid: Trying New Foods Teachers can challenge students to try new healthy foods and share their experiences with classmates. Students can help create a large bulletin board of MyPyramid (www.mypyramid.gov). When students try a new food, they can cut out a picture or make a drawing of the food to add to the bulletin board in the appropriate category. In this way, students can make a public statement about their openness to trying new foods and have a positive influence on classmates. (Note: If some students don't have access to a variety of foods, teachers can make sure new foods are introduced during the school day as healthy snacks and for tasting parties.)

ASSESSMENT | The MyPyramid students create is the assessment task for this activity. For assessment criteria, all students should try at least two new foods during the course of the activity and make a health-enhancing statement about trying new foods. (Constructs: Subjective norms, perceived behavioral control.)

Five a Day the Color Way The Produce for Better Health Foundation sponsors the Five a Day the Color Way campaign (www.5aday.com/) to promote fruit and vegetable consumption for adequate intake of vitamins, minerals, and phytochemicals. The site includes links both for educators and for kids. Teachers can teach healthy habits with "There's a Rainbow on My Plate," which includes lesson ideas and recipes. The kids' page offers 5 a Day friends including Brandon and Bronwyn Blueberry, activities, coloring sheets, links, and recipe tips. The linked sites offer a wide variety of colorful materials students can use to launch a 5 a Day campaign, in collaboration with the meal program in their school. Additional materials for teachers and students are available at the website for the government's "Eat 5 to 9 a Day for Better Health" initiative (www.5aday.gov).

ASSESSMENT | For an assessment task, students can use the 5 a Day tracker to monitor their fruit and vegetable intake. Teachers, cafeteria managers, administrators, and parents can help ensure that all students have the opportunity to eat and sample more fruits and vegetables during the campaign (and after). For assessment criteria, students should develop a health-enhancing message about eating fruits and vegetables. (Construct: Intention to act in healthy ways.)

Grades 3–5

DGA Letters Home Students can investigate the latest *Dietary Guidelines for Americans* (DGAs) (www.usda.gov) and brainstorm ways to let their parents and caregivers know more about the DGAs in a letter (the content of the guidelines, DGA hints for healthier eating, one specific suggestion for families, ways students can help). After students have contributed ideas, each can write a letter to his or her parents or caregivers. Students can report back to the class on the response of their families.

ASSESSMENT | The letters to families are the assessment task for this activity. For assessment criteria, students should state a positive position toward using the DGAs, back it up with evidence, design their letters to appeal to family members, and show strong conviction about the importance of improving nutrition. (Construct: Intention to act in healthy ways.)

Vitamin and Mineral Personalities Many teachers remember memorizing charts about vitamins and minerals. We may remember the memorizing itself more than what we learned. To learn about vitamins and minerals, students can make "sandwich boards" to wear at school on a given day. Students can choose the vitamin or mineral they want to portray and design their signs accordingly.

ASSESSMENT | The students' signs are the assessment task for this activity. For assessment criteria, students should design a clear message, back it up with facts, target their audience, and show strong conviction. (Constructs: Attitudes toward behavior, subjective norms.)

Grades 6–8

Fight Bac! Campaign—Clean, Separate, Chill, and Cook Students and teachers can use materials from the Partnership for Food Safety Education (www.fightbac.org). Students can learn to keep foods safe from bacteria and advocate for others to do the same. Students can teach about the four steps (clean, separate, chill, and cook), safe produce handling, and food-borne illnesses. Students might want to put their performing arts and puppetry skills to work to help the Fight Bac! characters come alive at school.

ASSESSMENT | The campaign students plan and carry out is the assessment task for this activity. For assessment criteria, students should have a clear, health-enhancing message, back it up with facts, target their audience, and show strong conviction. (Constructs: Intention to act in healthy ways, subjective norms.)

Healthier School Lunches Students can invite the school cafeteria manager and staff to participate with them on this project. Teachers can ask the cafeteria manager to discuss the requirements and restrictions he or she deals with in planning and preparing school lunches and to provide a month's school lunch menus for class members. Students can work in small groups to classify the different weeks' menus into the groups of MyPyramid and compare them with pyramid recommendations. What do students notice about the lunch menus for a week at a time? For a month at a time? Students can arrange time with the cafeteria manager to discuss their findings and to make specific recommendations for making school meals balanced and appealing.

ASSESSMENT | The students' analysis and recommendations are the assessment tasks for this activity. For assessment criteria, students should advocate for specific improvements in school meals, back up their recommendations with research on good nutrition, target their audience (cafeteria manager and staff), and show strong conviction in a respectful way. (Constructs: Subjective norms, perceived behavioral control.)

Raps for Nutrition Students can work in small groups to create a rap, poem, or song about a particular nutrient, one of the food groups in MyPyramid, the *Dietary Guidelines for Americans,* or food labels. Students should include factual information (NHES 1, core concepts) and a persuasive message for healthy dietary practices. To illustrate, a group of teachers in American Samoa created this nutrition rap as an example to prepare for a summer lab school with elementary and middle school students:

> We eat fruits and vegetables and things like that,
> We stay away from oily foods that make you fat.
>   It's like that, and that's the way it goes!
> We eat fish and drink our water,
> It's not healthy if you only eat butter.
>   It's like that, and that's the way it goes!
> Eat a healthy food, take a walk, and exercise.
> It's like that, and that's the way it goes!
> Boo Yaa!!

ASSESSMENT | The raps, poems, or songs students create are the assessment task for this activity. For assessment criteria, students should provide a clear advocacy message, back it up with facts, target their audience, and perform with conviction. (Constructs: Intention to act in healthy ways, subjective norms.)

EVALUATED CURRICULA AND INSTRUCTIONAL MATERIALS

The Health Education Curriculum Analysis Tool (HECAT) provides a list of programs that federal agencies consider exemplary, promising, or effective (www.cdc.gov/HealthyYouth/HECAT/pdf/HECAT_Append_2.pdf).

The National Cancer Institute, U.S. Department of Health and Human Services, provides these school-based programs related to healthy eating (http://rtips.cancer.gov/rtips/index.do):

- *5 a Day Power Plus.* School-based program designed to increase fruit and vegetable consumption.
- *Bienestar.* School-based program designed to promote healthy dietary habits and increase physical activity among elementary school students.

- *Coordinated Approach to Child Health (CATCH)*. Designed to promote healthy eating habits and increase physical activity among children and adolescents.
- *Eat Well and Keep Moving*. School-based program designed to increase physical activity and promote healthy dietary habits among fourth- and fifth-grade students.
- *Gimme 5*. School-based program designed to increase fruit and vegetable consumption.

- *High 5 Fruit and Vegetable Intervention for 4th Graders*. School-based program designed to increase fruit and vegetable consumption.
- *Middle School Physical Activity and Nutrition (MSPAN)*. Designed to increase physical activity and promote healthy dietary habits among Grade 6–8 level students.
- *Planet Health*. School-based program designed to increase physical activity and promote healthy dietary habits among sixth-, seventh-, and eighth-grade students.

INTERNET AND OTHER RESOURCES

Visit the Online Learning Center (www.mhhe.com/telljohann6e) for links to these sites, quizzes and other study aids, and many additional resources.

WEBSITES

American Dietetic Association
www.eatright.org

Dietary Guidelines for Americans, 2005
www.health.gov/dietaryguidelines

Dole 5 a Day
www.dole5aday.com

Fast Food Nutrition Fact Explorer
www.fatcalories.com

Fight Bac!
www.fightbac.org

Food Labeling and Nutrition
www.cfsan.fda.gov/label.html

Government Nutrition Facts Label
www.cfsan.fda.gov/~dms/foodlab.html

MyPyramid Food Guidance System
www.mypyramid.gov

National Cancer Institute, 5 to 9 a Day for Better Health
www.5aday.gov

National Dairy Council
www.nationaldairycouncil.org

Nutrition Data (ND)
www.nutritiondata.com

PBS Kids (Don't Buy It!)
www.pbskids.org/dontbuyit

School Strategies to Promote Healthy Eating
www.cdc.gov/HealthyYouth

OTHER RESOURCES

Action for Healthy Kids. *The Learning Connection: The Value of Improving Nutrition and Physical Activity in Our Schools.* (www.ActionForHealthyKids.org; 2004)

Centers for Disease Control and Prevention. "Guidelines for School Health Programs to Promote Lifelong Healthy Eating." *Morbidity & Mortality Weekly Report* 45, no. RR-9 (1996): 1–41.

Food and Nutrition Service, U.S. Department of Agriculture; Centers for Disease Control and Prevention, U.S. Department of Health and Human Services; and U.S. Department of Education. *Making It Happen! School Nutrition Success Stories.* Alexandria, VA: FNS-374, 2005.

U.S. Department of Health and Human Services, U.S. Department of Agriculture. *Dietary Guidelines for Americans 2005.* Washington, DC: U.S. Department of Health and Human Services, U.S. Department of Agriculture, 2005. (www.health.gov/dietaryguidelines)

CHILDREN'S LITERATURE

AGES 5–8

Aliki. *Milk: From Cow to Carton.* HarperTrophy, 1992.

Anderson, Derek. *Gladys Goes Out to Lunch.* Simon & Schuster Books for Young Readers, 2005.

Baer, Edith. *This Is the Way We Eat Our Lunch: A Book About Children Around the World.* Scholastic, 1995.

Blevins, Wiley. *Where Does Your Food Go?* Children's Press, 2004.

Blumenthal, Deborah. *Don't Let the Peas Touch!* Arthur A. Levine Books, 2004.

Brandenberg, Alexa. *Chop, Simmer, Season.* Harcourt, 1997.

Brown, Marc. *D.W. the Picky Eater.* Little, Brown, 1997.

Brown, Marcia. *Stone Soup: An Old Tale.* Atheneum, 1947.

Carle, Eric. *Pancakes, Pancakes!* Aladdin, 1998.

Carle, Eric. *Today Is Monday.* Putnam, 1997.

Carle, Eric. *The Very Hungry Caterpillar.* Philomel, 1981.

Carle, Eric. *Walter the Baker.* Aladdin, 1998.

Child, Lauren. *I Will Never NOT EVER Eat a Tomato.* Candlewick, 2000.

Chocolate, Deborah M. Newton. *My First Kwanzaa Book.* Scholastic, 1999.

Cocca-Leffler, Maryann. *Clams All Year.* Boyds Mills Press, 2001.

Cooper, Helen. *Pumpkin Soup.* Farrar, Straus & Giroux (BYR), 1999.

Demi. *One Grain of Rice: A Mathematical Folktale.* Scholastic, 1997.

DePaola, Tomie. *Pancakes for Breakfast.* Voyager Books, 1990.

DePaola, Tomie. *Tony's Bread: An Italian Folktale.* Paperstar Book, 1996.

Devlin, Wende, and Harry Devlin. *Cranberry Thanksgiving.* Aladdin, 1990.

Dooley, Norah. *Everybody Bakes Bread.* Carolrhoda Books, 1995.

Dooley, Norah. *Everybody Cooks Rice.* Carolrhoda Books, 1992.

Doyle, Malachy. *Jody's Beans.* Candlewick, 2002.

Ehlert, Lois. *Eating the Alphabet: Fruits and Vegetables from A to Z.* Voyager Books, 1993.

Ehlert, Lois. *Growing Vegetable Soup.* Voyager Books, 1990.

Ehlert, Lois. *Pie in the Sky.* Harcourt Children's Books, 2004.

Falwell, Cathryn. *Feast for 10.* Clarion Books, 1995.

Flanagan, Alice K. *A Busy Day at Mr. Kang's Grocery Store.* Children's Press, 1996.

French, Vivian. *Oliver's Fruit Salad.* Orchard Books, 1998.

French, Vivian. *Oliver's Milk Shake.* Hodder Children's Audio, 2000.

French, Vivian. *Oliver's Vegetables.* Orchard Books, 1998.

Freymann, Saxton, and Joost Elffers. *How Are You Peeling? Foods with Moods.* Arthur A. Levine Books, 1999.

Galdone, Paul. *Little Red Hen.* Clarion Books, 1985.

Gelman, Rita G. *Biggest Sandwich Ever.* Scholastic, 1981.

Gershator, David. *Bread Is for Eating.* Henry Holt, 1998.

Gray, Kes. *Eat Your Peas.* Dorling Kindersley, 2000.

Gretz, Susanna. *Rabbit Food.* Candlewick, 2001.

Hall, Zoe. *The Apple Pie Tree.* Blue Sky, 1999.

Hoban, Russell. *Bread and Jam for Frances.* HarperTrophy, 1993.

Hoberman, Mary Ann. *The Seven Silly Eaters.* Voyager Books, 2000.

Kann, Victoria, and Elizabeth Kann. *Pinkalicious.* HarperCollins, 2006.

Koster, Gloria, and Maryann Cocca-Leffler. *The Peanut-Free Café.* Albert Whitman & Company, 2006.

Kottke, Jan. *From Seed to Pumpkin.* Children's Press, 2000.

Krull, Kathleen. *Supermarket.* Holiday House, 2001.

Kuklin, Susan. *How My Family Lives in America.* Aladdin, 1998.

Landry, Leo. *Eat Your Peas, Ivy Louise.* Houghton Mifflin, 2005.

Lee, Brenda Cartee. *Lunch at the Zoo.* Little Cottage Books, 2003.

Lewis, Paeony. *No More Cookies!* Chicken House, 2005.

McMillan, Bruce. *Eating Fractions.* Scholastic, 1991.

Morris, Ann. *Bread, Bread, Bread* (Around the World Series). HarperTrophy, 1993.

Munson, Derek. *Enemy Pie.* Chronicle Books, 2000.

Murphy, Stuart J. *Just Enough Carrots: Comparing Amounts.* HarperTrophy, 1997.

Nolen, Jerdine. *In My Momma's Kitchen.* Amistad, 2001.

O'Donnell, Sallie. *Animals, Vegetables, Minerals from A to Z.* Legacy Publishing Services, 2005.

Palacios, Argentina. *Peanut Butter, Apple Butter, Cinnamon Toast: Food Riddles for You to Guess.* Heinemann Library, 1990.

Palatini, Margie. *Sweet Tooth.* Simon & Schuster Children's Publishing, 2004.

Peterson, Cris. *Harvest Year.* Boyds Mills Press, 1996.

Priceman, Marjorie. *Princess Picky.* Roaring Books, 2002.

Rabe, Tish. *Oh, the Things You Can Do That Are Good for You: All About Staying Healthy.* Random House Books for Young Readers, 2001.

Rattigan, Jama Kim. *Dumpling Soup.* Meagen Tingly, 1998.

Rosenthal, Amy Krouse. *Little Pea.* Chronicle Books, 2005.

Ruurs, Margriet. *Emma's Eggs.* Fitzhenry & Whiteside, 2003.

Seuss, Dr. *Green Eggs and Ham.* Random House Books for Young Readers, 1960.

Sharmat, Mitchell. *Gregory the Terrible Eater.* Scholastic, 1989.

Shields, Carol Diggory. *Food Fight!* Handprint Books, 2002.

Soto, Gary. *Too Many Tamales.* Paperstar Book, 1996.

Titherington, Jeanne. *Pumpkin Pumpkin.* Greenwillow Books, 1986.

Waber, Bernard. *Fast Food! Gulp! Gulp!* Houghton Mifflin/Walter Lorraine Books, 2001.

Watson, Pete. *The Market Lady and the Mango Tree.* HarperCollins, 1994.

Wellington, Monica. *Apple Farmer Annie.* Dutton Children's Books, 2001.

Wells, Rosemary. *Bunny Cakes.* Viking, 2000.

Wells, Rosemary. *The Gulps.* Little, Brown Young Readers, 2007.

Wells, Rosemary. *Yoko.* Hyperion, 1998.

Wiesner, David. *June 29, 1999.* Clarion Books, 1995.

Woodson, Jacqueline. *We Had a Picnic This Sunday Past.* Hyperion, 1998.

Zamorano, Ana. *Let's Eat.* Rebound by Sagebrush, 2001.

AGES 8–12

Adoff, Arnold. *EATS: Poems.* Lothrop, Lee & Shepard Books, 1979.

Barrett, Judi. *Cloudy with a Chance of Meatballs.* Aladdin, 1982.

Barrett, Judi. *Pickles to Pittsburgh.* Aladdin, 2000.

Burns, Marilyn. *Spaghetti and Meatballs for All.* Scholastic, 1997.

De Groat, Diane. *Annie Pitts, Artichoke.* Seastar Books, 2001.

Haduch, Bill. *Food Rules! What You Munch, Its Punch, Its Crunch and Why Sometimes You Lose Your Lunch.* Puffin, 2001.

Johanson, Paula. *Processed Food (What's In Your Food? Recipe for Disaster).* Rosen Central, 2008.

Jacobson, Michael F., Jayne G. Hurley, and the Center for Science in the Public Interest. *Restaurant Confidential: The Shocking Truth About What You're Really Eating When You're Eating Out.* Workman Publishing, 2002.

Jukes, Mavis, and Lilian Wai-Yin. *Be Healthy! It's a Girl Thing: Food, Fitness, and Feeling Great.* Crown Books for Young Readers, 2003.

Kovalski, Maryann. *Pizza for Breakfast.* William Morrow, 1991.

Priceman, Marjorie. *How to Make an Apple Pie and See the World.* Dragonfly Books, 1996.

Riccio, Nina. *Five Kids and a Monkey Solve the Great Cupcake Caper.* Creative Attic, 1997.

Rockwell, Lizzy. *Good Enough to Eat.* HarperCollins, 1999.

Rosen, Michael J. *The Greatest Table: A Banquet to Fight Against Hunger.* Harcourt, 1994.

Schlosser, Eric. *Fast Food Nation.*

Schlosser, Eric. *Fast Food Nation Tie-in: The Dark Side of the All-American Meal (P.S.)* Harper Perennial, 2006.

Schlosser, Eric, and Charles Wilson. *Chew On This: Everything You Don't Want to Know About Fast Food.* Houghton Mifflin, 2007.

Shanley, Ellen, and Colleen Thompson. *Fueling the Teen Machine.* Bull, 2001.

Showers, Paul. *What Happens to a Hamburger?* Trumpet Club, 1985.

Sturges, Philemon. *The Little Red Hen Makes a Pizza.* Puffin Books, 2002.

Swanson, Diane. *Burp! The Most Interesting Book You'll Ever Read About Eating.* Kids Can Press, 2001.

Wood, Audrey. *Sweet Dream Pie.* Scholastic, 2002.

ENDNOTES

1. T. G. Thompson and A. Veneman, *Dietary Guidelines for Americans: Message from the Secretaries* (Washington, DC: U.S. Department of Health and Human Services, 2005).

2. U.S. Department of Health and Human Services, U.S. Department of Agriculture, *Dietary Guidelines for Americans 2005* (Washington, DC: U.S. Department of Health and Human Services, U.S. Department of Agriculture, 2005). (www.health.gov/dietaryguidelines/)

3. W. H. Dietz, "Overweight: An Epidemic," in *About Children: An Authoritative Resource on the State of Childhood Today,* eds. A. G. Cosby, R. E. Greenberg, L. H. Southward, and M. Weitzman (American Academy of Pediatrics, 2005), 110–13.

4. Ibid.

5. Ibid.

6. P. H. Casey, "Food Insecurity," in *About Children: An Authoritative Resource on the State of Childhood Today,* eds. A. G. Cosby, R. E. Greenberg, L. H.

Southward, and M. Weitzman (American Academy of Pediatrics, 2005), 96–99.

7. Ibid.
8. Food and Nutrition Service, U.S. Department of Agriculture; Centers for Disease Control and Prevention, U.S. Department of Health and Human Services; and U.S. Department of Education, *Making It Happen! School Nutrition Success Stories* (Alexandria, VA: FNS-374, 2005).
9. National Center for Chronic Disease Prevention and Health Promotion, *Anemia and Iron Status*. (www.cdc.gov/nccdphp/dnpa/anemiron.htm)
10. Economic Research Service, U.S. Department of Agriculture. (www.ers.usda.gov/)
11. Council of Chief State School Officers, *Policy Statement on School Health, 2004* (www.ccsso.org).
12. Action for Healthy Kids, *The Learning Connection: The Value of Improving Nutrition and Physical Activity in Our Schools*. (www.ActionForHealthyKids.org; 2004)
13. Ibid
14. Ibid
15. Ibid.
16. H. Taras and W. Potts-Datema, "Obesity and Student Performance at School," *Journal of School Health* 75(8): 291–95.
17. Ibid.
18. Action for Healthy Kids, *The Learning Connection*.
19. Ibid.
20. Ibid.
21. H. Taras and W. Potts-Datema, "Obesity and Student Performance at School."
22. Ibid.
23. P. H. Casey, "Food Insecurity."
24. Ibid.
25. Ibid.
26. Ibid.
27. Ibid.
28. National Center for Health Statistics. *Prevalence of Overweight Among Children and Adolescents: United States, 1999–2002*. (www.cdc.gov/nchs/products/pubs/pubd/hestats/overwght99.htm)
29. Action for Healthy Kids, *The Learning Connection*.
30. Ibid.
31. W. H. Dietz, "Overweight: An Epidemic."
32. Ibid.
33. School Nutrition Association. (www.schoolnutrition.org)
34. Kids' Health, Inc., *Improving Academic Achievement Through a Quality School Food Service Program*. (www.kidshealthga.org; 2004).
35. Ibid.
36. School Nutrition Association, *House Education and Labor Committee Requests Study on ERP*. (www.schoolnutrition.org/Index.aspx?id=2750)
37. Action for Healthy Kids, *The Learning Connection*.
38. Ibid.
39. Ibid.
40. L. Kann, S. K. Telljohann, and S. F. Wooley, "Health Education: Results from the School Health Policies and Programs Study 2006," *Journal of School Health*, 77 (8): 408–434, 2007.
41. Centers for Disease Control and Prevention, "Guidelines for School Health Programs to Promote Lifelong Healthy Eating," *Morbidity & Mortality Weekly Report* 45, no. RR-9 (1996): 1–41.
42. Ibid.
43. Ibid.
44. Ibid.
45. Food and Nutrition Service, U.S. Department of Agriculture; Centers for Disease Control and Prevention, U.S. Department of Health and Human Services; and U.S. Department of Education. *Making It Happen! School Nutrition Success Stories*.
46. U.S. Department of Health and Human Services, U.S. Department of Agriculture, *Dietary Guidelines for Americans 2005*.
47. Ibid.
48. Ibid.
49. Ibid.
50. Ibid.
51. Ibid.
52. Ibid.
53. Ibid.
54. Ibid.
55. U.S. Department of Agriculture, MyPyramid Plan. (www.mypyramid.gov)
56. Ibid.
57. U.S. Department of Health and Human Services and U.S. Department of Agriculture, *Finding Your Way to a Healthier You: Based on the Dietary Guidelines for Americans*. (www.healthierus.gov/dietaryguidelines)
58. Ibid.
59. Centers for Disease Control and Prevention, "Guidelines for School Health Programs to Promote Lifelong Healthy Eating."
60. Centers for Disease Control and Prevention, *Health Education Curriculum Analysis Tool* (Atlanta: CDC, draft).
61. Kids' Health, *Kids Can Be Taught to Eat Healthy Foods, Study Finds*. (kidshealth.org/breaking_news/nutrition_habits.html)
62. National Heart, Lung, and Blood Institute, *Portion Distortion: Keep an Eye on Portion Size*. (http://hin.nhlbi.nih.gov/portion/keep.htm)
63. University of Michigan Health System, *Resources on Media and Media Literacy*. (www.med.umich.edu/1libr/yourchild/media.htm)
64. J. Bauer, *The Complete Idiot's Guide to Total Nutrition* (New York: Penguin Group, 2005).

Promoting Physical Activity

DESIRED LEARNER OUTCOMES

After reading this chapter, you will be able to . . .

- Describe the prevalence and cost of inactivity among youth.

- Explain the relationship between physical inactivity and compromised academic performance.

- Identify factors that influence physical activity.

- Summarize current guidelines and practices for schools and teachers related to promotion of physical activity and the prevention of inactivity.

- Summarize developmentally appropriate physical activity concepts and skills for K–8 students in the context of the National Health Education Standards and target healthy behavior outcomes.

- Demonstrate developmentally appropriate learning strategies and assessment techniques that incorporate concepts and skills that have been shown to promote physical activity among youth.

- Identify effective, evaluated commercial physical activity curricula.

- Identify websites and children's literature that can be used in cross-curricular instructional activities promoting physical activity.

TABLE 7–1

Youth Risk Behavior Survey Data Related to Participation in Physical Activity, 2007

Risk Behavior	Percent Reporting Behavior		
	Total	Females	Males
Met currently recommended levels of physical activity	34.7	25.6	43.7
Enrolled in physical education class	53.6	49.4	57.7
Attended physical education class daily	30.3	27.3	33.2
Played on one or more sports teams (in the twelve months preceding the survey)	56.3	50.4	62.1
Watched three or more hours/day of TV	35.4	33.2	37.5
Used computers three or more hours/day	24.9	20.6	29.1

SOURCE: Centers for Disease Control and Prevention, "Youth Risk Behavior Surveillance—United States, 2007," *Morbidity and Mortality Weekly Report 57*, no. SS-4 (6 June 2008): 1–131.

INTRODUCTION

Although many reasons are offered for failure to participate in consistent patterns of physical activity, there is no question of the benefits of such pursuits for all age groups. Robust physical activity is particularly important for young learners who are establishing personal health promotion habits. Schools must organize a range of learning opportunities to meet the fitness needs of students of all abilities and interest levels. Such developmentally appropriate and well-designed instruction contributes to a sound foundation for maintaining health and promoting school success.

Prevalence and Cost

A growing body of literature has emerged that confirms the public health benefits of increasing physical activity as a way to reduce the effects of a sedentary lifestyle. These findings were summarized in the 1996 *Physical Activity and Health: A Report of the Surgeon General.* Updated research has documented that participation in a pattern of consistent physical activity is associated with very positive health outcomes for all age groups. Specifically, physical activity

- Reduces the risk for heart attack, colon cancer, diabetes, and high blood pressure, and may reduce the risk for stroke
- Helps to control weight
- Contributes to healthy bones, muscles, and joints, and helps relieve the pain of arthritis
- Helps to reduce falls among older people
- Reduces anxiety and depression
- Is associated with fewer hospitalizations, physician visits, and medications
- Provides therapeutic benefits for people with chronic conditions, including heart disease, high cholesterol, and osteoporosis[1]
- Supports congnitive function[2]

Subsequent studies confirm the assertions in Surgeon General's report that regular participation in moderate physical activity is an essential element of a healthy lifestyle for all Americans.[3]

Although further research is necessary to fully define the relationship between physical activity and health among young people, documented benefits for school-age children and youth who participate in regular physical activity include

- Reduces total body fat in overweight children and adolescents[4]
- Improves metabolic syndrome (clustering of high blood sugar, high blood pressure, high cholesterol, and abdominal obesity)[5]
- Helps reduce high blood pressure in youth with mild hypertension[6]
- Improves fitness among youth with asthma[7]
- Helps reduce anxiety and depression[8]
- Enhances self-concept[9]
- Improves muscular strength and endurance[10]

Although science has confirmed that many positive outcomes are associated with consistent patterns of physical activity, many American adults remain inactive. More than 50 percent of adults don't participate in enough physical activity to produce health benefits, and 24 percent are not active at all during their leisure time. These data prompted then U.S. Secretary of Health and Human Services Michael Leavitt to assert that, "changing the culture from treating sickness to staying healthy calls for small steps and good choices to be made each and every day."[11]

Although children and youth are more physically active than adults, activity levels begin to decline as children approach adolescence and continue to decline throughout the teen years.[12] Table 7–1 provides Youth Risk Behavior Survey data that identify activities in which students in grades 9 through 12 participated in 2007.[13] Clearly, these data signal an inactivity problem among older youth.

Unfortunately, the data do not paint a much more optimistic picture of the physical activity patterns among younger children. Findings confirm that

- The U.S. is facing a potentially devastating crisis of overweight and obesity. Nearly ⅓ of American adults are classified as obese, a figure that has more than doubled over the last 30 years. Among children ages 2–5, obesity rates have more than doubled and among those aged 6–19 years old they have more than tripled. These data confirm that approximately 17 percent of today's children and youth are overweight, with estimates projecting that 20 percent will be obese by 2010.[14,15] Though science has confirmed that the obesity epidemic is a complex problem influenced by many economic, biomedical, social, and environmental factors, there is no question of the contribution made by physical inactivity and unhealthy eating. In fact, some researchers have asserted that childhood obesity is largely the result of a decline in regular participation in physical activity.[16] As discussed in Chapter 1, the consequences of the childhood obesity crisis of today will threaten American longevity in the future.[17]

• Urban and suburban community design has exerted a negative influence over the availability of safe and accessible play spaces and opportunities for active transportation (walking and biking) for youth in many communities.

• Research has documented that walking or biking for transportation can burn many calories, but use of such active modes of transportation is uncommon among youth. Children and young adolescents have averaged less than ten minutes per day using active transportation over the past several decades, approximately equal to the energy expenditure required to burn the calories in 1/2 can of a soft drink.[18]

• Travel to school has changed dramatically over the last 40 years. Due to factors including increased distance, safety and security concerns, family reliance on before- and after-school childcare, and inclement weather, far fewer children now walk or ride their bikes to school. Research has confirmed that children who live less than 1/4 mile from school are likely to be active travelers, but those living farther than 1/4 mile away are likely to be driven by parents or transported by school bus. Many students are thus missing an opportunity to increase their daily physical activity participation.[19]

• Children of today spend more time away from home than their counterparts in the past. As a result, formal opportunities for physical activity in school, in after-school programs, and in daycare settings have become more important. Unfortunately, little is known about the amount and type of physical activity that is available to children in nonschool settings.[20]

• Although many organizations and government agencies, including the Centers for Disease Control and Prevention (CDC), recommend that all schools require daily physical education for all students from kindergarten through grade 12, research has confirmed that typical school-based physical education instruction is far from the ideal. Despite this, physical education in today's elementary schools has been demonstrated to play an important role in containing excess weight gain among girls in elementary grades, even in its current form.[21]

In context of these findings, it is clear that physical inactivity has become a health and economic issue of importance. The consequences of physical inactivity have implications for every segment of society, including the health care industry, the American workforce, and even the military.

Regular physical activity promotes lifelong health and is associated with improved academic performance.

Schools currently bear avoidable or reducible costs specifically related to the combined effects of poor nutrition and physical inactivity among students. This economic burden is a result of reduced funding in states where attendance influences the amount of state dollars that local schools receive. In these states, a single day of absence can cost a local school district between $9 and $20 per student. Research has confirmed that severely overweight students miss an average of one day of school per month. Combining estimates of absenteeism with the prevalence of overweight students indicates a potential loss of state aid of $95,000 per year in an average-size Texas school district and $160,000 per year to a similar-size district in California. Obesity-related income losses could be larger among urban districts. It has been estimated that New York City schools could lose about $28 million, Chicago schools could lose about $9 million, and the Los Angeles Unified School District could lose up to $15 million each year as a result of weight-related student absences.[22]

In addition to this obesity-related economic burden confronted by schools, there are growing concerns that obesity disproportionately affects children from families who are least likely to be able to afford medical care, those covered by public health insurance including Medicaid. Obesity-related statistics include

- Children treated for obesity are about three times more expensive for medical care providers than the average child.
- Children diagnosed with obesity are two to three times more likely to be hospitalized than other children.
- Children treated for obesity are far more likely than their nonobese counterparts to be diagnosed with a mental health disorder or a bone or joint problem.
- Children covered by Medicaid are nearly six times more likely to be treated for a diagnosis of obesity, more likely to visit the doctor, and more likely to enter the hospital than comparable children with private insurance.
- However, the national cost of childhood obesity is estimated at about $11 billion for children with private insurance but only $3 billion for those with Medicaid.[23]

Healthy People 2010 specifies several national health promotion objectives related to encouraging physical activity among youth. Review Table 7–2, which contains specific objectives developed to address this issue.[24]

For the purpose of defining healthy levels of physical activity for young people, the International Consensus Conference on Physical Activity Guidelines for Adolescence has suggested that "all adolescents . . . be physically active daily, or nearly every day, as part of play, games, sports, work, transportation, recreation, physical education, or planned exercise, in the context of family, school, and community activities."[25] In support of these recommendations, the most recent research has concluded that "school-age youth should participate every day in 60 minutes or more of moderate to vigorous physical activity that is enjoyable and developmentally appropriate."[26]

Physical Activity and Academic Performance

Of particular interest to education professionals and parents is the growing body of literature confirming that participation in physical activity also is associated with improved academic outcomes for students. Participation in school-based physical activity programs has been linked to improved concentration; better scores on tests of math, reading, and writing skills; and reduced disruptive behaviors. Participation in vigorous physical activity also has been associated with improved student attitudes toward themselves and school.[27]

Physical activity is essential for maximum brain function. While the brain makes up only 2 percent of the body's weight, it uses more than 20 percent of the body's oxygen supply. When children sit for long periods, the blood that carries essential oxygen pools, respiration becomes shallow and slow, and brain function becomes inefficient. As a result, learning can be hindered. Conversely, when children are active, their heart rate is faster, breathing becomes faster and deeper, oxygen-rich blood reaches the brain more quickly, and student performance and learning can improve.

HEALTHY PEOPLE

TABLE 7–2

Healthy People 2010 Objectives Related to Promoting Physical Activity Among Youth

Because physical activity is so important to promoting health and preventing disease, the 2010 national health objectives call for schools to collaborate with families and communities to increase activity opportunities for children and youth. The following specific objectives focus on such an agenda:

Objective 15-31	Increase the proportion of public and private schools that require use of appropriate head, face, eye, and mouth protection for students participating in school-sponsored physical activities.
Objective 22-6	Increase the proportion of adolescents who engage in moderate physical activity for at least thirty minutes on five or more of the previous seven days.
Objective 22-7	Increase the proportion of adolescents who engage in vigorous physical activity that promotes cardiorespiratory fitness three or more days per week for twenty or more minutes per occasion.
Objective 22-8	Increase the proportion of the nation's public and private schools that require daily physical education for all students (particularly in middle and junior high schools).
Objective 22-9	Increase the proportion of adolescents who participate in school physical education daily.
Objective 22-10	Increase the proportion of adolescents who spend at least 50 percent of school physical education class time being physically active.
Objective 22-11	Increase the proportion of children and adolescents who view television two or fewer hours per school day.
Objective 22-12	Increase the proportion of the nation's public and private schools that provide access to their physical activity spaces and facilities for all persons outside of normal school hours.
Objective 22-14	Increase the proportion of trips made by walking (particularly among children and adolescents ages 5–15).
Objective 22-15	Increase the proportion of trips made by bicycling (particularly among children and adolescents ages 5–15).

SOURCE: U.S. Department of Health and Human Services, *Healthy People 2010: Understanding and Improving Health*, 2nd ed. (Washington, DC: U.S. Government Printing Office, 2000).

Research shows that brain development is related to movement as well as the development of motor skills. As motor skills develop, neurons in the brain form synapses (connections) that enable the brain to function better.[28] In addition, physical activity reduces stress, improves mood, and promotes a calming effect among students. These psychosocial benefits might be related to evidence confirming that adolescents who are physically active are less likely to attempt suicide, adopt risk behaviors, and become pregnant. Clearly, such positive health outcomes are related to improved academic prospects.[29,30]

Physical activity has been shown to improve behavior even among children (ages 5–12) diagnosed with attention deficit–hyperactivity disorder (ADHD). Children with

ADHD who exercised about forty minutes five days per week showed improved behavior in as little as three weeks.[31]

These findings received powerful reinforcement in a study conducted by the California Department of Education. In this study, researchers matched individual scores on tests of reading and math proficiency from the spring 2001 administration of state standardized tests of fifth-grade (353,000), seventh-grade (322,000), and ninth-grade (279,000) students with scores from state-mandated fitness tests.

The results of this analysis revealed that higher achievement was associated with higher levels of fitness in all grade levels tested. The relationship between fitness and achievement was greater in math than in reading, particularly among children with the highest fitness levels. In addition, students who met minimum fitness levels in three or more physical fitness areas showed the greatest gains in academic achievement at all three grade levels, and girls at the highest fitness levels demonstrated higher achievement than their male counterparts. In the words of State Superintendent of Public Instruction Delaine Eastin, "We now have the proof we've been looking for: Students achieve best when they are physically fit;" and, she asserted, "Every student [in California] should have quality physical education experiences from kindergarten through high school."[32]

Given the national focus on improving proficiency test outcomes for students, such a broad change in school programming and policy is warranted but unlikely in the near future. In light of this reality, Eric Jensen suggests that active learning has advantages over sedentary learning. Benefits include outcomes that are longer-lasting, better remembered, more fun, and age-appropriate. He urges simply that classroom teachers integrate a better blend of sitting and moving into daily classroom practice. Teachers are encouraged to consider the following strategies to exploit the relationship between physical activity and academic outcomes:

- Engage students in a greater variety of postures (walking, lying, moving, leaning, perching, or squatting) during classroom instruction.
- Engage students in movement.
- Encourage students to use their bodies to learn (demonstrate concepts, words, or rhythms).
- Incorporate daily or weekly role-plays as a way to dramatize key concepts.
- Take stand-and-stretch breaks every twenty minutes to energize the class.[33]

These recommendations are based on brain research that shows students learn best in time segments no longer than twenty minutes, followed by a two- to five-minute period of movement of some kind. Deviations from such a routine are likely to produce less than desirable outcomes. For example, during a forty-minute lesson in which no opportunity for gross motor activity has been provided, retention is very high for the first eight to ten minutes and again during the last three to five minutes. This is an example of the *primary–recency factor,* in which retention declines sharply between peak periods at the start and end of the lesson.

Having fun at physical activities while young helps promote continuing patterns of physical activity throughout the life span.

When teachers increase the length of a lesson, retention levels remain stable at the beginning and the end of the time period. The only difference between a twenty-minute lesson and a forty-minute lesson is the greater length of the "downtime" in the middle of the longer lesson.

In addition to increasing the number and variety of active learning strategies across the school day, teachers are encouraged to keep time parameters, particularly for younger students, as close to a twenty-minute ideal as possible. Such a time management strategy will support consistently high levels of retention at the beginning and end of lessons and minimize the length of downtime.[34]

Factors That Influence Physical Activity

Research has identified many factors that are associated with the patterns of physical activity among children and youth. Demographic variables, including sex, age, and race or ethnicity, have been demonstrated to account for variations in students' exercise behaviors. For example, girls are less physically active than boys, and adolescents are less active than younger children. Also, white students tend to be more physically active than their Hispanic and black counterparts.[35]

In addition to identified demographic variables, a number of individual variables have been shown to influence participation in physical activity. Students who perceive benefits from participating in physical activity or sports (having fun, learning or refining new skills, staying in shape, improving appearance, and improving strength, endurance, or flexibility) are more likely to engage in a range of physical activities. Conversely, students who perceive barriers to participating in physical activities, particularly a lack of time, are less likely to engage in exercise behaviors.[36]

Also, physical activity among children and adolescents is influenced by interpersonal and environmental factors. In particular, both the support and the physical activity behaviors of friends, siblings, and parents have been shown to influence the exercise behaviors of youth.[37] Finally, convenient play spaces, well-functioning sports equipment, and transportation to sports or fitness activities also have been demonstrated to positively influence student participation in physical activities.[38]

In this regard, many young people are confronted with barriers to establishing and maintaining a physically active lifestyle. In particular, educators and other advocates must acknowledge the following impediments:

1. In many communities, patterns of housing and urban development have centered on the use of the automobile. In such locales, walking and bicycling are discouraged, making it difficult for children to meet and participate in active play.
2. Increased concerns about safety have limited the time and locations in which children can play outside.
3. Appealing technology and electronic media (video- and computer games, cable and satellite TV) encourage a sedentary lifestyle for many young people.
4. Unfortunately, despite the evidence that active children learn better, many states and school districts have cut recess programs and reduced the requirements for participation in physical education classes. This problem is compounded in districts in which an unreasonable teacher–student ratio in physical education classes contributes to a risky or ineffective learning environment.
5. Due to budget constraints or other priorities, many communities have failed to invest in the development and maintenance of facilities, including parks and recreation centers, that are close to home for children and youth.[39]

These circumstances largely are beyond the control of most young people, but they conspire against the physical activity pursuits among even the most highly motivated youth. Recognition of such issues is critical if communities, schools, and families are to intervene with well-planned and collaborative solutions.

GUIDELINES FOR SCHOOLS

State of the Practice

As discussed earlier in this chapter and in Chapter 6, on promoting healthy eating, the majority of American youth are sedentary and do not eat well. These unhealthy practices

TABLE 7–3

Percent of U.S. Schools That Require Physical Education in Elementary and Middle Grades

Grade	Percent of Schools
Kindergarten	49.7
1	57.2
2	57.7
3	58.0
4	58.2
5	61.1
6	68.1
7	67.1
8	65.5

Source: S. Lee, C. Burgeson, J. Fulton, and C. Spain, "Physical Education and Physical Activity: Results from the School Health Policies and Programs Study 2006," *Journal of School Health* 77, no. 8 (October 2007): 449.

can lead to academic difficulties and to health problems that continue into adulthood. In addition to other associated problems, one of the most significant consequences of poor eating and physical inactivity is the risk of becoming overweight. Nearly 80 percent of overweight children and adolescents remain overweight or become obese adults with the potential to develop elevated cholesterol and blood pressure, gallbladder disease, joint problems, Type 2 diabetes, and depression.[40] Unfortunately, as discussed in Chapter 2, schools are making the choice to reduce physical activity opportunities for students. The recommendations are clear. In addition to the previously discussed research recommending that children engage in at least sixty minutes and as much as several hours of age-appropriate physical activity on all or most days of the week for best health outcomes, the Institute of Medicine has suggested that students be given the opportunity to participate in at least 30 minutes of physical activity each school day.[41]

As a foundation for promoting physical activity for children, it is important to understand where and when they accumulate their activity time. During the typical school day, students have three distinct opportunities to be active: in physical education classes, during recess or lunch periods, and either before or after school. Of these opportunities, schools can exercise the most control over the amount of activity embedded in physical education classes. Because the others are considered to be more discretionary periods, children are freer to make choices about the amount and types of activities in which they participate.[42]

Unfortunately, few schools meet optimal targets for formal physical education programming. The National Association of Sport and Physical Education (NASPE) recommends that elementary schools offer a minimum of 225 minutes, and secondary schools a minimum of 150 minutes, of physical education instruction per week. At present, only about 3.8 percent of elementary schools and 7.9 percent of middle schools provide daily physical education.[43]

Review Table 7–3 to gain a better understanding of the prevalence of required physical education instruction in the nation's elementary and middle schools.[44] In addition,

TABLE 7–4

SHPPS

School Health Policies and Programs Study 2006 Data Related to Physical Education Topics

Topic	Percent of Schools Teaching Topic in a Required Course	
	Elementary Schools	Middle/Junior High Schools
Balancing food intake and physical activity	64.3	60.1
Dangers of using performance-enhancing drugs	28.6	51.2
Developing an individualized physical activity plan	NA	46.7
Health-related fitness	87.4	91.9
How to find valid physical activity information and services	40.7	46.1
How much activity is enough	67.4	73.2
Monitoring progress toward personal goals (from individualized plan)	NA	54.7
Physical activity opportunities in the local community	73.4	74.5
Phases of a workout	88.9	88.3
Benefits of physical activity	85.6	86.3
Preventing injuries during physical activity	91.3	92.8
Role of physical activity in reducing disease risk	75.9	75.6

SOURCE: Centers for Disease Control and Prevention, *School Health Policies and Programs Study 2006* (SHPPS) (Atlanta, GA: CDC, 2007). www.cdc.gov/HealthyYouth/shpps

Table 7–4 presents data from the School Health Policies and Programs Study (SHPPS), providing insight into the variety of issues addressed during physical education classes.[45] While SHPPS 2006 results for teaching physical education topics are encouraging, they demonstrate the need for increased and more consistent school-based efforts to promote physical activity across the school community.

State of the Art

Given the unfortunate reality about the amount of current programming to promote physical activity among youth, researchers have developed four developmentally appropriate guidelines to improve the fitness and health

Children should accumulate a minimum of sixty minutes of daily physical activity. Activity can be spread throughout the day—recess, physical education class, after-school play, and sport practices all count towards total activity time.

prospects of youth. These guidelines focus on improving physical activity types, amounts, and opportunities for young people.

- *Guideline 1: Children should accumulate at least sixty minutes, and up to several hours, of age-appropriate physical activity on all or most days of the week.* This daily accumulation should include both moderate and vigorous types of activities, with the majority of activity time being devoted to intermittent activities.[46] Though sixty minutes is the recommended minimum for daily activity for children, they need to accumulate more than this amount for optimal health benefits. Daily activities should be both moderate (equal in intensity to brisk walking) and vigorous (more intense than brisk walking). Among children, the majority of the physical activity accumulated throughout the day will come in intermittent activity bursts of a few seconds to several minutes in length. Children should *not* be expected to participate in periods (longer than several minutes) of continuous vigorous activity.[47]

- *Guideline 2: Children should participate in several longer bouts of physical activity each day (lasting fifteen minutes or more).*

Most of the activity in which children participate will come in short bursts that accumulate over the day. If optimal benefits are to be achieved however, as much as one-fourth of activity time should be accumulated across longer (fifteen minutes or more) exercise periods. Children should balance longer or more frequent activity bursts with time for rest and recovery.[48]

- *Guideline 3: Children should participate in a variety of age-appropriate types of physical activity each day as a foundation for optimal health, fitness, and performance benefits.*

Daily activity for children should be varied but should include some lifestyle, active aerobics, and active sports and recreation types of pursuits. Review the discussion of the Physical Activity Pyramid in the next section; it was developed to meet the activity needs of children.[49]

- *Guideline 4: Extended periods (lasting two hours or longer) of inactivity are discouraged for children.*

According to research, students who watch excessive amounts of TV, play computer games, or engage in other low-energy activities are not likely to meet these activity guidelines.[50] Although devoting time to positive but less active pursuits (studying, reading, thinking, family time) is important, students are encouraged to avoid accumulating extended periods of inactivity (two hours or longer). Children are encouraged to be active when opportunities are available to them, including before and after school, at appropriate times during the school day, and on weekends or other nonschool days.[51]

GUIDELINES FOR CLASSROOM APPLICATIONS

Schools and communities have the potential to increase the amount of healthy physical activity among students through the provision of instruction, programming, and services. As noted in Chapter 1, school-based efforts to promote physical activity among young people should be formalized as part of the Coordinated School Health Program. In addition, community-based physical activity programs are essential since most physical activity among young people occurs during discretionary time away from the school setting.[52] In this context, schools and communities would be wise to coordinate efforts to make the best use of personnel and resources.

While the efforts of physical educators and classroom teachers are critical, in "Guidelines for School and Community Programs to Promote Lifelong Physical Activity Among Young People," the CDC has published a comprehensive agenda for school and community programs to promote physical activity among young people. This agenda is based on four key principles that suggest physical activity programs for young people are more likely to be effective when they

- Emphasize enjoyable participation in physical activities that are easily done throughout life
- Offer a range of diverse competitive and noncompetitive activities that are developmentally appropriate for different ages and abilities
- Provide the skills and confidence that young people need to be physically active
- Promote physical activity throughout all elements of the Coordinated School Health Program and cultivate links between school and community programs.[53]

To support program development and coordination, the CDC has provided the following ten broad recommendations and clarifying elements to help schools and communities promote physical activity among youth:

1. Establish policies that promote enjoyable, lifelong physical activity.
   - Require daily physical education and comprehensive health education (including lessons on physical activity) for all students in grades K through 12.
   - Provide adequate funding, equipment, and supervision for programs that meet the needs and interests of all students.
2. Provide physical and social environments that encourage and enable young people to engage in safe and enjoyable physical activity.
   - Provide access to safe spaces and facilities and implement measures to prevent activity-related injuries and illnesses.
   - Provide school time, such as recess, for unstructured physical activity, such as rope jumping.
   - Discourage the use or withholding of physical activity as punishment.
   - Provide health promotion programs for school faculty and staff.
3. Implement sequential physical education curricula and instruction in grades K through 12.
   - Emphasize enjoyable participation in lifetime physical activities, including walking and dancing, not just competitive sports.
   - Help students develop the knowledge, attitudes, and skills they need to adopt and maintain a physically active lifestyle.
   - Follow the National Standards for Physical Education developed by the National Association for Sport and Physical Education.
   - Keep students active for most of class time.
4. Implement health education curricula.
   - Feature active learning strategies and follow the National Health Education Standards.
   - Help students develop the knowledge, attitudes, and skills they need to adopt and maintain a healthy lifestyle.
5. Provide extracurricular activity programs that offer diverse, developmentally appropriate activities (competitive and noncompetitive) for all students.
6. Encourage parents and guardians to support their children's participation in physical activity, to be physically active role models, and to include physical activity in family events.
7. Provide training for teachers, coaches, recreation and health care personnel, and other school and community professionals to enable them to promote enjoyable, lifelong activity to young people.
8. Assess the physical activity patterns of youth, refer them to appropriate physical activity programs, and advocate for physical activity instruction and programs for young people.
9. Provide a range of developmentally appropriate community sports and recreation programs that are attractive to all young people.
10. Evaluate physical activity instruction, programs, and facilities regularly.[54]

Consider This 7.1

Elements of Health-Related Fitness

CARDIORESPIRATORY (AEROBIC) ENDURANCE

1. Aerobic endurance is the ability of the cardiovascular system (heart, blood, blood vessels, and lungs) to transport and utilize oxygen efficiently.
2. Aerobically healthy people can perform required tasks for extensive periods of time.
3. Inefficient cardiovascular fitness results in shortness of breath, fatigue, and the inability to work at normal tasks over time.
4. Long-term chronic diseases, such as diabetes, obesity, high blood pressure, and heart disease, are associated with poor cardiorespiratory fitness.
5. The process of cardiorespiratory disease starts in early childhood.
6. Aerobic endurance is enhanced by regular participation in such activities as running, bicycling, swimming, fast walking, and aerobic dance.

MUSCULAR STRENGTH AND ENDURANCE

1. Muscular strength is the amount of force one can exert to accomplish a task.
2. Endurance is the ability to use muscles over time without fatigue.
3. The likelihood of injury is reduced with increased muscle strength.
4. Muscular strength and endurance are developed through use of the muscles.
5. Although weight training may be appropriate for adolescents and adults, weight lifting is not recommended for students in elementary grades.

6. Younger children are encouraged to participate in activities such as push-ups (strengthen the triceps and chest muscles) chin-ups (biceps), and curl-ups (back and abdominal muscles).
7. Proper instruction is important to achieve the greatest benefit.

FLEXIBILITY

1. Flexibility is the range of movement of body joints and involves the ability to bend, stretch, and twist.
2. Inactivity can result in loss of flexibility, which is associated with risk for injury, poor posture, and discomfort.
3. Healthy levels of flexibility increase the ability to perform daily tasks and reduce injury risks.
4. Flexibility can be improved by slow, sustained stretching of the muscles and joints.
5. Quick, bouncing, or ballistic stretching exercises should be avoided.
6. Developmentally appropriate flexibility exercises include toe touches, sitting and curling of the back with the head between the knees, trunk-twists, and reach-and-stretch exercises.

BODY COMPOSITION

1. Body composition is the percentage of fat present in the body.
2. Risk factors associated with high body fat can be reduced by modifying body composition through diet and exercise.
3. School screening activities are helpful in early identification of children with potential weight problems (weight/growth charts and triceps skinfold thickness testing).

SOURCE: C. Caspersen, K. Powell. and G. Christenson, "Physical Activity, Exercise, and Physical Fitness: Definition and Distinctions for Health-Related Research," *Public Health Reports* 100, no. 2 (1985): 126–31.

In conclusion, coordinated school and community programs that promote a pattern of ongoing physical activity among young people are regarded as highly effective health promotion strategies. Such collaborative initiatives have shown promise in reducing the public health burden of chronic diseases associated with sedentary lifestyles. The attributes of the most successful programs include a focus on equipping students with knowledge, attitudes, motor and behavioral skills, and the confidence to be physically active during youth. With this foundation, lifelong physical activity patterns are likely to be established.[55]

Important Background for K–8 Teachers

As a foundation for advocacy and health promotion, teachers must be fluent in basic science and the terminology of physical activity and fitness. A discussion of important concepts and issues follows.

Fundamental Concepts and Definitions

As a foundation for promoting student activity, understanding the scientific literature, and supporting their professional physical education colleagues, elementary and middle school classroom teachers would be wise to review the distinctions among physical activity, exercise, and physical fitness. *Physical activity* is defined as any movement produced by skeletal muscles that results in the expenditure of energy. Physical activity is a broad term that includes exercise, sport, dance, and other forms of movement. In this context, *exercise* is defined as a subset of physical activity—planned, structured, and repetitive movement done with the purpose of improving or maintaining physical fitness. Consistent with this definition, *physical fitness* includes a set of attributes that are either health-related or motor skill–related and provides a foundation for daily living, leisure activities, and reduction of chronic disease.[56]

The elements of physical fitness that are health-related or have been demonstrated to have health benefits include cardiorespiratory (aerobic) endurance, muscular strength and endurance, flexibility, and body composition. Further information about each of these four elements of health-related fitness appears in Consider This 7.1.[57]

In this context, it is very healthy for students to participate in a range of moderate (walking to school, bicycling, dancing, hopscotch, some chores or yardwork) and vigorous (active games, jumping rope, running, in-line or rollerskating) physical activities. Students participate in physical activity and exercise in a variety of settings, including their homes, schools, playgrounds, public parks and recreation centers, private clubs or sports facilities, hiking/biking trails, summer camps, dance studios, and religious facilities.[58]

Developmentally Appropriate Concepts and Skills

As with all health promotion content, administrators, teachers, and parents are reminded of the importance of organizing physical activity programming based on the developmental abilities and interests of learners. Rather than attempting to adapt adult activity models, parents and professionals are encouraged to start program planning with a review of the following twelve elements that influence children's interest in and fidelity to participation in physical activity programs:

1. *Young animals, including humans, are inherently active.* Young children are considerably more active than teens and adults. The most dramatic drop in activity levels occurs in the teen years. However, young children will take full advantage of opportunities to be active. If opportunities for physical activity for children decrease, a drop in activity levels for all age groups is likely.

2. *Compared to their adult counterparts, children have a relatively short attention span.* As children get older, the length of time they can maintain interest in any one activity increases. As a result, parents, teachers, and physical activity programmers are reminded that activities that are long in duration are not likely to capture the attention of younger learners.

3. *Children are more likely to be concrete rather than abstract thinkers.* Children need concrete reasons, feedback, and evidence of success to persist in an activity. To increase the likelihood that children will participate in physical activity consistently, professionals must offer tangible rationales and benefits beyond the potential for improved health at a future time.

4. *Children need frequent periods of rest following bursts of intermittent activity.* Alternating bursts of activity followed by periods of rest or recovery are developmentally appropriate for children. This pattern may persist over a long time and may be necessary for stimulating growth and development.

5. *There is not a strong relationship between physical activity and measures of physical fitness in young children.* High scores on measures of physical fitness among children and youth are influenced by many variables, including chronological age, physiological age (maturation), and hereditary potential. Although consistently physically active, some children might not receive high fitness scores. The associated frustration experienced by some children can become a disincentive for persisting in physical activity.

6. *Physical activity provides a significant medium for learning among children and youth.* Children and youth are highly intrinsically motivated to seek control over their physical environment. Young children gain mastery of their physical environment through the successful performance of physical tasks. Learning to walk leads to mobility and increased control over the environment, and manipulating objects is related to feelings of power and achievement for young children.

7. *Numerous skills involved in adult recreation and leisure are learned during the school-age years.* While it is never too late to learn, most of the motor skills used in adult recreation and leisure are learned during youth. People who do not acquire requisite skills early in life are less likely to learn and use them during adulthood.

8. *Although high-intensity physical activity has benefits, it may be associated with reduced persistence in many adults and children.* Both moderate- and high-intensity physical activities are associated with many short- and long-term benefits. However, high-intensity activity may reduce exercise adherence in some people. This is particularly true of children who have little time to rest and recover and those who perceive such activities to be too difficult for the benefits they receive.

9. *Inactive children and youth are much more likely to become sedentary adults than are active children.* Childhood activity patterns tend to be closely related to physical activity practices in adulthood. Although a high level of childhood activity is not a direct predictor of adult behaviors, inactivity in childhood is very closely associated with inactivity in adulthood.

10. *Self-efficacy (feeling that one can be successful) is a powerful predictor of lifelong participation in physical activity.* People who believe they can experience success in physical activity are more likely to pursue such activities than are their counterparts. Consequently, parents and teachers should organize activities that reinforce self-efficacy about exercise participation.

11. *Youth who have active parents and family members with whom they can participate in consistent exercise are more likely to be physically active than are their counterparts.* Parental and family engagement and reinforcement are critical elements for establishing regular physical activity patterns for children and youth.

12. *Just as habits of regular physical activity can be established, inactivity also can become habitual if youth are not provided with developmentally appropriate opportunities for activity.* Parents and teachers must integrate ongoing physical activity into daily routines as a foundation for establishing health-enhancing exercise habits.[59]

The Physical Activity Pyramid

As a foundation for reinforcing developmentally appropriate participation in a range of physical activities, scholars have developed MyActivity Pyramid (Figure 7–1). Similar

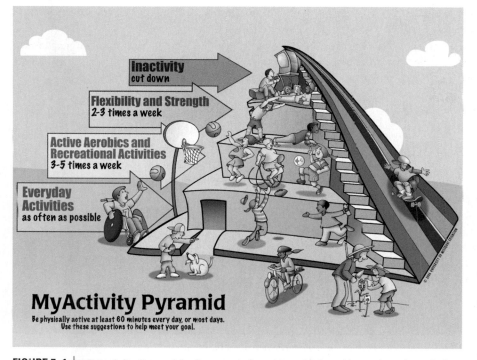

Inactivity
cut down

Flexibility and Strength
2–3 times a week

Active Aerobics and Recreational Activities
3–5 times a week

Everyday Activities
as often as possible

MyActivity Pyramid

Be physically active at least 60 minutes every day, or most days.
Use these suggestions to help meet your goal.

FIGURE 7–1 | MyActivity Pyramid For more information, visit http://extension.missouri.edu. SOURCE: University of Missouri Extension, Department of Nutritional Sciences (Family Nutrition Education Programs), Adapted from USDA's MyPyramid and funded in part by USDA's Food Stamp Program. *MyActivity Pyramid*. N386, July 2006, (http://extension.Missouri.edu/explore/hesguide/foodnut/n00386.htm)

to the MyPyramid food guidance system (see Chapter 6), the MyActivity Pyramid provides a visual representation of the recommended types and amounts of healthy exercise behavior. Five types of physical activities make up the bottom three levels of the pyramid:

- Base level – Everyday activities (to do as often as possible)
- 2nd level – Active aerobics and recreational activities (to do 3–5 times each week for at least 20 minutes)
- 3rd level – Flexibility and strength (to do 2–3 times each week for at least 20 minutes)[60]

Within the levels of the pyramid are identified activities that are important elements of any personal physical activity plan. Also, it is important to participate in a variety of activities within each of the activities categories. The tip of the pyramid, activities to cutdown on, reinforces the importance of avoiding periods of rest and inactivity. MyActivity Pyramid can serve as an excellent starting point for developing educational activities for students in elementary and middle schools. Not only does it provide direction for teachers, but Figure 7–1 also can help children learn the kinds of activities that are necessary to maintain health, and identify activity suggestions to do alone and with others.[61]

The base level of the MyActivity Pyramid shows recommended participation in everyday activities. These activities form the foundation of the pyramid because research has confirmed the positive health benefits of daily participation in them. Children are encouraged to accu-

mulate as many of their sixty minutes or more a day of any activity from this category. Activities done as part of a typical daily routine that require involvement of the large muscles of the body are considered to be everyday activities. Activities such as walking to school, climbing stairs, raking leaves, and doing vigorous household chores fit into this category. These are types of activities in which children commonly participate. Adults whose daily routine includes physical work, such as digging or lifting, are engaging in everyday activities.[62]

The second level of the MyActivity Pyramid includes two categories of activities. The active aerobics category includes those activities that can be done for long periods of time without stopping. For optimal health benefits, activities such as walking, jogging, biking, swimming, and hiking should be done at least at moderately vigorous levels. The recreation category includes tennis, soccer, basketball, racquetball, and skiing. Although activities such as bowling and golf generally require relatively low energy output, they are considered to have health benefits when they are part of a more comprehensive physical activity program. Many other recreational or leisure activities (playing cards or chess) do not fit into this physical activity category because they involve little calorie expenditure.[63]

The third level of the MyActivity Pyramid also comprises two categories of physical activities. Some leisure and playtime activities that increase body strength, such as swinging and canoing, make up one part of this level. In addition, flexibility exercises are exercises and physical activities performed to increase the length of muscles and connective tissue. Flexibility exercises increase the range of motion of joints and help reduce the likelihood of injury. In general, children are more flexible than adults are. While many activities in other categories of the pyramid might contribute to increased flexibility, even the most active adults must participate in specific exercises to gain the benefits associated with improved flexibility.[64]

The tip of the pyramid highlights those activities to cut down on. These activities include completely sedentary (passive) activities and activities that require little large-muscle activity (playing computer games). It must be noted that activities such as reading and television viewing have been shown to have some health benefits in the areas of stress management and relaxation. It is not necessary for students to abstain from such activities unless they limit participation in other, more physical, activities. Rest and inactivity are valuable only as a supplement to participation in activities from the other three levels in the MyActivity Pyramid.[65]

Promoting Physical Activity: The Role of Physical Education

A high-quality physical education program is the cornerstone of a school's physical activity programming, and a well-written curriculum is the foundation for such a program.[66] As for other content areas, the National Association for Sport and Physical Education (NASPE) has developed content standards to improve school-based physical education programs for students (Teacher's Toolbox 7.1).[67] Though a sound physical education program taught by qualified instructors whose practice is consistent with NASPE standards for professional practice is a critical foundational element of a school-based commitment to promoting physical activity, advocates of such a categorical approach are reminded of the complexity of promoting any health-enhancing behavior.

The ways in which fitness activities are taught and reinforced contribute to student attitudes about the value of being active for a lifetime. Because children spend a large percentage of their waking hours at school, it is more educationally sound to develop a coordinated approach to promoting participation in physical activities. In a coordinated approach, a formalized physical education curriculum, planned recess, and short activity periods are supplemented by a range of opportunities for activity during the school day. Classroom teachers should integrate physical activities into cross-curricular instructional approaches. Through such an agenda, many professionals are sending a consistent message about the value of daily physical activity.[68]

As a foundation, researchers have identified the following guidelines for promoting physical activity in the physical education setting. However, classroom teachers are encouraged to examine ways they can collaborate with their physical education colleagues to extend this agenda beyond the confines of the gymnasium. In conclusion, all education professionals are encouraged to

1. Provide time for activity in the school setting.
2. Encourage self-monitoring of physical activity.
3. Provide opportunities in which activities can be individualized.
4. Expose students to a variety of activities.
5. During instruction, focus feedback on the value of regular participation and personal accomplishment,

Classroom teachers can promote physical activity in many ways, including integrating activity time into the daily classroom routine and using cross-curricular instructional strategies.

Teacher's Toolbox 7.1

National Standards for Physical Education

A physically educated person meets the following standards:

Standard 1: Demonstrates competency in motor skills and movement patterns needed to perform a variety of physical activities

Standard 2: Demonstrates understanding of movement concepts, principles, strategies, and tactics as they apply to the learning and performance of physical activities

Standard 3: Participates regularly in physical activity

Standard 4: Achieves and maintains a health-enhancing level of physical fitness

Standard 5: Exhibits responsible personal and social behavior that respects self and others in physical activity settings

Standard 6: Values physical activity for health, enjoyment, challenge, self-expression, and/or social interaction

SOURCE: *Moving Into the Future: National Standards for Physical Education*, 2nd edition (2004). Reprinted with permission from the National Association for Sport and Physical Education (NASPE), 1900 Association Drive, Reston, VA 20191–1599.

---

rather than on factors such as how fast, how many, or how difficult.

6. Reinforce physical skills.

7. Be an active role model.

8. Pay attention to student attitudes about the value of a lifetime of activity.

9. Reinforce successful accomplishment and minimize self-criticism.

10. Promote participation in activities outside the school environment.

11. Encourage participation in activities that can endure for a lifetime.[69]

Classroom teachers who are concerned that promoting such an agenda might require too much time and equipment may review the suggestions in Teacher's Toolbox 7.2.

Recommendations for Concepts and Practice

Healthy Behavior Outcomes

The goal of health education is to help students adopt or maintain health-enhancing behaviors. School districts and teachers should identify the health-enhancing behaviors they would like their students to maintain or adopt. The following list identifies some possible healthy behavior outcomes related to promoting physical activity. Although not all the suggestions are developmentally appropriate for students in grades K–8, this list can help teachers understand how the learning activities they plan for their students support both short- and long-term desired behavior outcomes.

Ways to Promote Healthy Behavior Outcomes for Physical Activity

Engage in moderate to vigorous physical activity for at least sixty minutes every day.

Regularly engage in physical activities that enhance cardiorespiratory endurance, flexibility, muscle endurance, and muscle strength.

Engage in warm-up and cool-down activities before and after exercise.

Drink plenty of water before, during, and after physical activity.

Avoid injury during physical activity.[70]

Developmentally Appropriate Concepts and Skills

As with other health topics, teaching related to promoting physical activity should be developmentally appropriate and be based on the physical, social, emotional, and language characteristics of specific students. Teacher's Toolbox 7.3 contains a list of developmentally appropriate concepts and skills to help teachers create lessons that will encourage students to practice the desired behavior outcomes by the time they graduate from high school.[71] Note that these grade-level spans are aligned with the 2007 National Health Education Standards discussed in Chapter 3.

Teacher's Toolbox 7.2

A Little Bit of Equipment, a Lot of Physical Activity

Teachers don't need a lot of complex or expensive equipment to promote physical activity among their students. Here are a few tips:

- Integrate physical activity into daily classroom practice. Think of physical activity in the same way you think about reading. Every child needs a book, and everyone needs to read—not just those students who are good at it or who enjoy it. Similarly, all children need lots of activity, not just the talented and/or interested students.

- Change the format of games in which children are "out" if they don't perform with success. Rather than sitting out for the rest of the game, children who would be considered "out" can create another group (perhaps called "lost and found") for the remainder of the ongoing round of activity.

- Look at games like "Duck-Duck Goose," "Drop the Handkerchief," and relays with new eyes. In all these games, only a few students are moving as many others stand and wait, rather than practicing, participating, and learning. Teachers would never consider using such activities to promote skill development in reading. Similarly, it is not an effective way to promote physical activity.

- Find new ways to move students into groups rather than having students pick teams. Often, the same students get picked last—no wonder they dislike activities for which they need the most practice.

- Play games with many smaller teams (e.g., lots of small games of volleyball like on the beach, or many smaller teams involved in kickball or softball games).

- Use many jump ropes (no more than three children per rope, two to turn the rope and one to jump) to avoid having children wait in lines.

- Use music and dance whenever possible to reinforce academic concepts and promote fun and activity.

- Set up activity learning centers in the classroom (see a description in Chapter 4). A small amount of equipment can go a long way, and many children can rotate through many kinds of activities in very little time.

- Finally, just a few cautions concerning physical activity in the classroom:

  Never use physical activity as punishment for poor academic performance or problem behavior!

  Reinforce positive attitudes toward activity rather than cultivating negative or punishment associations about being active.

  Never withhold recess as punishment for behavior problems, and never use recess, physical education, or other activity times as an opportunity for making up late or missed work.

Developmentally Appropriate Concepts and Skills for Promoting Physical Activity

Grades K–2 Concepts	Grades 3–5 Concepts	Grades 6–8 Concepts

NHES 1: Core Concepts

Grades K–2 Concepts	Grades 3–5 Concepts	Grades 6–8 Concepts
• Describe the recommended amount of physical activity for children. • Explain ways to be active every day. • Describe behaviors that are physically active and physically inactive. • Describe the benefits of being physically active.	• Summarize the recommended amount of physical activity for children. • Describe the importance of choosing a variety of ways to be physically active. • Identify short-term and long-term benefits of moderate and vigorous physical activity, such as improving cardiovascular health, strength, endurance, and flexibility and reducing the risks for chronic diseases. • Describe how both eating habits and level of physical activity can affect a person's weight. • Identify ways to increase daily physical activity. • Identify behaviors that contribute to maintaining a healthy weight. • Identify safety precautions for physical activities in different kinds of weather and climates. • Identify basic safety precautions to help prevent injury during physical activity. • Discuss the benefits of drinking water before, during, and after physical activity. • Describe how to ride a bike, skateboard, scooter, and inline skate safely. • Identify personal protection equipment needed for sports and recreational activities, such as mouthpieces, pads, and helmets.	• Explain that incorporating daily moderate or vigorous physical activity into one's life does not require a structured exercise plan or special exercise equipment. • Differentiate between physical activity, exercise, health-related fitness, and skill-related fitness. • Analyze the short-term and long-term physical benefits of moderate and vigorous physical activity, including improving cardiovascular health, strength, endurance, and flexibility and reducing the risks for chronic diseases. • Analyze the mental and social benefits of physical activity. • Describe the recommended amounts and types of moderate and vigorous physical activity for adolescents and adults. • Identify ways to increase daily physical activity and decrease inactivity. • Summarize how physical activity and eating habits can contribute to maintaining a healthy body weight. • Describe physical activities that contribute to maintaining or improving the components of health-related fitness, such as cardio-respiratory fitness, muscular strength, endurance, flexibility, and body composition. • Summarize the benefits of drinking water before, during, and after physical activity. • Discuss climate-related physical conditions that affect physical activity, such as heat exhaustion, sunburn, heat stroke, and hypothermia. • Discuss how an inactive lifestyle contributes to chronic disease. • Explain the importance of warming up before and cooling down after physical activity. • Describe how using tobacco could hurt one's goals for physical fitness and athletic performance. • Describe the health risks of using performance-enhancing drugs. • Identify healthy and risky approaches to weight management. • Describe the use of safety equipment for specific physical activities. • Describe ways to reduce risk of injuries from participation in sports and other physical activities. • Summarize how to safely ride a bike and scooter, and use a skateboard or inline skates. • Analyze the importance of using helmets and other safety gear for biking, riding a scooter, skateboarding, and inline skating.

Grades K–2 Skills	Grades 3–5 Skills	Grades 6–8 Skills

NHES 2: Analyze Influence

Grades K–2 Skills	Grades 3–5 Skills	Grades 6–8 Skills
• Explain how television viewing can decrease an individual's level of physical activity. • Describe how peers can help an individual be physically active. • Describe activities an individual's family can do that would increase physical activity.	• Describe factors that influence a person to be physically active or inactive. • Describe how television, computer, and video games can influence an individual's level of physical activity. • Describe how family and cultural traditions influence physical activity. • Describe how peers can influence physical activity. • Identify strategies used in the media to influence the selection of products related to physical activity, such as sport shoes and equipment.	• Describe how personal and family values influence decisions about physical activity. • Discuss the influence of television, computers, and video games on physical activity behavior. • Discuss the influence of the physical environment on a person's interest in and ability to be physically active. • Discuss how cultural traditions influence physical activity. • Analyze how peers and family can influence a person's physical activity level. • Analyze how media can influence decisions to be physically active. • Demonstrate the influence of media on the selection of physical activity products. • Explain that physical activity does not require the purchase of expensive equipment or gear.

NHES 3: Accessing Information, Products, and Services

Grades K–2 Skills	Grades 3–5 Skills	Grades 6–8 Skills
• Identify people who can provide accurate information about physical activity.	• Identify reliable sources of information about physical activity. • Demonstrate the ability to access accurate information about physical activity. • Identify places where young people and families can be physically active. • Identify places to get physical activity equipment.	• Summarize reliable sources of information about physical activity. • Demonstrate the ability to access accurate sources of information about physical activity and fitness planning. • Evaluate the accuracy of fitness-related information. • Analyze places where youth and families can be physically active. • Locate accurate information about physical activity equipment. • Locate sources that encourage youth participation in physical activity. • Demonstrate the ability to access sources of accurate information about healthy and safe weight management. • Analyze the accuracy of claims of performance-enhancing products and supplements.

NHES 4: Interpersonal Communication

Grades K–2 Skills	Grades 3–5 Skills	Grades 6–8 Skills
• Demonstrate how to ask for help from trusted adults to improve physical activity.	• Demonstrate interpersonal skills for dealing with peer influence to be physically inactive. • Demonstrate effective negotiation skills to avoid unsafe physical activity.	• Demonstrate interpersonal skills to help deal with negative peer influences on physical activity. • Demonstrate effective negotiation skills to avoid sedentary leisure activities.

NHES 5: Decision Making

Grades K–2 Skills	Grades 3–5 Skills	Grades 6–8 Skills
• Choose active over inactive behaviors. • Identify physically active alternatives to watching television or playing video games.	• Choose active over inactive behaviors. • Explain positive outcomes for being physically active. • Identify physically active alternatives to watching television or playing video games.	• Choose active over inactive behaviors. • Summarize positive outcomes for being physically active.

(continued)

Grades K–2 Skills *(continued)*	Grades 3–5 Skills *(continued)*	Grades 6–8 Skills *(continued)*

NHES 6: Goal Setting

• Describe how being physically active can help a person feel better.	• Explain positive outcomes for being physically active. • Set a goal to increase daily physical activity. • Identify barriers to being regularly physically active. • Describe strategies to overcome barriers to being physically active. • Make a personal commitment to be physically active. • Make a personal commitment to use appropriate protective gear during physical activity. • Monitor progress in attaining a physical activity goal.	• Assess personal physical activity level. • Set a goal to increase physical activity. • Analyze barriers to being regularly physically active. • Develop a plan for overcoming barriers to physical activity. • Make a personal commitment to be physically active. • Monitor progress in attaining a physical activity goal.

NHES 7: Self-Management

• Demonstrate ways to be physically active in cooperation with others. • Demonstrate the ability to follow playground rules.	• Express intentions to be physically active regularly. • Express intentions to use protective gear to avoid injuries. • Demonstrate a variety of ways to be physically active. • Demonstrate how to do different types of developmentally appropriate physical activity. • Describe precautions for physical activity in weather and climate conditions such as very high or low temperatures, wet or snowy play surfaces, and direct sunlight. • Demonstrate the correct use of protective equipment during sports and physical activity. • Demonstrate the ability to follow playground safety rules.	• Express intentions to be physically active regularly. • Express intentions to use protective gear to avoid injuries during physical activity. • Demonstrate how to warm up and cool down in order to maximize the benefits of physical activity and minimize injury. • Demonstrate a variety of activities for cardio-respiratory fitness, muscular strength and endurance, and flexibility. • Analyze precautions for physical activity in weather and climate conditions such as very high or low temperatures, wet or snowy play surfaces, and direct sunlight. • Demonstrate the use of safety equipment for physical activity. • Demonstrate how to determine target heart rate. • Demonstrate the proper way to use a variety of safety gear for physical activity. • Demonstrate the use of safety equipment for physical activity.

NHES 8: Advocacy

• Ask parents, guardians, and other caretakers to be physically active. • List ways you can help friends become physically active.	• Explain to others what is enjoyable about physical activity. • Encourage parents to provide more opportunities for personal and family physical activity. • Provide support to peers and family members for being physically active.	• Advocate to others about how physical activity enhances personal health and wellness. • Advocate for increased physical activity for students and school personnel. • Advocate for family members to increase their physical activity. • Advocate for adequate facilities and time to improve physical activity programs at school. • Provide support to peers for being physically active.

SOURCE: Centers for Disease Control and Prevention, *Health Education Curriculum Analysis Tool (HECAT)* (Atlanta, GA: CDC, 2007). www.cdc.gov/HealthyYouth/Hecat/index.htm

STRATEGIES FOR LEARNING AND ASSESSMENT

Promoting Physical Activity

This section provides examples of standards-based learning and assessment strategies for promoting physical activity. The sample strategies begin with a restatement of the standard and a reminder of the assessment criteria, drawn from the RMC rubrics in Appendix B. Strategies are written as directions for teachers and, where applicable, include theory of planned behavior (TPB) constructs in parentheses (intention to act in healthy ways, attitudes toward behavior, subjective norms, perceived behavioral control). Additional strategies for learning and assessment for Chapter 7 can be found at the Online Learning Center. Appendix D, a complete list of all the strategies, is also available at the Online Learning Center. These learning and assessment strategies provide building blocks for standards-based lessons and units that can be tailored to local needs. Assessment criteria are used with permission from the Rocky Mountain Center for Health Promotion and Education (RMC). See Appendix B for Scoring Rubrics.

NHES 1 | Core Concepts

Students will comprehend concepts related to health promotion and disease prevention to enhance health.

ASSESSMENT CRITERIA

- Connections—Describe relationships between behavior and health; draw logical conclusions about connections between behavior and health.
- Comprehensiveness—Thoroughly cover health topic, showing breadth and depth; give accurate information.

Grades K–2

PE Central for Grades PreK–2 Lower-elementary teachers can find a wealth of ideas for teaching physical education and physical activity at PE Central (www.pecentral.org). The site includes lesson and assessment ideas, tips for creating a positive learning climate, and many other resources. Teachers also can find "activity cues" to help them teach specific skills in kid-friendly terms, for example, these cues about chasing:

- Definition: Chasing is moving quickly to catch up, tag, or overtake a moving object or person.
- Move quickly.
- Keep eye on the person's middle (waist) if chasing someone.
- Be ready to make quick changes of direction.

Many lower-elementary teachers are responsible for planning, implementing, and assessing their own physical education. PE Central offers one-stop shopping for tips on helping students get healthy through physical activity.

My Heart Is a Strong Muscle! Ask children to give their ideas about what muscles are and where they are located. Children likely will indicate muscles in their arms and legs. Ask if they think their hearts might be muscles, too. Ask children to locate their hearts by pointing to the protective sternum in the center of the chest. Ask children if they know what a pulse is and where they can feel it. Have them try feeling for their carotid arteries on either side of their neck below the jaw line. Ask children what happens to the heart and pulse when we exercise. Ask them to stand and participate in an experiment. First, have children walk in place. Call time and ask them to feel for their pulse. What happened? Next, ask them to jog in place or in a small space. What happens to their pulse? Now ask them to run to a certain point and back. What happens? Children can check their pulse again in five or ten seconds to see if it has slowed. What's happening in there? How is exercise good for the heart? It makes it work and grow stronger, as it does any other muscle.

ASSESSMENT | Anyone who has worked with young children knows that asking them to count their pulse rate makes for wild and hilarious answers. Rather than having them count, simply ask them to feel the difference in pulse rates as they are more, or less, active. For an assessment task, children can describe the kinds of exercise that make their hearts strong. For assessment criteria, their information should be correct, and they should make a connection between exercise and healthy hearts. (Construct: Attitudes toward behavior.)

Flexibility—Smo-o-o-oth Stretching Ask children whether they have seen older students or adults stretching. How do they do it? Children might answer that the adults stretch and hold the position, or they might answer that the adults bounce as they stretch. The important core concept is to stretch slowly, without any bouncing. Have children try several gentle, slow stretches of their arms, legs, and backs. Stretching our muscles and connective tissue improves *flexibility* (a new vocabulary word) and helps prevent injuries.

ASSESSMENT | For an assessment task, ask children to show at least one way to stretch their legs, arms, and backs. Ask them to explain what they are doing. For assessment criteria, children should provide correct information and explain how stretching can help prevent injuries. (Construct: Perceived behavioral control.)

Active or Sedentary? Teachers can ask students to define two words that might be new to them: *active* and *sedentary*. Students can consult dictionaries and talk to family members to help them define the words. Students will find that *sedentary* refers to a lot of sitting and little physical exercise. Students can brainstorm a list of things that are active (playing soccer, going for a walk, walking up the stairs) and sedentary (watching TV, sleeping on the couch, sitting at a desk). Students can also distinguish between activities that are somewhat or very active.

ASSESSMENT | For an assessment task, students can plan a variety of ways to get more physical activity into their day both at school and at home. For assessment criteria, students should identify at least five health-enhancing ways to increase physical activity. (Construct: Perceived behavioral control.)

Grades 3–5

PE Central for Grades 3–5 Upper-elementary teachers can find a wealth of ideas for teaching physical education and physical activity at PE Central (www.pecentral.org). The site includes lesson and assessment ideas, strategies for creating a positive learning environment, and many other resources. Teachers sometimes are hesitant about taking their students outdoors or to an indoor activity area for physical education. Following are some tips for successful physical education lessons:

- Use children's names, and notice and ask about what they are doing.
- Set clear boundaries for the lesson; for example, we will stay inside the area between the sidewalk and the cafeteria today.

- Post class rules clearly in all places in which you teach. A student can carry a laminated poster outside for physical activity lessons.
- When instructing, keep your "back to the wall" as much as possible. (Circulate outside of the group, with the children facing you.)
- While helping individual students with a task or skill, position yourself so you can see the rest of the class.
- Keep your eyes up and looking across the class so you can see what is going on with all the students, not just the students in front of you. Think of it as defensive driving—you don't look at the hood when driving but instead look out in front so you can anticipate and avoid potential problems.
- Have students practice and perfect the procedures and protocols you set for management tasks such as entering and leaving the classroom, lining up, getting out equipment, getting drinks, what to do on the "go" and "stop" signals, and so on.
- Enjoy the students! Physical activity lessons are a time to get to know students and learn about their talents, interests, and abilities in different ways. Let them know you see them.

Muscular Strength and Endurance   Ask children how we make our muscles stronger. We can make our muscles stronger by exercising more (doing more push-ups or abdominal crunches) or longer (exercising for longer periods of time). Elementary children should not participate in weight training. Rather, young students become stronger through appropriate physical activity. Ask students whether they know the meaning of the word *endurance*. To try it out, have students place the back of one hand on their desks or a table top. Ask them to open and close their fist on a "go" signal as many times as they can, counting as they go, for a selected period of time (two to three minutes). When time is called, ask students to write down the number of fists they made and words to describe the feeling of muscle fatigue. Ask students to think of other activities that cause muscle fatigue in other parts of the body (arms, legs, abdominal muscles). Endurance activities make muscles stronger, but be sure students can explain why "no pain, no gain" is the wrong approach. Have students exercise until muscles feel mildly fatigued, but have them stop immediately if they feel any pain.

ASSESSMENT | The students' explanations of building muscle strength and endurance are the assessment task for this activity. For assessment criteria, students should provide correct information and make connections between building strength and endurance and good health. (Construct: Attitudes toward behavior.)

We Got the Beat! Taking Pulse Rates   Teach students the correct technique for taking their carotid pulse. Have students take and record their resting heart rate. On your start and stop signals, students count their heart beats for six seconds, stop, and multiply by ten (the equivalent of sixty seconds). Then have students participate in several kinds of aerobic activity (jumping rope, running in place, jogging to a certain point and back) and record postexercise pulse rates. *Aerobic* may be a new word for students. Have students record their pulse rates again in five or ten seconds to notice how quickly their heart rates return to resting rates. Emphasize the importance of a cooldown period after exercising hard.

ASSESSMENT | For an assessment task, have students record their resting, postexercise, and cooldown pulse rates and explain what is happening to their heart rates. For assessment criteria, students should provide correct information and make connections between aerobic exercise and health. (Constructs: Attitudes toward behavior, perceived behavioral control.)

Why Exercise Is Cool!   Teachers and students can visit the Kids' Health website (www.kidshealth.org) to find out why exercise is cool and what counts as exercise. Students can investigate topics such as the following:

- Exercise makes your heart happy.
- Exercise strengthens muscles.
- Exercise makes you flexible.
- Exercise keeps the balance.
- Exercise makes you feel good.

Students can work in pairs or small groups to investigate these and other exercise-related topics on the Kids Health website. This activity links to NHES 3, access information, products, and services.

ASSESSMENT | For an assessment task, students can research and report on their topics to classmates. For assessment criteria, students should report accurate information and draw conclusions about the connections between behavior (being physically active) and good health. (Constructs: Perceived behavioral control, attitudes toward behavior, subjective norms.)

Grades 6–8

PE Central for Grades 6–8   Middle-level teachers can find a wealth of ideas for teaching physical education and physical activity at PE Central (www.pecentral.org). The site includes lesson and assessment ideas, strategies for creating a positive learning environment, and many other resources. The Best Practice link provides strategies such as "Building Fit Kids for Life—Fitness Portfolios." This strategy includes instructions for having students participate in a six- to eight-week unit for building fitness portfolios. Although many middle schools have physical education specialists, PE Central provides ideas for classroom teachers to help students dig deeper into connections between physical activity and health.

Fishbone Diagrams for Sports Skills   In *Children Moving,* Graham, Holt/Hale, and Parker organize children's physical education by generic skills themes: traveling; chasing, fleeing, and dodging; jumping and landing; balancing; transferring weight and rolling; kicking and punting; throwing and catching; volleying and dribbling; striking with rackets and paddles; and striking with long-handled implements.[72] To begin this activity, have students name as many generic skills as they can. List them for the class, with the idea of adding to the list as needed. Next, have students name all the sports they can (track-and-field events, volleyball, soccer, gymnastics, softball, basketball, ice-skating, roller-blading, swimming, diving, water skiing, snow skiing, surfing, skateboarding, tennis, badminton, archery, golf, bowling, football, wrestling). Provide or have students draw fishbone diagrams (see Chapter 4). Have students work in twos or threes to diagram the skills involved in one sport of their choosing. Name a sport as the head of the fishbone. Next, list the skills that are necessary for successful participation in the sport on the bones of the diagram. Have students share their diagrams, demonstrations, and explanations with the class, adding more skills to the original class list, if needed. Ask class members to help out if they think of skills that groups didn't include for their sports. Display the diagrams around the skills list on a bulletin board. As an extension, students can categorize the skills according to health-related fitness categories (cardiorespiratory or aerobic endurance, muscular strength and endurance, flexibility, body composition).

ASSESSMENT | The students' fishbone diagrams are the assessment task for this activity. For assessment criteria, students should provide correct information and make connections between participating in regular physical activity and health. (Construct: Attitudes toward behavior.)

BAM! Getting FITT, Looking Good, Feeling Fine! Teachers and students can visit the BAM! (Body and Mind) website (www.bam .gov) to learn about being "FITT." Students will learn that FITT stands for:

Frequency: Get active at least five times a week.
Intensity: Get your body revved up and your heart pumping.
Time: Spend at least sixty minutes doing a variety of activities.
Type: Do a variety of activities that work your body and fit your style—and have some fun while you're at it!

The website includes a quiz to assess students' knowledge and a fitness calendar to help them get started with being FITT. This activity links to NHES 3, access information, products, and services; NHES 6, goal setting; and NHES 7, self-management.

ASSESSMENT | For an assessment task, students can work in small groups to learn about the four components of FITT and to make class posters, presentations, and demonstrations about their topics. For assessment criteria, students should provide accurate information and draw conclusions about connections between behaviors (FITT) and good health. (Construct: Attitudes toward behavior.)

Fitness Spider Webs: Moderate and Vigorous Physical Activities with No Cost or Equipment On a sheet of paper with two columns, students brainstorm a list of all moderate physical activities that they can do within walking or biking distance of their homes that have no associated cost and require no equipment (in column #1). In column #2, students repeat this task identifying all vigorous physical activities that meet the same criteria. Then the class is divided into teams of no more than eight students. One student from each team is given a ball of yarn. As this person verbalizes an example of a moderate physical activity from their list, they unroll and toss (or roll) the ball of yarn to a classmate in the circle. The activity is continued until all group members have contributed a unique activity. Students are asked to note the shape of the "spider web" that the yarn has created. The process is reversed as the last person to have received the ball of yarn is asked to identify a vigorous physical activity from their written list. As they make their contribution they roll up the yarn and pass/carry it to the person from whom they received it. This reversing process is continued until all yarn is rolled back into balls. Students are asked to return to their desks, and turn their sheets to the blank back side. Here, they recreate two drawings of the spider web created by their group. On each line, in the first drawing they must write an example of a moderate physical activity. They repeat this process on the second drawing, indicating vigorous physical activity examples on each line.

ASSESSMENT | The students' spider web drawings are the assessment task for this activity. For assessment criteria, students must have identified a minimum of eight examples of each type of activity that meet criteria identified for the original brainstorming phase of the activity. (Construct: Attitudes toward behavior.)

BAM! Survival Skills: Playing It Safe The BAM! website (www .bam.gov) includes information for students about staying safe while doing a variety of physical activities. Students will find safety and survival tips for activities such as cycling, basketball, hiking, skiing, and swimming. Students can work in pairs or small groups to investigate survival skills and safety tips for their topic of interest. This activity links to NHES 3, access information, products, and services, and NHES 7, self-management.

ASSESSMENT | For an assessment task, students can demonstrate for classmates the survival skills and safety tips they learn. For assessment criteria, students should provide accurate information and draw conclusions about connections between safe behaviors and good health. (Construct: Attitudes toward behavior.)

NHES 2 | Analyze Influences

Students will analyze the influence of family, peers, culture, media, technology, and other factors on health behaviors.

ASSESSMENT CRITERIA

- Identify both external and internal influences on health.
- Explain how external and internal influences interact to impact health choices and behaviors.
- Explain both positive and negative influences, as appropriate.

Grades K–2

My Family's Favorite Activities Have students write and illustrate a page or short story about their families' favorite physical activities. As an alternative, have students write about physical activities they did while they were on vacation or visiting relatives. Have students share their pages or stories with the class. Students can bind pages into a class book about physical activity to share with other classes or to place in the library.

ASSESSMENT | The students' pages or short stories are the assessment task for this activity. For assessment criteria, students should write about how they feel about participating with their families. Does family involvement contribute to their enjoyment of physical activity and make them more likely to participate? (Construct: Subjective norms.)

My Personal Favorites Have students share their personal favorite physical activities. Make a class list on one side of a piece of chart paper or on the board. Students should explain what they like about particular activities and why. List the students' responses beside their activities. Ask students to consider how liking an activity makes them more likely to participate regularly.

ASSESSMENT | For an assessment task, students can describe a favorite physical activity and when and how often they participate in the activity. For assessment criteria, students should explain what they like about this activity and why and how this influences them to participate. (Construct: Subjective norms.)

You Can't Say You Can't Play Kindergarten teacher and author Vivian Paley wrote *You Can't Say You Can't Play* about her experiences working with children in kindergarten through grade 5.[73] Paley introduced this new rule to her kindergarten class and invited older children to share their opinions about the fairness of the rule. Teachers might introduce this rule to early elementary students and ask them to debate what it means and whether it's fair. What does it mean if some children are left out? How can everyone be included? How can children be sure everyone gets to play?

ASSESSMENT | For an assessment task, students can discuss ways they can practice the idea of you can't say "You can't play" for one week. For assessment criteria, students should identify three ways they can carry out the idea with their classmates. Students should assess their progress at the end of each day and at the end of the week. Students should explain how the new rule influenced their play time and their feelings about playing with others at school and in the community. (Constructs: Intention to act in healthy ways, subjective norms, attitudes toward behavior.)

Grades 3–5

Supports for and Barriers to Physical Activity Have students brainstorm a list of their favorite physical activities. Next, ask them to think about people, places, feelings, and conditions that help them participate more often (supports) and those that prevent their participation (barriers). Students should discuss ways to build their supports and overcome their barriers. Have students choose one strategy to put into practice during the coming week and report back to classmates. This activity links to NHES 5, decision making, and NHES 6, goal setting.

ASSESSMENT | For an assessment task, students can identify at least one personal support for and one personal barrier to physical activity. For assessment criteria, students should discuss or write about how these supports and barriers influence them and identify at least two strategies for building supports or overcoming barriers. (Construct: Subjective norms.)

Environmental Cues In a continuation of their discussion of supports for physical activity, have students identify environmental cues they can establish to help them stay active. For example, students might place their athletic shoes or sports equipment in a particular place (lightweight hand weights on the television set) in their house so they'll see them and remember to exercise. Students might also want to establish environmental cues for their families.

ASSESSMENT | For an assessment task, students can identify and track the usefulness of an environmental cue for a week. For assessment criteria, students should write about how environmental cues did or did not influence their decisions to participate in physical activity. This activity links to NHES 5, decision making, and NHES 6, goal setting. (Constructs: Subjective norms, perceived behavioral control.)

Selling It! Students can collect advertisements for sports clothing, shoes, drinks, and equipment and keep a record of billboard, poster, and television commercial advertisements they see for sporting goods. Students can use the list of advertising techniques in Chapter 3 to identify the methods advertisers use to persuade young people to buy their products.

ASSESSMENT | For an assessment task, students can work individually, in pairs, or in small groups to analyze an advertisement for an activity- or sport-related product. For assessment criteria, students should identify the advertising techniques used and explain how they might influence young people. Students also should explain how the advertisements might be misleading. (Construct: Perceived behavioral control.)

Grades 6–8

Media Messages About Physical Activity and Gender Students can go through newspapers and magazines to find pictures of people who are involved in physical activities of all kinds. Have students work in small groups to make two-sided collages that depict media messages to males and females about physical activity. What conclusions do students draw from the media images they find? Do men and women get similar messages to be strong and active? Students should share their collages and conclusions with classmates. How can students talk back to media images that they find false or misleading? Students might want to turn their talking back to media images into truth ads about physical activity for boys and girls.

ASSESSMENT | The students' collages and conclusions are the assessment task for this activity. For assessment criteria, students should explain how media images might affect young people's impressions and

decisions about physical activity and should provide at least two ways to talk back to false or misleading media messages. (Constructs: Perceived behavioral control, subjective norms.)

Puberty and Physical Activity Ask students to talk in same-gender groups about the changes males and females go through in puberty and how those changes can affect attitudes about and decisions to participate in physical activity. Then have the class "jigsaw" to form different mixed-gender groups. The new groups should share their previous discussions and ask for comments from new group members. What conclusions do students draw about how the onset of puberty might affect males' and females' attitudes about and decisions to participate in physical activity? What happens to early developers? What happens to late developers? How can students support and encourage their classmates to be physically active? What behaviors do students want stopped (teasing a girl about her developing breasts or hips, disparaging a boy who is small, making fun of students who are heavy or tall)?

ASSESSMENT | For an assessment task, students can make a two-column chart to show their analysis of how puberty can be a support for or a barrier to participating in physical activity for boys and for girls. For assessment criteria, students should identify at least three supports and three barriers and explain how to build on supports and overcome barriers. (Construct: Perceived behavioral control.)

NHES 3 | Access Information, Products, and Services

Students will demonstrate the ability to access valid information and products and services to enhance health.

ASSESSMENT CRITERIA

- Access health information—Locate specific sources of health informaton, products, or services relevant to enhancing health in a given situation.
- Evaluate information sources—Explain the degree to which identified sources are valid, reliable, and appropriate as a result of evaluating each source.

Grades K–2

Health Helpers for Physical Activity Children can name people in their homes, neighborhoods, schools, and communities who can help them learn more about fitness, physical activity, and safety (family member, athletic trainer, coach, athlete, teacher). Have children develop a class list of questions they would like to ask about physical activity. Children can interview individuals and report back to the class, or students might want to invite a guest speaker for the class to interview.

ASSESSMENT | For an assessment task, children can describe their interviews. For assessment criteria, students should explain why their interviewees are valid sources of information about physical activity. (Construct: Attitudes toward behavior.)

Places and Spaces for Family Physical Activity Students can brainstorm a list of places they and their families can go to be physically active. Teachers can help students see everyday places in new ways. For example, families can be active right in their own backyards. Students can make a list of physical activities they can do at home and others they can do in the community. Students also can find out more about physical activity opportunities in their communities at VERB, Places to Play (www.verbnow.com).

ASSESSMENT | For an assessment task, students can create pages for a class book on physical activity for families. For assessment criteria, students should decide as a group what would make "great pages." Use these criteria to assess and help students assess their work. At a minimum, students should identify a safe place where families can be active. (Construct: Subjective norms.)

Grades 3–5

Collecting Information on Family Heart Rates In class, have students take and record their resting heart rates (count their carotid pulse for six seconds and multiply by ten). As a homework activity, have students take and record the resting heart rates of at least six family members of different ages. Send home a note to parents or caregivers with a place to record data. Someone will need a watch with a second hand. When students return to class, have them graph their findings according to the ages of family members. What do they notice? Is there a connection between age and heart rate? What other factors influence heart rate (fitness, health status, weight)? As an extension, students might want to investigate the heart rates of different types of animals. They might be surprised at what they find.

ASSESSMENT | The graph or graphic organizer students make is the assessment task for this activity. For assessment criteria, students should explain their data and draw conclusions about the information they collected. Teachers and students can access a variety of graphic organizers from the North Central Regional Educational Laboratory (www.ncrel.org) by typing "graphic organizers" into the search line. (Construct: Attitudes toward behavior.)

Ask an Expert on Activity and Fitness Help students write a letter of invitation to a local sports figure or sports medicine professional to come to class to talk about staying fit and healthy. Students can develop a list of interview questions for the visit. In particular, students can ask about activities and practices that are *contraindicated* (a new vocabulary word), such as straight-legged sit-ups, ballistic stretching, and hard stretching while muscles are still cold.

ASSESSMENT | For an assessment task, students can work in small groups to make posters about recommendations for physical activity and safety. For assessment criteria, students should provide the sources of their information, including any research they do in addition to hearing the guest speaker. (Construct: Attitudes toward behavior.)

Use Your Head—Wear a Helmet! Teachers and students can visit the Bicycle Helmet Safety Institute website (www.bhsi.org) to learn more about bicycle helmet safety. Teachers and students can investigate topics such as how helmets work and how to fit them correctly; classroom materials are also available. Students also will find unusual topics that might pique their interest, such as whether helmets can be worn with braids or baseball caps.

Teachers should know that persuading students to wear bicycle helmets has been a difficult safety campaign, especially in low-income neighborhoods. Professor Gary Winn, the author of the first study on helmet use and poor children, remarked, "Anything that is not part of the local culture will die. Same thing with any safety program: If the recipients see that it's one shot, it's DOA."[74] In addition to helping students learn about bicycle helmets, teachers might have students take on the project of finding out what students in their school and community say about bicycle helmets and why. Based on their own school and community cultural findings (NHES 2), students might design their own advocacy campaign for wearing helmets (NHES 8).

ASSESSMENT | For an assessment task, students can investigate and report on a bicycle helmet topic of interest. For assessment criteria, students should explain where they obtained their information and why their sources were valid ones. (Constructs: Attitudes toward behavior, subjective norms.)

Grades 6–8

Field Trips for Activity and Fitness Help students arrange to visit a local sport or activity facility (fitness club, athletic arena, ball field). Have a staff member talk with the students about the training regimens and practices that individuals and team members follow. Students can prepare a list of questions in advance.

ASSESSMENT | Have students design a fitness plan for themselves, based on what they learned and other research. For assessment criteria, students should justify their plans and information sources. (Construct: Attitudes toward behavior.)

Designing a Fitness Course This activity can range from the imaginary to the actual. Have students talk with experts and do their own research on designing a fitness course of some kind for their school or community. Students should determine the equipment needs, estimate costs, and provide a final diagram and budget. Students can work on their project as a whole class or in small groups and present their work to classmates, staff members, and parents or caregivers.

ASSESSMENT | The students' designs and accompanying explanations are the assessment task for this activity. For assessment criteria, students should provide and justify all information sources. (Construct: Perceived behavioral control.)

Bogus Claims and Scams for Physical Activity Products Students and teachers will find that bogus and half-truth claims on "miracle products" abound in the area of physical activity. Students can participate in a scavenger hunt to find these products and claims in print media and on television. Students should note what the product is (a nutritional supplement, an exercise device, a diet pill), what claims are being made, the cost of the product, and the "fine print." In many cases, students will find that the fine print begins with the words "results not typical." Students also can investigate further to learn whether "miracle products" have caused harm to users.

ASSESSMENT | Students can work in pairs or small groups to investigate and report on the product of their choice. For assessment criteria, students should describe the product, state the claims, determine the cost, report the fine print or disclaimers, and determine whether the product has harmed anyone. Students also should explain where they obtained their information and why their sources are valid. (Construct: Perceived behavioral control.)

NHES 4 | Interpersonal Communication

Students will demonstrate the ability to use interpersonal communication skills to enhance health and avoid or reduce health risks.

ASSESSMENT CRITERIA
- Use appropriate verbal/nonverbal communication strategies in an effective manner to enhance health or avoid/reduce health risks.
- Use appropriate skills (negotiation skills, refusal skills) and behaviors (eye contact, body language, attentive listening).

Grades K–2

Simon Says for Physical Activity and Communication Skills Most of us have played the game "Simon Says." The leader prefaces verbal and visual cues for movements with the words "Simon Says." For example, the leader might say, "Simon says march in place. Simon says move your arms in big circles. Simon says hop on one foot." Students should follow and imitate the leader whenever they hear "Simon Says" before a movement. If the leader doesn't say "Simon Says," students should continue the previous movement and not change. The object is for the leader ("Simon") to catch people not listening or to mislead them through body movements. This familiar activity is a fun way to combine physical activity with verbal, nonverbal, and listening skills. In the traditional form of this game, children are "out" when they make a mistake. Change the rules. When someone misses, ask the leader to tell his or her strategy for being Simon and immediately start a new game with the same or a different leader. Have everyone play all the time. Alternatively, have children play in small groups of four or five. Each group has a Simon leader, and that role keeps changing so that all children have lots of turns to participate.

ASSESSMENT | For an assessment task, after playing this game, students can talk about the best strategies they observed for tricking classmates into moving when "Simon didn't say." For assessment criteria, students should identify two smart ways to communicate (in at least one verbal and one nonverbal way) as Simon. (Construct: Perceived behavioral control.)

Communicate Through Activity: Building Nonverbal Skills Lessons about interpersonal communication often focus on verbal skills. In the content area of physical activity, have students focus on nonverbal communication through movement. For example, read or tell a story and have children act out the movements required of the characters in the story (a trip to the zoo, a jungle adventure, an exploration for dinosaurs). Students also might use their bodies to show numbers, letters, and shapes they have learned. Combine the kinesthetic with the academic to reinforce learning and provide opportunities for children to move in the classroom.

ASSESSMENT | For an assessment task, students can act out a story as the teacher reads or make a display of numbers, letters, and shapes for other students to guess. For assessment criteria, students should identify at least two ways they can communicate through movement without needing to speak aloud. (Construct: Perceived behavioral control.)

Communicating About Physical Activity with Children's Books Teachers can read a variety of children's books with students to get them talking about physical activity. The booklist at the end of the chapter includes books that address many themes related to physical activity, such as dealing with a bully on the playground, overcoming disappointment, and learning to work as a member of a team. Teachers can use these books to spark discussion about physical activity and the way students treat others and want to be treated in physical activity settings.

ASSESSMENT | For an assessment task, students can work in small groups to retell and act out the story, using verbal and nonverbal communication. For assessment criteria, students should demonstrate clear verbal and nonverbal communication to depict the story accurately. (Construct: Perceived behavioral control.)

Grades 3–5

Mime Time Have students work in small groups to plan and tell a story to classmates entirely through mime. No speaking parts are allowed. Allow students time to rehearse. If possible, videotape their performances. Allow them to make simple props or bring props to school. After each performance, have classmates try to tell in words the story they think they saw in mime.

ASSESSMENT | The students' mime performances are the assessment task for this activity. For assessment criteria, students should identify

at least two nonverbal communication strategies they used to tell their stories. (Construct: Perceived behavioral control.)

Fitness Spelling Have students get active to spell. Students should sit on the floor in groups of five. Call out various words with five letters, and have the groups simultaneously demonstrate the spelling with their bodies. Students in a group can all make a different letter, or the group can make all the letters in unison—or students can work as a group to make each letter in sequence. Alternatively, give each group a written word to spell. Classmates must guess the word. As an extension, challenge students to spell out a simple sentence for classmates.

ASSESSMENT | The students' creative ways of using their bodies to spell are the assessment task for this activity. For assessment criteria, ask students to discuss the ease or difficulty of communicating by using physical movements alone (without words). (Construct: Perceived behavioral control.)

Communicating and Modeling Mathematical Patterns with Physical Activity: Mirroring, Matching, and Shadowing Students can apply the ideas of mathematical patterning and communication to physical activity by mirroring, matching, and shadowing a partner or a small group leader. Mirroring involves standing face-to-face with a partner or leader and following movements as if looking in a mirror. For example, if the leader raises her right hand, the mirroring student raises his left hand. In matching, students stand side-by-side and duplicate movements on the same side of the body. Shadowing is similar to matching, but the shadowers stand behind the leader. Students can vary their movements by changing speed, level, and quality (sharp, smooth). Students can add an extra challenge by matching and shadowing a partner while moving around the room.

ASSESSMENT | For an assessment task, students can work with a partner to communicate through mirroring, matching, and shadowing. Students begin by facing a partner, with one partner beginning the mirroring. On signal, students change the roles of leader and follower, trying to keep the transition as smooth as possible. Students also can try leading and following—changing roles on signal—with matching and shadowing movements. For assessment criteria, students should explain how they communicated with their partners nonverbally to keep their movements synchronized. (Construct: Perceived behavioral control.)

Grades 6–8

Walk and Talk for Fitness Have students walk or jog and talk with a buddy for a certain period of time during recess or physical education. The idea is to walk or jog and talk continuously—aerobic exercise should permit students to carry on a conversation. Afterward, have students discuss the pros and cons of exercising with someone else. Do students prefer exercising by themselves or with others?

ASSESSMENT | For an assessment task, students can make posters about exercising with a buddy. For assessment criteria, students should identify at least two ways that movement enhanced or detracted from their communication and enjoyment of exercise. (Construct: Perceived behavioral control.)

Talk Back to Obstacles and Barriers Ask students to name obstacles and barriers they have encountered that prevent their participation in physical activity. Their answers may range from unexpected rain to procrastination about doing homework (and thus not being able to go out to play). Students also might identify friends or family members who prefer to be inactive and want company. Students can demonstrate ways to talk back to obstacles and barriers to maximize opportunities for physical activity.

ASSESSMENT | Students can demonstrate talking back to obstacles and barriers to physical activity for an assessment task. For assessment criteria, students should be able to demonstrate at least two communication strategies to overcome barriers. (Construct: Perceived behavioral control.)

BAM! Motion Commotion Activity Cards   Students (or teachers) can visit the BAM! (Body and Mind) website (www.bam.gov) to print motion commotion activity cards. The site includes cards for baseball, basketball, bicycling, canoeing/kayaking, cheerleading, diving, figure skating, fishing, football, golf, gymnastics, hiking, horseback riding, in-line skating, jump rope, martial arts, skateboarding, snorkeling, snow skiing, soccer, softball, surfing, swimming, tennis, volleyball, water skiing, white-water rafting, and yoga. Students can select or draw a card to read and represent. On signal, students can walk (or jog, slide, skip, or gallop) around the room. On the next signal, they should find a partner and explain their activity card. Students should start moving again on signal and talk with a new partner on signal. Students can keep the communication and movement going. This activity allows students to practice their communication skills in a nonthreatening environment and to learn about many types of physical activity options.

ASSESSMENT | For an assessment task, students can communicate with classmates about their sport or activity. For assessment criteria, students should explain their activity clearly and concisely to each new partner. Teachers can debrief students by asking them about new activities they want to try. (Construct: Attitudes toward behavior.)

NHES 5 | Decision Making

Students will demonstrate the ability to use decision-making skills to enhance health.

ASSESSMENT CRITERIA
Reach a health-enhancing decision using a process consisting of the following steps:
- Identify a health-risk situation.
- Examine alternatives.
- Evaluate positive and negative consequences.
- Decide on a health-enhancing course of action.

Grades K–2

Playing Indoors or Outdoors?   Have students brainstorm a list of physical activities they can do indoors and outdoors, at home and at school. Have them list the pros and cons of doing each activity (pro—out of the sun indoors, con—not enough room indoors). Have students make a decision about an indoor or outdoor activity they want to participate in during the coming week. Students should report back to the class on their decisions.

ASSESSMENT | For an assessment task, students can describe how their physical activity went. For assessment criteria, students should write or tell about why their decision did or did not work well and their plans for future activity, based on their experiences. (Construct: Perceived behavioral control.)

Stress-Busting Through Physical Activity   Students can brainstorm a list of physical activities that help them feel better when they are stressed out. Students should list activities of all kinds and intensities (stretching, running, dancing). Each student can select a particular activity from the list to try as a stress-buster for the week. Students should report back to the class on how their stress-busting physical activity goal worked for them.

ASSESSMENT | The students' stress-buster reports are the assessment task for this activity. For assessment criteria, students should assess their progress and identify supports and barriers to practicing their stress-busters. (Construct: Perceived behavioral control.)

Grades 3–5

Make the Healthy Way the Easy Way   A European colleague shared the slogan "Make the healthy way the easy way." Students can work in pairs or small groups to identify ways to put this slogan into practice for students and their families. For example, students can list activities that don't require lots of equipment or special clothing. Students also might list environmental cues (the dog leash hanging over the kitchen doorknob to remind the family to go for a walk when the dog needs a walk). This activity links to NHES 7, self-management, and NHES 8, advocacy.

ASSESSMENT | For an assessment task, each student can decide on one strategy for making the healthy way the easy way and track progress for one week. For assessment criteria, students should report on their progress and identify supports for and barriers to making the healthy way the easy way. (Construct: Perceived behavioral control.)

Grades 6–8

The Best Activities for Me   Have students brainstorm a class list of all the kinds of physical activities they can name. Ask students to name the pros and cons of each activity (certain equipment is needed to play). Have each student choose three activities for themself. Beside each activity, students should list the positive and negative consequences of participating in the activity. Have students choose one activity to participate in regularly for the next two weeks, keep a journal of progress, and report back to the class.

ASSESSMENT | The students' plans and reports are the assessment task for this activity. For assessment criteria, students should be able to work through a simple decision-making process, showing choices, consequences, decisions, and progress. (Construct: Perceived behavioral control.)

NHES 6 | Goal Setting

Students will demonstrate the ability to use goal-setting skills to enhance health.

ASSESSMENT CRITERIA
- Goal statement—Give goal statement that identifies health benefits; goal is achievable and will result in enhanced health.
- Goal setting plan—Show plan that is complete, logical and sequential, and includes a process to assess progress.

Grades K–2

Recess Success   The lure of computers and other technology sometimes results in children wanting to stay indoors for recess rather than going out to play and be active. Ask students to talk about ways they can be active during recess, and have students set a simple goal for themselves ("During recess this week, I will walk around the play yard four times"). Have students draw and write their goal on a sheet of paper, making a note each day about what they did during recess to be active.

ASSESSMENT | The students' activity plans for recess are the assessment task. For assessment criteria, students should track their progress and identify at least one way to maintain or improve their activity during the following week. (Construct: Perceived behavioral control.)

Grades 3–5

Going the Distance   Have students try this activity in a place where distance can be determined (at a track or in a play area that has distance markers). Have students walk at their own pace for ten minutes. At the end of that time, students should record on their own record sheets the distance they were able to walk in ten minutes. Repeat the ten-minute walks each day for one week, recording distance each day. Have students set a distance goal for the next week and record their distance each day. Repeat each week for a month. Have students graph their distance for each day or week to show progress and write a paragraph about increasing fitness.

ASSESSMENT | The students' graphs and paragraphs are the assessment task for this activity. For assessment criteria, students should identify a goal for each coming week, identify supports and barriers, and assess their progress over time. (Construct: Perceived behavioral control.)

Estimating for Activity   Correlate physical activity with mathematics by having students make individual estimates about how they will perform at various activity stations—for example, the number of free-throws out of twelve, the number of volleyball serves over the net out of seven, the distance of a standing broad jump, the distance of a running broad jump, the number of seconds balancing on one foot out of sixty seconds, and the number of soccer goals kicked out of eight. Have students record their estimates and their actual scores on an individual record sheet. Have older students convert their scores to percentages. Provide opportunities for students to practice the activities for a period of days and have them set goals and record their scores again. (Most people can jump a standing broad jump distance equal to their height. Have students test this idea.)

ASSESSMENT | The students' record sheets, complete with their plans to practice for improvement, are the assessment task for this activity. For assessment criteria, students should specify the goal they have set for each activity and their plans to practice and achieve it. (Construct: Intention to act in healthy ways.)

Grades 6–8

Staying Active in Middle School   Students' lives tend to get busier in middle school—more responsibility, more opportunity, and more demands. Have students design a personal plan for staying active during the school year. Students should state their goal, name steps to achieve it, identify supports and barriers, and design a way to monitor progress. Have students share their progress with class members.

ASSESSMENT | The students' plans and progress reports are the assessment task for this activity. For assessment criteria, students should be able to demonstrate all parts of a simple goal-setting process. (Construct: Perceived behavioral control.)

My Own Activity Pyramid   After the previous activity (Staying Active in Middle School) has been completed, each student will develop a personal Activity Pyramid for each month of the school year. This activity should be completed in the first week of the month. Students' pyramids should be hung around the room as a reminder. A model for this activity can be found at The University of Missouri-Columbia Outreach and Extension (www.madison.k12 .al.us/nutrition/gh1800.pdf).

ASSESSMENT | The students' monthly pyramids are the assessment task for this activity. For assessment criteria, students must have completed all elements of their model and included a minimum of three examples

of activities that they could do alone, three that they could do with their friends, and three that they could do with a family member. (Construct: Perceived behavioral control.)

NHES 7 | Self-Management

Students will demonstrate the ability to practice health-enhancing behaviors and avoid or reduce health risks.

ASSESSMENT CRITERIA

- Application (transfer)—Initiate health-enhancing behaviors; apply concepts and skills appropriate and effectively.
- Self-monitoring and reflection—Monitor actions and make adjustments; accept feedback and make adjustments; ale to self-assess, reflect on, and take responsibility for actions.

Grades K–2

Defining Boundaries for Activity   Sometimes, elementary teachers are apprehensive about taking their young students out for physical activity and physical education. They fear the children will go too far or run away! Settle this concern from the beginning. Before going out, ask children if they know the word *boundary*—probably a new vocabulary word for most. Explain that the walls in a room are a boundary and that a fence in a yard is a boundary. When the students go outside for activity, teachers can use natural boundaries (tall trees, the sidewalk) or markers (orange traffic cones). After the boundaries are defined, have children practice running to touch the boundaries and coming back on your signal. Children enjoy this activity, and teachers can put their minds at ease. As a variation in the classroom, have students move around the room to find and touch specific colors and shapes.

ASSESSMENT | Having the children touch the boundaries and go back to place is the assessment task for this activity. For assessment criteria, children should explain why boundaries are necessary and important at school, at home, and in the community.

Get Moving! How Many Ways?   In a large space, challenge children to move in different ways without bumping anyone else. Designate a "go" signal and a "stop" (or "freeze") signal (drumbeat, claps, verbal signal) first; then have children practice with different locomotor movements (walking, jogging, galloping, sliding, skipping, leaping). Whenever children stop, or freeze, they should check to be sure that they have their own space, or "bubble," around them and are not standing close to anyone else. Then add levels of complexity. Have the children move at different speeds to a drumbeat, tambourine, or music. Have them move in different pathways (straight, curved, zigzag), at different levels (high, medium, low), and in different directions (forward, sideways, backward) as they try to perform a variety of locomotor movements. Have children try different kinds of arm movements (fast, slow, smooth, strong). Ask children to think of other ways they can change how they move. (Here's an easy way to help young children learn to skip: Have them walk around a large space. As they continue to walk, ask them to make their walking "bouncy." Have them bounce more and more as they walk. With a little practice, most will find that their bouncy walking soon becomes skipping.)

ASSESSMENT | For an assessment task, students can demonstrate at least two kinds of movement. For assessment criteria, students should demonstrate that they can change from one type of movement to the next and back again smoothly, not stopping until the end of the pattern. (Construct: Perceived behavioral control.)

Drawing Playground Rules—What Safety Looks Like Students are asked to fold a piece of paper in half and draw a line down the crease to divide it into two windows. Number each window. In window #1 students are asked to draw a picture of students violating the playground rule that they think makes the most important contribution to playground safety. In window #2, they are to draw students engaged in following this important playground safety rule. Drawings should be hung in the school cafeteria or hallway to the playground as a reminder for other students.

ASSESSMENT | The assessment task for this activity is students' drawings with contrasting depictions of playground rules. For assessment criteria, the drawings must contain a clear depiction of violation and compliance with playground rules. (Construct: Perceived behavioral control.)

Grades 3–5

Physical Activity Learning Stations Use cards or simple posters to number and label physical activity stations around a large space, indoors or out. Base stations on the generic skills identified by Graham et al. (chasing, fleeing, and dodging; jumping and landing; throwing and catching; kicking and volleying; striking with rackets and paddles; transferring weight and rolling) with a variety of soft, light equipment in different sizes (nerf balls, light plastic balls, balloons).[75] A "jumping and landing" station might include short and long jump ropes. A "throwing and catching" station might include nerf balls, plastic balls, Frisbees, and throwing rings. A "chasing, fleeing, and dodging" station might include playing a small-group dodgeball game with a nerf ball or chasing a partner to aim at a nerf ball. A "transferring weight and rolling" station might include trying cartwheels, walking on hands, and doing forward and backward rolls on the grass or a mat. A "dribbling and volleying" station might include volleying balloons or light plastic balls and dribbling basketballs or soccer balls. See www.pecentral.org for more ideas on children's physical activity. If possible, use recorded music as a cue to start and stop. Assign small groups to each station. When the music starts, begin. When the music stops, students should clean up the station and move on to the next. As students get the idea of the learning station, assign small groups a generic skill for designing a learning station for their classmates, complete with equipment selection and cards or posters. As a culminating activity, students can set up and explain their station and have the entire class participate.

ASSESSMENT | The students' designs for learning stations can serve as the assessment task for this activity. For assessment criteria, students should include a list of all equipment and steps to performing the activity on their station card or poster safely. (Construct: Perceived behavioral control.)

Obstacle Course for Activity In an area, lay out a simple obstacle course that includes many different types of activities. For example, students might jump over or climb under simple equipment (two milk crates and a bamboo pole), step or jump from hula hoop to hula hoop, run or dribble a ball in a zigzag pathway through plastic cones, jump across two jump ropes, and skip to end the course. Make simple posters to help children remember the activities. Have students try the course from the opposite direction, but remember that small children are concrete thinkers. For example, one kindergarten teacher asked her students to "go backward" through an obstacle course and was astounded when they began crawling backward. Incorporate natural features ("Run around the big tree") and constructed features ("Run and touch the fence and come back") of the school where appropriate. When students have the idea, they can

help design portions of an obstacle course as a class effort. Have each group make a simple sign for its portion and then help lay out the course for participation.

ASSESSMENT | For an assessment task, children can work in pairs or small groups to draw and lay out a simple obstacle course for class participation. For assessment criteria, students should draw and write about how staying active can help them be healthy. (Construct: Perceived behavioral control.)

Safe Physical Activity in All Kinds of Weather Depending on the local climate, students can investigate safe practices for physical activity in various kinds of weather. For cold weather and rain, students can research frostbite and hypothermia. For hot weather, students can research heat stress, heat exhaustion, heatstroke, and sunburn. Students should learn about prevention, proper clothing, hydration, signs and symptoms, and how to get help. Students can learn about weather precautions during physical activity by talking with a physical educator or medical professional or by conducting a Web search.

ASSESSMENT | For an assessment task, students can demonstrate safety procedures for physical activity in different kinds of weather conditions. For assessment criteria, students should correctly explain and demonstrate the steps involved in their safety procedures. (Construct: Attitudes toward behavior.)

Grades 6–8

Shop Around for Fitness Print a wide range of simple ideas for physical activity on strips of paper (toss and catch a beanbag ten times; jump rope for one minute; dribble a ball in and around legs; dribble two balls at once; serve a volleyball or plastic ball across a net or rope; dribble a soccer or playground ball around a set of cones; kick a goal through two cones; shoot a basketball ten times; throw a ball with a partner to play "one step," stepping back one step each time both partners make a catch). Scatter the strips of paper around a large play area, with needed equipment readily available. Students will participate in small groups of three or four. Have multiple strips of paper for each activity. To begin the activity, give each group a shopping or grocery bag. On signal, students pick up slips of paper and complete the activity. When they finish, they put the slip of paper in their bag and choose another. If possible, play music while the students participate. At the end of a given period of time, ask groups to count the number of activities they have completed. There's no winner. Participation and fun are the goals for this activity. Have groups aim to complete more activities the next time. (This activity is not a relay with winners and losers. Relays often cause blame of team members, hurt feelings, and deterioration of skills as students hurry. Teachers can place the emphasis on being active and having personal and group goals, rather than on beating others.)

ASSESSMENT | For an assessment task, students can describe activities they particularly like as well as activities that are challenging for them. For assessment criteria, students should select goals for the next round of the game. (Construct: Perceived behavioral control.)

VERB: It's What You Do Students will enjoy the VERB: It's What You Do website (www.verbnow.com), created especially for them by the Centers for Disease Control and Prevention (CDC) to promote physical activity. The site features a variety of resources and activities, including sport skill tips and a directory of places to play (students enter their zip code). One of the most interesting features of the website is the Game Generator. Students make three choices and click on the "make it" button to get an idea for a new game. Teachers will find that this site truly was created for kids! Students can visit the site and report on what they find there for kids on the move.

ASSESSMENT | For an assessment task, students can work in small groups to generate a new game to teach to other students. For assessment criteria, students should teach the steps for a healthy way to be active to other students. (Construct: Perceived behavioral control.)

NHES 8 | Advocacy

Students will demonstrate the ability to advocate for personal, family, and community health.

ASSESSMENT CRITERIA

- Health-enhancing position—Give clear, health-enhancing position.
- Support for position—Support position with facts, concepts, examples, and evidence.
- Audience awareness—Show awareness of target audience; choose words, tone, and examples to suit audience.
- Conviction—Display conviction for position.

Grades K–2

Physical Activity in Many Cultures: Games and Sports Around the World   Students can investigate the kinds of games and sports that children play in other countries and other cultures. Students can work with their school librarian or media specialist to access this information (NHES 3). Students can work in pairs or small groups to learn and teach a new activity to classmates. Learning about other cultures can help children expand their horizons, correct misperceptions, and become more educated world citizens. For example, one of the authors found while teaching summer school in American Samoa that a group of young boys were constantly pushing each other, shoulder to shoulder, during physical education class and recess. She redirected the boys to other activities several times before realizing that they were imitating the scrum movement in rugby, a popular sport in Samoan culture. The boys certainly must have wondered what was wrong with this visitor who didn't recognize a scrum when she saw one!

ASSESSMENT | For an assessment task, students can learn and teach a new type of physical activity to classmates. For assessment criteria, students should express a clear, health-enhancing position for learning about physical activity from cultures around the world. (Constructs: Intention to act in healthy ways, subjective norms.)

Equipment Drive for Recess   Many elementary classrooms don't have adequate or appropriate play equipment for recess. Students sometimes are inactive because they lack equipment to play with or because the equipment they have hurts their hands (hard, regulation-size balls). Have students brainstorm a list of inexpensive equipment they would like to have for their recess and physical education periods (short and long jump ropes, hula hoops, beanbags, nerf balls, lightweight plastic balls, plastic bats, wiffle balls, plastic scoops). Help students organize a drive for parents, community members, or Parent-Teacher-Student Associations (PTSAs) to collect equipment for classrooms. Be sure to list large, lightweight plastic barrels to transport and collect equipment before and after recess. Some schools don't make play equipment available for recess because they claim the children argue over it or misuse it. Use these situations as a teaching opportunity. Having plenty of equipment available will help with arguments. Who can blame children for not wanting to be "out" in a long jump rope activity when they have had to stand in a line of twenty-five children for a turn? The simple solution is to have plenty of long jump ropes—ideally, three children per rope,

with two children turning while one jumps, changing places when someone misses. If children misuse equipment, use this as a time to teach them to use equipment properly—and do so with each new piece of equipment before it is introduced.

ASSESSMENT | The plan for the equipment drive is the assessment task for this activity. For assessment criteria, students should design a flyer or posters to appeal to parents, community members, or the PTSA. Flyers and posters should give a clear message, back it up with reasons, target a particular audience, and show strong conviction. (Constructs: Perceived behavioral control, subjective norms.)

How Many Ways to Be Active Campaign   Have students brainstorm a list of ways they and their families can be more active. Have students design flyers or posters to advocate for more physical activity at home and at school. Post students' work in the school and community.

ASSESSMENT | The students' flyers and posters are the assessment task for this activity. For assessment criteria, students should give a clear message, back it up with reasons, target a particular audience, and show strong conviction. (Construct: Subjective norms.)

Grades 3–5

Inclusive Physical Activity: Participation for All   Graham, Holt/Hale, and Parker[76] recommend this strategy for helping children develop acceptance and empathy for peers who have disabilities. Teachers can coordinate with special education teachers to help children learn about the nature of the disability, its correct name, any limitations it imposes, and the potential for activity. In addition, children should have opportunities to work and talk with children who have disabilities. To help children become more sensitive, Graham, Holt/Hale, and Parker suggest the following activities:

- Forming a circle, standing with legs shoulder-width apart, and rolling a playground ball across the circle with eyes closed
- Playing a simple game with no verbal sound—no verbal clues for directions, rules, or stopping the action
- Executing simple ball-handling skills with the students' nondominant hand

ASSESSMENT | For an assessment task, students can describe ways they can include children with disabilities in their physical activity at school. For assessment criteria, students should state a clear, health-enhancing position and back it up with reasons. (Construct: Subjective norms.)

Teach a Classmate   Have students share physical activity skills they have with the class. For example, some students might be experts at using a yo-yo, demonstrating hula hoop or fancy jump rope routines, or line-dancing. Have a certain number of students volunteer to be instructors on given days. Students can work with their teachers in small groups to learn a new skill.

ASSESSMENT | Having students teach others is the assessment task for this activity. For assessment criteria, students should make their explanations and demonstrations clear and encourage other students to keep trying. (Constructs: Perceived behavioral control, subjective norms.)

Get Your Family Moving   Have students brainstorm a list of activities they can participate in with their families. Students should design a plan for their families to get everyone active for at least three days per week. Have students implement their plans and report back to the class.

ASSESSMENT | Students' plans and reports are the assessment task for this activity. For assessment criteria, students should make a clear plan for their families, back it up with reasons, target their proposal to their family members, and show strong conviction. (Construct: Subjective norms.)

Grades 6–8

The H₂O Connection Students can investigate the importance of drinking plenty of water during physical activity at Kids' Health (www.kidshealth.org) and BAM! (Body and Mind) (www.bam.gov). Topics include

- Is it important to drink a lot of water?
- Dehydration
- Keeping your cool!

After students have the facts on physical activity and hydration, they can inspect their school to ensure that plenty of water (water fountains, bottled water) is available to students during physical activity times. If students find that water is in short supply, they can plan a presentation on the importance of hydration for their classmates, teachers, administrators, and parents or caregivers to try to increase water availability at school.

ASSESSMENT | The students' presentation is the assessment task for this activity. For assessment criteria, students should state a clear health-enhancing position, back it up with data, target their audience, and speak with conviction. (Constructs: Attitudes toward behavior, subjective norms.)

Paint It for Physical Activity Have students design and sketch a layout for several types of physical activities that can be painted on sidewalks or other paved surfaces at school. Examples include Four-Square and Hop-Scotch. Have students determine measurements and supplies needed to paint these games for their own schools or for neighboring elementary schools. Help students arrange time and supplies to put their plan into action.

ASSESSMENT | The students' plans and calculations for measurements and supplies are the assessment task for this activity. For assessment criteria, students should present their plan to decision makers, including a clear message, reasons, a targeted audience, and conviction. (Construct: Perceived behavioral control.)

Teach Activity for Elementary Students Have students brainstorm a list of activities they can teach to elementary-age students. Students should choose an activity and work together to design a lesson plan for teaching younger students to be active. Help students arrange visits to work with younger children.

ASSESSMENT | Students' lesson plans are the assessment task for this activity. For assessment criteria, students should be able to show all the steps they need to take to teach their lessons and justify their plans to decision makers. (Construct: Perceived behavioral control.)

EVALUATED CURRICULA AND INSTRUCTIONAL MATERIALS

In 2005, *Child* published the results of an extensive analysis of activities to support physical fitness within each state in the United States. In collaboration with credible organizations including Action for Healthy Kids, the Center for Health and Health Care in Schools, the National Association of State Boards of Education, the American Academy of Pediatrics, the American Heart Association, and the Centers for Disease Control, measures such as school fitness and nutrition policies, the availability of safe playgrounds, rates of participation in youth sports, and physical activity opportunities for children of preschool age were analyzed. This research identified the "10 best and worst states for fit kids" in the United States (Table 7–5). This research shows that physical activity participation among youth is a complex matter influenced by personal, family, community, and broader social and psychological variables.[77]

While recognizing that the range and complexity of influential variables is important, advocates for evidence-based approaches to increasing physical activity in schools become frustrated with criteria that appear to be cumbersome or beyond their control. In response, Action for Healthy Kids, supported by a grant from the Robert Wood Johnson Foundation, has identified ten essential criteria to help administrators, teachers, parents, and concerned others evaluate physical activity programs of interest. These criteria ask stakeholders to evaluate whether the school-based approach

1. Is based on professional theories and is consistent with professional and/or national standards of practice

2. Is practical and realistic
3. Has a goal or purpose that is clearly stated and easy to understand by interested audiences
4. Has specific measurable objectives that address one or more of the following: knowledge, attitudes, skills, behaviors, policies, school environment
5. Is age- or developmentally appropriate and culturally relevant
6. Is engaging to students, interactive, and skills-based
7. Can be adapted to a variety of situations and environments

TABLE 7–5

The Ten Best and Worst States for Fit Kids

Ten Best States	Ten Worst States
1. Connecticut	41. Iowa
2. New York	42. Wyoming
3. Vermont	43. Idaho
4. Massachusetts	44. Alabama
5. Missouri	45. South Dakota
6. Maine	46. Kansas
7. West Virginia	47. Mississippi
8. Wisconsin	48. Nevada
9. Arkansas	49. Nebraska
10. Illinois	50. Alaska

Readers interested in locating states not listed or in information about specific criteria and attributes of state programming that contributed to these rankings are encouraged to go to www.child.com/web_links.

SOURCE: K. Cicero, "The 10 Best and Worst States for Fit Kids," *Child* (April 2005), 106–12.

8. Can be assessed and monitored with an evaluation component
9. Includes goals that are supported by evaluation data
10. Supports easy implementation by providing clearly written and user-friendly instructions, training resources, contact information for technical support, and instructions and/or materials available in languages in addition to English.[78]

In addition to these criteria specifically related to curricular or program elements, the developers from Action for Healthy Kids recognized that school-based approaches need to be adoptable and usable. They developed "critical" evaluation criteria to help clarify the potential for users to implement the approach in a real-world context. These criteria focus on important attributes such as cost-effectiveness, potential fit with school mandates, support of student achievement, feasibility for implementation within the time constraints of the school day, potential to be supported by critical stakeholders, and potential sustainability.[79]

Readers can review the "What's Working" database at www.afhk.org for a complete and updated list of positively evaluated programs. A brief description of selected successful programs is provided in Teacher's Toolbox 7.4.[80] Any school community trying to establish a new school-based approach to improving physical activity or revising or updating current practice will find the Action for Healthy Kids criteria a valuable place to begin.

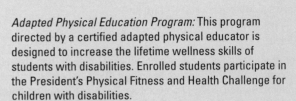

Teacher's Toolbox 7.4

What Works: Applying the Action to Healthy Kids Criteria

- *Adapted Physical Education Program:* This program directed by a certified adapted physical educator is designed to increase the lifetime wellness skills of students with disabilities. Enrolled students participate in the President's Physical Fitness and Health Challenge for children with disabilities.
- *Fine Arts Interdisciplinary Resource School:* This school for students in grades 4 through 8 is located in Crystal, Minnesota. Focused on an integrated approach to policies and programs, the school has made food choices and physical activity an integral part of the school day.
- *Healthy Hearts:* This instructional Internet e-module is designed to teach intermediate-grade children about cardiovascular health, with a particular focus on physical activity and nutritional choices. Participants read, write, and problem solve while learning to make healthy choices that will affect them throughout their life.

SOURCE: Action for Healthy Kids, *An Action for Healthy Kids Report: Criteria for Evaluating School-Based Approaches to Increase Good Nutrition and Physical Activity* (Skokie, IL: Action for Healthy Kids, Fall 2004). (www.actionforhealthykids.org)

INTERNET AND OTHER RESOURCES

Visit the Online Learning Center (www.mhhe.com/telljohann6e) for links to these sites, quizzes and other study aids, and many additional resources.

WEBSITES

Active Lifestyle, Presidential Champions
www.presidentschallenge.org

BAM! Body and Mind
www.bam.gov

Bicycle Helmet Safety Institute
www.bhsi.org

Cartoon Network—Rescuing Recess (in conjunction with PTA)
www.rescuingrecess.com

Center for Screen-Time Awareness
www.screentime.org

GirlsHealth.gov
www.4girls.gov

Health Finder for Kids
www.healthfinder.gov/kids

Kids' Health
www.kidshealth.org

Kids Walk to School
www.healthierus.gov/exercise.html

PE Central
www.pecentral.org

Playground Safety for Kids!
www.kidchecker.org/main.htm

U.S. Consumer Product Safety Commission
www.cpsc.gov/cpscpub/pubs/playpubs.html

VERB: It's What You Do
www.verbnow.com

We Can! Energize Our Families Ways to Enhance Children's Activity and Nutrition
http://wecan.nhlbi.nih.gov

OTHER RESOURCES

Boehmer, T., R. Brownson, D. Haire-Joshu, and M. Dreisinger, "Patterns of Childhood Obesity Prevention Legislation in the United States," *Preventing Chronic Disease* 4, no. 3 (July 2007): 3–21.

Centers for Disease Control and Prevention, *Physical Education Curriculum Analysis Tool* (Atlanta, GA: CDC, 2006).

DeBate, R., Y. Zhang, and S. Thompson, "Changes in Commitment to Physical Activity among 8- to-11-Year-Old Girls Participating in a Curriculum-Based Running Program," *American Journal of Health Studies* 38, no. 5 (October 2007): 276–283.

Ginsburg, K. "The Importance of Play in Promoting Healthy Child Development and Maintaining Strong Parent-Child Bonds," *Pediatrics* 119, no. 1 (January 2007): 182–191.

Joyner, A. "The Healthy Approach," *American School Board Journal* (June 2007): 42–44.

National Association for Sport and Physical Education, *Comprehensive School Physical Activity Programs: A Position Statement from the National Association for Sport and Physical Education* (Reston, VA: NASPE, May 2008).

National Association for Sport and Physical Education and American Heart Association, *2006 Shape of the Nation Report: Status of Physical Education in the USA* (Reston, VA: NASPE, 2006).

Hall, G., and D. Gruber, *Healthy Choices Afterschool: Investigation of the Alignment of Physical Activity and Nutrition Programs/Curricula and the National Afterschool Association Program Standards* (New York, NY: Robert Wood Johnson Foundation, 2006).

Ohio Action for Healthy Kids, *Make Positive Changes in your Schools: Parent Guide to Creating Nutrition and Physical Activity Changes in Schools* (Columbus, OH: OAHK, 2006).

Zapata, L., C. Bryant, R. McDermott, and J. Hefelfinger, "Dietary and Physical Activity Behaviors of Middle School Youth: The Youth Physical Activity and Nutrition Survey," *Journal of School Health* 78, no. 1 (January 2008): 9–18.

CHILDREN'S LITERATURE

AGES 5–8

Ackerman, Karen. *Song and Dance Man.* Alfred A. Knopf, 1988. (Caldecott Medal)

Andreae, Giles. *Giraffes Can't Dance.* Orchard, 1999.

April, Elyse, and Regina Sara Ryan. *We Like to Move: Exercise Is Fun.* Hohm Press, 2007.

Bateman, Teresa. *Hamster Camp: How Harry Got Fit.* Albert Whitman & Co., 2005.

Bolam, Emily, and Harriet Ziefert. *Murphy Meets the Treadmill.* Houghton Mifflin, 2001.

Brown, Marc. *Arthur and the Race to Read.* Little, Brown, 2001.

Carle, Eric. *From Head to Toe.* HarperCollins, 1999.

Carlson, Nancy. *Get Up and Go!* Viking Juvenile, 2006.

Corey, Shana. *Players in Pigtails.* Scholastic, 2003.

Cosby, Bill. *The Best Way to Play.* Scholastic, 1997.

Couric, Katie. *The Blue Ribbon Day.* Doubleday, 2004.

Craemer, Michele Bredice. *Pellie Runs a Marathon.* Power Pack Presentations, 2003.

Dunn, Opal. *Acka Backa Boo! Playground Games from Around the World.* Henry Holt, 2000. (Multicultural)

Glazer, Byron, and Sandra Higashi. *Bonz Inside Out: A Rhythm, Rhyme, and Reason Bonanza!* Harry N. Abrams, 2003.

Hamm, Mia. *Winners Never Quit!* HarperCollins, 2004.

Harwayne, Shelley. *Jewels: Children's Play Rhymes.* Mondo, 1995. (Multicultural)

Krull, Kathleen. *Wilma Unlimited: How Wilma Rudolph Became the World's Fastest Woman.* Harcourt, 2000.

Martin, Bill, and Michael Sampson. *Swish.* Henry Holt, 1997.

Miller, Edward. *The Monster Health Book: A Guide to Eating Healthy, Being Active and Feeling Great for Monsters and Kids!* Holiday House, 2008.

O'Neill, Alexis. *The Recess Queen.* Scholastic, 2002.

Paley, Vivian. *You Can't Say You Can't Play.* Harvard University Press, 1993.

Patrick, Denise. *Red Dancing Shoes.* William Morrow, 1993. (Multicultural)

Rockwell, Lizzy. *The Busy Body Book: A Kid's Guide to Fitness.* Dragonfly Books, 2008.

Royston, Angela. *A Healthy Body.* Heinemann, 1999.

AGES 8–12

Adler, David. *Lou Gehrig: The Luckiest Man.* Harcourt Brace, 1997.

Adler, David. *A Picture Book of Jesse Owens.* Holiday House, 1994.

Adoff, Arnold. *Sports Pages.* HarperCollins, 1986. (Multicultural)

Douglas, Ann, and Julie Douglas. *Body Talk: The Straight Facts on Fitness, Nutrition, and Feeling Great About Yourself.* Maple Tree Press, 2006.

Holt, Kimberly Willis. *When Zachary Beaver Came to Town.* Bantam Doubleday Dell Books for Young Readers, 1999. (1999 National Book Award for Young People's Literature)

Petersen, P. J. *White Water.* Simon & Schuster, 1997.

Prelutsky, Jack. *Good Sports.* Knopf Books for Young Readers, 2007.

Spilsbury, Louise. *Why Should I Get off the Couch? and Other Questions About Health and Exercise.* Heinemann Library, 2003.

Spinelli, Jerry. *Maniac Magee.* HarperCollins, 1990. (Newbery Medal; Multicultural)

Voigt, Cynthia. *The Runner.* Atheneum, 1995.

Yamaguchi, Kristi. *Always a Dream.* Taylor, 1998.

Yoshizumi, Carol. *Real Fitness: 101 Games and Activities to Get Girls Going!* American Girl, 2006.

ENDNOTES

1. Centers for Disease Control and Prevention, *Physical Activity and Good Nutrition: Essential Elements to Prevent Chronic Diseases and Obesity, At a Glance 2007.* (www.cdc.gov/nccdphp/publications/aag/dnpa.htm).

2. C. B. Corbin, R. P. Pangrazi, et al., *Physical Activity for Children: A Statement of Guidelines for Children Ages 5–12* (Reston, VA: National Association for Sport and Physical Education, 2004), 8–10.

3. U.S. Department of Health and Human Services, *Physical Activity and Health: A Report of the Surgeon General* (Atlanta: U.S. Department of Health and Human Services, Centers for Disease Control and Prevention, National Center for Chronic Disease Prevention and Health Promotion, 1996).

4. B. Gutin et al., "Effects of Exercise Intensity on Cardiovascular Fitness, Total Body Composition, and Visceral Adiposity of Obese Children," *American Journal of Clinical Nutrition* 75, (2002): 818–26.

5. M. A. Ferguson et al., "Effects of Exercise Training and Its Cessation on Components of the Insulin Resistance Syndrome in Obese Children," *International Journal of Obesity Related Metabolic Disorders* 23 (1999): 889–95.

6. C. K. Ewart, D. R. Young, and J. M. Hagberg, "Effects of School-Based Aerobic Exercise on Blood Pressure in Adolescent Girls at Risk for Hypertension," *American Journal of Public Health* 88 (1998): 949–51.

7. N. H. van Veldhoven et al., "Children with Asthma and Physical Exercise: Effects of an Exercise Programme," *Clinical Rehabilitation* 15 (2001): 360–70.

8. R. Norris, D. Carroll, and R. Cochrane, "The Effects of Physical Activity and Exercise Training on Psychological Stress and Well-Being in an Adolescent Population," *Journal of Psychosomatic Research* 36 (1992): 55–65.

9. B. D. Kirkcaldy, R. J. Shephard, and R. G. Siefen, "The Relationship Between Physical Activity and Self-Image and Problem Behaviour Among Adolescents," *Social Psychiatry and Psychiatric Epidemiology* 37 (2002): 544–50.

10. G. P. Beunen et al., "Physical Activity and Growth, Maturation, and Performance: A Longitudinal Study," *Medical Science in Sports and Exercise* 24 (1992): 576–85.

11. Centers for Disease Control and Prevention, *Physical Activity and Good Nutrition: Essential Elements to Prevent Chronic Diseases and Obesity, At a Glance 2007.*

12. P. Gordon-Larsen and M. C. Nelson, "Longitudinal Physical Activity and Sedentary

Behavior Trends: Adolescence to Adulthood," *American Journal of Preventive Medicine* 27, no. 4 (2004): 277–283.

13. Centers for Disease Control and Prevention, "Youth Risk Behavior Surveillance—United States, 2007," *MMWR Surveillance Summaries* 57, no. SS-4 (6 June 2008): 25–27.

14. National Heart, Lung, and Blood Institute, *We Can! Ways to Enhance Children's Physical Activity and Nutrition.* (www.nhlbi.nih.gov/health/public/heart/obesity/wecan/whats-we-can/background .htm).

15. U.S. Government Accountability Office, *Childhood Obesity: Factors Affecting Physical Activity, GAO-07-260R* (Washington, DC: GAO, December 6, 2006).

16. Ibid.

17. Olshansky, S. J. et al., "A Potential Decline in Life Expectancy in the United States in the 21st Century," *The New England Journal of Medicine* 352, no. 11 (March 17, 2005): 1138–1145.

18. R.C. Porter, *Economics at the Wheel: The Costs of Cars and Drivers* (London: Academic Press, 1999).

19. U.S. Department of Transportation, *National Household Travel Survey Brief—Travel to School: The Distance Factor* (Washington, DC: NHTS, January 2008).

20. R. Sturm, "Childhood Obesity—What We Can Learn from Existing Data on Societal Trends, Part 2," *Preventing Chronic Disease* 2, no. 2 (April 2005). (www.cdc.gov/pcd/issues/2005)

21. A. Datar and R. Sturm, "Physical Education in Elementary School and Body Mass Index: Evidence from Early Childhood Longitudinal Study," *American Journal of Public Health* 94, no. 9 (September 2004): 1501–6.

22. Action for Healthy Kids, *The Learning Connection: The Value of Improving Nutrition and Physical Activity in Our Schools* (Skokie, IL: Action for Healthy Kids, fall 2004). (www.ActionforHealthyKids.org)

23. T. Marder and S. Chang, *Childhood Obesity: Costs, Treatment Patterns, Disparities in Care and Prevalent Medical Conditions* (Stamford, CT: Thomson Medstat, 2006).

24. U.S. Department of Health and Human Services, *Healthy People 2010, Conference Edition, in Two Volumes* (Washington, DC: U.S. Department of Health and Human Services, January 2000).

25. J. Sallis and K. Patrick, "Physical Activity Guidelines for Adolescents: Consensus Statement," *Pediatric Exercise Science* 6 (1994): 434–47.

26. W. B. Strong et al., "Evidence Based Physical Activity for School-Age Youth," *Journal of Pediatrics* (June 2005): 736.

27. L. Kolbe et al., "Appropriate Functions of Health Education in Schools: Improving Health and Cognitive Performance," in *Child Health Behavior: A Behavioral Pediatrics Perspective*, eds. N. Krairweger, J. Arasteli, and M. Cataldo (New York: John Wiley, 1986).

28. B. McCracken, "Creating an Environment for Learning," *Education Standard* (autumn 2002): 46–51.

29. D. R. Patel and E. F. Luckstead, "Sport Participation, Risk Taking, and Health Risk Behaviors," *Adolescent Medicine* 11 (2000): 141–55.

30. H. Taras, "Physical Activity and Student Performance at School," *Journal of School Health* 75, no. 8 (August 2005).

31. B. McCracken, "Creating an Environment for Learning."

32. California Department of Education, "State Study Proves Physically Fit Kids Perform Better," 10 December 2002. (www.cde.ca.gov/cyfsbranch/lsp/health/pecommunications.htm.Families)

33. Eric Jensen, "Moving with the Brain in Mind," *Educational Leadership* (November 2000): 34–37.

34. B. McCracken, "Creating an Environment for Learning."

35. S. M. Lee, C. Burgeson, J. E. Fulton, and C. Spain, "Physical Education and Physical Activity: Results from the School Health Policies and Programs Study 2006," *Journal of School Health* 77, no. 8 (October 2007): 435–463.

36. M. Tappe, J. Duda, and P. Menges-Ehrnwald, "Personal Investment Predictors of Adolescent Motivational Orientation Toward Exercise," *Canadian Journal of Sport Science* 15, no. 3 (1990): 185–92.

37. J. Zakarian et al., "Correlates of Vigorous Exercise in a Predominately Low SES and Minority High School Population," *Preventive Medicine* 23 (1994): 314–21.

38. R. Stucky-Ropp and T. DiLorenzo, "Determinants of Exercise in Children," *Preventive Medicine* 22 (1993): 880–89.

39. U.S. Department of Health and Human Services and U.S. Department of Education, *Promoting Better Health for Young People Through Physical Activity and Sports* (Washington, DC: U.S. Department of Health and Human Services and U.S. Department of Education, Fall 2000): 11.

40. Action for Healthy Kids, *The Learning Connection.*

41. Institute of Medicine of the National Academies, *Preventing Childhood Obesity: Health in the Balance* (Washington, DC: The National Academies Press, 2004).

42. A. Beighle, C. F. Morgan, G. Le Masurier, and R. Pangrazi, "Children's Physical Activity During Recess and Outside of School," *Journal of School Health* 76, no. 10 (December 2006): 516.

43. S. M. Lee, C. Burgeson, J. E. Fulton, and C. Spain, "Physical Education and Physical Activity: Results from the School Health Policies and Programs Study 2006."

44. Ibid., 449.

45. Ibid., 456.

46. C. B. Corbin, R. P. Pangrazi, et al., *Physical Activity for Children*, 7.

47. C. B. Corbin, R. P. Pangrazi, et al., *Physical Activity for Children*, 7.

48. Ibid., 8.

49. Ibid.

50. P. Gordon-Larsen, R. G. McMurray, and B. M. Popkin, "Determinants of Adolescent Physical Activity and Inactivity Patterns, *Pediatrics* 105 (2000): E83.

51. C. B. Corbin, R. P. Pangrazi, et al., *Physical Activity for Children*, 8.

52. A. Beighle, C. F. Morgan, G. Le Masurier, and R. Pangrazi, "Children's Physical Activity During Recess and Outside of School."

53. Centers for Disease Control and Prevention, "Guidelines for School and Community Programs to Promote Lifelong Physical Activity Among Young People," *MMWR* 46, no. RR-6 (1997): 6–10.

54. Centers for Disease Control and Prevention, *Guidelines for School Health Programs to Promote Physical Activity: Summary* (Atlanta, GA: CDC/Division of Adolescent and School Health, May 2004). (www.cdc.gov/healthyyouth/PhysicalActivity).

55. Centers for Disease Control and Prevention, *Guidelines for School and Community Programs to Promote Lifelong Physical Activity Among Young People*, 24.

56. C. B. Corbin, R. P. Pangrazi, et al., *Physical Activity for Children*, 5–7.

57. C. Caspersen, K. Powell, and G. Christenson, "Physical Activity, Exercise, and Physical Fitness: Definitions and Distinctions for Health-Related Research," *Public Health Reports* 100, no. 2 (1985): 126–31.

58. Centers for Disease Control and Prevention, *Guidelines for School Health Programs to Promote Physical Activity: Summary.*

59. C. B. Corbin, R. P. Pangrazi, et al., *Physical Activity for Children*, 11–13.

60. University of Missouri-Columbia, *Children's Activity Pyramid* (Columbia: MO: Outreach and Extension University of Missouri-Columbia). (http://extension.missouri.edu/explore/hesguide/foodnut/n00386.htm).

61. Ibid.

62. C. B. Corbin et al., *Physical Activity for Children*, 14–16.

63. Ibid.

64. Ibid.

65. Ibid.

66. Centers for Disease Control and Prevention, *Physical Education Curriculum Analysis Tool* (Atlanta, GA: CDC, 2006).

67. National Association for Sport and Physical Education, *Moving into the Future: National Standards for Physical Education*, 2nd Edition (Reston, VA: NASPE). (www.aahperd.org/naspe/publications-nationalstandards.html).

68. C. B. Corbin, R. P. Pangrazi, et al., *Physical Activity for Children*, 16–19.

69. Ibid.

70. Centers for Disease Control and Prevention, *Health Education Curriculum Analysis Tool* (Atlanta, GA: CDC, 2007).

71. Ibid.

72. G. Graham, S. A. Holt/Hale, and M. Parker, *Children Moving: A Reflective Approach to Teaching Physical Education* (Mountain View, CA: Mayfield, 2001).

73. V. Paley, *You Can't Say, You Can't Play* (Cambridge, MA: Harvard University Press, 1993).

74. S. Meiers, "Promoting Helmet Use in Low Income Neighborhoods," *Bicycle Safety Institute* (www.bhsi .org/poorkids.htm).

75. G. Graham, S. A. Holt/Hale, and M. Parker, *Children Moving.*

76. Ibid.

77. K. Cicero. "The 10 Best and Worst States for Fit Kids," *Child* (April 2005), 106–12.

78. Action for Healthy Kids, *An Action for Healthy Kids Report: Criteria for Evaluating School-Based Approaches to Increase Good Nutrition and Physical Activity* (Skokie, IL: Action for Healthy Kids, fall 2004). (www.actionforhealthykids.org)

79. Ibid.

80. Ibid.

(Echo, age 12)

Promoting Safety and Preventing Unintentional Injury

DESIRED LEARNER OUTCOMES

After reading this chapter, you will be able to . . .

- Describe the prevalence and cost of unintentional injuries among youth.

- Explain the relationship between unintentional injuries and compromised academic performance.

- Identify factors that influence unintentional injuries.

- Summarize current guidelines and practices for schools and teachers related to safety promotion and unintentional injury prevention.

- Summarize developmentally appropriate safety promotion and unintentional injury prevention concepts and skills for K–8 students in the context of the National Health Education Standards and target healthy behavior outcomes.

- Demonstrate developmentally appropriate learning strategies and assessment techniques that incorporate concepts and skills that have been shown to promote safety and prevent unintentional injury among youth.

- Identify effective, evaluated commercial safety promotion and unintentional injury prevention curricula.

- Identify websites and children's literature that can be used in cross-curricular instructional activities promoting safety and the prevention of unintentional injuries.

INTRODUCTION

The risk of injury is so great in American society that most people sustain a significant injury sometime during their lives. However, the belief that injuries happen by chance as a result of unpreventable accidents is mistaken. Many injuries are neither accidents nor random, uncontrollable acts of fate. Most injuries are predictable and preventable.

Prevalence and Cost

Each day in America, 32 children or teens die from unintentional injuries.[1] The National Center for Injury Prevention and Control (NCIPC), Centers for Disease Control and Prevention (CDC), reported that unintentional injury is the leading cause of death among youth ages 5–14 in the United States. Motor vehicle injuries are the single leading cause of death for this age group.[2]

Unintentional injuries, or injuries that occur without specific intent of harm, are a leading cause of death and disability for children in the United States. Each year, approximately 3,600 children die, 20,000 children become permanently disabled, 550,000 children are hospitalized, and 15 million children visit the emergency room because of unintentional injuries. The implications of these injuries for children and their families are widespread. Consequences include time lost from school, decreased ability to participate in normal activities, and early loss of life.[3]

Injuries are the most common cause of death and disability among children and adolescents in the United States and in all industrialized countries. Nearly 150,000 Americans of all ages die from trauma each year. For infants under 1 year, the number of traumatic deaths is higher than the next ten leading causes of death combined.[4]

The NCIPC reported that 1,451 children age 14 and younger died as occupants in motor-vehicle crashes in 2005 and approximately 203,000 were injured—an average of 4 deaths and 556 injuries each day. Of the children age 14 and younger who were killed in motor-vehicle crashes during 2005, nearly half were unrestrained.[5]

The encouraging news is that the death toll from injuries is decreasing. The United States must continue to improve its injury prevention efforts for children and adolescents.

The overall death rates do not reflect the serious disparity in injury death rates between minority and white children. White children age 19 and younger experience more than twice the number of deaths as Asian American children, and death rates for African American children are nearly three times higher than for Asian American children. In addition, American Indians and Alaska Natives have profoundly higher death rates from injury than do whites. Injury rates for males are two to three times greater than those for females in all ethnic groups.[6]

Injury-related data from the Youth Risk Behavior Survey (YRBS) appear in Table 8–1.[7] Despite laws mandating seat-belt use, more than 11 percent of high school students across the United States reported rarely or never wearing a seat belt while riding in a car driven by someone else. Among students who rode bicycles, more than 85 percent rarely or never wore a helmet. More than 29 percent of students had ridden with a drinking driver during the past month, and 10.5 percent reported driving a car after drinking. Nine percent of males reported carrying a gun during the past thirty days, placing themselves and others at risk for unintentional as well as intentional injury. (YRBS data also are available by state and for many large cities at www.cdc.gov/HealthyYouth.)

Although the greatest impact of injury is human suffering and loss of life, the financial cost is also staggering. The costs of direct medical care and rehabilitation, as well as lost income and productivity, are included in the costs associated with injuries. Preventing injuries costs far less than treating them. For example,

- Every child safety seat saves $85 in direct medical costs and an additional $1,275 in other costs.
- Every bicycle helmet saves $395 in direct medical costs and other costs.[8]

Table 8–2 describes the wide range of public health concerns related to unintentional injury prevention. An important public health objective calls for an increase in the proportion of schools that provide school health education to prevent health problems in the area of unintentional injury. This chapter addresses the ways families, schools, and communities can work together to

---

| | YRBS |

TABLE 8–1

Youth Risk Behavior Survey Data Related to Unintentional Injuries, 2007

Risk Behavior	Percent Reporting Behavior		
	Total	Females	Males
Rarely or never wore seat belts when riding in a car driven by someone else	11.1	8.5	13.6
Rarely or never wore bicycle helmets (among the 66.8 percent of students who rode bicycles during the twelve months preceding the survey)	85.1	82.2	87.4
Rode with a driver who had been drinking alcohol during the past thirty days	29.1	28.8	29.5
Drove after drinking alcohol	10.5	8.1	12.8
Carried a gun on one or more of the thirty days preceding the survey	5.2	1.2	9.0

SOURCE: Centers for Disease Control and Prevention. "Youth Risk Behavior Surveillance—United States, 2007," *Morbidity and Mortality Weekly Report* 57, no. SS-4 (6 June 2008): 1–131.

TABLE 8–2

HEALTHY PEOPLE

Healthy People 2010 Objectives Related to Unintentional Injury

Objective 7-2	Increase the proportion of middle, junior high, and senior high schools that provide school health education to prevent health problems in the following areas: unintentional injury; violence; suicide; tobacco use and addiction; alcohol and other drug use; unintended pregnancy, HIV/AIDS, and STD infection; unhealthy dietary patterns; inadequate physical activity; and environmental health.
Objective 15-5	Reduce nonfatal firearm-related injuries to 10.9 injuries per 100,000 population.
Objective 15-8	Reduce deaths caused by poisonings to 1.8 deaths per 100,000 population.
Objective 15-9	Reduce deaths caused by suffocation to 2.9 deaths per 100,000 population.
Objective 15-14	Reduce nonfatal unintentional injuries.
Objective 15-15	Reduce deaths caused by motor vehicle crashes to 9.0 deaths per 100,000 population and 1 death per 100 million vehicle miles traveled.
Objective 15-16	Reduce pedestrian deaths on public roads to 1 pedestrian death per 100,000 population.
Objective 15-20	Increase use of child restraints to 100 percent of motor vehicle occupants aged 4 years and under.
Objective 15-23	Increase use of helmets by bicyclists.
Objective 15-25	Reduce residential fire deaths to 0.6 death per 100,000 population.
Objective 15-26	Increase functioning residential smoke alarms to 100 percent of residences, with a functioning smoke alarm on every floor.
Objective 15-29	Reduce drownings to 0.9 drowning per 100,000 population.
Objective 15-31	Increase the proportion of public and private schools that require use of appropriate head, face, eye, and mouth protection for students participating in school-sponsored physical activities.

SOURCE: U.S. Department of Health and Human Services, *Healthy People 2010: Understanding and Improving Health*, 2nd ed. (Washington, DC: U.S. Government Printing Office, 2000).

promote safety and prevent and reduce injuries among children and adolescents.

Safety and Unintentional Injury and Academic Performance

Every year between 20 and 25 percent of all children sustain an injury sufficiently severe to require medical attention, missed school, and/or bed rest.[9] Young children are at greater risk for many injuries. This increased risk may be attributable to many factors. Children are curious and like to explore their environment. This characteristic may lead children to sample the pills in the medicine cabinet, play with matches, or venture into the family pool. Young children have limited physical coordination and cognitive abilities. This can lead to a greater risk for falls from bicycles and playground equipment and make it difficult for them to escape from a fire. And their small size

and developing bones and muscles may make them more susceptible to injury in car crashes if they are not properly restrained.[13] When childhood and adolescent injuries result in days missed from school, academic performance is affected.

Factors That Influence Safety and Unintentional Injury

Several important factors play a role in unintentional injury morbidity and mortality. Racial disparities have already been mentioned. Rates of injuries among males are two to three times higher than among females, indicating risk-taking behavior by males and Western society's acceptance of it. Risk-taking behavior seems to begin early in the first decade of life and continues into adulthood, evidenced by behaviors such as drinking and driving, speeding, carrying a weapon, and using illicit drugs. All these behaviors can lead to an increased risk of injury.[11]

The science of injury prevention and control has moved away from a focus on "accident proneness" and parental supervision to an emphasis on the role of the environment as a modifiable risk or a protective factor for injury. Perhaps the most important environmental risk factor for injury among children is poverty.[12] Children living in poverty have a greater risk of almost every type of injury, including pedestrian–motor-vehicle collisions, fires and burns, drowning, falls, and violence. Poverty and parental educational differences account for nearly all of the increased risk of fatal injury among African American and Latino children. Poor children often live in firetraps and dilapidated housing, in tenements without heat or air conditioning, and in neighborhoods built for motor vehicles rather than for pedestrians or bicyclists. Poverty also can mean that children live in neighborhoods with high crime rates and easy access to guns, as well as low levels of neighborhood cohesion and little sense of self-efficacy. Lower levels of parental education make poor children less likely to use protective gear such as bike helmets, car seats, and personal flotation devices.[13]

At times, children and adolescents are powerless over situations that lead to injury (a small child who is held in an adult's arms, rather than being placed in a child safety seat, while riding in a car). However, many young people behave in ways that increase their risk of injury. These behaviors sometimes occur in combination. For example, among high school and college students, associations have been reported among thinking about suicide, not using seat belts, driving after drinking alcohol, carrying weapons, and engaging in physical fights.[14]

William M. Kane and Marcia Quackenbush explain that taking risks is part of growing up. They state,

> Children have a natural desire to grow up. They want to act like older kids. They want to feel like older kids. They like to look good in front of their peers, which often means looking more grown up. This is a normal, healthy developmental process, and every child does it to some degree. One of the places this process is played out is through risk taking.[15]

Helmets for bicycle safety should be a family habit.

Despite these factors, serious child and adolescent injuries are not inevitable. Frederick P. Rivara, a world-renowned expert in the field of injury prevention, stated,

> One of the most important tasks for education and health professionals, parents, and community members to undertake is to implement fully the strategies that have been shown to reduce injuries to children and adolescents. As many as one-third of injury fatalities in this age group could be prevented through strategies such as motor vehicle occupant protection, traffic calming to prevent pedestrian injuries, use of bicycle helmets, safe storage of guns, adequate pool fencing and use of personal flotation devices, and use of smoke detectors. . . . Some of these interventions require behavior change on the part of individuals, while others require behavior change at the level of communities and legislatures. . . . It is time for the United States to take the necessary steps to achieve the low injury rates seen in many other counties. Perhaps the most important change is in attitudes. All injuries to children must be viewed as preventable if the United States is to reduce disparities and the toll of trauma.[16]

GUIDELINES FOR SCHOOLS

State of the Practice

The CDC conducts the School Health Policies and Programs Study (SHPPS) every six years to monitor efforts to improve school health policies and programs.[17] Table 8-3 provides SHPPS 2006 data on the safety and unintentional injury concepts and skills that elementary and middle teachers reported teaching in at least one required class or course.

The percentage of schools that teach about safety topics in elementary and middle school classrooms has dropped dramatically since the previous SHPPS conducted in 2000. For example, the percentage of schools that taught about resisting peer pressure that would increase the risk of injuries went from 91.9 percent to 69.9 percent in elementary schools, and from 92.5 per-

cent to 60.9 percent in middle schools during the six-year interval. In another example, the percentage of schools that taught about fire safety went from 97.5 percent to 72.4 percent in elementary schools, and from 66.4 percent to 52.2 percent in middle schools. Injuries are the leading cause of death and disability among elementary and middle school youth. However, school subjects other than those on standardized tests increasingly are excluded from the K–8 curriculum.

State of the Art

Injury prevention efforts are most effective when schools and communities work in partnership. Students, teachers, parents and caregivers, school staff, and community members all play important roles.

The CDC's *School Health Guidelines to Prevent Unintentional Injuries and Violence* assist state and local education agencies and schools in promoting safety and help schools serve as safe places for students to learn.[18] The guidelines were developed in collaboration with experts from universities and national organizations and with federal, state, local, and volunteer agencies. They are based on extensive reviews of research, theory, and current practice in unintentional injury, violence, and suicide prevention; health education; and public health. The eight major recommendations for preventing injuries are

1. A social environment that promotes safety
2. A safe physical environment
3. Health education curriculum and instruction
4. Safe physical education, sports, and recreational activities
5. Health, counseling, psychological, and social services for students
6. Appropriate crisis and emergency response
7. Involvement of families and communities
8. Staff development to promote safety and prevent unintentional injuries, violence, and suicide

Teacher's Toolbox 8.1 summarizes the guidelines related specifically to safety and unintentional injury prevention.

Kane and Quackenbush, authors of *Teach and Talk: Safety and Risk,* recommended three steps for keeping young people safe:

- Prevent injury events.
- Prevent injury when events occur.
- Prevent disability and promote healing when injury occurs.[19]

These prevention principles occur at all levels—individual students, classrooms, schools, families, and communities. Thus, prevention efforts include teaching children to apply safety rules and skills and to assess risky situations as well as calling on adults to make the home, school, and community environments safer. Kane and Quackenbush stated,

> To help all kids be safe kids, injury prevention education must provide a foundation for children that enables them

TABLE 8–3

School Health Policies and Programs Survey 2006 Data Related to Unintentional Injury

Topic and Skills	Percent of Schools Teaching Topic/Skill in a Required Class	
	Elementary Schools	Middle and Junior High Schools
Emergency preparedness	63.6	56.4
Fire safety	72.4	52.2
First aid	49.3	56.2
CPR	15.2	37.1
Gun safety	26.9	18.5
Influence of families on behaviors related to safety	51.1	47.0
Influence of media on behaviors related to safety	39.7	43.5
Motor vehicle occupant safey (seat belt use)	68.5	54.3
Pedestrian safety	68.6	35.0
Playground safety	79.9	NA
Poisoning prevention	47.0	39.8
Relationship between alcohol or other drug use and injuries	51.3	60.0
Social or culture influences on behaviors related to safety	37.8	41.8
Use of protective equipment for biking, skating, or other sports	69.2	55.4
Water safety	54.6	42.8
How students can influence or support others to prevent injuries	68.6	58.7
How to find valid information or services to prevent injuries	31.3	47.7
Resisting peer pressure that would increase risk of injuries	69.9	60.9

SOURCE: Centers for Disease Control and Prevention *School Health Policies and Programs Study 2006 (SHPPS)* (Atlanta, GA: CDC, 2007). www.cdc.gov/HealthyYouth/shpps

to make smart, safe choices when they face risky situations. Activities and projects that build a sense of community and belonging are among the most important. A connected community protects its own, speaks up to get help when needed, and knows that every individual in the community is important. This is a powerful perspective to have when assessing risky situations or thinking about ways to support friends.[20]

Similarly, the National Injury Prevention Foundation explained that elementary school–age children are at an impressionable stage of development, during which they enjoy learning new responsibilities and decision-making skills and attempting to influence their family members and peers. Teachings directed to this age group have the potential to increase safety behaviors that will be maintained through the high-risk adolescent years and become lifelong habits.[21]

The Centers for Disease Control and Prevention released the Health Education Curriculum Analysis Tool (HECAT), an exciting new resource to help educators consider state-of-the-art practice in health education. The S module uses the National Health Education Standards as the framework for the tools to analyze and determine the extent to which the curriculum is likely to enable students to master the essential knowledge and skills that promote safety. Educators will find curriculum fundamentals, such as teacher materials, instructional design, and instructional strategies and materials analyses. This chapter includes

healthy behavior outcomes and developmentally appropriate concepts and skills for promoting safety provided in the HECAT. The HECAT is available at the Healthy Youth website of the Division of Adolescent and School Health (DASH) at CDC (www.cdc.gov/HealthyYouth/HECAT/index.htm).

GUIDELINES FOR CLASSROOM APPLICATIONS

Important Background for K–8 Teachers

The CDC defines *injury* as "unintentional or intentional damage to the body resulting from acute exposure to thermal, mechanical, electrical, or chemical energy or from the absence of such essentials as heat or oxygen." Injuries further can be classified based on the events and behaviors that precede them as well as the intent of the persons involved. At the broadest level, injuries are classified as either *violence* (intentional) or *unintentional injuries.*[22]

The events that lead to unintentional injuries often are referred to as accidents, although scientific evidence indicates that many of these events can be predicted and prevented. Students can learn to keep themselves safe by internalizing core concepts and practicing injury prevention skills such as self-management, communication, decision making, and peer resistance. Students need opportunities to determine solutions to a range of safety scenarios.

Recommendations for the Prevention of Unintentional Injuries

Establish a social environment that promotes safety and prevents unintentional injuries.

- Ensure high academic standards and provide faculty, staff members, and students with the support and administrative leadership to promote the academic success, health, and safety of students.
- Encourage students' feelings of connectedness to school.
- Designate a person with responsibility for coordinating safety activities.
- Establish a climate that demonstrates respect, support, and caring.
- Develop and implement written policies regarding unintentional injury.
- Infuse unintentional injury prevention into multiple school activities and classes.
- Establish unambiguous disciplinary policies; communicate them to students, faculty, staff members, and families; and implement them consistently.
- Assess unintentional injury prevention strategies and policies at regular intervals.

Provide a physical environment, inside and outside school buildings, that promotes safety and prevents unintentional injuries.

- Conduct regular safety and hazard assessments.
- Maintain structures, playground and other equipment, school buses and other vehicles, and physical grounds; make repairs immediately following identification of hazards.
- Actively supervise all student activities to promote safety and prevent unintentional injuries.
- Ensure that the school environment, including school buses, is free from weapons.

Implement health and safety education curricula and instruction that help students develop the knowledge, attitudes, behavioral skills, and confidence needed to adopt and maintain safe lifestyles and to advocate for health and safety.

- Choose prevention programs and curricula that are grounded in theory or that have scientific evidence of effectiveness.
- Implement unintentional injury prevention curricula consistent with national and state standards for health education.
- Use active learning strategies, interactive teaching methods, and proactive classroom management to encourage student involvement in learning about unintentional injury prevention.
- Provide adequate staffing and resources, including budget, facilities, staff development, and class time to provide unintentional injury prevention education for all students.

Provide safe physical education and extracurricular physical activity programs.

- Develop, teach, implement, and enforce safety rules.

- Promote unintentional injury prevention through physical education and physical activity program participation.
- Ensure that spaces and facilities for physical activity meet or exceed safety standards for design, installation, and maintenance.
- Hire physical education teachers, coaches, athletic trainers, and other physical activity program staff members who are trained in injury prevention, first aid, and CPR and provide them with ongoing staff development.

Provide health, counseling, psychological, and social services to meet the physical, mental, emotional, and social health needs of students.

- Coordinate school-based counseling, psychological, social, and health services and the education curriculum.
- Establish strong links with community resources and identify providers to bring services into the schools.
- Identify and provide assistance to students who have been seriously injured.
- Assess the extent to which injuries occur on school property.
- Develop and implement emergency plans for assessing, managing, and referring injured students and staff members to appropriate levels of care.

Establish mechanisms for short- and long-term response to crises, disasters, and injuries that affect the school community.

- Establish a written plan for responding to crises, disasters, and associated injuries.
- Prepare to implement the school's plan in the event of a crisis.
- Have short-term responses and services established after a crisis.
- Have long-term responses and services established after a crisis.

Integrate school, family, and community efforts to prevent unintentional injuries.

- Involve parents, students, and other family members in all aspects of school life, including planning and implementing unintentional injury prevention programs and policies.
- Educate, support, and involve family members in child and adolescent unintentional injury prevention.
- Coordinate school and community services.

For all school personnel, provide regular staff development opportunities that impart the knowledge, skills, and confidence to effectively promote safety and prevent unintentional injury; support students in their efforts to do the same.

- Ensure that staff members are knowledgeable about unintentional injury prevention and have the skills needed to prevent injuries at school, at home, and in the community.
- Train and support all personnel to be positive role models for a healthy and safe lifestyle.

SOURCE: Centers for Disease Control and Prevention, Guidelines for School Health Programs to Prevent Unintentional Injuries and Violence, *MMWR Recommendations and Reports* 50, no. RR-22 (7 December 2001): 1–46.

Safety instruction should include active learning strategies, interactive teaching methods, and proactive classroom management techniques that encourage calm, orderly classrooms. Active learning strategies engage students in learning and help them develop the concepts, attitudes, and behavioral skills they need to act safely.[23]

Teachers should remember that young students often do not fully understand abstract concepts or different perspectives. For example, young children might assume that drivers can see them and will stop simply because the children see the car coming. Safety instruction for younger students must focus on concrete experiences, such as practicing—not just hearing about—skills such as crossing the street or feeling a door to find out whether it's hot or cold to the touch. More abstract associations among behaviors, environment, and injury risk become appropriate as students enter the upper-elementary and middle-level grades. Although families play an important role in children's safety decisions, peer pressure to engage in risky behaviors becomes a strong motivator as students grow older. By the time children enter middle school, they are far more capable of understanding and acting on the connection between behaviors and injury risks.[24]

Educational programs must be appropriate for the cultures in the community. Students within the same school and even within the same classroom have diverse experiences, knowledge, attitudes, abilities, and behaviors with respect to health and safety. Rather than adopting a one-size-fits-all approach to safety, educators should take this diversity into account to increase the likelihood of reaching students in meaningful ways. For example, if the streets in a particular community don't have street names or road signs, students must learn other ways to tell someone how to get to their house in an emergency (We live at the end of the road that runs by the creek).

In busy classrooms, teachers often want to know exactly what their students should be learning for their age or developmental level. In truth, teachers cannot know this without first getting to know their students, their students' families, and their students' communities. As an experienced teacher aptly put it to a group of preservice teachers, "Don't think of your students as one class of twenty-five—think of them as twenty-five classes of one." Teachers must take the time to find out what their students know and want to know about safety and unintentional injury topics as they plan instruction appropriate for the particular children in their classrooms.

The National Center for Injury Prevention and Control (Injury Center) targets injuries related to transportation, home, and recreation activities. The types of injury and violence that pose the greatest threat to American youth are child passenger safety, fireworks-related injuries, playground injuries, poisonings, residential fire-related injuries, traumatic brain injury, and water safety. This section also includes information on pedestrian and bicycle safety, sports and recreation activities, and children home alone.[25]

Children under age 12 should ride in the backseat; younger children may need booster seats. Everyone in the vehicle should be secured with a seat belt.

Child Passenger Safety

Motor-vehicle injuries, the leading cause of death and the greatest public health problem for today's children, often stem from the behavior of drivers rather than from the behavior of children. One out of four occupant deaths among children from birth to age 14 involves a drinking driver. More than two-thirds of fatally injured children were riding with drinking drivers. In addition, use of restraints (car seats, seat belts) among young children often depends on the driver's own use of a restraint. Almost 40 percent of children riding with unbelted drivers are themselves unrestrained.[26]

Most motor-vehicle injuries can be prevented. Children should be properly restrained in car seats or with seat belts, and children age 12 and younger should ride in the backseat of a car to avoid possible serious injury from airbag deployment. Community awareness campaigns, school-based programs, public service announcements, billboard campaigns, and booster-seat distribution events and car-seat checkpoints have resulted in a significant increase in booster-seat use in targeted communities. Laws that mandate the use of child safety seats and safety belts and programs that distribute child safety seats and educate parents about their proper use also have been effective.[27]

At the classroom level, teachers can involve students and their families in education and awareness efforts to increase proper child restraint in motor vehicles. At a minimum, students should know that they should

- Always wear a seat belt, or sit in a booster seat if appropriate for their size, every time they ride in a car.
- Ride in the backseat if they are 12 years of age or younger.

Fireworks-related Injuries

Teachers may be surprised to see fireworks-related injuries on the list of priority prevention behaviors. However, depending on the community in which children live, fireworks can be a real danger. Of course, the safest way to prevent fireworks-related injuries is to leave fireworks displays to trained professionals. About 60 percent of all fireworks-related injuries in 2005 occurred between June 18 and July 18. During that time period,

- About 45 percent of persons injured from fireworks were children ages 14 years and younger.
- Males were injured by fireworks more than twice as often as females.
- Children ages 10 to 14 years had the highest injury rate.

The National Center for Injury Prevention and Control reports that despite federal regulations and varying state prohibitions, many types of fireworks are accessible to the public. It is not uncommon to find fireworks distributors near state borders, where residents of states with strict fireworks regulations can take advantage of more lenient state laws. Among the various types of fireworks, sold legally in some states, bottle rockets can fly into the face and cause eye injuries, sparklers can ignite clothing, and firecrackers can injure the hands or face if they explode at close range.

Injuries can result from being too close to fireworks when they explode. Younger children often lack the physical coordination to handle fireworks safely. In addition, children are often excited and curious around fireworks, which can increase their chances of being injured. In particular, homemade fireworks can lead to dangerous explosions.[28]

If appropriate to the community, teachers can engage their students in discussions about safety around fireworks before holidays, such as New Year's Eve and the Fourth of July. Students can access information about fireworks danger—for example, sparklers can burn at more the 1000 degrees Fahrenheit. Decision-making and self-management scenarios also make for lively discussion about fireworks safety.

Playground Injuries

Each year in the United States, emergency departments treat more than 200,000 children ages 14 and younger for playground-related injuries. About 45 percent of playground-related injuries are severe—fractures, internal injuries, concussions, dislocations, and amputations. Although all children who use playgrounds are at risk for injury, girls sustain injuries slightly more often than boys. Children ages 5 to 9 have higher rates of emergency department visits for playground injuries than any other age group. Most of these injuries occur at school.[29]

A lack of supervision often is associated with playground injuries. In addition to providing close adult supervision, teachers can help students learn and apply the following basic information about fall prevention:

- Play safely by taking turns on equipment. Help everyone remember not to push.

Playground safety: Take care of yourself, take care of others, take care of this place.

- Talk with parents, caregivers, and teachers about playground rules and safety.
- Ask adults if your playground has the right kind of soft surface to prevent injuries.
- Be careful on stairs and ladders (on sliding boards). Take your time in order to stay safe and prevent falls.
- Ask for help from adults if you see an unsafe situation on the playground.

Poisonings

The National Center for Injury Prevention and Control defines poison as any substance that is harmful to the body when ingested (eaten), inhaled (breathed), injected, or absorbed through the skin. Any substance can be poisonous if enough is taken. For this reason, "poisoning" implies that too much of some substance has been taken. This definition does not include adverse reactions to medications taken correctly.

Poisonings are either intentional or unintentional. Intentional poisoning is the result of a person taking or giving a substance with the intention of causing harm. Suicide and assault by poisoning fall into this category. If the person taking or giving a substance did not mean to cause harm, then it is an unintentional poisoning. Unintentional poisoning includes the use of drugs or chemicals for recreational purposes in excessive amounts, such as an overdose. It also includes the excessive use of drugs or chemicals for non-recreational purposes, such as by a toddler. When the distinction between intentional and unintentional is unclear, poisonings are usually labeled undetermined in intent.

Nonfatal poisonings treated in emergency departments that involve "accidentally" taking prescription or over-the-counter drugs primarily affect children. Among such incidents in 2004, pain and cardiovascular medications, antidepressants, and sedative/hypnotics were most commonly ingested. Acetaminophen-containing drugs, nonsteroidal anti-inflammatory drugs, and opioids were the leading types of pain medications.[30]

Teachers can help students learn and apply the following basic information about poison prevention:

- Call 9-1-1, the operator (dial 0), or the national poison control hotline (800-222-1222) in a poisoning emergency.
- Work with your family to be sure all poisonous materials are out of sight and out of the reach of young children.
- Check inside and outside the home for potential hazards, including poisonous plants, to protect small children and pets.
- Work with your family to be sure all medications are out of the reach of small children.
- Take medications only with adult supervision.

Residential Fire-related Injuries

Deaths from fires and burns are the fifth most common cause of unintentional injury death in the United States and the third leading cause of fatal home injury. The U.S. mortality rate from fires ranks sixth among the twenty-five developed countries for which statistics are available. Although the number of fatalities and injuries caused by residential fires has declined gradually over the past several decades, many residential fire-related deaths remain preventable and continue to pose a significant public health problem.

Small children and those living in substandard housing are at increased risk of fire-related injury and death. Approximately half of home fire deaths occur in homes without smoke alarms. Most residential fires occur during the winter months.[31]

At the classroom level, teachers can involve students and their families in education and awareness efforts to increase fire safety in the home. Teachers can help students learn that they should

- Check with their families to be sure they have a working smoke detector in the home and to check the batteries once every month.
- Plan a home fire escape route with their families.
- Keep matches and lighters out of the reach of young children.
- Work with their families to inspect their homes for potential fire hazards, such as frayed electrical cords, overloaded outlets, curtains or towels hanging over the stove, and improper storage of flammable liquids.
- Keep the handles of pots and pans turned toward the back of the stove, out of the reach of young children.
- Practice the "stop, drop, and roll" method for putting out clothing fires. Students should learn that "roll" may mean to rock back and forth to put out the fire—some teachers teach children to "stop, drop, and rock."
- Stay away from fallen electrical wires, and notify adults right away.

Traumatic Brain Injury

A traumatic brain injury (TBI) is defined as a blow or jolt to the head or a penetrating head injury that disrupts the function of the brain. Not all blows or jolts to the head result in TBI. Severity may range from mild (a brief change in mental status or consciousness) to severe (an extended period of unconsciousness or amnesia after the injury). A TBI can result in short- or long-term problems with independent functioning. Major causes of TBI are falls, motor-vehicle crashes, and assaults.[32]

An excellent resource for teachers and students related to TBI prevention is the ThinkFirst National Injury Prevention Foundation (www.thinkfirst.org). The ThinkFirst for Kids Program was developed to increase knowledge and awareness among elementary school children about the causes and consequences of brain and spinal-cord injury, injury prevention, and safety habits that reduce the risk of injury. ThinkFirst includes lessons on water, bicycle, vehicle, and playground safety. The site includes information for kids, youth, teens, and teachers.

Water Safety

For every child 14 years and younger who died from drowning in 2004, five received emergency department care for nonfatal submersion injuries. More than half of these children were hospitalized or transferred to another facility for treatment. Nonfatal drownings can cause brain damage that results in long-term disabilities ranging from memory problems and learning disabilities to the permanent loss of basic functioning (permanent vegetative state). Although drowning rates have slowly declined, fatal drowning remains the second-leading cause of unintentional injury-related death for children ages 1 to 14 years.[33]

Adult supervision is the key to drowning prevention. In addition, children can learn more about water safety at sites such as Kids' Health (www.kidshealth.org). The site offers information on staying safe in swimming pools, around lakes and ponds, at beaches, and at water parks—and on learning to swim.

Pedestrian and Bicycle Safety

The Safe Kids Worldwide campaign (www.safekids.org) sponsors an annual International Walk to School Day (www.walktoschool.org) in early October. The campaign includes walking and biking to school. According to Safe Kids, child pedestrians are at great risk of being seriously injured or killed, despite a sharp decline in the death rate during the past ten years, and children age 9 and younger have the highest death rate from pedestrian injuries. Safe Kids also found that nearly 60 percent of parents and kids encounter serious hazards on their route to school, including a lack of sidewalks or crosswalks, wide roads, complicated traffic conditions, improper parking, and speeding drivers.[34]

Teachers can find educational materials on International Walk to School Day at www.walktoschool.org. The

Children younger than age 10 should cross the street with an adult.

immature or undeveloped coordination, skills, and perception.[37]

Students participate in many kinds of sports, recreation, and exercise, depending on availability in the community. Participation varies widely. Children in some parts of the United States participate in winter activities such as snow skiing and ice-skating. In other parts of the country, children surf, boogie-board, and swim in the open ocean. In many communities, children participate in activities such as skateboarding, in-line skating, and bicycling.

More information on SRE safety can be found in Chapter 7, on promoting physical activity. Teachers and students also can access a number of websites with information on sports, recreation, and exercise safety. Students can conduct their own investigations into safety for different kinds of SREs; see the recommended websites.

campaign is designed to increase safety as well as physical activity among children and their families.[35] The website contains a link to the downloadable National Highway Traffic Safety Administration (NHTSA) Safe Routes to School Toolkit. Simple steps suggested in the toolkit for staying safe include

- When walking, stop at every curb or edge.
- Always look and listen, especially while crossing. Look left, look right, and then look left again before stepping past any curb or edge.
- Always wear a helmet when riding a bike.
- Always ride in the same direction as traffic.
- Know what signs say. When walking or riding, follow all traffic signs and signals.
- When riding, always stop; look left, look right, and then look left again before pulling out of a driveway.[36]

Sports and Recreation Activities

Participation in sports, recreation, and exercise (SRE) is increasingly popular and widespread in American culture. SRE activities include organized sports (school or club) and unorganized sports (backyard or pickup), such as basketball, football, and hockey; recreational activities, such as boating, biking, skiing, swimming, and playground activities; and exercise and training activities, such as weight-lifting, aerobics, and jogging. Participation in SRE activities contributes to health-related fitness; however, the risk of injury is inherent in any physical activity. Risk of injury varies depending on many factors, including the specific activity and the participant's age. Children younger than age 15 account for 25 percent of all drownings and about 40 percent of all SRE-related emergency room visits. They might be at greater risk because of

Children Home Alone

Every day thousands of children arrive home from school to an empty house. The American Academy of Child and Adolescent Psychiatry estimates that more than 40 percent of children are left home alone at some time, though rarely overnight. In more extreme situations, some children spend so much time at home without their parents or caregivers that they are called "latch key children," referring to the house or apartment key strung visibly around their neck.[38]

The National Child Care Information Center notes that most states do not have regulations or laws about when a child is considered old enough to care for him/herself or to care for other children. Illinois and Maryland do have laws on this topic, and some other states have guidelines or recommendations, often distributed through Child Protective Services or at the county level.[39]

Parents and caregivers should work carefully with children to teach them about safety issues, such as not opening the door, staying in the house, answering the phone properly, practicing what to do if something goes wrong, knowing emergency numbers, and practicing what to say if they need to call 9-1-1.

Being home alone can be a frightening and stressful experience for children. In addition to the important teaching that parents and caregivers must do with their children to minimize danger and keep them safe, teachers can talk with students about safety issues after school. KidsHealth (www.kidshealth.org) provides an excellent overview for students, entitled "When It's Just You After School." The site provides ideas for ground rules, staying safe, and strategies for dealing with feeling lonely.[40]

Other Safety Topics

Teacher may want to address other safety topics with their students, depending on the needs of the children and families of the local community. Example topics include

- Safety around animals
- Holiday safety
- First aid
- CPR
- Safety around strangers
- Natural disasters
- School bus safety
- Field trip safety
- Internet safety
- Safety for children with special needs

Safe Kids USA (www.usa.safekids.org/index.cfm) provides information and strategies on sixteen safety topics and is a very useful resource for teachers and parents/caregivers.[41]

Recommendations for Concepts and Practice

Healthy Behavior Outcomes

The goal of health education is to help students adopt or maintain health-enhancing behaviors. School districts and teachers should identify the health-enhancing behaviors they would like their students to maintain or adopt. The following list identifies some possible healthy behavior outcomes related to promoting safety and preventing unintentional injury. Though not all suggestions are developmentally appropriate for students in grades K–8, this list can help teachers understand how the learning activities they plan for their students support both short- and long-term desirable behavior outcomes.

> **Ways to Promote Safety and Prevent Unintentional Injury**
>
> Wear safety belts in motor vehicles.
>
> Sit in booster seats in the rear of the vehicle when age-appropriate.
>
> Sit in the backseat of the vehicle when age-appropriate.
>
> Avoid using alcohol and other drugs when driving a motor vehicle.
>
> Avoid riding in a car with a driver who is under the influence of alcohol or other drugs.
>
> Use appropriate safety equipment.
>
> Refuse to dare others or accept dares to engage in risky behaviors.
>
> Practice safety rules and procedures to avoid injury.
>
> Plan ahead to avoid dangerous situations and injuries.
>
> Seek help for poisoning, sudden illness, and injuries.
>
> Provide immediate help to others experiencing a sudden illness or injury.[42]

Developmentally Appropriate Concepts and Skills

As with other health topics, teaching related to promoting safety and preventing unintentional injury should be developmentally appropriate and be based on the physical, cognitive, social, emotional, and language characteristics of specific students. Teacher's Toolbox 8.2 contains a list of suggested developmentally appropriate concepts and skills to help teachers create lessons that encourage students to practice the desired healthy behavior outcomes by the time they graduate from high school.

STRATEGIES FOR LEARNING AND ASSESSMENT

Promoting Safety and Preventing Unintentional Injury

This section provides examples of standards-based learning and assessment strategies for promoting safety and preventing unintentional injury. The sample strategies begin with a restatement of the standard and a reminder of the assessment criteria, drawn from the RMC rubrics in Appendix B. Strategies are written as directions for teachers and include applicable theory of planned behavior (TPB) constructs in parentheses (intention to act in healthy ways, attitudes toward behavior, subjective norms, perceived behavioral control). These learning and assessment strategies provide building blocks for standards-based lessons and units that can be tailored to local needs. Assessment criteria are used with permission from the Rocky Mountain Center for Health Promotion and Education (RMC). See Appendix B for Scoring Rubrics.

Additional strategies for learning and assessment for Chapter 8 can be found at the Online Learning Center. Appendix D, a complete list of all the strategies, is available at the Online Learning Center.

NHES 1 | Core Concepts

Students will comprehend concepts related to health promotion and disease prevention to enhance health.

ASSESSMENT CRITERIA

- Connections—Describe relationships between behavior and health; draw logical conclusions about connections between behavior and health.
- Comprehensiveness—Thoroughly cover health topic, showing breadth and depth; give accurate information.

Grades K–2

Safety Rules and Practices   Provide opportunities for children to learn the most important facts and ideas relevant to early elementary students about these safety topics:

- Safety hazards in the home, school, and community
- Behaviors that can lead to injury
- Calling for and getting help in case of an injury or emergency
- Poisoning prevention (household products, medicines, help from adults)
- Fire safety

Developmentally Appropriate Concepts and Skills to Promote Safety and Prevent Unintentional Injury

Grades K–2 Concepts	Grades 3–5 Concepts	Grades 6–8 Concepts

NHES 1: Core Concepts

Grades K–2 Concepts

- Identify safety hazards in the home.
- Explain safe behaviors when getting on and off and while riding on school buses.
- Identify safety hazards in the community.
- Recognize that injuries can be prevented.
- Identify safety rules for being around fire.
- State how to safely take medications.
- Explain the importance of using safety belts and motor vehicle booster seats.
- State safety rules for being around firearms.
- State how to be a safe pedestrian.
- Identify ways to reduce injuries on the playground.

Grades 3–5 Concepts

- List ways to prevent injuries at home.
- List ways to prevent injuries at school.
- List ways to prevent injuries in the community.
- Explain how injuries can be prevented.
- List examples of dangerous or risky behaviors that might lead to injuries.
- Identify ways to reduce risk of injuries around water.
- Identify ways to reduce risk of injuries in case of fire.
- Explain why household products are harmful if ingested or inhaled.
- Explain the harmful effects of medicines when used incorrectly.
- Describe the use of safety equipment for specific physical activities.
- Identify ways to reduce risk of injuries while riding in a motor vehicle.
- Identify ways to reduce injuries from firearms.
- Identify ways to reduce risk of injuries as a pedestrian.
- Identify ways to reduce risk of injuries from animal and insect bites and stings.
- Identify ways to reduce injuries from falls.
- Identify ways to prevent vision or hearing damage.
- Identify safety precautions for physical activities in different kinds of weather and climates.
- Describe how to ride a bike, skateboard, ride a scooter, and/or in-line skate safely.
- Explain what to do if someone is poisoned (e.g., by household cleaning or paint products) or injured and needs help (e.g., calling 9-1-1, poison control center, or other local emergency number).
- Identify basic safety precautions to help prevent injury during physical activity.

Grades 6–8 Concepts

- Describe actions to change unsafe situations at home.
- Describe actions to change unsafe situations at school.
- Describe actions to change unsafe situations in the community.
- Explain how the interaction of individual behaviors, the environment, and characteristics of products cause or prevent injuries.
- Describe situations that could lead to unsafe risks that cause injuries.
- Describe ways to reduce risk of injuries around water.
- Describe ways to reduce risk of injuries in case of fire.
- Describe potential risks associated with over-the-counter medicines.
- Determine the benefits of reducing the risks for injury.
- Describe ways to reduce risk of injuries from participation in sports and other physical activities.
- Describe ways to reduce risk of injuries while riding in or on a motor vehicle (e.g., automobile, snowmobile, jet ski).
- Explain the importance of helmets and other safety gear for biking, riding a scooter, skateboarding, and in-line skating.
- Describe ways to reduce risk of injuries from firearms.
- Describe ways to reduce risk of injuries as a pedestrian.
- Describe ways to reduce risk of injuries from falls.
- Identify actions to take to prevent injuries during severe weather (e.g., thunderstorms, tornadoes, blizzards).
- Describe the relationship between using alcohol and other drugs and injuries.
- Explain the risks associated with using alcohol or other drugs and driving a motor vehicle.
- Discuss climate-related physical conditions that affect physical activity, such as heat exhaustion, sunburn, heat stroke, and hypothermia.
- Describe first response procedures needed to treat injuries and other emergencies.
- Identify personal protection equipment needed for sports and recreational activities (e.g., mouthpieces, pads, helmets).
- Describe the behavioral and environmental factors associated with the major causes of death in the United States.

Grades K–2 Skills	Grades 3–5 Skills	Grades 6–8 Skills

NHES 2: Analyze Influence

• Explain the influence of family in preventing injuries. • Describe how rules at school can help prevent injury.	• Describe internal influences that could lead to unintentional injury. • Explain the influence of family and peers in preventing injuries. • Describe external influences that could lead to unintentional injury. • Describe factors that influence a person's decision to engage in safe or unsafe behaviors.	• Describe how personal values and feelings influence choices. • Analyze the role of peers and family in causing or preventing injuries. • Examine the role of the media and its possible effects on safety-related behavior. • Analyze the relationship between alcohol and other drugs and unintentional injury. • Describe federal, state, or local laws intended to prevent injuries.

NHES 3: Accessing Information, Products, and Services

• Identify sources for accurate information about medicines. • Demonstrate ability to access appropriate school and community resources for safety information. • Demonstrate how to dial 911 or other emergency numbers and provide appropriate information. • Identify a trusted adult who can help read and follow directions on medicine labels.	• Identify sources for accurate information about potentially poisonous household products. • Identify accurate sources of information about how to prevent injury. • Demonstrate the ability to access accurate sources of information about how to prevent injuries. • Demonstrate how to seek help from a trusted adult. • Demonstrate the ability to access important phone numbers to get help in emergencies. • Demonstrate how to access a trusted adult who can help someone who may have been injured or poisoned. • Demonstrate the ability to read and follow labels of common household products about dangers, safe use, storage, and proper disposal.	• Demonstrate how to follow directions for correct use of over-the-counter and prescription medications. • Analyze sources for accurate information about how to prevent injury. • Demonstrate the ability to access accurate information about safety and unintentional injury. • Demonstrate the ability to access injury prevention programs and services provided in the school and community. • Demonstrate how to report situations that could lead to unintentional injury. • Demonstrate how to access a trusted adult who can help someone who may have been injured or poisoned.

NHES 4: Interpersonal Communication

• Demonstrate effective refusal skills to avoid unsafe situations. • Demonstrate verbal and nonverbal ways to ask an adult for help about an unsafe situation.	• Demonstrate what to say when calling 9-1-1 or other emergency numbers. • Demonstrate verbal and nonverbal ways to ask an adult for help about an unsafe situation. • Demonstrate peer resistance skills to refuse to participate in unsafe or dangerous behaviors. • Demonstrate effective negotiation skills to avoid riding in a car with someone who has been using alcohol or other drugs.	• Demonstrate verbal and nonverbal communication to avoid unsafe situations. • Demonstrate effective negotiation skills to avoid riding in a car with someone who has been using alcohol or other drugs. • Demonstrate how to communicate clear expectations, boundaries, and personal safety strategies. • Demonstrate how to report situations that could lead to unintentional injury.

NHES 5: Decision Making

• Explain the steps to follow to use medications appropriately and correctly. • Demonstrate how to make a decision to call 911 or other emergency numbers for help.	• Demonstrate safe decisions to prevent injuries (e.g., wear a bicycle helmet, wear a seat belt). • Demonstrate how to make a decision to call 911 or other emergency numbers for help. • Suggest alternatives to unsafe behaviors. • Make a personal commitment to use appropriate protective gear during physical activity. • Discuss methods for making decisions to avoid injuries.	• Develop and apply a decision-making process for avoiding situations that could lead to injury. • Suggest alternatives to unsafe situations at home, at school, and in the community. • Make a personal commitment to always wear a safety belt when riding in a motor vehicle.

(continued)

Grades K–2 Skills *(continued)*	Grades 3–5 Skills *(continued)*	Grades 6–8 Skills *(continued)*

NHES 6: Goal Setting

• Set a goal to remain injury-free during recess at school or during play at home.	• Set goals to remain injury-free during recesses at school and at play in the home and community. • Monitor behaviors related to safety (e.g., wearing seat belts and bicycle helmets). • Make a personal commitment to be safe.	• Set a personal goal to remain injury-free. • Demonstrate the ability to monitor behaviors related to safety (e.g., wearing seat belts and protective gear). • Make a personal commitment to be safe. • Describe how personal goals can be affected by unsafe practices and injury.

NHES 7: Self-Management

• Demonstrate ability to follow playground safety rules. • Demonstrate safe pedestrian behaviors. • Apply strategies to avoid fires and burns. • Demonstrate actions to avoid accidental poisoning by household products. • Demonstrate ways to stay safe while participating in a variety of activities. • Acknowledge personal responsibility for asking an adult for help when taking medications.	• Demonstrate safe pedestrian behaviors. • Demonstrate ability to develop and execute a fire escape plan. • Demonstrate how to store dangerous chemicals and materials safely. • Demonstrate the use of safety equipment for physical activity. • Express intentions to use protective gear to avoid injuries. • Explain how to use medicines safely. • Demonstrate safety practices around motorized vehicles.	• Demonstrate the ability to test smoke alarms. • Demonstrate the ability to identify and correct safety hazards in the home, at school, and in the community. • Demonstrate the correct use of protective equipment during sports and physical activity. • Demonstrate the proper way to use a variety of safety gear. • Demonstrate how to warm up and cool down in order to maximize the benefits of physical activity and minimize injury. • Demonstrate basic first responder first aid (e.g., calling for assistance, controlling bleeding). • Express intentions to wear a safety belt whenever riding in a motor vehicle.

NHES 8: Advocacy

• Demonstrate the ability to influence safety practices of family members.	• Demonstrate the ability to influence others' safety practices (e.g., wearing bicycle helmets and seat belts). • Demonstrate ways to publicly campaign to help promote safety and prevent unintentional injuries.	• Demonstrate the ability to influence others' safety behaviors (e.g., wearing bicycle helmets, using seat belts, using shop equipment safely). • Advocate for changes in the home (e.g., testing smoke detectors, implementing a fire escape plan, erecting fencing around swimming pools). • Advocate for a safe school environment (e.g., using non-slip floor materials, building handrails on stairs, maintaining athletic equipment).

SOURCE: Centers for Disease Control and Prevention, *Health Education Curriculum Analysis Tool (HECAT)* (Atlanta, GA: CDC, 2007). www.cdc.gov/HealthyYouth/Hecat/index.htm

- Water safety
- Motor-vehicle safety (seat belts, booster seats, sitting in the backseat)
- School bus safety
- Pedestrian safety
- Insect bites and stings
- Safety around animals
- Playground safety
- Safety around firearms (tell an adult)
- Safety around fireworks (leave to professionals)
- Safety on bicycles, skateboards, scooters, and in-line skates
- Wearing protective equipment for sports and athletics
- Safety during physical activity (warm-up and cooldown)
- Safety in different kinds of weather

To begin, find out what children already know and can tell about safety rules and practices. Children may know a great deal that they've learned at home, in preschool, or in earlier grades. By sharing in the children's discussions, teachers have the opportunity to correct misperceptions. Other ideas are to (1) use Know-Wonder-Learn (KWL) charts, (2) have children work in small groups to list what they know about a particular safety topic and then share with the class, (3) invite guest speakers to talk about safety topics, (4) make field trips, such as to the fire department, and (5) have older children share with younger children about safety topics.

ASSESSMENT | For an assessment task, children can write, create drawings, or present skits to demonstrate their knowledge. For assessment criteria, students should present information that is accurate and show connections between behaviors and safety. (Construct: Attitudes toward behavior.)

Safe and Unsafe Behaviors and Situations In the context of various safety topics, children can identify safe and unsafe behaviors and situations. Children enjoy acting out scenarios and using puppets to show what is safe and unsafe. Children can make connections between behaviors and safety.

ASSESSMENT | The children's dramatizations are the assessment task for this activity. For assessment criteria, children should provide correct information and make connections between behaviors and safety. (Construct: Attitudes toward behavior.)

Grades 3–5

Please Play Safely on the Playground! Margery Cuyler's book, *Please Play Safe! Penguin's Guide to Playground Safety* (see the book list at the end of the chapter) is a child-friendly guide to playground behaviors. Children hear about playground behaviors (climbing up the slide, jumping off a seesaw too quickly), followed by the question, "Is that right?" as Penguin explains the safe way to behave. Teachers can involve children right away in this story about how to act safely when they are playing with others. Children can work with a partner or group of three to develop scenarios for their own school playground, as well as going to and from the playground. Teachers might want to videotape the live action scenes to make a class movie about playing safely, or take pictures to make a class book.

ASSESSMENT | The scenarios are the assessment task. For assessment criteria, children should demonstrate unsafe ways to act, followed by safe behavior. Children should explain, in writing or for the camera, the connections between safe and unsafe behavior and health. (Construct: Attitudes toward behavior.)

Telling Fact from Fiction Teachers can ask children to brainstorm a list of safety topics. Teachers should add to the list as needed. Children can work in small groups to investigate a safety issue of their choosing. Their assignment is to help classmates review and update their knowledge about safety by making fact-or-fiction statements for classmates to discuss and distinguish among. This activity links to NHES 3, access information, products, and services. Students can use the list of topics for the activity "Safety Rules and Practices" to help them choose a safety issue or topic.

ASSESSMENT | The children's fact-or-fiction statements and the students' responses are the assessment task for this activity. For assessment criteria, students should provide accurate information and make connections between behaviors and safety. (Construct: Attitudes toward behavior.)

Web Search! Safety Resources for Elementary Students Students can find a wealth of information on the World Wide Web to help them with their research on safety topics. Checking out websites links to NHES 3, access information, products, and services. The "Internet and Other Resources" section at the end of the chapter includes an extensive list of safety websites for students and teachers.

ASSESSMENT | The reports and presentations students make are the assessment task for this activity. For assessment criteria, students should provide accurate information and draw conclusions about connections between behaviors and health. For NHES 3, they also should cite their sources and explain why they are valid. (Construct: Attitudes toward behavior.)

Safe and Unsafe Behaviors in New Situations and Settings As children grow older, their responsibilities for safe behavior grow as they encounter new situations and opportunities for autonomy (using public transportation, riding their bikes to a friend's house). Children can make a list of the kinds of recreational and other

situations in which they are involved as third, fourth, and fifth graders and then identify and role-play safe behaviors in these situations.

ASSESSMENT | The children's role-plays of safe and unsafe behaviors are the assessment task for this activity. For assessment criteria, students should provide accurate information, display appropriate depth and breadth of information, and make connections between behaviors and safety. (Construct: Attitudes toward behavior.)

Don't Touch That! Staying Clear of Icky Plants and Critters. Jeff Day's book, *Don't Touch That! The Book of Gross, Poisonous, and Downright Icky Plants and Critters* (see the book list at the end of the chapter) offers helpful and humorous advice on avoiding bites, scratches, rashes, and more in the natural world around us. The book also helps students know what to do if the unexpected happens. Teachers can use this book to have small groups dig deeper into learning about the plants and critters in their own community. Students can work in small groups to investigate a plant or critter.

ASSESSMENT | For an assessment task, students can make a poster presentation about their investigation. Students should provide accurate information and make connections between safe behaviors and staying healthy. (Construct: Attitudes toward behavior.)

Grades 6–8

Web Search! Safety Resources for Middle-Level Students Middle-level students can find a wealth of information on the World Wide Web to help them with their research on safety topics. Checking out websites links to NHES 3, access information, products, and services. The "Internet and Other Resources" section at the end of the chapter includes an extensive list of safety websites for students and teachers.

ASSESSMENT | The reports and presentations students make are the assessment task for this activity. For assessment criteria, students should provide accurate information and draw conclusions about connections between behaviors and health. For NHES 3, they also should cite their sources and explain why they are valid. (Construct: Attitudes toward behavior.)

Safety Presentations for Younger Students Students can work in small groups to create dramatic presentations on various safety topics for younger students. Students must gather their own information and verify its accuracy (NHES 3). Teachers can help students make arrangements with teachers in other classes to present their work.

ASSESSMENT | The students' presentations are the assessment task for this activity. For assessment criteria, students should present accurate information, show appropriate depth and breadth of information, and make connections between behaviors and safety for their younger audiences. (Construct: Attitudes toward behavior.)

Expert Speakers on Safety Topics Have students identify activities and issues that interest them from a safety perspective. Have students develop letters to invite expert guest speakers to the classroom. For example, students this age often are interested in skateboarding and in-line skating. What should they know about staying safe while participating in these activities? Students also might want to know about upkeep and repair of bicycles. This activity links to NHES 3, access information, products, and services, in that students are accessing information from their expert speakers.

ASSESSMENT | For an assessment task, students can write, make posters about, or demonstrate what they learn from guest speakers. For assessment criteria, students should provide accurate information, show appropriate depth and breadth of information, and make connections between behaviors and safety. (Construct: Attitudes toward behavior.)

NHES 2 | Analyze Influences

Students will analyze the influence of family, peers, culture, media, technology, and other factors on health behaviors.

ASSESSMENT CRITERIA
- Identify both external and internal influences on health.
- Explain how external and internal influences interact to impact health choices and behaviors.
- Explain both positive and negative influences, as appropriate.

Grades K–2

Curiosity Teachers can use stories from the *Curious George* books, by H. A. Rey, to introduce this discussion on curiosity (see the book list at the end of the chapter). Children can define curiosity in their own words. Next, children can think about how to handle curiosity to stay safe in various unintentional injury prevention areas (fire, traffic, water). For example, children might be curious about fires and matches or lighters or about how deep the water is in a lake. What are safe and unsafe ways to handle this curiosity?

ASSESSMENT | Students can write and draw about ways to stay safe when they are curious. For assessment criteria, students should be able to explain how curiosity can affect behavior. (Construct: Perceived behavioral control.)

Family Children can brainstorm family practices that help everyone stay safe at home (locking cabinets that contain cleaning products, regularly checking smoke detectors). Teachers can read the book *Lizzy's Do's and Don'ts,* by Jessica Harper, and ask children to make a list of "do's" (rather than "don'ts") for safety in their homes (see the book list at the end of the chapter). Children can take their lists home to share with their families. Children also can make a class book about home and family safety, with each child contributing a page.

ASSESSMENT | The students' lists and book pages are the assessment tasks for this activity. For assessment criteria, students should explain and illustrate how families influence safety practices. (Construct: Perceived behavioral control.)

Grades 3–5

Likes and Dislikes An important internal influence on injury prevention is what people like and dislike doing. For example, some children might like to go fast or climb to very high places. They might dislike having to walk in a line at school or remain quiet during a fire drill. Teachers can have an open discussion with students about what they like and dislike related to safety issues at school, at home, and in the community and what they need to do regardless for the protection of everyone. Children can list important reasons for safe behavior and plans to manage their likes and dislikes for personal safety and the safety of others. Some safety rules are nonnegotiable. No one would want to cause someone else to get hurt. This activity links to NHES 7, self-management.

ASSESSMENT | For an assessment task, children can create a page for a class book or a poster on likes, dislikes, and safety. For assessment criteria, students should identify criteria for "great" pages or posters. Teachers can use these criteria to assess and to help children assess their work. (Construct: Subjective norms.)

Friends and Peers As children move into the upper-elementary grades, the influence of friends and peers becomes increasingly important. Students can talk about the things they like to do with their friends (skateboarding, roller-blading, biking) and discuss safety issues in their activities. For example, do friends wear bicycle helmets? How do friends' decisions influence what they do? Do friends walk their bikes across intersections or do they ride in front of traffic? How can they do the courageous thing (wearing a bike helmet even if others don't) and influence their friends to act safely? To think more about peer pressure, students can visit the BAM! website (www.bam.gov) to check out "Grind Your Mind," an animated quiz on peer pressure. The site includes helpful tips for students, such as being aware of situations, trusting gut feelings, and respecting choices.

ASSESSMENT | For an assessment task, students can identify and demonstrate at least one situation in which they can try to influence friends to act safely. For assessment criteria, students should explain the strategies they will use to influence their friends and why they selected these particular strategies. (Construct: Subjective norms.)

Grades 6–8

Feelings Middle-level students experience new and intense feelings as they go through puberty. Feelings are normal. However, the ways we behave in response to those feelings can influence our safety. For example, if Mary is angry with her best friend and storms away down the hall, she might run right into someone if she is not looking where she is going. Similarly, if Joe is daydreaming about a new student at school, he might not pay attention to what's around him while he rides his bike. At the most serious and damaging level, people sometimes deliberately hurt others when they are angry (violence in schools, homes, and communities). Students can work in small groups to brainstorm scenarios in which feelings might affect attention to safety and injury prevention. Students can rehearse and role-play their scenarios for classmates, with recommendations for managing feelings in safety situations and for helping others who are experiencing strong feelings. Students can find lots of information on dealing with feelings at www.kidshealth.org. This activity links to NHES 7, self-management.

ASSESSMENT | The students' role-plays are the assessment task for this activity. For assessment criteria, students should explain and demonstrate how feelings can influence behavior and how they can manage feelings for safety and well-being. (Construct: Perceived behavioral control.)

Media Movies, television shows, and commercials are filled with action heroes and extraordinary risk taking. What is real and what is simply media hype to increase product or ticket sales? Have students work in small groups to talk about media images they have seen that involve thrill seeking and over-the-top risk taking. How do students believe the media affect their decisions or the decisions of others? Teachers can provide examples in the news and in the community. What constitutes acceptable and unacceptable risk taking? How can students talk back to media images that promote unacceptable risk? Students can find media-savvy information about entertainment at PBS Kids—Don't Buy It! (www.pbskids .org/dontbuyit/entertainment).

ASSESSMENT | For an assessment task, students can make posters, design a comic book, write stories, or create scripts about media influences on risk taking, examining what various individuals do. For assessment criteria, students should identify at least two influences on safety behaviors and explain how various influences can work together to influence behaviors. (Construct: Perceived behavioral control.)

Celebrations and Fireworks-Related Injuries Many students live in communities where fireworks are a part of the culture of celebration. The CDC Injury Center (www.cdc.gov/ncipc) reports that more than 9,000 people were treated for fireworks-related injuries in emergency departments in 2003. About 45 percent of those injured were age 14 or younger. The CDC lists fireworks-related injuries as one of the types of injury that pose the greatest threat to youth. Teachers can ask students to talk about their experiences around fireworks, if these types of celebrations are part of the community. Students can investigate fireworks safety from the U.S. Consumer Product Safety Commission (www.cpsc.gov/cpscpub/pubs/july4/safetip.html). Injuries usually occur on and around holidays such as the Fourth of July and New Year's Eve. The CDC says that the safest way to prevent fireworks injuries is to leave the displays to trained professionals. Students can find even more information at www.cpsc.gov/cpscpub/pubs/july4/4thjuly.html. In particular, students should check out Kidd Safety's message on using fireworks: *Kids should never play with fireworks!* Kidd Safety also says that fireworks are dangerous and can cause serious burns and eye injuries. Students also can take a quiz on fireworks safety and read stories about students who have been injured playing with fireworks. Students can discuss how fireworks celebrations are conducted in their communities and the influences that might lead to injury among children and youth.

ASSESSMENT | For an assessment task, students can combine their discussion of influences with an advocacy newsletter (NHES 8) to families for fireworks safety in their communities, if appropriate. For assessment criteria, students should explain how fireworks celebrations can lead to injuries and advocate for safe holidays in the community by providing safety guidelines. (Construct: Subjective norms.)

NHES 3 | Access Information, Products, and Services

Students will demonstrate the ability to access valid information and products and services to enhance health.

ASSESSMENT CRITERIA

- Access health information—Locate specific sources of health information, products, or services relevant to enhancing health in a given situation.
- Evaluate information sources—Explain the degree to which identified sources are valid, reliable, and appropriate as a result of evaluating each source.

Grades K–2

School and Community Helpers Teachers can have children brainstorm a list of people who can help in various types of safety situations (fire, water, traffic, school, home). Help children invite (assist them with letter writing) school and community helpers to the classroom or arrange field trips to visit school and community helpers. Children should prepare a list of interview questions in advance.

ASSESSMENT | For an assessment task, students can write and draw in their journals about what they learn. For assessment criteria, students should justify their information sources (why the school and community helpers they invited were valid and reliable sources of information). (Construct: Attitudes toward behavior.)

Getting Help in Emergencies Children can identify school and community helpers who can assist in emergency situations. Children can role-play the steps they would take to get the help they need. For example, children can use a disconnected telephone to role-play

calling the 9-1-1 operator (teacher or guest speaker). Children might need assistance in learning to use cell phones. Children can locate emergency telephone numbers in the phone directory (inside front cover). This activity links to NHES 7, self-management.

ASSESSMENT | The children's role-plays and demonstrations are the assessment task for this activity. For assessment criteria, students should explain why their school and community helpers are valid and reliable service providers. (Construct: Perceived behavioral control.)

The Adventures of Kidd Safety The U.S. Consumer Product Safety Commission introduced Kidd Safety and his pals (www.cpsc.gov/kids/kidsafety/) to help students learn about safety topics such as playground safety, bike helmets, and scooter safety; the website includes posters, games, and a comic book. Teachers and students can access the website to learn about safety related to products of all kinds. Students can work in pairs or small groups to investigate one of the Kidd Safety topics and report to class members.

ASSESSMENT | The students' reports are the assessment task for this activity. For assessment criteria, students should present accurate information and draw conclusions about the connections between safety and health (NHES 1). They also should explain where they got their information and why their information source is valid. (Construct: Attitudes toward behavior.)

Grades 3–5

Information Sources Students can work in small groups to investigate a variety of safety topics. Students might use resources in the school or public library, write or call safety organizations and agencies, e-mail an expert, and access Internet sites related to safety. Students can identify and document their sources, justify their selections, and make presentations to the class about their findings. See the list of websites at the end of the chapter for sources.

ASSESSMENT | The students' presentations are the assessment task for this activity. For assessment criteria, students should identify, document, and justify their sources. (Construct: Attitudes toward behavior.)

Products and Equipment for Safety Students can investigate various products and equipment that are important for injury prevention in activities of interest to them (bicycle helmets, sunscreen products, thermal clothing, mouth guards). Students can plan and make presentations to their classmates and to other classes. If students locate an expert in the community, teachers can assist them in writing a letter of invitation to have that person visit the classroom. Students can find information from the U.S. Consumer Product Safety Commission (www.cpsc.gov) and the National Youth Sports Safety Foundation (www.nyssf.org).

ASSESSMENT | The students' presentations are the assessment task for this activity. For assessment criteria, students should identify, document, and justify their sources. (Construct: Attitudes toward behavior.)

Learn About Chemicals Around Your Home The U.S. Environmental Protection Agency provides a virtual house tour for students (www.epa.gov/kidshometour/) to learn about safety related to household products used around the home. Students select a room in the house or go into the backyard to see how many products they can find. For example, when students click on the picture of drain cleaners under the bathroom sink, they can learn what chemicals are in drain cleaners, what health and safety precautions they need to think about with drain cleaners, and what to do if they or someone they're with has an accident with a household product. Teachers can have students visit the site or print material for them in advance.

Students can work in pairs or small groups to investigate and report on the kinds of chemicals found in and around the home.

ASSESSMENT | The reports and presentations students make are the assessment task for this activity. For assessment criteria, students should present accurate information and draw conclusions about the connections between safety and health (NHES 1). They also should explain where they got their information and why their information source is valid. (Construct: Attitudes toward behavior.)

USFA Fire Safety for Kids   U.S. Fire Administration for Kids (www.usfa.fema.gov/kids/flash.shtm) provides information for students and teachers on topics such as smoke alarms and how to escape from a fire. Students can access puzzles, coloring book pages, and a study guide to prepare to become a Junior Fire Marshal.

ASSESSMENT | For an assessment task, students can take the Junior Fire Marshal quiz. When students pass the quiz, they can download a Junior Fire Marshal Certificate. For assessment criteria, students should explain accurate information and draw conclusions about the connections between safety and health (NHES 1). They also should explain where they got their information and why their information source is valid. (Construct: Attitudes toward behavior.)

Grades 6–8

WISQARS: Accessing Data About Injuries   Middle-level students can challenge their accessing information skills by visiting the WISQARS website (www.cdc.gov/ncipc/wisqars). WISQARS stands for Web-Based Injury Statistics Query and Reporting System. Students can access data on categories of fatal and nonfatal injuries. This activity links to mathematics—students might want to work with their mathematics teachers as they investigate the charts and tables. Students might be interested in the concept of "Potential Years of Life Lost" or premature death from injury.

ASSESSMENT | For an assessment task, students can work in small groups to investigate a category of interest and report to classmates. For assessment criteria, student should explain how they accessed their data and why their data source is a reliable one. (Construct: Attitudes toward behavior.)

Mapping Safe Walking and Biking Routes   Starting from their homes, students can map safe routes for walking or biking to places they go frequently (school, soccer practice). Students can use actual community maps to mark the safest routes. Students should justify their choices and explain why they eliminated other routes, based on the information they gathered about their neighborhood or community. Students can access information on developing safe walking and biking routes to school at www.walktoschool.org/ (International Walk to School Day).

ASSESSMENT | The students' routes are the assessment task for this activity. For assessment criteria, students should provide and justify the sources of information about their neighborhoods and communities. (Construct: Attitudes toward behavior.)

Using Youth Risk Behavior Survey (YRBS) Data   Students can go online (www.cdc.gov/HealthyYouth/yrbs/index.htm) to access information from the YRBS about unintentional injury–related behaviors among youth in their state or city and in the nation (the percentage of high school students who always or almost always wear seat belts while riding in cars, the percentage of students who did not ride with a drinking driver during the past thirty days). Alternatively, teachers can print tables from the website for students to use. Students can report the data from the healthy perspectives (the percentage of students who practice the healthy behavior, such as wearing a bicycle helmet).

ASSESSMENT | The students' data reports are the assessment task for this activity. For assessment criteria, students should show how they used the data tables to find their information and explain why the YRBS is a valid and reliable source of data. (Construct: Subjective norms.)

Kidz Privacy: Surfing the Net   The Federal Trade Commission provides safety tips for kids and families on surfing the Web (www.ftc.gov/bcp/conline/edcams/kidzprivacy). Important things to know about surfing, privacy, and personal information include

- Never give out your last or family name, your home address or your phone number in chat rooms, on bulletin boards, or to online pen pals.
- Don't tell other kids your screen name, user ID, or password.
- Look at a website's Privacy Policy to see how the site uses the information you give them.
- Surf the Internet with your parents. If they aren't available, talk to them about the sites you're visiting.
- Talk about the site's Privacy Policy with your parents so that you and your parents will know what information the site collects about you and what it does with the information.
- Websites must get your parent's permission before they collect many kinds of information from you.
- If a website has information about you that you and your parents don't want it to have, your parents can ask to see the information—and they can ask the website to delete or erase the information.
- Sites are not supposed to collect more information than they need about you for the activity you want to participate in. You should be able to participate in many activities online without having to give any information about yourself.
- If a site makes you uncomfortable or asks for more information than you want to share, leave the site.

Students can find additional information on safe Web surfing at these sites:

- www.healthfinder.gov/kids
- www.netsmartzkids.org/indexfl.htm
- http://disney.go.com/surfswell/index.html

ASSESSMENT | For an assessment task, students can create a list of safe surfing rules for their classroom. Students can take the list home for their parents or caregivers to read and sign. For assessment criteria, students should provide a list of rules that help promote safety and explain the valid sources of information they used to create the rules. (Construct: Attitudes toward behavior.)

How Are Your H₂O Smarts? BAM! on Water Safety   BAM!, the CDC Body and Mind website (www.bam.gov) for kids provides important tips on staying safe around water. BAM's top ten tips for kids are

- *DO* learn to swim.
- *DO* take a friend along.
- *DO* know your limits.
- *DO* swim in supervised (watched) areas only, and follow all signs and warnings.
- *DO* wear a life jacket when boating, jet skiing, water skiing, rafting, or fishing.
- *DO* stay alert to currents.
- *DO* keep an eye on the weather.
- *DON'T* mess around in the water.
- *DON'T* dive into shallow water.
- *DON'T* float where you can't swim.

Students also can access information on water pollution, water plants and animals, wearing sunscreen, water parks, personal flotation devices, currents, boating, jet skiing, swimming, white water rafting, surfing, and diving.

ASSESSMENT | For an assessment task, students can research, design, and prepare a presentation on water safety for other students in the school. The presentation might include skits, props, scenery, artwork, and costumes. For assessment criteria, students should provide accurate information and draw conclusions about connections between water safety and health (NHES 1). They should explain where they found their information and why their sources are valid. (Construct: Perceived behavioral control.)

NHES 4 | Interpersonal Communication

Students will demonstrate the ability to use interpersonal communication skills to enhance health and avoid or reduce health risks.

ASSESSMENT CRITERIA
- Use appropriate verbal/nonverbal communication strategies in an effective manner to enhance health or avoid/reduce health risks.
- Use appropriate skills (negotiation skills, refusal skills) and behaviors (eye contact, body language, attentive listening).

Grades K–2

Communicating to Ask for Help Young children can practice communicating clearly to get help from adults in a safety situation at home, at school, or in the community. Children can brainstorm a list of dangerous situations (a fallen electric wire) that might occur and practice asking an adult for help (say "I need your help," tell what happened and where, tell what you or others did, repeat "I need your help").

ASSESSMENT | Students can role-play asking for help as an assessment task for this activity. For assessment criteria, students should communicate information clearly and correctly. (Construct: Perceived behavioral control.)

Recognizing Signs and Signals for Safety In addition to using verbal communication, people communicate through signs and signals. Children can identify and respond to traffic signs and signals, such as stop, yield, pedestrian or school crossing, railroad crossing, and traffic lights. Children can help make signs and signals for practice in the classroom. Children also should be able to identify symbols that indicate poison. Teachers can find a Traffic Sign Quiz for Kids at www.nysgtsc.state.ny.us/Kids/kidssign.htm. Teachers can find other materials on the Traffic Safety Kids Page from the New York State Governor's Traffic Safety Committee (www.nysgtsc.state.ny.us/kids.htm).

ASSESSMENT | The students' correct responses to signs and signals are the assessment task for this activity. For assessment criteria, students should correctly identify safety signs and signals and respond to them appropriately. (Construct: Perceived behavioral control.)

Grades 3–5

Peer Resistance Skills in Safety Situations Children can brainstorm a list of situations in which other children might dare or challenge them to try something dangerous (going into the ocean when danger flags are posted, jumping a bike over a very deep ditch). Children can work in pairs or small groups to demonstrate and compare effective and ineffective peer resistance skills, demonstrating a minimum of three skills. Teachers can find a list of peer resistance

strategies for students to try in Chapter 3. Here is a sample scenario to get students started:

> Donna and Rich are meeting on Saturday morning to bicycle to the park with a group of classmates for a holiday picnic. As the group takes off, one of the riders says he knows a short-cut through a new housing development. The kids can get in through a gate that's been left open for deliveries, but there are big danger signs warning that the site is a hard-hat area and that only authorized personnel are allowed on the property. Donna thinks it's a good idea to save time and go through the construction site with the other kids. Rich knows that there are nails, loose pieces of board, deep ditches, and heavy machinery they would have to watch for on the ride. In addition, the developers might call their parents or even the police if the kids trespass. Rich doesn't want to ride through. What examples of effective communication strategies can he use and still keep his friends? Contrast these with ineffective strategies.

ASSESSMENT | The students' demonstrations of peer resistance skills are the assessment task for this activity. For assessment criteria, students should be able to demonstrate a minimum of three peer resistance skills. (Construct: Perceived behavioral control.)

Community Safety Signs Hunt Students can make a list of all safety signs, symbols, and signals they see in their communities for one week. In addition to finding traffic lights and signs, students might also see marking on the sidewalk telling people to use caution in stepping down, to enter a construction site only with a hard hat, or to use caution on a wet floor in a public building. Students can compile a list of all the signs they see and share it with other classes. Students can add to this project by making drawings and posters of the signs they find.

ASSESSMENT | The students' drawings and posters of the signs they find are the assessment task for this activity. Students might want to display their work for other classes as a safety advocacy project (NHES 8). For assessment criteria, students should explain what safety message the signs communicate and give the reason for the sign. (Construct: Subjective norms.)

Grades 6–8

Communicating to Avoid Riding with Impaired Drivers Unfortunately, young children often are not in a position to have a say about the adults, siblings, or family friends who drive them from place to place. However, as students reach middle school age, they can have more of a voice in refusing to ride with impaired drivers, whether they are adults or teenage friends with a new driver's license. Teachers can provide students with a variety of scenarios in which they are faced with the dangerous situation of riding with an impaired driver ("Your older sister's boyfriend offers you a ride, but you suspect he's been drinking"). Students can work in pairs or small groups to demonstrate a minimum of three refusal skills. For help in communicating in situations that involve drinking and driving, students might access the website for Students Against Destructive Decisions (SADD; www.sadd.org). For example, SADD partners with the National Highway Traffic Safety Administration (NHTSA) to sponsor "Think About It . . . Prom and Graduation Season."

ASSESSMENT | The students' role-plays and demonstrations are the assessment task for this activity. For assessment criteria, students should demonstrate a minimum of three refusal skills. (Construct: Perceived behavioral control.)

Calling 9-1-1 and Designating a Bystander as a Helper In first aid classes, students are taught to speak directly to a bystander in an emergency situation to ask for help—for example, "You in the purple shirt, please go and call 9-1-1!" Students can practice this important tip for getting help, explaining that when no one is designated everyone might assume that someone else will make the call. Students can learn more about calling 9-1-1 from Kids' Health (www.kidshealth.org/teen/safety/safebasics/911.html). Students will learn that when they call 9-1-1, the emergency dispatch operator might ask questions such as these:

- "*What* is the emergency?" or "*What* happened?"
- "*Where* are you?" or "*Where* do you live?"
- "*Who* needs help?" or "*Who* is with you?"

The operator needs to know the answers to these and other questions to determine what emergency workers should be sent and where to send them. Callers should give the operator all the relevant information they can about what the emergency is and how it happened. If the person is unconscious or has stopped breathing, the 9-1-1 operator might give instructions for providing immediate help, such as administering CPR or clearing the person's breathing passage. It's important to stay calm and to speak slowly and clearly so the 9-1-1 operator knows what kind of help is needed. Callers need to stay on the phone and *not hang up* until the operator says its OK to do so—that way, the operator will have all the information needed to get help on the way fast.

ASSESSMENT | For an assessment task, students can write a short story about a scenario in which they appeal to a bystander for help in an emergency situation. For assessment criteria, students should clearly communicate their message to a specific individual. The story should include the bystander's calling 9-1-1 correctly. (Construct: Perceived behavioral control.)

NHES 5 | Decision Making

Students will demonstrate the ability to use decision-making skills to enhance health.

ASSESSMENT CRITERIA

Reach a health-enhancing decision using a process consisting of the following steps:

- Identify a health-risk situation.
- Examine alternatives.
- Evaluate positive and negative consequences.
- Decide on a health-enhancing course of action.

Grades K–2

Children's Literature for Safety Decisions Many children's books contain decision-making themes for safety (*It's OK to Say No,* by Amy Baker; *Sheila Rae, the Brave,* by Kevin Henkes). Teachers can read the stories to children up to the point at which a character must make a decision. Teachers can stop and have the children discuss good decisions and why they are good. Teachers can finish the stories and compare the children's solutions with what happens in the stories.

ASSESSMENT | The students' solutions for the story characters are the assessment task for this activity. For assessment criteria, students should explain why they recommended their decisions and how they compare with what the characters actually did. (Construct: Attitudes toward behavior.)

Grades 3–5

What Do You Do, Dear? Teachers can read Sesyle Joslin's book *What Do You Do, Dear?* to begin this activity. Next, teachers can read scenarios to the children about safety in their own school ("A classmate wants you to climb a ladder that was left leaning against the side of the school building by workers repairing a leak in the roof"), ending each statement with "What do you do, dear?" Children respond with ideas for making safe and smart decisions. Here are other sample scenarios for children to decide "What do you do, dear?":

- You find a book of matches and a lighter in a cigarette case on the playground.
- You and your friend kick a ball that rolls out into the street.
- You get outside with your bicycle and realize you've forgotten your helmet.
- You are at your friend's house and find her father's gun cabinet unlocked.
- You are working on an art project in the classroom when you hear the fire alarm.
- You are upstairs at your friend's house when the smoke detector goes off.
- You go outside to the swimming pool before your older sister gets there.

ASSESSMENT | The students' solutions are the assessment task for this activity. For assessment criteria, students should explain why they made their decisions and the likely consequences of their decisions. (Construct: Intention to act in healthy ways.)

Grades 6–8

Decisions About Alcohol and Other Drugs Alcohol and other drugs (AOD) play a tremendous role in unintentional injuries, especially motor-vehicle crashes. Students can work through a decision-making process about alcohol and other drug use related to various safety situations (drinking beer while boating). They can use their visual arts skills to create cartoon panels or posters illustrating the potential hazards of AOD use in various situations and their decisions to remain AOD-free. Students can find more information about making decisions about alcohol at websites listed at the end of this chapter and in Chapter 12.

ASSESSMENT | The students' cartoon panels are the assessment task for this activity. For assessment criteria, students should illustrate characters thinking through a decision-making process. (Constructs: Attitudes toward behavior, perceived behavioral control.)

The Courageous Thing to Do A recurring theme in personal and social skills for health is acting with courage, or doing the courageous thing, in the face of pressure to the contrary. Nan Stein's work in bullying prevention presents ideas for teaching about courage.[43] As students reach middle school age, peer pressures to act in certain ways to be popular increase. However, students of this age also can be quite idealistic and respond to the idea of acting courageously. Students can write individually about situations that require courage to prevent injury and share their scenarios in small groups. Groups can work through a decision-making process to act courageously. Groups can then share with the class. Students might also enjoy hearing the story *Courage,* by Bernard Waber, as an introduction to this activity.

ASSESSMENT | The students' sharing with the class is the assessment task for this activity. For assessment criteria, students should demonstrate all the steps in a decision-making process. (Constructs: Subjective norms, perceived behavioral control.)

NHES 6 | Goal Setting

Students will demonstrate the ability to use goal-setting skills to enhance health.

ASSESSMENT CRITERIA
- Goal statement—Give goal statement that identifies health benefits; goal is achievable and will result in enhanced health.
- Goal setting plan—Show plan that is complete, logical and sequential, and includes a process to assess progress.

Grades K–2

School Safety Goals   Students can invite their principal to the classroom to ask about the kinds of injuries that are most common at their school. If they find that a certain kind of injury occurs often (bloody noses, fingers caught in doors, falls), students can set a safety goal and steps to achieve the goal for students in their school. Students can assess the school's progress periodically. This activity links to NHES 8, advocacy.

ASSESSMENT | The students' plan is the assessment task for this activity. For assessment criteria, students should clearly define their plan and ways to communicate it to schoolmates. (Construct: Intention to act in healthy ways.)

Grades 3–5

Personal Goals to Prevent Athletic and Activity Injuries   Children increasingly are involved in physical activity, such as dance and sports, as they reach the upper-elementary grades. Students can discuss the common injuries in the kinds of physical activities in which they are involved and prevention for those injuries. Teachers can invite an athletic trainer or a dancer from the local high school or community to talk with the children about injury prevention in physical activity and about practices that are helpful and harmful (hard stretching at the beginning of a workout is not recommended; instead, do a general body warm-up and stretch at the end of the workout). Teachers can assist the students in setting personal goals and listing the steps to achieve their goals to remain injury-free. Making a plan of this type links to NHES 7, self-management. Students can set goals and create their own fitness calendar at BAM! (Body and Mind) (www.bam.gov).

ASSESSMENT | For an assessment task, children can develop a goal and a plan to remain injury-free. For assessment criteria, children should identify an achievable goal, steps to reach it, plans to build support for it and to deal with obstacles, and a means for assessment. (Construct: Intention to act in healthy ways.)

Grades 6–8

New Responsibilities: Babysitting Basics   Middle-level students might find themselves in a position to begin babysitting, a decision that carries a great deal of responsibility. The Kids' Health website (www.kidshealth.org) offers guidelines on babysitting for kids. Students can learn about important rules such as be prepared, know what to expect, and stay focused on the kids at all times. Students also can learn about babysitting basics and safety by contacting the local chapter of the American Red Cross or visiting www.redcross.org.

ASSESSMENT | For students interested in becoming babysitters, making a plan for babysitting is an assessment task. For assessment criteria, students should explain all the decisions they need to make in advance

Protective equipment helps everyone enjoy sports and activities safely.

and while carrying out their babysitting responsibilities. (Construct: Perceived behavioral control.)

NHES 7 | Self-Management

Students will demonstrate the ability to practice health-enhancing behaviors and avoid or reduce health risks.

ASSESSMENT CRITERIA
- Application (transfer)—Initiate health-enhancing behaviors; apply concepts and skills appropriate and effectively.
- Self-monitoring and reflection—Monitor actions and make adjustments; accept feedback and make adjustments; able to self-assess, reflect on, and take responsibility for actions.

Grades K–2

Children's Literature for Safety   This chapter and the other content chapters include a list of children's books that can be used for health education lessons. Suggestions for children's books related to safety and self-management can be found in the book list at the end of the chapter. Teachers can read these books with children to spark discussions on self-management issues such as making and following safety rules and practices.

ASSESSMENT | Students can make and act out a list of class safety rules as an assessment task for reading children's literature. For assessment criteria, students should create rules that are health enhancing and should explain the correct steps for following the rules in various situations. (Construct: Perceived behavioral control.)

Safety Plans and Simulations   Students can work individually or in small groups to make safety plans for various situations (home fire safety plan, safe biking plan, pool safety plan, home poisoning prevention plan). Researching topics by going to the library and talking to parents, teachers, and school health helpers links to NHES 3, access information, products, and services. To illustrate their self-management skills, students should identify and demonstrate the steps for safety. For example, students might arrange desks or chairs to simulate a "classroom bus" to show safe behaviors in planning for a field trip. Students need regular practice for school fire drills and weather emergency drills.

ASSESSMENT | Students' demonstrations are the assessment task for this activity. For assessment criteria, students should demonstrate safety steps correctly. (Construct: Perceived behavioral control.)

Safety Around Blood (Universal Precautions)   Students in the early elementary grades frequently experience nosebleeds or minor cuts and scrapes. Other children often want to help. Have children demonstrate how to stop their own nosebleeds and bleeding from cuts or scrapes. In addition, have children demonstrate how to behave around the blood of others (don't touch blood, get help from the teacher or another adult). To stop nosebleeds, students should learn these tips:

- If you get a nosebleed, sit down and lean slightly forward. Keeping your head above your heart will make your nose bleed less. Lean forward so the blood will drain out of your nose instead of down the back of your throat. If you lean back, you might swallow the blood. This can cause nausea, vomiting, and diarrhea.
- Use your thumb and index finger to squeeze together the soft portion of your nose—the area located between the end of your nose and the hard, bony ridge that forms the bridge of your nose. Keep holding your nose until the bleeding stops. Hold it for at least five minutes. If it's still bleeding, hold it for another ten minutes straight.
- You can also place a cold compress or an ice pack across the bridge of your nose.
- Once the bleeding stops, don't do anything that might make it start again, such as bending over or blowing your nose.[44]

ASSESSMENT | For an assessment task, students can demonstrate how to stop their own nosebleeds. For assessment criteria, students should follow all the steps correctly and in order. In addition, they should explain why it's not safe to touch the blood of others and how to get help from an adult is someone is bleeding. (Construct: Perceived behavioral control.)

Grades 3–5

Stress and Anger Management   Stress and anger management skills are an important part of injury prevention. Children sometimes see adults behaving unsafely when they are angry (driving too fast, throwing things), rather than using self-management skills to calm themselves. Children can brainstorm a list of their favorite stress busters that they use to help themselves calm down. Children can make colorful stress buster posters as reminders for the classroom. Teachers might also want to use children's books to talk with students about ways to calm down when they are feeling angry or upset; see the books listed in Chapter 5 under "Moods and Strong Feelings" for ideas.

ASSESSMENT | The students' stress and anger management strategies and posters are the assessment tasks for this activity. For assessment criteria, students should be able to demonstrate specific steps for their strategies. (Construct: Perceived behavioral control.)

Learn to Swim   If there are nonswimmers in the class or grade, teachers can help students arrange swimming lessons or practice at a school or community pool. Students also should demonstrate skills for helping someone who is having difficulty in the water (use a ring buoy, kickboard, shepherd's crook, lifejacket, towel). Invite a lifeguard to talk with the class. Students can learn more from the American Red Cross Learn-to-Swim program (www.redcross .org/services/hss/aquatics/lts.html). The new American Red Cross Learn-to-Swim classes provide instruction to help swimmers of all ages and abilities develop their swimming and water safety skills. The classes are designed to give students a positive learning experience. Learn-to-Swim teaches aquatic and safety skills in a logical progression, from safely entering the water to helping others. The objective is to teach people to swim and to be safe in, on, and around the water.

ASSESSMENT | For an assessment task, students can describe important steps for water safety. For assessment criteria, students should provide safety steps accurately and in the correct order. (Construct: Perceived behavioral control.)

Welcome to Safety City   The National Highway Traffic Safety Administration (NHTSA) posts a website for kids called Safety City (www.nhtsa.dot.gov/kids). Vince and Larry, the NHTSA's crash test dummies, teach students about safety through games, movies, and other resources. Teachers can visit the Teacher's Lounge for a variety of lesson materials; teachers also can get complimentary materials by participating in the Department of Transportation's Auto Safety Hotline Outreach Program.

ASSESSMENT | Teachers can use the games from the Teacher's Lounge as an assessment task for this activity. For assessment criteria, students should provide accurate information and tell the correct steps, in order, for safe behavior. (Construct: Perceived behavioral control.)

Grades 6–8

Simple First Aid   Students can work in pairs or small groups to investigate and demonstrate simple first aid techniques for dealing with cuts, scrapes, burns, insect and animal bites, choking, and suspected broken bones. Students might want to invite a Red Cross instructor to class for more information. Students can develop a checklist of steps as a handout for their classmates. These checklists could be bound into a class book to duplicate and share with other classes. For more in-depth first aid instruction, teachers can help students arrange an evening course for interested students and families. Students can learn more about first aid by contacting their local chapter of the American Red Cross and by visiting www .redcross.org.

ASSESSMENT | The students' demonstrations and checklists are the assessment task for this activity. For assessment criteria, students should demonstrate first aid procedures accurately and in the correct order. (Construct: Perceived behavioral control.)

Role-Play Safety Skills   Students can develop their language arts and health education skills by writing a script for a role-play or skit about a safety topic or issue. Students should present a scenario in which the characters demonstrate their self-management skills by avoiding, leaving, or refusing risk situations (taking a dare, riding bicycles on a busy street, swimming when the ocean is too rough, taking someone else's moped for a joyride). Students can try new dramatic techniques, such as having the main character think things over while voices in the background speak aloud as if in his or her head. Students should emphasize doing the "courageous thing" in risk situations. This activity links to NHES 4, interpersonal communication.

ASSESSMENT | The students' role-plays and skits are the assessment task for this activity. For assessment criteria, students should present specific steps students can take for safety. (Construct: Perceived behavioral control.)

Motion Commotion—BAM! on Safety in Physical Activity CDC's BAM! (Body and Mind) website (www.bam.gov) features activity cards on how to play it safe while participating in diverse activities, including cycling, swimming, basketball, cheerleading, skating, fishing, football, martial arts, skiing, yoga, and many others. Students can work individually or with a partner to investigate and report on playing it safe in various kinds of activities.

ASSESSMENT | The reports and presentations students make are the assessment task for this activity. For assessment criteria, students should provide accurate information on self-management strategies for playing it safe in sports, recreation, and exercise. (Construct: Perceived behavioral control.)

NHES 8 | Advocacy

Students will demonstrate the ability to advocate for personal, family, and community health.

ASSESSMENT CRITERIA

- Health-enhancing position—Give clear, health-enhancing position.
- Support for position—Support position with facts, concepts, examples, and evidence.
- Audience awareness—Show awareness of target audience; choose words, tone, and examples to suit audience.
- Conviction—Display conviction for position

Grades K–2

Buckle Up America: Click It or Ticket! Students might have heard public service announcements about the National Highway Transportation Safety Administration's and the state highway safety offices' campaign to increase seat belt use during May and June of each year. The campaign goes by the catchy slogan "Click It or Ticket!" Teachers can learn more to share with their students at www.buckleupamerica.org/. The website includes stories about how seat belts save lives. Students can plan and carry out a Click It or Ticket! campaign for their school and families, making presentations and posters. Students should be sure to include the reminder that students age 12 and younger should ride in the backseat of the car.

ASSESSMENT | The student's posters/presentations are the assessment task. For assessment criteria, students should present a clear message, back it up, target their audience, and speak with conviction. (Construct: Subjective norms.)

Smart Kids Stay Safe Campaign Students can make posters or banners for the school about the "Smart Kids Stay Safe" way to handle safety issues at home, at school, and in the community.

ASSESSMENT | The students' posters are the assessment task for this activity. For assessment criteria, posters should present a clear, health-enhancing message. (Construct: Subjective norms.)

Grades 3–5

Safety Raps Children can work in small groups to create safety raps, songs, or poems for a safety issue of their choice. Children enjoy having classmates clap and rap their desks in time with the beat while they perform. Children also might want to perform for other classes.

ASSESSMENT | The students' raps or other creations are the assessment task for this activity. For assessment criteria, students should provide a clear, health-enhancing message. (Construct: Subjective norms.)

National SAFE KIDS Campaign The Safe Kids campaign (www.safekids.org) tells students "There are lots of ways you can help keep yourself, your friends, and your family safe from injury. Explore this page to find out more." Students and teachers can download puzzles, mazes, and games to crack the safety codes. The Safe Kids Challenge is full of experiments, puzzles, and activities that show students how injuries happen and what they can do to protect themselves and others. Safe Sam has students do these activities:

- Search for a sneaky poison.
- Check out the commotion about motion.
- Learn how to do cool stuff like stay afloat and reflect light.
- See how gravity, air resistance, and seat belts work.

The site also provides materials for teachers at the Teacher's Desk.

ASSESSMENT | For an assessment task, students can complete the Safe Kids Challenge and plan a presentation to share their results with others. For assessment criteria, students should present a clear message, back it up, target their audience, and speak with conviction. (Construct: Subjective norms.)

Project Safe Neighborhoods: Making America Safer Through Youth Students and teachers can learn more about Project Safe Neighborhoods at www.psn.gov. The website offers these ten important tips for children:

1. Settle arguments with words, not fists or weapons. Don't stand around and form an audience when others are arguing.
2. Learn safe routes for walking in the neighborhood, and know good places to seek help. Know how to contact your parents in the event of an emergency.
3. Learn to work out your problems without fighting. If you're feeling angry toward someone, talk it out, walk away, stick with friends, or speak with a trusted adult. Try to think of some new ways to settle your problems without violence.
4. If you find a gun—stop, don't touch the gun, get away, and tell a grown-up you trust.
5. Report any crimes or suspicious activities to the police, school authorities, and parents.
6. Never go anywhere with (or open the door to) someone you or your parents don't know and trust. If someone touches you in a way that makes you feel uncomfortable, say no, get away, and tell a trusted adult.
7. Don't use alcohol or other drugs, and stay away from people and places associated with them.
8. Stick with friends who are also against violence and drugs, and stay away from known trouble spots.
9. Get involved to make school safer and better—conduct a poster contest against violence, hold anti-drug rallies, counsel peers, settle disputes peacefully. If there is no program, help start one!
10. Help younger children learn to avoid being crime victims. Set a good example, and volunteer to help with community efforts to stop crime.

ASSESSMENT | For an assessment task, students can work in small groups to dramatize each of the safety tips and create a slogan that's easy to remember. Students might want to perform for others in the school as well as for classmates. For assessment criteria, students should present a clear message, back it up, target their audience, and speak with conviction. (Construct: Subjective norms.)

Grades 6–8

Think First! Voices for Injury Prevention (VIP) to Prevent Brain and Spinal Cord Injuries Middle-level students might be especially interested in the National Injury Prevention Foundation's ThinkFirst campaign to prevent brain and spinal cord injuries (www.thinkfirst .org/home.asp). Each year an estimated 500,000 persons in the United States sustain brain and spinal cord injuries. The most frequent causes of these injuries are motor-vehicle crashes; falls; sports and recreation accidents, especially diving accidents; and violence. Children and teens are at high risk for these devastating injuries, many of which are preventable. ThinkFirst, the National Injury Prevention Program's award-winning public education effort, targets this high-risk age group. The upbeat programs educate young people about personal vulnerability and risk taking. The message is that you can have a fun-filled, exciting life without hurting yourself if you "Think-First" and use your mind to protect your body. More than 8 million young people have heard the ThinkFirst message. Teachers also can access curriculum materials through the website.

ASSESSMENT | For an assessment task, students can become VIPs (Voices for Injury Prevention) by designing and implementing a Think-First campaign in their school. For assessment criteria, students should present a clear message, back it up, target their audience, and speak with conviction. (Construct: Subjective norms.)

Local Radio or Television Broadcast Students can create a public service announcement (PSA) for local radio or television. Students can work with technology specialists to develop a recording or videotape—or invite local radio or television personalities to work with them or their message.

ASSESSMENT | The students' PSAs are the assessment task for this activity. For assessment criteria, students should provide a clear, health-enhancing message; back it up with data or reasons; target a specific audience; and demonstrate conviction. (Construct: Attitudes toward behavior.)

Safety Fair or Safety Night Students can plan a safety fair or safety night for students and families. Students should choose the issues they want to include and designate committees to take responsibility for all aspects of the project.

ASSESSMENT | The students' safety night or safety fair is the assessment task for this activity. For assessment criteria, students should provide clear, health-enhancing messages; back up the messages with data and reasons; target a specific audience; and demonstrate conviction. (Construct: Attitudes toward behavior.)

Speak Out and Make NOYS: National Organizations for Youth Safety The mission of NOYS (www.noys.org), sponsored by the National Highway Traffic Safety Administration, is to promote youth empowerment and leadership and build partnerships that save lives, prevent injuries, and enhance safe and healthy lifestyles among all youth. Students can learn about youth projects such as "Speak Out and Make NOYS." NOYS developed *Yough Changing the World Project Manual* to help students set goals for, plan, and carry out injury prevention projects.

ASSESSMENT | Students can plan a NOYS injury prevention project as an assessment task for this activity. For assessment criteria, students should present a clear message, back it up, target their audience, and speak with conviction. (Construct: Subjective norms.)

INTERNET AND OTHER RESOURCES

Visit the Online Learning Center (www.mhhe.com/telljohann6e) for links to these sites, quizzes and other study aids, and many additional resources.

American Academy of Pediatrics
www.aap.org/parents.html

American Red Cross
www.redcross.org

BAM! (Body and Mind)
www.bam.gov

California Department of Transportation Kids' Page
www.dot.ca.gov/kids

Centers for Disease Control and Prevention
www.cdc.gov/HealthyYouth (Healthy Youth)
www.cdc.gov/ncipc (National Center for Injury Prevention and Control)
www.cdc.gov/ncipc/bike (National Bicycle Safety Network)
www.cdc.gov/ncipc/wisqars (Web-Based Injury Statistics Query and Reporting System)

Coastie's Homepage for Water Safety
www.coastie.auxpa.org

Disney Surf Swell Island Adventures in Internet Safety
www.disney.go.com/surfswell/index.html

Children's Safety Network
www.childrenssafetynetwork.org

Farm Safety 4 Just Kids
www.fs4jk.org

Federal Bureau of Investigation Safety Tips for Kids
www.fbi.gov/kids/k5th/safety1.htm

Federal Emergency Management Agency for Kids
www.fema.gov/kids/index.htm

Federal Trade Commission: Kidz Privacy (surfing the Internet)
www.ftc.gov/bcp/conline/edcams/kidzprivacy

FirstGov for Kids
www.kids.gov/

Girl Power
www.girlpower.gov

GirlsHealth.gov
www.4girls.gov

HealthFinder for Kids
www.healthfinder.gov/kids

National Youth Sports Safety Foundati
www.nyssf.org

Net Smartz Kids
www.netsmartzkids.org/indexFL.htm

Operation Lifesaver (railroad crossing s
www.oli.org/for_kids/kids_overview.h

PBS Kids: Don't Buy It!
www.pbskids.org/dontbuyit/entertain

Police Notebook for Kid Safety
www.ou.edu/oupd/kidsafe/start.htm

Safe Kids Worldwide
www.safekids.org

Safe Ride News
www.saferidenews.com

School Safety
www.nea.org/schoolsafety

Smokey the Bear Smokey Kids
www.smokeybear.com/kids

ThinkFirst for KIDS
www.thinkfirst.org/kids

Traffic Safety Kids' Page (New York State
Safety Committee)
www.nysgtsc.state.ny.us/kids.htm

U.S. Consumer Product Safety Commiss
www.cpsc.gov/kids/kidsafety/main.ht
Safety)

U.S. Department of Agriculture Forest S
www.fs.fed.us/

U.S. Environmental Protection Agency
www.epa.gov/kidshometour (home ch

U.S. Fire Administration for Kids
www.usfa.dhs.gov/kids/flash.shtm

For sites related to alcohol use and drunk
Internet listing for Chapter 12.

Home Safety Council: Code Red Rover (home safety)
www.coderedrover.org

Indian Health Service Kids' Page
www.ihs.gov/PublicInfo/Publications/Kids/index.cfm

Injury Control Resource Information Network
www.injurycontrol.com/icrin

International Walk to School Day
www.walktoschool.org

Kids' Health
www.kidshealth.org
www.kidshealth.org/watch/out/bike_safety.html
www.kidshealth.org/watch/out/car_safety.html
(bicycle safety)
www.kidshealth Prevention Council)
(car and bus s

McGruff (N—ion Association
www.r
N—www.n—Traffic Safety Administration

National and Atmospheric Administration (weather
preparedness)
Natin.noaa.gov

sa—zation for Youth Safety

am for Playground Safety
u/playground

Boating Council
oatingcouncil.org

ety Council
org

chool Safety Center
hoolsafety.us

Transportation Safety Board
w.ntsb.gov

CHILDREN'S LITERATURE

AGES 5–8

Bang, Molly. *When Sophie Gets Angry—Really, Really Angry . . . .*
Blue Sky Press, 1999.

Berenstain, Stan, and Jan Berenstain. *The Berenstain Bears and No
Guns Allowed.* Random House, 2000.

Borden, Louise. *Albie the Lifeguard.* Scholastic, 1993.

Brillhart, Julie. *Molly Rides the School Bus.* Albert Whitman, 2002.

Brown, Marc. *Arthur's Fire Drill.* Random House, 2000.

Brown, Marc. *Dinosaurs Beware: A Safety Guide.* Little, Brown,
1982.

Carter, Sharon. *The Little Book of Choices.* Island Heritage, 2004.

Curtis, Jamie Lee, and Laura Cornell. *It's Hard to Be Five: Learning
How to Work My Control Panel.* Joanna Cotler, 2004.

Cuyler, Margery. *Please Play Safe! Penguin's Guide to Playground
Safety.* Scholastic Press, 2006.

Cuyler, Margery. *Stop, Drop and Roll: A Book About Fire Safety.*
Simon & Schuster, 2001.

Davidson, Martine. *Maggie and the Emergency Room.* Random
House, 1992.

Evans, Lezlie. *Sometimes I Feel Like a Storm Cloud.* Mondo, 1999.

Feldman, Heather. *My School Bus: A Book About School Bus Safety.*
Rosen, 1998.

Franklin, Kristine. *Iguana Beach.* Crown, 19

Gobbell, Phyllis, and Jim Laster. *Safe Sally S
Click.* Children's Press, 1986.

Haan, Amanda. *I Call My Hand Gentle.* Peng
for Young Readers, 2003.

Hallinan, P. D. *Let's Be Safe.* Ideals Childre

Harper, Jessica. *Lizzy's Do's and Don'ts.* Harp

Henkes, Kevin. *Lilly's Purple Plastic Purse.* G

Henkes, Kevin. *Sheila Rae, the Brave.* Willian

Hogan, Paul Z. *Sometimes I Get So Mad.* Raint
1991.

Kelley, Marty. *The Rules.* Zino Press Childre

Kurtz, Jane. *Do Kangaroos Wear Seatbelts?* D
Books, 2005.

Levete, Sarah. *Looking After Myself.* Millbroo

Moore, Eva. *Franklin's Bicycle Helmet.* Schol

Pendziwol, Jean. *Once Upon a Dragon: Strang
Can Press, Ltd., 2007.

Pendziwol, Jean. *No Dragons for Tea: Fire Saf
Dragons).* Kids Can Press, 2001.

Rathman, Peggy. *Officer Buckle and Gloria.*
1995. (Caldecott Medal)

Prevalence and Cost

The Children's Defense Fund cites these moments in the
life of America that pertain to the personal health and wellness of children:

Every thirty-six seconds in America, a child is confirmed
as abused or neglected.

Every thirty-five seconds, a baby is born into poverty.

Every forty-one seconds, a baby is born without health
insurance.

Every minute, a baby is born to a teen mother.

Every two minutes, a baby is born at low birth weight

Every eighteen minutes, a baby dies before his first
birthday.[2]

These sobering statistics point to an importa— fact:
Although the health of Americans overall has improve
dramatically during the past fifty years, children who
born into poverty—with its associated lower educa—
health care, and opportunity—are among those at h—
risk for serious health problems.

In *About Children*, from the American Academ
atrics, Bernard Guyer and Alyssa Wigton describ
ments in the health status of American childre—
twentieth century as spectacular.[3] During th—
life expectancy of Americans increased by —
overall age-adjusted death rate declined b—
—atest single contribution to the —
—cans was the decline in inf—
—ately, these impressi—
—hild health ob—

health
include

ng an out-
unselor about
area of personal
oung people learn to
and services from valid

t, also plays a major role in
previous example, students who
s actually use the sunscreen and seek
unselor. In addition, they practice basic
such as brushing and flossing teeth, wash-
d managing stress. NHES 3 and 7 are a major
the learning and assessment strategies included in
hapter.

Rey, H. A. *The Original Curious George.* Houghton Mifflin, 1941.

Spelman, Cornelia. *Your Body Belongs to You.* Albert Whitman, 2008.

Vail, Rachel. *Sometimes I'm Bombaloo.* Scholastic, 2002.

Viorst, Judith. *Alexander and the Terrible, Horrible, No Good, Very Bad Day.* Atheneum Books for Young Readers, 1972.

AGES 8–12

Cleary, Beverly. *Lucky Chuck.* Morrow, 1984.

Day, Jeff. *Don't Touch That! The Book of Gross, Poisonous, and Downright Icky Plants and Critters.* Chicago Review Press, 2008.

DeFelice, Cynthia. *Weasel.* William Morrow, 1991.

Harrison, Jean. *Sa...fety.* Smart Apple Media, 2004.

O'Dell, Scott. *Island of the Blue Dolphins.* Houghton Mifflin, 1960.

Park, Barbara. *Mick Harte Was Here.* Alfred A. Knopf, 1995.

Raatma, Lucia. *Fire Safety.* Child's World, 2003.

Raymer, Dottie. *Staying Home Alone: A Girl's Guide to Sta... and Having Fun.* Pleasant ...

Taylor-Butler, Christine. *Food Sa...* ny, 2002.

Waber, Bernard. *Courage.* Hough... Children's Press, 2... Books, 2002. ...flin/Walter Lor...

ENDNOTES

1. Children's Defense Fund. (www.childrensdefense.org)
2. Centers for Disease Control and Prevention (CDC), National Center for Injury Prevention and Control (NCIPC). (www.cdc.gov/ncipc)
3. E. M. Lewit and L. S. Baker, *Child Indicators: Unintentional Injuries.* (www.futureofchildren.org/information2826/information_show.htm?doc_id=79899)
4. F. P. Rivara, "Impact of Injuries," in *About Children: An Authoritative Resource on the State of Childhood Today,* eds. A. G. Cosby, R. E. Greenberg, L. H. Southward, and M. Weitzman (American Academy of Pediatrics, 2005), 122.
5. National Center for Injury Prevention and Control, CDC, *Child Passenger Safety: Fact Sheet.* (www.cdc.gov/ncipc/factsheets/childpas.htm)
6. F. P. Rivara, "Impact of Injuries," 122–23.
7. D. K. Eaton et al., "Youth Risk Behavior Surveillance—United States, 2007," *Morbidity and Mortality Weekly Report* 57, no. SS-4 (2008):1–131.
8. U.S. Department of Health and Human Services, *Healthy People 2010: Understanding and Improving Health,* 2d ed. (Washington, DC: U.S. Government Printing Office, November 2000).
9. National Center for Injury Prevention and Control, CDC, *Childhood Injury Fact Sheet.* (www.cdc.gov/ncipc)
10. National Center for Injury Prevention and Control, *CDC Injury Fact Book, 2006.* (www.cdc.gov/ncipc/fact_book/factbook.htm)
11. F. P. Rivara, "Impact of Injuries," 122–23.
12. F. P. Rivara, "Impact of Injuries," 123–24.
13. F. P. Rivara, "Impact of Injuries," 122–24.
14. ...for Disease Control and Prevention (CDC), ...th Guidelines to Prevent Unintentional ...ce, MMWR Recommendations and ...22 (7 December 2001): 1–46.
15. ...uackenbush, *Teach and Talk:* ...: ETR Associates,

16. F. P. Rivara, "Impact of Injuries," 125.
17. L. Kann, S. K. Telljohann, and S. F. Wooley, "Health Education: Results from the School Health Programs and Policies Study 2006," *Journal of School Health* 77, no. 8 (2007): 408–34.
18. CDC, *School Health Guidelines to Prevent Unintentional Injury and Violence.*
19. W. M. Kane and M. Quackenbush, *Teach and Talk: Safety and Risk.*
20. Ibid.
21. National Injury Prevention Foundation, *ThinkFirst for Kids.* (www.thinkfirst.org/About/Kids2/asp)
22. CDC, *School Health Guidelines to Prevent Unintentional Injury and Violence.*
23. Ibid.
24. Ibid.
25. National Center for Injury Prevention and Control, *Injuries Among Children and Adolescents.* (www.cdc.gov/ncipc/factsheets/children.htm).
26. National Center for Injury Prevention and Control, *Child Passenger Safety.* (www.cdc.gov/ncipc/factsheets/childpas.htm).
27. National Center for Injury Prevention and Control, *CDC's Unintentional Injury Activities—2004.*
28. National Center for Injury Prevention and Control, *Fireworks-related Injuries.* (www.cdc.gov/ncipc/factsheets/fworks.htm).
29. National Center for Injury Prevention and Control, *Playground Injuries.* (www.cdc.gov/ncipc/factsheets/playgr.htm).
30. National Center for Injury Prevention and Control, *Poisoning in the United States.* (www.cdc.gov/ncipc/factsheets/poisoning.htm).
31. National Center for Injury Prevention and Control, *Fire Death and Injuries.* (www.cdc.gov/ncipc/factsheets/fire.htm).
32. National Center for Injury Prevention and Control, *What Is Traumatic Brain Injury?* (www.cdc.gov/ncipc/tbi/TBI.htm).

33. National Center for Injury P... Control, *Water-related Injuries.* (...factsheets/drown.htm).
34. National Safe Kids Campaign, *P... Safety to Prevent Unintentional Inju...*
35. Walk and Bike to School Day. (w... .org)
36. National Highway Traffic Safety ... (NHTSA), *Safe Routes to School.* (w... people/injury/pedbimot/bike/Sa...
37. National Center for Injury Preve... Control, *Preventing Injuries in Sp... and Exercise.* (www.cdc.gov/ncip... research_agenda/05_sports.htm...
38. American Academy of Child & ... Psychiatry, *Home Alone Children ...* page.ww?name=Home+Alone+... Facts+for+Families).
39. National Child Care Informati... *Children Home Alone and Babysit...* Administration for Children & ... Department of Health and Hu... (www.nccic.org/poptopics/ho...
40. KidsHealth, *When It's Just You A...* kidshealth.org/kid/watch/ho... .html).
41. Safe Kids USA, *Safety Tips.* (w... index.cfm).
42. Centers for Disease Control a... *Education Curriculum Analysis ...* HealthyYouth/HECAT/index...
43. N. Stein, E. Gaberman, and ... *Bullyproof: A Teacher's Guide ... for Use with Fourth and Fifth G...* MA: Wellesley College Center ... Women, 1996).
44. American Academy of Fami... *Nosebleeds: What to Do When ...* (http://familydoctor.org/13...

INTRODUCTION

Scarcely one half of the children of our country continue in school much beyond the fifth grade. It is important, therefore, that so far as possible the knowledge which has most to do with human welfare should be presented in the early years of school life. . . . The health of a people influences the prosperity and happiness of a nation more than any other one thing. The highest patriotism is therefore the conservation of health.[1]

This quotation introduces the book *Health Lessons,* published in 1910. At that time, the author, Alvin Davison, was concerned with "infectious diseases and . . . serious cases of sickness from contagious maladies, with all their attendant suffering, largely sacrifices on the altar of ignorance." In 1910, the leading cause of death in children age 11 and older was tuberculosis.

Things certainly have changed during the almost hundred years since *Health Lessons* was published. Many infectious diseases are well controlled with immunizations and other public health measures. To continue these gains, effective public and school health education related to and children is needed. In a tremendous change since 1910, chronic diseases, such as heart disease and cancer, and unintentional and intentional injuries now claim the greatest number of lives. Efforts to prevent chronic disease and injury must include public and school health education.

When people think of school health education, they often think first of personal health habits—washing hands, bathing regularly, brushing and flo...

In the content area of personal health, two of the National Health Education Standards are especially important. NHES 3, access information, products, and services, provides opportunities for students to investigate and practice finding sources of information, products, and services to meet their health-related needs. For example, accessing information about the management of diabetes might mean searching the websites of the American Diabetes Association, the Centers for Disease Control Prevention (CDC), and the National Institutes of ... (NIH). Accessing products and services might ... selecting an appropriate sunscreen to wear ... door volleyball game or talking to a school ... a problem. The diversity of topics in th... health emphasizes the need to help ... get health information, produc... and reliable sources.

NHES 7, self-managem... personal health. In th... are good self-manag... out the school co... health habits, ... ing hands, ... focus in ... this ...

...TENTIONAL INJURY

DEVELOP SKILLS FOR POSITIVE HEALTH HABITS

Home Safety Council: Code Red Rover (home safety)
www.coderedrover.org

Indian Health Service Kids' Page
www.ihs.gov/PublicInfo/Publications/Kids/index.cfm

Injury Control Resource Information Network
www.injurycontrol.com/icrin

International Walk to School Day
www.walktoschool.org

Kids' Health
www.kidshealth.org
www.kidshealth.org/kid/watch/out/bike_safety.html
(bicycle safety)
www.kidshealth.org/kid/watch/out/car_safety.html
(car and bus safety)

McGruff (National Crime Prevention Council)
www.mcgruff.org

National Fire Protection Association
www.nfpa.org

National Highway Traffic Safety Administration
www.nhtsa.gov

National Oceanic and Atmospheric Administration (weather safety, emergency preparedness)
www.education.noaa.gov

National Organization for Youth Safety
www.noys.org

National Program for Playground Safety
www.uni.edu/playground

National Safe Boating Council
www.safeboatingcouncil.org

National Safety Council
www.nsc.org

National School Safety Center
www.schoolsafety.us

National Transportation Safety Board
www.ntsb.gov

National Youth Sports Safety Foundation
www.nyssf.org

Net Smartz Kids
www.netsmartzkids.org/indexFL.htm

Operation Lifesaver (railroad crossing safety)
www.oli.org/for_kids/kids_overview.htm

PBS Kids: Don't Buy It!
www.pbskids.org/dontbuyit/entertainment

Police Notebook for Kid Safety
www.ou.edu/oupd/kidsafe/start.htm

Safe Kids Worldwide
www.safekids.org

Safe Ride News
www.saferidenews.com

School Safety
www.nea.org/schoolsafety

Smokey the Bear Smokey Kids
www.smokeybear.com/kids

ThinkFirst for KIDS
www.thinkfirst.org/kids

Traffic Safety Kids' Page (New York State Governor's Traffic Safety Committee)
www.nysgtsc.state.ny.us/kids.htm

U.S. Consumer Product Safety Commission
www.cpsc.gov/kids/kidsafety/main.html (Adventures of Kidd Safety)

U.S. Department of Agriculture Forest Service Woodsy Owl
www.fs.fed.us/

U.S. Environmental Protection Agency
www.epa.gov/kidshometour (home chemical information)

U.S. Fire Administration for Kids
www.usfa.dhs.gov/kids/flash.shtm

For sites related to alcohol use and drunk driving, see the Internet listing for Chapter 12.

CHILDREN'S LITERATURE

AGES 5–8

Bang, Molly. *When Sophie Gets Angry—Really, Really Angry . . . .* Blue Sky Press, 1999.

Berenstain, Stan, and Jan Berenstain. *The Berenstain Bears and No Guns Allowed.* Random House, 2000.

Borden, Louise. *Albie the Lifeguard.* Scholastic, 1993.

Brillhart, Julie. *Molly Rides the School Bus.* Albert Whitman, 2002.

Brown, Marc. *Arthur's Fire Drill.* Random House, 2000.

Brown, Marc. *Dinosaurs Beware: A Safety Guide.* Little, Brown, 1982.

Carter, Sharon. *The Little Book of Choices.* Island Heritage, 2004.

Curtis, Jamie Lee, and Laura Cornell. *It's Hard to Be Five: Learning How to Work My Control Panel.* Joanna Cotler, 2004.

Cuyler, Margery. *Please Play Safe! Penguin's Guide to Playground Safety.* Scholastic Press, 2006.

Cuyler, Margery. *Stop, Drop and Roll: A Book About Fire Safety.* Simon & Schuster, 2001.

Davidson, Martine. *Maggie and the Emergency Room.* Random House, 1992.

Evans, Lezlie. *Sometimes I Feel Like a Storm Cloud.* Mondo, 1999.

Feldman, Heather. *My School Bus: A Book About School Bus Safety.* Rosen, 1998.

Franklin, Kristine. *Iguana Beach.* Crown, 1997. (Multicultural)

Gobbell, Phyllis, and Jim Laster. *Safe Sally Seat Belt and the Magic Click.* Children's Press, 1986.

Haan, Amanda. *I Call My Hand Gentle.* Penguin Putnam Books for Young Readers, 2003.

Hallinan, P. D. *Let's Be Safe.* Ideals Children's Books, 2007.

Harper, Jessica. *Lizzy's Do's and Don'ts.* HarperCollins, 2002.

Henkes, Kevin. *Lilly's Purple Plastic Purse.* Greenwillow, 1996.

Henkes, Kevin. *Sheila Rae, the Brave.* William Morrow, 1982.

Hogan, Paul Z. *Sometimes I Get So Mad.* Raintree Steck-Vaughn, 1991.

Kelley, Marty. *The Rules.* Zino Press Children's Books, 2000.

Kurtz, Jane. *Do Kangaroos Wear Seatbelts?* Dutton Children's Books, 2005.

Levete, Sarah. *Looking After Myself.* Millbrook, 1998.

Moore, Eva. *Franklin's Bicycle Helmet.* Scholastic, 2000.

Pendziwol, Jean. *Once Upon a Dragon: Stranger Safety for Kids.* Kids Can Press, Ltd., 2007.

Pendziwol, Jean. *No Dragons for Tea: Fire Safety for Kids (and Dragons).* Kids Can Press, 2001.

Rathman, Peggy. *Officer Buckle and Gloria.* Putnam & Grosset, 1995. (Caldecott Medal)

Rey, H. A. *The Original Curious George*. Houghton Mifflin, 1941.

Spelman, Cornelia. *Your Body Belongs to You*. Albert Whitman, 2008.

Vail, Rachel. *Sometimes I'm Bombaloo*. Scholastic, 2002.

Viorst, Judith. *Alexander and the Terrible, Horrible, No Good, Very Bad Day*. Atheneum Books for Young Readers, 1972.

AGES 8–12

Cleary, Beverly. *Lucky Chuck*. Morrow, 1984.

Day, Jeff. *Don't Touch That! The Book of Gross, Poisonous, and Downright Icky Plants and Critters*. Chicago Review Press, 2008.

DeFelice, Cynthia. *Weasel*. William Morrow, 1991.

Harrison, Jean. *Safety*. Smart Apple Media, 2004.

O'Dell, Scott. *Island of the Blue Dolphins*. Houghton Mifflin, 1960.

Park, Barbara. *Mick Harte Was Here*. Alfred A. Knopf, 1995.

Raatma, Lucia. *Fire Safety*. Child's World, 2003.

Raymer, Dottie. *Staying Home Alone: A Girl's Guide to Staying Safe and Having Fun*. Pleasant Company, 2002.

Taylor-Butler, Christine. *Food Safety*. Children's Press, 2008.

Waber, Bernard. *Courage*. Houghton Mifflin/Walter Lorraine Books, 2002.

ENDNOTES

1. Children's Defense Fund. (www.childrensdefense.org)
2. Centers for Disease Control and Prevention (CDC), National Center for Injury Prevention and Control (NCIPC). (www.cdc.gov/ncipc)
3. E. M. Lewit and L. S. Baker, *Child Indicators: Unintentional Injuries*. (www.futureofchildren.org/information2826/information_show.htm?doc_id=79899)
4. F. P. Rivara, "Impact of Injuries," in *About Children: An Authoritative Resource on the State of Childhood Today*, eds. A. G. Cosby, R. E. Greenberg, L. H. Southward, and M. Weitzman (American Academy of Pediatrics, 2005), 122.
5. National Center for Injury Prevention and Control, CDC, *Child Passenger Safety: Fact Sheet*. (www.cdc.gov/ncipc/factsheets/childpas.htm)
6. F. P. Rivara, "Impact of Injuries," 122–23.
7. D. K. Eaton et al., "Youth Risk Behavior Surveillance—United States, 2007," *Morbidity and Mortality Weekly Report* 57, no. SS-4 (2008):1–131.
8. U.S. Department of Health and Human Services, *Healthy People 2010: Understanding and Improving Health*, 2d ed. (Washington, DC: U.S. Government Printing Office, November 2000).
9. National Center for Injury Prevention and Control, CDC, *Childhood Injury Fact Sheet*. (www.cdc.gov/ncipc)
10. National Center for Injury Prevention and Control, *CDC Injury Fact Book, 2006*. (www.cdc.gov/ncipc/fact_book/factbook.htm)
11. F. P. Rivara, "Impact of Injuries," 122–23.
12. F. P. Rivara, "Impact of Injuries," 123–24.
13. F. P. Rivara, "Impact of Injuries," 123–24.
14. Centers for Disease Control and Prevention (CDC), *School Health Guidelines to Prevent Unintentional Injury and Violence*, MMWR Recommendations and Reports 50, no. RR22 (7 December 2001): 1–46.
15. W. M. Kane and M. Quackenbush, *Teach and Talk: Safety and Risk* (Santa Cruz: ETR Associates, 2001), 19.
16. F. P. Rivara, "Impact of Injuries," 125.
17. L. Kann, S. K. Telljohann, and S. F. Wooley, "Health Education: Results from the School Health Programs and Policies Study 2006," *Journal of School Health* 77, no. 8 (2007): 408–34.
18. CDC, *School Health Guidelines to Prevent Unintentional Injury and Violence*.
19. W. M. Kane and M. Quackenbush, *Teach and Talk: Safety and Risk*.
20. Ibid.
21. National Injury Prevention Foundation, *ThinkFirst for Kids*. (www.thinkfirst.org/About/Kids2/asp)
22. CDC, *School Health Guidelines to Prevent Unintentional Injury and Violence*.
23. Ibid.
24. Ibid.
25. National Center for Injury Prevention and Control, *Injuries Among Children and Adolescents*. (www.cdc.gov/ncipc/factsheets/children.htm).
26. National Center for Injury Prevention and Control, *Child Passenger Safety*. (www.cdc.gov/ncipc/factsheets/childpas.htm).
27. National Center for Injury Prevention and Control, *CDC's Unintentional Injury Activities—2004*.
28. National Center for Injury Prevention and Control, *Fireworks-related Injuries*. (www.cdc.gov/ncipc/factsheets/fworks.htm).
29. National Center for Injury Prevention and Control, *Playground Injuries*. (www.cdc.gov/ncipc/factsheets/playgr.htm).
30. National Center for Injury Prevention and Control, *Poisoning in the United States*. (www.cdc.gov/ncipc/factsheets/poisoning.htm).
31. National Center for Injury Prevention and Control, *Fire Death and Injuries*. (www.cdc.gov/ncipc/factsheets/fire.htm).
32. National Center for Injury Prevention and Control, *What Is Traumatic Brain Injury?* (www.cdc.gov/ncipc/tbi/TBI.htm).
33. National Center for Injury Prevention and Control, *Water-related Injuries*. (www.cdc.gov/ncipc/factsheets/drown.htm).
34. National Safe Kids Campaign, *Promoting Child Safety to Prevent Unintentional Injury*.
35. Walk and Bike to School Day. (www.walktoschool.org)
36. National Highway Traffic Safety Administration (NHTSA), *Safe Routes to School*. (www.nhtsa.dot.gov/people/injury/pedbimot/bike/Safe-Routes-2004/)
37. National Center for Injury Prevention and Control, *Preventing Injuries in Sports, Recreation, and Exercise*. (www.cdc.gov/ncipc/pub-res/research_agenda/05_sports.htm)
38. American Academy of Child & Adolescent Psychiatry, *Home Alone Children*. (http://aacap.org/page.ww?name=Home+Alone+Children&section=Facts+for+Families).
39. National Child Care Information Center, *Children Home Alone and Babysitter Guidelines*, Administration for Children & Families, U.S. Department of Health and Human Services. (www.nccic.org/poptopics/homealone.html).
40. KidsHealth, *When It's Just You After School*. (http://kidshealth.org/kid/watch/house/homealone.html).
41. Safe Kids USA, *Safety Tips*. (www.usa.safekids.org/index.cfm).
42. Centers for Disease Control and Prevention, *Health Education Curriculum Analysis Tool*. (www.cdc.gov/HealthyYouth/HECAT/index.htm).
43. N. Stein, E. Gaberman, and L. Sjostrom, *Bullyproof: A Teacher's Guide on Teasing and Bullying for Use with Fourth and Fifth Grade Students* (Wellesley, MA: Wellesley College Center for Research on Women, 1996).
44. American Academy of Family Physicians, *Nosebleeds: What to Do When Your Nose Bleeds*. (http://familydoctor.org/132.xml)

9

(Amberly, age 13)

Promoting Personal Health and Wellness

DESIRED LEARNER OUTCOMES

After reading this chapter, you will be able to . . .

- Describe the status of personal health and wellness among youth and the costs associated with poor personal health.

- Explain the relationship between personal health and wellness and compromised academic performance.

- Identify factors that influence personal health and wellness.

- Summarize current guidelines and practices for schools and teachers related to promotion of personal health and wellness.

- Summarize developmentally appropriate personal health and wellness promotion concepts and skills for K–8 students in the context of the National Health Education Standards and target healthy behavior outcomes.

- Demonstrate developmentally appropriate learning strategies and assessment techniques that incorporate concepts and skills that have been shown to promote personal health and wellness among youth.

- Identify effective, evaluated commercial personal health and wellness promotion curricula.

- Identify websites and children's literature that can be used in cross-curricular instructional activities promoting personal health and wellness.

INTRODUCTION

> Scarcely one half of the children of our country continue in school much beyond the fifth grade. It is important, therefore, that so far as possible the knowledge which has most to do with human welfare should be presented in the early years of school life. . . . The health of a people influences the prosperity and happiness of a nation more than any other one thing. The highest patriotism is therefore the conservation of health.[1]

This quotation introduces the book *Health Lessons,* published in 1910. At that time, the author, Alvin Davison, was concerned with "infectious diseases and . . . serious cases of sickness from contagious maladies, with all their attendant suffering, largely sacrifices on the altar of ignorance." In 1910, the leading cause of death in children age 11 and older was tuberculosis.

Things certainly have changed during the almost hundred years since *Health Lessons* was published. Many infectious diseases are well controlled with immunizations and other public health measures. To continue these gains, effective public and school health education related to communicable disease prevention and control for adults and children is needed. In a tremendous change since 1910, chronic diseases, such as heart disease and cancer, and unintentional and intentional injuries now claim the greatest number of lives. Efforts to prevent chronic disease and injury must include public and school health education.

When people think of school health education, they often think first of personal health habits—washing hands, bathing regularly, brushing and flossing teeth, eating nutritiously, exercising, and getting plenty of rest. Learning personal health care is extremely important. Many of today's communicable and chronic diseases could be largely prevented or controlled through just such simple, consistent measures. Illness from other conditions can be shortened or ameliorated through coordinated personal, family, school, and medical care. This chapter focuses on helping children learn basic personal health care skills and preventing and managing the common health problems school-age children experience.

In this chapter, educators will notice a departure from traditional personal health education approaches that emphasize learning about body systems. Learning about body systems, one after another outside a health context, more appropriately belongs in science or biology classes. To link learning about the body to health, teachers should help students apply their knowledge about priority health-risk behaviors to effects on body systems. For example, what are the effects of tobacco use on the respiratory and cardiovascular systems? What are the effects of healthy nutrition and regular physical activity on the muscular and skeletal systems? What are the effects of alcohol and other drug use on the nervous system? With these core concepts (NHES 1) in mind, students should go on to practice the personal and social skills they need to promote health and prevent illness and injury.

In the content area of personal health, two of the National Health Education Standards are especially important. NHES 3, access information, products, and services, provides opportunities for students to investigate and practice finding sources of information, products, and services to meet their health-related needs. For example, accessing information about the management of diabetes might mean searching the websites of the American Diabetes Association, the Centers for Disease Control and Prevention (CDC), and the National Institutes of Health (NIH). Accessing products and services might include selecting an appropriate sunscreen to wear during an outdoor volleyball game or talking to a school counselor about a problem. The diversity of topics in the area of personal health emphasizes the need to help young people learn to get health information, products, and services from valid and reliable sources.

NHES 7, self-management, also plays a major role in personal health. In the previous example, students who are good self-managers actually use the sunscreen and seek out the school counselor. In addition, they practice basic health habits, such as brushing and flossing teeth, washing hands, and managing stress. NHES 3 and 7 are a major focus in the learning and assessment strategies included in this chapter.

Prevalence and Cost

The Children's Defense Fund cites these moments in the life of America that pertain to the personal health and wellness of children:

> Every thirty-six seconds in America, a child is confirmed as abused or neglected.
>
> Every thirty-five seconds, a baby is born into poverty.
>
> Every forty-one seconds, a baby is born without health insurance.
>
> Every minute, a baby is born to a teen mother.
>
> Every two minutes, a baby is born at low birth weight.
>
> Every eighteen minutes, a baby dies before his first birthday.[2]

These sobering statistics point to an important fact: Although the health of Americans overall has improved dramatically during the past fifty years, children who are born into poverty—with its associated lower education, health care, and opportunity—are among those at highest risk for serious health problems.

In *About Children,* from the American Academy of Pediatrics, Bernard Guyer and Alyssa Wigton describe improvements in the health status of American children during the twentieth century as spectacular.[3] During this period, the life expectancy of Americans increased by 56 percent. The overall age-adjusted death rate declined by 74 percent, and the greatest single contribution to the increased longevity of Americans was the decline in infant and child death rates. Unfortunately, these impressive improvements in overall measures of child health obscure the confounding

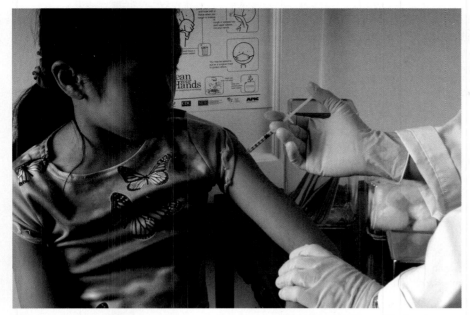

Regular medical checkups are an important part of personal health and wellness. Vaccinations have contributed to a significant decline in child mortality during the twentieth century.

disparities associated with race, class, and geography and the continuing and emerging health problems of American children.[4]

The infant mortality rate (IMR), or death in the first year of life, declined greatly during the twentieth century. In 1998, the IMR was 7.2 deaths per 1,000 live births, compared with 100 deaths per 1,000 births in 1915. Many factors influenced this 95 percent decline, including improvements in the environment, a safe milk supply, parenting information, improved housing, medical advances, blood banks, modern family-planning methods, and neonatal intensive care. However, little of the decline in the IMR resulted from a reduction in the number of births of low-birth-weight, high-risk infants. The birth-weight distribution of American infants has changed little during the past century.[5]

For children older than 1 year, the decline in mortality during the twentieth century was tremendous. Today, fewer than two children die between their first and twentieth birthdays, compared with thirty in 1900. These advances are due largely to improved sanitation and living standards during the first part of the century and to modern antibiotics, vaccines, and medications during the latter part. However, the decline in child mortality has not been uniform. Adolescents continue to be at high risk for death, primarily due to preventable causes such as injuries.[6]

Child mortality rates from infectious diseases have declined 99 percent, even with the emergence of HIV/AIDS, while injuries have emerged as the leading cause of child deaths. Injuries accounted for only 6 percent of child deaths in 1900 but 44 percent in 1998. At the beginning of the century, child injury deaths occurred mainly on farms, in factories, and from burns. Today, motor-vehicle-related deaths account for more than half of all child injury deaths, with children as passengers or pedestrians. In addition to motor-vehicle-related deaths, child deaths from violence (homicide, suicide) increased by the end of the twentieth century.[7]

Approximately 20 million children live with a chronic health condition, with asthma among the most severe. On average, American children miss 14 million school days each year because of asthma, which has become the third leading cause of hospitalization among children younger than 15. Childhood obesity also affects many American children. The number of overweight children has more than doubled since 1980, and the number of overweight adolescents has tripled during that time. Being overweight increases the risk of suffering severe chronic diseases such as heart disease, Type 2 diabetes, high blood pressure, some cancers, stroke, and depression.[8]

The health of American children also is impacted by HIV/AIDS. The rate of HIV/AIDS cases among children younger than 13 varies by race and ethnicity. In 2001, white children made up 61 percent of the population of U.S. children but only 19 percent of HIV/AIDS cases in children. In contrast, African American children made up 14 percent of the child population but 65 percent of HIV/AIDS cases in children. Hispanics made up 19 percent of U.S. children but 15 percent of HIV/AIDS cases in children. Of all HIV infections reported in the United States for youth ages 13 to 24, African Americans accounted for 56 percent. Gender differences also exist. Females represented 61 percent of HIV infections among young people ages 13 to 19, whereas males represented 39 percent.[9]

Other personal health and wellness issues affect children. Millions of children today grow up completely free of the dental problems that their parents experienced.[10] These children are the beneficiaries of better understanding of the decay process, healthier diets, fluoride use, dental sealants, and preventive dental care. However, for too many other children, dental caries is a daily nightmare of pain, eating difficulties, unsightly smiles, and distraction from play and learning. Tooth decay remains the single most common chronic disease of childhood, five times more common than asthma.[11]

In many ways, children today are better off than they have ever been, but new and emerging child health problems—such as asthma, obesity, ADHD, and HIV/AIDS—warrant special attention. Important disparities related to race and income continue to exist and in some cases have increased. To a large extent, these health disparities result from differences in access to health services and in the broader socioeconomic context in which minority and low-income children live. Guyer and Wigton state,

TABLE 9–1

Healthy People 2010 **Objectives Related to the Personal Health and Wellness of Children and Adolescents**

Access to Quality Health Services

| Objective 1-1 | Increase the proportion of persons with health insurance. |
| Objective 1-4 | Increase the proportion of persons who have a specific source of ongoing care. |

Cancer

| Objective 3-9 | Increase the proportion of persons who use at least one of the following protective measures that may reduce the risk of skin cancer: Avoid the sun between 10 A.M. and 4 P.M., wear sun-protective clothing when exposed to sunlight, use sunscreen with a sun-protective factor (SPF) of 15 or higher, and avoid artificial sources of ultraviolet light. |

Diabetes

| Objective 5-2 | Prevent diabetes. |

Educational and Community-Based Programs

| Objective 7-1 | Increase high school completion. |
| Objective 7-2 | Increase the proportion of middle, junior high, and senior high schools that provide school health education to prevent health problems in the following areas: unintentional injury; violence; suicide; tobacco use and addiction; alcohol and other drug use; unintended pregnancy, HIV/AIDS, and STD infection; unhealthy dietary patterns; inadequate physical activity; and environmental health. |

Environmental Health

| Objective 8-16 | Reduce indoor allergen levels. |
| Objective 8-20 | Increase the proportion of the nation's primary and secondary schools that have official school policies ensuring the safety of students and staff from environmental hazards, such as chemicals in special classrooms, poor indoor air quality, asbestos, and exposure to pesticides. |

Immunization and Infectious Diseases

Objective 14-1	Reduce or eliminate indigenous cases of vaccine-preventable diseases.
Objective 14-19	Reduce the number of courses of antibiotics prescribed for the sole diagnosis of the common cold.
Objective 14-22	Achieve and maintain effective vaccination coverage levels for universally recommended vaccines among young children.
Objective 14-27	Increase routine vaccination coverage levels for adolescents.

Oral Health

| Objective 21-1 | Reduce the proportion of children and adolescents who have dental caries experience in their primary or permanent teeth. |
| Objective 21-10 | Increase the proportion of children and adults who use the oral health care system each year. |

Respiratory Diseases

| Objective 24-1 | Reduce asthma deaths. |
| Objective 24-2 | Reduce hospitalizations for asthma. |

Vision and Hearing

Objective 28-2	Increase the proportion of preschool children age five years and under who receive vision screening.
Objective 28-9	Increase the use of appropriate personal protective eyewear in recreational activities and hazardous situations around the home.
Objective 28-14	Increase the proportion of persons who have had a hearing examination on schedule.
Objective 28-17	Reduce noise-induced hearing loss in children and adolescents age 17 years and under.

SOURCE: U.S. Department of Health and Human Services. *Healthy People 2010: Understanding and Improving Health,* 2nd ed. (Washington, DC: U.S. Government Printing Office, 2000).

As we embark on a new century certain to provide further advancements in child health, considerations must be given to ensuring that these disparities become a part of the past. In the 21st century, all American children should be able to achieve their optimal health and well-being.[12]

Table 9–1 describes the wide range of public health issues related to children's personal health and wellness. The *Healthy People 2010* objectives call for an increase in the proportion of schools that provide school health education in the content areas presented in this text. School health programs can make an important contribution to the achievement of the national health objectives.

Personal Health and Wellness and Academic Performance

The Institute of Medicine (IOM) reported that schools with large numbers of children who live in poverty have higher rates of absenteeism and grade retention among their student populations. These children often have more health problems and inadequate nutrition. The families of poor and at-risk children move frequently. Changing schools often disrupts education, making learning and achievement difficult.[13]

Schools with higher percentages of children living in poverty often are inferior structurally, might be unsafe, and might even be harmful to children's health. Billions of dollars are needed to bring schools into compliance with federal mandates to make all programs accessible to all students; to remove or correct hazardous substances, such as asbestos, lead in water or paint, materials in underground storage tanks, and radon; or to meet other requirements. Far too many children attend schools that have leaky roofs, unsanitary bathrooms, and inadequate plumbing, which make them unsafe and even harmful to children's health.[14]

Howard Taras and William Potts-Datema published an important series of articles reviewing the state of research on the association between academic outcomes among school-age children and health issues. Three of the articles concerned sleep, chronic health conditions, and asthma.[15-17] Research revealed a high prevalence of suboptimal amounts of sleep and poor-quality sleep among young people. Suboptimal sleep has been shown to affect how well students are able to learn and possibly to adversely affect school performance; academic achievement improved after corrective measures were taken (surgery, tonsillectomy/adenoidectomy). The onset of adolescence appears to be accompanied by a decrease in sleep among many youth, but the academic consequences of these changes in sleep habits are inconclusive. Still, students with learning and/or attention disorders would be justified in suspecting that poor sleep might be a contributing factor.[18]

With regard to chronic health conditions, Taras and Potts-Datema reviewed published studies that investigated the association of school attendance, cognitive ability, and achievement. The research revealed evidence that diabetes, sickle-cell anemia, and epilepsy affected students' achievement and ability. The association of school performance with chronic diseases other than diabetes, sickle-cell anemia, epilepsy, and asthma is not as well studied. Most studies showed an association between poor cognitive functioning and either early onset of diabetes or a history of severe hypoglycemic episodes (dangerously low blood sugar levels, sometimes resulting in seizure). Despite differing research methodologies, there is an emerging consensus that children with diabetes are more likely to be at an academic disadvantage.[19]

In the United States, sickle-cell anemia affects approximately 72,000 people, predominantly African Americans. Sickle-shaped red blood cells often block the flow of blood in narrow blood vessels, resulting in fever, pain, and swelling. One of the biggest threats to cognitive functioning from sickle-cell anemia is a narrowing of small blood vessels in the brain that results in strokes. A meta-analysis indicated small decrements in cognitive functioning as measured by components of IQ tests for children with sickle-cell anemia. Families should be encouraged to keep medical appointments and remain vigilant with regard to medical management.[20]

Taras and Potts-Datema reported these difficulties involved in describing the direct effects of epilepsy on school performance: Epilepsy is highly linked to other conditions that affect school functioning, such as mental retardation and cerebral palsy; there are many forms of epilepsy; and differentiating the effects of a seizure from the effects of medications used to manage seizures is difficult with regard to measuring academic functioning.[21]

Rates of absenteeism are higher among students with asthma, although the exact magnitude of absenteeism is difficult to determine. Studies thus far have shown either a weak or no association between asthma and school achievement. Further studies are needed to determine whether certain groups of children with asthma (those with severe or ongoing symptoms, those with disturbed sleep, or children in kindergarten) are at higher risk for poor school achievement.[22]

Many states have made tremendous strides in developing higher standards for their education system. Despite this progress, however, some states are struggling to improve student achievement. As indicated in Chapter 2, students' health and its impact on students' ability to perform well academically are receiving more attention.[23] Policymakers need to focus on eliminating the barriers that affect students' readiness to learn. Physical and mental health conditions impact students' school attendance and ability to pay attention in class, control their anger, and restrain self-destructive impulses. To help ensure that students come to school ready to learn, policymakers should provide technical assistance to help schools incorporate health into their curricula and increase interagency partnerships between the health and the education communities.[24]

Factors That Influence Personal Health and Wellness

The U.S. Public Health Service stated that the leading causes of death in the United States generally result from a mix of unhealthy behaviors; injury, violence, and other environmental factors; and the unavailability or inaccessibility of quality health services. Understanding and monitoring behaviors, environmental factors, and community health systems might prove more useful in assessing the nation's true health—and in driving health improvement activities—than death rates, which reflect the cumulative impact of these factors. This more complex approach served as the basis for development of the leading health indicators:

Physical activity

Overweight and obesity

Tobacco use

Substance abuse

Responsible sexual behavior

Mental health

Injury and violence

Environmental quality

Immunization

Access to health care[25]

Thus, poor health, particularly among children, is not necessarily a matter of choice.

The Institute of Medicine cited several important sources of health problems for children. The poverty rate for children under age 18 is the highest of any age group in the nation. The increasing number of poor and at-risk students requires schools to contend with more students who are potentially low achievers and who have health and other problems that interfere with learning. Lack of prenatal care and inadequate care and nurturing after birth place some children at a tremendous disadvantage for learning and health. Poor children have more health problems than other children, their health problems often are more severe, and they are less likely to receive regular health care.[26]

Changing family structures and lack of access to health care also pose risks to children's health. Economic stresses often require parents and caregivers to work outside the home, sometimes at more than one job. Many children live in one-parent families or with family members other than parents. Time devoted to employment can limit parents' and caregivers' ability to take sick children to the doctor or to spend time at home with them. Further, many children do not have adequate health insurance to cover basic preventive services and medical needs.[27]

The Annie E. Casey Foundation's *2007 Kids Count Data Book* reiterated that the risk of child injury and death is highest for children living in poverty.[28] Poor children in the United States are more likely to die at every age and from every cause. Despite the enormous wealth in the United States, the child poverty rate is among the highest in the developed world. Growth in the ranks of poor children during the past decades has been due not to an increase in the number of welfare-dependent families but to an increase in the number of the working poor. More than half (56 percent) of American children with incomes below the poverty threshold live in households where someone works full-time.[29]

Despite the enormous wealth in the United States, the child poverty rate is among the highest in the developed world. The gap in the child poverty rate between the United States and other developed countries is partly a product of differences in private-sector income, but differences in governmental efforts to alleviate child poverty greatly accentuate the disparities. The *2007 Kids Count Data Book* predicts that the lack of investment in children will put the United States at a competitive disadvantage in the international marketplace of the twenty-first century.[30]

GUIDELINES FOR SCHOOLS

State of the Practice

The Centers for Disease Control and Prevention (CDC) conducts the School Health Policies and Programs Study (SHPPS) every six years to monitor efforts to improve school health policies and programs.[31] Table 9–2 provides SHPPS 2006 data about the personal health and wellness concepts and skills elementary and middle school teachers

TABLE 9–2 SHPPS

School Health Policies and Programs Study 2006 Data Related to Personal Health and Wellness

Topic	Percent of Schools Teaching Topic in a Required Class	
	Elementary Schools	Middle and Junior High Schools
Benefits of rest and sleep	92.3	86.1
Consumer health (choosing sources of health-related information, products, and services wisely)	44.1	63.8
Dental and oral health	74.5	54.6
Difference between infectious and chronic diseases	42.1	67.8
Environmental health (how air and water quality can affect health)	67.5	66.3
Growth and development	73.3	80.8
Hand washing or hand hygiene	90.4	77.4
How common infectious illnesses such as the flu are transmitted	82.6	77.9
How positive health behaviors can benefit people throughout their life span	88.0	88.6
Immunizations	39.0	55.3
Importance of health screenings and checkups	57.5	53.5
Potential health and social consequences of popular fads and trends	52.8	76.1
Sun safety or skin cancer prevention	68.3	75.9
Ways to prevent vision and hearing loss	49.8	44.5
Compassion for persons living with HIV or AIDS	11.0	57.9
How HIV affects the human body	12.2	68.9
How HIV is diagnosed and treated	6.4	58.2
How HIV is transmitted	14.8	71.6
How to find valid information or services related to HIV or HIV counseling or testing	7.6	50.9
How to prevent HIV infection	15.4	69.5
Signs and symptoms of HIV and AIDS	9.6	63.7

SOURCE: Centers for Disease Control and Prevention, *School Health Policies and Programs Study 2006 (SHPPS)* (Atlanta, GA: CDC, 2007). www.cdc.gov/HealthyYouth/shpps

reported teaching in at least one required class or course. At the elementary level, more than 80 percent of teachers taught about the benefits of rest and sleep, hand washing or hand hygiene, common infectious disease transmission, and positive health behaviors. More than 68 percent taught about sun safety, but only about 15 percent taught about HIV prevention. More than 80 percent of middle school teachers taught about rest and sleep, growth and development, and positive health behaviors. At least three-quarters taught about hand washing, disease transmission, fads and trends, and sun safety. However, fewer than three-quarters of middle school teachers taught about

HIV prevention. The data indicate a need for increased and consistent school-based efforts to teach about personal health and wellness topics and skills.

State of the Art

Personal health and wellness efforts are most effective when schools and communities work in partnership. Students, teachers, parents, school staff, and community members all play important roles. To assist schools, the Centers for Disease Control and Prevention has published three sets of school health guidelines related to personal health and wellness promotion:

- *Guidelines for School Programs to Prevent Skin Cancer*[32]
- *Helping the Student with Diabetes Succeed: A Guide for School Personnel*[33]
- *Strategies for Addressing Asthma Within a Coordinated School Health Program*[34]

The Centers for Disease Control and Prevention released the Health Education Curriculum Analysis Tool (HECAT), an exciting new resource to help educators consider state-of-the-art practice in health education. The PEW module contains the tools to analyze and score curricula that are intended to promote personal health and wellness. The module uses the National Health Education Standards as the framework for determining the extent to which the curriculum is likely to enable students to master the essential knowledge and skills that promote personal health and wellness. Educators will find curriculum fundamentals, such as teacher materials, instructional design, and instructional strategies and materials analyses. This chapter includes healthy behavior outcomes and developmentally appropriate concepts and skills for promoting personal health and wellness provided in the HECAT. The HECAT is available at the Healthy Youth website of the Division of Adolescent and School Health (DASH) at CDC (www.cdc.gov/HealthyYouth/HECAT/index.htm).

GUIDELINES FOR CLASSROOM APPLICATIONS

Important Background for K–8 Teachers

A wide range of issues falls under the heading of personal health and wellness. Topics related to specific content areas, such as nutrition, physical activity, mental and emotional health, and injury prevention, are discussed in other topic-specific chapters. The background for teachers in this section focuses on the following issues:

- Hand washing and personal hygiene
- Dental and oral health
- Sleep and rest
- Skin cancer prevention and sun safety
- Communicable diseases
- Immunization
- Chronic diseases

Hand washing is an essential part of disease prevention.

Hand Washing and Personal Hygiene

Hand washing often is the first thing people think of when they hear the words *health* or *health education*. Indeed, thorough hand washing can prevent many communicable diseases. Children—and many adults—need instruction and practice in effective hand washing. Teachers can provide opportunities for children to wash their hands often and to demonstrate that they know how to do it well. Sometimes children and teachers report that their rest rooms are not stocked with soap and paper towels, either because of economics or because "the children make a mess." Teachers can use any mess making as a teaching opportunity to help children learn to wash their hands properly and to take care of their school rest rooms. Children can practice the take cares: take care of yourself, take care of others, and take care of this place.

Children should learn that one of the most common ways people catch colds is by rubbing their nose or their eyes after their hands have been contaminated with the cold virus. People pick up germs from other people and from contaminated surfaces and infect themselves when they touch their eyes, nose, or mouth. Germs can be spread directly to others or onto surfaces that people touch. In addition to colds, serious diseases (hepatitis A, meningitis, and infectious diarrhea) can be prevented when people make a habit of washing their hands.[35] The CDC's National Center for Infectious Diseases provides educational resources for K–12 teachers (www.cdc.gov/ncidod/teachers_tools/index.htm). At Kids' Health (www.kidshealth.org), students can learn about "Why do I need to wash my hands?"

Personal hygiene is an issue that teachers often want to address with students, especially with early adolescents. Teachers will find the Kids' Health website (www.kidshealth.org) especially helpful on hygiene issues (oily hair and skin, sweat and body odor). Teachers also must remember that poor hygiene on the part of some students may be linked to poor living conditions or to homelessness. A male middle school teacher related the story of being asked by several female faculty members to talk with a student about his body odor and dirty clothes, even though he didn't have the student in any of his classes. As he got to know the young man and brought up the topic, the student began to cry. His family simply didn't have the soap, shampoo, laundry, and home conditions that most other students took for granted. The teacher and the school were able to help the young man get the products and clothes he needed, and access to the kinds of facilities he needed, without his classmates being the wiser.

Dental and Oral Health

Professor Burton Edelstein of the School of Dental and Oral Surgery at Columbia University stated that childhood is an important time to prevent dental disease through positive health behaviors.[36] Tooth decay typically is established during the first two years of life. It is a completely preventable disease that causes suffering for far too many children.[37]

Children who develop early tooth decay or early childhood caries (ECC) remain at higher risk for cavities throughout childhood and into adulthood. Exposure to optimally fluoridated water is the single most effective public health method for reducing caries occurrence. However, ECC occurs even in fluoridated areas if destructive bacterial (from an adult's mouth who shares a spoon with a child) and feeding conditions (frequent sources of sugar) are present. Dental health professionals support initiating dental care for children at the time of their first birthday.[38]

Ideally, every child would have an identified dentist of his or her own who provides ongoing, comprehensive care throughout a child's growing years. The idea of a "dental home" parallels the idea of a "medical home" for all children. However, children at greatest need for dental care often have the least access to it. Preschoolers in poor families are more than twice as likely to experience tooth decay. On average, they experience twice the number of cavities, and their parents are twice as likely to report that their children have had toothaches or other dental problems. Edelstein explained that these young, disadvantaged children are only half as likely to visit the dentist, largely because Medicaid (the health insurance program for low-income children covering nearly one in four children in the United States) too often fails to deliver on its legal requirement to ensure the availability of dental care to low-income children. Access is compromised by the low number of dentists participating in Medicaid, overburdened health center dental programs, and inadequate funding for Medicaid dental insurance. An estimated 25 million children lack dental insurance.[39]

Regular visits to the dentist are an important part of good dental health.

The American Dental Association (ADA) notes that the news has been filled with frightening stories that link oral bacteria and oral disease to a variety of serious and potentially life-threatening illnesses. Dentists have long known that there is a strong relationship between oral health and general health. For example, tobacco, alcohol, and illicit drugs not only affect overall health but oral health as well. In addition, some researchers have found that periodontitis (the advanced form of gum disease that can cause tooth loss) is associated with cardiovascular disease, stroke, and bacterial pneumonia. Other research has found that pregnant women with periodontitis may be at increased risk for delivering babies that are pre-term, have low birth weight, or both. Although reports suggest that periodontitis may contribute to these conditions, the ADA states that the fact that two conditions occur at the same time doesn't necessarily mean that one causes the other. Disease relationships are complex.[40]

Given the potential link between periodontitis and systemic health problems, however, preventing periodontitis may turn out to be an important step in maintaining overall health. In most cases, that can be done with good daily oral hygiene (brushing and flossing) and regular professional care. Adults and children should tell their dentist about changes in oral health, including recent illnesses or chronic conditions.[41]

Teachers can help students learn the basics about dental care (brush twice a day, use fluoride toothpaste, floss, eat a balanced diet, and visit the dentist regularly) and can provide students with new toothbrushes and toothpaste from local dentists or health departments. The American Dental Association (www.ada.org/public/education/teachers/index .asp) offers a variety of classroom activities for teachers.

Sleep and Rest

The National Heart, Lung, and Blood Institute (NHLBI) reports that sleep is something all humans need to do. Sleep is a necessity, not an option. During sleep, many of the body's major organ and regulatory systems continue to work actively. Sleep, like diet and exercise, is important for minds and bodies to function normally. Sleep appears to be required for survival.[42]

Children and adolescents need at least nine hours of sleep each night to do their best. Most adults need approximately eight hours of sleep each night. When people get less sleep (even one hour less) than they need, they develop a sleep debt. Sleep debt can lead to problem sleepiness that occurs when people should be awake and alert, interferes with daily routines and activities, and reduces the ability to function. Even if people do not feel sleepy, sleep debt can have a powerful negative effect on their daytime performance, thinking, and mood and can cause them to fall asleep at inappropriate and even dangerous times.[43]

Problem sleepiness has serious consequences, putting adolescents and adults at risk for drowsy driving or workplace accidents. In children, problem sleepiness also increases the risk of accidents and injuries. Lack of sleep can have a negative effect on children's performance in school, on the playground, in extracurricular activities, and in social relationships. Inadequate sleep can decrease performance, concentration, reaction time, and consolidation of information and learning, as well as increase memory lapses, accidents and injuries, behavior problems, and mood problems.[44]

Teachers can help children learn about getting enough sleep by using a variety of children's books to prompt discussions on bedtime and going to sleep; some suggestions are included in "Children's Literature" at the end of the chapter. The NHLBI provides lessons and activities on healthy sleep at the Garfield Star Sleeper website (www .nhlbi.nih.gov/health/public/sleep/starslp).

Skin Cancer Prevention and Sun Safety

The CDC's *Guidelines for School Programs to Prevent Skin Cancer* state that skin cancer is the most common type of cancer in the United States. The two most common kinds of skin cancer—basal cell carcinoma and squamous cell carcinoma—are highly curable. Melanoma, the third most common type of skin cancer and one of the most common among young adults, is more dangerous. Melanoma accounts for more than three-fourths of all skin cancer deaths. The incidence of melanoma and mortality from melanoma has increased substantially during the past thirty years.[45]

Exposure to ultraviolet (UV) radiation in childhood and adolescence plays an important role in the development of skin cancer. Thus, preventive health behaviors can play an

Skin cancer prevention among students involves a coordinated effort between schools and families.

important role in reducing skin cancer when the behaviors are initiated early and practiced consistently throughout life. Schools are in an important position to teach and model healthy behavior about sun safety and skin cancer prevention, including offering sun safety lessons that involve families. Skin cancer protective behaviors schools can teach include the following:

- Minimize exposure to the sun during peak hours (10:00 A.M.–4:00 P.M.).
- Seek shade from the midday sun (10:00 A.M.–4:00 P.M.).
- Wear clothing, hats, and sunglasses that protect the skin.
- Use a broad-spectrum sunscreen (UV-A and UV-B protection) with a sun protective factor (SPF) of 15 or higher.
- Avoid sunlamps and tanning beds.[46]

Sun safety measures should not reduce student participation in physical activity. If physical activity must be scheduled during the middle of the day, teachers and children can focus on sun safety measures such as wearing a hat, protective clothing, or sunscreen and seeking shade.[47]

Because UV radiation plays a role in the synthesis of vitamin D, teachers might have heard that limiting UV exposure might be cause for concern, perhaps leading to a decrease in levels of vitamin D and increasing the likelihood that rickets, a disorder involving a weakening of the bones, will develop in susceptible infants and children. However, the average age for presentation of rickets is 18 months; thus, the age groups of concern typically are infants and toddlers, not school-age children between 5 and 18. Also, although the major source of vitamin D is skin exposure to sunlight, supplementing the diet with foods (fatty fish, vitamin D–fortified milk and breakfast cereal) can provide enough vitamin D to meet intake requirements.[48]

The CDC recognizes that skin cancer prevention measures vary in both their ease of adoption and their relevance. Schools should not allow an all-or-nothing approach to undermine the effectiveness of their skin cancer prevention efforts. For sun safety protection, a short-sleeve shirt and cap might be better than no hat and a sleeveless top. Flexibility is important while schools move in the direction of optimal skin cancer prevention environments, policies, and programs.[49] Teachers can find sun safety educational information from the American Cancer Society (www.cancer.org), the CDC (www.cdc.gov), and the National Safety Council (www.nsc.org).

Communicable Diseases

Communicable diseases are infectious diseases caused by various types of microscopic organisms, including viruses, bacteria, parasites, and fungi. These organisms cause illnesses ranging from colds and flu to deadly diseases such as HIV/AIDS. Infectious diseases vary in how they are spread. Some are spread through person-to-person contact, others are spread through the air, water, contaminated food, insects, and animals. Teachers and students can learn about infectious diseases from the National Center for Infectious Diseases (www.cdc.gov/ncidod) and the National Institutes of Health (www.nih.gov).

Many previously common childhood diseases now are controlled through immunization. Communicable diseases that teachers continue to encounter in school settings include chicken pox, colds and flu, eye and ear infections, scabies, ringworm, pediculosis (head lice), hepatitis, and human immunodeficiency virus (HIV). Children who become ill at school or return to school while they are still ill should be referred to the school nurse, a health aide, or a designated school staff member. Teachers can access information on infectious diseases as needed from government agencies such as the CDC and NIH. This section includes a discussion of four communicable disease issues: immunization, colds and flu, head lice, and HIV.

Immunization

Children are born with a full immune system composed of cells, glands, organs, and fluids that are located throughout the body to fight invading bacteria and viruses. The immune system recognizes germs that enter the body as foreign invaders, or *antigens,* and produces protein substances called *antibodies* to fight them. A normal, healthy immune system has the ability to produce millions of these antibodies to defend against thousands of attacks every day, doing it so naturally that people are not even aware they are being attacked and defended so often. Many antibodies disappear once they have destroyed the invading antigens, but the cells involved in antibody production remain and become *memory cells.* Memory cells remember the original antigen and then defend against it when the antigen attempts to re-infect a person, even after many decades. This protection is called *immunity.*[50]

Vaccines contain the same antigens or parts of antigens that cause diseases, but the antigens in vaccines are either killed or greatly weakened. When they are injected into fatty tissue or muscle, vaccine antigens are not strong enough to produce the symptoms and signs of the disease but are strong enough for the immune system to produce antibodies against them. The memory cells that remain prevent re-infection when they encounter that disease in the future. Thus, through vaccination, children develop immunity without suffering the actual disease.[51]

Children in the United States routinely receive vaccines that protect them from more than a dozen diseases such as measles, polio, and tetanus. Most childhood communicable diseases are now at their lowest levels in history, thanks to years of immunization. Children must get at least some vaccines before they may attend school.[52]

Most parents today have never seen a case of diphtheria, measles, or other once-common diseases now preventable by vaccines. As a result, some parents wonder why their children must receive shots for diseases that do not seem to exist. Myths and misinformation about vaccine safety abound and can confuse parents who are trying to make sound decisions about their children's health care. Thus, scientific research that attempts to distinguish true vaccine side effects from unrelated, chance occurrences is important.[53]

Vaccines are held to the highest standard of safety. The United States currently has the safest, most effective vaccine supply in history. The Centers for Disease Control and Prevention (CDC) and the Food and Drug Administration (FDA) continually work to make already safe vaccines even safer. Laws require extensive testing before a vaccine can be licensed. Once in use, vaccines are monitored continually for safety and efficacy. Immunizations, like any medication, can cause side effects. However, putting children and others who come into contact with them at risk of contracting a disease through failing to immunize could be dangerous or deadly.[54]

Two vaccines in particular have been in the news during the past several years. Educators and parents likely are aware of controversies related to childhood vaccines and autism, specifically that the measles-mumps-rubella (MMR) vaccine and thimerosal-containing vaccines are associated causally with autism.[55] The Centers for Disease Control and Prevention, the American Academy of Pediatrics, the U.S. Food and Drug Administration, and the Institute of Medicine state that childhood vaccines are safe and that the dangers of not vaccinating children far outweigh any potential risks.[56-59]

Another vaccine that has attracted media attention is Gardasil® the first vaccine developed to prevent cervical cancer and other disease in females caused by certain types of genital human papillomavirus (HPV). Gardasil® protects against four HPV types, which together cause 70 percent of cervical cancers and 90 percent of genital warts. The U.S. Food and Drug Administration (FDA) licensed the vaccine for use in girls/women ages 9-26 years. The vaccine is given as three injections over a six-month period. Immunization is expected to prevent most cases of cervical cancer due to HPV types included in the vaccine. Females, however, are not protected if they have been infected with the HPV types prior to vaccination. Also, Gardasil® does not protect against less common HPV types not included in the vaccine; therefore, regular Pap screening remains critically important to detect precancerous changes in the cervix to allow treatment before cervical cancer develops. The Advisory Committee on Immunization Practices (ACIP) voted to recommend the vaccine in June 2006.[60, 61]

Colds and Flu   Colds and flu are caused by viruses. Colds are minor infections of the nose and throat caused by several different viruses. They usually last for about a week but can last longer, especially in children and elderly people. Colds are extremely contagious and often are spread when droplets of fluid containing a cold virus are transferred by touch or inhaled. Avoiding close contact with other people during the first few days of a cold is important. Symptoms of a cold include runny nose, congestion, sneezing, weakened sense of taste and smell, scratchy throat, and cough. *Antibiotics are not effective for treating colds.* In fact, one of the *Healthy People 2010* objectives (see Table 9-1) is to decrease the number of prescriptions for antibiotics to treat colds. Colds get better in a week or so whether or not people take medications, although over-the-counter products can alleviate symptoms. To prevent the spread of colds, people should keep their hands away from their nose and eyes, wash their hands often, and cover their mouth and nose with a tissue when they cough or sneeze.[62]

The flu is an infection of the respiratory system caused by the influenza virus. Flu symptoms, such as fever, cough, or aches, are more severe than those of colds and come on abruptly. People who become sick with the flu often say they feel as if they have been hit by a truck. A person catches the flu by inhaling droplets full of flu particles that are released when someone who has the flu sneezes, coughs, or speaks. Specific symptoms include a temperature of 101 degrees Fahrenheit or above, cough, body and muscle aches, headache, sore throat, chills, tiredness, and feeling lousy all over. People who develop the flu should see their doctor. Over-the-counter medications can relieve symptoms, but they do not treat the viral infection. *Children younger than 18 should not take aspirin for the flu.* Aspirin might play a role in causing Reye syndrome, a rare but severe liver and central nervous system condition. Ade-

quate liquids and nutrition are essential for rapid recovery and to prevent dehydration. Bed rest is recommended, and people should not resume full activity until all flu symptoms are gone. The best tool for preventing the flu is the flu vaccine, and the best time to get a flu shot is from early October to mid-November. People do not get the flu from a flu shot.[63] Teachers and students can learn more about preventing colds and flu from the American Lung Association (www.lungusa.org).

Head Lice   Myths abound about the origin and treatment of head lice. Head lice are small, wingless insects about the size of a sesame seed that feed on human blood, do not live on pets, and survive only twenty-four hours off of their human host. Head lice leave an itchy feeling, like a mosquito bite. A head louse can lay up to ten nits (eggs) per day, and nits can be found anywhere on the head. Daily shampooing does not prevent head lice. Head lice can be spread through infested clothing or hats; infested combs, brushes, or towels; or infested bedding, couches, pillows, carpet, or stuffed animals that recently have been in contact with an infested person. Lice do not jump or fly—they crawl from place to place and person to person.[64]

Preschool and elementary school children become infested with head lice more often than older children. Lice typically are found on the scalp behind the ears and near the neckline at the back of the head. Parents should screen their children frequently for lice by looking closely through the hair and scalp for nits, baby lice, or adult lice. Finding lice can be difficult—they move quickly. Health care providers, school nurses, or local health department professionals can confirm an infestation.[65]

Teachers and school staff should be especially careful not to embarrass children or their families if an infestation occurs. Teasing by other children should not be permitted. Children typically are allowed to return to school after an approved treatment for head lice and when all lice and nits have been removed from the head. Families should contact a health care professional for advice on treating head lice. Many products designed for treating lice contain strong chemicals that can be dangerous to children.[66] Students and teachers can find more information about head lice from the National Pediculosis Association (www.headlice.org).

Human Immunodeficiency Virus (HIV)   HIV stands for human immunodeficiency virus, the virus that causes AIDS. HIV is different from most other viruses because it attacks the body's ability to fight infections by targeting the immune system. HIV finds and destroys a type of white blood cell (T cells or CD4 cells) that the immune system must have to fight disease. AIDS stands for acquired immunodeficiency syndrome, the final stage of HIV infection. A person infected with HIV, even without treatment, can take years to reach this stage. Having AIDS means that the virus has weakened the immune system to the point that the body has a difficult time fighting infections. When someone has one or more of these infections and a low number of T cells, he or she has AIDS. The Centers for Disease Control and Prevention provides a wealth of information on HIV and AIDS online (www.cdc.gov/hiv/topics/basic/index.htm).[67]

Young people in the United States are at persistent risk for HIV infection. CDC defines young people or youth as persons who are 13–24 years of age. Risk for this group is especially notable for minority races and ethnicities. Continual HIV prevention outreach and education efforts, including programs on abstinence and on delaying the initiation of sex, are required as new generations replace the generations that benefited from earlier prevention strategies.[68]

Vaginal, anal, and oral intercourse place young people at risk for HIV infection and other sexually transmitted diseases (STDs). High rates of use of alcohol and other drugs renders adolescents more likely to engage in high-risk behaviors, such as unprotected sex. Abstinence from vaginal, anal, and oral intercourse is the only 100 percent effective way to prevent HIV and other STDs. The correct and consistent use of a male latex condom can reduce the risk of STD transmission, including HIV infection. However, no protective method is 100 percent effective, and condom use cannot guarantee absolute protection against any STD.[69]

The Division of Adolescent and School Health, CDC, recommends that HIV/STD prevention education should be developed with the active involvement of parents, be locally determined, and be consistent with community values. It should address the needs of youth who are not engaging in sexual intercourse and youth who are currently sexually active, while ensuring that all youth are provided with effective education to protect themselves and others from HIV/STD infection.[70]

HIV prevention education provides an excellent opportunity to integrate health education with other subjects. For example, upper-elementary and middle-school students might be especially interested in what scientists know about the origins of HIV and how the virus works in the body. However, knowing factual information about this retrovirus does not necessarily help students protect themselves against infection. Health education must address issues such as how the virus is and is not transmitted (see Figure 9–1 for a pictorial summary). In addition, health education must help students deal with issues such as setting personal boundaries and resisting pressure to participate in risk behaviors (using alcohol and other drugs and engaging in sexual activity).

Teachers must consider additional issues with regard to HIV infection. Educators must know local regulations regarding the confidentiality rights of children and staff members with regard to HIV status. Teachers potentially might deal with issues of gossip, discrimination, prejudice, misinformation, and mistreatment related to those who are infected or thought to be infected. Just as important, teachers must be aware of safety for themselves and

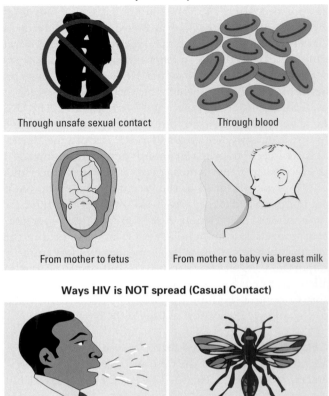

Ways HIV is spread

Through unsafe sexual contact

Through blood

From mother to fetus

From mother to baby via breast milk

Ways HIV is NOT spread (Casual Contact)

Coughs/sneezes

Insects

Food

Handshakes

FIGURE 9–1 | **How HIV Is and Is Not Transmitted**

for children when dealing with blood or other body fluid (urine, vomit, fecal matter) spills.

States and school districts require training on *universal precautions* for staff members. The CDC defines universal precautions as a set of precautions designed to prevent transmission of human immunodeficiency virus (HIV), hepatitis B virus (HBV), and other bloodborne pathogens when providing first aid or health care. Under universal precautions, blood and certain body fluids of all patients are considered potentially infectious for HIV, HBV, and other bloodborne pathogens.[71] *The Health, Mental Health and Safety Guidelines for Schools* provide important information on universal precautions and body substance isolation (BSI) at www.nationalguidelines.org/portal.cfm. A bloodborne pathogen exposure control plan for schools is mandated by the Occupational Safety and Health Administration (OSHA).

Chronic Diseases

Chronic diseases such as heart disease, cancer, and diabetes are the leading causes of adult death and disability in the United States. Chronic diseases are not contagious, but they are very costly and highly preventable. Adopting healthy behaviors such as healthy eating, exercising regularly, and avoiding tobacco use can prevent or control many chronic diseases. Teachers and students can learn more about chronic diseases through the CDC's National Center for Chronic Disease Prevention and Health Promotion (www.cdc.gov/nccdphp). Information about conditions that affect children and adolescents is available through the CDC's Healthy Youth website (www.cdc.gov/HealthyYouth/index.htm). This section includes a discussion of four chronic diseases: asthma, allergies, diabetes, and epilepsy.

Asthma Asthma, the most common chronic disease among American children today, affects approximately 5 million children. Asthma has become an epidemic in the United States.[72] Predictions are that the number of people affected with asthma will reach 20 million by the year 2010.

Asthma is a chronic inflammatory disorder of the airways that results in variable degrees of obstruction—leading to coughing, wheezing, labored breathing, and shortness of breath. Asthma symptoms can be intermittent or persistent, creating significant, ongoing disability. Although asthma can be diagnosed at any time, it is primarily a pediatric disease; most patients are diagnosed by age 5. Up to 80 percent of children with asthma have allergies. Although heredity plays a role in the risk for developing asthma, the disorder seems to develop from a combination of inherited risk and environmental factors. Exposure to secondhand tobacco smoke in infancy is one of many environmental factors associated with asthma.[73]

Both African American and white children in urban settings, regardless of income, are at greater risk of asthma than children in nonurban settings. African American children are four to five times more likely to die from asthma than either white or Hispanic children. Therapy for asthma has evolved over the past fifteen years to emphasize the use of preventive, anti-inflammatory medication instead of bronchodilators that treat the symptoms. However, studies consistently have found underuse of appropriate controller medication among African American and Hispanic children compared to white children of similar socioeconomic status. The lack of quality primary care for those with asthma is a leading contributor to the poor outcomes seen in some populations.[74]

The American Lung Association (www.lungusa.org) is an excellent resource for teachers and students. The association explains that children with asthma might feel scared and different from their classmates. The teacher, by knowing what to do and by treating children with asthma with understanding and kindness, can empower them and reduce their fear. Without embarrassing children with asthma, teachers should explain to the class what asthma

Many students have allergies, and allergies account for many lost school days each year. Common allergens include pollen, dust mites, and animal dander.

is, its effects on breathing, and how classmates can be helpful. To assist in this effort, the American Lung Association's Open Airways for Schools program provides asthma education and management skills specifically for children with asthma that can help create a supportive environment and a comprehensive approach to asthma management at school. For more information on this program, teachers can contact their local American Lung Association by calling 1-800-LUNG-USA (1-800-586-4872).[75]

Allergies In addition to dealing with asthma, colds, and flu, teachers often have students who suffer from various kinds of allergies. Up to 50 million Americans, including 2 million children, have some type of allergy. For most people, allergies are just an inconvenience. However, the National Institute of Allergy and Infectious Diseases (NIAID) (www.niaid.nih.gov) states that allergies are a major cause of disability in the United States. Allergies account for the loss of over 2 million school days per year.[76]

Kids Health for Parents (www.kidshealth.org) explains that some of the most common allergies are those to food and to airborne allergens such as pollen, mold, dust mites, and animal dander. Allergies can be seasonal (pollen or certain molds) or year-round (dust mites). Regional differences also exist—different allergens are more prevalent in different parts of the country or the world. The type and severity of allergy symptoms vary from allergy to allergy and from child to child. Some children experience a combination of symptoms.[77]

Airborne allergens can cause allergic rhinitis, characterized by sneezing, itchy nose and/or throat, nasal congestion, and coughing. These symptoms often are accompanied by itchy, watery, and red eyes (allergic conjunctivitis) or dark circles around reddened eyes (allergic shiners). Allergic rhinitis and conjunctivitis can range from minor or major seasonal annoyances to year-round problems. If they occur with wheezing and shortness of breath, the allergy might have progressed to asthma.[78]

Common foods that can cause allergies include cow's milk, soy, egg, wheat, seafood, tree nuts (such as walnuts and pistachios) and peanuts. Peanuts are one of the most severe food allergens, often causing life-threatening reactions. In rare instances, if the sensitivity to an allergen is extreme, a child can develop a life-threatening condition called anaphylactic shock. Severe reactions to any allergen require immediate medical attention. Fortunately, severe or life-threatening allergies occur only among a small percentage of children.[79]

All warm-blooded, furry animals, such as the average household pet, can cause allergic reactions, usually due to proteins in their saliva, dander, and urine. When the animal licks itself, the saliva is transferred to the fur. As the saliva dries, protein particles become airborne and work their way into fabrics in the home. Cats are the worst offenders, because their salivary protein is extremely tiny and cats tend to lick themselves as part of their grooming more than do other animals.[80]

Teachers must be alert to signs and symptoms among their students of allergies related to pollens, animals, foods, and insect bites. Teachers should be informed about any known allergies their students have. If this information is not already available, teachers should be sure to obtain it from parents and caregivers. Teachers and students can learn more about allergies from NIAID (www.niaid.nih.gov) and from Kids' Health (www.kidshealth.org).

Diabetes Few other pediatric health problems have increased as rapidly or have posed such grave concerns as the epidemic of overweight among children and adolescents.[81] The recent emergence of Type 2 diabetes among children and adolescents represents a consequence of obesity that previously was thought to occur only in adults. Newly diagnosed Type 2 diabetes in adolescence accounts for up to 45 percent of all new cases of diabetes in some settings.[82]

Diabetes is a serious chronic disease that impairs the body's ability to use food for energy. It is the sixth leading cause of death by disease in the United States. Long-term complications include heart disease, stroke, blindness,

kidney disease, and amputation of the foot or leg. Although there is no cure, the disease can be managed and complications delayed or prevented.[83]

Type 1 diabetes is a disease of the immune system, the body's system for fighting infection. In people with Type 1 diabetes, the immune system attacks the insulin-producing cells of the pancreas and destroys them. Because the pancreas no longer can produce insulin, people with Type 1 diabetes need to take insulin daily to live. Type 1 diabetes can occur at any age but is most common in children and young adults.[84]

Type 2 diabetes, the most common form of diabetes, occurs when the pancreas produces too little insulin and/or the body's cells are resistant to insulin (Figure 9–2). Excess body fat is a major factor in the development of insulin resistance, and rising rates of obesity underlie the recent dramatic increases in the incidence of Type 2 diabetes among Americans of all ages. People with Type 2 diabetes may need to take insulin or other medications to manage their disease, although lifestyle changes such as weight loss and exercise are also extremely beneficial.

Students with diabetes must check their glucose levels throughout the day with a blood glucose meter, which gives a reading of the current level of glucose in the blood. If blood glucose levels are too low (hypoglycemia) or too high (hyperglycemia), students can take corrective action, such as eating, modifying their activity level, or administering insulin. Low blood glucose levels, which can be life-threatening, present the greatest immediate danger to people with diabetes. Many students will be able to handle all or almost all of their diabetes care by themselves. Others, because of their age, developmental level, or inexperience, will need help from school staff.[85]

The school nurse is the most appropriate person in the school setting to provide care for a student with diabetes. Many schools, however, do not have a full-time nurse, and sometimes a single nurse must cover several schools. Moreover, even a nurse who is assigned to a school full time might not always be available during the school day, during extracurricular activities, or on field trips. Because diabetes management is needed at all times and diabetes emergencies can happen at any time, school personnel should be prepared to provide diabetes care at school and at all school-sponsored activities in which a student with diabetes participates.[86] Teachers who have diabetic students in their classes can learn more from the American Diabetes Association (www.diabetes.org) and the National Diabetes Education Program (1-800-438-5383 or www.ndep.nih.gov).

Epilepsy Epilepsy is a neurological condition that from time to time produces brief disturbances in the normal electrical functions of the brain. Brain function is interrupted by intermittent bursts of electrical energy that are much more intense than usual. These can affect a person's consciousness, bodily movements, or sensations for a short time. Children with epilepsy can have different kinds of

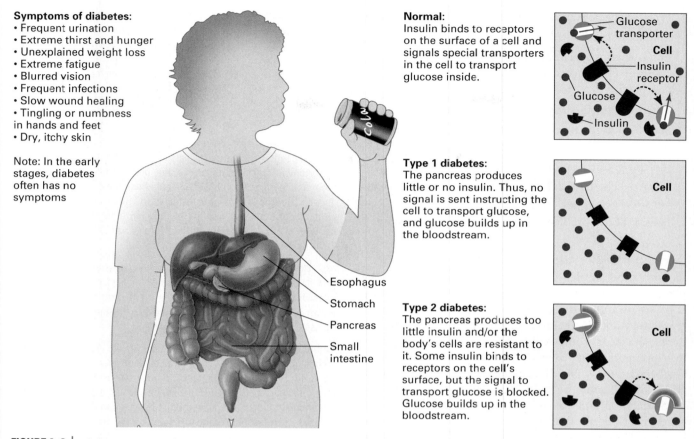

Symptoms of diabetes:
- Frequent urination
- Extreme thirst and hunger
- Unexplained weight loss
- Extreme fatigue
- Blurred vision
- Frequent infections
- Slow wound healing
- Tingling or numbness in hands and feet
- Dry, itchy skin

Note: In the early stages, diabetes often has no symptoms

Esophagus
Stomach
Pancreas
Small intestine

Normal:
Insulin binds to receptors on the surface of a cell and signals special transporters in the cell to transport glucose inside.

Glucose transporter
Cell
Insulin receptor
Glucose
Insulin

Type 1 diabetes:
The pancreas produces little or no insulin. Thus, no signal is sent instructing the cell to transport glucose, and glucose builds up in the bloodstream.

Cell

Type 2 diabetes:
The pancreas produces too little insulin and/or the body's cells are resistant to it. Some insulin binds to receptors on the cell's surface, but the signal to transport glucose is blocked. Glucose builds up in the bloodstream.

Cell

FIGURE 9–2 | **Diabetes** During digestion, carbohydrates are broken down in the small intestine into glucose, a simple sugar that enters the bloodstream. The presence of glucose signals the pancreas to release insulin, a hormone that helps cells take up glucose; once inside a cell, glucose can be converted to energy. In diabetes, this process is disrupted, resulting in a buildup of glucose in the bloodstream.

Source: Paul M. Insel and Walton T. Roth. *Core Concepts in Health*, 10th ed. (New York: McGraw-Hill, 2006, 417.) Reproduced with permission of the McGraw-Hill Companies.

seizures—absence, single partial seizures, complex partial seizures, or generalized tonic clonic seizures.[87]

If a child suffers convulsions in the classroom, teachers should protect the child from injury while the seizure runs its course. Teachers should ease the child to the floor and clear the area of anything that could hurt the child, put something flat and soft, such as a folded jacket, under the child's head and turn the child gently onto his or her side to keep the airways clear and allow fluids to drain from the mouth. Teachers should *not* try to force the mouth open, hold on to the tongue, put anything in the mouth, or restrain movements. The seizure triggers mechanisms in the brain that will bring it safely to an end. The child should rest until full consciousness returns. No other first aid steps can hasten that process.[88]

Other children might feel afraid for their classmate and for themselves. Teachers should provide factual information appropriate to the age of the children to alleviate their fears and help them support their classmate. If fears are not handled appropriately, children might come to fear, shun, or tease the child who had the seizure. Children who have epilepsy pose no danger to themselves or others.[89]

Students might be interested to know that Napoleon, Vincent van Gogh, Danny Glover, and Marion Clignet (an Olympic cyclist) are among well-known people with epilepsy. Teachers and students can learn more about epilepsy

at Health Finder for Kids (www.healthfinder.gov/kids) and at the Epilepsy Foundation (www.epilepsyfoundation.org).

Recommendations for Concepts and Practice

Healthy Behavior Outcomes

The goal of health education is to help students adopt or maintain health-enhancing behaviors. School districts and teachers should identify the health-enhancing behaviors they would like their students to maintain or adopt. The following list identifies some possible healthy behavior outcomes related to promoting personal health and wellness. Although not all the suggestions are developmentally appropriate for students in grades K–8, this list can help teachers understand how the learning activities they plan for their students support both short- and long-term desired behavior outcomes.

Ways to Promote Personal Health and Wellness

Brush and floss teeth daily.

Practice appropriate hygiene habits.

Get appropriate amount of sleep and rest.

Prevent vision or hearing loss.

Prevent damage from the sun.

Practice behaviors that prevent communicable diseases.

Practice behaviors that prevent chronic diseases.

Prevent serious health problems that result from common chronic diseases and conditions among youth, such as asthma, diabetes, and epilepsy.

Practice behaviors that prevent food-borne illnesses.

Seek help for common chronic diseases and conditions.

Seek out medical professionals for appropriate screenings and examinations.

Practice behaviors that support and improve the health of others.

Prevent health problems that result from fads or trends.[90]

Developmentally Appropriate Concepts and Skills

As with other health topics, teaching about promoting personal health and wellness should be developmentally appropriate and be based on the physical, cognitive, social, emotional, and language characteristics of specific students. Teacher's Toolbox 9.1 contains a list of suggested developmentally appropriate concepts and skills to help teachers create lessons that encourage students to practice the desired healthy behavior outcomes by the time they graduate from high school. Note that some of these concepts and skills are reinforced in other content areas (the concept "Describe how to keep food safe from harmful germs" is also found in promoting healthy eating).

STRATEGIES FOR LEARNING AND ASSESSMENT

Promoting Personal Health and Wellness

This section provides examples of standards-based learning and assessment strategies for promoting personal health and wellness. The strategies begin with a restatement of the standard and a reminder of the assessment criteria, drawn from the RMC rubrics in Appendix B. Strategies are written as directions for teachers and include applicable theory of planned behavior (TPB) constructs in parentheses (intention to act in healthy ways, attitudes toward behavior, subjective norms, perceived behavioral control). These learning and assessment strategies provide building blocks for standards-based lessons and units that can be tailored to local needs. Assessment criteria are used with permission from the Rocky Mountain Center for Health Promotion and Education (RMC). See Appendix B for Scoring Rubrics.

Additional strategies for learning and assessment for Chapter 9 can be found at the Online Learning Center. Appendix D, a complete list of all the strategies, is available at the Online Learning Center.

NHES 1 | Core Concepts

Students will comprehend concepts related to health promotion and disease prevention to enhance health.

ASSESSMENT CRITERIA

- Connections—Describe relationships between behavior and health; draw logical conclusions about connections between behavior and health.
- Comprehensiveness—Thoroughly cover health topic, showing breadth and depth; give accurate information.

Grades K–2

Parts and Even More Parts   Teachers can read the picture book *Parts*, by Tedd Arnold, to the class. This delightful book provides an opportunity to discuss children's questions about what happens to them as they grow older. For example, losing a tooth is natural—it doesn't mean children are falling apart. Have children draw and write about their experiences of growing older. If students enjoy the book, Tedd Arnold has written *More Parts* (2001) and *Even More Parts* (2004).

ASSESSMENT | The children's writing and drawings are the assessment task for this activity. For assessment criteria, students should accurately describe at least one change they have experienced as they have grown older and make connections between changes and good health. (Construct: Attitudes toward behavior.)

HeadLice.Org for Kids   Children can visit the website www .headlice.org/kids. The National Pediculosis Association displays news, FAQs, reports, projects, a catalog, and kids' head games and bug fun activities. Children can visit the site in the computer lab or at a learning station in the classroom. Children can discuss what they learned with classmates and write and draw about it.

ASSESSMENT | The children's discussions, drawings, and writing are the assessment task for this activity. For assessment criteria, students should provide correct information and describe at least two ways to prevent head lice infestation. (Construct: Attitudes toward behavior.)

Grades 3–5

Join the Scrub Club!   Teacher and students can check out The Scrub Club at www.scrubclub.org. The Scrub Club program is the first of its kind—a fun, interactive and educational website that teaches children the proper way to wash their hands. The site consists of a Webisode (*The Good, the BAC, and the Ugly*), interactive games, educational music, downloadable activities for kids, educational materials for teachers and program information for parents. Students can meet The Scrub Club and check out villains, such as Bac, E. Coli, Flu, Sal monella, Shigella, and Campy Lobacter. There's a Five Finger Alert for the Flu and a Hand-Washing Song. The Scrub Club Kids represent the six steps of the handwashing process.

ASSESSMENT | For an assessment task, students can explore different parts of The Scrub Club website and report back to classmates. For assessment criteria, students should provide accurate information and make connections between handwashing and health. (Construct: Attitudes toward behavior.)

Dental Health for Kids from the American Dental Association   The American Dental Association provides teaching ideas at www.ada .org/public/education/teachers/ideas.asp. Resources include lesson plan ideas, games, coloring activities, writing tasks, and hands-on activities. One of the hands-on activities suggests that teachers do the following:

> Make a hole one-inch deep in an apple. Put it in a paper bag and set aside for a few days. Cut through the place where the hole was

Developmentally Appropriate Concepts and Skills to Promote Personal Health and Wellness

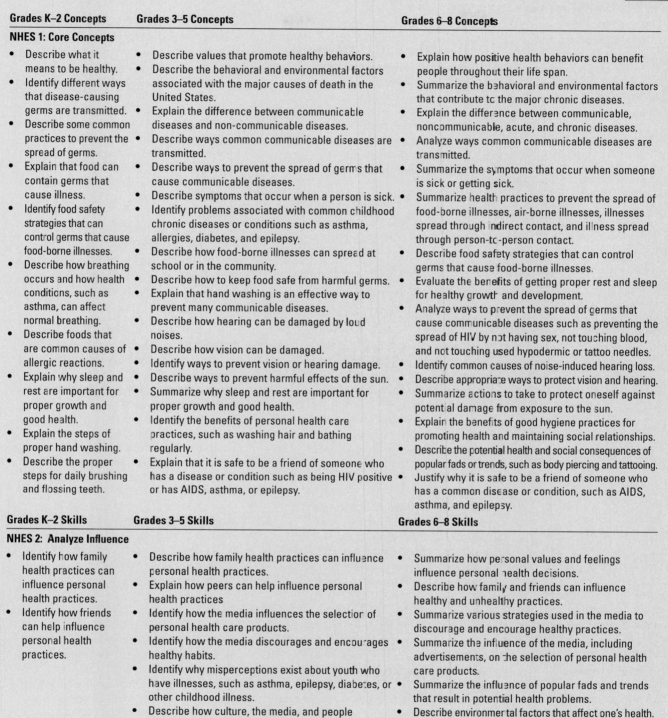

Grades K–2 Concepts	Grades 3–5 Concepts	Grades 6–8 Concepts

NHES 1: Core Concepts

• Describe what it means to be healthy. • Identify different ways that disease-causing germs are transmitted. • Describe some common practices to prevent the spread of germs. • Explain that food can contain germs that cause illness. • Identify food safety strategies that can control germs that cause food-borne illnesses. • Describe how breathing occurs and how health conditions, such as asthma, can affect normal breathing. • Describe foods that are common causes of allergic reactions. • Explain why sleep and rest are important for proper growth and good health. • Explain the steps of proper hand washing. • Describe the proper steps for daily brushing and flossing teeth.	• Describe values that promote healthy behaviors. • Describe the behavioral and environmental factors associated with the major causes of death in the United States. • Explain the difference between communicable diseases and non-communicable diseases. • Describe ways common communicable diseases are transmitted. • Describe ways to prevent the spread of germs that cause communicable diseases. • Describe symptoms that occur when a person is sick. • Identify problems associated with common childhood chronic diseases or conditions such as asthma, allergies, diabetes, and epilepsy. • Describe how food-borne illnesses can spread at school or in the community. • Describe how to keep food safe from harmful germs. • Explain that hand washing is an effective way to prevent many communicable diseases. • Describe how hearing can be damaged by loud noises. • Describe how vision can be damaged. • Identify ways to prevent vision or hearing damage. • Describe ways to prevent harmful effects of the sun. • Summarize why sleep and rest are important for proper growth and good health. • Identify the benefits of personal health care practices, such as washing hair and bathing regularly. • Explain that it is safe to be a friend of someone who has a disease or condition such as being HIV positive or has AIDS, asthma, or epilepsy.	• Explain how positive health behaviors can benefit people throughout their life span. • Summarize the behavioral and environmental factors that contribute to the major chronic diseases. • Explain the difference between communicable, noncommunicable, acute, and chronic diseases. • Analyze ways common communicable diseases are transmitted. • Summarize the symptoms that occur when someone is sick or getting sick. • Summarize health practices to prevent the spread of food-borne illnesses, air-borne illnesses, illnesses spread through indirect contact, and illness spread through person-to-person contact. • Describe food safety strategies that can control germs that cause food-borne illnesses. • Evaluate the benefits of getting proper rest and sleep for healthy growth and development. • Analyze ways to prevent the spread of germs that cause communicable diseases such as preventing the spread of HIV by not having sex, not touching blood, and not touching used hypodermic or tattoo needles. • Identify common causes of noise-induced hearing loss. • Describe appropriate ways to protect vision and hearing. • Summarize actions to take to protect oneself against potential damage from exposure to the sun. • Explain the benefits of good hygiene practices for promoting health and maintaining social relationships. • Describe the potential health and social consequences of popular fads or trends, such as body piercing and tattooing. • Justify why it is safe to be a friend of someone who has a common disease or condition, such as AIDS, asthma, and epilepsy.

Grades K–2 Skills	Grades 3–5 Skills	Grades 6–8 Skills

NHES 2: Analyze Influence

• Identify how family health practices can influence personal health practices. • Identify how friends can help influence personal health practices.	• Describe how family health practices can influence personal health practices. • Explain how peers can help influence personal health practices • Identify how the media influences the selection of personal health care products. • Identify how the media discourages and encourages healthy habits. • Identify why misperceptions exist about youth who have illnesses, such as asthma, epilepsy, diabetes, or other childhood illness. • Describe how culture, the media, and people influence what a person thinks about people who have infectious or chronic diseases, such as HIV infection, AIDS, and cancer.	• Summarize how personal values and feelings influence personal health decisions. • Describe how family and friends can influence healthy and unhealthy practices. • Summarize various strategies used in the media to discourage and encourage healthy practices. • Summarize the influence of the media, including advertisements, on the selection of personal health care products. • Summarize the influence of popular fads and trends that result in potential health problems. • Describe environmental factors that affect one's health. • Identify a role model that conveys healthy practices. • Analyze why misperceptions exist about youth who have illnesses, such as asthma, epilepsy, diabetes, or other childhood illness. • Explain why stereotypes exist about people with infectious diseases, such as HIV and tuberculosis.

(continued)

Grades K–2 Skills *(continued)*   **Grades 3–5 Skills** *(continued)*   **Grades 6–8 Skills** *(continued)*

NHES 3: Accessing Information, Products, and Services

- Demonstrate how to get help from a trusted adult when sick or hurt.
- Demonstrate how to get help from a trusted adult when someone is having an asthma episode, allergic reaction, or other emergency health problem.

- Identify sources of accurate information about personal health products, such as sunscreen, toothbrushes, soap, shampoo, and dental floss.
- Demonstrate the ability to access accurate information about personal health issues.
- Identify persons who can provide accurate information and help related to health issues.
- Demonstrate how to access a trusted adult who can help someone experiencing a potentially life-threatening health condition, such as an asthma episode, allergic reaction or seizure.

- Identify sources of accurate information about personal health problems.
- Distinguish accurate personal health information from inaccurate information.
- Demonstrate how to access and evaluate information about personal health issues and concerns.
- Demonstrate the ability to access and evaluate information about personal health products.
- Demonstrate how to access information about preventing common communicable and chronic diseases.
- Demonstrate how to access a trusted adult who can help someone experiencing a potentially life-threatening health condition, such as an asthma episode, allergic reaction, or seizure.
- Demonstrate the ability to access a health care professional who can assist with health-related issues.

NHES 4: Interpersonal Communication

- Demonstrate how to talk to a parent or caregiver about personal health problems or concerns.
- Demonstrate how to refuse foods that cause an allergic reaction.

- Demonstrate communication skills to help deal with negative peer influences on personal health practices.
- Demonstrate how to ask for assistance with a health-related problem.
- Demonstrate appropriate ways to talk to someone about personal health problems, issues, and concerns, such as a parent or health care provider.
- Demonstrate how to refuse foods that cause an allergic reaction.
- Communicate with parents and family about ways to protect against hearing damage.
- Demonstrate empathy for others.
- Demonstrate how to convey empathy for people with chronic diseases and conditions such as asthma, epilepsy, diabetes, and emphysema.

- Demonstrate communication skills to help deal with negative peer influences on personal health practices.
- Demonstrate how to ask for assistance with a health-related problem.
- Demonstrate appropriate ways to talk to someone about personal health problems, issues, and concerns.
- Demonstrate how to communicate clear expectations, boundaries, and personal safety strategies.
- Communicate with parents and family about ways to protect their hearing and vision.
- Demonstrate empathy for others.
- Demonstrate how to convey empathy for people with chronic diseases and conditions, such as asthma, epilepsy, diabetes, and emphysema.

NHES 5: Decision Making

- Explain positive outcomes from washing hands regularly.
- Explain positive outcomes from brushing and flossing teeth daily.
- Explain positive outcomes for being healthy.

- Summarize positive outcomes for washing hands regularly.
- Explain positive outcomes for getting adequate rest and sleep.
- Explain positive outcomes for avoiding prolonged exposure to the sun or using sunscreen when exposed to the sun.
- Identify strategies for avoiding exposure to communicable diseases.
- Describe factors to consider when determining whether or not to eat food that has been unrefrigerated.

- Explain the positive outcomes from exposure to direct ultraviolet rays, such as from the sun or tanning beds.
- Analyze the negative consequences of one choosing to expose friends and family to a contagious or communicable disease.
- Summarize factors to consider when determining whether or not to eat food that has been unrefrigerated.
- Describe factors that should be considered in choosing health care products.

NHES 6: Goal Setting

- Set a personal goal to improve a personal health practice, such as brushing and flossing teeth daily, washing hands regularly.
- Monitor progress in meeting personal health practice goal.
- Identify ways to overcome barriers to achieving personal health practice goal.

- Assess personal health practices.
- Establish short-term goals for improving personal health practices such as brushing and flossing teeth daily, washing hands regularly, handling and storing food safely, wearing sun protection, avoiding or minimizing exposure to loud noises, including amplified music.
- Identify ways to implement changes to meet a personal health practice goal.
- Monitor progress in meeting a personal health practice goal.
- Identify incentives and reinforcements to promote personal health practices.

- Discuss plans for the future and how personal health and wellness might affect those plans.
- Assess and evaluate personal health practices.
- Develop a personal plan to improve personal health practices, such as brushing and flossing teeth daily, washing hands regularly, avoiding or minimizing exposure to loud noises including amplified music, getting adequate amount of sleep, preventing the spread of a contagious or communicable disease.
- Determine ways to implement changes to meet a personal health practice goal.
- Monitor progress toward achieving a personal health practice goal.
- Identify barriers to maintaining good personal health practices and ways to address them.
- Summarize incentives and reinforcements to promote personal health practices.

NHES 7: Self-Management

- Demonstrate the steps for proper hand washing.
- Demonstrate steps for proper brushing and flossing of teeth.
- Express intentions to develop a healthy practice such as brushing and flossing teeth daily, washing hands regularly.

- Demonstrate the steps for proper hand washing.
- Demonstrate steps for proper brushing and flossing of teeth.
- Demonstrate proper ways to select and apply sunscreen.
- Demonstrate safe food handling and storage practices.
- Demonstrate the ability to recognize and avoid situations that can detract from a healthy future.
- Express intentions to develop a healthy practice such as brushing and flossing teeth daily, washing hands regularly, handling and storing food safely, wearing sun protection, avoiding or minimizing exposure to loud noises, including amplified music.

- Express intentions to remain tobacco free.
- Demonstrate ways to avoid second-hand smoke.
- Demonstrate the ability to recognize and avoid situations that can detract from a healthy future.
- Explain why health is an important personal priority.
- Express intentions to develop a healthy practice such as brushing and flossing teeth daily, washing hands regularly, avoiding or minimizing exposure to loud noises including amplified music, getting adequate amount of sleep, and preventing the spread of a contagious or communicable disease.

NHES 8: Advocacy

- Demonstrate ways to support friends and family who are trying to maintain or improve healthy practices.
- Advocate for friends to brush and floss teeth daily.
- Describe the benefits of proper hand washing to others.
- Demonstrate the ability to support other students who have common childhood chronic diseases and conditions, such as asthma, allergies, diabetes, and epilepsy.

- Demonstrate ways to support friends and family who are trying to maintain or improve health practices.
- Describe the benefits of proper hand washing to others.
- Advocate for proper hand washing facilities at school.
- Demonstrate the ability to support other students who have common childhood chronic diseases and conditions, such as asthma, allergies, diabetes, and epilepsy.

- Demonstrate ways to support friends and family who are trying to maintain or improve health practices.
- Demonstrate effective persuasion skills that encourage friends and family to reduce exposure to loud noises, including amplified music and protect vision.
- Educate family and peers to protect against skin damage from the sun.
- Advocate for proper hand washing facilities at school.
- Articulate, to others, the healthy practices that prevent spread of communicable diseases.
- Advocate that others properly prepare and handle food.
- Express compassion and support for people living with disease, such as cancer and AIDS.

Source: Centers for Disease Control and Prevention, *Health Education Curriculum Analysis Tool (HECAT)* (Atlanta, GA: CDC, 2007). www.cdc.gov/HealthyYouth/Hecat/index.htm

made and have the children look at the effect of decay. This shows how decay spreads through a tooth. Explain why oral hygiene (brushing twice a day with fluoride toothpaste and flossing once a day) is important.

ASSESSMENT | For an assessment task, children can make a class book about taking care of the teeth and about tooth facts. Each child can make a page, or children can work in pairs. For assessment criteria, children can decide what would make a "great" page for the class book. Teachers can use the criteria the children set to assess and to help them assess their work. At a minimum, information must be correct, and connections should be made between behaviors and health. (Construct: Attitudes toward behavior.)

Disease Detectives Children can consult the CDC's BAM! (Body and Mind) website for kids (www.bam.gov) to investigate topics of interest. For example, students can check out The Buzz on West Nile Virus, Disease Detectives, The Immune Platoon, Operation Infection Detection, and Stalking SARS. Students can select a topic of interest from this or other sites (www.kidshealth.org or www.healthfinder.org/kids) to research and report back to the class.

ASSESSMENT | The students' reports to the class are the assessment task for this activity. For assessment criteria, all information must be correct, and students should make at least two connections between behaviors and health. (Construct: Attitudes toward behavior.)

Grades 6–8

The Faces of Influenza. Middle school students can investigate *Faces of Influenza*—an educational website of the American Lung Association. This site is designed to put a face on influenza in the United States and show firsthand the seriousness of this potentially deadly infectious disease. This site features special portraits of famous and not-so-famous Americans, who represent each of the influenza high-risk groups—persons health officials recommend receive an influenza vaccination each and every year. Students and teachers can find information at www.facesofinfluenza.org. Students can visit the Portrait Gallery to learn more about people who have been affected by influenza. Along with their portraits are compelling stories about their experiences with influenza that highlight the importance of annual immunization.

ASSESSMENT | The Portrait Gallery features thirty portraits. For an assessment task, students can work as individuals or with a partner to investigate the story behind a particular portrait and report their findings to classmates. For assessment criteria, students should make connections between behaviors and health. (Construct: Attitudes toward behavior.)

Cool and Uncool Stuff Students can investigate Health Finder for Kids (www.healthfinder.gov/kids/coolstuff.htm) for a list of topics that are "cool" and "uncool." The list includes alcohol and other drugs, environmental health, exercise, feelings, nutrition, safety, and smoking. Students can work in pairs or small groups to investigate a topic and make posters and presentations for classmates. This site provides thirty-seven links to other U.S. government websites just for kids.

ASSESSMENT | The students' posters and presentations are the assessment task for this activity. Students can specify criteria for "great" posters and presentations. Teachers can use the criteria to assess and help students assess their work. At a minimum, all information must be correct, and students must make at least three connections between behaviors and health. (Construct: Attitudes toward behavior.)

Linking Health-Risk Behaviors and Body Systems Teachers can put a different spin on learning about body systems by having students work in small groups to investigate a body system of their choice. Their challenge is to find out how each of the six CDC priority health-risk areas (unintentional and intentional injury, alcohol and other drug use, sexual behaviors, tobacco use, nutrition, and physical activity) affect the body systems they are studying. Students can report their findings to the class, with illustrations for a visual representation.

ASSESSMENT | The students' presentations and illustrations are the assessment task for this activity. For assessment criteria, students should provide accurate information and make at least three connections between behaviors and health. (Construct: Attitudes toward behavior.)

NHES 2 | Analyze Influences

Students will analyze the influence of family, peers, culture, media, technology, and other factors on health behaviors.

ASSESSMENT CRITERIA

- Identify both external and internal influences on health.
- Explain how external and internal influences interact to impact health choices and behaviors.
- Explain both positive and negative influences, as appropriate.

Grades K–2

Bear Feels Sick: Getting Well in My Family Students can identify and discuss things their families do when someone is sick. What practices or traditions do families have? For example, do family members eat or drink certain things when they have a cold (chicken soup)? Do family members lie down in a certain place when they are sick, such as on the sofa? Children can talk about how their families influence the health practices of family members. Teachers can read the book *Bear Gets Sick* by Karma Wilson and Jane Chapman (see the book list at the end of the chapter) to begin the discussion about how family members and friends take care of each other when someone gets sick.

ASSESSMENT | For an assessment task, students can write and draw about what their families do when someone doesn't feel well. For assessment criteria, students should identify at least one family practice they like when someone is sick (that person gets to lie on the sofa during the daytime). (Construct: Subjective norms.)

Sun Safety and Friends Students can interview friends to find out what they do to stay safe in the sun and to avoid sunburn and skin damage. Students can report their findings to the class and answer the question "What do my friends do to stay safe in the sun?" Students can then make recommendations for sun safety that they want to share with friends who aren't being safe in the sun.

ASSESSMENT | For an assessment task, students can compare and contrast their own sun safety behaviors with those of their friends. For assessment criteria, students should identify how they and their friends influence each other. In a link to NHES 8, advocacy, students should explain how they can be a positive influence on their friends for sun safety. (Construct: Subjective norms.)

Grades 3–5

Personal Health Products in the Media Students can work in small groups to make posters or collages of all the personal health products and claims they can find in advertisements and on packaging. If they like, students can divide their posters into two sides—products and claims that are probably true and those that are probably not true. Students can show their posters to the class and discuss the claims they found that they think are exaggerated or untrue. Display the posters on a bulletin board or in the school hallways.

ASSESSMENT | Students can use the list of advertising strategies in Chapter 3 to identify techniques manufacturers and advertisers use to try to get people to purchase products. For assessment criteria, students should name at least two ways they can refute advertising claims. (Construct: Subjective norms.)

Freaky Flakes The Public Broadcasting Service (PBS) has a special website for kids (http://pbskids.org/dontbuyit). Students and teachers can find a variety of projects and activities to help students become smart about media. In "Design a Cereal Box," students can select a color, a character, a cereal name, a description, and a prize. When students are finished, they learn more about product placement—specifically, the placement of children's cereals on lower shelves so kids can see them. Students can print their cereal boxes to share with class members.

ASSESSMENT | For an assessment task, students can share their cereal boxes and explain what they learned about advertising to children. For assessment criteria, students should make a list of tips for kids to be smart about advertising. In the words of PBS, don't buy it! (Construct: Perceived behavioral control.)

Grades 6–8

Investigating Family History for Health. CDC's School Health Education Resources (SHER) (http://apps.nccd.cdc.gov/sher) provides information for teaching about personal and consumer health. Middle school students might be interested in investigating the importance of family history and health. CDC states that family members share their genes, as well as their environment, lifestyles, and habits. Everyone can recognize traits that run in their family, such as curly hair, dimples, leanness, or athletic ability. Risks for diseases such as asthma, diabetes, cancer, and heart disease also run in families. Students can talk with their families about their own health history and investigate topics of most relevance.

ASSESSMENT | For an assessment task, students can investigate and report to class members on issues of most importance in their own families. For an assessment task, students should provide accurate information, make connections between family history and health, and verify the accuracy of their information resources. (Construct: Subjective norms.)

PBS Kids—Don't Buy It! Students can explore more about being media smart with PBS Kids (http://pbskids.org/dontbuyit). Students can check out these topics:

- Secrets of a magazine cover model revealed! (rubbing hemorrhoid cream on the face to reduce puffiness)
- Food advertising tricks (how to make the perfect burger, with vegetable oil, brown food coloring, tweezers, superglue, and waterproof spray in addition to the burger)
- Buying smart (the cost of cool; hot or not—did it sell?)
- Your entertainment (money and music; the TV vs. life quiz)
- What you can do (get involved; learn more)

Students can put themselves in the driver's seat by making a video commercial or print advertisement for an imaginary product. Students can use the advertising techniques in Chapter 3 or the information from http://pbskids.org/dontbuyit or to try to "sell" their product to class-

mates. Teachers will find many more teaching ideas from the Education Development Center (www.youthlearn.org/).

ASSESSMENT | Students' advertisements are the assessment task. For assessment criteria, students should identify the advertising techniques they are using and their potential influence on middle school consumers of health-related products. (Construct: Perceived behavioral control.)

NHES 3 | Access Information, Products, and Services

Students will demonstrate the ability to access valid information and products and services to enhance health.

ASSESSMENT CRITERIA

- Access health information—Locate specific sources of health information, products, or services relevant to enhancing health in a given situation.
- Evaluate information sources—Explain the degree to which identified sources are valid, reliable, and appropriate as a result of evaluating each source.

Grades K–2

Ask a School or Community Health Helper Children can create a Know-Wonder-Learn chart about personal health topics of interest to them. Children can invite (write a letter) to various school and community health helpers who can answer their questions.

ASSESSMENT | Students can write and draw about what they learned for an assessment task. For assessment criteria, students should explain where they got their information and why the information source is one they can trust. (Construct: Attitudes toward behavior.)

How Loud Is Too Loud? Many children begin their love affair with music at an early age—and many youngsters like their music loud. The National Institute on Deafness and Other Communication Disorders (NIH) provides an Interactive Sound Ruler on its website to help answer the question "How loud is too loud?" (www.nidcd.nih.gov/health/education). Students will learn that soft talking is about 30 decibels and normal speaking is about 60 decibels. But an airplane, a boom box, or a rock concert can be 100 to 140 decibels—loud enough to cause permanent hearing loss.

ASSESSMENT | For an assessment task, children can draw pictures about at least one sound that does and one sound that does not have the potential to damage hearing. For assessment criteria, students should explain where they got their information and why the source is one they can trust. (Construct: Attitudes toward behavior.)

Grades 3–5

Getting Help in an Emergency Students can brainstorm a list of emergency situations in which they might need to get help. Students can work in groups of three to create a short skit about how they would get help in the situation they've chosen. Teachers should ensure that children know what to do if they need to call 9-1-1.

ASSESSMENT | The students' skits are the assessment task for this activity. For assessment criteria, in addition to showing the correct steps for getting emergency help, students should explain why their method of accessing emergency services is a good one. (Construct: Perceived behavioral control.)

Yucky, Cool Body Information—Your Gross and Cool Body A favorite website for kids is Your Gross and Cool Body: The Yuckiest

Site on the Internet http://yucky.discovery.com/flash. Kids can investigate how the human body works, in kid terms—with a list of topics that include belches and gas, bad breath, snot and boogers, dandruff, zits, ear wax, eye gunk, vomit, spit, hiccups, funnybones, stinky pits, scabs and pus, gurgling stomach, pee, poop, and ankle sprains. Students can work in small groups to investigate a particular topic and report back to classmates. There's also a teacher center at this site.

ASSESSMENT | The students' reports are the assessment task for this activity. For assessment criteria, students should explain where they got their information and why the information sources are trustworthy. (Construct: Attitudes toward behavior.)

Grades 6–8

Getting the Scoop on MSRA at School. The Centers for Disease Control and Prevention features online information about Methicillin-Resistant *Staphylococcus aureus* (MRSA) in Schools at www.cdc .gov/Features/MRSAinSchools. CDC, along with parents and school officials, wants to do everything possible to protect students from MRSA skin infections. Middle school students can investigate commonly asked questions, such as

- What type of infection does MRSA cause?
- How is MRSA transmitted?
- In what settings do MRSA skin infections occur?
- How do I protect myself from MRSA?
- Should schools close because of a MRSA infection?
- Should students with MRSA skin infections be excluded from attending school?
- I have a MRSA skin infection. How do I prevent spreading it to others?

ASSESSMENT | For an assessment task, students can make reports to classmates on what they learn about MRSA. For assessment criteria, students should report accurate information and make connections between behaviors and health. (Construct: Attitudes toward behavior.)

Who You Gonna Call? Health Resource Guide for Kids and Families Students can make a health resource guide to their community for classmates and families. Students should decide on the topics they want to include and work in small groups to investigate. Students can decide on a format for their guide and the information each group should collect. Teachers can make copies of the completed guide for students and families—and for other classes, if appropriate.

ASSESSMENT | The health resource guide the class produces is the assessment task for this activity. Students can set criteria for information gathering. Teachers can use these criteria to assess and help students assess their work. (Construct: Perceived behavioral control.)

Personal Health Newsletters Teachers can have students design and create a personal health newsletter for students and families. Students can decide on the format and a list of topics for each month, with small groups assigned a particular month to produce the newsletter. Students must do their own research and artwork. Teachers can make copies for classmates and families.

ASSESSMENT | The newsletters are the assessment task for this activity. For assessment criteria, students can set the specifications for the appearance and level of information that should appear in the newsletter. Teachers can use these specifications to assess and help students assess their work. (Construct: Attitudes toward behavior.)

NHES 4 | Interpersonal Communication

Students will demonstrate the ability to use interpersonal communication skills to enhance health and avoid or reduce health risks.

ASSESSMENT CRITERIA
- Use appropriate verbal/nonverbal communication strategies in an effective manner to enhance health or avoid/reduce health risks.
- Use appropriate skills (negotiation skills, refusal skills) and behaviors (eye contact, body language, attentive listening).

Grades K–2

Body Language and Health Students can use body language instead of words to show different ways people might be feeling at school. Students can show with gestures and facial expressions how a person might appear if he or she is sleepy, is hungry, has a headache, has a fever, or has a cold. Students can be asked to explain how they can recognize when a family member or friend isn't feeling well and how they might help.

ASSESSMENT | For an assessment task, students can finish two sentences and draw two pictures to illustrate "When I feel well, I . . ." and "When I don't feel well, I . . .". For assessment criteria, students should be able to communicate a clear difference between feeling well and not feeling well.

Grades 3–5

Medical Alert Jewelry Teachers can ask a health care provider to visit the class, show children various kinds of medical alert jewelry, and explain how it can help when the person who wears it is ill. If a class member or staff member in the school wears medical alert jewelry, that person might be willing to share with class members. Children can talk about how the message on the jewelry can be used to communicate with health care providers when the wearer cannot communicate his or her needs.

ASSESSMENT | Students can create a drawing or short story about a situation in which health care providers are able to help someone because of medical alert jewelry. For assessment criteria, students should explain how such jewelry can be used to communicate.

Grades 6–8

Talking with Parents About HIV To get students talking with parents, classmates, and other adults about HIV, students can research and design an HIV questionnaire for other students, teachers, and parents or caregivers. Each student should interview an agreed-on number of students and adults and bring their findings back to class for collation and discussion. Teachers can ask students if their questionnaires led to any further discussions in their families and what they discussed. Students can identify the three leading misperceptions they found during their survey. Make copies of the students' final results for them to take home to their families.

ASSESSMENT | The students' final report on their findings is the assessment task for this activity. For assessment criteria, students should write a paragraph about how it felt to talk with their parents or caregivers about HIV and advice they have for other kids on talking with adults about this topic. (Construct: Subjective norms.)

NHES 5 | Decision Making

Students will demonstrate the ability to use decision-making skills to enhance health.

Reach a health-enhancing decision using a process consisting of the following steps:
- Identify a health-risk situation.
- Examine alternatives.
- Evaluate positive and negative consequences.
- Decide on a health-enhancing course of action.

Grades K–2

Being a Friend Sometimes people hesitate to be around someone with a chronic illness (diabetes, epilepsy, HIV) because they don't understand the condition. Chronic diseases are not contagious—people won't catch the illness from being around another person. Students can discuss ways they can be kind to a student or adult who has a chronic condition and list steps to making a decision to be a good friend.

ASSESSMENT | Identifying the steps to being a good friend is the assessment task for this activity. For younger children, teachers can use a simple model that includes stating a problem, identifying alternatives, naming positive and negative consequences of each alternative, choosing an action, and evaluating the action. For assessment criteria, students should be able to discuss each step in the decision process and how they could carry it out, as their teacher names the steps. (Construct: Perceived behavioral control.)

Grades 3–5

Choosing Personal Health Products Students can build on the work they did in identifying advertising techniques and becoming media-wise by demonstrating a decision-making process about buying a particular health product. Students can select a product advertised in print media or commercials and work through simple decision-making steps to decide whether the product is worth buying. The PBS Kids website (http://pbskids.org/dontbuyit) has a helpful section called "Don't Buy It" to assist students in their decision making. Students can use the decision-making steps in Chapter 3 to help them work through the process.

ASSESSMENT | Applying a decision-making model is the assessment task for this activity. For assessment criteria, students should be able to explain each step of the model to make a health-enhancing decision about various personal health products. (Construct: Intention to act in healthy ways.)

Grades 6–8

Decision Trees for Personal Health Students in the middle-level grades are beginning to make personal health decisions for themselves. Students can identify a personal health issue of interest and make a decision tree about various alternatives, positive and negative consequences, and the decision that's best. Examples include what kind of drink to have after a soccer game (water, soda, juice, a nutrition drink), how to prepare for a big exam (go to bed on time, stay up late the night before to study, start studying several days ahead of the test), and what kind of deodorant to purchase (the expensive one with a designer name, the generic product at the drug store, the one that has the most impressive claims). Students can share their decision trees with the class. An important aspect of this activity is helping students realize that they often have more than two alternatives and should consider as many positive and negative consequences as possible.

ASSESSMENT | The students' decision trees are the assessment task for this activity. For assessment criteria, students should write a paragraph about three ways the decision tree helped them see their decisions in new ways. (Construct: Subjective norms.)

NHES 6 | Goal Setting

Students will demonstrate the ability to use goal-setting skills to enhance health.

- Goal statement—Give goal statement that identifies health benefits; goal is achievable and will result in enhanced health.
- Goal setting plan—Show plan that is complete, logical and sequential, and includes a process to assess progress.

Grades K–2

Preventing Colds and Flu at School and at Home Students can invite the school nurse or another health care provider to the classroom to talk about preventing colds and flu. Children can make a list of things they can do at school and at home to prevent colds and flu. Children can set a class goal of doing at least two of those things consistently (washing hands, not rubbing eyes) for a given period of time during cold and flu season.

ASSESSMENT | The students' goal for two practices to prevent colds and flu is the assessment task for this activity. For assessment criteria, children should list people, practices, and situations that will help them reach their goal (reminding each other to wash hands and cover sneezes) and those that might keep them from reaching their goal (being in too much of a hurry to wash hands). (Construct: Intention to act in healthy ways.)

Grades 3–5

Preventing Type 2 Diabetes Students can investigate Type 2 diabetes and the risk behaviors related to its development. Students will find that one of the major risk factors is physical inactivity. Students can design ways they can be more active throughout the day at school and at home. Students can then set personal or class goals for staying active during a certain period of time (two weeks). Students can report back to the class on their progress and on conclusions about supports for and barriers to physical activity.

ASSESSMENT | For an assessment task, students can keep a record of their participation in physical activity for the time period selected by the class. They can record what they did, how they felt, and what helped or hindered their progress. For assessment criteria, students should identify at least two important supports for and barriers to physical activity and specify how staying physically active can help keep them healthy. (Construct: Intention to act in healthy ways.)

Grades 6–8

Identifying Supports and Barriers Recognizing and managing supports for and barriers to achieving personal health goals is an important aspect of successful goal setting. Students can select a personal health goal of interest to them (being physically active for thirty minutes each day) and identify the supports they have in place to meet their goal. Students then can list ways they will use these supports to meet their goals. Examples of supports might be family members and friends who like to work out and living in a neighborhood conducive to regular physical activity. Next, students can identify potential barriers to meeting their goals and ways to manage them. Examples of barriers might be friends who don't want to be physically active and a neighborhood that doesn't have places for students to participate in physical activity.

ASSESSMENT | For an assessment task, students can explain or write a summary of their assessment of supports and barriers. For assessment criteria, students should name at least two potential supports and barriers and how they will use or manage them for reaching their goals. (Construct: Subjective norms.)

NHES 7 | Self-Management

Students will demonstrate the ability to practice health-enhancing behaviors and avoid or reduce health risks.

ASSESSMENT CRITERIA

- Application (transfer)—Initiate health-enhancing behaviors; apply concepts and skills appropriate and effectively.
- Self-monitoring and reflection—Monitor actions and make adjustments; accept feedback and make adjustments; able to self-assess, reflect on, and take responsibility for actions.

Grades K–2

Washing Hands   The importance of hand washing for people of all ages is key in preventing disease transmission. Teachers can provide a memorable experience for children as they practice their hand-washing skills. Children can rub a light coating of cooking oil or petroleum jelly on their hands. Next, teachers can sprinkle glitter lightly on the children's hands, using several different colors and sprinkling only one color on each child. Then, students can circulate to talk with others in the classroom, shaking hands as they do. Call the students back to their seats or to the circle after several minutes. Ask if they have glitter from other hands on their hands. Explain that, even though we can't see germs, they can rub off from one hand to another and from surfaces onto our hands. Next, children can conduct a hand-washing experiment. Some children can try washing off the oil and glitter using cold water only, while another group tries with warm water. Finally, another group tries with soap and water. Which worked best? All children can demonstrate their hand-washing skills with soap and water. Teachers can use children's books to extend this lesson, such as *Germs Make Me Sick,* by Melvin Berger, and *I Know How We Fight Germs,* by Kate Rowan.

ASSESSMENT | Students can write and draw in their journals or make pictures for a class bulletin board about hand washing. Students also can make posters about hand washing for school restrooms. For assessment criteria, students should name all the important steps learned in class for getting hands clean. (Construct: Perceived behavioral control.)

Going to the Dentist with Children's Literature   Teachers will find an extensive list of books at the end of this chapter that deal with children's health issues; for this activity, suggested books appear under "Dental Health." Teachers can ask students to discuss their experiences of going to the dentist to reassure students who might be anxious about dental visits. Students can write a class story about going to the dentist to help other children learn what to expect.

ASSESSMENT | The students' class book is the assessment task for this activity. For assessment criteria, students should provide accurate information about what happens at the dentist's office and how to take care of their own teeth at home. (Construct: Perceived behavioral control.)

Don't You Feel Well, Sam?   Teachers can read Amy Hest's book *Don't You Feel Well, Sam?* and other children's books to talk about getting sick and getting well. Additional books appear under "Getting Sick and Getting Well" at the end of the chapter. Teachers can use these books to begin a discussion with children on how people can tell that they might be getting sick and important things to do to feel better soon. Students also can discuss important self-management strategies (washing hands, covering coughs and sneezes) to prevent themselves and others from getting sick.

ASSESSMENT | For an assessment task, students can create a class list of tips for staying well and getting well. For assessment criteria, students should be able to list at least ten self-management strategies for staying and getting well. (Construct: Perceived behavioral control.)

Grades 3–5

Preventing Droplet Spread: Stopping Germs at Home and School.   The CDC states that the main way that colds and flu are spread is from person to person in respiratory droplets of coughs and sneezes, called droplet spread. This spread can happen when droplets from a cough or sneeze of an infected person move through the air and are deposited on the mouth or nose of people nearby. Sometimes germs also can be spread when a person touches respiratory droplets from another person on a surface such as a desk and then touches his or her own eyes, mouth, or nose before washing their hands. Some viruses and bacteria can live two hours or longer on surfaces such as cafeteria tables, doorknobs, and desks. To stop the spread of germs, students should remember to

- Cover mouth and nose.
- Clean hands often.
- Remind others to practice healthy habits.

Students and teachers can learn more about self-management strategies at www.cdc.gov/germstopper/home_work_school.htm.

ASSESSMENT | For an assessment task, students can design and illustrate posters or four-panel cartoons to help others learn to take steps to stop droplet spread. These can be placed around the school to help promote disease prevention during cold and flu season. For assessment criteria, students should provide accurate and specific steps for preventing droplet spread. (Construct: Intention to act in healthy ways.)

Be a Star Sleeper   Investigate the National Heart, Lung, and Blood Institute's partnership with Garfield the Cat for the *Sleep Well, Do Well Star Sleeper* campaign (www.nhlbi.nih.gov/health/public/sleep/starslp). Children might want to participate in the How I Get a Heap of Sleep contest. After discussing ways to get a good night's sleep, children can choose a particular strategy they want to try for one week and report back to the class day by day on their progress. Garfield uses delightful cartoons to teach students these tips:

1. Most kids need at least nine hours of sleep each night.
2. Go to bed at the same time each night.
3. Drinking sodas with caffeine before bed can keep you from sleeping.
4. A warm bath before bed helps you relax.
5. Make sure you're in a quiet place at bedtime, because noises can keep you awake.
6. Getting enough sleep helps you do your best in whatever you do.
7. During sleep, your brain sorts and stores memories.
8. Eating big meals before bedtime can ruin your sleep.
9. You might become too jumpy to sleep if you exercise too close to bedtime.

ASSESSMENT | For an assessment task, children can design posters for a class bulletin board or the school hallways, or make a class book for the library about being a Star Sleeper. For assessment criteria, students should show at least two strategies they can use to get a good night's sleep. (Construct: Perceived behavioral control.)

Slip! Slop! Slap! Wrap! for Sun Safety   Students can investigate the American Cancer Society's Sun Basics for Kids (www.cancer .org). Children can work in small groups to create a skit about going out in the sun for an activity of their choosing, demonstrating all the ways they can protect themselves from overexposure. Students can demonstrate their skits for classmates.

ASSESSMENT | The students' skits are the assessment task for this activity. For assessment criteria, students should correctly demonstrate at least three steps to protect themselves from sun exposure. (Construct: Perceived behavioral control.)

Achoo! Cold, Flu, or Allergies?   Students can work in groups to investigate colds, flu, and allergies and how to tell the difference. Students should explain self-management strategies for avoiding colds, flu, and allergies and tell what they should do to get better if they are ill. Students can find help at Kids' Health (www .kidshealth.org) under "Everyday Illnesses and Injuries." They also can explore the websites of the National Center for Infectious Diseases (www.cdc.gov/ncidod) and the National Institute for Allergy and Infectious Diseases (www.niaid.nih.gov/default .htm).

ASSESSMENT | For an assessment task, students can make a brochure or pamphlet for classmates and families about preventing and managing colds, flu, and allergies. For assessment criteria, students should provide health-enhancing self-management strategies. (Construct: Perceived behavioral control.)

Grades 6–8

Why Don't We Do It in Our Sleeves?   Middle school students really will enjoy the five-minute video entitled, "Why Don't We Do It in Our Sleeves?" Available on the web from OtoRhinoLounsburgology Productions at www.coughsafe.com, the video states that its goal is to make coughing and sneezing into one's sleeve or other fabric "fashionable." The video features several individuals' coughing and sneezing behavior, which is evaluated by a panel of "international judges." The humor makes the video very memorable.

ASSESSMENT | After viewing the video, students can create their own skits or videos to illustrate these ideas for other students in their schools. For assessment criteria, students should show specific steps to take to prevent the spread of germs. (Construct: Attitudes toward behavior.)

Preventing and Dealing with Injuries   Students can investigate the KidsHealth website (www.kidshealth.org) to learn self-management skills for a wide range of topics. Topics at the site include bug bites and stings, fireworks safety, concussions, farm safety, and sports injuries. Students can work in small groups to research and report their findings to classmates.

ASSESSMENT | The students' presentations are the assessment task for this activity. For assessment criteria, students can decide as a group what would make a "great" presentation. For example, students might want to see a demonstration and illustration, rather than just being told information. Teachers can use the criteria the students set to assess and help them assess their work. (Construct: Perceived behavioral control.)

Being a Friend: Asthma, Epilepsy, Diabetes   Teachers can help children learn the concept of a chronic health condition—one that is recurring but not contagious to others. Examples of chronic conditions are asthma, epilepsy, and diabetes. Students can investigate websites and talk to medical personnel to learn what people with various conditions need to do for themselves and what students need to do as supportive friends. If a student in the class has a chronic health condition, teachers can provide the opportunity (with the student's and parents' or caregivers' permission) for that child to talk openly with other students about managing the condition and what students can do to be supportive. Students can check out these websites:

American Diabetes Association (www.diabetes.org)
National Diabetes Education Program (www.ndep.nih.gov)
Epilepsy Foundation (www.epilepsyfoundation.org)
American Lung Association (www.lungusa.org)

ASSESSMENT | For an assessment task, students can write a short story about being a friend to someone who has a chronic health condition. For assessment criteria, students should include at least three ways they can act supportively to help a friend manage his or her condition. (Construct: Attitudes toward behavior.)

HealthTeacher.Com   The website www.healthteacher.com contains a wealth of standards-based teaching and assessment ideas for personal health and other health topics. In the personal health area, students can find out more about personal health care, preventing disease and infection prevention, and the selection and use of health care products and services. Students in the middle-level grades will be especially interested in lessons about personal health care and the selection of products and services during puberty. Schools or teachers must subscribe to HealthTeacher.com to access lesson plans. Information on subscription rates is provided on the website.

ASSESSMENT | For an assessment task, students can work in small groups to develop questions and answers on particular topics related to puberty. Teachers can provide each group with a turn to quiz classmates on what they learned. For assessment criteria, teachers can continue the class discussions and investigations until all information provided is correct. (Construct: Perceived behavioral control.)

NHES 8 | Advocacy

Students will demonstrate the ability to advocate for personal, family, and community health.

ASSESSMENT CRITERIA
- Health-enhancing position—Give clear, health-enhancing position.
- Support for position—Support position with facts, concepts, examples, and evidence.
- Audience awareness—Show awareness of target audience; choose words, tone, and examples to suit audience.
- Conviction—Display conviction for position.

Grades K–2

Get Moving for Good Health   Students can brainstorm ways they, their classmates, their families, and their teachers can be more physically active at school and at home. Being physically active on a regular basis is tremendously important in preventing chronic disease. Students can make posters to display their ideas around school and make a class bulletin board of drawings to encourage physical activity.

ASSESSMENT | The students' posters and drawings are the assessment tasks for this activity. For assessment criteria, students should show a clear, health-enhancing message that is targeted to classmates, teachers, and families. (Construct: Subjective norms.)

Grades 3–5

Open Airways for Schools Students can investigate the American Lung Association's Open Airways for Schools project (www.lungusa .org/site/pp.asp?c=dvLUK900E&b=44142) and design an advocacy campaign to make their school asthma-friendly.

ASSESSMENT | The students' campaign is the assessment task for this activity. For assessment criteria, students should show a clear, health-enhancing message; back it up with facts; target their audience (other students, administrators, teachers); and demonstrate conviction about what they believe. (Construct: Subjective norms.)

Grades 6–8

Advocacy Ideas from Voluntary Health Organizations Students can begin with websites to investigate the advocacy activities of various national and local voluntary health organizations. For example, the American Cancer Society sponsors the Great American Smokeout each November, and the American Diabetes Association sponsors the Walk for Diabetes. Students can select one of the advocacy activities or one of their own to organize for their school.

ASSESSMENT | The advocacy campaign the students design and carry out is the assessment task for this activity. For assessment criteria, students should show a clear, health-enhancing message, back it up with data and reasons, target their audience, and show conviction in their message. (Construct: Subjective norms.)

EVALUATED CURRICULA AND INSTRUCTIONAL MATERIALS

The Health Education Curriculum Analysis Tool (HECAT) provides a list of programs that federal agencies consider exemplary, promising, or effective (www.cdc .gov/HealthyYouth/HECAT/pdf/HECAT_Append_2.pdf).

The National Registry of Evidence-based Programs and Practices (www.modelprograms.samhsa.go) and the Compendium of HIV Prevention Interventions with Evidence of Effectiveness (www.cdc.gov/hiv/resources/reports/hiv compendium/index.htm) include programs on HIV/AIDS prevention.

INTERNET AND OTHER RESOURCES

Visit the Online Learning Center (www.mhhe.com/telljohann6e) for links to these sites, quizzes and other study aids, and many additional resources.

WEBSITES

American Academy of Allergies, Asthma, and Immunology
www.aaaai.org

American Cancer Society (Sun Basics for Kids)
www.cancer.org

American Dental Association
www.ada.org/public/education/teachers/index.asp

American Diabetes Association
www.diabetes.org

American Lung Association (Open Airways for Schools)
www.lungusa.org

Asthma and Allergy Foundation of American
www.aafa.org

BAM! (Body and Mind)
www.bam.gov/teachers/index.htm

Center for Health and Health Care in Schools
www.healthinschools.org

Children's Defense Fund
www.childrensdefense.org

Education Development Center
www.youthlearn.org

Epilepsy Foundation
www.epilepsyfoundation.org

Health Finder for Kids
www.healthfinder.gov/kids

Healthy Youth (Division of Adolescent and School Health, CDC)
www.cdc.gov/HealthyYouth

KidsHealth
www.kidshealth.org

Learning to Give Project
www.learningtogive.org

National Center for Chronic Disease Prevention and Health Promotion, CDC
www.cdc.gov/nccdphp

National Center for Infectious Diseases, CDC
www.cdc.gov/ncidod/teachers_tools/index.htm

National Diabetes Education Program
www.ndep.nih.gov

National Eye Institute, National Institutes of Health
www.nei.nih.gov/education/visionschool

National Institute of Allergy and Infectious Diseases
www3.niaid.nih.gov

National Institute on Deafness and Other Communication Disorders
www.nidcd.nih.gov/health

National Pediculosis Association
www.headlice.org/kids

PBS Kids (Don't Buy It)
http://pbskids.org/dontbuyit

The Scrub Club
www.scrubclub.org

Star Sleeper (National Heart, Lung, and Blood Institute)
www.nhlbi.nih.gov/health/public/sleep/starslp

AGES 5–8

BATHS AND BATHING

Krosoczka, Jarrett J. *Bubble Bath Pirates*. Viking, 2003.

Puttock, Simon. *Squeaky Clean*. Little, Brown, 2002.

Shannon, Terry Miller. *Tub Toys*. Tricycle, 2002.

Timberlake, Amy. *The Dirty Cowboy*. Farrar, Straus & Giroux, 2003.

Tucker, K. *Do Pirates Take Baths?* Albert Whitman, 1997.

Van Laan, Nancy. *Scrubba Dub*. Atheneum Books for Young Readers, 2003.

Zion, Gene. *Harry the Dirty Dog*. HarperCollins, 1984.

DENTAL HEALTH

Barber, T. *Open Wide!* Chrysalis Children's Books, 2004.

Brown, Marc. *Arthur's Tooth*. Little, Brown, 1985.

DeSantis, Kenny. *A Dentist's Tools*. Dodd, Mead, 1988.

Johnson, Arden. *The Lost Tooth Club*. Tricycle, 1998.

Laminack, Lester. *Trevor's Wiggly-Wobbly Tooth*. Peachtree, 1998.

Linn, Margot. *A Trip to the Dentist*. Harper & Row, 1988.

Mayer, Mercer. *Just Going to the Dentist*. Western, 1990.

Miller, Edward. *The Tooth Book: A Guide to Healthy Teeth and Gums*. Holiday House, 2008.

Munsch, Robert. *Andrew's Loose Tooth*. Scholastic, 1998.

Palatini, Margie. *Sweet Tooth*. Simon & Schuster Books for Young Readers, 2004.

Rosenberry, Vera. *Vera Goes to the Dentist*. Henry Holt, 2002.

Simms, Laura. *Rotten Teeth*. Houghton Mifflin, 1998.

Vrombaut, An. *Clarabella's Teeth*. Clarion, 2003.

GETTING SICK AND GETTING WELL

Bateman, Teresa. *Farm Flu*. Albert Whitman, 2001.

Berger, Melvin. *Germs Make Me Sick*. HarperCollins, 1985.

Brown, Marc. *Arthur's Chicken Pox*. Little, Brown, 1994.

Civardi, Anne. *Going to the Doctor*. Usborne, 2000.

Collins, Ross. *Germs*. Bloomsburg, 2004.

Dealey, E. *Goldie Locks Has Chicken Pox*. Atheneum Books for Young Readers, 2002.

Kornberg, Arthur. *Germ Stories*. University Science Books, 2007.

Neitzel, Shirley. *I'm Not Feeling Well Today*. Greenwillow Books, 2001.

Wilson, Karma, and Jane Chapman. *Bear Feels Sick*. Margaret K. McElderry Books, 2007.

Yolen, Jane. *How Do Dinosaurs Get Well Soon?* Blue Sky, 2003.

SLEEP

Gay, Marie Louise. *Good Night, Sam*. Groundwood Books, 2003.

Krosoczka, Jarrett J. *Good Night, Monkey Boy*. Knopf Books for Young Readers, 2001.

Parr, Todd. *Otto Goes to Bed*. Little, Brown, 2003.

Saltzbert, Barney. *Cornelius P. Mud, Are You Ready for Bed?* Candlewick, 2005.

Thomas, Scott. *The Yawn Heard Round the World*. Tricycle, 2003.

Wood, Audrey. *The Napping House*. Harcourt, 1984.

Yolen, Jane, and Mark Teague. *How Do Dinosaurs Say Good Night?* Blue Sky, 2000.

OTHER PERSONAL HEALTH AND WELLNESS TOPICS

Aliki. *My Five Senses*. HarperCollins, 1989.

Arnold, Tedd. *Even More Parts*. Dial Books for Young Readers, 2004.

Arnold, Tedd. *More Parts*. Dial Books for Young Readers, 2001.

Arnold, Tedd. *Parts*. Dial Books for Young Readers, 1997.

Brown, Marc. *Arthur's Eyes*. Little, Brown, 1979.

Glaser, Byron. *Bonz Inside-Out!* Harry N. Abrams, 2003.

Hobbie, Holly. *Charming Opal*. Little, Brown, 2003.

Kotzindle, William. *Walter, the Farting Dog*. Frog, 2001.

Lombardo, Michelle. *The Organwise Guys: How to Be Smart from the Inside Out*. The Organwise Guys Inc., 2006.

London, Jonathan. *The Lion Who Had Asthma*. Albert Whitman, 1992.

MacDonald, Amy. *Rachel Fister's Blister*. Houghton Mifflin, 1990.

Miller, Margaret. *My Five Senses*. Simon & Schuster, 1994.

Nassau, Elizabeth Sussman. *Peanut Butter Jam*. Health Press NM, 2001.

Pirner, Connie White. *Even Little Kids Get Diabetes*. Albert Whitman, 1991.

Sweeney, Joan. *Me and My Amazing Body*. Crown, 1999.

AGES 8–12

Avison, Brigid. *I Wonder Why I Blink and Other Questions About My Body*. Kingfisher, 1993.

Barner, Bob. *Dem Bones*. Chronicle, 1996. (Parent's Choice Silver Award)

Bendell, Norm. *Care and Keeping of Me: The Body Book Journal*. Pleasant Company, 2001.

Blume, Judy. *Blubber*. Bradbury, 1974.

Cheung, Lilian. *Be Healthy! It's a Girl Thing: Food, Fitness and Feeling Great*. Crown, 2003.

Cobb, Vicki. *Keeping Clean*. Harper, 1989.

Hawkins, Frank C., and Greta Laube. *The Boy's Body Guide: A Health and Hygiene Book for Boys 8 and Older*. Boys Guide Books, 2007.

Keller, Laurie. *Open Wide*. Scholastic, 2000.

Lowry, Lois. *The Giver*. Laurel Leaf, 1999.

Shannon, David. *A Bad Case of Stripes*. Scholastic, 1998.

Tatchell, Judy. *How Do Your Senses Work?* Scholastic, 1997.

True, Kelly. *I've Got Chicken Pox*. Penguin, 1994.

ENDNOTES

1. A. Davison, *Health Lessons: Book One* (New York: American Book Company, 1910), 5.
2. Children's Defense Fund, *Moments in America for Children*. (www.childrensdefense.org)
3. B. Guyer and A. Wigton, "Child Health: An Evaluation of the Last Century," in *About Children: An Authoritative Resource on the State of Childhood Today*, eds. A. G. Cosby, R. E. Greenberg, L. H. Southward, and M. Weitzman (American Academy of Pediatrics, 2005), 102–5.
4. Ibid.
5. Ibid.
6. Ibid.
7. Ibid.
8. Ibid.
9. Ibid.
10. B. L. Edelstein, "Tooth Decay: The Best of Times, the Worst of Times," in *About Children: An Authoritative Resource on the State of Childhood Today*, eds. A. G. Cosby, R. E. Greenberg, L. H. Southward, and M. Weitzman (American Academy of Pediatrics, 2005), 106–9.
11. Ibid.
12. B. Guyer and A. Wigton, "Child Health."
13. D. Allensworth, E. Lawson, L. Nicholson, and J. Wyche, eds., *Schools and Health: Our Nation's Investment* (Washington, DC: National Academy Press, 1997).
14. Ibid.

15. H. Taras and W. Potts-Datema, "Sleep and Student Performance at School," *Journal of School Health* 75, no. 7 (2005): 248–54.

16. H. Taras and W. Potts-Datema, "Chronic Health Conditions and Student Performance at School," *Journal of School Health* 75, no. 7 (2005): 255–66.

17. H. Taras and W. Potts-Datema, "Childhood Asthma and Student Performance at School," *Journal of School Health* 75, no. 8 (2005): 296–312.

18. H. Taras, "Sleep and Student Performance at School."

19. H. Taras, "Chronic Health Conditions and Student Performance at School "

20. Ibid.

21. Ibid.

22. H. Taras, "Childhood Asthma and Student Performance at School."

23. Center for Health and Health Care in Schools, *Improving Academic Performance by Meeting Student Health Needs.* (www.healthinschools.org/education.asp)

24. National Governor's Association, *Improving Academic Performance by Meeting Student Health Needs.* (www.nga.org/)

25. U.S. Department of Health and Human Services, Public Health Service, *Healthy People 2010 Online Documents.* (www.healthypeople.gov/document/)

26. D. Allensworth et al., *Schools and Health.*

27. Ibid.

28. Annie E. Casey Foundation, *2007 Kids Count Data Book* (Baltimore, MD: Annie E. Casey Foundation, 2007).

29. Ibid.

30. Ibid.

31. L. Kann, S. K. Telljohann, and S. F. Wooley, "Health Education: Results from the School Health Programs and Policies Study 2006," *Journal of School Health* 77, no. 8 (2007): 408–34.

32. Centers for Disease Control and Prevention (CDC), *Guidelines for School Programs to Prevent Skin Cancer.* (www.cdc.gov/HealthyYouth/publications/Guidelines.htm)

33. Centers for Disease Control and Prevention, *Helping the Student with Diabetes Succeed: A Guide for School Personnel.* (www.cdc.gov/HealthyYouth/publications/Guidelines.htm)

34. Centers for Disease Control and Prevention, *Strategies for Addressing Asthma Within a Coordinated School Health Program.* (www.cdc.gov/HealthyYouth/publications/Guidelines.htm)

35. National Center for Infectious Diseases, CDC, *An Ounce of Prevention: Keeps the Germs Away.* (www.cdc.gov/ncidod/op/)

36. B. L. Edelstein, "Tooth Decay "

37. Ibid.

38. Ibid.

39. Ibid.

40. American Dental Association, "Can What's in Your Mouth Really Make You Sick?" (www.ada.org/public/topics/oralsystemic_gumdisease.asp)

41. Ibid.

42. National Heart, Lung, and Blood Institute, *For Teachers: Why Sleep Is Important.* (www.nhlbi.nih.gov/health/public/sleep/starslp/teachers/whysleep.htm)

43. Ibid.

44. Ibid.

45. CDC, *Guidelines for School Programs to Prevent Skin Cancer.*

46. Ibid.

47. Ibid.

48. Ibid.

49. Ibid.

50. Centers for Disease Control and Prevention, *How Do Vaccines Protect Children from Diseases?* (www.cdc.gov/vaccines/vac-gen/howprotectkids.htm)

51. Ibid.

52. National Institutes of Health, *Childhood Immunization.* (www.nlm.nih.gov/medlineplus/childhoodimmunization.html)

53. Centers for Disease Control and Prevention, *Vaccine Safety Concerns.* (www.cdc.gov/od/science/iso/concerns/)

54. Centers for Disease Control and Prevention, *Vaccine Safety Information for Parents.* (www.cdc.gov/od/science/iso/basic/parents.htm)

55. Institute of Medicine, *Immunization Safety Review: Vaccines and Autism (2004).* (www.nap.edu/openbook.php?isbn=030909237X)

56. Ibid.

57. Centers for Disease Control and Prevention, *Measles, Mumps, and Rubella (MMR) Vaccine and Autism Fact Sheet.* (www.cdc.gov/od/science/iso/concerns/mmr_autism_factsheet.htm)

58. American Academy of Pediatrics, *The AAP Childhood Immunization Support Program.* (www.cispimmunize.org/aap/aap_main.html)

59. U.S. Food and Drug Administration, *Thimerosal in Vaccines.* (www.fda.gov/cber/vaccine/thimfaq.htm#q4)

60. U.S. Food and Drug Administration, *New Vaccine Prevents Cervical Cancer.* (www.fda.gov/fdac/features/2006/506_cervical.html)

61. Centers for Disease Control and Prevention, *Recommendations and Guidelines: Advisory Committee on Immunization Practices (ACIP).* (www.cdc.gov/vaccines/recs/acip/default.htm)

62. American Lung Association, *The Common Cold.* (www.lungusa.org)

63. Ibid.

64. National Pediculosis Association (www.headlice.org)

65. Ibid.

66. Ibid.

67. Centers for Disease Control and Prevention, *HIV Basic Information.* (www.cdc.gov/hiv/topics/basic/index.htm)

68. Centers for Disease Control and Prevention, *HIV/AIDS Among Youth.* (www.cdc.gov/hiv/resources/factsheets/youth.htm)

69. Centers for Disease Control and Prevention, *Sexual Risk Behaviors.* (www.cdc.gov/HealthyYouth/sexualbehaviors/index.htm)

70. Ibid.

71. Centers for Disease Control and Prevention, *Universal Precautions for Prevention of Transmission of HIV and Other Bloodborne Infections.* (www.cdc.gov/ncidod/dhqp/bp_universal_precautions.html)

72. H. W. Kelly, "Asthma," in *About Children: An Authoritative Resource on the State of Childhood Today,* eds. A. G. Cosby, R. E. Greenberg, L. H. Southward, and M. Weitzman (American Academy of Pediatrics, 2005), 114–17.

73. Ibid.

74. Ibid.

75. American Lung Association, *Open Airways.* (www.lungusa.org)

76. Kids' Health, *All About Allergies.* (www.kidshealth.org/parent/medical/allergies/allergy.html)

77. Ibid.

78. Ibid.

79. Ibid.

80. Ibid.

81. W. H. Dietz, "Overweight: An Epidemic," in *About Children: An Authoritative Resource on the State of Childhood Today,* eds. A. G. Cosby, R. E. Greenberg, L. H. Southward, and M. Weitzman (American Academy of Pediatrics, 2005), 110–13.

82. Ibid.

83. CDC, *Helping the Student with Diabetes Succeed.*

84. Ibid.

85. Ibid.

86. Ibid.

87. Epilepsy Foundation, *About Epilepsy.* (www.epilepsyfoundation.org)

88. Ibid.

89. Ibid.

90. Centers for Disease Control and Prevention, *Health Education Curriculum Analysis Tool.* (www.cdc.gov/HealthyYouth/HECAT/index.htm)

Helping Students Translate Their Skills to Manage Health Risks

Section III focuses on the health risks students can avoid or reduce to help them live a healthy life. It contains the content and personal and social skills that make up the National Health Education Standards. Each chapter in this section has an introduction that provides the reader with information about the prevalence and cost of not practicing the positive health behavior, the relationship between the healthy behavior and academic performance, and the risk and protective factors related to the behavior. Information is then provided about what schools are currently doing and what they should be doing in relation to the health behavior. Each chapter in this section also provides background information for the teacher, developmentally appropriate strategies for learning and assessment, sample student questions with suggested answers (Chapters 11–14), and children's literature, Internet, and other resources related to each content area.

10

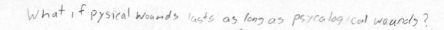

Preventing Intentional Injuries and Violence

DESIRED LEARNER OUTCOMES

After reading this chapter, you will be able to . . .

- **Describe the prevalence and cost of violence among youth.**

- **Explain the relationship between violence and compromised academic performance.**

- **Identify factors that influence violence.**

- **Summarize current guidelines and practices for schools and teachers related to violence prevention.**

- **Summarize developmentally appropriate violence prevention concepts and skills for K–8 students in the context of the National Health Education Standards and target healthy behavior outcomes.**

- **Demonstrate developmentally appropriate learning strategies and assessment techniques that incorporate concepts and skills that have been shown to prevent violence among youth.**

- **Identify effective, evaluated commercial violence prevention curricula.**

- **Identify websites and children's literature that can be used in cross-curricular instructional activities promoting violence prevention.**

INTRODUCTION

In recent years, educators, parents, and other concerned advocates have realized that the issue of violence and the risks associated with the range of intentional injuries extend far beyond the boundaries of the criminal justice system. High-profile school shootings and attendant media coverage of violence have focused the attention of many professionals on the types and costs of violence confronting American youth. In particular, an emerging body of science has confirmed that intentional injuries are much more than criminal acts. They are a serious threat to public health. Violence also is a threat to academic achievement and school success. As a foundation for understanding the impact of violence on students, teachers must be equipped to separate fact from myth in addressing this important social, political, academic, and health issue.

Prevalence and Cost

The National Academy of Sciences has defined violence as including those behaviors that intentionally threaten, attempt, or inflict physical harm on others.[1] In addition to their physical consequences, the fear associated with violent acts can infringe on our sense of personal freedom and compromise our basic and shared need to feel safe.[2] Because this epidemic affects all elements of society, intentional injury risk reduction has become more than a criminal justice priority. Violence risk reduction is now recognized as a public health priority in the United States.

Violence is pervasive and can change our quality of life. Shocking reports of school violence cause parents to fear for the safety of their children in educational environments. Accounts of gang activity threaten the sense of confidence and safety in neighborhoods. Dating violence among teens, a manifestation of the power or control that one partner exerts over the other, can take physical, sexual, or psychological forms. Child abuse and other forms of family violence that youth experience at home also are of concern to educators.[3]

As part of an agenda to improve the health of all Americans, particular emphasis has been placed on confronting the incidence and consequences of intentional injury risks among children and youth. It is important to remember that a young person can be the victim of a violent act, the perpetrator of it, or both. Aggressive behaviors among youth can include verbal abuse, bullying, intimidation, hitting, or fist fighting, among other acts. Although these behaviors have serious consequences, generally they do not result in serious injury or death. However, youth violence also can take the form of delinquent or criminal acts, including aggravated assault, robbery, rape, and homicide committed by and against youth.[4] Research has shown that even the youngest children are not immune from being victimized by murder, child abuse and neglect, or other nonfatal assaults.

The Children's Defense Fund, a national advocacy organization for children, youth, and families, confirmed the following findings related to the incidence and consequences of youth violence in the United States:

Every thirteen seconds, a public school student is corporally punished.

Every twenty seconds, a child is arrested.

Every thirty-five seconds, a child is confirmed as abused or neglected.

Every eight minutes, a child is arrested for committing a violent crime.

Every three hours, a child or teen is killed by a firearm.

Every five hours, a child or teen commits suicide.

Every six hours, a child is killed as a result of abuse or neglect.[5]

As shocking as these data are, they are consistent with 2005 Youth Risk Behavior Survey (YRBS) data related to intentional injuries (Table 10–1). These findings provide insight into the kinds of violence to which U.S. high school students were exposed in 2007.[6]

In addition to the social and emotional costs of abuse and victimization in the United States, an enormous health and economic burden is associated with violence. Violence-related costs associated with nonfatal injuries and deaths exceed $70 billion each year. Of these costs, over 90 percent are related to lost productivity. In addition, over $5.5 billion is spent each year on medical care to manage the over 2.5 million injuries caused by interpersonal and self-directed violence. Though people aged 15–44 years make up only 44 percent of the population, this age group of Americans accounts for nearly 75 percent of the injuries and 83 percent of the costs due to interpersonal violence. Victims of violence are more likely to experience a range of problems not reflected in these estimates, including depression, post-traumatic stress disorder, cardiovascular disease, and diabetes.[7]

Though violence committed by juveniles is recognized as being particularly costly, it has been the subject of relatively few economic evaluations. The combined direct and indirect costs associated with youth violence include expenses related to medical care, lost productivity, and reduced quality of life. Available data suggest that such costs might exceed $158 billion each year.[8]

Following the highly publicized shooting at Columbine High School in Colorado that resulted in the deaths of fourteen students and a teacher, then President Clinton and the U.S. Congress requested a report on the body of research about youth violence. In January 2001, then Surgeon General Dr. David Satcher issued the *Report of the Surgeon General on Youth Violence.*

This landmark document summarized information to challenge common myths and misconceptions about youth violence. Erroneous perceptions can be both dangerous and wasteful. Failing to recognize the existence of a problem and neglecting to confirm the extent to which individuals are affected by it can obscure the need for

TABLE 10–1

Youth Risk Behavior Survey Data Related to Intentional Injuries, 2007

Risk Behavior	Percent Reporting Behavior		
	Total	Females	Males
Carried a weapon (gun, knife, or club) (on one or more of the thirty days before survey)	18	7.5	28.5
Carried a gun (on one or more of the thirty days before survey)	5.2	1.2	9
Were injured in a physical fight (one or more times in the year before survey)	4.2	2.9	5.5
Experienced dating violence (hit/slapped/physically hurt on purpose) (in the year before survey)	9.9	8.8	11
Were forced to have sexual intercourse (in the year before survey)	7.8	11.3	4.5
Carried a weapon on school property	5.9	2.7	9
Were threatened or injured on school property with a weapon	7.8	5.4	10.2
Engaged in a physical fight on school property	12.4	8.5	16.3
Had property stolen or damaged on school property	27.1	23.7	30.4
Seriously considered suicide	14.5	18.7	10.3
Attempted suicide	6.9	9.3	4.6

SOURCE: Centers for Disease Control and Prevention, "Youth Risk Behavior Surveillance—United States, 2007," *Morbidity and Mortality Weekly Report* 57, no. SS-4 (6 June 2008): 1–131.

informed policy or developmentally appropriate interventions. Unfounded beliefs can lead to misplaced fears and to implementation of misguided policies that waste human and financial resources. The *Report of the Surgeon General* refuted a number of myths about youth violence, including the following:

- *Myth: The epidemic of violent behavior that marked the early 1990s is over. Young people and adults in the United States are much safer today.*
  Fact: Although arrest and victimization data show significant reductions in violence since the peak of the epidemic in 1993, self-reports of youth violence reveal that some violent behaviors remain at high levels.
- *Myth: Most future offenders can be identified in early childhood.*
  Fact: Uncontrolled behavior or a diagnosis of a conduct disorder among young children does not predetermine violence in adolescence. The majority of violent adolescents were not aggressive or out of control as young children. The majority of children diagnosed with mental or behavioral disorders do not become violent adolescents.
- *Myth: African American and Hispanic youth are more likely to become involved in violence than youth in other race or ethnic groups.*
  Fact: Race and ethnicity have little bearing on the proportion of youth engaged in nonfatal violent behavior. There are racial and ethnic differences, however, in homicide rates and in the timing and continuity of violence over the life span. These variables might account for the overrepresentation of certain groups in U.S. jails and prisons.

- *Myth: A breed of young and violent "superpredators" threatens the United States.*
  Fact: At the peak of the 1990s' violence epidemic, there was a claim that increasingly callous youth engaged in frequent, vicious offenses. There is no evidence to support this notion. Increased lethality was due to gun use, which has since decreased dramatically.
- *Myth: Trying juvenile offenders in adult courts reduces the likelihood that they will commit more crimes.*
  Fact: Youth who are transferred to adult courts have significantly higher rates of reoffending and a greater likelihood of committing subsequent felonies than youth who remain in the juvenile justice system. Youth referred to the adult criminal justice system are more likely to be both physically and sexually victimized.
- *Myth: In the 1990s, school violence affected mostly white students or those who attended suburban or rural schools.*
  Fact: African American and Hispanic males attending large urban schools that serve poor neighborhoods faced and still face the greatest risk of becoming victims or perpetrators of school violence.
- *Myth: Weapon-related injuries in schools have increased dramatically over the past decade.*
  Fact: Incidence of such injuries has not changed significantly over the past twenty years. Compared to neighborhoods and homes, schools are safe places for students.
- *Myth: Most violent youth will be arrested for a violent crime.*
  Fact: Most youth who participate in violent behavior will never be arrested for a violent crime.[9]

TABLE 10–2

Healthy People 2010 Objectives to Reduce Intentional Injuries (Violence and Abuse) Among Youth

Objective 15-32	Reduce homicides.
Objective 15-33	Reduce maltreatment and maltreatment fatalities of children.
Objective 15-34	Reduce the rate of physical assault by current or former intimate partners.
Objective 15-35	Reduce the annual rate of rape or attempted rape.
Objective 15-36	Reduce sexual assault other than rape.
Objective 15-37	Reduce physical assaults.
Objective 15-38	Reduce physial fighting among adolscents.
Objective 15-39	Reduce weapon carrying by adolescents on school property.

SOURCE: U.S. Department of Health and Human Services, *Healthy People 2010: Understanding and Improving Health*, 2nd ed. (Washington, DC: U.S. Government Printing Office, 2000).

Based on a review of the scientific literature, the *Report* concluded the following:

Youth violence is not just a problem of the cities, isolated rural areas, or selected segments within ~iety—it is our nation's problem.

~ation, we have access to credible knowledge that ~ translated into programs documented to be ~ preventing youth violence.

strategies exist that can be tailored to ~f youth at every stage of development, ~d to late adolescence.[10]

~ople 2010 has specified several objectives targeting violence ~ool-age children and youth ~ demonstrate the range ~y risks to which chil-~e exposed. Although ~t by the isolated ~s, this chapter ~s and class-~tary and

in brain development and the ability to function among children exposed to violence depend on a number of factors, including the nature of the violent experiences, the child's response to the threat, and a host of family and community variables.[12]

Students who have experienced trauma are likely to exhibit attendance problems, frequent suspensions from school, failing grades in at least half their subjects, performance that is two or more grade levels below age level, and poor performance on standardized tests. While many students are compromised, others who are under threat can demonstrate temporary or subject-specific overachievement.[13]

Students normally survive violence in their homes, communities, or schools, but they tend to lose interest in academic activities and are likely to manifest persistent behavior problems. Typically, these young people earn lower grades and have higher truancy and dropout rates than those who have not been exposed to violence.[14] Research also has shown that children who witness chronic violence tend to exhibit limited concentration and short attention spans.[15]

Abuse of children and youth by adult caregivers can cause children to be cautious and withdrawn. Abused children often manifest delayed language development, express feelings of powerlessness, and have a general inability to set goals or plan for meaningful futures.[16] Most compromised academic achievement among abused children is not due to general problems with intellectual development. Rather, academic problems among abused students are likely to be related to the difficulty these children have in forming bonds with peers and teachers or to a common difficulty engaging in classroom learning activities.[17]

Factors That Influence Violence

Risk factors for intentional injuries are evident in every area of the lives of students. These risk factors include internal attributes of the child and external variables within the family, school, social networks, and community. Some experts believe that violent images are so common in the media that children have become desensitized to their intense and devastating effects. Other experts suggest that violence can be linked to the complex social and economic changes that affect families and communities. They attribute youth violence to the actions of overworked and financially strapped parents who vent their frustrations at home. When frequent yelling or ~her aggressive or abusive acts become common in the ~e, children receive the message that such behaviors ~eptable or even necessary. Children who have not ~d skills to control their impulses and behav-~ght grow accustomed to using violence as a way ~solve conflicts or gain desired possessions. Students ~o have not learned that nonviolence is a better—or even possible—option view violence as an expedient and effective way to gain respect when confronted with frustrating circumstances.[18]

Risk and Protective Factors Associated with Youth Violence

INDIVIDUAL RISK FACTORS

History of violent victimization
History of early aggressive behavior
Attention deficits or learning disorders
Exposure to violence/conflict in the family

FAMILY RISK FACTORS

Authoritarian child-rearing attitudes
Harsh/lax/inconsistent discipline practices
Low attachment to parents/caregivers
Parental substance abuse/criminality

PEER/SCHOOL RISK FACTORS

Association with delinquent peers
Social rejection by peers
Low involvement in conventional activities
Low commitment to school
Poor academic performance

COMMUNITY RISK FACTORS

Diminished economic opportunities
High level of transience

High level of family disruption
Low levels of community participation
Socially disorganized neighborhoods

INDIVIDUAL PROTECTIVE FACTORS

Intolerant attitude toward deviance
High IQ/grade point average
Positive social orientation
Religiosity

FAMILY PROTECTIVE FACTORS

Connectedness to family/other
Ability to discuss problems w
Frequent shared activities w
High parent expectations f

PEER/SCHOOL PROTECT

Commitment to school
Involvement in social

SOURCE: Centers for Disease Control and Prevention, 19 April 2007: Youth Violence: Fact Sheet. (www/cdc/g

Research has increased our understanding of factors that make some youth more vulnerable to victimization and others to perpetration of violence. Although risk factors are not direct causes of youth violence, they increase the likelihood that a young person will become violent.[19]

Protective factors include variables demonstrated to buffer youth from risks of becoming violent, but protective factors have not been studied as extensively or rigorously as risk factors. Much less is known about protective than risk factors associated with youth violence.[20] Readers are encouraged to review available information about risk and protective factors for youth violence identified by the Centers for Disease Control and Prevention that can be foun in Consider This 10.1.[21]

Examination of these lists of risk and protective tors will reinforce that it is the interaction among pers characteristics, other people, and environmental tions that is important. The *Report of the Surgeon on Youth Violence* confirmed that the development of childhood and adolescence are very influenti development of risk and/or protective factors fo As children grow from infancy to adulthood factors become more influential while others so. For example, substance use among per greater risk factor for violence to children age those age 14.[22]

Rega
operate
are ex
lent.
fac
co
g

do not teach functional knowledge or enable students to practice essential skills to avoid and manage conflicts.[28]

Characteristics of Programs That Show Promise for Preventing Violence

An extensive review of school-based violence prevention programs conducted by the U.S. General Accounting Office has revealed common characteristics associated with the most promising interventions.[29] Educators, community leaders, and concerned parents are encouraged to review the following foundational elements of promising intentional injury risk reduction programs.

1. *Comprehensive approach.* Research shows that the most successful programs are undergirded by the recognition that youth violence evolves from a complex set of variables. Like the Coordinated School Health Program (see Chapter 1), promising interventions tend to address multiple problem areas and link a variety of services, both in school and in the community. Learn

2. *Early start and long-term commitment.* Learn and prevention activities are organized i scope and sequence activities designed to help accurate information, examine important skills. Sustained students reinforces the e

3. *Strong leadership* gram quality, orate with staff. In and

sound approaches to promoting an alcohol- and other drug-free lifestyle.

State of the Art

In light of the need to use finite resources in the most productive and evidence-based ways, an important body of literature has emerged that confirms attributes of school-based policies, programs, and practices with no or low potential to prevent violence. Although common in many school communities, the following activities should be avoided as they have been demonstrated to have very little potential to reduce youth violence. In addition, research has confirmed that some of these practices might actually increase the likelihood of aggression or violent acting-out behaviors among youth.[27]

1. *Using scare-tactic approaches based on pictures or videos depicting violent scenes or consequences.* There is a large body of research confirming that people who watch violence in the media are more likely than their counterparts to behave violently.

2. *Adding a violence prevention agenda to a school district that is overwhelmed with other activities.* It is important for schools to have an organizational structure and a climate that support violence prevention. Too often, school administrators try to add violence prevention programming to a school community that has not established intentional injury risk reduction as a priority. Although common, this practice can increase the burden on teachers, parents, and education ultimately backfire for students, professionals.

Segregating aggressive or antisocial students into separate maps: Integrating delinquent youth into a positive, no quent peer group can have a positive effect. Compelling evidence that efforts to separate v composed exclusively of aggressive yo tribute to a reduction in problem ctice actually might e haviors. ng brie

RECOMMENDATION 1

Establish a social environment that prevents violence and suicide.

Guiding Principles

- Ensure high academic standards and provide faculty, staff members, and students with the support and administrative leadership to promote the academic success (achievement), health, and safety of all students.
- Encourage students' feelings of connectedness to school.
- Establish a climate that demonstrates respect, support, and caring and that does not tolerate harassment or bullying.
- Develop and implement written policies regarding violence and suicide prevention.
- Infuse violence and suicide prevention into multiple school activities and classes.
- Establish unambiguous disciplinary policies; communicate them to students, faculty, staff members, and families; and implement them consistently.
- Assess violence and suicide prevention strategies and policies at regular intervals.

RECOMMENDATION 2

Provide a physical environment, inside and outside school buildings, that prevents violence.

Guiding Principles

- Actively supervise all student activities to prevent violence.
- Ensure that the school environment, including school buses, is free from weapons.

RECOMMENDATION 3

Implement health education curricula and instruction that help students develop the knowledge, attitudes, behavioral skills, and confidence needed to adopt and maintain safe lifestyles and to advocate for health and safety.

Guiding Principles

- Choose prevention programs and curricula that are grounded in theory or that have scientific evidence of effectiveness.
- Implement violence prevention curricula consistent with national and state standards for health education.
- Use active learning strategies, interactive teaching methods, and proactive classroom management to encourage student involvement in learning about violence prevention.
- Provide adequate staffing and resources, including budget, facilities, staff development, and class time, to provide violence prevention education for all students.

RECOMMENDATION 4

Provide health, counseling, psychological, and social services to meet the physical, mental, emotional, and social health needs of students.

Guiding Principles

- Coordinate school-based counseling, psychological, social, and health services and the education curriculum.
- Establish strong links with community resources and identify providers to bring services into the schools.
- Identify and provide assistance to students who have witnessed violence and who have been victims of violence.

RECOMMENDATION 5

Establish mechanisms for short- and long-term responses to crises and disasters that affect the school community.

Guiding Principles

- Establish a written plan for responding to crises and disasters.
- Prepare to implement the school's plan in the event of a crisis.
- Have short-term responses and services established after a crisis.
- Have long-term responses and services established after a crisis.

RECOMMENDATION 6

Integrate school, family, and community efforts to prevent violence and suicide.

Guiding Principles

- Involve parents, students, and other family members in all aspects of school life, including planning and implementing violence and suicide prevention programs and policies.
- Educate, support, and involve family members in child and adolescent violence and suicide prevention.
- Coordinate school and community services.

RECOMMENDATION 7

For all school personnel, provide regular staff development opportunities that impart the knowledge, skills, and confidence to prevent violence and suicide and to support students in their efforts to do the same.

Guiding Principles

- Ensure that staff members are knowledgeable about violence and suicide prevention and have the skills needed to prevent violence at school, at home, and in the community.
- Train and support all personnel to be positive role models for a healthy and safe lifestyle.

SOURCE: U.S. Department of Health and Human Services, *School Health Guidelines to Prevent Unintentional Injuries and Violence* (Atlanta, GA: Centers for Disease Control and Prevention, 7 December 2001), 13–46.

GUIDELINES FOR CLASSROOM APPLICATIONS

Important Background for K–8 Teachers

While many educators share a general concern about violent acts confronting children, few recognize the breadth of the kinds of violent acts and locations in which they occur. Teachers must be aware of the impact of violence in the world, homes, local communities, and schools on their students.

Violence in Their World: Helping Children Manage Trauma Associated with Catastrophic Events

In light of recent school shootings, terrorist acts and war, and natural disasters, educators need to update and refine skills to recognize and manage the effects of catastrophic events on students. Trauma occurs when an individual is exposed to an overwhelming event beyond the realm of normal human experience. Exposure to such events results in excessive stress to the body, mind, and psyche. The National Institute of Mental Health suggested that trauma characterized as more than simple loss is associated with exposure to or involvement in either of two kinds of events:

- Events that result in serious physical injuries or wounds
- Circumstances that are emotionally painful, distressful, or shocking[32]

Exposure to such events can have lasting mental or physical effects. Trauma can result from a broad range of conditions, including natural disasters, severe and constant criticism or bullying, divorce, car crashes, abuse or neglect, death of a family member or close friend, chronic exposure to violence, and terrorist acts or war.[33]

The impact of a catastrophe on children depends on a number of factors, including their physical proximity to the event and the support systems to which they have access, but trauma can pose particular challenges for younger learners. Depending on their stage of development, children often are not cognitively prepared to understand either the impact or the magnitude of the situation. In addition, they might not be equipped to cope with the intensity of emotions associated with the event or its impact on their caregivers.[34]

Children react to trauma in a way that is unlike that of their adult counterparts. It is common for children to have immediate and instinctive reactions to danger or the threat of it. Limited in their physical strength and cognitive capacity, children often will use withdrawal skills, including hiding, running away, and pretending, when they feel threatened. It is not uncommon for firefighters to find a young child hiding in a cupboard or closet in a house fire. Or, a child who is being sexually abused might pretend to be asleep as a way not to provoke or stimulate the offender. Quite often, children freeze and/or become speechless in the face of danger. This reaction can be manifested in adults, but it is an instinctive and primary coping mechanism among powerless children.[35]

Following their initial reaction, children often demonstrate a range of cognitive, emotional, behavioral, and physical responses to trauma. Although some children are particularly resilient, it is common for teachers to note fairly consistent manifestations of trauma among the majority of their students. Specifically, teachers might observe the following in students confronted by a catastrophic event:

1. Avoidance: In the wake of trauma, children might
   - Avoid feelings and memory of the trauma
   - Remain quiet about the experience
   - Lie as a way to avoid a similarly traumatic situation
2. Disassociation: As a result of an instinctive gating mechanism, the brain numbs the body and mind, so that the child does not feel the full physical, emotional, or psychological impact of the trauma. In severe cases, disassociation can
   - Be powerful enough to shut down normal body reactions to stimuli
   - Alter perceptions and memories of the event in the brain
3. An inability to build or maintain friendships or relationships with teachers that manifest as
   - Inappropriate expressions of feelings (laughing or crying at unusual times)
   - Expressions of aggressive or sexual behaviors or related verbalizations
   - A tendency to develop physical symptoms or fears (stomachaches or frequent headaches)
   - Regression to behaviors or language patterns that had formerly disappeared[36]

Though the symptoms and manifestations of traumatic events vary a great deal from child to child, teachers play a critical role in helping students manage such events. Education professionals must recognize that their responses to a traumatic event can influence the reactions of their students. Children tend to react much more calmly if this is the reaction among the adults around them.

Unfortunately, while attending to the needs of children, many adult caregivers fail to make time to reflect and implement self-care strategies to help with their own management of the trauma. This can compromise the supportive quality of the interactions they have with their students.

Another problem occurs when well-meaning adult caregivers attempt to protect children by minimizing the impact of a catastrophic event. Some teachers in elementary and middle schools choose to proceed with typical classroom activities. Some teachers even extend this practice to the point that they fail to acknowledge that the event ever took place.

As a foundation for effective practice, education professionals and caring adults are encouraged to continue to explore ways to help children work through their reactions to catastrophic events. Often, this can best be accomplished by maintaining a safe, stable classroom environment. Many

A safe and stable classroom environment can help children cope with traumatic events.

simple activities and support networks can be incorporated into classroom practice to promote a sense of security and ease among students. Following are general guidelines to help teachers prepare the learning environment:

1. From the beginning of the school year, encourage student participation in maintaining a positive and healthy classroom environment.
2. Teach nonviolent conflict resolution skills as an effective means of dealing with differences and problems.
3. Use life experiences and current events from children's lives as teaching resources.
4. Create a caring and nurturing learning environment for students.
5. Establish and maintain routines.
6. Cultivate peer mentorship among students.
7. Discuss academic problems and brainstorm solutions with the class.
8. Confront negative comments or actions that occur in the classroom.[37]

For further information, readers should review the additional information found in Chapter 14 on managing loss, death, and grief. Readers will find content that provides further clarification about the impact of catastrophic events on students and provides suggestions for educators.

Violence at the School Site

In an effort to present an accurate and comprehensive picture of the nature and scope of crime and violence on school property, the U.S. Departments of Education and Justice issue annual reports entitled Indicators of School Crime and Safety. The most recent of these reports confirmed that although the number of students carrying guns has declined and the victimization rate of violent crime has stabilized since 1990, there is a growing gang presence on school campuses. In addition, more of today's students than those of the past are fearful while they are at school.[38] This report confirmed the following findings about the risks for intentional injury on school property:

- In general, schools are safe places.
- Despite the concerns of many, schools are not especially dangerous places in most communities. Most crimes at the school site involve theft and are not of a serious, violent nature (physical attacks, fights with a weapon, rape, robbery, murder, or suicide).
- Homicides are extremely rare events on school property.
- The concerns teachers have about their own safety are not without foundation. Secondary teachers are more likely to be threatened with injury, whereas those in elementary schools are more likely to have been physically attacked by a student.
- Today's students are not significantly more likely to be victimized than were students in previous years.
- Since 1993, fewer students have been taking weapons to school. In addition, consequences for carrying weapons on school property have been formalized.
- The presence of gangs in schools makes students and teachers more vulnerable to the risks of intentional injuries.
- Nearly all American schools have implemented some type of campus-security measures (zero-tolerance policies for guns, alcohol, and other drugs; controlled access to buildings and grounds; required sign-in or escort policies for all guests).[39]

In response to particular concern about school shootings, a 2002 federal document provided a summary of findings from a study of school shootings that had occurred over time and in a number of states. This exhaustive research revealed the following:

- Incidents of targeted violence at schools rarely are impulsive. Such attacks are the culmination of an understandable and often traceable process of thinking and behavior, often in response to loss or failures.
- Prior to most incidents, the attacker(s) had told one or more people about the idea and the plan.
- Most attackers did not threaten targets directly prior to an attack.
- Many attackers had considered or attempted suicide at some time prior to attacks.
- Unfortunately, there is no useful profile of the "school shooter."
- Most attackers had experience using guns and had access to them.
- Most shooting incidents were not resolved by law enforcement action.
- In many cases, other students were involved in some capacity, including providing encouragement or participating in a cover-up.
- In a number of cases, retaliating for having been bullied by others was an important motivation for the attack.

- Most attackers engaged in some behavior prior to the incident that caused adults or other students to express concern or indicate that the student needed help.[40]

Though schools generally are very safe places, school violence can lead to a disruptive and threatening environment, physical injury, and emotional stress. All of these can threaten student achievement, the primary focus of educators. In response, school leaders have implemented a range of programs to prevent, deter, and respond to the potential for violence. In support of the agenda to reduce youth violence, the No Child Left Behind Act emphasized the importance of safe learning environments by requiring schools to have a safety plan in place and to fund programs and practices intended to prevent violence in schools.

Though there is variety in the kinds of policies and programs implemented to reduce violence in schools, the three most common types include

- Efforts to involve parents in preventing and reducing violence,
- Safety and security procedures (random metal detector checks, random dog sniffs to check for drugs, random sweeps for contraband, security cameras and guards) and
- Disciplinary policies.

Teachers are encouraged to work with school leaders to merge classroom policies and practices with those implemented to prevent violence throughout the local school community.[41]

Violence in the Home: Recognizing and Managing Child Maltreatment

Child maltreatment is manifested in the form of physical, sexual, or emotional abuse or neglect. Though children might be the targets of a single form of maltreatment, it is common for a child to experience several types of abuse simultaneously. For example, for a physically abused child also to be neglected and/or emotionally victimized is not uncommon.

Child abuse is a growing problem in the United States; the number of cases of abuse reported each year has increased steadily since the 1970s. It has been estimated that 1,100 children die each year from the combined effects of child abuse and neglect. The effects of child abuse are evident in every aspect of development. Research has confirmed the following:

- Maltreated children have a distorted view of their environment.
- The effects of child abuse influence a child's ability to interact with others and make friends.
- Abuse reinforces inappropriate reactions in social settings.
- Child abuse is related to poor school performance.[42]

Abuse is more likely to occur in families and communities enduring the stress of poverty and/or substance abuse. However, the maltreatment of adolescents and children can occur in any home on any street—it is a tragedy that crosses all cultures and socioeconomic levels.[43]

Researchers have confirmed that adults who perpetrate physical abuse and neglect are more likely to be female than male. Conversely, male parents are the perpetrators of the highest percentage of sexual abuse. It has been documented that the most common patterns of maltreatment include children being victimized by a female parent who is acting alone. In such cases, the most common forms of abuse are neglect and physical abuse.[44]

Perpetrators often attempt to convince children that they are to blame or in some way have contributed to their victimization. Because children are led to believe either that they are at fault for the abuse or that they will be punished further for revealing it, most young victims will not talk about abuse in their families. Thus, it is important that teachers and other adult caregivers not be misled by the silence of a child about such matters. Child advocates and educators must note the following characteristics that have been documented to be among the most common in young victims of maltreatment:

Chronic or frequent illness

ADHD/other hyperactivity disorders

Depression

Bowel or bladder control problems

Disabilities or special needs

Impulsivity, aggressiveness, or defiance

Academic difficulties

Limited self-management skills[45]

The issue of child abuse is confounded by the fact that there is no universally accepted set of parenting rules or strategies. As a result, the boundaries of child abuse are blurred by cultural or community values. Among many Pacific Islanders, for example, it is regarded as cruel and dangerous to leave a young child in a separate bed for the night. Tolerance for the notion of "spare the rod, spoil the child" has contributed to debate over the legitimacy of corporal punishment for children in the United States. Regardless of other influential variables, *hurting children is never acceptable, even if it is delivered in the name of love, care, or discipline.*[46]

Physical abuse, defined as a nonaccidental injury or pattern of injury to a child, receives the most attention from criminal justice, education, and child welfare professionals. This type of maltreatment is characterized by any type of physical trauma to a child and often is the result of disciplinary or punishment strategies.

Neglect occurs in cases in which a caregiver fails to provide for the basic emotional, medical, safety, and/or educational needs of a child. Although it is more common than physical abuse, neglect receives much less attention. This may be because neglect might not have easily observable manifestations, or it might result from other adult conditions, including poverty or depression. In addition, some parents are unaware that their behaviors constitute neglect. For example, a single parent who is working multiple jobs might view this circumstance as sacrificing for survival rather than as neglect. Thus, teachers must be careful not to make quick judgments about parents and conditions that might appear to be resulting in neglect. As in all cases, the best interests of students must be the first priority.

Though most of us think of sexual abuse in the context of physical acts, it can involve photographing children or exposing them to sexual activity or pornography. Emotional or psychological abuse involving excessive demands, harassment, criticism, rejection, belittlement, or withdrawn parenting is very difficult to quantify or diagnose. Unlike physical abuse, the connection between sexually and emotionally abusive acts and their effect on the child might not be immediate and/or might be difficult to prove. Teacher's Toolbox 10.2 provides detailed information about child abuse indicators.[47]

The Role of the "Mandated Reporter"   Detecting abuse or neglect is difficult because many children are too young or afraid to reveal what is happening to them. Maltreatment most often occurs behind closed doors or under circumstances in which no other adult or advocate is present. Also, many kinds of abuse leave no obvious sign of harm. In an effort to identify and help as many young victims as possible, each state has enacted laws requiring many kinds of professionals to act as "mandated reporters."

Specifically, these laws require certain individuals who suspect abuse or neglect to report their suspicions to state or county authorities. Reports can be made to the Childhelp National Child Abuse Hotline (800-4-A-CHILD or 800-422-4453) or to local child protection professionals or police. Though each state has its own laws governing mandated reporting protocol, in most cases any person who works with children on a regular basis is charged with the responsibility. In all states, this list of professionals includes counselors, lawyers, nurses, physicians, social workers, and teachers.[48]

If abuse is suspected, all concerned adults are encouraged to make a report to child protective service professionals, but mandated reporters are required to do so. It is important to note that such reports do not constitute an accusation. Rather, reports of such suspicions serve as a formal request for an investigation to be made on behalf of the child. In most states, reporters can remain anonymous and are immune from the legal actions of the unhappy parents or caregivers under investigation. However, teachers or other advocates who make reports are contributing significantly to the welfare of young people. In any case, teachers always should make a record of any abuse report, detailing to whom the report was made, the time and date of the report, and the information that was communicated. Although the most important thing for teachers to communicate is concern for the child, the following kinds of information might be helpful to the investigation process:

- The reporter's name, address, and relationship to the child
- The name of and contact information for the child
- Contact information for the parents, guardians, and/or siblings of the child
- Details leading to the suspicion of maltreatment
- Symptoms of abuse or neglect that have been observed
- Other information that might expedite contact with parents or other custodial caregivers[49]

The majority of teachers hope they will never have to manage a disclosure of any kind of maltreatment of a child. Unfortunately such revelations, although rare, are made to these trusted adults. Teachers must be equipped to respond as student advocates. In particular, when a child reveals an allegation of sexual abuse, the teacher must accept the disclosure at face value. Although it might be difficult for a teacher to believe that such an incident has occurred to a student in their class, educators must remember that most children do not have a frame of reference for describing sexual abuse unless it has happened to them.

After the child has revealed any information about abuse, it is important for teachers to respond in a calm manner. Education professionals are encouraged to thank the child for talking about this important matter. Teachers are cautioned not to react in an overtly emotional manner to the disclosure or ask questions such as "Are you telling the truth?" or "Did you see that on television?" Such inquiries indicate to students that their disclosure is not believed. Conversely, four important advocacy skills—observing, making referrals, gathering information, and following up—must be mastered by teachers and other professionals who have been designated as mandated reporters of suspected child abuse within their states.

1. *Observing Students—a Foundation for Advocacy.* As a foundation for advocacy on behalf of child and adolescent health, teachers and other concerned adults must train themselves to be critical observers of the students with whom they come into contact. Such professionals might be more able to notice the subtle signs or symptoms of abuse than nonabusive parents or other family members. Because teachers have the opportunity to observe students in the context of the child's age-cohort peers, any anomalies, changes, or injuries might be more conspicuous to them. In addition, teachers are charged with the responsibility of keeping records about a range of student performance measures. In this context, changes in student health, social interaction patterns, or academic performance could be noticeable over a period of time. Finally, teachers, physicians, and other mandated reporters often are better able than a child's relatives to maintain professional objectivity about potential problems.

In all cases in which teachers suspect that students are being abused or that violence is eminent, action must be taken. The best course of action is to make an immediate referral or report of these suspicions.

Signs and Symptoms of Child Maltreatment

PHYSICAL ABUSE

1. A child who is being *physically abused* might have
   a. Unexplained or unusually shaped injuries
   b. Recurring physical marks or injuries
   c. Bruises, welts, or adult-size bite marks
   d. Injuries in various stages of healing
   e. Lacerations or abrasions, particularly to the face, genitalia, arms, legs, or torso
   f. Injuries to both sides of the face (injuries tend to affect only one side of the face)
   g. Grab marks on the arms or shoulders
   h. Burns from cigarettes or cigars
   i. Immersion burns from scalding water
   j. Burns that resemble an object
   k. Rope burns
   l. Head and face injuries (hair loss from pulling) and/or
   m. Broken bones or other internal injuries
2. In the classroom, children being *physically abused* might
   a. Complain of severe punishment at home
   b. Exhibit behavioral extremes (aggression/withdrawal)
   c. Attempt to run away from home
   d. Arrive early for school and/or be reluctant to go home
   e. Show extreme anxiety or fear
   f. Refuse to change clothes for physical education or athletic activities
   g. Have a poor self-image and/or
   h. Self-mutilate and/or attempt suicide

NEGLECT

1. A child who is *neglected* might exhibit signs such as
   a. Delayed physical development
   b. Constant hunger or the tendency to hoard food or overeat
   c. Inappropriate dress for the season
   d. Lack of medical care
   e. Chronic or extreme fatigue
   f. Lags in emotional and/or cognitive development
   g. Speech disorders
   h. Underweight
   i. Untreated physical or dental problems
   j. Poor hygiene, dirty skin, or matted hair
   k. Frequent absences or late arrivals for school
   l. Substance abuse
   m. Flat affect (emotionally unresponsive)
   n. Listlessness or apathy and/or
   o. Parental behaviors toward younger siblings
2. In the classroom, *neglected* children might
   a. Have anxious or insecure attachments with caregivers
   b. Interact less with peers
   c. Appear helpless or passive
   d. Be less attentive or involved in learning

   e. Perform poorly on cognitive tasks and class assignments
   f. Have poor grades and performance on standardized tests and/or
   g. Rarely express humor, laugh, or tell or understand jokes

SEXUAL ABUSE

1. Children who are being *sexually abused* might have
   a. Difficulty walking or sitting
   b. Pain, itching, bleeding, or bruising in or around the genitalia
   c. Torn, stained, or bloody underclothing
   d. Pain during urination or bloody underclothing
   e. Vaginal or penile discharge
   f. Bruising to the oral cavity
   g. Sexualized play
   h. Sexually transmitted infections
   i. Frequent touching or fondling of the genitals or masturbation
   j. Pregnancy at a very young age
   k. Inappropriate sexual expression with trusted adults
   l. Developmentally age-inappropriate sexual knowledge or simulations of adult sexual behaviors
   m. Significant social isolation
   n. Fears and/or extreme avoidance of specific persons, places, or things and/or
   o. Statements suggesting sexual abuse
2. Classroom manifestations of *sexual abuse* include
   a. Withdrawn and often aggressive behaviors
   b. Uncharacteristic attachment to the teacher and/or
   c. Extreme need for approval

EMOTIONAL ABUSE

1. Children who are *emotionally abused* might behave
   a. In a nice and pleasant manner or strive to be people pleasers
   b. Very aggressively
   c. In a "take-charge" manner as a way to define and control their environment
   d. By rejecting praise or compliments
   e. By acting out against conventional norms
   f. In a socially isolated way and/or
   g. In a withdrawn or depressed manner
2. Classroom manifestations of *emotional abuse* include
   a. Demonstrations of little respect for the feelings or rights of others
   b. Inconsistency, emotional instability, and/or impulse control problems
   c. Speech disorders or other developmental delays
   d. Academic performance below ability
   e. Frequent physical health problems and/or
   f. Substance abuse, eating disorders, and/or self-mutilation

Source: CIVITAS, *Right on Course: How Trauma and Maltreatment Impact Children in the Classroom and How You Can Help* (Chicago: CIVITAS, 2002), 31, 33, 37, 39, 43.

Through interaction and careful observation, teachers can notice changes in students' health, social interactions, or academic performance that might be signs of abuse.

2. *Making Referrals—Reporting Abuse.* Children who are being abused need access to appropriate medical and social services. The principal agency that responds to child abuse in most communities is the child protective or children's service agency. Professional personnel, including social workers, are trained to provide the counsel, help, and legal advocacy needed by children who are being treated badly. Many agencies provide assistance to parents of abused children for the purpose of preventing further occurrences.

Schools have a significant role to play in the early identification of children who have been abused. Every state has a child abuse (including sexual abuse) reporting statute. Most of these laws mandate that teachers report any suspicions of abuse. This is not a particularly easy task for teachers. It is important to note that it is not the responsibility of the teacher to determine whether the child is actually being abused. Further, educators are not responsible for determining the identification of the perpetrator of the abuse. Instead, it is the job of teachers and other mandated reporters to report any suspicions of abuse. Teach-

ers always have the concern that maybe their "hunch" is wrong. Also, many teachers are afraid that they can be sued by the parents or caregivers of the child for reporting their suspicions. However, in most states, the mandated reporter statutes provide legal immunity from liability for those who report suspected child abuse, neglect, or sexual abuse in the context of job responsibilities.

3. *Gathering Information.* Many teachers are of the opinion that, once they make a referral, they turn the responsibility for problematic issues confronting the child over to protective service professionals. In many cases, however, the child continues to attend the same school and work with the same teacher and classmates while the case is being investigated and resolved. Once teachers have reported their suspicions in a way that is consistent with current interpretations of state law, it is important that they gather information about ways to support the child and to continue to integrate the student into daily classroom practice. School counselors, psychologists, and social workers are good sources of such information. Teachers are encouraged to seek their support.

4. *Following Up.* Referral networks often move slowly, due in part to the fact that child protective service professionals often must interact with the legal system. In addition, many departments of child protective services are grossly understaffed and stretched beyond their capacity. Teachers who become frustrated with delays or with concerns that the system has abandoned a student are urged to pursue follow-up activities. Teachers are advised to avoid making contact with family members about such matters. Rather, information can be clarified and the best interests of the children and their families preserved through telephone contacts, updates, or follow-up contacts with caseworkers or other child protective service professionals to whom initial reports have been made.

Though teachers must be equipped to serve as advocates for all students, there are some actions that are not advised. Teachers who suspect abuse are encouraged *not to*

- Call the parents or caregivers to discuss suspicions.
- Conduct an examination of unexposed areas of the child's body.
- Assert that the report is an emergency unless the danger appears to be immediate.
- Conduct an investigation.
- Wait to see if the situation improves.
- Discuss suspicions with colleagues, friends, or siblings of the child.
- Promise the child that the teacher will not share information that has been revealed.
- Ignore what the child reports about maltreatment and allow others to determine if reports should be made.[50]

Sexual Abuse Prevention and Education Developing meaningful prevention education strategies focused on sexual abuse is particularly challenging for most teachers. Often, educators feel uncomfortable with the topic or might be uninformed about developmentally appropriate approaches to managing instruction and/or questions about sexual matters. Many teachers believe that sexual issues are best managed within the family rather than in the academic environment. Increasingly, however, teachers are being called on to integrate sexual abuse risk reduction activities into classroom practice.

How should teachers teach the topic of sexual abuse to their students? It is important for teachers to examine their own feelings about teaching sexuality education and about reporting suspicions of sexual abuse. Educators must recognize that children who are empowered with information and skills are better equipped to tell an adult that they or a sibling is being sexually abused. Children are not to blame for being victimized and cannot defend themselves against adult perpetrators. They can only tell a concerned grown-up. Following are five main points that children should be taught regarding sexual abuse:

1. Children should be taught about the meaning and implications of having a problem. The word *problem* should be defined, and children should be given the opportunity to share examples of problems they or their friends might be having. Typically, examples include fighting, teasing, homework, and sibling rivalries. Some children might bring up abuse or other problems that occur in their homes. If they do, teachers should thank them for sharing that information with the class and agree that abuse is a problem. The teacher should talk to individual students about any abuse in a one-on-one situation at a later time. Teachers then should ask the students how problems make them feel. Typical responses include "sad," "angry," "confused," and "mad." The next task is to discuss appropriate but specific strategies that will help children solve problems. Teachers should emphasize that children should always tell an adult when they have a problem and reinforce that, when problems are not revealed or managed, they tend to grow or get worse.

2. Children should be taught about the availability of support systems. Teachers should explain the concept and identify the two categories of support systems to which children have access: the community and the family. Because a high percentage of abusers are family members, teachers should emphasize community support systems. Teachers must emphasize that people in support systems can help when a problem exists, and that although other children might be part of a support system, it is best to tell an adult when there is a problem. It is also important for teachers to separate family and community support systems because of the high percentage of abusers who are family members. Students should be encouraged to identify specific adults in their personal support system to whom they can turn.

3. Children should be taught the concept of different touches. Teachers should define three different touches: safe, unsafe, and secret. Safe touches are those that make a person feel good. Teachers should ask students to give examples of some safe touches that make students feel comfortable and supported, including hugging, holding hands, a pat on the back, and giving a "high five."

Unsafe touches are those that make a person feel uncomfortable. Teachers should ask students for examples of unsafe touches, including kicking, hitting, pinching, and tripping. Some students might ask if sexual abuse is an unsafe touch. If this happens, teachers can simply tell students that sexual abuse is another type of touch called a secret touch. It is important that teachers define a secret touch in the following way: "A secret touch occurs when an adult or older person touches your genitals, or 'private body parts' (those covered by your bathing suit), or when they encourage or trick you into touching their genitals, or 'private body parts.'" Some school districts encourage teachers to use correct anatomical terminology for body parts, whereas other districts are more comfortable using the term *private body parts.*

After discussing each type of touch, it is important to ask students how each of these touches would make a person feel. Most students respond that safe touches make them feel happy, and unsafe and secret touches might make them feel weird, confused, or mad. After the three types of touches have been defined and discussed, teachers should continue with a discussion of what to do if someone tries to give them a secret touch. Students should be taught the following rules: Say "no"; get away; and tell someone. It is important for teachers to emphasize that children can and should tell someone, because children might be too afraid to say no, or to get away, or to believe they can tell someone. The concept of support systems can be reinforced when discussing who can or should be told in the event that sexual abuse is occurring.

4. Children should be taught the concept of secrets. Teachers should emphasize that students should never keep a problem about any unsafe or secret touches a secret. It should be stressed that, even if students are afraid to tell, the problem will not go away unless they reveal the problem to a grown-up. Teachers can discuss the concept of secrets that are appropriate to keep, such as a surprise birthday party, versus secrets that are not appropriate to keep, including things that make the child uncomfortable or afraid.

5. Children should be taught the concept of blame or fault associated with sexual abuse. The concept of fault is often very difficult for students to understand. Teachers would be wise to devote adequate time to this topic. Teachers should stress that, as is the case with other forms of maltreatment, any sexual abuse problem is never a child's fault, even if he or she did not follow the rules, say no, get away, and tell someone. Students need to understand that sexual abuse is *always* the fault of the adult. Consequently, children should be supported in not feeling guilty if they have a problem that involves any form of sexual abuse.

In conclusion, the roles for teachers in managing abuse matters in general, and sexual abuse risk reduction in particular, can be challenging. Teachers and all school employees are encouraged to participate in pertinent staff development activities. Only in this way will they be prepared to act as effective advocates and be equipped to organize developmentally appropriate learning activities to meet the needs of the broadest range of learners.

Bullying

Although bullying often is considered to be an inevitable part of growing up, it can be traumatic, depending on variables such as the consistency and severity of the acts, the systems developed to support bullied children, and the internal capacity of a child to manage it. Bullying is defined as aggressive behavior that is carried out repeatedly in a relationship characterized by an imbalance of power.[51] Specifically, three conditions exist that can help teachers identify even the least obvious forms of bullying among students:

- The negative behaviors toward the target student are intentional and usually unprovoked,
- The bullying behaviors are repeated over time, and
- There is some imbalance of power or perceived inequity between the perpetrator and the target.[52]

In addition to these defining criteria, researchers classify bullying into two overarching categories. *Direct bullying* includes overt attacks on the target. These open attacks can take the form of physical bullying (hitting, kicking, pushing, or punching) or verbal bullying (name calling, taunting, threatening, or yelling). The other category, *indirect bullying*, is more difficult to detect as it is characterized by manipulation of peer relationships or friendships with intent. Perpetrators of indirect bullying spread rumors, gossip, and isolate victims from other students.[53]

Concerned advocates must be aware of a growing form of indirect bullying, cyberbullying, the use of communication technology to torment others. Hiding behind the relative anonymity of some form of communication technology, cyberbullys post text messages or images that threaten, spread rumors, and trash reputations, and do so usually without being caught. Because the bullying takes place on a computer screen, the cyberbully can be emboldened to say things that they would never say face to face. Sometimes free from seeing the consequences of their behavior, cyberbullys may lack any feeling of sympathy for the victim or remorse for the act.[54]

Research has confirmed that bullying is particularly common among students in the middle grades, whether carried out by an individual or by a group. As many as 40 percent of students ages 9 to 13 reported that they sometimes or frequently bully others.[55]

There is no question that bullying is a school safety issue. At its core, bullying is an act of violence. Whether it takes the form of physical or verbal aggression, bullying contributes to a hostile school environment and compromises school success among its victims.[56] Most people recognize that bullying is a violation of the safety rights of students, and that unchecked it can generate serious and costly consequences for a school community. Bullying has

Bullying behavior can lead to more serious acts of violence.

been identified as a common thread in school shootings, student suicides, and costly litigation. In addition, visible incidents and ongoing patterns of more covert bullying can compromise the reputation of a school as a safe place conducive to learning.[57]

The manipulation, intimidation, empowerment, and personal satisfaction experienced by many bullies can lead to more serious acts of violence. Many school bullies go on to commit acts of violence as adults. In addition, victims of bullying have been known to retaliate in serious and/or violent ways.[58]

Interestingly, many school communities continue to underestimate the prevalence and consequences of bullying despite a number of highly visible catastrophes associated with bullying and the accompanying outcry from concerned adults. It is not uncommon for educators and community residents to reflect attitudes that enable such violence to continue, including these:

- *Denial.* "We don't have a problem with violence in our community, but that other school district certainly does."
- *Minimization.* "Name-calling, pushing, and shoving are just normal behaviors for kids."
- *Rationalization.* "It is important for all kids to learn to stand up for themselves."

Teacher's Toolbox 10.3

A Coordinated Approach to Preventing and Managing Bullying

Recommendations for professional members of the school community:

- Treat all staff and students fairly and with respect.
- Come to consensus about a definition of bullying.
- Come to consensus about consequences for bullying behaviors.
- Encourage students to come forward when they or someone they know is being bullied. Reinforce that disclosing bullying is a courageous act that helps maintain a safe environment where everyone can learn.
- When bullying is observed, immediately bring it to a stop. Follow the school's policy for management of bullying with consistency.
- Collaborate to improve supervision at times and in locations where bullying is likely to occur (recess, lunch, in the gym, hallway transitions, on buses).[59]

Recommendations for administrators:

- Work on creating a safe and caring school where relationships between and among students and staff are supportive and civil and where an ethic of nonviolent conflict resolution is the norm. Reinforce all adults in the school for modeling civility and respect.
- Create a school-wide code of conduct that describes in concrete terms how students should and should not treat each other.
- Have clear and nonviolent consequences for bullying and other unacceptable behaviors.
- Ensure that students are supervised carefully.[60]

Recommendations for school counselors and other mental health providers:

- Offer direct and indirect support for students who have been the target of bullying.
- Do not have aggressors and victims work together in a mediated counseling context.
- Provide support and referrals for teachers to implement evidence-based bullying prevention strategies in their classrooms.

- When the victim of bullying needs help beyond the scope of school-based providers, refer the student and family to community mental health resources.[61]

Recommendations for school nurses:

- Be on the alert for overt and subtle signs of bullying (patterns of absences, complaints of nonspecific ailments, poorly explained wounds).
- Follow up with students who experience psychosomatic illnesses to determine if bullying or other child abuse might be involved.
- When bullying is suspected, communicate with school staff to ensure that school policies are implemented immediately and with consistency.
- Communicate and collaborate with counselors and teachers to identify and manage bullying before the onset of complex manifestations that could threaten academic success.[62]

Recommendations for school resource officers:

- Communicate to students and staff that any behavior intended to make someone feel unsafe is unacceptable and will not be allowed.
- When bullying occurs, inform the victim, the aggressor, and their parents or caregivers about school policies and consequences for such behavior.
- Intervene with participants in bullying incidents. Make sure to talk with the victim and the aggressor separately.
- Talk with students about what makes them feel unsafe in and around school.[63]

Recommendations for teachers:

- Work with students to develop classroom codes of behavior that communicate respect to all.
- Enforce classroom codes of conduct with consistency.
- Create developmentally and culturally appropriate instructional activities focused on bullying prevention.
- Following a bullying incident, do not use peer mediation or ask the aggressor and the target to meet and talk things out.[64]

- *Justification.* "Our classes are just too big to do something about bullying."
- *Blame.* "Bullying and other forms of violence are the result of single-parent families and mothers who work outside of their homes."
- *Avoidance.* "My job is to teach; managing violence is an administrative responsibility."[65]

What appears to work best in preventing or at least reducing bullying is a comprehensive approach that incorporates the strategies and interventions of many levels and types of participants. All school staff share in

the task of recognizing and intervening in bullying when they see it, implementing a consistent evidence-based plan to prevent school bullying. In this way, adults can participate in coordinated activities to address bullying and improve young people's chances for academic and social growth. Review Teacher's Toolbox 10.3 for specific action steps to be taken by for all stakeholders in the school community.

Administrators, teachers, law enforcement professionals, students, and parents must join together to reduce the incidences and effects of school bullying and its consequences. To this end, all concerned child advocates must take a stand against all forms of school violence, make a commitment to protect all students from emotional and physical injury, and promote school safety as a foundation for reaching the academic mission of the school community. Only in this way can the dignity and worth of all students be validated.[66]

Sexual Harassment: Violence, Not Humor or Attraction

Sexual harassment includes unwelcome sexual advances that affect a student's well-being. It can compromise a student's ability to feel safe and to succeed in school.[67] Specific acts that constitute sexual harassment include jokes, sexual text messages or e-mail comments, graffiti, sexually degrading skits or artistic depictions, bra snapping, pulling pants down, attempted sexual assault, and rape.[68]

Sexual harassment often happens in public and frequently is witnessed by teachers, coaches, or other adults in supervisory positions. Unfortunately, it is common for adults to fail to intervene or to respond with a wink or a nod upon observing acts that constitute sexual harassment. Such reactions communicate to victims, perpetrators, and any students who might have witnessed the behavior that sexual harassment is developmentally predictable, normal, and/or acceptable. In this way, young people are led to think that such behaviors must be equally acceptable in private.[69]

It is important to note that such behaviors, in addition to having unintended educational consequences, are illegal. Emerging from the civil rights movement of the 1960s and the equal employment rights movement of the 1960s and 1970s, federal law as promulgated in Title IX prohibits sexual discrimination and requires schools to provide equal access to all educational opportunities regardless of sex. Thus, schools have a legal responsibility to prevent and manage sexual harassment as one element of ensuring a safe and nurturing learning environment for all students.[70, 71] Though school communities commonly consider sexual harassment a form of bullying, bullying that is "sexual in nature—sexual harassment, in other words—is illegal."[72]

As for all activities that threaten the safety and potential for academic success of students, schools must develop prevention and intervention policies and practices that are consistently applied. Approaches that coordinate all the school's resources and expertise are most effective. Review Chapter 1 for a reminder of the elements of a Coordinated School Health Program.

Cooperation, respect, and conflict resolution skills help students maintain positive peer relationships as well as reduce the risk of violence.

Conflict Resolution Education: A Questionable Approach

All too often, small incidents and minor disagreements between young people escalate into destructive or violent acts. Individuals who have not cultivated the necessary skills to resolve conflicts efficiently and effectively will exchange harsh words, tempers will flare, the conflict will evolve, and violence can result.[73]

In response, schools, churches, and community organizations offer training programs to help young people master a range of self-management and conflict resolution skills. In such programs, individuals practice how to

- Figure out what strategies work best for them to control their anger and how to use them before they lose control.
- Identify adults (parents, teachers, counselors) with whom they can share anger, fears, and concerns.
- Anticipate consequences of potential responses to conflicts.
- Refuse to carry a gun or other weapon and avoid people who carry weapons.
- Avoid or use caution in places or situations in which conflict is common (cafeterias, crowded halls, bathrooms, unsupervised areas outside the school),
- "Reject the bait" for a fight.
- Treat others with respect.
- Weigh options to confront problems and manage conflicts that arise.[74]

Although there is great value in developing a range of self-management and interpersonal skills to resolve conflicts in nonviolent ways, peer-based approaches adopted by many school communities to mediate conflicts are questionable. In such programs, students are selected and trained to mediate conflicts between and among students. Although popular, there is no evidence that conflict resolution or peer mediation is effective, particularly when it is applied to stopping bullying. Further, mediation that requires the target of bullying to confront the tormentor can be frightening for the victim and can cause perpetrators to escalate violent acts off school grounds or out of sight of adult supervisors.[75]

It is important to remember that bullying is a form of victimization, not peer conflict. Rather than communicating that bullying is a problem to be resolved between two individuals, school staff must take the lead in managing all bullying as a critical element of maintaining a safe environment for all students. School staff must be consistent in communicating that bullying must stop and that they will protect any student who is being victimized rather than delegate this responsibility to peers.

Youth Suicide

The transition from childhood to adolescence is a stressful developmental stage for many young people. In addition to dealing with predictable developmental challenges, many young people are confronted with mental health concerns, problematic relationships with adults and peers, and family discord. Educators and researchers have concluded that "growing-up today is an achievement rather than an expectation for many children."[76]

Though the pain experienced by youth is translated into news stories and made-for-TV movies, insufficient attention has been paid to strengthening the ability of significant adults to identify early risks and warning signs of mental heath disorders and potential violence and suicide. In addition, little is known about how to cultivate community foundations that optimize youth development and increase young people's resilience.[77]

Suicide refers to self-chosen behavior to end one's life that might reveal itself as expressed thoughts (ideation), suicidal gestures (attempts of suicide that do not result in death), and suicide (a death accomplished with intent). Most of what is known about youth suicide comes from three sources:

- Psychological autopsies that gather information about the youth from family and friends
- School-based surveys
- Emergency-room reports of treatment for intentional injuries

Most of the existing research about youth suicide was gathered after the suicidal attempt or death occurred. Because suicide attempts that do not require medical attention are unlikely to be reported and a stigma is attached to suicide, it is difficult to get accurate estimates of the scope of the problem among American youth. The problems associated with underreporting are exaggerated because classification of a death as suicide requires others to draw conclusions about the intent of the deceased.[78]

There is no simple answer to why youth commit suicide. Many adults conclude that youth suicide attempts are associated with attention seeking or motivations

for revenge ("You'll be sorry when I'm gone), but the research does not support this conclusion. Rather, evidence suggests that most adolescent suicides are associated with pursuit of escape or a desire to end painful life circumstances.[79]

To reduce and prevent suicide successfully, concerned adults must learn to recognize suicidal youth and refer them to professionals with specific expertise. In addition, parents, teachers, and community resource professionals must develop strategies to maximize protective factors and reduce risks for intentional injuries among youth.[80] In support of such outcomes, a bill signed into law in 2004 (the Garrett Lee Smith Memorial Act) provides federal funds to implement prevention efforts in schools and other educational institutions and in juvenile justice systems, substance abuse and mental health programs, and foster care systems.[81] Specific suggestions to support the work of administrators and teachers in this regard are discussed in Chapter 14.

Recommendations for Concepts and Practice

Healthy Behavior Outcomes

The goal of health education is to help students adopt or maintain health-enhancing behaviors. School districts and teachers should identify the health-enhancing behaviors they would like their students to maintain or adopt. The list below identifies some possible behavioral outcomes related to preventing violence. Although not all of these suggestions are developmentally appropriate for students in grades K–8, the list can help teachers understand how the learning activities they plan for their students support both short- and long-term desired behavior outcomes.

Ways to Promote Healthy Behavior Outcomes by Preventing Violence

- Engage in positive, helpful behaviors.
- Manage interpersonal conflict in nonviolent ways.
- Manage emotional distress in nonviolent ways.
- Avoid bullying, being a bystander to bullying, or being a victim of bullying.
- Avoid engaging in violence, including coercion, exploitation, physical fighting, and rape.
- Avoid situations where violence is likely to occur.
- Avoid associating with others who are involved in or who encourage violence or criminal activity.
- Get help to prevent or stop violence including harassment, abuse, bullying, hazing, fighting, and hate crimes.
- Get help to address inappropriate touching.
- Get help to stop being subjected to violence or physical abuse.
- Get help for self or others who are in danger of hurting themselves.
- Argue persuasively against the use of violence.[82]

Developmentally Appropriate Concepts and Skills

As with other health topics, teaching related to preventing violence should be developmentally appropriate and based on the physical, cognitive, social, emotional, and language characteristics of specific students. Teacher's Toolbox 10.4 contains a list of suggested developmentally appropriate concepts and skills to help you create lessons that will encourage your students to practice the desired behavior outcomes by the time they graduate from high school.[83] Note that these grade level spans are aligned with the 2007 National Health Education Standards discussed in Chapter 3.

STRATEGIES FOR LEARNING AND ASSESSMENT

Preventing Violence

This section provides examples of standards-based learning and assessment strategies for preventing violence. The strategies begin with a restatement of the standard and a reminder of the assessment criteria, drawn from the RMC rubrics in Appendix B. Strategies are written as directions for teachers and include applicable theory of planned behavior constructs in parentheses (intention to act in healthy ways, attitudes toward behavior, subjective norms, perceived behavioral control). These learning and assessment strategies provide building blocks for standards-based lessons and units that can be tailored to local needs. Assessment criteria are used with permission from the Rocky Mountain Center for Health Promotion and Education (RMC). See Appendix B for Scoring Rubrics.

Additional strategies for learning and assessment for Chapter 10, including a complete list of all the strategies, is available at the Online Learning Center.

NHES 1 | Core Concepts

Students will comprehend concepts related to health promotion and disease prevention to enhance health.

ASSESSMENT CRITERIA

- Connections—Describe relationships between behavior and health; draw logical conclusions about connections between behavior and health.
- Comprehensiveness—Thoroughly cover health topic, showing breadth and depth; give accurate information.

Grades K–2

Feelings on Faces: Exploring Children's Picture Books   Learning to recognize and respond to the feelings of others is an important core concept for young children. Teachers can use picture books to talk with children about "reading" what characters are expressing and about recognizing feelings and emotions in facial expressions and body language. Examples of books teachers might use can be found in Chapter 5, where books about moods and other strong feelings are discussed. Other appropriate books are suggested at the end of this chapter. Teachers can help children build their vocabulary of words to describe a wide variety of feelings and emotions and ask students to demonstrate feelings using their own faces. Students can guess the feelings different children are showing. Students might want to follow up by drawing faces depicting different kinds of feelings to display around the classroom. This activity links to NHES 4, interpersonal communication, and NHES 7, self-management, when teachers ask children what they do to handle their feelings in healthy ways.

ASSESSMENT | For an assessment task, students can draw at least two different kinds of feelings or emotions or demonstrate them through their facial expressions and body language. For assessment criteria, students should explain what they look for in facial expressions and body language to recognize these feelings and emotions in others. (Construct: Attitudes toward behavior.)

People Portraits: Celebrating Our Class of Friends   In the videotape *Starting Small: Teaching Tolerance in Preschool and the Early Grades,* a teacher has her children make "people portraits" of themselves to display in the classroom.[84] The children look in hand mirrors to study their features and then choose colors of paper, markers, and yarn (for hair) to make portraits of themselves. The children's portraits can be displayed on a bulletin board as a "class picture." The intent of this activity is to help children recognize those special characteristics of themselves and their classmates that make them who they are. The *Starting Small* videotape has many teaching ideas and is available at no cost to schools from the Southern Poverty Law Center (www.tolerance.org/teach).

ASSESSMENT | The people portraits students create are the assessment task for this activity. For assessment criteria, students should explain what their portraits tell about them and two ways they contribute to the community of learners. (Construct: Attitudes toward behavior.)

Words, Hands, and Feet: Talking with Children About Pro-Social Behavior   Teachers can read Elizabeth Verdick's books *(Hands Are Not for Hitting, Feet Are Not for Kicking, Words Are Not for Hurting)* and Amanda Haan's *I Call My Hand Gentle* with children to discuss behavior at school and at home. See Chapter 5 for information about these two books and "Children's Literature" at the end of this chapter for other children's books about how students treat each other. After reading the books, students should be able to describe ways to use their words, hands, and feet to help others.

ASSESSMENT | For an assessment task, teachers can make a three-column chart that students complete by telling how they can use their words, hands, and feet in healthy ways. For assessment criteria, students should be able to identify at least three healthy ways each to use words, hands, and feet. (Construct: Attitudes toward behavior.)

Grades 3–5

Feeling Angry Is Normal: What We Do About It Can Keep Us Healthy   An important core concept for violence prevention is that anger is a normal human feeling and feeling angry is okay. We must think about our responses to anger to determine whether we remain safe and healthy. Children can list some of the things that make them angry, without using anyone's name. Teachers can record the children's list on the left side of a piece of chart paper and then ask what they or others do when they feel angry. Children will give a range of responses. Children can go back to the list they made earlier in the lesson. For each item on the list, children can name a healthy way people can handle their anger. List these healthy ways of managing anger on the chart. This activity links to NHES 7, self-management. Teachers might also want to read children's books,

Developmentally Appropriate Concepts and Skills for Preventing Violence

Grades K–2 Concepts	Grades 3–5 Concepts	Grades 6–8 Concepts

NHES 1: Core Concepts

Grades K–2 Concepts	Grades 3–5 Concepts	Grades 6–8 Concepts
• Identify "appropriate" and "inappropriate" touches. • State that inappropriate touches should be reported to a trusted adult. • Explain that a child is not at fault if someone touches him or her in an inappropriate way. • State that everyone has a right to tell others not to touch his or her body. • Identify the importance of respecting the personal space and boundaries of others. • Explain what to do if someone is being bullied. • Describe the difference between bullying and teasing. • Explain why it is wrong to tease others.	• Distinguish between "appropriate" and "inappropriate" touch. • Explain that inappropriate touches should be reported to a trusted adult. • Discuss why it is not a child's fault if someone touches him or her in an inappropriate way. • Explain that everyone has a right to tell others not to touch his or her body. • Explain the importance of respecting the personal space and boundaries of others. • Describe appropriate ways to express emotions and feelings. • Examine the importance of being aware of one's own feelings and of being sensitive to the feelings of others. • Explain the importance of talking with trusted adults about feelings. • List healthy ways to express affection, love, friendship, and concern. • List physical and emotional reactions to stressful situations. • List causes and effects of stress. • Identify positive and negative ways of dealing with stress. • Describe what to do if self or someone else is being bullied. • Explain the differences between tattling and reporting aggression, bullying, or violence. • State short- and long-term consequences of violence to perpetrators, victims, and bystanders. • Identify situations that might lead to violence. • Identify strategies to avoid physical fighting and violence. • Identify ways to reduce injuries from firearms. • Define prejudice, discrimination and bias. • Explain that anger is a normal emotion. • Describe nonviolent ways to manage anger. • Give examples of pro-social behaviors (e.g., helping others, being respectful of others, cooperation, consideration). • Identify examples of self-control. • Recognize techniques that are used to coerce or pressure someone to use violence.	• Describe appropriate ways to express and deal with emotions and feelings. • Explain how the expression of emotions or feelings can help or hurt oneself and others. • Summarize the benefits of talking with trusted adults about feelings. • Describe healthy ways to express affection, love, friendship, and concern. • Describe physical and emotional reactions to stressful situations. • Explain causes and effects of stress. • Explain positive and negative ways of dealing with stress. • Describe the similarities between types of violent behaviors (bullying, hazing, fighting, dating violence, sexual assault, family violence, verbal abuse, acquaintance rape). • Explain the role of bystanders in escalating, preventing, or stopping bullying, fighting, and violence. • Describe short- and long-term consequences of violence to perpetrators, victims, and bystanders. • Describe situations that could lead to physical fighting and violence. • Describe strategies to avoid physical fighting and violence. • Describe how the presence of weapons increases the risk of serious violent injuries. • Describe ways to reduce risks of injuries from firearms. • Describe how prejudice, discrimination and bias can lead to violence. • Describe the behavioral and environmental factors associated with the major causes of death in the United States. • Describe the relationship between using alcohol and other drugs and other health risks such as injuries, violence, suicide, sexual risk behaviors, and tobacco use. • Describe ways to manage interpersonal conflict nonviolently. • Explain why it is important to understand the perspectives of others in resolving a conflict situation. • Analyze the risks of impulsive behaviors. • Identify a variety of nonviolent ways to respond when angry or upset. • Describe how mental and emotional health can affect health-related behaviors (e.g., how anger contributes to violence). • Explain how intolerance can affect others. • Describe pro-social behaviors (e.g., helping others, being respectful of others, cooperation, consideration) that help prevent violence. • Describe examples of self-control. • Analyze techniques that are used to coerce or pressure someone to use violence. • Determine the benefits of using nonviolence to solve interpersonal conflict.

Grades K–2 Concepts *(continued)*	Grades 3–5 Concepts *(continued)*	Grades 6–8 Concepts *(continued)*
	• Explain why it is wrong to tease others based on their body type or other personal characteristic. • Describe the benefits of using nonviolent means to solve interpersonal conflict. • List examples of dangerous or risky behaviors that might lead to injuries. • Identify qualities of a healthy relationship. • Explain the importance of telling an adult if someone is in danger of hurting themselves or others. • Identify feelings of depression, sadness, and hopelessness for which someone should seek help.	• Describe examples of dangerous or risky behaviors that might lead to injuries. • Compare and contrast healthy and unhealthy relationships. • Identify models of healthy relationships. • Describe how changing behavior or changing the environment interacts to increase or decrease the likelihood of violence. • Describe how power and control differences in relationships (e.g., peer, dating, or family relationships) can contribute to aggression and violence. • Explain the importance of telling an adult if there are people who are in danger of hurting themselves or others. • Describe the signs and symptoms of people who are in danger of hurting themselves or others. • Describe actions to change unsafe situations at home. • Describe actions to change unsafe situations at school. • Describe actions to change unsafe situations in the community. • Explain the causes, signs, and effects of depression. • Explain that acquaintance rape and sexual assault are illegal. • Recognize techniques that are used to coerce or pressure someone to have sex. • Describe situations that could lead to pressures for sex. • Explain why individuals have the right to refuse sexual contact. • Explain that a person who has been sexually assaulted or raped is not at fault. • Explain that rape and sexual assault should be reported to a trusted adult.

Grades K–2 Skills	Grades 3–5 Skills	Grades 6–8 Skills
NHES 2: Analyze Influence • Identify why making fun of others is harmful to self and others.	• Identify internal influences that could lead to violence (e.g., curiosity, assertiveness, fears). • Identify external influences that could lead to violence. • Explain the differences between fantasy and reality violence in the media. • Explain how peer behaviors can influence future violence (e.g., children who are rejected by their peers are more likely to join gangs later). • Explain why making fun of others is harmful to self and others. • Explain that most young people do not use violence to deal with problems. • Describe the factors that influence a person's decision to use violence to solve interpersonal conflict.	• Describe how personal values and feelings influence choices. • Describe internal influences on behavior that could lead to violence (e.g., curiosity, aggression, and fear). • Describe external influences that could lead to violence. • Examine the presence of violence in the media and its possible effects on violent behavior. • Describe individual, community, and societal factors that contribute to the likelihood of violence. • Explain the risks associated with choosing friends who use violence to solve problems. • Identify media and cultural messages that could lead to different types of violence. • Recognize that most young people do not engage in violent behaviors. • Describe the role of alcohol and other drug use in violence-related situations (e.g., fighting, sexual assault, suicide). • Explain how sexual exploitation can occur via the Internet.

(continued)

Grades K–2 Skills *(continued)* | **Grades 3–5 Skills** *(continued)* | **Grades 6–8 Skills** *(continued)*

NHES 3: Accessing Information, Products, and Services

- Identify how to report unsafe, scary, or hurtful situations in the home or school.
- Identify a trusted adult to tell if inappropriate touching occurs.
- Demonstrate how to dial 9-1-1 or other emergency numbers and provide appropriate information.

- Identify how to report unsafe, scary, or hurtful situations in the home, school, or community.
- Demonstrate how to seek help from a trusted adult if inappropriate touching occurs.
- Identify safe people and places to go to if feeling unsafe or threatened (e.g., police department, fire department, school counselor).
- Identify safe people or adults to report to if people are in danger of hurting themselves or others.
- Identify when a person would benefit from asking for help for an emotional health problem.
- Demonstrate the ability to access important phone numbers to get help in emergencies.
- Demonstrate ways to seek help from trusted adults.

- Describe ways to seek help to report sexual harassment, sexual assault, child abuse, and other types of violence.
- Demonstrate the ability to access accurate sources of information about abuse, violence, or bullying.
- Demonstrate the ability to access existing laws and policies designed to protect young people from being sexually exploited.
- Demonstrate the ability to access safe people and places to go to if feeling unsafe or threatened (e.g., police department, fire department, school counselor).
- Demonstrate the ability to access safe people or adults to report to if people are in danger of hurting themselves or others.
- Describe when a person would benefit from asking for help for an emotional health problem.
- Demonstrate the ability to locate reliable school and community resources to assist with problems related to violence.
- Demonstrate ways to seek help from trusted adults or friends.
- Demonstrate appropriate strategies for avoiding and reporting weapons.
- Identify trusted adults to whom to report suspected plans for school violence.
- Demonstrate the ability to access school and community resources to help with mental and emotional health concerns.

NHES 4: Interpersonal Communication

- Demonstrate verbal and nonverbal ways to refuse inappropriate touch.
- Demonstrate how to report an inappropriate touch to an adult.
- Demonstrate how to express feelings to prevent conflict from starting.
- Explain nonviolent conflict resolution strategies to others.
- Demonstrate what to say when witnessing bullying.

- Demonstrate verbal and nonverbal ways to refuse or report inappropriate touch.
- Demonstrate verbal and nonverbal ways to ask an adult for help about a threatening situation.
- Demonstrate how to express feelings to prevent conflict from starting or escalating.
- Demonstrate a variety of communication skills and peer resistance skills to avoid violent situations.
- Demonstrate simple conflict resolution techniques to diffuse a potentially violent situation.
- Demonstrate what to say and do when witnessing bullying.

- Demonstrate ways to appropriately deal with a conflict with another person that might result in violence.
- Demonstrate verbal and nonverbal ways to ask a parent or other trusted adult for help with a threatening situation.
- Demonstrate verbal and nonverbal ways to refuse pressure to engage in violence.
- Demonstrate verbal and nonverbal communication to avoid potentially violent situations.
- Demonstrate nonviolent conflict resolution strategies.
- Demonstrate effective ways to address bullying.
- Identify verbal and nonverbal communication that constitutes sexual harassment.
- Explain how effective communication skills might decrease the risk of acquaintance or date rape.
- Demonstrate assertiveness skills in dealing with sexually aggressive behavior.
- Demonstrate effective communication skills to express feelings.

NHES 5: Decision Making

- Describe the steps of a decision-making model to avoiding a physical fight or other violent situation.
- Describe the importance of thinking about the effects of one's actions on other people.

- Apply steps of a decision-making model to avoiding a physical fight or other violent situation.
- Explain the positive alternatives to using violence.
- Discuss the importance of thinking about the effects of one's actions on other people.

- Develop and apply a decision-making process for avoiding violence-related situations.
- Discuss the short- and long-term consequences of the decision to choose a violent or nonviolent solution to a problem.
- Evaluate the reasons why some students decide to be bullies.

Grades K–2 Skills (continued)	Grades 3–5 Skills (continued)	Grades 6–8 Skills (continued)
	• Discuss methods for making decisions to avoid conflicts or violence.	• Develop and apply a decision model for responding to witnessing bullying.
	• Demonstrate the steps for determining if a touch is appropriate.	

NHES 6: Goal Setting

• Set a goal to show consideration, respect, and caring for classmates.	• Demonstrate the ability to set goals to prevent and manage stress. • Demonstrate the ability to monitor personal stressors and reactions to stress. • Make a personal commitment to be nonviolent. • Demonstrate the ability to monitor personal behaviors related to avoiding violence. • Make a personal commitment to avoid persons, places, or activities that encourage violence or delinquency.	• Demonstrate the ability to set goals to prevent and manage stress. • Demonstrate the ability to monitor personal stressors and techniques for managing them. • Demonstrate the ability to set goals to prevent and manage difficult relationships. • Make a personal commitment to be nonviolent. • Demonstrate the ability to monitor personal behaviors related to avoiding violence. • Describe how personal goals can be affected by using violence to solve problems. • Make a personal commitment to avoid persons, places, or activities that encourage violence or delinquency.

NHES 7: Self-Management

• Demonstrate the ability to avoid bullying. • Demonstrate how to express feelings in a healthy way.	• Demonstrate techniques to manage stress. • Demonstrate ways to prevent violence and unsafe situations. • Demonstrate the ability to use multiple nonviolent alternatives to conflict (e.g., walking away, negotiation). • Demonstrate how to avoid or prevent bullying. • Express intentions to resolve conflicts nonviolently. • Demonstrate how to express feelings appropriately. • Demonstrate how to use self-control when angry. • Demonstrate strategies to manage loss and grief.	• Demonstrate strategies that could be used to prevent a conflict from starting. • Demonstrate ways to avoid and manage stress. • Demonstrate strategies for avoiding situations and persons with a high risk for violence. • Describe the perspectives of all sides in a conflict situation. • Demonstrate ways of solving conflicts nonviolently (e.g., conflict resolution, diffusion). • Demonstrate how to prevent or stop bullying (as a bystander, perpetrator, or victim). • Accept that refraining from acts of violence is a personal responsibility. • Express intentions to resolve conflicts nonviolently. • Demonstrate strategies for expressing feelings appropriately. • Demonstrate tolerance for individual differences. • Demonstrate the ability to use self-control. • Demonstrate methods for coping with disappointment and loss. • Identify behaviors that are perceived as sexually coercive.

NHES 8: Advocacy

• Demonstrate ways to encourage peers not to bully.	• Advocate for a positive and respectful school environment that prevents or stops bullying. • Object to teasing of peers based on their body type or other personal characteristic. • Stand up for those being bullied. • Demonstrate support and respect for people with differences (e.g., cultural, disabilities, gender, religious). • Demonstrate the ability to influence others' violence-related behaviors. • Educate others about ways to prevent inappropriate touch.	• Advocate for a positive and respectful school environment that prevents or stops bullying and harassment. • Advocate for a violence-free school. • Object to teasing of peers based on their body type or other personal characteristic. • Stand up for those being bullied. • Demonstrate support and respect for people with differences (e.g., cultural, disabilities, gender, and sexual orientation). • Demonstrate how to influence others to report acts of violence to appropriate adults. • Advocate for a positive and respectful school environment that supports pro-social behavior.

Source: Centers for Disease Control and Prevention, *Health Education Curriculum Analysis Tool (HECAT)* (Atlanta, GA: CDC, 2007). www.cdc.gov/HealthyYouth/Hecat/index.htm

such as those suggested at the end of Chapter 5 and this chapter, in which characters experience and express strong negative feelings. Children can discuss the healthy ways the characters managed being angry or upset.

ASSESSMENT | The assessment task for this activity is the students' list of healthy ways to manage anger. For assessment criteria, students should be able to explain why the ways they have selected are healthy and to draw conclusions about connections between behaviors (healthy anger management) and good health. (Construct: Attitudes toward behavior.)

Crime Prevention Scavenger Hunt Teachers can ask students to define the concepts of crime and crime prevention. Students might want to use their dictionaries to check their definitions. Next, students can list crime prevention strategies that people use in their homes, schools, and communities. Children can take their lists home to check with their families. What kinds of strategies do different families use to prevent crime at home? Have students report back to their classmates and work in small groups to create a drawing or model of a safer home, school, or community that integrates crime prevention strategies from their lists and discussions. Teachers and students can learn more about crime prevention from the National Crime Prevention Council and McGruff the Crime Dog (www.ncpc.org). The website includes a toolkit section for educators on preventing crime, including sample lesson plans and activities on respecting differences and calling 9-1-1.

ASSESSMENT | The drawings or models of safe homes, schools, and communities students create are the assessment task for this activity. For assessment criteria, students should provide health-enhancing strategies and draw conclusions about the connections between behaviors (crime prevention strategies) and good health. (Construct: Perceived behavioral control.)

Prevent Child Abuse America Teachers and students can find information on preventing child abuse at www.preventchildabuse.org. Click on "About Us" and then on "Publications/Comics." Students can check out Spider Man comics that depict preventing bullying and contain other information for kids, including hotline numbers, tips for conflict resolution, and advice on what to do when parents drink too much. Teachers might also want to use Lucille Clifton's book *One of the Problems of Everett Anderson,* which tells about a boy who doesn't know what to do when one of his friends comes to school with bruises and scars. Everett tells a trusted adult, his mother, who is able to help him understand how to help his friend. Another book that involves domestic abuse within the family is Stephen Cosgrove's *Squabbles.* See "Children's Literature" at the end of this chapter.

ASSESSMENT | For an assessment task, students can check out Spidey's Tips on Conflict Resolution (www.preventchildabuse.org/learn_more/kids/spidey.html) and work in small groups to discuss and explain each tip. For assessment criteria, students should provide at least two examples of using their tips for conflict resolution and draw conclusions about connections between behaviors and health. (Construct: Attitudes toward behavior.)

Grades 6–8

No Name-Calling Week: No Sticks, No Stones, No Dissing Students and teachers can learn more about No Name-Calling Week at www.nonamecallingweek.org. No Name-Calling Week is an annual week of educational activities aimed at ending name-calling of all kinds and providing schools with the tools and inspiration to launch

an ongoing dialogue about ways to eliminate bullying in their communities. Teachers and students can join the network, plan an event, and learn about resources. This activity links to NHES 8, advocacy. Lesson plans and other resources available at the site include posters, stickers, tips for creating classroom and school policies about bullying, and specific advice for students, parents, and teachers.

ASSESSMENT | For an assessment task, students can work in small groups to investigate one of the topics on the website. For assessment criteria, students should present their topics to the class, explaining how to implement "no name-calling" strategies and drawing conclusions about connections between behavior (no name-calling) and health. (Construct: Subjective norms.)

Targets, Perpetrators, Bystanders, and Problem Solvers This activity is based on a curriculum titled *Victims, Aggressors, and Bystanders,* developed as part of the Teenage Health Teaching Modules.[85] Teachers should begin by describing a conflict situation from literature, the news, or a fictional event. After students have heard the situation, they should try to identify these roles:

- Target: Who was the object of the conflict?
- Perpetrator: Who started, caused, or carried out the conflict?
- Bystander: Was anyone else present who didn't help?
- Problem solver: Who, if anyone, worked to solve the problem?

Students should discuss how the conflict could have been avoided. After students have identified the roles, they can work in small groups to describe true or fictional conflicts they have seen on television or in the movies, heard about, or created. Students should be careful not to use the name of anyone in the school or community. Teachers should encourage students to use the term *target* rather than *victim,* a word that can denote powerlessness. Students can identify the roles of target, perpetrator, bystander, and, if present, problem solver in their scenarios.

ASSESSMENT | Students' role identifications are the assessment task. For assessment criteria, students should explain why they assigned these roles based on behavior, tell how the characters could have avoided the conflict, and draw conclusions about the connections between behavior (avoiding or preventing conflict) and health. (Construct: Perceived behavioral control.)

What Does My School Say About Harassment? Students can investigate the definitions and consequences of harassment of any kind in their school system. In most cases, students can find this information on state or local education websites. A sample policy states,

Harassment means a person acts with intent to harass, bully, annoy or alarm if he or she

1. Strikes, shoves, kicks, or otherwise touches a person in an offensive manner or subjects another person to offensive physical contact;
2. Insults, taunts, or challenges another person in a manner likely to provoke a violent response;
3. Makes verbal or nonverbal expressions related to race, color, national origin, ancestry, sex, religion, disability, or sexual orientation, creating an intimidating, hostile or offensive school environment, or interfering with the education of a student, or otherwise adversely affecting the educational opportunity of a student;
4. Name calls, makes rude gestures, insults, or constantly teases another person who feels humiliated, intimidated, threatened and/or embarrassed;

5. Makes a telephone call without purpose of legitimate communication;
6. Makes repeated communications anonymously, or at extremely inconvenient hours, or in offensively coarse language;
7. Causes fear as to prevent others from gaining legitimate access to or use of school buildings, facilities or grounds such as, but not limited to, restroom facilities;
8. Causes others to feel uncomfortable, pressured, threatened, or in danger as a result of sexually related verbal or physical activity (sexual harassment); or
9. Displays or possesses a "look-alike" gun or weapon.[86]

Students should note in item 4 that harassment occurs if another person "feels humiliated, intimidated, threatened and/or embarrassed." In other words, excuses such as "I was only kidding" or "I wasn't talking to him" provide no protection for perpetrators. Students should examine the anti-harassment policies in their schools and districts carefully to understand how students are protected at school. They can invite an administrator to the classroom to help them understand the policies and the consequences of harassment. One school superintendent stated, "No student should feel threatened at school because of his or her race, color, national origin, ancestry, sex, religion, disability, or sexual orientation—or for any other reasons relating to personal identity or beliefs."[87] Teachers also can refer to the curriculum *Flirting or Hurting?* for more information on preventing or responding to harassment at school.[88] This activity links to NHES 3, access information, products, and services.

ASSESSMENT | For an assessment task, students can define and provide examples of the anti-harassment policy at their school. For assessment criteria, students should provide accurate information and draw conclusions about connections between behaviors (a harassment-free campus) and good health. (Construct: Attitudes toward behavior.)

NHES 2 | Analyze Influences

Students will analyze the influence of family, peers, culture, media, technology, and other factors on health behaviors.

ASSESSMENT CRITERIA
- Identify both external and internal influences on health.
- Explain how external and internal influences interact to impact health choices and behaviors.
- Explain both positive and negative influences, as appropriate.

Grades K–2

The Grouchy Ladybug, Alexander, and Our Own Books of Days   One of the internal influences students deal with is moods and feelings, including that getting-up-on-the-wrong-side-of-the-bed feeling of being grouchy. Eric Carle's *The Grouchy Ladybug* provides an engaging way to discuss the topic. The point of this conversation with small children is to talk about how they feel and what they do when they are having a bit of a bad day. Everyone has those days—how they handle them makes the difference in the way the rest of the day goes. Other books teachers like to use on this topic are Judith Viorst's *Alexander and the Terrible, Horrible, No Good, Very Bad Day* and Stephen Sanzo's *Cranky Pants* (see the books on moods and strong feelings in "Children's Literature" in Chapter 5).

ASSESSMENT | For an assessment task, one student teacher had her first graders make pages for a class book about responding to feelings. For each page, the students wrote a few sentences about feelings they chose ("When I feel happy, I smile and show all my teeth!" "When I feel sad, I talk to my Mom."). The student teacher took color photographs of the students demonstrating their feelings and made a class book for students to read and share with others. For assessment criteria, students should demonstrate health-enhancing responses to feelings. This activity links to NHES 7, self-management. (Construct: Subjective norms.)

What Do Big Kids Do?   Teachers can ask children to think about what their older brothers, sisters, other relatives, friends, and students at school do when they get mad or stressed. Children might think of positive and negative examples of behavior. Invite several older students to talk with younger students about their stress and anger management strategies. Older students can role-play scenarios for younger students. This activity can be especially meaningful for older students, who see themselves as role models for younger children. This activity builds on the idea of positive models as an important influence in students' lives. Students can brainstorm positive and negative responses to stress or anger ("My grandpa says take a deep breath"; "My brother kicked the dog"). Teachers shouldn't express critical opinions of children's families but instead should focus on ways to handle stress and anger that don't hurt anyone. Having older students demonstrate various kinds of healthy anger or stress management strategies and explain why they chose them provides an excellent source of positive models for younger children.

ASSESSMENT | For an assessment task, younger students can describe or write about a healthy anger or stress management strategy that they saw modeled or heard discussed. For assessment criteria, students should explain how the older person they saw or individual influenced their selection. (Construct: Subjective norms.)

Grades 3–5

Personal Relationship Web   Students can draw a circle (about the size of a quarter) in the middle of a page and label the circle "Me." Depending on the age of the students, they should draw from five to ten other circles scattered around the "Me" circle and label these with the initials of the people with whom they have most regular contact (parents or caregivers, siblings, other relatives, classmates, teachers). Students should draw different kinds of lines from their circle to the circles of the other people to indicate the nature of their relationship. For example, a straight line might indicate a peaceful, solid relationship. A curvy line might indicate a relationship with ups and downs. A jagged line might indicate a relationship with conflicts or problems. For each of the relationships they identify, students can write a three-word description and one strategy they can use to maintain or improve the relationship. Students can reexamine their relationship page over time and write about ways their relationships are progressing.

ASSESSMENT | The relationship webs students create are the assessment task for this activity. For assessment criteria, students should explain how these relationships influence their feelings and behaviors and give strategies for maintaining or improving their relationships. (Construct: Perceived behavioral control.)

Television and Movie Conflict Analysis   Students can work in small groups to discuss television programs or movies, including animated features, they have seen that involve various types of conflict situations. Students also can watch a clip from a show or movie in class for discussion. Students should note the precipitating events (what led up to the conflict), the motivation of different characters, and the resolution (what happened). Students should be alert to depictions of alcohol and other drug use in relation to conflict and violence. Students can discuss how they believe these types of media scenarios do and do not influence students. Students also might want to rewrite the endings for some of the situations.

ASSESSMENT | For an assessment task, students can discuss or write about the ways they think television and movie situations influence the behavior of students their age and other ages. For assessment criteria, students should explain at least two ways media could influence behavior and offer more health-enhancing resolutions, if needed. (Constructs: Attitudes toward behavior, subjective norms.)

Celebrate the Beautiful Skin You Live In Teachers can read Michael Tyler's book *The Skin You Live In* to talk with students about friendship, acceptance, and the beauty of diversity. Children will learn that everyone looks different on the outside but people are the same on the inside. Teachers also can talk with children about the damage done by bias, prejudice, fear, and hate directed toward people perceived as different. Other books teachers can read with children to talk about these ideas can be found under "Diversity" in "Children's Literature" in Chapter 5.

ASSESSMENT | For an assessment task, students can design and create a classroom mural to celebrate the diversity of children in their class, school, and community. For assessment criteria, students should explain how friendship, acceptance, and valuing diversity influence the health of their school and community. (Constructs: Attitudes toward behavior, subjective norms.)

Grades 6–8

Socialization Collages Students can work in mixed-sex small groups to find magazine pictures that illustrate the different ways males and females are depicted as they communicate, solve problems, resolve conflicts, dress, and express their sexuality. Students can use the pictures to make a split-image collage of male and female socialization in the United States. Students can show their collages to the class, discuss the media messages, and respond to the media messages they find misleading or false. As students compare media images of what males and females do and how they "are," they likely will find stereotypes they disagree with for both sexes.

ASSESSMENT | The collages students create are the assessment task for this activity. For assessment criteria, students should identify and explain stereotypes they encounter about males and females and respond to the stereotypes with alternative and health-enhancing ways males and females behave and respond to others. In particular, students should be alert for depictions of alcohol use in relation to male and female behavior. (Construct: Subjective norms.)

Courage Continuum This activity is based on a lesson titled "Courage by Degrees" from Nan Stein's *Bullyproof* curriculum.[89] It invites students to think deeply about the varying degrees of courage required to respond to different types of teasing and bullying. To analyze influences, students must scratch beneath the surface of what happens at school to understand those factors—particularly the perceived opinions as well as the responses of peers—that influence students' actions. Teachers can create a list of sentences that describe various teasing and bullying situations at school. (Teachers might need help from students if they have trouble making such a list.) The question to ask about each scenario is how hard would it be (or how much courage would it take) to

- Invite a new kid at school who has been left out all week to play a game at recess?
- Join a girl who is considered somewhat of an outcast at lunch?
- Run away from some mean older kids who yell for you to come there right now?
- Tell a teacher a fight is being planned for recess?

As teachers read each sentence, students should stand along a continuum or line labeled "very hard to do" at one end and "very easy to do" at the other. Students can discuss the factors that influence their choices (popularity, whether public or private, what friends do during the activity). Teachers might want to read Bernard Waber's book *Courage* and Maya Angelou's poem *Life Doesn't Frighten Me* to the class as part of this activity (see the books on courage in "Children's Literature" in Chapter 5).

ASSESSMENT | For an assessment task, students can discuss or write about the situation they thought took the very most and very least courage. For assessment criteria, students should explain at least two factors in each scenario that made it difficult or easy to deal with from their perspective. In particular, students should explain how other students influenced them during the activity. Being influenced by friends is normal, but sometimes students need to make decisions for themselves that differ from those of friends. Students also might want to make their own "Courage" class book. (Construct: Subjective norms.)

Hand Tracings: Acquaintances vs. Friends As students get older, they are better able to analyze how the attributes of acquaintances and friends differ. After a class discussion in which definitions, characterizations, and parameters of these kinds of relationships are discussed, students are asked to trace their left hand on one side of the paper and their right hand on the other side. Fingers on their left hand tracing are to be numbered 1–5, and those on the right numbered 6–10. In each finger of the left hand students are to specify a characteristic of a personal acquaintance relationship (things they do, places they see this person, relationship qualities). In each finger of their right hand they are to list a unique characteristic that distinguishes someone as a friend. Starting in the palm of the hand and extending onto the bottom of each side of the page, students then write a brief poem or song lyric using the identified attributes to clarify the different roles and importance of each type of relationship in our lives.

ASSESSMENT | For an assessment task, students can hang hand tracings around the room after they read their poems/lyrics aloud. For assessment criteria, students must have listed a minimum of ten characteristics and completed their poem/lyrics about both types of relationships. (Construct: Perceived behavioral control).

Multicultural Approaches to Conflict Resolution In some communities, students will have a strong sense of how conflicts are resolved in their cultures. For example, in Hawaiian culture, families practice "ho'oponopono," which means to set or make right, to correct and restore, and to maintain proper relationships among family members. Students can investigate conflict resolution practices in their own or other cultures. Students might find it helpful to interview older members of their families and communities to learn more.

ASSESSMENT | For an assessment task, students can report on the conflict resolution practices they learn about in the cultures they investigate. For assessment criteria, students should explain how these practices influence middle-level students' responses to conflict situations. (Construct: Subjective norms.)

NHES 3 | Access Information, Products, and Services

Students will demonstrate the ability to access valid information and products and services to enhance health.

ASSESSMENT CRITERIA
- Access health information—Locate specific sources of health information, products, or services relevant to enhancing health in a given situation.

- Evaluate information sources—Explain the degree to which identified sources are valid, reliable, and appropriate as a result of evaluating each source.

Grades K–2

Asking for and Getting Help   An important skill for young children across many of the priority content areas is learning how to get help from an adult or from emergency services. Children can role-play various situations in which they need to get help from an adult (someone isn't feeling well on the playground, an odd smell is coming from an electrical appliance) or to call 9-1-1 in an emergency (a fire, someone is hurt). Children should practice these skills so that they will know what to do when unexpected situations arise.

ASSESSMENT   For an assessment task, students can demonstrate how to get help in various situations (school, home, or community situations in which they or others are afraid or uncomfortable or need help). For assessment criteria, students should explain how to contact helpers and tell why these are good choices. (Construct: Perceived behavioral control.)

My Secret Bully: **Getting Help from Supportive Adults**   Trudy Ludwig's book *My Secret Bully* (see "Children's Literature" at the end of this chapter) tells the story of Monica, who is bullied by a friend. This story about relational aggression explains the often hidden problem of emotional bullying within a network of friends. Instead of physical bullying, this story describes bullying that uses relationships, words, and gestures as weapons of attack. Name-calling, humiliation, exclusion, and manipulation are some of the bullying tactics Monica's friend Katie uses. Monica learns how to face her fears and reclaim her power with the help of a supportive adult, her mother, who helps her find ways to deal with Katie without acting like a bully herself. Teachers can read this book with students to talk about the importance of talking with a parent, caregiver, teacher, or other trusted adult when they need help. As contrast, teachers can read *The Recess Queen* by Alexis O'Neill. The main character in this story, Katie Sue, solves the problem by herself, without adult help, by making a friend of "Mean Jean." Students can discuss the similarities and differences between the two stories and tell when they need to get adult help.

ASSESSMENT   For an assessment task, students can describe times when children need help from adults and how they can go about getting it. For assessment criteria, students should identify at least three supportive adults who can help them and tell why they are good sources of help. (Constructs: Intention to act in healthy ways, perceived behavioral control.)

Grades 3–5

Finding Community Helpers for Violence Prevention or Response   Students can use old telephone books to find the names and phone numbers of organizations and agencies that deal with problems related to violence prevention. Students will find some of these phone numbers on the inside cover of the phone book. Students can make a list of community helpers who can help with different kinds of violence prevention problems. Students also can visit the McGruff website (www.ncpc.org) for information on community helpers. Students can click on "Problem Solver" to access information on strangers, staying home alone, and other topics.

ASSESSMENT   For an assessment task, students can make a directory of community helpers for class members and other students. For assessment criteria, students should provide contact information and explain why the helpers are good choices. (Construct: Perceived behavioral control.)

Collecting Data on Safe and Unsafe Places at School   The idea for this activity is based on a lesson in Dr. Nan Stein's *Bullyproof* curriculum called "On the Lookout."[90] In this data collection, students play the role of observers and researchers to look for safe and unsafe places at their school. Students might decide to make mental notes everywhere they go at school, or different students might take responsibility for observing certain areas (cafeteria). Students should write down their observations when they have a chance to do so without being noticed by others—they should not draw attention to themselves as observers. Students should not use real names in their notes but should describe the grade level of the students involved, the incident, and where it occurred. Students should watch for teasing, bullying, conflicts, name-calling, negative written words and drawings, and fighting. Students should collect their data for a certain period of time and then share their reports with the class.

ASSESSMENT   The students' analyses and reports are the assessment task for this activity. For assessment criteria, students should explain how they collected their data (NHES 3) and provide an analysis of who, what, where, when, why, and how for the incidents they observed. Students should make recommendations to their teachers and administrators for improving school safety, based on their findings (NHES 8). (Construct: Perceived behavioral control.)

Grades 6–8

Accessing Information on Preventing Violence   Students can estimate and check the actual data for students' answers to violence-related questions on the Youth Risk Behavior Survey. These data are available online (www.cdc.gov/healthyyouth/yrbs/index.htm). Students can check data for the national high school survey and for state and local surveys. Alternatively, teachers can provide a printout of the data. Students can discuss the statistics and the kinds of violence-related problems some students face. In addition, teachers should be sure to point out that most students make healthy choices and are not involved in violent behaviors.

ASSESSMENT   For an assessment task, students can work in pairs or small groups to research the answers to various violence-prevention Youth Risk Behavior Survey questions. For assessment criteria, students should present their findings, tell where they obtained their information (NHES 3), and explain how learning about what older students do can influence their own behavior choices (NHES 2). (Constructs: Subjective norms, perceived behavioral control.)

Love Doesn't Have to Hurt Teens: Accessing Information from the American Psychological Association   Students can access information on dating violence from the American Psychological Association (APA; www.apa.org/pi/pii/teen/homepage.html). This website is a powerful one for early adolescents, who might know about or even be experiencing dating violence. During these discussions, teachers need to be especially open to the fact that some students might disclose problems to them. Teachers should thank the student for telling them and let the student know that they will help them find help. Teachers can't promise not to tell. If a student is in danger, students should know that the law requires teachers to get help for them.

ASSESSMENT   Students can work in pairs or small groups to research one of the topics on the website and report to the class. For assessment criteria, students should focus their reports on helping classmates identify abusive and dangerous behaviors and getting help. (Constructs: Attitudes toward behavior, perceived behavioral control.)

ASSESSMENT | For assessment criteria, students should report health-enhancing strategies for stopping bullying and demonstrate how to carry them out successfully. (Construct: Perceived behavioral control.)

Enemy Pie Derek Munson's book *Enemy Pie* tells the story of a young boy who was looking forward to a perfect summer until his number one enemy moved into the neighborhood. His father assures him that he will make a pie to take care of enemies, but in the meantime the main character must spend the whole day with his enemy and even be nice to him. Pamela Duncan Edward's book *Gigi and Lulu's Gigantic Fight* tells the story of two friends who have a huge falling out. Teachers can read these and other stories with children to discuss things that come between friends and how friends can resolve their differences. The list of books on family and friends in "Children's Literature" in Chapter 5 includes many books appropriate for this activity.

ASSESSMENT | For an assessment task, students can draw a cartoon story about a real or imagined time when they had a disagreement with a friend and then made up. For assessment criteria, students should show the steps the friends took to work things out to become friends again. (Construct: Perceived behavioral control.)

What to Do When You're Scared and Worried: A Guide for Kids Teachers can read James Crist's book *What to Do When You're Scared and Worried: A Guide for Kids* (see "Children's Literature" in Chapter 5 for this and related titles) to talk about fears and worries and how to manage them. The book provides an example of ten "fear chasers and worry erasers" (self-management strategies) kids can use to feel safer, stronger, and calmer:

- "Get real" about your fears and worries.
- Flip the switch from negative to positive.
- Get your mind off your worries.
- Get active.
- Be aware of what you eat.
- Practice deep breathing and visualization.
- Relax those muscles.
- Write about your feelings.
- Be aware of your "red alerts."
- Tell others what you've learned.

Learning healthy self-management strategies can help students stop bullying and other violence-related behaviors. The authors would add to the list "Talk with trusted adults."

ASSESSMENT | For an assessment task, students can work in pairs or in small groups to investigate and discuss one of the fear chasers and worry erasers and report to classmates. For assessment criteria, students should demonstrate the self-management strategy in health-enhancing ways in at least two situations. (Construct: Perceived behavioral control.)

Grades 6–8

Sticks and Stones Can Break Your Bones, but Words Can Break Your Heart Middle-level students are very familiar with the rumor or gossip mill that goes on around them. Students can talk about the kinds of rumors and gossip that get spread by and about students their age, without mentioning anyone's name. Students can tell how this type of talk makes others feel and how it leads to misunderstandings, hurt feelings, and even fights. Teachers can ask students what they can do to prevent the problems associated with rumors and gossip, even when it's tempting to join in. Students can make a list of strategies for stopping this kind of hurtful talk as soon as they hear it. Students can find out more on the Kids' Health website page "The Scoop on Gossip" (www.kidshealth.org/kid/feeling/friend/gossip.html).

ASSESSMENT | The list of strategies students make for stopping gossip is the assessment task for this activity. For assessment criteria, students should provide three or more concrete examples of using their strategies, including at least one situation in which students should tell an adult what is being said. (Constructs: Attitudes toward behavior, perceived behavioral control.)

Calming a Volatile Situation Teachers can ask students to discuss whether they have either seen or found themselves in situations in which students their age were so angry or upset that they thought there would be a physical fight. Unfortunately, middle-level students do find themselves in or around such situations. What kinds of words and behaviors help in such situations—and what kinds just make things worse? For example, has anyone ever seen students around the edge of a disagreement taunt two angry students to fight? These situations are difficult, and each calls for judgment on the part of those involved and bystanders. Students should talk frankly about how to help and their commitment to helping classmates stay out of violent situations. Students can work in small groups to write a detailed scenario and script of a conflict situation at school or in the community that could lead to a fight. The scenarios should include three or more characters and describe what they do and say. When the scenarios are complete, students can exchange them with other groups. Groups should respond by explaining what each character in the scenario could do to prevent a physical fight. Students also should talk about when adult help is needed and how to get it. The school counselor can be invited to join these discussions on solving problems nonviolently.

ASSESSMENT | For assessment criteria, students should explain how the strategies they propose can work and why the strategies are realistic ones for middle-level students to use. (Construct: Perceived behavioral control.)

Try to See It My Way: Walk a Mile in My Shoes Students might not be familiar with the old songs the title refers to, but they can try out the ideas. Teachers might want to start with an entertaining children's book, such as *The True Story of the Three Little Pigs* by Jon Sciezka (see the books on communication in "Children's Literature" in Chapter 5). In this book, Alexander T. Wolf explains, from his perspective, how he was framed in the incident depicted in the famous children's story. The purpose of this activity is to invite students to realize that there are different perceptions and points of view in any situation, including some that could lead to fighting or violence. Students can practice taking other points of view by assuming the roles of characters in other well-known stories. When students understand the idea of looking at different points of view, they can apply their thinking skills to real-life scenarios that middle-level students face. Students can work in groups of three or more to write a real-life scenario that involves at least three characters. After reading the scenario to the class, each student should assume the role of one of the characters and explain what led up to the situation.

ASSESSMENT | For assessment criteria, students should explain how the characters can use health-enhancing self-management strategies, even when they are under stress or dealing with situations that others don't understand.

NHES 8 | Advocacy

Students will demonstrate the ability to advocate for personal, family, and community health.

ASSESSMENT CRITERIA
- Health-enhancing position—Give clear, health-enhancing position.
- Support for position—Support position with facts, concepts, examples, and evidence.

- Audience awareness—Show awareness of target audience; choose words, tone, and examples to suit audience.
- Conviction—Display conviction for position.

Grades K–2

Celebrating Our School's Rainbow   Children can make banners and posters to celebrate diversity among the students and staff members at their school—the rainbow of cultures, races, and ethnicities that makes up the students' unique school population. The rainbow signifies differences that work together for harmony and beauty.

ASSESSMENT | The banner and posters students create are the assessment task for this activity. For assessment criteria, students should state a clear message targeted to classmates. (Construct: Subjective norms.)

Words of the Day   Students can work on a campaign to put words or phrases of the day into action in their school. Words and phrases include *please, thank you, excuse me, why don't you go first?* and *I'm glad to see you.* Students can publicize their campaign and assess their efforts.

ASSESSMENT | The Word of the Day campaign students plan and carry out is the assessment task for this activity. For assessment criteria, students should state a clear, health-enhancing message and target it to two audiences—students and adults in the school. (Construct: Subjective norms.)

Grades 3–5

Posters for Younger Students   Upper-elementary students can work in groups to make posters for lower-elementary students' classrooms to advocate for healthy problem solving and conflict resolution. Students can visit the younger students' classrooms to present the posters and provide in-person instructional time. Students also might want to display their posters at local businesses and elsewhere in the community.

ASSESSMENT | The poster campaign and presentations students make for younger children are the assessment task for this activity. For assessment criteria, students should state a clear, health-enhancing message, back it up, target their audience, and show strong conviction. (Construct: Subjective norms.)

Who Can Help at Our School?   Students can make a list of the kinds of problems students might have in upper-elementary school and a corresponding list of school helpers and how to contact them. Students should advocate for the position "It's smart to get help when we need it."

ASSESSMENT | The students' presentation to other students of their list of school helpers is the assessment task for this activity. For assessment criteria, students should state a clear, health-enhancing message, back it up, target their audience, and show strong conviction. (Construct: Subjective norms.)

Grades 6–8

Anonymous Cards: What Can We Do to Help Keep Our School Safe?   In Chapter 4, the anonymous cards strategy is discussed as a way to formalize and apply brainstorming to a specific problem or issue. Students are given 3 × 5 cards and asked to label one side "A" and the other side "B." The teacher presents a common prob-

lem that is a challenge to the safety in their school (lack of compliance with playground rules, disagreements between students, etc.) and asks students to identify and rank order three things that they could do to help solve the problem on side "A" and three things that they see students doing to contribute to the problem on side "B" of their card (students should be reminded to not place any identifying marks on the card). Teachers proceed by collecting all cards, shuffling them, and returning them to students (students should be reminded that although they might receive their own card by mistake, they should pretend that the responses that they share were provided by a classmate). As students share responses that appear on the card that they receive, a master list of contributors and helping strategies is generated on the board. The activity is concluded by having each student write a brief letter to the principal that identifies important ways that student behavior contributes to, but could intervene to solve, the identified problem. Finally, after the principal reads the letters, he/she is invited to the classroom to discuss implementation of student-generated advocacy strategies.

ASSESSMENT | The assessment task for this activity is student letters to the principal and the discussion with that school leader. For assessment criteria, the letters must contain a minimum of three contributors and interventions. During the conversation with the principal, the specifics of an action plan for the class should be finalized. (Construct: Perceived behavioral control).

No Name-Calling and No Bullying: Videos for Younger Students   Middle-level students can work in teams to write and videotape healthy problem-solving and conflict resolution scenarios for upper-elementary school students. As part of the scripts, students should show what led to the conflict and the deliberations someone involved might make about how to solve the problem. Students should stop the scripts at different points to allow younger students to decide what to do. Students should videotape different endings for various scenarios. Older and younger students can discuss the scenarios and resolution together, with the guidance of teachers from both classes. Students can use websites such as www.stopbullyingnow.com and www.nonamecallingweek.org to help with their planning.

ASSESSMENT | The videos or presentation students make to younger students are the assessment task for this activity. For assessment criteria, students should state a clear, health-enhancing message, back it up, target their audience, and show strong conviction. (Constructs: Subjective norms, perceived behavioral control.)

Advocacy for Mental Health Services   Students can investigate and create a booklet of resources for mental health and other health services at school and in the community. Students should design their booklet to promote a positive attitude toward getting help when it's needed and to do away with the stigma often associated with needing mental health services. Students might want to include information about problems such as depression—how to recognize it and how to get help. This activity links to NHES 3, access information, products, and services.

ASSESSMENT | The booklet or handout of mental health resources students make is the assessment task for this activity. For assessment criteria, students should state a clear, health-enhancing message, back it up, target their audience, and show strong conviction for the value of mental health services. (Construct: Perceived behavioral control.)

EVALUATED VIOLENCE PREVENTION CURRICULA

Regardless of the implementation of a well-planned and collaborative approach to violence risk reduction, many local school districts have established policies and implemented practices that dictate that specific violence risk reduction content be covered as part of the instructional program in the school district. In all school districts facing competing budget priorities and time limitations, educators must carefully direct their energies and resources, implementing only those policies and programs documented to reduce risks for youth violence.

In this regard, the *Report of the Surgeon General on Youth Violence* has identified selected school-based programs that have been documented to be effective. All of these programs and strategies are defined to focus on primary prevention of youth violence. All are implemented with students of all ages and target the prevention of violence and related risk factors. Several of these evidence-based programs have been developed to target specific risk factors that may emerge among students, whereas others focus on reducing the impact of environmental risk factors. Readers are reminded that tobacco, alcohol, and other drug use among students is a risk factor for violence. Substance use risk reduction is targeted in a number of effective youth violence risk reduction programs. None of the programs discussed here were developed to intervene in specific risks that are identified among a particular group of students.[101]

Model Programs

In general, programs based on skill development are among the most effective general strategies for reducing youth violence and the risks for youth violence. Two programs have been rated as model programs, based on stringent evaluation criteria.

1. *Life Skills Training (LST)* is designed to prevent or reduce the use of gateway drugs. This program targets students in middle schools and has three major components:
   a. Self-management skills
   b. Social skills
   c. Information and skills specifically related to drug use risk reduction

Teachers use a variety of teaching techniques, including instruction, demonstration, feedback, and practice, to support learning in these three core areas. Evaluations have confirmed that the program can reduce tobacco, marijuana, and alcohol use. In addition, the program has produced impressive long-term outcomes.

2. *The Midwestern Prevention Project* targets students in middle schools (grade 6 or 7). The goal of this program is to reduce the risk of gateway drug use associated with the transition from early through middle to late adolescence. Specifically, the program empowers youth to avoid drug use and situations in which drugs are likely to be used. This program has five components implemented sequentially over several years:
   a. Mass media campaign
   b. School program
   c. Parent education and organization
   d. Community organization
   e. Community health policy

The project has demonstrated positive effects on youth violence risk reduction. Reduced rates of tobacco and marijuana use, that carry over through age 23, have been demonstrated. Improved parent–child communication about drug use and the development of programs, activities, and services within communities have been demonstrated as positive program outcomes.[102]

Promising Programs

Two school-based programs that focus on teaching important social skills have yielded promising results.

1. *Promoting Alternative Thinking Strategies (PATHS)* is a curriculum for students in grades K–5. Lessons target emotional competence indicators such as expression, understanding, and regulation, as well as social competence, self-control, and interpersonal problem solving. Evaluation outcomes suggest that participants engage in reduced rates of aggressive behavior and conflict problems. The positive outcomes of this program have been demonstrated for students in both regular and special education learning environments.

2. *I Can Problem Solve* has been used effectively with students in pre-primary learning environments through grade 6. The goal of this program is to train students to use problem-solving skills to find solutions to interpersonal conflicts. This program is most effective with children living in poor and/or urban areas. Positive effects on classroom behavior and problem solving have been maintained for up to four years after participation.[103]

In addition to complete risk reduction programs, several school-based strategies have been demonstrated to have positive, consistent effects on reducing violence, delinquency, and other related risks. Activities such as behavior monitoring, reinforcement of attendance, academic progress and school behavior, and behavioral techniques for classroom management show particular promise in reducing violence. Evaluations of the following strategies have been encouraging:

• *Behavior monitoring and reinforcement.* Studies suggest that enhancing positive student behavior, attendance, and academic achievement through consistent rewards and monitoring can reduce substance use, self-reported criminal activity, and arrests. In addition, improved academic achievement in middle school students has been demonstrated up to five years after the conclusion of the program.

• *Behavioral techniques for classroom management.* Activities that make up part of a general strategy for changing the classroom environment include the establishment of clear rules and directions, the use of praise and approval, behavior modeling, token reinforcement, and self-specification of contingencies. Strategies targeting reductions in negative student behaviors also have been shown to be effective, including ignoring of misbehavior, relaxation methods, soft reprimands, time-outs, and point loss.

- *Seattle Social Development Project, the Bullying Prevention Program, the Good Behavior Game, and the School Transitional Environmental Program (STEP)* are programs that use a classroom-based behavioral management approach to risk reduction.[104]

Several other school-level environmental approaches are effective in reducing youth violence and related out-comes. Strategies that focus on building the capacity of the school to plan, implement, and sustain positive changes can significantly reduce student delinquency. In addition, some classroom approaches have been demonstrated to reduce the risk of academic failure and promote violence risk reduction. Continuous progress is being made in developing programs designed to allow students to pro-ceed through a hierarchy of skills shown to be particularly effective. A robust body of science has confirmed the posi-tive outcomes associated with cooperative learning. Read-ers are encouraged to review the discussion of cooperative learning in Chapter 4.[105] Finally, a list of websites for gov-ernmental agencies responsible for program evaluation can be found in the Internet and Other Resources section at the end of Chapter 2.

INTERNET AND OTHER RESOURCES

Visit the Online Learning Center (www.mhhe.com/telljohann6e) for links to these sites, quizzes and other study aids, and many additional resources.

WEBSITES

American Association of Suicidology (AAS)
www.suicidology.org/index.cfm

American Psychological Association: Love Doesn't Have to Hurt Teens
www.apa.org/pi/cyf/teen.pdf

Association for Supervision and Curriculum Development
www.ascd.org

Center for Substance Abuse Prevention (CSAP): The ABC's of Bullying (an online course)
http://pathwayscourses.samhsa.gov/bully/bully_intro_pg1.htm

Center for the Study and Prevention of Violence
www.colorado.edu/cspv

Child Welfare Information Gateway
www.childwelfare.gov

Cyberbullying
www.cyberbully.org

Family Violence Prevention Fund
www.endabuse.org

Federal Emergency Management Agency
www.fema.gov/kids

Federation of Families for Children's Mental Health
www.ffcmh.org

Kentucky Center for School Safety
www.kysafeschools.org

Kids' Health
www.kidshealth.org

Minnesota Center Against Violence and Abuse
www.mincava.umn.edu

National Association for the Education of Young Children
www.naeyc.org

National Crime Prevention Council
www.ncpc.org

National Data Archive on Child Abuse and Neglect
www.ndacan.cornell.edu/index.html

National Middle School Association
www.nmsa.org

National PTA
www.pta.org

National Youth Violence Prevention Resource Center
www.safeyouth.org

No Name-Calling Week
www.nonamecallingweek.org

Prevent Child Abuse America
www.preventchildabuse.org

SAMHSA's National Mental Health Information Center
www.mentalhealth.org

Take a Stand. Lend a Hand. Stop Bullying Now Campaign
www.stopbullyingnow.hrsa.gov

Teaching Tolerance
www.teachingtolerance.org/teach/

OTHER RESOURCES

BULLYING AND HARASSMENT

Brown, S. L., D. Birch, and V. Kancherla, "Bullying Perspectives: Experiences, Attitudes, and Recommendations of 9–13-Year-Olds Attending Health Education Centers in the U.S." *Journal of School Health* (December 2005): 384–92.

Conn, K. *Bullying and Harassment: A Legal Guide for Educators* (Alexandria, VA: Association for Supervision and Curriculum Development, 2004).

National Middle School Association, Research Summary: Bullying (Columbus, OH: NMSA, 2006).

Prevention Researcher. *Juvenile Bullying* 11, no. 3 (September 2004).

Storey, K., et al. *Eyes on Bullying . . . What Can You Do?* (Newton, MA: Education Development Center, 2008).

CHILD ABUSE AND NEGLECT

Prevention Researcher. *Domestic Violence and Youth* 12, no. 1 (February 2005).

"Sports, Parents, and Violence: What Can Schools Do?" *American School Board Journal* (June 2005): 8–10.

U.S. Department of Health and Human Services. *Child Maltreatment, 2003* (Washington, DC: U.S. Government Printing Office, 2005).

U.S. Department of Health and Human Services. Child Neglect: A Guide for Prevention, Assessment, and Intervention (Washington, DC: Office on Child Abuse and Neglect, 2006).

SAFE SCHOOLS: POLICIES AND PRACTICES

Colgan, C. "Emerging Security Strategies Begin with Collaboration and Motivation." *American School Board Journal* (March 2005): 11–13.

Inlay, L. "Safe Schools for the Roller Coaster Years." *Educational Leadership* (April 2005): 41–43.

National Institute of Mental Health. *Helping Children and Adolescents Cope with Violence and Disasters* (Rockville, MD: NIMH, 2006).

Sallee, M. W. "The Red Lake Tragedy Is a Wake-up Call for America." *American School Board Journal* (May 2005).

Stueve, A., et al. "Rethinking the Bystander Role in School Violence Prevention." *Health Promotion Practice* 7, no. 1 (January 2006): 117–124.

SUICIDE

Center for Mental Health in Schools at UCLA. *A Technical Assistance Sampler on School Interventions to Prevent Youth Suicide* (Los Angeles: Center for Mental Health in Schools at UCLA, 2003).

Evans, D. W., et al. *Treating and Preventing Adolescent Mental Health Disorders* (New York: Oxford University Press, 2005).

National Adolescent Health Information Center. Fact Sheet on Suicide: Adolescents and Young Adults (San Francisco, CA: University of California, San Francisco, 2006).

Prevention Researcher. Teen Suicide Prevention 13, no. 3 (September 2006).

CHILDREN'S LITERATURE

Many relevant books are listed in "Children's Literature" at the end of Chapter 5; see especially the sections "Moods and Strong Feelings," "Communication," "Friends and Family," "Courage," and "Diversity and Uniqueness." Books with violence prevention themes are listed below.

AGES 5–8

Baker, Amy C. *It's OK to Say No.* Grosset & Dunlap, 1986.

Clifton, Lucille. *One of the Problems of Everett Anderson.* Henry Holt, 2001.

Cohn, Janice. *Why Did It Happen?* William Morrow, 1994.

Cosgrove, Stephen. *Squabbles.* Price Stern Sloan, 2003.

Fox, Mem. *Feathers and Fools.* Harcourt Brace, 1989.

Hansen, Diane. *These Are My Private Parts.* Empowerment Productions, 2007.

Henson, Jim. *My Wish for Tomorrow.* Tambourine, 1995.

Ludwig, Trudy. *My Secret Bully.* RiverWood Books, 2004.

O'Neill, Alexis. *The Recess Queen.* Scholastic, 2002.

Petty, Kate, and Charlotte Firmin. *Being Bullied.* Barron's Educational Series, 1991.

Spelman, Cornelia, M. *Your Body Belongs to You.* Albert Whitman, 2000.

Thomas, Shelly Moore. *Somewhere Today: A Book of Peace.* Albert Whitman, 1998.

Woodson, Jacqueline. *Our Gracie Aunt.* Hyperion, 2002.

AGES 8–12

Bunting, Eve. *Your Move.* Harcourt Brace, 1998.

Castelucci, Cecil. *The Plain Janes.* Minx, 2007.

Comen, Carolyn. *What Jamie Saw.* Front Street, 1995.

Cormier, Robert. *We All Fall Down.* Bantam, 1991.

Ewing, Lynne. *Drive-By.* HarperCollins, 1998.

Flinn, Alex. *Breathing Underwater.* HarperCollins Children's Books, 2002.

Foltz, Linda Lee. *Kids Helping Kids Break the Silence of Sexual Abuse.* Lighthouse Point Press, 2003.

Greenberg, Keith Elliot. *Out of the Gang.* Lerner, 1992.

Klass, David. *You Don't Know Me.* HarperCollins, 2002.

McCormick, Patricia. *Cut.* Scholastic, 2000.

Myers, Walter Dean. *Scorpions.* HarperCollins, 1988. (Newbery Medal, American Library Association Notable Children's Book, American Library Association Best Book for Young Adults, American Library Association Recommended Book for Reluctant Readers)

Paulsen, Gary. *The Rifle.* Harcourt Brace, 1995.

Spinelli, Jerry. *Wringer.* HarperCollins, 1995. (Newbery Medal)

Teague, Mark. *Dear Mrs. LaRue: Letters from Obedience School.* Scholastic, 2002.

White, Ruth. *Tadpole.* Farrar, Straus & Giroux, 2003.

Winter, Jeanette. *September Roses.* Farrar, Straus & Giroux, 2004.

ENDNOTES

1. National Research Council, "Summary," in *Understanding and Preventing Violence* (Washington, DC: National Academy Press, 1993), 1–27.

2. M. Forouzesh and D. Waetjen, "Youth Violence," in *Promoting Teen Health* (Thousand Oaks, CA: Sage, 1998), 166–68.

3. U.S. Department of Health and Human Services, *Healthy People 2010: Conference Edition, in Two Volumes* (Washington, D.C.: U.S. Department of Health and Human Services, 2000), 15-5, 15–49.

4. National Adolescent Health Information Center, *Fact Sheet on Violence: Adolescents & Young Adults* (San Francisco, CA: NAHIC, University of California, San Francisco, 2007).

5. Children's Defense Fund, 2007: *Moments in the Lives of America's Children.* (www.childrensdefense.org/site/PageServer?pagename=Why_CDF_ExistsMoments: retrieved 16 February 2008)

6. Centers for Disease Control and Prevention, "Youth Risk Behavior Surveillance—United States, 2007," *MMWR Surveillance Summaries* 57, no. SS-4 (6 June 2008): 6–11.

7. P. S. Corso et al., "Medical Costs and Productivity Losses Due to Interpersonal Violence and Self-Directed Violence," *American Journal of Preventive Medicine* 32, no. 6 (2007): 474–82.

8. Centers for Disease Control and Prevention, 19 April 2007: *Youth Violence: Fact Sheet.* (www.cdc.gov/ncipc/factsheets/yvfacts.htm; retrieved 16 February 2008)

9. U.S. Department of Health and Human Services, *Youth Violence: A Report of the Surgeon General* (Rockville, MD: U.S. Department of Health and Human Services, 2001).

10. Ibid.

11. U.S. Department of Health and Human Services, *Healthy People 2010,* 15-44–15-51.

12. B. D. Perry, "The Neurodevelopmental Impact of Violence in Childhood," in *Textbook of Child and Adolescent Forensic Psychiatry,* eds. D. Schetky and E. Benedek (Washington, DC: American Psychiatric Press, Inc., 2001b), 221–38.

13. CIVITAS, *Right on Course: How Trauma and Maltreatment Impact Children in the Classroom and How You Can Help* (Chicago, IL: CIVITAS, 2002), 13.

14. A. T. Lockwood, *Preventing Violence in Our Schools* (Madison: Wisconsin Center for Educational Research, 1993), 1–12.

15. R. S. Lorion and W. Saltzman, "Children Exposed to Community Violence: Following a Path from Concern to Research Action," *Psychiatry* 56, no. 1 (1993): 55–65.

16. D. Prothrow-Stith and S. Quaday, *Hidden Casualties: The Relationship Between Violence and Learning* (Washington, DC: National Consortium for African American Children, Inc., and the National Health Education Consortium, 1996).
17. CIVITAS, *Right on Course*, 23.
18. C. Remboldt, "Making Violence Unacceptable," *Educational Leadership* (September 1998): 32–38.
19. Centers for Disease Control and Prevention, *Youth Violence: Fact Sheet*.
20. Ibid.
21. Ibid.
22. U.S. Department of Health and Human Services, *Youth Violence*.
23. Ibid.
24. Kann, L., S. Telljohann, and S. Wooley, "Health Education: Results from the School Health Policies and Programs Study 2006," *Journal of School Health* 77, no. 8 (2007): 431.
25. U.S. Department of Health and Human Services, *Youth Violence*.
26. Ibid.
27. L. Dusenbury et al., "Nine Critical Elements of Promising Violence Prevention Programs," *Journal of School Health* 67, no. 10 (December 1997): 409–14.
28. Ibid.
29. U.S. General Accounting Office, *School Safety: Promising Initiatives for Addressing School Violence* (Washington, DC: U.S. General Accounting Office, 1995).
30. Ibid.
31. U.S. Department of Health and Human Services, *School Health Guidelines to Prevent Unintentional Injuries and Violence* (Atlanta, GA: Centers for Disease Control and Prevention, 7 December 2001), 13–46.
32. CIVITAS, *Right on Course*, 6.
33. Ibid., 9.
34. Ibid., 6–7.
35. Ibid., 9.
36. Ibid., 13–14.
... *Course*, 59.

51. Bul'ying," *American Journal of Health Behavior* 26, no. 4 (2002): 266.
52. D. Olweus, "Bully/victim Problems Among School Children: Basic Facts and Effects of a School-based Intervention Program," in *The Development and Treatment of Aggression*. eds. D. Pepler and K Rubin (Hillsdale, NJ: Erlbaum, 1991).
53. D. Olweus, *Bullying at School*.
54. C. Giannetti and M. Sagarese, "The Newest Breed of Bully: The Cyberbully," *PTA Our Children Magazine*. (www.pta.or/pr_magazine_article_details_1117639656218.html: retrieved 28 August 2007)
55 National Association of Health Education Centers, *Kids Health Kids Poll*. (www.nahec.org/KidsPoll/)
55. National School Safety Center, *Understanding, Preventing, and Responding to School Bullying* (Westlake Village, CA: National School Safety Center, December 2001): 5–6.
57. Ibid.
58. Ibid.
59. American School Health Association, "All Members of the School Community: Who Does What?" *Health in Action: Bullying in the School Community: Everyone Has a Role to Play in Preventing Bullying* 3, no. 4 (May/June 2005): 12.
60. M. J. Elias and D. I. Neft, "Administrators: Who Does What?" *Health in Action: Bullying in the School Community: Everyone Has a Role to Play in Preventing Bullying* 3, no. 4 (May/June 2005): 12.
61. T. Feinberg, "School Counselors and Other Mental Health Providers: Who Does What?" *Health in Action: Bullying in the School Community: Everyone Has a Role to Play in Preventing Bullying* 3, no. 4 (May/June 2005): 12–13.
62. A. Cebulski, J. Vessey, and W. F. Connell, "School Nurses: Who Does What?" *Health in Action: Bullying in the School Community: Everyone Has a Role to Play in Preventing Bullying* 3, no. 4 (May/June 2005): 13.
63. L. Piculell, "School Resource Officers: Who Does What?" *Health in Action: Bullying in the School Community: Everyone Has a Role to Play in Preventing Bullying* 3, no. 4 (May/June 2005): 13.

76. A. Doucette, "Youth Suicide," in *About Children: An Authoritative Resource on the State of Childhood Today* (Elk Grove Village, IL: American Academy of Pediatrics, 2005), 146–49.
77. Ibid.
78. Ibid.
79. C. M. Kienhorst et al., "The Adolescents' Image of Their Suicide Attempt," *Journal of the American Academy of Child and Adolescent Psychiatry* 34, no. 5 (1995): 623–28.
80. A. Doucette, "Youth Suicide."
81. Center for Health and Health Care in Schools, *President Signs Youth Suicide Prevention Law*. (www.healthinschools.org/2004/oct26_alert.asp)
82. Centers for Disease Control and Prevention, *Health Education Curriculum Assessment Tool* (Atlanta, GA: CDC, pending).
83. Ibid.
84. Teaching Tolerance, *Starting Small: Teaching Tolerance in Preschool and the Early Grades* (Montgomery, AL: Southern Poverty Law Center, 1997).
85. R. G. Slaby, R. Wilson-Brewer, and K. Dash, *Aggressors, Victims, and Bystanders: Thinking and Acting to Prevent Violence* (Newton, MA: Education Development Center, 1994), 28–29.
86. P. Hamamoto, "Letter to Editor Clarifies DOE's Rule on Harassment," *Honolulu Advertiser*, 13 June 2001.
87. Ibid.
88. N. D. Stein and L. Sjostrom, Flirting or Hurting: *A Teacher's Guide on Sexual Harassment in Schools, Grades 6–12* (Wellesley, MA: Wellesley College Center for Research on Women, 1994).
89. N. Stein, E. Gaberman, and L. Sjostrom, *Bullyproof: A Teacher's Guide on Teasing and Bullying for Use with Fourth and Fifth Grade Students* (Wellesley, MA: Wellesley College Center for Research on Women, 1996).
90. Ibid.
91. Teaching Tolerance, *Starting Small*.
92. A. W. Coffee, J. Coffee, and J. N. Elizalde, *Peace Signs: A Manual for Teaching School Children Anger Management and Communication Skills* (Honolulu: CoffeePress, 2000).
93. N. Stein and D. Cappello, *Gender Violence, Gender Justice* (Wellesley, MA: Wellesley College Center for Research on Women, 1999).
... Tolerance, *Starting Small*.
... Mullin-Rindler, N. ...

GUIDELINES FOR SCHOOLS CONCERNING PREVENTING VIOLENCE

It is clear that the kinds of violence to which children and youth are exposed are varied and involve girls and boys as both perpetrators and victims. Acts of aggression and violence range from bullying and verbal abuse to physical intimidation and assault and include acts of rape and other forms of sexual violence, homicide, and suicide. Though it must be noted that violence is relatively rare at the school site, weapon possession, gang activity, shootings, and other serious acts of youth violence have captured the attention

Research has increased our understanding of factors that make some youth more vulnerable to victimization and others to perpetration of violence. Although risk factors are not direct causes of youth violence, they fac-... the likelihood that a young person will become violent.[19] Protective factors include variables demonstrated to buffer youth from risks of becoming violent, but protective factors have not been studied as extensively or rigorously as risk factors. Much less is known about protective than risk factors associated with youth violence.[20] Readers are encouraged to review available information about risk and protective factors for youth violence identified by the Centers for Disease Control and Prevention that can be found in Consider This 10.1.[21]

Examination of these lists of risk and protective factors will reinforce that it is the interaction among personal characteristics, other... ...tions that...

Regardless of age, it is rare that risk factors for violence operate in isolation. The more risk factors to which youth are exposed, the more likely it is that they will become violent. It is important to note, however, that no single risk factor or combination of factors can predict youth violence with complete accuracy. The majority of youth exposed to single or even multiple risk factors will not behave violently. Although no indicator is absolute, there is strong evidence that selected risk factors can point to the likelihood of youth violence. Attention to these risks can enable advocates to identify vulnerable young people. In this way, targets for intervention efforts can be applied in the most effective ways.[23]

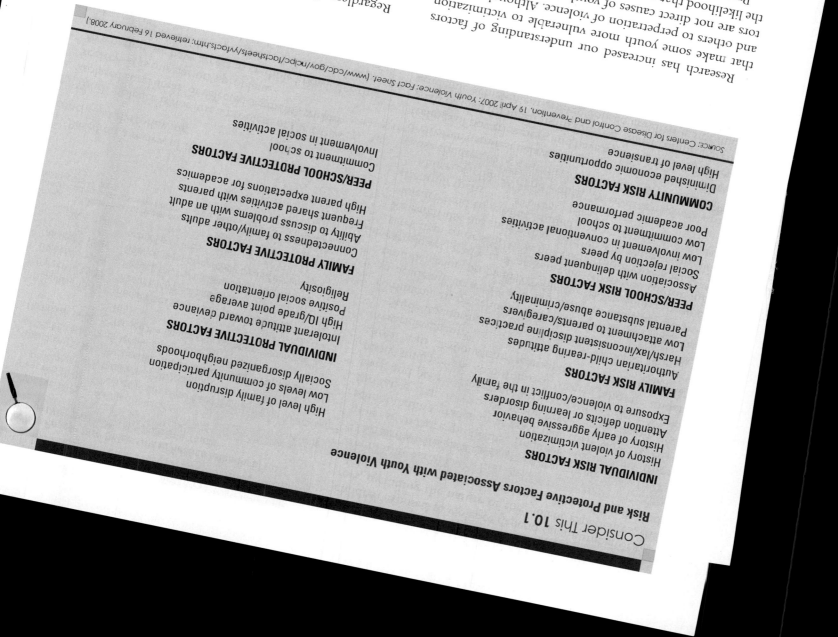

Consider This 10.1
Risk and Protective Factors Associated with Youth Violence

INDIVIDUAL RISK FACTORS
History of violent victimization
Attention deficits or learning disorders
Exposure to violence/conflict in the family

FAMILY RISK FACTORS
Authoritarian child-rearing attitudes
Harsh/lax/inconsistent discipline practices
Low attachment to parents/caregivers
Parental substance abuse/criminality

PEER/SCHOOL RISK FACTORS
Association with delinquent peers
Social rejection by peers
Low involvement in conventional activities
Poor academic performance
Low commitment to school

COMMUNITY RISK FACTORS
Diminished economic opportunities
High level of transience
High level of family disruption
Low levels of community participation
Socially disorganized neighborhoods

INDIVIDUAL PROTECTIVE FACTORS
Intolerant attitude toward deviance
High IQ/grade point average
Positive social orientation
Religiosity

FAMILY PROTECTIVE FACTORS
Connectedness to family/other adults
Ability to discuss problems with an adult
Frequent shared activities with parents
High parent expectations for academics

PEER/SCHOOL PROTECTIVE FACTORS
Commitment to school
Involvement in social activities

SOURCE: Centers for Disease Control and Prevention, 19 April 2007. Youth Violence: Fact Sheet. (www.cdc/gov/ncipc/factsheets/yvfacts.htm: retrieved 16 February 2008.)

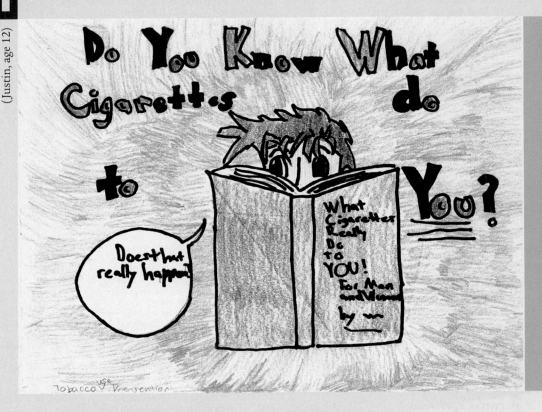

(Justin, age 12)

Promoting a Tobacco-Free Lifestyle

DESIRED LEARNER OUTCOMES

After reading this chapter, you will be able to . . .

- Describe the prevalence and cost of tobacco use among youth.

- Explain the relationship between tobacco use and compromised academic performance.

- Identify factors that influence youth tobacco use.

- Summarize current guidelines and practices for schools and teachers related to tobacco use prevention.

- Summarize developmentally appropriate tobacco prevention concepts and skills for K–8 students in the context of the National Health Education Standards and target healthy behavior outcomes.

- Demonstrate developmentally appropriate learning strategies and assessment techniques that incorporate concepts and skills that have been shown to reduce tobacco risks among youth.

- Identify effective, evaluated commercial tobacco use prevention curricula.

- Identify websites and children's literature that can be used in cross-curricular instructional activities promoting tobacco use prevention.

Research has increased our understanding of factors that make some youth more vulnerable to victimization and others to perpetration of violence. Although risk factors are not direct causes of youth violence, they increase the likelihood that a young person will become violent.[19] Protective factors include variables demonstrated to buffer youth from risks of becoming violent, but protective factors have not been studied as extensively or rigorously as risk factors. Much less is known about protective than risk factors associated with youth violence.[20] Readers are encouraged to review available information about risk and protective factors for youth violence identified by the Centers for Disease Control and Prevention that can be found in Consider This 10.1.[21]

Examination of these lists of risk and protective factors will reinforce that it is the interaction among personal characteristics, other people, and environmental conditions that is important. The *Report of the Surgeon General on Youth Violence* confirmed that the developmental stages of childhood and adolescence are very influential for the development of risk and/or protective factors for violence. As children grow from infancy to adulthood, some risk factors become more influential while others become less so. For example, substance use among perpetrators is a greater risk factor for violence to children age 9 than to those age 14.[22]

It is clear that the kinds of violence to which children and youth are exposed are varied and involve girls and boys as both perpetrators and victims. Acts of aggression and violence range from bullying and verbal abuse to physical intimidation and assault and include acts of rape and other forms of sexual violence, homicide, and suicide. Though it must be noted that violence is relatively rare at the school site, weapon possession, gang activity, shootings, and other serious acts of youth violence have captured the attention

GUIDELINES FOR SCHOOLS CONCERNING PREVENTING VIOLENCE

Regardless of age, it is rare that risk factors for violence operate in isolation. The more risk factors to which youth are exposed, the more likely it is that they will become violent. It is important to note, however, that no single risk factor or combination of factors can predict violence with complete accuracy. The majority of youth exposed to single or even multiple risk factors will not behave violently. Although no indicator is absolute, there is strong evidence that selected risk factors can point to the likelihood of youth violence. Attention to these risks can enable advocates to identify vulnerable young people. In this way, targets for intervention efforts can be identified and limited resources can be applied in the most effective ways.[23]

Consider This 10.1

Risk and Protective Factors Associated with Youth Violence

INDIVIDUAL RISK FACTORS
History of violent victimization
History of early aggressive behavior
Attention deficits or learning disorders
Exposure to violence/conflict in the family

FAMILY RISK FACTORS
Authoritarian child-rearing attitudes
Harsh/lax/inconsistent discipline practices
Low attachment to parents/caregivers
Parental substance abuse/criminality

PEER/SCHOOL RISK FACTORS
Association with delinquent peers
Social rejection by peers
Low involvement in conventional activities
Low commitment to school
Poor academic performance

COMMUNITY RISK FACTORS
Diminished economic opportunities
High level of transience
High level of family disruption
Low levels of community participation
Socially disorganized neighborhoods

INDIVIDUAL PROTECTIVE FACTORS
Intolerant attitude toward deviance
High IQ/grade point average
Positive social orientation
Religiosity

FAMILY PROTECTIVE FACTORS
Connectedness to family/other adults
Ability to discuss problems with an adult
Frequent shared activities with parents
High parent expectations for academics

PEER/SCHOOL PROTECTIVE FACTORS
Commitment to school
Involvement in social activities

Source: Centers for Disease Control and Prevention, 19 April 2007: *Youth Violence: Fact Sheet.* (www.cdc/gov/ncipc/factsheets/yvfacts.htm; retrieved 16 February 2003.)

Based on a review of the scientific literature, the *Report* concluded the following:

- Youth violence is not just a problem of the cities, isolated rural areas, or selected segments within society—it is our nation's problem.
- As a nation, we have access to credible knowledge that has been translated into programs documented to be effective at preventing youth violence.
- Intervention strategies exist that can be tailored to meet the needs of youth at every stage of development, from early childhood to late adolescence.[10]

To this end, *Healthy People 2010* has specified several national health promotion objectives targeting violence and abuse prevention for school-age children and youth (Table 10-2).[11] These objectives demonstrate the range and complexity of intentional injury risks to which children and youth in the United States are exposed. Although none of these objectives can be fully met by the isolated efforts of families, schools, or communities, this chapter contains suggestions for school administrators and classroom teachers working with children in elementary and middle schools.

Intentional Injury Risks as a Threat to Academic Performance

Of particular interest to educators is the growing body of literature confirming that exposure to violence and the risk for intentional injuries threatens academic success. Research has confirmed that exposure to violence activates a set of threat responses in the brain, and excess activation of the parts of the brain involved in responding to threatening circumstances can alter the developing brain of a child. These alterations can produce changes in the emotional, behavioral, and cognitive functioning of children forced to adapt to threats associated with violent experiences. Teachers must note that the specific changes in brain development and the ability to function among children exposed to violence depend on a number of factors, including the nature of the violent experiences, the child's response to the threat, and a host of family and community variables.[12]

Students who have experienced trauma are likely to exhibit attendance problems, frequent suspensions from school, failing grades in at least half their subjects, performance that is two or more grade levels below age level, and poor performance on standardized tests. While many students are compromised, others who are under threat can demonstrate temporary or subject-specific overachievement.[13]

Students normally survive violence in their homes, communities, or schools, but they tend to lose interest in academic activities and are likely to manifest persistent behavior problems. Typically, these young people earn lower grades and have higher truancy and dropout rates than those who have not been exposed to violence.[14] Research also has shown that children who witness chronic violence tend to exhibit limited concentration and short attention spans.[15]

Abuse of children and youth by adult caregivers can cause children to be cautious and withdrawn. Abused children often manifest delayed language development, express feelings of powerlessness, and have a general inability to set goals or plan for meaningful futures.[16] Most compromised academic achievement among abused children is not due to general problems with intellectual development. Rather, academic problems among abused students are likely to be related to the difficulty these children have in forming bonds with peers and teachers or to a common difficulty engaging in classroom learning activities.[17]

Factors That Influence Violence

Risk factors for intentional injuries are evident in every area of the lives of students. These risk factors include internal attributes of the child and external variables within the family, school, social networks, and community. Some experts believe that violent images are so common in the media that children have become desensitized to their intense and devastating effects. Other experts suggest that violence can be linked to the complex social and economic changes that affect families and communities. They attribute youth violence to the actions of overworked and financially strapped parents who vent their frustrations at home. When frequent yelling or other aggressive or abusive acts become common in the home, children receive the message that such behaviors are acceptable or even necessary. Children who have not developed skills to control their impulses and behaviors might grow accustomed to using violence as a way to resolve conflicts or gain desired possessions. Students who have not learned that nonviolence is a better—or even possible—option view violence as an expedient and effective way to gain respect when confronted with frustrating circumstances.[18]

TABLE 10-2   HEALTHY PEOPLE

Healthy People 2010 Objectives to Reduce Intentional Injuries (Violence and Abuse) Among Youth

Objective 15-32	Reduce homicides.
Objective 15-33	Reduce maltreatment and maltreatment fatalities of children.
Objective 15-34	Reduce the rate of physical assault by current or former intimate partners.
Objective 15-35	Reduce the annual rate of rape or attempted rape.
Objective 15-36	Reduce sexual assault other than rape.
Objective 15-37	Reduce physical assaults.
Objective 15-38	Reduce physical fighting among adolescents.
Objective 15-39	Reduce weapon carrying by adolescents on school property.

SOURCE: U.S. Department of Health and Human Services, *Healthy People 2010: Understanding and Improving Health*, 2nd ed. (Washington, DC: U.S. Government Printing Office, 2000).

of the national media and concerned citizens. The result has been a call for schools to assume a large share of the responsibility for developing and implementing violence prevention policies and programs.

State of the Practice

Recognizing that any act of violence, particularly one that occurs at school, is unconditionally unacceptable, educators have done their best to develop and implement effective violence prevention programming. The result of these efforts has been the emergence of policies, security strategies, and instructional activities as diverse as the school communities in which they have been implemented. Table 10-3 provides information from the School Health Policies and Programs Study (SHPPS) 2006 on the range of violence prevention topics and skills being addressed in the nation's elementary and middle schools.[24] The SHPPS 2006 data are encouraging but demonstrate the need for increased and more consistent school-based efforts to promote violence risk reduction across the school community.

In addition to taking instructional approaches to violence prevention identified in SHPPS 2006, many school communities have invested considerable time and money in broader policies and programs that have not been demonstrated to produce the desired outcomes. Many of these well-intentioned but ineffective practices persist because powerful stakeholders believe that "doing something is better than doing nothing." Research confirms that this often is not the case.

Although popular in many communities, peer counseling, peer mediation, and peer leader programs targeting all students have been demonstrated to be ineffective as primary prevention strategies. Administrators and other school leaders should note that no scientific evidence indicates that these activities produce violence risk reduction. Such activities are an unwise use of limited resources, but they are not likely to harm younger students; however, findings show that they do have the potential to harm high school students.

Some communities have applied a curious strategy in an attempt to reduce youth violence; specifically, some local boards of education have adopted a universal policy of restricting promotion to succeeding grades for violent students. Studies of this approach reveal very negative effects on achievement, attendance, behavior, and attitudes toward school.[25]

The most widely implemented youth drug prevention program in the United States, Drug Abuse Resistance Education (DARE), has been extended in some communities to include violence prevention elements. Based on the conventional approach taken to implement DARE in grades 5 and 6, there is little evidence of its effectiveness in either substance use or violence risk reduction. Researchers suggest that the program's lack of effectiveness might be related to its lack of skill development. In addition, it is developmentally and culturally inappropriate to confront students with drug and violence situations that they have not encountered as part of daily living in their neighborhood or community.[26] Interestingly, despite such findings, DARE remains popular in many school communities. Readers can examine the evidence-based recommendations for violence risk reduction in this chapter, as well as review Chapter 12 for

---

TABLE 10-3   **SHPPS**

School Health Policies and Programs Study 2006 Data Related to Preventing Violence and Suicide

	Percent of Schools Teaching Topic/Skill in a Required Class	
	Elementary Schools	Middle and Junior High Schools
Topics		
Anger management	76.3	65.9
Bullying	81.4	67.4
Dating violence	N/A	48.7
Gun safety	28.8	19.1
Personal safety (dealing with strangers)	74.2	N/A
Pro-social behaviors	84.0	67.2
Recognizing signs and symptoms of people who are in danger of hurting themselves	34.5	47.2
Sexual assault and rape	N/A	43.4
Skills		
Techniques to avoid conflicts and fights	83.3	67.1
What to do if someone is thinking about hurting him/herself	35.7	50.1
What to do if someone is thinking about hurting others	53.9	52.0

Source: Centers for Disease Control and Prevention, School Health Policies and Programs Study 2006 (SHPPS) (Atlanta, GA: CDC, 2007), www.cdc.gov/HealthyYouth/shpps

sound approaches to promoting an alcohol- and drug-free lifestyle.

State of the Art

In light of the need to use finite resources in the most productive and evidence-based ways, an important body of literature has emerged that confirms that attributes of school-based policies, programs, and practices with no or low potential to prevent violence. Although common in many school communities, the following activities should be avoided as they have been demonstrated to have very little potential to reduce youth violence. In addition, research has confirmed that some of these practices might actually increase the likelihood of aggression or violent acting-out behaviors among youth.[27]

1. *Using scare-tactic approaches based on pictures or videos depicting violent scenes or consequences.* There is a large body of research confirming that people who watch violence in the media are more likely than their counterparts to behave violently.

2. *Adding a violence prevention agenda to a school district that is overwhelmed with other activities.* It is important for schools to have an organizational structure and a climate that support violence prevention. Too often, school administrators try to add violence prevention programming to a school community that has not established intentional injury risk reduction as a priority. Although common, this practice can increase the burden on teachers, increase stress, and ultimately backfire for students, parents, and education professionals.

3. *Segregating aggressive or antisocial students into separate groups.* Integrating delinquent youth into a positive, non-delinquent peer group can have a positive effect. There is compelling evidence that efforts to separate or create groups composed exclusively of aggressive young people do not contribute to a reduction in problem behaviors. In fact, such a practice actually might contribute to an increase in criminal behaviors.

4. *Implementing brief instructional programs that are not reinforced by school climate variables.* Even instructional programs of sufficient duration to be educationally sound cannot sustain outcomes in a climate that is not supportive. More comprehensive approaches to prevention and intervention have proven to result in better outcomes.

5. *Focusing instructional programming exclusively on self-esteem enhancement.* Narrowly focused self-esteem programs have been determined to be largely ineffective. It is important to note that many gang-affiliated youth have a very highly developed sense of self-esteem. Those programs in which self-esteem enhancement is contextual to a broader agenda that promotes personal and social competency are more likely to produce desired outcomes.

6. *Focusing instructional programs only on knowledge acquisition.* Intentional injury programs focused on disseminating information, like those that have been evaluated in other health-risk content areas, do not succeed. Such programs

do not teach functional knowledge or enable students to practice essential skills to avoid and manage conflicts.[28]

Characteristics of Programs That Show Promise for Preventing Violence

An extensive review of school-based violence prevention programs conducted by the U.S. General Accounting Office has revealed common characteristics associated with the most promising interventions.[29] Educators, community leaders, and concerned parents are encouraged to review the following foundational elements of promising intentional injury risk reduction programs.

1. *Comprehensive approach.* Research shows that the most successful programs are undergirded by the recognition that youth violence evolves from a complex set of variables. Like the Coordinated School Health Program (see Chapter 1), promising interventions tend to address multiple problem areas and link a variety of services, both in the school and in the community.

2. *Early start and long-term commitment.* Learning strategies and prevention activities are organized in an instructional scope and sequence designed to help young students learn accurate information, examine attitudes, and practice important skills. Sustained programming targeting older students reinforces the earlier program of studies.

3. *Strong leadership and disciplinary policies.* To ensure program quality, principals and other school leaders collaborate with others to sustain funding and hire qualified staff. In addition, student disciplinary policies are reviewed and updated regularly, are made clear to all stakeholders, and are applied in a consistent manner.

4. *Staff development.* An ongoing program of staff development helps prepare administrators, teachers, and staff to manage disruptive students, mediate conflicts, and integrate evidence-based prevention activities into daily routines.

5. *Parental involvement.* In more successful programs, schools work to increase parental involvement by offering parent education activities, making home visits, and engaging parents or caregivers as tutors or volunteers.

6. *Culturally sensitive and developmentally appropriate materials and activities.* The most effective program materials and activities are developed to be compatible with students' cultural values, language, and experiences with leadership and role models. In addition, all school community intentional injury risk reduction activities and materials must be developmentally appropriate for all grades of participating students.[30]

Teacher's Toolbox 10.1 offers guidelines to prepare school and community advocates to prevent and/or manage a range of risks for youth violence. These recommendations are excerpted from the CDC's *School Health Guidelines to Prevent Unintentional Injuries and Violence.* These recommendations and strategies clarify the elements of a comprehensive approach to preventing and intervening in youth violence.[31]

16. D. Prothrow-Stith and S. Quaday, *Hidden Casualties: The Relationship Between Violence and Learning* (Washington, DC: National Consortium for African American Children, Inc., and the National Health Education Consortium, 1996).
17. CIVITAS, *Right on Course*, 23.
18. C. Remboldt, "Making Violence Unacceptable," *Educational Leadership* (September 1998): 32–38.
19. Centers for Disease Control and Prevention, *Youth Violence: Fact Sheet.*
20. Ibid.
21. Ibid.
22. U.S. Department of Health and Human Services, *Youth Violence.*
23. Ibid.
24. Kann, L., S. Telljohann, and S. Wooley, "Health Education: Results from the School Health Policies and Programs Study 2006," *Journal of School Health* 77, no. 8 (2007): 431.
25. U.S. Department of Health and Human Services, *Youth Violence.*
26. Ibid.
27. L. Dusenbury et al., "Nine Critical Elements of Promising Violence Prevention Programs," *Journal of School Health* 67, no. 10 (December 1997): 409–14.
28. Ibid.
29. U.S. General Accounting Office, *School Safety: Promising Initiatives for Addressing School Violence* (Washington, DC: U.S. General Accounting Office, 1995).
30. Ibid.
31. U.S. Department of Health and Human Services, *School Health Guidelines to Prevent Unintentional Injuries and Violence* (Atlanta, GA: Centers for Disease Control and Prevention, 7 December 2001), 13–46.
32. CIVITAS, *Right on Course*, 6.
33. Ibid., 9.
34. Ibid., 6–7.
35. Ibid., 9.
36. Ibid., 13–14.
37. CIVITAS, *Right on Course*, 59.
38. U.S. Departments of Education and Justice, *Indicators of School Crime and Safety: 2006.* (http://nces.ed.gov/programs/crimeindicators/crimeindicators2006/; retrieved 16 February 2008)
39. Ibid.
40. Vossekuil, B. et al., *The Final Report and Findings of the Safe School Initiative: Implications for the Prevention of School Attacks in the United States* (Washington, DC: U.S. Department of Education and U.S. Secret Service, National Threat Assessment Center, 2002).
41. U.S. Department of Education, *Public School Practices for Violence Prevention and Reduction: 2003–2004 NCES 2007-010* (Jessup, MD: ED Pubs, September 2007).
42. CIVITAS, *The Effects of Child Abuse are Painful.* (www.civitas.org/abuse.html; retrieved 17 February 2008)
43. CIVITAS, *Right on Course*, 26.
44. Ibid., 29.
45. Ibid., 25, 28.
46. Ibid., 26.
47. Ibid., 31, 33, 37, 39, 43.
48. Ibid., 90.
49. Ibid., 91.
50. Ibid., 93.
51. M. S. Stockdale et al., "Rural Elementary Students', Parents', and Teachers' Perceptions of Bullying," *American Journal of Health Behavior* 26, no. 4 (2002): 266.
52. D. Olweus, "Bully/victim Problems Among School Children: Basic Facts and Effects of a School-based Intervention Program," in *The Development and Treatment of Aggression*, eds. D. Pepler and K Rubin (Hillsdale, NJ: Erlbaum, 1991).
53. D. Olweus, *Bullying at School.*
54. C. Giannetti and M. Sagarese, "The Newest Breed of Bully: The Cyberbully," *PTA Our Children Magazine.* (www.pta.or/pr_magazine_article_details_1117639656218.html: retrieved 28 August 2007)
55. National Association of Health Education Centers, *Kids Health Kids Poll.* (www.nahec.org/KidsPoll/)
56. National School Safety Center, *Understanding, Preventing, and Responding to School Bullying* (Westlake Village, CA: National School Safety Center, December 2001): 5–6.
57. Ibid.
58. Ibid.
59. American School Health Association, "All Members of the School Community: Who Does What?" *Health in Action: Bullying in the School Community: Everyone Has a Role to Play in Preventing Bullying* 3, no. 4 (May/June 2005): 12.
60. M. J. Elias and D. I. Neft, "Administrators: Who Does What?" *Health in Action: Bullying in the School Community: Everyone Has a Role to Play in Preventing Bullying* 3, no. 4 (May/June 2005): 12.
61. T. Feinberg, "School Counselors and Other Mental Health Providers: Who Does What?" *Health in Action: Bullying in the School Community: Everyone Has a Role to Play in Preventing Bullying* 3, no. 4 (May/June 2005): 12–13.
62. A. Cebulski, J. Vessey, and W. F. Connell, "School Nurses: Who Does What?" *Health in Action: Bullying in the School Community: Everyone Has a Role to Play in Preventing Bullying* 3, no. 4 (May/June 2005): 13.
63. L. Piculell, "School Resource Officers: Who Does What?" *Health in Action: Bullying in the School Community: Everyone Has a Role to Play in Preventing Bullying* 3, no. 4 (May/June 2005): 13.
64. American School Health Association, "All Members of the School Community," 13.
65. C. Remboldt, "Making Violence Unacceptable."
66. Ibid.
67. C. Blaber, "Sexual Harassment in Schools," *Health in Action: Bullying in the School Community: Everyone Has a Role to Play in Preventing Bullying* 3, no. 4 (May/June 2005).
68. N. Stein, "Bullying or Sexual Harassment? The Missing Discourse of Rights in an Era of Zero Tolerance," *Arizona Law Review* 45, no. 783 (2003): 783–99.
69. Ibid.
70. Ibid.
71. C. Blaber, "Sexual Harassment in Schools."
72. N. Stein, *Harvard Education Letter* (January/February 2000).
73. National Youth Violence Prevention Resource Center, *Conflict Resolution.* (www.safeyouth.org/scripts/teens/conflict.asp)
74. W. Schwartz, *How to Help Your Child Avoid Violent Conflicts* (ERIC Clearinghouse on Urban Education).
75. C. Blaber and L. F. Hergert, "Flash Points," *Health in Action: Bullying in the School Community: Everyone Has a Role to Play in Preventing Bullying* 3, no. 4 (May/June 2005).
76. A. Doucette, "Youth Suicide," in *About Children: An Authoritative Resource on the State of Childhood Today* (Elk Grove Village, IL: American Academy of Pediatrics, 2005), 146–49.
77. Ibid.
78. Ibid.
79. C. M. Kienhorst et al., "The Adolescents' Image of Their Suicide Attempt," *Journal of the American Academy of Child and Adolescent Psychiatry* 34, no. 5 (1995): 623–28.
80. A. Doucette, "Youth Suicide."
81. Center for Health and Health Care in Schools, *President Signs Youth Suicide Prevention Law.* (www.healthinschools.org/2004/oct26_alert.asp)
82. Centers for Disease Control and Prevention, *Health Education Curriculum Assessment Tool* (Atlanta, GA: CDC, pending).
83. Ibid.
84. Teaching Tolerance, *Starting Small: Teaching Tolerance in Preschool and the Early Grades* (Montgomery, AL: Southern Poverty Law Center, 1997).
85. R. G. Slaby, R. Wilson-Brewer, and K. Dash, *Aggressors, Victims, and Bystanders: Thinking and Acting to Prevent Violence* (Newton, MA: Education Development Center, 1994), 28–29.
86. P. Hamamoto, "Letter to Editor Clarifies DOE's Rule on Harassment," *Honolulu Advertiser*, 13 June 2001.
87. Ibid.
88. N. D. Stein and L. Sjostrom, Flirting or Hurting: *A Teacher's Guide on Sexual Harassment in Schools, Grades 6–12* (Wellesley. MA: Wellesley College Center for Research on Women, 1994).
89. N. Stein, E. Gaberman, and L. Sjostrom, *Bullyproof: A Teacher's Guide on Teasing and Bullying for Use with Fourth and Fifth Grade Students* (Wellesley, MA: Wellesley College Center for Research on Women, 1996).
90. Ibid.
91. Teaching Tolerance, *Starting Small.*
92. A. W. Coffee, J. Coffee, and J. N. Elizalde, *Peace Signs: A Manual for Teaching School Children Anger Management and Communication Skills* (Honolulu: CoffeePress, 2000).
93. N. Stein and D. Cappello, *Gender Violence, Gender Justice* (Wellesley, MA: Wellesley College Center for Research on Women, 1999).
94. Teaching Tolerance, *Starting Small.*
95. M. Froschl, B. Spring, N. Mullin-Rindler, N. Stein, and N. Gropper, *Quit It! A Teacher's Guide on Teasing and Bullying for Use with Students in Grades K–3* (Wellesley, MA: Wellesley College Center for Research on Women, 2002).
96. T. Jackson, conversation with author, November 2004.
97. D. Catrow, *We the Kids: The Preamble to the Constitution of the United States* (New York: Dial Books for Young Readers, 2002).
98. M. Bang, *When Sophie Gets Angry—Really, Really Angry* (New York: Blue Sky Press, 1999).
99. M. Froschl et al., *Quit It!*
100. A. O'Neill and L. Luliska-Beith, *The Recess Queen Angry* (New York: Scholastic, 2002).
101. U.S. Department of Health and Human Services, *Youth Violence.*
102. Ibid.
103. Ibid.
104. Ibid.
105. Ibid.

11

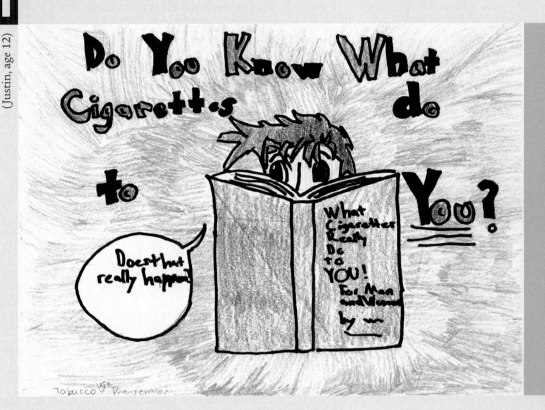

Promoting a Tobacco-Free Lifestyle

DESIRED LEARNER OUTCOMES

After reading this chapter, you will be able to . . .

- Describe the prevalence and cost of tobacco use among youth.

- Explain the relationship between tobacco use and compromised academic performance.

- Identify factors that influence youth tobacco use.

- Summarize current guidelines and practices for schools and teachers related to tobacco use prevention.

- Summarize developmentally appropriate tobacco prevention concepts and skills for K–8 students in the context of the National Health Education Standards and target healthy behavior outcomes.

- Demonstrate developmentally appropriate learning strategies and assessment techniques that incorporate concepts and skills that have been shown to reduce tobacco risks among youth.

- Identify effective, evaluated commercial tobacco use prevention curricula.

- Identify websites and children's literature that can be used in cross-curricular instructional activities promoting tobacco use prevention.

INTRODUCTION

Tobacco use is an issue that young people will frequently face; many will be tempted to try tobacco products as they advance through late elementary and middle school. Teachers can help students avoid tobacco products and ultimately prevent premature death. This section introduces teachers to the number of young people who use tobacco, how much tobacco costs society, the relationship between tobacco use and performance, and the factors that influence tobacco use.

Prevalence and Cost

Cigarette smoking and/or use of other tobacco products is the single most preventable cause of death in the United States today. One in every five deaths in the United States is tobacco-related. Each year, more than 440,000 people die of smoking-related illnesses (Figure 11–1).[1]

There is a definite need for tobacco use prevention programs in today's elementary and middle schools—nine out of ten adult smokers began smoking at or before the age of 18 (Figure 11–2).[2] Each day in the United States, 4,000 youth between ages 12 and 17 try their first cigarette, and approximately 1,140 youth become regular smokers.[3] In 2006, there were 769,421 youth who became regular smokers, and it is predicted that 246,215 will die prematurely from their addiction.[4] Unless current trends are reversed, more than 5 million children who are alive today will eventually die from smoking-related diseases.[5] Even with all of the negative information about the health consequences of tobacco use documented through research, the number of adolescents who smoke is too high. Currently, 14.3 percent of ninth-grade students, 19.6 percent of tenth-grade students, 21.6 percent of eleventh-grade students, and 26.5 percent of twelfth-grade students are smokers (Table 11–1).[6] Total current cigarette use among middle school students (grades 6–8) is 10.1 percent with 10.2 percent of males and 10.0 percent of females reported as being current smokers.[7]

Besides loss of life, there are economic costs related to smoking. Each pack of cigarettes sold in the United States costs the nation an estimated $7.18 in medical care and lost productivity, or about $3,702 per adult smoker per year.[8,9] Estimates indicate that smoking caused over $167 billion in annual health-related economic losses from 1997 to 2001, including $75 billion in direct medical costs, and $92 billion in lost productivity.[10]

Because of the prevalence of diseases related to tobacco use in the United States, the 2010 national health objectives encourage schools to provide a Comprehensive Health Education Program to prevent tobacco use; several of the *Healthy People 2010* objectives are tobacco-related (Table 11–2).

Tobacco Use and Academic Performance

The few research studies that have been conducted in the area of tobacco use and academic performance all show similar results. Preadolescents and adolescents who smoke

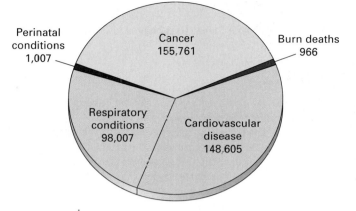

FIGURE 11–1 | **Annual Deaths Among Smokers Attributable to Smoking-Related Diseases**

Source: Centers for Disease Control and Prevention. "Annual Smoking-Attributable Mortality, Years of Potential Life Lost, and Economic Costs." *Morbidity and Mortality Weekly Report* 51, no. 14 (2002): 300–303.

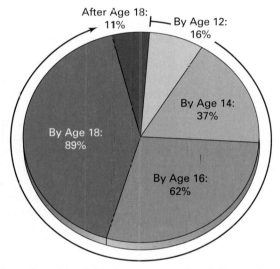

Age of smoking initiation among adult daily smokers: cumulative percent who began smoking by age 18

FIGURE 11–2 | **Tobacco Use Begins Early** Note that only 11 percent of adults who are daily smokers began smoking after age 18.

Source: Centers for Disease Control and Prevention (www.cdc.gov/tobacco). Institute of Medicine, *Growing Up Tobacco Free* (Washington, DC: National Academy Press, 1994).

tend to perform less well academically than their non-smoking peers. For example, a study in Canada found that 28 percent of middle school students who smoked said they were doing poorly in school compared to only 6 percent of nonsmoking students.[11] A longitudinal study, conducted with eighth-grade students found that high school failure was directly predicted by earlier tobacco use.[12] A study with high school seniors found that those with a low grade-point average were more likely to smoke cigarettes.[13] Another study, conducted with fourth- to seventh-grade students, found that students reporting school difficulties were 1.4 to 5.6 times more likely to report a history of tobacco use than were students who did not report school difficulties.[14] Most recently, a study examining Mississippi

TABLE 11–1

Youth Risk Behavior Survey Data Related to Tobacco Use, 2007

Risk Behavior	Percent Reporting Behavior		
	Total	Females	Males
Smoked a whole cigarette for the first time before age 13	14.2	11.9	16.4
Ever tried cigarette smoking, even one or two puffs	50.3	48.8	51.8
Ever smoked one or more cigarettes every day for thirty days	12.4	11.8	13.0
Smoked cigarettes on more than one of the past thirty days	20.0	18.7	21.3
Used chewing tobacco, snuff, or dip on more than one of the past thirty days	8.0	2.2	13.6
Smoked cigars, cigarillos, or little cigars on at least one of the past thirty days	13.6	7.6	19.4
Smoked cigarettes or cigars or used chewing tobacco, snuff, or dip on more than one of the past thirty days	25.7	21.0	30.3
Students less than 18 years of age who were current smokers and purchased cigarettes at a store or gas station during the past thirty days	16.0	11.3	20

SOURCE: Centers for Disease Control and Prevention, "Youth Risk Behavior Surveillance—United States, 2007," *Morbidity and Mortality Weekly Report* 57, no. SS-4 (6 June 2008): 1–131.

TABLE 11–2

Healthy People 2010 Objectives Related to Tobacco Use Among Children and Adolescents

Objective 7-2	Increase the proportion of middle, junior high, and senior high schools that provide school health education to prevent health problems in the area of tobacco use and addiction.
Objective 27-1	Increase the average age of first use of tobacco products by adolescents and young adults.
Objective 27-2	Reduce tobacco use by adolescents.
Objective 27-3	Reduce the initiation of tobacco use among children and adolescents.
Objective 27-7	Increase tobacco use cessation attempts by adolescent smokers.
Objective 27-9	Reduce the proportion of children who are regularly exposed to tobacco smoke at home.
Objective 27-1?	Increase smoke-free and tobacco-free environments in schools, including all school facilities, property, vehicles, and school events.
Objective 27-14	Reduce the illegal sales rate to minors through enforcement of laws prohibiting the sale of tobacco products to minors.
Objective 27-16	Eliminate tobacco advertising and promotions that influence adolescents and young adults.
Objective 27-17	Increase adolescents' disapproval of smoking.
Objective 27-18	Increase the number of tribes, territories, and states and the District of Columbia with comprehensive, evidence-based tobacco control programs.

SOURCE: U.S. Department of Health and Human Services, *Healthy People 2010: Understanding and Improving Health,* 2nd ed. (Washington, DC: U.S. Government Printing Office, 2000).

high school students found that frequent smoking was identified as a significant factor associated with low academic performance.[15] These studies determine only that there is a relationship between tobacco use and poor academic performance. They do not determine whether students started using tobacco and then their academic performance declined *or* students' academic performance declined and then they started to use tobacco—or whether in some cases some third factor influenced both behaviors. Regardless, the relationship exists, and the results of these studies should motivate school administrators and teachers to include tobacco use prevention in their health education curriculum.

Factors That Influence Tobacco Use

Several factors differentiate those who use tobacco from those who do not. The factors associated with reduced potential for tobacco use are protective factors and those associated with greater potential for tobacco use are risk factors. A summary of the most common protective and risk factors for tobacco use is given in the following lists.[16-18]

Protective Factors

• *Parent and family connectedness.* Adolescents who experience a high degree of closeness, caring, and satisfaction with parents are less likely to use tobacco. Another protective factor for adolescents is feeling understood, loved, wanted and paid attention to by family members.

• *Parental/adolescent activities.* Adolescents who participate in activities with their parents on a consistent basis are less likely to use tobacco products.

• *Parental academic expectations.* Adolescents whose parents expect them to graduate from high school or college are less likely to use tobacco products.

• *Behavioral and social skills.* Adolescents who can demonstrate and use effective refusal and stress management skills are less likely to use tobacco.

Risk Factors

- *Household access to tobacco.* Adolescents who live in households where there is easy access to tobacco are more likely to begin to use tobacco products than are adolescents who do not have easy access.
- *Family suicide or attempt of suicide.* Adolescents with a family member who has completed or attempted suicide in the past twelve months are at risk for tobacco use.
- *Low socioeconomic status.* Low socioeconomic adolescents are at increased risk for the initiation of tobacco use.
- *Tobacco availability.* When tobacco is easily accessible, adolescents are more likely to use tobacco. Unfortunately, most adolescents can easily access tobacco products. Even though it is illegal to sell cigarettes to anyone younger than 18, 48.5 percent of students under the age of 18 who purchased or attempted to purchase cigarettes in a store or gas station in the preceding thirty days were not asked to show proof of age.[19] About 15 percent of high school smokers usually buy their cigarettes directly from a store.[20] However, it is clear that enforcement of youth access laws can reduce tobacco sales to minors. For example, when California and Massachusetts started enforcing their youth access laws, they saw a substantial reduction in illegal cigarettes sales to minors. Although every state forbids retail sales of cigarettes to minors, most states do not proactively enforce these laws.[21]
- *Tobacco acceptability.* There is an increased risk of tobacco use among adolescents with a perception of acceptance among family, peers, and the community. Acceptability is influenced by the tobacco industry through advertising and other promotional activities. The tobacco industry currently spends over $13.4 billion a year, or over $36 million a day, to advertise cigarettes.[22] Cigarette companies increased their spending on point-of-sale marketing by almost $19 million between 2004 and 2005. Tobacco companies claim they do not target their advertising toward youth, but the evidence does not support their claim. The cigarette and spit-tobacco companies continue to advertise at retail outlets near schools and playgrounds.[23] In a recent study, Wellman and colleagues found that exposure to tobacco marketing, including advertising, promotions, and cigarette samples, and to pro-tobacco depictions in films, television, and videos more than doubles the odds that children under 18 will become tobacco users. They also found that pro-tobacco marketing and media depictions lead children who already smoke to increase their progression to heavier use by 42 percent.[24]
- *Parental smoking.* Most research has shown a relationship between parental and adolescent smoking. Adolescents with one or both parents who smoke are more likely to also smoke. This relationship seems stronger for females than for males, and for whites than for African Americans, Hispanics, or Asians.
- *Sibling smoking.* A synthesis of most research shows that adolescents who have an older sibling who smokes were more likely to also smoke.

- *Peer smoking.* Almost all studies have shown a strong relationship between adolescent smoking and having friends who smoke. In a review of sixteen prospective studies, peer smoking was predictive of some phase of smoking in all but one study.
- *Perceived norms.* Perceived norms, defined as people's perceptions of others' beliefs and behaviors, often can be inaccurate. It has been found that when adolescents believe most of their peers smoke or overestimate the percentage of their peers who smoke, they are more likely to begin and continue to smoke.
- *Academic achievement.* As discussed in the previous section, a positive relationship has been found between low academic achievement and the onset of smoking among adolescents.
- *Risk taking, rebelliousness, and deviant behavior.* Several studies have found that when adolescents are considered to be risk takers, rebellious, or likely to participate in deviant behaviors (unconventional or antisocial behaviors) they are more likely to use tobacco.
- *Behavioral and social skills.* Adolescents who do not have effective refusal and stress management skills are more likely to use tobacco.
- *Self-esteem.* Most studies show that students with lower self-esteem are more likely to smoke than are adolescents with higher self-esteem.
- *Body image concerns.* Girls who are concerned about weight and weight gain are at increased risk to initiate tobacco use.

GUIDELINES FOR SCHOOLS

This section provides information about current tobacco prevention programs and policies for elementary and middle schools. The first part of this section includes data about the actual programs and policies in use in schools today. The second part provides information for teachers and administrators about what should be happening in schools to help children and adolescents stay tobacco free.

State of the Practice

The Centers for Disease Control and Prevention (CDC) periodically conducts the School Health Policies and Programs Study (SHPPS) to assess current school health policies and programs at the state, district, school, and classroom levels.[25] Because tobacco use contributes to the most preventable causes of death in the country today, it is important for states and school districts to have policies that reflect zero tolerance for tobacco use. Unfortunately, the results of SHPPS 2006 found that only 38 percent of states, 55.4 percent of school districts, and 63.6 percent of schools have a "tobacco-free policy," that is, a policy that prohibits tobacco use by students, faculty, staff, and visitors in school buildings, on school grounds, on school buses, or at off-campus school-sponsored events.[26]

States and school districts are doing a better job in the area of tobacco prevention programs. As many as

TABLE 11–3

School Health Policies and Programs Study 2006 Data Related to Tobacco Use Prevention

Tobacco-Use Prevention Topic	% of All Elementary Schools	% of All Middle Schools
Addictive effects of nicotine in tobacco products	63.8	79.5
Benefits of not smoking cigarettes	75.9	80.5
Benefits of not smoking cigars	32.6	49.1
Benefits of not using smokeless tobacco	48.9	74
Health effects of environmental tobacco smoke or secondhand smoke	67.6	77.9
How many young people use tobacco	36.3	66.8
How students can influence or support others in efforts to quit using tobacco	58	72.5
How students can influence or support others to prevent tobacco use	65.7	76.6
How to avoid environmental tobacco smoke or secondhand smoke	60	74.2
How to find valid information or services related to tobacco use prevention or cessation	32.4	64.1
Importance of quitting tobacco use	66.9	78.3
Influence of families on tobacco use	59.9	75.3
Influence of the media on tobacco use	52.3	74.9
Long-term health consequences of cigarette smoking	73.9	80.3
Long-term health consequences of cigar smoking	32.6	48
Long-term health consequences of using smokeless tobacco	46.3	74.3
Making a personal commitment not to use tobacco	71.5	72
Resisting peer pressure to use tobacco	73.4	78
Risks of using other tobacco and tobacco-like products (eg., pipes, kreteks, or bidis)	25.5	53.3
Short-term health consequences of cigarette smoking	68.8	78.5
Short-term health consequences of cigar smoking	31.4	49.7
Short-term health consequences of using smokeless tobacco	46.3	73.1
Social or cultural influences on tobacco use	52.9	73.4

SOURCE: Centers for Disease Control and Prevention, *School Health Policies and Programs Study 2006 (SHPPS)* (Atlanta, GA: CDC, 2007). www.cdc.gov/HealthyYouth/shpps

72.5 percent of states, 81.1 percent of school districts, and 75.8 percent of schools require tobacco use prevention education at the elementary level. Elementary teachers who were required to teach tobacco prevention spent a median of 1.9 hours a year teaching the topic. There is a slight increase at the middle school level. Currently, 70.6 percent of states, 87.7 percent of school districts, and 84 percent of schools teach tobacco use prevention at the middle school level. Middle school teachers who were required to teach tobacco prevention spent a median of 3.5 hours a year teaching the topic.[27] SHPPS also provides important data related to the tobacco prevention topics and skills being taught at elementary and middle schools; Table 11–3 summarizes the findings. The topic taught most often by elementary and middle school teachers was the benefits of not smoking cigarettes.[28]

State of the Art

Even more important than the state of the practice in tobacco prevention, however, is for elementary and middle school teachers to understand what should be included in a successful schoolwide tobacco prevention program. The Centers for Disease Control and Prevention examined all the current research about successful smoking prevention programs and developed seven recommendations for school health programs to prevent tobacco use and addiction:[29]

1. Develop and enforce a school policy on tobacco use. The policy should
   - Prohibit students, staff, parents, and visitors from using tobacco on school premises, in school vehicles, and at school functions.
   - Prohibit tobacco advertising (on T-shirts or caps or through sponsorship of school events) in school buildings, at school functions, and in school publications.
   - Require that all students receive instruction on avoiding tobacco use.
2. Provide instruction about the short- and long-term negative physiological and social consequences of tobacco use, about social influences on tobacco use, about peer norms regarding tobacco use, and about refusal skills.
   - Decrease the social acceptability of tobacco use and show that most young people do not smoke.
   - Help students understand why young people start to use tobacco, and identify more positive activities to meet their goals.
   - Develop students' skills in assertiveness, goal setting, problem solving, and resisting pressure from the media and their peers to use tobacco.
   - Avoid programs that only discuss tobacco's harmful effects or attempt to instill fear, as they do not prevent tobacco use.

3. Provide tobacco use prevention education in kindergarten through twelfth grade.
   - Tobacco use prevention instruction should be introduced in elementary school.
   - Instruction should be intensified in middle school, when students are exposed to older students who typically use tobacco at higher rates, and should be reinforced in high school.
4. Provide program-specific training for teachers.
   - The training should include reviewing the curriculum, modeling instructional activities, and providing opportunities to practice implementing the lessons.
5. Involve parents or families in support of school-based programs to prevent tobacco use.
   - Promote discussions at home about tobacco use by assigning homework and projects that involve families.
   - Encourage parents to participate in community efforts to prevent tobacco use.
6. Support cessation efforts among students and all school staff who use tobacco.
   - Schools should provide access to cessation programs that help students and staff stop using tobacco rather than punishing them for violating tobacco use policies.
7. Assess the tobacco use prevention program at regular intervals.
   - Schools can use the CDC's *School Health Index* to assess whether they are providing effective policies, curricula, training, family involvement, and cessation programs.

As important as knowing what concepts to teach at each grade level is knowing what not to teach. Following are some guidelines for teachers to follow when teaching tobacco prevention:

1. Do not imply that kids are "bad" if they smoke. Although this approach might work with some youth, it has been found to backfire, especially with high-risk students. The more smoking is labeled bad by authority figures, the more some high-risk students want to rebel.
2. Do not say that smoking is "dumb." Children need to maintain respect for their parents and other adults in their life, whether or not they smoke.
3. Do not encourage children, even indirectly, to denounce smoking at home. Smoking remains a personal choice. If the school is perceived as intruding in the home, parents might become alienated from the school's smoking prevention efforts.
4. Do not tell young children that smoking leads to deadly diseases. This approach can provoke anxiety in children whose parents or relatives smoke. This information should be taught in upper-elementary grades when children can understand that these risks generally are long-term and that quitting can reverse the trend.
5. Do not warn older students that they will die an early death if they smoke. This "threat" approach is not

The vast majority of smokers began smoking as teenagers. In surveys, about 75 percent of teen smokers state that they wish they had never started smoking.

effective. It is far more effective to focus on immediate consequences.
6. Do not give mixed messages. A teacher who smokes should not try to hide this fact from students but should indicate the intention to help them avoid similar unhealthy decisions. The concept of nicotine addiction can also be discussed.

GUIDELINES FOR CLASSROOM APPLICATIONS

Important Background for K–8 Teachers

Tobacco is addictive and is responsible for more than one out of every five deaths in the United States. Because the use of tobacco is related to so many health problems, preventing tobacco use has become a major focus over the past several years. *Preventing Tobacco Use Among Young People* was the first surgeon general's report to focus on tobacco as it relates to adolescents. Following are some of the major conclusions of that report:

- Tobacco use usually begins in early adolescence, typically by age 16.
- Most young people who smoke are addicted to nicotine and report that they want to quit but are unable to do so.
- Tobacco often is the first drug used by young people who use alcohol and illegal drugs.
- Among young people, those with poorer grades and lower self-images are most likely to begin using tobacco.
- Cigarette advertising appears to increase young people's risk of smoking by implying that smoking has social benefits and is far more common than it really is.[30]

These conclusions highlight the importance of beginning tobacco use prevention education at a young age. Teachers must understand background information about tobacco before they can teach students about the dangers of tobacco use. Not all of this information is developmentally appropriate for all elementary and middle school students, but teachers should have a basic understanding of the negative side effects of tobacco use.

Smokeless or Spit Tobacco

The use of smokeless tobacco is common among many of today's youth. For example, the 2007 Youth Risk Behavior Survey found that 8 percent of high school students (13.6 percent of males and 2.2 percent of females) had used smokeless tobacco in the previous thirty days.[31] Of high school seniors who were smokeless tobacco users, almost three out of four had begun using by ninth grade.[32] Because young people begin using smokeless tobacco at a young age, it is important for elementary and middle school teachers to focus on all forms of tobacco use.

There are three principal methods of using smokeless or spit tobacco: chewing, dipping snuff, and smoking. Chewing tobacco is made of tobacco leaves that are either dried and shredded and sold in a pouch or made into plugs or strands that are mixed with molasses, sugar, licorice, and other products. As the name "chewing tobacco" suggests, a portion of the loose leaf, plug, or strand is placed in the mouth and chewed, while excess juices periodically are spit out. Chewing tobacco is the least popular form of tobacco among today's youth. The dangers of chewing tobacco are similar to those of snuff.

Snuff is made from finely cut tobacco leaves and mixed with various products. There are two kinds of snuff: dry snuff and moist snuff. Dry snuff is made from finely ground, dried tobacco leaves and usually is sniffed through the nose. This type of snuff is not popular in most parts of the United States. Moist snuff also is made of finely ground tobacco leaves, but it is packaged while it is still damp. A small amount of moist snuff, known as a "pinch," is held between the lip or cheek and the gum and sucked, while excess juices periodically are spit out. This activity is commonly referred to as "dipping." Although many persons believe smokeless tobacco to be a safe form of tobacco, it has numerous dangerous side effects. Some of the more common negative side effects are

- *Nicotine addiction.* Nicotine is a powerful, addictive substance found in all tobacco products. Although nicotine is absorbed more slowly from smokeless tobacco than from cigarettes, the amount of nicotine absorbed from smokeless tobacco is three to four times the amount absorbed from a cigarette. Also, the nicotine stays in the bloodstream for a longer time. Nicotine may contribute to cardiovascular disease, high blood pressure, ulcers, and fetal problems. Like most users of stimulants, tobacco users build a tolerance for nicotine, resulting in a need to use more of the drug to get the same effect.[33] Unfortunately, adolescents who use smokeless tobacco are more likely to become cigarette smokers.[34]
- *Oral cancer.* Snuff tobacco contains 29 carcinogens or cancer-causing agents. The most harmful carcinogens in smokeless tobacco are the tobacco-specific nitrosamines

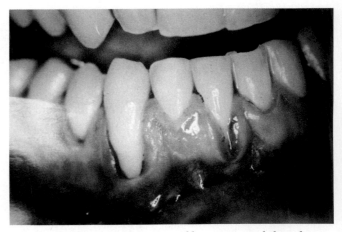

Receding gum lines are a common problem among smokeless tobacco users.

(TSNAs).[35] Because snuff stays in the mouth for a relatively long time, the nitrosamines may contribute to the high risk for oral cancer for tobacco snuff users. Oral cancers can form within five years of regular use of smokeless tobacco.[36] Many snuff users first experience a white, thick, hard patch of tissue in their mouths. Known as leukoplakia, this is considered to be a precancerous lesion. Studies have found that 60 to 78 percent of spit tobacco users have oral lesions.[37] Oral cancer has a tendency to spread to the body's lymph system, where it becomes very difficult to treat.

- *Gum and tooth problems.* Because sugar is added to smokeless tobacco and the tobacco is held in the mouth for long periods of time, users also tend to have more dental caries. One study found chewing tobacco users were four times more likely than non-users to have decayed dental root surfaces. Spit tobacco also causes gingivitis, a gum disease that can lead to bone and tooth loss. Receding gums at the site of tobacco placement are common among smokeless tobacco users. Gum recession exposes the teeth to disease, and, because the gum will not grow back, this condition can be corrected only by surgery.[38]

Smoking Tobacco

There are three ways persons smoke tobacco: pipes, cigars, and cigarettes. Because cigarettes are the most popular way for adults and adolescents to smoke tobacco in the United States, the majority of tobacco information in this chapter focuses on cigarettes.

Young people who use tobacco are more likely to progress to using other drugs. For example, among youth who have used both tobacco and marijuana by twelfth grade, 65 percent smoked tobacco before using marijuana, and 98 percent of those who had used both cocaine and tobacco by twelfth grade smoked tobacco first.[39] This does not mean that cigarette smoking causes other drug use but rather that cigarette smokers are more likely to use other drugs, such as marijuana and cocaine. If the number of teenagers who begin smoking can be reduced through educational prevention programs, then the prevalence of smoking and other drug use among adults can be decreased.

When tobacco is burned or smoked, it produces hundreds of toxic chemicals. When these chemicals condense, they form a brown, sticky substance called tar. Some of the chemicals in tar are carcinogens. Nicotine, the main chemical or drug found in tobacco, is the addictive part of tobacco that causes increased heart rate, blood pressure, and breathing rate, as well as constriction (narrowing) of the blood vessels. Cigarette smoke also contains carbon monoxide, the deadly gas found in automobile exhaust. It is considered to be one of the most harmful components of tobacco smoke. When carbon monoxide is inhaled, it quickly bonds with hemoglobin and reduces red blood cells' ability to transport oxygen. Because of the reduced oxygen, smokers tend to experience shortness of breath. For youth, the short-term consequences of smoking include respiratory and nonrespiratory effects, decreased physical fitness, adverse changes in cholesterol, and reduced rates of lung growth and function. In addition, the younger people are when they begin to smoke, the more likely they are to become strongly addicted to nicotine.[40] Teen smokers suffer from shortness of breath almost three time more often than teens who don't smoke.[41] Because of tar, nicotine, carbon monoxide, and many of the other chemicals and gases in tobacco, its use has many negative short-term consequences, including the following:

- *Increased heart rate.* After smoking just one cigarette, the heart rate increases by as many as thirty-three beats per minute. Although the heart rate will decrease over time, smokers generally have a higher resting heart rate than nonsmokers. This means that every day a smoker's heart has to work harder than does a nonsmoker's heart. This higher heart rate is attributed to the increased carbon monoxide levels and the constricted blood vessels caused by nicotine, which make it harder for the heart to pump blood throughout the body.[42] The resting heart rate for young adult smokers is two to three beats per minute faster than that of nonsmokers.[43]
- *Increased blood pressure.* After smoking just one cigarette, blood pressure increases. This increase is caused by the constricted blood vessels.[44]
- *Decreased skin temperature.* When persons smoke, their skin temperature quickly decreases. This is caused by nicotine, which reduces blood flow to the peripheral vessels.
- *Decreased hand steadiness.* Although some smokers believe that smoking relaxes them, it actually increases nervousness and tension and reduces hand steadiness. This is the result of the stimulant effect of nicotine. Decreased hand steadiness can affect athletic and art ability and other activities that require fine-motor skills.
- *Increased carbon monoxide levels.* Only about 5 percent of the smoke a person inhales is carbon monoxide; however, even this amount can be dangerous. When excess carbon monoxide is inhaled into the lungs, the oxygen-carrying capacity of the blood is reduced. The reduced amount of oxygen in the blood makes it more difficult for the body's

organs, such as the heart and brain, to do their work. This is why many smokers get out of breath easily, which can affect athletic and musical performance.[45]
- *Bad breath.* Smoking causes bad breath. This is one short-term effect that should be stressed to students, especially when upper-elementary and middle-level students become more interested in social interactions with classmates.
- *Fires and burns.* Other short-term effects of smoking cigarettes are fires related to smoking. Smoking is the leading cause of fire-related deaths.[46] Each year, over 1,300 deaths are associated with fires started by cigarettes. Most of these fatalities are caused by smokers who are careless about how, when, and where they smoke.[47]

Though students should understand all of the effects associated with smoking cigarettes, attention to the short-term side effects of smoking is more developmentally appropriate for younger learners than are long-term consequences. However, because some students will be curious about the long-term effects of smoking, it is important for teachers to have some general knowledge about this topic. Although smoking has numerous long-term effects, only the most common are discussed next.

- *Lung cancer.* Lung cancer is the leading cancer killer for both men and women. Smoking is responsible for about 80 percent of all lung cancer cases, over 130,000 deaths each year.[48] The risk of developing lung cancer increases with the number of cigarettes smoked per day, the number of years of smoking, and the age at which the person started smoking. People who stop smoking before age 35 may avoid 90 percent of the health risks related to tobacco.[49] Smoking also increases the long-term risk of getting cancer of the larynx, bladder, esophagus, pancreas, uterus, kidney, cervix, stomach, pharynx, and mouth.[50]
- *Cardiovascular disease.* Smoking is the most important recognized, modifiable risk factor for cardiovascular disease. Smoking causes atherosclerosis (hardening and narrowing of the arteries), stroke, and coronary artery disease. Cigarette smokers are two to four times more likely to develop coronary artery disease than nonsmokers and are at twice the risk for strokes. Young people who smoke already show greater deposits of fat in the blood vessels leading to and from the heart. A person who quits smoking reduces the risk of cardiovascular disease by about 50 percent after 1 year. After 15 years, the risk of cardiovascular disease is similar to that of a person who has never smoked.[51]
- *Chronic obstructive lung disease.* Smoking accounts for 90 percent of all chronic obstructive lung disease.[52] Chronic obstructive lung disease includes two related diseases: chronic bronchitis and emphysema. Both of these diseases are related to cigarettes because of the damage smoking does to the airways and the alveoli sacs, the sites of carbon monoxide and oxygen exchange in the lungs. Chronic bronchitis predisposes the smoker to emphysema, increasing risk. Chronic bronchitis is a persistent inflammation and infection of the smaller airways within the lungs.

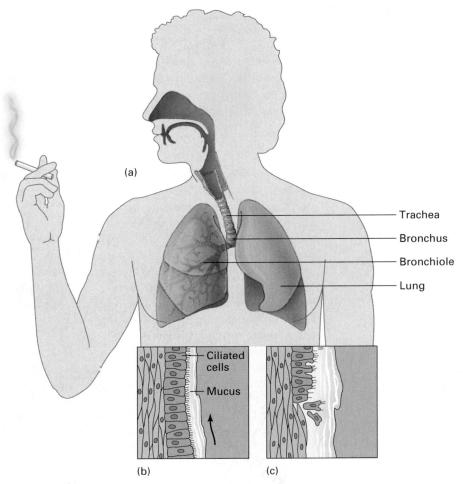

adults, secondhand smoke exposure increases the risk for lung cancer, respiratory problems, heart disease, and eye and nasal irritation.[54] In an analysis of thirty-seven research studies, lifelong nonsmokers living with smokers had an average 24 percent higher chance of contracting lung cancer than did those living with nonsmokers.[55] It is important that teachers not scare children with this information but instead inform parents about the dangers of secondhand smoke.

• *Aesthetic effects.* Numerous aesthetic effects are also associated with the long-term use of cigarettes. Smokers generally have bad breath and stains on their teeth and fingers. Smoking also destroys much of a person's sense of smell and taste, meaning that foods do not taste as good and flowers and other nice scents do not smell as good. Also, smoking causes the skin to wrinkle because of the constant constriction and relaxation of the surface blood vessels, which eventually makes people look much older.

FIGURE 11–3 | **Damage to the Lungs Caused by Smoking** (a) The respiratory system. (b) The inside of a bronchiole of a nonsmoker. Foreign particles are collected by a thin layer of sticky mucus and transported out of the lungs, up toward the mouth, by the action of cilia. (c) The inside of a bronchiole of a smoker. Smoking irritates the lung tissue and causes increased mucus production, which can overwhelm the action of the cilia. A smoker develops a chronic cough as the lungs try to rid themselves of foreign particles and excess mucus. Eventually the cilia are destroyed, leaving the delicate lung tissue exposed to injury from foreign substances.

SOURCE: P. M. Insel and W. T. Roth, *Core Concepts in Health,* 10th ed. (New York: McGraw-Hill, 2006, 310). Reproduced with permission of the McGraw-Hill Companies.

Recommendations for Concepts and Practice

Healthy Behavior Outcomes

The goal of health education is to help students adopt or maintain health-enhancing behaviors. School districts and teachers should identify the health-enhancing behaviors they would like their students to maintain or adopt. The following list identifies possible behavioral outcomes related to promoting a tobacco-free lifestyle. Though not all these suggestions are developmentally appropriate for students in grades K–8, this list can help teachers understand how the learning activities they plan for their students support both short- and long-term desired behavior outcomes.

Ways to Promote a Tobacco-Free Lifestyle

Avoid using (or experimenting with) any form of tobacco.

Avoid secondhand smoke.

Support others in being tobacco-free, including support for a tobacco-free environment.

Seek help for stopping the use of tobacco for self and others.

Quit using tobacco if already using it.[56]

Emphysema is an irreversible disease in which the alveoli are destroyed. Even quitting smoking will not regenerate the alveoli. Healthy adults have about 100 square yards of interior lung surface, created by the lungs' thousands of alveoli sacs. When a person gets emphysema, the walls between the sacs break down, creating larger and fewer sacs and thus gradually diminishing the interior lung surface. Eventually, the lung surface is so small that people with emphysema spend most of their time gasping for air and carrying an oxygen tank along with them (Figure 11–3).

• *Secondhand smoke health effects.* Secondhand tobacco smoke has a long-term effect on children and adults who live in homes with smokers. Children exposed to secondhand smoke are at higher risk for sudden infant death syndrome (SIDS), acute lower respiratory tract infections, asthma induction and exacerbation, chronic respiratory symptoms, and middle ear infections.[53] In

Developmentally Appropriate Concepts and Skills

As with other health topics, teaching related to promoting a tobacco-free lifestyle should be developmentally appropriate and be based on the physical, cognitive, social, emotional, and language characteristics of specific students. Teacher's Toolbox 11.1 contains a list of suggested developmentally appropriate concepts and skills to help teachers create lessons that will encourage students to practice the desired behavior outcomes by the time they graduate from high school.[57] Note that these grade-level spans are aligned with the 2007 Natural Health Education Standards.

Sample Students' Questions and Suggested Answers Regarding Tobacco

When learning about tobacco, students formulate many questions about the topic. Some commonly asked questions about tobacco and some suggested answers follow. It is not enough to just read the suggested answers—teachers should actually practice saying them aloud. Teachers should think of other questions students might ask and practice answering them as well.

1. *What's in a cigarette?*

A lot is in a cigarette besides tobacco. In fact, the smoke produced by a burning cigarette contains more than 4,000 chemicals. Of these 4,000 chemicals, 50 cause cancer.

2. *What do cigarettes do to the body?*

Besides causing cancer, lung disease and heart disease, cigarettes have immediate effects. The carbon monoxide absorbed by the body from one cigarette stays in the blood for as long as six hours. This means the heart has to work harder to supply the body with enough oxygen.

3. *Most kids my age smoke, don't they?*

It might look that way, because tobacco companies pay lots of money to fill magazines and billboards with pictures of people smoking. But, according to the latest surveys, only 10 percent of middle school students have smoked in the past thirty days. That means most kids—90 percent—are smart enough to not smoke.

4. *We don't need to worry—smoking won't affect our health until we're a lot older, right?*

You already know that smoking can cause long-term problems such as cancer and heart disease over time, but symptoms start to develop as soon as you smoke your first cigarette—no matter how young you are. Symptoms include shortness of breath, coughing, nausea, dizziness, and phlegm production. Pretty gross, huh?

5. *But, if you smoke only a little bit, that can't hurt, can it?*

Symptoms such as wheezing and coughing have been found in kids who smoke just one cigarette a week.

6. *Kids who smoke think they're cool—are they?*

Only if by "cool" you mean kids who probably aren't doing well in school. Studies have found that students with the highest grades are less likely to smoke than those with the lowest grades. Kids who smoke have lower self-images. They smoke because they think it will give them a better

More than 3,000 children become smokers every day. However, it is important to emphasize to students that most kids are smart enough to not smoke.

image—cooler, maybe, or more attractive or more popular. And, because their self-image is low, they don't have the confidence to say no when someone urges them to use tobacco.

7. *Why do some kids smoke or use smokeless tobacco?*

There are no physical reasons to start smoking; people don't need tobacco the way they need food, water, and sleep. Most people say they start smoking because of social reasons. One common reason is to try to look older. Some kids may think that smoking or chewing tobacco makes them look more hip or glamorous, like a movie star or a famous baseball player. Actually, smoking does make you appear older if stained teeth and wrinkled skin are the look you're going for. Some kids say that smoking helps them relax, but smoking actually raises your blood pressure and makes your heart beat faster. Other kids might think it's okay to smoke because other people in their family do. If you ask your mom, dad, uncle, or aunt about their tobacco use, chances are they will tell you not to start and that they wish very much that they could quit. It's always much easier to not start smoking than to quit.

Developmentally Appropriate Concepts and Skills for Promoting a Tobacco-Free Lifestyle

Grades K–2 Concepts	Grades 3–5 Concepts	Grades 6–8 Concepts
NHES 1: Core Concepts		
• Identify a variety of tobacco products.	• Identify the short- and long-term physical effects of using tobacco.	• Describe the short- and long-term physical effects of using tobacco.
• Identify the short-term effects of using tobacco.	• Identify the short- and long-term physical effects of being exposed to others' tobacco use.	• Summarize the short- and long-term physical effects of being exposed to others' tobacco use.
• Identify the short- and long-term physical effects of being exposed to tobacco smoke.	• Describe the benefits of abstaining from or discontinuing tobacco use.	• Discuss the social, economic, and cosmetic consequences of tobacco use.
• Describe the benefits of not using tobacco.	• Identify the effects of tobacco use on social relationships.	• Evaluate the dangers of experimenting with tobacco products.
• Explain the dangers of experimenting with tobacco.	• Summarize the dangers of experimenting with tobacco.	• Summarize the benefits of being tobacco free.
• Identify family rules about tobacco use.	• Summarize family and school rules about tobacco use.	• Explain that tobacco is addictive.
	• Explain that tobacco use is an addiction that can be treated.	• Describe the effects of secondhand smoke.
		• Analyze the effects of tobacco use on social relationships.
		• Explain school policies and community laws related to the sale and use of tobacco products.
		• Explain reasons most individuals do not use tobacco products.
		• Explain why using tobacco, alcohol, or other substances is an unhealthy way to manage stress.
		• Describe situations that could lead to the use of tobacco.
		• Describe the relationship between using tobacco and alcohol or other drugs.

Grades K–2 Skills	Grades 3–5 Skills	Grades 6–8 Skills
NHES 2: Analyze Influence		
• Identify parent and caregiver influence on the use of tobacco.	• Identify family and societal influences on tobacco use and exposure to secondhand smoke.	• Analyze the factors that influence a person's decision to use or not use tobacco.
	• Identify the influence of peers on tobacco use.	• Describe how personal and family values influence decisions about using tobacco.
	• Identify various strategies the media use, including advertisements, to encourage or discourage tobacco use.	• Explain family and societal influences on tobacco use and exposure to secondhand smoke.
	• Identify strategies used by tobacco distributors to encourage tobacco use among youth.	• Summarize how peers influence tobacco use.
	• Recognize that most young people and adults do not use tobacco.	• Analyze various strategies the media use, including advertisements, to encourage or discourage tobacco use.
	• Describe the factors that influence a person's decision to use or not use tobacco.	• Delineate advertising techniques used to promote tobacco use among adolescents.
		• Discuss how peers can support being tobacco free.
		• Explain that most young people and adults do not use tobacco.
		• Identify a role model who demonstrates non-use of tobacco products.
NHES 3: Accessing Information, Products, and Services		
• Identify trusted adults who can help prevent exposure to secondhand smoke.	• Identify sources of accurate information about the effects of tobacco use and exposure to secondhand smoke.	• Demonstrate how to access accurate sources of information about tobacco use.
	• Demonstrate the ability to access accurate information about preventing tobacco use.	• Analyze warning labels on tobacco products.
		• Demonstrate how to access successful smoking cessation programs.

Grades K–2 Skills (continued)	Grades 3–5 Skills (continued)	Grades 6–8 Skills (continued)
	• Identify the information found on the warning labels of tobacco products. • Identify a trusted adult, such as a parent, school nurse or counselor, who can provide helpful information about preventing and stopping tobacco use.	• Describe people in school and in the community who can help prevent tobacco use or help others to stop using tobacco. • Analyze the accuracy of images conveyed in the media, including advertisements, about tobacco use.
NHES 4: Interpersonal Communication • Describe how to ask for help in staying away from secondhand smoke.	• Demonstrate effective verbal and nonverbal ways to refuse pressures to use tobacco. • Communicate personal reasons to be tobacco free. • Describe how to ask for help in staying away from secondhand smoke. • Describe ways to help others who are trying to stop smoking.	• Demonstrate verbal and nonverbal ways to refuse tobacco use. • Describe how to ask someone effectively and respectfully not to smoke. • Demonstrate ways to support friends and family members who are trying to stop smoking. • Demonstrate how to ask for help from a parent, other trusted adult, or friend when pressured to use tobacco. • Communicate with parents and family about ways to avoid tobacco use. • Demonstrate ways to help others who are trying to stop smoking.
NHES 5: Decision Making • Explain positive outcomes from avoiding secondhand smoke.	• Explain positive outcomes for being tobacco free. • Summarize positive outcomes from avoiding secondhand smoke.	• Predict how not using tobacco products produces positive health outcomes. • Identify health-enhancing alternatives to tobacco use. • Analyze positive outcomes for avoiding secondhand smoke. • Analyze positive and negative choices about using tobacco and how these choices can affect friends and family.
NHES 6: Goal Setting	• Set a goal to avoid using tobacco. • Develop a plan for avoiding offers to use tobacco. • Make a commitment to be tobacco free. • Describe how using tobacco can harm personal goals for physical fitness and athletic performance.	• Discuss plans for the future and how the use or nonuse of tobacco might affect those plans. • Develop a personal plan to improve health by staying tobacco free or quitting the use of tobacco. • Make a commitment to remain tobacco free.
NHES 7: Self-Management • Demonstrate ways to avoid secondhand smoke.	• Express intention to remain tobacco free. • Demonstrate ways to avoid secondhand smoke. • Demonstrate ways to avoid use of tobacco products.	• Express intentions to remain tobacco free. • Demonstrate ways to avoid secondhand smoke. • Demonstrate ways to avoid use of tobacco products. • Express intentions to get help in quitting tobacco use if currently using.
NHES 8: Advocacy • Ask parents and others for help in avoiding secondhand smoke.	• Explain to others why it is important to be tobacco free. • Explain to others the benefits of a tobacco-free environment. • Advocate for friends to be tobacco free.	• Demonstrate effective persuasion skills that encourage friends and family not to use tobacco. • Advocate for a tobacco-free school environment. • Articulate to others why clean indoor air is important. • Demonstrate ways to support friends and family who are trying to stop using tobacco.

SOURCE: Centers for Disease Control and Prevention. *Health Education Curriculum Analysis Tool (HECAT)* (Atlanta, GA: CDC, 2007) www.cdc.gov/HealthyYouth/Hecat/index.htm

8. *What happens when a kid first tries smoking or using smokeless tobacco?*

No one likes smoking or chew at first. Your body is smart, and it knows when it's being poisoned. When people try smoking, they often cough a lot and feel pain or burning in their throat and lungs. This is your lungs' way of trying to protect you and telling you to keep smoke out of them. Also, many people feel sick to their stomach or even throw up to try to get the poison out of their system. If chewing tobacco is accidentally swallowed, some kids are sick for hours.

9. *What can I do to help a friend who is smoking?*

If you know someone who is using tobacco, you should tell your friend that you don't want him or her to become addicted to cigarettes. Not only is nicotine a drug, but kids who smoke are more likely to become drinkers and use other drugs, such as marijuana or cocaine. You also can tell your friend that you avoid smoking so that you can do your best on the sports field and earn good grades.

10. *How can I get my mom to quit smoking?*

You might not be able to get your mom to quit smoking. Remember, it is her choice and by now she may be very addicted. You can tell her what you have learned about tobacco and that you would like her to quit because you don't want her to get sick from smoking, but the bottom line is that it is her choice.

STRATEGIES FOR LEARNING AND ASSESSMENT

Promoting a Tobacco-Free Lifestyle

This section provides examples of standards-based learning and assessment strategies for promoting a tobacco-free lifestyle. The sample strategies begin with a restatement of the standard and a reminder of the assessment criteria, drawn from the RMC rubrics in Appendix B. Strategies are written as directions for teachers and include applicable theory of planned behavior (TPB) constructs in parentheses (intention to act in healthy ways, attitudes toward behavior, subjective norms, perceived behavioral control). These learning and assessment strategies provide building blocks for standards-based lessons and units that can be tailored to local needs. Assessment criteria are used with permission from the Rocky Mountain Center for Health Promotion and Education (RMC). See Appendix B for Scoring Rubrics.

Additional strategies for learning and assessment for Chapter 11 can be found at the Online Learning Center. Appendix D, a complete list of all the strategies, is available at the Online Learning Center.

NHES 1 | Core Concepts

Students will comprehend concepts related to health promotion and disease prevention to enhance health.

ASSESSMENT CRITERIA

- Connections—Describe relationships between behavior and health; draw logical conclusions about connections between behavior and health.

- Comprehensiveness—Thoroughly cover health topic, showing breadth and depth; give accurate information.

Grades K–2

KWL on Tobacco Students can talk about their knowledge of tobacco use by making a Know-Wonder-Learn (KWL; three-column) chart. Teachers can use a large piece of chart paper to list all the things students say they know (or think they know) about tobacco in a "Know" column, listing the children's names beside the facts they provide. Next, ask students what they wonder about tobacco (the "Wonder" column). Combine this activity with NHES 3, access information, products, and services, to have children check out their facts. Students might look up information in resource books, surf the Internet, e-mail an expert, talk to family and community members, or invite guest speakers to the classroom. When students have confirmed their facts and answered their questions, they can list their new knowledge in the "Learn" column.

ASSESSMENT | Completing the "Learn" column of the KWL chart is the assessment task for this activity. For assessment criteria, students should provide accurate information and describe relationships between and draw conclusions about connections between behaviors and health. (Constructs: Attitudes toward behavior, perceived behavioral control.)

Smoking Stinks—There's Nothing Good About Smoking! Read the book *Smoking Stinks* by Kim Gosseling to help students learn about the detrimental effects of smoking and the seriousness of addiction (see "Children's Literature" at the end of this chapter). Maddie and Alex prepare for their school health report about smoking and learn from Maddie's grandfather why he started smoking and why he hasn't been able to quit. The story stresses the importance of never using tobacco products and the dangers of secondhand smoke, particularly for children with asthma and allergies. This book has received positive reviews from the American Cancer Society, the American Lung Association, and health care professionals. After reading to students, teachers can ask them to recall the health effects of smoking discussed in the book, such as coughing and trouble with allergies, and write them on a piece of newsprint as the children speak. The children should tell why they think Maddie's grandfather says, "There's nothing good about smoking."

ASSESSMENT | The students' list of health effects of smoking is the assessment task for this activity. For assessment criteria, the children should provide correct information and be able to describe relationships between smoking and health and draw conclusions about those connections. Each student should contribute one answer to the question of why Maddie's grandfather says, "There is nothing good about smoking." (Construct: Attitudes toward behavior.)

Grades 3–5

Smoking Machine The "smoking machine" is a popular teaching strategy for upper-elementary and middle-level students. Smoking machines help students see how tar accumulates in the lungs after smoking only a few cigarettes. *Because of school tobacco-free policies and the dangers of secondhand smoke, the authors recommend that teachers show and explain four unused smoking machines to students and then take the machines off campus to "smoke cigarettes" in them.* Bring the used smoking machines back to the classroom to allow students to compare the evidence of smoking one (machine 1), three (machine 2), six (machine 3), and ten (machine 4) cigarettes in the smoking machines. For their own safety, teachers should go outdoors to use cigarettes in the smoking machines. Teachers can purchase commercial smoking machines or make their own from simple materials. To make the machines, teachers need four clear plastic dish-soap bottles, cotton balls, clay or putty, one package of cigarettes, and a lighter or matches.

1. Thoroughly rinse and dry four clear plastic dish-soap bottles. Label the bottles 1: One cigarette, 2: Three cigarettes, 3: Six cigarettes, and 4: Ten cigarettes.
2. Insert loosely packed cotton balls into the bottles and replace the caps.
3. Remove the nozzles from the caps of the bottles.
4. Insert a cigarette into the opening of each cap and make an airtight seal around the cigarette with clay or putty.
5. The smoking machine is ready for use, outdoors and away from houses and other buildings.
6. Press firmly on the plastic bottle to force out the air before lighting the cigarettes. After lighting the cigarettes, proceed with a slow and regular pumping action. When the cigarette is completely smoked, remove the cigarette filter from the cap.
7. Use an entire package of twenty cigarettes. Smoke one cigarette in bottle 1, three cigarettes in bottle 2, six cigarettes in bottle 3, and the remaining ten cigarettes in bottle 4. (Note: To show students the result of smoking one pack of cigarettes per day, smoke twenty cigarettes in one additional smoking machine.)
8. Back in the classroom, show the students the four smoking machines, labeled with the number of cigarettes smoked. Explain to students that the cotton balls represent the lungs of a smoker. Ask the students what they notice has happened to the cotton balls after smoking one, three, six, and ten cigarettes. Students should compare the cotton balls in the bottles with clean cotton balls.
9. Unscrew the caps on the smoking machines to show students the tar buildup on the caps and the cotton balls. Emphasize the difference between the clean cotton balls and the tar-stained cotton balls in the bottles. Allow the students to smell the bottles and caps. Ask students what they think about the appearance and smell of the cap and the cotton balls. What connections can they make to what happens to people when they smoke?
10. To add to this activity, place clean cotton balls in a dish in a room where people smoke, and leave the dish there for one week. Have students compare these cotton balls, exposed to secondhand smoke, with the cotton balls from the smoking machine and with clean cotton balls.

ASSESSMENT | For an assessment task, students can draw a cartoon to show what happens to the lungs of a smoker, based on their observations of the cotton balls. Students should write a caption for their cartoons, with a warning label about smoking. For assessment criteria, the students' cartoons should show an accurate depiction of what happens to a smoker's lungs and the warning labels should describe a relationship between tobacco use and health. (Construct: Attitudes toward behavior.)

KidsHealth.Org—Check Out Tobacco The Kids' Health website (www.kidshealth.org) provides core concepts information for elementary students and adults. Students can visit the website and click on "For Kids." They can type "tobacco" into the search line to learn about topics such as what tobacco is and the links between tobacco use and problems such as asthma and bad breath. Alternatively, teachers can print out the information for students to use in the classroom.

ASSESSMENT | As an assessment task, students can work in pairs to study and report on one of the tobacco topics on the Kids' Health website. For assessment criteria, students should be sure that all their information

is correct and should draw conclusions about connections between tobacco use and health. This activity links to NHES 3, access information, products, and services. (Constructs: Attitudes toward behavior, perceived behavioral control.)

Grades 6-8

Analyzing a Mystery Product Don't mention tobacco to the students as you begin this activity. The product is a mystery. This lesson requires two inflated balloons, a small glass or jar of flour, a small glass or jar of clear syrup, and a small glass or jar of molasses.

1. Begin by telling students that they are going to break down the ingredients in a mystery product (but don't mention tobacco). Have the students guess the product after they see all the ingredients.
2. Explain to students that this mystery product is associated with more than 500 gases and several thousand chemicals. Hold up one of the balloons and explain that one of the gases, carbon monoxide, is in the balloon. Carbon monoxide is colorless and odorless and can be deadly by depleting the amount of oxygen in the body.
3. Hold up the other balloon and explain that one of the other gases produced by the mystery product is hydrogen cyanide. Hydrogen cyanide is a gas that is used sometimes in gas chambers when a prisoner is executed.
4. Hold up the jar of flour and explain that one of the chemicals found in the mystery product is arsenic. Arsenic is used as a rat poison and is dangerous when ingested in large amounts.
5. Hold up the clear syrup and explain that this ingredient is too dangerous in its pure form and has been mixed with syrup. The syrup represents nicotine, but don't tell the students—that probably would give away the name of the mystery product. Explain that just two or three drops of the pure ingredient can kill a person instantly and it causes the heart to beat fast and the blood vessels to constrict.
6. Hold up the molasses and explain that this ingredient can cause cancer. Again, don't tell students that the molasses represents tar, another giveaway.
7. Ask the students if they know what the mystery product is. After the students guess, discuss each ingredient in more detail.[58] Ask students how their new knowledge affects their ideas about tobacco use.

Students can design a skit in which they play the ingredients of the mystery product. Thus, the characters are ingredient 1 (carbon monoxide), 2 (hydrogen cyanide), 3 (arsenic), 4 (nicotine), and 5 (tar). So that all students can participate, groups of five can create their own skits or different students can play different roles in designing one skit (script writer, costume designer, product designer, actor). Remind students that they should be careful not to give away the names of the last two ingredients, nicotine and tar. Students can perform their skits for other students in the school and have the audience guess the mystery product.

ASSESSMENT | The skit is the assessment task. For assessment criteria, students should make sure all information in the skit is accurate and should help others describe relationships between and draw conclusions about connections between tobacco use and health. This activity links to NHES 8, advocacy, because students are trying to convince others not to smoke. (Construct: Attitudes toward behavior.)

Carousel Activity After discussing the short-term physical, long-term physical, social, economic, and cosmetic effects of smoking, conduct a carousel activity with students. Divide students into five groups. Tape five large pieces of chart paper or newsprint around the room with the headings "Short-Term Physical," "Long-Term Physical," "Social," "Economic," and "Cosmetic." Have each group start at one of the papers to brainstorm the consequences of that type that could result from using tobacco. After a short time, students should rotate to the next piece of paper, read, and add new consequences. After each group returns to their original paper, have them decide on the five consequences they would least like to have.

ASSESSMENT | Students should write a paper indicating why they don't want to smoke. For assessment criteria, students should include at least five consequences in their paper from the carousel activity. (Construct: Attitudes Towards Behavior)

NHES 2 | Analyze Influences

Students will analyze the influence of family, peers, culture, media, technology, and other factors on health behaviors.

ASSESSMENT CRITERIA
- Identify both external and internal influences on health.
- Explain how external and internal influences interact to impact health choices and behaviors.
- Explain both positive and negative influences, as appropriate.

Grades K–2

The Feel Good Book   Read aloud Todd Parr's *The Feel Good Book* (see "Children's Literature" at the end of this chapter) to help children create a class book of activities that make them feel good inside. Examples in the Parr book include these:

Giving a great, big hug feels good.
Sharing your treats feels good.
Making a new friend feels good.
Saying "I love you" in sign language feels good.

Analyzing influences is an abstract idea for young children. Teachers can introduce this idea by having children identify caring things they do for others and for themselves that make them feel good inside. This activity builds on children's positive capabilities and links indirectly to tobacco use prevention. Children can share their ideas first with a partner and then with classmates. If children repeat the ideas in the Parr book at first, teachers can ask questions about things they have seen or heard children do to help them formulate their own ideas.

ASSESSMENT | For an assessment task, children can create individual pages for a class book about things that make them feel good inside. Students can draw a picture to express their idea and then write a sentence that explains their picture. Their pictures can be bound together into a book that they can read in the classroom and share with other classes. For assessment criteria, students should show ideas that are health-enhancing and that they can describe in words. (Construct: Attitudes toward behavior.)

Healthy Role Model   To reinforce the idea that both boys and girls (and men and women) play important roles in all aspects of life, ask students to think about the people in their lives who are "he-roes" and "she-roes" to them. Students should name the he-roes and she-roes in their own lives—people who are there for them and who help them. Ask the children what they admire about these people and in what ways they want to be like them. Healthy, positive role models are important for the prevention of risky behaviors.

ASSESSMENT | For an assessment task, students can share a few sentences about their he-roes and she-roes with the class. For assessment criteria, students should tell at least two things they admire in the person they name and explain how that person helps them be the kind of person they want to grow up to be. (Construct: Subjective norms.)

Grades 3–5

Tobacco Advertising   Approximately 1,200 smokers die each day in the United States. Thus, the tobacco industry needs to find 1,200 new smokers every day to replace them. Although the tobacco industry claims that tobacco advertising does not target young people, many of the advertising techniques are highly attractive to adolescents. Tobacco advertisements portray smoking as fun, sophisticated, cool, popular, attractive, and sexy. Help students analyze the external influence of tobacco advertising on the decisions and behaviors of young people.

1. Ask students to clip cigarette advertisements from magazines and bring them to class.
2. Have students examine the ads for techniques that make cigarette smoking seem attractive and appealing. (See Chapter 3 for a list of advertising techniques.)
3. Ask students to create new counter or "spoof" ads that depict more realistic outcomes of smoking. Sample spoof ads are available on the website Adbusters/Culture Jammers (www.adbusters.org/spoofads/tobacco). Students might want to use graphs or other data alongside their ads to emphasize their points.
4. Display students' work in the classroom and throughout the school.

ASSESSMENT | The spoof ads students create are the assessment task for this activity. In addition to the ads on the Adbusters website, students and teachers can access ads from Tobacco-Free Kids (www.tobaccofreekids.org; click on "Tobacco Ad Gallery") and from the surgeon general's website for kids (www.cdc.gov/tobacco/sgr/sgr4kids/adbust.htm). For assessment criteria, students should identify the advertising techniques used in the real ads and the techniques they use in their spoof ads (see the list of advertising techniques in Chapter 3). (Construct: Subjective norms.)

Family   Students can interview an adult family member about his or her feelings and attitudes toward youth smoking. Students can ask,

- How would you feel if I started smoking?
- What are our family rules and consequences about smoking?
- What advice can you give me about how to deal with pressures to smoke?

Knowing the attitudes and beliefs of their families is important for young people. Students can report on their interviews to the rest of the class and tell what their family attitudes and beliefs mean to them.

ASSESSMENT | The reports students make on their interviews are the assessment task for this activity. For assessment criteria, students should discuss how their family members' attitudes and beliefs influence their ideas about smoking. (Construct: Subjective norms.)

Grades 6–8

Truth Ads   Moving beyond print ads, students can create and videotape antitobacco commercials, popularly known as truth ads. Students might have seen truth ads on television. One of the most popular ads, "Body Bags," portrayed young people piling up body bags outside a famous tobacco maker's headquarters to represent the number of deaths each day from smoking. Students can portray the kinds of advertising techniques the tobacco industry uses in print ads (smoking is fun, sophisticated, and sexy) and deliver a truthful message to counter the claims. (See Chapter 3 for a list of advertising techniques.) Students can end their commercials with a tobacco statistic and the words "Brought to you by The Truth." Show the truth ads to other classes and on closed-circuit school television. Students can view examples of truth ads at www.thetruth.com. The website tells students, "Maybe there's no such thing as a bad question, but there sure are a ton of pretty bunk answers out there. But that won't stop us from calling out the tobacco industry and trying to get some quality responses, because without questions there are *no* answers. Period. Ask questions. Seek the truth." State and local health departments also might have videotapes or DVDs of antitobacco television spots available for classroom use on request.

ASSESSMENT | The truth ads students create are the assessment task for this activity. Students should base their ads on factual information about tobacco use to counteract the way smoking is portrayed in advertisements and movies. Link this activity to language arts and performing arts by inviting teachers in those content areas to get involved with the project. Students should script, rehearse, and perform their truth ads and videotape them, if possible, to share with other classes and parents. For assessment criteria, students' truth ads should refute at least one misleading idea about smoking portrayed in advertisements and the media. This activity links to NHES 8, advocacy. (Constructs: Attitudes toward behavior, subjective norms.)

Tobacco Warnings   Have students look at different warnings on tobacco products and ask them to discuss how effective they think the warnings are with young people and adults. Most students probably will say that they don't think the warnings are strong enough. Based on their knowledge of the short- and long-term effects of tobacco use, students can create and illustrate more effective warnings to deter youth smoking. Display these in the classroom and the hallways of the school. If possible, have students find examples of tobacco warnings that other countries use, which in some cases are more direct and graphic than American warnings. Students can conduct a general web search (www.google.com) of "tobacco warnings" or warnings for particular countries. For example, a Google search of "Australia tobacco warnings" reveals that Australia has some of the most graphic tobacco health warnings in the world on cigarette packets. Australia's tobacco industry must display warnings in color and text warnings that occupy 30 percent of the front and 90 percent of the back of cigarette packets. A set of fourteen health warnings ("Smoking causes mouth and throat cancer," "Smoking causes peripheral vascular disease," and "Smoking causes blindness") composed of graphic images and explanatory messages provide updated information on a range of adverse health effects of smoking. The more familiar warnings such as "Smoking kills" and "Smoking causes lung cancer and emphysema" are also included.

ASSESSMENT | For an assessment task, students can create posters that provide direct and graphic antitobacco warnings and display them on a drawing of tobacco products or as large print and picture ads. Showcase the students' work around the school. For assessment criteria, students should explain at least three ways tobacco warnings can influence young people's beliefs and attitudes about using tobacco. (Constructs: Attitudes toward behavior, subjective norms.)

Looking at Tobacco Inside and Out   Students can really show the difference between the way tobacco use is portrayed in the media and the effects it has inside the body by making a shoebox or diorama display. Students can bring old shoeboxes from home and ask family, friends, and colleagues to donate old shoeboxes for this project.

As students learn more about tobacco, they can design the inside of the shoebox to show tobacco's effects on the body, while designing the outside of the shoebox to show how advertising and other media glamorize tobacco use. Students can design the lid to give instructions to the user about viewing the inside and outside of the box. Display the boxes for other classes or in the school library.

ASSESSMENT | The shoebox display or diorama is the assessment task for this activity. Students should decide what would make a "great tobacco inside and out shoebox display." Use the students' criteria to assess and help them assess their work. (Constructs: Attitudes toward behavior, subjective norms.)

Multicultural Tobacco Marketing for Equal Opportunity Illness
This activity invites students to dig beneath the surface of tobacco advertising to examine strategies that target members of various racial, ethnic, and other groups. To learn more about how tobacco advertising targets specific groups, students can visit the Smoking Stops Here website to view "Big Tobacco: An Equal Opportunity Manipulator" (www.smokingstopshere.com/BigTobacco/equal.cfm). The website provides examples such as the study that found that three major African American publications—*Ebony, Jet,* and *Essence*—had 12 percent more advertisements for cigarettes than magazines targeted to the general public. Several cigarette brands have Spanish names (Rio and Dorado) created to appeal to Latinos. A study in San Diego, California, found that the highest proportion of tobacco billboards were posted in Asian American communities, and the lowest proportion in white communities. Several cigarette brands have names created to appeal specifically to women: Virginia Slims, Capri, Eve, Misty. Students can look for targeted ads in magazines and public places and discuss them in class.

ASSESSMENT | For an assessment task, students can create spoof ads or posters to challenge the messages portrayed in tobacco advertising targeted to various groups of people. For assessment criteria, students should explain how their truthful messages counteract the claims of tobacco advertising to influence people not to smoke. (Constructs: Attitudes toward behavior, subjective norms.)

NHES 3 | Access Information, Products, and Services

Students will demonstrate the ability to access valid information and products and services to enhance health.

ASSESSMENT CRITERIA

- Access health information—Locate specific sources of health information, products, or services relevant to enhancing health in a given situation.
- Evaluate information sources—Explain the degree to which identified sources are valid, reliable, and appropriate as a result of evaluating each source.

Grades K–2

Interview Older Kids   Younger students often model their behavior after older siblings, friends, and students in their school. Arrange for a group of upper-elementary students to visit younger students for the purpose of being interviewed about their knowledge of and views on tobacco. The children can prepare a list of questions they want to ask. Younger students will learn that most of the older students don't smoke and don't like to be around smokers.

ASSESSMENT | For an assessment task, the younger students can provide their own answers to all the questions on their list after the older students have finished talking with them. For assessment criteria, the older students should make sure the younger students provide accurate answers and tell why the older students are a valid source of information. (Construct: Subjective norms.)

What's Up, Doc?   Invite a local physician or nurse (or help children write a letter of invitation) to come to the classroom to be interviewed about how tobacco use affects his or her patients and the advice he or she gives to patients (especially young people) about smoking. Students can prepare questions in advance to conduct their interview.

ASSESSMENT | Students can discuss their findings with the doctor or nurse they interview. For an assessment task, students can write, draw, or act out what they have learned. For assessment criteria, children should explain why they think the information sources are vaild. (Construct: Attitudes toward behavior.)

Grades 3–5

Short-Term Effects of Smoking   Students relate more to what happens after smoking just one cigarette than to what happens after smoking for thirty years. Use the following strategy to help students access information about short-term effects:

1. Invite an adult smoker (parent, teacher, or administrator) to come to class to assist with a demonstration.
2. Ask the school nurse, or a nurse from the community, to take the volunteer's heart rate, blood pressure, and skin temperature before the volunteer smokes a cigarette. Record the data in a "Before Smoking" column on a chalkboard or chart paper so that students can see the numbers.
3. Ask the volunteer to step off school grounds and smoke one cigarette. While the smoker is gone, ask students to predict what will happen to the measurements after one cigarette.
4. Ask the nurse to retake the volunteer's heart rate, blood pressure, and skin temperature after smoking one cigarette. Record these numbers alongside the first set of numbers in an "After Smoking" column. Ask students to compare the measurements.
5. If measuring instruments are available from the American Lung Association, take two additional short-term measurements: carbon monoxide levels and hand steadiness. An ecolyzer measures carbon monoxide levels, and a tremor-tension tester measures hand steadiness.
6. The most important part of this activity is to ask students to identify the activities they like to do that would be affected by these short-term effects of smoking. Help students relate the results of the class experiment to their own lives. For example, students would have difficulty playing a musical instrument if their hands were unsteady.

ASSESSMENT | For an assessment task, students can make a list of activities they like to do that would be affected by smoking. Each student should contribute an activity to the list and tell how it would be adversely affected by smoking. For assessment criteria, students should explain how they know about the short-term effects of smoking (something they observed in class today) and tell why their own observations are a good source of information. (Construct: Attitudes toward behavior.)

Community Resources on Tobacco   Students can use phone books (ask friends and colleagues to save them for your class) to find community resources on tobacco use (American Lung Association, American Cancer Society, American Heart Association). Small groups of students can write to different agencies to request class materials on tobacco use prevention.

ASSESSMENT | For an assessment task, students can create a directory of tobacco education and cessation resources. For assessment criteria, students should identify the sources of their information and explain why their sources are valid. (Construct: Perceived behavioral control.)

Grades 6–8

Accessing YRBS and GYTS Data on Youth Tobacco Use   Teachers can use data from the CDC Youth Risk Behavior Survey (YRBS) and the Global Youth Tobacco Survey (GYTS) to help students get a true picture of tobacco use among school-age youth. These data are available on CDC websites at www.cdc.gov/HealthyYouth/yrbs/index.htm and www.cdc.gov/tobacco/Global/GYTS.htm. Have students estimate their answers to the survey questions on tobacco use. Then have students access the data online, or provide a printed summary for students to use. In most cases, students overestimate use among other young people. Learning the true prevalence of tobacco use among peers can be an important external influence (NHES 2) to support healthy behavior.

Students can compile their answers to make posters or charts to help other students learn about tobacco use among youth in the United States and around the world. Students should state their findings in a positive sense (the percentage of students who have remained tobacco-free during the past thirty days, the number and percentage of students who have never used smokeless tobacco or smoked cigars). Students can show their findings with different kinds of graphics or graphic organizers. For example, students could use small repeated symbols (♥ ♥ ♥) to show the number of students in a class of twenty-five who remained tobacco-free during the past thirty days.

ASSESSMENT | Students' posters are the assessment task. For assessment criteria, students should provide accurate information (NHES 1) and cite the sources of their data and tell why their sources are valid. (Construct: Subjective norms.)

Check Out TobaccoFreeKids.org   Middle-level students can access all kinds of information on tobacco by visiting www.tobaccofreekids.org. The site contains reports on topics such as candy-flavored cigarettes, cigarette taxes, smoke-free laws, and Kick Butts Day. Students can click on links such as "Youth Action," "Research and Facts," and "Tobacco Ad Gallery." Students can use the website to launch a wide variety of standards-based tobacco prevention projects, including core concepts (NHES 1), analyze influences (NHES 2), and advocacy (NHES 8).

ASSESSMENT | For an assessment task, allow students to take charge of designing the different kinds of tobacco prevention projects they would like to complete using this website as a starting point. For assessment criteria, students should discuss and agree on a list of expectations for "great project presentations." Use the students' criteria to assess and help them assess their work. At a minimum, students should identify their information sources and explain why they are valid. (Constructs: Attitudes toward behavior, perceived behavioral control, subjective norms.)

The Tobacco Industry Is Messing with You: More Links   The State of Maryland sponsors a website called Smoking Stops Here (www.smokingstopshere.com). The site provides the following links to other websites that allow students to learn more about "how the tobacco industry is messing with you." Students can investigate these and other state tobacco use prevention sites to report on the practices of the tobacco industry and on what states are doing to counteract those practices.

- *Big Tobacco Sucks* (California Department of Health Services) www.bigtobaccosucks.com

Learn about animal cruelty, child labor, ecological destruction, racial profiling, sexist marketing, public health epidemics, and other reasons why Big Tobacco just plain sucks.

- *WhiteLies.tv* (Indiana Tobacco Prevention and Cessation) www.whitelies.tv
  Learn about the ways tobacco companies manipulate residents of Indiana, what their dishonesty costs the state, and what you can do about it.
- *Just Eliminate Lies* (Iowa Department of Public Health) www.jeliowa.org
  Find graphic and honest portrayals of the health effects of tobacco use—definitely not the kind of images you see in tobacco ads.

ASSESSMENT | The students' reports are the assessment task for this activity. Students could each research a different state's tobacco use prevention efforts through Google. For assessment criteria, students should report the source of their information and tell why the information source is valid. (Constructs: Attitudes toward behavior, perceived behavioral control.)

NHES 4 | Interpersonal Communication

Students will demonstrate the ability to use interpersonal communication skills to enhance health and avoid or reduce health risks.

ASSESSMENT CRITERIA

- Use appropriate verbal/nonverbal communication strategies in an effective manner to enhance health or avoid/reduce health risks.
- Use appropriate skills (negotiation skills, refusal skills) and behaviors (eye contact, body language, attentive listening).

Grades K–2

Supporting Family Members Who Want to Stop Smoking Children shouldn't be told that people who smoke are bad or stupid, and children shouldn't be sent home to nag their parents or caregivers about smoking. These tactics usually backfire on the children and their teachers. However, sometimes children know that a family member is trying to stop smoking, and children can be supportive of these efforts. Ask children to imagine that their parents, caregivers, aunt, uncle, or grandparents have said they want to stop smoking. What can children say to let these relatives know that they are on their side? Children can role-play supportive communication without nagging or scolding.

ASSESSMENT | For an assessment task, pairs or small groups of children can create short skits to show what they can say to support a particular family member who wants to stop smoking. For assessment criteria, students should demonstrate appropriate communication behaviors, such as eye contact, a respectful tone, attentive listening, and expressions of empathy, understanding, and support. (Construct: Subjective norms.)

Asking to Get Away from Secondhand Smoke Young children learn that secondhand smoke is dangerous to them. However, they often have little control over what adults do around them. In this activity, children should brainstorm a list of things they can say and do to get away from secondhand smoke without being disrespectful to adults who are smoking. The list might include asking to go outside or into another room to play. Students might also consider saying to a smoker, "Tobacco smoke makes me cough and feel sick. Would you put your cigarette out for now or smoke outside?" Ask students what their experiences have been and what they have done to try to get away from secondhand smoke. Students can select the strate-

gies they feel are best from their list. Remember that a brainstorm list includes everything students say, even if teachers think the ideas won't work very well.

ASSESSMENT | The students' list of strategies is the assessment task for this activity. For assessment criteria, the students' strategies should make a clear, respectful request to be excused from a place where there is smoking or for the smoker to put out the cigarette or go outside to smoke. Students should demonstrate their strategies in class. (Construct: Perceived behavioral control.)

Grades 3–5

Letters: Communicating with People We Care About Although teachers don't teach students to nag or scold adults in their family who smoke, teachers often encounter the genuine concern many children feel about the health and well-being of smokers in their families. Some teachers and children have found a healthy compromise by having children who are concerned write a simple, caring letter to the smokers in their families. In the letter, children express their concern, support, and love. Writing a letter lets children express what they are feeling while recognizing that people make their own choices about smoking and no one else can control those choices.

ASSESSMENT | The letters students write are the assessment task for this activity. This activity can be a voluntary one that involves only some members of the class, or all students can choose to participate. Link this project to language arts by involving teachers who teach letter writing. For assessment criteria, students should express their own needs, wants, and feelings in a clear way while writing respectfully to the smoker. (Construct: Subjective norms.)

Resist the Pressure This activity is good to use after discussing the negative consequences of tobacco. Educators should emphasize the addicting qualities of nicotine, so students understand the dangers of experimenting with tobacco. This activity gives students the opportunity to practice how they would get out of a peer pressure situation that encourages experimentation with tobacco.

1. Ask students to write a short, realistic scenario depicting being pressured to experiment with tobacco. Allow some students to read their scenario aloud and provide feedback.
2. Brainstorm with the class some ways they could respond to a peer who is pressuring them to use tobacco. List these responses on the board.
3. Place students into groups of four. Assign each student in the group a role: two students will apply pressure, one student will resist, and one student will judge the skills of the resistor. Have the two students who will apply the pressure determine which scenario they will use.
4. The teacher should then tell students when to begin their role-play. The two students should apply pressure, and the resistor should use a variety of resistance skills to get out of the pressure situation.
5. After a few minutes, the teacher should provide time for the judges to give feedback to the resistor.
6. The students should rotate roles four times so that every student has the opportunity to practice the resistance skills one time.

ASSESSMENT | The feedback the judge gives the resistor is the assessment for this activity. For assessment criteria, students should use two resistance techniques to get out of the pressure situation. (Construct: Perceived behavioral control)

Grades 6–8

Restaurant Manager   In this activity, students get the chance to project their communication skills beyond the classroom and beyond the world of peers and family. Have children imagine that they are the owner of a popular restaurant. They have made a decision to make the restaurant entirely smoke-free. The challenge is to explain the new rules to customers who want to smoke, communicate that the decision is a healthy one, and persuade customers to stay and eat in the restaurant, even though they can't smoke. This is a real-world problem in many communities. The challenge is to communicate a decision without losing customers, just as students want to communicate a decision without losing friendships. How would students handle this situation?

ASSESSMENT | For an assessment task, students can work in small groups to create and perform a scenario in their restaurant. Students might want to make scenery and gather props to make their scenes convincing (no-smoking signs and table tents, tables and chairs, menus). Students should first write their scripts, practice the scenario, and then perform it for class members. Videotaping will help students analyze their communication skills. For assessment criteria, students should demonstrate appropriate verbal and nonverbal strategies for communicating the new policy and communication behaviors such as eye contact, clear "no" messages, repeated refusals, attentive listening to customers, restatement of other points of view, and statements of needs, wants, and feelings (a nonsmoking restaurant protects the staff and other customers). (Constructs: Attitudes toward behavior, perceived behavioral control.)

Comparing Communication Skills   Like other content areas, communication skills are important—but they might vary for refusing tobacco compared to other content areas. Students can compare resistance skills for tobacco with the communication skills they would use in pressure situations for alcohol and other drugs, sexual involvement, or risk taking that could result in injury. How would they use the skills in similar and in different ways, depending on the context? Students can work in small groups to create pressure situations in three different content areas of their choice (safety, violence, tobacco, alcohol and other drugs, sexual health, nutrition, physical activity). Students should demonstrate one kind of communication skill (repeated refusal, suggest an alternative) across all three content areas. (See Chapter 3 for a list of peer pressure resistance skills.)

ASSESSMENT | Comparing communication across different content areas provides students with the chance to examine their skills in depth. For assessment criteria, students should be able to identify and demonstrate the communication skill of their choice and explain how they are using it similarly and differently in three pressure situations. (Construct: Perceived behavioral control.)

NHES 5 | Decision Making

Students will demonstrate the ability to use decision-making skills to enhance health.

ASSESSMENT CRITERIA

Reach a health-enhancing decision using a process consisting of the following steps:

- Identify a health-risk situation.
- Examine alternatives.
- Evaluate positive and negative consequences.
- Decide on a health-enhancing course of action.

Grades K–2

Decision Making for Safety   Use the following story to help children think about decisions to stay away from matches, lighters, and cigarettes. Read the story to students. You also might want to use puppets or role-playing.

> Susan and Alex are visiting Tom at his house. Tom's dad is a smoker, and the children find his lighter and matches in the family room. They know they are not supposed to touch these items, but Susan picks up the lighter and begins to play with it.

- Ask students what they think Alex and Tom should do.
- Have students brainstorm and discuss all the possible solutions and then vote on the best way for the problem to be solved. Also ask the students to brainstorm different ways to avoid this situation.
- Have students draw pictures depicting what they should do when they find matches, lighters, or cigarettes. Display the pictures in the classroom and at open house sessions with parents.

ASSESSMENT | The discussions and pictures are the assessment task for this activity. At this grade level, students don't need to be able to name steps in a decision-making model. However, they should be able to discuss alternatives and explain a decision that they think is best. For assessment criteria, students should give two or more alternatives about what to do and choose and give a reason for their decision on how to act. (Construct: Perceived behavioral control.)

Reasons to Be Tobacco-Free   Focus health education strategies on what students should do, rather than what they should not do. Students should brainstorm a list of reasons to be tobacco-free and then list the positive and negative consequences of their reasons. Students can use their list and its consequences to counter the reasons people give for starting to smoke. Young children might not know the word *consequences.* Teachers can help them by asking, "What could happen if you . . . ?" In relation to a decision to be tobacco-free, students might list as positive consequences that they could hang out and do things with other kids who don't smoke and that they could save money for other purchases. A negative consequence might be that students who are smokers could leave them out of their plans.

ASSESSMENT | For an assessment task, students can state a reason to be tobacco-free and discuss the consequences of their decisions. For assessment criteria, students should identify two positive consequences of their decisions. (Construct: Attitudes toward behavior.)

Grades 3–5

Fortunately and Unfortunately: Thinking About Consequences   Students probably are accustomed to thinking about the short-term consequences of tobacco use in terms of physical outcomes. Have students expand their thinking about short-term consequences to social, emotional, financial, and family categories. Post five large pieces of paper, such as newsprint or chart paper, around the room. Label each with one category: "Physical," "Social," "Emotional," "Financial," "Family." Send a group of students to each of the papers to start.

First, ask students to write the words *Fortunately* or *Unfortunately* at the top of each of two columns on their paper. Students should tell what these words mean before starting the activity. Teachers can use examples to be sure students understand the concept. Next, have students list "Fortunately" and "Unfortunately" things that might happen applicable to their category if they do or don't smoke. For example, under "Social, Fortunately," students might list "Fortunately, I will be with most of my friends if I don't smoke, because most students don't smoke." Under "Social, Unfortunately," students might list "Unfortunately, I might be unpopular with a small group of smokers—but people who pressure me aren't really my friends." On signal, students rotate to the next paper, read, and add to it. Continue until all groups have visited all papers. When the original groups gets back to their papers, the group members can read, discuss, and share with the larger group. This type of activity is called a carousel.

ASSESSMENT | The Fortunately/Unfortunately charts students make are the assessment task for this activity. Students should identify the three most important points on their charts when they get back to the place they started. For assessment criteria, students should explain how these three most important points would influence their decisions about tobacco use and share their answers with the class. (Constructs: Attitudes toward behavior, subjective norms.)

Grades 6–8

Cost of Smoking   Determining the cost of smoking serves as a good prevention technique. Students can calculate the cost of smoking for a week, a month, and a year, basing the calculations on the cost of one pack of cigarettes per day and then two packs per day. When students have their answers, ask them what they would rather do with that amount of money than spend it on tobacco. The potential cost of a smoking habit is a major insight and an important deterrent for some students.

Students can identify the cost of something they would like to purchase for the classroom (a DVD player or sports equipment) and calculate the number of packs of cigarettes that would equal the cost of the item they wish to purchase. How many days would it take to collectively accumulate the money if each member of the class saved the cost of one pack of cigarettes per day?

ASSESSMENT | This activity is a good link with mathematics. For assessment criteria, students should calculate how much money they would spend on cigarettes for one year if they smoked one pack per day. They could then write how they would spend that money. (Construct: Attitudes toward behavior.)

Laws, Rules, and Policies on Tobacco Use   Students can invite a school administrator and a community official, such as a police officer, to class to explain the laws, rules, and policies on tobacco use by minors in the school and in the community. The police officer also might be able to share information about tobacco sales compliance checks of community merchants. Have students prepare a list of questions in advance. Students can discuss the consequences of underage smoking from a school-rule and legal standpoint. How do these consequences affect their decision making about tobacco?

ASSESSMENT | For an assessment task, students can share their thinking about how tobacco laws, rules, and policies affect their decisions about tobacco use. For assessment criteria, students should describe the laws, rules, and policies in terms of alternatives and consequences that affect their decisions. (Construct: Subjective norms.)

NHES 6 | Goal Setting

Students will demonstrate goal-setting skills to enhance health.

ASSESSMENT CRITERIA

* Goal statement—Give goal statement that identifies health benefits; goal is achievable and will result in enhanced health.
* Goal setting plan—Show plan that is complete, logical and sequential, and includes a process to assess progress.

Grades 3–5

Class Goals   Students can work together to set a class goal about smoking for their graduating group—for example, "By the time we

graduate from middle school, all of us will still be tobacco-free." Students should list the steps they will need to take, ways to overcome barriers they might encounter, ways they can support each other, and a method for assessing their progress.

ASSESSMENT | Working through a simple goal-setting process is the assessment task for this activity (see Chapter 3 for goal-setting steps). For assessment criteria, students should (1) state their class goal in measurable terms (they will be able to tell whether they accomplished the goal), (2) make a plan for reaching their goal, stating specific steps they will carry out, (3) identify sources of support they can count on and barriers they will need to overcome and how, and (4) design a way to assess their progress along the way. (Construct: Subjective norms.)

Grades 6–8

Personal Commitment   Making a public, personal commitment not to smoke is meaningful for some young people. Following are two ideas for students to make commitments:

1. Prepare a large piece of chart paper with the header "I promise not to use any tobacco products in middle and high school" at the top of the page. Invite students who want to make this commitment to sign the paper. Post the paper in a prominent place in the classroom so that students can see their classmates' commitments for the entire school year.
2. Students can also make commitments on individual pieces of paper. Have students write on their papers (or give the students preprinted papers) "I pledge to stay tobacco-free in middle and high school because _____."
   Signed: _____ Date: _____

Making commitments encourages students not to use tobacco and to think about why they won't use tobacco. The commitments also encourage peers not to use tobacco. Post the papers in the classroom or hallways, or send them home to parents and caregivers.

Remember from Chapter 3 that student pledges alone aren't necessarily sufficient to affect behavior. Teachers should bring the other components of the theory of planned behavior (intention to act in healthy ways, attitudes toward behavior, subjective norms, perceived behavioral control) into classroom discussions about making pledges. For example, students can discuss what their own attitudes toward tobacco use are, what they believe their families and friends think about tobacco use, and how successful they think they will be in remaining tobacco-free. Teachers also should assure students that signing pledges is voluntary. In fact, students might want to sign during a recess or break period rather than one by one in class. Students should not experience any pressure to sign from their teachers or classmates. Students might ask what would happen if a student breaks a pledge. Teachers can respond by saying that students can choose to take their name off the pledge poster at any time or sign it later. The reason for making the pledges "in middle and high school" is that most young people who remain tobacco-free during their school years do not begin smoking as adults. Limiting the pledges to middle and high school also provides a time frame that students can relate to realistically.

ASSESSMENT | This assessment is a bit more complicated than it might appear. Teachers assess students not on whether they sign a pledge but on their reasoning process. For an assessment task, students can write a short paper that answers these questions: (1) What are my plans about using tobacco in middle and high school? (2) What do I think about tobacco use? (3) What do my family and friends think about tobacco use? (4) How successful do I think I can be in remaining tobacco-free? Why? For assessment criteria, students should provide in-depth answers to all the questions. (Constructs: Intention to act in healthy ways, subjective norms, perceived behavioral control.)

NHES 7 | Self-Management

Students will demonstrate the ability to practice health-enhancing behaviors and avoid or reduce health risks.

ASSESSMENT CRITERIA

- Application (transfer)—Initiate health-enhancing behaviors; apply concepts and skills appropriate and affectively.
- Self-monitoring and reflection—Monitor actions and make adjustments; accept feedback and make adjustments; able to self-assess, reflect on, and take responsibility for actions.

■ Grades K–2

Managing Stress and Strong Feelings   Learning to manage feelings and stress in healthy ways is a constant theme across all the content areas. These self-management skills make sense in that young people need to choose healthy rather than unhealthy alternatives when they feel pressured, upset, or discouraged. In the content area of tobacco, ask students what kinds of feelings and events cause people to feel stressed. What kinds of stress management activities are healthy (relaxing, listening to music, shooting hoops, riding a bike) versus unhealthy (smoking, drinking, shouting, hitting)? Students can choose stress management strategies they think will work for them and show how they would use them.

ASSESSMENT | For an assessment task, students can work in pairs or small groups to create and perform a pantomime (no speaking allowed) to show an event that causes a person to feel stress and demonstrate a healthy way to respond to the stress. Teachers might want to participate in the pantomime with younger children. For assessment criteria, students should accurately demonstrate at least one healthy strategy for responding to stress. (Construct: Perceived behavioral control.)

Growing Healthy and Strong   Students can make a class list of things they do that help them grow healthy and strong. The students might list eating fruits and vegetables, exercising, getting enough sleep, spending time with their families, and brushing their teeth. Then ask students to make another list—things that could keep them from growing healthy and strong. Students probably will list tobacco use, among other detrimental habits. Help students emphasize the positive things they can do for their health. Ask them whether smoking might make it hard for them to do some of these things (running fast and for a long time to play a game).

ASSESSMENT | This and the preceding activity deal indirectly with tobacco use, which might or might not come up in the students' discussions. The emphasis is on positive self-management strategies for health rather than on what not to do. The two lists the students make are the assessment task for this activity. For assessment criteria, each student should describe or demonstrate a habit they practice for growing healthy and strong. (Construct: Attitudes toward behavior.)

Grades 3–5

Avoiding Risk Situations   Sometimes students don't realize that they will be faced with a difficult situation, such as refusing tobacco. Other times there are warning signs that tobacco will be part of the scene. Students can give examples of how they might know that tobacco could be used in a particular situation (an invitation to go to someone's home when his or her parents, who are smokers, aren't there). Next, ask students to strategize about how to avoid these situations altogether, rather than having to maneuver to get out of

them. These self-management skills involve communication and the physical act of going elsewhere.

ASSESSMENT | For an assessment task, students can illustrate "Don't Even Go There" posters showing strategies for avoiding risk situations that involve possible tobacco use. Students can make their posters individually or in small groups. For assessment criteria, students' posters should show a logical sequence of steps for avoiding tobacco risk situations. (Construct: Perceived behavioral control.)

A Bunch of Reasons Not to Smoke!   The American Heart Association website (www.americanheart.org) provides tobacco-related activities for students in grades 3–5. In one activity, called "A Bunch of Reasons Not to Smoke," students brainstorm and make a list of reasons not to smoke. The students then use markers to carefully write their reasons on balloons. Students display the balloons in a large bunch in the classroom or on the school grounds. To go a step further, students could write alternatives to smoking (self-management strategies) on a different-color balloon and mix the two balloons together to make a larger bunch. This activity links to NHES 8, advocacy.

ASSESSMENT | For an assessment task, students write reasons to not smoke and alternatives to smoking on their balloons. For assessment criteria, students' alternatives to smoking, their self-management strategies, should be health-enhancing. (Constructs: Attitudes toward behavior, subjective norms.)

Grades 6-8

A Little Help from My Friends   Students might not be familiar with the old song about getting by with "a little help from my friends." However, the principle applies strongly to preventing and reducing risk behaviors. Students need a support group of family, friends, and other caring individuals in their lives. For this activity, students identify at least three people they can call on to help them stand their ground if they are pressured to smoke or engage in other risk behaviors. Students can make a drawing to show how they and their support group connect.

ASSESSMENT | For an assessment task, students can create a graphic organizer or illustration that shows their name and the names of at least three people they can count on to back them up in a pressure situation. For assessment criteria, students should write a short sentence next to each name saying why they can count on that person in their support system. Students should share their illustration with the people they named to reinforce their support. (Constructs: Subjective norms, perceived behavioral control.)

Bumper Stickers for Healthy Alternatives   Ask students whether they have seen the popular bumper stickers that begin with the phrase "I'd rather be . . . ." Depending on the part of the country, the bumper stickers state that the driver would rather be skiing, surfing, skating, sailing, or fishing. Students can create a bumper sticker for their locker or notebook to remind them of things they would rather be doing than smoking. This activity links to NHES 8, advocacy.

ASSESSMENT | The locker or notebook stickers students create are the assessment task for this activity. For assessment criteria, students should share their stickers with classmates, explaining how and why their self-management strategies will help them resist pressure to engage in unwanted activities. (Construct: Subjective norms.)

NHES 8 | Advocacy

Students will demonstrate the ability to advocate for personal, family, and community health.

- Health-enhancing position—Give clear, health-enhancing position.
- Support for position—Support position with facts, concepts, examples, and evidence.
- Audience awareness—Show awareness of target audience; choose words, tone, and examples to suit audience.
- Conviction—Display conviction for position.

Grades K–2

Letters of Appreciation Help students write class thank-you letters to their favorite restaurants that are totally smoke-free. Have all students sign the letters, with parents' and caregivers' permission, and mail them to the restaurants. Students will be excited to see if they receive reply letters or if the restaurants post their letters. Students also can write a class thank-you letter to the local newspaper, listing the restaurants they visit that are smoke-free.

ASSESSMENT | The students' letters are the assessment task for this activity. For assessment criteria, students should express appreciation for the healthy decision the restaurants have made to go tobacco-free and show strong conviction for why they are appreciative. (Construct: Subjective norms.)

Rap to Be Tobacco-Free Elementary students are fond of slogans, raps, and rhymes, especially those that have a strong beat. Small groups of students can create simple slogans, raps, or rhymes about staying tobacco-free and teach them to the class. For example, an elementary teacher found that her first graders liked the beat of the popular song "We Will Rock You." Her students used that beat to chant "No more, no more smoking!" with accompanying claps and beats on their desks.

ASSESSMENT | The rhyme or rap students create is the assessment task for this activity. For assessment criteria, the student should teach the rhyme or rap to other students their age or younger and should have a clear, antitobacco message that they state with conviction. (Construct: Subjective norms.)

Grades 3–5

Letter-Writing Campaign to Big Tobacco Students can compose a class letter to a leading cigarette maker, indicating students' knowledge of tobacco advertising techniques that appeal to young people and of tobacco-related *morbidity* and *mortality* (new vocabulary words). Students should end their letter by stating their positions on tobacco advertising and marketing to youth and should ask the tobacco company for a reply letter. Have students sign the letter, with parents' and caregivers' permission, and mail it to the tobacco company. Students will be interested to see whether they receive a reply.

ASSESSMENT | The students' letter is the assessment task for this activity. For assessment criteria, students should state a clear, health-enhancing position, back it up with data, target their audience (a tobacco company), and write with conviction. (Construct: Subjective norms.)

Turning the Tables Challenge students to use the same techniques the tobacco industry uses to make antitobacco banners to post in school and local businesses. Students might want to also make kites, buttons, or T-shirts to promote tobacco-free lives.

ASSESSMENT | Share the list of advertising techniques in Chapter 3 with students to help them turn the tables on tobacco advertising. The banners, kites, buttons, or T-shirts the students make are the assessment task for this activity. For assessment criteria, students should give a clear, health-enhancing message and communicate it with conviction by making a strong statement. (Construct: Subjective norms.)

I'm Glad I Don't Smoke This is a good activity to do after reviewing the negative consequences of smoking. On a large sheet of chart paper or newsprint, write the heading "I'm Glad I Don't Smoke Because . . .". Give each student a marker and ask them to write down a response to the sentence stem. The newsprint should then be displayed in a prominent hallway in the school so that other students can read the responses.

ASSESSMENT | The student response to the sentence stem is the assessment task for this activity. For assessment criteria, the students should read their responses to the class and explain how it will help them remain tobacco free. (Construct: Subjective norms)

Grades 6–8

Social Norms Middle school students want to feel that their behaviors are respected by the people whose opinions they value—usually, their peers. If they believe that everyone smokes cigarettes, they might be more inclined to smoke. Young adolescents tend to greatly overestimate the *prevalence* (new vocabulary word) and acceptability of tobacco use among their peers. Help students get the real picture of smoking among their peers. Ask students to write "Yes" or "No" on a piece of paper to indicate whether they currently use tobacco. Students should not sign their names. Next, ask students to write the number and percentage (mathematics review) of students in class who they think currently use tobacco. A couple of volunteers can collect the papers and record the responses on the board or a piece of chart paper. In most cases, students make higher estimates than the actual number and percentage of tobacco users in their class. Ask students to think about why they tend to overestimate and how they can spread the word—advocate—to help classmates understand that the actual percentage of smokers in middle school is low. How can they publicize their findings? Students could conduct the same type of survey with other students in their school and publicize those results as well.

ASSESSMENT | For an assessment task, students can design a brief presentation and/or posters for their school about what they learn about the prevalence of smoking among students. For assessment criteria, students should display their survey data to make a strong case for staying tobacco-free. Their presentations/posters should focus on influencing the target audience (peers). (Construct: Subjective norms.)

Tobacco-Free Advocacy Campaign Begin class by asking students to sign a class pledge about not smoking. (Do not pressure students to sign if they do not want to.) Explain that one of the best ways they can help keep their peers tobacco free is to become an advocate. Brainstorm ways to be an advocate (posters, computer screen saver messages, songs, announcements). Allow students to work in groups to determine the advocacy project they would like to do. Have students create a list of steps to complete their project. Allow one to two weeks to implement their advocacy project.

ASSESSMENT | The advocacy campaign that the students create is the assessment task for this activity. For assessment criteria, students should provide factual information about the benefits of being tobacco free and the message should be convincing and appealing to same-age peers. (Construct: Subjective norms)

EVALUATED CURRICULA AND INSTRUCTIONAL MATERIALS

Following are three middle-level, school-based tobacco prevention programs effective for reducing tobacco use among students who participate.

- *Life Skills Training.* The Life Skills Training (LST) program is ideally designed for students in sixth or seventh grade and focuses on tobacco, alcohol, and other drug prevention. The curriculum has an impact on social risk factors, including media influence and peer pressure, as well as personal risk factors, such as anxiety and low self-esteem. The curriculum teaches resistance skills, knowledge, attitudes, self-management skills, and general social skills. One study found that at post-test, there was a 61 percent lower level of smoking in students at schools where the Life Skills Training program was implemented compared to students in the control schools.[59] Teachers can purchase LST materials or arrange for training by calling (800) 293-4969 or by visiting the website www.lifeskillstraining.com/order/php.

- *Project ALERT.* Project ALERT is a drug prevention curriculum for middle school students (ages 11 to 14). The two-year, fourteen-lesson program focuses on the substances adolescents are most likely to use: alcohol, tobacco, marijuana, and inhalants. Project ALERT uses participatory activities and videos to help motivate adolescents against drug use, teach adolescents the skills and strategies they need to resist pro-drug pressures, and establish non-drug-using norms. Guided classroom discussions and small-group activities stimulate peer interaction and challenge students' beliefs and perceptions, while intensive role-playing activities help students learn and master resistance skills. Homework assignments that involve parents extend the learning process by facilitating parent–child discussions of drugs and how to resist using them. The lessons are reinforced through videos that model appropriate behavior. Evaluation results show that current and occasional cigarette use was 20–25 percent lower and regular and heavy cigarette use 33–55 percent lower than among baseline experimenters. Teachers can find information on how to purchase the curriculum by contacting Project ALERT at (800) 253-7810 or www.projectalert.com.[60]

- *All Stars.* All Stars is a multiyear school-based program for middle school students (11 to 14 years old) designed to prevent or delay the onset of high-risk behaviors such as tobacco use, drug use, violence, and premature sexual activity. The program focuses on five topics important to preventing high-risk behaviors: (1) developing positive ideals that do not fit with high-risk behavior; (2) creating a belief in conventional norms; (3) building strong personal commitments; (4) bonding with school, prosocial institutions, and family; and (5) increasing positive parental attentiveness. The All Stars curriculum includes highly interactive group activities, games and art projects, small group discussions, one-on-one sessions, a parent component, and a celebration ceremony. The All Stars Core program consists of thirteen 45-minute class sessions delivered on a weekly basis by teachers, prevention specialists, or social workers. The All Stars Booster program is designed to be delivered one year after the core program and includes nine 45-minute sessions reinforcing lessons learned in the previous year. Multiple program packages are available to support implementation by either regular teachers or prevention specialists. All Stars participants reported significantly lower average levels of cigarette use at post-test compared with students who did not receive the program.[61] More information about the All Stars program can be found at www.allstarsprevention.com or by calling (336) 662-0090.

- *Keepin' It REAL.* Keepin' It REAL is a multicultural, school-based substance use prevention program for students aged 12 to 14 years. Keepin' It REAL uses a 10-lesson curriculum taught by trained classroom teachers in 45-minute sessions over ten weeks, with booster sessions delivered in the following school year. The curriculum is designed to help students assess the risks associated with substance abuse (including tobacco use), enhance decision-making and resistance strategies, improve antidrug normative beliefs and attitudes, and reduce substance use. The narrative and performance-based curriculum draws from communication competence theory and a culturally grounded resiliency model to incorporate traditional ethnic values and practices that protect against substance use. The curriculum places special emphasis on resistance strategies represented in the acronym "REAL" (Refuse offers to use substances, Explain why you do not want to use substances, Avoid situations in which substances are used, and Leave situations in which substances are used). Study results found that curriculum participants reported significantly lower cigarette use than students who did not receive the program. Effects lasted up to eight months for cigarette use.[62] More information about the Keepin' It REAL curriculum can be found at customerservice@etr.org or at (800) 321-4407.

INTERNET AND OTHER RESOURCES

Visit the Online Learning Center (www.mhhe.com/telljohann6e) for links to these sites, quizzes and other study aids, and many additional resources.

WEBSITES

Action on Smoking and Health (ASH)
   www.ash.org

Adbusters/Culture Jammers (Note: Teachers should download spoof ads for students rather than having students visit the site. Some of the language on the home page may be inappropriate for students.)
   www.adbusters.org/spoofads/tobacco/

American Cancer Society
   www.cancer.org

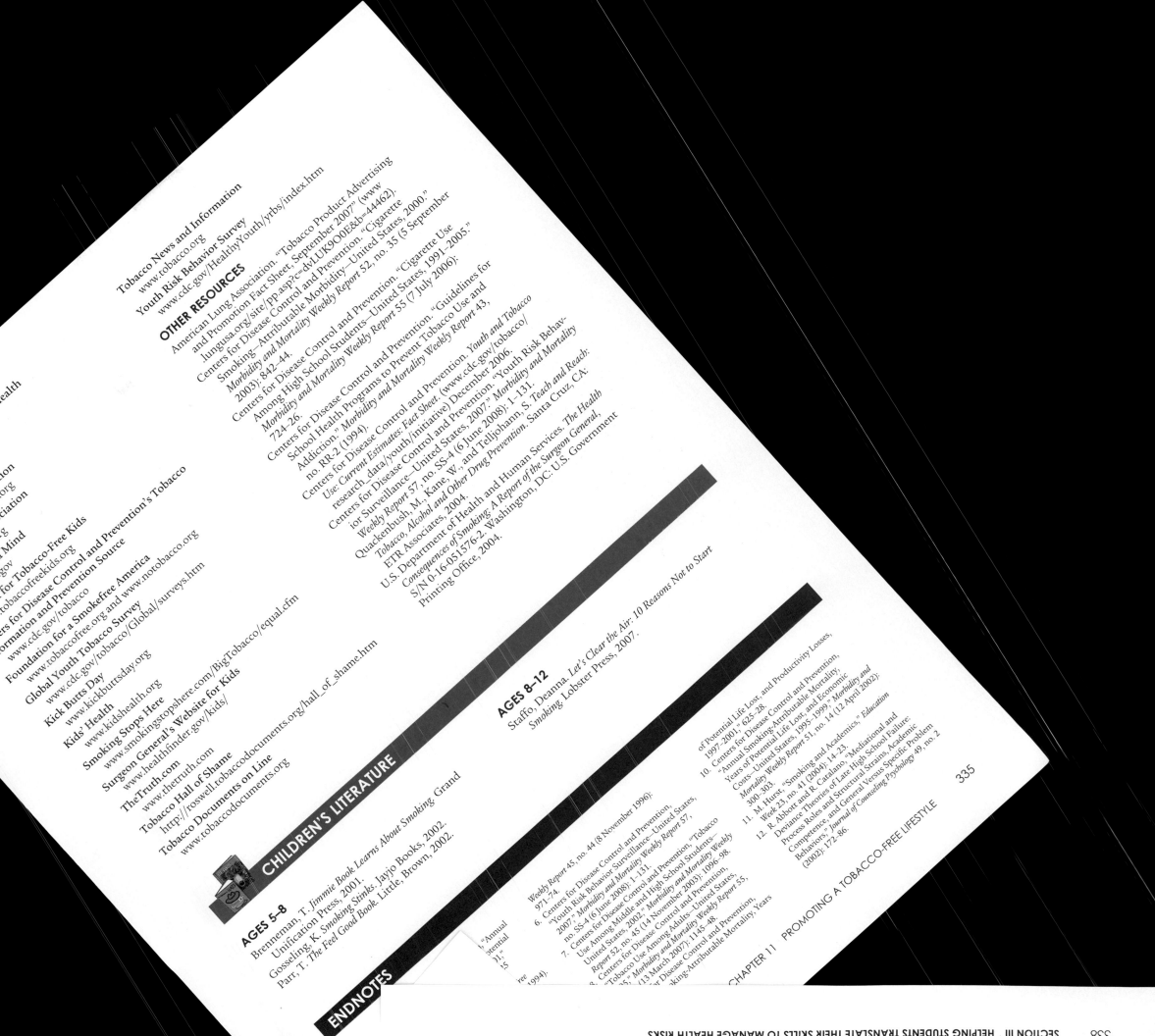

Tobacco News and Information

www.tobacco.org

Youth Risk Behavior Survey
www.cdc.gov/HealthyYouth/yrbs/index.htm

OTHER RESOURCES

American Lung Association. "Tobacco Product Advertising and Promotion Fact Sheet, September 2007" (www.lungusa.org/site/pp.asp?c=dvLUK9O0E&b=44462).

Centers for Disease Control and Prevention. "Cigarette Use ... United States, 2000." Morbidity and Mortality Weekly Report 52, no. 35 (5 September 2003): 842–44.

Centers for Disease Control and Prevention. "Cigarette Use Among High School Students—United States, 1991–2005." Morbidity and Mortality Weekly Report 55 (7 July 2006): 724–26.

Centers for Disease Control and Prevention. "Guidelines for School Health Programs to Prevent Tobacco Use and Addiction." Morbidity and Mortality Weekly Report 43, no. RR-2 (1994).

Centers for Disease Control and Prevention. Youth and Tobacco Use: Current Estimates: Fact Sheet. (www.cdc.gov/tobacco/research_data/youth/initiative) December 2006.

Centers for Disease Control and Prevention. "Youth Risk Behavior Surveillance—United States, 2007." Morbidity and Mortality Weekly Report 57, no. SS-4 (6 June 2008); 1–131.

Quackenbush, M., Kane, W., and Telljohann, S. Teach and Reach: Tobacco, Alcohol and Other Drug Prevention. Santa Cruz, CA: ETR Associates, 2004.

U.S. Department of Health and Human Services. The Health Consequences of Smoking. A Report of the Surgeon General, S/N 0-16-051576-2. Washington, DC: U.S. Government Printing Office, 2004.

...health
...ion
...org
...ciation
...ing
...Mind
...for Tobacco-Free Kids
...tobaccofreekids.org
...rmation and Prevention's Tobacco
...rs for Disease Control and Prevention Source
www.cdc.gov/tobacco
Foundation for a Smokefree America
www.tobaccofree.org and www.notobacco.org
Global Youth Tobacco Survey
www.cdc.gov/tobacco/Global/surveys.htm
Kick Butts Day
www.kickbuttsday.org
Kids' Health
www.kidshealth.org
Smoking Stops Here
www.smokingstopshere.com/BigTobacco/
Surgeon General's Website for Kids
www.healthfinder.gov/kids/
TheTruth.com
www.thetruth.com
Tobacco Hall of Shame
http://roswell.tobaccodocuments.org/hall_of_shame.htm
Tobacco Documents on Line
www.tobaccodocuments.org

CHILDREN'S LITERATURE

AGES 5–8

Brenneman, T. Jimmie Book Learns About Smoking. Grand Unification Press, 2001.

Gosseling, K. Smoking Stinks. Jayjo Books, 2002.

Parr, T. The Feel Good Book. Little, Brown, 2002.

AGES 8–12

Staffo, Deanna. Let's Clear the Air: 10 Reasons Not to Start Smoking. Lobster Press, 2007.

ENDNOTES

Weekly Report 45, no. 44 (8 November 1996); 971–74.

6. Centers for Disease Control and Prevention. "Youth Risk Behavior Surveillance—United States, 2007." Morbidity and Mortality Weekly Report 57, no. SS-4 (6 June 2008); 1–131.

7. Centers for Disease Control and Prevention. "Tobacco Use Among Middle and High School Students—United States, 2002." Morbidity and Mortality Weekly Report 52, no. 45 (14 November 2003) 1096–98.

8. Centers for Disease Control and Prevention, ... Morbidity and Mortality Weekly Report 55, ... (13 March 2007); 1143–48; ... Disease Control and Prevention, ...king-Attributable Mortality, Years of Potential Life Lost, and Productivity Losses, 1997–2001," 625–28.

10. Centers for Disease Control and Prevention, "Annual Smoking-Attributable Mortality, Years of Potential Life Lost, and Economic Costs—United States, 1995–1999," Morbidity and Mortality Weekly Report 51, no. 14 (12 April 2002); 300–303.

11. M. Hurst, "Smoking and Academics," Education Week 23, no. 41 (2004) 14–23.

12. R. Abbott and R. Catalano "Mediational and Deviance Theories of Late High School Failure: Process, Roles and Structural Strains Academic Competence," Journal of Counseling Psychology #9, no. 2 (2002): 172–86.

TABLE 12-1
National Summary of the Parent's Resource Institute for Drug Education (PRIDE) Survey, Grades 4–8, 2006–2007

Use of Selected Alcohol and Other Drugs

Frequency of Use of Risk Behavior	Grade 4–6			Grades 6–8		
	Annual Use %	Monthly Use %	Weekly Use %	Annual Use %	Monthly Use %	Weekly Use %
Drank Alcohol	5.5	1.7	0.6	31.0	10.8	5.5
Used Marijuana	1.0	0.6	0.3	8.2	4.9	3.5
Used Inhalants	2.5	1.1	0.5	5.4	2.5	1.7

SOURCE: PRIDE Questionnaire Report for Grades 4–6, 2006–2007 National Summary Grades 4–6 (www.pridesurveys.com), 2008; PRIDE Questionnaire Report for Grades 6–12, 2006–2007 National Summary (www.pridesurveys.com), 2008.

Although the rate of youth alcohol and other drug use has decreased over the past decade, it is still too high. For example, a study by the Substance Abuse and Mental Health Services (SAMHSA) found that every day 7,000 youth under age 16 have their first drink of alcohol.[5] Studies also show that students are more likely to use drugs and alcohol as they get older. The Parent's Resource Institute for Drug Education's (PRIDE) annual survey of a sample of students in grades 4–12 illustrates this trend (Table 12-1). For example, monthly consumption of beer is only 1.3 percent for students in grades 4–6 but 10.5 percent for students in grades 6–8. Monthly marijuana use also increases dramatically from late elementary (0.3 percent) to middle school (4.8 percent).[6,7]

Young people give many reasons for using alcohol and other drugs, including the following:

- Everybody's doing it
- Escape and self-medication
- Boredom and instant friends

These media and other influences contribute to the idea that young people already have that "everyone" uses alcohol and other drugs. Why is alcohol and other drug use in our society a big deal? The cost of substance abuse to the U.S. economy is estimated at over $414 billion annually. This cost includes productivity losses caused by premature death as well as the costs associated with the treatment of substance abusers, crime, and destruction of property. Alcohol abuse is the most costly, at $166.5 billion, with illicit drugs at $109 billion and smoking at $138 billion. The costs associated with alcohol and illicit drugs are disproportionately attributed to people between ages 15 and 44 because of higher prevalence rates and greater number of related deaths.[12] Because of the costs of alcohol and other drugs and the health problems related to their use, the federal government included several alcohol and other drug prevention objectives in Healthy People 2010 (Table 12-2).[13]

Alcohol advertising also has an effect on underage drinking. A recent study found that for each additional alcohol advertisement young people viewed (above the monthly youth average of 23 advertisements), they drank 1 percent more. That same study found that for each additional dollar per capita spent on alcohol advertising in a local market (above the national average of $6.80 per capita), young people drank 3 percent more.[11]

...about them. Alcohol was consumed in 71 percent of the episodes, including 65 percent of the top teen-rated episodes.[10]

13. M. Diego, T. Filed, and C. Sanders, "Academic Performance, Popularity, and Depression Predict Adolescent Substance Abuse," *Adolescence* 38, no. 149 (2003): 35–42.

14. D. Lee, E. Trapido, and R. Rodriguez, "Self-Reported School Difficulties and Tobacco Use Among Fourth- to Seventh-Grade Students," *Journal of School Health* 72, no. 9 (2002): 368–73.

15. R. Cox, L. Zhang, W. Johnson, and D. Bender, "Academic Performance and Substance Use: Findings from a State Survey of Public High School Students," *Journal of School Health* 77, no. 3 (2007): 109–15.

16. M. Resnick et al., "Protecting Adolescents from Harm: Findings from the National Longitudinal Study on Adolescent Health," *Journal of the American Medical Association* 278, no. 10 (1997): 823–32.

17. U.S. Department of Health and Human Services, *Preventing Tobacco Use Among Young People: A Report of the Surgeon General*, S/N 017-001-00491-0 (Washington, DC: U.S. Government Printing Office, 1994).

18. U.S. Department of Health and Human Services, *Reducing Tobacco Use: A Report of the Surgeon General*, S/N 017-023-00204-0 (Washington, DC: U.S. Government Printing Office, 2000).

19. Centers for Disease Control and Prevention, "Youth Risk Behavior Surveillance—United States, 2005."

20. Ibid.

21. Campaign for Tobacco-Free Kids, "Where Do Kids Get Their Cigarettes," 2007. (www.tobaccofreekids .org/research/factsheets/pdf/0127.pdf)

22. Campaign for Tobacco-Free Kids, "The Toll of Tobacco in the United States of America," 2007. (www.tobaccofreekids.org/research/factsheets/pdf/0072.pdf)

23. U.S. Federal Trade Commission (FTC), *Cigarette Report for 2004 and 2005*, 4 June 2007. (www.ftc.gov/reports/tobacco/2007cigarette2004-2005.pdf)

24. R. Wellman et al., "The Extent to Which Tobacco Marketing and Tobacco Use in Films Contribute to Children's Use of Tobacco: A Meta-Analysis," *Archives of Pediatrics and Adolescent Medicine* 160, no. 12 (2006): 1285–96.

25. L. Kann, S. Telljohann, and S. Wooley, "Health Education: Results from the School Health Policies and Programs Study 2006," *Journal of School Health* 77, no. 77 (2006): 408–34.

26. Ibid.

27. Ibid.

28. Ibid.

29. Centers for Disease Control and Prevention, "Guidelines for School Health Programs to Prevent Tobacco Use and Addiction," *Morbidity and Mortality Weekly Report* 43, no. RR-2 (1994): 1–18.

30. U.S. Department of Health and Human Services, *Preventing Tobacco Use Among Young People: A Report of the Surgeon General.*

31. Centers for Disease Control and Prevention, "Youth Risk Behavior Surveillance—United States, 2007."

32. Ibid.

33. National Cancer Institutes, *Smokeless Tobacco and Cancer: Questions and Answers, 2007.* (www.cancer.gov/cancertopics/factsheet/Tobacco/smokeless)

34. S. L. Tomar, "Snuff Use and Smoking in U.S. Men: Implications for Harm Reduction," *American Journal of Preventive Medicine* 23, no. 3 (2002): 248–54.

35. National Cancer Institutes, *Smokeless Tobacco and Cancer: Questions and Answers, 2007.*

36. Ibid.

37. Ibid.

38. S. L. Tomar, "Chewing Tobacco Use and Dental Caries Among U.S. Men," *Journal of the American Dental Association*, 130, no. 11 (1999): 1601–10.

39. U.S. Department of Health and Human Services, *Preventing Tobacco Use Among Young People.*

40. Ibid.

41. Centers for Disease Control and Prevention, "What Youth Should Know about Tobacco," 2007. (www.cdc.gov/tobacco/youth/information_sheets/00_pdfs/KIDTIPS4sm2.pdf)

42. U.S. Department of Health and Human Services, *Preventing Tobacco Use Among Young People.*

43. Ibid.

44. Ibid.

45. Ibid.

46. J. Hall, *The Smoking-Material Fire Problem* (Quincy, MA: National Fire Protection Agency, 2004).

47. Centers for Disease Control and Prevention, "Cigarette Smoking–Related Mortality," 2001. (www.cdc.gov/tobacco/research_data/health_consequences/mortali.htm)

48. American Cancer Society, "Overview: Lung Cancer: What Causes Lung Cancer? 2005. (www.cancer .org/docroot/CRI/content/CRI_2_2_2X_What_causes_lung_cancer_26.asp?sitearea=)

49. American Cancer Society, *Guide for Quitting Smoking*, 2003. (www.cancer.org/docroot/PED/content/PED_10_13X_Quitting_Smoking.asp)

50. U.S. Department of Health and Human Services, *Reducing Tobacco Use: A Report of the Surgeon General.*

51. U.S. Department of Health and Human Services, *The Health Consequences of Smoking: A Report of the Surgeon General*, S/N 0-16-051576-2 (Washington, DC: U.S. Government Printing Office, 2004).

52. Centers for Disease Control and Prevention, "Smoking and Tobacco Use," 2007. (www .cdc.gov/tobacco/health_effects/respiratory.htm)

53. National Institutes of Health, *Health Effects of Exposure to Environmental Tobacco Smoke, the Report of the California Environmental Protection Agency* (Bethesda, MD: U.S. Government Printing Office, 1999).

54. National Cancer Institute, *Secondhand Smoke: Questions and Answers*, 2005. (http://cis.nci.nih.gov/fact/10_18.htm)

55. A. K. Hackshaw, M. R. Law, and N. J. Wald, "The Accumulated Evidence on Lung Cancer and Environmental Tobacco Smoke," *British Medical Journal* 315 (1997): 980–88.

56. Centers for Disease Control and Prevention, "Health Education Curriculum Analysis Tool (HECAT): Model T Tobacco Free Curriculum," 2007, (www.cdc.gov/HealthyYouth/HECAT/pdf/HECAT_Module-T.pdf)

57. Ibid.

58. D. White and L. Rudisill, "Analyzing Cigarette Smoke," *Health Education* 18, no. 4 (August/September 1987): 50–51.

59. T. Zollinger, R. Saywell, C. Muegge, J. Wooldrige, S. Cummings, and V. Caine, "Impact of the Life Skills Training Curriculum on Middle School Students Tobacco Use in Marion County, Indiana, 1997–2000," *Journal of School Health*, 73, no. 9 (2003): 338–46.

60. R. Bell, P. Ellickson, and E. Harrison, "Do Drug Prevention Effects Persist into High School? How Project ALERT Did with Ninth Graders," *Preventive Medicine* 22 (1993): 463–83.

61. N. Harrington, S. Giles, R. Hoyle, G. Feeney, and S. Yungbluth, "Evaluation of The All Stars Character Education and Problem Behavior Prevention Program: Effects on Mediator and Outcome Variables for Middle School Students." *Health Education and Behavior*, 28, no. 5 (2001); 533–46.

62. S. Kulis, F. Marsiglia, E. Elek-Fisk, P. Dustman, P. Wagstaff, and M. Hecht, "Mexican/Mexican American Adolescents and Keepin' It REAL: An Evidence-Based, Substance Abuse Prevention Program," *Children and Schools*, 27 (2005): 133–45.

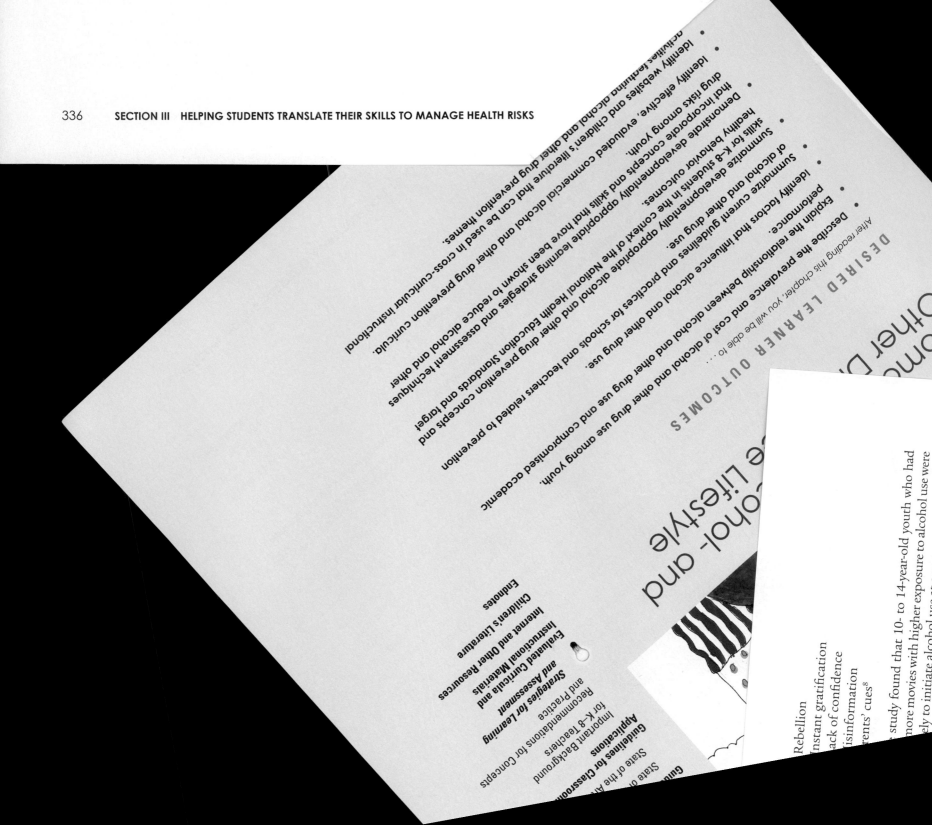

TABLE 12–2	HEALTHY PEOPLE

Healthy People 2010 Alcohol and Other Drug Prevention Objectives

Objective 26-6	Reduce the proportion of adolescents who report that they rode, during the previous thirty days, with a driver who had been drinking alcohol.
Objective 26-9	Increase the age and proportion of adolescents who remain alcohol- and drug-free.
Objective 26-10a	Increase the proportion of adolescents not using alcohol or any illicit drugs during the past thirty days.
Objective 26-10b	Reduce the proportion of adolescents reporting use of marijuana during the past thirty days.
Objective 26-11a	Reduce the proportion of high school seniors engaging in binge drinking of alcoholic beverages.
Objective 26-14	Reduce steroid use among adolescents.
Objective 26-15	Reduce the proportion of adolescents who use inhalants.
Objective 26-16	Increase the proportion of adolescents who disapprove of substance abuse.
Objective 26-17	Increase the proportion of adolescents who perceive great risk associated with substance abuse.

SOURCE: U.S. Department of Health and Human Services, *Healthy People 2010: Understanding and Improving Health*, 2nd ed. (Washington, DC: U.S. Government Printing Office. 2000).

Alcohol and Other Drug Use and Academic Performance

The education community has begun to recognize the relationship between drug use/abuse and learning and education. The National Survey on Drug Use and Health, found that frequency of the use of alcohol and marijuana during the prior month was related to academic performance. Results showed that 72.2 percent of students who had not used marijuana in the past reported an A or B average, compared with 58 percent of those who had used marijuana on one to four days in the past month, and 44.9 percent of those who had used marijuana on five or more days. The study found similar results for alcohol, with 72.5 percent of students who had not used alcohol during the past month reporting an A or B average, compared with 67.1 percent of those who used (but did not binge on) alcohol in the past month, and 57.7 percent of those who engaged in past month binge alcohol use.[14] Another study found that low academic performance (high school students with mostly Cs or below) during the twelve months preceding the survey was more prevalent among binge drinkers and marijuana users.[15] One study found that high school students who use alcohol or other drugs frequently are up to five times more likely than other students to drop out of school.[16]

As a result of the many academic performance problems, economic costs, and health consequences related to alcohol and other drug use, Americans have consistently identified drug abuse as one of the leading problems facing our schools.[17]

Factors That Influence Alcohol and Other Drug Use

The factors associated with greater potential for drug use are called risk factors. Before teachers and school districts can decide on their alcohol and other drug use prevention program or curriculum, they first must understand the risk factors associated with alcohol and other drug use.

These risk factors should be interpreted in the same way as risk factors for heart disease. That is, if a child or family has one of these risk factors, the child's chance of developing a problem with alcohol or other drug use increases. Having one of these risk factors does not mean that a child will become a drug abuser—only that the risk is increased. Seventeen identified risk factors can be categorized as school, individual/peer, family, and community risk factors.[18-24] Teachers should pay special attention to the school and the individual/peer risk factors.

School Risk Factors

Academic Failure Beginning in Late Elementary School There is an increased risk for adolescent drug abuse when a child receives low or failing grades in fourth, fifth, and sixth grades. Poor school performance increases the likelihood of an early start of substance use as well as subsequent use. Academic failure can have many causes, including a lack of parental support, boredom, a learning disability, and a poor match between student and teacher. Whatever the cause, children who have poor school performance are more likely to turn to drugs than are students who succeed in school.

Little Commitment to School Students who are not committed to education are more likely to engage in drug use. Fundamentally, this means that the child does not perceive school as meaningful or rewarding. Regardless of the reason, students in grades 4 through 7 who lose interest in school have a greater risk of getting into trouble with drugs. By way of confirmation, students who expect to attend college have significantly lower usage rates of drugs such as cocaine, stimulants, and hallucinogens.

Individual/Peer Risk Factors

Rebelliousness In middle or junior high school, students who do not adhere to the dominant values of society and who have a low religious affiliation tend to be at higher risk for drug abuse than students who are bonded to societal institutions of family, school, and church. Students who rebel against authority, particularly parents and school officials, are also at increased risk for substance abuse.

Antisocial Behavior in Early Adolescence A consistent relationship has been found between adolescent drug abuse and male aggressiveness in kindergarten through second grade. The risk is especially significant when this aggressiveness is coupled with shyness and withdrawal. Hyperactivity, nervousness, inattentiveness, and impulsiveness are

Aggressive or antisocial behavior is a risk factor for alcohol and other drug use.

Favorable Attitudes Toward Drug Use Specific favorable attitudes toward drug use are a risk factor for initiation of use. Having negative attitudes toward the use of alcohol or other drugs inhibits initiation. When children are in elementary school, they may carry strong, adult-supported feelings against drugs, but by the time they reach middle school many have developed more favorable attitudes. This shift in attitude often comes just before children begin to experiment with tobacco, alcohol, and other drugs.

Early First Use of Drugs Abusers of alcohol and other drugs tend to begin drinking or using at an early age. Generally, students begin using gateway drugs (tobacco and alcohol) and then progress to other, illegal, drugs. Early initiation into drug use increases the risk for extensive and persistent involvement in the use of more dangerous drugs. Children who begin to use tobacco, alcohol, or other drugs before age 15 are twice as likely to develop problems with drugs than are children who wait until they are older. Delaying first use until age 19 or older dramatically decreases the risk for subsequent abuse. In fact, young people who have not used tobacco, alcohol, or other drugs by age 21 are unlikely to ever become addicted.

Family Risk Factors

Family History of Alcoholism or Addiction to Other Drugs Current research continues to demonstrate a link between family drinking problems and adolescent alcohol and other drug abuse. Boys, in particular, have a high risk of abusing alcohol when they have alcoholic fathers. Alcoholics are more likely than nonalcoholics to have a history of parental or sibling alcoholism. In fact, 50 percent of today's alcoholics are the children of alcoholics.

Family Management Problems Family management problems have been a consistent predictor of adolescent alcohol and other drug abuse. These problems include poorly defined rules for behavior, poor monitoring of children's behavior, inconsistent consequences for breaking rules, excessively severe discipline, negative communication patterns (including constant criticism), and absence of praise. In order to make good decisions about their own behavior, children need to be given clear guidelines for acceptable and unacceptable behavior by their families (Teacher's Toolbox 12.1). They need to be taught basic skills, and they need to be provided with consistent support and recognition for acceptable behaviors as well as consistent but appropriate punishment for unacceptable behaviors.

Favorable Parental Attitudes Toward Alcohol and Other Drug Use Research confirms not only that child behaviors are related to family alcohol addiction but also that there is an increased risk that children will initiate drug use when their parents are users of alcohol and other drugs. If the parents involve their children in drug use, such as asking them to get a beer from the refrigerator, to light their

also characteristics of early antisocial behavior. Whatever the cause of the antisocial behavior and hyperactivity, students who exhibit these behaviors are at increased risk for abusing drugs as they get older. This risk factor includes a wide variety of behaviors, including school misbehavior and a low sense of social responsibility. Fighting, skipping school, and exhibiting general aggressiveness have been shown to be related to drug abuse. A consistent pattern of inappropriate classroom behaviors, including acting-out behaviors, is related to increased abuse of alcohol and other drugs.

Friends Who Use Drugs Association with drug-using friends during adolescence is one of the strongest predictors of adolescent drug use. Associating with friends who are involved in drug use operates independently of other risk factors. The evidence is clear that friends, rather than strangers, influence children to experiment with and continue to use drugs. This means that even children who grow up without other risk factors but who associate with children who use drugs are at an increased risk for drug use and/or abuse.

Gang Involvement The influence of gang involvement on alcohol and other drug use is even more pronounced than that of simply having drug-using friends. Being a gang member is a significant risk factor for alcohol and other drug use.

cigarette, or to mix them a drink, the likelihood that the children will use drugs increases.

Family Conflict   Serious, persistent conflict between children and their caregivers increases the risk for alcohol and other drug use, regardless of the type of family structure.

Community Risk Factors

Economic and Social Deprivation   Children from families who experience social isolation, extreme poverty, and poor living conditions are at elevated risk for delinquency. When extreme poverty accompanies childhood behavior problems, there is an increased risk for drug problems and alcoholism.

Transitions and Mobility   Transitions, such as residential moves and the move from elementary to middle school, are associated with increased rates of drug use and abuse. This is important for teachers who teach in transitional grades. For example, if a middle school begins at grade 5, fifth-grade teachers should focus more attention on drug abuse prevention. If a new child enters a class during the middle of the year, teachers should make sure that he or she has positive support from classmates.

Community Laws and Norms Favorable Toward Drug Use   Communities with laws that are favorable toward drug use, such as low taxes on alcohol, have higher rates of alcohol consumption and alcohol-related traffic fatalities. Greater availability of drugs in schools, combined with inadequate policies against alcohol and other drug use, leads to a higher use of drugs among students.

Availability of Alcohol and Other Drugs   When alcohol and other drugs are easily available in the community, the risk of use increases among youth. Risk is increased even when teens only perceive that alcohol and other drugs are easily available.

Low Neighborhood Attachment and Community Disorganization   There are higher rates of drug problems when people have little attachment to their neighborhood and community. Low neighborhood attachment can be present when people do not feel that they can make a difference in their community, when there is little involvement in area schools, and when voter turnout is low.

GUIDELINES FOR SCHOOLS

This section provides information about current alcohol and other drug prevention programs and policies in elementary and middle schools. The first part of the section includes data about the actual programs and policies in schools today; the second part provides ideas for teachers and administrators about what should be happening in schools to help children and adolescents stay drug free.

State of the Practice

The CDC periodically conducts the School Health Policies and Programs Study (SHPPS) to assess current school health policies and programs at the state, district, school, and classroom levels.[25] This study is important to determine the progress toward reaching the *Healthy People 2010* objectives; to help states determine technical assistance, funding needs, and priorities among their districts and schools; and to help school personnel determine how their school health policies and programs compare to those of other schools. Because alcohol and other drug use contributes to many deaths and injuries among young people, it is important that states and school districts have policies that reflect zero tolerance for alcohol and other drug use among students. Most school districts are doing a good job in this area. For example, 99.9 percent of school districts have a policy prohibiting alcohol use by students on school ground and 98.8 percent have a policy prohibiting alcohol use by students at all off-campus, school-sponsored events.[26]

States and school districts also are doing a good job of mandating alcohol and other drug prevention programs. For example, 76.5 percent of states, 79.0 percent of school districts, and 76.5 percent of schools require alcohol and other drug use prevention education at the elementary level. Elementary teachers who were required to teach alcohol and other drug prevention spent a median of 2.6 hours a year teaching the topic. Similar mandates are in force at the middle school level. Currently, 76.5 percent of states, 89.7 percent of school districts, and 84.6 percent of schools require alcohol and other drug use prevention education at the middle or junior high school level. Middle-level teachers who were required to teach alcohol and other drug use prevention spent a median of 5.5 hours a year teaching the topic.[27]

SHPPS also provides important data related to the alcohol and other drug prevention topics and skills being taught at the elementary and middle school levels.

TABLE 12–3

School Health Policies and Programs Study 2006 Data Related to Alcohol and Other Drug (AOD) Use Prevention

Alcohol-Use or Other Drug-Use Prevention Topic	% of All Elementary Schools	% of All Middle Schools
Benefits of not using alcohol	68.8	80.4
Benefits of not using illegal drugs	70.7	79.4
Distinguishing between medicinal and nonmedicinal drug use	66.4	75.1
Drink equivalents and blood alcohol content	17.1	62.9
Effects of alcohol or other drug use on decision making	70.2	81.5
How many young people use alcohol or other drugs	34.0	66.3
How students can influence or support others in efforts to prevent alcohol or other drug use	66.9	79.2
How students can influence or support others in efforts to quit using alcohol or other drugs	55.4	74.6
How to find valid information on services related to alcohol-use or other drug-use prevention or cessation	29.2	66.0
Influence of families on alcohol or other drug use	62.5	79.2
Influence of the media on alcohol or other drug use	51.0	77.9
Long-term health consequences of alcohol use and addiction	61.9	80.2
Long-term health consequences of illegal drug use and addiction	63.8	78.1
Making a personal commitment not to use alcohol or other drugs	70.2	72.2
Resisting peer pressure to use alcohol or other drugs	71.4	81.6
Short-term health consequences of alcohol use and addiction	68.8	79.7
Short-term health consequences of illegal drug use and addiction	66.9	77.5
Social or cultural influences on alcohol or other drug use	54.9	76.8

SOURCE: Centers for Disease Control and Prevention, *School Health Policies and Programs Study 2006 (SHPPS)* (Atlanta, GA: CDC, 2007) www.cdc.gov/HealthyYouth/shpps

Table 12–3 summarizes the findings. The concepts and skills taught most often by elementary teachers were resisting peer pressure to use alcohol and other drugs, the benefits of not using alcohol and illegal drugs, making a commitment not to use alcohol and other drugs, and the effects of alcohol or other drugs on decision making. Middle school teachers were most likely to teach resisting peer pressure to use alcohol and other drugs, effects of alcohol or other drugs on decision making, the benefits of not using alcohol, and the long-term health consequences of alcohol use and addiction.[28]

State of the Art

The previous discussion describes the state of the practice in alcohol and other drug prevention. It is even more important, however, for elementary and middle school teachers to understand what should be included in a successful, comprehensive alcohol and other drug prevention program. Before teachers can decide what to do in their classrooms to help prevent substance abuse, they must first understand what does and doesn't work in preventing young people from using alcohol and other drugs. To clarify what doesn't work, it is important to examine historical drug prevention programs that have not been successful.

History of Unsuccessful Drug Use Prevention Programs

Over the years, educators and health professionals have learned how to be more effective in promoting health-enhancing behaviors with students. Consequently, many changes in teaching strategies have occurred. This is espe-

cially true for drug prevention programs. It is important, however, to learn from past mistakes and to understand why some drug prevention strategies have been unsuccessful. Consistently incorporating successful drug prevention strategies into our schools and communities will likely result in a decrease in the rates of drug use by students.

In the 1960s, when there was a tremendous increase in drug usage, many teachers used scare tactics to try to deter their students from using drugs.[29] For instance, they taught their classes that, if students took LSD, they would experience a bad trip and either jump off a building or feel as though spiders were crawling all over them. Although this technique might have scared some students at first, it took only one student in the class to have a brother or sister who experienced a "good" LSD trip to make that teacher lose all credibility. Other inquisitive students might have read credible information on LSD and learned that bad trips did not always occur. Other teachers tried to scare their students by telling them they would become hooked on drugs after the first time they used them or that, if they were drinking and driving, they would be involved in a car crash. It is important for teachers to be truthful to students to maintain their credibility. Once teachers lose their credibility, students become skeptical of anything the teachers say. Another problem with scare tactics is that they tend to have short-lived outcomes. In other words, the effects of scare tactics might last for a few weeks, but then students return to their prior belief system.

In the early 1970s, a very popular component of a drug prevention program was to invite recovering addicts to class to discuss the problems they experienced with their addiction. Although this technique is still commonly used and might sound effective, many times students internalize messages that are different from those intended by the speaker. The intended message from the recovering addicts is not to get involved with drugs. Some students, however, conclude, "If I do get involved with drugs, I can get off of them, just as the speaker did." Another misinterpretation is "I am stronger than the speaker, and I won't get hooked on drugs."[30] Yet another problem with this strategy is that, if the recovering addicts are significantly older than the students, the students have difficulty relating to the intended message. Many athletes, actors, actresses, and musicians who are recovering addicts are used in antidrug commercials. These commercials give students the message that, if they use drugs and quit, they can recapture their original goals or become popular.

Later in the 1970s, many health professionals started using a different strategy for drug prevention. They believed that if the students were taught all of the facts about drugs, they would certainly choose not to try them or use them. These programs did increase knowledge about drugs; however, students' behavior was unaffected.[31] Individuals do not base their decisions about how to behave on information alone but also on their feelings, values, beliefs, and skills. Even adults do not make decisions based on information alone, even when that information is reinforced by law. This is shown by the number of adults who are involved in drinking and driving incidents and who do not wear seat belts. Information is the foundation for health-enhancing decisions, but other topics need to be included in effective drug prevention programs.

Another popular initiative is the "Just Say No" campaign. The "Just Say No" public service announcement campaign is not developmentally appropriate for many upper-elementary and middle-level students and is an ineffective way to deal with the drug problem in our country. In these public service announcements, children and adolescents are told to "Just Say No" but are not told how or why to say no to drugs. There are, however, "Just Say No" clubs in many school systems that have components of effective substance use prevention programs. These encourage students to say no to drug use and allow students to practice getting out of negative peer-pressure situations by using various peer resistance techniques. "Just Say No" clubs also provide social support for kids who do not use drugs and a positive alternative way to meet and make friends.

Another popular, though unsuccessful, program that is still being used is the "one-shot approach." In this model, schools organize a schoolwide assembly in which an expert addresses all students about the dangers of drugs and the wisdom of abstinence. Drug use, abuse, and refusal are very complex behaviors. Therefore, even the most entertaining or spectacular one-shot program cannot begin to have an impact on the use of tobacco, alcohol, and other drugs.[32]

Another popular elementary drug prevention program is the DARE program (Drug Abuse Resistance Education).

A father and son work together on a drug use prevention homework assignment.

DARE is the most widely used school-based drug prevention program in the United States. However, the results from multiple studies that have been conducted to determine the DARE program's effectiveness are disappointing. In fact, the United States General Accounting Office conducted six longitudinal evaluations of the DARE program and determined that the DARE program had no statistically significant long-term effect on preventing youth illicit drug use. Because of the results of these multiple evaluations, the DARE program has redesigned their elementary curriculum and is in the process of evaluating its effectiveness.[33]

The substance abuse prevention methods of the 1960s and 1970s were unsuccessful because they did not focus on the causes of drug use and abuse. Unfortunately, many teachers are still using these outdated methods. Every profession makes mistakes, but the key is to learn from those mistakes and make the necessary changes to be successful.

Key Alcohol and Other Drug Principles for Schools and Communities

The U.S. Department of Health and Human Services has identified a comprehensive list of principles that schools and communities should apply to help prevent alcohol and other drug use among youth (Teacher's Toolbox 12.2). These sixteen principles are intended to help parents, educators, and community leaders think about, plan for, and deliver research-based drug abuse prevention programs at the community level. The principles are divided

Principles for Preventing Alcohol and Other Drug Use Among Youth

RISK AND PROTECTIVE FACTORS

Principle 1: Alcohol and other drug prevention programs should enhance protective factors and reverse or reduce risk factors because the risk of becoming a drug abuser increases as the number of risk factors (e.g., deviant attitudes and behaviors) increases, and decreases as the number of protective factors (e.g., parental support) decreases. The possible impact of specific risk and protective factors changes with age. For example, risk factors within the family have greater impact on a younger child, whereas association with drug-abusing peers may be a more significant risk factor for an adolescent. Early intervention with risk factors (aggressive behavior and poor self-control) often has a greater impact than later intervention, by changing a child's life path (trajectory) away from problems and toward positive behaviors.

Principle 2: Prevention programs should address all forms of drug abuse, alone or in combination. These forms include the underage use of legal drugs (tobacco or alcohol); the use of illegal drugs (marijuana or heroin); and the inappropriate use of legally obtained substances (inhalants), prescription medications, or over-the-counter drugs.

Principle 3: Prevention programs should address the type of drug abuse problem in the local community, target modifiable risk factors, and strengthen identified protective factors.

Principle 4: Prevention programs should be tailored to address risks specific to population or audience characteristics, such as age, gender, and ethnicity, to improve program effectiveness.

PREVENTION PLANNING

Family Programs

Principle 5: Family-based prevention programs should enhance family bonding and relationships and include parenting skills; practice in developing, discussing, and enforcing family policies on substance abuse; and training in drug education and information. Family bonding is the foundation of the relationship between parents and children. Bonding can be strengthened through skills training on parent supportiveness of children, parent–child communication, and parental involvement.

Parental monitoring and supervision are critical for drug abuse prevention. These parenting skills can be enhanced with training on rule setting; techniques for monitoring activities; praise for appropriate behavior; and moderate, consistent discipline that enforces defined family rules.

Drug education and information for parents or caregivers reinforce what children are learning about the harmful effects of drugs and open opportunities for family discussions about the abuse of legal and illegal substances.

School Programs

Principle 6: Prevention programs can be designed to intervene as early as preschool to address risk factors for drug abuse, such as aggressive behavior, poor social skills, and academic difficulties.

Principle 7: Prevention programs for elementary school children should target improving academic and social-emotional learning to address risk factors for drug abuse, such as early aggression, academic failure, and school dropout. Education should focus on the following skills:

- Self-control
- Emotional awareness

- Communication
- Social problem solving
- Academic support, especially in reading

Principle 8: Prevention programs for middle or junior high and high school students should increase academic and social competence in the following skills:

- Study habits and academic support
- Communication
- Peer relationships
- Self-efficacy and assertiveness
- Drug resistance skills
- Reinforcement of antidrug attitudes
- Strengthening of personal commitments against drug abuse

Community Programs

Principle 9: Prevention programs aimed at general populations at key transition points, such as the transition to middle school, can produce beneficial effects even among high-risk families and children. Such interventions do not single out risk populations and therefore reduce labeling and promote bonding to school and community.

Principle 10: Community prevention programs that combine two or more effective programs, such as family-based and school-based programs, can be more effective than a single program alone.

Principle 11: Community prevention programs reaching populations in multiple settings (schools, clubs, faith-based organizations, and the media) are most effective when they present consistent, community-wide messages in each setting.

PREVENTION PROGRAM DELIVERY

Principle 12: When communities adapt programs to match their needs, community norms, or differing cultural requirements, they should retain core elements of the original research-based intervention, including

- Structure (how the program is organized and constructed)
- Content (the information, skills, and strategies of the program)
- Delivery (how the program is adapted, implemented, and evaluated)

Principle 13: Prevention programs should be long-term with repeated interventions (booster programs) to reinforce the original prevention goals. Research shows that the benefits from middle school prevention programs diminish without follow-up programs in high school.

Principle 14: Prevention programs should include teacher training in good classroom management practices, such as rewarding appropriate student behavior. Such techniques help to foster students' positive behavior, achievement, academic motivation, and school bonding.

Principle 15: Prevention programs are most effective when they employ interactive techniques, such as peer discussion groups and parent role-playing, that allow for active involvement in learning about drug abuse and reinforcing skills.

Principle 16: Research-based prevention programs can be cost-effective. Like earlier research, recent research shows that each dollar invested in prevention can result in a savings of up to $10 in treatment for alcohol or other substance abuse.

SOURCE: National Institute on Drug Abuse, *Preventing Drug Use Among Children and Adolescents: A Research-Based Guide For Parents, Educators, and Community Leaders*, 2nd ed. (Bethesda, MD: U.S. Department of Health and Human Services, 2003).

Teacher's Toolbox 12.3

Minimum Elements of a School Drug Policy Statement

A school's policy statement ought to contain at least the following elements:

1. A clear definition, based on state law, of what types of drugs and drug use are covered by the policy (making clear, for example, that prescribed medication is not covered but that drinking alcohol is)
2. A clear statement that the defined drugs and drug use are prohibited on school grounds, at school-sponsored functions, and while students are representing the school
3. A description of the consequences to be expected on violating the policy
4. An explanation of the process for referral to treatment—with a guarantee that self-referral will be treated in confidence and will not result in punishment

Source: *Drug Prevention Curricula: A Guide to Selection and Implementation* (Washington, DC: U.S. Department of Education, 1988).

into three categories: risk and protective factors, prevention planning (family, school, and community programs), and prevention program delivery.[34] Additional information about school drug policy is presented in Teacher's Toolbox 12.3.

GUIDELINES FOR CLASSROOM APPLICATIONS

Important Background for K–8 Teachers

This section presents basic information about alcohol, marijuana, inhalants, and prescription and over-the-counter drugs, the drugs that elementary and middle school students are most likely to use and abuse. There are too many drugs to discuss every one, and the majority of students do not use the other illicit drugs. Teacher's Toolbox 12.4 lists the most common drugs, along with their trade or slang names, the likelihood of physical and psychological dependence, their effects, and how long the drugs' effects last. Most of the information about illicit drugs in Teacher's Toolbox 12.4 is not developmentally appropriate for elementary and middle school children (see the section "Developmentally Appropriate Concepts and Skills"). However, teachers should possess basic literacy about these drugs, because students might ask questions about them. The common terms used in drug education and their definitions are listed in Teacher's Toolbox 12.5.

Alcohol

Alcoholic drinks contain ethyl alcohol, which is a depressant. Ethyl alcohol is not the same as isopropyl alcohol (rubbing alcohol) or methyl alcohol (wood alcohol). Methyl alcohol, even in small amounts, is dangerous. Isopropyl alcohol is found in antifreeze and some cosmetics and can be dangerous if ingested. Every year a small number of people die from drinking methyl alcohol, thinking it is the same as ethyl alcohol.

There are three main types of ethyl alcohol: beer, wine, and distilled spirits. Although some people believe beer is a less dangerous type of ethyl alcohol, all forms of ethyl alcohol are dangerous if misused. It is important to note that there is the same amount of ethyl alcohol in a 12-ounce beer, a 5-ounce glass of table wine, and a 1.5-ounce shot of 80 proof distilled spirits (Figure 12–1).[35]

Alcohol, along with tobacco, is a gateway drug. That is, those children who use tobacco and alcohol are more likely to use "hard" drugs later. It is important to delay the onset of alcohol use because it has been found that the younger the age of the beginning drinker, the more likely he or she will later turn to illegal drugs.[36] Unfortunately, 75 percent of high school students have had at least one drink of alcohol in their life and 44.7 percent have had at least one drink of alcohol in the past month. More disturbing, however, is that 26 percent of high school students have participated in heavy episodic drinking (five drinks in a row) in the past month.[37] Today, the estimated annual average consumption of alcoholic beverages per person in the United States is 2.17 gallons of pure ethanol: 57 percent from beer, 27 percent from liquor, and 14 percent from wine.[38]

Alcohol is the most commonly abused substance during adolescence.[39] Drinking has acute effects on the body, especially on the body of an adolescent who is not used to drinking alcohol. Researchers are beginning to recognize

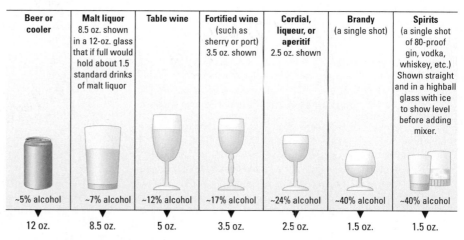

A standard drink is any drink that contains about 14 grams of pure alcohol (about 0.6 fluid ounces or 1.2 tablespoons). Above are standard drink equivalents. These are approximate, as different brands and types of beverages vary in their actual alcohol content.

FIGURE 12–1 | **How Much Is One Drink?**

Source: U.S. Department of Health and Human Services, *The Surgeon General's Call to Action to Prevent and Reduce Underage Drinking* (Washington, DC), 2007.

Commonly Abused Drugs

Category	Representative drugs	Street names	Potential short-term effects	Potential health effects
Opioids	Heroin	Dope, H, junk, brown sugar, smack	Relief of anxiety and pain; euphoria; lethargy, apathy, drowsiness, confusion, inability to concentrate; nausea, constipation, staggering gait.	Respiratory depression and arrest, tolerance, addiction, withdrawal, unconsciousness, coma, death.
	Opium	Big O, black stuff, hop		
	Morphine	M, Miss Emma, monkey, white stuff		
	Oxycodone, codeine, hydrocodone	Oxy, O.C., killer, Captain Cody, schoolboy, vike		
Central nervous system depressants	Alcohol	Booze, brewskies, cold one, hooch, hard stuff, sauce	Reduced anxiety, mood changes, (irritability, abusiveness), lowered inhibitions, impaired muscle coordination, reduced pulse rate, dizziness, slurred speech, drowsiness, loss of consciousness	Fatigue, confusion, impaired memory and judgment, tolerance, addiction, withdrawal, respiratory depression, death.
	Barbiturates	Barbs, reds, red birds, yellows, yellow jackets		
	Benzodiazepines (e.g., Valium, Xanax, Rohypnol)	Candy, downers, tranks, roofies, forget-me pill		
	Methaqualone	Ludes, quad, quay		
	Gamma hydroxy butyrate (GHB)	G, Georgia home boy, grievous bodily harm		
Central nervous system stimulants	Amphetamine, methamphetamine	Bennies, speed, black beauties, uppers, chalk, crank, crystal, ice, meth	Increased heart rate, blood pressure, metabolism; increased mental alertness and energy; nervousness, impulsive behavior; reduced appetite, loss of coordination	Rapid or irregular heartbeat, weight loss, heart failure, stroke, seizures, insomnia, delirium, panic attacks, paranoia, liver damage, memory loss, tolerance, addiction, withdrawal.
	Cocaine, crack cocaine	Blow, C, candy, coke, flake, rock, toot		
	Ritalin	JIF, MPH, R-ball, Skippy		
Marijuana and other cannabis products	Marijuana	Dope, grass, joints, Mary Jane, reefer, skunk, weed	Euphoria, slowed thinking and reaction time, confusion, anxiety, impaired balance and coordination, increased heart rate	Frequent respiratory infections, impaired lung function, precancerous changes in lungs, sperm abnormalities, impaired memory and learning, anxiety, panic attacks, tolerance, withdrawal.
	Hashish	Hash, hemp, boom, gangster		
Hallucinogens	LSD	Acid, boomers, blotter, yellow sunshines	Altered states of perception and feeling; nausea; increased heart rate, blood pressure; delirium; impaired motor function; numbness; weakness	Memory loss, depression, respiratory depression and arrest, persisting perception disorder (flashbacks), tremors, paranoia, tolerance.
	Mescaline (peyote)	Buttons, cactus, mesc		
	Psilocybin	Shrooms, magic mushrooms		
	Ketamine	K, special K, cat Valium, vitamin K		
	PCP	Angel dust, hog, love boat, peace pill		
	MDMA (ecstasy)	X, peace, clarity, Adam		
Inhalants	Solvents, aerosols, nitrites, anesthetics	Laughing gas, poppers, snappers, whippets	Stimulation, loss of inhibition, slurred speech, loss of motor coordination, loss of consciousness	Cramps, weight loss, muscle weakness, memory impairment, hearing loss, bone marrow damage, increased risk of cancer, damage to cardiovascular and nervous systems, sudden death.

SOURCES: National Institute on Drug Abuse, *Commonly Abused Drugs* (www.drugabuse.gov/DrugPages/DrugsofAbuse.html; retrieved 9 December 2004); U.S. Drug Enforcement Agency, *Photo Library* (www.usdoj.gov:80/dea/photo_library.html; retrieved 9 December 2004); U.S. Drug Enforcement Agency, *Drug Briefs and Backgrounds* (www.usdoj.gov:80/dea/concern/concern.htm; retrieved 9 December 2004).

the significant negative consequences of drinking on the adolescent brain. One area of the brain that is vulnerable to alcohol-related damage is the cerebral cortex, the region largely responsible for our higher brain functioning such as problem solving and decision making. Other areas of the brain negatively affected by alcohol are the hippocampus, which is important for memory and learning, and the cerebellum, which is important for coordination.[40] Heavy use of alcohol by adolescents may interfere with brain activity and brain development, leading to memory loss and the diminishment of other skills.[41] Magnetic resonance imaging (MRI) of brains shows that adolescents who abuse alcohol or are alcohol-dependent have smaller memory areas in the brain than do same-age nondrinking adolescents.[42]

Alcohol use can also alter judgment, vision, coordination, and speech, and its use often leads to dangerous risk-taking behavior. Because young people have lower body weight than adults, they absorb alcohol into their blood system faster and exhibit greater impairment for a longer time. Alcohol use not only increases the likelihood of being involved in a motor-vehicle crash but also increases the risk of serious injury in a crash because of its harmful effects on numerous parts of the body. Motor-vehicle crashes are the leading cause of death for 15- to 20-year-olds, and one-third of these crashes involve alcohol.[43] Alcohol use among

young people is also associated with fighting, crime, risky sexual behavior, depression, and suicide. Each year, approximately 5,000 people under the age of 21 die as a result of underage drinking. This includes 1,900 deaths from motor vehicle crashes, 1,600 as a result of homicide, 300 from suicide, and hundreds of others from injuries such as falls, burns, and drownings.[44]

When a person drinks alcohol, it takes time for the body to oxidize it. Alcohol always takes the same pathway in the body (Figure 12–2). First, alcohol travels through the esophagus to the stomach. The stomach is able to absorb about 20 percent of the alcohol, depending on how much and what kind of food is in the stomach. The rest of the alcohol, about 80 percent, travels to the small intestine and is absorbed into the bloodstream. The bloodstream then carries alcohol to all parts of the body, and it continues to circulate through the body until it is broken down and excreted. The brain is one of the organs influenced by alcohol. The more a person drinks, the more the control centers of the brain become depressed. In the short term, alcohol depresses the following functions sequentially: judgment, inhibitions, reaction time, coordination, vision, speech, balance, walking, standing, consciousness, breathing, and heartbeat—all affecting life itself. Alcohol is also transported to the liver, where it undergoes oxidation. The liver is able to oxidize about 0.5 ounce, or one drink, of alcohol per hour. If there is more than 0.5 ounce of alcohol in the body, the remainder circulates throughout the body until the liver can oxidize more alcohol. The amount of alcohol that circulates in the body and blood is known as the blood alcohol concentration, or BAC. As the BAC rises in the blood and reaches the brain, predictable changes occur (Table 12–4). The last organs to be affected by alcohol are the lungs and the kidneys, where about 10 percent of the alcohol is eliminated by breath and urine.[45]

Eight factors influence the absorption of alcohol into the bloodstream:

1. *Concentration of the alcoholic beverage.* The stronger the concentration of alcohol in the beverage, the faster the rate of absorption. If one person drinks 5 ounces of beer and another person drinks 5 ounces of wine, the person who drinks 5 ounces of wine will have a higher BAC, because wine has a higher concentration of alcohol (review Figure 12–1).

2. *Number of alcoholic beverages consumed.* The more alcoholic beverages a person consumes, the more alcohol there is in the body to absorb. There is a direct relationship between the amount of alcohol consumed and the BAC.

3. *Rate of consumption.* The faster alcohol is consumed, the higher the BAC. It is important to remember that the liver can oxidize only about 0.5 ounce of alcohol per hour; any additional alcohol stays in the blood and other organs in the body.

4. *Amount of food in the stomach.* The more food in the stomach, especially fatty foods, meat, and dairy products, the slower the absorption rate of alcohol.

TABLE 12–4

Alcohol Intoxication: Progressive States of Impairment with Increasing Blood Alcohol Concentration (BAC)

BAC	Possible Effects of Alcohol
0.01%	Usually mild effects, if any; slight changes in feeling; heightening of moods
0.03%	Feelings of relaxation and slight exhilaration; minimal impairment of mental function
0.06%	Mild sedation; exaggeration of emotion; slight impairment of fine-motor skills; increase in reaction time; poor muscle control; slurred speech
0.08%	Legal evidence of driving under the influence of alcohol in many states
0.09%	Visual and hearing acuity reduced; inhibitions and self-restraint lessened; increased difficulty in performing motor skills; clouded judgment
0.10%	Legal evidence of driving under the influence of alcohol in many states
0.12%	Difficulty in performing gross-motor skills; blurred vision; unclear speech; definite impairment of mental function
0.15%	Major impairment of physical and mental functions; irresponsible behavior; general feeling of euphoria; difficulty in standing, walking, talking; distorted perception and judgment
0.20%	Mental confusion; decreased inhibitions; gross-body movements can be made only with assistance; inability to maintain upright position; difficulty in staying awake
0.30%	Severe mental confusion; minimum of perception and comprehension; difficulty in responding to stimuli; general suspension of sensibility
0.40%	Almost complete anesthesia; depressed reflexes; likely state of unconsciousness or coma
0.50%	Complete unconsciousness or deep coma, if not death
0.60%	Death most likely now, if it has not already occurred at somewhat lower BACs, following depression of nerve centers that control heartbeat and breathing; person is "dead drunk"

SOURCE: From Charles Carroll and Dean Miller, *Health: The Science of Human Adaptation*, 4th ed. Copyright © 1986 Wm. C. Brown Publishers, Dubuque, IA. All rights reserved. Reprinted with permission.

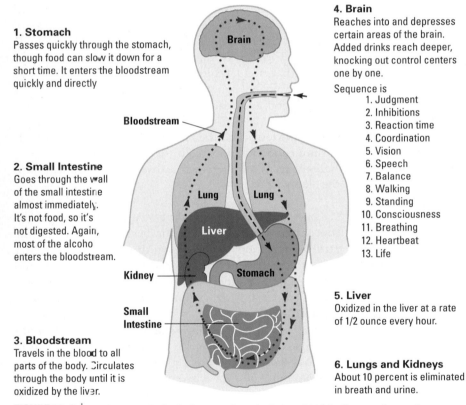

1. Stomach
Passes quickly through the stomach, though food can slow it down for a short time. It enters the bloodstream quickly and directly

2. Small Intestine
Goes through the wall of the small intestine almost immediately. It's not food, so it's not digested. Again, most of the alcohol enters the bloodstream.

3. Bloodstream
Travels in the blood to all parts of the body. Circulates through the body until it is oxidized by the liver.

4. Brain
Reaches into and depresses certain areas of the brain. Added drinks reach deeper, knocking out control centers one by one.

Sequence is
1. Judgment
2. Inhibitions
3. Reaction time
4. Coordination
5. Vision
6. Speech
7. Balance
8. Walking
9. Standing
10. Consciousness
11. Breathing
12. Heartbeat
13. Life

5. Liver
Oxidized in the liver at a rate of 1/2 ounce every hour.

6. Lungs and Kidneys
About 10 percent is eliminated in breath and urine.

FIGURE 12–2 | Pathways of Alcohol How does alcohol work? This diagram shows what happens to that drink after it's swallowed.

6. *Type of alcoholic drink.* Carbonated alcoholic beverages, such as champagne, and alcohol mixed in warm drinks, such as a hot rum toddy, are absorbed faster than other kinds of alcoholic beverages.

7. *Body weight and build.* Greater body weight allows a higher volume in which alcohol can be distributed. This means that a person who weighs more will be less affected by the same amount of alcohol ingested by a smaller person. Also, the greater the person's muscle mass, the lower the BAC.[46]

8. *Gender.* On average, females weigh less and have a higher proportion of body fat than do males. This means that females generally have a lower proportion of body water in which to distribute alcohol.

Alcohol has several negative short-term side effects.[47] Because students deal with the present, it is important to stress these negative short-term side effects. Students will identify better with the immediate consequences.

5. *Drinking history.* People who have been heavy drinkers for an extended period of time build a tolerance to alcohol, which means they have to drink more alcohol than before to get the same desired effects.

1. *Perception and motor skills.* As indicated in Table 12–4, even a BAC of 0.06 percent (one or two drinks) begins to impair fine-motor skills, reaction time, speech, and muscle control. These perception and motor skills are important

in many sport, art, and music skills, as well as in riding a bike or driving a car. Over 50 percent of the motor-vehicle deaths that occur each year are related to alcohol use. At higher BAC levels, there is a decrease in visual and hearing acuity, balance, and estimation of time.

2. *Heart and blood vessels.* Alcohol temporarily increases both heart rate and blood pressure. Alcohol also constricts the arteries that supply the heart. Although persons who drink alcohol feel warm, they are actually losing body heat, because alcohol causes the peripheral blood vessels to dilate, or expand. This can be extremely dangerous in cold weather and can lead to hypothermia, the extreme loss of body heat.

3. *Sleepiness.* Because alcohol is a depressant, it causes a person to become tired. Many persons believe

The combination of drinking and driving accounts for over 50 percent of the motor-vehicle deaths that occur each year.

alcohol is a stimulant because of the way alcohol users act; however, those actions result from alcohol initially depressing the part of the brain that controls inhibitions. Alcohol might help a person fall asleep more quickly, but the sleep is often light, making the person feel tired and unrefreshed even after eight hours of sleep.

4. *Emotions.* Alcohol depresses the prefrontal lobe of the brain, which controls judgment. With lack of judgment, persons under the influence of alcohol tend to have poor decision-making skills. This tends to increase risk taking and reduce inhibitions, temporarily decrease fears, and increase feelings of relaxation. Increased risk taking, combined with decreased motor skills and perception, causes many motor-vehicle crashes each year.

5. *Hangovers.* Hangovers can have many signs and symptoms, including headache, nausea, stomach distress, and generalized discomfort. These symptoms are caused by drinking too much alcohol, and only time can take away the unpleasant feelings. Theories attribute hangovers to an accumulation of acetaldehyde (a toxic chemical), dehydration, the depletion of important enzymes, and the metabolism of congeners (toxins) in the alcohol. Vodka tends to be low in congeners, whereas red wine and bourbon are high. The higher the concentration of congeners, the greater the probability of a hangover.

6. *Overdose.* Alcohol can depress the central nervous system to the point at which the heart and lungs quit functioning, resulting in cardiac or respiratory arrest. This occurs when large amounts of alcohol have been consumed over a short period of time. Approximately 4,500 people under the age of 21 die from alcohol poisoning or an alcohol overdose each year.[48]

7. *Lack of nutritional value.* Alcohol provides only empty calories, which means it does not have any nutritional value. Alcohol has a high caloric content—9 calories/gram. Persons who are trying to watch their weight should avoid alcohol.

Although many young students have a difficult time dealing with future outcomes, they should know that prolonged, heavy use of alcohol has several negative long-term side effects. For instance, longtime alcohol abusers shorten their life span by ten to twelve years. Other, more common, long-term side effects include the following:[49,50]

• Cirrhosis of the liver is commonly associated with alcohol consumption. With a person's continued use of alcohol, liver cells are damaged and gradually destroyed. The destroyed cells often are replaced by fibrous scar tissue, a condition known as cirrhosis of the liver. This disease is the leading cause of death among alcoholics and is the twelfth leading cause of death in the United States.

• Heavy drinkers also can experience gastrointestinal system disorders, which cause irritation and inflammation of the esophagus, stomach, small intestine, and pancreas. Alcohol use and cancer also have been correlated. Clinical and epidemiological studies have implicated excessive use of alcohol in the development of cancers of the mouth, pharynx, esophagus, and pancreas.

• Another problem for heavy drinkers is that they fulfill their caloric intake from alcoholic beverages instead of from food. Even though alcohol is high in calories, it has little nutritional value, such as vitamins and minerals. Decreased appetite, vomiting, and diarrhea contribute to nutritional imbalances. The diuretic properties of alcohol also cause a loss of water-soluble vitamins.

• Hypoglycemia is another problem associated with heavy alcohol use. Hypoglycemia is a condition in which blood sugar levels are lower than normal. Because heavy drinkers put such stress on the liver, it has a difficult time producing glucose and storing it as glycogen.

• Long-term, heavy use of alcohol can lead to cardiovascular disease. Long-term use of alcohol damages the heart muscle, leading to a condition known as cardiomyopathy, which can be fatal. It also can lead to premature heartbeats or total loss of rhythm in the heartbeat.

• Long-term heavy drinking increases the risk of developing high blood pressure, some kinds of stroke, and some types of cancer.

• Alcohol abuse is an additional long-term consequence of using alcohol. Alcohol abuse is a pattern of drinking that is linked to problems such as the inability to meet work, school, or family responsibilities; involvement in drunk-driving arrests; car crashes related to alcohol use; and relationship difficulties.[51]

• Alcoholism or alcohol dependence can be another negative consequence of long-term alcohol use. Alcoholism is a disease that has formal diagnostic criteria, with four symptoms:

1. Craving alcohol—a craving sometimes as strong as the need for food or water
2. Not being able to stop drinking once it has started
3. Physical addiction, characterized by withdrawal symptoms such as sweating, shakiness, nausea, and anxiety
4. Tolerance, or the need to drink greater amounts of alcohol to feel high, or intoxicated

Research shows that the risk for developing alcoholism runs in families. In fact, studies show that children of alcoholics are about four times more likely than the general population to develop problems related to alcohol. However, that does not mean that a child of an alcoholic will also become an alcoholic—50 percent of children of alcoholics do not become alcoholics themselves. It is also important for students to understand that some people develop alcoholism in the absence of any associated family history.[52–54]

Nearly one out of thirteen American adults is an alcoholic or abuses alcohol.[55] Because teachers will be dealing with children of alcoholics (COAs), it is important that they have factual information regarding these children. Alcoholism affects the entire family. Living with a nonrecovering alcoholic can contribute to stress for all family members, including children.

A child in such a family may have a variety of problems:

• *Guilt.* The child may see himself or herself as the main cause of the parent's drinking.
• *Anxiety.* The child may worry constantly about the situation at home. He or she may fear fights and violence between the parents or that the alcoholic parent will become sick or injured.
• *Embarrassment.* Parents may give the child the message that there is a terrible secret at home. The ashamed child does not invite friends home and is afraid to ask anyone for help.

• *Inability to have close relationships.* Because the child has been disappointed by the drinking parent many times, he or she often does not trust others. In addition, because the child may not invite friends home, it may be difficult to develop friendships with others.
• *Confusion.* The alcoholic parent will change suddenly from being very loving to being angry, regardless of the child's behavior. Additional confusion exists because there is no regular daily schedule in the child's life (bedtimes and mealtimes). A routine is very important for a child.
• *Anger.* The child feels anger at the alcoholic parent for drinking, and may be angry at the nonalcoholic parent for lack of support and protection.
• *Depression.* The child feels lonely and helpless to change the situation.

Although the child tries to keep the alcoholism a secret, teachers may sense that something is wrong. Mental health professionals advise that the following behaviors may signal a drinking or other problem at home:

• Failure in school; truancy
• Lack of friends; withdrawal from classmates
• Delinquent behavior, such as stealing or violence
• Frequent physical complaints, such as headaches or stomach aches
• Abuse of drugs or alcohol
• Aggression toward other children
• Risk-taking behaviors
• Depression or suicidal thoughts or behavior[56]

These children deserve special attention, because they most likely come from a home that lacks warmth, security, and even physical care. COAs can benefit when teachers help these students

Develop autonomy and independence

Develop a strong social orientation and social skills

Engage in acts of "required helpfulness"

Develop a close bond with teachers

Develop day-to-day coping strategies[57]

The National Association for Children of Alcoholics (NACoA) has prepared a kit entitled "Children of Alcoholics: A Kit for Educators" that provides basic information about family addiction and its impact, and about ways to help the children who are affected by this pervasive but often unrecognized public health problem. This 31-page kit contains information for teachers and handouts for students. It can be downloaded at http://nacoa-stage.shs .net/pdfs/EDkit_web_06.pdf.[58]

Marijuana

Marijuana is most likely to be the first illicit drug young people will use. It is a drug that is easy for many young people to get. In fact, 37 percent of students surveyed thought they could get marijuana within a day.[59]

Young people believe that marijuana is not very harmful. They think that it is natural, has a medical use, is harmless, and is not addictive.[60] Therefore, it is important that teachers understand the dangers associated with marijuana so that they can counteract their students' beliefs about the drug.

Marijuana is a green or gray mixture of dried and shredded flowers and leaves of the hemp plant *Cannabis sativa*. The marijuana plant contains over 400 chemicals, but the main active chemical in marijuana is delta-9-tetrahydrocannabinol (THC). When smoked, THC passes from the lungs and is quickly absorbed into the bloodstream and then transported to the brain. It is redistributed to the rest of the body, so that within thirty minutes much of the THC is gone from the brain. All forms of marijuana have immediate and negative physical and mental effects.

The immediate short-term effects of smoking marijuana include

- Problems with memory and recalling events
- Impaired attention, judgment, and other cognitive functions
- Impaired coordination and balance
- Increased heart rate
- Dry mouth
- Occasional anxiety, fear, or panic[61]

Because several of these short-term consequences are related to driving ability, marijuana use is associated with an increase in car crashes. Marijuana is second only to alcohol as the drug most detected in impaired drivers, fatally injured drivers, and motor vehicle crashes.[62] For more on the signs of drug use, see Teacher's Toolbox 12.6.

Smoking marijuana also has long-term negative effects. Research shows that marijuana use increases users' difficulty in trying to quit smoking cigarettes. In addition, memory and learning skills are affected longer than with intoxication. The adverse effects can last for days or weeks, even after the drug has worn off. Long-term marijuana use also can increase the risk of chronic cough, bronchitis, and emphysema. The risk of head, neck, and lung cancer also increases with long-term use, because marijuana smoke contains 50 to 70 percent more carcinogenic hydrocarbons than tobacco smoke. Marijuana users usually inhale more deeply and hold their breath longer than do tobacco smokers, which increases users' risk of lung cancer. Finally, long-term marijuana use can lead to addiction in some people. Currently more than 2 million people in the United States meet the diagnostic criteria for dependence on marijuana. More than 22,000 people recently entering drug abuse treatment programs reported that their primary drug of abuse was marijuana.[63,64]

Inhalants

Inhalants are legal, everyday products that have a useful purpose, but can be misused. Inhalant abuse is the intentional inhalation of a volatile substance for the purpose of achieving a mind-altering effect or a euphoric state. One national survey indicated that about 6 percent of U.S.

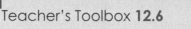

Teacher's Toolbox 12.6

Signs and Symptoms of Drug Use

Changing patterns of performance, appearance, and behavior might signal the use of drugs. The items in the first category provide direct evidence of drug use; the items in the other categories may indicate drug use. Adults should watch for extreme changes in children's behavior, changes that together form a pattern associated with drug use.

SIGNS OF DRUGS AND DRUG PARAPHERNALIA

- Possession of drug-related paraphernalia, such as pipes, rolling papers, small decongestant bottles, eye drops, or small butane torches
- Possession of drugs or evidence of drugs, such as pills, white powder, small glass vials, or hypodermic needles; peculiar plants or butts, seeds, or leaves in ashtrays or in clothing pockets
- Odor of drugs, incense, or other cover-up scents

IDENTIFICATION WITH DRUG CULTURE

- Drug-related magazines, drug-related slogans on clothing
- Conversation and jokes that are preoccupied with drugs
- Hostility in discussing drugs
- Collection of beer cans

SIGNS OF PHYSICAL DETERIORATION

- Memory lapses, short attention span, difficulty in concentration
- Poor physical coordination, slurred or incoherent speech
- Unhealthy appearance, indifference to hygiene and grooming
- Bloodshot eyes, dilated pupils

DRAMATIC CHANGES IN SCHOOL PERFORMANCE

- Marked downturn in student's grades—not just from Cs to Fs but from As to Bs and Cs; assignments not completed
- Increased absenteeism or tardiness

CHANGES IN BEHAVIOR

- Chronic dishonesty (lying, stealing, cheating), trouble with the police
- Changes in friends, evasiveness in talking about new ones
- Possession of large amounts of money
- Increasing and inappropriate anger, hostility, irritability, secretiveness
- Reduced motivation, energy, self-discipline, self-esteem
- Diminished interest in extracurricular activities and hobbies

---

children have tried inhalants by the time they reach fourth grade. Inhalants also are one of the few substances abused more by younger children.[65] Inhalants can be divided into four categories:

- *Volatile solvents* are liquids that vaporize at room temperature. They are found in a multitude of inexpensive, easily available products used for common household and industrial purposes. These include paint thinners and removers, dry-cleaning fluids, degreasers, gasoline, glues, correction fluids, and felt-tip marker fluids.

- *Aerosols* are sprays that contain propellants and solvents. They include spray paints, deodorant and hair sprays, vegetable oil sprays for cooking, and fabric protector sprays.
- *Gases* include medical anesthetics, as well as gases used in household and commercial products. Medical anesthetic gases include ether, chloroform, halothane, and nitrous oxide, commonly called laughing gas. Nitrous oxide, the most abused of these gases, can be found in whipped cream dispensers and products that boost octane levels in racing cars. Household and commercial products containing gases include butane lighters, propane tanks, whipped cream dispensers, and refrigerants.
- *Nitrites* often are considered a special class of inhalants. Unlike most other inhalants, which act directly on the central nervous system (CNS), nitrites act primarily to dilate blood vessels and relax the muscles. Other inhalants are used to alter mood, but nitrites are used primarily as sexual enhancers. Nitrites include cyclohexyl nitrite, isoamyl (amyl) nitrite, and isobutyl (butyl) nitrite. Cyclohexyl nitrite is found in room odorizers. Amyl nitrite is used in certain diagnostic procedures and is prescribed to some patients for heart pain. Illegally diverted ampules of amyl nitrite are called "poppers" or "snappers" on the street. Butyl nitrite is an illegal substance that is often packaged and sold in small bottles.[66,67]

Inhalants can be breathed in through the mouth or the nose in the following ways:

- Sniffing or snorting fumes from containers
- Spraying aerosols directly into the mouth or nose
- Sniffing or inhaling fumes from substances sprayed or deposited inside a plastic or paper bag (known as "bagging")
- "Huffing" from an inhalant-soaked rag stuffed in the mouth
- Inhaling from balloons filled with nitrous oxide[68,69]

Nearly all abused inhalant products produce effects similar to those of anesthetics, which slow down the body's functions. When inhaled via the nose or mouth into the lungs in sufficient concentrations, inhalants can cause intoxicating effects. Intoxication can last only a few minutes or up to several hours if the inhalant is taken repeatedly. Initially, users might feel slightly stimulated; with successive inhalations, they might feel less inhibited and less in control. Ultimately, a user can lose consciousness. A strong need to continue using inhalants has been reported among some individuals, particularly those who have used inhalants for prolonged periods over several days.[70]

Sniffing highly concentrated amounts of the chemicals in solvents or aerosol sprays can directly induce heart failure and death, known as sudden sniffing death syndrome. Other irreversible effects caused by inhaling specific solvents are

- Hearing loss—from paint sprays, glues, dewaxers, cleaning fluids, and correction fluids

- Limb spasms—from glues, gasoline, whipped cream dispensers, and gas cylinders
- Central nervous system or brain damage—from paint sprays, glues, and dewaxers
- Bone marrow damage—from gasoline
- Short-term memory loss—from a variety of inhalants

Serious but potentially reversible effects include

- Liver and kidney damage—from correction fluids and dry-cleaning fluids
- Blood oxygen depletion—from organic nitrites, such as poppers, rush, varnish removers, and paint thinners[71-73]

Many teachers include the topic of inhalants when teaching about alcohol and other drugs. Most experts, however, believe that the topic should be included in teaching about safety and label reading. The following concepts about inhalants, developed by Isabel Burk, a drug prevention consultant, should be taught for the specified age groups.[74]

Ages 4–7

- Teach about oxygen's importance to life and body functioning.
- Discuss the need for parental supervision and adequate room ventilation for cleaning products, solvents, glues, and other products.
- Be a good role model; let students see you reading labels and following instructions.

Ages 7–10

- Define and discuss the term *toxic;* students can practice reading labels and following instructions.
- Teach about oxygen's importance to life and body functioning, with emphasis on body systems and brain functions.
- Discuss the need for parental supervision, following directions, and adequate room ventilation.
- Discuss and discourage "body pollution" and introducing poisons into the body.
- Be a good role model; let students see you reading labels and following instructions.

Ages 10–14

- Discuss negative effects of oxygen deprivation.
- Teach/reinforce peer resistance skills.
- Discuss environmental toxins and personal safety issues.

Over-the-Counter and Prescription Drugs

Medicines, or legal drugs, are used to cure illness, relieve pain, prevent the spread of disease, and prolong life. They can be prescription drugs or over-the-counter (OTC) drugs. Prescription drugs can be obtained only through a licensed professional practitioner, whereas OTC drugs can be bought in a store without a prescription. Medicines can cause harm if misused. Drug misuse is the use of a legal drug in an improper way, such as taking more than the recommended

Caregivers should always assist children with prescription and over-the-counter medications.

dosage, taking a medicine longer than needed or prescribed, not taking the medication long enough, or using someone else's prescribed medication. Students need to be taught that all medicines should be taken under adult supervision and that the directions should be read and followed.

A number of recent studies indicate that the intentional abuse of prescription drugs—pain relievers, tranquilizers, stimulants, and sedatives—to get high is a growing concern, particularly among teens, in the United States. In fact, among people aged 12 to 17, prescription drugs have become the second most abused illegal drug, behind marijuana. Though overall teen drug use is down nationwide and the percentage of teens abusing prescription drugs is still relatively low compared to those using marijuana, there are troubling signs that teens view prescription drug abuse as safer than illegal drugs, and parents are unaware of the problem. In fact, for the first time, there are just as many new abusers (12 and older) of prescription drugs as there are for marijuana. Pain relievers are currently the most abused type of prescription drug, followed by stimulants, tranquilizers, and sedatives. One of the big concerns with the abuse of prescription drugs is that adolescents are more likely than young adults to become dependent on prescription medication.[75]

Over-the-counter (OTC) drugs are also problematic. For example, it has been reported that some young people are abusing OTC cough medicines containing dextromethorphan (DXM), an effective and safe cough-suppressant ingredient. If the directions are followed, products containing DXM produce few side effects and have a long history of safety and effectiveness. Some teens, however, are attempting to get high by taking much larger than recommended doses of DXM in OTC cough syrups, tablets, and gel caps. In high doses, DXM can have hallucinogenic and dissociative effects.[76] The most recent Monitoring the Future survey found that 4 percent of eighth-grade students used DXM in the last year to get high.[77] Regardless of the type of legal drug, teachers should stress the importance of reading and following the directions on both OTC and prescription medications.

Recommendations for Concepts and Practice

Healthy Behavior Outcomes

The goal of health education is to help students adopt or maintain health-enhancing behaviors. School districts and teachers should identify the health-enhancing behaviors they would like their students to maintain or adopt. The following list identifies some possible healthy behavior outcomes related to promoting an alcohol- and other drug-free lifestyle. Though not all of the suggestions are developmentally appropriate for students in grades K–8, this list can help teachers understand how the learning activities they plan for their students support both short- and long-term desired behavior outcomes.

Ways to Promote an Alcohol- and Other Drug–Free Lifestyle

Use over-the-counter and prescription drugs properly and safely.

Avoid experimentation with alcohol and other drugs.

Avoid the use of alcohol.

Avoid the use of illegal drugs.

Avoid driving while under the influence of alcohol and other drugs.

Avoid riding in a car with a driver who is under the influence of alcohol and other drugs.

Quit using alcohol and other drugs if already using.

Seek help for stopping the use of alcohol and other drugs (for self and others).[78]

Developmentally Appropriate Concepts and Skills

As with other health topics, teaching related to promoting an alcohol- and other drug–free lifestyle should be developmentally appropriate and be based on the physical, cognitive, social, emotional, and language characteristics of specific students. Teacher's Toolbox 12.7 contains a list of suggested developmentally appropriate concepts and skills to help teachers create lessons that encourage students to practice the desired behavior outcomes by the time they graduate from high school. Note that some of these concepts and skills are reinforced in other content areas (the concept "explain why household products are harmful" also applies to safety and unintentional injury).

Developmentally Appropriate Concepts and Skills for Promoting an Alcohol- and Other Drug–Free Lifestyle

Grades K–2 Concepts	Grades 3–5 Concepts	Grades 6–8 Concepts
NHES 1: Core Concepts		
• Explain why household products are harmful if ingested or inhaled.	• Summarize why household products are harmful if ingested or inhaled.	• Explain the dangers of alcohol and experimenting with other drugs, including inhalants.
• Explain the harmful effects of medicines when used correctly.	• Explain the benefits of medicines when used correctly.	• Differentiate between proper use and abuse of over-the-counter medicines.
• Describe the potential risks associated with over-the-counter medicines.	• Explain how to use medicines correctly.	• Differentiate between proper use and abuse of prescription medicines.
• Identify family rules about medicine use.	• Summarize the potential risks associated with inappropriate use of over-the-counter medicines.	• Summarize the negative consequences of using alcohol and other drugs.
	• Summarize the potential risks associated with inappropriate use and abuse of prescription medicines.	• Describe the relationship between using alcohol and other drugs and other health risks, such as unintentional injuries, violence, suicide, sexual risk behaviors, and tobacco use.
	• Explain the difference between medicines and illicit drugs.	• Determine reasons why people choose to use or not to use alcohol and other drugs.
	• Identify short- and long-term effects of alcohol use.	• Describe situations that could lead to the use of alcohol and other drugs.
	• Identify family and school rules about alcohol use.	• Describe how mental and emotional health can affect alcohol or other drug-use behaviors.
		• Explain why using alcohol or other substances is an unhealthy way to manage stress.
		• Discuss the harmful effects of using weight loss pills.
		• Describe the health risks of using performance-enhancing drugs.
		• Explain the dangers of drug dependence and addiction.
		• Explain the risks associated with using alcohol or other drugs and driving a motor vehicle.
		• Explain school policies and community laws about alcohol and other drugs.
		• Determine the benefits of being alcohol and drug free.
		• Describe positive alternatives to using alcohol and other drugs.
		• Describe the relationship of alcohol and other drug use to the major causes of death and disease in the United States.
		• Explain the relationship between intravenous drug use and transmission of bloodborne diseases, such as HIV and hepatitis.

Grades K–2 Skills	Grades 3–5 Skills	Grades 6–8 Skills
NHES 2: Analyze Influence		
	• Identify internal influences on alcohol and other drug use.	• Analyze the factors that influence a person's decision to use or not use alcohol and other drugs.
	• Identify external influences on alcohol and other drug use.	• Describe how personal and family values influence decisions about using alcohol and other drugs.
	• Identify various strategies used in the media that encourage and discourage the use of over-the-counter and prescription drugs.	

Grades K–2 Skills *(continued)*	Grades 3–5 Skills *(continued)*	Grades 6–8 Skills *(continued)*
	• Identify various strategies used in the media that encourage and discourage the use of alcohol. • Explain why friends ask friends to use alcohol. • Identify common missed messages about alcohol in the media. • Explain that most elementary and middle school students do not use alcohol.	• Explain family and societal influences on alcohol and other drug use. • Describe how peers can influence choices about using alcohol and other drugs. • Analyze positive and negative displays of alcohol and other drug use on television and in movies. • Analyze various strategies used in the media to encourage or discourage alcohol use. • Explain that most middle school students do not use alcohol. • Explain that most adolescents do not use illicit drugs.

NHES 3: Accessing Information, Products, and Services

• Identify trusted adults who can help read and follow directions on medicine labels.	• Identify sources of accurate information about medicines. • Demonstrate the ability to read and follow labels of common household medicines. • Identify sources of accurate information about alcohol.	• Evaluate a variety of sources of information about medicines. • Describe how to follow directions for correct use of over-the-counter and prescription medicines. • Distinguish accurate information about alcohol from inaccurate information. • Demonstrate the ability to access and evaluate sources of information about alcohol and other drug use. • Demonstrate the ability to access school and community resources to help if someone is affected by the drug use of another person. • Demonstrate the ability to locate school and community resources to assist with problems related to alcohol and other drug use. • Analyze the information found on the warning labels of alcohol products.

NHES 4: Interpersonal Communication

• Demonstrate what to say when calling 9-1-1 or other emergency numbers when someone has taken too much medicine.	• Demonstrate what to say when calling 9-1-1 or other emergency numbers when someone has taken too much medicine. • Demonstrate effective verbal and nonverbal ways to refuse alcohol. • Explain personal reasons for choosing to be alcohol free.	• Demonstrate effective refusal skills when pressured to use alcohol or other drugs. • Demonstrate how to ask for help from a trusted adult for someone with an alcohol or drug problem. • Demonstrate effective negotiating skills to avoid riding in a car with someone who has been using alcohol or other drugs. • Summarize personal reasons for choosing to remain alcohol and drug free. • Demonstrate how to ask for help from a parent, other trusted adult, or friend when pressured to use alcohol or other drugs.

NHES 5: Decision Making

	• Explain positive outcomes of being alcohol free. • Identify positive alternatives to using alcohol.	• Demonstrate decision-making skills to be alcohol and drug free. • Explain how decisions about alcohol and drug use will affect relationships with friends and family. • Predict how not using alcohol or other drugs contributes to positive health outcomes. • Summarize positive alternatives to using alcohol and other drugs.

(continued)

Grades K–2 Skills *(continued)*	Grades 3–5 Skills *(continued)*	Grades 6–8 Skills *(continued)*
NHES 6: Goal Setting		
	• Set a goal to avoid using alcohol. • Develop a plan for avoiding offers to use alcohol. • Make a commitment to be alcohol and drug free. • Describe how personal goals can be affected by alcohol and other drug use.	• Discuss how the use or nonuse of alcohol or other drugs might affect plans for the future. • Make a commitment to be alcohol and drug free. • Make a commitment to avoid riding in a motor vehicle with a driver who has been drinking alcohol or using other drugs. • Develop a personal plan to improve health by staying alcohol and drug free.
NHES 7: Self-Management		
• Acknowledge personal responsibility for asking an adult for help when taking medicines.	• Express intention to be alcohol free.	• Express intentions to be alcohol and drug free. • Express intentions to avoid riding in a motor vehicle with a driver who has been drinking alcohol or using other drugs.
NHES 8: Advocacy		
	• Demonstrate how to communicate the benefits of being alcohol and drug free to others. • Demonstrate ways to encourage friends to be alcohol free.	• Articulate to others the benefits of remaining alcohol and drug free. • Demonstrate how to effectively persuade and encourage others not to use alcohol and other drugs. • Demonstrate ways to support friends and family members who choose not to drink alcohol. • Demonstrate ways to support friends and family who are trying to stop using alcohol or other drugs.

Source: Centers for Disease Control and Prevention, *Health Education Curriculum Analysis Tool (HECAT)* (Atlanta, GA: CDC, 2007). www.cdc.gov/HealthyYouth/Hecat/index.htm

Sample Students' Questions and Suggested Answers Regarding Alcohol and Other Drugs

A list of some commonly asked questions about alcohol and other drugs and some suggested answers follows. It is not enough to just read the suggested answer—teachers should actually practice saying them aloud. Teachers are encouraged to think of other questions students might ask and to practice answering them as well.

1. *Why do people take illegal drugs?*
There are lots of reasons. They might not know how dangerous they are. They also might not know how to handle their problems, so they take drugs to forget about them. Many times, young people take drugs because of outside pressure from peers or from what they see in the media. None of these are good reasons to take drugs.

2. *Why are some drugs good for you and some drugs bad for you?*
When you get sick, the drugs the doctor gives you will help you get better. But if you take these drugs when you're healthy, they can make you sick. Also, some drugs, such as LCD, are never good for you. To be safe, never take any drugs unless your parent, your caregiver, or the doctor says it's okay.

3. *Is alcohol addictive?*
A person who drinks alcohol on a regular basis can become addicted. This usually happens to people who have been drinking for several years and who drink almost every day. However, some people can become addicted much faster—even after just a few months of regular drinking. It is important to wait until you are 21 to begin drinking alcohol, because people who wait until that age almost never become addicted.

4. *Can you get hooked on marijuana?*
Long-term marijuana abuse can lead to addiction in some people. They abuse the drug even though it interferes with family, school, and recreational activities. Long-term marijuana users can experience cravings and withdrawal symptoms when they try to quit.[79]

5. *What does it mean to get high?*
Being high is the feeling a person gets when taking a drug. It is usually a good feeling, followed by a complete letdown, or crash. These temporary highs are not worth it, because a person will want to feel that way always and usually will have to take more and more of a drug to get that high feeling.

6. *Why do people sell drugs?*

People sell drugs for many reasons. Some people sell drugs just to make money, others sell drugs so they have enough money to buy drugs for themselves. Regardless of the reason, it is against the law and hurts many young people.

7. *Are drugs really that bad for you?*

Yes. People who use drugs usually say they feel great at first, but that feeling doesn't last long. Over time, they need more and more of the drug to get the same high. This really increases the risk for addiction and, in some cases, overdose. Drugs can ruin people's health, make them drop out of school, cause them to lose friends, and hurt their judgment so that they do some really dangerous things.

8. *What should I do if I have a friend who wants to start sneaking his or her parent's beer?*

This is a difficult situation, but you do have influence over other people. First, don't agree to join your friend. Second, try to convince your friend not to do it by explaining some of the health and legal problems related to alcohol and pointing out that, if your friend gets caught, he or she will lose his or her parents' trust. Ask other friends to help you convince your friend that this is a bad idea.

9. *Can I make an alcoholic in my family stop drinking?*

No. It is important to know that an alcoholic needs help to stop drinking, but no one can be forced to accept the help, no matter how hard you try or what you do. It is also important to know that you cannot provide the help that an alcoholic needs. An alcoholic needs the help of people trained to treat the disease. Also, it is important to remember that it is not your fault that someone in your family is an alcoholic. If you want to talk to someone about the problem, remember that you can talk to the school counselor.

10. *Why can't kids drink if their parents can?*

Kids' bodies and brains are still developing, and alcohol has a greater effect on their physical and mental well-being, compared with its effect on adults. For example, people who begin drinking before age 15 are four times more likely to develop alcoholism than those who begin at age 21.

11. *Aren't beer and wine safer than liquor?*

No. One 12-ounce bottle of beer or 5-ounce glass of wine has as much alcohol as 1.5 ounces of liquor. Regardless of the type of drink, alcohol can cause you problems.

STRATEGIES FOR LEARNING AND ASSESSMENT

Promoting an Alcohol- and Other Drug–Free Lifestyle

This section provides examples of standards-based learning and assessment strategies for promoting an alcohol- and other drug–free lifestyle. The strategies begin with a restatement of

the standard and a reminder of the assessment criteria, drawn from the RMC rubrics in Appendix B. Strategies are written as directions for teachers and include applicable theory of planned behavior (TPB) constructs in parentheses (intention to act in healthy ways, attitudes toward behavior, subjective norms, perceived behavioral control). These learning and assessment strategies provide building blocks for standards-based lessons and units that can be tailored to local needs. Assessment criteria are used with permission from the Rocky Mountain Center for Health Promotion and Education (RMC). See Appendix B for Scoring Rubrics.

Additional strategies for learning and assessment for Chapter 12 can be found at the Online Learning Center. Appendix D, a complete list of all the strategies, is available at the Online Learning Center.

NHES 1 | Core Concepts

Students will comprehend concepts related to health promotion and disease prevention to enhance health.

ASSESSMENT CRITERIA

- Connections—Describe relationships between behavior and health; draw logical conclusions about connections between behavior and health.
- Comprehensiveness—Thoroughly cover health topic, showing breadth and depth; give accurate information.

Grades K–2

Medicine Cabinet Safety   Students can draw pictures of places in the home where storing medicines is safe and appropriate. Students can add words or pictures to illustrate rules about taking medicines at home and at school ("Take only your own medicine" and "Take medicine under the supervision of an adult, such as a parent, nurse, or doctor"). Students should tell why the proper use and storage of medicines is important.

ASSESSMENT | For an assessment task, students can draw a picture about using medicine safely and write a sentence to explain their picture. For assessment criteria, students should give correct information and describe a relationship between behavior (safe use of medication) and health. Meeting this criterion requires that students' sentences have a "because" statement to explain the relationship (Take your medicine the way the doctor says, because too much can make you sick). (Construct: Attitudes toward behavior.)

Safe and Unsafe Products   Ask students to explain their ideas about the words *safe* and *unsafe*. Students can make a class list of safe or unsafe products found in and around homes. Ask students to think about products that would or would not harm them if they swallowed them or got them on their skin. Safe items include milk, orange juice, water, coffee, and tea. Unsafe items include gasoline, bleach, bathroom cleaners, insecticides, and pills from a medicine cabinet. Ask students to think a little harder about products such as sunscreen, which would be safe on the skin but unsafe to swallow. Next, have students classify pictures or empty, clean containers of safe or unsafe items by placing them in one of two large boxes labeled "safe" and "unsafe." Students might want to draw on, color, or decorate the boxes to illustrate their ideas about safe or unsafe products. Provide enough product containers and pictures so that every child has a turn to place an item in one of the boxes.

ASSESSMENT | The assessment task for this activity is the students' categorization (placing products in a box or bag) of products as safe or unsafe. For assessment criteria, students should make correct decisions and be able to explain their decisions accurately. Students should explain why the unsafe products would be dangerous if used incorrectly. (Construct: Attitudes toward behavior.)

Grades 3–5

Short-Term Effects of Alcohol Use   Students can make a class list of things they like to do that require good balance (walking, running, playing tag games, dancing, doing gymnastics, playing sports, riding a bicycle, skateboarding, and in-line skating). Next, ask for a volunteer to demonstrate walking a straight line. Tape down a long piece of masking tape (15 feet) to guide the student. After the demonstration, spin the student around several times and ask him or her to try to walk the straight line again. The student will not be able to succeed at the task this time because of the balance difficulties that result from spinning. Identify loss of balance as one of the short-term effects of alcohol use. Students should discuss how loss of balance from alcohol use would affect the things they like to do now (riding a bicycle) and want to do in the future (driving a car). Help students think about this activity. While it's fun to spin around and even feel dizzy when students are playing, they wouldn't choose to feel dizzy while they are doing something that requires good balance. Make the distinction between spinning around for fun in a safe situation and being off-balance in a situation that could cause someone to get hurt.

ASSESSMENT | For an assessment task, students can identify activities they like to do that require good balance and explain how alcohol use could keep them from doing the activities well or could cause them or others to get hurt. For assessment criteria, each child should identify at least one activity and draw a conclusion about connections between alcohol use and health. (Construct: Attitudes toward behavior.)

Drawing the Line   Bring old magazines to class for this activity. (Ask others to save magazines for you. Also check with your librarian, doctor, or dentist to get the old magazines they discard.) Students can look through the magazines and cut out pictures of products and activities that are healthful and products and activities that are harmful. Students can display their selections by gluing them onto a piece of paper or a poster, with one side of the sheet labeled "healthy for me" and the other labeled "harmful to me." Students are "drawing the line" between these concepts. Create a gallery around the room, so that students can see and discuss each other's pictures. Students should tell why they made selections for both sides of their poster. Students probably will choose pictures of people using tobacco and alcohol for the harmful side.

ASSESSMENT | For an assessment task, students can work in pairs or small groups to make their healthy/harmful posters. For assessment criteria, students should categorize correctly and explain their decisions, drawing conclusions about connections between behaviors and health. (Constructs: Attitudes toward behavior, subjective norms.)

Remaining Drug Free   Ask students to brainstorm a list of why adolescents use drugs. Answers may include

- To feel grown-up
- Out of boredom
- Everyone else is doing it
- Curiosity
- To feel good

Divide students into small groups and assign one of the reasons to each group. Instruct students to create a poster that counteracts their assigned reason to use drugs. For example, the group who is assigned "out of boredom" could create a list of fun or constructive activities that they can do in their free time that will help them feel better emotionally and physically.

ASSESSMENT | The group poster is the assessment task for this activity. For assessment criteria, students should present their posters to the class and explain how their ideas successfully counteract the reason to use drugs. (Construct: Attitudes toward the behavior)

Grades 6–8

Short-Term Effects of Alcohol Use   For this activity, bring old sunglasses or eyeglasses, Vaseline, a pitcher of water, and a drinking glass to class. Prepare the eyeglasses before the lesson by smearing Vaseline over both lenses. To begin the lesson, set the drinking glass on a table and ask a volunteer to pour water from the pitcher into the glass without touching or picking up the glass. This task should be easy to perform. Next, have the volunteer put on the glasses and try pouring the water into the glass again. This time, the task will be difficult because vision is distorted. Identify blurred or distorted vision as a short-term effect of alcohol use. Talking with students about this activity is important. Not being able to see how to pour the water is funny for the volunteer and the classmates who are watching. Teachers should acknowledge this. Remind students that the classroom is a safe place to try these kinds of experiments, but blurry or distorted vision wouldn't be funny in a situation where clear vision is important (crossing a street, riding a skateboard, catching or hitting a baseball).

ASSESSMENT | For an assessment task, students can brainstorm a list of things they like to do now (riding a bike) and would like to do in the future (drive a car) that would be affected if they couldn't see well because of drinking alcohol. For assessment criteria, each student should name an activity and draw conclusions about the connection between alcohol use and vision and how this short-term effect could cause harm to self and others. (Construct: Attitudes toward behavior.)

Help Us Learn What *We* Want to Know: Real AOD Questions from a Real Seventh-Grade Classroom   Seventh-grade health education teacher Donna Rodenhurst shared this learning strategy for alcohol and other drugs from her standards-based classroom in Kaneohe, Hawaii. Rodenhurst asked her students to put their heads together to decide exactly what *they* wanted to know about various kinds of alcohol and other drugs. After class discussions, the students compiled the following list of questions:

When was it made? How long has it been around?

Where did it come from?

Who created it?

What are the effects on the body? What happens when you take it?

Why do people use it?

What are other names (street names) for the drug?

Who uses it? What percentage of people use it?

How much does it cost?

How is it taken?

What may have influenced people to take the drug?

What age are most people who take it?

What form does it come in?

Why do people need it?

How do they get it?

What's its *real* purpose?

How can you tell users from others?

The students worked together in groups of four or five to access information (NHES 3) to learn core concepts (links to NHES 1) about the drug name they pulled from a bowl (Rodenhurst prepared slips of paper in advance). By working this way, no drugs were repeated, and the students were able to learn about a wide variety of AOD topics of interest to them. The students were excited to see which drug their group would draw. Rodenhurst arranged for the students to work with the school librarian to find resources and websites to answer their questions. The students created posters and presented their information orally to the class. Each group chose eight to ten questions to answer with their poster and presentation. The students said that they enjoyed this project because they had a say in what they wanted to learn.

ASSESSMENT | For an assessment task, teachers and students can work together to identify the kind of end products students could prepare to demonstrate their learning. The students in this class created posters and prepared oral presentations. For assessment criteria, students should decide what would make a "great presentation" (answering eight to ten questions in the class list). Students should provide accurate information, draw conclusions about the connections between behavior and health, cite their resources, and explain why their resources are valid sources of information. (Constructs: Attitudes toward behavior, perceived behavioral control.)

NHES 2 | Analyze Influences

Students will analyze the influence of family, peers, culture, media, technology, and other factors on health behaviors.

ASSESSMENT CRITERIA
- Identify both external and internal influences on health.
- Explain how external and internal influences interact to impact health choices and behaviors.
- Explain both positive and negative influences, as appropriate.

Grades K–2

Advertising in the World Around Us Analyzing influences is an abstract concept that older students process more easily than younger students. However, advertising often is aimed at young children, and they can learn to be more aware of the constant messages in the world around them. Ask students to name television commercials that they remember well and to tell what makes the ads easy to remember. Children might, in fact, mention some of the beer commercials that feature animation and humorous situations. Ask children why commercials are on television (to try to get them to buy a certain product). Ask students if they ever have been disappointed with a purchase that wasn't quite like the commercial promised? What does that tell students about advertising and commercials?

ASSESSMENT | For an assessment task, students can describe a commercial they have seen and what made the product look like a good thing to buy. Explain to students that companies work very hard to make their products attractive. For assessment criteria, students should name at least one way the commercial tried to make the product look inviting to

young people. Do students think they could see through these commercials in the future? (Construct: Attitudes toward behavior.)

What Does Stress Have to Do with Alcohol? As in other content areas, help students realize that some people use alcohol to cope with stress and problems. However, using alcohol doesn't make the stress or problem go away—it is still there. Students can give examples of stress or problems people might try to solve with alcohol and come up with healthy ways people can cope that do not involve using alcohol. This activity links to NHES 7, self-management.

ASSESSMENT | For an assessment task, students can describe the ways they know they are feeling stress or having a problem (nervous, headache, scared, frustrated, heart beats fast). For assessment criteria, students should identify three ways they know they are experiencing stress or a problem and three healthy ways to cope. (Construct: Perceived behavioral control.)

Grades 3–5

Why Are All the People in the Alcohol Ads So Good-Looking? Collect or have students collect color alcohol advertisements from magazines. Students can work in small groups to discuss what the people portrayed in the ads seem to have in common. The students might say that the people all seem to be relaxed and having fun—and they all are very attractive. Students can use the list of advertising techniques in Chapter 3 to spot the kinds of strategies alcohol makers use to make their products appear inviting. Students might note techniques such as bandwagon, snob appeal, fun and friendship, and romance. Ask students their opinions on whether the advertisements are telling the whole story of alcohol use. What kinds of problems do real people have with alcohol (alcoholism, losing a job for not showing up for work, not having enough money for food because of spending on alcohol, violent behavior in families)? What are the ads leaving out? Having students examine misleading portrayals of alcohol use is especially important, because some students might mistakenly believe that alcohol is safer than the drugs they see antiuse commercials about on television.

ASSESSMENT | As with tobacco advertising, for an assessment task students can make truth ads that mock the original alcohol ads and provide a more truthful depiction of alcohol use. Students can explain and display their advertisements in the classroom and around the school. For assessment criteria, students should point out the false claims of the original ads and how they have counteracted them with their advertisements. This activity links to NHES 8, advocacy. (Construct: Perceived behavioral control.)

Getting Support Have a discussion about the influences that encourage use of alcohol (media, friends, older siblings). Ask students to create their list of five people who will help them stay alcohol free. Next to each person's name, students should write how that person can help them stay alcohol free. Encourage students to share the list with each person they wrote down.

ASSESSMENT | The list of people is the assessment task. For assessment criteria, students should indicate how the people will help them stay drug free. (Construct: Subjective norms)

Grades 6–8

Carousel Divide students into five groups. Tape five large pieces of chart paper or newsprint around the room with the headings "Social," "Family," "Educational," "Financial," and "Emotional."

NHES 4 | Interpersonal Communication

Students will demonstrate the ability to use interpersonal communication skills to enhance health and avoid or reduce health risks.

ASSESSMENT CRITERIA

- Use appropriate verbal/nonverbal communication strategies in an effective manner to enhance health or avoid/reduce health risks.
- Use appropriate skills (negotiation skills, refusal skills) and behaviors (eye contact, body language, attentive listening).

Grades K–2

Asking Adults for Help Health educators recommend teaching peer resistance/refusal skills in upper-elementary and middle-level grades. In lower-elementary grades, students should practice skills for clear communication to get the help they need. Students can practice calling 9-1-1 and staying on the line in emergency situations. They also can practice asking adults for help (say "I need your help," tell what happened, tell what they did, repeat "I need your help"). Students can practice and role-play their communication skills. Although this activity is not specific to alcohol and other drug use, students might encounter AOD situations in which they need to get help for someone.

ASSESSMENT | For an assessment task, give students various scenarios in which they need to ask or call for help. For example, the students see an older student push a classmate. How would they ask a teacher for help? In another example, the students see an elderly neighbor collapsed on the front steps of her apartment. How would they get help? Students can work in pairs to demonstrate what they would do to get the help they need. For assessment criteria, students should give a clear message about needing help and provide accurate answers to questions (location, what happened). (Construct: Perceived behavioral control.)

Nonverbal Communication Skills Small children understand and enjoy the idea of nonverbal communication—body language. Students can demonstrate different messages without saying anything aloud ("Stop," "No," and "I'm sad"). Students can stand and practice as a group. They also might enjoy portraying a particular idea they have chosen and having their classmates guess what they are saying. Although this activity is not specific to alcohol and other drug use, learning to use nonverbal communication is a building block for communicating clear refusal skills as children grow older.

ASSESSMENT | For an assessment task, students can work in pairs to demonstrate a nonverbal message to their classmates. Classmates can try to guess the message that is being communicated. Teachers can write different messages on slips of paper for students to pick (We need you to come with us, We're confused, We're so tired), or students can decide on their own messages. For assessment criteria, students should communicate their message clearly to others without using any words. (Construct: Perceived behavioral control.)

Grades 3–5

Effective and Ineffective Refusals Students might have learned and practiced peer resistance/refusal skills in other content areas. Now they can apply their skills to alcohol and other drug use. Students can work in groups to write scenarios in which they are pressured to try alcohol or other drugs. Have them exchange their scenarios with other groups, who will rehearse and demonstrate effective and ineffective refusals for dealing with the situations. Each group can read their scenario to the class and then demonstrate both effective

and ineffective peer pressure resistance techniques. For example, repeated refusals (no, not interested . . . no thanks . . . no, not for me . . .) can be an effective technique, while giving a mixed message (well, okay . . . no, stop . . . well, maybe . . .) can be ineffective.

ASSESSMENT | Students can use the peer pressure resistance techniques in Chapter 3 in their demonstrations of communication strategies. For assessment criteria, students should demonstrate and explain the difference between effective and ineffective techniques. (Construct: Perceived behavioral control.)

Talking with Friends About AOD Decisions Students might find themselves in situations in which they want to talk with friends about decisions their friends are about to make. How can students help their friends make a healthy decision without turning them off? Create or have students create scenarios in which a friend is considering alcohol or other drug use or is going to a location where AOD likely will be used. Students can work in pairs to write a scenario in which they know that a friend will be making a decision about using alcohol or other drugs (being invited to ride with a group of students who smoke pot on the way to and from school). As a class, students can discuss ways of communicating that are agreeable, as well as ways of communicating that turn them off. With this discussion in mind, students should decide on a way to talk to their friends about making a healthy decision in a way they think their friends will hear and consider tuning out. Students can explain their scenarios and communication plans to the class and ask for feedback.

ASSESSMENT | For assessment criteria, students should demonstrate a clear message and appropriate communication behaviors (eye contact, a respectful tone, attentive listening, restatement of friends' points of view, alternatives, and expression of needs, wants, and feelings). (Constructs: Subjective norms, perceived behavioral control.)

Grades 6–8

Saving Face One of the important aspects of communication and resistance skills is staying safe while maintaining relationships—saving face for oneself and for others. Middle-level students do not want to call attention to themselves as being different. Resistance skills should allow them to take healthy actions without appearing foolish or uncool to their friends and peers. Students can brainstorm situations they want to avoid or get out of while still appearing to be just like other kids. For example, a new student at school gets offered a drink of alcohol at the first party he or she attends. How can the student maintain new relationships and still say no? Teachers need to express their understanding that saving face is important for adolescents. Ask students what "saving face" means to them, and ask them to talk about verbal and nonverbal communications that do and do not help save face. What kind of communication works with kids their age? What turns them off or makes them potential targets of ridicule?

ASSESSMENT | For an assessment task, small groups of students can demonstrate a scenario that shows different ways to avoid or get out of a difficult situation. For assessment criteria, students should demonstrate communication that saves face and communication that does not, explain the difference, and make recommendations on communication to classmates. (Construct: Perceived behavioral control.)

Compare and Contrast Communication Skills Middle-level students enjoy the challenge of comparing and contrasting the use of communication and resistance skills in different risk areas. For example, students might politely say to a favorite aunt that they are just too full to eat another piece of pie. However, that particular resistance statement would hardly work for refusing alcohol or tobacco. In that case, students might say "Nah, not right now. Let's go shoot some hoops." That statement might work well for refusing substances, but what would work best for refusing sexual pressures or not wanting to gossip about or fight with another student? Students can try communication statements from one scenario in another. Do they still work? How can communication be changed and targeted to be most effective?

ASSESSMENT | For an assessment task, students can select one of the peer pressure resistance skills (give an excuse or reason, strength in numbers, suggest alternatives) from Chapter 3 and plan a demonstration of the skill in three different pressure situations (pressure to try marijuana, to shun another student, to shoplift). For assessment criteria, students should compare and contrast the use of the skill across the three situations. How was the skill the same or different in the way they used it in each situation? (Construct: Perceived behavioral control.)

NHES 5 | Decision Making

Students will demonstrate the ability to use decision-making skills to enhance health.

ASSESSMENT CRITERIA
Reach a health-enhancing decision using a process consisting of the following steps:
- Identify a health-risk situation.
- Examine alternatives.
- Evaluate positive and negative consequences.
- Decide on a health-enhancing course of action.

Grades K–2

Everyday Decisions Young children need to see themselves as being able to make a difference in what happens in their lives—to have some responsibility and power to make decisions and act on them. Introduce the idea of decision making by asking students to name decisions they make each day. Many decisions are made for children (what to eat, where to go). However, children should be able to think of decisions they make for themselves, such as choosing the clothes they wear to school, the books they read for pleasure, the colors and paints they use in a picture, and the games they play at recess and after school. Provide young children with various opportunities to make decisions for themselves, such as deciding which of two tasks to do first, with the understanding that both must be completed, and choosing between joining a game of tag, playing catch with different-size balls, or jumping rope during recess. Although this activity isn't related specifically to alcohol and other drugs, children should begin acquiring the skill and responsibility of decision making at an early age.

ASSESSMENT | For an assessment task, students can make a class list of decisions they are allowed to make at home and at school. Teachers might need to help students realize that they make more decisions than they think they do. For assessment criteria, students should describe what they think makes a smart decision or a not-so-smart decision. Students also should describe healthy and not-so-healthy decisions and explain the difference. Students should be able to describe at least two smart or healthy decisions they make on a daily basis and explain how they know their decisions are smart or healthy. (Construct: Perceived behavioral control.)

Grades 3–5

The Cost of Drinking Students can use their math and calculator skills to figure out the cost of supporting a drinking habit for a week, a month, and a year. Teachers can designate a price for one drink of alcohol. Students can calculate the amount of money spent on one drink per day for a week (7 days), a month (30 days), and a year (365 days). Next, students can brainstorm about things they would like to use that money for instead of alcohol. Students can double or triple the amount they could save for two or three drinks per day. Ask students how their calculations might affect their decisions about using alcohol.

ASSESSMENT | For assessment criteria, students should discuss how their new knowledge about the cost of drinking alcohol could affect their decisions about alcohol use and explain how the cost of alcohol is a negative consequence of drinking. (Construct: Attitudes toward behavior.)

Grades 6–8

Ask the Expert After teaching about the negative consequences of marijuana, provide students with a list of decisions that young people need to make about marijuana. Ask students to write a response that will help each person make a healthy decision. Examples include

- My best friend just started smoking pot. She is trying to get me to smoke it too. I really don't want to, but don't know how to say no to her. What should I do? Signed, Help
- I heard people who have cancer use marijuana, so it must be a safe drug to use. Is that true? Signed, Hoping for an Answer
- All of my classmates smoke pot, so why shouldn't I? Signed, Join the crowd
- I heard that smoking pot will help my memory. Is that true? Signed, I forget

ASSESSMENT | The written response is the assessment task for this activity. For assessment criteria, students include factual information about marijuana to help influence the person to make a healthy decision. (Construct: Perceived behavioral control)

Decisions Puzzle—How Do the Pieces Fit? The Substance Abuse and Mental Health Services Administration (SAMHSA) reported that young people who were involved in heavy alcohol use during the past month were most likely to have participated in at least one of the six risk behaviors assessed in the National Survey on Drug Use and Health (NSDUH; http://oas.samhsa.gov/2k5/alcDelinquent/alcDelinquent.cfm). Heavy drinking was defined as drinking five or more alcoholic beverages on the same occasion on each of five or more days in the past thirty days. Similarly, SAMHSA (http://oas.samhsa.gov/2k5/inhale/inhale.cfm) reported that young people age 12 or 13 who used inhalants were more than twice as likely to have been in a serious fight at school during the past year compared with youths the same age who had never used inhalants. Teachers can share these data with students to begin a discussion on how alcohol and other drug use might be connected to risk behaviors in other content areas (the titles of Chapters 5–14). Students can work in small groups to discuss their ideas about how decisions about alcohol and other drug use might be connected to risk behaviors or problems in other content areas. Groups can work on a particular content area or across all the content areas. Students might say, for example, that a person who uses alcohol and other drugs might forget or might not have the money to eat properly (content area: promoting healthy eating). Students might also say that people who drink alcohol and drive are at increased risk for motor-vehicle crashes that result in injury or death (content areas: promoting safety; managing loss, death, and grief). Students should share their possible connections with the class. Teachers should remind students not to use anyone's real name if they share a situation they know about personally.

ASSESSMENT | For an assessment task, students can design a graphic of some kind to illustrate the possible connections they have made between decisions to use alcohol and other drugs and behaviors in other content areas. For an extension, students can conduct a Web search to find out whether any of their hypotheses have been documented in studies on alcohol and other drug use. For assessment criteria, students should work through the decision-making model in Chapter 3 to discuss how alternatives and consequences related to one decision (alcohol and other drug use) can affect alternatives and consequences in other content areas. (Construct: Attitudes toward behavior.)

NHES 6 | Goal Setting

Students will demonstrate the ability to use goal-setting skills to enhance health.

ASSESSMENT CRITERIA
- Goal statement—Give goal statement that identifies health benefits; goal is achievable and will result in enhanced health.
- Goal setting plan—Show plan that is complete, logical and sequential, and includes a process to assess progress.

Grades K–2

Healthy Goals Begin building the idea of setting and reaching goals over a short period of time. During the morning, have children choose a goal for the day. The goals can be individual or group goals. For example, the entire class might set a goal of using kind words for the entire day. Have children assess their progress at the end of the day. For a whole week, individual children might choose brushing their teeth each day before school or eating breakfast every morning. Have children assess their progress at the end of the week and talk about how they feel about how things went for them. How did they feel when they did or didn't reach their goal? What would they do next time? Although this activity isn't related specifically to alcohol and other drugs, setting and reaching goals that children select for themselves can help build healthy habits.

ASSESSMENT | For an assessment task, students can select a class goal for the day. Students should state the goal in clear terms (so they will know whether they've achieved it) and identify steps they will take during the day to reach their goal, people who can help them meet their goal (supports), and people or situations that might make it hard for them to meet their goal (barriers). At the end of the day, students should reflect on how they did in meeting their goal. For assessment criteria, students should be able to answer questions about steps they took to meet their goal, supports and barriers, and how they did. (Construct: Perceived behavioral control.)

Grades 3–5

In the News Students can look through newspapers with their parents or caregivers, for two weeks, and bring in articles related to alcohol and other drug use. Alternatively, teachers can provide newspapers for students to search for articles in class, or can clip articles for students to review in class. Teachers should be mindful of students' family and community connections and omit articles that could affect class members personally. Students can share their articles with class members. Students likely will find articles related to motor-vehicle crashes, pedestrian injuries, violence, and arrests. Ask students how the consequences they found in the articles could affect their short-term goals (playing in a soccer match this week).

ASSESSMENT | For assessment criteria, students should identify the consequences of alcohol and other drug use in the articles and explain how the articles affect their decision making about alcohol and other drug use. In addition, students should describe how their important goals (playing sports, becoming an artist) could be adversely affected by the outcomes in the articles if they were involved in the situations under discussion. (Construct: Attitudes toward behavior.)

Grades 6–8

Legal Perspectives on Alcohol Teachers can invite, or have children write a letter to invite, a police officer or judge to class to discuss the laws related to alcohol use, including issues such as underage drinking and fake identification use. Students can reflect on how these legal consequences might affect their decisions about using alcohol as middle school students. Students should be allowed to ask the questions they really want to ask. For example, they might want to know more about the legal drinking age and how it was established. Students also might wonder about terms such as *decriminalization* and *legalization* and about the new federal focus on student drug testing in schools. Ask students to set personal goals about staying alcohol free throughout their school years.

ASSESSMENT | For an assessment task, students can develop a list of questions in advance that they want to ask about laws and regulations pertaining to alcohol and other drug use. For assessment criteria, students should provide accurate answers to their questions after the interview and explain how alcohol and other drug use could adversely affect their future plans. (Constructs: Attitudes toward behavior, perceived behavioral control.)

AOD and Families Students can talk in small groups about how alcohol and other drug use can affect family life. Teachers should make an agreement with students that no one will identify individuals or families by name. Students can share their group discussion with the rest of the class. Have students reflect on how the consequences of AOD use on families might affect their decisions about AOD use. Ask students to set personal goals about staying alcohol free throughout their school years.

Students can work in small groups to complete a Lōkahi Wheel (see Chapter 1) showing how alcohol and other drug use can affect families in terms of the following areas: physical/body, friends/family, thinking/mind, spiritual/soul, work/school, and feelings/emotions. Students can share and compare their wheels with other groups. Alternatively, the six parts of the wheel can be used in a carousel activity in which students rotate to different posters on signal.

ASSESSMENT | Some students will have experienced problems in their families or in families close to them related to alcohol and other drug use. Be sure to set ground rules that no one will refer to a family member or other individual by name. For an assessment criteria, students should discuss each component of the Lōkahi Wheel in relation to how it would affect their decisions about using alcohol and other drugs and the possibility of reaching important goals in the future. (Constructs: Attitudes toward behavior, perceived behavioral control.)

NHES 7 | Self-Management

Students will demonstrate the ability to practice health-enhancing behaviors and avoid or reduce health risks.

ASSESSMENT CRITERIA

- Application (transfer)—Initiate health-enhancing behaviors; apply concepts and skills appropriate and effectively.
- Self-monitoring and reflection—Monitor actions and make adjustments; accept feedback and make adjustments; able to self-assess, reflect on, and take responsibility for actions.

Grades K–2

Poison-Proof Your Home   As a homework assignment, have students take home a checklist (Figure 12–3) to complete with their parents or caregivers. This activity provides an opportunity for parents and caregivers to reinforce medicine and product safety at home and to take corrective action as needed. Students can report back to classmates on the results of this activity.

ASSESSMENT | The Poison-Proof Your Home checklist is the assessment task for this activity. For assessment criteria, students should explain the safety precautions that were and were not in place in their homes and the actions their families will take to make improvements. (Construct: Perceived behavioral control.)

Role-Play Actions for Safe Cleanup   Children might encounter spilled household, automobile, or gardening products. Have children role-play various scenarios for reporting spills to adults, being careful not to touch or taste the spilled products or try to do the cleaning by themselves. Also ask students to include actions they would take if pets or younger children were near the spill. What would they do first?

ASSESSMENT | The students' acting out of what to do in case of a chemical spill is the assessment task for this activity. Students can demonstrate their self-management strategies in pairs or small groups in response to the type of spill the teacher designates. For assessment criteria, students should be able to explain the steps they would take, in the appropriate order. For example, if pets or small children were near the spill, they would need to remove them from the area before contacting an adult to help clean up the spill. (Construct: Perceived behavioral control.)

Grades 3–5

Avoiding or Getting Out of Pressure Situations   In upper-elementary school, some students begin to experience pressures to use alcohol and other drugs. Students find themselves in situations they perhaps could have avoided or gotten out of by thinking through various scenarios in a safe classroom environment. Dealing with pressure situations often involves NHES 4, interpersonal communication. However, avoiding and getting away from risky situations also involves actions, such as going elsewhere or getting a ride home with someone who isn't drinking. Ask students to describe AOD pressure situations that students their age might encounter. For each pressure situation, students can brainstorm and discuss various self-management strategies they could plan in advance and use in situations that arise. Students should talk about what they believe will work in real situations. Teachers should acknowledge that sometimes adults have ideas about what works and students have other ideas. Teachers should listen to students' ideas about what is real and relevant to them.

ASSESSMENT | For an assessment task, students can work in small groups to participate in a behavioral rehearsal. Each group should identify a realistic situation that might occur related to alcohol and other drug use. Students should script and rehearse the self-management strategies they choose (carry money for a phone call or a cell phone). Students can perform their behavioral rehearsals up until the point at which a self-management strategy is needed and then freeze the action (some performing arts educators call this a tableau) while classmates give advice on what to do. After classmates have given advice, the group should finish their dramatization to demonstrate the self-management strategy they chose during rehearsal. For assessment criteria, the performing students should explain which self-management strategy they think would work best for them and why. (Construct: Perceived behavioral control.)

Preventing Inhalant Use: Reading Labels and Following Instructions   The National Inhalant Prevention Coalition (www.inhalants.org) offers a link called "Tips for Teachers," designed to help educators talk with different age groups about inhalant use. The site recommends starting prevention efforts by age 5 and linking inhalants to safety and environmental issues. Teachers must be especially careful not to give details on "how to use" or trendy products being abused. For grades 3–5, teachers are encouraged to try strategies such as discussing the term *toxic*, teaching about the importance of oxygen to life, and reading labels and following instructions. For this activity, bring a variety of empty, and clean, product containers to class for students to practice reading labels and to discuss how to follow instructions. Students should note the warnings the labels include and discuss why these are important to follow for their own health and a healthy environment.

ASSESSMENT | Students are learning self-management skills when they read labels and follow directions. They also are accessing information (NHES 3) from labels in this activity. For an assessment task, students can work in pairs to explain a label to the class. For assessment criteria, students should tell their classmates the correct steps for using the product and any warnings they should be aware of about harm to their health or the environment. (Construct: Perceived behavioral control.)

Grades 6–8

Changing a Habit   To help students understand how difficult it is to change a behavior, such as drinking alcohol, have students start by defining the word *habit*. Then have students choose a current habit that they want to change, such as nail biting, procrastinating in doing homework, or drinking soda each day after school. Teachers should be sure that the habits students choose are appropriate targets for change. Have students design a daily log sheet to record the steps they take and their progress. Link this activity to NHES 5 and 6, decision making and goal setting, in setting clear and measurable steps for achieving their goals. Students can record their progress for a given period of time (two weeks) and report back to the class on what helped (supports) and what hindered (barriers) their progress. Although stopping alcohol use is much more difficult for an alcoholic than students' projects will be for them, their experiences can help students grasp the idea that preventing a negative behavior is easier than trying to change a behavior that has become a habit.

ASSESSMENT | The records students keep and their reflection on their experiences are the assessment task for this activity. Ask students to share with each other throughout the designated time period and offer

Name _____ Date _____

Note to Parents

Dear Parent or Guardian,

Today in my class we learned about SAFE things and UNSAFE things. I have several "SAFE" and "UNSAFE" labels for us to properly label various substances in our home. I also have a checklist to help us keep our home safe.

Please help me complete the checklist and sign this form so I can return them both to school tomorrow.

Thank you very much.

Signature of parent or guardian

WE'RE PUSHING FOR A DRUG-FREE STATE
TEXAS EDUCATION AGENCY

Name _____ Date _____

Poison Proof Your Home

With your parents' help, check your house for unsafe areas.

☐ Keep drugs, poisons, and other dangerous substances (such as paint, charcoal lighter fluid, gasoline, and cleaning supplies) out of reach of children and pets. If possible, store these items in locked cabinets

☐ Read all labels carefully.

☐ Clearly label all poisonous substances.

☐ Store poisonous substances away from food or food containers.

☐ Protect utensils and food when spraying chemicals such as bug spray and cleaning solutions.

☐ Date all drug supplies when you buy them.

☐ Keep medicines in original labeled bottles; do not transfer them into unlabeled bottles.

☐ Clean out the medicine cabinet regularly to remove outdated medicines and prescriptions.

☐ When you throw away drugs and medicines, flush them down the toilet or discard them in containers that cannot be reached by children or pets.

☐ Keep a poison control kit in the house in case an accidental poisoning happens.

☐ Make sure that all family members know what to do in case of a poisoning emergency.

WE'RE PUSHING FOR A DRUG-FREE STATE
TEXAS EDUCATION AGENCY

FIGURE 12–3 | A Homework Assignment to Be Done by Parents and Children Together to Teach Medicine and Product Safety

support for each other. For assessment criteria, students should reflect on and write about (1) the habit they chose and why; (2) the plan they made, with specific steps; (3) the supports and barriers they prepared for and those they encountered unexpectedly; and (4) an assessment of their progress, including any next steps. (Construct: Perceived behavioral control.)

Real-World Strategies for Staying Safe   Middle school students can consider more complex scenarios involving alcohol and other drug use that they might have to manage. For example, what if they get to a party and unexpectedly find alcohol on the scene? What if the person they are supposed to ride home with is drinking? Students can plan ahead by visualizing scenarios that might put them at risk and taking actions to stay safe. Students can make agreements with parents, caregivers, or other adult family friends to come and get them if they are stranded. To do this, students need to carry money for a phone call at all times or carry a cell phone. Students also might say that they should carry money for bus or cab fare. Enlisting the support of friends who don't drink or use drugs is another self-management strategy students might use (using strength in numbers).

ASSESSMENT | An important aspect of this activity is allowing students to explain situations that have happened to them or that they know have happened to others. The idea is to try to think ahead to envision tough situations they might have to manage. For an assessment task, students can work in pairs to draw a cartoon of a situation and a self-management strategy for getting out of the situation safely. For assessment criteria, students should illustrate all the steps they would take to put their self-management strategy into action. (Constructs: Subjective norms, perceived behavioral control.)

NHES 8 | Advocacy

Students will demonstrate the ability to advocate for personal, family, and community health.

ASSESSMENT CRITERIA
- Health-enhancing position—Give clear, health-enhancing position.
- Support for position—Support position with facts, concepts, examples, and evidence.
- Audience awareness—Show awareness of target audience; choose words, tone, and examples to suit audience.
- Conviction—Display conviction for position.

Grades K–2

Taking Care of Our Minds and Bodies   Young children can begin learning the skill of advocacy by planning a health-promoting event at school. For example, children might plan a daily walking program at recess, inviting everyone in their grade (students and teachers) to participate. When children invite others to participate, they should explain what they want to do, explain why they want to do it, and target their presentation to other students their age. First-grade teacher Diane Parker's students chose keeping their school grounds litter-free. The students collected the litter on the school grounds for one week and made posters and graphs (with the litter actually glued to the poster) to show the other students exactly what they wanted to change. Students might try their activity for two weeks, assessing their progress at the end of each week.

ASSESSMENT | For an assessment task, children can select a healthy idea they would like to promote in their class, grade, or school (eating fruit for snacks, walking every day, using kind words). Students should decide

how they want to promote their idea and then try it for a certain period of time (one or two weeks). For assessment criteria, students should communicate a clear message about what they want other students to do and should make their presentation one that other students will listen to (target their audience). (Constructs: Subjective norms, perceived behavioral control.)

Safe Home Week Campaign   As a homework assignment, students can inspect their homes, inside and out, with their parents or caregivers to make sure that all medicine, poisons, cleaners, and automobile products are locked away or out of the reach of small children and pets. Students can report back to classmates on any changes they made at home as a result of their advocacy campaign for safety.

ASSESSMENT | For an assessment task, students can make posters for their grade or school about Safe Home Week. Students can help design a checklist for other students to use with their families to check around their homes. For assessment criteria, students should communicate a clear message about what they want other students to do and target their message to their schoolmates. (Construct: Perceived behavioral control.)

Grades 3–5

Drug-Free Posters   Upper-elementary children can practice their advocacy skills specifically in relation to alcohol and other drugs. Students can work in pairs to design posters for the classroom and school that illustrate a drug-free message. Students can show healthy alternatives to AOD use and the consequences of AOD use. Arrange to have the posters displayed around the school.

ASSESSMENT | The posters the students make are the assessment task for this activity. For assessment criteria, students should communicate a clear message, back it up with accurate information, target their audience, and show conviction. (Construct: Subjective norms.)

Ready—Action!   Students can work as individuals, pairs, or small groups to design a drug-free message through some type of performing art: raps, songs, poems, dance, skits, commercials, game shows, public service announcements. Provide ample time for students to rehearse before their performances. For example, students might work on this project for a certain amount of time each day for a week. Having students take the time to plan and rehearse will result in better performances than having students perform on the spur of the moment. They can make and select props or scenery that they think will add to their performance. Videotape their performances, if possible, to share with families and other classes. (Some students might be hesitant to perform in front of others. Provide alternative formats for their presentations, or work with them to find a performance format that is comfortable for them.)

ASSESSMENT | The drug-free message students present is the assessment task for this activity. For assessment criteria, students should communicate a clear message, back it up with accurate information, target their audience, and show conviction. (Construct: Subjective norms.)

Grades 6–8

Reality Check   Middle-level students need to feel accepted and part of a group. Thus, if they believe that everyone is drinking alcohol, they are inclined to want to be like their friends and the students they admire. Early adolescents tend to overestimate the prevalence and acceptability of alcohol use among their peers. This activity provides an important reality check. Give each student a small slip of paper (make sure that all papers look alike) and ask students simply to write "yes" or "no" in answer to the question of whether they currently drink alcohol. Collect the pieces of paper and ask the class to predict the response (how many "yes," how many "no"). A couple of students can count the actual responses. In most cases, students' predictions will be an overestimate. Students can discuss the reasons middle-level students overestimate drinking and other risk behaviors. Teachers can ask students how they can share with other students what they learned in their reality check.

ASSESSMENT | Students might have made similar estimates when they discussed tobacco use among peers. These kinds of reality checks are important in all the content areas. For an assessment task, students can use their results to make a slogan about refusing alcohol or other drugs, including the social norm for nonuse in their class or grade. For assessment criteria, students should communicate a clear message, back it up with accurate information, target their audience, and show conviction. (Construct: Subjective norms.)

Youth in Action (YIA) Students can visit the website www.youthinaction.org to learn more about an advocacy group that looks for community solutions to teenage drinking by considering the whole environment that seems to condone underage alcohol use. Sponsored by Mothers Against Drunk Driving (MADD), YIA teams focus on "laws and policies that affect people's behavior because that's the best place to make changes." Students can arrange to receive the YIA Quarterly (e-newsletter) in their classroom.

ASSESSMENT | For an assessment task, students can investigate and discuss the community solutions approach of YIA. For assessment criteria, students should determine whether the YIA approach has the hallmarks of a standards-based advocacy project: having a clear message, backing it up with accurate information, targeting the audience, and showing conviction. Students should give examples to explain why YIA does or does not meet these standards. (Construct: Subjective norms.)

EVALUATED CURRICULA AND INSTRUCTIONAL MATERIALS

Several evaluated commercial alcohol and drug prevention programs are available to school districts. These curricula should complement, not replace, a Comprehensive School Health Education curriculum. The evaluation results of these curricula have been reviewed by many organizations (e.g., Substance Abuse and Mental Health Services Administration [SAMHSA]) and have been shown to be effective in reducing the number of students who use alcohol and other drugs or in reducing the number of students who intend to use alcohol and other drugs. Effective, research-based prevention programs can be cost effective: each dollar invested in prevention can result in a $10 savings in alcohol and other drug treatment.[81] This section does not provide information about commercial programs that target high-risk youth; instead, it provides information on selected commercial curricula targeted toward all elementary and/or middle school youth and a summary of the evaluation results.

• *All Stars*. All Stars is a multiyear school-based program for middle school students (11 to 14 years old) designed to prevent or delay the onset of high-risk behaviors such as tobacco use, drug use, violence, and premature sexual activity. The program focuses on five topics important to preventing high-risk behaviors: (1) developing positive ideals that do not fit with high-risk behavior; (2) creating a belief in conventional norms; (3) building strong personal commitments; (4) bonding with school, pro-social institutions, and family; and (5) increasing positive parental attentiveness. The All Stars curriculum includes highly interactive group activities, games and art projects, small group discussions, one-on-one sessions,

a parent component, and a celebration ceremony. The All Stars Core program consists of thirteen 45-minute class sessions delivered on a weekly basis by teachers, prevention specialists, or social workers. The All Stars Booster program is designed to be delivered one year after the core program and includes nine 45-minute sessions reinforcing lessons learned in the previous year. Multiple program packages are available to support implementation by either regular teachers or prevention specialists. All Stars participants reported significantly lower average levels of inhalant use and alcohol use at post-test compared with students who did not receive the program.[82] More information about the All Stars program can be found at www.allstarsprevention.com or by calling (336) 662-0090.

• *Life Skills Training*. The Life Skills Training curriculum focuses on resistance skills training within the context of broader personal and social skills. There are fifteen core sessions in sixth or seventh grade, with ten booster sessions the second year and five booster sessions the third year. The program focuses primarily on drug resistance skills and information, self-management skills, and general social skills. It has more published evaluations than any other curriculum.

The evaluations of the program showed a reduction in tobacco, alcohol, and marijuana use by 50 to 87 percent. Long-term evaluation found significantly lower smoking, alcohol, and marijuana use six years after the initial baseline assessment. The prevalence of cigarette smoking, alcohol use, and marijuana use for students who received the program was 44 percent lower than for control students, and their weekly use of multiple drugs was 66 percent lower.[83,84]

• *Project Alert*. The Project Alert curriculum is a two-year curriculum for grades 6 through 8 that covers information on alcohol, tobacco, marijuana, and inhalants. Consisting of eleven sessions the first year and three sessions the second year, this program emphasizes the development of resistance skills (both perceived or internal pressure and overt peer pressure) and helps establish nondrug-using norms.

The evaluation of this program showed a reduction in marijuana use initiation by 30 percent, a decrease in current and heavy smoking by participants of 33 to 55 percent, a 60 percent decrease in current marijuana use, and a reduction in pro-drug attitudes and beliefs; the curriculum also helped current smokers quit.[85]

• *Project Northland.* Project Northland is a curriculum for grades 6 through 8 that focuses on alcohol use and abuse. This program has eight sessions a year and emphasizes resistance skills and decision making. The whole program sets the norm that it is not cool to drink. The curriculum presents many opportunities for role-plays. In addition, the sixth-grade curriculum includes many family take-home assignments.

The evaluation of this program showed a reduction in tobacco and alcohol use by 27 percent and a reduction in marijuana use by 50 percent three years after the completion of the program.[86]

• *Lions-Quest Skills for Adolescence (SFA).* Lions-Quest Skills for Adolescence (SFA) is a comprehensive prevention program designed for school-wide and classroom implementation in grades 6 through 8. The program focuses on developing social and emotional competencies, good citizenship, drug prevention skills and attitudes, and community service. The forty-session program can be delivered daily, two or three times a week, or weekly with equal effectiveness, depending on the implementation model. The curriculum presents the opportunity for inquiry, presentations, discussions, group work, guided practice, and reflections to build positive social behaviors of self-discipline.

The evaluation of this program showed significantly lower rates of initiation of regular cigarette smoking and marijuana use.[87]

INTERNET AND OTHER RESOURCES

Visit the Online Learning Center (www.mhhe.com/telljohann6e) for links to these sites, quizzes and other study aids, and many additional resources.

WEBSITES

Freevibe
www.freevibe.com

Get It Straight—the Facts About Drugs
www.usdoj.gov/dea/pubs/straight/cover.htm

Indiana Prevention Resource Center
www.drugs.indiana.edu

Just One Night
www.pbs.org/justone

Kids' Health—Teens
www.kidshealth.org/teen

KidSpace @ the Internet Public Library
www.ipl.org/youth/poisonsafe

National Center on Addiction and Substance Abuse at Columbia University
www.casacolumbia.org

National Clearinghouse for Alcohol and Drug Information
www.ncadi.samhsa.gov

National Inhalant Prevention Coalition
www.inhalants.org

National Institute on Alcohol Abuse and Alcoholism
www.niaaa.nih.gov

National Institute on Drug Abuse
www.nida.nih.gov

Partnership for a Drug-Free America—Kids and Teens
www.drugfree.org

Pride Surveys
www.pridesurveys.com

Stop Underage Drinking: Portal of Federal Resources
www.stopalcoholabuse.gov

Teen Health and the Media
http://depts.washington.edu/thmedia

The Cool Spot: The Young Teen's Place for Info on Alcohol and Resisting Pressure
www.thecoolspot.gov

OTHER RESOURCES

Center on Alcohol Marketing and Youth. *Underage Drinking in the United States: A Status Report, 2004* (Washington, DC: Center on Alcohol Marketing and Youth, 2005).

National Institute on Drug Abuse, *Drugs, Brains and Behaviors— The Science of Addiction* (Washington, DC: National Institutes of Health, 2007).

National Research Council and Institute of Medicine. *Reducing Underage Drinking: A Collective Responsibility,* eds. R. Bonnie and M. O'Connell. (Washington, DC: National Academies Press, 2004).

Office of National Drug Control Policy, *Teens and Prescription Drugs: An Analysis of Recent Trends on the Emerging Drug Threat* (Washington, DC: Office of National Drug Control Policy, 2007).

Soledad, S., and F. Springer. "Risk, Protection, and Substance Use in Adolescents: A Multi-Site Model." *Journal of Drug Education* 3, no. 1 (2003): 91–105.

U.S. Department of Health and Human Services, *The Surgeon General's Call to Action to Prevent and Reduce Underage Drinking* (Rockville, MD: Office of the Surgeon General, 2007).

U.S. Department of Health and Human Services, *The Surgeon General's Call to Action to Prevent and Reduce Underage Drinking: A Guide to Actions for Educators* (Rockville, MD: Office of the Surgeon General, 2007).

AGES 5–8

Birdseye, T. *Tucker.* Holiday, 1990.

Byars, B. *The Pinballs.* HarperCollins, 1977.

Cosgrove, S. *Crickle Crackle.* Price Stern Sloan, 2001.

Daly, N. *My Dad.* McElderry, 1995.

Hughes, D. *The Trophy.* Alfred A. Knopf, 1994.

Langsen, R. *When Someone in the Family Drinks Too Much.* Penguin, 1996.

Thomas, J. *Daddy Doesn't Have to Be a Giant Anymore.* Clarion, 1996.

Vigna, J. *I Wish Daddy Didn't Drink So Much.* Albert Whitman, 1988.

AGES 8–12

Aretha, David. *On the Rocks: Teens and Alcohol.* Franklin Watts, 2007.

Brooks, B. *No Kidding.* HarperCollins, 1989.

Bunting, E. *A Sudden Death.* Harcourt, 1990.

Gantos, J. *Joey Pigza Loses Control.* First HarperTrophy, 2004.

Kehret, P. *Cages.* Puffin, 2001.

KidsPeace. *I've Got This Friend Who: Advice for Teens and Their Friends on Alcohol, Drugs, Eating Disorders, Risky Behavior and More.* Hazelden, 2007.

Osborne, M. *Last One Home.* Dial, 1986.

Packer, Alex J., and Pamela Espeland. *Wise Highs: How to Thrill, Chill and Get Away from It All Without Alcohol or Other Drugs.* Free Spirit Publishing, 2006.

Service, R. *The Shooting of Dan McGrew.* David Godine, 1995.

Taylor, C. *The House That Crack Built.* Chronicle, 1992. (American Bookseller Pick of the Lists; American Library Association Best Books for Young Readers; American Library Association Best Books for Reluctant Readers)

Voigt, C. *Izzy Will Nilly.* Ballantine, 1986.

Wood, J. *A Share of Freedom.* Putman, 1994. (School Library Journal Best Books, 1994)

Zindel, P. *The Pigman.* Harper and Row, 1968.

ENDNOTES

1. Centers for Disease Control and Prevention, "Alcohol-Attributable Deaths and Years of Potential Life Lost—United States, 2001," *Morbidity and Mortality Weekly Report* 53, no. 37 (24 September 2004): 866–70.

2. Substance Abuse and Mental Health Services Administration. *Results from the 2006 National Survey on Drug Use and Health: National Findings* (Rockville, MD: Office of Applied Studies, NSDUH Series H-32, DHHS Publication No. SMA 07-4293, 2007).

3. National Highway Traffic Safety Administration, *Traffic Safety Facts 2003* (Washington, DC: National Center for Statistics and Analysis, U.S. Department of Transportation, 2005).

4. Centers for Disease Control and Prevention, "Alcohol-Attributable Deaths and Years of Potential Life Lost—United States, 2001."

5. Substance Abuse and Mental Health Services Administration, *Overview of Findings from the 2003 National Survey on Drug Use and Health.* (http://oas.samhsa.gov/NHSDA/2k3NSDUH/2k3OverviewW.pdf; 2004)

6. PRIDE Surveys, "PRIDE Questionnaire Report for Grades 4 thru 6, 2005–2006 PRIDE Surveys National Summary, September 19, 2006." (www.pridesurveys.com/customercenter/us05ns.pdf)

7. PRIDE Surveys, "PRIDE Questionnaire Report for Grades 6 thru 12, 2005–2006 National Summary, September 18, 2006." (www.pridesurveys.com/customercenter/ue05ns.pdf)

8. Partnership for a Drug Free America, *Why Teenagers Use—and Abuse—Alcohol and Other Drugs.* (www.drugfree.org/Parent/Knowing/Why_Teenagers_Use_and_Abuse; February 2005)

9. J. D. Sargent, T. A. Wills, M. Stoolmiller, J. Gibson, and F. X. Gibbons, "Alcohol Use in Motion Pictures and Its Relation with Early-Onset Teen Drinking," *Journal of Studies on Alcohol* 67 (2006): 54–65.

10. P. Christenson, L. Henriksen, and D. Roberts, *Substance Use in Popular Prime-Time Television* (Rockville, MD: Office of National Drug Control Policy and Department of Health and Human Services, 2000).

11. L. B. Snyder, F. F. Milici, M. Slater, H. Sun, and Y. Strizhakova, "Effects of Alcohol Advertising Exposure on Drinking Among Youth," *Archives of Pediatrics and Adolescent Medicine* 160 (2006): 18–24.

12. Schneider Institute for Health Policy, *Substance Abuse: The Nation's Number One Health Problem—Key Indicators for Policy* (Waltham, MA: Schneider Institute for Health Policy, 2001).

13. U.S. Department of Health and Human Services, *Healthy People 2010 Online Documents.* (www.health.gov/healthypeople/document/; May 2002)

14. Substance Abuse and Mental Health Services Administration, "Academic Performance and Substance Use among Students Aged 12 to 17: 2002, 2003, and 2004," *The NSDUH Report, 18* (2006): 1–4.

15. R. Cox, L. Zhang, W. Johnson, and D. Bender. "Academic Performance and Substance Use: Findings from a State Survey of Public High School Students" *Journal of School Health* 77, no. 3 (2007): 109–15.

16. The National Center on Addiction and Substance Abuse at Columbia University, *Malignant Neglect: Substance Abuse and America's Schools* (New York: Columbia University, 2001).

17. R. Lowell and A. Gallup, "The 39th Annual Phi Delta Kappa/Gallop Poll of the Public's Attitude Towards Public Schools." (www.pdkintl.org/kappan/k_v89/k0709pol.htm, 2007)

18. National Institute on Alcohol Abuse and Alcoholism, "Why Do Adolescents Drink, What Are the Results, and How Can Underage Drinking Be Prevented?" *Alcohol Alert, 67* (2006): 1–10.

19. J. Hawkins, R. Catalano, and R. Miller, "Risk and Protective Factors for Early Alcohol and Other Drug Problems in Adolescence and Early Adulthood," *Psychological Bulletin* 112, no. 1 (1992): 64–105.

20. U.S. Department of Health and Human Services, *The Surgeon General's Call to Action to Prevent and Reduce Underage Drinking: A Guide to Actions for Educators* (Rockville, MD: Office of the Surgeon General, 2007).

21. R. Svensson, "Risk Factors for Different Dimensions of Adolescent Drug Use," *Journal of Child and Adolescent Substance Abuse* 9, no. 3 (2000): 67–90.

22. National Institute on Drug Abuse, *Preventing Drug Use Among Children and Adolescents: A Research-Based Guide for Parents, Educators, and Community Leaders,* 2d ed. (Washington, DC: U.S. Department of Health and Human Services, 2003).

23. S. Soledad and F. Springer, "Risk, Protection, and Substance Use in Adolescents: A Multi-Site Model," *Journal of Drug Education* 3, no. 1 (2003): 91–105.

24. Channing Bete, *About the Risk and Protective Factors.* (http://preview.channing-bete.com/CTC/5558OJ_RandP.pdf; 2004)

25. L. Kann, S. Telljohann, and S. Wooley, "Health Education: Results from the School Health Policies and Programs Study 2006," *Journal of School Health* 77, no. 77 (2006): 408–34.

26. S. E. Jones, C. Fisher, B. Greene, M. Hertz, and J. Pritzl, "Healthy and Safe School Environment, Part I: Results from the School Health Policies and Programs Study 2006," *Journal of School Health* 77, no. 77 (2006): 522–43.

27. L. Kann, S. Telljohann, and S. Wooley, "Health Education: Results from the School Health Policies and Programs Study 2006."

28. Ibid.

29. R. Towers, *How Schools Can Help Combat Student Drug and Alcohol Abuse* (Washington, DC: National Education Association, 1987).

30. U.S. Department of Education, *Drug Prevention Curricula: A Guide to Selection and Implementation* (Washington, DC: U.S. Government Printing Office, 1988).

31. R. E. Glasgow and K. D. McCaul, "Life Skills Training Programs for Smoking Prevention: Critique and Directions for Future Research," in *Prevention Research: Deterring Drug Abuse Among Children and Adolescents,* eds. C. Bell and R. Battjes (Washington, DC: NIDA Research Monograph no. 63, DHHS publication number (ADM) 85-1334, 1985).

32. M. Goodstadt, "School-Based Drug Education in North America: What Is Wrong? What Can Be Done?" *Journal of School Health* 56, no. 7 (1986): 278.

33. United States General Accounting Office, *Youth Illicit Drug Use Prevention: DARE Long-Term Evaluations and Federal Efforts to Identify Effective Programs.* (Washington, DC: 2003).

34. National Institute on Drug Abuse, *Preventing Drug Use Among Children and Adolescents.*

35. U.S. Department of Health and Human Services, *The Surgeon General's Call to Action to Prevent and*

Reduce Underage Drinking (Rockville, MD: Office of the Surgeon General, 2007).

36. National Institute on Alcohol Abuse and Alcoholism, *Alcohol: What You Don't Know Can Harm You.* (www.niaaa.nih.gov/publications/harm-al.htm; May 2002)

37. Centers for Disease Control and Prevention, "Youth Risk Behavior Surveillance—United States, 2007," *Morbidity and Mortality Weekly Report* 57, no. SS-4 (6 June 2008): 1–131.

38. J. Kinney, *Loosening the Grip: A Handbook of Alcohol Information* (New York: McGraw-Hill, 2003).

39. Ibid.

40. National Institute on Drug Abuse, *Drugs, Brains and Behaviors—The Science of Addiction* (Washington, DC: National Institutes of Health, 2007).

41. National Research Council and Institute of Medicine, *Reducing Underage Drinking: A Collective Responsibility,* eds. R. Bonnie and M. O'Connell (Washington, DC: National Academies Press, 2004).

42. M. Bellis et al., "Hippocampal Volume in Adolescent-Onset Alcohol Use Disorders," *American Journal of Psychiatry* 157, no. 5 (2000): 737–44.

43. National Highway Traffic Safety Administration, *Traffic Safety Facts 2003* (Washington, DC: National Center for Statistics and Analysis, U.S. Department of Transportation, 2005).

44. U.S. Department of Health and Human Services. *The Surgeon General's Call to Action to Prevent and Reduce Underage Drinking: A Guide to Actions for Educators* (Rockville, MD: Office of the Surgeon General, 2007).

45. J. Kinney, *Loosening the Grip.*

46. Ibid.

47. P. Insel and W. Roth, *Core Concepts in Health,* 9th ed. (New York: McGraw-Hill, 2004).

48. L. Mkdanik et al., "Alcohol-Attributable Deaths and Years of Potential Life Lost—United States, 2001," *Morbidity and Mortality Weekly Report* 53, no. 37 (2004): 866–70.

49. P. Insel and W. Roth, *Core Concepts in Health.*

50. National Institute on Alcohol Abuse and Alcoholism, *Understanding Alcohol: Investigations into Biology and Behavior—Teacher's Guide.* (http://science.education.nih.gov/supplements/nih3/alcohol/guide/guide_toc.htm; 2003)

51. National Institute on Alcohol Abuse and Alcoholism, *Frequently Asked Questions.* (www.niaaa.nih.gov/faq/faq.htm; 2002)

52. Ibid.

53. National Institute on Alcohol Abuse and Alcoholism, *A Family History of Alcoholism: Are You at Risk?* (www.niaaa.nih.gov/publications/Family/famhist.htm; 2004)

54. National Institute on Alcohol Abuse and Alcoholism, *Alcoholism: Getting the Facts.* (www.niaaa.nih.gov/publications/booklet.htm; 2004)

55. Ibid.

56. American Academy of Child and Adolescent Psychiatry, "Children of Alcoholics." (www.aacap.org/cs/root/facts_for_families/children_of_alcoholics, 2002)

57. Resource Center, State of California, *Children of Alcoholics: Important Facts,* Publication no. ADP 99-2567 (Sacramento, CA: Resource Center, State of California, 1999).

58. National Association for Children of Alcoholics (NACoA), "Children of Alcoholics: A Toolkit for Educators." (http://nacoa-stage.shs.net/pdfs/EDkit_web_06.pdf, 2001)

59. National Center on Addiction and Substance Abuse at Columbia University, *CASA National Survey of American Attitudes on Substance Abuse XII: Teens and Parents* (New York: National Center on Addiction and Substance Abuse at Columbia University, 2007).

60. M. Quackenbush, W. Kane, and S. Telljohann, *Teach and Reach: Tobacco, Alcohol and Other Drug Prevention* (Santa Cruz, CA: ETR Associates, 2004).

61. National Center on Addiction and Substance Abuse at Columbia University, *Non-Medical Marijuana II: Rite of Passage or Russian Roulette? A CASA White Paper* (New York: National Center on Addiction and Substance Abuse at Columbia University, 2004).

62. Ibid.

63. National Institute on Drug Abuse, *NIDA Infofacts: Marijuana.* (www.nida.nih.gov/infofacts/marijuana.html; 2006)

64. National Institute on Drug Abuse, *Research Report Series: Marijuana Abuse.* (www.nida.nih.gov/ResearchReports/Marijuana/default.html; 2005)

65. National Institute on Drug Abuse, *NIDA Infofacts: Inhalants.* (www.nida.nih.gov/infofacts/inhalants.html; 2006)

66. Partnership for a Drug-Free America, *New Findings on Inhalants: Parent and Youth Attitudes—a Special Report.* (www.drugfree.org/Portal/DrugIssue/News/New_Findings_on_Inhalants_Parent_and_Youth; 2005)

67. National Inhalant Prevention Coalition, *About Inhalants.* (www.inhalants.org/about.htm; 2004)

68. Ibid.

69. Partnership for a Drug-Free America, *New Findings on Inhalants.*

70. National Institute on Drug Abuse, *NIDA Infofacts: Inhalants.*

71. Ibid.

72. National Inhalant Prevention Coalition, *Potential Long Term Effects of Chronic Inhalant Use.* (www.inhalants.org/lngtrm.htm; 2005)

73. National Inhalant Prevention Coalition, *Damage Inhalants Can Do to the Body and Brain.* (www.inhalants.org/damage.htm; 2005)

74. National Inhalant Prevention Coalition; Isabel Burk, The Health Network; *Tips for Teachers.* (www.inhalants.org/teacher.htm; 2005)

75. Office of National Drug Control Policy, *Teens and Prescription Drugs: An Analysis of Recent Trends on the Emerging Drug Threat* (Washington, DC: Office of National Drug Control Policy, 2007).

76. Partnership for a Drug-Free America, *What Every Parent Needs to Know About Cough Medicine Abuse.* (www.drugfree.org/Parent/Resources/Cough_Medicine_Abuse; 2005)

77. L. D. Johnston, P. M. O'Malley, J. G. Bachman, and J. E. Schulenberg, *Monitoring the Future National Results on Adolescent Drug Use: Overview of Key Findings, 2006* (Bethesda, MD: National Institute on Drug Abuse, 2007).

78. Centers for Disease Control and Prevention, "Health Education Curriculum Analysis Tool (HECAT): Module AOD Alcohol and Other Drug-Free Curriculum." (www.cdc.gov/HealthyYouth/HECAT/pdf/HECAT_Module-AOD.pdf; 2007)

79. National Institute on Drug Abuse, *NIDA Infofacts: Marijuana.* (www.nida.nih.gov/infofacts/marijuana.html; 2006)

80. Public Broadcasting System, "Targets." (www.pbs.org/inthemix/educators/lessons/alcohol1/; 2008)

81. National Institute on Drug Abuse, *Preventing Drug Use Among Children and Adolescents.*

82. N. Harrington, S. Giles, R. Hoyle, G. Feeney, and S. Yungbluth, "Evaluation of the All Stars Character Education and Problem Behavior Prevention Program: Effects on Mediator and Outcome Variables for Middle School Students," *Health Education and Behavior,* 28, no. 5 (2001): 533–46.

83. G. Botvin, J. Epstein, E. Baker, T. Diaz, and M. Ifill-Williams, "School Based Drug Abuse Prevention with Inner City Minority Youth," *Journal of Child and Adolescent Substance Abuse* 6, no. 5 (1997): 5–19.

84. G. Botvin, K. Griffin, E. Paul, and A. Macaulay, "Preventing Tobacco and Alcohol Use Among School Students Through Life Skills Training," *Journal of Child and Adolescent Substance Abuse* 12, no. 4 (2003): 1–18.

85. Substance Abuse and Mental Health Services Administration, *Project Alert.* (www.modelprograms.samhsa.gov/; accessed 2005)

86. Ibid.

87. Ibid.

13

(Nicolette, age 12; Marlo, age 12)

Promoting Sexual Health

DESIRED LEARNER OUTCOMES

After reading this chapter, you will be able to . . .

- Describe the prevalence and cost of early sexual involvement and sexual risk-taking behaviors among youth.

- Explain the relationship between early sexual involvement and sexual risk-taking behaviors and compromised academic performance.

- Describe how to deal with individuals and groups who oppose sexuality education.

- Identify factors that influence early sexual involvement and sexual risk-taking behaviors.

- Summarize current guidelines and practices for schools and teachers related to sexuality education.

- Summarize developmentally appropriate sexuality education concepts and skills for K–8 students in the context of the National Health Education Standards and target healthy behavior outcomes.

- Demonstrate developmentally appropriate learning strategies and assessment techniques that incorporate concepts and skills that have been shown to reduce early sexual involvement and sexual risk-taking behaviors among youth.

- Identify effective, evaluated commercial sexuality education curricula.

- Identify websites and children's literature that can be used in cross-curricular instructional activities promoting healthy sexuality.

INTRODUCTION

Teaching sexuality education can be interesting, exciting, and sometimes anxiety producing for teachers. It is important that teachers have a good grasp of why sexuality education is an important subject to include as part of a comprehensive health education curriculum. This introduction provides teachers with an understanding of the prevalence and cost of risky sexual behavior, how teen pregnancy can affect academic performance, the risk and protective factors associated with early risk-taking sexual activity, opposition to sexuality education, and reasons to include sexuality education at the elementary and middle levels.

Prevalence and Cost

Today's children and adolescents are faced with many serious issues and decisions regarding their sexuality. Unfortunately, they often receive mixed messages from the media about sexuality, which can contribute to confusion about their sexual development and related behaviors. Between the ages of 8 and 18, children and adolescents spend more hours viewing TV each year than interacting directly with their parents or teachers.[1] Approximately eight hours each day is devoted to the media, with three to four hours dedicated to television viewing alone.[2] Many of these media include messages related to sexuality. For example, a Kaiser Family Foundation study found that 64 percent of all network primetime television shows contained either talk about sexuality or sexual behavior. Those programs with sexual content averaged more than 4.4 scenes per hour with a reference to a sexuality-related topic.[3] Another study found that adolescents who viewed more television shows containing sexual content were more likely to initiate sexual intercourse at a younger age.[4]

New research found that heavy exposure to sexual content on television related strongly to teens' initiation of intercourse or their progression to more advanced sexual activities such as "making out" or oral sex. Teens who viewed the greatest amounts of sexual content were twice as likely as those who viewed the smallest amount to initiate sexual intercourse during the following year or to progress to more advanced levels of other sexual activity.[5]

Although sexual intercourse rates among youth have declined in the past decade, media messages and other factors contribute to the fact that a high number of preadolescents and adolescents participate in sexual intercourse and other risky sexual behaviors at a young age (Table 13–1). For example,

- 6.2 percent of U.S. teens had sexual intercourse before age 13
- 20 percent had sexual intercourse before age 15[6]
- 47.8 percent of students in grades 9 through 12 have had sexual intercourse[7]
- 36 percent of adolescents aged 15–17 reported having had oral sex[8]

Youth Risk Behavior Survey (YRBS) Data Related to Risky Sexual Behaviors, 2007

In 2007, high school students in the United States reported the following health-risk behaviors related to risky sexual behavior.

Sexual Risk Behavior	Percent Reporting Behavior		
	Total	Females	Males
Students who have ever had sexual intercourse	47.8	45.9	49.8
Students who are currently sexually active	35.0	35.6	34.3
Had sexual intercourse before age 13	7.1	4.0	10.1
Had four or more sexual partners during their lifetime	14.9	11.8	17.9
Used a condom during last sexual intercourse	61.5	54.9	68.5
Used alcohol or other drugs before their last sexual intercourse	22.5	17.7	27.5

SOURCE: Centers for Disease Control and Prevention, "Youth Risk Behavior Surveillance—United States, 2007," *Morbidity and Mortality Weekly Report* 57, no. SS-4 (6 June 2008): 1–131.

The results of early risky sexual behavior are teen pregnancy, HIV/AIDS, and other sexually transmitted diseases (STDs). Each year in the United States, almost 750,000 young women age 19 or younger become pregnant, more than double the teenage pregnancy rate of most Western industrialized countries.[9] In addition, teenagers have the highest rates of STDs of any age group.[10] Every year, 3 million teens—about one in four sexually active teens—get an STD.[11]

Nearly 420,000 children are born to teen mothers each year. This entails a considerable financial cost, with teen pregnancy costing society over $9 billion annually. Most of these costs are associated with negative consequences for the children of teen mothers including lack of health care, reliance on child welfare, and lower lifetime earnings.[12] The cost to society of STDs is also very high. It is estimated that the lifetime medical costs for new STD and HIV cases for 15–24 year olds reach $6.5 billion.[13]

Sexual Health and Academic Performance

Teen pregnancy also creates academic problems. Parenthood is a leading cause of high school dropout among teen girls. Less than one-third of teens who begin families before age 18 ever complete high school.[14] Early parenting also limits young mothers' chances of getting a postsecondary education, which increases the chances that they will live in poverty. Teen fathers tend to complete one less semester of school than fathers who delay parenthood until at least age 21. Numerous challenges also face the children of teen parents. For example, children of teen parents are 50 percent more likely to repeat a grade and to perform worse on standardized tests. They also are less likely to complete high school, compared to children with parents who delayed childbearing.[15]

Factors That Influence Sexual Health

Factors have been identified that differentiate those who participate in early risky sexual behaviors from those who do not. The factors associated with greater potential for engaging in early risky sexual behaviors, pregnancy, and STDs are called risk factors; the factors associated with a reduced potential for such activity are called protective factors. Some protective factors against early risky sexual behaviors include youth who

1. Live in a community where there is a high proportion of foreign-born residents.
2. Live with two parents.
3. Live with parents who have a high level of education.
4. Live in a home where there is a high quality of family interactions, connectedness, and satisfaction with relationships.
5. Live in a household where there is adequate parental supervision and monitoring.
6. Have parents who disapprove of premarital sex or teen sex.
7. Have parents who accept and support contraceptive use for sexually active teens.
8. Have good parent–child communication about sex and condoms or contraception, especially before the teen initiates sex.
9. Have peers who use condoms or have positive norms or support for condom or contraceptive use.
10. Have a partner who is supportive of condom or contraceptive use.
11. Are connected to school, as demonstrated by their positive attendance rates, good grades, and participation in extracurricular activities, and plan to go to college.
12. Are involved in the community.
13. Have a religious affiliation.
14. Are involved in sports (girls only).
15. Have a higher level of cognitive development.
16. Have a higher internal locus of control.
17. Take a virginity pledge.
18. Have a greater perceived male responsibility for pregnancy prevention.
19. Have a belief that condoms do not reduce sexual pleasure.
20. Believe that there are benefits to using condoms and are motivated to use condoms or other contraceptives.
21. Have confidence in the ability to demand condom use and use condoms or other contraceptives.
22. Have an intention to use condoms.
23. Perceive negative consequences of pregnancy.
24. Are motivated to avoid pregnancy and STD.
25. Are older at first voluntary sex.
26. Discuss sexual risks, pregnancy, and STD prevention with their sexual partner.[16]

Some risk factors for early risky sexual behaviors, pregnancy, and STDs include youth who

1. Live in a community where there is community disorganization (violence, substance abuse).
2. Live in a family that has experienced disruption (divorce, change to a single-parent household).
3. Live in a household where there is substance abuse.
4. Live in a household where there is physical abuse and general maltreatment.
5. Have a mother who first had sex at an early age or gave birth at an early age.
6. Have peers and close friends who are older.
7. Have an older sibling who has had sex or a sister who has given birth as an adolescent.
8. Have peers who drink alcohol, are sexually active, or have a permissive attitude toward premarital sex.
9. Have a romantic relationship with an older person.
10. Are black or Hispanic.
11. Are behind in school or having problems in school.
12. Are involved in delinquent behaviors including alcohol and drug use, being part of a gang, or carrying weapons.
13. Work in a paid job more than 20 hours a week.
14. Have depression or thoughts of suicide.
15. Have permissive attitudes toward premarital sex.
16. Date frequently.
17. Have a romantic relationship with a boyfriend or girlfriend.
18. Have a high number of sexual partners.
19. Have a history of prior sexual coercion or abuse.[17]

Opposition to Sexuality Education

Although problems regarding risky sexual behavior are well documented, not nearly enough students receive comprehensive K–12 sexuality education. In fact, only 49 percent of elementary schools, 59 percent of middle/junior high schools, and 61 percent of high schools have a state requirement to teach human sexuality.[18] Most states and school districts teach one unit of sexuality education during a one-semester ninth- or tenth-grade health class. Do these school districts assume that their students do not need developmentally appropriate sexuality education until this time? Studies show that sexuality education begun before youth are sexually active helps them stay abstinent and use protection when they do become sexually active.[19]

With all the sexuality issues and decisions facing young people today, why don't school districts mandate a K–12 sexuality education program? There is one main obstacle to such programming: controversy regarding sexuality education. A handful of vocal parents opposed to such instructional activities often have succeeded at keeping developmentally appropriate, quality, comprehensive sexuality education out of many school districts. Yet a variety of studies show that the majority of parents overwhelmingly support comprehensive sexuality education. One national survey found that 93 percent of junior high parents believe it is very important or somewhat important to have sexuality education as a part of the school curriculum. The same study found that 95 percent of parents of junior high students believe that birth control and other methods of preventing pregnancy are appropriate topics to teach in school.[20] Another study of low socioeconomic parents found that 81 percent were in favor of schools teaching comprehensive sexuality education, including birth control and STD prevention.[21] In another study, 88 percent of parents supported teaching all aspects of sexuality education in high school, over 50 percent of parents supported teaching all aspects of sexuality education in middle school, and 34 percent supported basic sexuality information for middle school students.[22] If the majority of parents are supportive of sexuality education in the schools, why are quality, comprehensive programs reaching only 5 percent of students? The main issue is that many administrators are nervous about the political and practical implications of teaching such a sensitive topic.

Sexuality education, or family life education, encompasses a broad scope of concepts and skills, including acquiring information about sexual development, reproductive health, interpersonal relationships, affection, body image, and gender roles and identity. It also includes skill development in areas such as communication, decision making, refusal techniques, and goal setting. Sexual health promotion programming is grounded in the premise that sexuality is a natural, ongoing process that begins in infancy and continues through life. From the moment of birth, children are learning about themselves as sexual people through the unintentional and informal messages of parents and caregivers. As children grow and explore more of their environment, they can learn about sexuality through television, friends, books, and newspapers. Given the speed of communication networks and information transfer, it is unrealistic to presume that students can be shielded from all information about sexuality until they reach adulthood. Parents and teachers cannot control a child's curiosity and desire to learn about sexuality. They can, however, empower children with formal, developmentally appropriate sexuality education experiences in the classroom environment that give students accurate, quality, and comprehensive information. Sexuality education should be a planned, intentional, and specific program of instruction that encourages parents and educators to identify the kinds of information, skills, and attitudes that are developmentally appropriate for children of different ages.

If school districts in the United States continue to be held captive by a few vocal minority groups who oppose such instruction, students likely will be forced to make sexual decisions without the benefit of the best information, skills, and support available to them. There will continue to be high rates of teenage pregnancy, STD, and HIV resulting from a lack of information, healthy attitudes, and appropriate skills regarding sexuality. Research shows that sexuality education programs do not hasten the onset of intercourse, nor do they increase the frequency of intercourse or the number of sexual partners. In fact, effective skill-based programs have been shown to delay significantly the onset of sexual intercourse and to increase contraceptive and condom use among sexually experienced adolescents.[23]

Concrete steps can be taken to minimize controversy and garner support for implementing a comprehensive sexuality education curriculum. First, determine the goals of the sexuality curriculum. For example, if the goal of the curriculum is to prevent teen pregnancies and sexually transmitted diseases, most parents would support that goal. It is important for school districts to focus the discussion around these common goals. Second, school districts should base their curriculum on sound research. Knowing current research can help support a well-written curriculum. Third, when writing a curriculum, form a broad-based, knowledgeable, and inclusive committee. This will help assure that people feel they have a voice in determining what will be included in the curriculum.[24,25]

Reasons to Include Sexuality Education in Elementary and Middle Schools

It is important for teachers to have a solid understanding of why sexuality education is important to include in an elementary and middle school health education curriculum. It is not uncommon for parents to contact teachers about their concerns on this topic. The following reasons should help teachers formulate their own rationale for teaching sexuality education.

1. Attitudes regarding sexuality are formulated early in life, which makes them difficult to change once a person has internalized them. Children begin forming opinions about their bodies, their gender identity, and their feelings about sexuality at a young age. If parents and teachers provide children with negative messages about their sexuality when children are young, these messages generally stay with them through adulthood. For instance, if a 6-year-old girl is taught to use slang terms for body parts and functions, such as *boobs* and *pee pee*, she will probably continue to use that terminology as she gets older. Some parents and teachers feel this is not a problem, but it gives children a message that something is wrong with those body parts.

When children ask adults questions about sexuality and the adults respond, "I never want to hear you talk like that again," or "Wait until you get older," children quickly get the message that there must be something wrong with their concerns or questions about their sexuality. In contrast, when children grow up in an open and honest environment regarding sexuality and are reinforced for seeking information from significant adults rather than from peers, they have a better chance of developing healthy attitudes and appropriate sexual communication skills as they get older.

2. If factual information and skills are presented in a positive manner throughout the elementary and middle grades, negative attitudes, apprehensions, and fears about sexuality can be reduced and superseded by a positive understanding that people live as sexual beings. Unfortunately, many school districts limit sexuality education to discussing puberty and the menstrual cycle through a one- or two-day presentation during the fifth or sixth grade. Outside experts sometimes give the presentation, with the girls and boys in separate classrooms. At this age, many students have already begun going through puberty, making the presentation developmentally inappropriate. Also, students might feel uncomfortable with an outsider, might not have a question concerning puberty on that day, or might be more curious about what is happening in the opposite gender's presentation. Again, the message that students get from this type of presentation is that there is something wrong or embarrassing about sexuality because the classroom teacher is too embarrassed to talk about puberty. Further, such a strategy sends messages about communication between girls and boys on sexual issues. How are mutual respect and appropriate sexual communication to be reinforced if boys and girls are not allowed to listen to the same presentation?

If student questions are not answered by trained professionals during that one- or two-day presentation in the fifth or sixth grade, students typically have to wait until sexuality is again formally discussed during a high school health class. Again, that gives students the message that sexuality is not important enough to discuss or that there is something wrong with developmentally appropriate curiosity and concern about the topic.

3. Information and skill development are the greatest defenses against the negative aspects of sexuality, such as promiscuity, teen pregnancy, sexually transmitted diseases, and sexual abuse. Sexuality knowledge increases when students are instructed on the topic. Also, skill-based programs can significantly delay the onset of sexual intercourse and increase contraceptive and condom use among sexually experienced youth. No studies have revealed evidence that sexuality education leads to earlier or increased sexual experience, and several indicate that it is associated with the delay of sexual intercourse.[26]

4. Schools can provide a unique opportunity for students to exchange ideas and thoughts about sexuality with their peers, under the guidance of a trained teacher. Sexuality education should take place at home, because parents can add love, security, and values to the factual information and skills being taught. Without usurping this pivotal role of the family, school-based programs can formalize student interaction with their peers about sexuality issues. Many students talk about sexuality with their friends, but in an unsupervised arena. Encouraging students to share thoughts, feelings, and questions about sexuality with their peers and a trained teacher complements the learning taking place at home.

5. Students receive a distorted view of sexuality through the mass media (see the section "Prevalence and Cost").

6. Many parents do a wonderful job of teaching formal sexuality education to their children, but some parents are so uncomfortable talking to their children about sexuality that they ignore or avoid the topic. Every student is entitled to formal sexuality education as a means of learning correct information and developing health-enhancing attitudes and skills.

GUIDELINES FOR SCHOOLS

This section provides information about current sexuality education programs and policies in elementary and middle schools. The first part of the section includes data about the actual programs and policies in place in schools today, while the second part provides information for teachers and administrators about what should be happening in schools to help prevent risky sexual behaviors and to promote healthy sexuality among children and adolescents.

State of the Practice

The CDC conducts the School Health Policies and Programs Study (SHPPS) to assess current school health policies and programs at the state, district, school, and classroom levels. Because pregnancy, STDs, and HIV cause so many problems for young people, it is important for states and school districts to have policies that require prevention education in these areas. More states, school districts, and schools require pregnancy, STD, and HIV prevention education at the middle and high school levels than at the elementary level (see Table 13–2).

TABLE 13–2

	States	School Districts	Schools
Percentage requiring pregnancy prevention education			
at elementary level	27.5	27.2	16.4
at middle school level	58.8	70.0	61.3
Percentage requiring HIV prevention education			
at elementary level	60.8	48.6	39.1
at middle school level	74.5	79.0	74.5
Percentage requiring STD prevention education			
at elementary level	45.1	32.8	21.7
at middle school level	68.6	77.3	69.6

SOURCE: L. Kann, S. Telljohann, and S. Wooley, "Health Education's Results from the School Health Policies and Programs Study 2006," *Journal of School Health, 77,* vol. 8 (2007): 408–34.

TABLE 13-3

School Health Policies and Programs Study 2006, Data Related to Pregnancy, HIV, and STD Prevention Education

Human Sexuality Topic	% of All Elementary Schools	% of All Middle Schools
Abstinence as the most effective method to avoid pregnancy, HIV, and other STDs	12.3	75.8
Condom efficacy	NA	42.0
Dating and relationships	9.2	66.2
How students can influence or support others to make healthy decisions related to sexual behavior	13.8	67.1
How to correctly use a condom	NA	21.0
Human development issues (reproductive anatomy and puberty)	22.2	69.4
Influence of families on sexual behavior	6.5	45.2
Influence of the media on sexual behavior	12.4	60.3
Marriage and commitment	8.5	60.4
Resisting peer pressure to engage in sexual behavior	15.8	72.6
Risks associated with having multiple sexual partners	NA	65.2
Sexual identity and sexual orientation	NA	37.4
Social or cultural influences on sexual behavior	14.3	61.1

SOURCE: Centers for Disease Control and Prevention, *School Health Policies and Programs Study 2006 (SHHPS)* (Atlanta, GA: CDC, 2007). www.cdc.gov/HealthyYouth/shpps

SHPPS also provides important data related to the pregnancy, HIV, and STD prevention education topics and skills being taught at the elementary and middle school levels. Table 13–3 summarizes these findings. Resisting peer pressure to engage in sexual behavior is the most common skill taught at the elementary level. Middle school teachers are most likely to teach abstinence as the most effective method to avoid pregnancy, HIV, or STDs, and the skill of resisting peer pressure to engage in sexual behavior.[27]

State of the Art

Several guidelines are important to consider when teaching sexuality education. These guidelines can help school districts make decisions about their sexuality education and help teachers not be defensive with parents and students when teaching sexuality education.

School districts should establish sexuality education guidelines and policies with the input of parents, teachers, administrators, community members, and support staff. Policies might include topics such as the omission of specific students from sexuality education classes, how teachers should respond to questions about specific sexuality topics, and what teachers should do if a student questions his or her own sexual orientation. Without established guidelines and policies in place, teachers will have a difficult time determining how to manage these situations.

After creating a K–12 sexuality curriculum, it is important to determine whether it includes the information and skills that will help children and adolescents make positive sexual choices. The following ten characteristics of effective sexuality education programs can help school districts create their curriculum:[28]

1. Effective programs focus on reducing one or more sexual behaviors that lead to unintended pregnancy or HIV/STD infection.

2. Effective programs are based on theoretical approaches that have been demonstrated to influence other health-related behavior and identify specific important sex antecedents to be targeted.

3. Effective programs deliver and consistently reinforce a clear message about abstaining from sexual activity and/or using condoms or other forms of contraception. This appears to be one of the most important characteristics that distinguish effective from ineffective programs.

4. Effective programs provide basic, accurate information about the risks of teen sexual activity and about ways to avoid intercourse or use methods of protection against pregnancy and STDs.

5. Effective programs include activities that address social pressures that influence sexual behavior.

6. Effective programs provide examples of and practice with communication, negotiation, and refusal skills.

7. Effective programs use teaching methods designed to involve participants and have them personalize the information.

8. Effective programs incorporate behavioral goals, teaching methods, and materials that are appropriate to the age, sexual experience, and culture of the students.

9. Effective programs last a sufficient length of time (more than a few hours).

10. Effective programs select teachers or peer leaders who believe in the program and then provide them with adequate training.

Some states and school districts have ignored these ten characteristics and have adopted abstinence-only curricula. States and school districts have opted for these programs because of pressure from minority groups and legislation at the federal level. In 1996, the federal government added a new formula grant program to Title V of the Social Security Act; its purpose is to enable the states to provide funding for abstinence-only education.

Since 1997, the federal government has spent more than $1.5 billion on prescriptive abstinence-only and abstinence-until-marriage programs.[29] At best, these programs are ineffective. Research shows that they do not result in young people delaying sexual intercourse.[30] At their worst, they can be misleading and dangerous to young people. Many of the funded abstinence-only programs contain false, misleading, or distorted information. In fact, a 2004 investigation reviewed thirteen commonly used abstinence-only curricula taught to millions of school-age youth. The study concluded that two of the curricula were accurate but that eleven others blurred religion and science, and contained unproven claims and subjective conclusions or outright falsehoods regarding the effectiveness of contraceptives, gender traits, and when life begins.[31]

For their part, teachers should encourage proper terminology in the classroom. Beginning in kindergarten, students should learn the proper terms for their external body parts, including their reproductive organs. At that age, it is not important for students to know the names of their internal body parts (such as *fallopian tube* or *epididymis*), because they are concrete thinkers and have difficulty imagining what the inside of their body is like. However, as students get older, they should learn the proper terminology for internal reproductive body parts. If students are taught proper terminology at an early age, they will not be as embarrassed to say words such as *penis, testes, vulva,* and *vagina* when they get older. This will allow students to communicate about sexuality in a more comfortable manner.

Teachers do not have to know all the answers to every sexuality-related question. Students are capable of asking a variety of questions about sexuality. Because most elementary and middle school teachers do not receive adequate training in this area, they cannot be expected to know all the answers about this subject. It is appropriate for teachers to respond "I don't know" to a question, as long as they find out the answer and relay that information to the student as soon as possible. The teacher also can ask students to find the answer to the question. Perhaps a student can volunteer to find the correct answer.

Although teachers cannot be prepared for all questions asked by children, it is important for them to understand that students are capable of asking unexpected questions. If teachers act shocked when students ask questions about sexuality, the students will be less likely to ask another question in the future. A good way to overcome a shocked look is to practice answering common questions that children ask about sexuality. A sample list of questions with suggested answers can be found in the section "Recommendations for Concepts and Practice."

Teachers should teach only those topics in sexuality education that have been approved as part of their course of study by their board of education and administrators. Many teachers have felt so strongly about teaching all aspects of sexuality education that they have jeopardized their jobs because they did not have administrative support for teaching certain sexuality topics. Such a practice can jeopardize the credibility of the entire health education program. If teachers feel that more sexuality education should be included in their curriculum, they should seek the support of their administrators, boards of education, and parents in the community.

Teachers should not use handmade drawings of the reproductive system. Students have a difficult time imagining what the internal male and female reproductive systems look like. When teachers use handmade drawings, there is a better chance that the proportions or specific organs will be incorrect. There are enough good professional drawings of the male and female reproductive systems that handmade drawings are not necessary.

Activities should be structured to include parents or caregivers whenever possible. When teaching sexuality education topics, teachers should encourage students to discuss the information taught that day with parents. This will help bridge the gap among children, parents, and schools. Teachers might even want to have specific questions written out on a handout for parents and children to discuss.

GUIDELINES FOR CLASSROOM APPLICATIONS

Important Background for K–8 Teachers

Depending on the grade level, not all of the information presented in this section is relevant to all elementary and middle school students, but teachers should have background knowledge about relationships, families, the male and female reproductive systems, and puberty.

Relationships

Students develop many relationships throughout their elementary and middle school years. Relationships with family members, same-age friends, relatives, and teachers change as children continue through elementary and middle school. It is vital that teachers have a basic understanding of the importance children place on friends as they advance through elementary and middle school.

When children first enter school at age 5, they are very self-centered and more concerned about their own needs and identity than about the needs or characteristics of others. As they progress through kindergarten, they begin to develop an increasing awareness of others. They start to understand that other people have needs and rights, too. This recognition might conflict with their early attitudes of self-gratification and might be displayed by their throwing temper tantrums and not wanting to share. Friends, and their behaviors, are not that important to students at this age.[32]

Children from age 6 to 8 begin to redirect their personal concerns to intellectual concerns and group activities. They begin to expend more energy on friendships and the community around them. Children in this age group also become less dependent on their parents, although their parents are still important to them. Most 9- and 10-year-old children accept sexuality education as they do other subjects. Many children this age do not yet feel self-conscious about their bodies, making it an ideal time to discuss the reproductive system. At this age, boys and girls begin to regard the opinions of their friends as more important than those of their parents. Although same-sex friendships are more popular in this age group, children begin to become interested in the opposite sex. This interest typically is exhibited in the forms of teasing and aggressive behavior.[33]

Between ages 11 and 13, children become even more independent of their parents. Their friendships are increasingly more important as they try to emancipate themselves from their parents and other adult authority figures. This is a means of exploring the parameters of their own unique identities. Peer pressure becomes a major issue during this time because children are struggling with developing their own codes of morals and ethics. Preadolescents also are beginning to become more self-conscious about the physical changes to their bodies. Teachers might find it more difficult to discuss sexual issues with students of this age because of their self-consciousness. They also become more interested in the opposite sex as they get older.[34]

Another relationship issue that sometimes arises with preadolescents is being gay or lesbian. Teachers are sometimes nervous about addressing this topic because of fear of how parents and students will react, or they may be uncomfortable with this subject themselves. As with all areas of sexuality, it is important that the teacher know what is in the course of study or curriculum before teaching about a specific topic. If the issue of gays and lesbians is included in the curriculum, teachers should have some background information on the topic.

Students should understand that gays and lesbians are people who have a sexual and emotional relationship with others of the same sex. They should learn that females are referred to as lesbians and males as gays. It is important for young people to understand that being gay or lesbian is normal. Gay and lesbian adolescents need to feel that they are okay and it is important to help prevent violence against gays and lesbians. It is important teachers also explain that preadolescents sometimes have attractions toward individuals of the same sex, and that this may mean that their sexual orientation is homosexual or these feelings may be transitory. If a student has concerns about his or her sexual orientation, teachers should be supportive and refer the student to a gay-lesbian–friendly counselor within the school district. In addition, students should be encouraged to discuss their feelings with supportive family members. Teachers should feel secure in knowing that discussions about homosexuality will not make someone become gay or lesbian.

Families

When discussing the family structure and the role of the family during sexuality education, the teacher should not be judgmental about different types of families and the way they function. Today's families are quite different from the families of 50 to 100 years ago. For example, in the past, extended families were common. This meant that parents, children, grandparents, and other relatives lived in the same house or in close proximity. Children had several adult role models they could depend on for love, support, understanding, and protection. Various factors have contributed to the changing structure of the family. For example, the increased mobility of families has made it difficult to maintain extended families. It was once common to grow up in a town, marry someone from that town, and raise a family in that town. Today, many people move often because of career changes and no longer live close to the town in which they were raised.

Some people believe that the "typical" or "normal" family of today is the nuclear family. A nuclear family consists of children living with both of their natural parents. Of course, many nuclear families exist, but there are many other types of families as well. People can no longer assume that the nuclear family is the norm.

Today's families are more diverse than in the past. Types of families include single-parent families and families with stepparents and half-siblings. There are many single-parent families because of the high divorce rate, teenagers who become pregnant and decide not to marry, gays and lesbians who are raising children, and never-married single people who are raising children. It is important that elementary and middle school teachers not assume that all students are being raised in a nuclear family and recognize that some students might have special needs because of their family situation. Students also should be taught that members of a family might not be blood-related, such as in an adoption or a remarriage. It is important that children believe they belong to a family regardless of its structure.

Children also should be taught that family members have responsibilities to one another and to the overall functioning of the family unit. For example, certain tasks need to be accomplished by a family, such as buying groceries, cooking, cleaning, and helping each other. Teachers should discuss the concept of family roles and responsibilities with their students so that they understand that each person must contribute if the family is to be nurturing, mutually supportive, and happy.

Another issue that arises when discussing families is sex-role stereotypes. Some families still establish and reinforce clear gender roles for boys and girls—for example, the boys mow the lawn and the girls wash the dishes. It is not the teacher's role to judge the ways different families function. Teachers can, however, try to eliminate sex-role

Boys and girls should be encouraged to participate in opposite-gender activities and to play with opposite-gender toys.

stereotyping in their classrooms. For example, certain chores should not be identified as being for boys or for girls. Textbooks also should be reviewed with sex-role stereotyping in mind. These activities can help balance students' attitudes about sex-role stereotyping. Allowing students to participate in all types of activities also allows them to explore interests and talents without fear of negative judgment.

The Male and Female Reproductive Systems

A general understanding of the male and female reproductive systems is an important part of sexuality education. The reproductive system is the only system in the body that has different organs for the male and the female. The following information should provide enough background for the elementary and middle school teacher about the male and female anatomy and physiology of the reproductive system.

The Male Reproductive System The function of the male reproductive system is to produce sperm, which are the male cells that unite with female eggs to form fertilized eggs. Both external and internal organs make up the male reproductive system (Figure 13–1).

The external part of the male sex organs, called the genitalia, is composed of the penis and the scrotum. The penis is a tubelike organ composed mainly of erectile tissue and skin and is used for urination and sexual intercourse. Some males are circumcised and others are not. In circumcision the foreskin of the penis is removed. Approximately 65 percent of newborn males in the United States are circumcised (see Figure 13–1a).[35] When a male becomes sexually excited, the erectile tissue in the penis becomes filled with blood, which makes it become enlarged and erect. The scrotum is the pouchlike structure hanging behind and slightly below the penis.

The major internal organs of the male reproductive system are the testes, vas deferentia, seminal vesicles, prostate gland, Cowper's glands, and urethra.

The scrotum contains the testes and acts as a thermometer. Because the scrotum keeps the testes at a constant temperature, they can produce viable sperm. For example, if the body temperature rises, muscles in the scrotum relax to lower the testes away from the body, cooling the scrotum. Sperm are produced in a section of the testes called the seminiferous tubules. These tubules produce about 500 million sperm a day and can produce billions of sperm throughout a lifetime. After the sperm are produced, they are stored in the epididymis. After about sixty-four days, the sperm reach maturity and are capable of uniting with a female egg.

The vasa deferentia, two tubes connected to the epididymis, are used to store and transfer sperm to the seminal vesicles during ejaculation. The seminal vesicles are two small pouches near the prostate gland. Their function is to secrete a fluid, which mixes with the sperm. This fluid contains nutrients for the sperm, helps make the sperm mobile, and provides protection for them.

The prostate gland is about the size of a chestnut and is located near the bladder. It produces a thin, milky, alkaline fluid, which mixes with sperm to make semen. The alkaline fluid acts as an acid neutralizer and a coagulant.

The two Cowper's glands are about pea-size and open up into the urethra. These glands secrete a clear fluid, prior to ejaculation, that helps neutralize the urethra. This fluid can contain some sperm, and its release is not felt by the male.

The urethra is a tube that runs the length of the penis. The urethra allows both urine and semen to leave the body, but not at the same time. When semen enters the urethra, the internal and external urethral sphincters close the connection between the bladder and the urethra.

The Female Reproductive System The function of the female reproductive system is to release a mature egg, which unites with a sperm to make a fertilized egg. Both external and internal organs make up the female reproductive system.

The external part of the female sex organs, called the vulva, is composed of the clitoris, vaginal opening, hymen, and labia (Figure 13–2a).

The clitoris is a knob of tissue located in front of the vaginal opening. It contains many nerve endings and blood

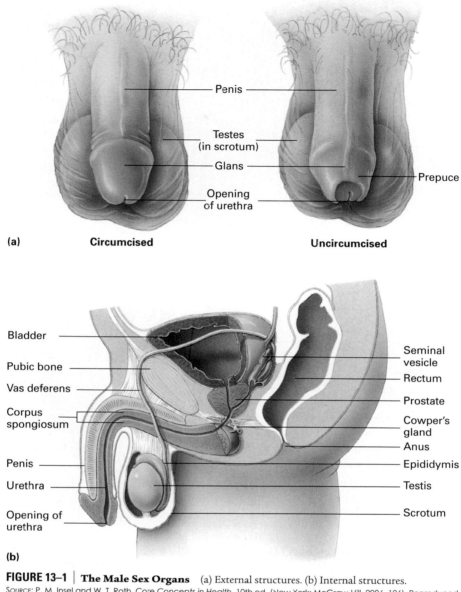

Penis

Testes
(in scrotum)

Glans

Opening
of urethra

Prepuce

(a)   **Circumcised**   **Uncircumcised**

Bladder

Pubic bone

Vas deferens

Corpus
spongiosum

Penis

Urethra

Opening of
urethra

Seminal
vesicle

Rectum

Prostate

Cowper's
gland

Anus

Epididymis

Testis

Scrotum

(b)

FIGURE 13–1 | **The Male Sex Organs**   (a) External structures. (b) Internal structures.

Source: P. M. Insel and W. T. Roth, *Core Concepts in Health,* 10th ed. (New York: McGraw-Hill, 2006, 126). Reproduced with permission of The McGraw-Hill Companies.

vessels. When the female gets sexually excited, the clitoris becomes engorged with blood and enlarges. The clitoris is the only part of the female sexual anatomy that does not have a reproductive function, but it does produce sexual arousal.

The hymen is a flexible membrane that partially covers the vaginal opening. It has no known function and is different in every female. For example, some females have a hymen that covers a large portion of the vaginal opening, some have a hymen that is barely visible. A common myth about the hymen is that an intact hymen is a sign of virginity. This is not true, because every female's hymen is unique and, in fact, some females do not have a hymen at birth.

The labia are folds of skin that protect the female genitals from germs entering the body. There are two labia: the

labia majora and the labia minora. The labia majora are large folds of skin that surround the opening of the vagina. The labia minora are smaller folds of skin located between the labia majora.

The internal reproductive organs in the female are the vagina, uterus, fallopian tubes, and ovaries (Figure 13–2b). The vagina is a muscular tube that goes from the outside of the body to the uterus. It has three main functions: It receives the penis during intercourse, it is the opening for menstrual flow to exit the body, and it serves as the birth canal. It is called the birth canal because, during birth, the baby is pushed from the uterus through the vagina and out of the mother's body.

The uterus is an elastic muscle the size of a fist and the shape of a pear. The tip of the uterus, which leads to the

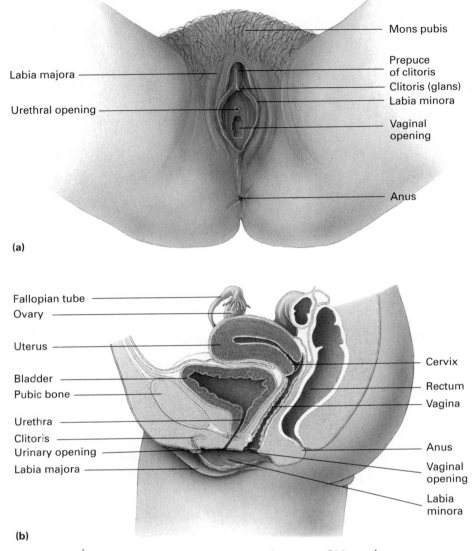

Mons pubis

Prepuce
of clitoris

Clitoris (glans)

Labia minora

Vaginal
opening

Labia majora

Urethral opening

Anus

(a)

Fallopian tube

Ovary

Uterus

Bladder

Pubic bone

Urethra

Clitoris

Urinary opening

Labia majora

Cervix

Rectum

Vagina

Anus

Vaginal
opening

Labia
minora

(b)

FIGURE 13–2 | **The Female Sex Organs**   (a) External structures. (b) Internal structures.
SOURCE: P. M. Insel and W. T. Roth, *Core Concepts in Health*, 10th ed. (New York: McGraw-Hill, 2006, 125).
Reproduced with permission of The McGraw-Hill Companies.

vagina, is called the cervix. The role of the cervix is to help keep the baby inside the uterus until the time of delivery. The lining of the uterus is composed of many blood vessels. About once every month, this lining thickens and turns into a nourishing place for a fertilized egg to develop into a baby. If an egg is not fertilized, the thickening material disintegrates because it is no longer needed. The fluid and membrane then leave the body through the vagina; this process is called menstruation.

There are two fallopian tubes, which curl around the ovaries and connect to the uterus. The fallopian tubes are narrow and are lined with tiny, hairlike projections called cilia. After an egg is released from an ovary, it travels through a fallopian tube for a few days, where it waits to be fertilized. If the egg is fertilized, it travels to the uterus, where it attaches itself. If the egg is not fertilized while it is in the fallopian tube, it disintegrates.

There are two ovaries, located on each side of the uterus and next to the fallopian tubes. The functions of the ovaries are to house the egg cells for maturation and to produce the hormones estrogen and progesterone. Though males manufacture sperm following puberty, females are born with all the egg cells they will ever have.

Puberty

Puberty is not a single event but rather a long process that includes many physical and emotional changes. Regardless of the age at which puberty begins, it takes four to five years for boys and three to four years for girls to complete. Puberty has been reached when males and females have the physical capability to reproduce.

Teachers should remember that not all students reach puberty at the same time. That is why some upper-elementary and middle-level students might seem both

Children grow at different rates while going through puberty

physically and emotionally mature for their age but others might seem very immature. Puberty changes can occur as early as age 7 and as late as age 18. However, about 50 percent of boys and girls reach puberty before age 13. The emotional changes that preadolescents experience are diverse because of their changing hormone levels and the developmentally consistent feeling of wanting to be independent. Shifts in certain hormones can trigger feelings of irritability, restlessness, anxiety, happiness, excitement, and frustration. For instance, students going through puberty might be happy and sensible one day but depressed and irrational the next. These mood swings are normal and should be expected throughout puberty. Whatever emotion students express, teachers should be patient and understanding when interacting with them.

Boys and girls also are curious about the physical changes that are happening to them during puberty. The physical changes that occur throughout puberty are called secondary sex characteristics. These changes occur because different hormones are being released in males and females.

When teaching students about the changes that accompany puberty, it is important to emphasize that these changes can begin anytime from age 7 to 18. When teachers say "The average age of puberty is 13," students tend to remember the number 13 and not the word *average*. It should be emphasized that there is no best time to go through puberty and that everyone will experience these changes when his or her body is ready.

Female Changes During Puberty   For girls, the secondary sex characteristics, produced by the release of estrogen,

that teachers and peers might observe include the following (Figure 13–3):

- A gain in height and weight
- Breast enlargement
- Growth of pubic and underarm hair
- Onset of menstruation
- Widening of hips

Females will notice the external changes that happen throughout puberty gradually, such as breast enlargement and pubic hair growth. During this time, internal changes also occur, which the female cannot see. The reproductive organs develop so that a female is able to bear children. Part of this internal process is menstruation. Menarche, which is the first period, or menstruation, is a sign that a female's reproductive system is beginning to function so that she can produce a baby.

The menstrual cycle begins at puberty and continues until a woman is in her middle to late forties. Before the cycle has begun and after it has ended, a woman is usually unable to bear children.

The number of days for the complete menstrual cycle varies from female to female. For adolescents, it is usually twenty-seven to thirty-one days, although it can be anywhere from twenty to forty-two days. Teenagers generally have an irregular cycle during the first year of menstruation.

The purpose of the menstrual cycle is to produce a mature egg and to develop the lining of the uterus so that it is ready to receive and nourish a fertilized egg. The menstrual cycle is complex, because many hormonal and physical changes occur each month. It is not necessary for the elementary or middle school teacher to understand every detail in the menstrual cycle; a general knowledge of the changes that occur is sufficient (Figure 13–4). The cycle begins when one egg in one of the ovaries develops, becomes larger, and is mature enough to produce a baby if it is joined by a sperm. This mature egg is called an ovum. An ovum is produced every month, usually in alternating ovaries. While the egg is growing, the lining of the uterus becomes thick with blood and other materials in preparation for a fertilized egg. As the uterine lining continues to thicken, the egg breaks through the wall of the ovary (called ovulation) into the fallopian tube, where it travels toward the uterus for a few days. If the egg is to be fertilized, it must be joined by a sperm while it is in the fallopian tube. While the egg is traveling through the fallopian tube, the uterine lining continues to get thicker and be filled with blood.

If the egg does not meet the sperm while it is in the fallopian tube, it disintegrates. The buildup in the uterus is no longer needed, so it begins to shed. The shedding of the uterine lining (menstruation) lasts for three to seven days. The cycle then continues with the maturing of another egg and the buildup of the lining of the uterus.

Male Changes During Puberty   Males also go through many physical changes during puberty. Their secondary

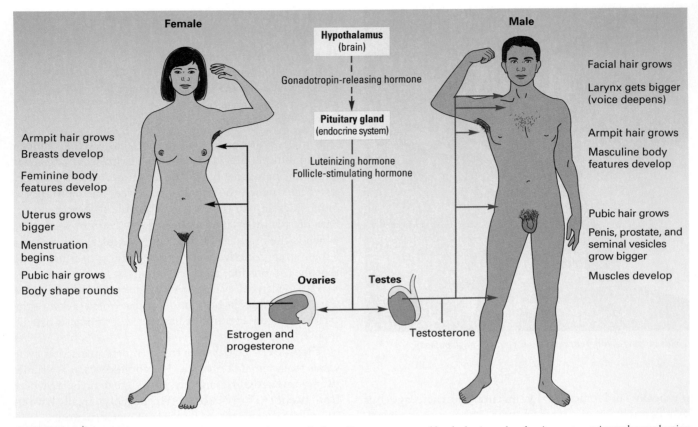

FIGURE 13–3 | **Female and Male Secondary Sex Characteristics**   Hormones secreted by the brain and endocrine system trigger the production of sex hormones by the ovaries and testes; these hormones in turn trigger the physical changes of puberty.

sex characteristics, produced by the release of the hormone testosterone, that teachers and peers might observe include the following (see Figure 13–3):

- A gain in height and weight
- Growth and added muscle strength
- Growth of body hair around the penis and scrotum, under the arms, and on the face, arms, legs, and chest
- An increase in the size of the penis and scrotum
- Broadening of the shoulders
- Deepening of the voice
- An increase in metabolic rate
- Possible nocturnal emissions (wet dreams)

As with girls, boys will notice some of the physical changes occurring gradually in their bodies throughout puberty. During this time, internal changes also are happening, which the male cannot see. Hormones are being released, making it possible for the male to produce sperm in the reproductive organs.

Before sperm are being produced, males can become sexually excited and have orgasms; however, no semen is ejaculated. Once a male is able to produce sperm, he ejaculates semen. When males go through puberty, many times they experience ejaculation while sleeping. This is called a nocturnal emission, or wet dream. There is no warning when this will occur, and it cannot be prevented. Wet

dreams are natural, and boys should be informed about wet dreams before they go through puberty so that they are not frightened by them.

Sexually Transmitted Diseases

Although most middle school students do not get sexually transmitted diseases (STDs), students will ask questions about them. In addition, some middle school health curricula include sexually transmitted disease prevention, so it is important for middle school health teachers to have basic understanding of the most common STDs, how to prevent them, and issues regarding treatment. STDs are infections that a person can get from having sex with someone who has the infection. The causes of STDs are bacteria, parasites, and viruses. These infections are usually passed by having vaginal intercourse, but they can also be passed through anal sex, oral sex, or skin-to-skin contact. There are more than twenty types of STDs including chlamydia, gonorrhea, herpes simplex, human immunodeficiency virus (HIV), human papillomavirus (HPV), syphilis, and trichomoniasis (Table 13–4).[36]

The only sure way to prevent STDs is by not having sex. If a person is sexually active, the risk for getting an STD can be lowered by only having sex with someone who isn't having sex with anyone else and who does not have an STD. Another way to reduce the risk of getting an STD

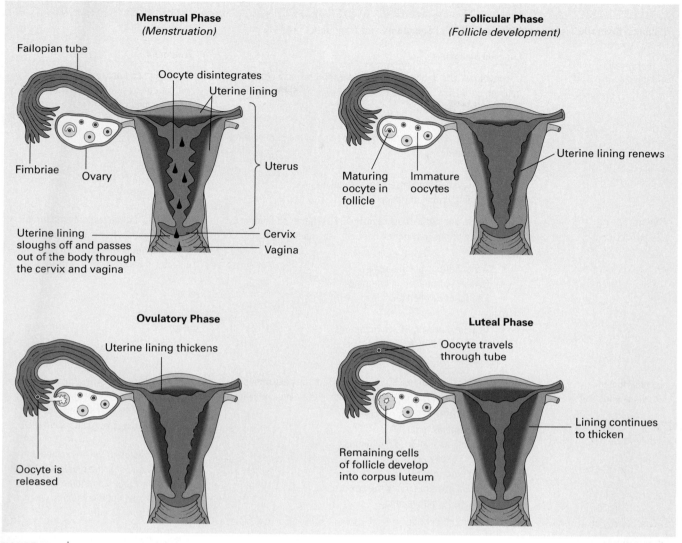

Menstrual Phase
(Menstruation)

Fallopian tube

Oocyte disintegrates

Uterine lining

Fimbriae

Ovary

Uterus

Uterine lining sloughs off and passes out of the body through the cervix and vagina

Cervix

Vagina

Follicular Phase
(Follicle development)

Uterine lining renews

Maturing oocyte in follicle

Immature oocytes

Ovulatory Phase

Uterine lining thickens

Oocyte is released

Luteal Phase

Oocyte travels through tube

Lining continues to thicken

Remaining cells of follicle develop into corpus luteum

FIGURE 13–4 | **The Stages of Menstruation**

is to use a male condom correctly and consistently. Condoms, however, are not 100 percent safe and they can't protect a person from coming into contact with sores that can occur with herpes simplex or warts. Other ways to reduce the risk of getting an STD are to limit the number of sex partners, get tested for STDs on a regular basis if sexually active, and to discuss STD testing with a sex partner.[37]

It is not important for middle school students to memorize every STD and their signs and symptoms. However, it is important to have an understanding of the common signs/symptoms of STDs. They include

- Itching around the vagina and/or discharge from the vagina for women
- Discharge from the penis for men
- Pain during sex or when urinating
- Pain in the pelvic area
- Sore throats in people who have oral sex

- Pain in or around the anus for people who have anal sex
- Chancre sores (painless red sores) on the genital area, anus, tongue and/or throat
- A scaly rash on the palms of your hands and the soles of your feet
- Dark urine, loose, light-colored stools, and yellow eyes and skin
- Small blisters that turn into scabs on the genital area
- Swollen glands, fever, and body aches
- Unusual infections, unexplained fatigue, night sweats, and weight loss
- Soft, flesh-colored warts around the genital area[38]

Treatment for an STD depends on the specific type. For some STDs, treatment may involve taking medicine or getting a shot. For other STDs that can't be cured, such as herpes, there is treatment to relieve the symptoms.

TABLE 13–4

Common Sexually Transmitted Diseases (STDs) Symptoms and Treatment

STD	Common Symptoms	Treatment
Chlamydia	Chlamydia can be dangerous because symptoms may not be noticed. Males • A discharge from the penis • Burning or itching around the opening of the penis during urination Females • An unusual discharge from the vagina • Burning during urination	Chlamydia can be treated and cured with antibiotics. It is important to finish all of the medication to make sure the disease is cured.
Gonorrhea	Gonorrhea is one of the most reported STDs. It can be dangerous because symptoms may not be noticed, especially in females. Males • A discharge from the penis • Pain or burning when urinating • Painful or swollen testicles Females • Vaginal bleeding between periods • Pain or burning during urination • Increased vaginal discharge	Gonorrhea can be treated and cured with antibiotics. It is important to finish all of the medication to make sure the disease is cured.
Genital Human Papillomavirus (HPV)	HPV is the most common STD. At least 50% of sexually active people will have genital HPV at some time in their lives. Individuals with HPV may not have any symptoms. Common symptoms include: • Burning sensation in the genitals • Lower back pain • Pain during urination • Painful blisters around the sex organs • Enlarged lymph glands • Flu-like symptoms	Because HPV is a virus, there is no cure. There are treatments for the health problems that some types of HPV can cause, like genital warts. The FDA has approved a vaccine that protects against some types of HPV. Experts on vaccines recommend that all girls should get the vaccine when they are 11 or 12 years old.
Genital Herpes	Most people who have genital herpes don't know it. The most common symptoms are painful blisters and sores around the sex organs. Some people might have flu symptoms when sores are present. Sores can disappear and then come back several times within a year.	There is no cure for genital herpes, but there are treatments for its symptoms. Some medications can prevent blisters or make them go away faster.
Human Immunodeficiency Virus (HIV)	There typically are no symptoms for HIV. HIV causes AIDS, which can cause the immune system to fail. On average, it takes 7–9 years for symptoms to develop.	There is no cure for HIV. There are treatments that can help an individual to live longer.
Syphilis	Many people infected with syphilis have no symptoms for years. The first symptom a person may see is a single sore (chancre) where syphilis entered the body. It is usually painless. If left untreated, more severe symptoms can appear later. Without treatment, individuals with syphilis can die.	Syphilis is easy to treat in its early stages with an antibiotic.
Trichomoniasis	Some people may not have symptoms, especially men. Males • A burning feeling or irritation inside the penis • A discharge from the penis Females • An unusual discharge from the vagina, which will have a strong odor • Discomfort during urination or sex • Irritation or itching around the genitals	Trichomoniasis can be treated and cured with antibiotics. It is important to finish all of the medication to make sure the disease is cured.

SOURCE: Centers for Disease Control and Prevention, *Sexually Transmitted Diseases, Brochures,* www.cdc.gov/STD/; 2008).

Recommendations for Concepts and Practice

Healthy Behavior Outcomes

The goal of health education is to help students adopt or maintain health-enhancing behaviors. School districts and teachers should identify the health-enhancing behaviors they would like their students to maintain or adopt. The following list identifies some possible behavior outcomes related to promoting sexual health. Although not all of the suggestions are developmentally appropriate for students in grades K–8, this list can help teachers understand how the learning activities they plan for their students support both short- and long-term desired behavior outcomes.

Ways to Promote Sexual Health

Establish and maintain healthy relationships.

Practice and maintain sexual abstinence.

Seek support to be sexually abstinent.

Avoid pressuring others to engage in sexual behaviors.

Return to sexual abstinence if sexually active.

Support others to avoid sexual risk behaviors.

Seek health care professionals to promote sexual health.

Limit the number of sexual partners if sexually active.*

Use condoms consistently and correctly if sexually active.*

Use birth control consistently and correctly if sexually active.*

Discuss contraception, disease prevention, and HIV and STD risk and status with sexual partners if sexually active or experienced.*[39]

(*This behavior is consistent with a risk-reduction approach and would not be addressed by a risk-avoidance or abstinence-only curriculum.)

Developmentally Appropriate Concepts and Skills

As with other health topics, teaching related to promoting sexual health should be developmentally appropriate and be based on the physical, cognitive, social, emotional, and language characteristics of specific students. Teacher's Toolbox 13.1 contains a list of suggested developmentally appropriate concepts and skills to help teachers create lessons that encourage students to practice the desired behavior outcomes by the time they graduate from high school. Note that some of these concepts and skills are reinforced in other content areas (the concept "identify the benefits of healthy family relationships" also applies to mental and emotional health).

Sample Students' Questions and Suggested Answers About Sexuality

A list of some commonly asked questions about sexuality and some suggested answers follows. It is not enough just to read the suggested answers—teachers should practice saying them out loud. Teachers are encouraged to think of other questions children might ask and to practice answering them as well.

Sample Questions Lower-Elementary Students Commonly Ask

1. *Where do babies come from?*
Babies come from their mothers' bodies. The baby grows inside the mother's body in a place called the uterus. [Do not tell the child that a seed has been planted in the mother's body, because the child might imagine a plant starting to grow.]

2. *How does a baby eat and breathe before it is born?*
Before a baby is born, it gets food and air from its mother's blood through a long tube, called the umbilical cord. One end of the cord is attached to the inside of the mother's uterus, and the other end is attached to the baby's navel, or belly button.

3. *Why do grown-ups have hair on their bodies, but I don't?*
When children grow up and go through puberty, many changes happen in their bodies. One of these changes is for hair to grow in different places on the body. As you get older, hair will grow on you, too.

4. *How long does a baby grow inside the mother?*
A baby grows for about nine months inside the mother.

5. *How does a baby get in a mother's body?*
A man and a woman make a baby. [If this answer does not satisfy the child, the teacher might have to give more detail.] When a man and woman want to have a baby, they put their bodies very close together. This feels good to both of them. When they are close, the man's penis becomes hard and is put into the woman's vagina. This is called sexual intercourse. In time, a fluid called semen comes out of the man's body. The semen has sperm cells in it. When one sperm meets with a woman's egg, the beginning of a baby is formed.

6. *What is gay?*
Gay is a term used to describe homosexuals. Homosexuals are people of the same sex who have a sexual and emotional relationship.

7. *When is a boy old enough to make a baby?*
A boy is old enough to make a baby when he is old enough to ejaculate [ejaculation may have to be discussed]. When a boy is able to ejaculate, it is called puberty. Boys go through puberty around age 10 to 15. Just because a boy can physically make a baby at this age does not mean he is responsible enough to take care of a baby.

8. *When is a girl old enough to make a baby?*
Girls are old enough to make babies when they begin to have their menstrual cycle. This usually happens when girls are around age 9 to 16. A girl may be physically ready to have a baby when she begins to menstruate, but she is probably not emotionally ready to care for it.

9. *Why do boys stand up to pee, but girls don't?*
Boys stand up to pee or urinate through an opening in the penis. Girls sit down to pee or urinate through an opening between their legs. These are the easiest and neatest ways for boys and girls to urinate.

10. *How does a baby get out of a mother?*
When the baby is big enough and is ready, the baby usually comes out of an opening between the mother's legs called the vagina.

Developmentally Appropriate Concepts and Skills for Promoting Sexual Health

Grades K–2 Concepts	Grades 3–5 Concepts	Grades 6–8 Concepts

NHES 1: Core Concepts

Grades K–2 Concepts	Grades 3–5 Concepts	Grades 6–8 Concepts
• Identify qualities of a healthy relationship. • Describe ways to prevent the spread of germs that cause common infectious diseases.	• Describe appropriate ways to express and deal with emotions and feelings. • List healthy ways to express affection, love, friendship, and concern. • Identify qualities of a healthy relationship. • Describe the benefits of healthy family relationships. • Identify characteristics of someone who has self-respect. • Describe values that promote healthy behaviors. • Describe basic male and female reproductive body parts and their functions. • Describe the physical and emotional changes that occur during puberty. • Explain that puberty and development can vary considerably and still be normal. • Describe the effects of HIV infection on the body. • Explain why HIV infection is not transmitted through casual contact. • Explain that it is safe to be a friend of someone who has HIV infection or AIDS.	• Describe appropriate ways to express and deal with emotions and feelings. • Summarize the benefits of talking with trusted adults about feelings. • Describe impulsive behaviors and strategies for controlling them. • Describe healthy ways to express affection, love, friendship, and concern. • Summarize basic male and female reproductive body parts and their functions. • Identify models of healthy relationships. • Compare and contrast healthy and unhealthy relationships. • Explain the qualities of a healthy dating relationship. • Describe the emotional effects of breaking up a dating relationship. • Describe effective strategies for dealing with difficult relationships with family members, peers, and boyfriends or girlfriends. • Describe situations that could lead to pressures for sex. • Explain why individuals have the right to refuse sexual contact. • Recognize techniques that are used to coerce or pressure someone to have sex. • Analyze the risks of impulsive behaviors. • Describe the relationship between using alcohol and other drugs and sexual risk behaviors. • Describe conception and its relationship to the menstrual cycle. • Identify the responsibilities of parenthood. • Explain how HIV and the most common STDs are transmitted. • Describe signs and symptoms of common STDs, including HIV. • Explain that some STDs are asymptomatic. • Explain the short- and long-term consequences of HIV and common STDs. • Summarize which STDs can be cured and which can be treated. • Analyze ways to decrease the spread of germs that cause communicable diseases, such as preventing the spread of HIV by not having sex, not touching blood, and not touching used hypodermic or tattoo needles. • Describe why sexual abstinence is the safest, most effective risk avoidance method of protection from HIV, other STDs, and pregnancy. • Determine the benefits of being sexually abstinent. • Describe the factors that contribute to one engaging in sexual risk behaviors. • Describe the factors that protect one against engaging in sexual risk behaviors. • Explain the importance of setting personal limits to avoid sexual risk behaviors. • Describe the effectiveness or lack of effectiveness of common contraceptive methods in reducing the risk of pregnancy. • Describe the effectiveness or lack of effectiveness of condoms in reducing the risk of pregnancy, HIV, and other STDs, including Human Papillomavirus (HPV). • Describe how to reduce the risk of pregnancy and the sexual transmission of HIV and other STDs.* • Justify why it is safe to be a friend of someone who has HIV infection or AIDS.

Grades K–2 Skills	Grades 3–5 Skills	Grades 6–8 Skills

NHES 2: Analyze Influence

	Grades 3–5 Skills	Grades 6–8 Skills
	• Describe how culture, the media, and people influence what one thinks about attractiveness and relationships. • Describe how culture, the media, and people influence what a person thinks about people who have infectious or chronic diseases, such as HIV infection, AIDS, and cancer.	• Describe how internal influences, such as curiosity, interests, desires, and fears, affect sexual behavior. • Describe how personal and family values influence decisions about sexual behavior and relationships. • Describe a variety of external influences, such as parents, the media, culture, peers, and society that affect sexual decision making and sexual behavior. • Analyze the influence of alcohol and other drugs, including "date rape" drugs, on sexual behavior. • Explain how sexual exploitation can occur on the internet. • Examine why stereotypes exist about people with infectious diseases, such as HIV and tuberculosis. • Explain that most students are not having sex.

NHES 3: Accessing Information, Products, and Services

		Grades 6–8 Skills
		• Identify adults, such as a parent, teacher, or health care provider, who can provide accurate information about puberty, sexual health, relationships, and responsible sexual behavior, including sexual risks. • Demonstrate the ability to access accurate and reliable data on abstinence and sexual risk behaviors among young people. • Demonstrate the ability to access appropriate community resources about puberty, sexual health, and family relationships. • Evaluate accuracy and usefulness of sources of information on sexual health. • Describe ways to seek help to report sexual harassment, sexual assault, child abuse, and other types to violence. • Demonstrate the ability to access existing laws and policies designed to protect young people from being sexually exploited.

NHES 4: Communication Skills

Grades K–2 Skills	Grades 3–5 Skills	Grades 6–8 Skills
• Demonstrate effective communication skills to express feelings appropriately.	• Demonstrate effective communication skills to express feelings appropriately. • Demonstrate communication skills necessary to maintain a healthy relationship.	• Demonstrate effective communication skills to express feelings appropriately. • Demonstrate actions that express personal values. • Demonstrate communication skills necessary to maintain a healthy relationship. • Demonstrate effective negotiation and refusal skills to avoid sexual risk behavior. • Demonstrate how to ask for help from a parent, other trusted adult, or friend when pressured to participate in sexual behaviors. • Demonstrate how to communicate clear expectations, boundaries, and personal safety strategies. • Demonstrate how to communicate clear limits on sexual behaviors. • Demonstrate verbal and nonverbal ways to ask a parent or other trusted adult for help with a threatening situation. • Demonstrate assertiveness skills in dealing with sexually aggressive behavior. • Identify verbal and nonverbal communication that constitutes sexual harassment.

(continued)

Grades K–2 Skills *(continued)*	Grades 3–5 Skills *(continued)*	Grades 6–8 Skills *(continued)*
NHES 5: Decision Making		
		• Describe the benefits of delaying romantic involvement.
		• Predict short- and long-term consequences of sexual behavior.
		• Explain the possible consequences of early sexual behavior and the emotional, social, and physical benefits for delaying sexual behavior.
		• Summarize the benefits of sexual abstinence.
		• Summarize the benefits of reducing the risk of HIV infection, other STD infection, and pregnancy.*
		• Summarize the options for reducing the risk of HIV infection, other STD infection, and pregnancy.*
NHES 6: Goal Setting		
		• Explain how early sexual behavior can affect achieving long-term goals.
		• Set a goal to reduce risk of pregnancy and transmission of HIV and other STDs.*
		• Set personal boundaries and limits related to sexual behavior.
		• Demonstrate the ability to set goals to prevent and manage difficult relationships.
		• Make a personal commitment to remain sexually abstinent.
NHES 7: Self-Management		
• Demonstrate how to express feelings in a healthy way.	• Demonstrate how to express feelings appropriately.	• Demonstrate strategies for expressing feelings appropriately.
		• Demonstrate the ability to use self-control.
		• Acknowledge personal responsibility for sexual abstinence.
		• Acknowledge personal responsibility for sexual and reproductive health.
		• Plan strategies for maintaining sexual abstinence.
		• Plan strategies for avoiding situations that place one at risk for engaging in sexual behavior.
		• Demonstrate setting personal limits to avoid sexual risk behavior.
		• Express intentions to be sexually abstinent.
		• Identify behaviors that are perceived as sexually coercive.
NHES 8: Advocacy		
		• Demonstrate ways to encourage friends to remain sexually abstinent or return to abstinence if sexually active.
		• Demonstrate ways to communicate the benefits of protecting oneself from pregnancy and infections from HIV and other STDs.*
		• Express compassion and support for people living with disease, such as cancer and AIDS.
		• Demonstrate how to influence others to report acts of violence to appropriate adults.

* This skill example promotes risk reduction and might not be included in a risk-avoidance curriculum.

Source: Centers for Disease Control and Prevention. *Health Education Curriculum Analysis Tool (HECAT)* (Atlanta, GA: CDC, 2007). www.cdc.gov/HealthyYouth/Hecat/index.htm

Sample Questions Upper-Elementary and Middle-Level Students Commonly Ask

1. *What is a rubber?*

A rubber is a type of contraceptive that is also called a condom. It is a rubber sheath that covers the penis when it is hard and keeps the sperm from getting into the vagina.

2. *What makes puberty happen?*

Glands in the body become more active and begin making different hormones. These hormones have specific functions, which make the body change and develop.

3. *Can urine and semen come out at the same time?*

No; when semen comes out of the urethra, muscular contractions shut off the valve that allows urine to leave the body.

4. *How does a girl know when she will start her period?*

Nobody knows when a girl will have her first period. When it happens, she may feel dampness in the vaginal area. When she goes to the bathroom, she will notice some menstrual blood in her panties. This means menstruation has begun.

5. *Does a penis have to be a certain size to work?*

No; there are different sizes to all body parts, including the penis; however, most erect penises are about the same size.

6. *Do boys have menstrual periods?*

No; when a boy goes through puberty, he does not have a menstrual cycle. Instead, his sex glands begin to produce sperm cells. Sperm can be released from the body at any time. At night, some of the sperm may pass out through the penis during sleep. When this happens, it is called a wet dream, or a nocturnal emission, because it is often associated with a sexually exciting dream.

7. *Can a woman have a baby without being married?*

Yes; a woman can have a baby when she is able to produce an egg and that egg meets with a sperm.

8. *Is wet dream another term for masturbation?*

No; masturbation is performed when a person is awake, but a wet dream happens involuntarily while a person is asleep.

9. *How do the sperm and egg get together?*

When a man puts his penis into a woman's vagina, some fluid, called semen, is released through the penis. There are many sperm in the semen. If one of them finds and fertilizes an egg in the woman's fallopian tube, a new life can begin to grow. This is called intercourse and should be done only by mature individuals who are ready to raise a child.

10. *What is semen?*

Semen is a white, milky fluid a man's body makes when he is having sex. Semen carries the sperm out of a man's body.

STRATEGIES FOR LEARNING AND ASSESSMENT

Promoting Sexual Health

This section provides examples of standards-based learning and assessment strategies for promoting sexual health. The sample strategies begin with a restatement of the standard and a reminder of the assessment criteria, drawn from the RMC rubrics in Appendix B. Strategies are written as directions for teachers and include applicable theory of planned behavior (TPB) constructs in parentheses (intention to act in healthy ways, attitudes toward behavior, subjective norms, perceived behavioral control). These learning and assessment strategies provide building blocks for standards-based lessons and units that can be tailored to local needs. Assessment criteria are used with permission from the Rocky Mountain Center for Health Promotion and Education (RMC). See Appendix B for Scoring Rubrics.

Additional strategies for learning and assessment for Chapter 13 can be found at the Online Learning Center. Appendix D, a complete list of all the strategies, is available at the Online Learning Center.

NHES 1 | Core Concepts

Students will comprehend concepts related to health promotion and disease prevention to enhance health.

ASSESSMENT CRITERIA

- Connections—Describe relationships between behavior and health; draw logical conclusions about connections between behavior and health.
- Comprehensiveness—Thoroughly cover health topic, showing breadth and depth; give accurate information.

Grades K–2

Family Members   Talking about family similarities and differences and the roles and responsibilities of family members is an important concept in sexual and family health for early elementary children. Teachers should be sure classmates treat each other with respect—no teasing or put-downs. Start a discussion by asking children to volunteer to tell how many people are in their family and who they are. As they tell who is in their family, have other children stand up, if they like, to represent each of the family members. Note that some families are larger and some are smaller—but all are families. Next, ask children to draw and color a picture of one of their family members. As a summary, children can volunteer to tell a story about the person they drew and how that person helps the family.

ASSESSMENT | For an assessment task, children can draw a picture of a family member (or all their family members) and share a story with classmates about how that person helps the family stay healthy and safe. Children also can write a sentence to go with their picture about how the person helps the family. For assessment criteria, students should be able to express the concept of family members helping one another stay healthy and safe. (Construct: Attitudes toward behavior.)

Families in Many Cultures   Books about families are listed at the end of this chapter. In addition to reading children's books, students can investigate family traditions around the world through library and Internet searches. Children can talk about what they learn about family traditions in different places and cultures, including the families represented in their own classroom.

ASSESSMENT | For an assessment task, students can work in small groups to plan and present a puppet show about family traditions they've investigated. Students can design paper-bag or sock puppets as a link to performing arts. For assessment criteria, students should explain how family traditions help keep families safe and healthy. (Construct: Attitudes toward behavior.)

Grades 3–5

We Come in All Sizes and Shapes (Grade 3)   Pair students and provide each child with a piece of butcher paper that is longer than the child's height. Ask one student to lie down on the butcher paper while the other student traces the outline of the partner's body. Have students switch roles. You might want to pair boys with boys and girls with girls for the tracing. After both partners have an outline of their own bodies, ask them to draw their face, hair, and clothing and hang the pictures around the room. Ask children what they notice about how the outlines are similar and different. Emphasize that people have different body sizes and shapes. Continue the discussion by asking students how they think their bodies will change as they get older.

ASSESSMENT | The students' completion and comparisons of their outline drawings are the assessment task for this activity. For assessment criteria, students should be able to explain at least two ways class members of similar age are the same and different and make predictions about how they will grow and change as they get older. Teachers should be sure students respect the sizes and shapes of their classmates—no teasing or put-downs. Teachers also can emphasize that the class members like one another just the way they are. A first-grade teacher was surprised when her students applauded for the tallest and heaviest students, saying "They won!" Teachers can help students understand that this activity is about accepting people as they are, rather than a competition for height and weight. (Construct: Subjective norms.)

What Kids Want to Know About Sex and Growing Up (Grade 4 or 5)   An excellent videotape on puberty is called *What Kids Want to Know About Sex and Growing Up*.[40] Teachers often show this video in grade 4 or 5, before most children actually begin puberty. Teachers always should preview any video in its entirety before showing it in class. The video covers male and female changes in puberty, nocturnal emissions, and menstruation and provides simple, straightforward answers to a variety of questions that students ask. The video provides good modeling for teachers in how to answer children's questions. Showing a video such as this one is a good way to help students begin to understand the changes they will experience in puberty and to help them formulate their own questions. Teachers can show the video and then have students write anonymous questions to turn in. Teachers can read through the cards and answer the questions in a following class. Teachers might want to do this activity with other teachers in the same grade level or with assistance from community health educators. Students can watch the video and have question-and-answer sessions together or in separate boy and girl groups. Having some time in separate groups and some time together is a good way for students to get all of their questions answered. (Teachers should follow parent and caregiver permission requirements for their school.)

ASSESSMENT | For an assessment task, students can work in groups to write question-and-answer cards (question on one side, answer on the other) to share with other groups. Students can use the cards as a quiz game within their group, keeping track of the answers they knew, didn't know, or have further questions about. Students can pass their cards from group to group, or groups can take turns reading a question to the whole class. Either way, students can answer within their groups. Alternatively, teachers can ask the students' questions and have each group respond by writing on a tablet or small erasable board. For assessment criteria, students should provide accurate answers and draw conclusions about connections between behavior and health. (Construct: Attitudes toward behavior.)

Grades 6–8

What Kids Want to Know About Sex and Growing Up   This videotape is recommended for grade 4 or 5 and for grades 6 through 8 because many students don't get information on puberty and growing up until they reach middle school. This video is a good one for middle school students as well as upper-elementary students. The early-adolescent moderators and the adult sexuality educators in the video provide good role models for students in asking questions and for teachers in answering questions. The video contains diagrams of and explains the male and female reproductive systems. The authors encourage teachers to show this video in sections, pausing to discuss each section in depth with students before moving to the next. Teachers might not want to use all the sections, depending on the objectives of the lesson. Teachers also should note that the video was produced in 1992. The information is accurate, but

teachers should acknowledge to students that the hair and clothing styles might seem out of date. The video is available from ETR Associates (www.etr.org). (Teachers should follow parent and caregiver permission requirements for their school.)

ASSESSMENT | For an assessment task, students can help design a written quiz on what they've learned for classmates to take. Students can work in groups to write quiz questions on assigned topics (puberty and boys, puberty and girls), focusing on the physical and emotional changes that occur in puberty. Students can read their quiz questions to the class or pass their questions from group to group for students to answer. For assessment criteria, students should provide correct answers and draw conclusions about connections between behaviors and health. (Construct: Attitudes toward behavior.)

Matching Game for the Reproductive System   After teaching upper-elementary students the names and functions of the reproductive organs, teachers can use this activity to reinforce that information. Write the name of one reproductive organ on an index card, and write its function on another card. For example, one index card might have "fallopian tube" written on it, and another card might have "a tubelike structure connected to the uterus where fertilization takes place" written on it. Make matching cards for every reproductive organ discussed in class. Give one index card to each student. Tell students that half of the cards contain the names of the reproductive organs and the other half contain the functions of the reproductive organs. Tell students to find the person who has the index card that matches the correct organ to its function. This activity allows students to say the reproductive organ names aloud and encourages students to interact with a variety of classmates. Repeat the activity several times so that students receive a different organ or function each time.

ASSESSMENT | For an assessment task, students can complete the activity several times, starting with a different card each time. For assessment criteria, students should match the cards correctly and consistently. (Construct: Attitudes toward behavior.)

A Wheel of Healthy Relationships   Middle-level students have a growing interest in relationships and what dating is all about. Ask students to describe the qualities of a healthy relationship, using the Lōkahi Wheel from Chapter 1. Students should think about healthy relationships in terms of these dimensions:

Physical/body
Friends/family
Thinking/mind
Spiritual/soul
Work/school
Feelings/emotions

Students might say that people in a healthy relationship respect the physical boundaries and limits of others and think in similar ways about important ideas. Help students dig beneath the surface to discuss what would (expressing enthusiasm for another person's success) and would not (behaving jealously and putting down another person's success) be part of a healthy relationship. In the physical and feelings areas, students should identify hitting or belittling as unhealthy behaviors in relationships.

ASSESSMENT | For an assessment task, students can work in small groups to complete one section of a large Lōkahi Wheel, identifying characteristics and examples of healthy and unhealthy relationships. Alternatively, students can rotate to different posters in a carousel activity. For assessment criteria, students should contrast healthy and unhealthy relationship qualities in each of the six Lōkahi areas. (Construct: Attitudes toward behavior.)

Preventing STDs   After providing an overview to students about STDS, divide students into groups of three or four. Assign each group a common STD. Instruct them to create a poster about their assigned STD. The poster should contain the following information:

- How the STD is transmitted
- The symptoms of the STD
- The treatment of the STD
- How to prevent the STD
- The responsibility of someone who has the STD

After the students have finished making their posters, allow time for them to present them. Process the presentations by asking students to identify the common concepts presented.

ASSESSMENT | The completed poster and presentation is the assessment task for this activity. For assessment criteria, students should provide accurate information about their assigned STD and communicate that information to the class. (Construct: Attitude toward the behavior).

NHES 2 | Analyze Influences

Students will analyze the influence of family, peers, culture, media, technology, and other factors on health behaviors.

ASSESSMENT CRITERIA
- Identify both external and internal influences on health.
- Explain how external and internal influences interact to impact health choices and behaviors.
- Explain both positive and negative influences, as appropriate.

Grades K–2

How We Do Things in My Family   Families are an important influence on how we do things (NHES 7, self-management skills) of all kinds—from brushing our teeth to handling our feelings when we are upset or angry. Students can write about the "way we do things to stay healthy in my family." Ask students to think about how the decisions they make and the things they do are influenced by family habits and self-management strategies. Students can make a list of the ways their families influence them to behave in healthy ways. Students can think through a typical day in their lives, from getting up to going to bed, to help them consider family habits and their influence on family members. Over time students internalize these habits.

ASSESSMENT | For an assessment task, students can draw a picture and write a sentence about "how my family helps me stay healthy." For assessment criteria, students should explain at least one healthy preference or habit they have developed (internalized) because of the way their family does things. (Construct: Subjective norms.)

Friendship Stories   Use a writing or drawing activity to help students think about friendship. Ask students to write a short story titled "What Would It Be Like to Live in a World Without Friends?" Ask students to share their stories with the rest of the class. After the students read their stories, they can discuss ways they can help everyone have friends. This activity focuses on the importance of having and maintaining friendships. Friends influence the health behaviors of other friends. This activity asks students to think about helping everyone have friends.

ASSESSMENT | The short stories students write are the assessment task for this activity. For assessment criteria, students can explain how their friends help (influence) them to stay safe and healthy. (Constructs: Attitudes toward behavior, subjective norms.)

Grades 3–5

Cultural and Family Traditions   Students can choose one of the following topics and write about it.

- A way your family celebrates a specific time of year
- A traditional food or eating pattern in your family
- How household chores are assigned in your family
- Traditional family trips or vacations
- Treatments for a cold or the flu in your family
- Visits with older relatives

Students can work in small groups to share their answers. Have students write a follow-up paragraph about how their family traditions influence their health and how their traditions are similar to and different from the traditions of other families. Elementary students might make connections between family and traditions more readily than they do between culture and traditions. Teachers can help students link some of their traditions to culture as well as family.

ASSESSMENT | The paragraphs students write are the assessment task for this activity. For assessment criteria, students should explain how their family and cultural traditions influence their behaviors related to health and safety. (Constructs: Subjective norms, attitudes toward behavior.)

Stereotypes—What Can We Really Tell from Looking?   In the upper-elementary grades, students become very conscious of how they and others look. Try an activity with students to have them think about what we actually can and can't tell about people just from looking at them. Bring magazine pictures of a variety of people to class (students can bring in magazine pictures, too). Have children work in small groups with a few pictures each. Ask, "What can we tell about the people by looking at them?" Be prepared for all kinds of responses. Have the groups share with the whole class, and introduce the idea of stereotypes. Ask children to give alternative explanations for the stereotypes that come up in the conversations. We can't really know about people until we get to know them and their life stories. How can assumptions and stereotyping cause problems? The word *stereotype* (or *bias*) might be new for students. Help students scratch beneath the surface to identify and challenge stereotypes they find in media portrayals (magazine pictures) of different kinds or groups of people. For example, students might comment on a picture of an athlete that he or she probably uses steroids, a stereotype. While acknowledging that some (but not all) athletes use steroids, students can provide alternative explanations for how athletes develop skill and fitness.

ASSESSMENT | For an assessment task, students can work individually or in pairs to select a magazine picture to "de-stereotype" for the class. For assessment criteria, students should explain the possible stereotypes communicated in the picture and challenge those biases with alternative explanations. Students also should explain how stereotypes can influence the way people behave toward others and why such assumptions should be questioned. (Construct: Subjective norms.)

Grades 6–8

Messages in the Media About "Ideal" Men and Women   Ideas about sexual attractiveness are reflected in and come from images in the media. Middle-level students enjoy this assignment of finding magazine pictures of what men and women are "supposed" to look like, according to media images—the "ideals." Students can make posters or collages. The images for males and females, side by side, are especially revealing. Women are encouraged to be thin (perhaps strong, but always thin). Men are encouraged to be strong and muscular. What do these images mean in terms of health? How realistic are the images? Are the pictures altered (air-brushed, touched up)? Share with students that a famous model answered a question about whether she dieted before a photo shoot by saying "No, I don't diet. That's what air-brushing is for!"

ASSESSMENT | For an assessment task, students can explain their media messages about men and women in terms of myths and misperceptions. For example, girls might say that it's a myth that women are attracted to men who have overdeveloped muscles. Boys might say that it's a misperception that men are attracted to women who are skinny. Students also might say that, in terms of health, the images portrayed in the media could lead to problems—eating disorders, steroid use, unbalanced nutrition, obsession with exercise and dieting, and obsession with appearance. For assessment criteria, students should identify at least five myths and misperceptions about media images of "ideal" men and women and provide healthy alternatives to the images. (Construct: Subjective norms.)

Coming of Age in Different Cultures Students might be interested to learn that many cultures celebrate the time in young people's lives when they go through adolescence, marking their growth to become an adult woman or man. Students can work with librarians or media specialists to access books and other information on how different cultures celebrate adolescence or coming of age. For example, in Australian Aboriginal culture, boys are sent on "walkabout" to test the tracking and survival skills they've learned while growing up. In some African tribes, young boys bring back a particular animal that they have hunted alone. In some Native American cultures, boys go away and survive special night adventures.[41] Judaism celebrates bar mitzvah for a boy when he turns thirteen and is recognized as a man and bat mitzvah for a girl when she turns twelve and is recognized as a woman. In Australia, New Zealand, and numerous other countries, a party known as the "Twenty First" has long celebrated coming of age. On their twenty-first birthdays, young people and their families and friends traditionally gather for parties where gifts are presented to the birthday young man and woman. The Quinceañera (Fifteenth Birthday) for a young Latina is a rite of passage signifying that she has reached adulthood; the event is marked by a large celebration and a candle-lighting ceremony that acts as a spiritual mark of the young woman's achievement.[42] Coming-of-age ceremonies have been held for centuries in Japan. In the past, boys marked their transition to adulthood when they were around 15, and girls celebrated their coming of age around 13. During the Edo period (1603–1868), boys had their forelocks cropped off and girls had their teeth dyed black. It wasn't until 1876 that 20 became the legal age of adulthood in Japan.[43] Many cultures celebrate a girl's first menstrual period, although other cultures isolate girls during this time.

ASSESSMENT | For an assessment task, students can work in pairs or small groups to investigate the coming-of-age traditions in different cultures or parts of the world. Students also can interview their own families about how they mark adolescence in their family or culture. For assessment criteria, students should reflect, orally or in writing, on how coming-of-age traditions might influence a young person's beliefs and attitudes about becoming a man or woman. For example, would a young person feel pride or shame? How could these feelings influence a young person's behaviors with regard to sexual health? (Construct: Attitudes toward behavior.)

NHES 3 | Access Information, Products, and Services

Students will demonstrate the ability to access valid information and products and services to enhance health.

ASSESSMENT CRITERIA
- Access health information—Locate specific sources of health information, products, or services relevant to enhancing health in a given situation.
- Evaluate information sources—Explain the degree to which identified sources are valid, reliable, and appropriate as a result of evaluating each source.

Grades K–2

Finding Out About Growth and Development A popular classroom activity for discussing growth and development with young children is hatching chicken eggs in an incubator. Watching the chicks grow and change lets children access information for themselves about growth and development. However, teachers should realize that sometimes the eggs don't hatch or the chicks die, and the children might raise questions about death and dying. Teachers must be prepared to explain this to children. Chapter 14 includes helpful ideas for discussing these topics with children. Teachers also can have guppies or small animals for classroom pets. If they reproduce, use the teachable moment to discuss reproduction, growth, and development with students. It is important that teachers think about a permanent home for any classroom animals.

ASSESSMENT | Learning about growth and development with classroom pets is a good link to science education. For an assessment task, students can keep journals to draw and describe the changes they observe each day or week. First grade teacher Diane Parker shared that one of her students said he was sad when their class butterfly emerged from its cocoon and flew away, saying "I miss the old Blackie!" For assessment criteria, students should report their findings accurately (links to NHES 1) and explain why their observations are a valid source of information. (Construct: Attitudes toward behavior.)

Adults I Can Count On Identifying trusted adults is an important skill for early elementary students. Students need to know they can count on adults if they have questions or need help with a problem. In particular, students need to identify adults they could turn to if they experience unwanted touching or other situations that make them feel scared or uncomfortable. Have students trace the outline of one hand and label each finger with the name of an adult at home, at school, or in the community that they can go to if they have a question or need help.

ASSESSMENT | The students' hand tracings are the assessment task for this activity. For assessment criteria, students should be able to identify five people they can count on in at least three different locations (home, school, community). (Construct: Perceived behavior control.)

Grades 3–5

Finding Out About Heredity Ask students whether they have ever been told that they look like another family member—a parent, an aunt, an uncle, a grandparent, or a sibling. Ask children to make a list of the characteristics of the people in their immediate and extended families. What do they notice? For example, a child might say, "Most people in my family have brown hair and brown eyes—but my little brother has red hair and blue eyes!" or "My sister and I are really tall, but my grandma is really short." Help children understand that they *inherit* (a new vocabulary word for some students) characteristics from both sides of their families and from relatives they might not remember or might never have met. That blue-eyed little brother—it turns out the great-grandmother on the mother's side had blue eyes. (Think carefully about the students in your class before doing this activity. Some children might be adopted or living with people who are not their relatives. Another way to talk about heredity is to talk about how a litter of puppies or kittens can look the same as or different from the parent animals.)

ASSESSMENT | This activity can help students find out more about their families and family members, increasing their sense of connectedness. For an assessment task, students can ask their parents or caregivers who they resemble from past generations. Students can make drawings of themselves and family members to explain the resemblances. For assessment criteria, students should explain what they learned (links to NHES 1),how they collected their information (who they interviewed), and why the information sources were valid. (Construct: Attitudes toward behavior.)

Finding Out About How Families Work Together Students can interview their parents or caregivers to find out what their families say "makes a caring and helpful family member" and "what kinds of jobs various family members do to help our family." Children can brainstorm a list of questions they want to ask and share their answers with classmates.

ASSESSMENT | The students' reports on their family interviews (what makes a caring family member, what jobs family members do to help the family) are the assessment task for this activity. For assessment criteria, students should report their information sources and tell why the sources are valid. (Construct: Perceived behavioral control.)

Grades 6–8

Interviews About Dating Parents and caregivers sometimes are uncomfortable about initiating conversation with their early adolescents about dating and relationships. Encourage these conversations by having students complete a homework assignment to interview parents or caregivers about dating. Students can talk together to decide on their interview questions as a class and report back to their classmates. Their questions might include the following:

- How old were you the first time you went out on a date?
- How did you feel about going on your first date?
- Where did you go and what did you do on your first date (go to a movie, eat out)?
- What kind of curfew did you have?
- What advice do you have for me to make dating safe and fun?

ASSESSMENT | For an assessment task, students can write up their interview results and share their findings with their classmates. As a class, students can create a poster of best advice from their parents and caregivers on dating. For assessment criteria, students should provide advice that is health enhancing (links to NHES 1) and explain why their interviews are valid sources of information. (Constructs: Subjective norms, perceived behavioral control.)

Finding Out About STDs A great way for middle-level students to learn about sexually transmitted diseases (STDs) is to have them interview other students, parents, and teachers about their STD knowledge. To begin, students need to look up information on various STDs so that they are knowledgeable. Then students can design a list of survey questions to investigate the knowledge level of other

students, parents, and teachers. Students can collect and compile the data and make a report to their class and to other classes. (Middle-level teacher Georgia Goeas shared that her students reported that some of their parents "didn't know about STDs." The students said that their parents called them "vinyl disease or something like that." The students' parents obviously remember the days when STDs were called venereal disease.)

ASSESSMENT | For an assessment task, students can research STDs, design a questionnaire, conduct their interviews, and compile their data to report to classmates. For assessment criteria, students should correct any misinformation that they discover in interviews (links to NHES 1) and explain why their interviews are a valid source of information on what students, teachers, and parents and caregivers know about STDs. (Constructs: Attitudes toward behavior, perceived behavioral control.)

4Girls Health Female students can access information on a website created just for them by visiting www.4girls.gov. Girls can check out topics such as physical changes during puberty, menstruation, hygiene, friendship, dating, and emotional and physical safety. Girls also can find out about "free stuff" they can obtain through this website, such as pocket planners and even 4Girls wallpaper. 4Girls.gov is sponsored by the office of the surgeon general—teachers and parents can feel safe about the information posted on the site.

ASSESSMENT | For an assessment task, female students can use this website for reports on puberty and sexual health. For assessment criteria, students should present accurate information and draw conclusions about connections between behaviors and health (links to NHES 1) and cite their information sources and explain why they are valid. (Constructs: Attitudes toward behavior, perceived behavioral control.)

NHES 4 | Interpersonal Communication

Students will demonstrate the ability to use interpersonal communication skills to enhance health and avoid or reduce health risks.

ASSESSMENT CRITERIA

- Use appropriate verbal/nonverbal communication strategies in an effective manner to enhance health or avoid/reduce health risks.
- Use appropriate skills (negotiation skills, refusal skills) and behaviors (eye contact, body language, attentive listening).

Grades K–2

Your Body Belongs to You: **Communicating About Your Body** Children often participate in games and songs to name their exterior body parts by touching their head, eyes, ears, nose, cheeks, mouth, neck, chest, arms, elbows, hands, wrists, fingers, abdomen, hips, legs, knees, feet, ankles, and toes. Thus, children can communicate easily about these body parts ("I fell and hurt my knee"). Teachers can use Cornelia Spelman's book *Your Body Belongs to You* to talk with children about the "private parts of their bodies or those covered by their bathing suits." By reading and discussing the book with students, teachers can help children understand that their bodies belong to them and that the only other people allowed to touch their private parts are (1) parents or other adults, such as teachers, who are helping them go to the bathroom or (2) doctors or nurses when they visit the doctor's office. Children should always tell a trusted adult if someone touches or tries to touch them in a way that makes them feel scared or uncomfortable. Children should say "Stop it!," get away as soon as they can, and tell a trusted adult as soon as possible, no matter who the person is or what the person doing the touching says to them about telling.

Discussing the parts of the body covered by a swimsuit is a good way to introduce students to the concept of the parts of their bodies that are private.

ASSESSMENT | For an assessment task, students can tell what they would say and do if someone touched or tried to touch them in a way that made them feel scared or uncomfortable. For assessment criteria, students should be able to list saying "Stop it!," getting away as soon as they can, and telling a trusted adult as soon as possible that someone touched or tried to touch them on their private parts. (Construct: Perceived behavioral control.)

Asking for Help Be sure that young children know how to ask for help from adults so that adults will listen. Family counselor Allana Coffee recommends that children take the following steps:

1. Say "I need your help."
2. Tell what happened.
3. Tell what you did to try to make the situation better.
4. Say again "I need your help."[44]

Have children demonstrate asking for help in different kinds of situations. Asking adults for help in ways that make adults stop and listen to them is an important communication skill for children. Teachers, in particular, sometimes become frustrated with what they perceive as tattling and tell children to "solve it yourself," even when children genuinely need help. Practicing the steps in asking for help can assist children in communicating more clearly when someone needs help or is in danger.

ASSESSMENT | For an assessment task, students can work in pairs to demonstrate their skills. One student can play the role of an adult (parent, teacher, crossing guard), and the other can play the student role. For assessment criteria, students should be able to communicate the four steps in this activity (saying "I need your help," telling what happened, telling what the student did to try to help, and saying again "I need your help." (Construct: Perceived behavioral control.)

Grades 3–5

Talking About Privacy Wilson, Quackenbush, and Kane state that discussions and questions about sexuality often can be handled more easily when children understand the concept of "privacy."[45] The examples the authors provide include teaching students that it's inappropriate to go through someone else's desk or to keep asking questions when someone has declined to answer. Teachers can ask students for other examples of "wanting privacy" or wanting to "keep things private." Students can communicate with their teachers through notes if they have questions or concerns they don't want to voice in front of the class. Teachers should be sure to respond to these questions. However, teachers must communicate clearly to students that teachers are required to get help for students if they are in danger or might endanger someone else. Teachers can't promise "not to tell," because they have to keep students safe. Students also can discuss when they should or shouldn't keep something private and ways to protect privacy. For example, first-grade students in Diane Parker's classroom devised an interesting solution to protect the privacy of their desks. Each student designed and decorated a paper cover ("lock") to fit across the opening in their desk. These locks, which were the students' own idea, ended "borrowing" from other people's desks.

ASSESSMENT | For an assessment task, students can make a "Respecting Privacy" list that tells ways they can respect the privacy of others (knocking on my sister's closed bedroom door before entering) and ways they want others to respect their privacy (not looking in my book bag while I'm away from my desk). For assessment criteria, students should explain when they should and shouldn't tell a trusted adult about "private" concerns a friend or family member might have. Students should always tell a trusted adult when they feel that they or others are unsafe or in danger. (Construct: Perceived behavioral control.)

Communicating About Boundaries and Limits Setting and respecting *limits* and *boundaries* is an important concept for upper-elementary students. Start by asking students how they would define these terms. The students might need to access information by looking in a dictionary or asking older students or adults about these words. Students can discuss the kinds of boundaries and limits their families set on various activities (watching television, eating snacks, letting someone know where they are and where they are going). Students also can discuss personal limits and boundaries they set for themselves. What's okay and what's not okay for them? Students can discuss effective and ineffective ways to communicate their limits and boundaries to others. What kind of communication is clear? What kind of communication might give a mixed message? Teachers can link this activity to various risk areas, including sexual health and responsibility.

Students can write and answer "Dear Abby"–type letters to ask advice about communicating boundaries and limits. Teachers can provide an example to start, such as a letter from a boy asking for help in telling a girl he likes that he wants to be friends but doesn't feel right about going to her house while her parents aren't at home. Students can discuss their communication advice in this example before writing their own letters about situations of their choosing. For added anonymity, students can type their letters on computers and not sign them.

ASSESSMENT | For assessment criteria, students should write a response to another person's letter giving advice on health-enhancing communication. Students can share their answers by reading the letters and responses aloud to the class. Students should recommend at least two effective communication strategies (see examples in Chapter 3). (Construct: Perceived behavioral control.)

Grades 6–8

Talking Back to Pressure Lines: Which Part of "No" Don't You Understand? In the safe environment of the classroom, students enjoy developing assertive things to say to pressure lines. Teachers can write pressure lines (one-sentence lines to pressure someone into doing something) and/or have students write them. Examples of pressure lines include "Everyone is doing it," "If you loved me you would," "No one will find out." Students can work in small groups to come up with replies to pressure lines, demonstrating different types of peer resistance/refusal skills (repeat the refusal, suggest an alternative, make an excuse, give a reason). Students can demonstrate different kinds of refusal skills to the same pressure line. Some of the refusal skills should deal with pressures to have sex. Teachers should remind students that their goal in communication is to give a clear message and to maintain relationships. Teachers can find excellent examples of pressure lines and answers in Joyce Fetro's book *Personal and Social Skills,* in the chapters on communication.[46]

ASSESSMENT | For an assessment task, students can work in small groups to demonstrate passive, aggressive, and assertive responses to pressure lines that they create or draw from a bowl (teachers can prepare slips of paper or have students write pressure lines and put them in a bowl). (See Chapter 3 for more information on these three types of responses.) For assessment criteria, students should explain why passive and aggressive responses usually are ineffective and how the assertive response, coupled with appropriate body language, can be most effective. (Construct: Perceived behavioral control.)

Communicating to Abstain Distribute index cards to each student. Instruct students to use a pencil (so that they will not be identified by ink color on their card) and write down what a person might say to a partner if they were being pressured to have sex. Collect the cards, read each one for appropriateness, and then distribute one to each student. Have students create two circles—an inner circle and an outer circle—where students are facing each other. Tell students to take turns reading their refusal statement to their partner. Have students pass their cards to the person on their right and repeat the process. After students have read all of the resistance statements, ask them to write the three statements that would work best for them.

ASSESSMENT | Writing the three resistance statements that will work best for them is the assessment task. For assessment criteria, students should explain why those statements would work best for them. (Construct: Perceived behavioral control).

R-E-S-P-E-C-T Teachers can use a recording of the song "R-E-S-P-E-C-T," by Aretha Franklin, to introduce the idea of respecting oneself and others. Begin the discussion by having students share their ideas about respect—for example, "When is a person respecting me?" "When is a person disrespecting me?" "What in my behavior could show respect or disrespect for others?" Students might be surprised to learn that they have different ideas about being respectful and disrespectful. Then turn the conversation to pressures on young people to have sex. What kind of communication shows respect? Disrespect? How do students respond to both kinds of communication in ways that give a clear message?

ASSESSMENT | For an assessment task, students can create their own version of an R-E-S-P-E-C-T song, a rap, or some other kind of reminder. For assessment criteria, students should list at least three examples of the respect they want ("R-E-S-P-E-C-T, find out what it means to me!") (Construct: Perceived behavioral control.)

NHES 5 | Decision Making

Students will demonstrate the ability to use decision-making skills to enhance health.

ASSESSMENT CRITERIA

Reach a health-enhancing decision using a process consisting of the following steps:

- Identify a health-risk situation.
- Examine alternatives.
- Evaluate positive and negative consequences.
- Decide on a health-enhancing course of action.

Grades K–2

What Do You Do, Dear? As recommended in the standards-based learning strategies in Chapter 3, children's literature can be used to discuss the concept of decision making. Characters in children's books often are faced with a problem or decision. What do they decide, and do students agree or disagree with that decision? Children can predict what might happen if other decisions were made. A book that examines decision making in a fun and fanciful way is Joslin and Sendak's *What Do You Do, Dear? Proper Conduct for All Occasions.*[47] For example, what do you do if

- A lady polar bear walks into your igloo in a white fur coat?
- You meet someone coming the other way on a circus tightrope?

Children can provide their own decisions about what to do and how to decide and then compare their answers with those in the book.

ASSESSMENT | For an assessment task, students can make up their own "What do you do, Dear?" questions and answers. For assessment criteria, students should explain what to do and why they chose to do it. All answers should be health enhancing. (Construct: Perceived behavioral control.)

Grades 3–5

Deciding for Me Students can think about decisions that other people make for them, along with decisions they get to make for themselves. In elementary school and at home, many decisions are made for children (what assignments to do, what time to go to bed). However, children do make some decisions for themselves (what book to read, what shirt to wear). Children can list decisions in two columns—decisions others make and those they make for themselves. Emphasize the importance of making good decisions in those areas where students get to decide for themselves. If feasible, follow this discussion with an activity in which the children get to make a decision (which assignment to do first, what to do for a class celebration).

ASSESSMENT | For an assessment task, students can make their two-column list of decisions that others make and that they make and explain how they can make good decisions. If the activity includes making individual or class decisions, students can explain how they make their decisions. For assessment criteria, students should explain three alternatives for a specific decision, name positive and negative consequences, choose a decision, and tell how they will know whether it was a good one. (Construct: Perceived behavioral control.)

Grades 6–8

Making the Hard Decisions: What If We Don't Want to Say NO? The idea for this discussion with middle-level students came from the classroom experiences of health educator Lynn Shoji. When she was working with her health education classes on refusal skills, a group of boys asked very honestly, "But, Mrs. Shoji—what if we don't want to say no?" That was a teachable moment and a time for conversation that was relevant and current in students' lives. In the area of sexual health and responsibility, students naturally become curious as they reach adolescence. In the area of sexuality, students get many messages, from parents, the school, friends, and the media. What are they to do with their curiosity and new feelings? These questions present an ideal opportunity to look honestly at alternatives and the positive and negative consequences of those alternatives: "How will my decisions affect my health and safety?" "How will they affect my family?" "How will they affect my friends or other people who are involved in my decisions?" "How will my decisions affect my goals for the future and the kind of person I want to be—and to be known as?" Providing an open forum for discussion helps students think through the short- and long-term outcomes of the decisions they are beginning to face.

Facilitating a discussion like this one requires a skillful teacher—one who can listen and help students think deeply without scolding or demanding that students say they think a certain way (even if they don't). Teachers can facilitate and guide the discussion by listening carefully, respecting what students say, and asking questions to help them scratch beneath the surface of short- and long-term outcomes.

ASSESSMENT | For an assessment task, students can work through the steps of a decision-making model (see Chapter 3). (To review the decision-making model, students can participate in a short session of "Balloon Up" from Chapter 5). Students can state a problem or decision they are interested in related to sexual health, name three or more alternatives, identify positive and negative consequences for each alternative, choose a decision, and then evaluate how they think this decision would work for them. For assessment criteria, students should work through all five steps of decision making and arrive at a health-enhancing conclusion. If students have difficulty arriving at a health-enhancing conclusion, teachers can continue to ask other students to talk about what they think and ask about consequences. (Constructs: Attitudes toward behavior, perceived behavioral control.)

Deciding on Abstinence Introduce the activity by emphasizing that not making a good decision about sex is one of the reasons teens can become pregnant or infected with HIV or other STDs. Explain that one decision teens can make about sex is to abstain until they are older. Post two pieces of newsprint with the word "Abstinence" on one piece and "Reasons to Remain Abstinent" on the other piece. Ask the class to define the word abstinence. Some possible responses might include avoiding something such as sweets, alcohol, meat, or sex. Emphasize that people choose to abstain from something for many reasons including health, religion, fear, or lack of interest.

Next, divide the class into groups of four or five students. Ask students to create a list of reasons why teens might decide not to have sex. Once they have created their list, create a master list on the second piece of newsprint. Some ideas might include fear of pregnancy, fear of an STD, want to graduate from high school, personal beliefs, or religious beliefs. After each reason is listed, discuss it with the class.

ASSESSMENT | For an assessment task, students can write down the reasons to remain abstinent that have the most meaning to them. For assessment criteria, students should be able to explain why their reasons have the most meaning and why those reasons would help them remain abstinent. (Construct: Attitudes towards behavior)

Ask the Expert Students can be given a variety of questions related to sexual decision making that have been asked by students their age or younger (these can be questions formulated by the teacher or ones that have been generated by real students). Students are to act as "experts" and apply their knowledge regarding STDs and pregnancy to help answer each question. Some examples include

- I heard that you can't get pregnant if you have sex just once. Is that true? Signed, Confused
- Is it OK to have sex with my boyfriend if I really love him? Signed, In True Love
- All of my friends are having sex. What is wrong with me? Signed, Left Out

ASSESSMENT | The answer students write is the assessment task for this activity. For assessment criteria, students should provide factual information in their answer and encourage the person asking the question to act in a healthy way. (Constructs: Attitudes towards behavior, perceived behavioral control.)

NHES 6 | Goal Setting

Students will demonstrate the ability to use goal-setting skills to enhance health.

ASSESSMENT CRITERIA
- Goal statement—Give goal statement that identifies health benefits; goal is achievable and will result in enhanced health.
- Goal setting plan—Show plan that is complete, logical and sequential, and includes a process to assess progress.

Grades K–2

Goals for Being a Good Friend Students can work in small groups to brainstorm the qualities of a good friend. The importance of friendship increases as children get older, and their responses will change through time. Ask the groups to share their responses with the rest of the class. Students should identify one way they could improve on being a good friend. Teachers can help them set a goal and make a plan to try to improve that quality.

ASSESSMENT | For an assessment task, students can set an individual or class goal for being a good friend or a better friend for one week. Students should discuss their progress day by day during the week. For assessment criteria, students should state a clear goal (I will be a better friend by using kind words at school), make a plan (I will listen to what I say and what others say), plan for supports and barriers (I will hang out with friends who use kind words; I will be especially careful of what I say if someone makes me mad), and evaluate results (I will check on how I'm doing at lunch and at the end of school each day). (Constructs: Subjective norms, perceived behavioral control.)

Grades 3–5

Goals to Help My Family Students can discuss ways they can be of help in their families without being asked. Students can set a personal goal to help in a certain way in their families for a week, without publicizing their goal at home. Ask students to keep a journal about their progress during the week and about the response of family members at their volunteering to help without being asked.

ASSESSMENT | The goals students set are the assessment task for this activity. For assessment criteria, students should set a clear goal, tell what steps they will take to achieve it, identify supports and barriers and ways to deal with barriers, and plan a way to assess their progress. (Construct: Perceived behavioral control.)

Grades 6–8

Teen Parenting—Not One of My Goals   Conduct this activity after discussing that one of the negative outcomes of becoming sexually active is becoming a teen parent. This carousel activity is a way to get students to think about how becoming a teen parent would affect them. Students can work in small groups to brainstorm on a sheet of newsprint about how their lives would change in each of five categories—financial, family, social, educational, and emotional—if they became a teen parent. After each group returns to its original sheet of newsprint, students should circle the three answers that would be the most persuasive reasons to not become a teen parent.

ASSESSMENT | For an assessment task, students can share with the class the three most persuasive reasons to not become a teen parent. During their presentation, students should share personal goals that would be affected if they became teen parents. For assessment criteria, students should list at least three goals that would be affected and explain how these goals affect their decisions related to sexual health. (Construct: Attitudes toward behavior.)

NHES 7 | Self-Management

Students will demonstrate the ability to practice health-enhancing behaviors and avoid or reduce health risks.

ASSESSMENT CRITERIA
- Application (transfer)—Initiate health-enhancing behaviors; apply concepts and skills appropriate and effectively.
- Self-monitoring and reflection—Monitor actions and make adjustments; accept feedback and make adjustments; able to self-assess, reflect on, and take responsibility for actions.

Grades K–2

My Family, My Support System   Children can draw and color pictures of their families and then share their pictures with the class and tell how their family members help each other. Sharing about families helps children understand that there are many different types of families and that all families are important. Counting on families as support systems helps students with healthy self-management in knowing where they can go for help and support.

ASSESSMENT | For an assessment task, students can explain or write about how the family members in their pictures help them—how family members make up a support system for them. For assessment criteria, students should name of least three family or extended family members who make up their special support system. (Construct: Attitudes toward behavior.)

Julius, Baby of the World: A New Brother or Sister in the Family   Kelvin Henke's book *Julius, Baby of the World* (Mulberry, 1990) is a favorite for talking with young students about what it's like to have a new baby brother or sister in the house. Big sister Lilly is excited about having a new baby in the family; however, her enthusiasm cools when her parents admire the baby rather more than she expected. The book allows new older brothers and sisters to identify with Lilly's rejection campaign ("If you were a number, you would be zero," she tells the baby) in the safe environment of the classroom. Children also will find that when a visiting relative insults the baby, Lilly displays tremendous loyalty to Julius. Teachers can ask students to share their experiences about having new siblings at home. Another book students will enjoy is Paula Danziger's *Barfburger Baby, I Was Here First*.

ASSESSMENT | For an assessment task, students might want to make new pages to add to *Julius, Baby of the World*, based on their own experiences. Students should report their feelings honestly, but they also should discuss healthy ways to deal with their feelings. For assessment criteria, students should be able to describe at least one feeling and explain a healthy way to manage it. (Construct: Attitudes toward behavior.)

Grades 3–5

Dealing with Feelings   An important part of learning the skill of self-management is learning how to deal with feelings. This theme is repeated throughout the content chapters because it's such an important one. The Kids' Health website (www.kidshealth.gov) offers a special link or dealing with feelings related to family life, school, and relationships. Students can learn more about topics related to sexual and family health, such as adoption, divorce, nontraditional families, running away, gossip and peer pressure, body image, self-esteem, and worrying. Students can check out these topics, focusing on self-management. What are healthy responses to difficult feelings and challenging situations?

ASSESSMENT | For an assessment task, students can select a topic to research and report on to the class. Students can brainstorm a list of possible presentation formats (story, poem, poster, skit, PowerPoint presentation). For assessment criteria, students should identify the challenges of the issue they are discussing and explain at least two healthy ways for dealing with the issue. (Constructs: Attitudes toward behavior, perceived behavioral control.)

Getting Help   For all priority content areas, students need to know how to get help when they need it. Getting help might include telling a safe adult about a problem, or it might mean calling 9-1-1 in an emergency. Students should know how to get the help they need should an uncomfortable, threatening, or emergency situation arise. Students need to know that it's important for them to tell an adult if someone bothers or hurts them, no matter what that person tells them. Similarly, it's important for adults to believe children who come to them for help and see that they get the assistance they need. Read more about preventing and reporting sexual assault in Chapter 10 on preventing violence.

ASSESSMENT | For an assessment task, students can describe and discuss situations in which they might feel uncomfortable or unsafe. Students can work in pairs or small groups to write a scenario in which they feel the need to get help and then share the scenario with the class. For assessment criteria, students should specify at least two ways to get help in the scenario they describe. (Construct: Perceived behavioral control.)

Grades 6–8

Role-Plays for Self-Management   Students can work in small groups to brainstorm challenging or risky situations they know that students their age face or might face in the future. Students can choose one of the situations and show a strong or courageous way to handle the situation, as well as a less decisive way that could lead to problems. Have students volunteer to demonstrate their two role-plays for the class. Classmates should identify the two strategies and discuss how difficult or easy they would be to carry out. Students might role-play pressures to smoke, use drugs, have sex, or brag about doing these things.

ASSESSMENT | For an assessment task, students can work in small groups to demonstrate a challenging situation with two self-management outcomes—one effective and one ineffective. Students can follow their demonstration by asking classmates which techniques were effective or ineffective and why. For assessment criteria, students should compare and contrast at least one effective and one ineffective self-management strategy for responding to the challenging situation they demonstrate for the class. (Construct: Perceived behavioral control.)

Healthy Ways to Handle New and Normal Feelings Ask students to talk about some of the feelings they have as they become adolescents and go through puberty. Students might say that they feel anxious or scared, different from one day to the next, stressed, or just plain weird. Help students understand that their feelings are normal and a natural part of growing up Ask students to talk about healthy ways to manage new feelings. The class might want to make a "tip sheet" or "survival sheet" of their favorite self-management strategies. Students can visit the BAM! (Body and Mind) website for kids (www.bam.gov) and click on "Head Strong" to learn about ten tips to help stay cool, calm, and collected: put your body in motion, fuel up, lots of laughing, have fun with friends, spill to someone you trust, take time to chill, catch some z's, keep a journal, get it together, lend a hand.

ASSESSMENT | For an assessment task, students can create their own class list of adolescent survival tips, using the BAM website to get them started. For assessment criteria, the students' list should expand the website ideas of healthy self-management strategies. Students also might want to list "dead end" strategies, such as tobacco or alcohol use and overeating. (Constructs: Attitudes toward behavior, perceived behavioral control, subjective norms.)

Sexual Abstinence: What Does It Mean and How Does It Work? Middle-level students often hear that they should be "sexually abstinent." What does that mean, and how does it work? Why is abstinence a smart self-management strategy for middle-level students? To answer these and other questions, students can visit the Kids' Health website (www.kidshealth.org) and click on "For Teens" and type "abstinence" into the search line to learn

- What is it?
- How does it work?
- How well does it work?
- How does it protect against STDs?
- How do you do it?

Students will learn that abstinence is the simplest form of birth control—if two people don't have sex, then sperm can't fertilize an egg and pregnancy can't occur. Students also learn that although abstinence protects against sexually transmitted diseases (STDs), some STDs spread through oral-genital sex or skin-to-skin contact without actual penetration. Thus, only complete and consistent abstinence protects against pregnancy and STDs. AIDS and hepatitis B can be transmitted through nonsexual activities such as using contaminated needles for drugs or tattooing or taking steroids. With regard to decisions about abstinence, the website talks about media messages, peer pressure, and other influences. When students are clear on what abstinence is and how it can protect them, they can discuss how and why it can be a smart self-management strategy for middle-level students.

ASSESSMENT | For an assessment task, students can work in small groups to make a list of pros and cons of practicing abstinence as a self-management strategy during their middle school years. Students can share and compare their lists with classmates. For assessment criteria, students should describe at least three reasons why abstinence is a smart self-management strategy for middle-level students and three ideas for helping students remain abstinent (hang out with other kids who have decided to remain abstinent in middle school, avoid situations where there could be pressure to have sex, express intentions to remain abstinent in middle school). (Construct: Attitudes toward behavior.)

NHES 8 | Advocacy

Students will demonstrate the ability to advocate for personal, family, and community health.

ASSESSMENT CRITERIA

- Health-enhancing position—Give clear, health-enhancing position.
- Support for position—Support position with facts, concepts, examples, and evidence.
- Audience awareness—Show awareness of target audience; choose words, tone, and examples to suit audience.
- Conviction—Display conviction for position.

Grades K–2

It's Okay to Be Different: **Treating Others with Friendliness and Compassion** Todd Parr's book *It's Okay to Be Different* is a good one for helping children think about the issues in this activity. After reading the book, teachers can ask students to define the words *friendliness* and *compassion*. Students might want to look in their dictionaries and check with parents and caregivers to learn what these words mean. Teachers then can ask students whom they treat with kindness and compassion in their everyday lives. Children might name their family members, classmates, and teachers. Teachers can ask students to think about other people who need their kindness and compassion, such as people who are sick with diseases like cancer or HIV or people they perceive to be different in some way. Teachers can help students understand that they don't need to be afraid of people who seem different in some way and that they can treat all people with friendliness and compassion.

ASSESSMENT | For an assessment task, students can make a list of ways they can treat others with friendliness and compassion (smile and say hello, ask other kids to come and play). For assessment criteria, students should explain why they would "take a stand" by doing these things. (Construct: Subjective norms.)

Grades 6–8

Easing the Teasing: Supporting Classmates Who Choose Abstinence In middle school, students are ready to discuss the pressures they encounter or expect to encounter for risky behaviors, such as sexual involvement. Students can think about ways they will support the healthy decisions of their classmates, such as remaining abstinent throughout school. One of the most daunting aspects of making a decision is the fear that others will make fun of it. Ask students to talk openly about how they can support each other and prevent or deflect the teasing or taunting of other students. Teachers can help students with concrete strategies to deal with teasing from the "Easing the Teasing" website (www.easingtheteasing.com). The site provides ten strategies, including using humor, responding to the teaser with a compliment, ignoring the teasing, and asking for help. In addition to thinking about their own experiences, students can identify how they can adapt the strategies to support and advocate for others who choose abstinence and other healthy behaviors in middle school. This activity links to NHES 4, interpersonal communication, and NHES 7, self-management.

ASSESSMENT | For an assessment task, students can work in small groups to demonstrate one of the ten strategies adapted for supporting friends who choose abstinence. Students can divide into at least ten groups to be sure all strategies are covered. For assessment criteria, students should show the characteristics of a good advocate—stating a strong position, backing it up, targeting the audience, and speaking with conviction. (Constructs: Subjective norms, perceived behavioral control.)

Spreading the Word: Most Kids Make the Healthy Choice   As with the other priority content areas, high school (and, in some locales, middle school) data are available on the sexual behaviors of young people. Students can review and publicize their findings from the Youth Risk Behavior Survey (YRBS) to other classes within their school. The bottom line is that most kids make the healthy choice. YRBS data are available at www.cdc.gov/HealthyYouth/yrbs/index.htm.

ASSESSMENT | For an assessment task, students can prepare pamphlets or PowerPoint presentations on what they learn about the sexual behavior of high school students. Students should present their data from the positive perspective (the percentage of students who are abstinent in high school). For assessment criteria, students should state a strong position, back it up, target the audience, and speak with conviction. (Construct: Subjective norms.)

EVALUATED CURRICULA AND INSTRUCTIONAL MATERIALS

There are many high school and a few evaluated middle school commercial pregnancy, STD, and HIV prevention programs available to school districts. These curricula should complement, not replace, a comprehensive school health education curriculum. The evaluation results of these curricula have been reviewed by many professionals and have been shown to be effective in reducing the number of students who engage in sexual intercourse or in increasing the number of students who use condoms or other contraceptives. Following are commercial curricula targeted toward all middle school youth:

• *Draw the Line—Respect the Line.* This middle school sexuality education program has twenty sessions: five in the sixth grade, eight in the seventh grade, and seven in the eighth grade. It includes instruction on the consequences of unplanned sex, personal sexual limit setting, and refusal skills. The evaluation showed that it had significant effects in reducing the initiation of intercourse for seventh- and eighth-grade boys, but no significant differences for girls.[48]

• *Postponing Sexual Involvement (PSI) Human Sexuality.* This eighth-grade curriculum is designed for low socioeconomic students and lasts ten hours. Its goal is to help students understand social and peer pressure to have sex and be able to apply resistance skills, postpone sexual involvement, develop decision-making skills, and learn about contraceptives. The evaluation showed that it had a significant impact on reducing the initiation of intercourse at the end of eighth and ninth grades.[49]

• *Be Proud! Be Responsible! A Safer Sex Curriculum.* The evaluation for this curriculum was conducted on sixth- and seventh-grade low-socioeconomic students. The program has eight one-hour sessions, which include information on delaying sexual intercourse, building skills, and using condoms. The evaluation showed that there was a significant decrease in the frequency of sexual intercourse at the end of twelve months and a significant increase in condom use by participants at the end of twelve months.[50]

• *Making Proud Choices.* This middle school curriculum emphasizes safer sex and includes information about both abstinence and condoms. The curriculum contains eight culturally appropriate sixty-minute lessons that include experiential activities to build skills to delay initiating sex and to communicate with partners to use condoms. The evaluation indicated there was a significant delay in initiation of sexual intercourse, a reduction in the frequency of sex, and a reduced incidence of unprotected sex and increased condom use.[51]

INTERNET AND OTHER RESOURCES

Visit the Online Learning Center (www.mhhe.com/telljohann6e) for links to these sites, quizzes and other study aids, and many additional resources.

WEBSITES

Advocates for Youth
www.advocatesforyouth.org

Alan Guttmacher Institute
www.guttmacher.org

Centers for Disease Control and Prevention
www.cdc.gov/HealthyYouth

Henry J. Kaiser Family Foundation
www.kff.org

National Campaign to Prevent Teen Pregnancy
www.teenpregnancy.org

Network for Family Life Education
www.sexetc.org

Office of the Surgeon General
www.surgeongeneral.gov/sgoffice.htm

Planned Parenthood
www.plannedparenthood.org

Sexuality Information and Education Council of the United States (SIECUS)
www.siecus.org

Tambrands
www.tampax.com

OTHER RESOURCES

Kirby, D. *Emerging Answers 2007: Research Findings on Programs to Reduce Teen Pregnancy and Sexually Transmitted Diseases* (Washington, DC: The National Campaign to Prevent Teen and Unplanned Pregnancy, 2007).

Kirby, D., and G. LePore, *Sexual Risk and Protective Factors—Factors Affecting Teen Sexual Behavior, Pregnancy, Childbearing and Sexually Transmitted Disease: Which Are Important? Which Can You Change?* (Washington, DC: The National Campaign to Prevent Teen and Unplanned Pregnancy, 2007).

Quackenbush, M., W. Kane, and S. Telljohann. *Teach and Reach: Human Sexuality.* Santa Cruz, CA: ETR Associates, 2004.

Sexuality Information and Education Council of the United States. *Guidelines for Comprehensive Sexuality Education.* 3d ed. New York: Sexuality Information and Education Council of the United States, 2004.

CHILDREN'S LITERATURE

AGES 5–8

Butler, Dori Hillstad. *My Mom's Having a Baby.* Albert Whitman, 2007.

Cooper, M. *I Got a Family.* Henry Holt, 1993. (American Bookseller Pick of the Lists, Booklist Editors Choice)

Cousins, L. *Za Za's Baby Brother.* Candlewick, 1995.

Curtis, Jamie. *Tell Me Again About the Day I Was Born.* HarperCollins, 1996.

Danziger, Paula. *Barfburger Baby, I Was Here First.* GP Putnam's Sons, 2004.

Davis, J. *Before You Were Born.* Workman, 1997.

Harris, Robie. *It's NOT the Stork!: A Book About Girls, Boys, Babies, Bodies, Families and Friends.* Candlewick, 2006.

Harris, Robie. *It's So Amazing! A Book About Eggs, Sperm, Birth, Babies, and Families.* Candlewick, 2004.

Hausherr, R. *Celebrating Families.* Scholastic, 1997. (Multicultural)

Henkes, K. *Julius, Baby of the World: A New Brother or Sister in the Family.* Mulberry, 1990.

Hoberman, M. *Fathers, Mothers, Sisters, Brothers.* Puffin, 1991.

Mayle, Peter. *Where Did I Come From? A Guide for Children and Parents.* Kensington, 1999. (Multicultural)

Nemiroff, Marc. *All About Adoption: How Families Are Made and How Kids Feel About It.* American Psychological Association, 2003.

Numeroff, L. *What Mommies Do Best/What Daddies Do Best.* Simon & Schuster, 1998.

Parr, Todd. *The Family Book.* Little, Brown, 2003.

Saltz, Gail. *Amazing You: Getting Smart About Your Private Parts.* Dutton Juvenile, 2008.

Spelman, Cornelia. *Your Body Belongs to You.* Albert Whitman, 2000.

AGES 8–12

American Medical Association. *American Medical Association Boy's Guide to Becoming a Teen.* Jossey-Bass, 2006.

American Medical Association. *American Medical Association Girl's Guide to Becoming a Teen.* Jossey-Bass, 2006.

Blackstone, Margaret, and Elissa Haden Guest. *Girl Stuff: A Survival Guide to Growing Up.* Harcourt Paperbacks, 2006.

Bourgeois, Paulette. *Changes in You and Me: A Book About Puberty Mostly for Boys.* Key Porter Books, 2005.

Bourgeois, Paulette. *Changes in You and Me: A Book About Puberty Mostly for Girls.* Key Porter Books, 2005.

Brown, L., and Marc Brown. *What's the Big Secret? Talking About Sex with Boys and Girls.* Little, Brown, 2000.

Cole, Joanna. *Asking About Sex and Growing Up: A Question-and-Answer Book for Boys and Girls.* William Morrow, 2001.

Conrad, P. *Staying Nine.* HarperCollins, 1988.

Dunham, Kelli. *The Boy's Body Book: Everything You Need to Know for Growing Up You.* Applesauce Press, 2007.

Gravelle, Karen. *The Period Book, Updated Edition: Everything You Don't Want to Ask (But Need to Know).* Walker Books for Young Readers, 2006.

Halse, Laurie. *Speak.* Puffin, 1999.

Harris, Robie H. *It's Perfectly Normal.* Candlewick, 2004.

Hoffman, M. *Boundless Grace.* Penguin, 1995. (Multicultural)

Holbrook, S. *I Never Said I Wasn't Difficult.* Boyds Mills, 1996.

Jukes, Mavis. *Growing Up: It's a Girl Thing.* Alfred A. Knopf, 1998.

Kindersley, Barnabas, and Anabel Kindersley. *Children Just Like Me: A Unique Celebration of Children Around the World.* Dorling Kindersley, 1995.

MacLacklan, P. *Journal.* Bantam, 1991. (American Library Association Notable Book for Children, American Library Association Best Book for Young Adults)

Madaras, Lynda. *What's Happening to My Body? Book for Girls.* Newmarket, 2007.

Madaras, Lynda. *What's Happening to My Body? Book for Boys.* Newmarket, 2007.

Madaras, Lynda. *My Body, My Self for Boys, Revised Third Edition.* Newmarket, 2007.

Madaras, Lynda. *My Body, My Self for Girls, Revised Third Edition.* Newmarket, 2007.

Meyers, W. *Won't Know Till I Get There.* Puffin, 1988. (Multicultural)

Strickland, D., and M. Strickland. *Families: Poems Celebrating the African-American Experience.* Boyds Mills, 1994. (Multicultural)

Vigna, J. *My Two Uncles.* Albert Whitman, 1995.

Willhoite, M. *Daddy's Roommate.* Alyson, 1990.

Willhoite, M. *Daddy's Wedding.* Alyson, 1996.

ENDNOTES

1. S. Hofferth and J. Sandberg, "How American Children Spend Their Time," *Journal of Marriage and the Family* 63 (2001): 295–308.

2. D. Roberts, U. Foehr, and V. Rideout, *Generation M: Media in the Lives of 8–18 Year Olds* (Menlo Park, CA: Henry J. Kaiser Family Foundation, 2005).

3. Kaiser Family Foundation, *Sex on TV3: A Biennial Report to the Kaiser Family Foundation* (Menlo Park, CA: Kaiser Family Foundation, 2003).

4. R. Collins, M. Elliott, S. Berry, D. Kanouse, D. Kunkel, S. Hunter, and A. Miu, "Watching Sex on Television Predicts Adolescent Initiation of Sexual Behavior," *Pediatrics* 11, no. 3 (2004): 280–89.

5. R. Collins, M. Elliott, S. Berry, D. Kanouse, D. Kunkel, S. Hunter, and A. Miu, "Watching Sex on Television Predicts Adolescent Initiation of Sexual Behavior," *Pediatrics* 114, no. 3 (2004): e280–e289.

6. National Campaign to Prevent Teen and Unplanned Pregnancy, *Science Says: The Sexual Behavior of Young Adolescents* (Washington, DC: National Campaign to Prevent Teen Pregnancy, 2003).

7. Centers for Disease Control and Prevention, "Youth Risk Behavior Surveillance—United States, 2007," *Morbidity and Mortality Weekly Report* 57, no. SS-4 (6 June 2008): 1–131.

8. T. Hoff et al., *National Survey of Adolescents and Young Adults: Sexual Health Knowledge, Attitudes, and Experiences* (Menlo Park, CA: Kaiser Family Foundation, 2003).

9. Guttmacher Institute, *U.S. Teenage Pregnancy Statistics National and State Trends and Trends by Race and Ethnicity* (New York, NY: Guttmacher Institute, 2006).

10. H. Weinstock, S. Berman, and W. Cates, "Sexually Transmitted Diseases among American Youth: Incidence and Prevalence Estimates, 2000," *Perspectives on Sexual and Reproductive Health,* 36, vol. 1 (2004): 6–10.

11. Centers for Disease Control and Prevention, *Tracking the Hidden Epidemics: Trends in STDs in the United States, 2000* (Atlanta, GA: Centers for Disease Control and Prevention, 2000).

12. S. Hoffman, *By the Numbers: The Public Costs of Teen Childbearing* (Washington, DC: National Campaign to Prevent Teen Pregnancy, 2006).

13. H. Chesson, J. Blandford, T. Gift, G. Tao, and K. Irwin, "The Estimated Direct Medical Cost of Sexually Transmitted Diseases Among American Youth, 2000," *Perspectives on Sexual and Reproductive Health,* 36, vol. 1 (2004): 11–19.

14. National Campaign to Prevent Teen Pregnancy, *Halfway There: A Prescription for Continued Progress in Preventing Teen Pregnancy* (Washington, DC: National Campaign to Prevent Teen Pregnancy, 2001).

15. G. Ehrlich and C. Vega-Matos, *The Impact of Adolescent Pregnancy and Parenthood on Educational Achievement: A Blueprint for Education Policymaker's Involvement in Prevention Efforts* (Alexandria, VA: National Association of State Boards of Education, 2000).

16. D. Kirby and G. LePore, *Sexual Risk and Protective Factors—Factors Affecting Teen Sexual Behavior, Pregnancy, Childbearing and Sexually Transmitted Disease: Which Are Important? Which Can You Change?* (Washington, DC: The National Campaign to Prevent Teen and Unplanned Pregnancy, 2007).

17. Ibid.

18. L. Kann, S. Telljohann, and S. Wooley, "Health Education: Results from the School Health Policies and Programs Study 2006," *Journal of School Health,* 77, vol. 8 (2007): 408–34.

19. D. Kirby, *Sexual Risk and Protective Factors—Factors Affecting Teen Sexual Behavior, Pregnancy,*

Childbearing and Sexually Transmitted Disease: Which Are Important? Which Can You Change?

20. Kaiser Family Foundation, *Sex Education in America: General Public/Parents Survey* (Washington, DC: Kaiser Family Foundation, 2004).

21. Lake, Snell, Perry, and Associates, *Lower Income Parents on Teaching and Talking with Children About Sexual Issues: Results from a National Survey* (New York: Sexuality Information and Education Council of the United States, 2002).

22. Kaiser Family Foundation, *Sex Education in America: A Series of National Surveys with Students, Parents, Teachers and Principals* (Menlo Park, CA: Kaiser Family Foundation, 2000).

23. D. Kirby, *Emerging Answers 2007: Research Findings on Programs to Reduce Teen Pregnancy and Sexually Transmitted Diseases* (Washington, DC: The National Campaign to Prevent Teen and Unplanned Pregnancy, 2007).

24. The National Campaign to Prevent Teen Pregnancy, *Get Organized: A Guide to Preventing Teen Pregnancy and While the Adults Are Arguing, the Teens Are Getting Pregnant: Overcoming Conflict in Teen Pregnancy Prevention* (Washington, DC: The National Campaign to Prevent Teen Pregnancy, 1999).

25. The National Campaign to Prevent Teen Pregnancy, *Fact Sheet: Overcoming Conflict in Teen Pregnancy Prevention Initiatives* (Washington, DC: The National Campaign to Prevent Teen Pregnancy, 2000).

26. D. Kirby, *Emerging Answers 2007: Research Findings on Programs to Reduce Teen Pregnancy and Sexually Transmitted Diseases.*

27. L. Kann, S. Telljohann, and S. Wooley, "Health Education: Results from the School Health Policies and Programs Study 2006."

28. D. Kirby, *Emerging Answers 2007: Research Findings on Programs to Reduce Teen Pregnancy and Sexually Transmitted Diseases.*

29. SIECUS. *No More Money: Spending on Abstinence-only-until-Marriage Programs (1982–2007).* (www.nonewmoney.org/historyChart.html; 2007)

30. D. Kirby, *Emerging Answers 2007: Research Findings on Programs to Reduce Teen Pregnancy and Sexually Transmitted Diseases.*

31. U.S. House of Representatives Committee on Government Reform—Minority Special Investigations Division, "The Content of Federally Funded Abstinence-Only Education Programs" (Washington, DC: Prepared for Rep. Henry A. Waxman, 2004).

32. Sexuality Information and Education Council of the United States, *Guidelines for Comprehensive Sexuality Education,* 3d ed. (New York: Sexuality Information and Education Council of the United States, 2004).

33. Ibid.

34. Ibid.

35. National Center for Health Statistics. *Trends in Circumcisions Among Newborns.* (www.cdc.gov/nchs/products/pubs/pubd/hestats/circumcisions/circumcisions.htm; 2007)

36. Medline Plus, *Sexually Transmitted Diseases.* (www.nlm.nih.gov/medlineplus/sexuallytransmitteddiseases.html; 2008)

37. American Academy of Family Physicians, *STIs: Common Symptoms & Tips on Prevention.* (http://familydoctor.org/online/famdocen/home/common/sexinfections/sti/165.printerview.html; 2007)

38. Ibid.

39. Centers for Disease Control and Prevention, *Health Education Curriculum Analysis Tool* (Atlanta, GA: CDC, 2008).

40. Children's Television Network, *What Kids Want to Know About Sex and Growing Up* (distributed by ETR Associates, Santa Cruz, CA, 1992).

41. Department for Jewish Zionist Education, *Adolescent Issues and Coming of Age Ceremonies.* (www.jafi.org.il/education/lifecycle/jewishlc/03-4.html; 2004)

42. Answers.com, *Coming of Age.* (www.answers.com/topic/coming-of-age; 2005)

43. Web Japan: Gateway for All Japanese Information, *Coming of Age Day.* (http://web-japan.org/kidsweb/calendar/january/seijinshiki.html; accessed 2005)

44. W. Coffee, J. Coffee, and J. N. Elizalde, *Peace Signs: A Manual for Teaching School Children Anger Management and Communication Skills* (Honolulu: CoffeePress Publications, 2000).

45. P. M. Wilson, M. Quackenbush, and W. M. Kane, *Teach and Talk: The Subject Is Sex* (Santa Cruz, CA: ETR Associates, 2001), 29.

46. J. Fetro, *Personal and Social Skills* (Santa Cruz, CA: ETR Associates, 2000).

47. S. Joslin and M. Sendak, *What Do You Do, Dear? Proper Conduct for All Occasions* (HarperTrophy, 1986).

48. K. Coyle, K. Basen-Enquist, D. Kirby, G. Parcel, S. Banspach, J. Collins, E. Baumler, E. Caravajal, and R. Harrist, "Safer Choices: Reducing Teen Pregnancy, HIV, and STDs," *Public Health Reports* 116, Suppl. 1 (2001): 82–93.

49. M. Howard and J. McCabe, "Helping Teenagers Postpone Sexual Involvement," *Family Planning Perspectives* 22, no. 1 (1990): 21–26.

50. J. Jermott, L. Jermott, and G. Fong, "Abstinence and Safer Sex: A Randomized Trial of HIV Sexual Risk-Reduction Interventions for Young African American Adolescents," *Journal of the American Medical Association* 279, no. 19 (1998): 1529–36.

51. Ibid.

14

(Tracy, age 12)

Managing Loss, Death, and Grief

DESIRED LEARNER OUTCOMES

After reading this chapter, you will be able to . . .

- Describe the reasons to include loss, death, and grief education in elementary and middle schools.

- Describe the developmental stages of understanding death.

- Explain the stages of grief.

- Explain the stages of dying.

- Summarize the current teacher's role when a student or a student's relative dies.

- Summarize the school's and teacher's role when dealing with a disaster or traumatic event.

- Explain the school's role when handling a suicide.

- Demonstrate developmentally appropriate learning strategies incorporating concepts and skills that help students deal with loss, death, and grief.

- Demonstrate developmentally appropriate loss, death, and grief assessment techniques that can be used with K–8 students.

- Use loss, death, and grief Internet and other resources.

- Provide examples of children's literature featuring loss, death, and grief themes that can be used in cross-curricular instructional activities.

INTRODUCTION

Loss, death, and grief affect everyone, regardless of race, gender, or age, yet they remain taboo topics of discussion in our society. To change this attitude, formalized instruction and informal discussion, particularly of critical incidents and events related to loss, death, and grief, need to be included in the elementary and middle school health education curriculum. The tendency is to try to protect children and preadolescents from these topics. This prevents those young people from obtaining accurate information, which in turn can exacerbate their fears and anxieties about these natural life processes.

Teaching about loss, death, and grief helps students deal effectively with their feelings when a loved one dies, but many adults find it difficult to discuss these things, particularly with children. For example, parents sometimes find it easier to evade the issue or even lie about a death because they want to protect their children from any uncomfortable feelings. Although parents who react to a death in this way are trying to help their children, in the long run avoidance can cause problems. Some parents use euphemistic language with their children, such as "Grandma is taking a long vacation" or "Grandpa is sleeping." Although the parents' intention is to ease the pain of loss, children at a more concrete developmental level might be frightened to take a vacation or go to sleep because they are confused about what happened to Grandma or Grandpa. Parents also might immediately replace a dead pet with a new one. Children typically do not want their pet replaced, but parents sometimes feel it will help the children forget the loss and get over the death.

Teachers who have researched the subject and have been trained in the various aspects of death and grief are able to satisfy the natural and developmentally consistent curiosities of young children. They can help children understand that their feelings about death are normal and even healthy. Teachers also can deal professionally and truthfully with other important issues of death and grief.

At the elementary and middle grades, professional instruction is important, because this is the time when many students first experience a loss, for example, when they move away from a best friend, when their parents divorce, or when an older brother or sister goes to college. Many elementary children experience a death, whether seen on television or experienced with a pet or a family member. It is estimated that one in twenty children will lose a parent by death by age 18, one in three American children will spend their first 18 years with only one parent, one in five families moves each year, and almost every child will experience the death of a pet, a friend, or a relative.[1-3] Children need to know the facts and issues surrounding death, dying, and loss so that any false impressions they have formed can be dispelled and so that they can deal with death in a healthy manner.

Readers might notice that this chapter is organized differently than the previous content-related chapters (Chapters 5–13). Unlike behaviors such as tobacco use or inactivity, loss and grief cannot be prevented. These are feelings and experiences that all children have, and teachers should be equipped to help students through the process. This chapter presents information about loss, death, and grief and ideas on teaching these topics to elementary and middle school students. Even with accurate information and suggested teaching activities in hand, teachers need to explore their own attitudes about loss, death, and grief before trying to teach the subject. Pronounced death anxiety or fears on the part of teachers might be conveyed to their students. Such well-meaning professionals can do more harm than good.

REASONS TO INCLUDE LOSS, DEATH, AND GRIEF EDUCATION IN ELEMENTARY AND MIDDLE SCHOOLS

Some administrators and teachers feel overwhelmed by the number of subjects and topics they are asked to teach their students during the school year. Loss, death, and grief education is an important topic to include within the elementary and middle school health education curriculum. Seventy to 100 years ago, loss, death, and grief would not have been an important topic to teach children, because families, churches, and the health care delivery system were different than they are today. During that time, it was common for children to experience the death of a sibling, parent, neighbor, or grandparent. Not only did deaths occur at a younger age, but the families were responsible for preparing the body and making all the funeral arrangements. There were no funeral homes as we know them today, and undertakers did not take care of all of the arrangements. Today, the living are isolated from the dying because the terminally ill typically are in hospitals, hospices, and nursing homes, whereas in the past dying people stayed at home. When a person dies, the funeral home takes care of all the details, from the preparation of the body for the funeral to the burial. Many parents totally isolate their children from the dying person and the funeral because they want to shelter them from pain. The changes have made death mysterious and, for some, more fearful. Many children do not have any real experiences with death and are only educated by the media. Because children are removed from death and do not understand what it is all about, teachers and other adults need to talk with them about death.

Although death is portrayed in the media, the portrayals are often misleading and confusing. According to Elisabeth Kübler-Ross, the media present "death in a two-dimensional aspect that tends to make it unreal and devoid of significant emotions."[4] A person is alive and then dead, and the emotions surrounding the death often are ignored. Because of these misleading portrayals, children once again are protected from the very real emotions that are connected with death. Children also might get confused about death when watching television because they might see a character get killed on one show and two days later see the same actor as a different character on another show.

Children, even those younger than age 6, are curious about death and typically have many questions about the topic.[5,6] Many parents do not feel comfortable talking about death, so they ignore the questions or lie to the child. For example, if a child asks what *dead* means, the parent might tell the child that he or she is too young to understand. The teacher can be an objective resource for answers to many of these sensitive questions.

Another reason to include loss, death, and grief education in the elementary and middle school curriculum is to allow students to express their feelings. Students should be taught the stages of grief so that, if they do experience a loss, they will know that they are not alone in how they feel. Students also might have a relative going through the dying process and, if allowed to discuss the stages of dying and the feelings associated with those stages, might feel less isolated.

It is healthy for children to gain an understanding of what people do for those who are grieving. Teachers should explain to children that loss or death is a topic that is out-of-bounds for teasing. Students should be taught how to respond to the grieving process. It should be explained to them that loss and grief might be a long process and a challenge for their classmates.[7] Sending sympathy cards and acknowledging another student who is grieving are important skills for students to master.

In the upper-elementary and middle-level grades, students might become more interested in death-related issues as a result of technology, such as euthanasia. Students will hear those issues being discussed on television, and they might need a forum in which to discuss them openly.

Some people might argue that the home or the church is the place to discuss the issues of loss, death, and dying. It would be wonderful if all children could discuss this topic openly with their parents; however, it just does not happen. As stated previously, many parents do not talk to their children about death because they are uncomfortable with the topic.[8] All children deserve the opportunity to discuss this relevant issue openly, which leaves the schools as the most practical place to teach about issues of loss, death, and grief.

IMPORTANT BACKGROUND FOR K–8 TEACHERS

There are a variety of topics about loss, death, and grief with which teachers should be both familiar and comfortable. These topics include the developmental stages of understanding death, the stages of grief, and the stages of dying. Depending on the grade level, not all of this information is developmentally appropriate; however, all teachers should have a basic understanding of these concepts.

Developmental Stages of Understanding Death

Several studies have been conducted with children to determine the developmental stages of understanding death. Perhaps the most widely cited study was published in 1948 by Maria Nagy.[9] Nagy maintained that children's ideas about death develop in three age-related stages. Although her work has been the standard for this topic, more current research suggests that the age of a child is not the best predictor of the child's understanding of death. Rather, individual development and experience more heavily influence how a child will understand the concept of death.[10] For instance, terminally ill children have a much more sophisticated understanding of death than do healthy, same-age children.[11] Likewise, children who have experienced the death of a pet or a relative seem to have a more mature understanding of death than do their peers. Deaths portrayed in the media and literature also influence a child's understanding of death. Although there are disagreements about Nagy's age-graded developmental model of understanding death, it still provides a foundation for elementary and middle school teachers as they work with their students.

- *Stage one (ages 3 to 5).* During this developmental stage, children do not understand the finality of death. They see death as a sleeplike, reversible state because their conceptions of time are concrete. They view the dead person as still being able to eat, work, laugh, and cry as if alive. Because of this view, children often seem matter of fact or callous about death. This is often demonstrated at funerals, when children in stage one show no signs of grief and, in fact, enjoy themselves with other stage one cousins and relatives. Parents are sometimes embarrassed when this type of behavior occurs; however, because these children believe the dead person will eventually return and continue to function, they see no reason to grieve. Children might also act this way if the person who died is not in their immediate circle of contact or support. It is not uncommon for children in this stage to ask questions such as "When is Daddy coming back?" It is especially important for adults *not* to explain death in terms of sleep or a vacation, because doing so reinforces some inaccurate beliefs. Although young children do not understand the finality of death, that lack of understanding does not negate the sense of grief that children might experience with any type of separation. Depending on experiences and maturity, many children in kindergarten through second grade will still view death as not final.
- *Stage two (ages 5 to 9).* Nagy found that children in stage two have an understanding of finality; however, they believe that an outside source, such as the "bogeyman" or "death man," causes death. Children often communicate with the bogeyman by asking him to leave their family alone or to go away. Many guilt feelings are associated with death during this stage, because stage two children believe the bogeyman is watching their actions. For instance, if a 7-year-old boy asks his grandfather to buy him a toy and the grandfather refuses, the boy might think negative thoughts about the grandfather. If the grandfather then dies, the boy might think that the bogeyman heard his negative thoughts about his grandfather and therefore he caused his grandfather's death. During this stage, it

It is appropriate for children to attend funerals and visit graves.

be more emotional and last longer because there was no preparation for the death.

During the grieving process, there are two main challenges for children. First, they need to process the actual event ("What is emphysema? Will I get it too?"). Second, they need to cope with the loss of the loved one ("I want to play with grandpa.")[13] Just as children go through developmental stages of understanding death, each person typically experiences stages of grief following the death of a loved one (Figure 14–1).[14] Adults and most schoolchildren follow these stages of grief. It needs to be emphasized that these are patterns, not strict steps that people should follow when they are grieving. Although timelines lay out these stages, they are rough estimates and are not prescriptions for appropriate behavior. Various factors, including how close a person was to the deceased and whether the death was expected, affect the length of time and intensity of each stage.

is important for teachers to be aware of potential guilt feelings and to try to alleviate them.

- *Stage three (age 9 and older).* During stage three, children fully understand the finality of death and know that it is something that happens within the body, not something strictly external. They are more likely to understand that death is universal and an inevitable end to everyone's life, including their own. Children in stage three do not associate death with themselves, however, but rather associate death with other, "old" people. During this stage, middle school students may experience a variety of feelings and emotions, expressed in ways such as acting out, crying, anger, or self-injurious behavior.[12]

Although these stages have been identified, it is important to remember that they are not prescriptive but instead should serve as guidelines. Children's behavior, depending on their personal experiences with death, might not conform to the suggested age parameters.

Stages of Grief

Grief is the psychological and sometimes physical response to the death of a loved one or to the loss or longing of someone due to transition (divorce of parents, a move). It consists of the feelings of sorrow, anger, depression, guilt, confusion, shock, and despair that occur after someone dies. Two terms are used to describe the intensity of grief related to death: *low-grief death* and *high-grief death*. A low-grief death results from a prolonged illness, an anticipated death, or the death of someone with whom there is little emotional connection. Following a low-grief death, the survivors might not show as many emotions because they have already grieved prior to the death. A high-grief death is an unexpected adult death or the death of a young person. Following a high-grief death, the grieving process might

- *Stage one—denial, shock, and disbelief.* This stage begins after hearing about the death of a loved one. Possible manifestations include crying, confusion, stress, and disbelief that the death has occurred. This stage typically lasts up to two weeks after the death. Some persons stay in this stage for a longer time, which may become unhealthy. Part of this stage includes denial, which might explain why survivors can act as though they are in control during the funeral or other commemorative ceremonies. Friends of the survivors should not mistake this calmness as an acceptance of the death and should not assume that the survivors do not need support after the funeral. After they accept the death, survivors desperately need support from their friends and loved ones.

- *Stage two—despair, numbness, guilt, sadness, and apathy.* This stage begins after the survivors have recognized the reality of the death and usually lasts up to one year. Because this stage generally expands over a long period of time, many feelings and degrees of feelings can be experienced: sadness, depression, guilt, preoccupation with thoughts of the deceased, anger, apathy, and numbness. It is not uncommon for survivors to experience loss of appetite, insomnia, crying spells, and restlessness and to deny themselves pleasure because of the guilt they feel over the death of loved ones. Children are more likely to express their grief in the form of anger, because they are angry that the person has died and left them behind. Often, this anger is expressed toward the surviving family members. Sometimes, adults find these expressions of anger difficult to accept because the children appear selfish and egocentric. Because anger is a major part of grief for children, adults

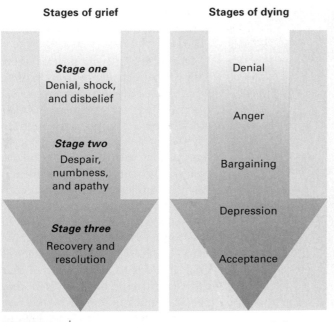

Stages of grief

Stage one
Denial, shock, and disbelief

Stage two
Despair, numbness, and apathy

Stage three
Recovery and resolution

Stages of dying

Denial

Anger

Bargaining

Depression

Acceptance

FIGURE 14–1 | Dying and grieving individuals share some feelings.

Children need to understand that grief is a normal and healthy response to loss.

can help them by accepting their feelings and not scolding them if they do express anger. It is important that survivors have the opportunity to share all feelings of grief and not be asked to hold them in or be brave. It is particularly important to stress this to boys, who might feel that they have to live up to the stereotype "boys don't cry." Another behavior sometimes exhibited by children during this stage is assumed mannerisms. This occurs when the grieving child begins to model the mannerisms of the dead person as if to take the place of that person. In addition, children tend to idealize the dead person by describing him or her in terms of perfection and excellence. Young children who are grieving over a parent's death might begin to act younger than they are. They might demand to be cuddled, might start to wet the bed, or might demand to be fed. During this stage, children also can experience feelings of loneliness, isolation, and abandonment. Children who feel this way need help in identifying significant people in their lives with whom they can talk.

• *Stage three—recovery and resolution.* Recovery and resolution begin approximately one year to fifteen months after the death. The name of this stage might suggest that the survivor is completely over the trauma and related emotions of the death; however, there are still times of depression during this stage. Sadness will occur occasionally, especially during holidays and on anniversaries and birthdays. Sometimes, this sadness occurs at an unconscious level; the person might not realize right away why he or she is feeling so bad. When individuals are taught that this sadness probably will be stronger during certain special times, they can prepare themselves to cope better. Survivors should be allowed to express their *grief* and not be asked to repress it. During this *stage,* the survivor has decreasing episodes of *sadness* and depression, recalls positive memories of *the* deceased, and is able to return to normal activities

and form new friendships. During this stage, the survivor accepts the death and tries to move on with life.

Children who understand that death is not reversible typically follow these stages of grief. The stages also can occur during divorce or separation. Besides the feelings associated with the stages of grief, children might experience other emotions and behaviors as they go through the grieving process.[15] For instance, children might become withdrawn from the family because they cannot stand to see their parents' pain. Another common reaction is for children to become hostile toward the deceased or any person whom they feel was responsible for the person's death. Children also might try to find a replacement for the deceased, so that they can maintain some of their normal routine. Don't assume that children always grieve in a predictable or orderly way. We all grieve in different ways and there is no one right way for children and pre-adolescents to move through the grieving process. However children express grief, the most important things for adults to remember are to allow them to grieve and to provide them with as much support as possible.

There are three dimensions of grief that school professionals should understand to help children successfully grieve:

• Grief is a normal, natural, and healthy response to loss.
• Grief is a unique, lifelong process for everyone who has experienced a loss.
• Everyone has the capability to heal in a supportive and emotionally safe environment.[16]

Many times, teachers are concerned about what is normal or abnormal grieving. The distinction is not easy to determine. It is not so much the emotions or behaviors that stand out, but their intensity and duration. What should be of concern is the continued denial or avoidance of reality, prolonged bodily distress, persistent panic, extended guilt, enduring anxiety, and unceasing hostility. If there is any doubt about whether a child needs professional attention, it is best to ask the school counselor for advice.

Stages of Dying

It is important for teachers and students to understand the stages of dying. Some students might have a relative who is dying, and it would be helpful for those students to understand why their relative acts the way he or she does. Elisabeth Kübler-Ross is the person most associated with research on the emotions of the dying. She interviewed about 200 terminally ill patients and found that most of them went through five psychological stages.[17] Not everyone with a terminal illness will experience all these stages, and not everyone progresses through these stages in the stated order. Some people fluctuate between two stages at the same time, whereas others skip various stages. These stages should not be valued as being good or bad but rather should be seen as guidelines to help a person interact with the dying. The stages are denial, anger, bargaining, depression, and acceptance.

- *Denial.* The first emotion that most persons experience when they are told they have a terminal illness is denial. This is a healthy response to a stressful situation, and it acts as a temporary buffer to help protect the individual. It is not uncommon for the terminally ill to return periodically to the denial stage, even after progressing to other stages. This stage becomes dangerous only when the terminally ill person seeks third and fourth opinions about an illness or spends money on quack cures.
- *Anger.* After terminally ill persons can no longer deny their approaching death, they typically become angry, resentful, and hostile. This is perhaps the most difficult stage for loved ones to deal with because the anger sometimes is directed at them. Anger might be expressed through shouting, complaining, and bitterness. For instance, the person might say, "I don't want to see anyone—go away." These emotions are understandable but not always easy to deal with. This is an especially important stage for children to understand, because a terminally ill grandparent might yell or express meanness to a child while in this stage. Children need to understand that the grandparent is angry not at them but at the situation.
- *Bargaining.* Bargaining typically occurs throughout most of the dying process. This stage is characterized by the terminally ill person's bargaining with someone in power, such as the physician or God, to prolong life. For instance, a terminally ill person might think, "If you let me live until my next birthday, I promise I will always be a kind person."

An outsider might not be aware of this stage, because many patients keep these bargains a secret.
- *Depression.* Many terminally ill people bounce back and forth among the bargaining stage, the depression stage, and the anger stage. After they determine that the bargaining has not worked, they become depressed. They begin to understand that death is certain, and feelings of sadness and depression become overwhelming. Although it might be frightening for a child to visit a terminally ill person, children should not be discouraged from doing so. Many times, children can help the patient deal with or temporarily forget about death. When visiting a terminally ill relative, children should be encouraged to take a small present, such as an art project from school. This can give the patient and the child something to talk about. The opportunity to bring some happiness to a dying person might also help children feel useful and helpful.
- *Acceptance.* The last stage of the dying process occurs when the person accepts the outcome of death. It does not mean that the person is happy; rather, there is a lack of feelings. During this stage, the dying person wants to make psychological and practical arrangements, such as funeral arrangements or the writing of a will. Those arrangements become difficult and frustrating if the relatives still deny the death; however, it is important to accommodate the dying person as much as possible.

Children should understand that one of the biggest fears of dying people is the fear of being alone. If children understand this and the stages of dying, they might be more inclined to make frequent visits or contacts with a terminally ill relative.

GUIDELINES FOR TEACHERS

When teaching about loss, death, and grief, it is important not only to identify activities that are useful for elementary teachers but also to understand the guidelines for teaching about loss and death, dealing with a grieving student, handling a traumatic event, and facing the aftermath of a student suicide. What follows are guidelines for teachers in dealing with all of these events. These guidelines can help teachers and administrators avoid becoming defensive with parents and students when teaching a controversial topic such as loss, death, and grief.

Teaching About Loss, Death, and Grief

Teachers must be honest with students—many times, parents and other adults try to shield children from any loss- or death-related experiences or emotions. Although shielding children might delay their pain, it will emerge at some point. For instance, while discussing death-related issues in college classes, some students express their anger about not being able to go to their grandparent's funeral when they were younger or not being told about a pet's or a relative's death. In fact, one study found that children who participated in funeral rituals had better emotional adjustment to the death of a loved one compared to those children who did not participate in funeral rituals.[18] Following are some guidelines for talking with students about loss, death, and grief.

- *It is important for teachers to be honest and open when answering children's questions about death.* If children are capable of asking a question, then they are capable of understanding an answer offered at the same level. Sometimes, teachers might not know the answer to a child's question. Instead of making up an answer, teachers should not hesitate to say "I don't know, but I will try to find an answer for you." As soon as the teacher obtains the answer, it should be relayed to the student.

- *When teachers are answering students' questions, it is important to be as factual as possible.* For instance, if a student asks, "What makes people die?" an appropriate response is "A person's heart stops beating." Although this seems concrete and simple, it is important to remember that most elementary students are concrete thinkers.

If a teacher does not understand a question, he or she can refer the question back to the child. For instance, if a child asks, "Do children die?" it might be a good idea to find out what the child thinks and why he or she has asked the question. The teacher might respond by asking, "Do you think children die?" or "What made you ask that question?" The responses to these questions can give the teacher more information and provide a framework to best answer the original question.

- *Teachers should avoid providing personal values on controversial issues related to death.* Parents become uncomfortable when teachers voice their views on controversial issues related to death. For instance, a teacher should not suggest that dead people go to heaven, that euthanasia should be legalized, or that reincarnation is possible. These beliefs should be discussed within the family unit. Death and grief education should focus on the facts and feelings surrounding grief and death. Children, however, will ask teachers their opinions about value-related issues, such as "What happens to people when they die?" The safest way for a teacher to respond to that question is to simply state, "There are many ideas about what happens to people when they die, and the best thing to do is to ask your parents or caregivers what their beliefs are about this question." Because there are numerous religious viewpoints about death, it is important for teachers not to promote any one viewpoint. Remember, teachers should not impose their philosophy of death on children, no matter how comforting they think it might be.[19]

- *Teachers should be especially good and supportive listeners when children are discussing their feelings about death.* Many children already will have experienced the death of a pet or a relative by the time they reach elementary school, but they might not have been given the opportunity to express their feelings about death. While discussing death or teaching a lesson about grief, many children want the opportunity to express their feelings about the death of someone they knew. It is important for teachers to listen and encourage the sharing of feelings so that students understand that other classmates have felt the same way in similar situations. It is also acceptable for teachers to share the feelings of grief they have experienced.

- *Teachers should ask children to explain what they have learned about death during class.* Although the developmental attributes of young children are consistent with concrete thinking, adults tend to use metaphorical explanations about death. Many teachers do not realize they are using metaphors or euphemistic language and can innocently confuse children. For example, if a euphemism such as *gone away* is used instead of *died*, children might view death as a person leaving for a while. Sentence stems can be offered at the end of a lesson to summarize what each student has learned:

> I learned . . .
>
> I was surprised . . .
>
> I feel . . .

The Teacher's Role When a Student or a Student's Relative Is Dying or Dies

If a person teaches long enough, he or she probably will experience the death of a student or the death of a student's close relative, such as a parent or sibling. Although it is best to discuss death before it occurs, sometimes this is not possible. Regardless of whether dying, death, and grief have been formally taught before a death occurs, several guidelines should be remembered when discussing the death of a classmate or the death of a classmate's relative with elementary and middle school students:

1. Teachers should be prepared to deal with a child in the class who is dying. For example, there might be frequent absences or hair loss due to therapeutic regimens. Children should participate in discussions of their feelings about dying as well as death. The class might vote to get a special hat for the child who has lost his or her hair and to wear hats also.

2. Teachers should feel comfortable in expressing their grief openly after the death of a child. When teachers share their grief with the class, students are able to see that it is acceptable to cry or feel sad. Many teachers are afraid they will say something wrong or act inappropriately, but the most important thing to children is the sincere care and concern their teachers show toward them.

3. If possible, talk with the grieving child before he or she returns to school. Ask the child what he/she wants the class to know about the death.

4. Talk to the class about how grief affects people. Discuss how difficult it may be for their classmates to return to school.

5. Teachers should acknowledge and discuss guilt feelings. Guilt is commonly felt by survivors of a loved one. A teacher can help by acknowledging the guilt and helping children understand that the death was not their fault. It might be helpful for upper-elementary and middle-level

Children can be encouraged to write sympathy cards.

students to write about their feelings if they are having a difficult time discussing them.

6. Teachers should encourage students to write personal sympathy cards to the parents or to a student who has had someone close die. This helps students deal with their grief, and the survivors appreciate it. Teachers can instruct students to emphasize their fond memories of the deceased and their sorrow. Teachers also can ask students how they want to commemorate a student who has died. They might create a memorial book, collect money for a charitable donation, or plant a tree to help them remember their friend.

7. Teachers should allow children to express their grief and sadness. Because grief always surfaces at some point, it is important for children to be allowed to grieve. Many times, adults tell children to be brave and be strong, but this causes students to repress their grief. Because the school might be the only place where children are allowed to express their sadness, teachers should give the students time to openly express their feelings.

8. If a classmate dies, teachers should not force a typical day on grieving students. It is important to have structured and planned activities; however, part of the day should revolve around sharing feelings and discussing death. For example, students should help decide what to do with the empty desk and possessions of a classmate who dies. Some daily routines should be maintained, because children can become agitated and disoriented when boundaries disappear in times of crisis.

9. Teachers should expect unusual behavior from students for several weeks or months after the death of a classmate or relative. Students might become aggressive, exhibit a lack of concentration, be withdrawn, have mood swings, become nervous, or experience headaches and nausea. These are normal behaviors for persons who are experiencing grief. If a teacher is concerned about a student's excessive behavior, it is important that the teacher refer the student to the school counselor. Teachers also should reassure children

that feelings of sadness, loneliness, anger, and anxiety are normal reactions to a death. Sometimes, just knowing that these reactions are normal is helpful to children.

10. Teachers should not focus on the details of death. For example, it is not important to describe an automobile crash or a deteriorating disease to students. This may frighten them needlessly and cause unwarranted stress.

11. In talking with students, teachers should use the words *dead* and *death,* avoiding phrases meant to soften the blow, such as "she went away" or "God took him." These phrases can be confusing and scary.

12. A touch sometimes can communicate more comfort than words can to children who are experiencing grief. If it is appropriate, a teacher can ask permission to give a child a hug.

13. Teachers should plan nonverbal activities to allow expressions of grief. For example, listening to music, drawing pictures, and writing journal entries allow nonverbal students an opportunity to express grief.

14. Teachers should not try to tell children how they feel. Teachers should ask them how they feel but should not say "I know how you must feel."

15. Teachers should encourage social interactions with peers. Children who are grieving need social interaction. Teachers can plan activities in which all students are required to interact with one another.

16. Teachers should have resources available in the classroom about death and grief or offer to read a book to children that helps explain grief.

17. Teachers should allow a distraught child to call home if necessary. A child who has experienced the death of a parent, sibling, or grandparent might need reassurance that a parent is still at home, waiting.[20-26]

These guidelines can help teachers who are faced with the death of a student or of a student's relative. If teachers have other concerns, funeral directors and school counselors are good resources on how to deal with children after a death has occurred.

The School's and Teacher's Roles When Dealing with Disasters or Traumatic Events

It is not uncommon for children to witness or experience a disaster or traumatic event. For example, past generations of children have witnessed or lived through the shooting of national leaders (J. F. Kennedy, Martin Luther King, Jr.) and the bombing of buildings (the Oklahoma City bombing) and have experienced tornadoes, hurricanes, fires, earthquakes, and other natural disasters. Most recently, this generation of pre-adolescents witnessed and/or experienced the terrorist attack on the World Trade Center in New York City on September 11, 2001.

It is important for school personnel to understand how to help children deal with disasters and traumatic events. For example, most children react in the following ways:

- They feel a loss of control—disasters and traumatic events are something over which we have little or no control. This feeling of loss of control can be overwhelming to children and adults alike.

- They experience a loss of stability—disasters and traumatic events threaten a child's routine and structure. They get scared that, if this event could happen once, it could happen again.
- They are very self-centered—these events can make children worry about their own safety and well-being, to an extent that some adults may think is unreasonable. Children need ongoing messages of comfort regarding their safety.[27]

Traumatic events can lead to painful emotions in children, including mild to severe posttraumatic stress reactions. If these signs and symptoms persist, it is advisable for teachers to refer students to a school counselor or another mental health professional. Some common stress symptoms that elementary teachers might observe or hear about include

Clinginess

Aggressiveness

Withdrawal from activities and friends

Increased fighting with friends

School avoidance

Loss of interest and poor concentration in school

Regressive behavior (acting much younger than their age—for example, asking for help to be fed or dressed)

Headaches or other physical complaints

Depression

Fear about safety

Irritability

Difficulty sleeping because of nightmares[28,29]

Some common stress symptoms that middle school teachers might observe or hear about include

Poor school performance

School problems (fighting, attention-seeking behaviors)

Physical complaints such as headaches and stomachaches

Withdrawal from friends

Agitation

Sleep disturbances

Loss of appetite

Rebellion at home (refusal to do chores, not obeying parents)[30,31]

There are many things school districts and teachers can do after students have experienced a natural disaster or a traumatic event:

1. School districts should have a plan in place as to how they will handle a natural disaster or traumatic event. For

example, counselors should be available to help students and teachers handle the event. Administrators should prepare a uniform announcement that teachers can use to tell children about an event if it happens while they are in school. Administrators should also prepare a typed message that can be sent home with students to communicate with parents about how the school dealt with the situation.

2. Teachers should provide opportunities for children to talk about the event and to ask questions. If the natural disaster or traumatic event is something that they are continually seeing on television, they might ask questions for several days or weeks. If teachers don't know the answer to their questions, they should not be afraid to admit it.

3. When a teacher does know the answers to students' questions, the teacher should answer them at an appropriate developmental level.

4. Teachers should practice emergency procedures at school so that children are confident they know what to do in case of an emergency (an intruder in the building, fire and tornado drills). Also, teachers should encourage children to practice emergency procedures at home with their families (fire escape routes, earthquake procedures)

5. Teachers should promote positive coping and problem-solving skills.

6. Teachers should assure children that there is a wide range of emotions that are appropriate, normal, and healthy and should encourage them to express their emotions.

7. Teachers should try to focus on some positive events that surround the natural disaster or traumatic event (identifying heroes and discussing organizations and people who have been helpful during and after these events).

8. Teachers should try to maintain a routine for children. Children need structure and routine to help them understand that not everything in the world has changed.[32,33]

The School's Role When Handling a Suicide

Dealing with student suicide is a difficult situation that might occur in some middle schools. Suicide is the third leading cause of death in 10- to 14-year-olds, with 270 deaths among children in this age group.[34,35] Although it is not common for middle school students to commit suicide, it can happen, and school districts and teachers should be prepared.

It is first important for teachers to understand the risk and protective factors associated with youth suicide. As with other risk factors for various health problems, the more risk factors that are present, the more likely a person is to participate in the risky behavior. The risk factors for suicide that teachers would most likely know about or be able to observe include

- A previous suicide attempt
- Mental disorders including depression, conduct disorders, and bipolar disorder
- A family history of suicide

- Feelings of hopelessness
- Impulsive or aggressive behaviors
- Easy access to lethal means, especially guns
- The influence of significant people who have died by suicide (movie star, best friend)
- A local epidemic of suicide that has a contagious influence
- Feelings of isolation
- Family stress and dysfunction
- Barriers to mental health treatment
- Loss of work, social status, or financial loss
- Unwillingness to seek help because of stigma attached to mental disorders and/or suicidal thoughts
- Alcohol and other drug use[36,37]

Protective factors, or things that can enhance resilience to suicide, include

- Easy access to help for emotional and mental health problems
- Restricted access to lethal means
- Family and community support
- Learned skills in problem solving, conflict resolution, and nonviolent handling of arguments
- Cultural and religious beliefs that discourage suicide and support self-preservation[38]

Teachers should be aware of these risk and protective factors and know the warning signs for suicide, which appear in Teacher's Toolbox 14.1. If teachers notice these warning signs in a student, they should refer that student to the school counselor. No one should keep a secret about suspected suicidal behavior. The parents of the suicidal student must be notified.

There is a lack of concrete evidence as to how schools can help prevent suicide. Approaches to suicide prevention that are encouraged include promoting overall mental health among students, encouraging seeking help when signs and symptoms of suicide are present, and detecting those youth most likely to be suicidal and referring them to professionals.[39]

If a middle school child does commit suicide, it is important that schools have a plan in place to deal with the suicide and help prevent copycat suicides. The principal of the school should try to get as much information as soon as possible. He or she should meet with teachers and staff to inform them of the proper way to announce the death, support the reactions of their students, and identify and refer close friends of the victim and other high-risk students for counseling. The teachers then should inform each class of students about the suicide. It is important that all the students hear the same thing. After they have been informed, they should have the opportunity to discuss their feelings. The school should have extra counselors available for students and staff who need to talk. Students who appear to be the most severely affected might need parental notification and outside mental health referrals.[40]

Schools also should be very careful not to glorify the victim and sensationalize the suicide. For example, school memorial services at which the victim is held in high esteem should be avoided. Schools should announce when and where the funeral is to be held but should not organize a memorial service.[41] By not glorifying the victim, schools can help prevent further suicides by students who have thought about committing suicide and see the positive attention paid to the victim. Teacher's Toolbox 14.2 summarizes the steps a school should and should not take when a suicide happens.

Recommendations for Concepts and Practice

Sample Students' Questions and Suggested Answers About Loss, Death, and Grief

A list of some commonly asked questions about loss, death, and grief and some suggested answers follows. It is not enough to just read the suggested answers—teachers should practice saying them aloud and adjust their answers to the age of the child asking the question. Teachers are encouraged to think of other questions students might ask and to practice answering them as well.

1. *Why do people die?*
It is sad, but dying is a very natural thing. All things that live will die one day. People, plants, insects, and animals all will die one day.

2. *Is dying like going to sleep?*
No, it's different. When someone dies, the person's body is no longer working. The heart stops beating, the person no longer needs to eat or sleep, and he or she no longer feels any pain. The person doesn't need the body any longer. That means we will never see that person again as we could before.

3. *Does dying hurt?*
Not normally; many people who are old just quietly die. Sometimes, people involved in accidents die so quickly they don't even know it has happened. Even when someone dies after being ill for a long time, the doctor gives him or her special medicine to stop any pain while the person is alive.

4. *Where do dead people go when they die?*
Well, different people believe different things. This is a very important question to ask your mom or dad to see what she or he thinks.

5. *Why did my grandma die and leave me?*
Your grandma didn't choose to leave you, and I know it doesn't seem fair. She loved you very much and would be with you if she could.

6. *Why didn't someone else die instead of my brother?*
All over the world, living things die every day. Someone else dying would not have prevented your brother from dying.

7. *When someone dies, is she being punished for being bad?*
No; people die because their bodies stop working, either because they have worn out or they have been damaged. Most people live for a long time, but sometimes younger people die because of an accident or a bad illness. Their death has nothing to do with being bad.

8. *Why can't the doctor stop people from dying?*
Doctors often can stop someone from dying, and most people who are ill do not die. Sometimes, though, when there are lots of things wrong with the body or it just wears out, the doctor cannot stop the person from dying.

9. *Why do we have funerals?*
A funeral is a chance for people to comfort each other and remember all the good things about the person who has died.

10. *What causes death?*
Many things can cause death. Injuries, illness, and disease can cause the body to stop working and die. Sometimes, growing very old results in death. Some things never cause death—wishes or thoughts will never cause death. Sometimes, we might not be sure why someone we love has died, and that can confuse us and leave us with many unanswered questions.

11. *My grandpa just died. What can I do when I feel really bad?*
After someone we love dies, it is natural to feel sad, scared, or angry. The best way to take care of yourself is to find a grown-up you trust and let him or her know how you are feeling. Sometimes, just letting someone know how we are feeling reminds us that we are not alone, and this can really help.

12. *What is death?*
Death is the end of living. All things that live eventually die. Just as flowers and animals die, so do people. When people die, they don't breathe, their heart stops beating, and they don't need to eat or drink. Death is not like sleeping. When someone dies, his or her body stops working forever.

STRATEGIES FOR LEARNING AND ASSESSMENT

Managing Loss, Death, and Grief

Learning strategies dealing with managing loss, death, and grief can be used successfully with a range of age groups. Some of the strategies in this section link to science education, as students discuss the characteristics of living and nonliving things. Teachers should be certain that children have opportunities to discuss and understand the range of normal emotions people are likely to experience when someone dies. Teachers should vary the topics and level of discussion to suit the needs and interests of their students. Teachers must know what is going on in their students' lives before initiating lessons related to loss, death, and grief. For example, lessons such as these would be inappropriate if a child has experienced a family death and is back in school for the first time. However, teachers might conduct lessons to help class members demonstrate understanding and empathy when the child returns to school. The anniversary of the September 11, 2001, attacks on the United States often brings up discussions about death, tragedy, and commemorations of people's lives. Teachers will want to know if any children in their classes lost relatives or loved ones during that time.

This section provides examples of standards-based learning and assessment strategies for managing loss, death, and grief. The strategies begin with a restatement of the standard and a reminder of the assessment criteria, drawn from the RMC rubrics in Appendix B. Strategies are written as directions for teachers. These learning and assessment strategies provide building blocks for standards-based lessons and units that can be tailored to local needs. Assessment criteria are used with permission from the Rocky Mountain Center for Health Promotion and Education (RMC). See Appendix B for Scoring Rubrics.

NHES 1 | Core Concepts

Students will comprehend concepts related to health promotion and disease prevention to enhance health.

ASSESSMENT CRITERIA

- Connections—Describe relationships between behavior and health; draw logical conclusions about connections between behavior and health.
- Comprehensiveness—Thoroughly cover health topic, showing breadth and depth; give accurate information.

Grades K–2

Living or Nonliving?   Early elementary students might have difficulty distinguishing the ideas of *living* and *nonliving*. They also might be unsure about what will and will not die. Discuss examples and characteristics of living and nonliving things with students. Make a two-column list. Next, ask them to work in groups of two or three to make a collage of pictures (have magazines on hand or a variety of precut pictures) and drawings of things that live and die and things that do not. Children should explain their categorizations, and teachers should help answer their questions. Experiment with "planting" various kinds of objects—such as seeds of various kinds, flower bulbs, lightbulbs, rocks, chalk—and compare the results. Students also might enjoy breathing or coughing on a piece of bread and sealing it in a plastic bag to see if anything "living" will grow. These experiments help clarify students' ideas about things that are and are not living (and thus cannot grow and cannot die).

ASSESSMENT | The students' categorization of items as living or nonliving is the assessment task for this activity. For assessment criteria, students should be able to categorize accurately and explain their categorizations. This activity links to science education.

Life Cycle   The concept of the life cycle links to science lessons. Students can describe what happens in their own yards or in the yards at school as the seasons pass. What happens when a seed is planted? What happens after flowers bloom? What happens to leaves in autumn in many parts of the country? Why? All during the school year, students can bring in plants in different stages to demonstrate the life cycle. Teachers can share a collection (seeds, buds, leaves, plants, dead leaves or plants, dried flowers). Also, children can investigate the life cycles of different types of insects and animals, including class pets. Older students can diagram these life cycles. Teachers might want to use the song "The Circle of Life" from the popular movie *The Lion King* to discuss this concept.[42] Children can talk about what the words to the song mean in relation to their discussions and investigations.

ASSESSMENT | For an assessment task, students can describe the life cycle of a particular plant, insect, or animal of their choosing. For assessment criteria, students should provide accurate information and draw logical conclusions about life cycles (various organisms have different life spans; all living things die).

Grades 3–5

Learning About Body Systems in a Health Context   Science lessons for upper-elementary and middle-level students often include study of human body systems. To make the link to health, children can discuss ways to keep the body systems healthy and functioning properly. How do different kinds of behaviors affect the body systems? For example, how do healthy nutrition and regular physi-

cal activity affect the muscular and skeletal systems? How does tobacco affect the circulatory and respiratory systems? How does alcohol and other drug use affect the nervous system? Teachers can make these links between behaviors and health to be sure health is part of these discussions. Ask students what kinds of diseases affect the body systems. Which have cures at this time? Which do not? What progress have scientists made in preventing and treating various diseases? Which do students think is more often successful—prevention or treatment? When? Why? What happens when there is no treatment? Link these discussions with the process of dying and death and ask students to express feelings about this outcome of some diseases.

ASSESSMENT | For an assessment task, students can work in groups to research and serve as "Tour Guides" for various body systems, with a strong emphasis on keeping those systems healthy and strong. ("All aboard—you are now entering the circulatory system. During our tour, we'll learn how to keep it healthy for a long life!") For assessment criteria, students should provide accurate information, describe relationships between behaviors and health, and draw logical conclusions about connections between behaviors and health (healthy body systems) and living a long, healthy life. This activity links to science.

Child and Adolescent Literature with a Loss, Death, or Grief Theme   Many children's books have themes that relate to loss, death, and grief. Some of these books can be used to teach an entire lesson on loss, death, and grief, whereas others would be more appropriately used to reinforce or support a lesson. For instance, before introducing the activity "Memory Book" to students, teachers might read a book that discusses the importance of memories during the grieving process. When reading a children's book with a loss, death, or grief theme, teachers should pause and ask questions. For example, ask students to describe how they think certain characters are feeling or how students would feel in the same situation. Ask students whether they identify with the characters and why. Some books might not be ideal to read to an entire class, but the books can be available as choices during silent reading or free time. Before reading a children's book with a loss, death, or grief theme to the class, teachers should evaluate the book to make sure the information is presented appropriately. For instance, a book might describe death as a sleeplike state, or it might discuss heaven and God. Teachers need to be sure that the information presented is accurate and avoids teaching about a particular religion. In addition, teachers must be highly aware of what is going on in their children's individual lives related to death or loss before using these books. A list of children's books that have a loss, death, or grief theme appears at the end of this chapter.

ASSESSMENT | For an assessment task, students can discuss the books in literature circles. Students can listen to a story being read, or groups of students can select a book for their circles. For assessment criteria, students should explain how the characters dealt with situations in healthy ways for themselves and others. This activity links to language arts.

How Do You Feel?   Teachers can begin the lesson by facilitating a discussion about famous people who have died both recently and in the more distant past. Next, have students brainstorm and discuss various ways of remembering someone who has died. Some possibilities include planting a tree or shrub, writing a poem, or composing a song. Then ask students to think of a person who was close to them, or a pet who has died. (If students do not have anyone in mind, allow them to complete this activity about a famous person who has died.) Tell the students that they will write a letter to a person or a pet who has died. The following is a list of things you might ask students to include in the letter:

- How you feel?
- What you miss about the pet or the person?
- What would you want to say to the pet or the person?
- How will you remember the person or pet?

Tell students to indicate on the back of their letter if they are willing to have their letter read aloud to the class. Collect the letters, and choose some to share with the class.

ASSESSMENT | The letter that the students write is the assessment task for this activity. For assessment criteria, students should explain how writing the letter helps them remember the person or pet and deal with their feelings in healthy ways.

Grades 6–8

What Is Hospice Care?   Students might be familiar with or have questions about the concept of hospice care. Middle school students can access information at Hospice Net (www.hospicenet.org) to learn more about hospice, caregiving, and coping with grief.

ASSESSMENT | For an assessment task, students can work individually, in pairs, or in small groups to investigate and report on a topic related to hospice care and dealing with the end of life. For assessment criteria, students should present information that is accurate and explain how family and caregivers can help one another deal with loss, death, and grief. This activity links to NHES 3, access information, products, and services.

NHES 2 | Analyze Influences

Students will analyze the influence of family, peers, culture, media, technology, and other factors on health behaviors.

ASSESSMENT CRITERIA
- Identify both external and internal influences on health.
- Explain how external and internal influences interact to impact health choices and behaviors.
- Explain both positive and negative influences, as appropriate.

Grades K–2

***My Mama Had a Dancing Heart:* The Influence of Parents and Other Special Adults**   Libba Gray's book *My Mama Had a Dancing Heart* begins with the words "My Mama had a dancing heart, and she shared that heart with me." A ballet dancer remembers her mother's enthusiasm for life and how her mother influenced and inspired her. Teachers can use this book to talk with students about how family members and other caring adults influence them to pursue their dreams.

ASSESSMENT | For an assessment task, students can select someone who influences and inspires them and tell or write about that person. For assessment criteria, students should explain how this person influences the way they live their lives and what they want to do with their lives.

Grades 3–5

Sentence Stems   Teachers can use sentence stems to begin a discussion of dying and death with upper-elementary students. Some examples of sentence stems are

- Death is like . . .
- A good thing about death is . . .

- The scariest thing about death is . . .
- When someone dies, I feel . . .
- A bad thing about death is . . .
- An important thing to remember about death is . . .

After students complete their sentences, they can share with each other in small groups and then with the rest of the class. These statements can act as a springboard for discussing some of the issues and feelings related to death.

ASSESSMENT | Students can use the completion of the sentence stems to initiate a conversation about where people learn their ideas about death and loss. For an assessment task, students can analyze whether their sentence completions come from internal (feelings, moods, curiosity, fear, likes, dislikes) or external influences (family, peers, culture, media) or both. For example, when students share their ideas about good, bad, or scary things about death, they can analyze how they might have learned these responses. For assessment criteria, students should specify and explain at least three influences on their and others' ideas about loss and death.

Grades 6–8

Dealing with Loss, Death, and Grief in Different Cultures   Teachers can ask students what they know about how different cultures deal with issues related to loss, death, and grief. Students can work in pairs or small groups to find out more about the culture of their family or a culture they want to know more about. For example, Mexicans observe the Day of the Dead (Dia de los Muertos) to remember members of their families who have died and to celebrate the continuity of life. The focus of students' research is how different cultures help their members deal with loss, death, and grief in healthy ways. To illustrate, the Day of the Dead is not a day of mourning but a festive time. Many other cultures honor their ancestors with ceremonies of respect.

ASSESSMENT | For an assessment task, students can investigate the culture of their families or a culture of interest to learn how traditions related to loss, death, and grief are observed. For assessment criteria, students should explain how the traditions help members of the culture deal with loss, death, and grief in healthy ways. This activity links to social studies.

Portrayals of Death in the Media   Middle school students can brainstorm about the ways they have seen death portrayed in movies, television shows, news, and commercials. Students can work as a class or in small groups to add to a brainstorm list with four columns (movies, television shows, news, commercials), saying all the things that pop into their minds, without editing. Students then can analyze their lists for themes and ideas that come up repeatedly. For example, students might say that movies often portray violent death or strong emotions about death. They might notice television commercials about buying life insurance for family members. Television shows might include jokes about or make fun of death (a weekly cartoon in which the same character is killed each week). Students can draw conclusions about the influences portrayed in the media related to ideas about loss, death, and grief.

ASSESSMENT | For an assessment task, students can identify themes or ideas they notice in their brainstorm list. For assessment criteria, students should explain how these themes or ideas might influence a young person's ideas about loss, death, and grief.

NHES 3 | Access Information, Products, and Services

Students will demonstrate the ability to access valid information and products and services to enhance health.

ASSESSMENT CRITERIA
- Access health information—Locate specific sources of health information, products, or services relevant to enhancing health in a given situation.
- Evaluate information sources—Explain the degree to which identified sources are valid, reliable, and appropriate as a result of evaluating each source.

Grades K–2

Talking Things Out One of the most important health education skills for children of all ages is knowing where to go for help and to ask for help when they need it. Children can talk about who can help them when they feel sad, angry, or depressed. Students can draw a support tree to show the people they can go to when they need to talk things out. Children should include at least two adults on their support tree.

ASSESSMENT | The support tree or other graphic (helping hand) students draw to illustrate the people in their support system is the assessment task for this activity. For assessment criteria, students should include at least two adults in their support system and explain how each person can help them if they need to talk to someone about questions or problems.

Grades 3–5

Survey Family Members Older children can survey their family members about their cultural traditions and family practices for commemorating death. Students can share what they learn with the class. Teachers should be sure to seek administrative approval before conducting this activity, because students might report on family religious practices and traditions. Teachers should send home a simple explanation of the assignment to parents and caregivers.

ASSESSMENT | The reports students make about their family and cultural traditions is the assessment task for this activity. Students can work together to create a list of questions they want to ask at home. For assessment criteria, students should tell with whom they talked and why those family members were valid resources for information on their family and cultural traditions.

Grades 6–8

Helping a Friend or Family Member Students need to know how to help or get help for a friend or family member who is experiencing sadness, anger, or other difficult emotions. Teachers can make a list of school and community health helpers with younger students. Older students can use phone books to identify community helpers and organizations.

ASSESSMENT | The list of school and community helpers students make for helping a family member or friend is the assessment task for this activity. For assessment criteria, students should explain how to contact the school and community helpers and tell why they are good sources of assistance.

The Hopeline Network Students can learn more about suicide prevention hotlines at www.suicidehotlines.com. At this site, students can find the toll-free phone numbers for suicide prevention hotlines in their states. Suicide prevention is a serious topic. From the site, students can learn how to get help for themselves and others in a crisis situation.

ASSESSMENT | For an assessment task, students can explain how to get help through a suicide hotline. For assessment criteria, students should explain how to determine whether a hotline is a valid source of assistance (has trained professional counselors).

NHES 4 | Interpersonal Communication

Students will demonstrate the ability to use interpersonal communication skills to enhance health and avoid or reduce health risks.

ASSESSMENT CRITERIA
- Use appropriate verbal/nonverbal communication strategies in an effective manner to enhance health or avoid/reduce health risks.
- Use appropriate skills (negotiation skills, refusal skills) and behaviors (eye contact, body language, attentive listening).

Grades K–5

Talking About Emotions To prepare for this activity, teachers can clip magazine pictures of people showing different types of facial expressions, gestures, and feelings. Elementary students sometimes do not understand what emotions are and how people express them. Students should try to explain the word *emotions*. They can use their dictionaries to check their definitions. As a homework assignment, students can try to find out what the word *emotions* means by talking with family members. The simplest definition that children probably will find is that emotions are feelings. Children can list all the kinds of feelings they can imagine. If pictures are available, children can describe the feelings or emotions they see the people expressing. Children can try to make connections about reasons the people might feel this way. For example, a student might say about a picture, "That little girl is smiling because she is happy."

After looking through the pictures, students should think of examples of times when people might express strong emotions. The children might state the example of feeling sadness, anger, or shock when a person or a pet dies. If a student does bring up the subject of death, teachers can continue the discussion about why people are sad or angry when a person or pet dies and ask whether the children ever have felt this way.

Discussing feelings and emotions is important, regardless of whether death is a specific topic. Students can select a picture from those at school or at home for a story-writing assignment and share their stories with classmates.

ASSESSMENT | In this activity, students focus on how to read the emotions that people communicate with their facial expressions and body language. Their stories about a picture they select are the assessment task for this activity. For assessment criteria, students should explain what the people in the picture are communicating and how they determined this (identify what facial expressions or body language appeared to indicate feelings).

Expressing My Feelings This is an activity that can be used with very young children who might have a difficult time expressing their feelings. It can be used with one child who is grieving or for a whole class who is grieving. Provide grieving students with a paper bag. Tell students to make a paper mask that shows how they are feeling.

ASSESSMENT | The paper mask is the assessment task for this activity. For assessment criteria, students should be able to describe the feeling that they drew on their mask.

Grades 6-8

Helpful vs. Hurtful Statements   Begin the lesson by asking students to think about their own experiences with grief. Ask them to think about helpful and hurtful things that were said to them after the death of someone close to them. Write the following statements on an individual card and then mix them up. Give one card to each student and ask them to read the statement. Have a discussion about whether the statement is helpful or hurtful.

> **Examples of Helpful Statements**
> "How can I be of help?"
> "Tell me how you are feeling."
> "It must be hard to accept."
> "That must be very painful."
> "I'm sorry."
> "I wish I could take the pain away."
>
> **Examples of Hurtful Statements**
> "I know how you feel."
> "Time heals all things."
> "She/he led a full life."
> "Don't worry, you will get over it."
> "Don't be such a baby."
> "Just try to forget about it."

ASSESSMENT | The response to each statement is the assessment task for this activity. For assessment criteria, students should be able to explain why the statement is either helpful or hurtful to a grieving person.

NHES 5 | Decision Making

Students will demonstrate the ability to use decision-making skills to enhance health.

ASSESSMENT CRITERIA

Reach a health-enhancing decision using a process consisting of the following steps:

- Identify a health-risk situation.
- Examine alternatives.
- Evaluate positive and negative consequences.
- Decide on a health-enhancing course of action.

Grades K–5

Planning a Funeral or Memorial   Many students have questions about funerals, wakes, and other types of services associated with death. Teachers can discuss the idea of remembering and honoring the life of a person as the reasons for these services, allowing students to discuss their experiences of these services with the rest of the class. If a class pet dies, students might want to plan a funeral for it, but it should be a generic service without any specific religious affiliations. An appropriate focus for the service is to allow students to share memories of the class pet with one another. For example, the students might plan a program that includes a song performed by a group of students, memory sharing, the burial, and another music selection.

ASSESSMENT | For an assessment task, students can use this activity to make decisions about planning a funeral or remembrance for a class pet (or a community member, if appropriate). For assessment criteria, students should decide how they will carry out their funeral or remembrance. Students can use the decision-making model described in Chapter 3 to help them work through the process (state the problem, identify alternatives, consider consequences, choose their action, evaluate how it went).

Grades 6-8

Decision Making About Living Wills   Students might have heard about "living wills" or "advanced health care directives" on the news during the past several years. These documents tell family members and medical personnel whether a person wants to be kept on artificial life support if he or she is ever permanently unconscious or otherwise dying and unable to speak for himself or herself. Living wills are created differently across the fifty states. Students can investigate living wills in various states through a Web search and report to class members on the kinds of decisions that must be made in establishing a living will.

ASSESSMENT | The reports students make on living wills are the assessment task for this activity. For assessment criteria, students should explain the decisions required for making a living will and discuss their ideas about establishing such a document.

NHES 6 | Goal Setting

Students will demonstrate the ability to use goal-setting skills to enhance health.

ASSESSMENT CRITERIA

- Goal statement—Give goal statement that identifies health benefits; goal is achievable and will result in enhanced health.
- Goal setting plan—Show plan that is complete, logical and sequential, and includes a process to assess progress.

Grades 6-8

How Will Others Remember Me?   Joyce Fetro uses a teaching activity called "Writing My Own Epitaph" to have students think about what they want to accomplish in life.[43] In this activity, students write their own epitaph—an inscription on a gravestone that contains a brief statement about the dead person. Students should consider what they want to accomplish before they die and what they want to be remembered for doing. Dr. Fetro has students draw a tombstone and write their epitaph. This activity truly is an example of "beginning with the end in mind" as students consider the kind of life they want to lead and how they want to be remembered.

ASSESSMENT | The epitaphs students write are the assessment task for this activity. For assessment criteria, students should identify three short- or long-term goals they would like to accomplish that would lead toward their being remembered in the way they write.

NHES 7 | Self-Management

Students will demonstrate the ability to practice health-enhancing behaviors and avoid or reduce health risks.

ASSESSMENT CRITERIA

- Application (transfer)—Initiate health-enhancing behaviors; apply concepts and skills appropriately and effectively.
- Self-monitoring and reflection—Monitor actions and make adjustments; accept feedback and make adjustments; able to self-assess, reflect on, and take responsibility for actions.

Grades K–2

Jenny Is Scared! When Sad Things Happen in the World   Teachers can read Carol Shuman's book *Jenny Is Scared! When Sad Things Happen in the World* to talk with young children about managing their fears related to terrorism, war, and other violent events. In this story, Jenny and her brother Sam know that something sad is on the news that has adults upset. There's no school, and Jenny and Sam want to know what's going on and how not to be scared. The book provides concrete suggestions for helping children feel safer and offers families and educators ideas for making the world a better place. This book is published by the American Psychological Association's Magination Press (Special Books for Children's Special Concerns; www.maginationpress.com).

ASSESSMENT | For an assessment task, teachers can help students make a list on chart paper of the ways the story recommends to help children feel better and not be scared (ask questions, talk about how I feel, send loving thoughts to other people). Each student can select a way to feel better to draw and write about. For assessment criteria, students should explain at least one way to feel better and less scared.

The Memory Box: **Loving a Grandparent Who Has Alzheimer's Disease** Mary Bahr's book *The Memory Box* tells the story of Zach, who learns during a summer vacation that his grandfather has Alzheimer's disease. Zack's grandfather tells him that it's time to start a special box for storing their family tales and traditions. In this book, children learn about a disease that can take away the memories of a beloved grandparent or family friend and discover how to preserve those memories in a special way. Teachers can use this book to talk with children about changes they might notice in an older relative or friend and positive ways to deal with those changes.

ASSESSMENT | For an assessment task, students can illustrate or describe the things they would put into their memory boxes of special relatives or friends. For assessment criteria, students should explain how making a memory box can help them deal with changes in healthy and positive ways.

Grades 3–5

Magic Circle Teachers can prepare discussion questions for this activity in advance to use in that all-important teachable moment—instances such as the death of a class pet, the death of a student's pet (with the student's permission), or the death of a public figure. The class should sit in a circle, in chairs, desks, or on the floor, so that children are face to face and can make eye contact with each other. Questions should be appropriate for the age of the students and the degree of feeling they have about the pet or person who died. The idea of the Magic Circle is to allow children to express their feelings, rather than to dwell on the details of the death. The teacher might simply say, "We want to spend some time talking about and remembering [name]. What do you remember?" As children contribute, the teacher might ask how students feel about the memory they shared. Diane Parker, a first-grade teacher, had her class watch a caterpillar ("Blackie") spin a cocoon and, over time, emerge from the cocoon and fly away.[44] As the children discussed these events, one student said with sadness, "I just miss the old Blackie!" Even though Blackie didn't die, the caterpillar the children had come to regard as part of their class was no longer with them, and they had feelings about that. The children talked about Blackie and shared their memories of watching Blackie change and grow.

After a loss, students need opportunities to express their feelings, ask questions, and clarify misconceptions about death. Teachers sometimes hesitate to conduct an activity such as this one, fearing that children will not want to share their feelings or that they will be overcome with grief. Teachers who build trust, respect, and a sense of community in their classrooms throughout the school year will find that students generally welcome the opportunity to talk about how they feel and what they remember. Teachers need to ask students' permission to talk about anything that involves them

personally. Teachers might need to seek parental permission, too. Invite the school counselor to sit in with the circle to help answer questions and respond to children's feelings.

ASSESSMENT | The focus of this activity is talking things out to help students deal with strong feelings, an important self-management strategy. Contributions are voluntary; students can skip their turn at any time. For an assessment task, students can write a paragraph or draw a picture with a sentence about the person or pet they are remembering. For assessment criteria, students should indicate how they use their memories to keep the person or pet in a special place in their minds and hearts.

Memory Book Children can make a memory book if a class pet dies. This activity can also be used if a classmate dies or if a friend of the class or school dies. Adults and children can find comfort and sometimes even pleasure in sharing memories of the deceased. Memories reaffirm that loved people and pets go on living in our minds and will always be an important part of us now and as we grow older. Students can make their own memory book from a stapled, construction paper booklet, or they might contribute a page to a class book. Students can write notes and draw pictures that remind them of the deceased. Students can share their memory books with the rest of the class. If students make a class book, they might want to give it to the family of the deceased. Students can complete a memory book as an individual project for children who have lost a pet or a loved one.

ASSESSMENT | The memory book students create is the assessment task for this activity. For assessment criteria, students should explain how creating the book helps them remember the person or pet and deal with their feelings in healthy ways.

Grades 6–8

Kids' Health on Dealing with Loss, Death, and Grief The Kids' Health website for teens (www.kidshealth.org/teen) provides assistance with managing the feelings and events associated with a loss or death. Topics students can investigate include coping with the death of a pet, coping with the death of a family member, visiting the school counselor, and going to a therapist. The Health Finder website for kids (www.healthfinder.gov/kids) also has information on these topics. This activity links to NHES 3.

ASSESSMENT | For an assessment task, students can work in pairs or small groups to research and report on these and related topics. For assessment criteria, students should identify healthy self-management strategies for dealing with their topics.

Kids' Health on Dealing with Depression and Suicide The Kids' Health website for teens (www.kidshealth.org/teen) provides information for students on the issues of depression and suicide. Topics students can investigate include dealing with moving, divorce, and break-ups; counseling and therapy; and what to do if they or someone they know is depressed or suicidal. This activity links to NHES 3.

ASSESSMENT | For an assessment task, students can work in pairs or small groups to research and report on these and related topics. For assessment criteria, students should identify healthy self-management strategies for dealing with their topics.

Kids' Health on Dealing with Terrorist Attacks The Kids' Health website for teens (www.kidshealth.org/teen) provides information for students on the aftermath of terrorist attacks, such as that on the World Trade Center in 2001. Topics students can investigate include dealing with terrorist attacks and posttraumatic stress disorder. This activity links to NHES 3.

ASSESSMENT | For an assessment task, students can work in pairs or small groups to research and report on these and related topics. For assessment criteria, students should identify healthy self-management strategies for dealing with their topics.

NHES 8 | Advocacy

Students will demonstrate the ability to advocate for personal, family, and community health.

ASSESSMENT CRITERIA

- Health-enhancing position—Give clear, health-enhancing position.
- Suppport for position—Support position with facts, concepts, examples, and evidence.
- Audience awareness—Show awareness of target audience; choose words, tone, and examples to suit audience.
- Conviction—Display conviction for position.

Grades K–2

Blow Me a Kiss, Miss Lilly Teachers can use Nancy White Carlstrom's book *Blow Me a Kiss, Miss Lilly* to talk with children about their reactions to people who are ill or dying. In this book, Sara is very sad when her elderly neighbor, Miss Lilly, goes to the hospital. Students can discuss how they might feel in Sara's place, but they can discuss other feelings as well. Sometimes children feel afraid to be around someone who is sick or dying. This activity provides a good opportunity to talk with children about expressing caring and compassion for those who are ill without being afraid.

ASSESSMENT | For an assessment task, students can create a card for Miss Lilly, as Sara did, or for family members and friends with their own messages. For assessment criteria, students should convey a supportive, caring message.

Grades 3–8

The AIDS Memorial Quilt (The NAMES Project) Students can learn more about the AIDS Memorial Quilt at www.aidsquilt.org/. The mission of this advocacy project is to preserve, care for, and use the AIDS Memorial Quilt to foster healing, heighten awareness, and inspire action in the struggle against HIV and AIDS. The goals of the AIDS Memorial Quilt are to

- Provide a creative means for remembrance and healing
- Effectively illustrate the enormity of the AIDS epidemic
- Increase the general public's awareness of HIV and AIDS
- Assist others with education on preventing HIV infection
- Raise funds for community-based AIDS service organizations

Students can learn about making panels for the quilt, view the quilt, and learn about the quilt's history.

ASSESSMENT | For an assessment task, students can discuss how the AIDS Memorial Quilt meets the expectations for an advocacy project. For assessment criteria, students should be able to explain the message, the background, the target audience, and the conviction of the project.

INTERNET RESOURCES

Visit the Online Learning Center (www.mhhe.com/telljohann6e) for links to these sites, quizzes and other study aids, and many additional resources.

WEBSITES

American Academy of Child and Adolescent Psychiatry
www.aacap.org/index.htm

Compassionate Friends
www.compassionatefriends.org

Dougy Center for Grieving Children and Families
www.dougy.org

Families and Work Institute
www.familiesandwork.org/911ah/911ashistory.html

GriefNet
www.griefnet.org

Hospice Net
www.hospicenet.org

National Association of School Psychologists
www.naspcenter.org

Parents Trauma Resource Center
www.tlcinstitute.org

Public Broadcast Service
www.pbs.org

Substance Abuse and Mental Health Services Administration
www.samhsa.gov

Suicide Hotlines
www.suicidehotlines.com

CHILDREN'S LITERATURE

AGES 5–8

Aliki. *The Two of Them.* Greenwillow Books, 1979.
Buscaglia, Leo. *The Fall of Freddie the Leaf.* Henry Holt, 1982.
Carick, C., and D. Carick. The Accident. Seabury, 1976.

Carlstrom, Nancy White. *Blow Me a Kiss, Miss Lilly.* HarperCollins Children's Books, 1999.
Clifton, L. *Everett Anderson's Goodbye.* Holt, Rinehart & Winston, 1973. (Multicultural)

Cohen, M. *Jim's Dog Muffin*. Greenwillow Books, 1984.

DeSalvo, Anne Ryan. *Dog Like Jack*. Holiday House, 1999.

Fox, Mem. *Sophie*. Harcourt Brace, 1989. (Parent's Choice Honor) (Multicultural)

Fox, Mem. *Tough Boris*. Harcourt Brace, 1994.

Gray, Libba. *My Mama Had a Dancing Heart*. Orchard Books, 1995.

Muller, Birte. *Felipa and the Day of the Dead*. North-South Books, 2004. (Multicultural)

Powell, S. *Geranium Morning*. Carolrhoda, 1990.

Shuman, Carol. *Jenny Is Scared!* Magination Press, 2003.

Viorst, Judith. *The Tenth Good Thing About Barney*. Atheneum, 1971.

White, E. B. *Charlotte's Web*. Harper Junior Books, 1952.

Zalben, Jane. *Pearl's Marigolds for Grandpa*. Simon & Schuster, 1997.

Zolotow, Charlotte. *My Grandson Lew*. Harper & Row, 1974.

AGES 8–12

Bahr, Mary. *The Memory Box*. Albert Whitman, 1992.

Coleman, H. *Suddenly*. William Morrow, 1987.

Creech, S. *Walk Two Moons*. HarperCollins, 1998. (Newbery Medal) (Multicultural)

Droyer, Ann L. *After Elaine*. Cricket Books, 2002.

Ellis, S. *A Family Project*. McElderry, 1988.

Fox, Mem. *Wilfred Gordon McDonald Partridge*. Kane Miller, 1985.

Gilbert, Sheri. *The Legacy of Gloria Russell*. Random House Children's Books, 2004.

Grimes, Nikki. *What Is Goodbye?* Hyperion, 2004.

Hesse, K. *Out of the Dust*. Scholastic, 1997. (Multicultural)

Koss, Amy Goldman. *Stolen Words*. Pleasant Company, 2001.

Mann, P. *There Are Two Kinds of Terrible*. Doubleday, 1977.

Mass, Wendy. *Jeremy Fink and The Meaning of Life*. Little, Brown Young Readers, 2006.

Munsch, R. *Love You Forever*. Firefly Books, 1989.

Patron, Susan. *The Higher Power of Lucky*. Atheneum/Richard Jackson Books, 2006. (Newbery Award, 2007)

Patterson, K. *Bridge to Terabithia*. Avon Books, 1972.

Rylant, C. *Missing May*. Orchard Books, 1992.

Silverstein, S. *The Giving Tree*. Harper & Row, 1970.

Smith, Doris. *A Taste of Blackberries*. Crowell, 1972.

Stepanek, Mattie J. T. *Journey Through Heartsongs*. Hyperion, 2002.

Thomas, J. *Saying Good-Bye to Grandma*. Ticknor & Fields, 1988.

White, E. B. *Charlotte's Web*. Harper Junior Books, 1952.

Wild, M. *The Very Best Friends*. Harcourt Brace, 1989.

Wilhelm, H. *I'll Always Love You*. Crown, 1985.

ENDNOTES

1. R. Hayes, "Coping with Loss: A Developmental Approach to Helping Children and Youth," *Counseling and Human Development* 17, no. 3 (1984): 1–12.

2. J. Glass, "Death, Loss and Grief Among Middle School Children: Implications for the School Counselor," *Elementary School Guidance and Counseling* 26, no. 2 (1991): 139–48.

3. K. Steen, "A Comprehensive Approach to Bereavement," *Nurse Practitioner* 23, no. 3 (1998): 54–62.

4. E. Kübler-Ross, *On Death and Dying* (New York: Macmillan, 1969).

5. C. Willis, "The Grieving Process in Children: Strategies for Understanding, Educating, and Reconciling Children's Perceptions of Death," *Early Childhood Education Journal* 29, no. 4 (2002): 221–26.

6. T. Granot, *Without You: Children and Young People Growing Up with Loss and Its Effects* (Philadelphia: Jessica Kingsley, 2005).

7. B. Perry, "Death and Loss: Helping Children Manage Their Grief," *Scholastic Early Childhood Today* 15, no. 4 (2001): 22–23.

8. D. Seibert, J. Drolet, and J. Fetro, *Helping Children Live with Death and Loss* (Carbondale, IL: Southern Illinois University Press, 2003).

9. M. Nagy, "The Child's Theories Concerning Death," *Journal of Genetic Psychology* 73 (1948): 3–27.

10. L. DeSpelder and A. Strickland, *The Last Dance* (New York: McGraw-Hill, 2004).

11. V. Slaughter, "Young Children's Understanding of Death," *Australian Psychologist* 40, no. 3 (2005): 179–86.

12. National Association of School Psychologists, *Helping Children Cope with Loss, Death & Grief: Tips for Teachers and Parents*. (www.nasponline.org/resources/crisis_safety/griefwar.pdf; 2003)

13. B. Perry, "Death and Loss."

14. L. DeSpelder and A. Strickland, *The Last Dance*.

15. M. Jackson and J. Colwell, *A Teacher's Handbook of Death* (Philadelphia, PA: Jessica Kingsley, 2002).

16. H. McGlauflin, "Helping Children Grieve at School," *Professional School Counseling* 1, no. 5 (1998): 46–49.

17. E. Kübler-Ross, *On Death and Dying*.

18. M. Fristad, J. Cerel, M. Goldman, E. Weller, and R. Weller, "The Role of Ritual in Children's Bereavement," *Omega* 42, no. 4 (2001): 321–39.

19. American Hospice Foundation, *Grief at School: A Guide for Teachers and Counselors* (Washington, DC: American Hospice Foundation, 1996).

20. D. Seibert, J. Drolet, and J. Fetro, *Helping Children Live with Death and Loss*.

21. T. Granot, *Without You*.

22. M. Jackson and J. Colwell, *A Teacher's Handbook of Death*.

23. H. McGlauflin, "Helping Children Grieve at School."

24. B. Perry, "Death and Loss."

25. The Dougy Center for Grieving Children and Families, *When Death Impacts Your School*. (www.dougy.org/default.asp?pid=725353; 2004)

26. J. Milton, "Helping Primary School Children Manage Loss and Grief: Ways the Classroom Teacher Can Help," *Education and Health* 22, no. 4 (2004): 58–60.

27. D. Waddell and A. Thomas, *Disaster: Helping Children Cope*; New York State Office of Mental Health, *Age-Related Reactions of Children to Disasters*. (www.omh.state.ny.us/omhweb/crisis/crisiscounseling3.html; 2001)

28. Ibid.

29. P. Lazarus, S. Jimerson, and S. Brock, *Responding to Natural Disasters: Helping Children and Families*. (www.nasponline.org/NEAT/naturaldisaster_teams_ho.html; 2003)

30. Ibid.

31. D. Waddell and A. Thomas, *Disaster*.

32. Ibid.

33. P. Lazarus, S. Jimerson, and S. Brock, *Responding to Natural Disasters*.

34. Centers for Disease Control and Prevention, *10 Leading Causes of Death, United States*, 2005. (www.webappa.cdc.gov/cgi-bin/broker.exe; 2005)

35. Centers for Disease Control and Prevention, "Suicide Trends Among Youths and Young Adults Aged 10–24 Years—United States, 1990–2004," *MMWR* 56, no. 35 (2007): 905–908.

36. U.S. Public Health Service, *The Surgeon General's Call to Action to Prevent Suicide* (Washington, DC: U.S. Public Health Service, 1999).

37. Suicide Prevention Resource Center, *Risk and Protective Factors for Suicide*. (www.sprc.org/library/srisk.pdf; 2001)

38. Ibid.

39. National Institute of Mental Health, *Frequently Asked Questions About Suicide*. (www.nimh.nih.gov/research/suicidefaq.cfm; 2000)

40. Centers for Disease Control and Prevention, *Youth Suicide Prevention Programs: A Resource Guide* (Atlanta, GA: CDC, 1992).

41. Ibid.

42. Walt Disney Records, "The Circle of Life," *The Lion King*, 1994.

43. J. Fetro, *Personal and Social Skills, Level 1* (Santa Cruz, CA: ETR Associates, 2000), 211–12.

44. D. Parker, conversation with author, Honolulu, HI, January 1997.

APPENDIX A

2007 National Health Education Standards for Grades Pre-K–8

NATIONAL HEALTH EDUCATION STANDARD 1

Students will comprehend concepts related to health promotion and disease prevention to enhance health.

Performance Indicators

As a result of health instruction, students will:

Grades Pre-K–2

1. Identify that healthy behaviors impact personal health.
2. Recognize that there are multiple dimensions of health.
3. Describe ways to prevent communicable diseases.
4. List ways to prevent common childhood injuries.
5. Describe why it is important to seek health care.

Grades 3–5

1. Describe the relationship between healthy behaviors and personal health.
2. Identify indicators of emotional, intellectual, physical, and social health.
3. Describe ways in which a safe and healthy school and community environment can promote personal health.
4. Describe ways to prevent common childhood injuries and health problems.
5. Describe when it is important to seek health care.

Grades 6–8

1. Analyze the relationship between healthy behaviors and personal health.
2. Describe the interrelationship of emotional, intellectual, physical, and social health in adolescence.
3. Analyze how the environment impacts personal health.
4. Describe how family history can impact personal health.
5. Describe ways to reduce or prevent injuries and other adolescent health problems.
6. Explain how appropriate health care can promote personal health.
7. Describe the benefits of and barriers to practicing healthy behaviors.
8. Examine the likelihood of injury or illness if engaging in unhealthy behaviors.
9. Examine the potential seriousness of injury or illness if engaging in unhealthy behaviors.

Performance Indicators

As a result of health instruction, students will:

Grades Pre-K–2

1. Identify how the family influences personal health practices and behaviors.
2. Identify how the school can support personal health practices and behaviors.
3. Describe how the media can influence health behaviors.

Grades 3–5

1. Describe how the family influences personal health practices and behaviors.
2. Identify the influence of culture on personal health practices and behaviors.
3. Identify how peers can influence healthy and unhealthy behaviors.
4. Describe how the school and community can support personal health practices and behaviors.
5. Explain how the media influence thoughts, feelings, and health behaviors.
6. Describe ways technology can influence personal health.

Grades 6–8

1. Examine how the family influences the health of adolescents.
2. Describe the influence of culture on health beliefs, practices, and behaviors.
3. Describe how peers influence healthy and unhealthy behaviors.
4. Analyze how the school and community can impact personal health practices and behaviors.
5. Analyze how messages from media influence health behaviors.
6. Analyze the influence of technology on personal and family health.
7. Explain how the perceptions of norms influence healthy and unhealthy behaviors.
8. Explain the influence of personal values and beliefs on individual health practices and behaviors.
9. Describe how some health-risk behaviors can influence the likelihood of engaging in unhealthy behaviors.
10. Explain how social and public health policies can influence health promotion and disease prevention.

NATIONAL HEALTH EDUCATION STANDARD 2

Students will analyze the influence of family, peers, culture, media, technology, and other factors on health behaviors.

NATIONAL HEALTH EDUCATION STANDARD 3

Students will demonstrate the ability to access valid information and products and services to enhance health.

Performance Indicators

As a result of health instruction, students will:

Grades Pre-K–2

1. Identify trusted adults and professionals who can help promote health.
2. Identify ways to locate school and community health helpers.

Grades 3–5

1. Identify characteristics of valid health information, products, and services.
2. Locate resources from home, school, and community that provide valid health information.

Grades 6–8

1. Analyze the validity of health information, products, and services.
2. Access valid health information from home, school, and community.
3. Determine the accessibility of products that enhance health.
4. Describe situations that may require professional health services.
5. Locate valid and reliable health products and services.

NATIONAL HEALTH EDUCATION STANDARD 4

Students will demonstrate the ability to use interpersonal communication skills to enhance health and avoid or reduce health risks.

Performance Indicators

As a result of health instruction, students will:

Grades Pre-K–2

1. Demonstrate healthy ways to express needs, wants, and feelings.
2. Demonstrate listening skills to enhance health.
3. Demonstrate ways to respond when in an unwanted, threatening, or dangerous situation.
4. Demonstrate ways to tell a trusted adult if threatened or harmed.

Grades 3–5

1. Demonstrate effective verbal and nonverbal communication skills to enhance health.
2. Demonstrate refusal skills to avoid or reduce health risks.
3. Demonstrate nonviolent strategies to manage or resolve conflict.
4. Demonstrate how to ask for assistance to enhance personal health.

Grades 6–8

1. Apply effective verbal and nonverbal communication skills to enhance health.
2. Demonstrate refusal and negotiation skills to avoid or reduce health risks.

3. Demonstrate effective conflict management or resolution strategies.
4. Demonstrate how to ask for assistance to enhance the health of self and others.

NATIONAL HEALTH EDUCATION STANDARD 5

Students will demonstrate the ability to use decision-making skills to enhance health.

Performance Indicators

As a result of health instruction, students will:

Grades Pre-K–2

1. Identify situations when a health-related decision is needed.
2. Differentiate between situations when a health-related decision can be made individually or when assistance is needed.

Grades 3–5

1. Identify health-related situations that might require a thoughtful decision.
2. Analyze when assistance is needed when making a health-related decision.
3. List healthy options to health-related issues or problems.
4. Predict the potential outcomes of each option when making a health-related decision.
5. Choose a healthy option when making a decision.
6. Describe the outcome of a health-related decision.

Grades 6–8

1. Identify circumstances that can help or hinder healthy decision making.
2. Determine when health-related situations require the application of a decision-making process.
3. Distinguish when individual or collaborative decision making is appropriate.
4. Distinguish between healthy and unhealthy alternatives to health-related issues or problems.
5. Predict the short-term impact of each alternative on self and others.
6. Choose healthy alternatives over unhealthy alternatives when making a decision.
7. Analyze the outcome of a health-related decision.

NATIONAL HEALTH EDUCATION STANDARD 6

Students will demonstrate the ability to use goal-setting skills to enhance health.

Performance Indicators

As a result of health instruction, students will:

Grades Pre-K–2

1. Identify a short-term personal health goal and take action toward achieving the goal.

2. Identify who can help when assistance is needed to achieve a personal health goal.

Grades 3–5
1. Set a personal health goal and track progress toward its achievement.
2. Identify resources to assist in achieving a personal health goal.

Grades 6–8
1. Assess personal health practices.
2. Develop a goal to adopt, maintain, or improve a personal health practice.
3. Apply strategies and skills needed to attain the personal health goal.
4. Describe how personal health goals can vary with changing abilities, priorities, and responsibilities.

NATIONAL HEALTH EDUCATION STANDARD 7

Students will demonstrate the ability to practice health-enhancing behaviors and avoid or reduce risks.

Performance Indicators

As a result of health instruction, students will:

Grades Pre-K–2
1. Demonstrate healthy practices and behaviors to maintain or improve personal health.
2. Demonstrate practices to avoid or reduce health risks.

Grades 3–5
1. Identify responsible personal health behaviors.
2. Demonstrate a variety of healthy practices and behaviors to maintain or improve personal health.
3. Demonstrate a variety of behaviors to avoid or reduce health risks.

Grades 6–8
1. Explain the importance of assuming responsibility for personal health behaviors.
2. Demonstrate healthy practices and behaviors that will maintain or improve the health of self and others.
3. Demonstrate behaviors to avoid or reduce health risks to self and others.

NATIONAL HEALTH EDUCATION STANDARD 8

Students will demonstrate the ability to advocate for personal, family, and community health.

Performance Indicators

As a result of health instruction, students will:

Grades Pre-K–2
1. Make requests to promote personal health.
2. Encourage peers to make positive health choices.

Grades 3–5
1. Express opinions and give accurate information about health issues.
2. Encourage others to make positive health choices.

Grades 6–8
1. State a health enhancing position on a topic and support it with accurate information.
2. Demonstrate how to influence and support others to make positive health choices.
3. Work cooperatively to advocate for healthy individuals, families, and schools.
4. Identify ways that health messages and communication techniques can be altered for different audiences.

SOURCE: Reprinted with permission from the American Cancer Society, *National Health Education Standards: Achieving Excellence*, Second Edition. Atlanta, GA: American Cancer Society, 2007. www.cancer.org/bookstore

APPENDIX **B**

Rocky Mountain Center for Health Promotion and Education Rubrics for the National Health Education Standards

Scoring Rubric for Core Concepts

NHES #1: Students will comprehend concepts related to health promotion and disease prevention to enhance health.

Connections	Score	Comprehensiveness	Score
Completely and accurately describes relationships between behavior and health. Draws logical conclusion(s) about the connection between behavior and health.	4	Thoroughly covers health topic, showing both breadth (wide *range* of facts and ideas) and depth (*details* about facts and ideas). Response is completely accurate.	4
Describes relationships between behavior and health with some minor inaccuracies or omissions. Draws a plausible conclusion(s) about the connection between behavior and health.	3	Mostly covers health topic, showing breadth and depth, but one or both less fully. Response is mostly accurate, but may have minor inaccuracies.	3
Description of relationship(s) between behavior and health is incomplete and/or contains significant inaccuracies. Attempts to draw a conclusion about the connection between behavior and health, but conclusion is incomplete or flawed.	2	Minimal coverage of health topic, showing some breadth but little or no depth. Response may show some inaccuracies.	2
Inaccurate or no description of relationship(s) between behavior and health. Inaccurate OR no conclusion drawn about the connection between behavior and health.	1	No coverage of health topic information. Little or no accurate information.	1

Goals or Action: _____

_____

Core Concepts Score: _____

SOURCE: Rocky Mountain Center for Health Promotion and Education (RMC). *RMC Analytic Rubrics for National Health Education Standards.* Copyright © 2007. Reprinted with permission. For information call 303-239-6494 or access the RMC website (www.rmc.org).

Scoring Rubric for Analyzing Influences

NHES #2: Students will analyze the influence of family, peers, culture, media, technology, and other factors on health behaviors.

	Score
Accurately identifies both external and internal influences. Effectively explains how external and internal influences interact to impact health choices and behaviors of individuals, families, and communities. The explanation may include both positive and negative influences.	4
Accurately identifies influences and explains how these influences impact health choices and behaviors of individuals, families, and communities. The explanation may distinguish between external and internal influences, but does not clarify how external and internal factors interact to impact health choices and behaviors.	3
Identifies one or more relevant influences, but does not provide an effective explanation of how the influence(s) impact(s) health choices and behaviors of individuals, families, and communities.	2
Does not identify relevant influences, OR offers no explanation, OR the explanation reveals a flawed analysis of the influences' impact on health choices and behaviors of individuals, families, and communities.	1

Goals or Action: _____

_____

Analyzing Influences Score: _____

SOURCE: Rocky Mountain Center for Health Promotion and Education (RMC). *RMC Analytic Rubrics for National Health Education Standards.* Copyright © 2007. Reprinted with permission. For information call 303-239-6494 or access the RMC website (www.rmc.org).

Scoring Rubric for Accessing Information

NHES #3: *Students will demonstrate the ability to access valid information and products and services to enhance health.*

Accessing Health Information	Score	Evaluating Information Sources	Score
Locates very specific sources of health information, products, or services especially relevant for enhancing health in a given situation.	4	Clearly and accurately explains the degree to which identified sources are valid, reliable, and appropriate as a result of a thorough evaluation of each source. The explanation includes specific and extensive evaluative criteria for determining validity, reliability, and appropriateness.	4
Locates general sources of health information, products, or services that may enhance health in a given situation.	3	Explains the degree to which identified sources are valid, reliable, and appropriate as a result of an evaluation of each source. However, the explanation does not include extensive or specific evaluative criteria used in determining validity, reliability, and appropriateness of the sources.	3
Locates general sources of health information, products, or services; however, the information does not specifically support health-enhancing behaviors in a given situation.	2	Attempts to explain whether identified sources are valid, reliable, and appropriate; however, the evaluation is incomplete or flawed, OR the explanation is ineffective.	2
No sources located OR the information does not support health-enhancing behaviors in a given situation.	1	Does not attempt to evaluate sources to determine validity, reliability, and appropriateness to the given health situation. No explanation is provided.	1

Goals or Action: _____

Accessing Information Score: _____

SOURCE: Rocky Mountain Center for Health Promotion and Education (RMC). *RMC Analytic Rubrics for National Health Education Standards.* Copyright © 2007. Reprinted with permission. For information call 303-239-6494 or access the RMC website (www.rmc.org).

Scoring Rubric for Interpersonal Communication

IC

NHES #4: *Students will demonstrate the ability to use interpersonal communication skills to enhance health and avoid or reduce health risks.*

Communication Strategies*	Score
Uses appropriate verbal/nonverbal communication strategies in a highly effective manner (in a given situation with a particular audience) to enhance health or avoid/reduce risk for the health of self and others.	4
Uses appropriate verbal/nonverbal communication strategies in a generally effective manner (in a given situation with a particular audience) to enhance health or avoid/reduce risk for the health of self and others.	3
Uses verbal/nonverbal communication strategies effectively, but the strategies may be inappropriate for a given situation or a particular audience, OR the use of the selected strategy may be ineffective. In either case, the effect may not enhance health or avoid/reduce risk for the health of self and others.	2
Uses inappropriate verbal/nonverbal communication strategies to the given situation and particular audience, OR the communication strategies are used ineffectively. In either case, the effect will not enhance health or avoid/reduce risk for the health of self and others.	1

*This rubric can be used to assess a variety of communication skills and strategies, including:

Skill Sets
- Negotiation skills
- Refusal skills
- Conflict management skills
- Advocacy skills

Behaviors
- Eye contact
- Body language
- Respectful tone
- Clear message
- "I" messages

- Expressing needs, wants, and feelings
- Attentive listening
- Restating other points of view
- Suggesting an alternative

Goals or Action: _____

Interpersonal Communication Score: _____

SOURCE: Rocky Mountain Center for Health Promotion and Education (RMC). *RMC Analytic Rubrics for National Health Education Standards.* Copyright © 2007. Reprinted with permission. For information call 303-239-6494 or access the RMC website (www.rmc.org).

NHES #5: Students will demonstrate the ability to use decision-making skills to enhance health.

Use of a Decision-Making Process	Score
Reaches a health-enhancing decision using a decision-making process consisting of the following steps: • Identifies a situation poses a health risk. • Examines a comprehensive set of alternative courses of action. • Effectively evaluates the positive and negative health consequences of each alternative course of action. • Decides on a health-enhancing course of action.	4
Reaches a health-enhancing decision using a decision-making process consisting of the following steps: • Identifies a situation that poses a health risk. • Examines some alternative courses of action. • Evaluates some of the positive and negative health consequences of each alternative course of action. • Decides on a health-enhancing course of action.	3
The decision-making process is incomplete or contains flaws. *For example:* • May not identify a situation that poses a health risk. • Does not examine alternative courses of action. • Fails to fully or effectively evaluate the positive and negative health consequences of alternative courses of action. • Presents a course of action that is vague, incomplete, or unlikely to enhance health.	2
Does not reach a health-enhancing decision due to an ineffective decision-making process. Steps of the decision-making process are ineffectively used or not evident.	1

Goals or Action: _____

Decision-Making Score: _____

SOURCE: Rocky Mountain Center for Health Promotion and Education (RMC). *RMC Analytic Rubrics for National Health Education Standards.* Copyright © 2007. Reprinted with permission. For information call 303-239-6494 or access the RMC website (www.rmc.org).

NHES #6: Students will demonstrate the ability to use goal-setting skills to enhance health.

Goal Statement	Score	Goal-Setting Plan	Score
Clear and complete goal statement that explicitly states health benefits. The goal is achievable and will result in enhanced health.	4	The goal-setting plan: • Is complete—all important steps are included. • Follows a logical, sequential process. • Includes a process for assessing progress.	4
Goal statement that suggests or implies health benefits. The goal is achievable and will result in enhanced health.	3	The goal-setting plan: • Is complete—all important steps are included. • Follows a sequential process but may contain minor flaws. • Includes a process for assessing progress but could be incomplete.	3
Goal statement, but with no reference to health benefits. The goal may be unrealistic or unlikely to lead to health benefits.	2	The goal-setting plan may be incomplete or difficult to implement because of one or more of the following: • Does not include all important steps. • Does not follow a logical, sequential, process. • Does not include a process for assessing progress.	2
No clear goal statement, OR the goal will not enhance health.	1	No goal-setting plan is stated, OR the plan is vague, illogical, or unrealistic.	1

Goals or Action: _____

Goal-Setting Score: _____

SOURCE: Rocky Mountain Center for Health Promotion and Education (RMC). *RMC Analytic Rubrics for National Health Education Standards.* Copyright © 2007. Reprinted with permission. For information call 303-239-6494 or access the RMC website (www.rmc.org).

NHES #7: Students will demonstrate the ability to practice health-enhancing behaviors and avoid or reduce health risks.

Application (Transfer)	Score	Self-Monitoring and Reflection	Score
• Consistently initiates health-enhancing behaviors to avoid or reduce risks without prompts or cues. • Applies learned concepts and skills appropriately and effectively in new situations to enhance health and avoid or reduce risks.	4	• Consistently monitors actions and makes adjustments as needed. • Openly accepts feedback and makes adjustments as needed. • Consistently able to self-assess, reflect on, and take responsibility for one's actions.	4
• Usually initiates health-enhancing behaviors to avoid or reduce risks without prompts or cues. • Applies learned concepts and skills appropriately and effectively in most new situations to enhance health and avoid or reduce risks.	3	• Usually monitors actions and makes adjustments as needed. • Is open to feedback and willing to make adjustments as needed. • Usually self-assesses, reflects on, or takes responsibility for one's actions.	3
• Rarely initiates health-enhancing behaviors to avoid or reduce risks without prompts or cues, OR requires prompts, cues, and reminders to initiate health-enhancing behaviors. • Seldom applies learned concepts and skills appropriately and/or effectively in new situations.	2	• Rarely monitors actions and makes needed adjustments. • Rarely accepts feedback and makes needed adjustments. • Rarely self-assesses, reflects on, or takes responsibility for one's actions.	2
• Never initiates health-enhancing behaviors to avoid or reduce risks without prompts or cues, OR requires prompts, cues, and reminders to initiate health-enhancing behaviors. • Unable to, or does not, apply learned concepts and skills to new situations.	1	• Does not monitor actions. • Fails to accept feedback and does not make adjustments. • Does not self-assess, reflect on, or take responsibility for one's actions.	1

Goals or Action: _____

_____

_____

_____

_____

Self-Management Score: _____

Source: Rocky Mountain Center for Health Promotion and Education (RMC). *RMC Analytic Rubrics for National Health Education Standards.* Copyright © 2007. Reprinted with permission. For information call 303-239-6494 or access the RMC website (www.rmc.org).

NHES #8: Students will demonstrate the ability to advocate for personal, family, and community health.

Health-Enhancing Position	Score	Support for Position	Score	Audience Awareness	Score	Conviction	Score
Extremely clear, health-enhancing position.	4	Thoroughly supports position using relevant and accurate facts, concepts, examples, and evidence.	4	• Strong awareness of the target audience (e.g., their background, perspective, interests). • Word choice, tone, examples, graphics, etc., are well suited for the target audience.	4	Displays strong and passionate conviction for position.	4
Generally clear, health-enhancing position.	3	Adequately supports position using facts, concepts, examples, and evidence; support may be incomplete and/or contain minor inaccuracies.	3	• Awareness of audience is evident. • Word choice, tone, examples, graphics, etc., are appropriate for the target audience.	3	Displays conviction for position.	3
Unclear or conflicting positions.	2	Inadequately supports position. Facts, concepts, examples, or evidence used contain significant inaccuracies and/or have little relevance.	2	• Some awareness of audience may be evident, however, word choice, tone, examples, graphics, etc., are not always appropriate for target audience.	2	Displays minimal conviction for position.	2
No position stated , OR position is not health-enhancing.	1	No accurate or relevant support for position is provided.	1	• No evidence of audience awareness. • Word choice, tone examples, graphics etc., are not appropriate for the audience.	1	No conviction for position is evident.	1

Goals or Action: _____
_____
_____
_____
_____

Advocacy Score: _____

Source: Rocky Mountain Center for Health Promotion and Education (RMC). *RMC Analytic Rubrics for National Health Education Standards.* Copyright © 2007. Reprinted with permission. For information call 303-239-6494 or access the RMC website (www.rmc.org).

APPENDIX C

Development Characteristics and Needs of Students in Elementary and Middle Grades: A Foundation for Age-Appropriate Practice

Attributes of Students in Grades K Through 3 (5–8 years old)

PHYSICAL CHARACTERISTICS

Growth relatively slow

Increase in large-muscle coordination, beginning of development of small-muscle control

Bones growing

Nose grows larger

Permanent teeth appearing or replacing primary teeth, lower part of face more prominent

Hungry at short intervals, may overeat and gain inappropriate weight if inadequate physical activity

Enjoys active play—climbing, jumping, and running

Susceptible to fatigue and limits self

Visual acuity reaches normal

Susceptible to respiratory and communicable diseases

NEEDS

To develop large-muscle control through motor skills

To have play space and materials

To use developmentally appropriate instructional tools and equipment

To establish basic health habits: appropriate use of bathroom facilities, eating, covering nose and mouth when coughing, etc.

To have snack time and opportunity to develop social graces

To have plenty of sleep and rest, exercise interspersed with rest

To have health examinations and follow-up

To have visual and auditory checks

To have dental attention

EMOTIONAL CHARACTERISTICS

Self-centered, desires immediate attention to his or her problem, wants to be selected first

Sensitive about being left out of activities

Sensitive about ridicule, criticism, or loss of prestige

Easily emotionally aroused

Can take responsibility but needs adult supervision

Parent image strong, also identifies with teacher

Readily express likes and dislikes

Questioning attitude about sex differences

NEEDS

To receive encouragement, recognition, ample praise, patience, and adult support

To express inner feelings, anxieties, and fears

To feel secure, loved, wanted, and accepted (at home and at school)

To be free from pressure to achieve beyond capabilities

To have a consistent, cooperatively planned program of classroom management

To develop self-confidence

To have some immediate, desirable satisfactions

To know limitations within which he or she can operate effectively

To develop realistic expectations of self

SOCIAL CHARACTERISTICS

Lacks interest in personal grooming

Engages in imitative play

Friendly, frank, sometimes aggressive, bossy, assertive

Generally tolerant of race, economic status, etc.

Gradually more socially oriented and adjusted

Boys and girls play together as sex equals but are aware of sex differences

NEEDS

To have satisfactory peer relationships, to receive group approval

To learn the importance of sharing, planning, working, and playing together—both boys and girls

To have help in developing socially acceptable behavior

To learn to assume some responsibility, to have opportunities to initiate activities and to lead

To work independently and in groups

To explore gender constructs

To develop an appreciation of social values, such as honesty, sportsmanship, etc.

INTELLECTUAL CHARACTERISTICS

Varied intellectual growth and ability

Interested in things that move, bright colors, dramatizations, rhythmics, making collections

Interested in the present, not the future

Learns best through active participation in concrete, meaningful situations

Can abide by safety rules

Wants to know "why"

Attention span short

NEEDS

To experience frequent success and learn to accept failure when it occurs

To have concrete learning experiences and direct participation

To be in a rich, stable, challenging environment

To have time to adjust to new experiences and new situations

To learn to follow through to completion

To develop a love for learning

To learn without developing feelings of hostility

To communicate effectively

(continued)

Attributes of Students in Grades K Through 3 (5–8 years old) *(continued)*

Cues for teachers working with this age group: Vigorous games emphasizing outdoor play with basic movement patterns and skills and singing games and rhythms. Parallel play and learning strategies that involve some component of self-selection tend to be more successful among the youngest children in this group.

Attributes of Students in Grades 4 Through 6 (8–11 years old)

PHYSICAL CHARACTERISTICS

Growth slow and steady
Girls begin to forge ahead of boys in height and weight
Extremities begin to lengthen toward end of this period
Muscle coordination improving
Continued small-muscle development
Bones growing, vulnerable to injury
Permanent dentition continues
Malocclusion may be a problem
Appetite good, increasing interest in food
Boundless energy
Tires easily
Visual acuity normal
Menarche possible toward end of this period

NEEDS

To develop and improve coordination of both large and small muscles
To have plenty of activities and games that will develop body control, strength, endurance, and skills/stunts (throwing, catching, running, bicycling, skating)
To have careful supervision of games appropriate to strength and developmental needs, protective equipment
To have sleep, rest, and well-balanced meals
To have health examinations and follow-up
To have visual and auditory checks
To have dental attention

EMOTIONAL CHARACTERISTICS

Seeks approval of peer group
Desire to succeed
Enthusiastic, noisy, imaginative, desire to explore
Negativistic (early part of period)
Begins to accept responsibility for clothing and behavior
Increasingly anxious about family and possible tragedy
Increasing self-consciousness
Sex hostility
Becomes modest but not too interested in details of sex

NEEDS

To begin seriously to gain a realistic image of self and appreciate uniqueness of personality
To be recognized for individual worth, to feel self-assurance and self-esteem
To receive encouragement and affection, to be understood and appreciated
To exercise self-control
To talk about problems and receive reasonable explanations
To have questions answered

SOCIAL CHARACTERISTICS

Learns to cooperate better in group planning and group play and abides by group decisions
Interested in competitive activities and prestige
Competition keen
Begins to show qualities of leadership
Developing interest in appearance
Strong sense of fair play
Belongs to a gang or secret club, loyal to group
Close friendships with members of own sex
Separate play for boys and girls

NEEDS

To be recognized and accepted by peer groups, to receive social approval
To have relationships with adults that give feelings of security and acceptance
To assume responsibilities, to have increased opportunities for independent actions and decisions
To develop appreciation for others and their rights
To learn to get along with others and accept those different from self
To cultivate friendships with both boys and girls
To explore gender constructs

INTELLECTUAL CHARACTERISTICS

Likes to talk and express ideas
High potential for learning—in science, adventure, the world
Eager to acquire skills
Wide range of interests; curious, wants to experiment
Goals are immediate
Demands consistency
Generally reliable about following instructions
Attention span short

NEEDS

To experiment, explore, solve problems, accept challenges, use initiative, select, plan, and evaluate
To receive individual help in skill areas without harmful or undue pressure
To have opportunities for creative self-expression
To have a rich environment of materials and the opportunity to explore it
To participate in concrete, real-life situations
To be able to accept oneself with strengths and weaknesses

Cues for teachers working with this age group: More formal games with emphasis on body mechanics. Equipment should be appropriately sized and placed at proper height to promote development of sound fundamental skills. Cooperative learning and other supervised group learning strategies contribute to learning and improved interpersonal skills. Students seek attention and reinforcement from both peers and significant adults. Potential tension between norms established by adult authority figures and those of self-selected friends. Emotionally fragile, high need for feeling successful in a variety of areas. Learning activities and planned repetition to develop conflict resolution, decision making, refusal, communication, and other critical skills.

Attributes of Students in Grades 7 Through 9 (11–14 years old)

PHYSICAL CHARACTERISTICS

Accelerated and often uneven growth

Individual differences most prominent, girls continue rapid growth and are taller and heavier than boys in early period

Muscular growth toward adult size begins toward end of period

Variable coordination

Bones growing, vulnerable to injury

Onset of puberty generally at the beginning of this age range for girls, and at the end of this range for boys

Dental caries common

Permanent dentition—28 teeth

Malocclusion may be present

Appetite ravenous but may be capricious

Enjoys vigorous play

Tires easily, particularly girls

Visual problems may increase

Variations in development of secondary sex characteristics, menarche

Skin problems, voice changes, etc.

Reproductive organs growing

NEEDS

To have adequate nourishment for growth spurt and daily energy

To understand development change of adolescence

To recognize wide physical differences among peers as normal

To have good protective equipment in games

To have physical activity interspersed with rest

To have health examinations and follow-up

To have visual and auditory checks

To have dental attention

EMOTIONAL CHARACTERISTICS

Emotional instability, sudden and deep mood swings

Strong feelings of like and dislike, negative and positive attitudes

Sensitive, self-critical but vulnerable to criticism

Overanxious about health, common to think he or she has a gruesome disease

Overconcerned about physical and emotional changes

Striving for independence from adults

Hero worship

Searching for sensational emotional experiences

Self-conscious

Shows growing restraint in expressing feelings

Unique sense of humor

NEEDS

To express volatile emotions, grief, anger, disappointment, likes, and dislikes in constructive ways

To assume responsibility for own conduct

To achieve more independence

To feel secure, wanted, loved, trusted, adequate, and capable

To have privacy respected

To exercise self-discipline

To experience success, receive individual recognition

To identify with a friendly adult (teacher, parent, older friend)

To be alone occasionally

To feel the support, firm guidance, and assurance of an adult

To differentiate between reality and fiction, fact and inaccuracy

To appreciate individuality

SOCIAL CHARACTERISTICS

Interested in competitive sports as participant and spectator

Developing good sportsmanship

Socially insecure

Very peer-conscious

Desires freedom with security

Argues against authority but wants it

Sensitive to appearance (clothes, skin)

Imitative fads in clothing, speech, etc.

Wishes to conform to defined pattern of good school citizenship

Assumes responsibility for personal and group conduct

Beginning to discriminate right from wrong

Aware of opposite sex, chivalry, rivalry, and teasing

Separating into groups by sex: boys into large groups, girls into small groups, then gradually mixed groups

NEEDS

To see oneself as a socially accepted, important person

To relate to members of the same and opposite sex

To receive recognition from and acceptance by peers

To work and play with different age groups

To recognize the importance of leadership as well as being a follower

To have congenial social settings

To appreciate diversity

To initiate relationship boundaries

To explore gender constructs

(continued)

Attributes of Students in Grades 7 Through 9 (11–14 years old) *(continued)*

INTELLECTUAL CHARACTERISTICS

Eager to learn, curious, and alert exploring
Reads widely
Wider range of abilities and interests
Wants to succeed
Wants precise assignments and meaningful experiences
Skeptical, demands facts
Unrealistic in passing judgment
Overconfident in own information
Increasing span of attention and concentration

NEEDS

To determine individual motives, goals, standards, and ideals
To satisfy curiosity, desire to know, and to experiment
To express oneself verbally, manually, and through activities such as dance, music, clubs, debate, etc.
To appreciate the value of work and products of work
To know the satisfaction of achieving to the extent of one's ability

Cues for teachers working with this age group: Games with moderate fatigue and emotional stress, involving development of a range of skills. Learning activities and planned repetition to develop conflict resolution, decision making, refusal, communication, and other critical skills. Develop opportunities for students to participate in developing rules, codes of conduct, and consequences. Reinforcement for requiring students to identify range of consequences and potential implications for self and others involved in various behaviors. Consistently demonstrate respect for diverse behavioral manifestations common in this stage of development. Provide formal and informal opportunities for discussion of concerns. Protect rights to privacy.

SOURCE: J. W. Lochner, "Growth and Development Characteristics," in *A Pocketguide to Health and Health Problems in School Physical Activities* (Kent, OH: American School Health Association, 1981). Reprinted with permission.

CREDITS

Page 1, © BananaStock/PunchStock; p. 9, © image100 Ltd; p. 20, Photodisc; p. 23, © BananaStock/PunchStock; p. 33, © Scott T. Baxter/Getty Images; p. 41, © image100 Ltd; p. 51, Photodisc Collection/Getty Images; p. 60, Courtesy of Nadine Marchessault; p. 72, Comstock/PictureQuest; p. 77, Thomas Barwick/Getty Images; p. 89, Photodisc Collection/Getty Images; p. 104, © Geostock/Getty Images; p. 110, EyeWire Collection/Getty Images; p. 113, © Brand X Pictures/PunchStock; p. 117, © Creatas/PunchStock; p. 119, Royalty-Free/CORBIS; p. 126, © BananaStock/PunchStock; p. 141, © D. Berry/PhotoLink/Getty Images;

p. 158, Ryan McVay/Getty Images; p. 164, © Pixland/PunchStock; p. 182, © PhotoLink/Getty Images; p. 184, © Creatas/PunchStock; p. 191, © Pixland/PunchStock; p. 193, © Creatas; p. 195, © Brand X Pictures/PunchStock; p. 200, Steve Stephens; p. 222, © Royalty-Free/CORBIS; p. 225, © Photodisc/PunchStock; p. 226, © Ryan McVay/Getty Images; p. 228, © Blend Images/Alamy; p. 239, PhotoLink/Getty Images; p. 247, © The McGraw-Hill Companies, Inc./Jill Braaten, photographer; p. 251, © BananaStock/PunchStock; p. 252, © Keith Brofsky/Getty Images; p. 253, © Ant Strack/Corbis; p. 257, Royalty-Free/CORBIS; p. 273, © Creatas/

PunchStock; p. 283, Getty Images, p. 287, © Creatas/PunchStock; p. 291, © BananaStock/PunchStock; p. 317, © image100/Corbis; p. 318, National Cancer Institute; p. 321, © Royalty-Free/CORBIS; p. 340, 343, Brand X Pictures/PunchStock; p. 349, U.S. Air Force photo illustration by Senior Airman Mike Meares; p. 353, © David Buffington/Getty Images; p. 380, © The McGraw-Hill Companies, Inc./Jill Braaten, photographer; p. 383, © Stockbyte/PictureQuest; p. 396, Jules Frazier/Getty Images; p. 407, Royalty-Free/CORBIS; p. 411, Geostock/Getty Images

All Stars, 334
allergens, 248*t, 257,* 257–258
American Academy of Pediatrics, 246, 254
American Cancer Society, 9–10
American Diabetes Association, 246, 258
American Federation of Teachers (AFT), 35
American Indians, 220
American Lung Association, 255
American School Board Journal, 109–110
amphetamine, 346
Analyze Influences (NHES Standard 2), 55, *57,* 57–58, 69, 83
    alcohol and other drug-free lifestyle, 354–355, 359–360
    healthy eating promotion/disease prevention, 171, 177–178
    loss, death, and grief, 416
    mental and emotional health promotion, 129–130, 133–135
    performance indicators, 423
    personal health and wellness, 261, 264–265
    physical activity promotion, 203, 207–208
    rubric for, 426
    safety and unintentional injury prevention, 231, 234–235
    sexual health promotion, 388, 393–394
    Teacher's Toolbox on advertising techniques, 59
    tobacco-free lifestyle, 322, 326–327
    violence prevention, 295–296, 299–300
anesthetics, abuse of, 346
angel dust, 346
anger management, 279*t*
Annie E. Casey Foundation, 250
anorexia nervosa, 116*t*
antisocial behavior, 280, 339–341, *340*
anxiety disorders, 127
    drug abuse causing, 346
appreciation activities, 91
Arkansas, 215*t*
The Art of Classroom Management: Building Equitable Learning Communities (Landau), 123
asbestos, 248*t,* 249
ASCD. *See* Association for Supervision and Curriculum Development
ASD. *See* autism spectrum disorders
Asian Americans, 220
aspirin, contraindication for, 255
assessment. *See also* rubric
    Checking for Understanding: Formative Assessment Techniques for Your Classroom, 74
    formative, 74
    HEAP, 55, 128
    lesson plan to include evidence for, 74
    NCTM statement on, 80
    RMC rubric, 79*f,* 80
    sample standards-based assessment task, 82
    State Collaborative on Assessment and Student Standards, 55
    students engaged in, 79
    summative, 74
    teacher- and student-created rubrics, 79*f,* 80–81, 81*f*
    Teacher's Toolbox approaches and methods of, 79
    Teacher's Toolbox strategies for, 75
    Wiggins and McTighe on, 77

Association for Supervision and Curriculum Development (ASCD), 10
    Position Statement on Health and Learning, 27
asthma, 190, 247, 249, 257
    absenteeism from, 249
Attention Deficit Hyperactivity Disorder (ADHD), 115, 116*t,* 117, 121, 127, 247
    child abuse/neglect and, 284–285
    physical activity improving symptoms, 192–193
authentic instruction and achievement, 40–41
autism spectrum disorders (ASD), 116*t*
avoidance (manifestation of trauma), 282

BAC. *See* blood alcohol concentration
barbiturates, 346
Bean, Reynold, 124
Bedworth, A., 3
Bedworth, D., 3
benzodiazepines, 346
Bernard, Bonnie, 125
bicycling
    helmets, 220–221, 220*t, 222*
    safety for, 192*t, 195,* 202, 225, 227–228
Bienestar, 185
binge-eating disorder, 116*t*
bipolar disorder, 116*t*
birth control, 256, 387. *See also* females
bladder or bowel problems, 284–285
blood alcohol concentration (BAC), 347–348, 348*f*
blood pressure, 154, 190
    drug abuse influencing, 346
    as part of school health service, 18*t*
bloodborne pathogens, 256
Blueprints for Violence Prevention, 147
BMI. *See* body mass index
Board of Pharmacy regulations, 17
body composition, 197
body image, 375
    "private parts," 396, *396*
body mass index (BMI), 157, 190
body substance isolation (BSI), 256
body-kinesthetic intelligence, 38
borderline personality disorder (BPD), 116*t*
boredom, 338
Born to Buy: The Commercialized Child and the New Consumer Culture (Schor), 59
boundary breaking, 90
bowel or bladder problems, 284–285
BPD. *See* borderline personality disorder
brain
    alcohol's physiological pathways, 348*f*
    -based research, 36–39, 192
    -development and emotional health, 63
    injury from trauma, 227
    stimulants influencing, 346
    Teenage Brain: A Work in Progress, 63
breakfast, school program, *158,* 158–159
BSI. *See* body substance isolation
bulimia nervosa, 116*t*
bullying, 121, 127, 275, 279*t,* 289–291
    as challenge to learning, 118
bus, school, 18–19, 281

calcium, 154, 167, 167*f*
California
    Health Framework for California Public Schools, 69
    Los Angles Unified School District, 191

calories, 162, 167, 167*f*
cancer
    American Cancer Society, 9–10
    cervical, 255
    death from, 6*t*
    National Cancer Institute, 185
    oral, 318
    skin, 150*t,* 248*t, 253,* 253–254
cannabis, 346. *See also* marijuana use
carbohydrates, 162, 164–165, 167, 167*f*
cardiopulmonary resuscitation (CPR), 223*t,* 224, 229
cardiopulmonary system
    alcohol's physiological pathways, 348*f*
    American Lung Association, 255
    cigarettes v., 318–320, 320*f*
    drug abuse influencing, 346
cardio-respiratory (aerobic) endurance, 197, 199*f,* 201
Carter, G. F, 3
CASEL. *See* Collaborative for Social and Emotional Learning
CATCH. See Coordinated Approach to Child Health
Caucasian Americans, 193, 276
    injury-related data, 220
    overweight in childhood, 154
CCSSO. *See* Council of Chief State School Officers
CDC. *See* Centers for Disease Control and Prevention
Centers for Disease Control and Prevention (CDC), 5, 7, 33. *See also* Health Education Curriculum Analysis Tool
    alcohol/drug use data related to school policies and programs, 342*t*
    chronic ill health conditions/diseases, 6*t*
    Coordinated School Health Program, 12–13, 13*f*
    Division of Adolescent and School Health, 121, 256
    Division of Nutrition and Physical Activity, 158
    guidelines for healthy eating promotion, 161
    Guidelines for School Health Programs to Promote Lifelong Healthy Eating, 159–160, 161, 196
    health instruction using priorities from, 15*t*
    National Center for Infectious Diseases, 251
    personal health and wellness, 250*t*
    on physical activity, 158, 190*t,* 191, 196
    Physical Activity Survey, 190*t,* 191
    School Health Education Resources, 70–72
    SHPPS data on mental/emotional health topics, 121
    unintentional injuries data, 220, 220*t*
    unintentional injuries prevention guidelines, 222
    Youth Risk Behavior Survey, 117–118, 117*t,* 155, 155*t,* 190*t,* 220
    2006 personal health/wellness study, 250*t*
central nervous system stimulants, 346. *See also* brain
charter school, 31
chat rooms, 106
Checking for Understanding: Formative Assessment Techniques for Your Classroom (Fisher and Frey), 74

chewing tobacco, 318. *See also* tobacco-free
 lifestyle
Chicago, 191
child abuse, 121, 284
 mandated reporting of, 285, 287
 signs and symptoms of, 286
child development, 42. *See also* brain; females;
 males
 brain development and emotional health, 63
 grades K through 3, 431–432
 grades K through 12, 55–68
 grades 4 through 6, 432
 grades 7 through 9, 433–434
 Maslow's Hierarchy of Needs, 123–125,
  124f, 124t
 mental/emotional disorder development,
  119–120
 pervasive developmental disorders, 116t
 stages of understanding death, 406–407
Child Nutrition Reauthorization Act of
 Congress (2004), 20
children home alone, 228
children of alcoholics (COAs), 350
 National Association for Children of
  Alcoholics, 350
 "Children of Alcoholics: A Kit for Educators,"
  350
Children's Defense Fund, 246
Children's Mental Health Resource List, 127
chlamydia, 386t
cholesterol, 167, 167f, 190
chronic ill health conditions/diseases, 251t,
 257–259. *See also* diseases
 linked to risk behaviors, 6–7, 6t
 sources of, 7
cigarettes. *See also* tobacco-free lifestyle
 cardiopulmonary system v., 318–320, 320f
 family connectedness v., 109
class contracts, 92–93
class meetings, 94
class picture inspection (for teachers), 91–92
classroom. *See also* emergency protocol
 building sense of community in, 122–123
 climate of civility, 37
 color, lighting, and air quality of, 18
 positive/safe/stable environment,
  282–283, 283
 sex education in, 378–387, 380, 381f, 382f,
  384f, 385f
 student convulsions in, 259
 tobacco-free, 317–318
Closing the Gap: A National Blueprint for Improving
 the Health of Persons with Mental Retardation
 (Surgeon General's report), 33
Club drug, 347
clustering, 89
COAs. *See* children of alcoholics
cocaine, 346
codeine, 346
cognitive disabilities
 interdisciplinary instruction with theme
  of, 103
 teaching to, 77
colds and flu, 251, 255, 261t. *See also*
 handwashing
Collaborative for Social and Emotional
 Learning (CASEL), 118
college readiness, 10

color, of classroom, 18
Columbine High School, 275
Commission on the Whole Child (2006), 10
communicable diseases, 254. *See also* diseases;
 HIV infection
 airborne pathogens, 258
 bloodborne pathogens, 256
 colds and flu, 251, 255, 261t
 hepatitis B virus, 256
 infectious agents, 6t, 7, 246
 microbial infection avoidance, 162,
  165–166, 165f
 National Center for Infectious Diseases, 251
 STDs, 6t, 7, 66, 67, 248t, 256, 373, 385, 386t
communication. *See also* Interpersonal
 Communication
 conversation v. one-directional, 41
 interpersonal, 55, 60, 60–62, 61
 nurses' responsibility of, 16
 real-time online, 106
 with students having cognitive disabilities,
  77, 103
 teacher's skillful, 110–111
 Teacher's Toolbox tips for, 111
 teacher-student interview, 41, 91, 126
community disorganization
 drug/alcohol usage compared to, 341
 youth violence v., 278
community involvement, 10, 13f 25, 25t, 26, 26t
 advocacy for healthy behavior, 55, 67, 67–68
 alcohol and drug prevention principles,
  343–345
 networking, 126
 violence prevention, 281
community laws and norms
 drug/alcohol abuse and, 341
 key principles for preventing alcohol
  consumption, 343
community school, 31
community service/service learning projects, 95
Compendium of HIV Prevention Interventions
 with Evidence of Effectiveness, 147
comprehensive school health education
 commercial pregnancy/STD/HIV prevention
  programs, 401
 Healthy People 2010 objectives for, 118t
 keys to, 15t
condoms, 256, 387
Conference on Health Disparities and Mental
 Retardation (2002), 33
confidence-building activities
 mental health promotion through, 128t
 safe environment via, 220
conflict resolution, 291, 291–292
Connecticut, 215t
contracts, 92–93
controversy management (over health education),
 106–108. *See also* conflict resolution
conversation, one-directional communication
 v., 41
convulsions, 249, 259. *See also* epilepsy
cool-down activities, 201
cooperative learning, 45
Coordinated Approach to Child Health (CATCH), 186
Coordinated School Health Program (CSHP),
 25–27, 26t, 33, 109
 CDC endorsement of, 12–13, 13f
 health services provided, 15–18

key concepts of, 11–12
 managing potential controversy, 106–108
 physical activity as part of, 197
Core Concepts (NHES Standard 1), 55–57, 56,
 69, 83, 423
 alcohol and other drug-free lifestyle, 354,
  357–359
 healthy eating promotion/disease prevention,
  171, 174–177, 176f
 loss, death, and grief, 415–416
 mental and emotional health promotion,
  129, 132–133
 performance indicators, 423
 personal health and wellness, 260, 261, 264
 physical activity promotion, 202, 205–207
 rubric for, 426
 safety and unintentional injury prevention,
  229–230, 233–234
 sexual health promotion, 388, 391–393
 tobacco-free lifestyle, 322, 324–326
 violence prevention, 293, 294–295, 298–299
corporal punishment, 275
Council of Chief State School Officers
 (CCSSO), 10, 55, 155
counseling, 26, 26t. *See also* school health
 services
 advocacy for healthy behavior, 55, 67, 67–68
 anger management, 279t
 antisocial behavior, 280, 339–341, 340
 anxiety disorders, 127, 346
 barriers to learning requiring, 21–22, 22t
 bullying prevention/management, 290
 conflict resolution, 291, 291–292
 National Association of School
  Psychologists, 118
 as part of coordinated services, 13f
 rape, 278, 279t, 291
 school as primary provider, 21
 suicide, 413
 suspected abuse victims requiring, 287
 traumatic event requiring, 128t
 violence victim requiring, 281
CPR. *See* cardiopulmonary resuscitation
crack, 346
crime rate, 275
 unintentional injuries v. neighborhood, 221
criterion-referenced feedback, 45
CSHP. *See* Coordinated School Health Program
cues, Teacher's Toolbox, 45
culturally sensitive health care, 16
curricula and instructional materials
 alcohol and other drug-free lifestyle,
  368–370
 disabilities/special needs, 103
 healthy eating, 185–187
 injury prevention, 242–244
 loss, death, and grief, 420–422
 mental and emotional health, 147–151
 personal health and wellness, 270–271
 physical activity promotion, 215–217
 physical fitness, 215–216, 215t
 sexual health, 401–402
 tobacco-free lifestyle, 334–335
 violence prevention, 308–310
curriculum, 15t. *See also* Health Education
 Curriculum Analysis Tool
 Association for Supervision and Curriculum
  Development, 10, 27